Essentials of Psychology

Saul Kassin
John Jay College of Criminal Justice

Gregory J. Privitera
St. Bonaventure University

Krisstal D. Clayton
University of North Texas

Los Angeles | London | New Delhi
Singapore | Washington DC | Melbourne

FOR INFORMATION:

SAGE Publications, Inc.
2455 Teller Road
Thousand Oaks, California 91320
E-mail: order@sagepub.com

SAGE Publications Ltd.
1 Oliver's Yard
55 City Road
London, EC1Y 1SP
United Kingdom

SAGE Publications India Pvt. Ltd.
B 1/I 1 Mohan Cooperative Industrial Area
Mathura Road, New Delhi 110 044
India

SAGE Publications Asia-Pacific Pte. Ltd.
18 Cross Street #10-10/11/12
China Square Central
Singapore 048423

Copyright © 2023 by SAGE Publications, Inc.

All rights reserved. Except as permitted by U.S. copyright law, no part of this work may be reproduced or distributed in any form or by any means, or stored in a database or retrieval system, without permission in writing from the publisher.

All third party trademarks referenced or depicted herein are included solely for the purpose of illustration and are the property of their respective owners. Reference to these trademarks in no way indicates any relationship with, or endorsement by, the trademark owner.

Printed in Canada

Library of Congress Cataloging-in-Publication Data

Names: Kassin, Saul, author. | Privitera, Gregory J., author. | Clayton, Krisstal D., 1978- author. Title: Essentials of psychology / Saul Kassin, Gregory J. Privitera, Krisstal D. Clayton. Description: Los Angeles : SAGE, [2022] | Includes bibliographical references and index. Identifiers: LCCN 2021013761 | ISBN 9781544348438 (paperback ; alk. paper) | ISBN 9781544348469 (epub) Subjects: LCSH: Psychology. Classification: LCC BF121 .K3352 2022 | DDC 150--dc23 LC record available at https://lccn.loc.gov/2021013761

Medical illustrations created by Body Scientific International.

This book is printed on acid-free paper.

21 22 23 24 25 10 9 8 7 6 5 4 3 2 1

Acquisitions Editor: Lara Parra

Content Development Editor: Emma Newsom

Project Editor: Veronica Stapleton Hooper

Copy Editor: Amy Marks

Proofreader: Dennis Webb

Typesetter: diacriTech

Cover Designer: Rose Storey

Marketing Manager: Victoria Velasquez

BRIEF CONTENTS

Preface	xix
Acknowledgments	xxvii
About the Authors	xxxi
Student Success Guide	xxxiii
Moments in Psychology Around the World	xli
Chapter 1 Psychology and Its Methods	1
Chapter 2 Behavioral Neuroscience	45
Chapter 3 Sensation and Perception	85
Chapter 4 Consciousness	131
Chapter 5 Learning	173
Chapter 6 Memory	211
Chapter 7 Thought, Language, and Intelligence	255
Chapter 8 Personality	303
Chapter 9 Life Span Development and Its Contexts	347
Chapter 10 Social and Cultural Influences	395
Chapter 11 Motivation and Emotion	449
Chapter 12 Health, Stress, and Wellness	489
Chapter 13 Psychological Disorders	525
Chapter 14 Treatment and Interventions	573
Appendix: Statistics in Psychology	A-1
Glossary	G-1
References	R-1
Name Index	I-1
Subject Index	I-5

DETAILED CONTENTS

Preface	xix
Acknowledgments	xxvii
About the Authors	xxxi
Student Success Guide	xxxiii
Moments in Psychology Around the World	xli

Chapter 1 Psychology and Its Methods — 1

- What Is Psychology? — 3
  - Historical Roots — 3
    - *Pioneers in the Study of the Mind* — 4
    - *The Behaviorist Alternative* — 7
    - *The "Cognitive Revolution"* — 8
  - Expansion of Psychology's Horizons — 9
    - *Psychology as a Multidimensional Science* — 10
    - *Psychology as a Responsive and Anticipatory Science* — 13
    - *Values, Ethics, and Social Responsibility* — 13
    - *Psychology Applied: When Protests Become Violent* — 14
    - *Moralization of a Cause* — 14
    - *Perceived Moral Convergence and Social Media* — 15
  - A Range of Perspectives — 16
- Scientific Methods — 17
  - The Research Process — 18
  - Research Settings — 19
  - Psychological Measurements — 20
    - *Physiological Measures* — 21
    - *Self-Reports* — 21
    - *Behavioral Observations* — 22
    - *Archival Records* — 22
  - Research Designs — 23
    - *Descriptive Research* — 23
    - *Correlational Studies* — 27
    - *Experiments* — 28
    - *Literature Reviews* — 30
  - Ethical Considerations — 32
    - *Ethical Considerations in Human Research* — 32
    - *Ethical Considerations in Animal Research* — 34
- Psychology Today — 35
  - Emerging Branches of Psychology — 37
  - Sociocultural Perspectives — 38
  - Thinking Like a Psychologist About Psychology and Its Methods — 39

Chapter 2 Behavioral Neuroscience — 45

- The Body's Communication Networks — 49
  - The Nervous System — 49
  - The Endocrine System — 50
- The Neuron — 51
  - Structure of the Neuron — 53
  - The Neuron in Action — 54
  - How Neurons Communicate — 54
  - Neurotransmitters — 55
- The Brain — 57
  - Tools of Behavioral Neuroscience — 58
    - *Clinical Case Studies* — 58
    - *Experimental Interventions* — 58
    - *Electrical Recordings* — 59
    - *Brain-Imaging Techniques* — 60
  - Regions of the Brain — 61
    - *The Brainstem* — 63
    - *The Limbic System* — 64
    - *The Cerebral Cortex* — 65
  - The Split Brain — 69
    - *Split-Brain Studies* — 69
    - *Cerebral Lateralization* — 71
- Prospects for the Future — 74
  - The Brain's Capacity for Growth and Reorganization — 75
    - *The Benefit of Plasticity: Growth Through Experience* — 75
    - *What's Your Prediction?* — 76
    - *The Cost of Plasticity: The Case of the Phantom Limb* — 76
  - Repairing the Damaged Brain: New Frontiers — 76
    - *Neurogenesis* — 77
    - *Psychology Applied: Head Injury in Contact Sports* — 77
    - *Neural Transplantation* — 79
  - Thinking Like a Psychologist About Behavioral Neuroscience — 80

Chapter 3 Sensation and Perception — 85

- Measuring the Sensory Experience — 88
  - Absolute Thresholds — 89
  - Signal-Detection Theory — 89
  - Difference Thresholds — 90
- Sensation — 91
  - Vision — 91
    - *Light* — 91
    - *The Visual System* — 92
    - *Color Vision* — 98
  - Hearing — 102
    - *Sound Waves* — 102
    - *The Auditory System* — 103
    - *Hearing Abilities* — 104
    - *Hearing Loss* — 105
    - *Psychology Applied: When Is Loud Too Loud?* — 106
  - Other Senses — 106
    - *Smell* — 106
    - *Taste* — 108
    - *Touch* — 109
    - *What's Your Prediction?* — 110

Temperature	111
Pain	111
Coordination	113
Keeping the Signals Straight	114

Perception — 115
- Perceptual Organization — 116
  - *Figure and Ground* — 116
  - *Gestalt Laws of Grouping* — 117
- Perceptual Constancies — 118
- Depth and Dimension — 120
  - *Binocular Depth Cues* — 120
  - *Monocular Depth Cues* — 120
  - *Origins of Depth Perception* — 120
- Perceptual Set — 124
- The World of Illusions — 124
- Thinking Like a Psychologist About Sensation and Perception — 126

Chapter 4 Consciousness — 131

Attentional Processes — 133
- Selective Attention — 133
- Divided Attention — 134
- Influence Without Awareness — 136
  - *Mere Exposure* — 136
  - *Priming* — 136

Sleep and Dreams — 137
- The Sleep-Wake Cycle — 137
- Night Work, Sleeping, and Health — 140
- The Stages of Sleep — 141
  - *Presleep* — 141
  - *Stages 1 to 4* — 142
  - *REM Sleep* — 143
  - *What's Your Prediction?* — 144
- Why Do We Sleep? — 144
- Dreams — 146
  - *The Nature of Dreams* — 146
  - *What Do People Dream About?* — 147
  - *Freud's Interpretation* — 148
  - *Activation-Synthesis Theory* — 148
  - *Comparing Perspectives* — 149
- Sleep Disturbances — 149
  - *Insomnia* — 149
  - *Hypersomnia* — 151
  - *Parasomnias* — 152

Hypnosis — 153
- The Seeds of Controversy — 154
- The Hypnotic Induction — 154
- Hypnotic Responsiveness — 155
- The Myths and Realities — 155
  - *Coercion* — 156
  - *Pain Relief* — 156
  - *Posthypnotic Suggestion* — 156
  - *Memory Enhancement* — 157
  - *Psychology Applied: Does Hypnosis Enhance Eyewitness Testimony?* — 157
- Is Hypnosis an "Altered" State? — 158
  - *Special-Process Theories* — 159
  - *Social-Cognitive Theories* — 159

Consciousness-Altering Drugs	161
Sedatives	163
Stimulants	165
Hallucinogens	165
Opiates	166
Consciousness and Control	167
Thinking Like a Psychologist About Consciousness	169

Chapter 5 Learning — 173

Nonassociative Learning	175
Fixed Action Patterns	175
Habituation	176
Classical Conditioning	178
Pavlov's Discovery	178
Basic Principles	180
Acquisition	180
Extinction	181
Generalization	182
Discrimination	182
Pavlov's Legacy	182
Theoretical Advances	183
Practical Applications of Classical Conditioning	185
Conditioned Fears	185
Social Attitudes and Behavior	187
Psychology Applied: Can the Immune System Be Classically Conditioned?	188
Operant Conditioning	189
What's Your Prediction?	189
The Law of Effect	190
The Principles of Reinforcement	190
Reinforcers and Punishers	191
Shaping and Extinction	192
Schedules of Reinforcement	193
Punishment	195
Stimulus Control	196
Self-Control	197
Practical Applications of Operant Conditioning	198
Developments in Operant Conditioning	199
Biological Constraints	199
Cognitive Perspectives	200
Observational Learning	204
Studies of Modeling	205
The Process of Modeling	206
Thinking Like a Psychologist About Learning	207

Chapter 6 Memory — 211

An Information-Processing Model	214
The Sensory Register	215
Iconic Memory	215
Echoic Memory	216
Short-Term Memory	216
Capacity	217
Duration	220
Functions of Short-Term Memory	221
Working Memory	221
The Serial-Position Effect	221

Long-Term Memory	223
Encoding	224
Storage	226
Formats of Long-Term Memory	226
Contents of Long-Term Memory	227
Neural Bases of Long-Term Memory	229
Retrieval	232
Explicit Memory	233
Implicit Memory	235
Forgetting	238
The Forgetting Curve	239
What's Your Prediction?	241
Why Do People Forget?	241
Reconstruction	244
The Misinformation Effect	245
The Creation of Illusory Memories	246
Autobiographical Memory	247
What Events Do People Remember?	248
Thinking Like a Psychologist About Memory	251

Chapter 7 Thought, Language, and Intelligence — 255

Concepts	257
Solving Problems	260
Representing the Problem	260
Mental Images	260
Mental Models	261
Generating Solutions	261
Trial and Error	261
Algorithms and Heuristics	262
Insight	263
"Blind Spots" in Problem Solving	264
Representation Failures	264
Mental Set	265
Functional Fixedness	265
The Confirmation Bias	265
The Representativeness Heuristic	266
The Availability Heuristic	267
Anchoring Effects	267
What's Your Prediction?	268
Language	269
Characteristics of Human Language	269
Semanticity	269
Generativity	270
Displacement	270
Emergence of Language	271
Developmental Sequence	271
Developmental Theories	272
The Relationship Between Thought and Language	273
The Linguistic-Relativity Hypothesis	273
Culture, Language, and the Way We Think	274
Intelligence	275
Intelligence Tests	275
The Stanford-Binet	276
The Wechsler Scales	277
Group Aptitude Tests	278

Are Intelligence Tests Accurate?	278
Are Intelligence Tests Biased?	280
The Nature of Intelligence	281
Crystallized and Fluid Intelligence	281
General Intelligence	282
Gardner's "Frames of Mind"	282
The Great Intelligence Debates	285
Nature and Nurture	386
The Racial Gap	388
Gender Differences	389
Education	293
The Self-Fulfilling Prophecy	293
Teacher Expectancies	293
Stereotype Threat	294
Thinking Like a Psychologist About Thought, Language, and Intelligence	296

Chapter 8   Personality   303

Psychoanalysis	307
The Birth of Psychoanalysis	307
Freud's Theory of Personality	308
The Unconscious	308
The Structure of Personality	309
Psychosexual Development	309
The Dynamics of Personality	312
Freud's Legacy	313
Neo-Freudian Theorists	313
Projective Personality Tests	315
Current Perspectives on Psychoanalysis	317
The Cognitive Social-Learning Approach	319
Principles of Learning and Behavior	319
Social-Learning Theory	321
Locus of Control	322
Self-Efficacy	324
Perspectives on Cognitive Social-Learning Theory	325
The Humanistic Approach	325
Carl Rogers	326
Rogers's Theory	326
Self-Esteem	327
What's Your Prediction?	330
Abraham Maslow	331
Maslow's Theory	331
The State of Self-Actualization	331
Perspectives on the Humanistic Approach	333
The Trait Approach	334
The Building Blocks of Personality	334
Construction of Multitrait Inventories	336
Introversion and Extraversion	338
Psychology Applied: Use of Personality Tests and Social Media Sites in Hiring	340
Perspectives: Do Traits Exist?	341
Thinking Like a Psychologist about Personality	342

Chapter 9   Life Span Development and Its Contexts   347

Genes	350
What Genes Are and How They Work	351
Genetic Building Blocks	352

Prenatal Development	353
The Growing Fetus	353
Germinal Stage	353
Embryonic Stage	354
Fetal Stage	354
Psychology Applied: How Does Alcohol Affect the Fetus?	355
Fertility	356
The Remarkable Newborn	357
Observing Infants	357
Reflexes	358
Sensory Capacities	358
Vision and Visual Preferences	358
Hearing and Auditory Preferences	360
Sensitivity to Number	360
The Infant and the Growing Child	361
Biological Development	362
Physical Growth	362
Motor Skills	362
Cognitive Development	362
Piaget's Theory	363
Piaget's Legacy	367
Social Development	368
Social-Cultural Influences on Cognitive Development	368
The Parent-Child Relationship	369
Peer Relationships	372
Adolescence	373
Puberty	374
Cognition and Moral Reasoning	375
Social and Personal Development	377
Parent Relationships	377
Peer Influences	379
Sexuality	380
Adulthood and Old Age	381
Physical Changes in Adulthood	381
The Adult Years	382
Old Age	382
Aging and Intellectual Functions	383
Memory and Forgetting	383
Alzheimer's Disease	384
Social and Personal Development	385
What's Your Prediction?	385
Ages and Stages of Adulthood	386
Critical Events of Adulthood	386
Changing Perspectives on Time	387
Dying and Death	388
Thinking Like a Psychologist About Life Span Development	388
Chapter 10 Social and Cultural Influences	**395**
Social Perception	398
Making Attributions	399
Attribution Theory	399
The Fundamental Attribution Error	399
Attributions as Cultural Constructions	400
Forming Impressions	401
Cognitive-Confirmation Biases	401
Behavioral-Confirmation Biases	402

Attraction	403
Similarity and Liking	403
Physical Attractiveness	404
Social Influence	**407**
Social Influence as "Automatic"	407
Conformity	408
The Early Classics	408
Majority Influence	410
Obedience to Authority	412
Attitude Change	414
Persuasive Communications	415
Cognitive Dissonance Theory	416
What's Your Prediction?	418
Psychology Applied: How Persuasion Fueled Fyre Festival	418
Group Processes	419
Social Facilitation	420
Social Loafing	420
Social Relations	**421**
Aggression	421
Biological Roots	422
Aversive Stimulation	423
Situational Cues	424
Altruism	426
Bystander Intervention	427
Cross-Cultural Perspectives	**431**
Cultural Diversity: A Fact of Life	432
Individualism and Collectivism: A Tale of Two Cultural Worldviews	433
Conceptions of the Self	434
Intergroup Discrimination	**435**
Stereotypes	436
Prejudice: The Motivational Roots	437
Realistic-Conflict Theory	438
Social-Identity Theory	438
Racism in America	439
The Problem	439
The Symptoms	440
The Intervention	443
Thinking Like a Psychologist About Social and Cultural Influences	444

Chapter 11 Motivation and Emotion   449

What Motivates Us?	**451**
General Theories of Motivation	452
Drive Theory	452
Arousal Theory	453
Incentive Theory	453
The Pyramid of Human Motivations	453
Basic Appetitive and Social Motives	**454**
Hunger and Eating	454
The Biological Component	455
Psychological Influences	456
What's Your Prediction?	457
Obesity	457
Eating Disorders	460
Belongingness Motives	461
The Need for Affiliation	461
The Need for Intimacy	462

Esteem Motives	462
The Need for Achievement	463
Psychology Applied: Finding Your Work-Health Balance	464
The Physiological Component of Emotion	**466**
A Historical Perspective	466
Brain Centers of Emotion	467
Generalized Autonomic Arousal	468
Specific Patterns of Arousal	469
The Expressive Component of Emotion	**470**
Nonverbal Communication	470
Sensory Feedback	472
The Cognitive Component of Emotion	**474**
Schachter's Two-Factor Theory of Emotion	475
Counterfactual Thinking	476
Is Cognition Necessary?	477
Human Emotion: Putting the Pieces Together	**479**
Types of Emotions	479
Are There Cultural Differences in Emotion?	480
Pleasure and the Pursuit of Happiness	481
The Roots of Happiness	481
Does Money Buy Happiness?	481
Thinking Like a Psychologist About Motivation and Emotion	483

Chapter 12   Health, Stress, and Wellness   489

Studying Health and Wellness	**491**
Illness-Wellness Continuum	492
Biopsychosocial and Biomedical Models	493
Health Belief Model	494
Illness Prevention and Health Promotion	495
Psychology Applied: Growing Up Transgender: When Is It Appropriate to Transition?	496
Mind Over Matter: The Placebo Effect	497
Stress and Health	**499**
Sources of Stress	501
Physiological Effects of Stress	503
The Stress Process	504
Types of Stressors	505
Effects of Stress	505
Personality Types and Stress	506
The Immune System	507
The Link Between Stress and the Immune Response	507
How Stress Impacts the Immune System	509
Coping With Stress	**511**
Coping Strategies	511
Problem-Focused and Emotion-Focused Coping	511
Relaxation	512
Physical Activity	513
The "Self-Healing Personality"	513
Hardiness	513
Optimism and Pessimism	514
Social Support	517
The Health Benefits of Social Support	517
What's Your Prediction?	518
Thinking Like a Psychologist About Health, Stress, and Wellness	519

Chapter 13 Psychological Disorders — 525

- Psychological Disorders: A General Outlook — 527
  - Defining Normal and Abnormal — 528
  - Models of Abnormality — 529
    - *Perspectives* — 529
    - *Combining Perspectives in a "Synthetic" Model* — 531
  - Diagnosis: A Necessary Step — 531
- Depressive Disorders — 533
  - Major Depressive Disorder — 534
  - Theories of Depression — 535
    - *Biological Factors* — 536
    - *Psychological Factors* — 537
    - *What's Your Prediction?* — 538
  - The Vicious Cycle of Depression — 538
  - Suicide — 539
- Anxiety Disorders — 540
  - Generalized Anxiety Disorder — 540
  - Panic Disorder — 541
  - Specific Phobia — 542
  - Social Anxiety Disorder — 544
  - Cultural Influences on Anxiety Disorders — 545
- Trauma- and Stressor-Related Disorders — 545
  - Posttraumatic Stress Disorder — 546
  - Theories of Posttraumatic Stress Disorder — 547
    - *Psychological History Factors* — 547
    - *Environment and Severity Factors* — 548
    - *Gender and Cultural Factors* — 548
- Obsessive-Compulsive and Related Disorders — 549
  - Obsessive-Compulsive Disorder — 549
  - Theories of Obsessive-Compulsive Disorder — 550
- Bipolar and Related Disorders — 552
  - Bipolar Disorder — 552
  - Theories of Bipolar and Related Disorders — 553
    - *Biological Factors* — 553
    - *Cognitive Factors* — 554
- Personality Disorders — 555
  - The Borderline Personality — 555
  - The Antisocial Personality — 556
  - Psychology Applied: The Insanity Defense — 557
- Schizophrenia Spectrum Disorders — 559
  - Symptoms of Schizophrenia Spectrum Disorders — 559
  - Theories of Schizophrenia Spectrum Disorders — 560
    - *Biological Factors* — 561
    - *Psychological Factors* — 562
- Dissociative Disorders — 563
  - Dissociative Amnesia — 563
  - Dissociative Identity Disorder — 564
  - Thinking Like a Psychologist About Psychological Disorders — 566

Chapter 14 Treatment and Interventions — 573

- Psychological Therapies — 576
  - Psychoanalytic Therapies — 577
    - *Orthodox Psychoanalysis* — 577
    - *Brief Psychoanalytic Therapies* — 580

Controversies in Psychoanalysis	580
Psychology Applied: Putting Repressed Memories on Trial	580
Behavioral Therapies	582
Classical Conditioning Techniques	582
Operant Conditioning Techniques	575
Eye Movement Desensitization and Reprocessing Therapy	588
Cognitive Therapies	589
Rational-Emotive Behavior Therapy	589
Beck's Cognitive Therapy	589
Cognitive-Behavioral Therapies	591
Schizophrenia and Cognitive-Behavioral Therapy	592
Humanistic Therapies	593
Person-Centered Therapy	593
Gestalt Therapy	593
Group-Therapy Approaches	595

Perspectives on Psychotherapy — 597

The Bottom Line: Does Psychotherapy Work?	597
Are Some Therapies Better Than Others?	598
What Are the Active Ingredients?	599
A Supportive Relationship	599
A Ray of Hope	600
An Opportunity to Open Up	600
What's Your Prediction?	600
What's the Future of Psychotherapy?	601
Eclectic Approach	601
Empirical Support	601
Treatment and Technology	602

Medical Interventions — 603

Drug Therapies	603
Antianxiety Drugs	603
Antidepressants	605
Mood Stabilizers	606
Antipsychotic Drugs	606
Perspectives on Drug Therapies	607
Electroconvulsive Therapy	608
Psychosurgery	608
Thinking Like a Psychologist About Treatment and Interventions	609

Appendix: Statistics in Psychology — A-1

Descriptive Statistics	A-1
What We Know About Data and Why It Is Important	A-1
Continuous and Discrete Data	A-3
Quantitative and Qualitative Data	A-3
Scales of Measurement	A-4
Why Summarize Data?	A-5
Frequency Distributions: Tables and Graphs	A-7
Frequency Distribution Tables	A-8
Frequency Distribution Graphs	A-9
Measures of Central Tendency	A-9
Mean	A-10
Median	A-10
Mode	A-11
Measures of Variability	A-11
Range	A-11
Variance	A-12
Standard Deviation	A-13

Graphing Means and Correlations	A-13
Graphing Group Means	A-14
Graphing Correlations	A-14
Ethics in Focus: Deception Due to the Distortion of Data	A-14
Inferential Statistics	**A-16**
What Are We Making Inferences About?	A-16
Null Hypothesis Significance Testing	A-16
Using the Criterion and Test Statistic to Make a Decision	A-17
Illustrating NHST: The Courtroom Analogy	A-18
Types of Error and Power	A-19
Decision: Retain the Null Hypothesis	A-20
Decision: Reject the Null Hypothesis	A-20
Parametric Tests: Applying the Decision Tree	A-20
t Tests and ANOVAs	A-21
Correlation and Regression	A-21
Nonparametric Tests: Applying the Decision Tree	A-22
Tests for Ordinal Data	A-22
Nonparametric Alternatives to Pearson r	A-23
Tests for Nominal (Categorical) Data	A-23
Effect Size: How Big Is an Effect in the Population?	A-24
Cohen's d	A-25
Proportion of Variance: η^2, R^2	A-25
Proportion of Variance: Cramer's V	A-26
Estimation: What Are the Possible Values of a Parameter?	A-26
Ethics in Focus: Full Disclosure of Data	A-27
Glossary	**G-1**
References	**R-1**
Name Index	**I-1**
Subject Index	**I-5**

ESSENTIAL. EXPERIENTIAL. ENGAGING.

Essentials of Psychology propels students into a clear, vibrant understanding of psychological science through concise explanations, real-life examples, and active practice. Introductory psychology may be a student's first exposure to the scientific method—or a step toward a career in the field. This book takes an integrative approach that meets individuals where they are and builds from there. Inside, you'll find:

- **What's Your Prediction?**—Clear accounts of classic or recent studies in each chapter invite you to take on the role of subject, experimenter, or observer, placing yourself into the details of each study and predicting results.

- **Psychology Experiment Exercise videos**—These videos bring to life classic studies so that you can discover, question, and experience psychological research methods and findings first-hand.

- **Concepts in Action videos**—More than a break from reading, these videos clarify and reinforce important foundational concepts and provide opportunities for greater critical synthesis.

- **Spaced, embedded study aids**—Visual and contextual learning hints empower classroom success and stronger critical thinking.

PREFACE TO THE STUDENT

WHAT'S YOUR PREDICTION? Can a better understanding of psychology change your life? Whether you're an aspiring psychologist or pursuing a different career, we believe the answer is yes. Technology is constantly moving the needle for how we live, interact, and engage. Greater access to information, virtual communication, and social media gives each of us more opportunities to connect. Psychology helps illuminate the forces driving our need to make those connections.

Hashtags like #MeToo, #WhyIStayed, #BlackLivesMatter, and #GivingTuesday bring to light not only the differences between us but also the aspects of human behavior that unite us. By immersing yourself in the principles of psychology, you can discover not only how these principles apply to your own life but also how they impact the world in which we live.

With psychology entering its third century as a formal discipline, we could easily offer you a huge text, piling new theories and discoveries on old ones from psychology's historical warehouse. Instead, we've tried to balance efficiency with depth of coverage that highlights the defining and distinguishing features of the field.

Think Like a Psychologist

Our primary goal with this book is to develop your ability to think critically about the human experience—in other words, to think like a psychologist.

If you look globally at countries, economies, and businesses, or more personally at marriages, partners, families, individuals, and even yourself, the world in which we live is really an interaction among people—a shared lived experience. Understanding the nature of this experience requires context and critical thinking. To that end, this material provides:

- **Historical connections.** Important moments in psychology, like the emergence of psychoanalysis as a behavioral therapy and the Jane Doe case study of repression that made it to the California Supreme Court, help you see how the field has evolved and grown.

- **Real people, real lives.** We introduce you to everyday people and stories in ways that help you constantly evaluate the lived experience of being human. Examples include a heroic first responder who was Muslim, an upper-middle-class family that was close to homelessness, and many more. These introductions help you see the world from many perspectives and think critically about your own place in it.

- **Behind the headlines.** The content is peppered with news stories ranging from politics and law to sports and entertainment. You'll see how athletes like Serena Williams, celebrities like Carrie Fisher, everyday people like Louise Ogborn, and social media are helping to reshape society's perception of issues such as pregnancy, mental health, coercion, and the field itself.

- **First-hand predictions.** Have you ever heard about a story and wondered if there was more to it? Or predicated an outcome and then checked it against what actually happened? This material presents you with frequent opportunities to make your own predictions, just as a psychologist would, about cases, examples, and ground-breaking scientific studies. The more you practice, the sharper your critical skills will become.

Embrace Experimentation

We hope you will embrace trial and error as part of your psychology journey. Research methods are central to psychology's identity as a science. The "data" or information we have—regarding psychological disorders, the impact of chemistry on behavior, how and why we feel, what stress does to the body, methods of persuasion, and other phenomena—is thanks to the deliberate task of testing predictions and building theories using the scientific method.

As those test results are revealed, they build on one another to present a more thorough understanding of psychology and human behavior. However, those cumulative effects are never static. Some ideas prove to be outdated or incorrect—like the perpetuated myth of gender-based cognitive performance. When an accumulation of science says otherwise, we must move forward and adapt better theories. This quest for better theories is why psychology is dynamic. This research process is introduced and fully presented in the first chapter.

See Yourself in the Field

Another goal is to connect with you as fellow members of a diverse and inclusive society. We believe that race, gender, sexual orientation, and socioeconomic status are crucial factors in how the field of psychology has evolved and where it needs to go. Therefore, we seek to address our own implicit biases and illustrate relevant events and developments, such as diversity and inclusion efforts in business. We feel that all this, and so much more, is worth talking about to support our goal of diversity and inclusion in the classroom and in the world.

Furthermore, we understand you want meaningful employment. The good news is, psychology has a lot to offer your career. Psychology majors thrive in many different settings, including human resources, teaching, research, sales, sports, marketing, social media, the arts, and law enforcement. In fact, can you name more than a few jobs where an understanding of human behavior won't serve you? To better prepare you for your job hunt, coverage in this material aims to demonstrate how useful psychology is in the workforce. For example, psychology plays an integral role in helping employees find their work-life balance, assisting employers with conducting interviews that can reveal promising applicants, and developing skills that translate into effective leadership, teamwork, and motivation.

Diversity, Equity, and Inclusion

As educators, authors, and people, we strive to celebrate diversity and practice inclusivity. Therefore, reflecting current research, we share a range of experiences, and use considerate language, including careful consideration for how we discuss sex, gender, ability, race, ethnicity, and other valued factors. Psychology is the study of human behavior—a topic we should all feel connected to. In this light, we are dedicated to presenting psychological science in a manner that allows all students to be represented and respected. As inclusive language and vocabulary evolve with our understanding of psychology, so also will our materials in subsequent editions.

You are the reason authors like us do what we do. Thank you for this incredible opportunity to connect with you and introduce you to psychology.

PREFACE TO THE INSTRUCTOR

WHAT'S YOUR PREDICTION? Can the right course material transform your classroom and improve learning outcomes?

We believe so. That's why we've built a product that solves common teaching challenges and sets students up for success. We packed it with examples students can sink their teeth into, activities to get them thinking like psychologists, and lessons learned—not just by us, but from some of the biggest names in the field. Then we refined each element, incorporating feedback from instructors, students, and specialists who are as passionate about psychology as we are. In addition to being mindful of our own implicit biases throughout the writing process, we engaged a diversity and inclusion specialist to read, validate, and strengthen each chapter.

The result: an objective, classic, and mainstream look at psychology today.

Remarkably Current

Included are discussions of the most recent work on the effects of racism, the value of diversity, awareness of implicit bias, challenges with fertility, the opioid crisis, domestic and international terrorism, public health crises such as global obesity and the coronavirus, equity and equality, wellness, the role of technology in our everyday lives, and even the relevance of psychology in politics.

As academics, we also strive to meaningfully integrate research and practice. Our choices are inspired and steered by the scholarship of teaching and learning research that empirically demonstrates the need for change in what is presented to students. For example, Ferguson, Brown, and Torres (2016) expressed concern with the myths and false stories published in texts such as the story that no one tried to help Kitty Genovese. Rodkey's (2015) historical work revealed that the visual cliff experiment as written in so many texts eliminated important pieces. We take a critical and deep dive into the psychological literature and further recognize and discuss findings, once accepted, that have since been debunked.

Refreshingly Practical

Psychology has a far-reaching impact across several careers, which is one reason an introductory psychology course is available to, and often required by, all majors at the college level. Therefore, in this content we aim to demonstrate the value of psychology, not only for its application in your students' lives but also in their careers.

Psychology majors will find references to organizational psychology, forensic psychology, educational and school psychology, clinical psychology, sports psychology, health psychology, and other exciting fields within the discipline.

Nonmajors will discover how psychology can have an impact on almost any career they might pursue. Search the latest job postings and you'll find calls for critical thinking, effective communication, strategic decision-making, and the ability to collaborate and work in diverse groups and settings. This content emphasizes the cultivation of these skills, benefiting students of all interests and experience levels.

Packed With Special Features

It is our goal to help you cultivate critical thinking, empowering each student to learn to think like a psychologist. To achieve this, we put much thought into features, organization, and readability. We added pedagogical elements designed to get readers questioning, reflecting, and discussing. Here are a few features we're most excited about:

- **What's Your Prediction?** Chapter openers describe a classic or contemporary psychological study and ask the student to predict the results. The results are then revealed, followed by a brief discussion. This activity, more than any other we have tried in the classroom, gets students to think critically about research methods and their own assumptions about human behavior.

- **Psychology Applied.** These spotlight some of the most exciting work being done in areas of health, education, law, sports, and current events, enabling students to see the relevance of psychology as an active participant.

- **Video Enrichment.** Bite-sized videos support understanding and the applications of foundational studies and concepts.
  - **Psychology Experiment Exercises** allows students to learn about experiments such as Gibson's Visual Cliff and Bandura's social learning theory, helping them understand the real-world significance and application of these well-known experiments.
  - **Concept in Action** dig deeper into tough concepts, such as differentiating between classical and operant conditioning, difficult biological functions, and types of stress.

- **Try This!** activities guide students through mini-experiments so that they can test intriguing psychological phenomena for themselves. For instance, the "Primacy Effect" activity provides materials to test how something as simple as the order of words can impact our attitudes toward a stranger.

- Periodic **Learning Checks** in each chapter enable students to review their knowledge by quizzing themselves on the material in a variety of formats, such as matching, sorting, recall, ordering, multiple-choice, and true-or-false.

- **Thinking Like a Psychologist** sections at the end of each chapter prompt students to assume the role of psychologist, considering scientific questions, a summary of related findings, challenging readers to critically consider key theories, studies, and pertinent contextual factors.

Organization

We believe the relationship between psychology and everyday life should be a part of every chapter's conversation. Therefore, we highlight mainstream and classical psychological topics in each chapter. You will notice these highlights throughout the content and in our "Psychology Applied" features, where real-world topics and issues in psychology are connected to content. As a team of authors committed to culture and diversity, we weave cross-cultural and diversity issues into the narrative. Some of the discussions we hope these highlights will spark include mental health in American Indians, wellness disparities in Black Americans versus White Americans, the need for wellness initiatives to support employees' work-life balance, and intimate partner violence toward men.

CHAPTER 1: PSYCHOLOGY AND ITS METHODS

In this chapter, we take a journey through the rich, albeit brief, history of psychology and how the field has evolved, particularly over the past few decades. Students are exposed to a range of perspectives and see how psychology has matured as a discipline. Also covered is the scaffolding that supports knowledge creation in psychology: science. Many introductory textbooks separate the introduction of psychology from its methods of inquiry, often presented in a parenthetical second chapter. We take a more integrated approach that presents psychology's research methods as part and parcel of its history, development, and current identity as a science.

- Explore how psychology can be applied across disciplines and professions.
- Take a deep dive into the science behind peaceful protests and why they turn violent.
- Gain a broad perspective of the science of psychology, to increase research methods fluency.

CHAPTER 2: BEHAVIORAL NEUROSCIENCE

In this chapter, we look inside the *person* to explore the biology and neuroscience that underlies behavior. Incredibly to some, behavior is possible due to the unique structure and function of our nervous system. Electrical potentials releasing chemicals from one cell to another at incredible speeds allow us to move, think, talk, and feel emotions. We take a first-person approach in this chapter to show not only what the nervous system is but also how it works, and why this is important to understanding the psychology of human behavior.

- Explore the structure of a neuron and how it allows us to think, act, learn, and behave.
- Learn the implications for a remarkable feature of the human brain: Each hemisphere of the brain is an exact copy of itself.
- Take a deeper look at the science of concussions and how psychology contributes to establishing safety protocols for professional athletes.

CHAPTER 3: SENSATION AND PERCEPTION

In this chapter, we delve into the parts of human biology that allow us to sense the world around us, and the experiences we need to process and understand those senses. Like many psychological phenomena, it is a combination of nature and nurture that empowers a person to recognize depth, locate an object solely based on sound, or connect a favorite food with its aroma. We also proceed with care to expose you to important reasons not to take the senses for granted.

- Investigate the intricacies of the eye, ear, nose, and tongue to learn how each unique type of cell collaborates to produce a neural signal.
- Recognize the importance of taking better care of the delicate hair cells of the inner ear; once we lose them, they never return.
- Experience the tricks our brains can play on us by trying out optical illusions, and then learn why they work.

CHAPTER 4: CONSCIOUSNESS

In this chapter, we explore the nature of our awareness of ourselves: consciousness. We begin with a look at attention and just how much processing goes on in the brain each moment, beyond our awareness. We then turn to ways that we alter our consciousness, from sleep and dreaming to hypnosis to drug use. We explore not only the importance of sleep but also how sleep relates to changes in our levels of consciousness. We take a critical look at the controversy surrounding the responsiveness we have during hypnosis and how drugs (legal and illegal) can alter our consciousness and our behavior.

- Explore how and why we dream, and whether dreams have meaning.
- Investigate the controversy of hypnosis and whether it can enhance eyewitness testimony.
- Learn about the effects of consciousness-altering drugs and their effects on our thoughts and behaviors.

CHAPTER 5: LEARNING

In this chapter, we discover one of the most remarkable aspects of human behavior: our ability to learn and adapt to a changing world. We explore many of the foundational theories in learning, which include those introduced by three of the most famous psychologists of the 20th century: Ivan Pavlov (and his dogs), B. F. Skinner (and his cages), and Albert Bandura (and his dolls). We look at the process of learning, how it affects behavior, and the ways in which learning applies to all aspects of our lives—especially in a world so closely connected through social media and the Internet.

- Explore how the immune system can be trained to be more responsive.
- Take a deep dive into the effectiveness (or lack thereof?) of punishment.
- See what a classic study of children abusing a doll taught researchers about how we learn from observation.

CHAPTER 6: MEMORY

In this chapter, we tackle something both frustrating and rewarding: memory. Our discussion covers foundations of current knowledge about memory, what we know about memory failures, and lessons learned from a world-famous patient by the name of Henry Molaison. From pills to mnemonics to simply paying attention, we consider the valid and invalid methods for memory improvement. Memory is a huge part of who we are, and we rely on it greatly. But relying on it can sometimes lead to consequences like the incarceration of Ronald Cotton, an innocent man. The problem is that we usually don't know when our memories are faulty; this chapter explains why.

- Learn about the importance of connecting our current memories with new memories we are trying to make.
- Understand different types of memory loss and how we can create false memories without even knowing it.
- Connect certain parts of the brain with memory storage and retrieval.

CHAPTER 7: THOUGHT, LANGUAGE, AND INTELLIGENCE

In this chapter, we bring together biology, environment, culture, and racial bias to present a unified understanding of the ways we think, how we speak, and our intelligence. We cover stages of development and how humans harness language to express themselves. Culture greatly influences the language we fluently speak, which in turn can impact our scores on an IQ test. Thus, we examine how psychologists are working to remove cultural bias from intelligence tests, better understand languages of different cultures, and tap into the decision-making process.

- Put problem-solving skills to the test with mind-bender exercises.
- Recognize the history of intelligence testing and how tests of the past are different from those of today.
- Understand the pieces of language that allow us to communicate complex thoughts.

CHAPTER 8: PERSONALITY

In this chapter, we focus on the many unique traits that make us who we are. From extraverted to introverted, we introduce the personality tests that are scientifically valid, and some that—perhaps surprisingly—aren't. The journey begins with Freud, where we learn about his theories of why we act the way we do. To appreciate how his theories still influence us today, we look at examples such as the case of Nicole Kluemper's repressed memories. This chapter also dissects other famous theories of personality, to provide a better understanding of the need for diverse perspectives about the field.

- Connect Freud's theory of personality with current events.
- Recognize a scientifically supported personality test.
- Learn about the benefits of personality tests and social network sites in the hiring process.

CHAPTER 9: LIFE SPAN DEVELOPMENT AND ITS CONTEXTS

In this chapter, we follow development from the miracle of birth to the psychological effects of aging and death. We begin with the growth of a fetus and explore complications that can arise with fertility (that is, the ability to reproduce). We take a deep look at early milestones, from the sensory abilities of a newborn to the language development of a child. In addition, we consider development from multiple viewpoints, including biological, cognitive, and social perspectives. We follow human development through death to see not only how we cope with aging but also how we thrive as we age.

- Explore how a fetus is capable of learning, even before birth.
- Take an honest look at fertility and the complications women experience.
- Learn not only how we cope with aging but also how we can thrive during this stage of life.

CHAPTER 10: SOCIAL AND CULTURAL INFLUENCES

In this chapter, we tackle some of the most difficult questions about human nature—one of which is, if humans are so similar, why do we see each other as so different? We present an array of scientific explanations to address racism, aggression, beauty standards, belongingness, and diversity. To provide important lessons learned from social psychology, we discuss classic studies, like Milgram's obedience experiment, and current ones, such as Bushman's investigation of TV violence and its connection with aggression. Furthermore, this chapter applies the principles of persuasion to social media advertising to demonstrate how the everyday person can be misled.

- Recognize the power of groups on thoughts and behavior.
- Connect social psychology's theories to current issues such as racism, medical care, and altruism.
- Understand why we stereotype and why we make false assumptions about others, and how to correct these behaviors.

CHAPTER 11: MOTIVATION AND EMOTION

In this chapter, we ask questions about why we do what we do and how we feel. Why do we eat foods that are not healthy for us? How can we gain control of our emotions? What strategies can we use? We use many foundational theories to introduce concepts related to hunger and fullness, feelings of belongingness and esteem, and expressing and thinking about our emotions. An appreciation of how culture and society influence us, and how we express emotion, helps us develop a more nuanced worldview.

- Explore the widely applied hierarchy of needs model developed by Abraham Maslow.
- Apply strategies we can use to find an elusive work-life balance.
- Follow the science on how we can realize our pursuit of happiness.

CHAPTER 12: STRESS, HEALTH, AND WELLNESS

In this chapter, we explore the illness-wellness continuum, which reveals the state of our health at any given moment. How we prioritize our health is important whether or not we are sick. We examine health behaviors across contexts—times of healthiness, illness, living through a pandemic, and even facing the reality of death. We take a further look at how stress affects health, and how the body naturally responds to it. Strategies for coping with stress and the benefits of social support during stressful times are also discussed from a cultural perspective.

- Explore the health belief model to understand why so many people disregarded public health guidelines during the coronavirus pandemic.
- Look at how the body's natural response to stress is healthy when stress is managed well over time.
- Gain insights into what it is like to grow up transgender and the complexities of transitioning.

CHAPTER 13: PSYCHOLOGICAL DISORDERS

In this chapter, we present and discuss eight major psychological disorders. Environmental, biological, and cultural contributors to psychological disorders are included to demonstrate their complexity. We attempt to remove the stigma from disorders such as depression, anxiety, and personality disorders by showing that they are common and that people who live with them—such as Mariah Carey, Pete Davidson, Ariana Grande, and Dr. Kay Redfield Jamison—can thrive. For those who have misconceptions about the role of psychological disorders in the courts, we provide a discussion of the insanity defense.

- Learn about the *DSM-5* symptoms of some major psychological disorders, and how common it is to experience them.
- Recognize the variables that contribute to the development of a psychological disorder.
- Apply what we know about psychological disorders to real examples of people who thrived and continue to thrive.

CHAPTER 14: TREATMENT AND INTERVENTIONS

In this chapter, we debunk the myth that all therapies and therapists are the same by introducing readers to a range of treatments and interventions. Dr. Eleanor Longden's true story of schizophrenia and cognitive-behavioral therapy offers a personal perspective on the importance of how we think about our experiences. However, we do not shy away from the controversies in the history of psychological treatment. We plainly ask, does psychotherapy work? If so, what are the winning ingredients? To illuminate the roles that culture, support, medicine, and accessible care play in mental wellness, we provide research on diverse populations, pharmaceuticals, client-to-practitioner rapport, and technology.

- Realize the need for psychological treatment and those who can provide it.
- Differentiate between types of treatment, and compare theoretical approaches.
- Learn how to find the right therapist using empirically based suggestions, and embrace the change that can come with treatments and interventions.

STATISTICAL APPENDIX

In this appendix, we survey the essentials of statistics, both descriptive and inferential. We reveal how psychologists crunch the numbers, enabling you to better evaluate the analyses behind many sales and marketing claims. A key aim of this appendix is to reinforce that you do not need to be a scientist to appreciate what you learn in this book. *Science* is all around us—for this reason, being a critical consumer of the information we come across each day is useful and necessary across professions.

- Learn about data and its usefulness in psychological research.
- Explore how researchers measure and summarize data to make sense of it.
- Gain insights into how researchers leverage statistics to make decisions about their observations.

ACKNOWLEDGMENTS

In a time of uncertainty, it was a tremendous gift to benefit from the unwavering dedication of incredibly talented people. Our SAGE team has been nothing short of brilliant, supportive, and compassionate. From Josh Perigo to Reid Hester to Katherine Hepburn, the journey has been filled with opportunities to take risks, address challenges, and be better educators. In particular, we wish to thank Lara Parra and Emma Newsom, who will forever be the scaffolding that supports the brick and mortar of this monumental build—the first of its kind at SAGE.

This book is an example of what it means to stand on the shoulders of giants. None of us would be here today without the efforts and risks of those who came before us to legitimize and question the field of psychological science. Dr. Saul Kassin, our leading author, is one such giant. Thank you, Saul, for trusting this team with your creation of curated knowledge.

To our students, past and present, we would not be successful pedagogues or authors without your bravery, inquisitiveness, and participation. You have shared your experiences, asked for numerous examples, posited questions we couldn't answer, forced us to grow, and, as a result, taught us more than you could imagine. May you always love the lifelong process of learning as much as we will always love the lifelong process of teaching.

From Dr. Kassin: In a 1982 issue of the *American Psychologist*, Albert Bandura wrote one of my all-time favorite articles. Titled "The Psychology of Chance Encounters and Life Paths," his thesis pertains to us all: No matter how hard we try to plot the future, our life trajectories are shaped by chance encounters. The take-home message: Be vigilant and brace for those *carpe diem* opportunities that come along.

For me, three mentors provided those opportunities. At Brooklyn College in the 1970s, I took a summer class on the history of psychology. Afterward, Arthur S. Reber, the professor, invited me to join his lab. Although the term *cognitive psychology* was brand new, he was forging into the cognitive unconscious against a behaviorist tide. Running subjects in his lab was electrifying; watching them learn an artificial grammar through mere exposure to letter strings, without awareness, stayed with me.

Riveted by the "orange attribution book" titled *Attribution: Perceiving the Causes of Behavior*, I entered the social psychology program at the University of Connecticut, where I was lucky enough to get adopted by attribution expert, teacher extraordinaire, and friend, Charles "Skip" Lowe. His guidance was immeasurable. Together, we published papers that served as a foundation for everything I have done since.

Then I accepted a postdoctoral research fellowship at the University of Kansas to work with Larry Wrightsman, newly funded to study jury decision-making. With my interest in attribution, the application to juries was a perfect fit. And Larry was the perfect mentor—prolific, boundless in his curiosity, and focused on matters of social justice. Together we explored the yet-to-be science of false confessions.

Having spent 35 years at a liberal arts college, I am secretly a teacher at heart—which is why the opportunity to bring forth this content with Greg and Krisstal, two talented teachers and writers, was one of those opportunities I could not pass up. I am thankful to SAGE for bringing us all together.

From Dr. Privitera: It cannot be understated how incredibly grateful I am to all those at SAGE who have supported and guided my development as an author for over a dozen years. Your contributions are immeasurable.

In no particular order, I also want to thank my family. To my wife, Alisha, for her love and support; my mother, Donna, for her resilient example of faith; my father, James, for his strength and positive spirit; my twin brother, Andrew, for being there for me from the beginning—I couldn't imagine this life without you; my sister, Rachel, who gracefully survived childhood with four brothers; my brother Stephen, whose work ethic has largely inspired my own; and my brother Joseph, who was in the gym with me every day as I prepared for Marine Corps boot camp many years ago—he was only five!

To my sons, Aiden Andrew (18) and Luca James (1), and my daughter, Grace Ann (14)—every moment I am with you is the greatest moment of my life. I often teach that confidence in the absence of humility is arrogance. It is in those moments that I share with my children that I find my humility each day.

As a veteran, I also want to thank all those who serve and have served—being a U.S. Marine was an experience that inevitably shaped my character and instilled in me the belief that there is no greater honor than to serve something greater than yourself. Semper Fi!

From Dr. Clayton: To my friend and forever mentor, Dr. David Trafimow, who believed in me like no other. During the past 18 years, you have taught me several valuable lessons, including the following: Approach teaching and science from the perspective of a third grader. Expect the best from people until they prove otherwise. Science is supposed to be fun. If it stops being fun, then you should stop engaging with science. Always look at the big picture first. When in doubt, choose integrity, music, and food. The best measure of an academic's success is the happiness and success of their students. Question everything. David, to know you is to embrace the beauty of wonder, the realization of not knowing, and the possibility of finding the answer all in the same breath. Here's to our innovation of science and teaching. May it be filled with long conversations and laughter for many years to come.

To my mother, Ladona; my dad, Mark; my brother, Joe; and my sweet canine companions, Phoebe and Arya. Thank you for the lessons in unconditional love, forgiveness, choosing words wisely, that no job is beneath me, and to keep dreaming big.

Thank you to the advisory board for *Essentials of Psychology*, First edition. We learn so much from your expertise, and we value your time and insights:

Amy Button, Alfred University
Bobby Hiep Bui, State University of New York, New Paltz
Jennifer Butler, Case Western Reserve University
Debra Hollister, Valencia Community College
Elgrie Hurd III, Brookhaven Community College
Stephanie Jimenez, University of Pittsburgh, Johnstown
Rachel Laimon, Mott Community College
Christine Lofgren, University of California, Irvine
Lynda Mae, Arizona State University
Dorothy Marsil, Kennesaw State University
Gregory Repasky, Texas Christian University
Sheldon H. Rifkin, Kennesaw State University
Tambra Riggs-Gutiérrez, Longwood University
Wendy Valentine, Ellsworth Community College
Brian J. Wiley, Florida State College, Jacksonville
Chrysalis L. Wright, University of Central Florida

SAGE also wishes to thank the following reviewers for their many contributions to the development of this book. You taught us so much, for which we are grateful:

Pilar Galiana Abal, Ottawa University
Angela Adame-Smith, Palm Beach State College
Viara Agars, California State University San Bernardino
Janet N. Ahn, William Paterson University
Debra Ahola, Schenectady County Community College
Christopher Alas, Houston Community College
William S. Altman, SUNY Broome Community College
Benjamin Anderson, SUNY Broome Community College
Roxanna Anderson, Palm Beach State College
Tessa Anderson, Idaho State University
Jaime M. Ascencio, Colorado State University
Elaine Augustine, Texas Christian University
Kevin S. Autry, California State Polytechnic University, Pomona
Marina Baratian, Eastern Florida State College

David Baskind, Delta College
Shane W. Bench, Utah State University Eastern
Deshanda Blair, Collin College
Debi Brannan, Western Oregon University
Alicia Briganti, Dalton State College
Salena Brody, University of Texas, Dallas
Allison Buskirk-Cohen, Delaware Valley University
Marguerite Capone, The University of Rhode Island
Jessica Carnevale, Purchase College, SUNY
Ellen Carpenter, Virginia Commonwealth University
Ken Carr, Northcentral University
Abigail J. Caselli, Syracuse University
Doreen Collins-McHugh, Seminole State College
W. Matthew Collins, Nova Southeastern University
Alita Cousins, Eastern Connecticut State University
Carmen M. Culotta, Wright State University
Nidal Daou, McNeese State University
Chris De La Ronde, Austin Community College
David Devonis, Graceland University
Theresa DiDonato, Loyola University Maryland
Stephanie B. Ding, Del Mar College
Camille Drake-Brassfield, Florida SouthWestern State College
Kerry Evans, Onondaga Community College
Rebecca Ewing, Western New Mexico University
Sue Fenstermacher, University of Vermont
Lisa Fozio-Thielk, Waubonsee Community College
Nathalie Franco, Broward College
Perry N. Fuchs, University of Texas at Arlington
Courtney L. Gosnell, Pace University
Carmela V. Gottesman, University of South Carolina, Salkehatchie
Christine L. Grela, McHenry County College
Mary T. Guerrant, State University of New York, Cobleskill
Tiffany Hardy, Florida State University
Haley N. Harris, University of Texas at Arlington

Michael Himle, University of Utah
Mark Holden, University of Nebraska, Lincoln
Robert S. Hoople, Bethune-Cookman University
Lourdes Humble, Broward College
Todd Allen Joseph, Hillsborough Community College
Kevin Keating, Broward College
Tabitha Kirkland, University of Washington
Andrew Knapp, Finger Lakes Community College
Samantha Kohn, Orange County Community College
Lauren Kois, University of Alabama
Dana Kuehn, Florida State College at Jacksonville
Shannon M. A. Kundey, Hood College
Don C. Larson, Utah State University
Juliana Leding, University of North Florida
Marvin W. Lee, Tennessee State University
Kristin Leimgruber, Franklin & Marshall College
Alison Levitch, County College of Morris
Mary M. Lewis, Columbus State Community College
Regina Luce-Hughes, Collin College
Karenna Malavanti, Baylor University
Nicole Martin, Kennesaw State University
Steven McCloud, Borough of Manhattan Community College
Tracy Meyer, Collin College
Kendra Miller, Anoka-Ramsey Community College
Greg Mullin, Bunker Hill Community College
Angela L. Nadeau, University of South Carolina, Columbia
Angela M. Neal, University of South Carolina, Lancaster
Vias Chris Nicolaides, George Mason University
LeighAnn Ostrowsky-Leonard, Valencia College
Cari J. Paterno, William Rainey Harper College

Michaela Porubanova, Farmingdale State College
Carolynn Pravatta, Collin College
Cynthia Prehar, Framingham State
Ellen Ratajack, Colorado State University
Clayton T. Ryan, Bunker Hill Community College
Genevieve Ryan, Bay Path University
Beverly Salzman, University of New Haven
Teresa Segelken, Coastal Carolina Community College
Dylan Selterman, University of Maryland
Melonie W. Sexton, Valencia College
Richard Shadick, Pace University
Shubam Sharma, University of Florida
Michelle Slattery, North Central State College
Kimberly Nelms Smarr, Houston Baptist University
Stephanie Smith, LaGrange College
Jennifer Spychalski, College of Charleston
Gillian S. Starkey, Goucher College
Melissa Streeter, University of North Carolina at Wilmington
Bradley Thurmond, Ivy Tech Community College
Angela Vergara, Valencia College
Kristie Veri, William Paterson University
Jovana Vukovic, Broward College
Naomi Wagner, San Jose State University
Christopher Walker, Santa Fe College
Christopher Warren, Utah State University
Manda Williamson, University of Nebraska, Lincoln
Theresa Wise, SUNY Empire State College
John Woodman, Nashville State Community College
Chit Yuen Yi, Florida International University

ABOUT THE AUTHORS

Saul Kassin is a Distinguished Professor of Psychology at John Jay College of Criminal Justice and Massachusetts Professor Emeritus at Williams College. Born and raised in New York City, he graduated from Brooklyn College in 1974. After receiving his PhD in personality and social psychology from the University of Connecticut in 1978, he spent time at the University of Kansas, Purdue University, the Federal Judicial Center, and Stanford University. He is an author or editor of several books—including *Social Psychology, Developmental Social Psychology, The American Jury on Trial*, and *The Psychology of Evidence and Trial Procedure*.

Interested in the psychological causes and consequences of wrongful convictions, Dr. Kassin pioneered the scientific study of false confessions. His work is cited all over the world—including by the U.S. Supreme Court. He has received several awards—including the APA Award for Distinguished Contribution to Research on Public Policy (2017) and the APS James McKeen Cattell Lifetime Achievement Award for Applied Research (2021). He has consulted on many high-profile cases, served as an analyst on all major news networks, and appeared in several podcasts and documentaries—including Ken Burns's film *The Central Park Five* (2012). Away from work, Dr. Kassin has an insatiable appetite for family, music, travel, and ethnic food.

Gregory J. Privitera is a professor of psychology at St. Bonaventure University, where he is a recipient of its highest teaching honor, the Award for Professional Excellence in Teaching, and its highest honor for scholarship, the Award for Professional Excellence in Research and Publication. He received his PhD in behavioral neuroscience in the field of psychology from the State University of New York at Buffalo and continued with his postdoctoral research at Arizona State University. He is a national award–winning author and research scholar. His textbooks span diverse topics in psychology and the behavioral sciences, including two introductory psychology texts (one upcoming), four statistics texts, two research methods texts, and multiple other texts bridging knowledge creation across health, health care, and well-being. In addition, he has authored more than three dozen peer-reviewed papers aimed at advancing our understanding of health and well-being. His research has earned recognition by the American Psychological Association and in media and the press, including in *O, The Oprah Magazine, Time* magazine, and the *Wall Street Journal*. In addition to his teaching, research, and advisement, Dr. Privitera is a veteran of the U.S. Marine Corps, is an identical twin, and is married with three children: a daughter, Grace Ann, and two sons, Aiden Andrew and Luca James.

Krisstal D. Clayton is a clinical associate professor and the director of undergraduate programs for the Department of Psychology at the University of North Texas. She received her PhD from New Mexico State University in 2009 under the advisement of Dr. David Trafimow. Her faculty career began at Western Kentucky University, where she received the College of Education and Behavioral Sciences Excellence in Teaching Award in 2015. She is passionate about pedagogy, and regularly provides invited talks and workshops about teaching. As a professor, Dr. Clayton is a student favorite known for her gamification techniques, storytelling, and application of fascinating real-world examples to psychology, many of which you will see in this book. Her research regularly includes student involvement and authorship, as she has supervised several student research projects, including those of National Science Foundation REU scholars. Her current research addresses shifts in perspectives as a result of higher education. She is a consulting editor for the *Journal of General Psychology*. Dr. Clayton isn't all work and no play. She is an avid yogi and cook who nerds out on documentaries; binges National Public Radio podcasts; collects vinyl records; roughhouses with her dogs Arya and Phoebe; and loses her voice at concerts (all hail Stevie Nicks!). When her students need a little pick-me-up, she makes them playlists. Music is her answer to just about everything.

STUDENT SUCCESS GUIDE

Suppose you are taking a college course for the first time. You purchase your course material and begin to peruse its contents. Within moments you realize that there is a lot of information to learn. You wonder how you are going to understand all this material by the end of the course. You might feel a mix of emotions, from intimidated to overwhelmed to excited. These emotions are all quite common among college students. Learning is a process of growth, and growth is not always comfortable. One reason is that learning is similar to exercising. You exercise to become stronger, faster, and more agile. Your goal is to be healthier, and this does not come without times of being tired or exhausted. But you work through it so that you can reach your goal of being healthier. Similarly, as a student, you learn to become more knowledgeable and capable, and to be smarter, and this also does not come without times of being tired or exhausted. But you work through it so that you can reach your goal of being educated. This parallel brings to light a key to your success in college: to set goals. Setting goals helps you to stay focused and motivated to "work through" the challenging times. Of course, it is also helpful to have a plan or guide that can help you achieve your goals. For this reason, we have prepared the following guide to help you achieve your academic goals and to support your success.

TIPS AND TRICKS FOR STUDENT SUCCESS: THE BASICS

Textbooks typically do not provide a "How-to-Rock-This-Class Manual," yet every student would love to have one. How do you study efficiently? How do you know what to say to your professors? Who can you reach out to for help? What strategies can you use to be a successful student? If these types of questions are what students seek answers for, then this guide is a great place to start. So, let's start at the very beginning—the basics:

- It is important to want to be a great student. Being a great student does not mean getting straight As, but it does mean that you are truly committed to learning. As a student, you should embrace the opportunity to learn, be genuinely curious about the information being taught, and take the time to study it, question it, and think critically about it. This perspective captures the spirit of what it means to be a great student.

- Take the time on the first day of class to introduce yourself to your professor and teaching assistants (if applicable). Whether your class is online, in person, or a hybrid course, go out of your way to introduce yourself. Your professors are more than just teachers. They are experts in their fields of study, and this makes them excellent people to connect with. Additionally, getting to know your professors can benefit your learning in class and even into your career as possible people you can reach out to for a professional recommendation.

- Attend each class session if it is in a synchronous or face-to-face format. What is taught in class is very often the bulk of the material that is tested and/or assessed. Not only are you putting your best foot forward by attending each class session, but you are also doing your due diligence to be a great student and setting yourself up for success. If your class is asynchronous (fully online), then make sure you watch each lecture. Professors who teach asynchronous classes offer good information in the recorded lectures, and it is important to watch the full lecture—from beginning to end—so that you are not missing important information.

- Be prepared—have your materials ready, put your distracting technology away, and read before attending class. If you are in a fully online class, the same rules apply. When you are ready to watch your lecture, put the technology away. Research has demonstrated that being distracted because of multitasking—specifically by looking at your phone at the same time you are listening to a lecture—lowers your performance and retention. Students often think they are good at multitasking, but the science says that's not accurate.

GETTING THE MOST OUT OF YOUR COURSE

On the first day, the professor is going to give you the owner's manual to the class: the **syllabus**. This document will give you all the information you need for the class. In general, the first bit of information you see on the syllabus is your professor's contact information. This information generally includes the professor's email address, office hours, office location (if applicable), and availability. When it comes to professors, there are a few things to remember:

- Be respectful when you email. This is a professional communication. Start the email with "Dear Professor _____."

- When you do email, make sure it does not sound like a text. You are conducting a formal business-like exchange.

- Use correct grammar and punctuation.

- Always let professors know what class you are in by typing it in the subject header, so that they can appropriately answer your questions—most professors teach multiple classes.

- Allow for at least 24–48 hours for a response from your professor. Allow a bit more time if you email on a Friday or the weekend.

- Ask questions. If you have questions, other students likely do too!

- If you have a few questions, consider making an appointment with your professor to meet during office hours. Having a conversation with your professor might answer many questions in one sitting; and, as most of us know, sometimes answers can be lost in translation in an email.

- Just a reminder—teachers love to teach—and they appreciate enthusiastic students. So, make an appointment with your professors and say hello.

Next, you need to sit down and *read all of the syllabus*. The syllabus is like your road map. You will be able to find *exactly* which textbook to obtain (never assume an older edition is going to be "good enough") and any other course requirements. Additionally, the syllabus will include course policies, course materials, a course calendar, and grading and assessment policies.

Helpful tip: Note in your calendar when you should start each assignment and when it is due. That will make it easier to keep on track (in other words, put it in your calendar RIGHT NOW). Multiple research studies have found that 80 to 95 percent of college students put off doing their work and studying on "a regular basis." Procrastination is not your friend, so start projects and assignments as early as possible. Life happens, and you do not want to turn in work late. Plan to start working on written work at least two weeks in advance if assignments are available to you that far in advance.

Also add to your calendar the dates for all quizzes and exams. A general rule of thumb is to start studying for quizzes and exams one week in advance. Never, ever cram. And get good sleep.

Many students color-code their schedules to keep all of their classes organized. This might sound like a lot of work, but you will be glad you did it!!

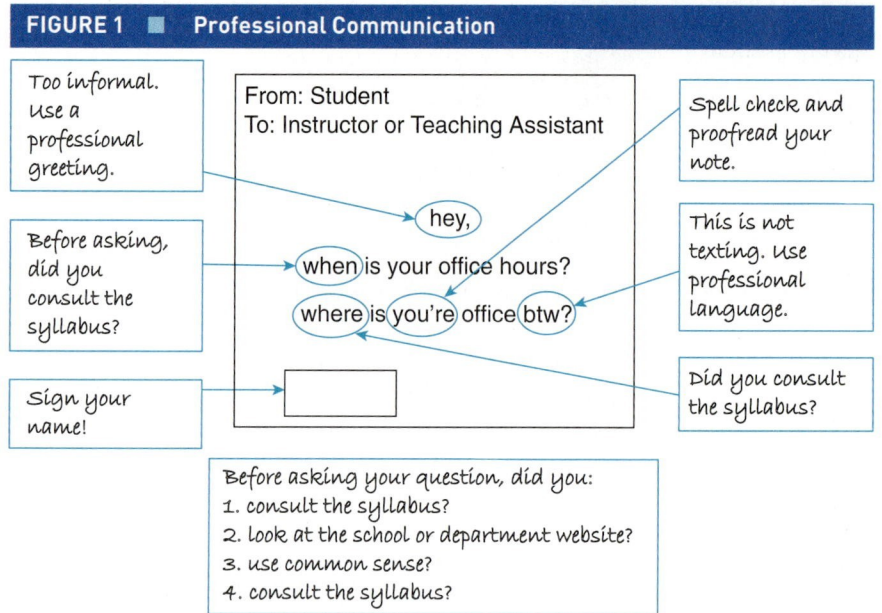

FIGURE 1 ■ Professional Communication

COURSE MATERIALS

It's important to have a plan—and to use science to help you out. Researchers have found that certain strategies work well for learning—particularly when it comes to reading the textbook. So, use them! For starters, many students do not read before class, and they often try to start reading without any real plan for reading a textbook efficiently. *Helpful tip*: Read BEFORE CLASS. It will save you time and improve your grades! Research has shown that if you have no idea what the professor is going to teach about, and then you sit down and try to take notes and listen, your brain will literally put you in a "time out." It is too much! *You will have cognitive overload*. So, be fair to your brain and give yourself the information you need to be able to absorb the material.

As part of your plan, figure out how to tackle your weekly reading, which is often approximately 40 pages of generally dense material. Use tools that will help you want to keep going rather than stop before you have even begun. So, make a plan of action:

- First, skim over the chapter that you are preparing to read. Whether your book is in a hard-copy format or a digital ebook, it's important to get a sense of the formatting of the book such as the illustrations, applied sections, questions, summaries, and text size. If this is your first time using an ebook, spend some extra time familiarizing yourself with the basics such as how to "turn" pages and enlarge the font if needed, as well as the general format of the book. Many students prefer digital ebooks, but if this is your first one, it can be a very different experience for you. It may take a bit of adjusting on your part. Also, no matter the format, get familiar with the interactive elements that are often included with the book.

- When you are ready to start working on a specific chapter, consider starting at the back of the chapter. The end of the chapter will give you a clear and concise **summary** of the chapter. You can also review **key words**, which will acquaint you with what the professor is going to discuss in class.

- Read over any **thought questions** at the end of each chapter. Obviously, you will not know the answers, but it'll give you an idea of what is important.

- When you begin a chapter, peruse the first page. Read the **chapter outline**, or scan the **section headings**, and, if present, review the **learning objectives**. The learning objectives state what you should be able to accomplish when you truly learn the material. They'll also give insight into the chapter.

- Divide your reading into reasonable portions. Researchers recommend setting a timer for 20–30 minutes (approximately 7–10 pages) to serve as a reminder to take a break. When the timer goes off, take a moment or two to stretch and move around a little. It is also recommended that you not have your phone close by or that you put it on silent mode, so that random alerts and messages won't interrupt you and break your flow.

- **Learning is not about being fast. Learning is about appropriately retaining important information.** When you read those 7–10 pages, try to understand the *main points*, not every point. Do not take notes initially. You don't want to break your cognitive flow. As you go back and review the pages you've read, notetaking can be beneficial. Research has shown that taking notes (pen-to-paper notetaking) can help students understand and retain the material better. *Helpful tip*: Paraphrase what the authors are saying and write it in your notes. This will help you articulate, and therefore understand, the material better. We call this approach *deep processing*, compared to memorizing, which is *surface processing*.

- It is highly recommended that you create a learning community (aka a study group) and then discuss the chapters with that group. This will help you with deep processing, and you are more likely to remember the material. *Helpful tip*: If you are unsure how to go about creating a learning community, consider discussing this with your professor. Professors can make announcements in class, start an online forum for the class, or offer you and your classmates other ways to connect. Many study groups create their own Google Docs so that they can exchange notes with others or post questions. Other study groups may use social media as a way to connect. No matter how you do it, be sure to do it *early* in the term. The sooner you have a study support team, the better.

STUDYING: NOW THAT YOU KNOW HOW TO READ THE MATERIAL, HOW DO YOU STUDY IT?

General Studying

We have talked about ways to tackle the book, but studying involves more than that. Reading, paraphrased notetaking, time with a learning community—all of those are great strategies, but sometimes (to use a saying from my grandfather) "you don't know what you don't know." Well, how are you ever going to *know* what you are supposed to *know*, then? Again, let's turn back to science for help. The cognitive psychologist Regan Gurung posits that, based on his extensive research, the ways people try to learn are not necessarily helpful. Yes, highlighting helps and rereading is good, but if you want GREAT results, start paying attention to what science is saying!!!

Gurung suggests three things you need to keep in mind if you want the best learning outcomes:

1. What do you **NEED** to know? This requires reviewing the syllabus.

2. What **DO** you know? This requires testing yourself and reviewing those tests.

3. What do you **NOT** know? Again, review the tests. Many books offer sets of knowledge checks and flashcards to help you in this process.

It is important for you to fully understand the professor's learning objectives. In other words, what exactly does the professor want you to know? Between the syllabus and the learning objectives in the textbook, you should have a pretty good idea what you need to know. If it's still not clear to you, ask your study group. At that point you should have it figured out, but if not, that is okay. *Helpful tip:* Do not spend more time trying to figure it out. It's time to write to the teaching assistant, or TA, if there is one. TAs are good "first contacts." If you're still unclear or there isn't a TA, then ask the professor. Do not be shy to ask questions. If you can't figure it out, many others students probably can't either. Too, there are great webinars and free materials available online from some of the best researchers out there. Search for reputable online resources on studying, notetaking, and test preparation.

Prepping for a Test

Never, ever, ever cram for a test! Cramming is bad in a multitude of ways:

- Cramming is associated with anxiety and stress, which results in lower scores.
- You will have cognitive overload, which means your brain is overworked.
- Learning takes *time*, and one night of cramming will not help you learn.
- Lack of sleep results in lower test scores.

You get the idea. Do not cram for a test. Here are a few scientifically supported practices for prepping for a test. Recent research by John Dunlosky and colleagues found that a key component for doing well on exams is **space practicing**:

- The idea of space practicing is to study the same content on different occasions. Think of it like this: If you were a softball player, you might practice catching and throwing three of the five days of the week (the same drill on different days). You would schedule these specific days and times to practice your throwing and catching. *Practicing the same thing over and over embeds it into your memory and recall.* It works for softball, and it works for psychology exams!

Next, work on **retrieval practicing**:

- Retrieval practicing involves bringing key information to mind to increase learning and retention.
- Test yourself frequently to make sure you know what you need to know.
- This can be done by using the flashcards and practice tests that go with your textbook. Many researchers believe that practice tests are the most underutilized resource that students have.
- Often, textbook authors work hard to provide the student resources to use in retrieval practicing. If you have them available, be sure to use them.

WHAT ABOUT YOU? SCHOOL-WORK-FAMILY BALANCE

Research has demonstrated that there is no simple, easy answer to balancing multiple roles such as being a student, an employee, a parent, a friend, a partner, and a family member, to name just a few roles. In fact, many psychologists have suggested that "balancing" these roles isn't the correct way to think about them. Is your life ever really balanced? And with one more major life role added to the list—student—it is important to keep expectations in check. This is going to be difficult, but that's okay. It can be done if you use the resources you have around you… and science:

- Time management is key to reducing stress and anxiety. Plan out your day and week, and stick to a schedule. *Helpful tip*: It's easy to lose track of time, so setting reminders on your phone or watch will help you to keep track of what you need to be doing and when you should be doing it. Set a timer when you are studying so that you remember to get up and move and take a break, but also set a timer to remind yourself to get back to studying.
- Pick your method of tracking (e.g., when assignments are due, when you should start studying for a test) and stick to it. Many people like to use paper calendars so that they can check off

- what they've done and color-code what needs to be done. If you choose this method, pick a calendar that fits in your bag and take it everywhere.

- You may choose to use an online calendar. That's a great method, too. You certainly can color-code assignments, due dates, and deadlines, as well as prioritize activities and set alerts. The key to using a calendar (electronic or paper) is to *remember to look at it… every day*. Without exception. Do not rely on your memory.

- Prioritize sleeping and exercising. These two activities go together; research has demonstrated that the relationship between sleep and exercise is bidirectional. More specifically, exercise helps you sleep better. And when you sleep better, you are more likely to exercise. Also, research has shown that increasing both activities increases recall. That is a win-win-win! You might think that it's more important to study than to sleep for a full 7 or 8 hours, or take a brisk walk, but that is a myth. The less sleep you get, the less efficient your brain will be. The same goes for exercise. Your brain needs oxygen to function at its best, and there is no better way to get oxygen to your brain than through exercise.

- Ask your academic advisor about your school's counseling center. The transition to college can be difficult. It's always a great idea to build a support system as early as possible, and counselors are trained to provide exactly that. They can also direct you to support groups on and off campus.

- You might be a first-generation college student or a student who is a caretaker of others. There will be times when you might feel pulled in different directions, or times when your family will not understand why you need to spend so many hours on your studies. *Helpful tip*: Keep the lines of communication open with your family, which will help them get a better grasp of what you need to succeed. If you must be in a quiet room for 3 hours a day to study, let them know. If you need to be on campus late that week to prepare for a big project, tell them! Many students who try to balance school and family have found that discussing needs and responsibilities can create a supportive environment.

- Practice mindfulness throughout the day. Many smartphone apps are available that provide guided meditation. Also, many smartwatches have a 2-minute mindfulness activity. For some, it might be praying. For others, it could just be sitting still and being fully present in the moment. There are many ways to practice mindfulness. Pick a technique that works for you and practice consistently. *Helpful tip*: Schedule "mindfulness moments" into your day.

EFFECTIVE DISTANCE LEARNING

More and more people are deciding to become distance learners, and they need a game plan, too. Not attending college in a more traditional manner can make students feel isolated and not connected to their peers or professors. There are ways to address those issues, many of which have already been mentioned. But here's a refresher:

- Ideally, try to designate a specific area for studying. Keep it organized and clean so that when you are ready to study, your study space is prepared. If you cannot do this, make sure you are studying in a nondistracting environment that has all the "tools" (e.g., computer, paper, pen) that you need for studying.

- Create a study community. If you are unsure how to go about it, talking to your professor is a great place to start.

- Study groups give you the opportunity to articulate what you are learning (paraphrasing the content), which helps with deep processing.

- Study groups allow you to test each other on the content.

- Because many people are deciding to take classes from home, try to keep distractions to a minimum when studying and testing. It's easy to get distracted when laundry and other chores need to be done. Also, other family members can be a distraction, so try to communicate what you need and how long you need it to the others in your home. Communication is key when it comes to keeping the distractions at bay.

SECRET WEAPONS

Sometimes it may feel that being a student is a solitary endeavor, but it should not be. A wealth of resources are available to you. Here are a few:

- **Teaching Assistants**. They know so much about the inner workings of the department, faculty, university, and your specific class. They are an amazing resource! If your class is not face-to-face, TAs will often have virtual office hours. Be sure to schedule a short appointment to introduce yourself, and if you have questions, come prepared. *Helpful tip*: Write down all your questions ahead of time so that you can use your time efficiently.

- **Librarians.** Each department has a dedicated librarian. Get to know those wonderful people! They can help you in so many ways. If you're not able to meet with them on campus, you can email them and ask for a quick phone call to introduce yourself. Or you can ask for an online video session to say hello and ask for any resources that you may need. Again, be prepared for the meeting.

- **Writing Center.** The people who work at your school's writing center are focused on helping students. Many writing centers are set up to help students by subject area, and then there are more "generalists" (people who can help in any discipline). Commonly, it is recommended that students go to subject-specific tutors, if possible. Be sure to bring your assignment with you. Writing center tutors do not know every assignment for every class, but they are great with helping you understand the writing component. Keep in mind that if you do not live on campus, most writing centers have evening hours, and most universities offer online sessions.

- **Other Students.** So many students are struggling with school-work-family balance, so creating a support and study group can be extremely beneficial. If you can't find one, ask your TA or professor. Research suggests that the more connections you have, the better you will do in school.

ATTEND OFFICE HOURS

One of the first things students should do at the beginning of the term is to attend their professors' office hours (whether in person or virtually). For many students, the idea of attending office hours can be a scary prospect, but that one-on-one time with the professor is priceless. Specifically, you can ask questions you might not want to ask in class. Additionally, it is a chance for you to find out how nice and caring your professors really are! To make the most of the time with your professors, do the following:

- Read the syllabus before you go and think about any questions you have.
- Write down your questions before you go. This will help you use the time effectively.
- Do not be late.
- Discuss "best practices" with your professor. This means, ask what your professor believes are the best study methods for the class and how long it might take to properly prepare for exams.
- Inquire about any additional resources. It never hurts to ask.
- If you have questions about a grade, now is the time to ask for clarity.

> **FIGURE 2 ■ Advice from an Undergraduate Advisor**
>
> - It is not recommended that students take classes back-to-back. It's better to have some time to absorb what you just learned, and then maybe write down a few more thoughts.
> - If possible, do not take classes at times when you know you cannot do your best. For example, if you are not an 8 AM person, do not take a class first thing in the morning.
> - Make sure you are a good fit for the instructor. Ask other students about the instructor and visit the instructor during office hours.
> - Do not overload your schedule. You are in college to learn, not to stress yourself out. Be realistic with what you can do.
> - We want you to be successful!

- Take notes during your meeting because you might be covering a lot of ground and you do not want to rely on your memory.

- If you are unsure about what the professor suggested or said, do not hesitate to ask for clarification. Professors appreciate it when you are honest about not understanding an explanation. They would rather clarify during this one-on-one time rather than you leave confused.

- Lastly, thank your professors for their time. That's the best way to leave your appointment.

LIMIT MEDIA EXPOSURE

Being a student is stressful. If you add in personal or global events, it can be downright unmanageable. It is important that you take care of yourself so that you can prosper as a student, friend, family member, and community member. To help manage stress today, the American Psychological Association offers some great tips. One of the best tips is to limit media exposure. Media are there to keep you interested, so they often focus on the negative so that viewers will have a more visceral reaction. Keep that in mind... and limit the amount of time you spend on social media and news outlets.

SUMMARY OF HELPFUL TIPS

- **Planning.** Note in your calendar when you should be starting assignments and when they are due.

- **Reading.** Read *before class*. It will save you time and improve your grades.

- **Studying.** Paraphrase what the authors are saying and write it in your notes.

- **Study group.** If you are unsure how to go about creating a learning community, discuss it with your professor or teaching assistant.

- **Course goals.** If you do not fully understand what the course learning goals are, write to the teaching assistant (if there is one) or the professor (if there is no teaching assistant).

- **Reminders.** Setting reminders on your phone or watch will help remind you what you need to be doing and when you should be doing it.

- **Communication.** Keep the lines of communication open with your family and/or roommates to help them get a better grasp of what you need to succeed.

- **Take a moment:** Schedule mindfulness moments into your day.

- **Questions.** Write down all of your questions for instructors, teaching assistants, or study groups ahead of time so that you can use your time efficiently.

College is an exciting time in a person's life, but it can be stressful at times. By practicing good study habits and connecting to your college community—online or in person—you will be well suited to handle any bumps in the road!

MOMENTS IN PSYCHOLOGY AROUND THE WORLD

Date	Milestone
BCE	
387	Plato argues that the brain is the center of mental process.
335	Aristotle argues that the heart is the center of mental process.
CE	
1637	René Descartes (France) publishes *A Discourse on Method*. Descartes asserts that ideas are innate to humans from birth.
1690	John Locke (England) publishes *An Essay Concerning Human Understanding*. Locke asserts that ideas come from experience and the human ability to reason.
1774	Franz Mesmer (Austria) presents a treatment for mental illnesses, originally called mesmerism and now known as hypnosis.
1794	Philippe Pinel (France) publishes *Memoir on Madness*. It argues for humane treatment of mentally ill patients. Pinel made significant contributions to the classification of mental disorders.
1808	Franz Joseph Gall (Germany) proposes the idea of phrenology, the belief that the shape of a person's skull reveals personality traits.
1848	Phineas Gage (United States) suffers massive brain damage when his brain is pierced by a large iron rod. This leaves his intellect intact, but his personality is changed. From this, researchers study how areas in the brain play a role in personality.
1856	Hermann von Helmholtz (Germany) publishes *Handbook of Physiological Optics*. His many works make important contributions, including reports on the physiology of vision and hearing, and measurement of nerve impulse speed.
1859	Charles Darwin (England) publishes *On the Origin of Species*. Darwin asserts that species evolve, and that living beings all share a common ancestor.
1861	Paul Broca (France) presents his findings regarding the area in the left frontal lobe of the brain that is critical for the production of spoken language. This is now called Broca's area.
1869	Francis Galton (England) publishes *Hereditary Genius*. He asserts that intelligence is inherited. Galton is credited with the expression "nature and nurture" to correspond with "heredity and environment."
1874	Carl Wernicke (Germany) presents his findings that damage to a specific area in the left temporal lobe damages the ability to comprehend or produce language. This is now called Wernicke's area.
1879	Wilhelm Wundt (Germany) founds the first formal laboratory for psychological study at the University of Leipzig. Wundt, the first person to refer to himself as a psychologist, helped to establish psychology as an independent field of study.
1883	The first formal U.S. psychology laboratory is established at Johns Hopkins University.
1885	Hermann Ebbinghaus (Germany) publishes *On Memory*. Ebbinghaus made numerous contributions to the areas of learning and memory.

(Continued)

(Continued)

Date	Milestone
1887	G. Stanley Hall (United States) founds the *American Journal of Psychology*. Hall was the first North American to receive a PhD in psychology.
1890	William James (United States) publishes *Principles of Psychology*. His research contributes to the study of functionalism. He is also the first person to teach a psychology course in the United States.
1892	The American Psychological Association (APA) is organized by G. Stanley Hall. The APA's stated mission is to promote the advancement, communication, and application of psychological science and knowledge to benefit society and improve lives.
1894	Margaret Floy Washburn (United States) is the first woman to receive a PhD in psychology. She made contributions in the fields of animal behavior and motor theory development.
1896	John Dewey (United States) publishes *The Reflex Arc Concept in Psychology*. He focused on the areas of education and helped develop the psychological philosophy of functionalism.
1898	Edward Thorndike (United States) publishes *Animal Intelligence*. His work proposes that animals and humans learn similarly and leads to the development of operant conditioning.
1900	Sigmund Freud (Austria, England) publishes *The Interpretation of Dreams*. Freud is considered the founder of psychoanalysis.
1901	Mary Whiton Calkins (United States) publishes *An Introduction to Psychology*. In 1905, she is the first female elected as president of the American Psychological Association.
1903	Alfred Binet (France) publishes *Experimental Studies of Intelligence*. Binet made contributions to the study of intelligence, including the creation, along with colleague Theodore Simon, of the Binet-Simon intelligence scale.
1906	Ivan Pavlov (Russia) publishes his first studies on classical conditioning.
1912	Carl Jung (Switzerland) publishes *Psychology of the Unconscious*. Jung is considered the founder of analytical psychology.
1912	Tsuruko Haraguchi (Japan) receives a PhD in psychology. She is the first Japanese woman to receive a PhD in any subject.
1913	John Watson (United States) publishes *The Behaviorist Manifesto*. This puts forth a new area called behaviorism. In 1920, he and his colleague and wife, Rosalie Raynor, conducted the controversial "Little Albert" experiment.
1920	Francis Cecil Sumner (United States) receives a PhD in psychology. He is the first African American to earn a PhD in psychology. His work focuses on race psychology and education reform.
1921	Hermann Rorschach (Switzerland) publishes *Psychodiagnostik*. This work introduces the Rorschach Inkblot Test.
1923	Jean Piaget (Switzerland) publishes *The Language and Thought of the Child*. Piaget contributed in the area of child development, and championed child education.
1926	Leta Stetter Hollingworth (United States) publishes *Gifted Children*. Her work in the psychology of women helped to dispel myths that had been used to argue against women's rights.
1927	Anna Freud (Austria, England), the sixth and youngest child of Sigmund Freud, publishes *Introduction to the Technique of Child Analysis*. Freud developed the field of child psychoanalysis.
1929	Christine Ladd-Franklin (United States) publishes *Color and Color Theories*. Ladd-Franklin makes contributions in the field of color vision, in addition to other fields.
1929	Wolfgang Köhler (Germany) publishes *Gestalt Psychology*. This work criticizes behaviorism.
1932	Walter B. Cannon (United States) publishes *The Wisdom of the Body*. This work introduces the term *homeostasis* and discusses the fight-or-flight response.
1933	Inez Beverly Prosser (United States) becomes the first African American woman to receive a doctoral degree in psychology from a U.S. institution.

Date	Milestone
1936	Anna Freud (Austria, England) publishes her influential book, *The Ego and the Mechanisms of Defense*.
1936	Egas Moniz (Portugal) publishes work on the first human frontal lobotomies.
1936	Herman George Canady (United States) publishes *The Effect of "Rapport" on the I.Q.: A New Approach to the Problem of Race Psychology*. He was the first psychologist to examine the role of the examiner's race as a bias factor in IQ testing. His work provided suggestions for establishing a more equal testing environment.
1938	Ugo Cerletti (Italy) and Lucio Bini (Italy) use electroshock treatment on a human patient.
1939	David Wechsler (Romania, United States) publishes the Wechsler-Bellevue intelligence test, which will later evolve into the Wechsler Intelligence Scale for Children (WISC) and the Wechsler Adult Intelligence Scale (WAIS).
1940	George I. Sanchez (United States) publishes *Forgotten People: A Study of New Mexicans*. Also in 1940, he receives a tenured, full professorship at the University of Texas, where he becomes the first professor of Latin American Studies.
1943	Starke Hathaway (United States) and J. Charnley McKinley (United States) publishes the Minnesota Multiphasic Personality Inventory (MMPI).
1945	Karen Horney (Germany, United States) publishes *Our Inner Conflicts*. Her work criticizes Freud's theory of female sexual development.
1946	Mamie Phipps Clark (United States) founds the Northside Center for Child Development. The first program of its kind in Harlem, it offers necessary therapy and assistance to children and families.
1948	Alfred Kinsey (United States) publishes *Sexual Behavior in the Human Male*, and then *Sexual Behavior in the Human Female* in 1953 with colleagues.
1948	B. F. Skinner (United States) publishes *Walden Two*. It describes a utopian community based on positive reinforcement and an experimental attitude. The book encourages the application of psychological principles to everyday life.
1949	Donald O. Hebb (Canada) publishes *The Organization of Behavior: A Neuropsychological Theory*. It offers a new and influential conceptualization about how the nervous system functions.
1950	Erik Erikson (Germany, United States) publishes *Childhood and Society*. He made contributions that advanced the study of human development across the lifespan.
1951	Carl Rogers (United States) publishes *Client-Centered Therapy*. His work advanced the humanist movement.
1952	The American Psychiatric Association publishes the first *Diagnostic and Statistical Manual of Mental Disorders (DSM)*, an influential text that is updated periodically.
1953	Janet Taylor Spence (United States) publishes her Taylor Manifest Anxiety Scale in the *Journal of Abnormal Psychology*. Her contributions advance the fields of anxiety and gender studies.
1954	Abraham Maslow (United States) publishes *Motivation and Personality*. It proposes a hierarchy of needs, ranging from physiological needs to self-actualization.
1954	Gordon Allport (United States) publishes *The Nature of Prejudice*. He was one of the first psychologists to study personality.
1955	Kenneth Clark (United States) publishes *Prejudice and Your Child*. His earlier research and experiments with his colleague and wife, Mamie Phipps Clark, explored issues of race for African American children. The findings of that research were included as evidence in the Supreme Court decision *Brown v. Board of Education* (1954) by proving that segregation psychologically harms children.
1957	B. F. Skinner (United States) publishes *Schedules of Reinforcement*. He contributed in the areas of behavior analysis and the experimental analysis of behavior.

(Continued)

(Continued)

Date	Milestone
1957	Leon Festinger (United States) proposes his theory of cognitive dissonance; in 1959, he and his colleague James Carlsmith conducts a landmark experiment to test this theory at Stanford University.
1958	Lawrence Kohlberg (United States) proposes his theory of moral development.
1960	Beatrice Ann Wright (United States) publishes *Physical Disability: A Psychological Approach*. Her contributions include developing appropriate and culturally relevant ways of working with differently abled people.
1961	Aaron Beck (United States) creates the Beck Depression Inventory, which is still used widely. Beck's contributions include the development of cognitive therapy and cognitive-behavioral therapy, along with making advances in the study of clinical depression and anxiety disorders.
1967	Zing-Yang Kuo (China) publishes *The Dynamics of Behavior in Development*. He contributed in the areas of animal and comparative psychology.
1967	Raymond Cattell (England, United States) publishes *Objective Personality and Motivation Tests*. He made contributions in the field of personality, putting forth a taxonomy of 16 different personality traits that could explain differences in peoples' personalities.
1969	Eleanor Gibson (United States) publishes *Principles of Perceptual Learning and Development*. With colleague Richard Walk (United States), Gibson conducts research on infant depth perception, known as "The Visual Cliff."
1971	Phillip Zimbardo (United States) conducts the Stanford Prison Experiment in the basement of an academic hall to examine the effects of authority in a prison environment.
1971	Albert Bandura (Canada, United States) publishes *Social Learning Theory*. His contributions advance the field of social cognitive psychology, and he is well known for his experiments regarding aggression.
1972	Elliot Aronson (United States) publishes *The Social Animal*. His contributions lead to advances in the theory of cognitive dissonance and explore the importance of situational factors on behavior.
1974	Eleanor Maccoby (United States) and Carol Jacklin (United States) publish *The Psychology of Sex Differences*. Their contributions lead to advances in the fields of gender studies and developmental psychology.
1974	Stanley Milgram (United States) publishes *Obedience to Authority: An Experimental View*. Milgram may be best known for his controversial experiments on obedience, which researched to what extent people would obey orders, even if the orders were dangerous or immoral.
1976	Robert V. Guthrie (United States) publishes *Even the Rat Was White*, the first history of African American psychologists in the United States.
1979	James J. Gibson (United States) publishes *The Ecological Approach to Visual Perception*. His contributions lead to advances in the field of visual perception.
1979	Elizabeth Loftus (United States) publishes *Eyewitness Testimony*. Her contributions lead to advances in the field of memory, misinformation, and eyewitness memory.
1983	Howard Gardner (United States) publishes *Frames of Mind*. This work outlines his theory of multiple intelligences.
1984	Hiroshi Azuma (Japan) publishes "Psychology in a Non-Western Country" in the *International Journal of Psychology*. He made contributions in the areas of cross-cultural psychology.
1986	Durganand Sinha (India) publishes *Psychology in a Third World Country: The Indian Experience*. He studied indigenous psychology; self, family, and social values; and human and socioeconomic development. He was central to the modern development of psychology from an Indian perspective.
1987	Marius Romme (Amsterdam) founds the Hearing Voices Network with Sandra Escher, a science journalist, and Patsy Hage, a person who hears voices. The network serves as a peer-mentor organization for persons who have auditory hallucinations and their supporters. The network soon spreads across the world.

Date	Milestone
1988	Muzafer Sherif (Turkey, United States) publishes *The Robbers Cave Experiment* with colleagues. One of the founders of modern social psychology, he advanced the fields of social judgment theory and realistic conflict theory.
1988	The Association for Psychological Science (APS), previously the American Psychological Society, is founded. Its stated mission is to promote, protect, and advance the interests of scientifically oriented psychology in research, application, teaching, and the improvement of human welfare.
1989	Kimberlé Williams Crenshaw (United States) publishes the paper "Demarginalizing the Intersection of Race and Sex." She is one of the founders of critical race theory, developing the theory of intersectionality.
1990	Reiko True (Japan, United States) publishes "Psychotherapeutic Issues with Asian American Women" in the journal *Sex Roles*. Her work has advanced mental health services for Asian Americans and other minorities.
1991	Martin Seligman (United States) publishes *Learned Optimism*. This work introduces the field of positive psychology.
1991	Qicheng Jing (China) publishes *Landmarks of Psychology: Contemporary Great Masters in Psychology*. He made contributions in highlighting the international aspect of psychology, advancing the exchange of international psychology, and lifting Chinese psychology onto the world stage.
1997	Beverly Daniel Tatum (United States) publishes *Why Are All the Black Kids Sitting Together in the Cafeteria?* This work examines the development of racial identity.
1997	U.S. president Bill Clinton apologizes for the Tuskegee Syphilis Study, an infamous study that violated human participant rights and led to the publishing of the Belmont Report in 1979, a U.S. code of ethics for human participants in research.
2003	Kuo-Shu Yang (China, Taiwan) publishes *Progress in Asian Social Psychology* with colleagues. A pioneer in indigenous Chinese and Taiwanese psychology, he also devoted his life to social reform in Taiwan.
2007	Alice Eagly (United States) publishes *Through the Labyrinth: The Truth about How Women Become Leaders* with colleague Linda Carli (United States). Her contributions have advanced the understanding of prejudice, sex differences, leadership styles, feminism, and stereotypes.
2008	U.S. president George W. Bush signs Mental Health Parity Act, requiring insurance to equally cover both mental and physical health.
2008	Lisa Diamond publishes *Sexual Fluidity: Understanding Women's Love and Desire*. Her research has advanced the understanding of sexual identity, sexual orientation development, and human bonding.
2010	Derald Wing Sue (United States) publishes *Microaggressions in Everyday Life: Race, Gender, and Sexual Orientation*. His contributions have advanced the fields of multicultural counseling and research.
2010	Claude Steele (United States) publishes *Whistling Vivaldi and Other Clues to How Stereotypes Affect Us*. He has advanced the areas of stereotype threat and its impact on the academic performance of minority students.
2010	The replication controversy impacts how a variety of disciplines, including psychology, validate existing studies.
2011	Michael Gazzaniga (United States) publishes *Who's in Charge? Free Will and the Science of the Brain*. His studies advance understanding of the functions of each brain hemisphere, and how they work independently and in collaboration.
2011	Daniel Kahneman (Israel) publishes *Thinking, Fast and Slow*. His contributions have advanced the fields of judgment and decision making. With colleague Amos Tversky (Israel), Kahneman has established a cognitive basis for common human errors that arise from heuristics and biases.
2013	*DSM*-5 is published by the American Psychiatric Association.

(Continued)

(*Continued*)

Date	Milestone
2014	A radio soap opera, "Musekeweya" is created by clinical psychologist Ervin Staub (Hungary, United States) and disseminated to Rwandan listeners to counteract hate speech and intolerance.
2015	The American Psychological Association bans psychologist participation in national security interrogations.
2015	Mona Amer (Egypt) and Germine Awad (United States) publish *The Handbook of Arab American Psychology*. It is the first major publication to comprehensively discuss the Arab American experience from a primarily psychological lens.
2015	David Trafimow (United States) bans null hypothesis significance testing for the journal *Basic and Applied Social Psychology*. This begins the debate about how to better determine if a hypothesis is supported or rejected.
2016	U.S. president Barack Obama signs the 21st Century Cures Act, which provides essential prevention services and treatments for populations in need and support.
2016	Mahzarin Banaji (India, United States) publishes *Blindspot: Hidden Biases of Good People* with colleague Anthony Greenwald (United States). Her work has advanced awareness of implicit or unconscious bias.
2017	Arkansas (United States) opens the first intimate partner violence shelter for men in the United States. The shelter also runs a domestic violence hotline for men.
2018	Mental Health at Work (United Kingdom) is launched by The Royal Foundation. The nonprofit provides support to employers and employees to help them improve well-being in their workplace and encourage conversations about mental health.
2019	Jennifer Eberhardt (United States) publishes *Biased: Uncovering the Hidden Prejudice That Shapes What We See, Think, and Do*. Her research advances the fields of race, bias, and inequality.
2020	In Mexico, a mental health bill that would have removed a person's right to consent to treatment was stopped by human rights activists.
2020	Telemental health availability broadens treatment options during the coronavirus pandemic.
2021	American Psychological Association apologizes for contributions to systemic racism, and vows to achieve the social equality, health equity, and fairness that all human beings deserve.

1 PSYCHOLOGY AND ITS METHODS

iStock.com/iMrSquid

LEARNING OBJECTIVES

Engage with the pioneers of psychology and become familiar with the trajectory of the field from its beginning until now.

Consider the methods, tools, types of participants, and ethical practices used to study psychology and evaluate its scientific rigor.

Identify the major organizations and emerging branches in psychology, and explain the need to study a diverse group of people.

WHAT'S YOUR PREDICTION: THINKING LIKE A PSYCHOLOGIST

The Situation

When you first signed up to take an introductory psychology course, you likely had some idea or conception of what you think psychology is. You may have read about Sigmund Freud or Ivan Pavlov and his dogs; you may have seen a psychologist, such as "Dr. Phil," on a television talk show; or you may have heard a therapist giving personal advice on a podcast. You may even have taken a psychology course in high school, had exposure to psychology in other classes, or done some reading on your own. Whatever your background, it's important to realize that you come into this course with many intuitive or commonsense theories about people. Everyone does. What are some of *your* theories? And are they correct in light of what psychologists know on the basis of scientific research?

Make a Prediction

Let's stop and evaluate some of your intuitive beliefs about people. The 10 statements below concern topics in psychology that you will find in this book (the chapters in which they appear are shown in parentheses). Read each statement carefully, and write down whether you think it is generally TRUE or FALSE. When you've finished, try to estimate the number of answers you got correct.

___ 1. The right and left sides of your brain are basically exact copies of one another. (2)
___ 2. Some people dream; others do not. (4)
___ 3. Getting what you want all of the time is more reinforcing than getting what you want occasionally. (5)
___ 4. Human memory capacity is limited, which is why we lose memories. (6)
___ 5. Intelligence is purely inherited. (7)
___ 6. Americans are getting married at younger ages today than in the past. (9)
___ 7. A smile has very different meanings in different cultures. (10)
___ 8. Any type of stress is bad for your health. (12)
___ 9. Suicide rates are highest among teenagers and younger adults. (13)
___ 10. Using social media is one of the most effective ways to reduce anxiety. (14)

The Results

Now that you have completed the commonsense psychology quiz, you are ready to read this section on how to score it. In fact, the scoring is easy: The first statement is true; the other nine statements are false. So how well did you do? This is a true-false quiz, so you could expect to get about five answers right just by guessing or flipping a coin. Did you do any better than that? Did you do worse?

What Does It All Mean?

Look back at the statements in this quiz, and you'll notice that they cover a broad spectrum of topics, including your brain, sleeping and dreaming, learning, memory, intelligence, marriage, cultural diversity, health and wellness, aging and development, and mental health. These topics represent a cross-section of psychology today—a remarkably diverse discipline with many areas of specialization.

If you did not get a perfect score on the test, you may also have noticed that at least some of the answers were not obvious as a matter of common sense. For example, later in this book we will find that the left and right sides of your brain are near copies of each other, that everyone dreams, (whether or not we remember it), that it is more rewarding to get what we want occasionally (it can be quite boring to get what we want all of the time), that our capacity to store memories is infinite (we do not "lose" memories per se; we can have greater difficulty retrieving them as we age), that intelligence is partly inherited and partly due to learning, that Americans who get married are marrying much later in life (waiting on average until their late 20s), that a smile has the same meaning all over the world, that some types of stress can be good for us (such as the stress of earning a college degree), that suicide is highest among older adults (rates increase around age 45), and that using social media more often can lead to increased anxiety—even if using it can also be fun. And there is a lot more. But for now, let us step back and define psychology and look at its history and its methods.

We live in a fast-paced world where the cause and effect of human behavior is as mainstream and critical to our lived experiences as its impact on the world around us. Human behavior and ingenuity move the needle for how we live, interact, and engage in the world, to include the technologies we develop. From our greater access to information (e.g., using Google), our increased ability to reach out and connect with people anywhere in the world (e.g., via video conferencing), to the everyday person having a stronger voice in the world in real time (e.g., via social media platforms)—understanding the psychology of human behavior is increasingly important. Why? Because human behavior is more closely connected worldwide now than ever before, and with continued advancements and human ingenuity, we are likely to become increasingly connected.

While psychology is still in its infancy, now in its third century as a formal discipline, it's easier than ever before to build an encyclopedic text by compiling new theories and discoveries, hot off the presses, with old ones from psychology's historical warehouse. Both the history of the field and the discoveries and issues today are relevant for developing an understanding of the contributions of psychology, both to fields of science and to our everyday lives. We begin this text with the most fundamental of questions: What is psychology?

iStock.com/ALLVISIONN

WHAT IS PSYCHOLOGY?

> ### LEARNING OBJECTIVES
>
> Engage with the pioneers of psychology and become familiar with the trajectory of the field from its beginning until now.
>
> - Define psychology.
> - Explain whether psychology is the study of the human mind or of human behavior.
> - Outline how the field of psychology has changed over the years.
> - Identify the important issues and areas of specialization in psychology.

Psychology is the scientific study of behavior and the mind, and its biological bases. If you dissect this definition, you'll find that it contains three elements. First, psychology is a *scientific* enterprise. At an intuitive level, everyone is a psychologist—you, me, the Uber driver who listens to the stories that their passengers share, the users on social media, and the novelist who paints exquisite verbal portraits of fictional characters. Unlike those who rely largely on their personal experience, however, psychologists employ systematic, objective methods of observation.

The second key element in the definition of psychology is that it is the study of *behavior*. The term *behavior* refers to any activity that can be observed, recorded, and measured. It may be as simple as the blink of an eye or as complex as making the decision to get married.

Third, psychology is the study of the *mind*. For many years, researchers flinched at the mere use of the term. It was like talking about spirits or souls or ghosts in the human machine. Today, the term *mind* is used to refer to all conscious and unconscious mental states. These states cannot be seen, but psychologists try to infer them from observable behavior.

psychology. The scientific study of behavior and the mind, and its biological bases.

Historical Roots

Having its origins in philosophy, psychology is said to have a long past but a short history. There is truth in this statement. The Greek philosopher Socrates (470–399 BCE) and his followers Plato and Aristotle wrote extensively about human nature. They wrote about pleasure and pain, the senses, imagination, desire, and other aspects of the "psyche." They also speculated about whether human beings were innately good or evil, rational or irrational, and capable of free will or controlled by outside forces. At about the same time, Hippocrates (460–377 BCE), the "father of modern medicine," referred to the human brain as an "interpreter of consciousness." He also tried to differentiate for the first time among psychological disorders. Years later, Roman physician Galen (130–200 CE) theorized that every individual is born with one of four personality types or "temperaments."

Other philosophers have planted more recent seeds. French mathematician and philosopher René Descartes (1596–1650) theorized that the body is a physical structure, that the mind is a spiritual entity, and that the two interact only through a tiny structure in the brain. This position, known as **dualism**, implied that although the body could be studied scientifically, the mind—as the product of a willful "soul"—could not. Thomas Hobbes (1588–1679) disagreed. He and other English philosophers argued that the entire human experience, including our conscious thoughts and feelings, are physical processes emanating from the brain—and therefore are subject to study. In this view, which later became known as **monism**, the mind and body are one and the same.

Psychology also has its origins in physiology (a branch of biology that scientifically studies living organisms) and medicine. In the 19th century, physiologists began studying the brain and nervous system. For example, German scientist Hermann von Helmholtz (1821–1894) studied sensory receptors in the eye and ear and investigated such topics as the speed of neural impulses, color vision, and space perception. Gustav Fechner (1801–1887), another German scientist, founded psychophysics, the study of the relationship between physical stimuli and our subjective sensations of those stimuli.

Within the medical community, there were two particularly notable developments. In an influential textbook, German psychiatrist Emil Kraepelin (1856–1926) likened mental disorders to physical illness and devised the first comprehensive system for classifying the various disorders. In Paris, neurologist Jean Charcot (1825–1893) discovered that patients suffering from nervous disorders could sometimes be cured through hypnosis, a psychological form of intervention. From philosophy, physiology, and medicine, then, psychology is deeply rooted in the past (Hilgard, 1987; Watson & Evans, 1991).

Pioneers in the Study of the Mind

The history of modern psychology is a history of great thinkers, but with a largely homogenous voice—one largely consisting of white men resulting from the social, cultural, and political climates in which they lived. Dean Keith Simonton (2002) thus said of psychology's history that it springs from a combination of individual genius and *zeitgeist*, which is German for "spirit of the times." More than this, initiatives to expand the inclusivity of the voice in psychology across race, gender, and more is of utmost importance to the field (American Psychological Association, 2021).

Modern experimental psychology was born in 1879, in Germany, at the University of Leipzig. It was there that physiologist Wilhelm Wundt (1832–1920) founded the first laboratory dedicated to the scientific study of the mind. At the time, no courses in psychology were being taught because the discipline did not exist on its own. Yet many students from Europe and the United States were drawn to Wundt's laboratory, comprising the first generation of scholars to call themselves psychologists. This distinguished group included G. Stanley Hall (who in 1891 founded the American Psychological Association, with 26 members), James McKeen Cattell (the first to study individual differences), Hugo Münsterberg (among the first to apply psychology to industry and the law), Edward Titchener (who introduced his system of **structuralism**); and Margaret Floy Washburn (Edward Titchener's first graduate student and the first woman to earn a PhD in Psychology in 1894). Overall, 186 students were awarded doctoral degrees under Wundt's supervision, including 33 from the United States (Benjamin, Durkin, Link, Vestal, & Acord, 1992). During his career, Wundt published 53,735 pages of material, edited psychology's first journal, and wrote its first book. His goal, as stated in the book's preface, was ambitious: "to mark out a new domain of science."

Wundt's approach to the study of the mind was a far cry from the "armchair speculation" of the philosophers of his time. He founded the first laboratory dedicated to the study of psychology—to the study of how the mind works in a more structured, systematic, scientific way with objective measurement and control. Among the methods he developed was intensive **introspection**, in which trained observers reported on their moment-to-moment reactions to tones, visual displays, and other stimuli presented to them. In this way, Wundt studied such topics as attention span, reaction time, color vision, and time perception. In one study, for example, he had an observer look at a block of 12 letters for a fraction of a second and

---

dualism. The assumption that the body and mind are separate, though perhaps interacting, entities.

monism. The assumption that the body and mind are the same; the mind and body are part of one synergistic entity.

structuralism. Developed by Wilhelm Wundt and his student Edward Titchener as a theory of consciousness by breaking down consciousness into elements that constitute the mind.

introspection. Wundt's method of having trained observers report on their conscious, moment-to-moment reactions.

Wilhelm Wundt (1832–1920) founded the first laboratory dedicated to the scientific study of the mind at a time when no courses in psychology were being taught because the discipline did not yet exist on its own.

Source: Wikimedia, Weltrundschau zu Reclams Universum 1902

Margaret Floy Washburn (1871–1939) became the first woman to receive a PhD in psychology. In 1908, she wrote *The Animal Mind*, a book that was important to the emerging study of animal behavior.

Source: Wikimedia Commons

then immediately report as many as he could remember. Six letters seemed to be his limit. What would happen if the number of letters in the array were varied? How would others do if given the same task? By recruiting people to serve as participants, varying stimulus conditions, and demanding that all observations be repeated, Wundt was laying the foundation for today's psychology experiment.

In the United States, this budding new field was hearing a second voice. That voice belonged to William James (1842–1910)—a medical school graduate who went on to become a professor at Harvard University. In 1875, James (whose brother Henry was the famous novelist) offered his first course in psychology. He was very different from Wundt, but he too was influential. While Wundt was establishing psychology as a rigorous new laboratory science, James was arousing interest in the subject matter through rich ideas and eloquent prose. Those who studied with James described him as an "artist" (Leary, 1992). This group included G. Stanley Hall (who had also worked with Wundt), Mary Whiton Calkins (a memory researcher who conducted one of the first studies of dreams and in 1905 became the first female president of the American Psychological Association), and Edward Thorndike (known for his work on animal learning and for the first textbook on educational psychology).

In 1890, James published a brilliant two-volume text entitled *The Principles of Psychology*, and in 1892 he followed it with a condensed version. In 28 chapters, James wrote about habit formation, the stream of consciousness, individuality, the link between mind and body, emotions, the self, and other deep and challenging topics. The original text was referred to as "James"; the brief version was nicknamed "Jimmy." For American psychology students of many generations, at least one of these books was required reading. Now, more than a hundred years later, psychologists continue to cite these classics. The brief version can still be found in the paperback section of many bookstores, and online.

A third prominent leader of the new psychology was Sigmund Freud (1856–1939), a neurologist from Vienna. Quite far removed from the laboratory, Freud was developing a very different approach to psychology through clinical practice. After graduating from medical school, he saw patients who seemed to

William James (1842–1910) a medical school graduate who went on to become a professor at Harvard University teaching courses in psychology. In 1890, James published the first textbook in psychology, titled *The Principles of Psychology*.

Source: Wikimedia Commons

be suffering from ailments that had no physical basis. These patients were not consciously faking, and they could often be "cured" under hypnosis. Based on his observations, Freud formulated **psychoanalysis**—a theory of personality, a form of psychotherapy, and one of the most influential schools of thought in modern history. Freud and his many followers (most notably, Carl Jung, Alfred Adler, and Karen Horney) left a permanent mark on psychology.

Freud (1900) introduced his theory in *The Interpretation of Dreams*, the first of 24 books he would write. In sharp contrast to Wundt and James, who defined psychology as the study of conscious experience, Freud argued that people are driven largely by *un*conscious forces. Indeed, he likened the human mind to an iceberg: The small tip above the water is the conscious part, and the vast region submerged beneath the surface is the unconscious. Working from this assumption, Freud and his followers developed personality tests and therapy techniques designed to penetrate this hidden but important part of the human mind (explored further in Chapter 8).

Despite the differences in their approaches, Wundt, James, and Freud were the pioneers of modern psychology. Indeed, they were ranked by 29 prominent historians as the first, second, and third most important psychologists of all time (Korn, Davis, & Davis, 1991). Many others also helped shape this new discipline (illustrated in Table 1.1). In 1885, German philosopher Hermann Ebbinghaus published the results of classic experiments on memory and forgetting, using himself as a subject. In 1886, American Lightner Witmer opened the first psychological clinic. He later established the first journal and training program in a new helping profession that he would call "clinical psychology" (McReynolds, 1997). In 1905, French psychologist Alfred Binet devised the first major intelligence test in order to assess the academic potential of schoolchildren in Paris. And in 1912, Max Wertheimer

Sigmund Freud (1856–1939) posited that people are driven largely by unconscious forces. From this perspective, Freud formulated a theory of personality called psychoanalysis, which is a form of psychotherapy, and one of the most influential schools of thought in modern history.

Hans Casparius / Stringer / Getty

psychoanalysis. Freud's theory of personality and method of psychotherapy, both of which assume that our motives are largely unconscious.

TABLE 1.1		Pioneers of Modern Psychology
Wilhelm Wundt	1879	At the University of Leipzig, Germany, established the first psychology laboratory.
Hermann Ebbinghaus	1885	In Germany, conducted classic experiments on memory and forgetting.
Lightner Witmer	1886	In the United States, established the first psychological clinic.
William James	1890	At Harvard University, published *The Principles of Psychology*.
G. Stanley Hall	1892	Founded the American Psychological Association.
Margaret Floy Washburn	1894	First woman to receive a PhD in psychology.
Edward Thorndike	1898	In the United States, reported on the first experiments on animal learning.
Sigmund Freud	1900	In Vienna, introduced psychoanalysis in *The Interpretation of Dreams*.
Alfred Binet	1905	In Paris, developed the first modern intelligence test for assessing schoolchildren.
Mary Whiton Calkins	1905	Became the first female president of the American Psychological Association.
Ivan Pavlov	1906	In Leningrad, discovered classical conditioning in research with dogs.
Max Wertheimer	1912	In Germany, discovered the illusion of apparent movement, which launched Gestalt psychology.
John Watson	1913	In the United States, defined psychology as the study of behavior, sparking behaviorism.

discovered that people see two stationary lights flashing in succession as a single light moving back and forth. This illusion paved the way for Gestalt psychology, a school of thought based on the idea that what people perceive is different from the sum of isolated sensations. In the emergence of psychology as the study of mental processes, there were many, many pioneers.

The Behaviorist Alternative

The first generation of psychologists was just beginning to explore conscious and unconscious mental processes when they were struck by controversy about the direction they were taking: Can a science really be based on introspective reports of subjective experience or on mental processes that supposedly reside in the unconscious? Should understanding how the mind works be the goal of this new science? There were those who did not think so.

In 1898, Edward Thorndike ran a series of novel experiments on "animal intelligence." In one study, he put cats into a cage, put food outside a door, and timed how long it took for them to learn how to escape. After several trials, Thorndike found that the cats, by repeating behaviors that "worked," became quicker with practice. Then in 1906, Russian physiologist Ivan Pavlov made another key discovery. Pavlov was studying the digestive system in dogs by putting food in their mouths and measuring the flow of saliva. After repeated testing, he found that the dogs would salivate in anticipation before the food was in the mouth. At first, Pavlov saw this "psychic secretion" as a nuisance. But soon he realized what it revealed: that a very basic form of learning had taken place.

Interesting. But what do puzzle-solving cats and salivating lab dogs have to do with psychology? Indeed, what's the relevance to people of *any* animal research? To answer these questions, John Watson—an American psychologist who experimented with dogs, cats, fish, rats, monkeys, frogs, and chickens—redefined psychology as the study of observable behavior, not of the invisible and elusive mind. Said Watson in his address given at Columbia University, "Psychology as the behaviorist views it is a purely objective experimental branch of natural science. Its theoretical goal is the prediction and control of behavior" (1913, p. 158). Sensations, thoughts, feelings, and motivations may fuel speculation for the curious philosopher, but if something can't be seen, then it has no place in psychology. Psychoanalysis, barked Watson, is "voodooism" (1927, p. 502). As for using animals, Watson—like others who were influenced by Darwin's theory of evolution—saw no reason to believe that the principles of behavior would differ from one species to the next.

American psychologists were immediately drawn to the hard-boiled approach of **behaviorism**. The behaviorist's research goals were clear: Vary a *stimulus* in the environment and observe the organism's *response*. There were no inferences made about mental processes inside the head, just stimulus-response connections. It was all neat, clean, and objective. One of Watson's more famous examples was that of Little Albert—a 9-month-old boy conditioned by John Watson and his research assistant, Rosalie Raynor, to fear objects that included a white rat, and even generalized to other furry objects, such as a rabbit, a furry dog, and white cotton balls as a beard (Watson & Rayner, 1920). Watson's academic career was cut short not long afterward after he was forced out of academic psychology in 1920 when it became public that he had an extramarital affair with his research assistant. He divorced his wife; married the assistant whom he loved, Rosalie Raynor; and left psychology as a result of this incident. (Watson then went into advertising, where he applied the principles of conditioning and became a leader in the industry.) But behaviorism was alive and well. Psychology was defined as the scientific study of behavior, and animal laboratories were springing up all over North America.

Behaviorism had many proponents and was popular for many years. After Watson, another leader emerged. B. F. Skinner, the psychologist who coined the term *reinforcement*, invented an apparatus for use in testing animals and demonstrated in numerous experiments with rats and

behaviorism. A school of thought that defines psychology as the scientific study of observable behavior.

Now he fears even Santa Claus

Rosalie Raynor with Little Albert, a 9-month-old boy conditioned to fear objects that included a white rat, and even generalized to other furry objects, such as a beard.

Source: Wikimedia, Akron psychology archives.

pigeons that behavior is controlled by reward contingencies in the environment. Skinner first reported on his experiments in 1938. Later, he and others used his findings to modify behavior in the workplace, the classroom, the clinic, and other settings. To the day he died, Skinner (1990) maintained that psychology could never be a science of mind.

The "Cognitive Revolution"

Behaviorism dominated psychology in the United States and Canada from the 1920s through the 1960s. Ultimately, however, psychologists were unwilling to limit their scope to the study of observable behavior. There was too much happening inside the human organism that was interesting and hard to ignore. Physiologists were locating new pathways in the brain that regulate thoughts, feelings, and behavior. Animal researchers were finding that inborn biological instincts often interfere with learning. Child development researchers were noticing that children pass through a series of cognitive stages in the way they think about the world. Those interested in social relations were finding that our interactions with other people are influenced by the way we perceive and interpret their actions. Those studying psychoanalysis were increasingly coming to appreciate the powerful influences of unconscious motivation. And psychologists who called themselves humanists argued that people strive not only for reward but also to achieve "self-actualization," a higher state of fulfillment. Among the foundational psychologists for the humanistic approach are Carl Rogers (who is also regarded as among the founding fathers of psychotherapy research) and Abraham Maslow (who developed the groundbreaking work of a hierarchy of needs focused on positive qualities in people).

The most dramatic change that took place in psychology was (and still is) the "cognitive revolution." The term **cognition** refers to the mental processes that intervene between a stimulus and response—including images, memories, expectations, and abstract concepts. At least in the United States, the cognitive psychologies of Wundt and James were swept under the proverbial rug for years during the rise of behaviorism. The subject matter was considered too "soft" and nonscientific. In the 1960s, however, the pendulum swung back and cognitive psychology reemerged, stronger than ever, in a trend that has continued to this day (Robins, Gosling, & Craik, 1999; Xiong & Proctor, 2018).

What rekindled this interest in mental processes? One source of inspiration was the invention of the computer. Built for information-processing purposes, computers provided a new and intriguing model of the human mind. The computer receives input in the form of symbols, converts the symbols into a special code, stores the information, and retrieves it from memory when directed to do so. Computer hardware was likened to the brain, and computer programs provided a step-by-step flowchart model of how information about a stimulus is processed to produce a response. Computers are at the cutting edge of science, so the metaphor is readily accepted (Neisser, 1967; Newell, Shaw, & Simon, 1958; Xiong & Proctor, 2018).

A second source of inspiration came from Swiss psychologist Jean Piaget. Beginning in the 1920s, Piaget studied the way children think. He developed various tasks that revealed how children of different ages reason about people, objects, time, nature, morality, and other aspects of the world. From dozens of studies described in his more than 40 books and 62,935 pages of writing, Piaget theorized that from infancy to adolescence, all children advance through a series of cognitive stages. Despite the dominance of behaviorism in the United States, Piaget had a large following in Europe, and his writings—which were translated into English in the 1950s and 1960s—were ultimately deemed too important to ignore.

The cognitive revolution was also fueled by developments in the study of language. B. F. Skinner (1957) had argued that the laws of learning control the acquisition of language in much the same way that they control the way a laboratory rat learns to press a metal bar to get food. However, linguist Chomsky (1959) charged that such an account was naive. Chomsky noted that children all over the world start to speak at roughly the same age and proceed at approximately the same rate without explicit training or reinforcement. He argued convincingly that our capacity for language is innate and that specialized cognitive structures are "hard-wired" into the human brain as a product of evolution. Chomsky's theory dealt a serious blow to behaviorism and sparked a great deal of interest in psycholinguistics—a topic that has played a key role in the cognitive revolution.

---

cognition. A general term that refers to mental processes such as thinking, knowing, and remembering.

Today, few psychologists identify themselves as strict behaviorists. Free to probe beneath the surface, researchers have thus made some fascinating discoveries. For example, psychologists now know that people all over the world smile when they're happy, that memories of the past can be altered by misinformation, that our views of one another are biased by first impressions, that personality traits are partly inherited, and that drugs can be used to treat certain psychological disorders. Behaviorism has had a profound, lasting, and positive impact, but psychology's horizons have expanded beyond it in exciting ways.

> **LEARNING CHECK**
>
> **Trail Blazers**
>
> Match each figure in the history of psychology to the term or topic most closely associated with him or her.
>
> 1. B. F. Skinner
> 2. Jean Piaget
> 3. Wilhelm Wundt
> 4. Sigmund Freud
> 5. Ivan Pavlov
> 6. William James
> 7. Mary Whiton Calkins
>
> a. Measured salivation in dogs
> b. First laboratory devoted to the study of the human mind
> c. Formulation of psychoanalysis
> d. Elected president of American Psychological Association in 1905
> e. Theorized that all children advance through cognitive stages
> f. Coined the term *reinforcement*
> g. Wrote *The Principles of Psychology*
>
> (Answers: 1. f; 2. e; 3. b; 4. c; 5. a; 6. g; 7. d.)

Expansion of Psychology's Horizons

Just over one hundred years ago, psychology was in its infancy. Since that time, it has grown larger and stronger, with more research published today in psychology than ever before. Indeed, the number of searchable articles in the largest database for finding psychological research, PsycINFO, has more than doubled just since the turn of the century (illustrated in Figure 1.1). Psychology has developed in four important ways.

First, there are many more areas of **basic research** today than in the past. The goals of basic research are to test theories, study processes, discover general principles, and build a factual foundation of knowledge for the field. Psychology now has many subfields, and each focuses on mind and behavior from a somewhat different perspective.

Second, psychology has expanded in the area of **applied research**. Although some psychologists believe that the discipline should remain a pure and basic laboratory science, others want to study people in real-world settings, using the results to solve practical human problems. Some specific areas of applied research include health, education, business, law, family, politics, engineering, military, and sports.

Third, psychology has become more open and inclusive as a profession and contains within its ranks a more diverse group of people than in the past. When psychology was forming as a new discipline, virtually all psychologists were white, male, and from North America or Europe. This has changed dramatically over time, particularly in recent years—a change that has both elevated the pool of talent within the field and brought in important new perspectives on the human condition. Today, there are more female and minority psychologists than ever before, as well as more psychologists from other parts of the world.

Fourth, psychology has strengthened over the years by refining its research methods. Human beings are complex and difficult to study. As individuals, we differ in our biological makeup, age, experience, and cultural background, for example. The way we behave in one setting may differ from the way we behave in another. The inner workings of the mind can never actually be "seen." In fact, we

basic research. "Pure science" research that tests theories and builds a foundation of knowledge.

applied research. Research that aims to solve practical human problems.

FIGURE 1.1 — Growth of Psychology

As measured by the number of searchable articles in PsycINFO, psychology has flourished over the years and is still in the midst of an enormous growth spurt.

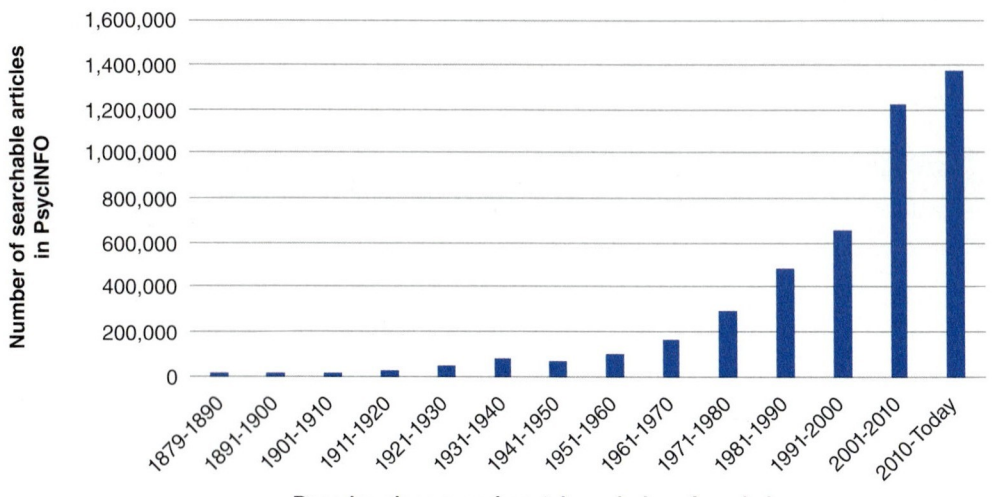

Decades since experimental psychology founded by Wilhelm Wundt in 1879

often lack insight even into ourselves. To meet these challenges, researchers use various tests, mazes, inkblots, shock-generating devices, computerized perception tasks, brain scans, and sophisticated instruments that record physiological states. Most important, as we'll soon explore, psychology stands high on the shoulders of the scientific method.

Psychology as a Multidimensional Science

Psychology is multidimensional, as illustrated in Figure 1.2. It is a highly specialized discipline in which researchers examine people from a number of different perspectives (outlined in Table 1.2).

From a **biological perspective**, human beings are, first and foremost, biological animals, genetically predisposed to behave in some ways rather than others. Many psychologists focus on these biological aspects of human nature. For some, this means studying the neuroscience of the human body, brain, and nervous system—and their influence on our behavior. Others evaluate how behaviors in turn influence a variety of biological and neuroscience functions, such as brain activity, the immune system, and general health. Still others bring biological perspectives into psychology through the study of animal behavior, the evolutionary origins of human behavior, behavioral genetics, and the influences of hormones and drugs.

Also important in psychology today is a focus on internal psychological processes and what goes on "inside the head." From this **cognitive perspective**, with computer-based models serving as a representation of the human mind, cognitive psychologists study the ways in which people are competent, rational, and objective in the way they process information about the world. They study such topics as sensation and perception, consciousness, learning, memory and forgetting, thought, and language. Also focused on inner processes, many researchers study the ways in which we warm-blooded humans are driven by motivations and emotions.

Psychology also has a focus on the ways in which people develop over the lifespan. From this **developmental perspective**, an important issue is the "nature-nurture" debate concerning evolutionary, genetic, and biological influences on us—and the ways in which these influences are tempered by environmental factors from parents, siblings, peers, and culture as a whole. Aspects of individual development, such as self-esteem, intelligence, trust, resilience, and personality, are interests, as well. Some developmental psychologists study prenatal development; some study infants, children, or adolescents; others, often called geropsychologists, specialize in various aspects of adulthood and old age.

---

biological perspective. A perspective in psychology for evaluating the physical basis of animal and human behavior. It involves topics such as the brain, immune system, nervous system, and genetics.

cognitive perspective. A perspective in psychology for evaluating how mental processes such as memory, perception, thinking, and problem solving are related to behavior.

developmental perspective. A perspective in psychology for evaluating change over the lifespan. It involves topics such as physical, cognitive, biological, and social development processes.

FIGURE 1.2 ■ Psychology as a Diverse, Intellectual Discipline

Psychology is a diverse discipline. Its interests span the social behavior of large crowds to the study of animal conditioning.

iStock.com/simonkr; iStock.com/gorodenkoff

TABLE 1.2 ■ Perspectives of Psychology

Perspective	Focus
Biological	Biological aspects of human nature
Cognitive	Inner processes
Developmental	Ways in which people develop over the lifespan
Social psychological	Influences of other people on the individual
Sociocultural	Dynamics of society and cultural on human behavior
Clinical	Understanding and treatment of "abnormal" behavior
Positive psychological	Promotion and maintenance of positive health and wellness; prevention of illness and disability
Health	Influences of the individual and health care on health
Educational	Human learning across the lifespan
School	Ways to improve education and learning via better diagnosis and treatment for students with behavioral and learning problems
Counseling	Ways to improve the health and wellness of patients (in general practice) and students (in education)
Forensic psychological	Applied issues related to law and the legal system
Industrial/organizational (I/O)	Issues related to individuals and groups in the workplace; regional, national, and global impacts of businesses and industries

Human beings are gregarious animals, not isolated hermits, so a **social psychological perspective** is necessary to fully understand the human experience. Drawn together by the belief that social situations sometimes cause us to behave in ways that are "out of character," social psychologists focus on the influences of other people on the individual. By observing people in carefully staged social settings, researchers in this area study a range of behaviors—including attraction, conformity, persuasion, aggression, altruism, and group dynamics. A critical perspective that has risen from the social psychological perspective is the **sociocultural perspective**, in which the focus is on the dynamics of society and culture on human behavior. Sociocultural psychologists study many cultural influences and the

social psychological perspective. A perspective in psychology for evaluating the dynamics of social interaction and its effects on groups and the individual.

sociocultural perspective. A perspective in psychology for evaluating the dynamics of society and culture on human behavior. It involves topics such as the dynamics of stereotyping, prejudice, and discrimination.

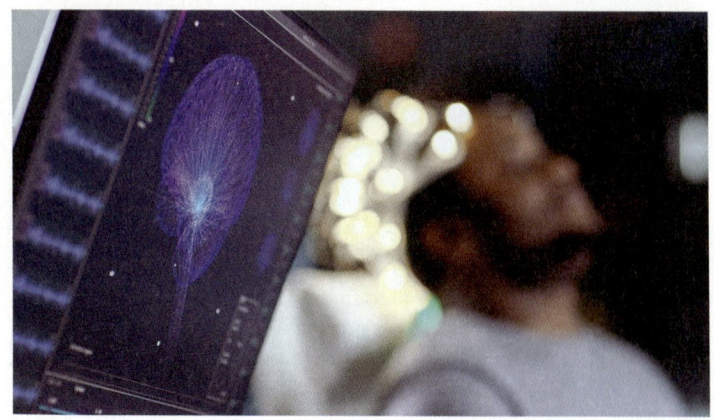

In a laboratory study, behavior is observed in a controlled environment—such as a sleep laboratory to study sleep disorders.

iStock.com/gorodenkoff

clinical perspective. A perspective in psychology for evaluating the nature and treatment of dysfunction in human behavior. It involves topics of mental and physical health.

positive psychological perspective. A perspective in psychology for evaluating human flourishing and wellness. It involves topics of maintaining optimal mental and physical health.

intergroup problems of stereotyping, prejudice, and discrimination.

Possibly the largest and most visible perspective in psychology comes from a **clinical perspective**. In contrast to those who strive to understand what's "normal," clinical psychologists study people who are "abnormal" in their perceptions, thoughts, feelings, and behavior. Based on the study of human personality and the belief that people have a capacity for change and renewal, clinical psychologists—and other mental health workers—routinely seek to diagnose and treat psychological disorders such as anxiety, depression, and schizophrenia.

Many other fields and perspectives in psychology have risen from these fundamental perspectives. For example, the clinical perspective focuses largely on mental and physical health—specifically, when such health needs treatment. However, around the beginning of the 21st century, a **positive psychological perspective** arose as a new perspective. Instead of evaluating human disorder, positive psychologists evaluate human flourishing and wellness, focusing on the promotion and maintenance of positive mental and physical health, as well as the prevention of illness and disability.

Many other fields in psychology have risen from these fundamental perspectives in applied settings. Consider, for example, your health. Psychologists who study health, called *health psychologists*, focus on factors associated with being healthy across the lifespan (part of a developmental perspective)—in terms of the individual (behavior, emotion, cognition, social interactions, motivation, and biological functioning) and the environment (access to gyms, health care, walkable communities, and health foods). Consider also the educational environment. Psychologists who study education, called *educational psychologists*, focus on human learning across the lifespan (part of a developmental perspective)—in terms of the individual (behavior, emotion, cognition, social interactions, motivation, and biological functioning) and the environment (classroom, school, family, education policy, and community) as well.

Drawn from clinical and developmental perspectives, psychologists who study schooling, called *school psychologists*, aim to improve education and learning. School psychologists are responsible for diagnosing and treating behavioral and learning problems in students—largely children and adolescents—in an educational environment. The school psychologists assess these students and develop plans for schools to support them. Similarly, psychologists who study counseling, called *counseling psychologists*, draw from cognitive, clinical, and developmental perspectives to improve the health and wellness of students and patients. Counseling psychologists in general practice provide marriage, family, individual, and career guidance; counseling psychologists in education provide individual, career, and guidance counseling to students and sometimes their families.

In other professional settings, psychology also has its imprint. For example, forensic psychology is an applied field that addresses issues related to law, the legal system, and those involved in the system—from the police and lawyers to the criminals (accused and convicted). *Forensic psychologists* address issues from individual, community, societal, policy, and legal approaches, including crime and drug prevention, prisons and rehabilitation, the dynamics in a courtroom, law enforcement, and even crime scene and criminal analysis. In workplace settings, industrial/

Counseling reflects the discipline of psychology as a multidimensional science that incorporate many perspectives and approaches to helping people live their best lives.

iStock.com/SDI Productions

organizational (I/O) psychology is an applied field that addresses issues related to individuals and groups in the workplace, and issues related to the regional, national, and global impacts of businesses and industries. *I/O psychologists* focus on issues such as employee motivation and management, organizational effectiveness, the well-being of employees, personality traits and their ability to predict job performance, and marketing.

Certainly, the perspectives and fields of psychology shared here do not represent an exhaustive list of all the perspectives and areas of focus in psychology. What should be clear is that the field of psychology is far reaching and has diverse applications across disciplines. From child development to education to work, health, culture, society, and more, psychology contributes to our understanding of the world and the people with whom we interact—and, maybe most important, to an understanding of ourselves.

Psychology as a Responsive and Anticipatory Science

Psychology is—and always has been—a science that is *responsive* to current events—in terms of both anticipating human problems and human exceptionality (e.g., promoting positive health in the community) and reacting to those events (e.g., helping survivors cope following a natural disaster). From the beginning, psychologists from all perspectives have sought to apply what they have learned in order to solve important human problems. As mentioned previously, early in the 20th century, French psychologist Alfred Binet developed the first modern intelligence test to help schools identify children needing special attention. After the Nazi horrors of World War II, psychologists began intensive study of obedience to authority, propaganda, prejudice, and aggression. Today, psychologists study factors influencing, among other things, health (e.g., traumatic stress, work-life balance), safety (e.g., foreign and domestic terrorism, natural disasters), the importance of diversity and inclusion in a range of settings (e.g., from movements such as BLM and #MeToo to issues of hate and discrimination), the impact of social media use in society, sports gambling and addiction, and the impact of politics on human behavior (e.g., immigration reform and climate). As with all other basic sciences, psychology has strayed from the laboratories of the ivory tower into the real world.

Values, Ethics, and Social Responsibility

The application of psychology—or any other science, for that matter—raises hard and sometimes tricky questions about values, professional ethics, and social responsibility (Johnson, Barnett, Elman, Forrest, & Kaslow, 2012). For example, should research be suppressed if it yields socially sensitive results? It's easy in the abstract for psychologists to assert that they must seek the truth regardless of where it may lead, but what about the policy implications? Why do peaceful protests turn violent? How does social media use impact protesting? What is the potential impact of human-like robots powered by artificial intelligence (AI)? Can these robots ultimately impact or even supplant human-to-human contact? Does giving mean generosity? Is a poor person's penny worth less than a wealthy person's dollar?

Additional questions confront those who apply psychology. Is it ethical to dispense mental health advice on television or radio? Should psychologists use their scientific credentials to promote drug company products or to lobby for LGBTQ+ rights, abortion rights, handgun control, racial justice, and other social and political causes? Should psychologists testify as experts in trials involving questions of competence or insanity? Working in a discipline that addresses many delicate topics, psychologists routinely must face these important questions. To illustrate some of these fascinating links between basic and applied psychology, every chapter of this text contains one or more special boxes designed to highlight relevant research in an

Many clinical psychologists collect patient health data. Tracking health outcomes can be critical for optimal patient health, but to what extent is it appropriate to record, store, and track such data in real time?

iStock.com/XiXinXing

The First Amendment to the U.S. Constitution states that "Congress shall make no law ... abridging the right of the people peaceably to assemble." Understanding how peaceful protests become violent is of great concern to psychologists and lawmakers.

JOSE LUIS MAGANA / Contributor / Getty

important and interesting domain of application. Whether the topic is health and medicine, education, business, law, sports, politics, world news, or the environment, these applications boxes will help to animate all aspects of the field.

Psychology Applied: When Protests Become Violent

You may have heard the phrase "There is nothing more American than peaceful protest," made popular by Russell Feingold, an American lawyer and former U.S. senator from Wisconsin. Yet protests are not always peaceful. Protests that turned violent in recent years include clashes between protesters and police in Ferguson, Missouri, after the death of Michael Brown in 2014, and in Baltimore, Maryland, after the death of Freddie Gray in 2015. In 2017, violence erupted between protesters and counterprotesters during a rally in Charlottesville, Virginia. The violence there resulted in the death of civil rights activist Heather Heyer, who was hit by a car that plowed into the crowd of counterprotesters she had joined.

Why did these protests, which began peacefully, turn violent? Can we not only predict the emergence of violence but also understand why it occurs? Researchers from Northwestern University, the University of Southern California, and Rensselaer Polytechnic Institute collaborated to find answers to these questions. Mooijman and colleagues (2018) evaluated more than 18 million tweets sent out during the Baltimore protests in 2015 and conducted independent experiments to test their hypothesis that protest violence can be understood as a function of what they called *moralization*, or the extent to which protesters consider their cause a moral issue, and *agreement*, or the extent to which protesters believe others in their social network think about that cause the same way they do.

To add context for the tweets evaluated by Mooijman and colleagues (2018), let's consider the case of Freddie Gray (NPR, 2015). On April 12, 2015, Freddie Gray, a 25-year-old African American resident of Baltimore, Maryland, was arrested by city police for possession of an allegedly illegal knife. During his transport in a police van, Gray sustained injuries to his neck and spine and subsequently fell into a coma. He was pronounced dead on April 19. Protests over the treatment Gray received during his arrest and while in police custody began on April 18, a day before his death. Protests were peaceful initially; however, they became increasingly tense as information regarding the arrest was made public—such as video evidence of the arrest, the police officers' insistence that excessive force was not used, and the failure of police officers to get medical attention for Gray in a timely manner. On April 25, after the funeral service for Gray, protests grew and violence ensued with at least 20 police officers injured, hundreds of arrests, hundreds of businesses damaged, and hundreds more vehicular and structural fires. Mooijman and colleagues evaluated tweets that circulated during this time. As the violence grew, a state of emergency was declared in the city of Baltimore; it was not lifted until May 6. Six police officers were ultimately charged with various offenses related to Gray's death, including second-degree murder—three officers were acquitted, and charges against the other three officers were dropped.

Why did the Freddie Gray protests turn violent? Can we use what we learn from them to predict the emergence of violence in future protests? That is exactly what Mooijman and colleagues tested. Let's look at the findings from their insightful study.

Moralization of a Cause

Many issues can have moral undertones. For example, political issues—such as abortion rights, physician aid in dying, immigration, and, in the case of the Baltimore protests, perceived racial inequality and police brutality—can reasonably be seen as moral issues. Evidence indicates that the more a cause is seen as a moral issue, the more willing people are to use violence to defend that cause (Skitka

& Morgan, 2014). When an issue is moralized, it is seen more as "right vs. wrong" or "good vs. evil" instead of, for example, as "approve vs. disapprove" or "support vs. do not support" (Rozin, 1999; Skitka, Hanson, & Wisneski, 2017). In this way, protests for a moral issue cause are considered more absolute, which can lead to attitudes that something can or should be done, and even to the endorsement of violence to defend a cause (Skitka & Morgan, 2014).

In the Mooijman et al. (2018) study, nearly 19 million tweets sent during the Baltimore protests were evaluated by three independent reviewers for the extent to which the tweets included moral content. The findings were quite interesting. In an analysis of the number of tweets per day, for example, the number of tweets with moral content did not exceed 8,000 tweets per day prior to the first violent protests on April 25 (illustrated in Figure 1.3). However, on April 25, nearly 10,000 tweets contained moral content, and the number of tweets containing such content grew exponentially as the violence grew, maxing out at nearly 25,000 tweets per day at the peak of the violence over the next few days. By the time the city of Baltimore lifted the state of emergency on May 6, the number of tweets containing moral content had fallen again below 8,000 tweets per day. The pattern was clear: As the moralization of the issue increased (measured by the number of tweets per day with moral content), the violence also increased.

Perceived Moral Convergence and Social Media

According to Mooijman et al. (2018), the acceptability of violence in protests can best be understood by *perceived moral convergence*: the moralization of an issue—seeing a cause as a moral issue—plus the degree of perceived agreement—the belief that others share one's moral attitude. In subsequent experiments, that is exactly what the researchers found: Moralization of an issue predicted violence only when participants believed that others shared their moral attitudes.

Consider the implications of these results for social media. Moralization alone—while showing a clear pattern in the Baltimore protests—does not predict violence unless the protesters also believe others share their moral views. Social media provides a unique platform by which protesters can gauge agreement, thereby enhancing perceived moral convergence, which was the best predictor for the acceptability of violence in protests. As the co-first author Joseph Hoover explains: "The risk of violent protest may not only simply be a function of moralization but also the perception that others agree with one's moral position, which can be strongly influenced by social media dynamics." Thinking ahead about the role of social media in protests, such as those following the killing of George Floyd in Minneapolis, Minnesota, on May 25, 2020, what will future protests look like? As world and community leaders seek to prevent violence in protests, often through increased security and force, psychologists seek to understand the reasons for the violence and its impact on us all.

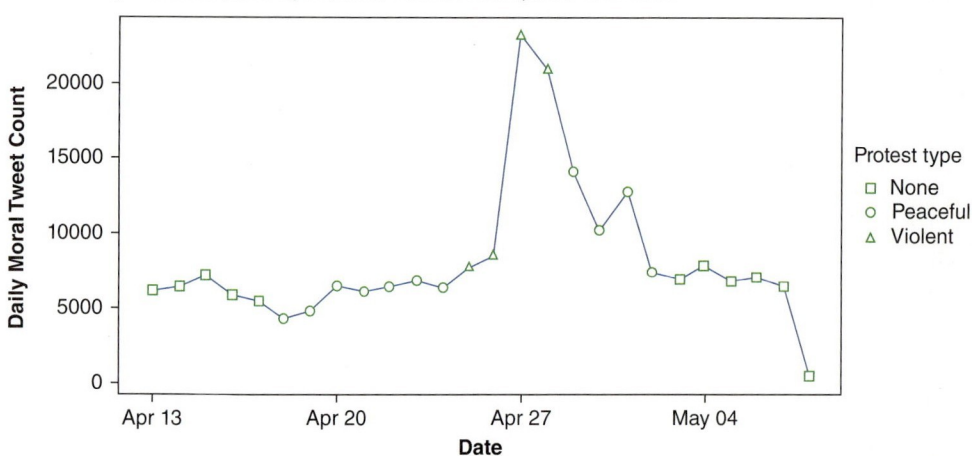

FIGURE 1.3 ■ Number of Tweets per Day during the Baltimore Protests

Tweets containing moral content spiked during the time frame when the Baltimore protests became violent.

A Range of Perspectives

When Wundt, James, Freud, and others were defining this new discipline in the late 19th and early 20th centuries, virtually all psychologists were white, male, and from North America or Europe. In part, this situation existed because of discrimination and other societal barriers that made it difficult for women and minorities to enter the professional ranks. Consider the distinguished career of Mary Whiton Calkins.

In the 1890s, Calkins successfully completed graduate coursework at Harvard to the acclaim of William James and her other professors there. She went on to write two textbooks and a number of important research articles, she founded one of the first psychology laboratories in the United States at Wellesley College, and in 1905 she was elected first female president of the American Psychological Association. Yet at the time, Harvard University would not grant her a PhD because she was a woman. The pages of psychology's history are filled with other important women who faced institutional obstacles (O'Connell & Russo, 1990). Today, things have changed. A majority of psychologists entering practice in North America are women (Association for Women in Psychology, 2019), and include significant contributions from psychologists such as Mary Ainsworth (attachment theory), and Karen Horney (neurosis and personality), Barbara Rolls (hunger and satiety), and Elizabeth Loftus (memory and eyewitness testimony).

Minorities were also highly underrepresented in the early years of psychology. In 1920, Francis Sumner, who studied at Clark University with G. Stanley Hall, became the first African American to earn a PhD in psychology. He went on to publish two articles about the higher education of African American youths (Sawyer, 2000). To pave the way for progress, consider the landmark case of *Brown v. Board of Education of Topeka* (1954), in which the U.S. Supreme Court ruled for the first time that racially separate schools were unequal and had to be integrated. In support of its opinion, the Court cited studies by Kenneth B. Clark, an African American psychologist whose research suggested that racial segregation makes Black schoolchildren feel inferior. Behind the scenes, Clark played a pivotal role in the application of psychology to the civil rights movement. This was also the first time that the U.S. Supreme Court had cited psychology research in an opinion. Cultural and political shifts in the 1960s continued this progress toward greater representation of minority psychologists. Cultural and political activism, such as the civil rights movement and Black nationalism, provided platforms by which to address institutional challenges. This activism paved the way for minority groups, including Asian, Black, and Latinx persons, to join the ranks—and many have made significant contributions.

The demographic makeup of psychology is more inclusive today than ever, as it includes more women, ethnicities, sexualities, gender identities, and those from the international community. Clearly, the more perspectives that are brought to bear on the study of mind and behavior, the better. As Association for Psychological Science fellow Robert M. Sellers stated in an address at the association's annual convention in New York City, "It's very difficult for one to think about how, as human beings, we can actually study human beings from an objective perspective.... [It's our goal] to try to understand the perspective that we bring to bear and to both value that perspective and put it into context." In the past, researchers typically observed the behavior of predominantly male college students because college students were convenient to sample and, in the mid- to early 1900s, college students tended to be mostly males; and an assumption was made that the results would apply generally to people all over the world. This assumption was largely unchallenged for many years until finally, in the 1960s and 1970s, a new generation of researchers, many of whom were female, identified important similarities and differences between men and women. Today, women have a greater voice than ever in the field of psychology, with women now earning more doctorates in psychology than men each year (since 2014, women have earned more college degrees than men). As we'll explore in later chapters, the study of sex and gender is now basic to all areas of psychology. Similarly, researchers of varying nationalities are now testing psychological theories in different parts of the world.

Mary Whiton Calkins (1863–1930) studied at Harvard University with William James and went on to have a distinguished career. She was never granted her PhD, however, because she was a woman. In 1905, Calkins was elected the first female president of the American Psychological Association.

Notman studio, Boston via Wikimedia Commons

In 1920, Francis Sumner became the first Black man to earn a PhD in psychology. Sumner was an American leader in education reform and is commonly regarded as the "Father of Black Psychology."

Kenneth B. Clark is a Black psychologist whose research was cited by the United States Supreme Court in Brown v. Board of Education (1954), a landmark ruling that outlawed the racial segregation of public schools.

Source: Kenneth Bancroft Clark, 1914-2005 Chicago Urban League Records, University of Illinois at Chicago Library. http://collections.carli.illinois.edu/u?/uic_cul,149

These studies enable us to determine the extent to which certain patterns of human behavior are "universal" or found only in certain populations. As we'll explore throughout this text, it could be said that everyone is basically the same, yet no two people are alike.

Considerations of diversity within the profession are also important in the mental health area. In countries with heterogeneous populations, such as the United States and Canada, many racial and ethnic minority groups have their own unique languages, worldviews, lifestyles, experiences, and problems. Some researchers now specialize in diagnosing and treating mental health problems in Asian American groups (Lor, 2018). Others focus on Latinx populations (Velasco-Mondragon, Jimenez, Palladino-Davis, Davis, & Escamilla-Cejudo, 2016). To be most helpful in providing treatment to individuals from diverse populations, psychotherapists need to understand the ways in which their clients are "culturally unique" (Anders et al., 2021; Cuellar & Paniagua, 2000).

SCIENTIFIC METHODS

LEARNING OBJECTIVES

Consider the methods, tools, types of participants, and ethical practices used to study psychology and evaluate its scientific rigor.

- Explain what scientific methods are and why they are important.
- Evaluate whether it is better to study people in laboratories or in natural settings.
- Justify why psychologists devise subtle measures of behavior when they can just ask people about themselves.
- Describe the various types of research designs.
- Discuss the ethical concerns raised about using humans and animals in research.

Psychology is a scientific endeavor aimed at the discovery of the principles of human behavior that connects each and every one of us.

iStock.com/PeopleImages

critical thinking. The process of solving problems and making decisions through a careful evaluation of evidence.

theory. An organized set of principles that describes, predicts, and explains some phenomenon.

hypothesis. A specific testable prediction, often derived from a theory.

operational definition. A concrete definition of a research variable in terms of the procedures needed to control and measure it.

It happens all the time. You may find a report on the evening news, a Twitter or Facebook feed, or an ad for a new product, and react with a mixture of curiosity and skepticism. For example, you may have heard that cell phone use during class lowers academic performance, that a full moon triggers bizarre behavior, that workaholics work themselves to an early grave, that pornography incites sexual assault, that young drivers are more likely to be involved in car accidents, and that girls start talking before boys. Some of these claims are true; others are not. For this reason, it is always best to keep a critical mind and look for the evidence.

Many of us are drawn to psychology because people are fascinating and the subject matter is important. What unifies the entire discipline, however, is its commitment to scientific methods. A basic goal in science is one that everyone should model: **critical thinking**. Critical thinking is a skill, and it's also an attitude. Psychologists are trained to practice critical thinking. This means that we challenge blind assumptions, distrust our intuition in favor of systematic observation, maintain a healthy air of skepticism, revise our theories in the light of evidence, scrutinize carefully the methods used to derive that evidence, and search for alternative explanations.

The objective of scientific inquiry is to generate creative ideas and entertain these ideas with an open mind—but, at the same time, to be cautious, to demand that all claims be tested, and then to scrutinize the results. The "art" in science is to achieve a balance among these competing objectives. It's good to be creative but not intellectually sloppy. Similarly, it's good to be critical, even skeptical, but not closed-minded. The key to thinking like a psychologist is learning how to walk these fine lines. And that means knowing something about the methods of research used in psychology.

The Research Process

The research process involves developing ideas and questions, and then proceeding through a series of steps designed to answer the questions in a systematic manner. The first step is to develop a theory, or at least a loose set of ideas. As discussed earlier, you already have many intuitive theories on psychological issues. Everyone does. When you chose a college to attend, you may have had to decide whether or not to leave your hometown—which possibly meant leaving behind a significant other. What should you do? What effect would distance have on your relationship? One friend might answer: "Absence makes the heart grow fonder." Those words of encouragement make sense, although a second friend might say with equal certainty, "Out of sight, out of mind." Just what you might expect. Two contradictory assumptions, both derived from common sense.

Psychological theories are more formal than the hunches we come up with in everyday conversation. A **theory** is an organized set of principles that describes, predicts, and explains a phenomenon. We can derive a theory from logic, a world event, a personal experience or an observation, another theory, a research finding, or an accidental discovery. Some theories are broad and encompassing; others account for only a thin slice of behavior. Some are simple; others contain a large number of interrelated propositions.

The second step in the research process is to formulate from one's theory specific testable predictions, or **hypotheses**, about the relationship between two or more variables. Researchers can then test these hypotheses to evaluate the theory as a whole. In a typical study, psychologists would test one or more specific hypotheses derived from the theory. If the results support the hypotheses, confidence in the theory is increased. If the results fail to support the hypotheses, the theory as a whole is revised, qualified, or discarded.

To formulate a testable hypothesis, researchers must provide **operational definitions** that specify, in concrete "how-to" terms, the procedures needed to control and measure the variables in the hypothesis. Over the years, for example, psychologists have tried to determine why we overeat, which can lead to obesity. To do so, researchers have conducted a variety of studies in which research participants consume a variety of foods in a buffet, with the amount consumed operationally defined as the number of calories consumed in these settings. It is possible, for example, that we measure the weight of food (in grams)—however, some people eat small amounts of high-calorie foods while others eat large amounts of low-calorie foods. So, is it often best to operationally define food consumption by measuring caloric intake, even if we can also operationally define it as weight of food consumed? Another example is mood. How do we know if someone is happy or unhappy? Well, one way to operationally define happiness is to give people a survey where they report their happiness. This can be done on a scale from 1 (least happy) to 5 (most happy). Another way to operationally define happiness is to measure behaviors—count the number of times the person smiles or laughs within a certain span of time. For how much time do you want to record smiles and laughs? The number of smiles and laughs can be measured for 5, 15, 60, or even 90 minutes. These specifications are all up to the researcher, and they also illustrate why operational definitions are important. We need to know exactly how the researchers decided to measure things like happiness and the amount of food consumed. Without these details, we cannot replicate experiments as they were themselves conducted, nor can a thorough critique of the experiment occur.

Once researchers have a theory, a hypothesis, and an operational definition in place, they are ready for the next and remaining steps—to design the study, collect data, analyze the results, and draw a conclusion (illustrated in Figure 1.4). There is no magic formula for determining how to test a hypothesis. In fact, as we'll learn, studies vary along at least three dimensions: (a) the setting in which observations are made, (b) the ways in which psychological variables are measured, and (c) the types of conclusions that can be drawn. Let's examine each of these dimensions.

Research Settings

There are two types of settings in which people can be studied. Sometimes, data are collected in a laboratory, usually located at a university, so that the environment can be regulated and the participant observed carefully. **Laboratory research** offers control, precision, and an opportunity to keep conditions uniform for different participants. For example, bringing volunteers into a sleep lab enables the psychologist to monitor their eye movements and brain waves, record the exact time they fall asleep, and get dream reports the moment they awaken. Likewise, bringing a caregiver and child into a special

laboratory research. Research conducted in an environment that can be regulated and in which participants can be observed carefully.

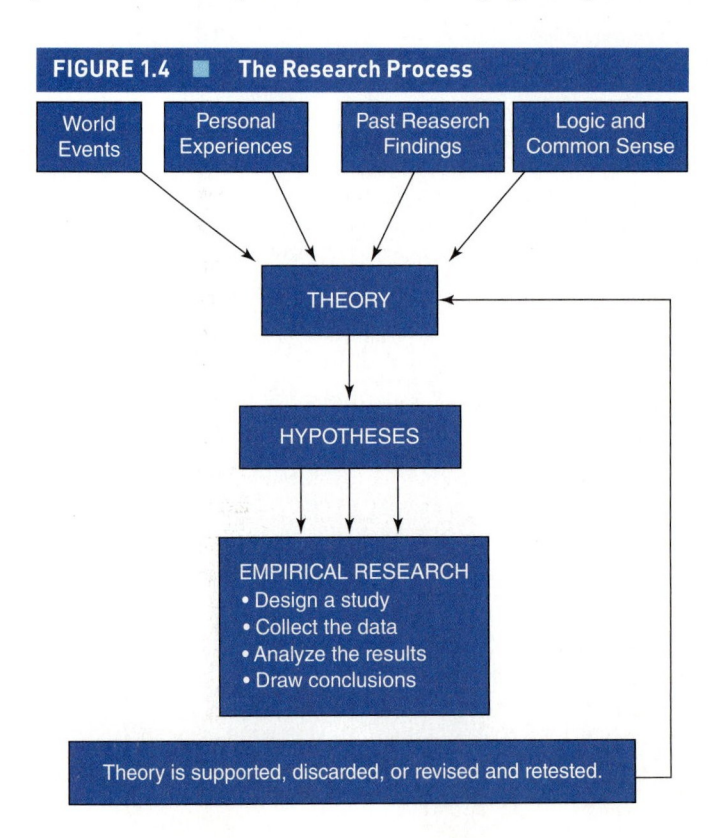

FIGURE 1.4 ■ The Research Process

World Events, Personal Experiences, Past Reaserch Findings, Logic and Common Sense → THEORY → HYPOTHESES → EMPIRICAL RESEARCH
- Design a study
- Collect the data
- Analyze the results
- Draw conclusions

→ Theory is supported, discarded, or revised and retested.

playroom equipped with hand-picked toys, two-way mirrors, a hidden camera, and a microphone enables the psychologist to record every word uttered and analyze every nuance of their interaction. To study the way juries make decisions, potential jurors can be recruited to serve on mock juries so that the researcher can videotape and analyze their deliberations.

Laboratory research is common in science. NASA physicists construct special chambers to simulate weightlessness in space; chemists spark chemical reactions in the test tube; botanists study plant growth in the greenhouse; and meteorologists use wind tunnels to mimic atmospheric conditions. Similarly, psychologists often find it necessary to simulate events in a laboratory. There is, however, a drawback. Can someone sleep normally in a strange bed with metal electrodes pasted to the scalp? Will a caregiver and child interact in the playroom the way they do at home? Do mock juries reach verdicts the same way real juries do? Being an artificially constructed world, the laboratory may at times elicit atypical behavior.

The alternative is **field research** conducted in real-world locations. The psychologist interested in sleep and dreams may have participants report back periodically on their experiences. The caregiver and child could be visited in their own home. And jurors could be questioned about their decision-making process after a trial is over. The setting chosen depends on the behavior to be measured. Indeed, psychologists have observed people on city streets and in classrooms, factories, offices, bars, subways, dormitories, elevators, and even public restrooms. To understand behavior in real-world settings, there is no substitute for field research. Unfortunately, the psychologists "out there" cannot control what happens to their participants or measure with precision all aspects of their experiences. That's why the most fruitful approach is to use both laboratory and field settings.

field research. Research conducted in real-world locations.

Psychological Measurements

Regardless of where observations are made, many different types of measurements can be taken. These types fall into four categories: physiological measures, self-reports, behavioral observations, and archival records. These four types of observations, and the advantages and disadvantages of each, are summarized in Table 1.3.

TABLE 1.3 ■ Four Ways to "Observe" People

Method	Description	Advantages	Disadvantages
Physiological measures	Record physical responses of the brain and body in a human or animal.	Measures are unbiased when careful collection procedures are used.	The equipment needed to make the measurements costs money and requires training.
Self-reports	Ask people to report on themselves in interviews, surveys, or questionnaires.	People often reveal inner states that cannot be "seen" by others.	People distort self-reports to present themselves in a favorable light. People are not always aware of their own inner states.
Behavioral observations	Observe behavior firsthand, openly or covertly, sometimes using special tasks or instruments.	Behavior can be measured objectively.	Inner states can only be inferred from behavior, not actually seen. People may behave differently if they know they are being observed.
Archival records	Observe behavior secondhand, using available records of past activities.	The behavior occurs without the biasing presence of an observer.	Records of past activities are not always complete or accurate.

Physiological Measures

Researchers can measure and compare the normal and disordered functioning of participants' physiological responses. A **physiological measure** is the recorded physical response of the brain or body in a human or animal. For example, researchers can measure stress and anxiety by measuring cortisol levels in a blood sample or by measuring a galvanic skin response; they can measure sleep and arousal using an electroencephalograph, which records brain activity, or by using an electrooculograph, which monitors eye movements. Other commonly used physiological measures include blood pressure (in systolic pressure over diastolic pressure, or millimeters of mercury), heart rate (in number of beats per minute), or body temperature (in degrees Fahrenheit).

The key advantage of physiological measures is that when careful collection procedures are used—for example, checking caffeine consumption or resting heart rate—these measures are unbiased. Physiological measures are particularly unbiased when they are not under conscious control, such as heart rate, blood pressure, body temperature, and skin conductance. Each physiological measure is an involuntary process of the body. The key disadvantage is largely the expense and training required to operate the equipment needed to make these measurements. Self-report and behavioral measures, for example, are often more affordable options.

> **physiological measure.** A type of measurement in which researchers record physical responses of the brain or body in a human or an animal.

Self-Reports

Another way to assess a person's thoughts, feelings, or behavior is to go right to the source and ask. This is the method of **self-report**. Through interviews, questionnaires, or diaries, people are asked to report on their behavior, perceptions, beliefs, attitudes, and emotions. Self-reports are quick and easy to get. The information, however, can be inaccurate and misleading, which is why an entire field, called *psychometrics*, is dedicated to the development of survey and self-reports that can be trusted.

> **self-report.** A method of observation that involves asking people to describe their own thoughts, feelings, or behavior.

Self-reports can be used with a single item or question. For example, Cooke, Emery, Brimelow, and Wollin (2016) had students complete a single-item measure for mood both before and following a therapeutic massage therapy in which participants rated their mood on a five-point Likert-type scale. Although single-item measures are commonly used, multiple-item measures are typically preferred when measuring a **construct** such as quality of life, depression, self-esteem, or disgust. A construct is a variable that can't be observed directly. For example, we can measure life satisfaction indirectly using the Quality of Life Enjoyment and Satisfaction Questionnaire (Endicott, Nee, Harrison, & Blumenthal, 1993); we can measure depression indirectly using the 17-item Hamilton Rating Scale for Depression (Hamilton, 1960; Kalali et al., 2002); we can measure self-esteem indirectly using the Rosenberg Self-Esteem Scale (Rosenberg, 1965); and we can measure disgust indirectly using the Disgust Propensity and Sensitivity Scale (Cavanagh & Davey, 2000). Each survey or measure includes multiple items to measure a construct or behavior.

> **construct.** A conceptual variable that is known to exist but cannot be observed directly.

The key advantage of using a self-report measure is that it is easy and cost-effective to administer and allows researchers to measure a lot of data in little time. Participants can respond to dozens of restricted items in minutes, providing researchers with a lot of data for a construct or behavior. However, the key disadvantage is that self-report items are often inaccurate. Participants can deliberately lie, be confused by the questions being asked, or simply guess if they do not know how to respond to items in a self-report measure.

There are many reasons why participant self-reports can be unreliable. Consider that people sometimes distort their responses in order to present themselves in a favorable light. It's hard to get anyone to admit to failures, mistakes, and shortcomings. Studies show, for example, that people overestimate their own contributions to a joint effort (Ross & Sicoly, 1979), report after the occurrence of an event that they knew all along it would happen (Hawkins & Hastie, 1990), and hide their feelings of prejudice (Crosby, Bromley, & Saxe, 1980). More than this, when respondents try to be accurate, they are often limited in their ability to do so. Long ago, Freud noted that people block certain thoughts and wishes from awareness. And studies show that people often lack insight into the causes of their own behavior (Nisbett & Wilson, 1977).

Behavioral observation is critical to psychology. In this study, children are being observed in a childcare setting.

Billy Hustace / Corbis / Getty

behavioral observation. A form of research based on the firsthand observation of a subject's behavior.

archival research. A form of research that relies on existing records of past behavior.

Self-report measures are common in psychology, sometimes even essential. As you read through this book, however, you'll find that researchers often go out of their way to collect data in more subtle, indirect ways, when possible or practical.

Behavioral Observations

It is said that actions speak louder than words—and many researchers would agree. Many years ago, the Nielsen ratings of television shows (which determine the cost of advertising and success of programs) were derived from the results of surveys and diary forms mailed to viewers. Realizing that these self-reports are flawed, however, Nielsen Media Research later installed "people meters" in thousands of sample households across the country to electronically record what viewers are watching, when, and for how long. Similarly, Internet marketing companies today measure the value of specific websites by monitoring the number of users who visit the site, the amount of time spent there, and the frequency with which users click on the advertising banners.

In psychology as well, the major alternative to self-reports is firsthand **behavioral observation**. To animal researchers, the pressing of a metal bar, the running of a maze, and the consumption of food pellets are important behaviors. Sucking, smiling, crying, moving the eyes, and turning the head are significant sources of information for those who study infants. As for those who study adults, psychologically relevant behaviors range from the blink of an eye to the choice of a marital partner or career. Even changes in internal states (such as respiration, heart rate, eye movements, brain waves, hormone levels, muscle contractions, and white blood cell activity) can be monitored with the use of special instruments.

Behavioral observation plays a particularly important role in the study of subjective experience. One cannot crawl under a subject's skin and literally see what is on the individual's mind. But researchers can try to infer various internal states from behavior. It is usually (though not always) safe to assume, for example, that recognition reveals the presence of a memory, that solving difficult problems reveals intelligence, and that the person who breaks into a cold sweat and runs at the sight of a snake has a fear of snakes.

Archival Records

Another way to collect information about people is to conduct **archival research** that involves examining records of past activities instead of ongoing behavior. Archival measures used in psychology include medical records, birth rates, literacy rates, newspaper stories, sports statistics, photographs, absenteeism rates at work, personal ads, and marriage and divorce records. A major advantage of these kinds of measures is that by observing behavior secondhand, researchers can be sure that they did not influence the participants by their presence. An obvious limitation is that existing and available records of human activity are not always complete or detailed enough to be useful.

For example, Hehman, Graber, Hoffman, and Gaertner (2012) analyzed how two U.S. presidents were portrayed by Internet media outlets to determine whether media outlets would preferentially depict images of presidents that aligned with their political leanings. The warmth and competence of the presidents depicted was evaluated because these qualities are highly prized in leadership and can be conveyed effectively in facial images. Images of the 43rd U.S. president (George W. Bush) and 44th U.S. president (Barack Obama) were collected in May 2010 from conservative-leaning (e.g., FOX.com, *Townhall*) and liberal-leaning (e.g., CNN.com, *Huffington Post*) media outlets. In this study, the existing data were images of the presidents from the Internet media outlets. Ratings of how each president was depicted were compared against the source of the image. The results showed that media outlets were in fact biased in their portrayal of presidents. Figure 1.5 provides a sample of images assessed.

FIGURE 1.5 ■ Depictions of Presidents George W. Bush and Barack Obama by Media Sources

Source: Hehman, E., Graber, E. C., Hoffman, L. H., & Gaertner, S. L. (2012). Warmth and competence: A content analysis of photographs depicting American presidents. Psychology of Popular Media Culture, 1(1), 46-52. doi:10.1037/a0026513

Images are a sample of those analyzed for media bias.

Overall, media outlets portrayed a president as warmer and more competent in the images if the president shared the same political orientation as the media outlet.

Research Designs

Regardless of where and how the information is obtained, researchers use **statistics** to summarize and then analyze the results. In some cases, statistical tests are used simply to describe what happened in terms of averages, percentages, frequencies, and other quantitative measures. In other cases, analyses are used to test inferences about people in general and their behavior. The Appendix of this book provides a closer look at the use of statistics in psychological research. For now, note that the types of conclusions that are drawn are limited by the way a study is designed. In particular, three types of designs are used in psychological research: descriptive studies, correlational studies, and experiments.

Statistics. A branch of mathematics that is used for analyzing research data.

Descriptive Research

The first purpose of research is simply to describe a person, a group, or a psychological phenomenon through systematic observation. This goal can be achieved through case studies, surveys, and naturalistic observations.

Case Studies. Sometimes it is useful to study one or more individuals in great detail. Information about a person can be obtained through tests, interviews, firsthand observation, and biographical material such as diaries and letters written. **Case studies** are conducted in the hope that an in-depth look at one individual will reveal something important about people in general. The problem with case studies is that they are time consuming and often are limited in their generality. To the extent that a subject is atypical, the results may say little about the rest of us but can often be quite informative for developing new theories about behavior.

Nevertheless, case studies have played an influential role in psychology. Sigmund Freud based his theory of personality on a handful of patients. Behaviorist John Watson used a case study involving an infant to try to debunk psychoanalysis. Jean Piaget formulated a theory of intellectual development by questioning his own children. Neuroscientists gain insights into the workings of the brain by observing and testing patients who have suffered brain damage. Cognitive psychologists learn about memory from rare individuals who can retain enormous amounts of information. Psycholinguists study language development by recording the speech utterances of their own children over time. Intelligence

case study. A type of research that involves making in-depth observations of an individual person.

researchers learn about human intellectual powers by studying child prodigies, chess masters, and other gifted individuals. Social psychologists pick up clues about leadership by analyzing biographies of great leaders. And clinical psychologists refine the techniques of psychotherapy through their shared experiences with patients. When an individual comes along who is exceptional in some way or when a psychological hypothesis can be answered only through systematic, long-term observation, the case study provides a valuable starting point.

survey. A research method that involves interviewing or giving questionnaires to a large number of people.

Surveys. In contrast to the in-depth study of one individual, **surveys** describe an entire population by looking at many cases. In a survey—which can be conducted in person, over the phone, through the mail, or over the Internet—people can be asked various questions about themselves. Surveys have become very popular in recent years and tell us all sorts of things about what humans believe. For example, using surveys on paranormal beliefs and fears, we learn that about 52 percent of Americans believe places can be haunted by spirits, 35 percent believe aliens have visited Earth, 25 percent believe that some people can move objects with their minds, 19 percent believe fortune-tellers and psychics can foresee the future, and 16 percent believe that Bigfoot is a real creature (Chapman University Survey of American Fears Wave 4, 2017). Common results from surveys on this topic are shown in Figure 1.6. Surveys are a useful way to quickly gather these kinds of insights into what we believe.

epidemiology. The study of the distribution of illnesses in a population.

Surveys are sometimes necessary to describe psychological states that are difficult to observe directly. For example, this method is a vital tool in **epidemiology**—the study of the distribution of illnesses in a population. How many children are awakened by nightmares? What percentage of college students are struck by test anxiety? How common are depression, drug use, and suicide? These kinds of questions are vital for determining the extent of a problem and knowing how to allocate health care resources. Surveys are also useful for describing sexual practices. With the prevalence of sexually transmitted diseases, it's important to know how sexually active people are, whether they use condoms, and whether some segments of the population are more at risk than others. Today, surveys are so common, and the results have such significant implications, that the methods (which, after all, rely on self-report) should be scrutinized carefully. Two factors are particularly important in this regard: who the respondents are and how the questions are asked (Jones, Baxter, & Khanduja, 2013; Privitera, 2020).

To describe a group, any group—males, females, college students, redheads, Americans, or all registered voters—researchers select a subset of individuals. The entire group is called the *population*; the subset of those questioned constitutes a *sample*. For a survey to be accurate, the sample must be similar to or representative of the population on key characteristics such as sex, gender, race, age, region, income, ability, education, and cultural background. For example, if the research question was about women in their 40s who had been diagnosed with breast cancer in the past five years, then a sample that

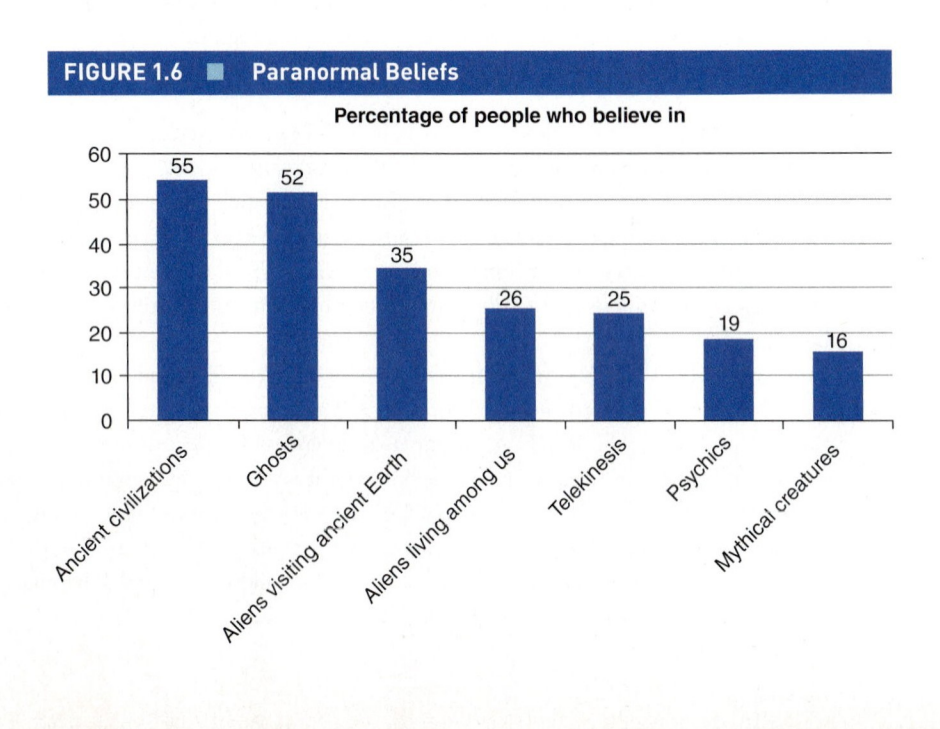

FIGURE 1.6 ■ Paranormal Beliefs

Percentage of people who believe in

Category	Percentage
Ancient civilizations	55
Ghosts	52
Aliens visiting ancient Earth	35
Aliens living among us	26
Telekinesis	25
Psychics	19
Mythical creatures	16

includes women in their 30s as part of the study would not be representative. Nor would a sample that included men, or women in their 50s. Short of questioning everyone in the population, the best way to ensure representativeness is to use a **random sample**, a method of selection in which everyone who meets the criteria for the research question has an equal chance of being chosen.

Most research studies include only a select group of participants (a sample), and not all participants who are members of a particular group of interest (a population). In other words, most psychologists have limited access to the phenomena they study, especially behavioral phenomena. For this reason, most science involves research in which researchers select a portion of all members of a group (illustrated in Figure 1.7). Imagine, for example, trying to identify every person who has experienced exam anxiety, depression, fatigue, happiness, or being in love. This is true for most behaviors—the population of all people who exhibit those behaviors is likely too large, making it more practical to select samples from which we can infer what is happening in the population.

Survey researchers usually pick names arbitrarily from a list or recruit volunteers. This seems like a reasonable strategy, but no sample is perfect. Not everyone has a listed phone number, some people's physical or email address is not up to date, and some people who are called upon to participate whether in person, via social media, or by phone may refuse to participate. Prior to the 1936 presidential election, pollsters for the magazine *Literary Digest* mailed postcards to more than 10 million people selected from telephone directories and automobile registration lists. The cards asked the respondents to indicate who they intended to vote for. Based on the more than two million cards that were returned, the *Literary Digest* predicted that Republican Alfred Landon would defeat Democrat Franklin D. Roosevelt in a landslide. In fact, the opposite occurred. The problem: At the time, more registered Republicans than Democrats owned telephones and automobiles, which skewed the poll results. For a sample to accurately reflect its given population, it must be selected in a manner that is random, not biased, and it must be representative of the population as a whole—across all demographics, or groups to which people belong, such as by race, ethnicity, class, sexuality, and gender.

A second factor to consider is the way in which survey questions are asked. Studies show that the answers people give are influenced by the wording of the questions, the context in which they are asked, and other extraneous factors (Schwarz, 1999). The following examples illustrate the point. When survey respondents were asked about "assisting the poor," only 23 percent said that too much money was being spent. Yet among those asked about "welfare," 53 percent gave this negative response (Geer, 2004).

random sample. A method of selection in which everyone in a population has an equal chance of being chosen.

FIGURE 1.7 ■ Distinguishing Between Populations and Samples

In this example, a sample of $n = 19$ was selected from a population of $N = 90$.

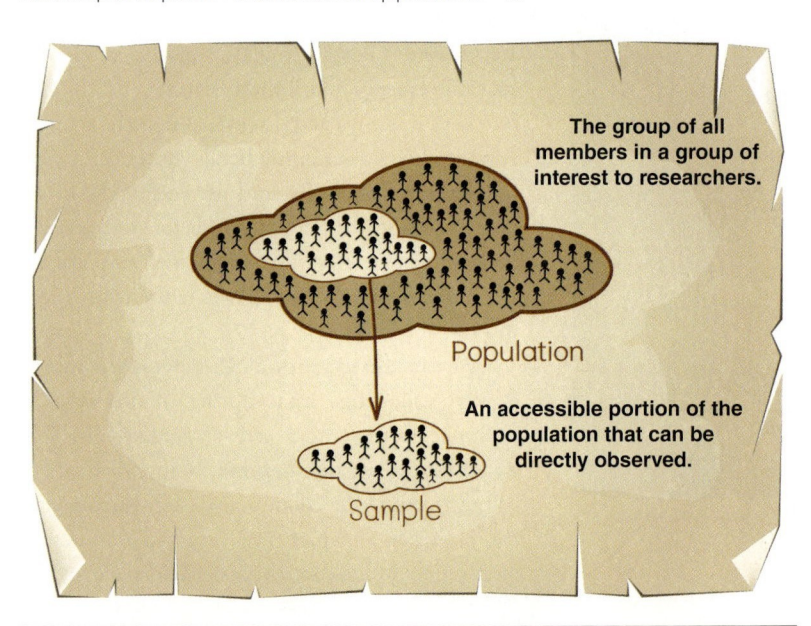

Population — The group of all members in a group of interest to researchers.

Sample — An accessible portion of the population that can be directly observed.

istock.com/lamnee

> ### TRY THIS!
>
> #### Survey Says...
>
> To explore how the wording of questions can affect survey results, **TRY THIS:** Ask three people at random one of the questions in the left-hand column. Then ask a second random group of three the corresponding question from the right-hand column:
>
> | | |
> |---|---|
> | Consider whether there are more than 100 calories in a medium-size slice of pizza. How many calories do you think there are? | Consider whether there are less than 400 calories in a medium-size slice of pizza. How many calories do you think there are? |
> | Consider whether there were more than 50 episodes made of the original *Star Trek* series. How many episodes do you think were made? | Consider whether there were less than 50 episodes made of the original *Star Trek* series. How many episodes do you think were made? |
> | Consider whether Taylor Swift is over 25 years old. How old do you think she is? | Consider whether Taylor Swift is under 25 years old. How old do you think she is? |
>
> Next, add up your two sets of answers and divide each by 3 to arrive at your survey respondents' average estimate. Was the second average higher or lower than the first? What does this say about how survey questions are phrased? How should these questions have been phrased to obtain the most objective result possible?
>
> (For the record: According to Pizza Hut, a medium slice of cheese pizza has 240 calories. The original *Star Trek* ran 79 episodes. And Taylor Swift was born December 13, 1989.)

naturalistic observation. The observation of behavior as it occurs naturally in real-world settings.

ethogram. A grid of predetermined behaviors to watch for when collecting data during naturalistic observation.

Naturalistic Observations. A third descriptive approach is to observe behavior as it occurs in the real world. **Naturalistic observations** are common in sociology and anthropology, where fieldworkers seek to describe a group, organization, or culture by "living" in it for long periods of time. Psychologists use this method as well to study caregivers and their children, corporate executives, factory workers, nursing home residents, and others.

Naturalistic observation is particularly common among ethologists, who study the behavior of animals in their natural habitats. For example, Jane Goodall (1986, 2000) has spent more than 40 years watching chimpanzees in African jungles. She has observed their social structure, courting rituals, struggles for dominance, and child-rearing practices. She observed cannibalism and a war between chimpanzee troops. She also saw the chimps strip leaves from twigs and use the twigs to fish termites out of nests—a finding that disproved the widely held assumption that only humans are capable of making tools. In another program of research, Dorothy Cheney and Robert Seyfarth (1990) observed vervet monkeys in Kenya and discovered that these monkeys behave as if they know the kinship bonds within the group, use deception to outsmart rivals, and use vocal calls in ways that are more sophisticated than anyone before had expected. To truly understand primates, and perhaps their similarities to humans, one has to observe their behavior in the wild—not in captivity in a zoo or laboratory.

We can also use naturalistic observation to study humans. When collecting data during naturalistic observation, researchers often use a grid of predetermined behaviors to watch for, called an **ethogram**. Ethograms contain rows and columns, with each column given a distinct behavior to track, and each row a span of time such as 5 minutes. As an example, you could look for three behaviors across the span of 30

Naturalistic observation is a common form of descriptive research. For many years, Jane Goodall has observed chimpanzees in the wild.

Everett Collection Inc / Alamy Stock Photo

minutes in increments of five. When you completed the 30 minutes, you would tally the number of marks in each column to find how many of each behavior was observed.

Correlational Studies

Description is a nice first step, but science demands much more. A second goal is to find connections, or correlations, between variables so that one factor can be used to predict another. Correlational research is reported in psychology—and in the news—with remarkable frequency. Consider a few examples: Higher levels of education are associated with higher lifetime incomes. The more optimistic people are, the less often they get sick. Adults who exercise regularly live longer than those who do not. The more satisfied you are with your job, the less psychological distress you experience. So, what do these statements of correlation *really* prove? The answer is that correlation does not *prove* anything; it cannot demonstrate *cause*. In other words, correlation can tell you that two things are related; it cannot tell you *why* they are related.

A **correlation** is a statistical measure of the extent to which two factors are associated. Expressed in numerical terms, *correlation coefficients* range from –1 to +1. A positive correlation exists when the two variables increase or decrease together, in the same direction. The link between education and income is positive—more of one means more of the other; so are the correlations between exercise and longevity. In contrast, a negative correlation exists when an increase in one variable is accompanied by a decrease in the other, and vice versa. The link between optimism and illness is in a negative direction, as is the one between job satisfaction and psychological distress.

Correlation coefficients vary not only in direction but also in strength. The higher a correlation is, regardless of whether it is positive or negative, the stronger the link is between variables. Correlations that are very low, near zero, indicate that two variables are independent. For example, contrary to popular opinion, research shows that there is no correlation between phases of the moon and criminal activity or between intelligence-test scores in infancy and adulthood. In short, full moons and infant test scores cannot be used to predict crime or adult IQ. As illustrated in Figure 1.8, the direction and strength of a correlation can be represented in a **scatterplot**.

Correlational studies serve an important function: Based on existing associations, researchers can use one variable (or more) to make *predictions* about another variable. Before interpreting correlations, however, two important limitations guide the cautious scientist. First, correlations between psychological variables are seldom perfect. Human beings are complex creatures, and their behavior is multidetermined. If you know a boy who spends 20 hours a week watching Ultimate Fighting Championship, or playing violent video games such as Fortnite, you might predict that he gets into fights at school. But the positive correlation between media violence exposure and aggressiveness is far from perfect, and you may well be wrong. Similarly, not every optimist is healthy and not every college graduate brings home a hefty paycheck. Unless a correlation is close to 1, it can be used only to make general statements of probability, not predictions about specific individuals.

correlation. A statistical measure of the extent to which two variables are associated.

scatterplot. A graph in which paired scores (X, Y) for many participants are plotted as single points to reveal the direction and strength of their correlation.

FIGURE 1.8 ■ Visualizing Correlations

Scatterplots provide a graphic representation of the observed relationship between two variables. The graphs illustrate a positive correlation (left), a negative correlation (center), and a zero correlation (right). Each point locates the position of a single subject on the two variables. The solid straight lines show what the correlations would look like if they were perfect.

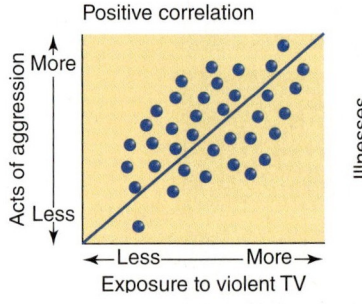

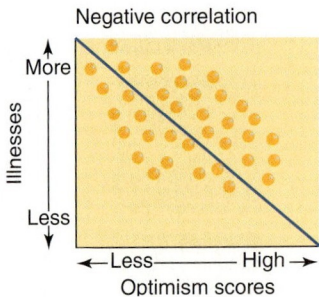

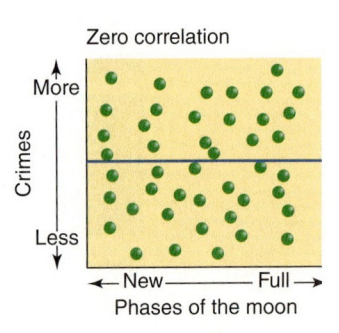

Correlation Is Not Causation. The types of conclusions that can be drawn from correlational evidence are limitless. It's tempting to assume that because one variable predicts another, the first must have caused the second. Not true. This interpretation is an error often committed by laypeople, college students, the news media, and sometimes even researchers themselves. Think about examples of *Spurious correlations*—correlations that can be shown but are clearly false. For example, data show that greater consumption of margarine is associated with increased divorce rates. Just sticking with dairy: Data also show that greater consumption of cheese is associated with a greater number of people dying by becoming tangled in their bedsheets. Now would you honestly believe that eating more margarine *causes* divorce or that eating more cheese *causes* more people to die by becoming tangled in their bedsheets? You can visit http://www.tylervigen.com/spurious-correlations to find many more examples of these types of spurious correlations. What these examples ultimately reinforce is a cardinal rule of statistics: *Correlation does not show causation.*

It's important to know and understand this rule. It does not mean that correlated variables are never causally related, only that *the link may or may not be causal*. Think again about our examples, and you'll find there are other ways to interpret these correlations. Sure, it's possible that optimism (X) reduces sickness (Y). But based solely on the observation that these two variables go hand in hand, it's also possible that the causal arrow points in the opposite direction—that being sick less often (Y) makes someone generally more optimistic (X). Or perhaps both variables—optimism and illness—are caused by a third factor (Z), such as the type of home a person is raised in.

Consider other examples and you'll further appreciate the point. Perhaps people become optimistic because they are healthy or are shy because they lack friends. As for college graduates earning more money than high school graduates, being smart or coming from an upper-middle-class family (Z) may both propel a student through college (X) and lead to the student's financial success (Y). In a similar vein, maybe adults who exercise live longer because they also tend to smoke less, drink less, and eat healthier foods (illustrated in Figure 1.9).

Experiments

To *explain* a relationship between variables, we need a more exacting method of research: the scientific experiment. In an **experiment**, the psychologist seeks to establish causal connections by actively controlling the variables in a situation and measuring the subject's behavior. The factor an experimenter manipulates (the proposed cause) is called the **independent variable**, so named because it can

---

experiment. A type of research in which the investigator varies some factors, keeps others constant, and measures the effects on randomly assigned participants.

independent variable. Any variable that the researcher manipulates in an experiment (the proposed cause).

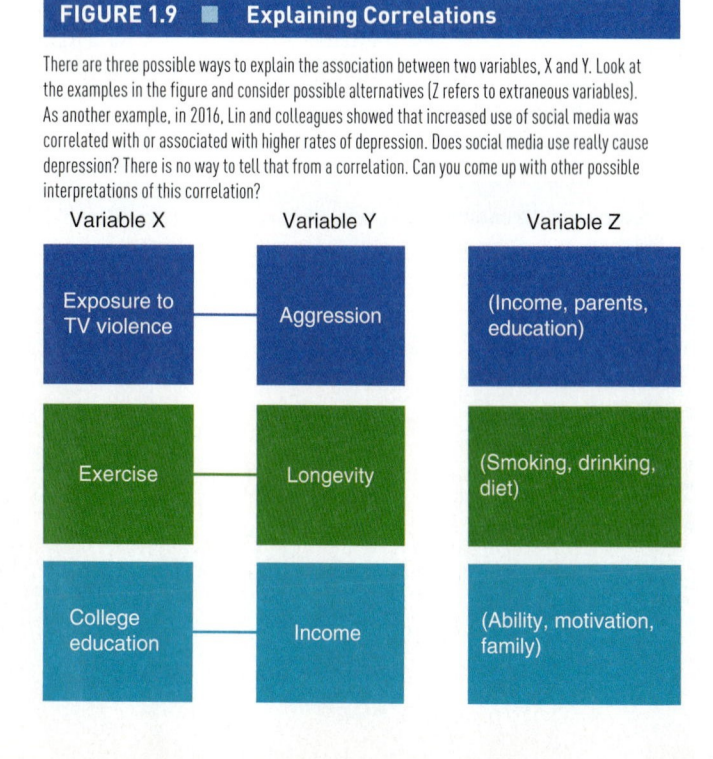

FIGURE 1.9 ■ Explaining Correlations

There are three possible ways to explain the association between two variables, X and Y. Look at the examples in the figure and consider possible alternatives (Z refers to extraneous variables). As another example, in 2016, Lin and colleagues showed that increased use of social media was correlated with or associated with higher rates of depression. Does social media use really cause depression? There is no way to tell that from a correlation. Can you come up with other possible interpretations of this correlation?

Variable X	Variable Y	Variable Z
Exposure to TV violence	Aggression	(Income, parents, education)
Exercise	Longevity	(Smoking, drinking, diet)
College education	Income	(Ability, motivation, family)

be varied on its own, "independent" of any other factors. The behavior that is being measured (the proposed effect) is known as the **dependent variable** because it is said to "depend" on the experimental situation. If you were to test the hypothesis that bolding key terms in a book improves recall of those words, bolding (yes, no) would be the independent variable, and recall would be the dependent variable.

The purpose of an experiment is to focus on a causal hypothesis by manipulating the independent variable, keeping other aspects of the situation constant, and observing behavior. A true experiment contains two essential sets of ingredients. The first is control over the independent variable and use of a comparison group. Second is the random assignment of participants to conditions. By means of these ingredients, any differences in behavior can logically be traced back to the independent variable (illustrated in Figure 1.10).

Control and Comparison. There was a report in the news recently that half of all couples who live together before marriage later get divorced. "Wow, that's high," you may think. You may wonder why, but then you realize, "Wait a second. Isn't there a 50 percent divorce rate in the United States?"

To evaluate the significance of any number, you have to ask the question "Compared to what?" In its most basic form, a typical experiment compares research participants who are exposed to the independent variable with others, similarly treated, who are not. Those who receive the treatment make up the **experimental group**; the others constitute the **control group**. To the extent that the two groups differ in behavior, the difference can then be attributed, with varying degrees of certainty, to the independent variable. The key is to *vary one factor, keep other aspects of the situation constant, and measure the effect.* To test the hypothesis that bolding key terms in a book improves recall of those words, for example, researchers bring participants into the laboratory, have half of them read a passage with key

dependent variable. A variable that is being measured in an experiment (the proposed effect).

experimental group. Any condition of an experiment in which participants are exposed to an independent variable.

control group. The condition of an experiment in which participants are not exposed to the independent variable.

FIGURE 1.10 ■ Basic Model of an Experiment

The structure of an experiment that meets the basic requirements for demonstrating cause and effect. In this study, a sample of students at a similar reading level was selected at random from a population of college undergraduates to test if bolding key terms in a short passage improves recall. To qualify as an experiment, (a) the researcher created each level of the bolding/not bolding independent variable (manipulation), (b) students were randomly assigned to read a passage with or without bolded key terms (randomization), and (c) a control group was present where the manipulation of bolding the key terms was absent (comparison/control).

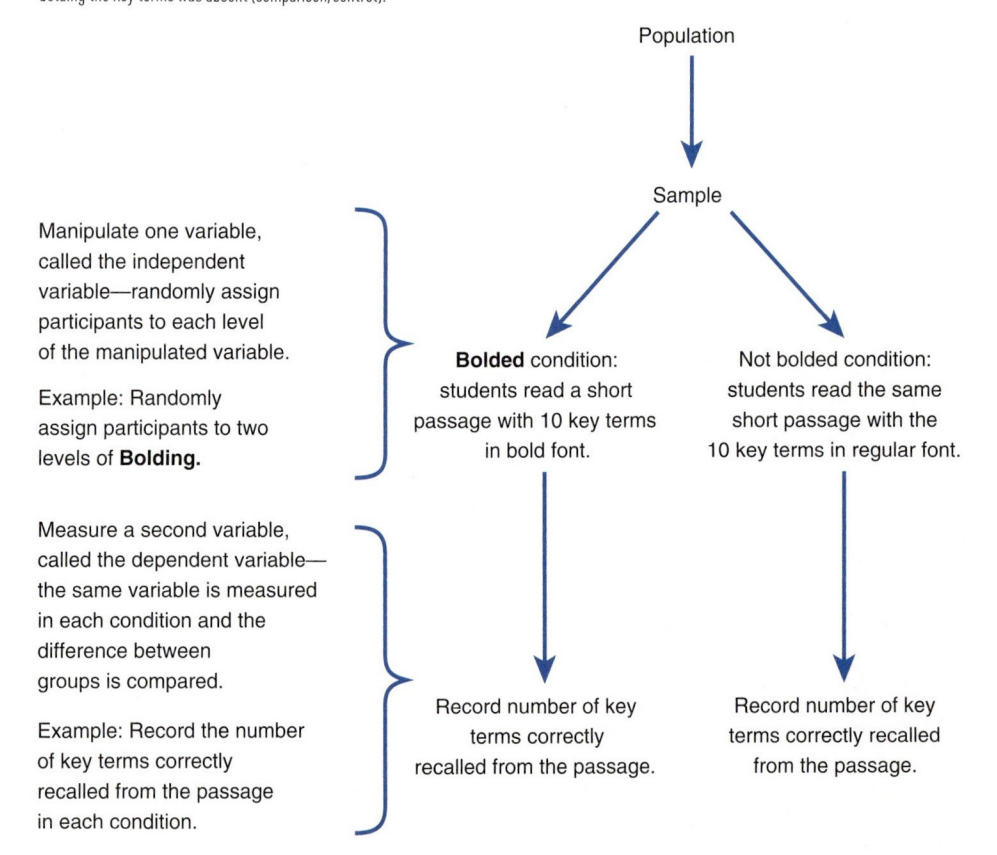

Population
↓
Sample

Manipulate one variable, called the independent variable—randomly assign participants to each level of the manipulated variable.

Example: Randomly assign participants to two levels of **Bolding.**

- **Bolded** condition: students read a short passage with 10 key terms in bold font.
- Not bolded condition: students read the same short passage with the 10 key terms in regular font.

Measure a second variable, called the dependent variable—the same variable is measured in each condition and the difference between groups is compared.

Example: Record the number of key terms correctly recalled from the passage in each condition.

- Record number of key terms correctly recalled from the passage.
- Record number of key terms correctly recalled from the passage.

terms bolded (the experimental group) while the other half read the same passage but without bolding (the control group), and then measure subsequent recall of the key words in a test (Privitera, 2018).

The comparison between an experimental and a control group provides the building blocks for more complex experiments. This basic two-group design can be expanded on in three ways. The first is to create more than two levels of the independent variable. Instead of comparing the presence and absence of bolded key terms, for example, one might form three groups by varying the color of the bolding (bolded-black, bolded-red, no bold words). Second, researchers can manipulate more than one independent variable in the same experiment. For example, in addition to bolding key terms, they might also vary the number of words bolded (few, many), or the length of the passage (short, long). The separate and joint effects of these variables can then be evaluated. The third way to increase the complexity of an experiment is to use more than one dependent variable, or to measure the dependent variable on more than one occasion. In our example, recall could be measured, as could time to complete the recall test.

Random Assignment. The second essential ingredient of an experiment is that participants be assigned to conditions in an arbitrary manner. **Random assignment** ensures that everyone in a study has an equal chance of being put into an experimental or control group. If we were to show *The Walking Dead* to children in one school and *Moana* to those in another school, it would later be impossible to know if observed differences in aggression were produced by this exposure or whether they reflect preexisting differences between the schools. Similarly, if I were to let the children pick their own condition ("Which show would you rather see?"), observed differences might mean that those who chose the violent show were more aggressive to begin with.

By flipping a coin to determine which children in a sample are in the experimental and control groups, a researcher can neutralize individual differences. Assuming that enough participants are recruited, the two conditions would contain roughly equal numbers of male and female participants as well as rich and poor, active and passive, and bright and dull. Similarly, to evaluate the health benefits of exercise, we might recruit volunteers and assign half of them randomly to take part in an experimental aerobics program. Chances are that both the exercise and the no-exercise groups would then have an equal mixture of men, women, smokers, health-food eaters, couch potatoes, and so on. Then if exercisers turn out to be healthier, the reason would be clear.

Literature Reviews

Seeking to describe, predict, and explain psychological phenomena, researchers use a diverse assortment of investigative tools—including single case studies, large-scale surveys, naturalistic observations, correlational studies, and experiments in laboratory and field settings. Yet regardless of the method used, there is a humbling lesson in this scientific enterprise. It is that knowledge accumulates slowly, in increments, one small step at a time. There are no "critical" experiments, and no single study can literally "prove" a hypothesis.

There *are* exciting new discoveries destined to become research classics. But each raises questions, the most important being: Will a finding replicate? **Replication** is an essential property of science. It refers to the process of conducting a second, nearly identical study to determine if the initial findings can be repeated. If the result does not replicate, the cautious scientist concludes that the findings may not be reliable enough to pursue further. If the result does replicate—in other words, if the result is consistent enough to stand the test of time—then attention shifts to a second important question, that of **generalizability**: Is a finding limited to a narrow set of conditions, or does it apply across a broad range of circumstances? Just how generalizable is the result? Suppose you found that media violence causes aggression. Would the result be the same if the study were

---

random assignment. The procedure of assigning participants to conditions of an experiment in an arbitrary manner.

replication. The process of repeating a study to determine if the results are reliable enough to be duplicated.

generalizability. The extent to which a finding applies to a broad range of subject populations and circumstances.

In an experiment, the selection of participants and the assignment of participants to groups is conducted using a random procedure, similar to flipping a coin.
iStock.com/LightFieldStudios

conducted in another culture or if children of a different age group were used? What if participants were shown different materials or if aggression were measured in a different way? Once replication is achieved, the next step is to establish the boundaries of the phenomenon. As with some fine wines, good science takes time.

Science demands replication and generalizability, but it is often difficult to make sense of the growing bodies of evidence. One study may show that exposure to media violence causes aggression in children, but another study may produce contradictory or ambiguous results. Why the disparity? Sometimes many studies are needed before clear patterns begin to emerge. There are two ways to discern these patterns. One is to conduct a review of the research literature, noting the strengths or weaknesses of various studies, making comparisons, and arguing for certain conclusions. In contrast to the interpretive, somewhat subjective style of a review, the second method is to use a quantitative technique known as **meta-analysis**. Meta-analysis is a set of statistical procedures that is used to review a body of evidence by combining the data and results from multiple studies (Cook et al., 1992; Hunt, 1997; Privitera, 2020). By "meta-analyzing" a sample of *studies* the way researchers "analyze" individual *participants*, reviewers can draw precise conclusions concerning the strength and breadth of support for a hypothesis. As you will learn, many of the conclusions drawn in this book were informed by the reviews and meta-analyses published by others.

To summarize, advances in psychological knowledge are made through primary research in the form of descriptive studies, correlational studies, and experiments. As the data from these efforts accumulate in the published literature, patterns begin to emerge. These patterns become revealed in reviews and statistical meta-analyses. The various tools of discovery discussed here are summarized in Table 1.4.

meta-analysis. A set of statistical procedures used to review a body of evidence by combining the results of individual studies.

TABLE 1.4 ■ The Tools of Discovery

Method	Purpose
Descriptive research	To *describe* the thoughts, feelings, and behaviors of an individual or group using case studies, surveys, and naturalistic observations
Correlational studies	To uncover links, or correlations, between variables so that one factor can be used to *predict* another
Experiments	To test hypotheses about cause and effect in order to establish that one factor can *cause* another
Literature reviews	To *summarize* an existing body of research in a narrative review or in a statistical meta-analysis of studies previously conducted

LEARNING CHECK

Define It!

Match each term from the left column to its closest description on the right.

1. Meta-analysis
2. Hypothesis
3. Control group
4. Theory
5. Experimental group
6. Correlation

a. A set of principles that describes a phenomenon
b. The extent to which two factors are associated
c. A testable prediction
d. Research participants not exposed to an independent variable
e. Research participants exposed to an independent variable
f. Research combined from multiple studies

(Answers: 1. f; 2. c; 3. d; 4. a; 5. e; 6. b.)

Ethical Considerations

Ethics is often thought of as the distinction between right and wrong, such as the Golden Rule: "Do unto others as you would have them do unto you." Sometimes ethics can even be confused with common sense; however, issues of ethics are far more difficult to resolve than are questions of common sense. Many concerns of ethics are universally recognized, but the interpretation or application needed to resolve these issues can vary based on an individual's perspective.

One's perspective is shaped in different ways often depending on one's values and life experiences. An individual's perspective can have a substantial impact on the actions the person takes to address ethical concerns. Consider academic dishonesty, for example. Being a dishonest student is an ethical concern; however, the debate over this concern can be approached from different perspectives. A student may assess the consequences of cheating in the classroom in terms of the pressure to secure academic scholarships and college enrollment status; a professor may assess the consequences of cheating on class grading; and an administrator may assess the fairness of awarding degrees to students who cheat. In each case, the issue of academic honesty is addressed but from divergent perspectives.

Researchers likewise have divergent perspectives regarding ethical conduct in behavioral research. The information obtained using the scientific method is typically important. For example, studying academic dishonesty is important. However, how we obtain information about academic dishonesty is also of ethical concern. For example, would it be ethical to tell a student to cheat in order to observe cheating? Is it ethical to video record a classroom to check for possible cheating during a test without making students aware that they are being recorded? These types of questions should be addressed prior to making observations.

Ethical Considerations in Human Research

The term *Ethics* describes appropriate human action in areas such as business, medicine, health, religion, and research. In addition, most schools have ethical guidelines about cheating, academic dishonesty, and showing respect to classmates. In behavioral research, the term has special meaning. The term **research ethics** is used to identify the actions that a researcher must take to conduct responsible and moral research. Engaging in responsible research requires a researcher to anticipate what might happen, react to what is happening, and reflect on what did happen. Researchers must be aware of how a study will affect others in any positive or negative way.

The research process begins with an idea or hypothesis from which researchers devise a research plan. In the plan, the researcher must make ethical considerations such as to anticipate what type of sample is needed (human or animal) and how to treat those in the sample. The difficulty of anticipating what will happen in a study is the biggest ethical challenge that researchers face. After all, the best-case scenario is to avoid ethical problems altogether, and the best way to do that is to fully anticipate concerns before the study is conducted.

What ethical issues are raised by research involving human participants, and how are these issues resolved? The American Psychological Association adopted three core recommendations drafted by the National Commission for the Protection of Human Subjects of Biomedical and Behavioral Research in a document called the Belmont Report.

- Respect for persons
- Beneficence
- Justice

Respect for persons means that participants in a research study are treated as autonomous agents. That is, participants in a study must be capable of making informed decisions concerning whether to participate in a research study. *Capable* participants are those with the physical and mental capacity to participate. *Informed* participants are those with the ability to comprehend their potential role in a research study.

---

research ethics. Identifies the actions that researchers must take to conduct responsible and moral research.

respect for persons. An ethical principle listed in the Belmont Report that states that participants in a research study must be autonomous agents capable of making informed decisions concerning whether to participate in research.

In addition to being capable and informed, all potential participants in research must be free of coercion or undue influence. To adhere to this recommendation, researchers must provide certain protections for special populations. For example, to protect children less than 18 years of age, a caregiver or guardian waiver to participate in a research study is required; caregivers or guardians give consent for underage children. This protection is especially important for children who participate in sensitive areas of research, such as research with people who abuse drugs (Souleymanov et al., 2016) or research requiring the disclosure of diagnoses such as HIV (Barfield & Kane, 2009; Dubé et al., 2017).

Beneficence means that it is the researcher's responsibility to minimize the potential risks and maximize the potential benefits associated with a research study. Anticipating the risks and benefits in a study is also called a *risk-benefit analysis*. To apply a risk-benefit analysis, you must determine whether the benefits of a research study outweigh the risks. If not, then the study is potentially unethical. The principle of beneficence can be subjective and difficult to assess. Researchers must anticipate potential risks, including the potential for physical and psychological harm, stress and health concerns, and loss of privacy or confidentiality. They must also anticipate potential benefits including the potential for monetary gain, the acquisition of new skills or knowledge, and access to treatments for psychological or physical illnesses. To meet the challenges of anticipating potential risks and benefits in research, all research institutions appoint ethics committees that consist of many trained professionals from diverse educational backgrounds who provide additional review of the risks and benefits anticipated in a study before any research is conducted.

Justice refers to the fair and equitable treatment of all individuals and groups selected for participation in research studies in terms of the benefits they receive and the risks they bear from their participation in research. Justice is applied to ensure equality in the selection of potential participants in research. Researchers often select participants based on such criteria as age, gender, level of education, ethnicity, or body weight. The principle of justice ensures that any decision to include or exclude certain individuals or groups from participating in a research study is scientifically justified. For example, a study on the effects of menstruation on mood can include only females. The scientifically justifiable reason to exclude males is that they do not have menstruation cycles.

The American Psychological Association (2017a), the largest association of psychologists worldwide, has adopted a method of assessing risk in its publication of the *Ethical Principles of Psychologists and Code of Conduct*. This code extends the ethical principles outlined in the Belmont Report to include two others related to scientific integrity:

- Fidelity and responsibility
- Integrity

The principles contained in these guidelines are important, and all investigators are responsible for the well-being of those who take part in their research. Consider, for example, the participant's right to privacy, the possible harm or discomfort caused by experimental procedures, and the use of **deception**. In response to these concerns, researchers must follow guidelines established by professional organizations, university ethics committees, and government granting agencies. For example, the American Psychological Association (2017a) urges its members to (a) tell prospective participants what they will encounter so that they can give their **informed consent**, (b) instruct participants that they're free to withdraw from the experiment at any time, (c) minimize all harm and discomfort, (d) keep the data obtained from participants confidential, and (e) if deception is necessary, "debrief" participants afterward by fully explaining the purposes and procedures of the study.

Some psychologists argue that these rules should be followed without exception. Others point out that many important issues could not then be investigated. In practice, ethical decisions are seldom clear-cut. For example, informed consent is necessary, and everyone agrees that deception is undesirable, but it's often impossible to test a hypothesis on a fully informed participant. As a matter of compromise in situations where deception is used, therefore, researchers describe to participants the procedures that they may encounter but withhold complete disclosure of the key variables and hypothesis until later, when participants are debriefed. Deception is generally acceptable in cases where the

---

beneficence. An ethical principle listed in the Belmont Report that states that it is the researcher's responsibility to minimize the potential risks and maximize the potential benefits associated with conducting a research study.

justice. An ethical principle listed in the Belmont Report that states that all participants should be treated fairly and equitably in terms of receiving the benefits and bearing the risks in research.

deception. A research procedure used to mislead participants about the true purposes of a study.

informed consent. The ethical requirement that prospective participants receive enough information to permit them to decide freely whether to participate in a study.

Social media is a part of the social fabric of society today. However, to what extent should companies be allowed to track and use your data? At the heart of an ethical debate is how you are informed about how your online social media data is used and why.
iStock.com/scyther5

deception (the information being withheld) does not put the participant in greater than minimal to no harm.

Other types of judgment calls also must be made from time to time. For example, is it ethical to put participants under stress—perhaps by presenting impossible problems to solve, showing a pornographic film, sharing the negative results of a test they took, or leading them to think temporarily that they inflicted harm on another person? Is it ethical to study pain tolerance or to ask participants to recount a traumatic episode? When the polio vaccine was tested in 1954, two million children were selected for study, but many received a placebo (a dummy medication that contains no active ingredients) instead of the real vaccine. In the 1990s, AIDS researchers in a number of developing countries administered placebos to hundreds of HIV-infected pregnant women instead of AZT—an expensive drug that would have prevented these women from passing on the virus to their babies.

A more recent example involved a study that manipulated the algorithms on "news feeds" of almost 700,000 Facebook users for one week in January 2012, to determine whether a mostly positive or negative news feed would elicit different types of status updates (Kramer, Guillory, & Hancock, 2014). The authors concluded: "When positive expressions were reduced, people produced fewer positive posts and more negative posts; when negative expressions were reduced, the opposite pattern occurred. These results indicate that emotions expressed by others on Facebook influence our own emotions" (p. 8788). The key ethical concern for this study was that, while the information collected "was consistent with Facebook's Data Use Policy" (Verma, 2014, p. 10779), participants were not able to opt out of participating in the study, which has ethical implications. Other ethical concerns were also evident. Indeed, the ethical concerns for this study were so apparent that the editor for the journal that published these findings formally printed an *expression of concern* regarding the ethics of the study, and the authors of the study issued a formal apology via popular media. Examples like this have led to substantial debate over the ethics of using social media outlets in the conduct of psychological research.

Were these studies ethical? The answer is not always easy to find and often leads to much debate. In making these kinds of decisions, researchers weigh the costs to the individual participants against the benefits to science and humanity. In weighing these outcomes, however, there is widespread disagreement among psychologists of differing values (Golder, Ahmed, Norman, & Booth, 2017; Kimmel, 1991; Rosnow, Rotheram-Borus, Ceci, Blanck, & Koocher, 1993).

Ethical Considerations in Animal Research

When Charles Darwin (1859) introduced his theory of evolution in *On the Origin of Species*, he not only revolutionized conceptions of human history but also set the stage for the use of animals in research. Human beings, said Darwin, are biologically related to other creatures on the planet. Hence, the study of animals has relevance for understanding people. Does it ever! Over the years psychology has made great strides using animals to study the brain and nervous system; vision and other senses; learning and reasoning; social behavior; anxiety, stress, and other psychological disorders; aggression; addiction; spinal cord injury; the workings of the immune system; and the impact of various drugs. Mice, rats, rabbits, cats, dogs, apes, monkeys, and even birds, fish, insects, and sea slugs have all proved valuable in this endeavor.

There are four reasons for using animals in research: to learn more about certain kinds of animals, to investigate ways to medically treat and/or house animals, to evaluate the cross-species generality of the principles of behavior, and to examine variables that cannot ethically be imposed on human participants.

Is it ethical to experiment on animals? Many animal rights activists say no—and are quite vocal in their opposition (Langley, 1989). To understand how psychologists respond to these charges, it helps to know what both sides stand for. Everyone, including those in the research community, consider themselves to be advocates for animal *welfare* and support the establishment of shelters for lost pets, inoculation programs, the prevention of cruelty to animals, and the protection of endangered species (Johnson, 1990). Indeed, researchers argue that although food deprivation, mild shock, drugs, and surgery are sometimes performed, allegations of mistreatment are exaggerated. Caroline Coile and Neil Miller (1984) analyzed 608 animal-based research articles published in the preceding five years and found that the charges were not supported in a single instance.

Psychologists and medical researchers defend their practices by pointing to the many ways in which their work has helped to improve the quality of human life and arguing that it would be immoral *not* to use animals for our most serious problems (Miller, 1985). Animal studies were instrumental in the development of a rabies vaccine, in organ transplants, and in understanding diseases such as cancer and diabetes. Animal studies have contributed to the treatment of anxiety, depression, and other mental disorders, and they have shed light on what is currently known about neuromuscular disorders, Alzheimer's disease, alcoholism, aggression, ulcers, and obesity. Indeed, recent animal research has played a pivotal role in helping us to understand Alzheimer's (a disorder associated with a loss of ability to retrieve memories), with researchers now collaborating to test a possible vaccine for the disease (Cummings et al., 2021; Fessel, 2021).

PSYCHOLOGY TODAY

LEARNING OBJECTIVES

Identify the major organizations and emerging branches in psychology, and explain the need to study a diverse group of people.

- List the major organizations in psychology.
- Identify the emerging branches of psychology.
- Explain why researchers study diversity.

Grounded in the older disciplines of philosophy, biology, and medicine, and firmly rooted in the conviction that mind and behavior can be studied only by using scientific methods, psychology has made enormous progress as a field of study. From the first subject to be tested in Wundt's original Leipzig laboratory, to the first patient to lie on Freud's couch, to the first psychologist hired to work in an applied setting, to the barrage of new discoveries concerning the links among mind, body, and health, psychology has come a long, long way.

Although psychologists study basic processes, psychology is also a responsive science, leading researchers to touch on some of the most important and socially sensitive topics of our generation. The similarities and differences between men and women; racial and ethnic diversity; sexuality; gender identity; abortion; adoption; terrorism; standardized testing; obesity and dieting; and the effects of Ritalin for attentional disorders, Prozac for mood disorders, and other drugs are among the topics now being addressed. If you're interested in the possibility of a future career in psychology, refer to the list of major subfields (what psychologists do) and employment settings (where they do it) presented in Figure 1.11 (American Psychological Association, 2017b).

Psychology has been growing for decades now, and we continue to find that growth emerge. At the college level, the popularity of the field is extraordinary. According to the U.S. Department of Education, psychology is the second largest college major, behind only business. There are more women in the field than ever before, more minorities, more articles being published, and more topics being studied. The American Psychological Association (APA) now has as members more than 117,000 researchers, educators, clinicians, consultants, and student members—and contains 54 divisions, each dedicated to a particular area of specialization. Across the northern border, the Canadian Psychological Association (CPA) was founded in 1939. In addition, a group of scientifically oriented psychologists recently established an organization dedicated solely to basic and applied *research* (the APA and the CPA also address the concerns of practicing clinical and counseling psychologists). This organization, founded in 1988, is called the Association for Psychological Science, or APS. It has more than 33,000 members. You can check for news updates on the latest advances in psychology at the APA, CPA, and APS websites.

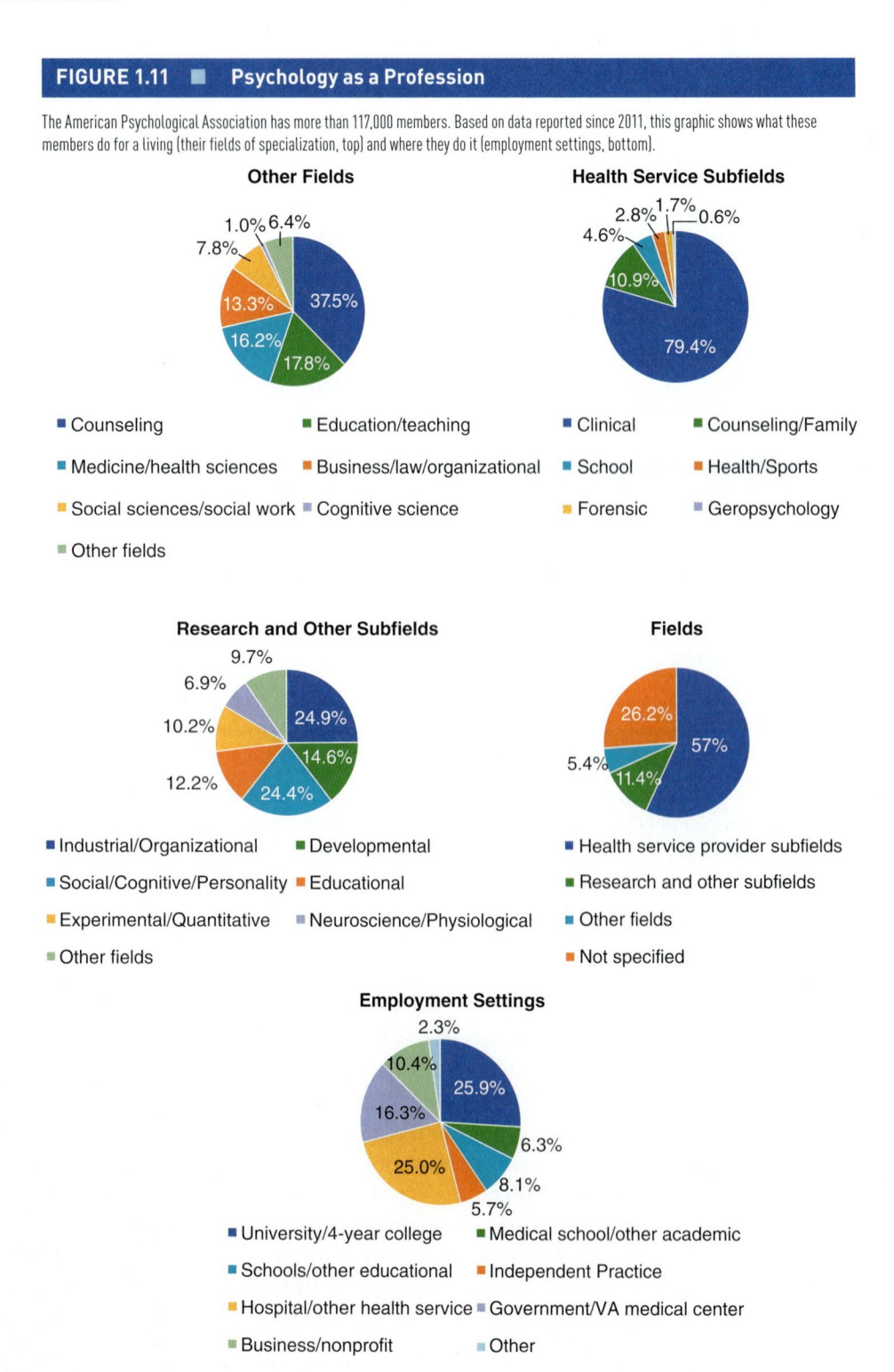

FIGURE 1.11 ■ Psychology as a Profession

The American Psychological Association has more than 117,000 members. Based on data reported since 2011, this graphic shows what these members do for a living (their fields of specialization, top) and where they do it (employment settings, bottom).

Other Fields
- Counseling: 37.5%
- Education/teaching: 17.8%
- Medicine/health sciences: 16.2%
- Business/law/organizational: 13.3%
- Social sciences/social work: 7.8%
- Cognitive science: 1.0%
- Other fields: 6.4%

Health Service Subfields
- Clinical: 79.4%
- Counseling/Family: 10.9%
- School: 4.6%
- Health/Sports: 2.8%
- Forensic: 1.7%
- Geropsychology: 0.6%

Research and Other Subfields
- Industrial/Organizational: 24.9%
- Developmental: 14.6%
- Social/Cognitive/Personality: 24.4%
- Educational: 12.2%
- Experimental/Quantitative: 10.2%
- Neuroscience/Physiological: 6.9%
- Other fields: 9.7%

Fields
- Health service provider subfields: 57%
- Research and other subfields: 11.4%
- Other fields: 5.4%
- Not specified: 26.2%

Employment Settings
- University/4-year college: 25.9%
- Medical school/other academic: 6.3%
- Schools/other educational: 8.1%
- Independent Practice: 5.7%
- Hospital/other health service: 25.0%
- Government/VA medical center: 16.3%
- Business/nonprofit: 10.4%
- Other: 2.3%

Emerging Branches of Psychology

Psychology is dynamic. It is a field that can adapt to changing environments and needs. This has never been truer than it is today. At the heart of this dynamic field is the ability for psychology to play increased roles in fields where the largest growth is being observed. This is likely one reason for the popularity of psychology in college: It is a growing, adaptive, "in demand" field (Clay, 2017). In terms of demand, psychology is projected to realize the greatest growth in three areas (Novotney, 2018). Let's briefly look at each area.

One growth area in psychology is **geropsychology**, a field dedicated to understanding and helping people with the mental and physical changes of aging. According to the U.S. Census Bureau (2017), the number of Americans 65 years and older is expected to double by 2060, and the number of Americans 85 and older may reach more than 19 million (approximately the population of New York state). This growth in older populations has led to substantial growth in majors, studies, trainings, certifications, and jobs aimed at caring for these populations. Many of the Americans in this population will be your own parents, grandparents, and if you are older than 25 today, then by 2060 this will include you too! In this way, psychology is taking the lead in meeting the increased demands of caring for older populations, particularly for those who are underserved.

A second growth area is provided by a large and growing body of research in **behavioral neuroscience**, the study of the links between the brain and behavior. Triggered by recent breakthroughs in biomedical technology, which enable researchers to observe the living brain in action, this area is generating a great deal of excitement. Two related areas are also making important contributions. One is *clinical neuroscience*, which focuses on how abnormalities in the brain and nervous system can alter perceptions, thoughts, language, memory, emotions, and motivations and can trigger the onset of various psychological disorders (Simonds et al., 2018; Yudofsky & Hales, 2002). The other related area is *cognitive neuroscience*, in which researchers record physical activity in different parts of the brain as a subject reads, speaks, looks at pictures, listens to music, or solves math problems. In this way, researchers are able to pinpoint regions and activities in the brain that correspond to different operations of the mind (Breedlove & Watson, 2017).

A third growth area for psychology is **industrial/organizational (I/O)**—an applied field introduced earlier in this chapter that addresses issues related to individuals and groups in the workplace, and issues related to the regional, national, and global impacts of businesses and industries. Globalization in business has led to an increased diversity of thought and demographics, and psychology is at the forefront of not only studying but also addressing head-on the challenges associated with these changes. Psychology plays a critical role in developing best practices and policies for optimizing employee motivation, management, organizational effectiveness, marketing, human resources, and even the well-being of employees. Across all of these challenges, understanding cultural influences is an important part of the growth process, not only in business but also across disciplines in psychology.

geropsychology. A subfield of developmental psychology dedicated to understanding and helping people with the mental and physical changes of aging.

behavioral neuroscience. A subfield of psychology that studies the links among the brain, nervous system, and behavior.

industrial/organizational (I/O). An applied field of psychology that addresses issues related to individuals and groups in workplace settings.

LEARNING CHECK

Playing the Fields

Match each question in the left column with the area of psychological study under which it falls.

1.	How are we affected by the aging process?	a.	Cognitive neuroscience
2.	How can abnormalities in the brain alter your perceptions?	b.	Clinical neuroscience
3.	How can we reduce harassment in the workplace?	c.	Geropsychology
4.	Which area of the brain is activated when you listen to music?	d.	Industrial/organizational psychology

(Answers: 1. c; 2. b; 3. d; 4. a.)

Sociocultural Perspectives

In an increasingly diverse world, sociocultural perspectives are increasing important. Now that we are well into the 21st century, communication satellites, cell phones, social media, and the Internet bring together people from vastly different cultures—and raise questions about the ways that we are all similar and different. Are there, psychologists ask, "universals" in human nature, ways in which everyone is fundamentally the same? In what ways are people from different parts of the world distinct from one another because of the regions and cultures in which they live?

Over the years, psychologists have tried to identify established patterns of behavior that are universally applicable to all members of the human species. People in general, we have been told, see better in daylight than in darkness, prefer reward to punishment, remember landmark events better than trivial ones, undergo an identity crisis in adolescence, strive to boost self-esteem, lash out at others when frustrated, and suffer depression after the loss of a loved one. Are these universal tendencies? Until recently, psychologists had studied only a small segment of the human population. All that has changed.

Today, more and more psychologists do **cross-cultural research**, by which they compare people from different regions of the world who have lived very different lives (Shiraev & Levy, 2016). Cross-cultural similarities and differences are discussed throughout the book. Table 1.5 provides a preview of the kinds of questions that psychologists ask and the chapters in which these questions are addressed.

In addition to comparing people from different parts of the world, psychologists also conduct **multicultural research**, the study of racial and ethnic groups within cultures. As in most countries, the populations of North America are heterogeneous and diverse—and are becoming more so with time. This diversity is an important fact of social life in all open societies, and it raises profound questions for psychologists in all areas of the discipline. How do immigrants torn between two cultures form a new identity, and what special problems do they face? Why are racism and other forms of prejudice so pervasive, and what can be done about them? What experiences do LGBTQ+ persons have

cross-cultural research. A body of studies designed to compare and contrast people of different cultures.

multicultural research. A body of studies designed to compare and contrast racial and ethnic minority groups within cultures.

This market in Mumbai is bustling with activity. In what ways are the people depicted in this scene similar to you and everyone else on the planet? In what ways are they different? Sociocultural perspectives focus on how people are influenced by culture, language, the region they live in, and other aspects of their surrounding environment.

iStock.com/HemantMandot

TABLE 1.5 ■ Cultural Similarities and Differences: Putting Your Common Sense to the Test

Roughly 90 percent of North Americans are right-handed. Are there human cultures in which this preference is not shown?
Do people in all regions of the world use "beds" for sleeping in a horizontal position?
Do people interpret experiences differently as a result of the language they speak?
Do babies all over the world start to walk and talk at the same age, or are these timetables culturally determined?
Do adolescents all over the world reach puberty at the same age, or are there marked differences?
Are eating disorders such as anorexia found among women in all cultures, or are they a uniquely Western affliction?
Is smiling a universal expression of joy, or are there cultures in which people do not smile when they are happy?
Do people in different cultures agree about what constitutes an attractive face, or is beauty culturally defined?
Do people all over the world suffer from depression, or are there cultures in which this problem is not found?

with their employers, families, and communities as a result of their sexual and gender identity? These topics are discussed throughout the book.

Thinking Like a Psychologist About Psychology and Its Methods

Psychology is a *broad* discipline that examines the biological roots of experience, internal cognitive and affective processes, the nature and nurture of human development, social and cultural influences, and the diagnosis and treatment of clinical disorders. Psychology is also a *dynamic* discipline. New theories are always being proposed, and old ones supported, revised, and discarded; new research methods are developed, and old ones are refined. On an ongoing basis, psychology is also a *responsive* discipline that tackles problems posed by world events and in such areas as health, education, race relations, and law. Finally, despite all the diversity and specialization, psychologists throughout the discipline value critical thinking and a commitment to *scientific* research methods as a mean of gaining knowledge about human behavior.

There are so many new developments, so many emerging areas of specialization, so many practical applications, and so many refinements in scientific methods, that it is impossible to cover the entire field in a single textbook. Also, because psychology is so dynamic, its knowledge evolves somewhat over time. To the extent possible, we have presented in this book the state of psychology *today*. Drawing on all of the areas, we will close with a "capstone" chapter on some of the fascinating new discoveries in health and well-being. As you'll learn, the theme of this final chapter, and of the book as a whole, is: "The mind is a powerful tool. The more we know about how to use it, the better off we'll be."

SUMMARY

WHAT IS PSYCHOLOGY?

Psychology can be defined as the scientific study of behavior and the mind.

HISTORICAL ROOTS

Psychology's origins can be traced to ancient Greek philosophers and physicians. During the Renaissance, Descartes developed **dualism**, a theory that the mind is spiritual and the body physical. This theory implied that the mind could not be studied scientifically. Thomas Hobbes and others disagreed, arguing that thoughts and feelings are physical processes.

Modern experimental psychology began in 1879 when Wilhelm Wundt established his laboratory in Germany. Wundt used a method of **introspection**, in which trained observers described their reactions to stimuli. In the United States, William James wrote his classic *The Principles of Psychology*; and in Vienna, Sigmund Freud developed **psychoanalysis** to examine the unconscious mind.

The emerging discipline faced a major controversy: Should psychologists speculate about the invisible mind, as Freud and Wundt did, or should they confine themselves to observable behavior? **Behaviorism**, as defined by John Watson, held that psychology should concentrate on what can be seen and measured. Studying the way organisms respond to stimuli, behaviorists such as B. F. Skinner refused to speculate about mental processes.

Behaviorism dominated American psychology from the 1920s through the 1960s. Then the focus shifted to **cognition**, the mental processes that intervene between a stimulus and a response. The computer, which offers a model of the human mind, helped inspire this "cognitive revolution." So did the child development theories of Jean Piaget and the linguistic theories of Noam Chomsky.

EXPANSION OF PSYCHOLOGY'S HORIZONS

Since its early days, psychology has expanded considerably. It now includes specialized areas of both **basic research** and **applied research**, it is more diversely represented, and it relies on sophisticated research methods.

The chapters of this textbook cover several broad areas of basic research. The **biological perspective** focuses on the links between the mind and body. The **cognitive perspective** considers whether human beings are generally competent in the way they learn, think, remember, and process information. The **developmental perspective** addresses changes from infancy through old age and tackles the nature-nurture debate. The **social psychological perspective** considers the extent to which social situations overpower individuals. And the **clinical perspective** deals with personality, disorders, treatment, and the question of whether people have the capacity for change.

Psychology is also a responsive science that has expanded in terms of its applications. Today, psychologists work in applied settings and use their theories and research to better understand such areas as health and medicine, education, business, law, sports, and current events.

A Range of Perspectives

Today there are more female, minority, and non-Western psychologists than in the past. This increased diversity within the professional ranks has strengthened psychology by providing new perspectives. These perspectives include those from biological, cognitive, developmental, social psychological, sociocultural, and positive psychological perspectives.

SCIENTIFIC METHODS

Connecting all strands of psychology is an emphasis on **critical thinking** and scientific methods.

The Research Process

Research is a multistep process that begins with a **theory**, an organized set of principles that describes, predicts, and explains an aspect of human behavior, and provides testable propositions known as **hypotheses** and **operational definitions** of key variables. Investigators must then plan the study, collect data, analyze the results, and draw a conclusion. Psychological studies vary in their settings, their ways of measuring variables, and the types of conclusions the research is designed to reach.

Research Settings

There are two types of research settings: **laboratory research**, valuable for its control and precision; and **field research**, conducted in real-world environments.

Psychological Measurements

Self-reports are interviews or questionnaires in which people report on their own thoughts, feelings, or behavior. These are easy to administer but are sometimes misleading. The alternatives are direct **behavioral observation** and the **archival research** that uses records of past behavior such as medical files and public documents.

Research Designs

No matter how the information is collected, researchers use **statistics** to analyze it and draw conclusions. The types of conclusions they reach depend on the research design.

There are three types of descriptive studies designed simply to describe a person, group, or phenomenon. **Case studies** collect detailed information about a particular person. **Surveys** use interviews or questionnaires to draw conclusions about an entire population. To make a survey as accurate as possible, researchers study a **random sample**, so that each individual in the group has an equal chance of being chosen. **Epidemiology**, the study of the distribution of illnesses in a population, is a particularly important form of survey research. The third type of descriptive study, **naturalistic observation**, involves the measurement of behavior in natural settings.

When description is not enough, researchers often employ correlational studies. A **correlation** is a statistical measure of the extent to which two factors are associated. In numerical terms, correlation coefficients range from –1 to +1 and can be shown on a **scatterplot**. Researchers use correlational studies to make predictions about one variable based on what they know about another variable. Correlation, however, does not prove causation.

To study causal links, researchers turn to the **experiment**, where the investigator manipulates an **independent variable** (the proposed cause) and measures a **dependent variable** (the proposed effect). Then the researcher compares the **experimental group** of participants to a **control group** that was not exposed to the independent variable. An effective experiment requires **random assignment** of participants, so that each participant has an equal chance of being in either group.

Finally, psychological research often includes reviews of the existing evidence. By summarizing the current state of knowledge, research reviews can help resolve the questions of **replication** (Would a new study produce the same results?) and **generalizability** (Is the finding applicable under other sets of conditions?). Various studies can be summarized through literature reviews and through **meta-analysis**, a set of statistical procedures for combining the results of individual studies.

Ethical Considerations

Like other professions, psychology faces ethical issues—questions, for example, about the use and treatment of research participants. For human participants, concerns include the subject's right to privacy, the harm or discomfort that may be caused, and the use of **deception**. Research guidelines stress the need to obtain **informed consent** from participants, to let them know they can withdraw at any time, to minimize discomfort, to keep data confidential, and to debrief participants afterward. When the experimental participants are animals, researchers must treat them humanely and minimize their suffering.

PSYCHOLOGY TODAY

Because of the richness of psychological research and its many applications, there are more people in psychology today than ever before, and their work touches on many vital public policy topics.

Emerging Branches of Psychology

Psychology is dynamic. At the heart of this dynamic field is psychology's flexibility and application to several areas. Thus, psychology is experiencing growth, with three areas projected to realize the greatest growth. One such area is **geropsychology**, a field dedicated to understanding and helping people with the mental and physical changes of aging. A second growth area is **behavioral neuroscience**, which examines the links between neural activity in the brain and behavior. Clinical neuroscience focuses on how abnormalities in the brain and nervous system can cause psychological disorders. And cognitive neuroscience examines the links between the brain and normal mental activities. A third growth area, **industrial/organizational (I/O)**, is an applied field that addresses issues related to the regional, national, and global impacts of business on individuals and groups in the workplace.

Sociocultural Perspectives

Increasingly, psychologists are testing the universality of their principles in **cross-cultural research** all over the world. With increasing diversity in the populations in many countries, there is also an increase in **multicultural research**, studies of racial and ethnic groups within cultures.

CRITICAL THINKING

Thinking Critically About Psychology and Its Methods

1. Historically, psychologists have been white males of North American or European descent. How might this fact have influenced the questions psychologists asked and/or the theories they developed?

2. Most psychologists, at one time or another, have had to defend the notion that psychology is a science. Why do you think it is important for psychologists to view psychology as a scientific enterprise? Do you agree that psychology is the *scientific* study of behavior and the mind? Why or why not?

3. In the past several years, we have seen a dramatic increase in violence in schools, including adolescents shooting teachers and classmates. How might the different theoretical perspectives discussed in this chapter (e.g., behaviorist, cognitive, biological) attempt to explain such behavior?

4. Suppose you wanted to study school violence. Design three separate studies—one descriptive, one correlational, and one experimental—that would allow you to examine this issue. Would you use a case study, survey, or naturalistic observation for your descriptive study? What variables would you measure in your correlational study? What would be the independent and dependent variables in your experiment? What type of measurements would you collect in your studies? What sorts of conclusions about school violence would each study allow you to make?

5. Do you personally believe that research should use animal participants? What are the arguments for and against using animals as research participants?

CAREER CONNECTION: PREPARING FOR A CAREER

College is a place for more than just learning in the classroom; it is preparing for life beyond the classroom. Throughout college you'll do more than just study. You may seek internships, engage in scholarship, volunteer in the community, join clubs or play sports, provide tutoring to your fellow students, get a job, make friends, and even enjoy a little fun along the way. Collectively, these experiences will allow you to grow personally and professionally. The goal of starting college, of course, is to graduate and, beyond that, to prepare for a career. While the career you choose is your own personal journey, in this section we'll explore how psychology can help prepare you for a variety of careers and skills.

More than ever, employers are looking for intangible qualities in their employees. In other words, they are looking for applicants who have honed their *21st century skills*. These skills include critical thinking, creativity, leadership, initiative, productivity, social skills, communication, and information/technology/media literacy. The American Psychological Association's Learning Outcomes map onto several of these skills. Therefore, graduates with psychology degrees can apply to jobs in almost every industry and in roles that involve understanding or guiding human behavior, such as in business, counseling, marketing, teaching, and social services. The skills graduates walk away with can be applicable in a number of different industries such as business, government, education, and health care. They also set the stage for students hoping to pursue graduate education and work as a psychologist.

Key skills for these roles that psychology students learn to develop:

- Develop a working knowledge of psychology's content domains
- Apply psychological content and skills to career goals
- Develop meaningful professional direction for life after graduation

KEY TERMS

applied research (p. 9)
archival research (p. 22)
basic research (p. 9)
behavioral neuroscience (p. 37)
behavioral observation (p. 22)
behaviorism (p. 7)
beneficence (p. 33)
biological perspective (p. 10)
case studies (p. 23)
clinical perspective (p. 12)
cognition (p. 8)
cognitive perspective (p. 10)

construct (p. 21)
control group (p. 29)
correlation (p. 27)
critical thinking (p. 18)
cross-cultural research (p. 38)
deception (p. 33)
dependent variable (p. 29)
developmental perspective (p. 10)
dualism (p. 4)
epidemiology (p. 24)
ethogram (p. 26)
experiment (p. 28)

experimental group (p. 29)
field research (p. 20)
generalizability (p. 30)
geropsychology (p. 37)
hypothesis (p. 14)
hypotheses (p. 18)
independent variable (p. 28)
industrial/organizational (I/O) (p. 37)
informed consent (p. 33)
introspection (p. 4)
justice (p. 33)
laboratory research (p. 19)
meta-analysis (p. 31)
monism (p. 4)
multicultural research (p. 38)
naturalistic observations (p. 26)
operational definitions (p. 18)

physiological measure (p. 21)
positive psychological perspective (p. 12)
psychoanalysis (p. 6)
psychology (p. 3)
random assignment (p. 30)
random sample (p. 25)
replication (p. 30)
research ethics (p. 32)
respect for persons (p. 32)
scatterplot (p. 27)
self-report (p. 21)
social psychological perspective (p. 11)
sociocultural perspective (p. 11)
statistics (p. 23)
structuralism (p. 4)
surveys (p. 24)

2 BEHAVIORAL NEUROSCIENCE

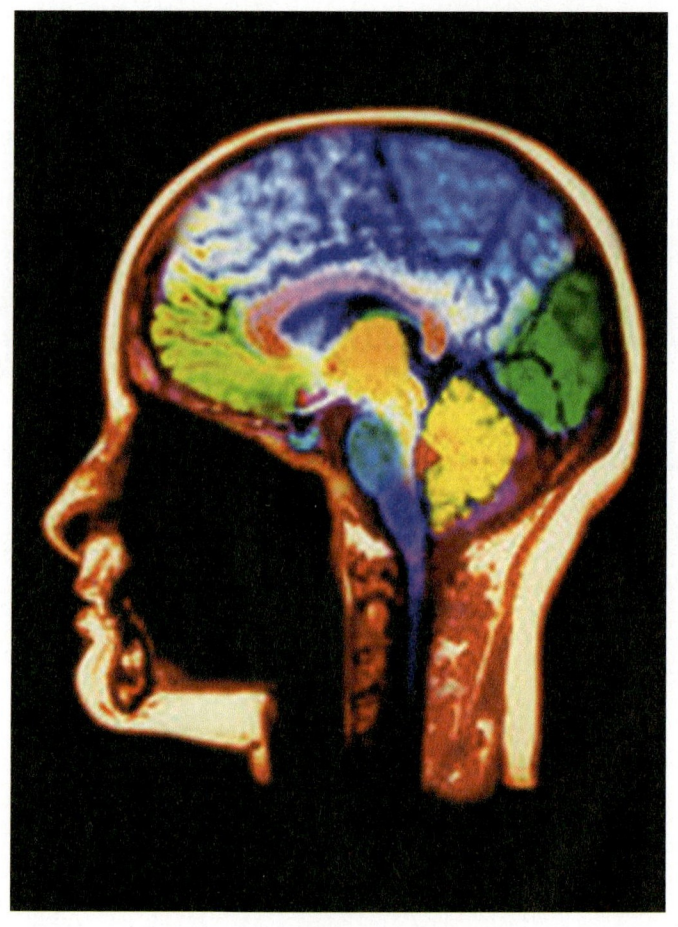

Scott Camazine & Sue Trainor/Science Source

LEARNING OBJECTIVES

Explain the steps taken by the brain and body to prepare for a reaction.

Apply the parts of a neuron and neurotransmitters to the process of electrochemical communication.

Summarize and synthesize the methods utilized to understand the parts and operation of the brain.

Identify the nature of plasticity in the brain and how it can be applied to understanding brain injuries.

WHAT'S YOUR PREDICTION: ONE BRAIN OR TWO?

The Situation

You've likely observed pictures or models of the human brain, so you may have a fairly good sense of what it looks like. The brain has two halves: a right hemisphere and a left hemisphere. Each is nearly a copy of the other, but as you may know, while the whole brain works together, the right and left sides (or hemispheres) have different strengths. The left side tends to be a literal interpreter (e.g., the literal meaning of the words you read in a novel), whereas the right side tends to be a more of a subjective interpreter (e.g., how you imagine the characters and setting as you read the novel). Incredibly, each hemisphere largely controls the opposite side of the body (the right hemisphere processes the left side of the body; the left hemisphere processes the right side of the body).

You're only mildly interested. But wait. What if the two halves of a person's brain were physically separated from each other? Would each side compensate for the loss and function on its own, or would the person flounder? This sounds like one of those hypothetical problems that philosophers like to ponder, but it's real. On rare occasions, people who suffer life-threatening seizures undergo a radical form of surgery in which the cable of nerves that connect the brain's right and left hemispheres is completely severed. In these "split-brain" patients, the two sides of the brain can no longer communicate. The question is: What is the effect?

Now imagine the following situation. The year is 1961 and a split-brain patient by the name of W.J. agrees to take part in a psychological experiment in which you are assisting. After introductions, you show W.J. a series of cards, each containing a red-and-white geometric pattern, and a set of cubes—each containing two red sides, two white sides, and two mixed sides divided along the diagonal. As illustrated in Figure 2.1, the task is to arrange the blocks in squares that match the patterns on the

FIGURE 2.1 ■ **The Block-Design Task Given to W.J.**

Monica Wierzbicki/Body Scientific Intl.

cards. Oh, there's one hitch. You tell W.J. that he can use only one hand to assemble the blocks. On some cards, you tell him to use his right hand and keep the left one tucked under the table. On other cards, you tell him to use only his left hand. Can W.J. match the patterns? Does it matter which hand he uses?

Make a Prediction

Reread the situation and examine the clues given earlier about the human brain, the type of surgery that W.J. had, and the nature of the task he is being asked to complete. Also keep in mind that W.J. is a normal and intelligent man—at least he was before the surgery. Putting all these pieces together, do you think he is able to complete the task with his right hand? What about with his left hand? Make two predictions, one for each hand.

	Yes	No
Left-hand success	_____	_____
Right-hand success	_____	_____

The Results

Before W.J. was tested, researchers Michael Gazzaniga and Roger Sperry were not sure what to expect. W.J. seemed normal in conversation, but perhaps both sides of an integrated brain are needed for complex mental activities. Or perhaps one side is sufficient if it's the one that specializes in the task at hand. The result was dramatic: W.J. could assemble the block patterns with his left hand, but not with his right hand. In fact, as his right hand struggled, the left hand occasionally sneaked up from under the table to help out!

What Does It All Mean?

W.J. was the first split-brain patient ever tested, but others later confirmed the basic result: The left hand succeeded at the spatial block-design task because the left hand is controlled by the "spatial" right hemisphere. Yet his right hand—because it is controlled by the left hemisphere and was unable, after the surgery, to receive signals from the right side—was clueless. This case study involving W.J. shows that the brain's two hemispheres specialize in different types of mental activities—something we normally don't notice because the hemispheres are connected and both sides are involved in everything we do. More important, this study shows that when the two halves are disconnected, they act as two separate brains. Reflecting on the implications, Gazzaniga (1992) notes that "each half brain seemed to work and function outside of the conscious realm of the other" (p. 122).

Case studies such as this one have played a major role in our understanding of the human brain and its links to the body and the mind. The brain is a complex anatomical structure, and researchers today have many tools at their disposal to study how it works. In this chapter, we'll examine the human brain, how it's built, its place in the nervous system, and the psychological functions that it serves.

At 25 years of age, Phineas Gage was a supervisor for the Rutland & Burlington Railroad in Vermont. He was bright, well liked, and energetic. On the afternoon of September 13, 1848, Gage and his coworkers were in Vermont blasting rock to pave the way for new railroad tracks. To do this, they drilled holes in the rock and packed the holes with gunpowder and sand, using a three-foot-long rod called a tamping iron. All of a sudden, a spark ignited the powder, causing an explosion that propelled the rod upward like a missile. As shown in Figure 2.2, the rod (which was an inch and a quarter in diameter at one end but came to a sharp point at the other end) pierced Gage's left cheek behind the eye, exited the front-top part of his skull, flew 50 feet into the air, and landed in a pile of dirt, covered with blood and brain matter.

FIGURE 2.2 ■ Phineas Gage's Skull

Using photographs and measurements of Gage's skull, and computerized images of normal brains, Damasio et al. (1994) plotted the possible paths of the tamping iron and produced this computerized reconstruction of the damage to the prefrontal cortex of Gage's skull. Gage's skull and the tamping iron are now on display on the fifth floor of the Harvard Medical School Library.

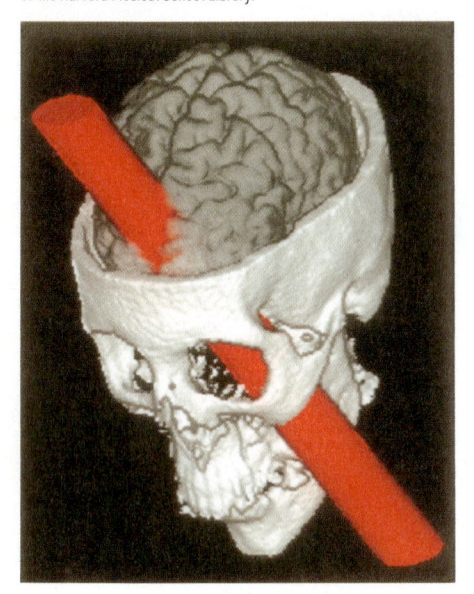

Reprinted with permission from H. Damasio, T. Grabowski, R. Frank, A. M. Galaburda, and A. R. Damasio, "The Return of Phineas Gage: Clues About the Brain From a Famous Patient," Science, 264, pp. 1102–1105. © 1994. Reprinted by permission from AAAS.

Gage was catapulted backward to the ground, where he began to shake. To everyone's amazement, he was still alive. Minutes later, with blood pouring down his face, Gage was sitting up, moving about, and talking to those around him. Doctors soon stopped the bleeding, cleaned out the loose bits of bone and brain tissue, and packed the wound. Within a few months, Gage was back at work. He showed no loss of intellectual ability. But the front part of his brain, the area known as the frontal lobes, was badly damaged. As a result, this normally soft-spoken, controlled, and considerate young man had become irritable, demanding, unable to plan for the future, and unrestrained—at times engaging in gross profanity. In many ways, Gage was not a social being. According to his doctor, the change in his personality was so profound that he was "no longer Gage." To complete the sad story: Gage lost his job, traveled with P.T. Barnum's circus, and exhibited his skull and tamping iron all over the country. Twelve years after the accident, at age 37, Gage died. To this day, however, his case remains important in the history of brain science (Fleischman, 2002; Harlow, 1868; MacMillan, 2000; Thiebaut de Schotten et al., 2015).

Psychologists now know that the frontal lobes are involved in thinking, planning, setting goals, and inhibiting impulses. But the case of Phineas Gage told us much more. It told us that the human brain and nervous system are not a single or simple entity but rather an integrated "system" consisting of different specialized parts. And it told us that the links among the brain, the mind, and behavior can be revealed by the effects of damage to specific structures. These points set the stage as we begin to explore the biological roots of the human experience. As we'll explore, all aspects of our existence—every sight, sound, taste, and smell, every twitch, every movement, every feeling of pleasure or pain, all our dreams, learned associations, memories, thoughts, emotions, and even our personalities and social interactions—are biological events. Behavioral neuroscience is the subfield of psychology that focuses on these links (Breedlove & Watson, 2017; Kandel, Schwartz, & Jessell, 2000).

FIGURE 2.3 ■ Phineas Gage

(A) A three-dimensional plaster life mask of Phineas Gage. Recognizing the historic value of his case, doctors in Boston made it, one year after the accident, by having Phineas close his eyes and inserting straws into his nose so that he could breathe while liquid plaster was poured over his face. Notice the large scar on his forehead. (B) In 1998, the small town of Cavendish, Vermont (72 miles north of one author's home in Williamstown, Massachusetts), memorialized Phineas Gage by dedicating a plaque in his honor. The plaque tells the story of what happened and its significance for the study of behavioral neuroscience.

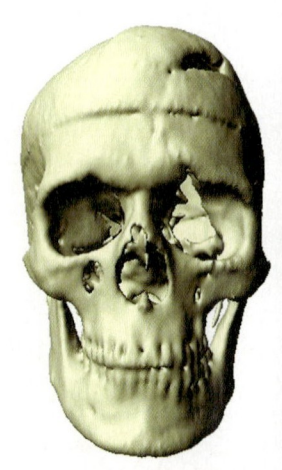

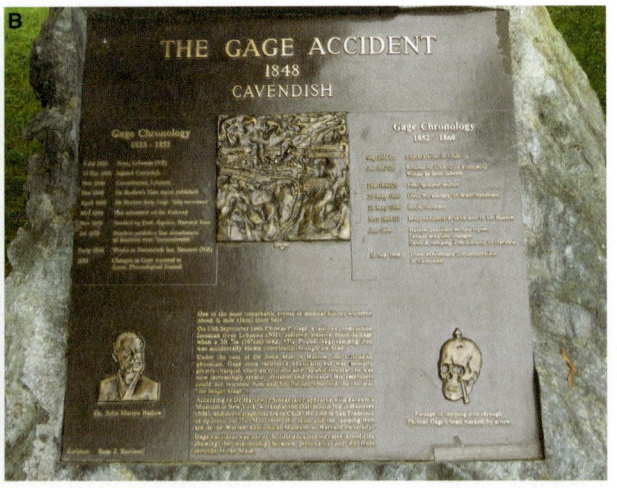

Source: Kelley DJ, Farhoud M, Meyerand ME, Nelson DL, Ramirez LF, et al. (2007) "Creating Physical 3D Stereolithograph Models of Brain and Skull." PLoS ONE 2(10): e1119. doi:10.1371/journal.pone.0001119. Licensed under Creative Commons CC BY 2.5

Roadside plaque in Cavendish, Vermont memorializing Phineas Gage by Daniel G. Axtell, licensed under CC BY-SA 4.0 https://creativecommons.org/licenses/by-sa/4.0/deed.en

THE BODY'S COMMUNICATION NETWORKS

> **LEARNING OBJECTIVES**
>
> Explain the steps taken by the brain and body to prepare for a reaction.
>
> - Outline how the sensory organs, muscles, and other parts of the body prepare for action.
> - Identify the body's communication networks, and discuss how the brain acts as a central command center.

The human brain weighs only about three pounds. With its gnarled mass of cells, it feels like a lump of jelly and looks like an oversized, wrinkled gray walnut. The brain is an extraordinary organ—capable of great feats and more complex than any computer. It is one of those "miracles" of life that inspire philosophers and scientists alike.

The Nervous System

The brain is the centerpiece of the body's nervous system, an elaborate electrochemical communication network that connects the brain and spinal cord to all sensory organs, muscles, and glands. The nervous system is divided into two major parts: central and peripheral. The **central nervous system (CNS)** consists of the brain and the spinal cord. The spinal cord is a long tubular column of neural tissue surrounded by a ring of bone that runs from the lower back up to the base of the skull. Basically, it is a transmission cable filled with nerve fibers and pathways—and it serves as an "information superhighway." Later in this chapter, we'll explain that the spinal cord transmits signals from sense organs and muscles below the head up to the brain and funnels signals from the brain to the rest of the body. Injury to the spinal cord can cause partial or complete paralysis.

The **peripheral nervous system (PNS)** consists of all the nerves that radiate from the CNS to the rest of the body—from the top of the head out to the fingers, toes, and skin. The peripheral nervous system is divided into two components: somatic and autonomic. The nerves of the **somatic nervous system** transmit signals (such as sights, sounds, tastes, smells, and pain) from the sensory organs and skin to the CNS. They also relay motor commands from the CNS to the skeletal muscles of the arms, legs, torso, and head, thus directing the body's voluntary movements. The nerves in the **autonomic nervous system** connect the CNS to all of the smooth *involuntary* muscles and organs (such as the heart, stomach, and liver) and to the body's many glands, which secrete hormones (defined in the next section). As the term *autonomic* implies, this system automatically regulates internal states such as heartbeat, blood pressure, body temperature, digestion, hormone levels, and glucose levels in the blood. As we'll explain later in this book, people can learn to use biofeedback, yoga, and other techniques to exert some control over these bodily functions.

The autonomic nervous system itself has two parts: sympathetic and parasympathetic. In light of the functions served by these subsystems, they may be thought of as the body's "departments of war and peace." The **sympathetic nervous system** energizes the body for action. In times of stress, it directs the adrenal glands, which rest atop the kidneys, to secrete more of the hormones epinephrine and norepinephrine (also known as *adrenaline* and *noradrenaline*)—thereby increasing the heart rate and heightening physiological arousal. The pupils dilate to let in more light, breathing speeds up to bring in more oxygen, and perspiration increases to cool down the body. When action is no longer necessary, as when the stress subsides, the **parasympathetic nervous system** takes over and restores the body to its preenergized state. The heart stops racing, the pupils contract, breathing slows down, and energy is conserved. The blood levels of epinephrine and norepinephrine diminish slowly, and the body relaxes, cools down, and returns to normal. These systems play a vital role in the experience of emotion.

To summarize, the nervous system is divided into two parts, central and peripheral. The CNS contains the brain and spinal cord. The PNS is subdivided further into the somatic and autonomic systems. In turn, the autonomic system contains both sympathetic (arousing) and parasympathetic (calming) divisions. This overview of the nervous system is presented in Figure 2.4.

---

central nervous system (CNS). The network of nerves contained within the brain and spinal cord.

peripheral nervous system (PNS). The network of nerves that radiate from the central nervous system to the rest of the body. The PNS comprises the somatic and autonomic nervous systems.

somatic nervous system. The branch of the peripheral nervous system that transmits signals from the sensory organs to the CNS, and from the CNS to the skeletal muscles.

autonomic nervous system. The branch of the peripheral nervous system that connects the CNS to the internal muscles, organs, and glands.

sympathetic nervous system. A branch of the autonomic nervous system that controls the involuntary activities of various organs and mobilizes the body for fight or flight.

parasympathetic nervous system. The division of the autonomic nervous system that reduces arousal and restores the body to its preenergized state.

FIGURE 2.4 ■ Divisions of the Nervous System

The Endocrine System

Closely linked to the nervous system is the body's second communication system. The **endocrine system** is a collection of ductless glands that regulate growth, sexual development, reproduction, metabolism, mood, and certain aspects of behavior by secreting chemical messengers called **hormones** (the word *hormone* means to "set in motion"). Hormones are produced in tissue and secreted into the bloodstream, which then carries them to "target organs" throughout the body. Compared to the speedy transmission of impulses through the nervous system, hormonal messages may take several seconds, hours, or even days to take effect. Once they do, however, the impact is often long lasting. Dozens of hormones are produced by the body. Some of the major glands, along with their locations and their functions, are illustrated in Figure 2.5.

As we'll explain later, a small but important structure in the brain called the hypothalamus controls the endocrine system through the **pituitary gland**, a pea-size gland that sits at the base of the brain. The pituitary can be thought of as the master gland of the endocrine system. Upon command from the control center in the brain, the pituitary releases a hormone that stimulates the production of hormones in other endocrine glands. In turn, many hormones flow from the bloodstream back to the brain—which sends a signal to the hypothalamus that more or less additional secretion is needed. The importance of hormone regulation for the maintenance of the body is apparent when an endocrine gland malfunctions in some way. For example, when a thyroid gland produces too little hormone, people become easily tired and sensitive to cold. When the thyroid produces too much of the hormone, people tend to get nervous and irritable and lose weight.

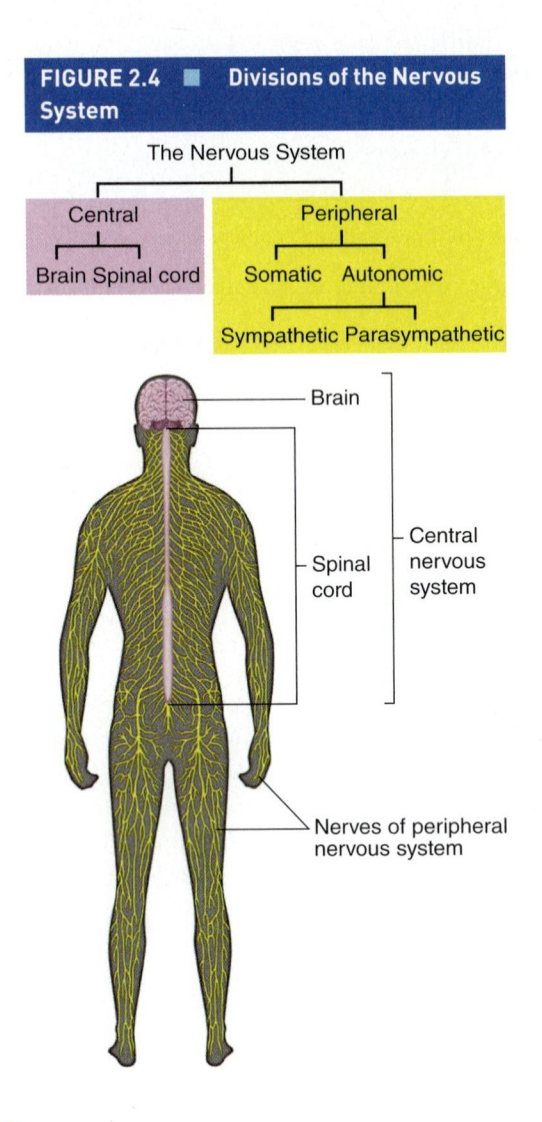

endocrine system. A collection of ductless glands that regulate aspects of growth, reproduction, metabolism, and behavior by secreting hormones.

hormones. Chemical messengers secreted from endocrine glands, into the bloodstream, to be carried to various organs throughout the body.

pituitary gland. A tiny gland in the brain that regulates growth and stimulates hormones in other endocrine glands at the command of the hypothalamus.

FIGURE 2.5 ■ Major Endocrine Glands

Taking commands from the hypothalamus, the glands of the endocrine system regulate growth, reproduction, metabolism, and behavior by secreting hormones into the bloodstream. These hormones are carried to certain "target organs" throughout the body.

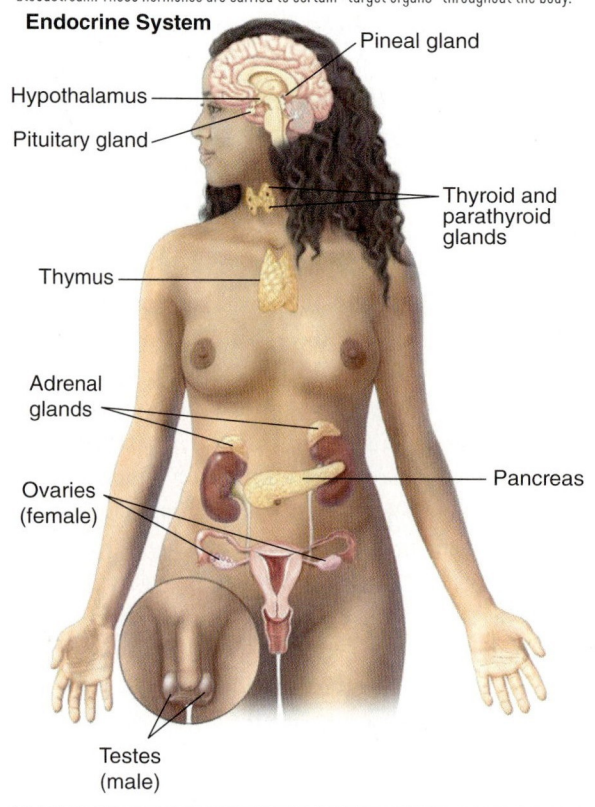

Endocrine System

- Pineal gland
- Hypothalamus
- Pituitary gland
- Thyroid and parathyroid glands
- Thymus
- Adrenal glands
- Ovaries (female)
- Pancreas
- Testes (male)

Carolina Hrejsa/Body Scientific Intl.

Notice that there is a constant flow of communication between the nervous system and the endocrine system. Indeed, the brain regulates the release of hormones the same way that a thermostat maintains the temperature of a room. If you set a thermostat at 70 degrees and the temperature dips below that level, the heat comes on until the room tops 70, at which point it shuts itself off. Similarly, if a hormone drops below a certain level, the hypothalamus signals the pituitary and other glands that more is needed. Then once the hormone levels are sufficient, the hypothalamus signals the pituitary gland to stop the additional release of hormones. With the brain in command, the nervous system and the endocrine system work together.

THE NEURON

LEARNING OBJECTIVES

Apply the parts of a neuron and neurotransmitters to the process of electrochemical communication.

- Explain what neurons are and how they are constructed.
- Discuss how neurons transmit information from one neuron to the other.
- Elaborate on how neurons transmit information throughout the body.
- Explain what neurotransmitters are and what they contribute to the process.

From a broad overview of the nervous system, we turn to its specific parts. We begin with the tiny but numerous building blocks and the electrical and chemical impulses that fire throughout the body. In humans and other animals, the nervous system consists of two main types of cells: nerve cells and glial cells.

Playing the lead role in this system are the nerve cells, known as **neurons**. Neurons send and receive information throughout the body in the form of *electrochemical signals*. There are three types of neurons. **Sensory neurons** send signals from the senses, skin, muscles, and internal organs to the central nervous system. When you view an awesome sunset, scrape your knee, or enjoy the flavor of a terrific meal, messages fire from your eyes, knee, and taste buds. These messages are then relayed up to the brain. **Motor (motion-producing) neurons** transmit commands the other way around—from the CNS to the muscles, glands, and organs. Once the sunset, injured knee, and delicious food "register," you and your body react. Finally, **interneurons** serve as neural connectors within the CNS. Among their functions is to link input signals from the sensory neurons to output signals from the motor neurons.

No one knows for sure how many neurons there are in the human brain, but researchers estimate that the number is about 86 billion (Herculano-Houzel, 2014). If you were to count one neuron every second, you would need nearly 3,000 years to count them all. Even more mind-boggling is the fact that each neuron is linked to more than a thousand other neurons, thus providing each of us with literally trillions of connections among the neurons in the brain. It's important to realize that individual neurons are not distributed evenly or haphazardly throughout the body. Rather, they cluster into interconnected working groups known as **neural networks**. Much like habits, neural cell connections are strengthened by usage and experience, allowing for fast and efficient communication within networks.

The nervous system also has a supporting cast of smaller cells that are called **glial cells**, or neuroglia. The word *neuroglia* is derived from the Latin and Greek words meaning "nerve glue." These cells are so named because they provide structural support, insulation, and nutrients to the neurons, thereby "gluing" the system together. They also play a role in the development and repair of neurons and the speed of the neural signals throughout the system. Glial cells are much smaller than the neurons they support and are almost as numerous with nearly 85 billion glial cells in the human brain (Herculano-Houzel, 2014).

To appreciate how various neurons work together within the nervous system, let's trace the neural pathway of a simple **reflex**, defined as an automatic response to external sensory stimulation. You are probably familiar with the "knee jerk" reflex elicited during a medical checkup. Using a rubber mallet, the doctor taps your patellar tendon, located just below the knee, causing your leg to kick forward. You don't have to think about it; the reaction is immediate and automatic. How? As shown in Figure 2.6, the knee stretches your thigh muscle, which sends a sensory signal to the spinal cord, which sends

---

neurons. Nerve cells that serve as the building blocks of the nervous system.

sensory neurons. Neurons that send signals from the senses, skin, muscles, and internal organs to the central nervous system.

Motor (motion-producing) neurons. Neurons that transmit commands from the central nervous system to the muscles, glands, and organs.

interneurons. Central nervous system neurons that connect sensory inputs and motor outputs.

neural networks. Clusters of densely interconnected neurons that form and strengthen as a result of experience.

glial cells. Nervous system cells, also called neuroglia, that provide structural support, insulation, and nutrients to the neurons.

reflex. An inborn automatic response to a sensory stimulus.

FIGURE 2.6 ■ The Knee Jerk Reflex and the Withdrawal Reflex

(a) The knee jerk reflex: A tap on the knee sends a sensory signal to the spinal cord, which sends a motor signal back to the muscle. Tap, kick! (b) The withdrawal reflex: Touch a hot object, and your hand will immediately pull away. In this case, sensory and motor neurons are linked by an interneuron.

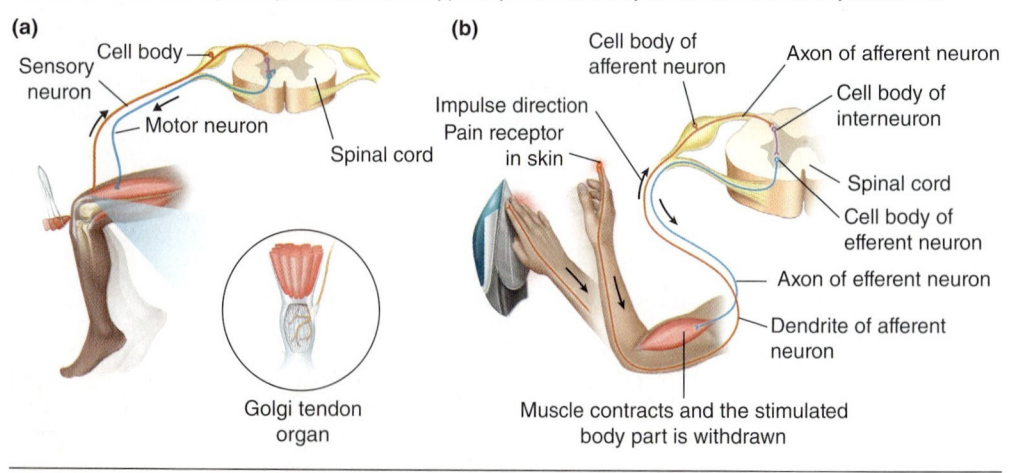

Amanda Tomasikiewicz/Body Scientific Intl.

a motor signal right back to the thigh muscle. Tap, kick! This two-step chain of events takes only 50 milliseconds because it does not involve higher mental processes in the brain.

Reflexive behaviors can be very adaptive. When your hand touches a hot iron or the thorn of a rose bush, a sensory neuron sends a quick message to the spinal cord and connects to an interneuron, which activates a motor neuron, causing your hand to pull away. The entire reaction takes place in the spinal cord—before you and your brain feel the pain and before too much damage is done.

In the case of more complex forms of behavior—say, driving a car, working on a math problem, playing a musical instrument, talking to a friend, or reading this fascinating sentence—more extensive activity is needed than is possible within the spinal cord. Sensory inputs travel toward the spinal cord (via the somatic nervous system), but they are then forwarded up to the brain and "processed" before a behavioral "decision" is reached. This decision is sent back down through the spinal cord and out to the muscles, which results in behavior. Most of the behaviors that interest psychologists are of this sort.

Structure of the Neuron

The neuron is a lot like other cells in the body. It is surrounded by a membrane and has a nucleus that contains genetic material. What makes the neuron so special is its ability to communicate. Everything that we do and all that we know depend on the transfer of signals from one neuron to another.

It's hard to describe the dimensions of a "typical" neuron because these cells come in hundreds of different shapes and sizes, largely depending on their specific function. But the various neurons do have certain structural features in common. As illustrated in Figure 2.7, every neuron has a roundish **soma**, or cell body, which stores the nucleus of the cell and maintains a chemical balance. Connected to the cell body are two types of branched fibers, or tentacles. The **dendrites** (derived from the Greek word for "tree") *receive* impulses from sensory organs or other neurons. The more dendrites there are, the more information can be received. The **axon** (so named because of its axlelike shape) *sends* the impulse from the neuron to other neurons. Some axons are short and stubby; others are several feet long and slender (some run from the spine down to the muscles of your big toe). At the end of each axon are branches with knoblike tips called axon terminals. As we'll explore, these tips contain vital chemical substances to be released onto other cells. Many axons are also covered with the **myelin sheath**, a shiny white layer of fatty cells. Produced by the glial cells, the myelin sheath is wrapped tightly around the axon to insulate it. This insulation helps to speed up the movement of electrical impulses by preventing leakage. The importance of this insulation can be seen in multiple sclerosis, a disease in which the myelin sheath degenerates, slowing signals to the muscles and resulting in the eventual loss of muscle control. To summarize, neural signals travel from the dendrites, through the (cell body) soma, down the axon, and into the axon terminals.

soma. The cell body of a neuron.

dendrites. Extensions from the cell body of a neuron that receive incoming impulses.

axon. The extension of the cell body of a neuron that sends impulses to other neurons.

myelin sheath. A layer of fatty cells that is wrapped tightly around the axon to insulate it and speed the movement of electrical impulses.

FIGURE 2.7 ■ How Neurons Communicate

Every neuron consists of a soma, or cell body, and two types of branched fibers. Dendrites receive electrical impulses from sensory organs or other neurons, and the axon relays these impulses to other neurons or muscles. As shown, many axons are insulated with the myelin sheath, a fatty layer that speeds the movement of the impulses.

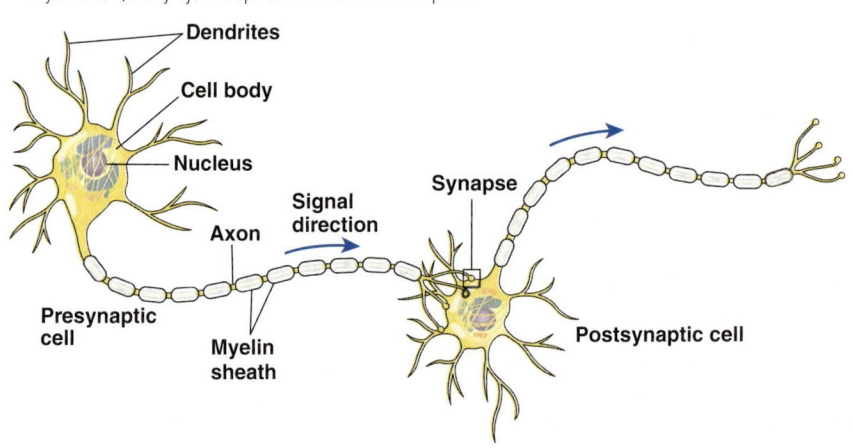

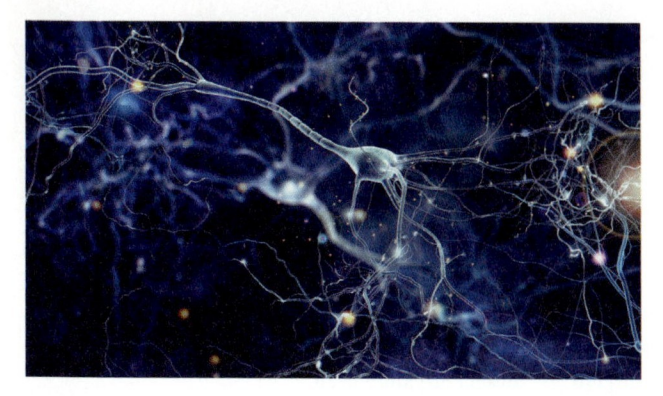

As shown, neurons transmit electrochemical signals throughout the body.
iStock.com/koto_feja

action potential. An electrical impulse that surges along an axon, caused by an influx of positive ions in the neuron.

threshold. The level of stimulation needed to trigger a neural impulse.

synapse. The junction between the axon terminal of one neuron and the dendrites of another.

neurotransmitters. Chemical messengers in the nervous system that transmit information by crossing the synapse from one neuron to another.

The Neuron in Action

To understand how messages are transmitted from the axon of one neuron to the dendrites of another, you need to know that these messages occur in the form of electrical impulses. Here is a brief lesson in the electricity of the nervous system.

Every neuron is covered by a membrane, a semipermeable skin that permits some chemicals to pass through more easily than others. Dissolved in fluid on both sides of the membrane are electrically charged particles called *ions*. Three kinds of ions are most important: sodium (positively charged ions that do not pass easily through the membrane and so remain concentrated outside the cell), potassium (positively charged ions that cross easily and are concentrated inside the cell), and negatively charged ions that are trapped permanently inside the cell. When a neuron is at rest, the inside of the cell has a negative charge relative to the outside, making it a store of potential energy.

When the dendrites of a neuron are stimulated, usually by other neurons, this delicate balance is suddenly altered. The semipermeable membrane opens ion channels, permitting the positively charged sodium ions outside the cell to rush in. For an instant, the charge inside the cell becomes less negative and, as a result, may trigger an **action potential**—a quick burst of electrical energy that surges through the axon like a spark along a trail of gunpowder. Depending on the neuron, most impulses travel at speeds ranging from 2 miles an hour up to 200 miles an hour, which is faster than a car but three million times slower than the speed of electric current passing through a wire. At top speed, then, it takes an action potential one-hundredth of a second to run along an axon from the spinal cord to a muscle in the finger or toe. Then after an impulse has passed, the positive ions inside the cell are pumped back to the outside of the membrane. The neuron returns to its resting state and is once again ready for action.

The stimulation of a neuron does not always trigger the firing of an electrical impulse. At any given moment, a neuron may be receiving signals at its dendrites from very few or from hundreds, even thousands, of other neurons. Whether the neuron fires depends on the sum total of signals impinging on it. Only if the combined signals exceed a certain minimum intensity, or **threshold**, does the neuron's membrane break down and begin to transmit an electrical impulse. If it does not, no impulse is created. In other words, the action potential is an *all-or-none response*. Either it fires or it does not. This effect is like firing a gun. If you squeeze the trigger past a certain point (the threshold), bang! The bullet is launched. If not, nothing happens. You can't half-shoot, and you can't vary the intensity of the shot.

The firing of an electrical impulse is as quick as the blink of an eye, but it has profound significance. Information in the nervous system is made up of action potentials. Every thought, dream, or emotion you have, every action you take, and every decision you make is coded in the form of action potentials. For neuroscientists, cracking the action potential code is a key to understanding the language of the nervous system and unlocking new discoveries about the biology of our minds and behavior.

How Neurons Communicate

A neural impulse races from the receiving dendrites (the starting line), through the cell body, and down the axon. What happens when the signal reaches the axon terminals? And how does it then get to the dendrites of the next neuron? The transmission of messages in the nervous system is like a relay race. When the impulse reaches the end of one cell, it passes the electrochemical baton to the next cell or to a muscle or gland. How is this accomplished? Scientists used to think that the branching axons and dendrites of adjacent neurons always touched, thus enabling impulses to travel seamlessly, the way an electrical current crosses two extension cords that are plugged together. We now know that this is not the main way it works. Rather, there is a narrow gap between neurons that is roughly one-millionth of an inch wide. This gap is called a **synapse**, from a Greek word meaning "point of contact." The question is: How does the impulse cross this synaptic gap to the next neuron?

The answer has to do with the action of **neurotransmitters**. When an electrical impulse reaches the knoblike axon terminal, it forces the release of chemical messengers called neurotransmitters—so

FIGURE 2.8 ■ How Neurons Communicate

When an impulse reaches the axon terminal, it forces the release of neurotransmitters, which are stored in tiny vesicles. These chemicals squirt across the synaptic gap and bind to receptors on the receiving neuron. There are different neurotransmitters. Each fits only certain receptors, the way a key fits only one lock.

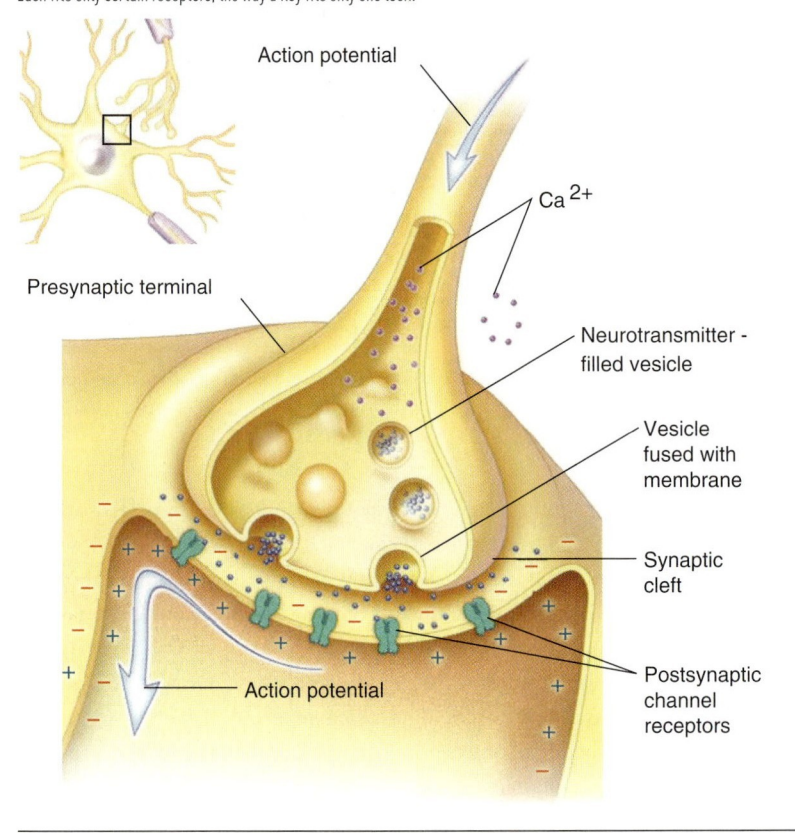

Carolina Hrejsa/Body Scientific Intl.

named because they aid in the *transmission* of information from one *neuron* to another. These chemical substances are manufactured by the neuron and stored in tiny round packets called synaptic vesicles. Upon release, the neurotransmitters literally squirt across the synaptic gap and bind to specialized **receptors** on the dendrites of the receiving neuron or on muscles or glands.

There are different types of neurotransmitters. Some will excite (fire) an action potential in the next neuron, whereas others will inhibit (restrain the firing of) the next action potential. It's a truly remarkable process. There are many different neurotransmitters and many different types of receptors, each with its own shape. This fact is significant because a neurotransmitter binds snugly only to certain receptors, the way a key fits only one lock. The electrochemical process is illustrated in Figure 2.8.

Neurotransmitters

Anxiety, feelings of calm, sadness and depression, pain, relief, memory disorders, drowsiness, hallucinations, paralysis, tremors, and seizures all have something in common: a link to the activity of neurotransmitters. The human nervous system is a prolific chemical factory. There are possibly as many as 100 different neurotransmitters in the human nervous system that provide extremely precise communication (Herculano-Houzel, 2009).

The activities of certain neurotransmitters—where in the body they're produced, their effects on mind and behavior, and their responsiveness to drugs—are well understood. (Table 2.1 describes many important neurotransmitters discussed in this book.)

The first substance identified as a neurotransmitter was **acetylcholine (ACh)**, which is found throughout the nervous system and is most concentrated in the parts of the brain that control motor behavior. Using powerful electron microscopes, researchers can see the sacs that store and release ACh

receptors. Specialized neural cells that receive neurotransmitters.

acetylcholine (ACh). A neurotransmitter found throughout the nervous system that links the motor neurons and muscles.

TABLE 2.1 ■ Major Neurotransmitters	
Neurotransmitter	**Function**
Acetylcholine (ACh)	Links motor neurons and muscles. Also facilitates learning and memory. Alzheimer's patients have an undersupply of Ach.
Dopamine	Concentrated in the brain, it is linked to muscle activity. A shortage can cause Parkinson's disease; an excess of dopamine receptors is linked to symptoms of schizophrenia.
Endorphins	Distributed throughout the CNS, these natural opiates relieve pain.
Norepinephrine	Widely distributed in the CNS, it increases arousal. Too much may produce a manic state; too little may lead to depression.
Serotonin	Produced in the brain, it lowers activity level and causes sleep. Too little is linked to depression.
GABA (gamma aminobutyric acid)	Produced in the brain, it lowers arousal and reduces anxiety. It is the main inhibitory neurotransmitter in the nervous system.

molecules and have found that ACh is the chemical key that links the motor neurons and muscles. Thus, whenever you walk, talk, ride a bike, dance, throw a ball, or take a breath, ACh is released. What would happen if you somehow blocked the release of all ACh in the system? Think about the link that would be severed, and you'll have the answer. Curare, a poison that some South American Indians put on the tips of their hunting arrows, blocks the ACh receptors, causing complete paralysis of the skeletal muscles. Consider the opposite condition. What would happen if you were to flood the synapses between motor neurons and muscles with ACh? The toxic bite of a black widow spider does just that, resulting in violent muscle contractions, sometimes even death. ACh may also play a role in the formation of new memories. As we will explain in Chapter 9, people with Alzheimer's disease, a degenerative brain disorder that destroys memory, have abnormally low levels of ACh.

dopamine. A neurotransmitter that is involved in voluntary movements and with reward-seeking behaviors, such as eating, sex, and drug use.

Another neurotransmitter, **dopamine**, is also involved in the regulation of movement. Parkinson's disease, a motor disorder characterized by hand tremors, stooped posture, slowness, and a loss of control over one's voluntary movements, is caused by the death of neurons that produce dopamine. For people with this disease, the symptoms can often be eased with L-dopa, a chemical substance that the neurons convert into dopamine, which replenishes the supply. We'll explain later in this chapter that a promising new treatment approach involves implanting healthy tissue containing dopamine into the brains of Parkinson's patients. As we'll explain in Chapters 13 and 14, many people who suffer with schizophrenia have an oversupply of dopamine receptors in the brain. Their symptoms can often be treated with drugs that block the activity of dopamine. Dopamine also plays an important role in reward-seeking behaviors, such as eating and drug use via a pathway called the *mesolimbic tract*, sometimes called the "reward region" of the brain. Dopamine appears to drive motivation to consume "comfort foods" and, among people with drug addiction, to increase drug use. Specifically, dopamine drives what is called *incentive salience*—making foods and drugs more salient or noticeable, which drives the desire or incentive to consume or use.

Another exciting discovery is that the brain produces its own morphine, a painkiller. As part of a research study, Candace Pert and Solomon Snyder (1973) injected laboratory animals with morphine, a powerful and addictive painkilling drug derived from opium. To their surprise, they found that the morphine bound to certain receptors in the brain the way neurotransmitters do. This discovery is only mildly interesting, you may think. But wait. Why would the brain have receptors for a chemical produced outside the body? Doesn't a special receptor for morphine mean that the brain produces its own morphinelike substance?

Micrograph of neurotransmitters in synaptic vesicles (top) squirting across the synaptic gap (center) to a receiving neuron (bottom).
ALFRED PASIEKA/Science Source

The answer is yes, and the neurotransmitter is called an **endorphin** (from the words *endogenous*, which means "internal," and *morphine*). Since this discovery, researchers have found that endorphins and their receptors, and other similar substances, are distributed throughout the central nervous system (Cooper, Bloom & Roth, 2002; Sheffler, Reddy, & Pillarisetty, 2021).

endorphin. A morphinelike neurotransmitter that is produced in the brain and is linked to pain control and pleasure.

LEARNING CHECK

Nerve Racking

Match each part of the nervous system in the left column with the activity it regulates.

1. Sensory neuron
2. Motor neuron
3. Myelin sheath
4. Sympathetic nervous system
5. Parasympathetic nervous system
6. Endocrine system
7. Neurotransmitter

a. Heightens arousal and energizes the body for action.
b. Regulates aspects of growth, reproduction, metabolism, and behavior by secreting hormones.
c. Transmits information by crossing the synapse.
d. Sends signals from the senses, skin, muscles, and internal organs to the central nervous system.
e. Insulates the axon and speeds electrical impulses.
f. Transmits commands from the central nervous system to the muscles, glands, and organs.
g. Reduces arousal and restores the body to its preenergized state.

(Answer: 1. d; 2. f; 3. e; 4. a; 5. g; 6. b; 7. c.)

What triggers the release of endorphins? Sensations of pain and discomfort—as triggered by physical injury, or by the labor pains that precede childbirth (Akil, 1982)? In fact, research has shown that females with higher endorphin levels in the bloodstream are less sensitive to pain and less likely to experience premenstrual mood complications such as tension, irritability, and depression (Barbosa, Guirro, & Nunes 2013; Straneva et al., 2002). Over the years, some researchers have speculated that the exhilarating and intense "runner's high" described by many long-distance runners and bicyclists might result from the release of endorphins (Farrell, Gates, Maksud, & Morgan, 1982). Yet others note that while exercise seems to be addictive for some people, factors such as genes, gender, training status, hormonal status, and more need to be considered to understand the possible role of endorphins (Heijnen, Hommel, Kibele, & Colzato, 2016). For now, the causes and effects of endorphins are not well understood. It is clear, however, that the human body comes equipped with a natural, built-in pharmacy for pain relief.

THE BRAIN

LEARNING OBJECTIVES

Summarize and synthesize the methods utilized to understand the parts and operation of the brain.

- Compare the methods psychologists use to study activity in the human brain.

- Evaluate whether different parts of the brain specialize in certain functions or operate as an integrated system.

- Interpret what it means to say we have two copies of the same brain. Explain how the two hemispheres uniquely process information.

Encased in a hard, protective skull, the brain is the crown jewel of the nervous system. It weighs only about three pounds and constitutes only 1/45th of the human body's average weight. But, as we saw earlier, it contains billions of neurons and trillions of synaptic connections. For those who are interested only in anatomy, it was easy to determine the physical *structure* of the brain by dissecting brains removed from dead animals and from humans who had donated their bodies to science. For behavioral and cognitive neuroscientists, however, the task is more challenging: to determine the *functions* of the living brain and to understand its influences on the way we think, feel, and behave.

Tools of Behavioral Neuroscience

Before the term *neuroscience* had ever been uttered, Viennese physician Franz Joseph Gall (1758–1828) founded **phrenology**, the pseudoscientific theory that psychological characteristics are revealed by bumps on the skull. Apparently, as a young boy, Gall "noticed" that his friends who had the best memories also had prominent eyes and large foreheads. From this he speculated that the brain structure involved in verbal memory must lie behind the eyes. Similarly, Gall believed that speech, math ability, aggression, and other traits are "localized" in certain regions of the brain. In believing that there were many parts to the brain and that the parts were involved in different mental functions, Gall was on the right track. In using bumps on the skull to find these links, however, he was very much on the wrong track (Damasio, 1994; Zola-Morgan, 1995).

To fully understand and evaluate what researchers currently know about the human brain, it helps to be aware of *how* they arrive at that knowledge—the methods they use and why they use them. Thanks in part to advances in medical and computer technology, today's behavioral neuroscientists are like explorers on a new frontier. As we'll explore, four types of research methods are commonly used: clinical case studies, experimental interventions, electrical recordings, and brain-imaging techniques.

phrenology. The pseudoscientific theory that psychological characteristics are revealed by bumps on the skull.

Clinical Case Studies

One approach to studying the brain is the clinical case study, in which researchers observe people with brain damage resulting from tumors, diseases, head injuries, or exposure to toxic substances. In the case of Phineas Gage, discussed earlier, massive damage to the frontal lobes was followed by changes in his personality (specifically, an inability to control impulses), yet his intellectual abilities remained unchanged. Thus, the case showed that the frontal lobes are involved in the control of behavior.

Clinical evidence is tantalizing and often enlightening, but it cannot provide the sole basis for behavioral neuroscience. One drawback is that when one part of the brain is damaged, nearby neurons sometimes sprout new branches, and other structures sometimes take over the function. Another drawback is that natural injuries are seldom localized, so the resulting deficit may not be traceable to a single structure. A third drawback of case studies in the brain and behavior is that they often cannot be used to establish cause and effect. In a fascinating use of the case study method, neuroscientist Sandra Witelson gained access to the brain of physicist Albert Einstein, one of the greatest geniuses of modern history. When Einstein died in 1955, the pathologist who did the autopsy removed the brain and preserved it in a jar. More than 40 years later, Witelson, Kigar, and Harvey (1999) compared Einstein's brain tissues with those of other males who had died at a similar age. They found that the overall size of Einstein's brain was about average, but a region used in visuospatial and mathematical thinking was 15 percent wider than the others tested. It may be tempting to conclude from this result that Einstein was born with a brain uniquely gifted for physics, but the researchers were quick to suggest another possibility—perhaps this region of Einstein's brain grew *because* he used it so often. Clinical evidence alone cannot solve the puzzle.

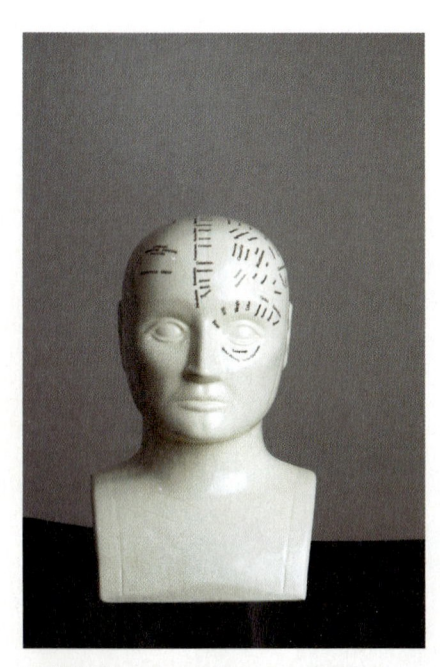

In 1873, Mark Twain visited Lorenzo Fowler, a phrenologist. "I found Fowler on duty," Twain wrote, "amidst the impressive symbols of his trade...marble white busts, hairless, every inch of the skull occupied by a shallow bump, and every bump labeled in black letters." Fowler sold hundreds of busts like these. The one shown here can be observed at the Smithsonian Institution in Washington, D.C.

iStock.com/Bohoe

Experimental Interventions

A second method of brain research is to "invade" the brain through an experimental intervention and then measure the effects on behavior. One invasive technique, often used by animal researchers, is to purposely disable, or "lesion," a part of the brain by surgically destroying it. Often this is done by anesthetizing an animal, implanting an electrode into a specific site in the brain, and passing a high-voltage current through it to burn the tissue.

Another technique is to administer drugs that are suspected of affecting neurotransmitters and other activity in the brain. Over the years, the effects of many substances on the brain and behavior have been tested in this manner, including alcohol, caffeine, adrenaline, nicotine, and the sex hormones testosterone and androgen.

Yet another form of intervention is through the use of electrical brain stimulation. In these studies, a microelectrode is inserted in the brain and a mild electrical current is used to "activate" the neurons in a particular site. Most of these experiments are conducted with animals, but on occasion clues are derived from human brain-surgery patients. How does this occur? Since no two brains are exactly alike, brain surgeons often must "map" a patient's brain so that they don't accidentally destroy key functions. Toward this end, the patient is given a local anesthetic and kept awake for the procedure.

Electrical Recordings

The most exciting advances in behavioral neuroscience arise from techniques that are not invasive to the human subject. In 1929, German psychiatrist Hans Burger invented a machine that could detect, amplify, and record waves of electrical activity in the brain using metal disc electrodes pasted to the surface of the scalp. The instrument, which is depicted in Figure 2.9, is called an **electroencephalograph (EEG)**, and the information it provides is in the form of line tracings called *brain waves*.

As we'll explain in later chapters, researchers using the EEG have found that brain waves differ depending on whether a person is excited, relaxed, pensive, drowsy, or asleep. It can also be used for diagnosing brain damage from tumors, strokes, infections, and various neurological disorders. For example, people with epilepsy have seizures because a certain portion of the brain is overexcitable and

electroencephalograph (EEG). An instrument used to measure electrical activity in the brain through electrodes placed on the scalp.

FIGURE 2.9 ■ The EEG

Through electrodes on a subject's scalp, the electroencephalograph records electrical activity in the brain and displays the output in line tracings called brain waves. Varying in their frequency (cycles per second) and amplitude (voltage), EEG patterns differ according to a person's mental state.

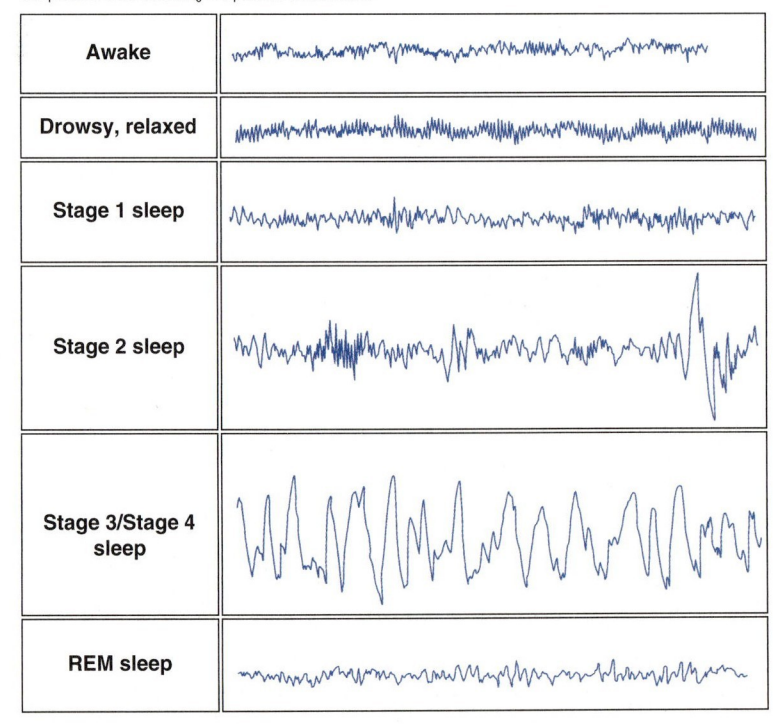

Awake	
Drowsy, relaxed	
Stage 1 sleep	
Stage 2 sleep	
Stage 3/Stage 4 sleep	
REM sleep	

Christopher M. Sinton, Robert W. McCarley. "Neurophysiological Mechanisms of Sleep and Wakefulness: A Question of Balance." Semin Neurol 2004; 24(3): 211-223. DOI: 10.1055/s-2004-835067

prone to fire in a wild manner, setting off electrical spikes, or "explosions." The EEG may even be useful for diagnosing psychological disorders such as attention-deficit/hyperactivity disorder (ADHD), schizophrenia, and depression (Howells et al., 2018; Lazarev, 2006).

There are limits, however, to what EEG recordings can tell us. The problem is that the EEG merely summarizes all the electrical activity of billions of neurons firing along the brain's surface. Thus, as one group of researchers put it, "we are like blind men trying to understand the workings of a factory by listening outside the walls" (quoted by Hassett, 1978). For greater precision, some animal researchers use microelectrodes, wires with tips so tiny that they can stimulate or record the activity of a single cell.

Brain-Imaging Techniques

When people think about the wonders of high technology, what comes to mind is global communication satellites and giant-size telescopes that can spy on the distant galaxies of the universe. But recent advances in technology have also enabled us to turn the scientific eye on ourselves, to inner recesses of the human brain never previously seen. Designed to provide visual images of the live human brain, without our ever having to lift a scalpel, this new technology uses computers to combine thousands of still "snapshots" into models of the brain in action. As described in *Images of Mind* (Posner & Raichle, 1997), there are several basic types of imaging techniques. Three of the most common, all popularly known by their initials, are CT, PET, and MRI.

First introduced to medicine in the 1970s, the **computerized tomography (CT) scan** is a computer-enhanced X-ray of the brain. In this technique, X-ray beams are passed through the head at 1-degree intervals over a 180-degree arc, and a computer is used to convert this information into an image that depicts a horizontal slice of the brain. This technique takes advantage of the fact that when a highly focused beam of X-rays is passed through the body, the beam is affected by the relative density of the tissue through which it passes. Although CT scans do use X-rays that can be harmful in certain doses, CT scans are invaluable for diagnosing tumors and strokes and for identifying brain abnormalities in people who suffer from schizophrenia and other psychological disorders.

A second revolutionary imaging technique, one that can be used to map activity of the brain over time, is the **positron emission tomography (PET) scan.** Because glucose supplies the brain with energy, the level of activity in a given region of the brain can be measured by the amount of glucose it burns. After a tiny amount of radioactive glucose is injected into the brain, the scanner measures the amount of glucose consumed in different regions. The results are then fed to a computer, which produces an enhanced color picture that can be used not only to infer mental processes but also to assist with understanding clinical and mental health outcomes (Silverman, Mosconi, Ercoli, Chen, & Small, 2008; Vaquero & Kinahan, 2015). Can the PET scan actually spy on our thought processes? In a way, yes. In the scans in Figure 2.10, "hot" colors such as red, orange, and yellow indicate more activity, whereas cool colors such as violet, blue, and green mean less activity.

Using the PET scan, psychologists have made some interesting discoveries. One is that it may be possible to distinguish among different types of psychological disorders by measuring brain activity (Masdeu, 2011; Vaquero & Kinahan, 2015). For example, researchers had patients with schizophrenia relax with their eyes closed and press a button whenever they started to hear imaginary voices and when they stopped hearing these voices. The result: On PET scans, hallucinating lit up certain areas of the brain more than others (Silbersweig et al., 1995). Today, researchers are using PET scans to identify anomalies in brain structure and function that can be used to identify and predict the severity of schizophrenia (Marques et al., 2017).

An advanced technique, called **magnetic resonance imaging (MRI)**, is similar to a CT scan, but instead of using an X-ray it passes the subject's head through a strong but harmless magnetic field to align the brain's atoms. A quick pulse of radio waves is then used to disorient the atoms, which give off detectable signals as they return to normal. As shown in Figure 2.11, the MRI can produce clear and detailed pictures of the brain's soft tissues (Grover et al., 2015).

Particularly important today is a high-speed version of MRI known as *functional MRI* (fMRI), used to take moving pictures of the brain in action. The method is noninvasive and does not involve the use of radioactive materials, so researchers can do hundreds of scans on the same person to get detailed information about a particular brain's activity.

---

computerized tomography (CT) scan. A series of X-rays taken from different angles and converted by computer into an image that depicts a horizontal slice of brain.

positron emission tomography (PET) scan. A visual display of brain activity, as measured by the amount of glucose being used.

magnetic resonance imaging (MRI). A brain-scanning technique that uses magnetic fields and radio waves to produce clear, three-dimensional images.

FIGURE 2.10 ■ PET Scans

After radioactive glucose has been injected into the brain, a scanner measures how much glucose is consumed in different regions. The results are displayed in a computer-enhanced picture in which hotter colors (red, orange, yellow) indicate more activity.

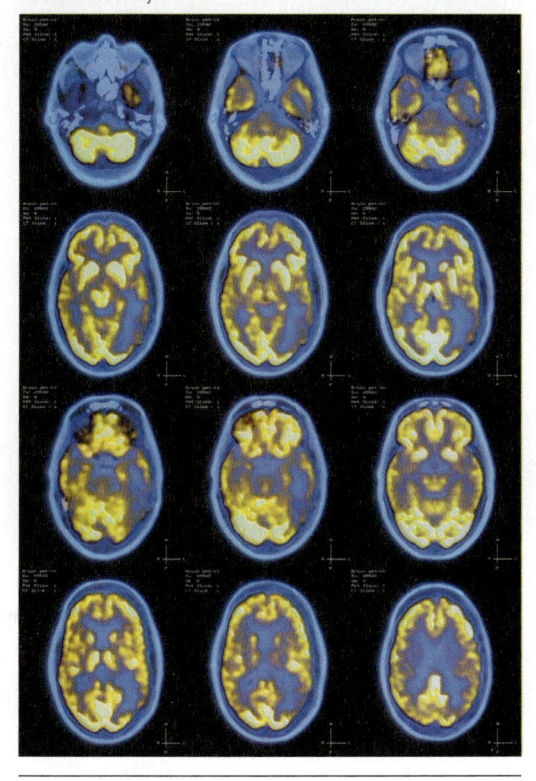

iStock.com/Cginspiration

This technology is generating tremendous excitement among psychologists who are interested in attention, perception, memory, and other cognitive processes (D'Esposito, 2002; Rana et al., 2016). Early in its use, researchers were saying, "This is the wonder technique we've all been waiting for," and calling it "the most exciting thing to happen in the realm of cognitive neuroscience in my lifetime" (Blakeslee, 1993). It is still just as exciting today.

Regions of the Brain

The human brain is a unique product of evolution. In some ways it is similar to the brains of "lower" animals; in other ways it is quite different. Salmon, caribou, and migrating birds have navigational abilities unparalleled in our own species. Dogs, cats, and certain other mammals have senses of hearing and smell that are downright superhuman. Yet no other animal on the planet can solve problems, think about itself and the future, or communicate as we do. As we'll explore, these relative strengths and weaknesses can be traced to the unique structure of the human brain.

Although the brain is a single organ containing interconnected pathways of nerve fibers, neuroscientists have found that there are really three mini-brains rolled into one. The *brainstem* is the old "inner core" that rests atop the spinal cord and helps to regulate primitive life-support functions such as breathing, heartbeat, and muscle movements. Surrounding the brainstem,

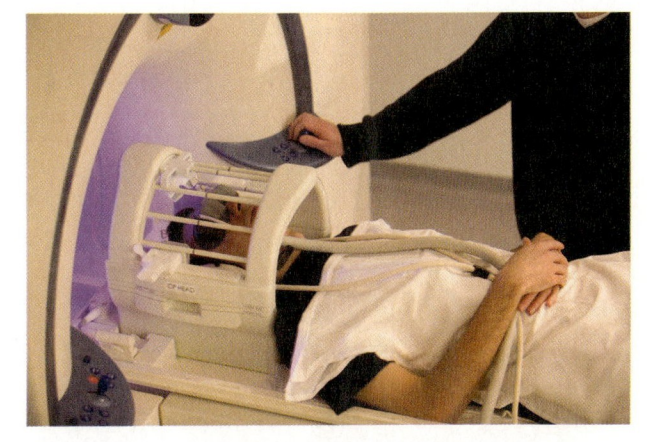

In this fMRI study, the participant is inside the magnet, and the result is a vivid picture of the brain's activity.

Mark Harmel / Alamy Stock Photo

FIGURE 2.11 ■ The MRI

Magnetic resonance imaging yields the best resolution for visualizing brain structures.

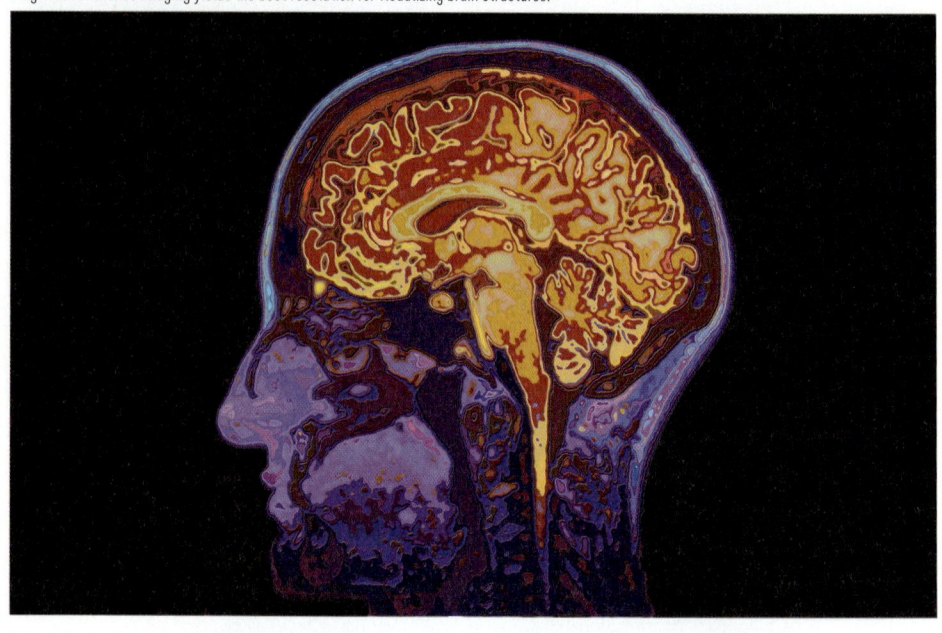

Ian Allenden / Alamy Stock Photo

FIGURE 2.12 ■ The Human Brain

There are three main regions of the human brain. The brainstem controls life-support and basic functions, such as sleep and arousal. The limbic system regulates motivation, emotion, and aspects of learning and memory. And the cerebral cortex, which is the outer layer of the brain, controls "higher" or advanced mental processes of learning, memory, thought, and language.

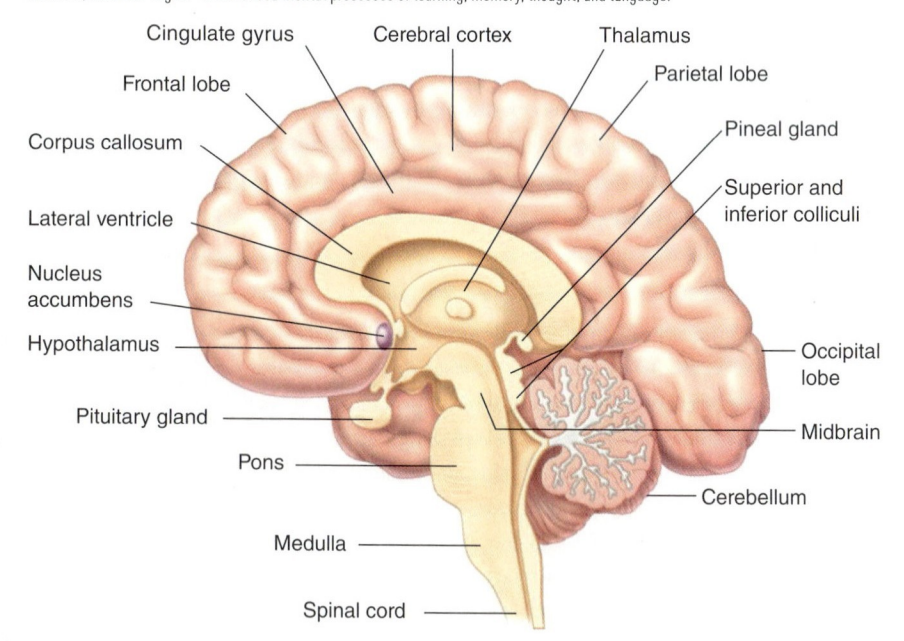

the *limbic system* provides an increased capacity for motivation, emotional responses, and basic forms of learning and memory. And in the *cerebral cortex*, the wrinkled outer layer of the brain, "higher" mental processes enable more complex forms of learning, memory, thought, and language. The cerebral cortex, depicted in Figure 2.12, is the last part of the brain to develop in the life of an individual. It also developed last in the species as a whole.

FIGURE 2.13 ■ The Brainstem

The brainstem is the most primitive structure of the brain. Resting atop the spinal cord, it contains the medulla, pons, and reticular formation and is attached to the cerebellum.

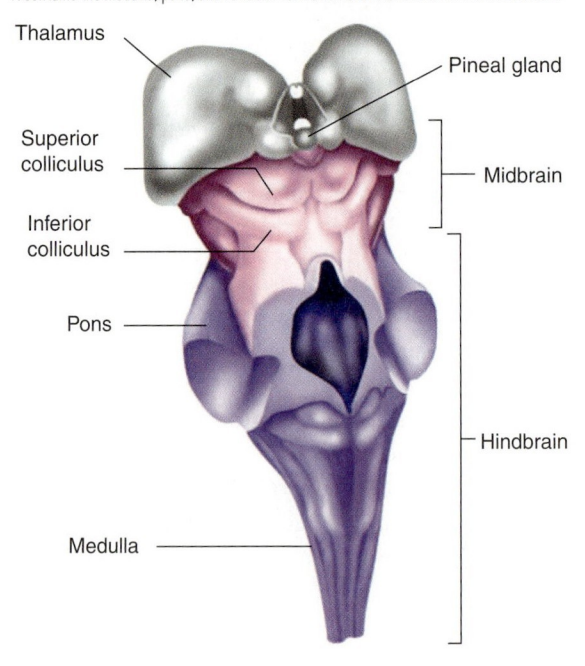

The Brainstem

As the spinal cord enters the skull, it enlarges into the **brainstem**, the primitive inner core. As illustrated in Figure 2.13, the brainstem contains three key structures: the medulla, the pons, and the reticular formation. Located just above the spinal cord, the **medulla** controls some of our most vital, involuntary functions—swallowing, breathing, and heart rate—and contributes to muscle control. It's also a "crossover" point where nerves from one side of the brain connect to the opposite side of the body. There's nothing particularly exotic about the medulla, but if it were severed, blood pressure would drop to zero, breathing would stop, and death would soon follow. Just above the medulla is a bulbous structure called the **pons** (meaning "bridge"), which helps to connect the lower and higher regions of the brain. The pons also has neurons that play a role in sleep and arousal. Damage to this area can put a person into a coma. Finally, the **reticular formation** is a netlike group of nerve cells and axons that project throughout the brain and help to control sleep, arousal, and attention. It is here that sensory information is filtered in or out of our consciousness.

Also attached to the back of the brainstem is the **cerebellum**, a peach-sized structure that means "little brain." Figure 2.12 shows that the cerebellum resembles a miniature brain attached to the brain, wrinkles and all. This structure is one of the oldest in the nervous system and is highly developed in fish, birds, and lower mammals. It plays a role in learning and memory, but its primary functions (like that of certain other structures distributed throughout the brain) is balance and the coordination of muscle movements. In this regard, the cerebellum is like a sophisticated computer. It receives and integrates information from all the senses, considers the positions of the limbs, and makes rapid-fire calculations as to which muscle groups must be activated in order to run, jump, dance, break a fall, or throw a ball (Houk, Buckingham, & Barto, 1996). The cerebellum is also activated by certain aspects of music. In a study of eight conductors listening to Bach, PET scans revealed that when the expected rhythm was altered, blood flow to parts of the cerebellum increased, even though the conductors had not moved a muscle (Parsons & Fox, 1998). Even among ordinary research participants, those trained to learn complex rhythms—compared to those exposed to random sequences—exhibit more activity in parts of the cerebellum (Ramnani & Passingham, 2001).

Alongside the cerebellum are the **basal ganglia**, large masses of gray matter that are involved in the coordination of slower, more deliberate movements such as turning the head or reaching for an object. Damage to the cerebellum and basal ganglia can make it difficult to coordinate various motor

brainstem. The inner core of the brain that connects to the spinal cord and contains the medulla, pons, and reticular formation.

medulla. A brainstem structure that controls vital involuntary functions.

pons. A portion of the brainstem that plays a role in sleep and arousal.

reticular formation. A group of nerve cells in the brainstem that helps to control sleep, arousal, and attention.

cerebellum. A primitive brainstem structure that controls balance and coordinates complex voluntary movements.

basal ganglia. Masses of gray matter in the brain that help to initiate and coordinate deliberate movements.

behaviors. The reason drunken drivers can't pass the roadside test given by the police ("Close your eyes, put out your arms, and touch your nose with the index finger") is that alcohol affects these areas.

The Limbic System

Continuing up from the brainstem is a ring of loosely connected structures collectively known as the **limbic system**. Just above the inner core, yet surrounded by the cerebral cortex, the limbic system contains several structures that play a role in the regulation of motivation, emotion, and memory. Brain researchers disagree as to which structures actually qualify as "limbic" and whether they really form a unified "system." Still, the key structures here include the thalamus, the amygdala, the hippocampus, and the hypothalamus (illustrated in Figure 2.14).

The Thalamus. Directly atop the brainstem, and buried like the pit inside a peach, is the **thalamus** ("inner chamber"). The thalamus is a sensory relay station that directs neural traffic between the senses and the cerebral cortex. All input from what you see, hear, taste, and touch is received in the thalamus and then sent for processing to the appropriate region of the cortex. For example, there's a special nucleus located in the thalamus that receives visual input from the optic nerve behind the eye and sends the information to the visual cortex. It's interesting that the sense of smell completely bypasses the thalamus because it has its own private relay station that directs input from the nose to the olfactory bulb, which sits near areas that control emotion. This may explain why perfume, cookies baking in the oven, freshly cut grass, and other scents often arouse powerful emotions in us.

The Amygdala. The **amygdala** is an almond-shape bulge that has at times been called an "aggression center." This phrase oversimplifies both the behavioral functions of the amygdala and the biological roots of aggression. But there is a link, and experiments have shown that stimulation of the amygdala can produce anger and violence, as well as fear and anxiety (Davis, 1992). In fact, experiments suggest that the amygdala plays a more general role in learning, memory, and the experience of both positive and negative emotions (Rolls, 1999; Tyng, Amin, Saad, & Malik, 2017).

In 1937, psychologists Heinrich Kluver and neurosurgeon Paul Bucy found that lesions of the temporal lobe, including the amygdala, calmed ferocious rhesus monkeys. Later experiments on other wild animals revealed the same mellowing effect. Can amygdala lesions be used to treat people who are uncontrollably violent? Case studies have suggested that they can (Mark & Ervin, 1970). As we'll

---

limbic system. A set of loosely connected structures in the brain that help to regulate motivation, emotion, and memory.

thalamus. A limbic structure that relays neural messages between the senses and areas of the cerebral cortex.

amygdala. A limbic structure that controls fear, anger, and aggression.

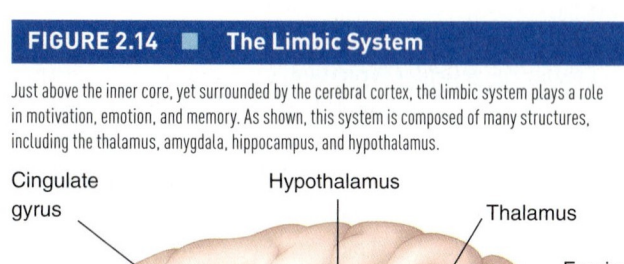

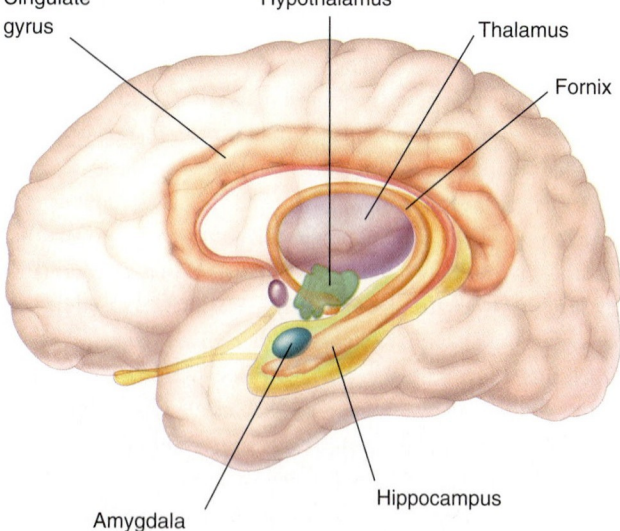

FIGURE 2.14 ■ The Limbic System

Just above the inner core, yet surrounded by the cerebral cortex, the limbic system plays a role in motivation, emotion, and memory. As shown, this system is composed of many structures, including the thalamus, amygdala, hippocampus, and hypothalamus.

explore in Chapter 14, however, the use of psychosurgery—operating on the brain as a way to alter behavior—raises profound ethical questions (Pressman, 1998; Valenstein, 1986).

The Hippocampus. The largest structure in the limbic system is the **hippocampus**, which is Greek for "seahorse," whose shape it roughly resembles. Research reveals that the hippocampus plays a key role in the formation of new memories. In rats, monkeys, and many other animals, hippocampal lesions cause deficits in memory. In fact, when the structure is removed from black-capped chickadees—food-storing birds whose brains have an unusually large hippocampus compared to nonstoring birds—they lose the natural ability to recover food they had stored previously (Hampton & Shettleworth, 1996). In humans, brain scans reveal that the hippocampal area is shrunken in people with severe memory loss, even while surrounding areas of the brain are intact (Squire, 1992). As we'll explore in Chapter 6, long-term memories are not necessarily stored in the hippocampus, but they may well be formed there (Opitz, 2014; Van Petten, 2004).

hippocampus. A limbic structure that plays a key role in the formation of new memories.

The Hypothalamus. At the base of the brain, there is a tiny yet extraordinary limbic structure called the **hypothalamus** (which means "below the thalamus"). The hypothalamus is the size of a kidney bean, weighs only about half an ounce, and constitutes less than 1 percent of the brain's total volume. Yet it regulates the body's temperature and the activities of the autonomic nervous system, controls the endocrine system by triggering the release of hormones into the bloodstream, helps regulate basic emotions such as fear and rage, and is involved in basic drives such as hunger, thirst, sleep, and sex. The hypothalamus is also home to one of the brain's true "pleasure centers," an area associated with regulating feelings of pleasure when it is stimulated (Rolls, 1999; Wise, 1996). If you had to sacrifice a half ounce of brain tissue, you wouldn't want to take it from the hypothalamus.

hypothalamus. A tiny limbic structure in the brain that helps regulate the autonomic nervous system, endocrine glands, emotions, and basic drives.

The Cerebral Cortex

The **cerebral cortex** is the outermost covering of the brain. Its name is derived from the words *cerebrum* (which is Latin for "brain") and *cortex* (which means "bark"). It is the newest product of evolution, overlaid on the older structures. If you were to examine the cerebral cortex of various species, you would observe that the more complex the animal, the bigger the cerebral cortex is relative to the rest of the brain. You would also notice that in complex animals, the cortex is wrinkled, or folded in on itself, rather than smooth, and is lined with ridges and valleys. This wrinkling allows for more tissue to fit compactly inside the skull (just as crumpling up a piece of paper allows one to squeeze it into a small space).

cerebral cortex. The outermost covering of the brain, largely responsible for higher order mental processes.

As shown in Figure 2.15, the cerebral cortex is virtually absent in all fish, reptiles, and birds. But it is present in mammals (particularly in primates, dolphins, and whales) and is the most highly developed in humans. In volume, it constitutes 80 percent of the human brain (Kolb & Whishaw, 1990). Whenever you read, write, count, speak, reflect on the past, think about the future, or daydream about being rich and famous, billions of neurons are firing in the cerebral cortex.

The cortex is divided into left and right hemispheres, and each hemisphere is further divided along deep grooves, called fissures, into four sections called lobes. These are the *frontal lobes* (in front, just behind the forehead), the *temporal lobes* (at the temples, above the ears), the *parietal lobes* (in the back, at the top of the skull), and the *occipital lobes* (in the back, at the base of the skull). Although these regions describe the

FIGURE 2.15 ■ The Cerebral Cortex in Animals

From fish and birds to mammals, primates, and humans, there is an increase in the relative size and wrinkling of the cerebral cortex.

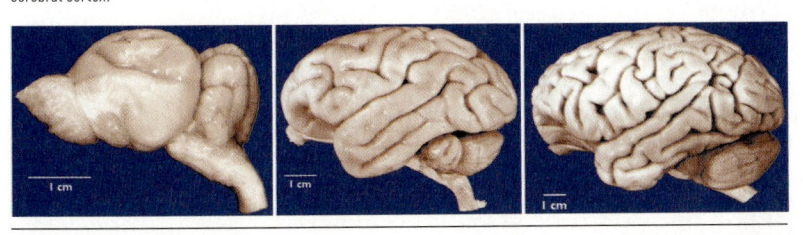

Used with permission from http://www.brains.rad.msu.edu, and http://brainmuseum.org, supported by the US National Science Foundation.

FIGURE 2.16 ■ The Cerebral Cortex

The cortex is divided along deep grooves, or fissures, into four lobes. Within these lobes, areas are further distinguished by their functions. These include the sensory areas (visual, auditory, and somatosensory), the motor area, the association areas, and two special areas—Broca's area and Wernicke's area—where language is processed and produced.

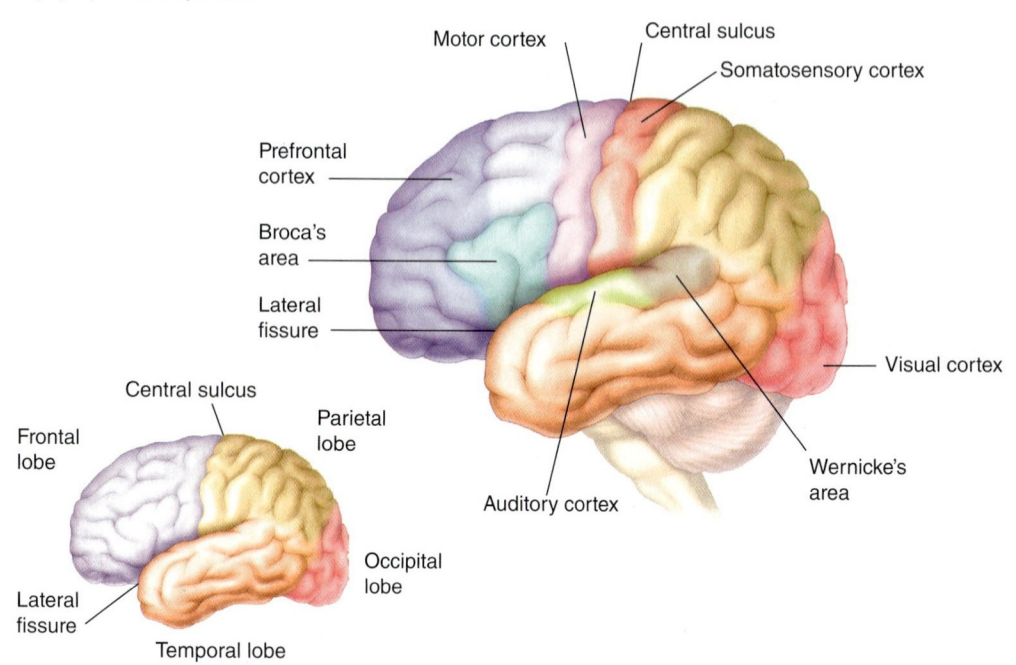

anatomy of the cerebral cortex, most psychologists prefer to divide the areas of the brain according to the functions they serve. As shown in Figure 2.16, the functional regions include the sensory areas of the cortex, the motor cortex, the association cortex, and two special areas where language is processed and produced.

Sensory and Motor Areas. While operating on his hundreds of epilepsy patients, Wilder Penfield, in 1947, stimulated exposed parts of the cortex with a tiny electric probe and thereby "mapped" the human cortex. One of Penfield's great discoveries was that certain areas of the brain specialize in receiving sensory information. When he touched the occipital lobe in the back of the brain, patients "saw" flickering lights, colors, stars, spots, wheels, and other visual displays. This area is the primary visual cortex—and damage to it can leave a person blind. Or damage to a specific part of it may result in a more specific visual deficit. For example, in *The Man Who Mistook His Wife for a Hat*, Oliver Sacks (1985) tells a story about a patient who suffered occipital lobe damage. As this patient looked for his hat while preparing to leave Sacks's office, he grabbed his wife's head and tried to lift it. Suffering from visual agnosia—an inability to recognize familiar objects—this patient had apparently mistaken his wife for a hat.

Penfield discovered other sensory areas in the cortex as well. When he stimulated a small area of the temporal lobe, called the auditory cortex, the patients "heard" doorbells, engines, and other sounds. Indeed, damage in this area can cause deafness. And when he stimulated a narrow strip in the parietal lobe, the **somatosensory cortex**, patients "felt" a tingling of the leg, hand, cheek, or other part of the body. In general, Figure 2.17 shows that the more sensitive to touch a body part is, the larger is the cortical area devoted to it. Today, researchers continue to study this system in an effort to uncover "the brain's own body image" (Bashford et al., 2021).

somatosensory cortex. The area of the cortex that receives sensory information from the touch receptors in the skin.

Mirroring the somatosensory cortex is another narrow strip that specializes in the control of motor functions. Once again, much of what we know came from Penfield's work. Stimulating different parts of this strip triggers movement in different parts of the body. Stimulate the top, and a leg twitches; stimulate the bottom, and the tongue or jaw moves. All 600 muscles of the human body are represented in this area, called the **motor cortex**. As in the somatosensory cortex, the greater the need for precise control over a body part, the larger is its area in this strip. Thus, Figure 2.17 shows more surface area devoted to the face, hands, and fingers than to the arms and legs.

motor cortex. The area of the cortex that sends impulses to voluntary muscles.

FIGURE 2.17 ■ The Somatosensory and Motor Areas

Each part of the body is represented in the somatosensory and motor cortex. Note that the amount of tissue devoted to a body part does not correspond to its actual size. Rather, more area is devoted to parts that are most sensitive to touch (such as the lips) and in need of fine motor control (such as the thumbs).

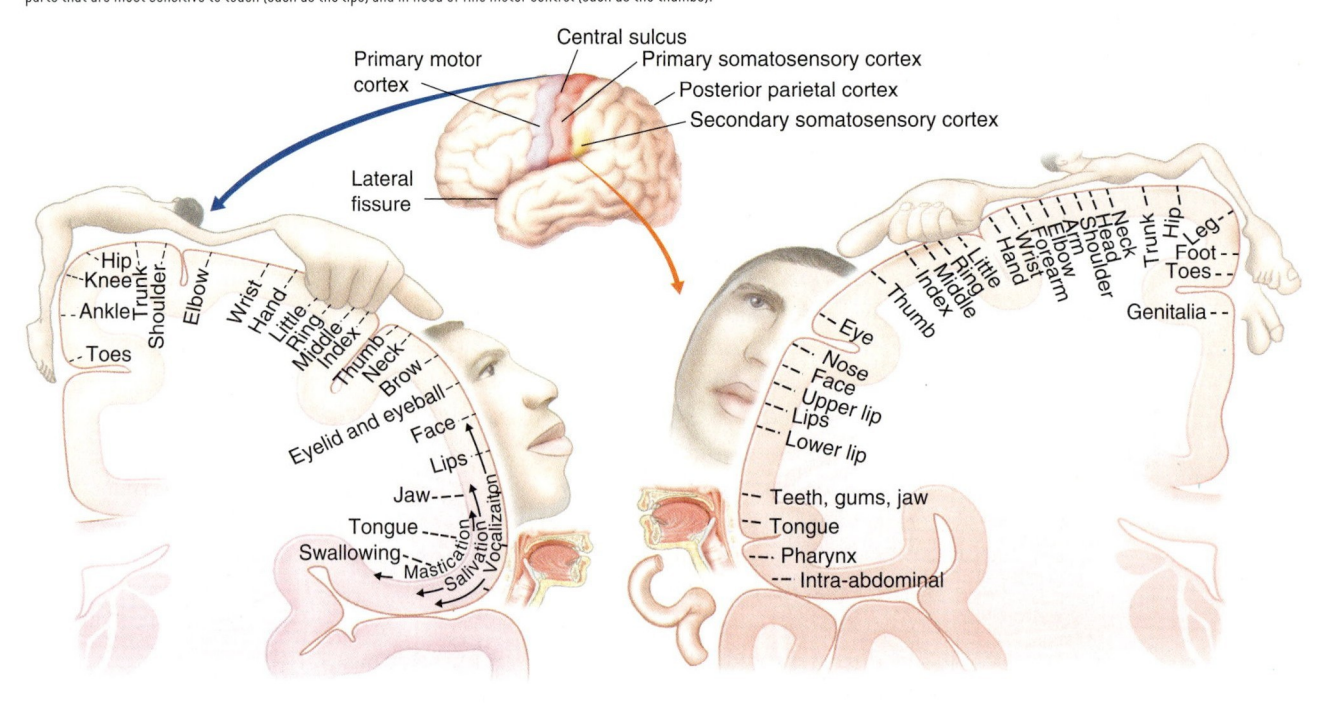

TRY THIS!

Autonomic Pilot

To explore how the autonomic nervous system (which regulates involuntary functions like heartbeat) can react to external stimuli, **TRY THIS:** Measure your typical heartbeat before starting the experiment. Next, sit silently in a darkened, candlelit room for half an hour. Choose a quiet time of day, turn off your phone, and try to reduce all possible distractions or interruptions. Empty your mind and try to concentrate on your own breathing, making it deep, slow, and even.

At the end of the half hour, test your pulse again. Was it lower than when you started? By how much? What other techniques would you suggest for slowing or accelerating your "automatic" functions?

Association Areas. The cerebral cortex does more than just process sensory information and direct motor responses. There are also vast areas that collectively make up the **association cortex**. These areas communicate with both the sensory and motor areas and house the brain's higher mental processes. Electrical stimulation of these sites does not elicit specific sensations or motor twitches in specific parts of the body, so it's hard to pin down these areas. But damage to the association cortex can have devastating results. In the frontal lobes, such damage can change someone's personality, as in the case of Phineas Gage. In other association areas, damage can impair specific kinds of memories, distort our spatial awareness, render us oblivious to emotions, or cause odd speech deficits (Saper, Iverson, & Frackowiak, 2000).

Language Areas. For the most part, our ability to adapt to life's demands through learning, memory, and thought processes is spread throughout the regions of the cortex. But language—a complex activity for which humans, and in some ways only humans, are uniquely prepared—is different. Carved within the cortex are two special areas dedicated to language. One plays a role in the production of speech; the other, comprehension. In 1861, French physician Paul Broca observed that people who have suffered damage in part of the frontal lobe of the left hemisphere lose the ability to form words to *produce* fluent speech. The

association cortex. Areas of the cortex that communicate with the sensory and motor areas and house the brain's higher mental processes.

Broca's area. A region in the left hemisphere of the brain that directs the muscle movements in the production and comprehension of speech.

Wernicke's area. A region of the brain that is involved in the comprehension of language.

words sputter out slowly, and what is said is often not grammatical ("Buy milk store"). This region of the brain—now known to be important for speech production and comprehension (Flinker et al., 2015)—is called **Broca's area** (Schiller, 1992). Interestingly, while Broca in a narrow sense, did "discover" this region in his research, it was another researcher, Ernest Auburtin (representing Jean-Baptiste Bouillaud) in 1861, who is credited with discovering Broca's area as being associated with speech (Thomas, 2001).

A few years later, German neurologist Carl Wernicke (1874) found that people with damage to the temporal lobe (subsequently called **Wernicke's area**) lose their ability to comprehend speech. In short, people with language disorders, or aphasias, demonstrate that there are at least two distinct cortical centers for language. Interestingly, these two areas are connected by a neural pathway, thus forming part of a language circuit within the brain (Brown & Hagoort, 1999; Geschwind, 1979).

The Integrated Brain. Even though Penfield was able to pinpoint or "map" various locations in the cortex that house sensory and motor functions, we mustn't overstate the case for localization. Although different cortical regions *specialize* in certain functions, the healthy human brain operates as an *integrated* system. This point is illustrated by the role of the brain in language, whereby different cortical areas are activated depending on whether a word is read, spoken, written, or presented in music—or even whether it is a verb or a noun (Caramazza & Hillis, 1991). Consider what it takes simply to repeat the written word *ball*. From the eyes, the stimulus must travel for processing to the visual cortex. The input must then pass through the angular gyrus to be recorded, to Wernicke's area to be understood, and then to Broca's area, where signals are sent to the motor cortex, which drives the muscles of your lips, tongue, and larynx so that you can repeat the word (illustrated in Figure 2.18).

It's also important to note that this model may not accurately describe the ways in which different brain regions interact to produce language. Figure 2.18 seems to suggest that the neural events related to language occur in serial fashion, one step at a time. In fact, evidence suggests that language and other complex mental processes may be more accurately represented by *parallel* models in which neural signals move along several routes at once and are processed simultaneously (Peterson, Fox, Mintun, Posner, & Raichle, 1989). As in an orchestra, it takes the coordinated work of many instruments, often playing together, to make music.

FIGURE 2.18 ■ Language Processing

Although different regions specialize in certain functions, the brain operates as an integrated system. The "simple" act of speaking a written word, for example, requires a coordinated effort of the eyes, the visual cortex, the angular gyrus, Wernicke's area, Broca's area, and the motor cortex.

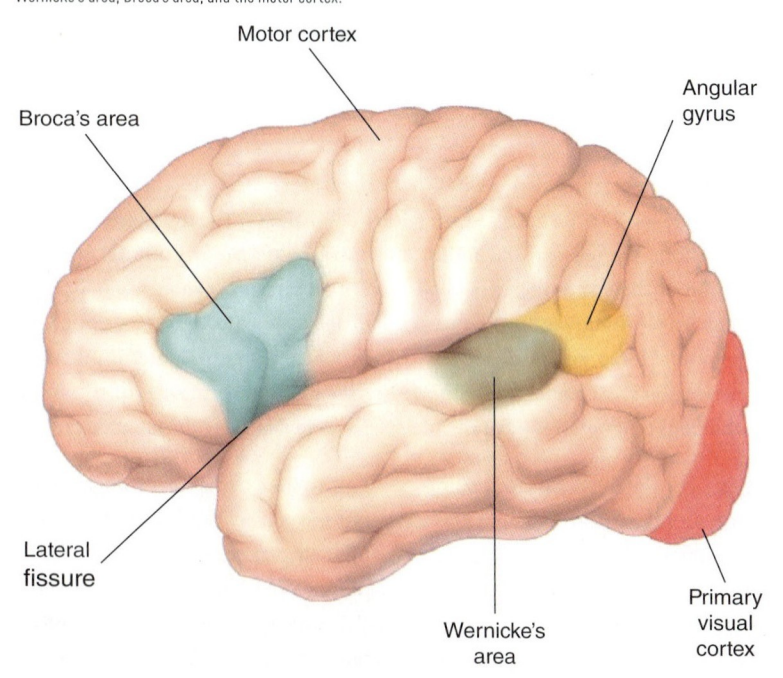

LEARNING CHECK

Brain Teasers

Match each part of the brain in the left column with its description in the right.

1.	Motor cortex	a.	Directs muscle movements in the production and comprehension of speech.
2.	Cerebral cortex	b.	Relays neural messages between the senses and areas of the cerebral cortex.
3.	Somatosensory cortex	c.	The outermost covering of the brain.
4.	Pons	d.	Region of the brain involved in the comprehension of language.
5.	Broca's area	e.	Brainstem structure that controls vital involuntary functions.
6.	Wernicke's area	f.	Receives sensory information from touch receptors in the skin.
7.	Thalamus	g.	Sends impulses to voluntary muscles.
8.	Medulla	h.	Portion of the brainstem that plays a role in sleep and arousal.

(Answers: 1. g; 2. c; 3. f; 4. h; 5. a; 6. d; 7. b; 8. e.)

The Split Brain

A remarkable feature of the human brain is that each hemisphere is basically a copy of itself. For each structure in the right brain, there is a corresponding structure in the left side of the brain. For example, we introduced many regions of the brain including the hippocampus, amygdala, hypothalamus, thalamus, association areas, language areas, and sensory and motor areas. For each structure, there is one region in the right brain and in the same corresponding stereotaxic location in the left brain. This organization has interesting implications, which we discuss in this section for split brain cases.

Split-Brain Studies

For people with severe epilepsy, seizures are the brain's equivalent of thunder-and-lightning storms. A seizure usually starts in one small area, but it quickly spreads across the brain from one side to the other. The experience can be terrifying, and at times life-threatening. In the past, neurosurgeons tried to control the problem by removing the overactive area, but these operations had only limited success. To prevent the seizures from spreading, a more radical approach was needed. The goal was to separate the two hemispheres. The method was to cut the **corpus callosum**, a four-inch-long, quarter-inch-thick bundle consisting of millions of white nerve fibers that join the two hemispheres (illustrated in Figure 2.19). This **split-brain** surgery often eliminates epileptic seizures, as hoped. But are there psychological side effects? Fechner (1860) proposed that a split brain, in which the link between the two hemispheres is severed, contains two separate minds. Was he right?

Before we examine the effects of split-brain surgery, let's consider the divisions of labor within the brain. Recall that the left hemisphere receives sensory input from, and sends motor commands to, the right side of the body (hand, leg, arm, and so on), whereas the right hemisphere communicates with the left side of the body. Processing visual and auditory input is somewhat more complex. Both eyes send information to both hemispheres, but images in the right half of the visual field are sent to the left hemisphere, and images in the left half of the visual field are sent to the right

corpus callosum. A bundle of nerve fibers that connects the left and right hemispheres of the brain.

split brain. A surgically produced condition in which the corpus callosum is severed, thus cutting the link between the left and right hemispheres of the brain.

FIGURE 2.19 ■ The Corpus Callosum

Containing millions of nerve fibers, the corpus callosum joins the left and right hemispheres of the brain.

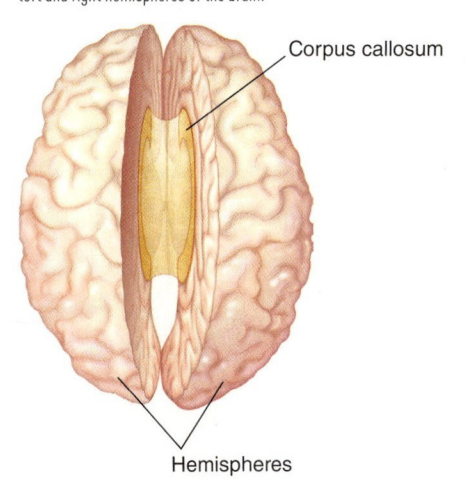

Carolina Hrejsa/Body Scientific Intl.

FIGURE 2.20 ■ Visual Processing

Both eyes send information to both hemispheres, but images in the right half of the visual field are sent to the left hemisphere, and images in the left half of the visual field are sent to the right hemisphere. Each image is instantly sent to the other side through the corpus callosum.

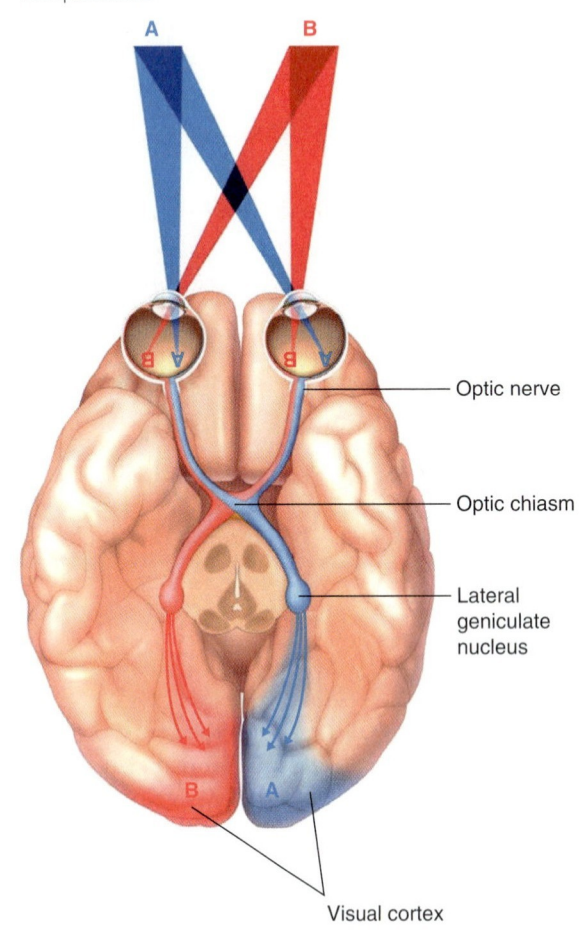

hemisphere. In other words, if you're looking straight ahead at someone, images on the left are sent by both eyes to the right hemisphere, and images on the right are sent by both eyes to the left hemisphere (illustrated in Figure 2.20). Auditory inputs are also sent to both hemispheres, but sounds received in one ear register in the opposite hemisphere first.

If your brain is intact, then this odd crossover arrangement poses no problem because information received by each hemisphere is quickly sent to the other side through the corpus callosum. By sharing information in this manner, the two sides of the brain work as a team. But what happens when the neuron-filled highway that connects the hemispheres is severed?

Roger Sperry (who was awarded a Nobel prize in 1981 and died in 1994), Michael Gazzaniga (his student), and others have helped bring this picture into focus through an ingenious series of studies, such as the one cited at the beginning of this chapter. Involving split-brain patients, the basic procedure was to present information to one hemisphere or the other, and then to measure what the subject "knew" by testing each hemisphere separately.

In one study, Sperry (1968) asked a female patient, identified as N.G., to stare at a black dot in the center of a screen. Then, for only a fraction of a second, he flashed a picture of a spoon either to the right or left of the dot and asked, "What do you see?" The result was fascinating. When the image was shown in the right visual field, and thus sent to the left hemisphere, N.G. was quick to reply that she saw a spoon. But when the image was presented on the left side and sent to the right hemisphere, she could not say what she saw. Why not? As noted earlier, speech is controlled by the left hemisphere. If an

FIGURE 2.21 ■ Sperry's Split-Brain Experiment

When the image of a spoon was projected to the right hemisphere, the split-brain patient could not say what she saw. Yet when she felt various objects with her left hand, she selected the spoon.

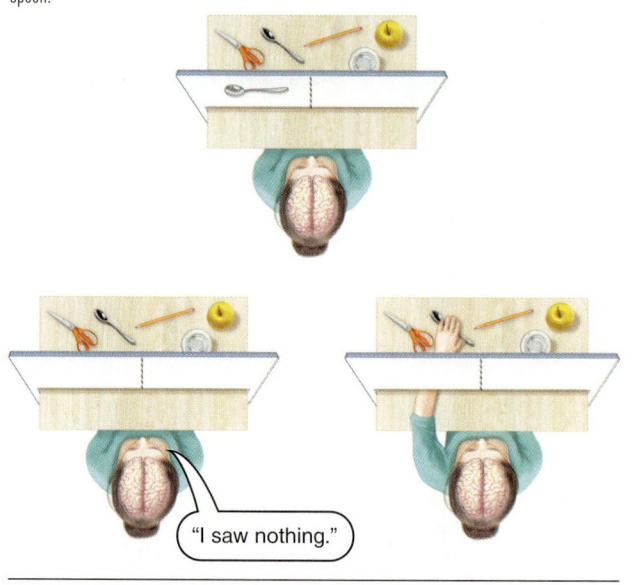

"I saw nothing."

Carolina Hrejsa/Body Scientific Intl.

image in the right side of the brain cannot cross over to the left side, then the person cannot transform what is seen into words. But wait. How do we know that N.G. actually saw the spoon? Maybe the right hemisphere is just stupid. To probe further, Sperry asked N.G. to reach behind a screen and feel an assortment of objects, such as a pencil, an eraser, a key, and a piece of paper. "Which of these did you see before?" Easy. Touching the objects with her left hand (which sent the sensations to the right hemisphere), she selected the spoon. The right side knew all along it had seen a spoon, but only the left side could say so (illustrated in Figure 2.21).

In a second, similar study, Gazzaniga (1967) had split-brain patients stare at a black dot and flashed the word *teacup* on the screen. The letters *tea* were presented to the left visual field (the right hemisphere), and *cup* was presented to the right visual field (the left hemisphere). If you were the subject—and if your corpus callosum was intact—you would see the full word, *teacup*. But the split-brain patients reported seeing only *cup*, the portion of the word that was flashed to the left hemisphere. Again, how do we know they actually saw the second part of the word? When told to choose between the two parts by pointing with the left hand, they pointed to tea, the letters sent to the right hemisphere. As in the spoon study, each hemisphere was in touch with only half of the total input. Under normal circumstances, stimuli reaching both hemispheres are blended to form a unified experience. Disconnected, each hemisphere has a mind of its own.

In a third study, Levy, Trevarthen, and Sperry (1972) took pictures of faces, cut them vertically in half, and pasted different right and left halves together. These composite photographs were then presented rapidly on slides. As in other studies, subjects stared at a center dot so that half of the image fell on either side. When asked what they saw, subjects who looked at the stimulus presented in Figure 2.22 said it was a child. Because they were forced to respond in words, the left hemisphere dominated, causing them to name the image in the right visual field. But when subjects were told to point to the face with the left hand, they pointed to the woman wearing glasses, whose image was projected on the left side. Remarkably, split-brain patients did not seem to know that the composite face was unusual.

Cerebral Lateralization

Split-brain research has generated tremendous excitement in behavioral neuroscience. When the corpus callosum is severed, most (though not all) input to one hemisphere is trapped, unable to pass to the other

FIGURE 2.22 ■ Levy's Split-Brain Experiment

Split-brain subjects stared at a dot and viewed a composite of two faces (a). When asked what they saw, subjects chose the child—the image sent to the verbal left hemisphere (b). But when subjects pointed to the face with the left hand, they chose the woman with glasses—whose image was received by the right hemisphere (c).

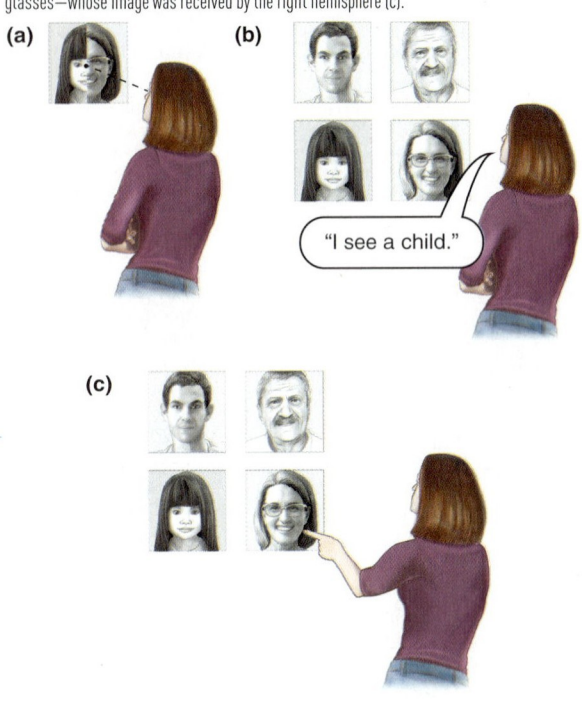

Carolina Hrejsa/Body Scientific Intl.

cerebral lateralization. The tendency for each hemisphere of the brain to specialize in different functions.

side. As a result, neither hemisphere knows quite what the other is doing. But what about the day-to-day operations of a normal and healthy brain, corpus callosum and all? We know that speech is usually located in the left hemisphere, but are there other asymmetries in the human brain? Are other functions similarly *lateralized*? Does one side or the other control math, music, or the ability to recognize faces?

Using an array of tools, researchers have uncovered many strands of evidence for **cerebral lateralization** in the normal human brain (Corballis, 2014; Davidson & Hugdahl, 1995; Springer & Deutsch, 1998). As we learned, the left hemisphere largely controls verbal activities—including reading, writing, speaking, and other aspects of language. Studies also show that people recognize words, letters, and other verbal stimuli faster when these stimuli are sent directly to the left hemisphere. Those who are deaf also appear to rely on the left hemisphere more than the right for reading sign language (Corina, Vaid, & Belugi, 1992; Sakai, Tatsuno, Suzuki, Kimura, & Ichida, 2005). Finally, PET scans show that different regions of the left hemisphere (and some areas of the right hemisphere as well) "light up" depending on whether subjects are listening to words that are spoken (hearing), reading words on a screen (seeing), saying words aloud (speaking), or coming up with related words (thinking). A sample PET scan appears in Figure 2.23 (Peterson & Fiez, 1993).

Whereas the left hemisphere is a verbal specialist, there is now converging evidence that the right hemisphere plays a vital role in nonverbal activities such as visual-spatial tasks, music, and the recognition of other people's faces and emotional states. Laboratory studies show that people are usually faster at locating dots, drawing three-dimensional objects, and recognizing faces when the material is presented to the right hemisphere than to the left (Bradshaw & Nettleton, 1981). Clinical case studies also illustrate this point (Corballis, Funnell, & Gazzaniga, 2002). For example, Gazzaniga (1985) instructed a split-brain patient to draw a cube and found that he produced a better drawing with the left hand than with the right—even though he was right-handed. Right hemisphere damage may also cause people to lose their sense of direction while driving, have trouble locating items in a familiar supermarket, or even get lost in their own homes (Newcombe & Ratcliff, 1990).

FIGURE 2.23 ■ The Talking Left Hemisphere

PET scans show that a single word activated different left-hemisphere areas depending on whether it was heard, seen, spoken, or thought about. Notice that these "lit-up" areas are in the visual cortex, auditory cortex, Broca's area, and frontal lobes, respectively.

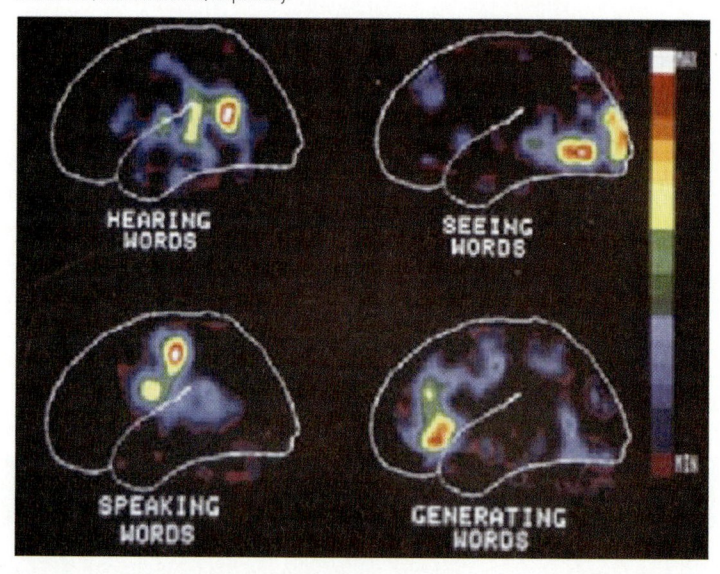

Adapted from Petersen, S., Fox, P., Posner, M. et al. Positron emission tomographic studies of the cortical anatomy of single-word processing. Nature 331, 585–589 (1988). https://doi.org/10.1038/331585a0

FIGURE 2.24 ■ Neglect Syndrome

A patient with a stroke in the right hemisphere was asked to copy model pictures. Like many neglect syndrome patients, he almost completely overlooked the left side of each drawing.

In some cases, right hemisphere damage caused by a stroke or an accident triggers a disruption of spatial awareness called "neglect" (Vallar, 1998). People with neglect syndrome lose all awareness of the left side of space—including the left side of their own bodies. When asked to bisect a horizontal line, these patients draw the line to the right of center. In life tasks, they may comb their hair only on the right side of the head, shave only the right side of the face, or eat food only if it's on the right side of the plate (illustrated in Figure 2.24).

But some researchers believe that the key difference between the two hemispheres is not in *what* kind of input is processed but in *how* that input is processed. In essence, research suggests that the left hemisphere processes information in analytical, piecemeal style—as used in word analogies, arithmetic, and logical problem solving—and that the right hemisphere processes information in a more global, holistic style—as used in music, art, and various forms of creative expression. In one study, for example, Gazzaniga tested a split-brain patient's perceptions of a painting that depicted a face made up of a pattern of small fruits. When the image was presented to the right hemisphere, the patient reported seeing the face, but when the same image was shown to the left hemisphere, he perceived only the fruits. The right side saw the whole; the left side saw the parts (Reuter-Lorenz & Miller, 1998).

Regardless of how the differences between left and right hemispheres are characterized, it's important not to overstate the case for lateralization. Neither hemisphere has exclusive control over certain functions, and both sides can process different kinds of information (Efron, 1990). As we'll explore in the coming pages, our brains are highly adaptive—and often capable of reorganization. If one side is damaged, the other often compensates for the lost functions. Even with old age, which brings about a decline in certain cognitive functions, people compensate by using both sides of the brain. As a result, older adults are more bilateral than younger adults, meaning older adults are less likely to exhibit left-right differences in specialization (Cabeza, 2002; Woytowicz, Sainburg, Westlake, & Whitall, 2020).

LEARNING CHECK

Right or Left?

How well do you know your right from your left (brain hemispheres, that is)? Indicate whether each question below is associated with the right or left brain hemisphere.

1. "Neglect syndrome" is a result of damage to which hemisphere?
2. Which hemisphere is the first to register sounds received in the right ear?
3. According to research, which hemisphere processes information in a more analytical, piecemeal style?
4. Which hemisphere processes information in a more global, holistic style?
5. Which hemisphere has more to do with music?
6. Which hemisphere has more to do with recognizing people's faces?
7. Which hemisphere sends motor commands to your right hand?
8. Damage to which hemisphere would be more likely to disrupt your sense of direction?

(Answers: 1. right; 2. left; 3. left; 4. right; 5. right; 6. right; 7. left; 8. right.)

PROSPECTS FOR THE FUTURE

LEARNING OBJECTIVES

Identify the nature of plasticity in the brain and how it can be applied to understanding brain injuries.

- Conclude whether the adult brain is fixed in its structure or has a capacity to change as a result of experience.
- Discuss whether it is possible for people to recover functions lost to brain damage.
- Summarize the evidence that healthy tissue can be transplanted from one brain into another.

The human brain is a remarkable organ. It is organized with a specificity that allows researchers to compare differences in brain structure and function across the human species. Yet it is also adaptive to change—to facilitate not only learning but also recovery of function when injuries occur. In this section, we introduce the human brain as an adaptive organ capable of changing over time and recovering from injury.

The Brain's Capacity for Growth and Reorganization

The human brain is an impressive organ. Encased in a hard, protective skull, it is complex and has a great deal of **plasticity** (from the word *plastic*)—a capacity to change as a result of usage, practice, and experience (Huttenlocher, 2002; Nelson, 1999).

plasticity. A capacity to change as a result of experience.

The Benefit of Plasticity: Growth Through Experience

Psychologists used to believe that the neural circuits of the adult brain and nervous system were fully developed and no longer subject to change. Then a series of provocative animal experiments showed that this is not so. Mark Rosenzweig (1984) built an "amusement park" for rats to examine the effects of an enriched environment on neural development. Some rats lived together in a cage filled with ladders, platforms, boxes, and other toys, whereas others lived in solitary confinement. The enriched rats developed heavier, thicker brains with more dendrites and synapses than those that were deprived. In fact, the growth can be quite specific. Rats flooded with visual stimulation formed 20 percent more synaptic connections per neuron in the visual cortex than those raised in darkness (Greenough, Black, & Wallace, 1987). "Acrobatic" rats trained to run between pylons on elevated runways formed new synaptic connections in the cerebellum, the structure involved in balance and motor coordination (Greenough, Withers, & Wallace, 1990). Similar results in birds, mice, squirrels, and monkeys of different ages have confirmed a basic point: Experiences spark the growth of new synaptic connections and mold the brain's neural architecture (Colangelo, Cirillo, Alberghina, Papa, & Westerhoff, 2019; Kolb & Whishaw, 1998).

Plasticity has profound practical implications for human development and adaptation. Reorganization within the brain can help people compensate for other types of loss as well. For example, brain-imaging studies have shown that in people who are blind, the visual cortex—which is deprived of visual input—is activated by other types of stimulation such as sound and touch (Sadato et al., 1999). Similarly, in people who are deaf, the auditory cortex becomes activated in response to touch (Levanen, Jousmaki, & Hari, 1998). Illustrating "cross-modal plasticity," these findings may help to explain a common observation, that when people lose their sight, or their hearing, other senses become sharpened as a result.

Neural plasticity has other implications, too. Avi Karni and Leslie Ungerleider (1996) tested the proposition that repeated stimulation of a body part would cause corresponding changes in the human brain. Every day these researchers had six males perform one of two finger-tapping sequences for 10 to 20 minutes. After five weeks, they had the males tap out both the practiced and nonpracticed sequences. Using fMRI, they found that tapping the practiced sequence lit up a larger portion of the primary motor cortex.

If sheer usage can spark the buildup of new synaptic connections among neurons, then individuals' life experiences should leave a permanent mark on their brains. In an interesting test of this hypothesis, researchers autopsied a number of human brains and measured the degree of synaptic branching in Wernicke's area of the left hemisphere. Then they probed into the backgrounds of these deceased subjects and found that the more educated they were, the more branching there was in this language-rich part of the brain (Jacobs, Schall, & Scheibel, 1993). Similarly, researchers played tones of varying frequencies for 37 professional musicians and nonmusicians and found that the part of the auditory cortex that responds to sound was more active in the musicians' brains—containing, on average, 130 percent more gray matter. Perhaps years of experience had stimulated the growth of extra neurons in this music-sensitive structure (Schneider et al., 2002).

The recent analysis of Albert Einstein's brain is a case in point (Witelson et al., 1999). We noted earlier that whereas Einstein's brain was average size overall, a highly specific region that is active in visual-spatial and mathematical thinking was 15 percent larger than normal. Einstein may well have been born with a brain uniquely gifted for physics. But it's possible, as the researchers were quick to point out, that this part of his brain bulked up in size as a result of constant usage (Witelson et al., 1999). "Practice may not always make perfect, but it is likely to make a lasting impression on your brain" (Azar, 1996).

What's Your Prediction?

Most people in the world are right-handed. Yet psychologist Lee Salk (1962) once noticed that mothers tend to hold their infants on the left side of their body. Is this true? Shouldn't most people, being right-handed, prefer the right arm for something as precious as a human baby? What about books, boxes, and other objects? Imagine you are holding a 3-month-old baby in one arm. Are you using your right arm or left? Now imagine that you're holding an antique vase, or a shoebox. Which arm are you using now? Almerigi, Carbary, and Harris (2002) tested 300 college students. What percentage do you think saw themselves using the right arm for a baby—25, 50, 75, more? What about for inanimate objects? The result confirmed Salk's observation: Although 76 percent said they'd use the right arm to hold objects, 66 percent said they'd use the *left* arm for an infant. This result is found consistently—not just for imaginary tasks, but in actual practice (Harris, 2002). How can this be explained? Is it possible that people hold infants on the left arm in order to free up the right hand? The preference is clear, but at this point more research is needed to determine the reason for it.

The Cost of Plasticity: The Case of the Phantom Limb

Plasticity is an adaptive feature of the nervous system. However, recent studies indicate that the brain's plasticity can also be a burden, as in the case of amputation. Psychologists have long been puzzled by phantom pain—the fact that amputees often feel excruciating pain in the area of their lost limb, sensations that would often last for years. To lessen the pain, puzzled physicians and their patients have sometimes resorted to desperate measures such as shortening the stump or cutting sensory tracts in the spinal cord, typically without success. In the past, some observers interpreted the pain as a form of denial, or wishful thinking; others believed that frayed nerve endings in the stump were inflamed and irritated, thereby fooling the brain into thinking that the limb was still there. It now appears that neither of these explanations is correct and that the phantom pain results, ironically, from the brain's own capacity for reorganization and growth.

This possibility was first raised when Michael Merzenich et al. (1983) severed the nerve of the middle finger in an adult monkey and found that the area of the somatosensory cortex dedicated to that finger did not wither away. Rather, nearby neurons activated by other fingers filled in the dormant region. The sensations produced by these neurons may thus fool the brain into thinking that the limb is still there. Consistent with this account, a study of human amputees revealed that the more cortical reorganization that had occurred, as detected in brain scans, the more pain the patients felt (Flor et al., 1995; Karl, Birbaumer, Lutzenberger, Cohen, & Flor, 2001).

Repairing the Damaged Brain: New Frontiers

The brain has great capacity for enrichment, but alas, we are mortal and our bodies are fallible. Strokes, spinal cord injuries, diseases that strike at the core of the nervous system, exposure to toxic substances, and addictions to alcohol and other drugs are just some of the causes of brain damage. The possible effects include paralysis, motor disorders, thought and speech disorders, blunted emotion, changes in personality, and a loss of sensory capabilities, consciousness, and memory.

The brain is capable of incredible feats, including the ability to adapt to a missing limb. Here a child with a prosthetic leg learns coordination in an occupational therapy setting.

iStock.com/FatCamera

Neurogenesis

Scientists used to believe that adult brains do not produce new neurons—that the death of brain cells results in permanent loss. It now appears, however, that the production of new brain cells—a process called **neurogenesis**—continues well beyond infancy. The human brain may acquire billions of new cells between birth and age 6, and those cells are incorporated into existing neural circuits and help to construct new ones (Blakeslee, 2000; Gilmore, Knickmeyer, & Gao, 2018). Neurogenesis may slow in adulthood, but it does not stop completely. The adult brain, too, has special cells that divide and produce new neurons. The discovery of neurogenesis in adults can be traced to the mid-1960s, when researchers studying adult mice found new brain cells in the hippocampus, the structure involved in forming new memories. Within a few years, scientists observed neurogenesis in the brains of other adult mammals, such as guinea pigs and rabbits, and in birds. For instance, new cells are created in the brains of adult canaries that learn new songs and in adult chickadees that store memories for where their winter seed stashes are hidden.

Does all this mean that neurogenesis occurs in the brains of adult humans? Although more evidence is needed, the possibilities are exciting. If you get an ulcer, break a finger, or scrape your knee, new cells will be produced to heal the wound. Scientists of the past assumed that the brain did not have this same capacity to heal itself. Once a neuron is damaged, after all, it is forever disabled. Yet every now and then, we hear stories of "miraculous" recoveries from brain damage. What makes this possible is the adaptive capacity to compensate for loss by strengthening old synaptic connections and by sprouting new axons and dendrites to form new connections. Earlier we saw that healthy brain tissue will sometimes pick up lost functions—which is why children with substantial damage to the left hemisphere learn to speak, and many adults who suffer strokes later recover their speech and motor abilities. Although methodological challenges have constrained the ability of investigators to reach a definitive answer, neurogenesis may also occur in the brains of adult humans, putting us on the verge of exciting new treatments for brain disorders (Kumar, Pareek, Faiq, Ghosh, & Kumari, 2019).

neurogenesis. The production of new brain cells.

Psychology Applied: Head Injury in Contact Sports

How often have you seen an athlete take a crushing blow to the head, go down, lie still for a few moments, and then stumble off the field looking dazed? Elite National Football League (NFL) quarterbacks Aaron Rodgers, Tom Brady, and Russell Wilson have all suffered from concussions. So do thousands of other athletes every year, professionals and amateurs, who play soccer, hockey, and other contact sports. What happens in a concussion, what are its effects, and can they be prevented?

A **concussion** is an alteration in a person's mental state caused by trauma to the head. From a neurological perspective, a concussion occurs when a jarring blow causes axons to become stretched, twisted, or sheared, interrupting signals between neurons (illustrated in Figure 2.25). The most common changes in mental state following a concussion are temporary confusion and amnesia, and these symptoms may occur right after the trauma or up to 15 minutes later.

concussion. An alteration in a person's mental state caused by trauma to the head.

Concussions vary a great deal in their severity. Mild "Grade 1" concussions tend to cause headaches, dizziness, disorientation, blurred speech, and a ringing in the ears. In sports, this type of concussion is difficult to diagnose and is commonly referred to as a "dinger" (athletes like to describe the state as "having their bell rung"). At the other extreme are severe "Grade 3" concussions, which are easy to spot because they cause unconsciousness for a brief or prolonged time. This type of injury can damage the brainstem and disrupt such autonomic functions as heart rate and breathing. Over time, it may also result in such symptoms as persistent headaches, vision problems, memory loss, sleep loss, an inability to concentrate, a lack of tolerance for loud noises and bright lights, fatigue, and anxiety or depressed mood. How can a coach or an athletic trainer know that an athlete has just suffered a concussion? Here are some common symptoms (American Academy of Neurology, 1997; Bailes, Lovell, & Maroon, 1998):

- Stares vacantly into space or looks confused
- Is slow to answer questions

- Is easily distracted and unable to follow instructions
- Slurs speech or talks in gibberish
- Stumbles and cannot walk a straight line
- Is disoriented, often walking in the wrong direction
- Doesn't know the current time, day, or place
- Repeatedly asks the same question and forgets the answer
- Becomes highly emotional, crying for no apparent reason

Doctors fear that people who suffer repeated concussions may face lasting cognitive declines. So what can be done to minimize the damage to athletes? There are three steps to be taken. The first is to require the use of safety equipment that would lessen the risk of getting a concussion. In the NFL, the focus has been largely on improving the safety of helmets, head gear, and mouth guards. Many testing methods are now being used to determine equipment safety. A second precautionary step is to change the rules of the game in order to reduce risks of concussions for plays or rules that create high-risk situations for concussions to occur. Changes for the NFL include moving the line where a team kicks off

FIGURE 2.25 ■ Anatomy of a Concussion

How often have you seen an athlete take a crushing blow to the head, go down, and leave the game? Featured NFL quarterbacks suffer repeated concussions. So do thousands of other athletes each year. But with what effect?

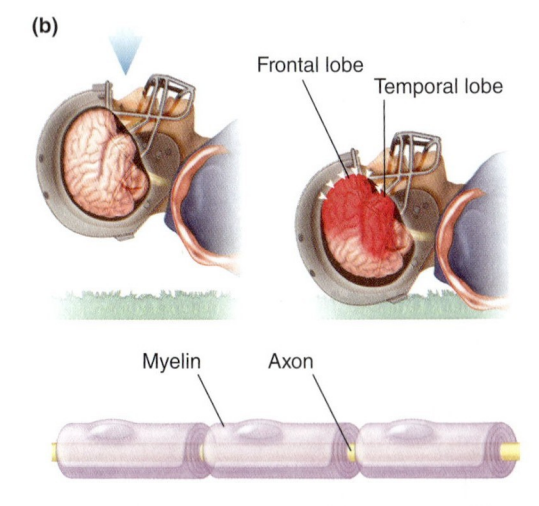

In a normal neuron, the axon, which is protected by a myelin sheath, is not broken or otherwise distorted.

After a concussive blow, an axon might twist or bend interrupting communication between neurons.

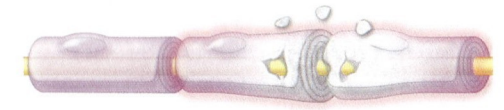

If a concussion is severe enough, the axon swells and disintegrates. Less severely damaged axons return to normal.

Michael Zagaris/Contributor/Getty Images; Carolina Hrejsa/Body Scientific Intl.

from the 30- to the 35-yard line to reduce the number of times a kickoff is returned, expanding the list of "defenseless players" to protect players in vulnerable positions, and reducing the length of overtime to 10 minutes. A third precautionary step appropriate to all sports is to ensure that any player who takes a blow to the head be sidelined immediately and carefully examined for concussion-like symptoms. For this step, standardized brief examination methods have been developed and a five-step concussion protocol is now implemented in the NFL. In fact, concussion protocols are now implemented in most contact sports—in college and in professional leagues (Deubert, Cohen, & Lynch, 2017; NCAA Sport Science Institute, 2020).

Today, neurologists are wondering if the newest roller-coasters can cause brain trauma by jostling the brain's soft tissue, causing it to press up against the skull. A few years ago, no roller-coaster surpassed 200 feet in height; today, "hypercoasters" reach up to 400 feet. A few years ago, roller-coasters gained speed by gravity; today, many are catapulted by motors designed to launch rockets. As thrilling as the rides can be, they subject riders to powerful physical forces—such as gravity, or G-force, as well as jerk, roll, pitch, and yaw. Research is under way to examine the effects of these rides on the brain (Pieles et al., 2017).

Neural Transplantation

Is it possible to more effectively restore the brain through medical intervention? For the millions of people each year who are struck by Parkinson's disease, Alzheimer's disease, and other degenerative nerve disorders, can the damaged brain and nervous system be repaired? One exciting development is that researchers have been busy trying to transplant healthy tissue from the central nervous system of one animal into that of another animal in a surgical procedure known as a **neural graft**. In amphibians and fish, researchers long ago demonstrated that it was possible to transplant neurons in cold-blooded animals. In classic experiments from the 1940s, Sperry transplanted eyeballs in frogs and found that these grafts formed new pathways to the brain and restored vision. Would neural grafting work as well in warm-blooded mammals? To find out, a team of researchers destroyed a dopamine-producing area of the brainstem (called the *substantia nigra*) in laboratory rats. As they had anticipated, the lack of dopamine caused severe tremors and other symptoms that mimicked Parkinson's disease. Next, they implanted healthy tissue from brains taken from rat fetuses and observed, after four weeks, a 70 percent decline in symptoms (Perlow et al., 1979). In later experiments with rats, mice, and primates, researchers also used neural grafting in other regions of the brain to reverse cognitive learning deficits, spatial deficits, and alcohol-induced memory loss (Brasted, Watts, Torres, Robbins, & Dunnett, 2000; Stoker, Blair, & Barker, 2017).

neural graft. A technique of transplanting healthy tissue from the nervous system of one animal into that of another.

News from animal laboratories is encouraging. But can brain grafts help people suffering from degenerative nerve disorders? In March 1982, a male Parkinson's patient in Stockholm, Sweden, agreed to serve as a human guinea pig. Barely able to move without medication, he underwent an experimental operation. The neurosurgeons removed part of his adrenal gland, which produces dopamine, and injected the tissue directly into his brain (Parkinson's disease results from a shortage of dopamine). But the result was disappointing. The patient showed some minor improvement during the first couple of weeks, but he soon reverted to his presurgery state (Backlund, Grandburg, & Hamberger, 1985). Undiscouraged, others pursued the use of brain grafts in Parkinson's patients with varying degrees of success.

Recent studies offer an exciting direction for future efforts to repair the damaged brain. Neuroscientists have long held that new nerve cells

In 1984, three years after retiring from boxing, Muhammad Ali was diagnosed with Parkinson's disease. Outside of his Hall of Fame boxing career, he played an instrumental role in the civil rights movement and was a world-recognized advocate raising awareness for those suffering with Parkinson's disease. Muhammad Ali passed away from complications of the disease on June 3, 2016, at the age of 74.

R. McPhedran/ Stringer/Hulton Archive/Getty Images

cannot be produced in the adult brain. New axons and dendrites may sprout, forming new synaptic connections. While the growth of new neurons was once considered impossible, neurogenesis researchers have since discovered that the adult human brain does spawn new nerve cells in the hippocampus, a structure that is important in learning and memory. This discovery, and the possibility that neuroscientists may some day find a way to stimulate the growth and migration of nerve cells, has led some researchers to speculate that the human brain harbors great potential for its own repair (Doidge, 2007; Fawcett, Rosser, & Dunnett, 2001).

Thinking Like a Psychologist About Behavioral Neuroscience

The study of the split-brain patient described at the outset of this chapter gave us a glimpse into the fascinating and developing world of behavioral neuroscience. This research illustrates why it is valuable to observe individuals who are exceptional in some way and tells us that each region of the brain is involved in different psychological processes. But as we have seen elsewhere in this chapter, researchers use other methods as well, including powerful brain scans, to discover linkages among the brain, the mind, and behavior. And although different areas of the brain act as "specialists," the healthy human brain operates as an integrated system—and has the capacity to change as a result of usage, practice, and experience.

To this day, the human brain and nervous system remain one of the great frontiers in science. From the trillions of tiny building blocks, consisting of axons, dendrites, synapses, and neurotransmitters, to the structures of the brainstem, limbic system, and cerebral cortex, there is a solid biological foundation for the study of mind and behavior. The goal, as we'll explore in later chapters, is to understand the links between the human body and psychological processes that range from visual perception to moral development, social aggression, and the health benefits of psychotherapy.

SUMMARY

Phineas Gage's dramatic brain injury showed that the human brain and nervous system form an integrated system of specialized parts—the concern of *behavioral neuroscience*.

THE BODY'S COMMUNICATION NETWORKS

The body has two communication networks: the nervous system and the endocrine system.

THE NERVOUS SYSTEM

The human nervous system has two basic parts. The **central nervous system (CNS)** includes the brain and the spinal cord. The **peripheral nervous system (PNS)** consists of the nerves that radiate from the CNS to the rest of the body.

The PNS is divided further into two components. The **somatic nervous system** transmits signals from the sensory organs and skin to the CNS. It also relays motor commands from the CNS to the skeletal muscles. The **autonomic nervous system** connects the CNS to the involuntary muscles, organs, and glands, thus regulating such functions as heartbeat and temperature. The autonomic nervous system has two parts: the **sympathetic nervous system**, which energizes the body for action, and the **parasympathetic nervous system**, which returns the body to its normal state.

THE ENDOCRINE SYSTEM

The **endocrine system** is a collection of ductless glands that regulate growth, metabolism, and other functions by secreting **hormones** into the bloodstream. These secretions are controlled in the brain by the hypothalamus, which signals the **pituitary gland**.

THE NEURON

Neurons, or nerve cells, transmit and receive information throughout the nervous system. **Sensory neurons** transmit information from the senses, skin, muscles, and internal organs to the CNS. **Motor neurons** send commands from the CNS to the muscles, glands, and organs. **Interneurons** serve as connectors within the CNS. Neurons cluster into interconnected working groups called **neural networks**. **Glial cells** help support, insulate, and nourish the neurons. A simple **reflex** like the knee jerk illustrates the speed of neural signals.

STRUCTURE OF THE NEURON
Each neuron has a rounded body, called the **soma**, and two types of branched fibers: **dendrites**, which receive impulses, and an **axon**, which sends impulses through its terminals. Many axons are covered with **myelin sheath**, a fatty insulating layer that speeds impulses.

THE NEURON IN ACTION
A neuron transmits messages by means of an electrical process. When dendrites receive signals of sufficient strength, the cell's membrane breaks down. Positively charged sodium ions rush in, altering the charge inside in such a way that a burst of electrical energy known as an **action potential** surges through the axon as soon as a certain necessary level of stimulation, or **threshold**, is reached.

HOW NEURONS COMMUNICATE
To transmit a signal across the **synapse**, the tiny gap between two neurons, the sending neuron releases chemical **neurotransmitters** from vesicles in its axon terminals. These chemicals bind to **receptors** on the dendrites of a receiving neuron. There are many neurotransmitters in the body, and each fits only certain receptors.

NEUROTRANSMITTERS
Acetylcholine (ACh) is a neurotransmitter that links motor neurons and muscles. ACh has an excitatory effect on muscles. **Dopamine**, in contrast, inhibits muscles and helps control voluntary movements. Alzheimer's disease, Parkinson's disease, and schizophrenia have all been linked to problems with these chemical messengers. Other neurotransmitters called **endorphins** serve as the body's own pain relievers.

THE BRAIN

The basic anatomy of the brain has long been known, but behavioral neuroscientists face the more difficult task of understanding how it functions.

TOOLS OF BEHAVIORAL NEUROSCIENCE
Although **phrenology** was misguided in linking mental characteristics to bumps on the skull, it correctly supposed that functions are localized in particular parts of the brain.

Today, neuroscientists use four methods to study brain functions: (a) clinical case studies of people with brain damage; (b) invasion of the brain through surgery, drugs, or electrical stimulation; (c) electrical recordings of activity using the **electroencephalograph (EEC)**; and (4) brain-imaging techniques, such as **computerized tomography (CT) scan**, **positron emission tomography (PET) scan**, and **magnetic resonance imaging (MRI)**.

REGIONS OF THE BRAIN
The brain consists of three main parts: the brainstem, the limbic system, and the cerebral cortex. Each of these comprises several important structures.

The **brainstem** is the inner core. It contains the **medulla**, which controls vital involuntary functions such as breathing; the **pons**, involved in sleep and arousal; and the **reticular formation**, a netlike group of cells that filter sensory information and help control sleep, arousal, and attention. Nearby are the **cerebellum** and **basal ganglia**, which play an important role in balance and coordination.

Above the brainstem is the **limbic system**, which helps govern motivation, emotion, and memory. It includes the **thalamus**, a relay station for sensory information; the **amygdala**, linked to fear, anger, and aggression; the **hippocampus**, which performs a key function in memory formation; and the **hypothalamus**, which helps regulate the autonomic nervous system, emotions, and basic drives.

The outermost 80 percent of the brain, the wrinkled **cerebral cortex**, controls higher order mental processes. Anatomically, it consists of two hemispheres and four lobes. It can also be divided into areas based on function: (a) Sensory areas specialize in receiving sensory information. For example, the **somatosensory cortex** receives information from the touch receptors in the skin. (b) The **motor cortex** controls the voluntary muscles. (c) The **association cortex** areas communicate with the sensory and motor areas and house higher mental processes. Within the association cortex, two areas specialize in language. **Broca's area** directs the production and comprehension of speech, and **Wernicke's area** is involved in language comprehension.

THE SPLIT BRAIN

Researchers have investigated Fechner's idea that each side of the brain has its own mind (Fechner, 1860). The studies rely on the fact that the left hemisphere communicates with the right side of the body, and the right hemisphere with the left side. The hemispheres are connected by, and share information through, the **corpus callosum**. Experiments with **split-brain** patients, in whom the corpus callosum has been severed, show that each hemisphere has a somewhat different version of experience.

Other research has tried to determine which functions have a tendency toward **cerebral lateralization**, or control by a single side of the brain. The key language centers are in the left hemisphere. The right hemisphere plays a crucial role in nonverbal functions. But the most important distinction may be the style of processing. The left hemisphere seems to rely on analytical processing, whereas the right hemisphere is more holistic.

Research supports the notion that the two hemispheres, when their links are cut, produce separate streams of consciousness. But in the healthy brain, they exchange information so quickly that our mental experience is a seamless whole.

PROSPECTS FOR THE FUTURE

Recent advances in the study of the brain have addressed two questions: Does the adult brain have a capacity to change and adapt as a result of experience, and is it possible to repair a damaged brain?

THE BRAIN'S CAPACITY FOR GROWTH AND REORGANIZATION

Research shows that the brain has **plasticity**, a capacity to change. Specifically, certain experiences can spark the branching of new dendrites and the growth of new synaptic connections. This enables the brain to compensate for damage. But it also causes people with amputated limbs to experience phantom pain.

REPAIRING THE DAMAGED BRAIN: NEW FRONTIERS

Advances in understanding the brain have shown that **neurogenesis** continues past infancy and have led to attempts at brain repair. With the **neural graft** procedure, researchers have transplanted brain tissue from one animal to another in an effort to reduce deficits in brain function. Among human beings, the greatest hope may involve the transplantation of fetal tissue, a highly controversial procedure. Contrary to what has been believed, recent studies show that new nerve cells can be produced in the mature brain.

CRITICAL THINKING

Thinking Critically About Behavioral Neuroscience

1. What is the difference between the "mind" and the "brain"?

2. Advances in brain-imaging technology allow us to observe the human brain at work. What kinds of questions do you think we might be able to answer with these sophisticated techniques?

3. Research investigating neural plasticity suggests that life experiences can alter the neural circuitry of the brain. What are the advantages and disadvantages of this phenomenon? What are some of the real-world implications of this research (e.g., for child rearing or the treatment of stroke victims)?

4. What is your opinion of the concussion protocols in sports? For example, should a sports league be forced to make changes if concussions are a known risk of the sport? Do athletes need to be better educated on the risks involved? In your answer, explain how science and, specifically, psychology can help inform how to protect athletes going forward.

CAREER CONNECTION: RESEARCH

Research Assistant

Research assistants aid in the collection and analysis of data at universities, think tanks, market research firms, consulting and polling companies, and other organizations. Pursuing a career as a research assistant is a great way to put a bachelor's degree in psychology to good use. Assistants who work in labs are heavily involved in research and experimental psychology. Those who work in government agencies and private-sector businesses that study human behavior put their understanding of psychology to work alongside many of the more general research and critical-thinking skills that are essential for a psychology major. Research assistants may review and summarize existing data, write or edit documents, conduct experiments, log data, organize materials and information, and generally assist the lead researchers for whom they work.

Key skills for this role that psychology students learn to develop:

- Scientific reasoning to interpret psychological phenomena

- Critical thinking and analysis

- Effective communication across a variety of contexts

KEY TERMS

acetylcholine (ACh) (p. 55)
action potential (p. 54)
amygdala (p. 64)
association cortex (p. 67)
autonomic nervous system (p. 49)
axon (p. 53)
basal ganglia (p. 63)
brainstem (p. 63)
Broca's area (p. 68)
central nervous system (CNS) (p. 49)
cerebellum (p. 63)
cerebral cortex (p. 65)
cerebral lateralization (p. 72)
computerized tomography (CT) scan (p. 60)
concussion (p. 77)
corpus callosum (p. 69)

dendrites (p. 53)
dopamine (p. 56)
electroencephalograph (EEG) (p. 59)
endocrine system (p. 50)
endorphin (p. 57)
glial cells (p. 52)
hippocampus (p. 65)
hormones (p. 50)
hypothalamus (p. 65)
interneurons (p. 52)
limbic system (p. 64)
magnetic resonance imaging (MRI) (p. 60)
medulla (p. 63)
motor (motion-producing) neurons (p. 52)
motor cortex (p. 66)
myelin sheath (p. 53)

neural graft (p. 79)
neural networks (p. 52)
neurogenesis (p. 77)
neurons (p. 52)
neurotransmitters (p. 54)
parasympathetic nervous system (p. 49)
peripheral nervous system (PNS) (p. 49)
phrenology (p. 58)
pituitary gland (p. 50)
plasticity (p. 75)
pons (p. 63)
positron emission tomography (PET) scan (p. 60)
receptors (p. 55)
reflex (p. 52)
reticular formation (p. 63)
sensory neurons (p. 52)
soma (p. 53)
somatic nervous system (p. 49)
somatosensory cortex (p. 66)
split brain (p. 83)
sympathetic nervous system (p. 49)
synapse (p. 54)
thalamus (p. 64)
threshold (p. 54)
Wernicke's area (p. 68)

3 SENSATION AND PERCEPTION

Lucas Vallecillos / Alamy Stock Photo

LEARNING OBJECTIVES

Distinguish between a stimulus and a sensation; recognize the interplay between the two that inspired some of the first psychologists to measure them.

Imagine what life would be like for one day without sensation.

Summarize the steps we take to perceive our world as adults.

WHAT'S YOUR PREDICTION: DOES CULTURE INFLUENCE PERCEPTION?

The Situation

You have always assumed that when it comes to vision, hearing, and other biological senses, people are basically the same. But you also suspect that the way each of us perceives the world is influenced by our life experiences and cultural backgrounds. So, which is it? Thinking about the problem, you realize that one possible way to tease apart biological and cultural influences is to select an important aspect of perception, create a task to measure it, and then compare people from different parts of the world.

In reading up on the visual system, you learn that images projected on the eye's retina are flat and two-dimensional. So, you wonder, how do people judge depth and distance? How do people know that one object in the visual field is closer than another? Is depth perception innate among humans, or are certain types of life experience necessary? To examine these questions, you create the drawings demonstrated in Figure 3.1 and ask the following question: Which animal is closer to the hunter:

the antelope or the elephant? The task seems easy. To you, the elephant looks farther away because its image is so small and because it stands either on a hill that is partly blocked (top) or at the top of a road with converging lines that form an upside-down V (bottom).

Make a Prediction

Determined to test people from very different backgrounds and cultural experiences, you show the drawings to English speakers. Then you travel to southern Africa and present the same pictures to both illiterate and educated Bantus living in a rural area. What will you find? Will everyone, as you do, see the pictures in three-dimensional terms and see the antelope as closer than the elephant? Which participant groups will see the antelope as closer than the elephant: educated Westerners, educated Bantus, or illiterate Bantus?

FIGURE 3.1 ■ Which Animal Is Closer to the Hunter?

Monica Wierzbicki/Body Scientific Intl.

The Results

This study, conducted by W. Hudson (1960), was one of the first to examine perception from a cross-cultural perspective. Using drawings like those shown, Hudson found that compared to Western adults, illiterate Bantu participants saw the pictures as flat and the elephant as closer to the hunter. And what about the school-educated Bantus? It is interesting that in this group, most participants saw the antelope as closer. Apparently, seeing three-dimensional depth in two-dimensional displays is a skill that people develop—probably from exposure to books, photographs, artwork, and other flat visual representations of reality.

What Does It All Mean?

Among researchers who study vision and other senses, certain aspects of perception—such as our ability to perceive depth and distance—seem biologically "hardwired" and universal. From the two eyes to the neural pathways that carry visual signals to the brain, most humans are similarly equipped. Yet other researchers, such as those who study people from different cultures, have come to realize that in some ways our perceptions are influenced by our experiences. For example, people living in urban environments that contain many edges and right angles are more susceptible than those living in open spaces to certain line-based optical illusions (Deregowski, 1989). So, are the processes of perception biologically based or learned? As we will see in this chapter, both views are correct.

Thud. Giggle. Thud. Giggle. Thud. Splat. Giggle.

Have you ever watched a baby in a highchair? The joys of dinnertime with a 10-month-old are numerous. You may have even wondered, "When will this baby tire of throwing stuff on the ground?" One can quickly get caught up in the "go fetch" game, especially if the baby rewards you with a fantastic giggle. But have you pondered what the baby might be thinking and experiencing with every toss of the object? Might the falling object be magical? Take a moment to drop something unbreakable from about 4 feet above the ground. What happens on the object's way down? Does the object appear to get smaller? When it stops on the ground below, what happens? Is there a noise and a wobbly movement? Now, do it again. Test for consistency. You will probably find that the movement changes. Sometimes it might wobble to the left, sometimes to the right, and sometimes, it might hit flat and not wobble at all. When you pick up the object, does it appear to grow back to the same size? What might be even more fun, but a total mess, would be to fill some random objects with tasty and colorful stuff that delivers a punch of great smells like spaghetti or macaroni and cheese. Now, imagine you are an infant with these food-filled objects. Red, orange, and green end up everywhere, like a Jackson Pollock painting, but the awesome part is that this amateur artwork is edible. Babies tend to love getting their hands in it. What does red and green mixed together look like? Taste like? Smell like? Does it feel different? And that splatting noise… Can I make that happen again? Yes, food is fun to play with!

An experience with baby dinnertime can make one appreciate what we might have been like while learning about the world. We often take for granted that it has a lot to offer, and our sensory systems bring some of it into the brain with radar-like sensitivity. However, our brains have to learn the rules of our world. When an object is far away, it looks small. As it gets closer, it looks as if it is growing. When it has an edge, the color of the object seems to change—a darker hue is present and a shadow is cast. In this chapter, we will examine the psychology of sensation and perception. These terms are used to describe different stages in the process by which we acquire information about the world. In **sensation**, our eyes, ears, and other sensory receptors absorb raw physical energy. Through the process of **transduction**, this raw energy is converted into neural signals that are sent to the brain. In **perception**, these signals are then selected, organized, and interpreted, as illustrated in Figure 3.2. We hope that, while you learn about these fascinating

sensation. The processes by which our sense organs receive information from the environment.

transduction. The process by which physical energy is converted into sensory neural impulses.

perception. The processes by which people select, organize, and interpret sensations.

FIGURE 3.2 ■ Processes of Sensation and Perception

Perception is the process of converting physical stimuli, such as light and sound energy, into neural signals within our sensory organs. (a) Light is reflected off the petals of the flowers and into the eyes. The eyes then transduce this light into a neural signal to be sent to the brain. (b) Sound is produced by the bird and reaches our ears. Special hair cells in the cochlea of the ear transduce the sound into a neural signal to be sent to the brain.

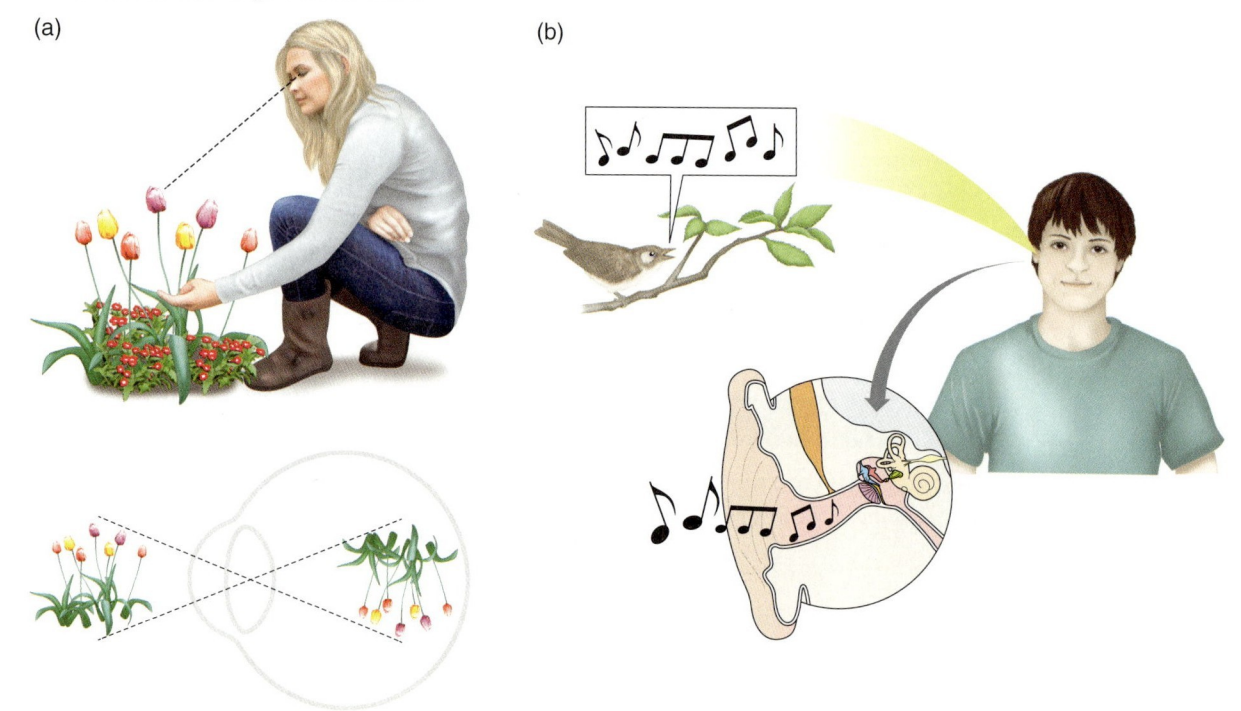

(a)

(b)

processes, you will appreciate the incredible complexity in how the world works in collaboration with our biology and psychology. The result of said collaboration? An infinite combination of experiences.

Psychologists used to treat sensation and perception as separate. Sensation was considered a strictly *physiological* process involving the various sense organs, receptors, neural pathways, and regions of the brain. Perception was considered a purely *psychological* process by which we derive meaning from these sensations. In this view, the body supplied the raw material and the mind made sense of that material. We now know, however, that in this continuous stream of events, there is no bright line dividing sensation and perception. As you will learn, the interaction between body and mind is seamless, but because different processes are at work, psychologists still find it useful to make the distinction.

This distinction comes to life in a poignant true story told by neurologist Oliver Sacks (1995). Virgil, a 50-year-old Oklahoma man, had been blind since the age of 6. Because Virgil could see light and faint shadows, a local ophthalmologist suggested that it might be possible to restore his eyesight through surgery. Starting with the right eye, the doctor removed a thick cataract that blanketed the retina, inserted a new lens implant, and bandaged the eye for 24 hours. The next day, the bandage was removed. It was the moment of truth, but Virgil did not cry out with joy or react in any other way. Instead, he stared blankly at the surgeon, silent and bewildered. As Sacks put it, "The dramatic moment stayed vacant, grew longer, sagged." Was the operation a success? Could Virgil see? In a manner of speaking, yes. He said he could detect light, forms, movement, and color, all mixed up in a confusing and cluttered blur. Only when the doctor started to speak did Virgil realize that he was staring at a face. His retina was alive and well, but his brain could not make sense of the information. There was sensation, but no perception.

Even as the weeks passed, Virgil remained disoriented. In the supermarket, he was overwhelmed, even stressed, by all the visual stimulation—the bright lights, the shelves lined with cans and jars, the fruits and vegetables, and the people wheeling carts up and down the aisles. "Everything ran together," he said. Virgil could not identify by sight common objects such as chairs and tables that he recognized easily by touching. He also lacked the ability to perceive depth. He was confused by shadows, often stopping to step over one. Yet he saw a staircase as a flat surface of parallel and crossing lines rather than as a three-dimensional solid object. Movement posed additional problems. He would recognize his dog one moment, but then wonder if it was the same animal when he saw it from a different angle.

For reasons that are unclear, Virgil suddenly became ill, collapsed, and almost died. He had a respiratory illness and needed a constant supply of oxygen. By the time he returned home from the hospital, he had to carry an oxygen tank wherever he went. Unable to work, Virgil lost his job, his house, and, once again, his eyesight. Extensive tests found no response to light whatsoever—and no electrical activity in the visual cortex. He was totally blind. But all was not lost. As Sacks (1995) put it, "Now, at last, Virgil is allowed to not see, allowed to escape from the glaring, confusing world of sight and space, and to return to his own true being, the intimate, concentrated world of the other senses that had been his home for almost fifty years" (p. 152).

It is the study of sensation that will start the chapter and allow us to examine the physiology of vision, hearing, smell, taste, touch, and other sensory systems. Then we will examine the psychological processes of perception that enable us to comprehend and interpret this raw material. As we will see, the world "out there" comes to us through an interaction of physical energy, the body, and the mind.

MEASURING THE SENSORY EXPERIENCE

LEARNING OBJECTIVES

Distinguish between a stimulus and a sensation; recognize the interplay between the two that inspired some of the first psychologists to measure them.

- Explain how physical energy becomes a psychological experience.
- Determine the minimum amount of stimulation needed to register on our senses.
- Differentiate between measurements for the smallest amount of stimulation detectable and the smallest change in stimulation detectable.

Light, vibration, odor-filled molecules, cold winds, warm breezes, and the collision of bodies. The first generation of psychologists, including Wilhelm Wundt, raised the most basic of questions: Whatever the stimulus, how does physical energy become a psychological experience? How much light is necessary to see? How can you hear a pin drop or detect minute variations in pitch well enough to tune a musical instrument? How different must two wines be for a wine taster to tell them apart? Inspired by the work of Gustav Fechner (1860), questions of this nature gave birth to psychology's first subfield, **psychophysics**: the study of the relationship between physical stimuli and subjective sensations. The key to psychophysics is measurement. Because sensation is subjective, it cannot be measured using objective instruments the way you assess height, weight, or time. There are no yardsticks, or scales, or stopwatches—only subjects and their self-reports. New procedures thus had to be devised to maximize the accuracy of these reports (Gescheider, 1997). Much of the material discussed in this chapter was derived from these psychophysical procedures.

psychophysics. The study of the relationship between physical stimulation and subjective sensations.

Absolute Thresholds

What is the minimum amount of light that we can see, the weakest vibration that we can hear, or the faintest odor that we can smell? How much sugar needs to be added to a food for us to taste more sweetness? What is the slightest amount of skin pressure, as in a tickle, that we can feel? Just how sensitive are our sensory systems? Researchers interested in a sensation begin by trying to determine an **absolute threshold**, the minimum level of stimulation that an organism can detect.

absolute threshold. The smallest amount of stimulation that can be detected.

Absolute threshold can be derived in different ways. One method is simply to ask a subject to adjust the intensity of a stimulus until it is barely detectable. A second method is to gradually increase the intensity level and ask subjects from one trial to the next if they detect the stimulus. A third method is to vary the stimulus presentation randomly, again checking with the subject on each trial. Over the years, research has shown that absolute thresholds are not "absolute." There is no single point on the intensity scale at which people suddenly detect a stimulus. Rather, detection rates increase gradually. Psychophysics researchers thus define absolute threshold as the point at which a stimulus can be detected 50 percent of the time. Defined in this way, some of our absolute thresholds are highly impressive, as summarized in Table 3.1.

Signal-Detection Theory

Imagine you are a subject in a classical psychophysics experiment. You are sitting in a darkened room staring at a blank wall, and the experimenter presents a series of flashes varying in brightness. Did you see it? What about the next one, and the one after that? On some trials, the flashes are clear, well above threshold, so you say *yes*. But on other trials, you are just not sure. With the experimenter waiting for a response, what do you say? Confronted with this dilemma, some subjects prefer to say yes (when in doubt, go for it). Others, more cautious, say no (unless it is clear, do not go out on a limb). These tendencies to respond yes or no in uncertain situations are individual response biases—and they have little to do with sensation. The problem for the researcher, then, is that a subject's responses are influenced not only by the strength of the signal but also by background factors such as the subject's personality, motivation, and expectations.

Enter signal-detection theory. Based on the assumption that performance is determined jointly by the strength of a signal and the subject's response criterion (that is, the subject's willingness to say yes

TABLE 3.1	Some Absolute Thresholds
Sensory System	**Absolute Threshold**
Vision	A lit candle 30 miles away on a dark, clear night
Hearing	The tick of a watch 20 feet away in total quiet
Smell	One drop of perfume dispersed throughout a six-room apartment
Taste	One teaspoon of sugar in 2 gallons of water
Touch	The wing of a bee falling on your cheek from a height of 1 centimeter

signal-detection theory. The theory that detecting a stimulus is jointly determined by the signal and the subject's response criterion.

rather than no), **signal-detection theory** gave rise to a more sophisticated method. On some trials, a weak stimulus is presented. On others, no stimulus is presented. By comparing a subject's "hit" versus "miss" rate on stimulus trials to the subject's tendency to commit "false alarms" by saying yes in blank trials, a researcher can mathematically separate the subject's detection performance from the response bias (Green & Swets, 1966; Wickens, 2001; Wickens, Hollands, Banbury, & Parasuraman, 2016). The method of establishing absolute thresholds was based on the assumption that a threshold is determined solely by the stimulus. But signal-detection theory recognizes that response biases are also at work. This approach provides the psychologist with a valuable tool for analyzing why air traffic controllers are so quick to detect danger signals on the radar screen (Wickens et al., 2009), why overeager witnesses identify innocent suspects in police lineups (Wixted & Mickes, 2014), or why doctors tend to over-diagnose certain diseases from available test results (Lynn & Barrett, 2014; Swets, 1996). Signal-detection theory has also been used to evaluate how clinical psychologists make the prediction that someone will suffer from a psychological disorder (Bardeen, Stevens, Clark, Lahti, & Cropsey, 2015), attempt suicide, or erupt in violence (McFall & Treat, 1999).

Difference Thresholds

Sensory capacities are measured not only by our ability to detect low levels of stimulation but also by the extent to which we can detect subtle differences. This ability is determined by asking subjects to compare the brightness of two light bulbs, the loudness of two tones, the weight of two blocks, and so on. Given one stimulus, subjects are asked to adjust the level of another stimulus so that the two are the same. Or subjects are given the two stimuli and asked to report whether they are the same or different. Either way, it is possible to pinpoint the smallest change in stimulation that subjects can detect 50 percent of the time. This point is called the difference threshold, or **just noticeable difference (JND)**.

just noticeable difference (JND). The smallest amount of change in a stimulus that can be detected.

While measuring difference thresholds, Ernst Weber (1834) quickly noticed that JNDs increase with the size or intensity of the stimulus—and that the magnitude of a JND is a constant proportion of the original stimulus. In other words, as the stimulus increases in magnitude, a greater change is needed before it can be detected. This general principle is known as **Weber's law**. To illustrate, the JND for weight is 1/50, or 2 percent. In other words, if you lift a 50-ounce object, and then a 51-ounce object, you will probably notice that the second one is heavier than the first. However, you would not feel a difference between one object that weighs 50 pounds and another that weighs 50 pounds, 1 ounce. Again, there is an absolute difference of 1 ounce; but a JND of 2 percent means that if your reference point is a 50-pound object, you would not detect a difference unless the second object is equal to or greater than 51 pounds. Except at the extremes, Weber's law provides a good estimate of our difference thresholds. It can also be applied to other senses—though each has a different threshold. For example, the JND is 10 percent for loudness. Consider, for example, the last time you turned up the volume. Imagine the manufacturer of your headphones did not know about the JND. As a result, turning up the volume one notch meant increasing the volume 1 percent. Would you notice the change? Unfortunately, you likely would not. It would take turning up the volume by 10 notches for you to notice a slight increase. Thus, those headphones would probably be returned not just by you but by many other consumers who believed the headphones did not work properly.

Weber's law. The principle that the just noticeable difference of a stimulus is a constant proportion despite variations in intensity.

Tuning a piano requires a heightened ability to detect subtle differences among tones.
iStock.com/syolacan

SENSATION

> ### LEARNING OBJECTIVES
>
> Imagine what life would be like for one day without sensation.
>
> - List the steps that occur when the human visual system converts light into meaningful color images.
> - Describe the structures in the auditory system that convert vibrating air molecules into meaningful sounds.
> - Compare and contrast the chemical senses of smell to taste.
> - Examine how those who have synesthesia experience the world.

In school, we are taught that there are five senses: vision, hearing, taste, smell, and touch. This simple notion can be traced to the writings of Aristotle (384–322 BCE). Even today, people who believe in "extrasensory" perception, or ESP, call it the "sixth sense." In fact, we have more than five sensory modalities. Vision has two subsystems, one for daylight and one for nighttime conditions. The chemical senses of taste and smell are easily distinguished, but touch is really a mixture of several skin senses—including pressure, pain, warmth, and cold. We also have a keen sense of balance and of the position and movement of our body parts. Combined, these various systems bring in a steady stream of information from the world around us.

Vision

Humans, with some exceptions, are visual creatures. How many times have you said, "Show me," "I'll believe it when I see it," "Out of sight, out of mind," or "My eyes are playing tricks on me"? Like other aspects of human anatomy, our visual system is a highly adapted product of evolution. The earliest forms of life could "see" in the sea through faint patches of membrane that were sensitive to light. They could tell brightness from dark and even turn toward the light source. In contrast, other features—such as shapes, textures, motion, and color—could be detected later, only by more advanced forms of life (Land & Fernald, 1992).

Light

For every sensory system, physical energy is the source of stimulation. The stimulus input for vision is light—a form of energy known as electromagnetic radiation that travels through empty space in oscillating waves. As illustrated in Figure 3.3, what we see as light comes from a narrow band in the spectrum of electromagnetic radiation. All matter gives off electromagnetic radiation of different wavelengths (a wavelength is measured by the distance between waves). The sun and other stars give off radiation that includes light. So do fires and electric lamps. Visible wavelengths range from about 380 to 760 nanometers (a nanometer is one billionth of a meter). Thus, some waves (such as X-rays, ultraviolet rays, and gamma rays) are too short for us to see and fall below our visible range. Others (such as infrared rays, TV signals, radio waves, and radar) are too long for us to see, so they exceed our visible range. Other organisms have sensory capabilities that are different from ours. For example, most insects can see shorter wavelengths in the ultraviolet spectrum, and most fish and reptiles can see longer wavelengths in the infrared spectrum.

The *length* of a light wave determines its hue, or perceived *color*. To the human eye, white light is made up of all visible wavelengths combined. Short wavelengths look bluish, medium wavelengths look greenish, and long wavelengths look reddish. The picturesque colors of the visible spectrum can be seen in a rainbow or in the spectrum of colors produced when white light passes through a glass prism. A second property of light is its intensity, or *amplitude*, as measured by the height of the peaks in the wave. As wavelength determines color, amplitude determines *brightness*. The higher the amplitude, the brighter the light

FIGURE 3.3 ■ The Electromagnetic Spectrum

The top part of the figure shows the visible spectrum of light on a continuum of electromagnetic radiation. The figure makes it clear that visible light is just a small range on this continuum. The bottom part of the figure shows the distribution of wavelengths across natural sunlight, incandescent light bulbs, and fluorescent bulbs.

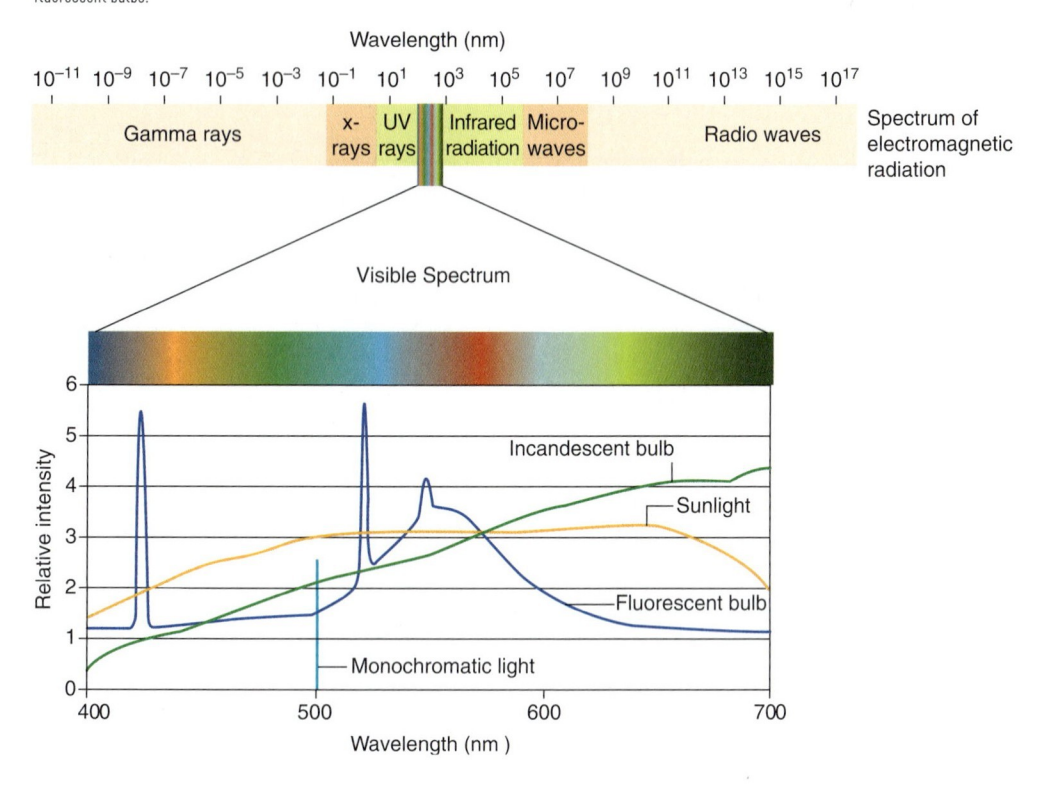

appears to be. A third physical property of light is its *purity*, as measured by the number of wavelengths that make up the light. Purity influences the *saturation*, or richness, of colors. The fewer wavelengths there are in a light (the purer it is), the richer or more saturated is the color. A pure red light made up of only a narrow band of wavelengths would give off a rich fire-engine or tomato-like color. In contrast, white light—which contains all visible wavelengths—is completely unsaturated and lacking in color.

The Visual System

The Eye. The fantastic journey of neural impulses through the human visual system begins with the eye—an extension of the brain and the most exposed part of the central nervous system. Lying in a protective bony socket within the skull, the eye converts, or transduces, light waves into electrochemical neural impulses. The major structures of the human eye are presented in Figure 3.4.

Light waves provide the stimulus input for vision, but what is seen depends on the capabilities of the visual system that is in place. Accordingly, different species see the world in different ways. Eagles can spot a tiny field mouse moving in the grass a mile away. Owls can see at night, in low levels of illumination. Cows and sheep have their eyes on the sides of the head, enabling them to spot predators sneaking up from behind. Each species has evolved visual systems uniquely suited to its way of life (Archer, Djamgoz, Loew, Partridge, & Vallerga, 1999; Nieder, 2012).

Light rays from the outside world first pass through the **cornea**, a clear, curved membrane, or "window." The cornea bends light so that it is sharply focused within the eye. Abnormalities in the shape of the cornea cause astigmatism, usually experienced as a selective blurring of parts of the image at a particular orientation, such as horizontal. Next comes the ring-shaped **iris**, which gives the eye its color. The iris is a muscle that is controlled by the autonomic nervous system. Its function is to regulate the size of the **pupil**—the small, round hole in the iris through which light passes. The iris causes the pupil to dilate (enlarge) under dim viewing conditions to let in more light and to contract (shrink) under brightness to let in less light.

cornea. The clear outer membrane that bends light so that it is sharply focused in the eye.

iris. The ring of muscle tissue that gives eyes their color and controls the size of the pupil.

pupil. The small round hole in the iris of the eye through which light passes.

FIGURE 3.4 ■ Structures of the Human Eye

In (a), the major parts of the eye are shown. In (b), the major pathway of visual information is shown (photoreceptor to bipolar cells to ganglion cells). Note how the connections to the cones "fan out" away from the fovea, making the cones there more accessible to light. (a) Refraction of light onto the lens (b) Focusing of light in the fovea.

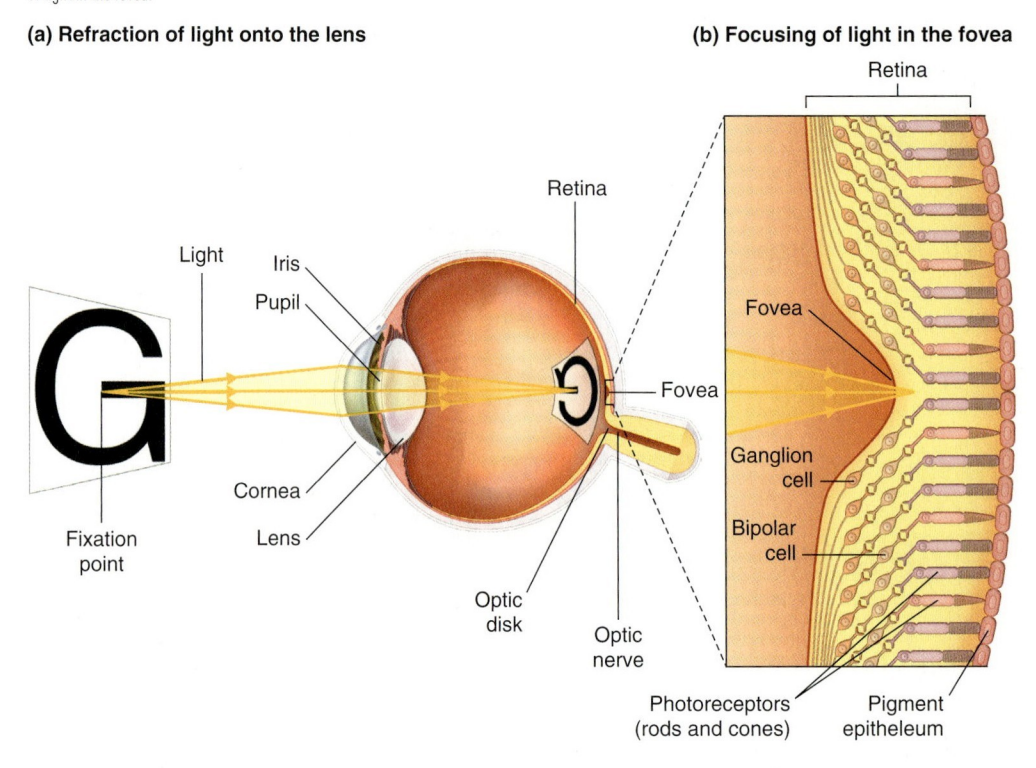

(a) Refraction of light onto the lens

(b) Focusing of light in the fovea

Behind the pupil, light continues through the **lens**, another transparent structure whose function is to fine-tune the focusing of the light. The lens brings an image into focus by changing its shape, in a process called **accommodation**. Specifically, the lens becomes more rounded for focusing on nearby objects and flatter for more distant objects (the cornea, which has a fixed shape, cannot make these adjustments for different distances). With age, the lens loses much of its elasticity and keeps the flatter shape appropriate for viewing at a distance—called presbyopia (Garner & Garner, 2016). As a result, many middle-aged people start to need corrective vision devices or procedures such as glasses or intraocular lens implants (Mesa & Monteiro, 2018).

Filling the central part of the eyeball is a clear jellylike substance called the vitreous humor. Light passes through this fluid before it reaches the retina. The **retina** is a multilayered screen of cells that lines the back inside surface of the eyeball (illustrated in Figure 3.5). It is one of the most fascinating tissues in the body—both because of its function, which is to transform patterns of light into images that the brain can use, and because of its structure, which illustrates many basic principles of neural organization. In an odd twist of nature, the image projected on the retina is upside down. That is, light from the top part of the visual field stimulates photoreceptor cells in the bottom part of the retina, and vice versa.

The retina has aptly been called an extension of the brain (Gregory, 1998). It has several relatively transparent layers and contains 130 million photoreceptor cells that convert light energy into neural activity. The layer closest to the back of the eyeball is lined with two specialized types of nerve cells called rods and cones. **Rods** are long, thin, cylindrical cells that are highly sensitive to light. They are concentrated in the sides of the retina and are active for black-and-white vision in dim light. Under impossibly ideal conditions, rods have the capacity to detect the light produced by one ten-billionth of a watt. **Cones** are shorter, thicker, more tapered cells that are sensitive to color under high levels of illumination. Cones are densely clustered in the center of the **fovea**, the pinhead-size center of the retina. Unlike the rest of the retina, the fovea contains only cones, and the ratio of rods to cones increases in

lens. A transparent structure in the eye that focuses light on the retina.

accommodation. In Piaget's theory, the process of modifying existing cognitive structures in response to new information.

retina. The rear, multilayered part of the eye where rods and cones convert light into neural impulses.

rods. Rod-shaped photoreceptor cells in the retina that are highly sensitive to light.

cones. Cone-shaped photoreceptor cells in the retina that are sensitive to color.

fovea. The center of the retina, where cones are clustered.

94 Essentials of Psychology

FIGURE 3.5 ■ The Retina

In Figure 3.5a, note the location of the retina relative to other anatomical structures in the eye. As you can see, the foveal region looks like a pit, as the top layers of the retina are swept aside so that there is no scatter of light reaching the receptor cells (that is, the cones). In Figure 3.5b, note a schematic of what the retina would look like if it were stretched out to reveal the layers. Oddly, the rods and cones form the back layer of the retina, even though they are the light-sensitive portion of the retina. The horizontal, amacrine, and bipolar cells serve as a middle layer and connect the photoreceptors to the retinal ganglion cells, which exit the retina and bring visual information to the brain.

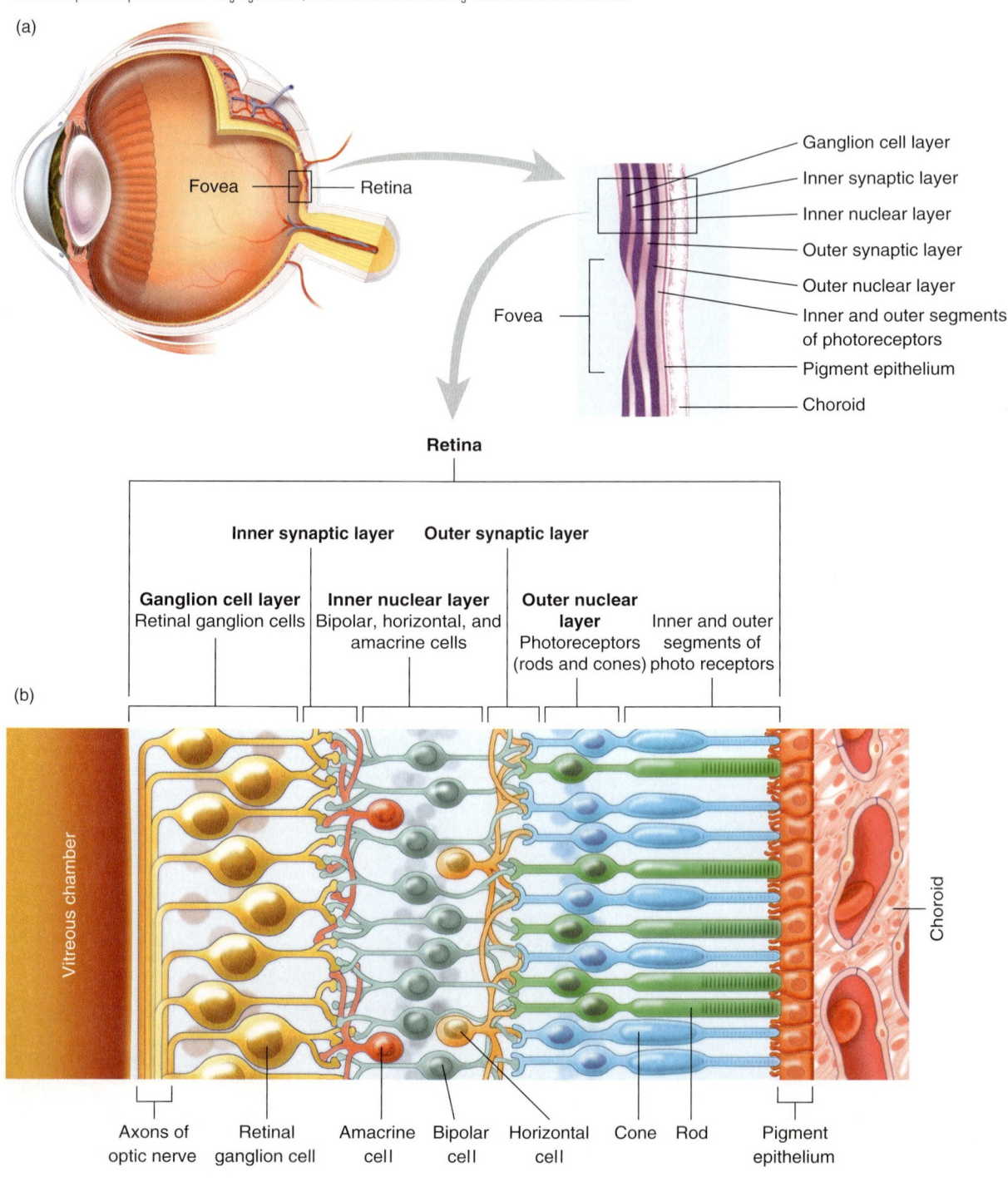

the outer edges of the retina. Therefore, cones are sprinkled throughout the retina; by contrast, the fovea contains a cluster of cones but has no rods.

In owls and other nocturnal (active only at night) animals, the retina contains only rods. Thus, they can see at night, but their vision is in black and white. In chipmunks, pigeons, and other diurnal (active only during the day) animals, the retina contains only cones. Thus, they are virtually blind at night. In animals that are active both day and night, the retina has a mixture of rods and cones. For example, the human retina has about 120 million rods and 7 million cones, enabling us to see colors under normal lighting and to make out forms under low levels of illumination. Individuals whose retinas contain no rods suffer from night blindness; those without cones lack all color vision.

Often, we need to adjust to radical changes in illumination. You step inside a darkened movie theater on a sunny day. As you start walking down the aisle, however, you have to put your arms out and inch forward slowly, stumbling around. After a few minutes, you can see again. This experience illustrates **dark adaptation**, the process by which eyes become more sensitive to light in a dark environment. It takes about 30 minutes for you to fully adapt to the dark—at which point the eyes become 10,000 times more sensitive. It also takes time to adjust to bright light. That is why, when you leave a movie theater during the day, everything seems so "washed out" that you have to squint at first to keep out the glare. This is an instance of **light adaptation**, the process by which our eyes become less sensitive to light under high levels of illumination.

When light strikes the rods and cones, it sparks a chain of events within a network of interconnected neurons that results in vision. Rods and cones contain photopigments, chemicals that break down in response to light, thus triggering neural impulses. These impulses activate bipolar cells, which, in turn, activate nearby ganglion cells. The axons of the ganglion cells form the **optic nerve**, a pathway that carries visual information from each eyeball to the brain. The area where the optic nerve enters the eye has no rods or cones, only axons. So each eye has a **blind spot**. We don't usually notice it because our eyes are always moving, but it's possible to find the blind spot through a simple exercise (illustrated in Figure 3.6).

Psychologists used to think that electrical impulses were delivered from the retina to the brain, as on an assembly line. It was as if there was a simple division of labor, whereby the retinal neurons "received" sensory information and passed it along on a conveyer belt to the visual cortex for perceptual "processing." We now know that the mechanisms of vision are more complex. Ultimately, signals from 130 million rods and cones are funneled through a mere 1 million axons in the optic nerve. This pattern of processing means that the bipolar and ganglion cells must be integrating and compressing signals from multiple receptors, and the number of bipolar and ganglion cells interacting with each rod and cone has an impact on visual detail detection.

As an analogy for this type of processing, consider having a conversation with a large group versus an individual. When attempting to converse with a large group of people at one time, you can get the general idea of what the people are saying, but much information can be lost. This is like the rods' relationship with bipolar and ganglion cells. Now, when you have a conversation with one or two people, much more information is heard and, in turn, less information is lost. This is akin to the cones' relationship with bipolar and ganglion cells. This is also why our cones are so much better at sending detailed visual information than our rods—fewer organisms are trying to have a conversation at once! The retina is a "smart" optical instrument. Not only does it receive light, but it also processes visual information (Casanova & Ptito, 2001; Hoffman, 1998; Palmer, 1999).

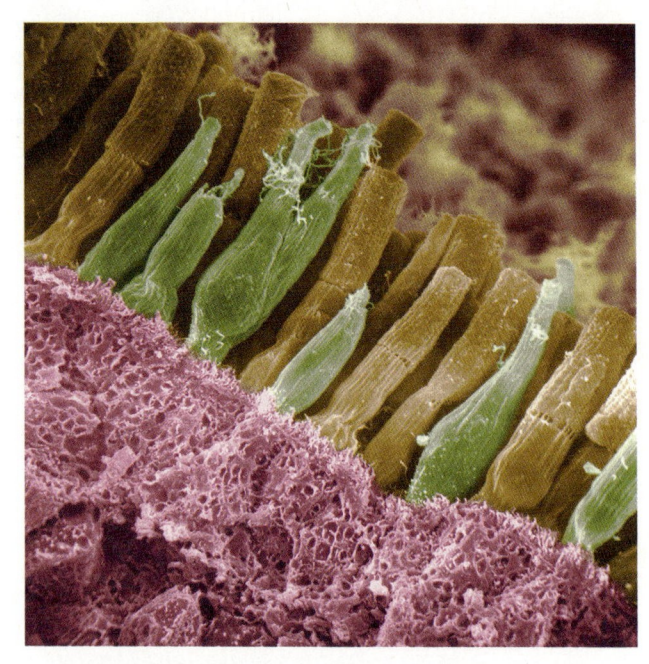

This photo shows how rods and cones, magnified approximately 14,000 times, line the back wall of the retina.
Omikron / Science Source

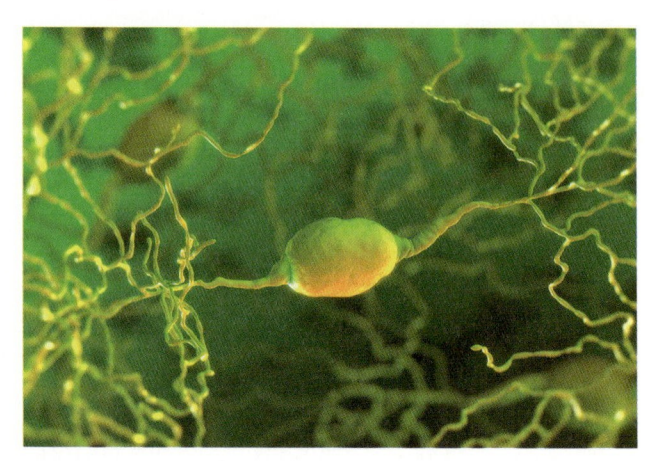

Bipolar cells activate ganglion cells, which send the information from the eyeball to the brain.
Science Picture Co / Alamy Stock Photo

dark adaptation. A process of adjustment by which the eyes become more sensitive to light in a dark environment.

light adaptation. The process of adjustment by which the eyes become less sensitive to light in a bright environment.

optic nerve. The pathway that carries visual information from the eyeball to the brain.

blind spot. A part of the retina through which the optic nerve passes. Lacking rods and cones, this spot is not responsive to light.

FIGURE 3.6 ■ The Blind Spot

Close your right eye and hold the book or your electronic device at arm's length. Slowly move the book or device toward you while looking at the orange circle with your left eye. At some point, the plus sign will disappear. The plus sign disappears when its image lands on the optic disc, where there are no receptor cells.

Any ganglion cell that represents a cluster of neighboring rods and cones receives input from a sizable portion of the retina. This region is called a **receptive field**. By recording the activity of individual ganglion cells, researchers have found many different types of receptive fields (Alitto & Usrey, 2015; Kuffler, 1953). The most common are circular "center-surround" fields in which light falling in the center has the opposite effect of light in the surrounding area. Some cells are activated by light in the center and inhibited by light in the surrounding area (center-on cells). Others work the opposite way; when light hits the center of the cell, it is inhibited but activated by light that hits the surrounding area (center-off cells). This arrangement makes the human eye particularly attuned to brightness-and-darkness contrasts in the visual field—contrasts that indicate corners, borders, and edges.

Visual Pathways. Axon fibers of ganglion cells form the optic nerve, which is the first part of the visual pathway that links each eyeball to the brain. The two optic nerves meet at the optic chiasm, where axons from the inside half of each eye cross over to the opposite half of the brain. This arrangement means that the left visual field of both eyes is projected to the right side of the brain, and the right visual field of both eyes is projected to the left side of the brain. After reaching the optic chiasm, the nerve fibers travel along two tracts, through the thalamus—the relay station where sensory signals are directed—to appropriate areas of the **visual cortex**, located in the back of the brain (illustrated in Figure 3.7). The visual cortex is the main information-processing center for visual information.

The Visual Cortex. Once information from the ganglion cells reaches the visual cortex, it is processed by **feature detectors**—neurons that are sensitive only to certain aspects of a visual image, such as lines or angles. This aspect of vision was first revealed by David Hubel and Torsten Wiesel (1962), who implanted microelectrodes in the visual cortexes of cats (and later monkeys). They projected different types of visual stimuli on a screen, and measured the electrical activity of single cells (illustrated in Figure 3.8). Do different neurons specialize in certain types of information? If neuronal specialization was the case, then the goal was to map or "decode" the visual cortex.

In a painstaking series of studies, Hubel and Wiesel (1979) discovered that three types of neurons service the visual cortex and that each type has its own specialists at work. *Simple cells* are activated by highly particular images. For example, some simple cells fire in response to a vertical line in the middle of the screen but not to a line that is off-center or tilted at a different angle. Other simple cells fire in response to horizontal lines, wider lines, or lines tilted at a 45-degree angle. The stimulus-response connection is that specific. *Complex cells* receive input from many simple cells. Although complex cells specialize in certain types of images, they react to those images anywhere in the visual receptive field—center, bottom, side, and so on. Finally, *hypercomplex cells* receive input from complex cells and respond to stimulus patterns. If one simple cell is activated by /, a second by \, and a third by -, the hypercomplex cell might react to a combination of these features, as in the letter A. When you consider the complexity of words, faces, landscapes, three-dimensional objects, skylines, and other images that enrich our lives, it is no wonder that the visual cortex is packed tightly with more than 100 million neurons.

---

receptive field. An area of the retina in which stimulation triggers a response in a cell within the visual system.

visual cortex. Located in the back of the brain, it is the main information-processing center for visual information.

feature detectors. Neurons in the visual cortex that respond to specific aspects of a visual stimulus (such as lines or angles).

Chapter 3 • Sensation and Perception 97

FIGURE 3.7 ■ Visual Pathways

From both eyes, the optic nerves meet at the optic chiasm, where the signals cross to the opposite half of the brain. The nerve fibers travel in two tracks through the thalamus, where they are directed to the visual cortex.

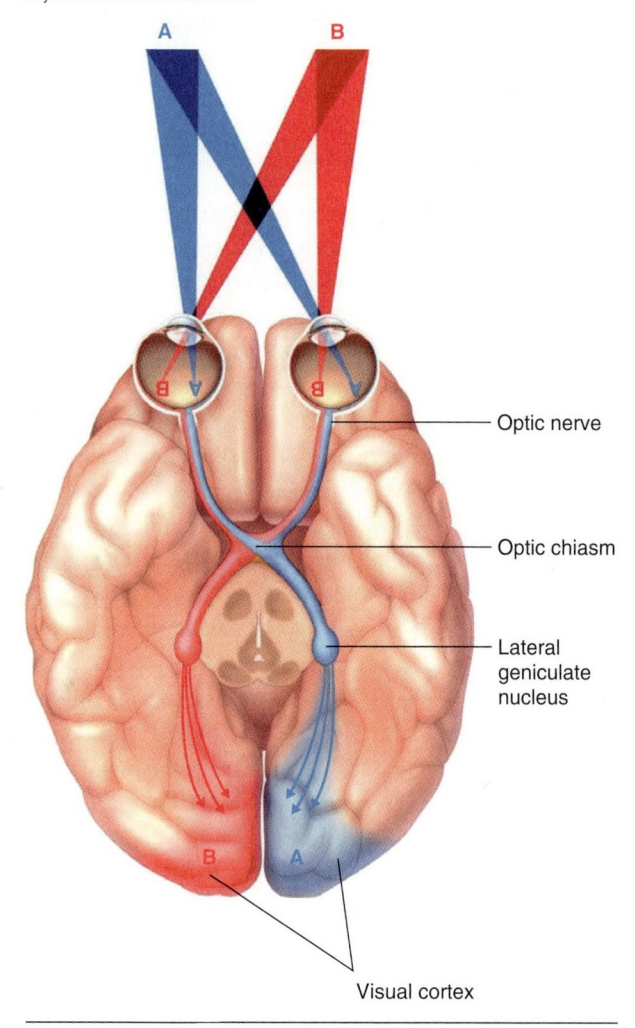

- Optic nerve
- Optic chiasm
- Lateral geniculate nucleus
- Visual cortex

Source: Garrett, Brain and Behavior, 5e, 2018, SAGE Publications, Inc.

FIGURE 3.8 ■ Hubel and Wiesel's Apparatus

Hubel and Wiesel implanted microelectrodes in a cat's visual cortex, projected visual stimuli, and measured single-cell activity. These signals were amplified and displayed on an oscilloscope.

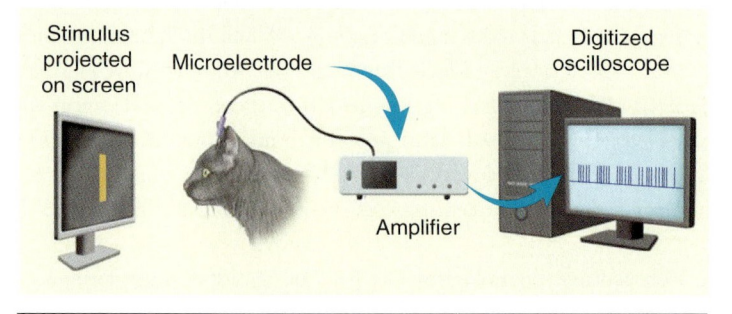

Monica Wierzbicki/Body Scientific Intl.

What colors of fabric do you see when you look at this dress? For a few days in 2015, people were divided over that question. The division highlighted an important lesson in perception—color is created in our brains.

picture alliance / Contributor / Getty

In 1981, Hubel and Wiesel were awarded a Nobel Prize for their work. In the years since their discovery of feature detectors in the visual cortex, others have identified neurons that fire primarily in response to highly specific features such as color, form, movement, navigation, and the depth of a visual stimulus (Hubel, 1996; Killian, Jutras, & Buffalo, 2012; Livingstone & Hubel, 1988).

Color Vision

Ruby-red apples. Lush green grass. Although some animals see the world in pale shades (including the bull, which is supposedly enraged by the sight of a matador's bright-red cape), all mammals have some form of color vision (Jacobs, 1993). For us humans, color is a particularly vital part of the visual experience and is also linked in interesting ways to emotion. Thus, sadness feels blue, anger makes us see red, death is mourned in black, and jealousy brings a visit from the green-eyed monster. Color perception even varies by gender. Abramov and colleagues (2012) and Murray and colleagues (2012), for example, both found that females are generally better than males at discriminating between various shades of colors.

In general, individual differences in color discrimination can exist because color is a property of the viewer, not the object. "The dress that broke the Internet" is a good example of this. On February 26, 2015, the dress in the accompanying photo stirred much controversy and was viewed more than 28 million times within 24 hours. Some viewers perceived the dress as blue and black, while others perceived the dress as white and gold. The debate became a phenomenon—to the extent that Ellen DeGeneres posted on Instagram, "From this day on, the world will be divided into two people: blue and black, or white and gold" (as cited by Weintraub, 2018). Years later, the debate has been settled—it is a blue and black dress. Neal Adams, an ophthalmologist, was asked about the optical illusion that caused some people to perceive it as white and gold. His explanation attributed the difference in perception to how light strikes the retina. "If light skews in one direction, a color looks blue-black. In another, it looks yellow-white" (Weintraub, 2018). What can skew the light coming toward the retina? Issues with the eye, like cataracts and aging of the lens; amber-hued glasses; the hue of the light in the store where the photo was taken; and the screen the image is displayed on can result in this illusion. What about color vision that isn't affected by such an illusion? The rose perceived as red is a good example. When sunlight shines on a red rose, only the long red rays in the spectrum are reflected into our eyes. All other wavelengths are absorbed in the flower's surface. (If no wavelengths were absorbed, then the rose would appear white.) Ironically, then, the rose holds everything but red. Most people can discriminate among 200 different colors and thousands of different shades. How do we do it? There are two major theories of color vision: the trichromatic theory and the opponent-process theory (Jacobs, 2014; Kaiser & Boynton, 1996; Lennie, 2000).

Early in the 19th century, physiologists Thomas Young (1802) and Hermann von Helmholtz (1852) argued that the human eye is receptive to three primary colors—red, blue, and green—and that all other colors are derived from combinations of these primaries. By recording the neural responses of individual cones to different wavelengths of light, 20th-century researchers later confirmed the

Young-Helmholtz **trichromatic theory** (Schnapf, Kraft, & Baylor, 1987; Wald, 1964). Specifically, there are three types of cones, each having a different photochemical that produces a particular response to light. One type fires most when struck by short wavelengths, so it picks up the color blue. The second type is most sensitive to the middle wavelengths, for the color green. The third type is most sensitive to long wavelengths, for the color red. In short, blue cones, green cones, and red cones serve as the building blocks for color vision. The different combinations of cones produce other colors in the eye's "palette." Activate both red and green cones, for example, and you will see the color yellow. Activate all three types of cones, and white is produced (illustrated in Figure 3.9).

German physiologist Ewald Hering (1878) was not completely satisfied with the trichromatic theory. As he saw it, yellow was a primary color, not a derivative of red and green. He also noticed that certain color combinations just do not seem to exist. A mix of red and blue gives rise to varying shades of purple, but what is reddish green? Another puzzling phenomenon that didn't fit was the occurrence of negative **afterimages**, sensations that persist after prolonged exposure to a stimulus.

FIGURE 3.9 ■ Trichromatic Theory

As shown, any color can be produced by mixing blue, green, and red light waves. When all three colors are combined, white is produced.

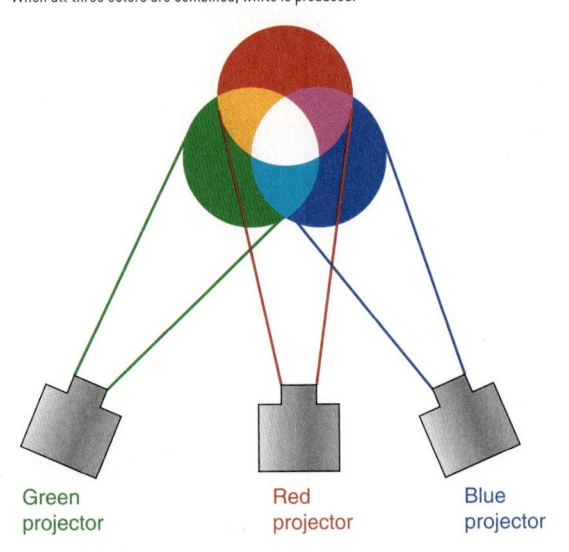

trichromatic theory. A theory of color vision stating that the retina contains three types of color receptors—for red, blue, and green—and that these combine to produce all other colors.

afterimage. A visual sensation that persists after prolonged exposure to and removal of a stimulus.

TRY THIS!

Afterimages

To observe the formation of an afterimage, **TRY THIS:** At the center of the accompanying image is a small white dot. Stare at it for 60 seconds with minimal blinking, and then look at a white sheet of paper or a white wall. According to the opponent-process theory, a negative afterimage should appear that converts into the face of a celebrity. If an afterimage doesn't appear right away, blink and look again.

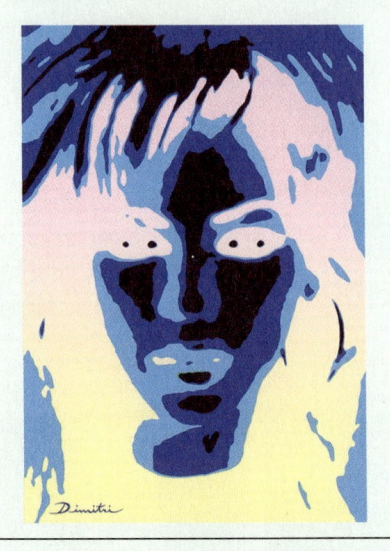

Source: Via Wikimedia Commons, Afterimage by Dimitri Parant, concentrate 30 seconds on the white dot and close your eyes 10 seconds. 2009, Flickr.

Putting the pieces together, Hering proposed the **opponent-process theory** of color vision. According to this theory, there are three types of visual receptors, and each is sensitive to a pair of complementary or "opponent" colors. One type reacts to the colors blue and yellow, a second type detects red and green, and a third type detects variations in brightness ranging from black to white. The color wheel in Figure 3.10

opponent-process theory. The theory that color vision is derived from three pairs of opposing receptors. The opponent colors are blue and yellow, red and green, and black and white.

illustrates how these primary colors and their "companions" line up on nearly opposite sides of the circle. Within each pair of red-green, blue-yellow, and black-white receptors, some parts fire more to one color whereas other parts react to its opposite. That is why we never see bluish yellow or reddish green, but we might see bluish green and reddish yellow. While seeing one color at a specific spot on the retina, you cannot also see its opposite on the same spot (Conway, 2002, 2013; Jacobs, 2014).

The opponent-process theory can explain two aspects of color vision that its predecessor theory could not. First, it explains afterimages. Think about what you saw when you completed the Try This! exercise. Staring at the blue areas of Beyoncé's altered image causes the blue-seeing cells to fire. Then, when the blue color is removed from view, these parts of the cells become temporarily fatigued, leaving only the yellow parts to fire normally (Vimal, Pokorny, & Smith, 1987). This process tips the neural balance to yellow, which produces a brief "rebound" effect (staring at green and black triggers a similar rebounding of red and white, respectively).

Second, opponent-process theory can explain color deficiency, usually a genetic disorder. In actuality, only about 1 in 100,000 people are color "blind," seeing the world in only black, white, and shades of gray (Nathans, 1989). Rather, color-deficient people tend to confuse certain colors. The most common problem, particularly among 2 percent of men (Álvaro, Moreira, Lillo, & Franklin, 2015), is red-green color deficiency, which is an inability to distinguish between red and green because both appear gray (illustrated in Figure 3.11). Though very rare, a second form of color deficiency is the inability to distinguish between—you guessed it—blue and yellow.

For many years, researchers debated the relative merits of the trichromatic and opponent-process theories of color vision. As often happens in either-or debates, it now appears that both theories are correct—and that the way people sense color is a two-step process. According to this view, the human retina contains red, blue, and green cones, as suggested by the trichromatic theory. But in the thalamus—where these signals are sent en route to the visual cortex—single-cell recordings reveal that the neurons operate in accordance with the opponent-process

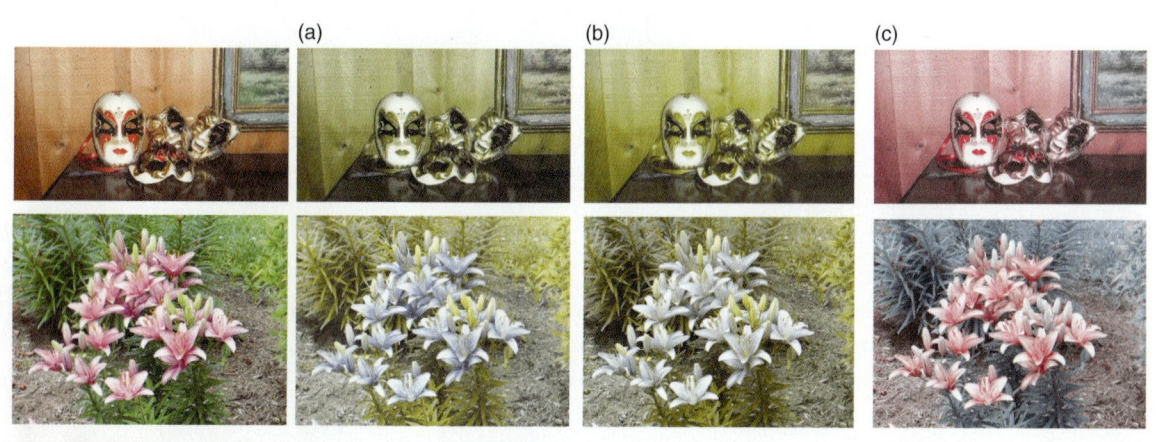

FIGURE 3.10 ■ The Color Wheel

Colors opposite each other are complementary; that is, equal amounts of light in those colors cancel each other out, producing a neutral gray.

Source: Garrett, Brain and Behavior, 5e, 2018, SAGE Publications, Inc

This is how these colored displays look to persons with (a) red-green color deficiency called protanopia, (b) a second form of red-green color deficiency called deuteranopia, and (c) blue-yellow color deficiency called tritanopia.

theory. That is, some cells are excited by red and inhibited by green, and vice versa. Other cells react to blue and yellow. Color vision is complex and still not fully understood (Conway, 2013; Jacobs, 2014; Simunovic, 2016).

FIGURE 3.11 ■ Test of Color Deficiency

In items like these, people with red-green color-deficiency have difficulty seeing the figures embedded in the pattern. The inability to distinguish between red and green, as in these patterns or in traffic signals, caused a 1996 train crash near Hoboken, New Jersey. According to the National Transportation Safety Board, the engineer, who had failed a color-vision test, failed to detect the red signal. New Jersey Transit now requires all of its engineers to pass a color-vision test consisting of 14 circular plates of polka dots in which numbers are formed by slightly contrasting colors.

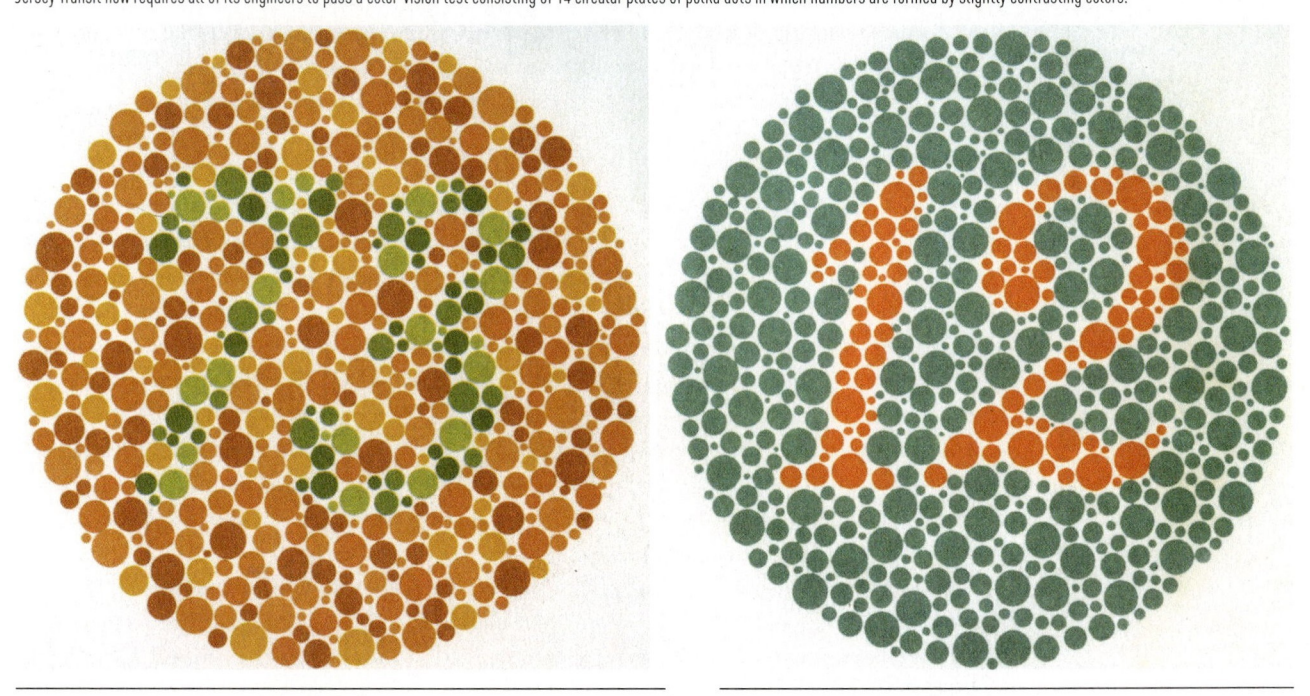

Album / Alamy Stock Photo

PRISMA ARCHIVO / Alamy Stock Photo

LEARNING CHECK

The Eyes Have It

Below are parts of the visual system, listed alphabetically. Rearrange them in the order in which they process visual input, starting with the first part of the eye to receive light and ending with the part of the brain that processes visual information.

| Cornea |
| Iris |
| Lens |
| Optic chiasm |
| Optic nerve |
| Pupil |
| Retina |
| Thalamus |
| Visual cortex |
| Vitreous humor |

(Answer: cornea, iris, pupil, lens, vitreous humor, retina, optic nerve, optic chiasm, thalamus, visual cortex.)

Hearing

If you had to lose your sense of either sight or sound, which would you choose? It is easy to take the sounds of everyday life for granted—and, indeed, we often say that "silence is golden." But auditory sensations surround us and inform us: the chatter of voices, music throbbing from stereo speakers, the trickling of water over pebbles, the crunching of potato chips, the hum of a fluorescent lamp, the crack of a wooden bat against a baseball, the clinking of champagne glasses on New Year's Eve, the screeching of brakes, and the chime of an incoming text message. In fact, we are so dependent on noise that U.S. regulators are requiring electric cars to make sounds when traveling at speeds over 18.6 miles per hour (Matousek, 2018). If you aren't sure why this is so important, think about trying to cross the street with nothing but your auditory senses to rely on. But what is sound, and how do we hear it?

Sound Waves

audition. The sense of hearing.

Every sensation is born of energy. For vision, or seeing, the stimulus is light. For **audition**, or hearing, the stimulus is sound. As in light, sound travels in waves. Physically, sound is *vibration*, a pattern of rapid wavelike movement of air molecules. First, something has to move—an engine, vocal cords, violin strings, or clapping hands. The movement jolts the surrounding molecules of air, and these collide with other air molecules. Like the ocean, sound ripples in waves that ebb and flow in all directions. It loses energy from one ripple to the next, however, which is the reason sound fades at a distance. Sound travels through air at 750 miles per hour—much slower than the speed of light, which is 186,000 miles per second. That is why, in thunderstorms, you see lightning before you hear the accompanying thunder.

Like light, sound waves can be distinguished by three major properties, as summarized in Table 3.2. The first is wavelength, or *frequency*. As molecules of air push outward from a source, they expand and compress in cycles. Frequency, measured by the number of cycles completed per second, is expressed as hertz (Hz). One cycle per second equals 1 Hz. Subjectively, the frequency of a sound wave determines its *pitch* (the highness or lowness of a sound). The higher the frequency, the higher the pitch. In May 2018, pitch became a popular Google search thanks to the "Yanny vs. Laurel debate." A viral tweet by YouTube personality Cloe Feldman played an audio track that divided listeners into two camps; people heard either "Yanny" or "Laurel" (Gutman, 2018). To demonstrate that all listeners could hear both names with a simple adjustment to pitch, software developer Steve Pomeroy created an audio file posted on SoundCloud (Gutman, 2018). When the pitch dropped by 30 percent, listeners most likely heard "Laurel." When the pitch raised by 30 percent, the listeners most likely heard "Yanny." Thus, the apparatus we use to play an audio file can make all the difference. This is why sound engineers and headphone settings have so much influence on what we hear.

Humans can hear frequencies ranging from about 20 Hz to 20,000 Hz—in music, the equivalent of almost 10 octaves. Homing pigeons and elephants can hear lower frequencies. Bats, dogs, and dolphins hear at higher frequencies (dogs can hear at 50,000 Hz, which is why a "silent" dog whistle is not silent to a dog). Most of the sounds we need to hear, and certainly those we enjoy hearing, are well within this range. The lowest note on a piano is 27.5 Hz, the highest note is 4,180 Hz, and the voices of conversation range from 200 to 800 Hz. When all frequencies of the sound spectrum are combined, they produce a hissing sound. This hissing is called **white noise**—named by analogy to the white light that results from the combination of all wavelengths in the visible light spectrum.

white noise. A hissing sound that results from a combination of all frequencies of the sound spectrum.

The second property of sound is *amplitude*. Amplitude refers to the intensity, or height, of each sound wave. In physical terms, the amplitude of a wave determines its *loudness*. The greater the

TABLE 3.2 ■ Physical and Sensory Dimensions of Sound

Physical Dimension	Sensory Dimension
Frequency	Pitch
Amplitude	Loudness
Complexity	Timbre

amplitude, the louder the sound. We may not be able to hear a pin drop, but our ears are responsive to a remarkably wide range of amplitudes. For variations within this range, amplitude is measured in decibels (dB). Figure 3.12 provides examples of the loudness of various sounds at different dB levels. You will see that dB levels over 120 are painful and can cause permanent damage to the ears (Kryter, 1994).

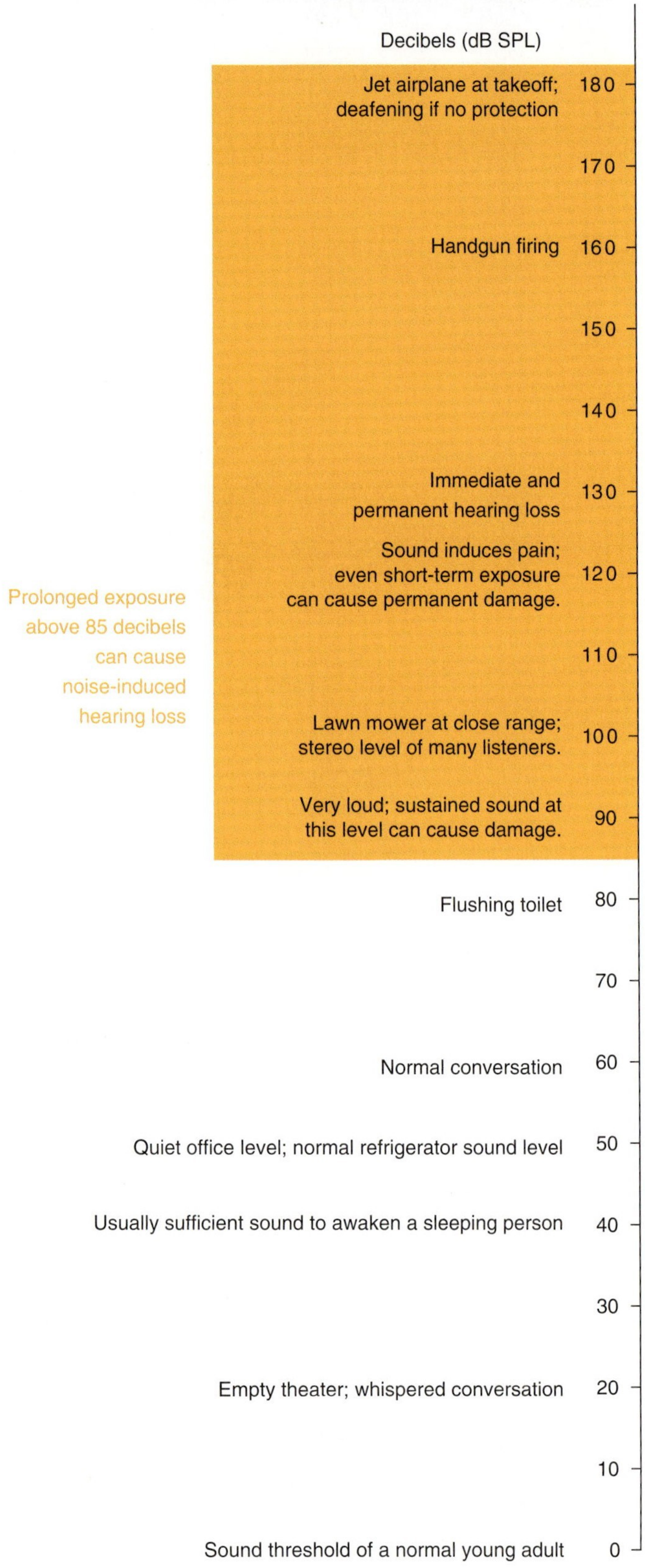

A third property of sound is purity, or *complexity*. Strike a tuning fork, and you will produce something rare: a pure tone consisting of a single frequency of vibration. In reality, most sounds are complex mixtures of waves of different frequencies. Speech, music, a ringing bell, and a breaking window are familiar examples (Bregman, 1990; Krumhansl, 1991). The complexity of a sound determines its *timbre*, or tonal quality. Play the same note at the same loudness on a piano, trumpet, saxophone, tuba, and violin, and what you will hear are differences in timbre.

The Auditory System

Philosophers like to ponder the age-old question, "If a tree falls in a forest, but no one is around to hear it, does it make a sound?" This really is a profound question. We know that the fall of a tree sends waves of molecules blasting through the air, but we also know that without an auditory system to catch these molecules—well, you make the call. As in vision, hearing requires that energy be detected, converted into neural impulses, and relayed to the brain. As shown in Figure 3.13, this complex process begins in the three-part (outer, middle, and inner) structure of the human ear.

Sound waves are collected in the *outer ear*, beginning with the fleshy pinna. Some animals, such as dogs, cats, and deer, can wiggle this structure like a radar dish to maximize the reception of sound (humans cannot). Research shows that the folds of the pinna enable people to pinpoint the location of sounds—for example, whether they come from above us or below, in front or behind. The sound waves are then funneled through the auditory canal to the eardrum, a tightly stretched membrane that separates the outer and middle portions of the ear. The eardrum vibrates back and forth to the waves, thereby setting into motion a series of tiny connecting bones in the *middle ear*—the hammer, the anvil, and the stirrup (for you trivia buffs, these are the three smallest bones in the body). This middle-ear activity amplifies sound by a factor of 30. The last of these bones, the stirrup, then vibrates against a soft *inner-ear* membrane called the oval window. This vibration is transmitted to the fluid that fills the canals of the cochlea, a snail-shape tube—and the resulting motion presses up against the basilar membrane, which brushes up against an array of 16,000 sensitive hair cells. These hair cells bend, exciting fibers in the auditory nerve—a bundle of axons that link to auditory centers of the

FIGURE 3.12 ■ **Common Sounds and the Amounts of Noise They Produce, in Decibels**

Decibels (dB SPL)	
Jet airplane at takeoff; deafening if no protection	180
	170
Handgun firing	160
	150
	140
Immediate and permanent hearing loss	130
Sound induces pain; even short-term exposure can cause permanent damage.	120
	110
Lawn mower at close range; stereo level of many listeners.	100
Very loud; sustained sound at this level can cause damage.	90
Flushing toilet	80
	70
Normal conversation	60
Quiet office level; normal refrigerator sound level	50
Usually sufficient sound to awaken a sleeping person	40
	30
Empty theater; whispered conversation	20
	10
Sound threshold of a normal young adult	0

Prolonged exposure above 85 decibels can cause noise-induced hearing loss

FIGURE 3.13 ■ The Human Ear

The process of hearing begins in the three-part (outer, middle, and inner) structure of the ear. From the auditory nerve, signals are relayed to the auditory cortex.

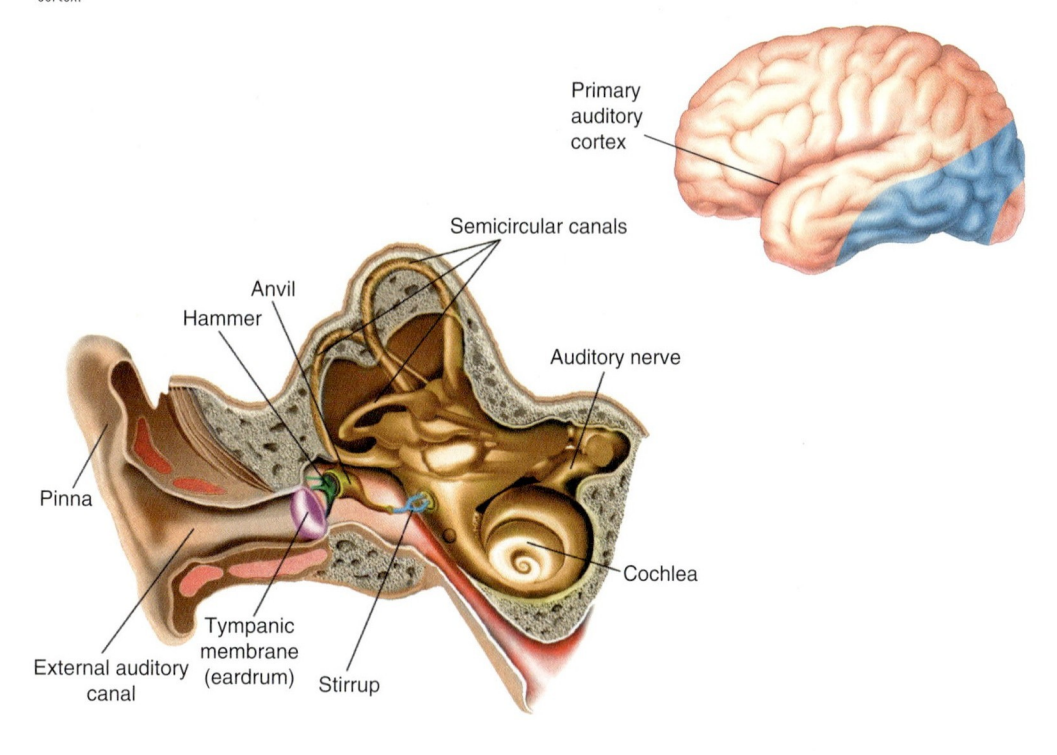

brain. Also in the inner ear are semicircular canals, which, as we will see later, play a critical role in balance (Hudspeth, 2000; Phillips et al., 2015).

To summarize, the "plumbing" and "wiring" that turn sound waves into meaningful input are fairly intricate. Sound waves collected in the outer ear are transmitted into a salt-watery fluid and then transformed into electrical impulses in the inner ear. From the auditory nerve, signals then cross to the other side of the brain. Next, they get routed to the thalamus, where the medial geniculate body transforms the signals en route to the auditory cortex (Bartlett, 2013) to assist with frequency discrimination. Once there, the signals are processed by cells that specialize in high, middle, or low frequencies of sound (Leaver & Rauschecker, 2016).

auditory localization. The ability to judge the direction a sound is coming from.

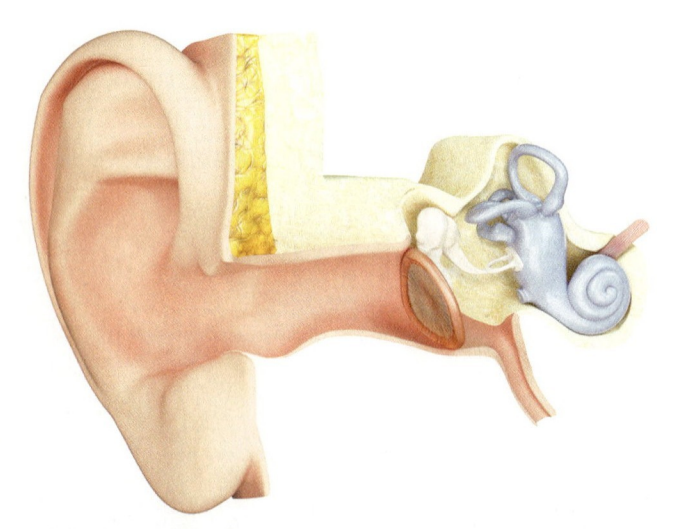

In this image of the middle ear, you can see the eardrum (left), hammer (top), anvil (center), and stirrup (right). The stirrup is connected to the cochlea, which houses the hair cells.

iStock.com/Didacta_produktionsbyra

Hearing Abilities

Hearing is not one sensory ability but many. People can detect sound, understand spoken language, and appreciate the acoustical qualities of music. Those with normal hearing can distinguish between sounds that are loud and soft or between those produced by horns and those produced by stringed instruments. Although only 1 in 10,000 people have "absolute pitch "(an ability to identify a musical note as middle C, F-sharp, or B-flat), we can all make judgments of "relative pitch"—enabling us to know, for example, that a child's voice is higher than a man's (Oxenham, 2018; Takeuchi & Hulse, 1993). In many ways, our auditory competence is impressive.

A particularly adaptive aspect of normal hearing that we take for granted is **auditory localization**—the ability to tell the *direction* a sound is coming from. Localization is needed to determine if the blaring siren you hear is coming from behind you on the road, or if the approaching footsteps are coming from your left or your right. This skill was vital to the survival of our primitive ancestors and is a matter of life and death to all animals of prey.

It is usually easy to tell if a sound is coming from your left or your right, and those who are not hard of hearing or deaf have auditory localization even as infants. In fact, if you stand to the left or right of an infant and shake a rattle, the baby will often turn its head in your direction, as if locating the source.

What makes auditory localization possible is that we hear in stereo, using two ears spaced about 6 inches apart. If you are at a noisy gathering and someone on your left calls your name, your left ear receives the signal before your right ear does (it is closer to the source) and more intensely (your head is a barrier to the more distant ear). The 6 inches of brain tissue and skull that separate your ears may seem too little to matter, but the auditory system is sensitive. Unless a sound is directly above, below, in front of, or behind you, the brain can detect small differences in timing and intensity between the ears—and use these differences to locate the source. This process is demonstrated in Figure 3.14 (Konishi, 1993; Middlebrooks & Green, 1991). Researchers are now suggesting that vision also plays a role in auditory localization, since congenitally blind participants demonstrate difficulty with some auditory localization tasks (Cappagli, Cocchi, & Gori, 2017; Vercillo, Burr, & Gori, 2016).

Hearing Loss

It is natural to take your sensory competence for granted—until you do not have it. Today, millions of people have hearing loss, ranging from a partial loss to profound deafness. There are two kinds of hearing loss. The symptoms are the same, but the causes and treatment are very different. One type is **conductive hearing loss**, in which damage to the eardrum or to the bones in the middle ear diminishes their ability to conduct sound waves. In this case, hearing can be partially restored through surgery or by means of a hearing aid that amplifies sound waves—provided that the inner-ear structures are intact (Ahmadi, Daramadi, Asadi-Samani, & Sani, 2017; Woods et al., 2015). By contrast, **sensorineural hearing loss** results from inner-ear damage to the cochlea, hair cells, or auditory nerve. Sensorineural hearing loss can be caused by certain diseases or genetic mutations, by biological changes due to old age, or by exposure to intensely loud noises (Tremblay, 2015). Some species can regenerate hair cells, but humans are not one of them (Burns & Corwin, 2013). However, genetic research on a mutation that causes hereditary deafness is tapping into hair cell regeneration with the hopes of bringing sound to people who either lost it or never had it (Mahmoodian-sani & Mehri-Ghahfarrokhi, 2017). Thanks to science, we are getting closer to making hair cell regeneration a reality for humans (Lefèbvre, Malgrange, & Moonen, 2008).

Although it is not currently possible to regenerate working auditory hair cells in humans and although conventional hearing aids do not fully restore hearing in sensorineural hearing loss, cochlear implants have the ability to bypass hair cell function (McCreery, Han, Pikov, Yadav, & Pannu, 2013). A cochlear implant uses a tiny microphone to transmit sound to a processor worn behind the ear (similar to a hearing aid). The processor then transmits the sound as an electrical signal to a miniature electrode implanted in the cochlea (National Institute on Deafness and Other Communication Disorders [NIDCD], 2018). The electrode stimulates the auditory nerve—and an

conductive hearing loss. Hearing loss caused by damage to the eardrum or bones in the middle ear.

sensorineural hearing loss. Hearing loss caused by damage to the structures of the inner ear.

FIGURE 3.14 ■ Auditory Localization

The brain is able to detect small differences in the timing and intensity of sound between the two ears—and can use these differences to localize the source.

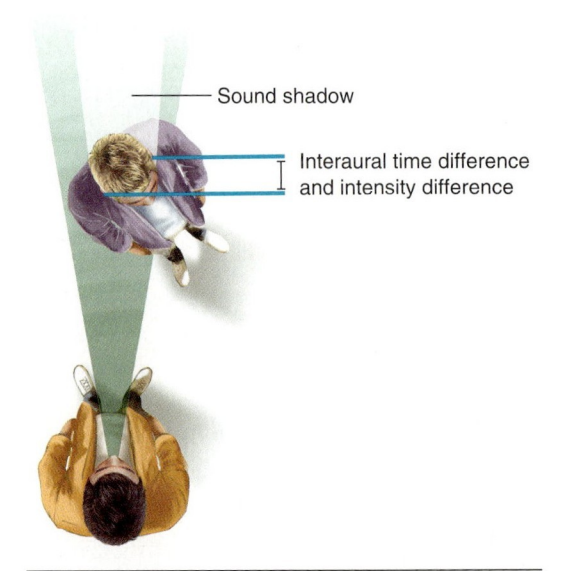

Source: Garrett, Brain and Behavior, 5e, 2018, SAGE Publications, Inc

impulse is fired to the brain. Cochlear implants may enable many people who are profoundly deaf or severely hard-of-hearing to detect the presence of sound. The NIDCD (2018) reports that, worldwide, more than 324,000 devices have been implanted in persons with hearing loss—adults and children—as of December 2012. The sensations produced by these devices seem to vary from one user to another. Some wearers derive little benefit from the implants, but researchers believe benefit is correlated with age at implantation (Bruijnzeel, Ziylan, Stegeman, Topsakal, & Grolman, 2016). A thorough literature review of improved speech and language performance post–cochlear implantation revealed that earlier is better; cochlear implantation before the age of 12 months resulted in better speech production, auditory performance, and receptive language scores (Bruijnzeel et al., 2016). In adults with hearing loss, quality of life for those with cochlear implants was reported to be higher than for those without (Crowson, Semenov, Tucci, & Niparko, 2017). However, these reviewed studies have limitations, and researchers suggest further testing with experimental rigor to determine the replicability and validity of these findings.

Psychology Applied: When Is Loud Too Loud?

My Bloody Valentine is an American rock band known for its high decibel levels. The band's music has been described as "painfully loud—terrifyingly loud" (Richards, 2008). But when does loud become *too* loud, and is loud dangerous only when it becomes painful? The amplitude of a sound, which determines its loudness to the human ear, is measured in terms of decibels (dB). To understand this scale, it is important to know that loudness increases in orders of magnitude (a 20 dB sound is 10 times as intense as a 10 dB sound, a 40 dB sound is 100 times as intense as a 20 dB sound, and so on). Constant daily exposure to sounds of over 85 dB (heavy street traffic, subways, jackhammers, snowmobiles, lawnmowers, and vacuum cleaners) can flatten the inner-ear hair cells over time and cause a gradual loss of hearing. It makes you wonder how many people experience ringing in the ears, which often occurs following exposure to loud sounds.

Ringing in the ears is common. The NIDCD (2016) estimates that 10 percent of Americans have experienced ringing in the ear—tinnitus—and 13 percent of Americans over 12 years of age have suffered from full or partial hearing loss, often because of noise. Even a brief assault by an ear-shattering sound that exceeds 140 dB (a gunshot, an explosion, or a rocket launch) can tear the delicate inner-ear tissues and cause permanent hearing loss. Review Figure 3.14, and you will see that danger to the ear is all around us. Current research on sound exposure focuses on the occupational hazards of noise in work settings and nonoccupational hazards such as power tools or loud music (Hoffman, Dobie, Losonczy, Themann, & Flamme, 2017). Spend 2 hours at a rock concert or turn the stereo volume up to full blast, and you may be putting your ears at risk (West & Evans, 1990). Many experts claim that if your headphones can be heard by someone near you, then you are damaging your ears. And the loss can be irreversible. Many famous musicians, such as Pete Townshend, Sting, Ozzy Osbourne, and Eric Clapton, are now partially deaf. My Bloody Valentine, whose founding member Kevin Shields suffers from tinnitus, provides free earplugs at every concert. This is a wonderful service, especially since hearing damage is a major concern for today's adolescents and young adults (Jiang, Zhao, Guderley, & Manchaiah, 2016). So, turn down the volume, and protect your ears whenever you can, whether while mowing the lawn, vacuuming, or relishing your next live music event.

Other Senses

Psychologists know more about seeing and hearing than about other sensory systems, but these other systems are also essential to the adaptive human package. You cannot see or hear the heat of a fire, the sting of a bee, the stench of a gas leak, or the bitter taste of a poisonous plant. Nor can you see or hear the sensuous pleasures of a scent-filled rose, creamy chocolate, or a soothing massage. Human beings have developed the ability to detect, process, and integrate information from many sources.

Smell

Dogs are known for their ability to sniff out faint scents and to track down animals, criminals, and illegal drugs over time and long distances. In fact, dogs have such a keen sense of smell that they can

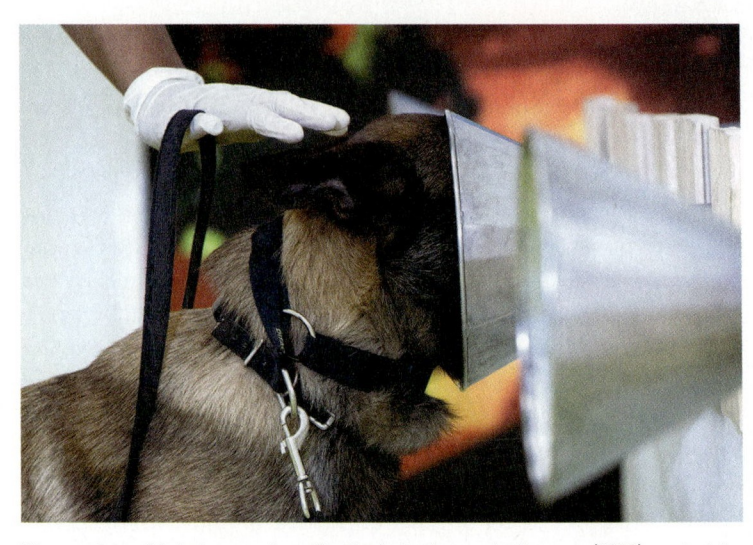

We cannot smell it, but researchers, like Paula Jendrny and colleagues (2020), are training dogs to detect the coronavirus before the most sophisticated technology can.
JOEL SAGET / Contributor/Getty

When airborne odor molecules dissolve in the nose, they are trapped by the hairlike olfactory receptors shown in this image.
Universal Images Group North America LLC / Alamy Stock Photo

detect signs of sleep apnea in urine samples (Koskinen et al., 2018) and harmful bacteria in cow's milk (Fischer-Tenhagen, Theby, Krömker, & Heuwieser, 2018)!

In a contest of smelling ability, we humans would have little to brag about compared to our canine buddies—who may well have the keenest noses in the animal kingdom (Marshall & Moulton, 1981). But our own sense of smell, the product of the body's **olfactory system**, is more sensitive than you may realize—and potentially more important. Since ancient times, medical doctors used the smell of sweat, breath, urine, and other body odors to diagnose illness. Recently it was even discovered that Joy Milne, a woman living in the United Kingdom, can detect Parkinson's disease by smell (Quigley, 2015). Milne is so accurate that, during one controlled trial, she corrected researchers when they presented her with an olfactory sample from a participant they thought was Parkinson's free; they were wrong, and Milne correctly diagnosed the disease with nothing but her sense of smell. The fact that she is a woman may not be a coincidence. Research has found that women tend to have greater olfactory acuity than men (Dalton, Doolittle, & Breslin, 2002; Lundstrom & Hummel, 2006; Tubaldi, Ansuini, Tirindelli, & Castiello, 2008).

All smells have a chemical origin (Buck, 2000). Depending on their molecular structure, substances emit odor-causing molecules into the air. Some objects, such as glass and metal, have no smell (any scent these objects may emit comes from impurities on the surface). Other objects, like the musk oil extracted from animal sweat glands, produce overpowering odors. By breathing through the nose and mouth, we inhale these airborne odorant molecules—which dissolve and become trapped by *olfactory receptors* in the moist yellow lining of the upper nasal passages just above the roof of the mouth. There are about 10 million of these hairlike receptors in the human nose (the average dog has 200 million). Certain molecules seem to fit certain types of receptors the way a key fits a lock. Once activated, they trigger an action potential in the *olfactory nerve*. This nerve connects the nose to the *olfactory bulb*, a bean-size organ that distributes information throughout the cortex and to the nearby limbic-system structures that control memory and emotion. Smell is the only sensation that is not routed to the cortex through the thalamus. As illustrated in Figure 3.15, the olfactory bulb is its own private relay station (Doty, 2001).

Unlike other animals, humans do not need a sense of smell to mark territory, track prey, signal danger, establish dominance hierarchies, or attract a mate. Also, language does not provide an adequate supply of olfaction words, which makes it hard for people to describe smells (Richardson & Zucco, 1989). Yet the millions of olfactory receptors in the nose enable us to distinguish among 10,000 different odor molecules—including the proposed "primary" odors of vinegar, roses, mint, rotten egg, mothballs, dry-cleaning fluid, and musk (Amoore, Johnston, & Rubin, 1964). Brain-imaging technology demonstrates that laboratory rats have a unique pattern of receptor activity in the olfactory bulb

olfactory system. The structures responsible for the sense of smell.

FIGURE 3.15 ■ The Olfactory System

Once in the nose, odorant molecules are trapped by olfactory receptors. These receptors send signals through the olfactory nerve to the olfactory bulb, which communicates with various parts of the brain.

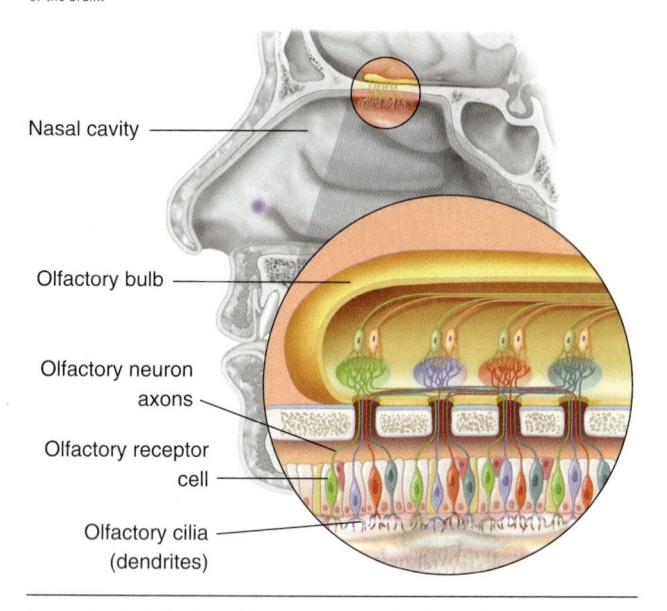

- Nasal cavity
- Olfactory bulb
- Olfactory neuron axons
- Olfactory receptor cell
- Olfactory cilia (dendrites)

Source: Garrett, Brain and Behavior, 5e, 2018, SAGE Publications, Inc

pheromones. Chemicals secreted by animals that transmit signals—usually to other animals of the same species.

gustatory system. The structures responsible for the sense of taste.

taste buds. Nets of taste-receptor cells.

and cortex in response to odors (Isaacson, 2010; Osmanski et al., 2014).

People from different cultures have the same olfactory capacity—and similar likes and dislikes when it comes to the smell of plants, fruits, spices, and body odors. Universally, people are drawn to flowers and other perfume-like fragrances and disgusted by foul and sulfurous odors (Miller, 1997). At the same time, people from different parts of the world are uniquely and adaptively attuned to the smells that surround them. In *Aroma: The Cultural History of Smell*, Classen, Howes, and Synnott (1994) illustrate the point in several cultures. In an Amazonian rain forest in Colombia, the Desana separate the musky smell of "deep forest" animals (such as the jaguar), and the sweet smell of "open field" animals (such as various rodents). They also say they can detect by nose the presence of different neighboring tribes—based on whether those tribes eat a steady diet of hunted game, fish, or roots and vegetables.

Smell is a primitive sense—yet so successful, suggests Diane Ackerman (1990), "that in time the small lump of olfactory tissue atop the nerve cord grew into a brain" (p. 20). Given this view, it is hardly surprising that researchers have tried to identify pheromones in human beings. **Pheromones** are chemicals secreted by animals that transmit signals to others, usually of the same species. Ants, bees, termites, and other insects secrete chemicals that attract mates and "release" other behaviors. Equipped with sensitive chemoreceptors on his antennae, for example, the male emperor moth can detect the scent of a virgin female more than 6 miles away. Many mammals are also sexually excited by scent, which is why female dogs in heat send neighboring male dogs into a state of frenzy. Are humans similarly aroused? If so, could the scent be bottled and manufactured? For perfumers, the potential is easy to imagine. At this point, however, the research evidence is scant. Human sexuality is far too complex to be chemically "controlled" by scent. However, some researchers have found evidence that human pheromone can attract our attention and impact emotional centers in the brain (Ferdenzi, Delplanque, Atanassova, & Sander, 2016; Hummer, Phan, Kern, & Mcclintock, 2017).

Taste

Taste is a product of the body's **gustatory system** (Doty, 1995; Santa-Cruz Calvo & Egan, 2015). Like smell, taste is a chemical sensation. Put a morsel of food or a drop of liquid on your tongue, and it will come into contact with clusters of hairlike receptor cells called **taste buds** (illustrated in Figure 3.16). There are about 10,000 taste buds in the mouth. Some cling to the roof and back of the throat, but most line the trenches and bumps on the surface of the tongue. Taste buds are packed most densely on the tip of the tongue but are virtually absent from the center of the tongue. Within each taste bud, between 50 and 150 receptor cells absorb the chemical molecules of food and drink—and trigger neural impulses that are routed to the thalamus and cortex. These cells are replaced every 10 days, so if you burn your tongue on hot soup, the damage to your receptors will be repaired.

There are five primary tastes: sweet, salty, sour, umami, and bitter (Calvo & Egan, 2015). Researchers have also found evidence that the tongue can detect fat (Fukuwatari et al., 1997; Martin et al., 2011). All of your taste buds can react to these primary tastes, regardless of their location on your tongue. However, the *flavor* of a food is determined not only by taste but by other factors as well. You may have noticed that after you have brushed your teeth in the morning, orange juice tastes bitter. Chemical residues from the substance already eaten mix with what you are currently eating to produce a new taste sensation. Temperature, texture, and appearance are also important factors, which is why no one likes warm soda or soggy potato chips and why the great chefs prepare dishes for the eye as well as for the palate. By far the most important determinant of flavor is odor; it accounts for about 80

FIGURE 3.16 ■ Taste Buds

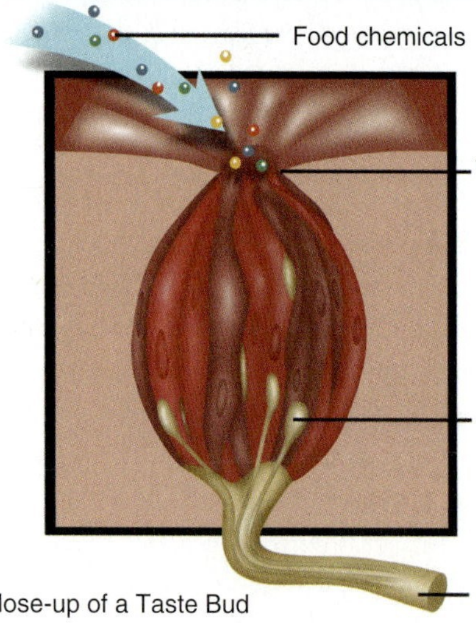

Close-up of a Taste Bud
- Food chemicals
- Taste bud pores
- Synapse
- Gustatory nerve to brain

This microphotograph is a section of the taste bud receptors of a human tongue, magnified 400 times.

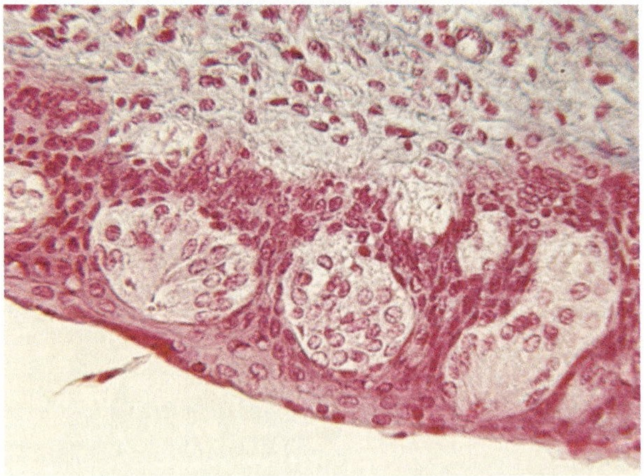

Gwen Shockey / Science Source; DE AGOSTINI PICTURE LIBRARY / Contributor/Getty

percent of the taste we experience (Chartier, 2012). When you have an illness that stuffs up your nose (Wolf, Renner, Tomazic, & Mueller, 2018), or COVID-19 (Parma et al., 2020), food does not quite taste the same. Indeed, research shows that people lose their ability to identify common flavors—such as chocolate, vanilla, coffee, wine, and even onion and garlic—when they are prevented from smelling the food (Mozell, Smith, Smith, Sullivan, & Swender, 1969). Furthermore, the flavors we become accustomed to are influenced by our culture (Spence, 2015). For example, Spence (2015) mentions that people from Japanese cultures are frequently exposed to almonds in savory dishes with pickled condiments, whereas those from Western cultures more often experience almonds in sweet dishes, like cakes and toffee.

The more taste buds that dot your tongue, the more sensitive you are likely to be to various tastes. Children have more taste buds than adults do, for example, which may explain why they are often so picky about eating "grown-up" foods. Even among adults, individuals differ in the number of taste buds they have—and in their sensitivity to taste (Herbert, Platte, Wiemer, Macht, & Blumenthal, 2014). Indeed, studies have shown that people can be divided into three groups: nontasters, medium tasters, and supertasters (Tepper et al., 2009). At one extreme, nontasters (30 percent of the population) are unable to detect certain sweet and bitter compounds and are in general less sensitive to taste. At the other extreme, supertasters (about 25 percent of the population) react strongly to certain sweet and bitter compounds. Compared to most, supertasters use half as much sugar or saccharin in their coffee or tea. They also are more likely to experience a burning sensation in response to the active ingredient in chili peppers. These differences in taste sensitivity correspond nicely to our physiological makeup. Using videomicroscopy to count the number of taste buds on the tongue, researchers have found that nontasters have an average of 96 taste buds per square centimeter, medium tasters have 184, and supertasters have 425. Put differently, the number of taste buds on the human tongue can range from a low of 500 to a high of 10,000 (Bartoshuk & Beauchamp, 1994; Miller & Reedy, 1990).

Touch

Every organism has a sense of touch. Sea snails withdraw their gills at the slightest pressure. Sponges sense an intruder by feeling the water around them quiver. As for us humans, often feeling is believing. Put up a "wet paint" sign, and you will find, paradoxically, that it seems to invite touching rather than inhibit it. Tactile sensations are unique in many ways. To begin with, touch is the only sensation with receptors that are not localized in a single region of the body. We need eyes to see, ears to hear, a nose to smell, and a tongue to taste. But the organ of touch, and the site of its sensory receptors, is *skin*.

Skin is by far the largest organ of the body. It covers two square yards and weighs 6 to 10 pounds. It is multilayered, waterproof, and elastic, and is filled with hair follicles, sweat-gland ducts, and nerve endings that connect to the central nervous system. When you consider all the sensations that emanate from your skin—feeling hot, cold, wet, dry, sore, itchy, scratchy, sticky, gooey, greasy, tingly, numb, and hurt—you can see that touch involves not one sensory system but many (Craig & Rollman, 1999; Heller & Schiff, 1991; Zimmerman, Bai, & Ginty, 2014).

The sensations of touch are vital for survival and socialization. Without it, you would not know that you are in danger of becoming frostbitten or burned; you would not know if you have been stung by a bee; you would be unable to swallow food; and, according to an interview with David Linden, it would be difficult to bond. David Linden, an expert on touch at Johns Hopkins University, states that humans have an emotional touch system that sends information to a part of the brain "crucial for socially-bonding touch. This includes things like a hug from a friend, to the touch you got as a child from your mother, to sexual touch" (Stromberg, 2015). Mammals deprived of touch during development have demonstrated psychological issues, higher than average levels of stress hormones, and immune deficiencies (Ardiel & Rankin, 2010).

When other sensory systems fail, touch takes on even more importance. For Virgil, the blind man whose eyesight was restored temporarily, shapes and textures were particularly important for recognizing objects. When Virgil was handed a bowl of fruit, he could easily distinguish among a slick plum, a soft fuzzy peach, a smooth nectarine, and a rough, dimpled orange. He was even able to "see" through the disguise of an artificial wax pear that had fooled everyone else. "It is a candle," he said, "shaped like a bell or a pear" (Sacks, 1995, p. 149).

It is important to distinguish between passive and active touch. In passive touch, a person's skin is contacted by another object, as when a cat rubs up against your leg. In active touch, it is the person who initiates the contact, as when you pet your cat. Psychologically, the effects are different. James Gibson (1962) tested subjects' ability to identify cookie cutters shaped like stars, triangles, circles, and so on. When the objects were pressed lightly onto the hand (passive), they were identified correctly 29 percent of the time. When subjects actively explored the shapes with their fingers, the accuracy rate increased to 95 percent. Other research, too, shows that people can make fine discriminations among common objects when they explore by grasping, lifting, holding, squeezing, rubbing, and tracing the edges. For example, merely touching an object reveals temperature, rubbing a finger across it reveals texture, and molding the hand around it reveals its shape and volume (Klatsky & Lederman, 1992).

Active touch is what allows Virgil to feel the differences among plums, peaches, oranges, and nectarines. It is also the key to *Braille*, the alphanumeric system that allows many blind people to read. Braille letters and numbers consist of coded patterns of raised dots on a page that readers scan with their fingertips. Some Braille readers achieve a reading rate as high as 200 words per minute—which is remarkable considering that the average rate among sighted readers is 250 words per minute (Foulke, 1991). In one experiment, people who were blind that used their Braille-reading fingers outperformed blindfolded sighted adults by 20 percent in their ability to discriminate different shapes by touch (Stevens, Foulke, & Patterson, 1996).

The skin contains a wide range of sensory neurons such as nociceptors for pain, pruriceptors for itch, thermoreceptors for temperature, and low-threshold mechanoreceptors for touch (Zimmerman et al., 2014). One of the most striking aspects of touch is that sensitivity to pressure or vibration is different from one part of the body to another. To determine the thresholds for touch (how much force it takes before a subject reports a feeling), researchers would apply a thin rod or wire to different areas of skin and vary the pressure (Weinstein, 1968). In all cases, pressure causes nerve endings to fire messages through the spinal cord, brainstem, and thalamus en route to the somatosensory cortex (Burton & Sinclair, 1996; Greenspan & Bolanowski, 1996).

What's Your Prediction?

People can distinguish objects by touch. Can we also identify live human faces in this way? If so, do we rely on "geometric" cues (like nose size and cheekbone structure) or "material" cues (like skin texture and temperature)? Andrea Kilgour and Susan Lederman (2002) had college students manually explore an unfamiliar live face up to the hairline. All the students wore blindfolds, headphones, and nasal ointment to ensure that they relied only on a sense of touch. Afterward, they tried to identify that face by hand from a group of three faces. Keeping in mind that they could guess correctly 33 percent of the time, how accurate do you predict the students were—33, 50, 75, 90, or 100 percent? What if they felt plaster masks of the same faces, which preserved geometric information but not material cues? Would that make them more accurate or less? The results were interesting. Students who felt live faces were accurate 79 percent of the time; those who felt masks were accurate in 59 percent of their identifications. Apparently, we *can* recognize faces by hand, by using both geometric and material cues.

Temperature

Normal human body temperature is 98.6 degrees Fahrenheit, or 37 degrees Celsius (temperatures at the surface of the skin are slightly lower). There are two striking facts about the sensation of temperature. First, temperature is, to a large extent, *relative* to your current state. To demonstrate, fill three buckets with tap water—one cold, one hot, and one at room temperature. Place your right hand into the cold water and your left hand into the hot water, and leave them there for a minute. Then place both hands together into the third bucket. You can probably predict the amusing result: Both hands are now in the same water, yet your right hand feels warm and your left hand feels cool. If you ever plunged into a cold pool or eased yourself into a hot tub, you know that the sensations are triggered by temperatures that are well above or below your own current "adaptation level" (Hensel, 1981).

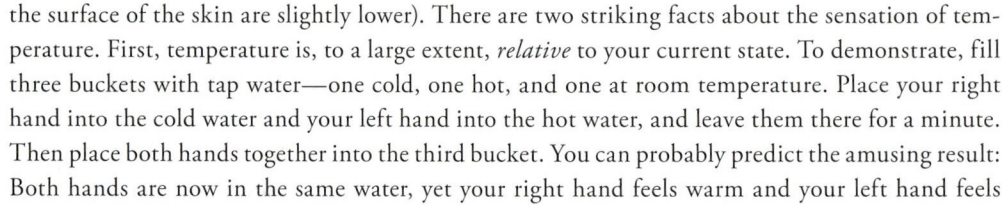

The second fact about temperature is that there are two separate sensory systems—one for signaling warmth, the other for signaling cold. Early studies showed that some spots on the skin respond more to warming and others more to cooling (Dallenbach, 1927). "Hot" is a particularly intriguing sensation in that it is triggered when these warm and cold spots are simultaneously stimulated. Thus, when people grasp two braided pipes—one with cold water running through it, the other with warm water—they will pull away, complaining that the device is literally too hot to handle, as illustrated in Figure 3.17. This effect of the "thermal grill," first described by Torsten Thunberg (Jutzeler, Warner, Wanek, Curt, & Kramer, 2017) is found not only among humans but also in other animals (Bach, Becker, Kleinbohl, & Holzl, 2011; Bouhassira, Kern, Rouaud, Pelle-Lancien, & Morain, 2005; Kammers, de Vignemont, & Haggard, 2010). Apparently,

Using Braille, persons who are blind can navigate a computer using their sense of touch.
iStock.com/zlikovec

FIGURE 3.17 ■ The Thermal Grill

When people use only a single hand to touch both cold and warm temperatures at once, the resulting sensation is "very hot" and painful. The apparatus used to create this sensation is called a thermal grill. Scientists have conducted thermal grill studies for decades, but they remained baffled by the phenomenon until now. Lindstedt and colleagues (2011) built their own thermal grill, much like the one you see here, and tested 20 participants' response to the grill while in an fMRI scanner. The result? Study participants had busy activity in the thalamus and the brain's pain matrix.

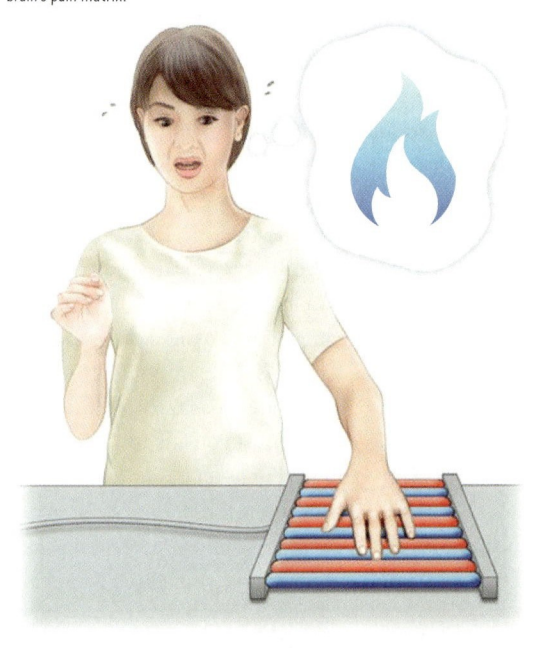

Carolina Hrejsa/Body Scientific Intl.

the brain interprets the dual firing of both types of temperature receptors as being caused by a burning hot stimulus. Is the sensation a mere illusion? No. Neuroimaging studies show that gripping the entire grill (but not the warm or cold bars alone) activates regions of the brain that process unpleasant stimuli (Casey & Bushnell, 2000; Craig, Reiman, Evans, & Bushnell, 1996; Hofbauer, Rainville, Duncan, & Bushnell, 2001).

Pain

Pain is a dentist's drill boring through a tooth. Pain is stepping on a thumbtack. Pain is a pulled muscle, a splitting headache, a backache, sunburn blisters, and stomach cramps. Ouch! Whatever the source, people are understandably motivated to avoid and escape from pain. Yet pain is crucial to survival because it serves as a red flag, a warning system that signals danger and the risk of tissue damage. Life without pain may sound great, but it would be a life unlikely to last very long. The case studies of children with a pain-specific genetic mutation illustrate the point. Born with a congenital indifference to pain, these children often injure themselves without realizing it. For example, these children are reported to repeatedly bang their heads on the floor, bite into their tongues, and cut their hands—all without a pain response. As a result, their bodies are often marked by burns, cuts, scrapes, and bruises (Mansouri et al., 2014; Restak, 1988; Shorer, Wajsbrot, Liran, Levy, & Parvari, 2014).

For those of us who do feel pain, it is a subjective, emotionally charged sensation. No single stimulus triggers pain the way that light does vision, no nerve endings in the skin are specially dedicated to pain over other sensations, and people with similar injuries often experience different degrees of pain. Clearly, the conditions that lead us to report pain include not only the threat of bodily harm but also culture, religion, personality, expectations, and other factors. Even gender plays a role, as male research subjects tend to have a greater tolerance for painful stimulation than do female subjects (Berkely, 1997; Keogh & Herdenfeldt, 2002). Why might this be? Some argue that it is the role our society places on males to be tough. When a male child cries, it is not abnormal to hear a caretaker say, "Boys don't cry." Others argue that it might be a biological, or sex, difference. Regardless, theories of pain must take into account all of these factors (Gatchel & Turk, 1999; Kruger, 1996) and, thus, lean toward a biopsychosocial model (Bartley & Fillingim, 2013; Gatchel, Peng, Peters, Fuchs, & Turk, 2007).

Gate-Control Theory. If you have a sore leg muscle or if you scrape your knee, nerve endings in the skin send messages to the spinal cord through one of two types of nerve fibers. Dull, chronic aches and pains—as in a sore muscle—are carried to the spinal cord by "slow," thin nerve fibers that also respond to nonpainful touch. Sharp, acute, piercing sensations—as when you scrape your knee—are relayed through "fast" myelinated fibers. In short, an express lane to the spinal cord is reserved for acute, emergency-like sensations. But how are these signals then sent from the spinal cord to the brain? And can they be blocked when the pain is too intense to bear?

In an attempt to answer these questions, Ronald Melzack and Patrick Wall (1965) proposed the **gate-control theory** of pain. According to this theory, the nervous system can process only a limited number of sensory signals at once. When the system is full, a neural "gate" in the spinal cord either blocks or allows the upward passage of additional signals to the brain (the gate is not an actual structure but a pattern of inhibitory neural activity). Research shows that although Melzack and Wall were wrong about the physiological details of their theory, and the gate seems to be a bit "leaky" instead of a perfect barrier (Sun et al., 2017), they were generally right about the key point: Strong pain signals to the brain can be blocked (Melzack & Wall, 2001; Mendell, 2014; Pereira & Lerner, 2017).

This theory has a valuable practical implication: that you can partially shut the gate on pain by creating competing sensations. If you fall and hurt your knee, rubbing it hard will send new impulses into the spinal cord—and inhibit other pain signals. That is one reason it often helps to put ice on a bruise or to scratch the skin near a mosquito bite. For chronic pain, such interventions as deep massage, electrical stimulation, and acupuncture may provide temporary relief in the same way. It seems paradoxical, but as the theory correctly suggests, you can ease the pain by causing additional pain.

---

gate-control theory. The theory that the spinal cord contains a neurological "gate" that blocks pain signals from the brain when flooded by competing signals.

Psychological Control. One psychological approach people often use is to block the pain from awareness. Just try not to think about it, okay? This advice sounds great, but beware: The strategy can backfire. Research shows that the more we try to suppress a particular thought, the more readily that thought pops to mind. Try not to think about the itch you are not supposed to scratch, and the harder you try, the less likely you are to succeed (Wegner, 1989). For adaptive reasons, pain sensations may be particularly hard to suppress. Almost regardless of where we are, whom we are with, and what we are doing, pain has a way of stealing the spotlight of our attention (Eccleston & Crombez, 1999). But too much attention to pain can lead to depression, so the person suffering from pain has to find a balance (Hulsebusch, Hasenbring, & Rusu, 2016).

One popular method believed to reduce a sufferer's pain experience during medical procedures is distraction (Ryckeghem, Damme, Eccleston, & Crombez, 2018). In studies of pain tolerance, researchers have found that people can best manage the effects of intense physical discomfort—and exhibit less activation in pain-responsive areas of the brain—by focusing their attention on something else, preferably something pleasant like a picture, music, film, odor, or even a virtual reality environment (Inal & Kelleci, 2012; Malloy & Milling, 2010; Villemure & Bushnell, 2002). This is why children are asked to play a game when given a shot. In terms of chronic pain, however, the findings across several studies demonstrate that distraction has no significant impact on the pain experience or distress (Ryckeghem et al., 2018). As we will learn in Chapter 4, hypnosis can also be used to combat pain, in part through a refocusing of attention (Martin et al., 2018). Mind over sensation.

Coordination

The five traditional senses and their subdivisions are vital adaptive mechanisms, but by themselves they do not enable us to regulate sensory input through movement. To bend, lean, stretch, climb, turn the head, maintain an upright posture, and run from danger, we need to sense the parts of our bodies as well as our orientation in space. The **kinesthetic system** monitors the positions of various body parts in relation to each other. Just as vision comes to us through sensory receptors in the eye, coordination of movement is provided by receptors in the joints, tendons, and muscles. These receptors are linked to motor areas of the brain. Without this system, an acrobat could not turn somersaults and cartwheels. Nor could gymnasts, dancers, and athletes perform their feats of bodily magic. Nor, for that matter, could we walk upright, deliver a firm handshake, aim food into our mouths, or touch our noses with the tip of the index finger.

A related sensory mechanism is provided by the **vestibular system**, which monitors head tilt and location in space. Situated in the inner ear, this system has two parts: the *semicircular canals*, three fluid-filled tubes that are set at right angles to one another; and two *vestibular sacs*, which are also filled with fluid. Whenever you move about, the movement rotates and tilts your head, causing the fluid to slosh back and forth, which pushes tiny hair cells. In turn, these hair cells send impulses to the cerebellum, which signals from moment to moment whether you are sitting, lying down, or standing on your head. The vestibular system provides us with the sense of equilibrium, or balance. But sometimes this delicate sense is disrupted by an excess of fluid, floating particles, an infection, or by certain types of motion. The result may be car sickness, sea sickness, or the dizzying aftereffects of twirling in circles (Filippopulos et al., 2017; Howard, 1986; Thompson & Amedee, 2009).

kinesthetic system. The structures distributed throughout the body that give us a sense of position and movement of body parts.

vestibular system. The inner ear and brain structures that give us a sense of equilibrium.

From hanging upside down, to seamlessly unraveling as they descend, aerial silk performers exhibit a remarkable sense of coordination and location in space thanks to the kinesthetic and vestibular systems.

iStockphoto.com/sundrawalex

Keeping the Signals Straight

In a world filled with lights and colors, voices and musical tones, smells and tastes, and feelings of cold, warmth, pressure, pain, and other sensations, our sensory abilities seem marvelously adaptive. How do we bring in so much information without becoming overwhelmed? With neural impulses flooding the brain from different receptors throughout the body, it is amazing that we do not get our signals crossed. Why is it that we see light and hear sound rather than the other way around?

There are, however, interesting exceptions. Exhibiting a very rare condition known as **synesthesia** ("joining the senses"), some individuals report that they experience sensory "crossovers"—that bright lights are loud, that the sound of a jazz trumpet is hot, that colors can be felt through touch, or that they can "enjoy the sweet smell of purple" or "taste the sound of raindrops" (Stein & Meredith, 1993). As described in Richard Cytowic's (1999) *The Man Who Tasted Shapes*, a number of fascinating cases have been reported over the years. Recent studies indicate that the condition is found in only 1 out of 2,000 people—and that most are women (Cytowic, 2002; Harrison, 2001).

Can the self-reports of those claiming to have synesthesia be trusted? Although there is reason to be skeptical, recent studies provide intriguing evidence. In one study, nine women with word-color synesthesia and nine control subjects were asked to report on the color sensations triggered by 130 letters, words, and phrases. When retested a year later, without warning, the synesthetic women reported the identical sensations 92 percent of the time—compared to only 38 percent in the control group. In a second study, six synesthetic women and six control subjects listened to words while blindfolded. PET scans revealed that this auditory stimulation activated the language areas of the brain in both groups. Among the synesthetic women, it also activated certain areas of the *visual* cortex (Paulesu et al., 1995). Other studies, too, have provided independent evidence of this rare condition in adults (Martino & Marks, 2001; Smilek, Dixon, Cudahy, & Merikle, 2002) and children (Simner & Bain, 2013; Simner, Harrold, Creed, Monro, & Foulkes, 2009). In fact, some argue that we are all born with synesthesia (Maurer & Maurer, 1988; Spector & Maurer, 2011), but the evidence is debatable (Deroy & Spence, 2013).

Although there are exceptions, our sensory systems generally do not cross. The reason is that different receptors are sensitive only to certain types of energy and stimulate only certain nerve pathways to the brain. Rods respond to light, not to sound, and they transmit impulses through the optic nerve, not the auditory nerve. There may be "normal" exceptions—as when pressing on a closed eyelid stimulates the optic nerve and causes you to "see" a flash of light—but each sensory system operates independent of the others (Gardner & Martin, 2000).

Two other aspects of sensation enable us to respond to volumes of information without confusion. First, all of our sensory systems are designed to detect novelty, contrast, and change—not sameness. After constant exposure to a stimulus, sensation fades. This decline in sensitivity is known as **sensory adaptation**. We saw earlier that the eyes gradually adapt to bright light and darkness. The same is true of the other senses. After a while, you simply get used to the new contact lenses in your eyes, the new watchband on your wrist, the noise level at work, or the coldness of winter. To those sensitive to smells that often pervade the hallways of apartment buildings (or dormitories), it is comforting to know that people also adjust to chronic odors (Dalton & Wysocki, 1996; Pellegrino, Sinding, Wijk, & Hummel, 2017; Yoder et al., 2014). By adapting to repeated stimulation, you are free to detect important changes in the environment.

A second adaptive mechanism is selective attention. People can choose to focus on some sensory input and block out the rest. This selective attention enables us to pick out a face or a voice in a crowded room or to find distractions from pain and discomfort. Parents thus can hear their baby cry over the sounds of a TV, traders on the floor of the stock exchange can hear orders to buy and sell amid all the noise, and commuters in a city can spot yellow cabs in the street through all the commotion of rush-hour traffic. People are not passive sensation-recording devices. We have a way of "zooming in" on sensations—such as pain—that are personally important.

---

synesthesia. A rare condition in which stimulation in one sensory modality triggers sensations in another sensory modality.

sensory adaptation. A decline in sensitivity to a stimulus as a result of constant exposure.

> **LEARNING CHECK**
>
> **Common Senses**
>
> Listed below are the five traditional senses, plus two additional sensory systems covered in this chapter. Choose among them for answers to the questions below.
>
> | a. Vision b. Hearing c. Smell d. Taste e. Touch f. Kinesthetic System g. Vestibular System |
> |---|
>
> 1. Which is the only sense to bypass the thalamus?
> 2. Which is the only sense whose receptors are not localized in a single area of the body?
> 3. Which sense uses the three smallest bones in the body?
> 4. Which sense uses rods and cones?
> 5. Which sense enables you to touch the tip of your nose with your eyes closed?
> 6. Which sense tells you if your soup is too salty?
> 7. Which sense enables you to keep your balance?
>
> (Answers: 1. smell; 2. touch; 3. hearing; 4. vision; 5. kinesthetic system; 6. taste; 7. vestibular system.)

PERCEPTION

> **LEARNING OBJECTIVES**
>
> Summarize the steps we take to perceive our world as adults.
>
> - List the ways that perception is an active mental process.
> - Discuss how we manage to identify objects despite apparent changes in their size, shape, and other features.
> - Describe how we perceive depth in three-dimensional space.
> - Examine whether our perceptual skills are inborn or learned from experience.
> - Critique why humans fall prey to perceptual illusions.

Our sensory systems convert physical energy from a multitude of sources into neural signals that are transmitted to the brain. But we do not see inverted retinal images, hear the bending and swaying of hair cells in the cochlea, or smell the absorption of odorant molecules in the nose. These and other sensations must be further processed to make sense. Perception is not a mere "copying" process, and the brain does more than just serve as a sensory screenshot. As perceivers, we must select, organize, and interpret input from the world in ways that are adaptive. Putting the sensory pieces together is a "constructive" mental process (Brown, 2017; Gibson, 2015; Palmer, 1999).

To illustrate this point, consider the image in Figure 3.18. Some people might see an elegant young woman looking over her right shoulder. But as the caption reveals, the picture is a **reversible figure**, and it could also be seen as an elderly woman with a very prominent nose and chin. Do you see both images? Look away for a few seconds, and then look back. Can you see the elderly woman and the young woman? The lines and shading have not changed, but if you look at the young woman's chin as a nose, the choker necklace as a mouth, and the ear as an eye, you might be able to switch your brain into perceiving the elderly woman.

Maybe not. The point is, visual input can often be processed in different ways, as illustrated in Figure 3.19. The sensation may be the same, but the perception can vary from one person and moment to the next.

reversible figure. A drawing that one can perceive in different ways by reversing figure and ground.

FIGURE 3.18 ■ A Reversible Figure

Is this a young woman or an older woman? Visual input can be perceived in different ways.

Source: This image is available from the United States Library of Congress's Prints and Photographs division under the digital ID ds.00175.

Gestalt psychology. A school of thought rooted in the idea that the whole (perception) is different from the sum of its parts (sensation).

FIGURE 3.20 ■ Figure and Ground

Depending on whether the light or dark areas are seen as figural, this drawing may be perceived as a vase or as two people facing each other.

iStock.com/Martin Janecek

FIGURE 3.19 ■ Perception and Interpretation

These drawings have different interpretations. Most people report seeing one interpretation and then the other but never both simultaneously.

When Virgil's eyesight was restored at the age of 50, he was able to detect lights, shadows, colors, shapes, and textures, but he could not separate one figure from another or identify common objects just by looking at them. In busy settings such as a supermarket, he was so overwhelmed by sensory information that "everything ran together." In this section, we examine the ways in which the brain organizes and interprets sensory input. As much of the research does, we will focus on visual perception.

Perceptual Organization

In 1912, Max Wertheimer discovered that people perceive two stationary lights flashing in rapid succession as a single light moving back and forth. This illusion of apparent motion explains why we see flashing neon signs as a continuous stream rather than as a series of separate lights. At the time, this illusion also paved the way for **Gestalt psychology**—a school of thought arising in Germany that was founded on the premise that the whole (perception) is different from the sum of its parts (sensations). The word *gestalt* is German for "pattern" or "whole," and Gestalt psychologists believed that humans have an inborn tendency to construct meaningful perceptions from fragments of sensory input. A classic example is the way we listen to music. A melody has a form that is different from the individual notes that make it up. So, if the melody is transposed to another key, even if that means changing every note, listeners would still recognize the music because its form would be the same. The perception of music is based on a gestalt, not on a particular set of notes (Koffka, 1935; Kohler, 1947; Schindler, Herdener, & Bartels, 2013). The same is true of the way people view and extract meaning from works of art and complex visual scenes (Livingstone, 2002; Wagemans et al., 2012).

Figure and Ground

The first gestalt principle of perceptual organization is that people automatically focus on some objects in the perceptual field to the exclusion of others. What we focus on is called the *figure*. Everything else fades into the *ground*. A teacher standing in front of a blackboard, the printed black words on a page or screen, the lights on the car ahead of us on a dark highway, a scream in the night, and the lead singer's voice in a rock band—all are common figures and grounds. Gestalt psychologists were quick to point out that these perceptions are in the eyes (or ears) of the beholder—but also that we are prone to "figurize" objects that are close to us, novel, intense, loud, and moving rather than still. Even ethnicity and culture are believed to play a role in what is perceived as figure versus ground (Valarmathi et al., 2021). As in the reversible figure in Figure 3.18, however, the image in Figure 3.20 demonstrates that we can mentally flip-flop the figure and ground from one moment to the next. It is as if each of us is shining a spotlight on a portion of the sensory field—and can move that spotlight if necessary.

FIGURE 3.21 ■ Gestalt Laws of Grouping

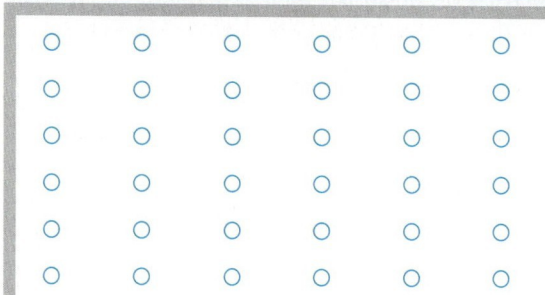

a. **The law of proximity.** You will see this arrangement as a set of columns—not a set of rows. Items that are near each other are grouped together. Now notice the typing in this book. You see rows of letters rather than columns because a letter is closer to the letters to the right and left than it is to the letters above and below.

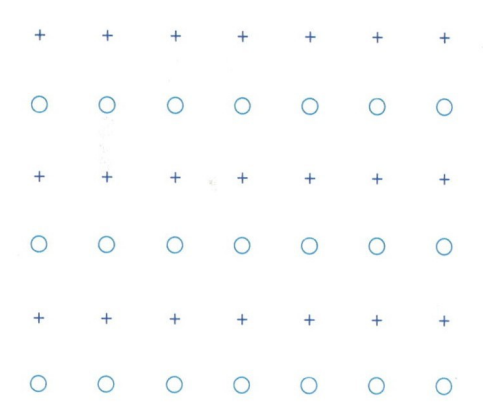

b. **The law of similarity.** You will see this arrangement as a set of rows rather than columns. Items that are similar to each other are grouped together. Now look at the two words at the end of this sentence that are in **boldface type**. Notice how these two words in heavier print cling together in a group, whereas the words in regular, lighter print form their own separate groups.

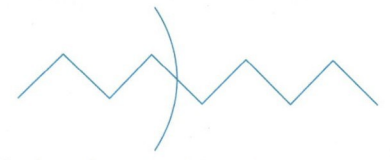

c. **The law of good continuation.** You will see a zigzag line with a curved line running through it, so that each line continues in the same direction it was going prior to intersection. Notice that you do not see the figures as being composed of the two elements below.

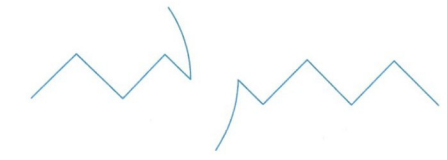

Look out the window at the branches of a tree, and focus on two branches that form a cross. You clearly perceive two straight lines, rather than two right angles touching each other.

d. **The law of closure.** You will see a circle here, even though it is not perfectly closed. A complete figure is simply more tempting than a curved line! Now close this book and put your finger across one edge, focusing on the shape of the outline of your book. You should still see your book as complete, but with a finger in front of it.

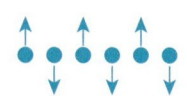

e. **The law of common fate.** If dots 1, 3, and 5 suddenly move up and dots 2, 4, and 6—at the same time—suddenly move down, the dots moving in the same direction will be perceived as belonging together. The next time you look at automobile traffic on a moderately busy street, notice how clearly the cars moving in one direction form one group and the cars moving in the opposite direction form another group.

Gestalt Laws of Grouping

Another principle of perceptual organization is that we tend to group collections of shapes, sizes, colors, and other features into perceptual wholes. The natural grouping tendencies are not arbitrary; rather, they follow simple rules like those shown in Figure 3.21. The Gestalt psychologists argued that these tendencies are inborn, and they may have been right. Research shows that even young infants "group" stimulus objects in the predicted ways (Bhatt & Quinn, 2011; Quinn, Burke, & Rush, 1993; White, Jubran, Heck, Chroust, & Bhatt, 2018). Some of these laws of grouping are as follows:

- **Proximity.** The closer objects are to one another, the more likely they are to be perceived as a unit.
- **Similarity.** Objects that are similar in shape, size, color, or any other feature tend to be grouped together.
- **Good Continuation.** People perceive the contours of straight and curved lines as continuous flowing patterns.
- **Closure.** When there are gaps in a pattern that resembles a familiar form, people mentally "close" the gaps and perceive the object as a whole. This tendency enables us to recognize imperfect representations in hand drawings, written material, and so on.
- **Common fate.** Extending on the static grouping principles of proximity and similarity, we find that objects moving together in the same direction, or sharing a "common fate," are perceived as belonging to a single group. Examples include marching bands, schools of fish, flocks of birds, and sports fans sending the "wave" around a stadium.

The principles of Gestalt psychology describe how people transform raw visual input—lights, shadows, lines, points, shapes, and colors—into meaningful displays. More recent research has focused as well on the question of how our brains combine these simple features into larger units, enabling us to identify common objects such as chairs, airplanes, bottles, and so on. According to Irving Biederman (1987), people can recognize common objects from a quick glance, based on exposure times as brief as one-tenth of a second. The reason, he says, is that we perceive objects by breaking them down into simple, three-dimensional component shapes called *geons* ("geometric ions") and then matching the unique pattern of shapes to "sketches" stored in memory. Biederman has identified 36 geons that, when combined (as illustrated in Figure 3.22), enable us to identify the essential contours of all objects—the way that an alphabet of 26 letters can be used to form thousands of words.

Theories of how people organize visual information and identify common objects help to explain the effortless nature of perception—and the confusion that results when figures are concealed from view through camouflage. But what happens to our perception of an object when its retinal image changes from one moment to the next? How do we know that objects have depth when the images projected on the retina are flat and two-dimensional? How are interpretations of input influenced by characteristics of the perceiver? As we will see, people are highly adept, yet often fooled, by disparities between sensation and perception.

Perceptual Constancies

Unlike a camera or microphone stationed on a tripod, the human perceiver is active and mobile. And unlike the portrait or landscape hanging on a wall, many of the objects that humans perceive are likewise active and mobile. As the perceiver and perceived move about, the image projected on the retina may change in size, shape, brightness, color, and other properties. But this is not a problem. Thanks to perceptual constancies, perceptions remain stable despite radical changes in sensory input (Dosher & Lu, 2017; Rock, 1997). As an example, consider **size constancy,** the tendency to view an object as constant despite changes in the size of its image on the retina. This is a common phenomenon. Imagine an observer watching from the ground as an airplane pokes its nose through a cloud to descend for a landing. As the plane approaches, its image looms larger and larger. Or another observer watches a friend walk away. As the friend walks away, the image gets smaller and eventually fades into the distance. The changing sensations might lead the observers to think that the airplane was growing and that the friend was shrinking right before their eyes.

size constancy. The tendency to view an object as constant in size despite changes in the size of the retinal image.

FIGURE 3.22 Identifying Objects

According to Biederman, people perceive objects by breaking them down into simple, three-dimensional component shapes called geons (a). Just as letters of an alphabet can be combined to produce a large number of words, combinations of geons create thousands of different objects (b).

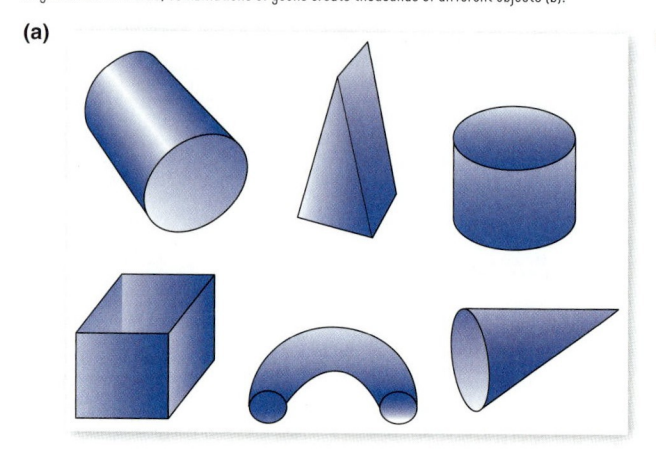

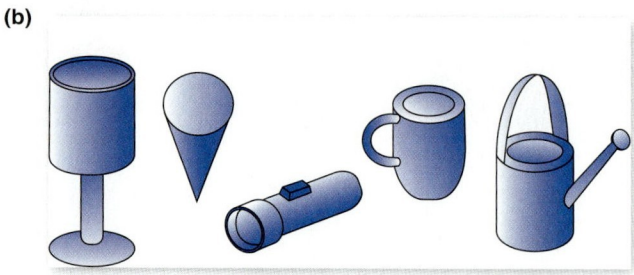

But we know better—for two reasons. One has to do with experience and familiarity. We know that airplanes are bigger than people and that people are bigger than insects, so our perceptions remain stable despite variations in retinal image size. Distance cues provide a second source of information. As objects move around in space, we perceive the change in distance and adjust our size perceptions accordingly. In other words, we know that the closer an object is, the larger the image it casts on the retina, so we make the adjustment.

This skill is so basic that it can be observed in infants at 4 months of age. Carl Granrud (2006) habituated 4-month-olds to an object: either a disk 6 centimeters in diameter at a distance of 18 centimeters or a disk 10 centimeters in diameter at a distance of 50 centimeters. After habituation, both objects were presented side by side to the infants at a distance of 30 centimeters. The goal was to determine if infants were able to differentiate between physical size and retinal size. Thus, during the objects' presentation, one test object had the same physical size that it did during habituation, but a novel retinal size, while the other test object had the same retinal size but a novel physical size. Infants looked longer at the object with the novel physical size, demonstrating that it was not the retinal image they were attending to.

Ponder the following question: Is a zebra a white horse with black stripes or a black horse with white stripes? What would you say? Neither color is figural in Gestalt terms, and answers tend to be split.

iStock.com/pchoui

As demonstrated by Granrud (2006), the capacity for size constancy may be present in infancy, but cultural and environmental experiences also play a role. In 1961, anthropologist Colin Turnbull studied Pygmies who lived in a densely wooded central African forest. At one point, he took a Pygmy named Kenge for a Jeep ride out of the forest. It was Kenge's first trip away from home—and he was disoriented. Standing on a mountain overlooking miles of open plain, Kenge saw buffaloes and thought they were insects. Then he saw a fishing boat in the middle of a lake and thought it was a floating piece of wood. The problem? Turnbull (1961) came to realize that "in the forest the range of vision is so limited that there is no great need to make an automatic allowance for distance when judging size" (p. 252).

Note that these cupcakes are the same size even though the images they project on your retina shrink with distance.
FOODSTUFF / Alamy Stock Photo

depth perception. The use of visual cues to estimate the depth and distance of objects.

convergence. A binocular cue for depth perception involving the turning inward of the eyes as an object gets closer.

binocular disparity. A binocular cue for depth perception whereby the closer an object is to a perceiver, the more different the image is in each retina.

monocular depth cues. Distance cues, such as linear perspective, that enable us to perceive depth with one eye.

Depth and Dimension

Perceptual constancies enable us to identify objects despite changes in sensory input. But there's another problem: How do we know that objects in three-dimensional space have depth, and how do we perceive distance when images projected on each retina are flat and only two-dimensional? Two types of information are used in **depth perception**: binocular cues and monocular cues.

Binocular Depth Cues

With eyes on the sides of their heads, deer, sheep, and other prey can use peripheral vision to see predators sneaking up from behind. By contrast, the eyes of lions, owls, and other predators are squarely at the front of the head, an arrangement that maximizes depth perception and enables them to track their prey. Human eyes are the eyes of a predator. Our binocular (two-eyed) vision, in turn, allows us to use two binocular depth cues: convergence and binocular disparity.

Convergence refers to the fact that the eyes turn in toward the nose or "converge" as an object gets closer, and move outward or "diverge" to focus on objects farther away. Hold your finger up at arm's length and slowly move it toward your nose. As you refocus, you can actually feel your eye muscles contracting. This signals the brain about the object's distance from the eyes.

The second cue is **binocular disparity**. With our eyes set about 2.5 inches apart on the face, each retina receives a slightly different image of the world. To demonstrate, hold your finger about 4 inches from your nose and shut your right eye. Then shut only your left eye and look at the finger. Right. Left. As you switch back and forth, you will see that each eye picks up the image from a slightly different vantage point. Now hold up your finger farther away, say at arm's length, and repeat the routine. This time you will see less image shifting. The reason: Binocular disparity decreases with distance. Special neurons located in the visual cortex use this retinal information to "calculate" depth, distance, and dimensionality (Cumming & DeAngelis, 2001).

If two eyes combine to give a three-dimensional look at the world, can flat pictures do the same? In the 19th century, British physicist Charles Wheatstone invented the first stereoscope—an optical instrument that brought two-dimensional pictures to life. To create the illusion, Wheatstone photographed a scene twice, using two cameras spaced inches apart. He then mounted both pictures side by side on the device, using mirrors to overlap the images. This technique underlies the View-Master—a toy that shows three-dimensional scenes in double-view cardboard slides. It is also used in virtual reality (VR) systems and the Nintendo 3DS (Tidbury, Black, & O'Connor, 2015).

Monocular Depth Cues

Binocular depth cues are useful at short distances. But for objects that are farther away, convergence and binocular disparity are uninformative. At such times, we can utilize **monocular depth cues**, which enable us to perceive depth, quite literally with one eye closed. These are cues that many artists use to bring a flat canvas to life. What are they? Figure 3.23 describes the cues and illustrates them with accompanying images.

Origins of Depth Perception

With normal vision, interpreting the layout of objects in an environment is easy and requires no conscious thought or effort. Why is depth perception so easy? Clearly, a rich array of depth cues is available to one or both eyes—especially when we are moving about (Gibson, 1979). But how do we know how to interpret these cues? Are we born with these skills, or do we learn them from experience?

FIGURE 3.23 ■ Monocular Depth Cues

Relative image size. We saw earlier that as the distance of an object increases, the size of its retinal image shrinks—and vice versa. Object size can thus be used to judge depth.

The Photo Works / Alamy Stock Photo

Texture gradient. As a collection of objects recedes into the horizon, they appear to be spaced more closely together, which makes the surface texture appear to become denser.

iStockphto.com/MikeMareen

Linear perspective. With distance, the parallel contours of highways, rivers, railroad tracks, and other rowlike structures perceptually converge—and eventually reach a vanishing point. The more the lines converge, the greater the perceived distance.

Vassilis Spiliotopoulos / Alamy Stock Photo

Interposition. As most objects are not transparent, those nearer to us will partly or completely block our view of more distant objects. This overlap provides a quick and easy way to judge relative distances.

National Geographic Image Collection / Alamy Stock Photo

Atmospheric perspective. The air contains a haze of dust particles and moisture that blurs images at a distance. This blurring, or atmospheric perspective, makes duller and less detailed objects appear farther away.

iStockphoto.com/Pgiam

Familiarity. Experience provides familiar reference points for judging distance. We know the approximate size of certain objects, and this knowledge helps us judge their distance. In fact, the presence of a familiar object in a scene helps us judge the sizes and distances of everything around it, like our familiarity with the famous Taj Mahal.

Marina Pissarova / Alamy Stock Photo

Virtual reality headsets contain two miniature screens for stereo vision. To simulate reality, they are most realistic at short distances when they display separate but overlapping images to each eye.

Drew Angerer / Staff/Getty

Perceptual Experience. The average person has an enormous amount of experience with depth perception. Is this experience necessary? Case studies of blind people who had their eyesight surgically restored during adulthood suggest that experience is critical to depth perception. Sacks (1995) observed that Virgil sometimes stepped over shadows so that he would not trip or failed to step up on a staircase that, for all he knew, was a flat surface consisting of parallel and crossing lines. Richard Gregory (1998) studied a similar patient by the name of S.B. and described his perception of depth as "peculiar." At one point, S.B. thought he could touch the ground below his hospital window with his feet—even though his window was on the fourth floor. The importance of perceptual learning and experience is also evident in cross-cultural studies. We saw earlier that when a Pygmy named Kenge was taken from his dense forest home to the open plain, he saw distant buffaloes as insects and a large boat as a floating log. As described at the start of this chapter, research also shows that people who lack exposure to three-dimensional representations in artwork find it difficult to judge relative distance from pictures (Deregowski, 1989).

Depth Perception as Inborn. Experience may seem necessary, but studies of infants suggest otherwise. Infants cannot tell us what they see, so Eleanor Gibson and Richard Walk (1960) devised the **visual cliff**, a clever nonverbal test of depth perception. As demonstrated in Figure 3.24, the apparatus consists of a glass-covered table top, with a shallow one-inch drop on one end and a steep "cliff" on the other end. Infants ages 6 to 14 months were placed in the middle of the table, and their mothers tried to lure them into crawling to one side or the other. The entire surface was covered by sturdy transparent glass, so there was no real danger. The result: Six-month-old babies would crawl to their mothers at the shallow end. But despite all the calling, clapping, waving, and encouragement, most did not crawl out over the cliff. Clearly, they had perceived the steepness of the drop.

visual cliff. An apparatus used to test depth perception in infants and animals.

Does the visual cliff experiment prove that depth perception is innate? Not necessarily, argued critics. Perceptual learning begins at birth, so by the tender age of 6 months an infant has already experienced over a thousand waking hours—and has experienced plenty of perceptual practice. What about younger babies? They may not be able to crawl, but their bodies can communicate to an astute researcher. Accordingly, Campos, Langer, and Krowtiz (1970) moved 2-month-old infants from one side of the glass top to the other and found that the infants exhibited a change in heart rate when placed over the deep side but not over the shallow side. These infants were too young to fear the situation as we would, but they "noticed" the difference.

The development of this famous study did not happen overnight (Rodkey, 2015). It took several animal studies conducted by Gibson and Walk to eventually evolve into the visual cliff study we talk about today. The intriguing experiment that inspired the visual cliff was one created by Gibson where rats were raised in an environment completely absent of light (Rodkey, 2015).

In an attempt to replicate the surprising results with other animals, Gibson and Walk also tested chicks, turtles, lambs, kid goats, pigs, kittens, dogs, and monkeys. Kittens raised in the dark did not avoid the cliff. However, a mere 6-day exposure to the light changed their response. Kittens exposed to light for this amount of time did avoid the cliff, and they did not need to experience a fall to learn said avoidance. Eventually, Walk (1981) published findings collected from other animals such as newborn lambs, chicks, ducklings, pigs, cats, and rats.

This begs the question, is depth perception innate or is it the product of visual experience? As the pieces of the puzzle have come together, it seems that both factors are at work. Using binocular

FIGURE 3.24 ■ The Visual Cliff

This apparatus is used to test depth perception in infants and animals.

Source: Levine, Laura E.; Munsch, Joyce, Child Development From Infancy to Adolescence: An Active learning Approach, 1e, SAGE Publications (2015).

FIGURE 3.25 ■ Perceptual Set

What someone sees in the middle drawings depends on the order in which they look at the pictures. Subjects who start at the far left see the drawings in the middle as a man's face; those who start at the far right see a woman's figure.

Adapted from Heuer Jr., Richards J., Psychology of Intelligence Analysis. Center for the Study of Intelligence. 1999.

cues—and, later, monocular cues—infants are capable of perceiving depth and dimension. But early experience is necessary for this skill to emerge. Thus, formerly blind humans have trouble making judgments of depth when their eyesight is surgically restored. As the saying goes, you have to "use it or lose it."

FIGURE 3.26 ■ Context Effects

Indicating the effects of context on perception, people see the middle item as *B* or *13* depending on whether it is surrounded by letters or numbers.

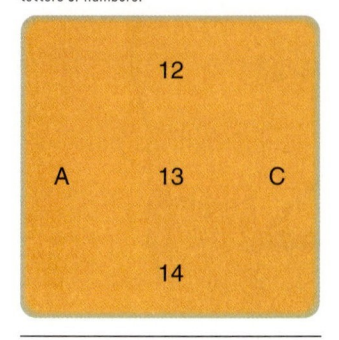

Jerome S. Bruner & A. Leigh Minturn (1955) Perceptual Identification and Perceptual Organization, The Journal of General Psychology, 53:1, 21-28, DOI: 10.1080/00221309.1955.9710133

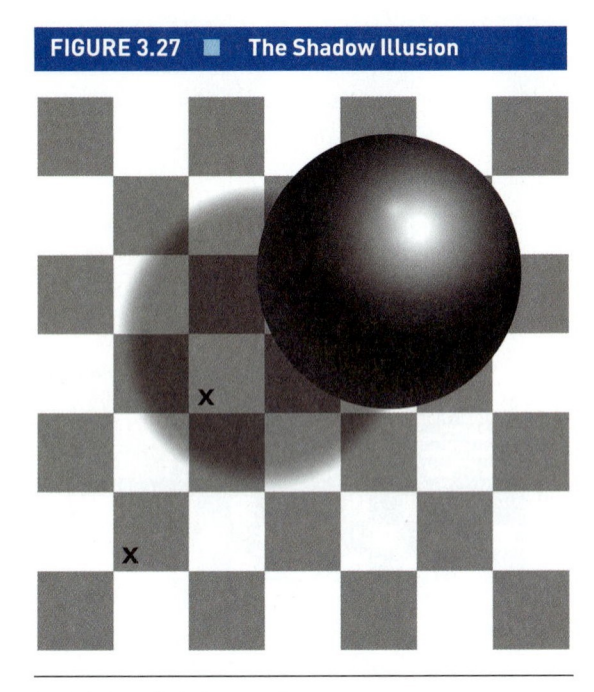

FIGURE 3.27 ■ The Shadow Illusion

iStockphoto.com/PeterHermesFurian

Perceptual Set

perceptual set. The tendency to perceive or notice some aspects of the available information due to our past experiences or the context

At any given moment, the interpretation of sensory input can be influenced by prior experiences and expectations, which create a **perceptual set**. To illustrate, review Figure 3.25. The middle drawings in this series are ambiguous: They can be seen as either a man's face or the figure of a kneeling young woman. Do people tend to see the man's face, or the kneeling young woman? It turns out that interpretations are biased by prior experience. Subjects who were first shown the drawing on the far left saw the middle pictures as a man's face, whereas those who were first shown the drawing on the far right saw the same pictures as a kneeling woman (Fisher, 1968). This finding highlights an important point about perception: At times, we see what we expect to see (Bruner & Potter, 1964).

Perceptual sets are established not only by past experience but also by the context in which a stimulus is perceived. In Figure 3.26, for example, the same physical pattern of black and white is used for the letter *B* as for the number *13*. Close inspection shows that the *B* and *13* are physically identical. Which of the two is "seen" depends on whether the surrounding context consists of letters or numbers.

The same phenomenon can influence perceptions of color. Review the shadow illusion presented in Figure 3.27. Two squares are marked with an "X." These two squares appear to be different shades of gray, even though they are the same shade of gray. The colors seen depend in part on the broader context in which they appear (Hoffman, 1998).

The World of Illusions

perceptual illusions. Patterns of sensory input that give rise to misperceptions.

The brain's capacity to transform sensations into accurate perceptions of reality is impressive. Without conscious thought, effort, or instruction, we often manage to perceive size, shape, depth, and other properties in an accurate manner. But the mind also plays tricks on us. Magicians, ventriloquists, and artists count on it. So do perception psychologists. Over the years, researchers have learned a great deal about how people perceive the world by probing the systematic ways in which they also *mis*perceive the world. From the mirage that glistens as wet on a highway to the fastball that looks as if it is rising, and whether we should avoid wearing horizontal stripes, **perceptual illusions** are all around us (Rodgers, 1998; Thompson & Mikellidou, 2011; Wade, 1990).

FIGURE 3.28 ■ The Müller-Lyer Illusion

FIGURE 3.29 ■ The Moon Illusion

Viewed low over the Tampa, Florida, skyline, the moon seems larger than when it is seen higher in the sky above the city of Abu Dhabi, in the United Arab Emirates.

iStock.com/mokee81

Anne Clark / Alamy Stock Photo

What is interesting about perceptual illusions is that they often stem from the overapplication of rules that normally serve us well. Review the two vertical lines on the left side of Figure 3.28. Which is longer? Most people believe that the line on the right is slightly longer than the one on the left. Measure them, however, and you will discover that they are the same length. As devised by Franz Müller-Lyer, in 1889, these comparisons illustrate the classic and pervasive **Müller-Lyer illusion**.

Why is the Müller-Lyer illusion so compelling? There are several possible explanations (Nijhawan, 1991). One is that the arrowed tips trick us into overapplying the linear-perspective depth cues and the principle of size constancy. In Figure 3.28, the vertical configuration depicted on the left resembles the near outside corner of a room or building, whereas the configuration on the right resembles a far inside corner. Because both lines cast equal-size retinal images, we assume that the farther one must be larger. Part of the problem, then, is that people mistakenly apply a rational rule of three-dimensional depth perception—that distance decreases image size—to a flat two-dimensional figure (Gregory, 1998). Interestingly, however, the illusion is not purely visual. It is also found in blindfolded people who make the line judgments by running their fingers along raised plastic lines with arrowed tips (Millar & Al-Attar, 2002).

A second illusion that seems to stem from depth-related cues is the most spectacular but also the most puzzling, as illustrated in Figure 3.29. A full moon appears larger when it is low on the horizon than when it is high in the sky. The moon is the moon, of course. It does not change in size or in its distance from the earth. So, what causes this **moon illusion**?

Müller-Lyer illusion. An illusion in which the perceived length of a line is altered by the position of other lines that enclose it.

moon illusion. The tendency for people to see the moon as larger when it is low on the horizon than when it is overhead.

> ### LEARNING CHECK
>
> **Perceptive Perspective**
>
> From the column on the right, choose the perceptual phenomenon that most closely answers each question:
>
> | | | | |
> |---|---|---|---|
> | 1. | How do you a know that a Frisbee being thrown to you is getting closer, not larger? | a. | Common fate |
> | 2. | Why do your eyes turn inward as that Frisbee gets closer? | b. | Linear perspective |
> | 3. | Why do parallel railroad tracks seem to converge in the distance? | c. | Monocular depth clues |
> | 4. | When you look at a painting, how can you tell which objects are supposed to be close and which are far away? | d. | Convergence |
> | 5. | Why does a steady noise seem to fade into the background after a while? | e. | Perceptual set |
> | 6. | When sports fans do "the wave," why does it look like a wave? | f. | Sensory adaptation |
> | 7. | Why do we often see only what we expect to see? | g. | Size constancy |
>
> (Answers: 1. g; 2. d; 3. b; 4. c; 5. f; 6. a; 7. e.)

Throughout history, scholars have tried to understand this phenomenon. Then in 1962, Lloyd Kaufman and Irvin Rock brought it to the attention of perception psychologists, which stimulated many theories and explanations. Some psychologists claim the illusion is caused by earth-bound depth cues that make the moon seem farther away and thus trick us into "seeing" a larger object. Indeed, if you peer at the low moon through a tube, apart from surrounding cues, it will appear smaller. Others have found that people sometimes perceive the horizon moon as closer, not more distant (Coren & Aks, 1990), and that the illusion does not occur when the target object is a star instead of the moon (Reed & Krupinski, 1992). Then there are those who have demonstrated that the illusion persists even when the moon is projected at different angles without depth cues, as in the total darkness of a planetarium (Suzuki, 1991), and that the illusion can also be created indoors by projecting a point of light straight ahead, horizontally, or elevated at an upward angle (Suzuki, 1998). Ralph Weidner and colleagues believe the explanation could be the unique firing of neural patterns. Their study, which employed fMRI, found that certain parts of the brain were involved in combining retinal size and distance when viewing a digital moon in a three-dimensional virtual environment (Weidner et al., 2014). To this day, the moon illusion—and other psychological phenomena—remains something of a perceptual mystery (Weidner et al., 2014). Psychology has come a long way to help us understand why we perceive the things we do, but there is so much more we still do not know.

Thinking Like a Psychologist About Sensation and Perception

Sensation and perception are processes by which we make sense of the world around us. The process begins with the raw stimuli that impinge on various sensory receptors, sending signals through neural pathways to specialized regions of the brain. In this way, light is converted to vision, vibration to sound, odorant molecules into smell, and so on. That is the physiological part. But the human mind is active, and people do not perceive stimuli the way a photocopy machine reproduces an image. As perceivers, people select, organize, and interpret input from the world in ways that are sensible and adaptive. Thus, perception is an active and constructive mental process.

Human beings are sometimes remarkable in their ability to convert raw sensations into an accurate representation of reality. Without conscious thought, effort, or instruction, we can perceive sizes, shapes, depths, distances, colors, the location of sounds, subtle odors, tastes, touches to the skin, and other properties of our surrounding environment. Yet at times the mind plays tricks on us, fooling us into misperceiving reality, sometimes in predictable ways—as shown in the many demonstrations of perceptual illusions. This dual portrait of human beings is evident in other chapters too. In many ways, we are supremely competent and yet subject to bias and distortion. The trick is to recognize our biases and remember that much of what we perceive is all in our heads.

SUMMARY

Through **sensation** we absorb raw energy with our sense organs. **Transduction** converts this energy into neural signals to the brain, and then we select, organize, and interpret the signals through **perception**. Sensation and perception are interconnected. But they involve different processes.

MEASURING THE SENSORY EXPERIENCE

Psychophysics uses special measuring procedures to study the link between physical stimuli and the sensations they arouse.

Absolute Thresholds
The **absolute threshold** is defined as the smallest amount of stimulation an organism can detect 50 percent of the time.

Signal Detection Theory
The original work on absolute thresholds assumed that the stimulus alone determined the threshold. But **signal-detection theory** takes into account the subject's response bias as well.

Difference Thresholds
Researchers also measure the ability to detect differences between two levels of a stimulus. The smallest detectable change is called the difference threshold, or **just noticeable difference (JND)**. According to **Weber's law**, the JND is a constant proportion of the stimulus, so it increases as the stimulus increases.

SENSATION

Humans have several distinct sensory modalities—more than the so-called five senses.

Vision
The light we see is only a small band in the spectrum of electromagnetic radiation. The physical properties of light waves—length, amplitude, and purity—correspond, respectively, to our sensations of color, brightness, and saturation.

The human eye translates light waves into neural impulses. Light passes through the **cornea**, which bends the light to focus it. Behind the cornea, the ring-shape **iris** controls the size of the **pupil**, the hole through which light enters the eye. The **lens** continues the task of focusing the light, becoming rounder for nearby objects and flatter for remote ones—a process called **accommodation**. After passing through the vitreous humor, the light hits the **retina**, a multilayer screen of photoreceptor cells. The **rods** in the retina are responsible for black-and-white vision in dim surroundings. The **cones**, which provide for color vision, are concentrated in the **fovea**, the center of the retina. With millions of photoreceptors, the eye can adjust to lighting changes through **dark adaptation** and **light adaptation**.

The rods and cones stimulate bipolar and ganglion cells that integrate the information they receive and pass it on to the **optic nerve**, composed of the axon fibers of the ganglion cells. Because the area where the optic nerve enters the eye has no rods or cones, each eye has a **blind spot**.

The two optic nerves meet at the optic chiasm, where the axons split up so that fibers from inside half of each eye cross to the opposite side of the brain. The fibers travel through the thalamus to the **visual cortex**. There the image is processed by specialized neurons called **feature detectors**.

There are two theories of color vision. According to the **trichromatic theory**, the human eye has three types of cones, sensitive to red, green, and blue. However, this theory cannot explain **afterimages**, the visual sensations that linger after prolonged exposure to a stimulus. The **opponent-process theory** also assumes that there are three types of photoreceptors, but it contends that each kind responds to a pair of "opponent" colors. Both theories are correct. The retina contains the types of cones described by the trichromatic theory, but neurons in the thalamus operate in accordance with the opponent-process theory.

Hearing

The stimulus for **audition**, or hearing, is sound—vibrations in air molecules caused by movement of an object. Our sensations of pitch, loudness, and timbre derive from the frequency, amplitude, and complexity of sound waves. **White noise** is the hissing sound we hear when all frequencies of the sound spectrum are combined.

Collected by the outer ear, sound waves travel through the auditory canal to vibrate the eardrum. The vibration continues through the bones in the middle ear, the oval window of the inner ear, the fluid of the cochlea, and the membrane that excites hair cells, which activate the auditory nerve. Like visual impulses, auditory signals cross to the opposite side of the brain and pass through the thalamus before reaching the auditory cortex.

The remarkable faculties of human hearing include **auditory localization**, our ability to judge a sound's direction. There are two types of hearing loss: **conductive hearing loss** (caused by damage to the eardrum or middle-ear bones) and **sensorineural hearing loss** (resulting from damage to the inner ear).

Other Senses

Our sense of smell derives from the **olfactory system**. Odor-causing molecules dissolve and become trapped by receptors in the upper nasal passages, triggering the olfactory nerve. Instead of passing through the thalamus like other sensory information, the impulse goes straight to the olfactory bulb, which distributes the information to the cerebral cortex and to limbic structures. Researchers are investigating whether humans secrete **pheromones**, chemicals that transmit signals to other humans.

Like smell, taste is a chemical sensation. The **gustatory system** begins with **taste buds** in the mouth, which absorb molecules in food or drink and trigger neural impulses to the thalamus and cortex. There are five primary tastes: sweet, salty, sour, umami, and bitter. The flavor of food depends in part on the number of taste buds that dot the tongue and in part on other factors such as odor.

Touch is based in the skin, the body's largest organ. Touch involves many sensory systems and the sensations of pressure, warmth, cold, and pain. Active touch, as used by Braille readers, provides much more information than passive touch.

Temperature is a sensation with two unusual aspects: It is generally relative to a person's current state, and it entails two separate sensory systems—one for signaling warmth and the other for signaling cold.

Pain is a subjective sensation with no single stimulus. The **gate-control theory** suggests that pain signals to the brain can be blocked when they become too intense. This theory explains why pain can often be eased by a competing sensation. Endorphins, the body's natural pain relievers, can also help control pain, as does the psychological technique of distraction.

Our sense of coordination derives from the **kinesthetic system**. Receptors in the joints, tendons, and muscles, linked to motor areas of the brain, help us register the body's position and movements. The related **vestibular system** includes structures in the inner ear that monitor the head's tilt and location in space, giving us our sense of equilibrium.

Keeping the Signals Straight

In the welter of sensations that confront us, three factors help us keep our signals straight. First, the different senses have different receptors—though some people have **synesthesia**, a very rare condition in which one sensory modality triggers sensations in another sensory modality. Second, our senses are built to detect novelty rather than sameness. As a result of **sensory adaptation**, our sensitivity to a stimulus declines as a result of constant exposure. Third, selective attention allows us to focus on one input and to block out the rest.

PERCEPTION

Perception is an active, "constructive" process. As simple **reversible figures** demonstrate, perception involves selecting, organizing, and interpreting sensory information.

Perceptual Organization
Based on the idea that the whole (perception) is different from the sum of its parts (sensation), **Gestalt psychology** studies the way we construct meaningful perceptions. In any perceptual field, we focus on the figure rather than the background. We also group features into perceptual wholes according to the rules of proximity, similarity, good continuation, closure, and common fate.

Perceptual Constancies
Although sensory inputs are always changing, perceptual constancies keep our perceptions stable. Because of **size constancy**, we see an object as retaining its size even when its retinal image grows or diminishes.

Depth and Dimension
Through **depth perception**, flat images on the retina are used to perceive distances in three-dimensional space. One binocular depth cue is **convergence**, the turning inward of the eyes when objects get closer. Another cue is **binocular disparity**, the difference in retinal image between the two eyes. The closer the object is, the greater the disparity. There are also **monocular depth cues** that permit depth perception, including relative image size, linear perspective, interposition, and atmospheric perspective.

Experiments with the **visual cliff** indicate that the capacity for depth perception may be inborn. But case studies of blind people whose eyesight was restored and cross-cultural evidence suggest as well that experience is needed to interpret depth cues correctly.

Perceptual Set
Our prior experience and expectations often create a **perceptual set** that leads us to see what we expect to see.

The World of Illusions
Despite the brain's astonishing feats of perception, it falls prey to various **perceptual illusions**. In the **Müller-Lyer illusion**, the perceived length of a line is changed by the position of other lines that enclose it. And in the **moon illusion**, the full moon looks larger when it is close to the horizon than when it is high in the sky.

CRITICAL THINKING

Thinking Critically About Sensation and Perception
1. Distinguish sensation and perception. Can we have sensation without perception? How about perception without sensation?
2. Gestalt psychologists assume that the whole is greater than the sum of its parts. What exactly does this mean, and what does it have to do with perception?
3. Children have more taste buds than adults, and we all have more taste buds at the tip of our tongues than at the center. From an evolutionary perspective, how might these differences be adaptive?

4. Suppose a friend wants to get a tattoo but is worried about the pain involved. Your friend decides to deal with the pain by trying to ignore it. Is this a good strategy for managing pain? What other strategies would you advise?

CAREER CONNECTION: EDUCATION

Childcare Worker

Daycare centers, nursery schools, preschools, after-school programs, and even individual families may employ childcare workers. These caregivers attend to the basic needs of children as well as enable children's social and emotional growth through play and learning. Administrators at care centers establish overall objectives and standards, provide supervision of the staff and children in their care, and resolve any disputes or disciplinary issues that may arise. Childcare workers are also needed in mental health settings, aiding children and their families in outpatient settings. Although some positions in daycare centers do not require a college degree, a background in childhood development or psychology is increasingly desirable.

Key skills for this role that psychology students learn to develop:
- Interpersonal relationship development
- Self-efficacy and self-regulation
- Innovative and integrative thinking and problem solving

KEY TERMS

absolute threshold (p. 89)
accommodation (p. 93)
afterimages (p. 99)
audition (p. 102)
auditory localization (p. 104)
binocular disparity (p. 120)
blind spot (p. 95)
conductive hearing loss (p. 105)
cones (p. 93)
convergence (p. 120)
cornea (p. 92)
dark adaptation (p. 95)
depth perception (p. 120)
feature detectors (p. 96)
fovea (p. 93)
gate-control theory (p. 112)
Gestalt psychology (p. 116)
gustatory system (p. 108)
iris (p. 92)
just noticeable difference (JND) (p. 90)
kinesthetic system (p. 113)
lens (p. 93)
light adaptation (p. 95)
monocular depth cues (p. 120)
moon illusion (p. 125)
Müller-Lyer illusion (p. 125)
olfactory system (p. 107)

opponent-process theory (p. 99)
optic nerve (p. 95)
perception (p. 87)
perceptual illusions (p. 124)
perceptual set (p. 124)
pheromones (p. 108)
psychophysics (p. 89)
pupil (p. 92)
receptive field (p. 96)
retina (p. 93)
reversible figure (p. 115)
rods (p. 93)
sensation (p. 87)
sensorineural hearing loss (p. 105)
sensory adaptation (p. 114)
signal-detection theory (p. 90)
size constancy (p. 118)
synesthesia (p. 114)
taste buds (p. 108)
transduction (p. 87)
trichromatic theory (p. 99)
vestibular system (p. 113)
visual cliff (p. 122)
visual cortex (p. 96)
Weber's law (p. 90)
white noise (p. 102)

4 CONSCIOUSNESS

iStock.com/RomoloTavani

LEARNING OBJECTIVES

Describe the nature of consciousness and the selectivity of what we attend to and are aware of in our environment.

Explain why sleep is a necessary function for many mammals, including humans.

Explain the phenomenon of hypnosis and how it is used in therapy.

Identify psychoactive and addictive drugs and the effects of drug use on consciousness and long-term health.

WHAT'S YOUR PREDICTION: DO SUBLIMINAL SELF-HELP RECORDINGS WORK?

The Situation

You saw a social media ad seeking volunteers for a study of subliminal (outside of conscious awareness) videos, and you could not resist. No money is offered for participating, but you've heard about the power of subliminal messages, so you sign up. During your first session, an experimenter plays for you an audio recording created by a company that specializes in subliminal materials. He asks you to listen to the recording once a day, every day, for five weeks. But first, you fill out some questionnaires, including some self-esteem scales and memory tests. When you've finished, you are handed a recording labeled either "Subliminal Building Self-Esteem" or "Subliminal Memory Improvement."

With the recording in hand, you go home and try it. All you can hear is classical music, but you know that the recording contains faint messages you cannot consciously detect, such as "I have high self-worth" or "My ability to remember is increasing daily." The recording is now part of your daily routine, and after five weeks, you return to the lab for testing. As before, you fill out some self-esteem scales and memory tests. Then depending on the group you're in, the experimenter asks, "Do you feel that the recording has improved your self-esteem (memory)?"

The procedure in this study is simple. Participants are exposed to positive subliminal messages concerning their self-esteem and memory. After five weeks, the experimenter measures both actual improvement on objective tests and self-rated improvement. There's just one hitch. Although half the participants are randomly assigned to receive recordings that are correctly labeled, the other half have recordings with the labels reversed (the self-esteem recordings have the memory label, and vice versa).

What's Your Prediction?

So what do you think happens? Let's focus on the potential for improvement in memory. To some extent, scores on objective tests should increase across the board simply because participants had practice taking such tests in the first session. But what about the added benefit to those who listened to the recording? In the first row of the table below, put an X in the box if you think the recording produced an *actual* increase in memory-test scores in that experimental condition. Then in the second row, put an X in each box where you think the participants *perceived* an improvement in their memory.

	Memory Recording		Self-Esteem Recording	
	M Label	SE Label	M Label	SE Label
Actual				
Perceived				

The Results

When Anthony Greenwald and his colleagues (1991) conducted this study—with cassette tapes at that time—they asked two questions: (a) Did the memory recording actually work, and (b) did participants perceive that they worked? The key results are presented in the table below. First, scores on the objective memory test were no higher for those who listened to the subliminal memory recording than for those given the self-esteem recording. Second, participants perceived that their memory had improved—but that perception was based on which label was on the recording, not on which message the recording actually contained. People may believe in the power of the hidden message, but the recordings themselves had no real effect. Other research has shown that subliminal weight-loss recordings also are ineffective (Merikle & Skanes, 1992).

	Memory Recording		Self-Esteem Recording	
	M Label	SE Label	M Label	SE Label
Actual	------	-----	-----	-----
Perceived	×	-----	×	-----

What Does It All Mean?

Ever since psychology was born as a discipline, questions have been raised about consciousness and the extent to which we are influenced by information that is not in awareness. If you predicted that the subjects in this study did not benefit from subliminal self-help messages, you were right. (You were also right if you predicted that they believed the recordings to be effective, illustrating the power of suggestion.) If you think, however, that people are not in other ways subject to influence without awareness, stay tuned to the rest of this chapter. To fully understand the human organism, we must account for both what we attend to in our normal waking lives and the effects of sleep, dreams, hypnosis, and other less conscious processes.

What does it mean to be conscious? Is consciousness achieved only during wakefulness? Are we conscious when we sleep or when we dream? In many ways, having consciousness is an incredible achievement. It relates to our recognition not only of the environment within which we live but also of ourselves and our actions within our environment. In this chapter, we'll find that human consciousness ranges on a continuum from an alert waking state of attention to varying depths of sleep, dreams, hypnosis, and the "altered" states produced by psychoactive drugs. We'll also find that the more we know about consciousness, the more able we will be to regulate our own states of mind.

ATTENTIONAL PROCESSES

LEARNING OBJECTIVES

Describe the nature of consciousness and the selectivity of what we attend to and are aware of in our environment.

- Define consciousness.
- Explain whether people can attend selectively to one stimulus among many and the mechanism by which stimuli we try to block out still register on the mind.
- Outline the mechanism that enables people to divide their attention so that they can engage simultaneously in more than one activity.
- Discuss how we are influenced by stimuli that never register in our awareness.

The word **consciousness** has many different meanings, but psychologists tend to define it in terms of **attention**—a state of awareness that consists of the sensations, thoughts, and feelings that a person is focused on at a given moment. As implied by this definition, consciousness has a limited capacity. Whether you are mentally focused on a memory, a conversation, a foul odor, this sentence, or your growling stomach, consciousness is like a spotlight. It can shift rapidly from one stimulus to another, but it can shine on only one stimulus at a time. Try free associating into a recording device some time, and you'll find yourself mentally straying in what William James (1890) called the stream of consciousness.

Consciousness may be limited and the mind may wander, but three important and adaptive processes are at work. First, attention is selective—so, to some extent, people can control consciousness the way they control the channels of a television set. Second, for tasks that require little conscious effort, people can divide their attention and simultaneously engage in more than one activity. Third, even when people are conscious of one stimulus, they are also capable of reacting to other stimuli in the environment, which suggests that we can process information outside of awareness. As we'll explore, these features enable us to widen, narrow, and move the spotlight of consciousness as needed (Pashler, 1998; Phillips, 2019).

Selective Attention

Picture this scene. You're standing at a cocktail party with a drink in one hand and a spring roll in the other. In the background, there's music playing, as well as the chatter of voices. You're in the middle of a conversation with a friend when suddenly you overhear two other people talking about someone you know. Can you tune into the gossip and still carry on a conversation? How easy is it to attend selectively to one stimulus among many?

In a classic test of this **cocktail party phenomenon**, Colin Cherry (1953) presented subjects wearing headphones with two different messages, played simultaneously, one to each ear. In this dichotic listening task, subjects were told to "shadow"—that is, follow and repeat aloud, word for word—only one of the two messages. Were they able to do it? Yes, especially when the competing messages were different,

consciousness. An awareness of the sensations, thoughts, and feelings that one is attending to at a given moment.

attention. A state of awareness consisting of the sensations, thoughts, and feelings that one is focused on at a given moment.

cocktail party phenomenon. The ability to attend selectively to one person's speech in the midst of competing conversations.

selective attention. The ability to focus awareness on a single stimulus to the exclusion of other stimuli, as in the cocktail party phenomenon.

as when one featured the voice of a man and the other the voice of a woman. But what happened to the message that subjects had filtered out and ignored? Later, subjects could not recall any of it. Even when they were stopped in the middle of the presentation and asked to repeat the unattended message, their ability to do so was limited. Through a process of **selective attention**, people can zoom in on a single auditory stimulus, but then they lose track of competing auditory stimuli.

To examine selective attention in another sensory modality, Ulric Neisser and Robert Becklen (1975) devised a visual analog of the dichotic listening task. They simultaneously showed subjects two videotapes, one superimposed over the other. One tape showed three people passing a basketball, and the other showed two people playing a hand-slapping game (illustrated in Figure 4.1). The task was to keep track of one game or the other. As in the shadowing study, subjects could attend to only one stimulus at a time. In fact, the filtering process was so complete that out of 24 subjects who were focused on the basketball players, all but one failed to notice that the hand slappers had stopped their game at one point to shake hands. When the researcher later replayed this segment, these subjects were shocked at what they had missed. This result illustrates that information may be included or excluded from consciousness through a process of selective attention.

Divided Attention

Our consciousness may be limited, but the filtering process does not immediately or completely block out all of the extraneous information. In dichotic listening experiments, for example, most subjects do manage to hear the mention of their own names (Moray, 1959). They also manage to hear sexually explicit words, and words they had learned to associate with electric shock—even when these are irrelevant stimuli spoken in the unattended ear. Many subjects in this situation could tell that something odd had occurred in the unattended ear when the speech in that ear was switched from ordinary English to English played backward (Wood & Cowan, 1995). Recent studies also show that people make rapid eye movements to examine the world around them, and that our eyes are naturally drawn to objects that are novel, bright, colorful, moving, and abrupt in their appearance—even, at times, when these stimuli intrude on another task in which we are engaged (Pashler, Johnston, & Ruthruff, 2001). As Jan Theeuwes and colleagues (1998) put it, "Our eyes do not always go where we want them to go" (p. 379).

Is it possible, despite our selective tendencies, to divide attention among competing stimuli? Can you simultaneously watch TV and read a book, or drive a car, listen to the radio, and carry on a conversation? It depends on how much conscious effort is needed for the various tasks. Consider driving. When first learning to drive, you have to concentrate on how to operate the steering wheel, gas pedal, and brake, and on how to monitor traffic and watch for pedestrians, signs, and lights. At that point, driving is so *effortful* an activity that even the radio is distracting. As you gain more experience behind

FIGURE 4.1 ■ Selective Attention

Shown here are drawings of the two videotapes (left and center) and the resulting superimposed image (right). Subjects who were focused on the basketball players did not see the hand slappers, and vice versa.

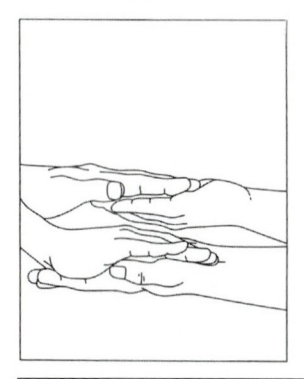

Source: Neisser, U., & Becklen, R. (1975). Selective looking: Attending to visually specified events. Cognitive Psychology, 7(4), 480–494. https://doi.org/10.1016/0010-0285(75)90019-5

the wheel, however, driving then becomes an *automatic* process that does not require high levels of effort or awareness or your undivided attention. Once that happens, you can drive, listen to music, and talk to others in the car all at the same time (Simons-Morton & Ehsani, 2016; Treisman, Viera, & Hayes, 1992).

The distinction between effortful and automatic processing explains how people are able to exhibit **divided attention** when at least one competing task is "on automatic." It's easy to walk, talk, and chew gum simultaneously, but for most of us it is difficult to play chess while watching TV. Consider the attention required to perform the complex motor behaviors needed in sports. When you first learn a sport—like baseball, basketball, hockey, or soccer—you tend to monitor every move you make. Then as you get better and more experienced, your movements become so automatic that you don't have to think about timing, breathing, head position, follow-through, and other mechanics. Experienced athletes should thus be able to divide their attention while performing in a way that novices cannot. To test this hypothesis, Sian Beilock and colleagues (2002) observed experienced and novice golfers putting on an indoor green, then experienced and novice soccer players dribbling through cones in a slalom course. In both studies, the experienced athletes were better able to maintain their performance while attending to a competing auditory task. Today, many sports teams use a variety of cognitive training methods to develop the working memory and attention of athletes to improve sporting performance and abilities in other tasks even outside of sports, although the effectiveness of such trainings is mixed (Harris, Wilson, & Vine, 2018).

A classic study on divided attention was devised in 1935 by John Stroop, using a test aptly called the **Stroop test**. When Stroop first presented his subjects with 100 colored items, he found that the task in which participants were presented with blocks of color to name took an average of 63 seconds, whereas the task in which participants were presented with words in colored font took 110 seconds—a 74 percent slowdown in performance time.

Researchers have used the Stroop test in hundreds of experiments, and they continue to debate the reasons for this effect (MacLeod, 1991; Scarpina & Tagini, 2017). Still, one conclusion is clear: Experienced readers process word meanings automatically, without effort or awareness. It just happens. And because the test words contradict the colors (when they don't, performance is quicker), reading interferes with the color-naming task (Brown, Gore, & Carr, 2002). Past experiments also show that personally relevant and emotionally provocative words interfere with color naming more than neutral words do. Thus, people diagnosed as having a fear of spiders are highly disrupted by words such as *crawl* and *hairy*, while those overly concerned about their health are disrupted more by *cancer* and *blood* (Williams, Mathews, & MacLeod, 1996). In a study of people who had been physically injured in a serious automobile accident, those who were traumatized by the experience were slowed more than those who were not by such words as *wreck, crashed*, and *totaled* (Beck, Freeman, Shipherd, Hamblen, & Lackner, 2001).

Is it safe to talk on the phone while driving? Researchers examined the phone records of 699 motorists who were in accidents and who had cellular telephones. The accident rate was four times higher when drivers were on the phone than when not—even with hands-free headsets. A recent large-scale survey of U.S. drivers found that texting while driving was associated with increased crash rates and while this was true across all age groups, it was highest among younger drivers. Driving may be a largely automatic process, but people need to stay alert to traffic and other changing conditions—which is why most states now prohibit motorists from talking on the phone while driving.

http://iStock.com/globalmoments

We have a canny ability to perform many skills at one time. Here a performer rides a unicycle and juggles at the same time.

iStock.com/double_p

divided attention. The ability to distribute one's attention and simultaneously engage in two or more activities.

Stroop test. A color-naming task that demonstrates the automatic nature of highly practiced activities such as reading.

Influence Without Awareness

Whereas Wilhelm Wundt and William James pioneered the study of conscious processes, Sigmund Freud theorized that people are driven more by *un*conscious forces. Freud argued that there are three levels of awareness in the human mind: *conscious* sensations, thoughts, and feelings that are currently in the spotlight of attention; *preconscious* material that is temporarily out of awareness but is easy to bring to mind; and an *unconscious* reservoir of material that is suppressed, banned from awareness. According to Freud, people are influenced by material that resides outside of awareness. Was he right?

For years, many researchers were skeptical of this claim. But then an outpouring of new studies brought unconscious processes to the forefront of modern psychology. These studies suggest that people can be influenced in subtle ways by **subliminal messages**—information that is presented so faintly or so rapidly that it is perceived "below" our threshold of awareness (Bornstein & Pittman, 1992; Merikle, Smilek, & Eastwood, 2001; Ruch, Züst, & Henke, 2016). Let's consider some examples that illustrate the point.

subliminal message. A stimulus that is presented below the threshold for awareness.

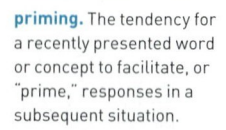

Mere Exposure

One powerful principle of attraction is called the mere exposure effect: The more often you see a stimulus—whether it's a word, an object, a melody, or a face—the more you come to like it (Zajonc, 1968). This type of learning begins even before birth, with mere exposure to the flavors of foods in a mother's diet being later preferred by newborns, and children learning to like novel (i.e., new) flavors simply by increased exposure to them (Trabulsi & Mennella, 2012). But must you be aware of the prior exposures for this effect to occur? Not always (Privitera, 2016; Yagi & Inoue, 2018). After all, as stated, even a fetus shows signs of mere exposure learning. In a typical study with children and adults, subjects are shown pictures of geometrical objects, each for only 1 to 5 milliseconds, which is too quick to register in awareness—and too quick for anyone to realize that some objects appear more often than others. After the presentation, subjects are shown each of the objects and asked two questions: Do you like it? Have you ever seen it before? Perhaps you can predict the result. The more frequently presented the object, the more subjects like it. And when asked if they've ever seen the liked objects before, they say *no*. This pattern of results demonstrates the mere exposure effect, even without awareness (Bornstein, 1992; Huang & Hsieh, 2013; Zajonc, 2001).

Priming

priming. The tendency for a recently presented word or concept to facilitate, or "prime," responses in a subsequent situation.

Have you ever noticed that whenever a novel word slips into conversation, it suddenly gets repeated over and over again? If so, then you have observed **priming,** the tendency for a recently presented concept to "prime" responses to a subsequent "target" question. Thus, when subjects are asked to decide if the letters *D-O-C-T-O-R* form a word, they are quicker to say *yes* if the previous item was *N-U-R-S-E* than if it was *A-P-P-L-E* (Meyer & Schvaneveldt, 1971). What if the prime word is presented subliminally, below our threshold of awareness? When that is done, the result is the same—even when the prime word is presented so quickly that subjects could only recall seeing a flash of light (Marcel, 1983). In fact, subliminal presentations of drawn objects, such as hammers, chairs, and dogs, can be used to prime the identification of similar objects that are shown up to 15 minutes later (Bar & Biederman, 1998).

In a series of provocative experiments, Tanya Chartrand and John Bargh (1999) found that motivations and emotions are also subject to automatic influence without awareness. In one study, subjects took part in a "word search" puzzle that contained either neutral words or words associated with achievement motivation (*strive, win, compete, succeed, master*). Afterward, they were left alone and given 3 minutes to write down as many words as they could generate from a set of Scrabble letter tiles. When the 3-minute limit was up,

Priming can be any stimulus, even images, that can influence your behavior. For example, images like the one shown here, depicting delicious-looking fruits and vegetables, can be used to prime healthy eating.

iStock.com/Aiselin82

subjects were signaled over an intercom to stop. Did subjects, driven to obtain a high score, stop on cue or continue to write? Through the use of hidden cameras, the experimenters observed that 57 percent of the subjects primed with achievement-related words continued to write after the stop signal—compared to only 22 percent in the control group.

In a second study by Chartrand and Bargh (1999), subjects took part in a "reaction-time" task in which they were subliminally exposed to words that evoked strongly positive emotional reactions (*music, friends*), strongly negative reactions (*cancer, cockroach*), or more neutral—only mildly positive and negative—reactions. Afterward, they described their current mood state as part of what was supposed to be an unrelated experiment. Subjects were not aware of the words they had "seen" in the first task. Yet compared to those in the neutral-word groups, those previously exposed to positive words were in a happier mood, and those exposed to negative words were in a sadder mood.

SLEEP AND DREAMS

LEARNING OBJECTIVES

Explain why sleep is a necessary function for many mammals, including humans.

- Discuss whether people, like animals, are influenced by biological rhythms or whether they are flexible in their sleeping schedules.
- Outline how researchers study sleep in the laboratory.
- Differentiate among the stages of sleep and identify what makes REM sleep so special.
- Explain what dreams are, why we have them, and what they mean.
- Distinguish among common sleep disturbances and approaches suggested to address them.

It may start with a deep yawn. Then the eyelids begin to fall. Then your head drops and you get that drowsy sense of calm before nodding off, tuning out, and calling it a day. For most people, falling asleep is a pleasurable experience. Why? What is sleep? Why do we need it? And what about dreams—what purposes do they serve and what, if anything, do they mean? The average person spends about 8 hours a day sleeping and 90 minutes dreaming. Given an average life expectancy of 75 years, that amounts to about 25 years of sleep and 5 years of dreaming in a lifetime. Yet until recently, we knew very little about this important aspect of our lives. Shakespeare once referred to sleep as "the death of each day's life." Others, too, think of sleep as a state of complete dormancy. They are wrong. As we'll learn, the sleeping brain is humming with activity (Dement & Vaughan, 1999; Grandner, 2019).

The Sleep-Wake Cycle

Many birds migrate south for the winter. Bears and raccoons hibernate. Certain plants open their leaves during the day and close them at night—even if kept in a dark closet. As biological organisms, humans are also sensitive to seasonal changes, the 28-day lunar cycle, the 24-hour day, and the 90-minute activity-rest cycle that is linked to variations in alertness and daydreaming. These and other regular fluctuations are forms of **biological rhythms**.

From a psychological standpoint, one internal clock is particularly important: Every 24 hours, we undergo a single sleep-wake cycle. This cycle and others that take roughly a day to complete are referred to as a **circadian rhythm**. Humans tend to be most active and alert during the middle of the day, when body temperature peaks, and least active and alert at night, when body temperature drops to its low point. The human circadian rhythm is also evident in fluctuations in blood pressure, pulse rate, blood sugar level, potassium level, growth hormone secretions, cell growth, and other physiological functions (Lavie, 2001; Pilorz, Helfrich-Förster, & Oster, 2018).

biological rhythm. Any periodic, more or less regular fluctuation in a biological organism.

circadian rhythm. A biological cycle, such as sleeping and waking, that occurs approximately every 24 hours.

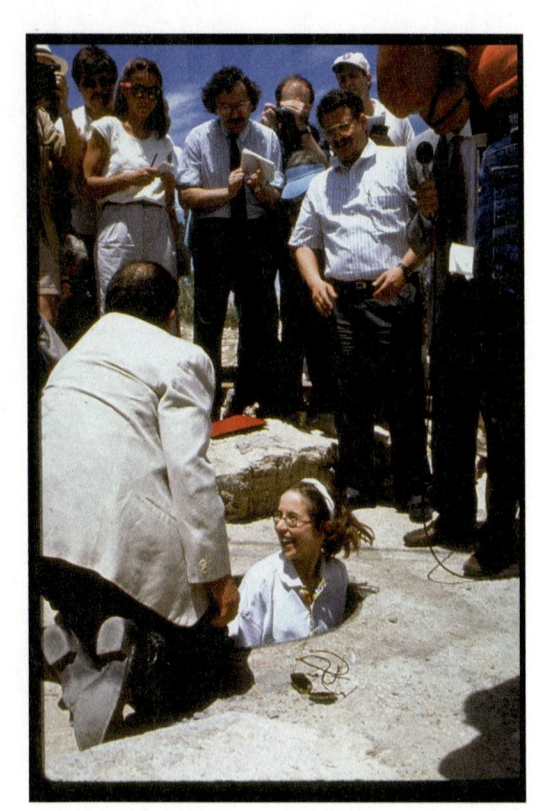

Stefania Follini steps inside the underground bunker where she lived alone for 131 days.

Thomas Ives / ContributorThomas Ives / Contributor

Everyone is influenced by circadian rhythms, but everyone's inner clock is set somewhat differently. Think about yourself. Are you a morning person or a night person, a lark or an owl? If you had a choice, would you rather wake up at 6, 8, or 10 o'clock in the morning? How easy is it for you to work late into the night? During what time of day are you most productive? These kinds of questions can be used to determine your circadian rhythm (Hasan et al., 2012). Although morning types fall asleep earlier at night and awaken earlier in the morning, most people adapt as needed to the schedules they must keep. Still, it helps to know when you're likely to be at your best. When subjects were tested for memory at 9 AM, 2 PM, and 8 PM, the larks performed worse as the day wore on, whereas owls performed better (Anderson, Petros, Beckwith, Mitchell, & Fritz, 1991; Malone, Patterson, Lozano, & Hanlon, 2017). Among college students, up to 60 percent suffer from poor quality sleep (Schlarb, Friedrich, & Claßen, 2017), although larks are more likely than owls to take early morning classes—and they earn higher grades in those classes (Guthrie, Ash, & Bendapudi, 1995). Among older people, who tend to prefer early-morning hours, performance on learning and memory tasks declines when they're tested late in the day (Intons-Peterson, Rocchi, West, McLellan, & Hackney, 1999). Across a whole range of cognitive activities that require vigilance, research shows that people perform better during their "preferred" time of day (Malone et al., 2017; May & Hasher, 1998).

Is the circadian rhythm endogenous (set by an inner clock), or is the human body responsive to outside patterns of lightness and darkness? Ask Stefania Follini, an Italian interior designer. In January 1989, she descended into a Plexiglas bunker buried in a cave in New Mexico. Sealed off from sunlight, outside noises, changes in temperature, schedules, and clocks, she lived alone in this underground home for 131 days—a "free-running" period of time that allowed her body to establish its own rhythm. Her only link to the world was a personal computer. When Follini emerged from her isolation in May, she thought it was only March. Her "day" had extended to 25 hours, then to 48. As time went on, she slept and woke up later and later. She stopped menstruating, ate fewer meals, and lost 17 pounds.

Other volunteers were similarly isolated for extended periods of time. Some settled naturally into a "short" day, but most free-ran on a longer cycle that averaged 25 hours. With each successive cycle, these subjects tended to go to sleep a little later and to wake up a little later (illustrated in Figure 4.2). Body temperature and hormone levels tended to follow the same rhythm. Like Follini, these subjects drifted toward a longer day—then underestimated the amount of time they had been isolated. When reexposed to sunlight, the subjects readjusted their biological clocks.

Where is this timing device? Animal experiments have shown that the circadian rhythm is controlled in the brain's hypothalamus, just above the optic nerves, by two pinhead-size clusters of neurons called the suprachiasmatic nuclei, or SCN. How do the SCN function? You may recall from Chapter 2 that light passing through the eye is converted to neural signals and sent to the cortex through the optic nerve. Apparently, some of these optic nerve axons—and the information they convey about light—are diverted to the SCN. Nestled in the center of the brain, the pea-shape pineal gland also plays an important role. As darkness falls, the pineal gland produces melatonin—a hormone that facilitates sleep by letting the body know that it's dark outside. When light strikes the retina, melatonin secretion is slowed down. As we'll explore later, melatonin is often used to treat chronic insomnia (Auld, Maschauer, Morrison, Skene, & Riha, 2017).

The circadian rhythm is synchronized like a fine watch by an interplay between the brain and environmental cues. But what happens when your rhythm is disrupted? One common source of disruption is air travel—specifically, flying across time zones, which throws your body out of sync with the new time of day and causes you to sleep at the wrong time. If you've ever flown from one coast to the other or overseas, then you may have suffered jet lag, a condition that makes you feel tired, sluggish, and grumpy. Most people find it easier to fly west, which lengthens the day, than to fly east, which shortens

FIGURE 4.2 The Inner Clock

Each dark bar indicates the timing and length of sleep during a day. During the unscheduled period (without time cues), the subject's activity assumed a 25-hour rhythm and began to advance around the clock. When light-dark periods were scheduled, he resumed a normal sleep and activity rhythm.

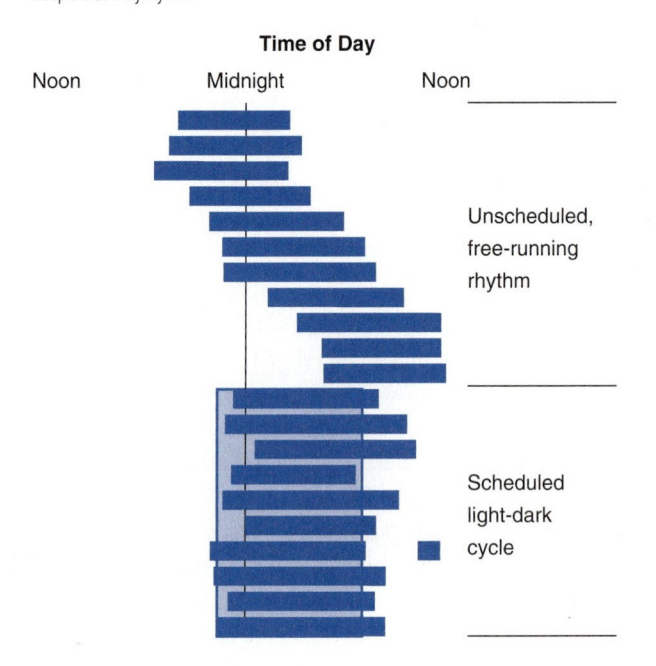

it. Because the body naturally drifts to a longer day, this makes sense. Flying westward goes "with the flow" rather than against it. Consistent with this analysis, research shows that long-distance travel within a time zone does not cause jet lag (Ambesh et al., 2018).

In recent years, researchers have tested various strategies that long-distance travelers can use to combat jet lag. Many tips and suggestions can help you get a full night's rest (National Sleep Foundation, 2018). For example, always get a full night's sleep before a long trip. Anticipate your new time zone. Drink lots of liquids to avoid dehydration, but avoid alcohol, which disrupts later sleep. If you plan to travel east—say, from Los Angeles to New York—you can facilitate the adjustment process by sleeping earlier than normal before you leave so that you more closely "fit" the light-dark cycle of the new time zone. As soon as you board the plane, set your watch to your destination's time zone and eat and sleep accordingly. Because of studies that indicate that bright-light exposure at night speeds the resetting of the inner clock, researchers also advise that, upon arrival, you spend the first day outdoors.

Can anything more be done to prevent jet lag from gripping us as we cross time zones in flight? In 1998, Scott Campbell and Patricia Murphy published an article in *Science* on a technique for combating jet lag by resetting our internal clock. They reported that by shining a light on the backs of people's knees, they were able to shift the clock that regulates the sleep-wake cycle. Because the backs of the knees contain blood vessels just under the skin, they reasoned, it was possible to send a chemical timing signal through blood circulating through the body, not just through the eyes. Subsequent research, however, casts doubt on the claim. In a study also published in *Science*, Kenneth Wright and Charles Czeisler (2002) measured changes in the levels of melatonin in 22 subjects over a 10-day period. Some subjects were exposed to bright light behind the knee but not in the eye; others were exposed to light in the eye but not behind

To combat jet lag, exposure to light can help to adjust the body clock to a new time zone through controlled exposure to bright light, and it can even improve your mood.

iStock.com/Rocky89

the knee; still others received no light. The result: The circadian clock was shifted by light to the eyes—but not by light to the back of the knee. Today, it is widely recognized that more research is needed to combat jet lag (Ambesh et al., 2018).

Night Work, Sleeping, and Health

We humans are diurnal creatures—active during the day and asleep at night. Thus, we like to work from 9 to 5 and then play, sleep, and awaken to the light of a new day. Yet an estimated 25 percent of all Americans—including truckers, emergency-room doctors and nurses, security guards, police officers, factory workers, and telephone operators—are often forced to work late-night shifts (American Psychological Association, 2020a). The question is, what is the effect? Do people adapt over time to shift work and other late-night activity, or does it compromise their health and safety?

Both biological and social clocks set the body for activity during the daytime and sleep at night, so it's no surprise that many shift workers struggle to stay alert. People who choose night work tend to fare better than those assigned on a rotating-shift basis (Barton, 1994). Still, shift workers in general get fewer hours of sleep than day workers, complain that their sleep is disrupted, and report being drowsy on the job. Often they blame their lack of sleep on ringing phones, crying babies, traffic, and other daytime noises. Part of the problem too is that the body's internal alarm clock tries to awaken the day sleeper. Either way, the adverse effects can be seen at work—where night-time energy levels are low, reaction times are slow, and productivity is diminished. In a survey of 52 flight controllers of the International Space Station, nearly half of night-shift workers sampled reported disordered sleepiness while on shift (Mizuno et al., 2016). Can anything be done to lessen the dangers posed by shift work? Koh Mizuno and colleagues (2016) recommend rotating shifts more often to maximize the number of days between shifts (to reduce the number of consecutive shifts), increasing the number of shorter breaks (5 to 10 minutes per hour), and improving working conditions (to reduce stressors during a shift). Consistent with these suggestions, studies show that it seems to take two days of rest, not one, for workers to fully recover from their nocturnal routine (Totterdell, Spelten, Smith, Barton, & Folkard, 1995). Charles Czeisler and colleagues (1990) found that the realignment of the circadian rhythm can also be speeded up by exposing shift workers to bright levels of light in the workplace and to 8 hours of total darkness at home during the day. Within a week, the body's biological clock can be reset and the health risks of night work reduced. It takes only 4 hours of bright-light exposure one night to improve performance the next night (Grønli & Mrdalj, 2018; Thessing, Anch, Muelbach, Schweitzer, & Walsh, 1994).

The National Highway Transportation Safety Administration estimates that up to 6,000 fatal traffic accidents a year are sleep related—and, according to the Traffic Safety Foundation, 37 percent of all drivers have dozed off at least once while behind the wheel. Overall, 1 to 3 percent of highway crashes in the United States are caused by driver sleepiness—a problem that most plagues young drivers, shift workers, drivers who use alcohol and other drugs, drivers with sleep disorders, and commercial truck drivers (National Highway Traffic Safety Administration, 2018). Drivers are 5 to 10 times more likely to have an accident late at night than during daytime hours. The reason is easy to find. Monitoring of EEG activity shows that those who drive in the middle of the night often take quick, 2- to 3-second **microsleeps**, which elevates the risk of accident (Al-Lawati, 2018; Kecklund & Akerstedt, 1993). A study of 80 long-haul truck drivers revealed that 56 percent had at least one episode of drowsiness and two drifted briefly into a light stage of sleep (Mitler, Miller, Lipsitz, Walsh, & Wylie, 1997). A study of 35 people in a driving simulator revealed a slowed heart rate and brain-wave patterns indicative of drowsiness. Over time, many subjects yawned, blinked quickly, closed their eyes, nodded off, drifted lanes, and made driving errors resulting in collisions (Lai & Craig, 2002). There are times when a person just can't avoid the situation. Often when I'm out of town and have to return for

microsleep. A brief episode of sleep that occurs in the midst of a wakeful activity.

To avoid traffic, many truckers drive at night. However, they are more likely to have an accident during nighttime hours than in the daytime.

Lee Rentz / Alamy Stock Photo

an early-morning class, I'll find myself driving late at night and fighting to keep my eyes open. Is there a way to counteract this tendency? Studies have shown that a brief nap and a cup of coffee will help drivers stay awake (Al-Lawati, 2018; Horne & Reyner, 1996).

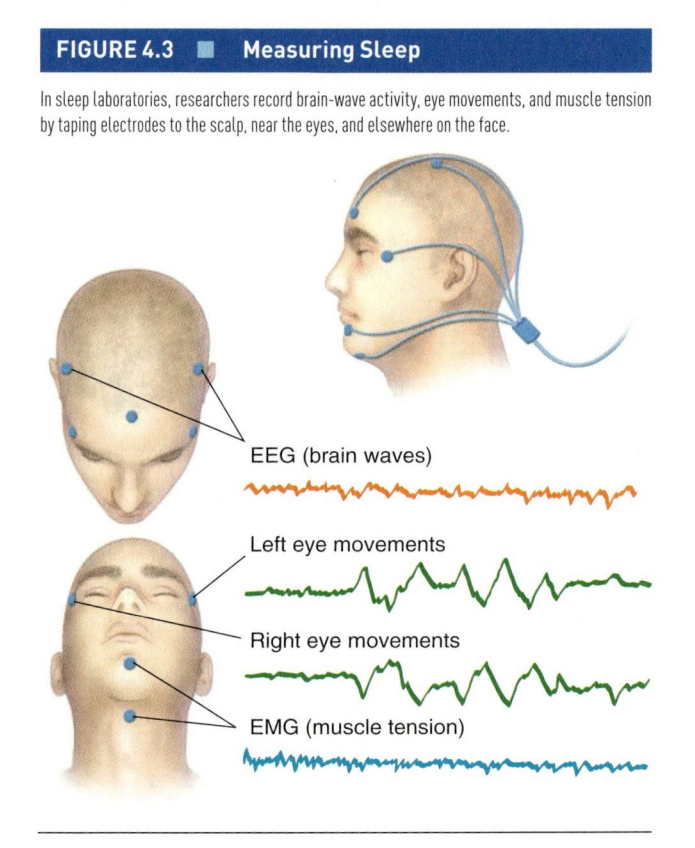

The Stages of Sleep

Just as activity levels follow a rhythm, so too does sleep. Every night, humans cycle through five distinct stages of sleep. Much of what is known about these stages first came to light in the 1950s, thanks to the pioneering collaborative work of Nathaniel Kleitman, Eugene Aserinksy, and William Dement. The scientific study of sleep is now highly active (American Psychological Association, 2020a; Grandner, 2019; Hobson, 2003).

To appreciate how these discoveries were made, imagine that you're a subject in a sleep study. As you enter the sleep lab, you meet an experimenter, who gives you some questionnaires to fill out, prepares you for the experience, and takes you to a carpeted, tastefully decorated, soundproof "bedroom." Electrodes are then taped to your scalp to record brain-wave activity, near your eyes to measure eye movements, and under your neck and chin to record muscle tension (illustrated in Figure 4.3). Other devices may also be used to measure your breathing, heart rate, and even genital arousal. The pillow is fluffy, the bed is okay, and the blanket is warm. But you know you're being watched, and you can feel the electrodes and wires on your skin, so you wonder how you'll ever manage to fall asleep. The experimenter reassures you that it may take a couple of nights to adapt to the situation.

Presleep

The experimenter departs, shuts off the lights, and leaves you alone. As you try to settle down, EEG recordings reveal that all is well (illustrated in Figure 4.4). Typical of a person who is awake and alert, your EEG shows short, quick *beta waves*. This pattern indicates that different parts of your brain are producing small bursts of electrical activity at different times—a sure sign of mental activity. Your eyes move rapidly up and down and from side to side, and many of your muscles are tensed.

FIGURE 4.3 ■ Measuring Sleep

In sleep laboratories, researchers record brain-wave activity, eye movements, and muscle tension by taping electrodes to the scalp, near the eyes, and elsewhere on the face.

Carolina Hrejsa/Body Scientific Intl.

FIGURE 4.4 ■ The Stages of Sleep

As recorded by the EEG, brain waves get larger and slower as sleep deepens from stages 1 to 4. As illustrated, REM sleep waves closely resemble those of the presleep state.

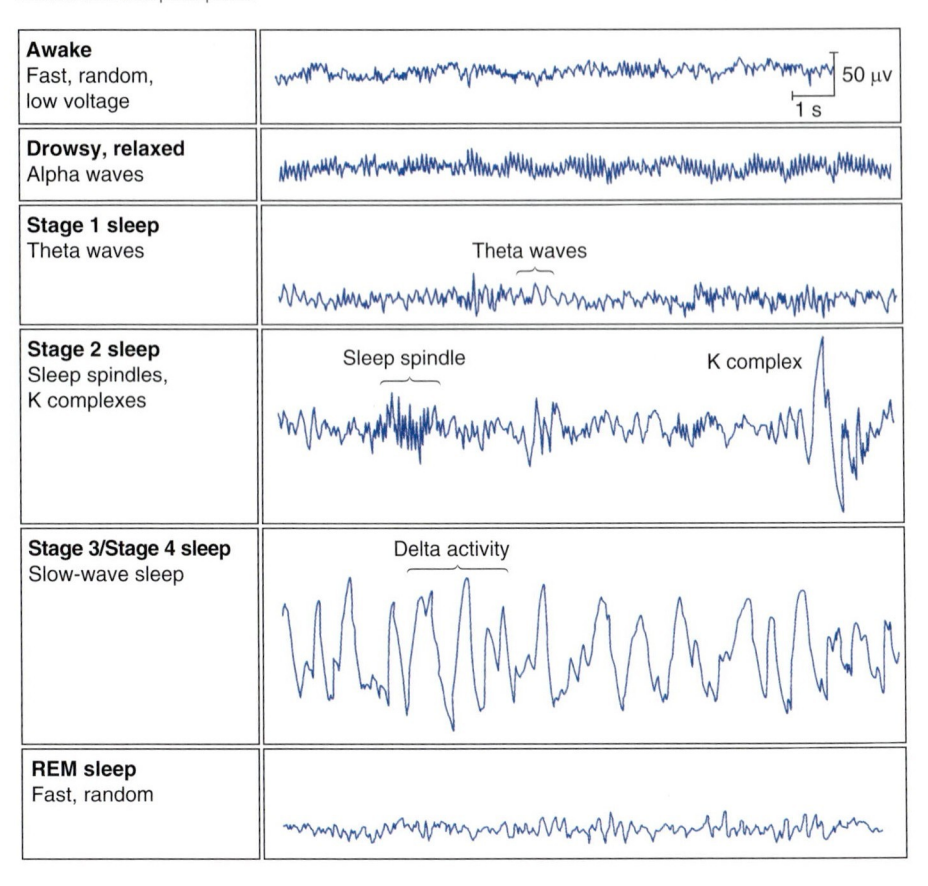

Awake Fast, random, low voltage	(EEG trace; 50 μV, 1 s)
Drowsy, relaxed Alpha waves	(EEG trace)
Stage 1 sleep Theta waves	Theta waves (EEG trace)
Stage 2 sleep Sleep spindles, K complexes	Sleep spindle — K complex (EEG trace)
Stage 3/Stage 4 sleep Slow-wave sleep	Delta activity (EEG trace)
REM sleep Fast, random	(EEG trace)

Stages 1 to 4

You start to become drowsy. Your breathing slows down, your mind stops racing, your muscles relax, your eyes move less, and EEG recordings show a slower, larger, and somewhat more regular pattern of *alpha waves* (alpha waves appear to occur when people are relaxed but not focused on something specific). For a minute or two, you drift into a "hypnogogic state" in which you may imagine seeing flashes of color or light, and perhaps you jerk your leg abruptly as you sense yourself falling. You are entering stage 1 sleep. Electrical activity in the brain slows down some more, in a pattern of *theta waves*. Your breathing becomes more regular, your heart rate slows, and your blood pressure drops. This is a period of very light sleep. No one makes a sound or calls your name, however, so you don't wake up.

After about 10 minutes in stage 1 sleep, your EEG pattern shows waves that are even slower and larger. As you slip into stage 2 sleep, you become progressively more relaxed, the rolling eye movements stop, and you become less easily disturbed. On the EEG, stage 2 is marked by periodic short bursts of activity called *sleep spindles*. If the experimenter in the next room makes a noise, your brain will register a response—but you probably will not wake up. In the laboratory, subjects detect a change in a tone 95 percent of the time while awake, 47 percent of the time in stage 1 sleep, and only 3 percent of the time in stage 2 sleep (Cote, De Lugt, & Campbell, 2002).

After about 20 minutes in stage 2, you fall into the deepest stages of sleep. Stages 3 and 4 are hard to distinguish because they differ only in degree. Both are marked by the onset of very slow waves with large peaks, called *delta waves*, which last for about 30 minutes (delta waves seem to indicate that increasing numbers of neurons are firing together, in synchrony). At this point, you are "out like a light" or "sleeping like a rock." If the phone rings, you may not hear it. If you do answer the call, you'll sound dazed and confused. It is during the very deep sleep of stages 3 and 4 when young children may wet the bed or when you may walk or talk in your sleep. It's this stage that Mark Twain had in mind when he said, "There ain't no way to find out why a snorer can't hear himself snore." Yet in keeping with the adaptive and very selective nature of attention, certain noises will penetrate consciousness. New parents may be oblivious to the sounds of traffic outside, for example, but they're quick to hear the baby cry.

REM Sleep

After an hour of deepening sleep, something odd happens—something first discovered in Kleitman's lab (Aserinksy & Kleitman, 1953; Dement & Kleitman, 1957; Kleitman, 1963). Rather than maintain your deep sleep, you begin to cycle backward to stage 3, then to stage 2. But then instead of returning to stage 1, you enter a new, fifth stage, marked by two dramatic types of changes. On the one hand, the EEG reveals a surge of short, high-frequency beta waves like those found when you were awake. Also indicating an increased level of activity, blood flow to the brain increases, your breathing and pulse rates speed up, and your genitals become aroused—even without sexual thoughts or dreams. At the same time, you have lost skeletal muscle tone throughout the body. In fact, your arms, legs, and trunk are so totally relaxed that, except for an occasional twitch, you are completely paralyzed. You're also hard to awaken at this stage. This odd combination—of being internally active but externally immobile—has led some researchers to refer to this stage of sleep as paradoxical.

The most prominent change occurs in the eyes. The eyelids are shut, but underneath, your eyeballs are darting frantically back and forth as if you were watching a world-class Ping-Pong match. These rapid eye movements are so pronounced that this stage has been named **REM sleep**—and it is contrasted with stages 1 through 4, which are lumped together as non-REM, or **NREM, sleep**. What makes rapid eye movements so special is what they betray about the state of your mind. When sleeping subjects are awakened during non-REM stages, they report on dreams about 50 percent of the time. Yet when subjects are awakened during REM, they report on dreams about 80 percent of the time—and that includes subjects who came into the lab saying they don't ever dream (Foulkes, 1962). Clearly, everyone dreams throughout the night, during both REM and NREM sleep (Squier & Domhoff, 1998). But compared to the fleeting thoughts and images reported during stages 1 through 4, REM dreams are more visual, vivid, detailed, and storylike. In the mind's late-night theater, the production of dreams can be seen in the resurgence of activity within the eyes and brain.

From the time you fall asleep, it takes about 90 minutes to complete one cycle. The contrasts within this cycle are striking. Coleman (1986) describes NREM sleep as "an idling brain in a moveable body" and REM as "an active brain in a paralyzed body." In a full night's sleep, you are likely to recycle through the stages four to six times. The first time through the cycle, you spend only about 10 minutes in REM sleep. As the night wears on, however, you spend less time in the deeper NREM periods and more time in REM sleep. During the last hour before you awaken in the morning, the REM period is 30 to 60 minutes long. This explains why people are so often in the middle of a dream when the mechanical tyrant we call an alarm clock rings. The sleep cycles and the progression of stages within each cycle are illustrated in Figure 4.5.

REM sleep. The rapid-eye-movement stage of sleep associated with dreaming.

NREM sleep. The stages of sleep not accompanied by rapid eye movements.

FIGURE 4.5 ■ A Typical Night's Sleep

People pass through four to six 90-minute sleep cycles per night. As shown, progressively more time is spent in REM sleep and progressively less is spent in the deeper stages.

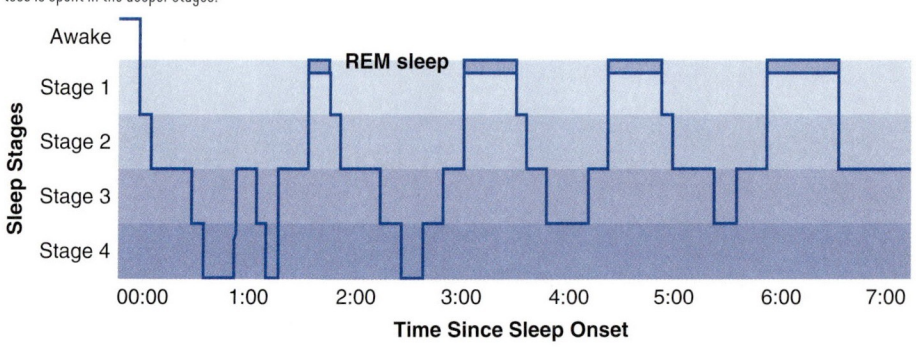

Garrett, *Brain and Behavior*, 5e, 2018, SAGE Publications, Inc

What's Your Prediction?

How much sleep do we need to function during the day and stay healthy? Clearly, people differ. Thomas Edison, inventor of the modern light bulb, required only about 4 hours a night. This fact is interesting given that Edison's 1913 light bulb precipitated a decline in the amount of sleep people get—from 9 hours a night, measured in 1910, to... well, you make the call. As part of its Sleep in America poll, the National Sleep Foundation (2018) asked a random sample of 1,000 adults to identify which of five items was most important to them personally. What are your predictions? Look at Figure 4.6, and you'll find that Americans do not tend to prioritize sleep compared to other parts of their lives. How much do *you* prioritize sleep? According to the poll, a majority of the public (65 percent) says that getting enough sleep makes them a more effective person, yet 41 percent admit to rarely considering how much sleep they need in planning for the next day.

Why Do We Sleep?

Because humans spend a third of their lives in this state, it's natural to wonder: Why do we sleep? When we are tired, the urge to doze is overwhelming and very hard to fight, regardless of what we're doing or where we are. And if we are still tired when the alarm clock rings, we might shut it off, clutch our pillows to our ears, or just pretend we didn't hear it—even if we have a schedule to keep. Our need for sleep is powerful and irresistible. But why?

One way to investigate this question is to deprive people of sleep and find out what happens. You may have pulled a few "all-nighters" but probably not for periods of time that are long enough to push the limits. A unique opportunity to observe the effects of sleep deprivation presented itself in New York City in 1959. As part of a fund-raising drive, disc jockey Peter Tripp forced himself to stay awake and on the air for 200 hours. By the fifth day, Tripp's speech was slurred, and he was hallucinating and showing signs of paranoia (he believed that "enemies" were trying to drug his coffee). It seemed that sleep was essential to his mental health. But after sleeping for 13 hours, Tripp had recovered completely.

A second highly publicized case came about in 1964, when 17-year-old Randy Gardner sought fame in the *Guinness Book of World Records.* As part of a high school science project, and with the help

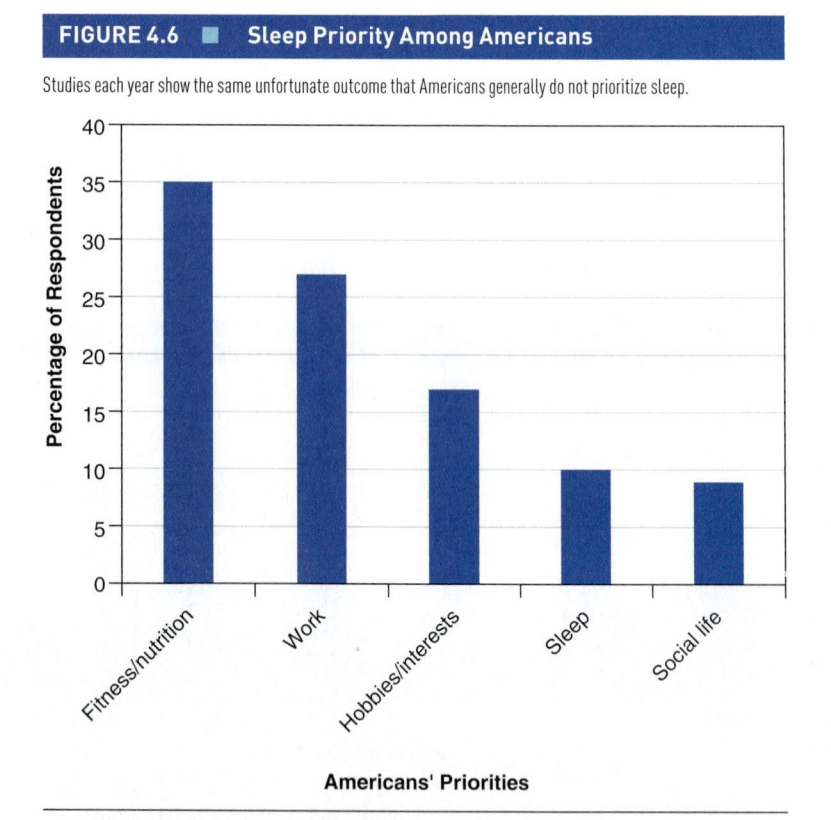

FIGURE 4.6 ■ Sleep Priority Among Americans

Studies each year show the same unfortunate outcome that Americans generally do not prioritize sleep.

Americans' Priorities	Percentage of Respondents
Fitness/nutrition	35
Work	27
Hobbies/interests	17
Sleep	10
Social life	9

Source: National Sleep Foundation's 2018 Sleep in America® Poll

of two friends, Gardner stayed awake for 264 hours—that's 11 straight days, a world record (which was later broken). When it was over, he held a news conference, during which he said, "It's just mind over matter." He went to sleep for 14 hours, woke up feeling fine, and resumed his normal schedule. Follow-up tests initially confirmed that Gardner suffered no long-term ill effects. For many years, the Gardner story was surrounded by the myth that he suffered no ill effects during the episode. But daily tests administered to Gardner showed that his thinking was fragmented, his speech was slurred, he couldn't concentrate, he had memory lapses, and toward the end, he was hallucinating. Then, in later years, Gardner suffered unbearable insomnia and reported being terrified of going even a single night without sleep (Coren, 1996; National Public Radio, 2017).

On the basis of these episodes and many studies, sleep researchers have concluded that sleep is a necessary function. There are four types of explanations for why this is so: restoration, circadian patterns, consolidation, and neural synthesis.

One explanation comes from *restoration theory*, which states that sleep recharges the battery, enabling us to recover from the day's physical, cognitive, and emotional demands. This theory explains why people feel run-down as the day wears on and refreshed after a night's sleep. Restoration is thought to be achieved largely in stages 3 and 4—or deep sleep.

A second explanation for why we sleep comes from the *circadian theory*, which focuses on the evolutionary significance of sleep. All animals sleep or undergo regular intervals of inactivity. According to this view, sleep is a neural mechanism that has evolved over time so that animals can conserve energy and minimize their exposure to predators when they are not foraging for food or seeking a mate. Circadian theory correctly predicts that there are species-specific differences in sleep patterns. As shown in Figure 4.7, animals that sleep the longest find food easily and are well hidden from predators while sleeping. In contrast, animals that sleep the shortest amount of time spend more hours foraging and can defend themselves only by running away. Seen from this perspective, we humans sleep at night because we're not very well adapted to searching for food in the dark or protecting ourselves from nocturnal predators (Allison & Cicchetti, 1976; Horne, 1988).

A third explanation comes from theories of *consolidation*—the process of converting short-term memory to long-term memory (Peever & Fuller, 2016). Consolidation occurs in the hippocampus, a region of the brain known to be associated with memory. This region is highly active during REM sleep, as are other regions in the brain where memory conversion is evident, to include the motor cortex (Li, Ma, Yang, & Gan, 2017; Sterpenich et al., 2014). In this way, sleep, particularly REM sleep, is a time for the brain to "organize" our memories.

A fourth explanation comes from activation-synthesis theory (Antrobus, 1991; Scarpelli et al., 2021), which explains that sleep functions to allow the synthesis (or merging) of random neural activity. *Neural synthesis* is a type of bottom-up processing in which processing, initiated in the hindbrain, causes activation in the cortex, leading to dreaming. Specifically, studies show that regions responsible

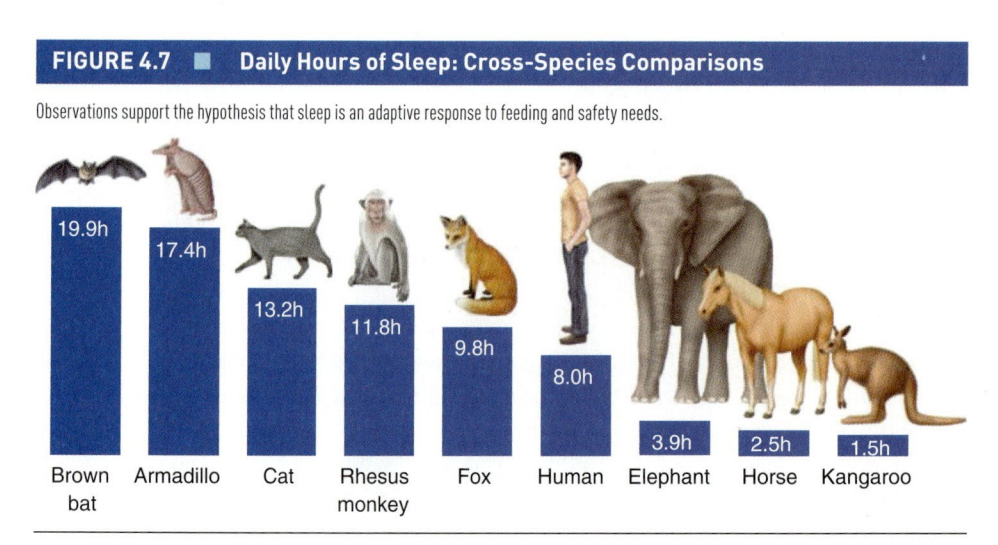

FIGURE 4.7 ■ Daily Hours of Sleep: Cross-Species Comparisons

Observations support the hypothesis that sleep is an adaptive response to feeding and safety needs.

Brown bat	Armadillo	Cat	Rhesus monkey	Fox	Human	Elephant	Horse	Kangaroo
19.9h	17.4h	13.2h	11.8h	9.8h	8.0h	3.9h	2.5h	1.5h

Monica Wierzbicki/Body Scientific Intl.

for processing visual information—but not the visual cortex specifically—are active during dreaming. During emotional dreams, limbic regions responsible for emotion (the amygdala) are also highly active (Perogamvros & Schwartz, 2012). Dreaming, then, is a by-product of this synthesis of random neural activity.

Dreams

Have you ever had a recurring dream? Some 75 percent of Americans report having recurring dreams; nearly 39 percent started in childhood. What is your recurring dream about? Maybe that you were falling? Being chased? Flying? Meeting a celebrity? Or maybe something more serious. . . like finding out a partner is cheating? Driving in an out-of-control vehicle? Or maybe something more taboo... like having sex with someone you shouldn't have? Being naked in public? Or maybe something more serious. . . like being paralyzed or unable to speak? Experiencing a death of yourself or a loved one? Or maybe something more off the wall. . . such as being unable to find a toilet? Going nowhere or moving in slow motion? If any of these recurring dreams sound familiar, then you are not alone. A recent poll of more than 2,000 Americans found that these are common recurring dreams (Hyde, 2020). More than 50 percent of respondents reported dreams about falling or being chased; nearly 33 percent reported flying; 32 percent, having sex with someone they shouldn't have; 30 percent, experiencing a death of themselves or a loved one; 26 percent, going nowhere or moving in slow motion; 24 percent, being paralyzed or unable to speak; 18 percent, finding out a partner is cheating; 15 percent, being naked in public; 14 percent, meeting a celebrity or driving in an out-of-control vehicle; and 13 percent, being unable to find a toilet. Other common dreams included being back in school (38 percent), being unprepared for a test or an important event (34 percent), having teeth fall out (27 percent), being lost (27 percent), drowning (9 percent), and even encountering aliens or UFOs (7 percent). So, what are dreams, why do we have them, and what, if anything, do they mean?

The Nature of Dreams

Dreams are less puzzling now than they were before the 1953 discovery of REM sleep. Psychologists used to think that the mind was idling in sleep and that dreaming was a rare, and therefore significant, event. But then EEG recordings revealed that the sleeping human brain is active and that everyone dreams, without exception, several times a night. We now know that dreams are electrochemical events involving the brainstem and areas of the cortex and that the eyes flutter back and forth. What more is known about this mysterious state of consciousness, a state in which the mind is active but the sleeper is immobilized and hard to awaken?

Researchers now believe that REM sleep and the dreaming that often accompanies it are biologically adaptive. This belief arises from three sources of evidence. The first is that all mammals have REM sleep (most birds do too, but reptiles, amphibians, and fish do not)—from a high of 57 percent of all sleep time in the platypus to a low of 2 percent in the dolphin (Siegel, 2001). Second, the amount of REM sleep is greatest early in life, while the brain is developing—and there is evidence to suggest that REM sleep is necessary for brain maturation (Marks, Shaffrey, Oksenberg, Speciale, & Roffwarg, 1995). Among premature infants, 60 to 80 percent of all sleep time is spent in the REM stage. That proportion drops to 50 percent in full-term newborns, 30 percent in 6-month-olds, 25 percent in 2-year-olds, and 20 percent in early childhood, before diminishing later in life. Third, when subjects are deprived of REM sleep one night, they exhibit a "rebound effect" by taking extra REM time the next night (Brunner, Kijk, Tobler, & Borbely, 1990).

Is there a linkage between a sleeper's eye movements and dreams? This is a tricky question. Research shows that the longer a REM episode is, the more words an awakened subject uses to describe the dream—and the more elaborate the story. Similarly, the more active the brain is during REM, the more eventful are the dreams that are later reported. But patterns of eye movements do not seem to correspond to the images and actions of a dream—as when we follow characters in a film (Chase & Morales, 1983).

What Do People Dream About?

What do people dream about? What do you dream about? Over the years, analyses of dream content have shown that certain themes seem to arise with remarkable frequency. Can you guess the three most commonly reported dreams? Figure 4.8 lists many of the most common recurring dreams. The first is of falling. The second is of being chased or attacked. The third is of being back in school. Also common are dreams of flying, being unprepared or late for a big event, being rejected, and interacting with someone who just passed (Hyde, 2020).

According to research, we tend to recognize most of the characters in our dreams with fewer than one-fifth of dream characters being unrecognizable to the dreamer (Kahn et al., 2008). Other research indicates that our waking lives influence what we dream. For example, women who are pregnant dream more about childbirth and musicians dream about music twice and often as non-musicians do (Lara-Carrasco et al., 2013; Uga et al., 2006). Still, our capacity for dreaming extends beyond our own experiences. For example, people born paralyzed dream of walking, swimming, and running as often as those without paralysis, and people born deaf often report that they hear in their dreams (Voss et al., 2011).

What influences the contents of our dreams? There are two documented sources. One is the concerns of everyday life. If you're struggling financially, if you've had a death in the family, or if you're studying for an important exam or are involved in an exciting new relationship, these issues may well slip into your dreams (Nikles, Brecht, Klinger, & Bursell, 1998). External stimuli are a second source of influence. Have you ever heard the radio alarm go off but slept through the music and dreamed you were at a concert? Dement (1992) sprayed water on subjects' hands during REM sleep, awakened them a short time later, and found that 42 percent—far more than normal—reported dreaming of rainfalls, leaking roofs, swimming pools, and the like. Similarly, 56 percent incorporated into their dreams the taped sounds of dogs, trains, bells, and other stimuli.

FIGURE 4.8 ■ Most Common Recurring Dreams

Many people report common recurring dreams. Indeed, Americans tend to have many recurring dreams in common.

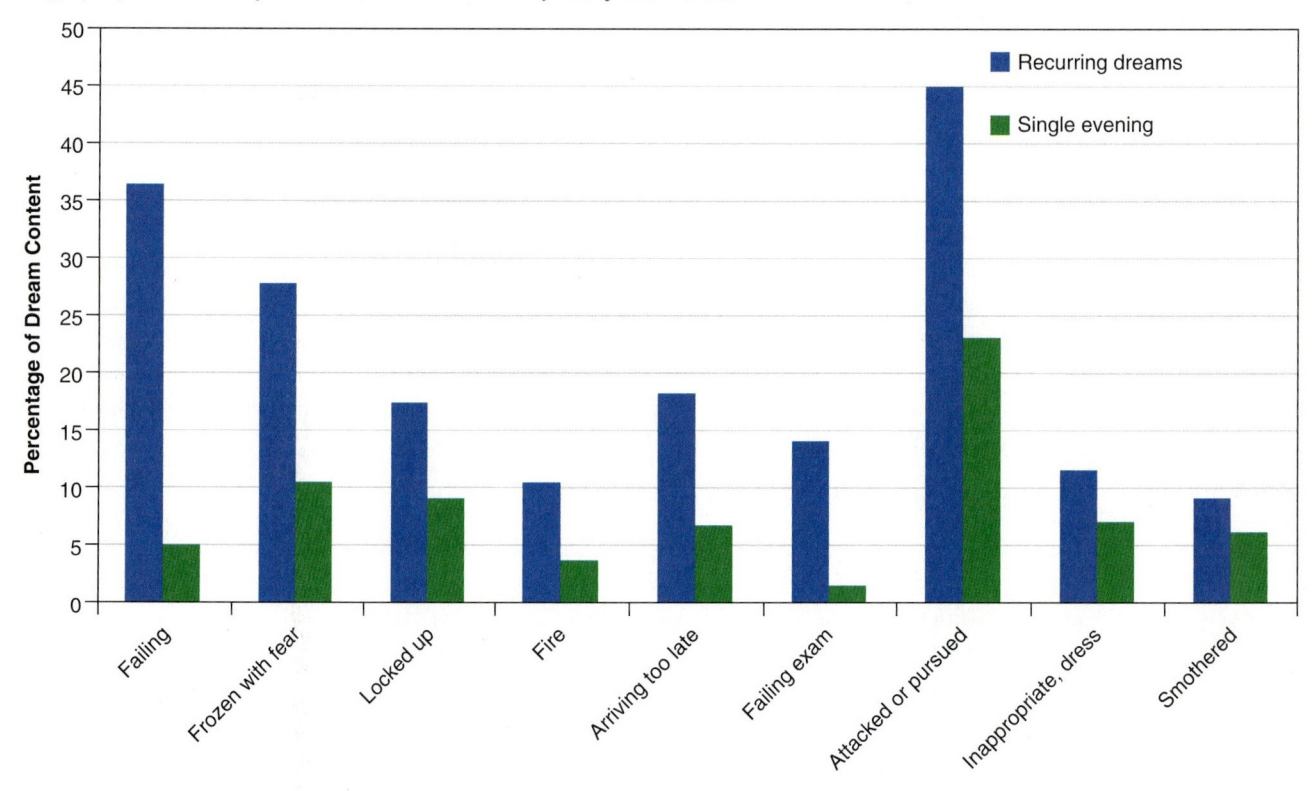

Source: Weinstein, N., Campbell, R. & Vansteenkiste, M. Linking psychological need experiences to daily and recurring dreams. Motiv Emot 42, 50–63 (2018). https://doi.org/10.1007/s11031-017-9656-0

Presumably, we all dream, whether we recall them or not. Understanding what dreams we have and why we have them is a focus of interest for many psychologists.

iStock.com/Adene Sanchez

lucid dreaming. A semiconscious dream state in which sleepers are aware that they are dreaming.

For some dreamers, there is a third source of influence that, in some ways, is the most interesting: themselves. As a general rule, people are not aware that they are dreaming *while* they are dreaming. But have you ever had the odd sensation of dreaming—and knowing that you were in a dream? This "half in–half out" state of consciousness is called **lucid dreaming**. Most people have experienced this state on only an occasional basis—as when a dream takes on such a bizarre quality that they know it cannot be real. But some people are frequent lucid dreamers, and it appears to be a skill that can be developed. In some studies, lucid dreamers were trained to signal the onset of a dream to an experimenter by moving their eyes and clenching their fists. Some lucid dreamers say that at times they can control the contents—and outcomes—of their own dreams. If true, then perhaps lucid dreaming can be used to resolve personal conflicts and tame the monsters in our nightmares (LaBerge, 1992; Rotenberg, 2015).

Our dreams may be influenced by inner concerns and external stimuli and even by our own will. And most dreams are fairly mundane (Cipolli, Bolzani, Cornoldi, DeBeni, & Fagioli, 1993). But sometimes our dreams have a bizarre, magical quality—whereby time seems to stand still or speed forward, shadowy figures appear and vanish on cue, or we fall into bottomless pits, soar like Superman, and float in utter defiance of gravity. How can these qualities be explained? And what do they tell us about why we dream? No one really knows for sure, but there are two major theories.

Freud's Interpretation

In 1900, Sigmund Freud published a classic book entitled *The Interpretation of Dreams*. According to Freud, all people are unconsciously motivated to satisfy sexual and aggressive urges. These ideas are too threatening to express or even to recognize, so we keep them from awareness through the use of psychological defense mechanisms. So far, so good. During sleep, however, our defensive guard is down, and pent-up drives can no longer be suppressed. It would be psychologically shattering to come face to face with our deepest, darkest urges. Such realizations would also disrupt our sleep. The solution: We construct dreams that express the fulfillment of these drives—but in ways that are too indirect and confusing to recognize. In short, the dream we remember in the morning is a disguised, scrambled expression of unconscious wishes. The drive is fulfilled, but in such a way that the psyche—and our sleep—is protected.

manifest content. According to Freud, the conscious dream content that is remembered in the morning.

latent content. According to Freud, the unconscious, censored meaning of a dream.

With his theory of psychoanalysis to guide him (refer to Chapter 14), Freud saw dreams as a "royal road" to the unconscious. He called the dream we remember in the morning the **manifest content**. The underlying thoughts, urges, conflicts, and needs that give rise to that dream constitute its **latent content**. According to Freud, the only way to uncover this unconscious latent material (which, after all, is the "true meaning") is to decode the dream and the symbols that disguise it. In the language of dreams, he said, kings and queens symbolize parents; small animals symbolize children; a house symbolizes the human body; and flying is the mental equivalent of having sex.

Activation-Synthesis Theory

activation-synthesis theory. The theory that dreams result from the brain's attempt to make sense of random neural signals that fire during sleep.

Freud's theory is hard to prove or disprove, and many psychologists worry that it leads us to "overinterpret" dreams. Recent theories take a more neuropsychological approach. The most influential is the **activation-synthesis theory** of J. Allan Hobson and Robert McCarley (1977), which was later revised by Hobson (1988). According to this two-process theory, random neural signals firing in the brainstem spread up to the cortex (activation). Drawing on past experiences stored in memory, the brain then creates images and stories in an effort to make sense out of these random signals (synthesis). According to this account, the brightness, color, and clarity of dream images are triggered by random bursts of sensory neurons during REM sleep (Antrobus, 1991; Hobson & Friston, 2012). Similarly, the physical-motion dreams that Freud described as typical (flying, climbing, falling) are triggered by the activity of motor neurons during REM sleep (Porte & Hobson, 1996).

Comparing Perspectives

Both Freud's account and activation-synthesis theory agree that the dream's manifest content is not meaningful. But they differ in two respects. The first concerns the interpretation of the manifest content. For Freud, the mind constructs bizarre dreams to disguise their true meaning from the dreamer. For Hobson, the brain constructs bizarre dreams because it has only limited information and operates on short notice. Thus, "the manifest content is the dream. There is no other dream" (Hobson, 1988, p. 258). The second key difference concerns the significance attached to the so-called latent content. Freud believed that dreams spring from deep unconscious wishes. Hobson and McCarley argued that dreams are the incidental by-product of neural overactivity.

Research continues to enlighten these dual perspectives on dreaming. For example, Allen Braun and colleagues (1998) used PET scans on sleeping subjects and found that the limbic regions of the brain—areas that control our motivations and emotions—were highly active during REM sleep. In contrast, the frontal lobes—involved in the processes of attention, planning, logical thinking, and short-term memory—were inactive. These results may help to explain why dreams often seem bizarre and illogical. They're also consistent with Freud's contention that dreams reflect deep-seated motivations and emotions—something of a "wishing system," in the words of neuropsychologist Mark Solms (Carpenter, 1999). At this point, there is not enough research to declare a winner between these theoretical approaches. In fact, new theories are still being proposed. Building on the work of Solms (1997), Foulkes (1999), and Domhoff (2001), Yvette Graveline and Erin Wamsley (2015) have proposed that dreaming is a natural extension of waking conscious experience. In this light, dreaming is a cognitive activity that involves a special neural network in the forebrain that develops through childhood, and the contents of our dreams are not that different from our waking thoughts, concerns, and feelings. At this point, all that is clear is that through a complex interplay of physiological and psychological processes, the mind is remarkably active during sleep.

Sleep Disturbances

At some point in life, nearly everyone suffers from a sleep-related problem. You lie in bed, tossing and turning, brooding over something that happened or worrying about something that might. Or you keep nodding off in class, at work, or in other embarrassing situations. Or you leap up in a cold sweat, with your heart pounding, from a realistic and terrifying nightmare. In general, there are three types of sleep disturbances: sleeping too little (insomnia), sleeping too much (hypersomnia), and having disturbed or troubled sleep (parasomnia).

Insomnia

The sleep disturbance known as **insomnia** is characterized by a recurring inability to fall asleep, stay asleep, or get the amount of sleep needed to function during the day. Very few of us adhere to the daily "ideal" of 8 hours for work, 8 for play, and 8 for sleep. On the contrary, people differ in the amount of sleep they want. Some are at their most alert after 6 hours a night, whereas others need 9 or 10 hours to get along. How much time is sufficient depends on who you are.

About one-third of the population complains of insomnia—and roughly half of these people consider the problem to be serious (American Psychiatric Association, 2020). It's not easy to know when someone has insomnia based on self-report, however. In a study that illustrates the point, Mary Carskadon brought 122 insomniacs into the laboratory and compared their self-perceptions to EEG measures of sleep. The next morning, the subjects estimated that it took them an hour to fall asleep and that they slept for 4.5 hours. But EEG tracings revealed that it took them only 15 minutes to fall asleep, which is average, and that they slept for 6.5 hours. More than 10 percent of all complaints are from "pseudoinsomniacs" who sleep normally but don't realize it. Part of the problem is that people with insomnia

insomnia. An inability to fall asleep, stay asleep, or get the amount of sleep needed to function during the day.

For many people, getting to sleep and staying asleep can be a challenge, affecting about a third of the population.

iStock.com/PeopleImages

worry so much about getting to sleep, and then getting enough sleep, that they monitor themselves closely and overestimate the extent of the problem (Harvey, 2002; Neubauer, Pandi-Perumal, Spence, Buttoo, & Monti, 2018).

Today, you can use wearable devices, such as an Apple Watch, a Fitbit, or even a basic phone app to monitor your own sleep. These devices and apps can track many characteristics of your sleep, including duration and quality of sleep and how often you woke up (that is, how often your sleep was interrupted). One caution, though, is that most evidence shows that sleep trackers on wearable devices and in apps can only help you identify patterns in your sleep and give you a good "guesstimate" as to how much sleep you are getting (Evenson, Goto, & Furberg, 2015; Gruwez, Bruyneel, & Bruyneel, 2019). To know exactly how much sleep you are getting, the quality of that sleep, and certainly whether or not your sleep is disordered, you'd have to participate in a medical sleep study or see a physician.

At times, everyone has trouble falling asleep. But what should you do if the problem persists? Research shows that many people can help themselves simply by altering their own sleep-related behavior (American Psychiatric Association, 2017; Maas, 1998). Some recommendations from physicians and psychologists include the following:

- Record how much sleep you get in a night, and set that total as a goal. If you sleep 4 or 5 hours, aim for a 4-hour schedule.

- Do not take naps during the day.

- Avoid all alcohol, caffeine, and cigarettes within 5 hours of bedtime; avoid exercise within 2 hours of bedtime; relax.

- Make sure the bedroom is dark, quiet, and comfortable when you go to bed. That also means not streaming videos or using your phone in bed. When you awaken, turn on the lights and lift the shades.

- Keep a rigid schedule. Get into bed at 1 AM, not earlier. Set the alarm for 5 AM—and get out of bed no matter what.

- If you're awake but relaxed, stay in bed.

- If you're awake and anxious, get out of bed and return when you are sleepy. Keep the alarm set, and get up when it rings.

- If you stick to this schedule, you should see results. If you want, you can then add 30 to 60 minutes to your schedule.

- Rest assured that you can get by on less sleep than you want and that a temporary loss of sleep will cause you no harm.

Can this advice get you to sleep better on your own, without the help of a professional? To answer this question, Veronique Mimeault and Charles Morin (1999) recruited 58 people complaining of insomnia. For a six-week period, one-third of participants were given a take-home course consisting of treatment booklets on sleep, insomnia, and the management of sleep problems. For a second group, the program included weekly phone calls from a therapist. In a third, no-treatment control group, subjects spent the time waiting for the program to begin. Before and after the treatment period, subjects recorded how long it took them to fall asleep each night as well as the total amount of time they slept. Did the self-help program work? Look at Figure 4.9, and you'll find that it did. Compared to subjects in the no-treatment control group, those who took part in the treatment program—regardless of whether or not they talked with a therapist—took less time to get to sleep and spent more time sleeping after the program than before.

Among people who have trouble falling or staying asleep, insomnia can have many causes. On average, psychiatric patients get less sleep than do people without mental disorders (Benca, Obermeyer, Thisted, & Gillin, 1992; Talih, Ajaltouni, Ghandour, Abu-Mohammad, & Kobeissy, 2018). Medical ailments, pain, stress, depression, jet lag, night work, shifting work schedules, old age, and

FIGURE 4.9 ■ **Self-Help Benefits for Insomnia**

In this study, 58 people with insomnia received a self-help program, additional care from a therapist, or no treatment. As shown, all treatment subjects—whether or not they had a therapist—took less time to fall asleep after the program than before it. With guidance, people can help themselves to overcome insomnia.

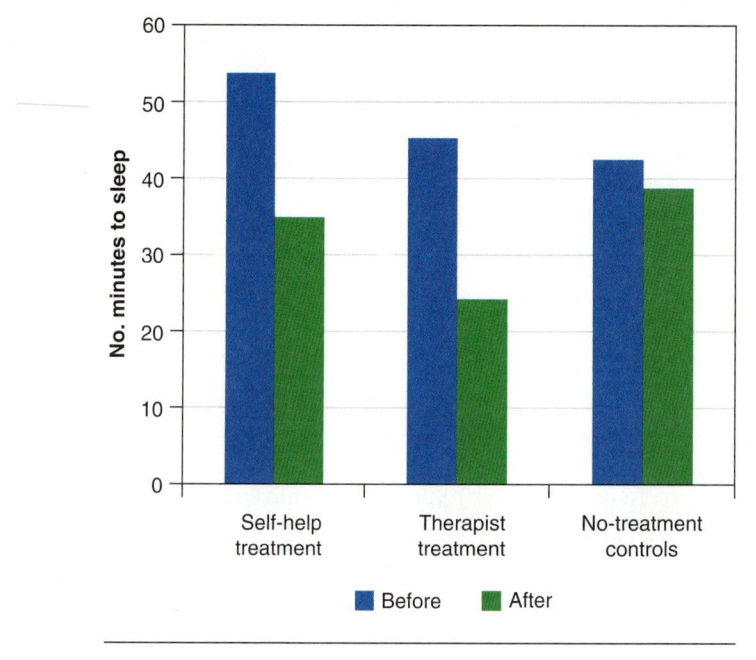

Source: Adapted from Mimeault, V., & Morin, C. M. (1999).

alcohol and drug abuse are also linked to insomnia. In some cases, the only "problem" is that people who think they should sleep 8 hours a night go to bed before they're really tired. The use of medications may also pose an ironic danger. Certain over-the-counter sleeping pills are not effective. Some prescription drugs will, at first, put the insomniac to sleep and prevent rude awakenings during the night, but sedatives may also inhibit certain stages of sleep and cause restlessness after the drug is terminated. Numerous studies have shown that most people can successfully overcome insomnia by altering their behavior—but that the benefits are smaller for those who take sleeping pills (Lichstein & Morin, 2000; Hu, Oh, Ha, Hong, & Oh, 2018).

Hypersomnia

Studies conducted in different countries show that between 5 and 18 percent of people complain of hypersomnia—being sleepy during the day and sleeping too much at night (Guilleminault & Roth, 1993; Slater & Steier, 2012). The most profound and most dangerous problem of this type is **narcolepsy** (meaning "sleep seizure"), an uncommon disorder characterized by sudden, irresistible attacks of drowsiness and REM sleep during the day (American Psychiatric Association, 2020; Materna et al., 2018).

A narcolepsy attack may strike without warning at any time—while playing basketball, eating a meal, having a conversation, working in an office, or having sex. The attack lasts from 5 to 30 minutes and plunges its victim into REM sleep. The narcoleptic's jaw will sag, the head will fall forward, the arms will drop, and the knees will buckle. This collapse is sometimes accompanied by the hypnogogic hallucinations that usher in the onset of sleep. As you might imagine, people with narcolepsy have problems at work and in their social lives. For example, they are often unfairly perceived to be lazy and uninterested (Douglas, 1998). Narcolepsy can be life threatening. In one study, 40 percent of the narcoleptics who were questioned admitted they had fallen asleep while driving (Siegel et al., 1991). Although there is no cure, daytime sleep attacks can be minimized by taking regularly scheduled naps (Mullington & Broughton, 1993) and stimulant drugs (Franceschini et al., 2021).

narcolepsy. A sleep disorder characterized by irresistible and sudden attacks of REM sleep during the day.

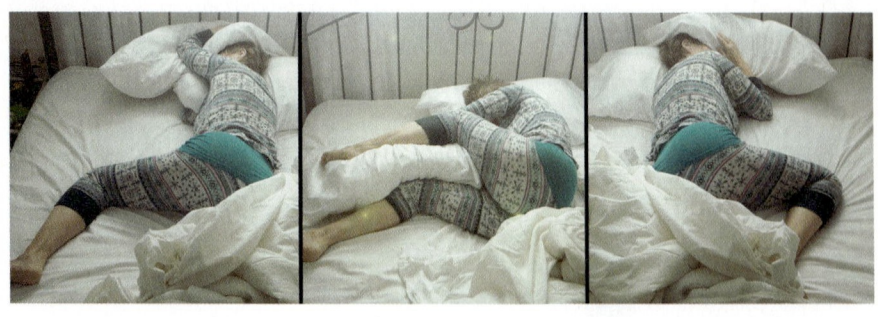

This photograph shows a person tossing and turning due to an insomnia disorder. Insomnia can be a frustrating experience that can have short- and long-term effects on health.

f:nalinframe / Alamy Stock Photo

Parasomnias

For some people, falling asleep at night and staying awake during the day are not a problem—but too often their sleep is disturbed. There are several specific disorders of this type. One particularly troublesome disturbance is **sleep apnea** (*apnea* means "to stop breathing"), which afflicts an estimated 22 million Americans (American Sleep Apnea Association, 2017). A person with sleep apnea will fall asleep normally but then stop breathing and awaken snorting like a buzz saw, choking, and gasping for air. Sleep-laboratory studies show that a person with sleep apnea will fall asleep again right away, but these partial awakenings can recur 400 times during the night, thus preventing slow-wave sleep and making the person excessively tired and irritable during the day (Langevin, Sukkar, Leger, Guez, & Robert, 1992). With some success, the problem can be treated surgically, or with a continuous positive airway pressure (CPAP) device—which pumps air through a tube and into a plastic mask worn during sleep. The air holds the person's throat open and prevents snoring (Bollu, Goyal, Thakkar, & Sahota, 2018; Piccirillo, Duntley, & Schotland, 2000). Of course, many people without apnea also snore while they sleep—much to the discomfort of roommates and bed partners.

Nightmares are vivid, anxiety-provoking dreams that sometimes haunt us during REM sleep—and awaken us. They are common, particularly among children, and should not be a source of concern unless they persist for long periods of time. Nightmares—albeit scary—are not dangerous, except for people with **REM sleep behavior disorder (RBD)**—a very rare condition in which the skeletal muscles do not become paralyzed, as they should, during REM sleep. People with RBD have mobility to act on their nightmares and often do so in violent ways. As a result, 85 percent of sufferers have injured themselves and 44 percent have hurt their bed partners, sometimes seriously (Bassetti & Bargiotas, 2018; Schenck, 1993).

There are also NREM sleep disruptions. In *night terrors*, the person jolts abruptly from a deep sleep, in a state of panic, and gives off a loud, bloodcurdling scream. As with nightmares, this problem is more common among children than among adults. It's also more frightening, particularly for others in the household. Because it occurs during NREM sleep, however, the night-terror victim will usually not recall a dream and by morning will have forgotten the whole episode.

Another NREM experience is *sleepwalking*, in which a sleeper quietly sits up, climbs out of bed, and walks about with eyes open and a blank expression. Sleepwalkers may start slowly, but soon they're going to the bathroom, dressing, eating, and opening doors. They are prone to accidents such as falling down stairs, so it is safer to gently awaken a sleepwalker than to allow the person to wander about. People used to think that sleepwalkers were acting out dreams. But that's not the case. These episodes occur early in the night, during the deep, slow-wave stages of sleep. Sometimes sleepwalkers will wake up and be disoriented, but most often they just go back to bed. Like night-terror victims, sleepwalkers seldom recall their travels in the morning. In a rare and particularly curious variant of the problem, some individuals are said to have engaged in "sleepsex"—sexual acts performed while asleep (Rosenfeld & Elhajjar, 1998). Cleary, the brain is active even during sleep—and, clearly, consciousness is complex and multilayered.

---

sleep apnea. A disorder in which a person repeatedly stops breathing during sleep and awakens gasping for air.

REM sleep behavior disorder (RBD). A condition in which the skeletal muscles are not paralyzed during REM sleep, enabling sleepers to act on their nightmares, often violently.

LEARNING CHECK

Sleeping Generalities

Presleep	
Non-REM sleep stage 1	
Non-REM sleep stage 2	
Non-REM sleep stages 3–4	
REM sleep	

Above, the stages of sleep are divided into five categories. Below are various characteristics and phenomena of sleep. Identify the sleep stages in which thee various sleep phenomena are likeliest to occur.

a. Alpha waves
b. Beta waves
c. Delta waves
d. Theta waves
e. Tensed muscles
f. Paralyzed muscles
g. Genital arousal
h. Sleepwalking
i. Talking in your sleep
j. Sleep spindles
k. Increased blood flow to the brain

(Answers: Presleep: a, b, e; non-REM sleep stage 1: d; non-REM sleep stage 2: j; non-REM sleep stages 3–4: c, h, i; REM sleep: f, g, k.)

HYPNOSIS

LEARNING OBJECTIVES

Explain the phenomenon of hypnosis and how it is used in therapy.

- Describe what hypnosis is and explain why it has always been controversial.
- Summarize the current thinking regarding susceptibility to hypnosis.
- Distinguish between common myths and realities related to hypnosis.
- Relate how hypnosis can be useful in therapy.
- Elaborate on the debate over whether hypnosis is an "altered" state of mind.

Many decades ago, Ernest Hilgard was demonstrating hypnosis in his psychology class. The student who volunteered to serve as a subject happened to be blind, so Hilgard hypnotized him and said that on the count of three he would become deaf—and would stay that way until touched on the right shoulder. One, two, three! Hilgard then banged blocks together and fired a starter's pistol that made everyone else leap from their seats. But the subject did not respond. His classmates shouted questions and taunted him, but still he did not respond. Then a hand went up. A student wanted to know if any part of the subject knew what was happening, because, after all, there was nothing really wrong with his ears.

It was a fascinating question. Hilgard said to the subject, "Perhaps there is some part of your mind that is hearing my voice and processing the information. If there is, I should like the index finger of your right hand to rise as a sign that this is the case." To everyone's surprise, even Hilgard's, the young man raised his finger and said, "Please restore my hearing so that you can tell me what you did." Hilgard then put his hand on the subject's shoulder and asked, "Can you hear me now?" The subject did. "I remember you telling me that I would be deaf at the count of three and have my hearing restored when you placed your hand on my shoulder. Then everything was quiet for a while. It was a little boring just sitting here so I busied myself with a statistical problem that I had been working on. I was still doing that when I felt my finger lift; that is what I want you to explain to me."

Next, Hilgard asked to speak with "that part of your mind that listened to me before, while you were hypnotically deaf." "Do you remember what happened?" The subject remembered it all—the count to three, the banging blocks, the starter pistol, and the questions from the class to which he did not respond. "Then one of them asked if I might really be hearing, and you told me to raise my finger if I did. This part of me responded by raising my finger, so it's all clear now." Hilgard lifted his hand from the subject's arm to restore the hypnotic state and said, "Please tell me what happened in the last few minutes." The subject replied, "You said... some part of me would talk to you. Did I talk?" The young man was assured that he would later recall everything, and the session was terminated (Hilgard, 1992). Hilgard called the aware part of this subject's mind a "hidden observer." This concept is controversial—and, as we'll learn, it has profound implications for the study of consciousness. But first things first. What is hypnosis, how is it induced, and what are its effects?

The Seeds of Controversy

hypnosis. Attention-focusing procedures in which changes in a person's behavior or mental state are suggested.

Hypnosis is a set of attention-focusing procedures in which changes in a person's behavior or state of mind are suggested. In one form or another, hypnosis has been around for centuries, but the earliest known reference to it is traced to Franz Anton Mesmer (1734–1815), a Viennese physician. Mesmer believed that illness was caused by an imbalance of magnetic fluids in the body—and could be cured by restoring the proper balance. Working in Paris, he would pass his hands across the patient's body and wave a magnetic wand over the infected area. Many patients would descend into a trance and then awaken feeling better. The medical community, however, viewed this treatment with skepticism, and in 1784 a French commission chaired by Benjamin Franklin found that there was no scientific basis for the "animal magnetism" theory, only "mere imagination." Mesmer was called a quack and run out of town. When he died, he was penniless. Yet to this day, we acknowledge his work whenever we describe ourselves as being mesmerized.

In the 19th century, the trancelike state Mesmer had created was called hypnotism, from the Greek word for "sleep." From that point on, hypnosis has had a rocky relationship with science (Forrest, 2001). On the one hand, stage hypnotists who swing pocket watches back and forth and try to make audience members cluck like chickens lead people to associate hypnosis with parlor games, carnivals, and magic shows. On the other hand, psychoanalysis originated with Freud's use of hypnosis to treat patients with various nervous disorders. Today, many health care specialists use hypnosis with reasonable success to control pain and help patients break bad habits (American Psychological Association, 2020b).

The Hypnotic Induction

Hypnosis consists of two stages: an *induction*, which guides the subject into a pliable, suggestible frame of mind; then a specific *suggestion*. The induction process is not like casting a spell. There are no magical words or incantations to be uttered, and there is no single technique. But there is one essential ingredient: a focusing of attention.

Hypnosis is important in the history of psychology. This 1780 engraving depicts treatment by animal magnetism as practiced by Franz Mesmer. "Mesmerism" is today considered a form of hypnosis.

duncan1890/Getty

Speaking in a slow, soft, monotonous tone of voice, the hypnotist asks the subject to concentrate on something. It could be anything. Hypnotists used to have subjects stare at a flame, a shiny object, or a swinging pendulum, but a spot on the wall will work just as well. So will the subject's imagination. "Imagine that you're lying on a quiet beach. You are so warm and relaxed on the soft white sand, under the sun. You're very tired, and your eyes are closed. You can hear the ocean waves crashing on the shore and the gulls flying overhead. And you can smell the warm, salt air. It's so sunny. Your skin is so warm. And you're so relaxed. Your eyes are growing tired. Very tired. Your eyelids are getting heavy. Heavy. They're starting to close." Whatever technique is used, the purpose is to help the subject filter out all distractions and focus a mental spotlight.

Once the subject is in a state of "relaxed alertness," the individual is ripe for the second stage, the suggestion. The hypnotist may begin with a quick test by suggesting that "your eyes are closed and your eyelids are shut so tight that you cannot open them no matter how hard you try." Sure enough, the subject's eyes remain closed. At that point, the subject is ready for more. The hypnotist may note that the subject's arm is filling with air like a balloon and that it's feeling lighter and lighter—and is rising in the air. The subject does not know why, but the arm rises, as if being pulled up on a string. The hypnotist may even invite the subject to enjoy the scent of "perfume"—and watch as he or she inhales the fumes from a jar of ammonia. Assuming the subject "passes" these preliminary tests, additional suggestions depend on the reasons for the hypnosis. Thus, a subject may be encouraged to block out pain, recall a traumatic past event, forget a past event, or break a bad habit when the session is over.

Hypnotic Responsiveness

Contrary to popular belief, you cannot be hypnotized against your will. Nobody can. People also respond differently. Over half a century ago, Hilgard (1965) developed the Stanford Hypnotic Susceptibility Scale (SHSS), a 12-item behavioral test that measures one's **hypnotic susceptibility**, or responsiveness to hypnosis. In this test, a brief induction is followed by suggestions for the subject to close his or her eyes, sway back and forth, stiffen an arm, lower a hand, see an imaginary person, and so on. Over the years, Hilgard has found that some people are highly susceptible to hypnosis and that others are invulnerable to hypnosis but that most fall somewhere between these extremes (Hilgard, 1982). In short, some types of people are more susceptible, and others are less susceptible, to hypnosis.

What accounts for these individual differences? Research has shown that college students who scored high or low in the early 1960s scored similarly when retested 25 years later (Piccione, Hilgard, & Zimbardo, 1989). This result tells us that there are stable personality differences between the highs and lows. But how are these differences to be interpreted? It's interesting that in discussions of hypnosis, students often seem eager if not proud to proclaim that they are too "independent" or too "strong-willed" to be hypnotized. But hypnotic responsiveness is not a sign of weakness. High scorers are not generally weaker or more conforming, compliant, or obedient. But they are more open to experience, have more vivid imaginations, and have an ability to become deeply absorbed in books, movies, and other activities (Nadon, Hoyt, Register, & Kihlstrom, 1991; Zhang et al., 2017). In one study, individuals highly responsive to hypnosis—often referred to as "virtuosos"—were led under hypnosis to experience themselves as members of the opposite sex (Noble & McConkey, 1995).

hypnotic susceptibility. The extent to which an individual is characteristically responsive to hypnosis.

The Myths and Realities

Can a stage hypnotist make you strip naked in front of an audience, clap your hands together, and bark like a seal? Popular portrayals of hypnosis are sometimes accurate, but often they are not. Based on the results of controlled research, let us examine the effects of hypnosis and try to separate the myths from the realities.

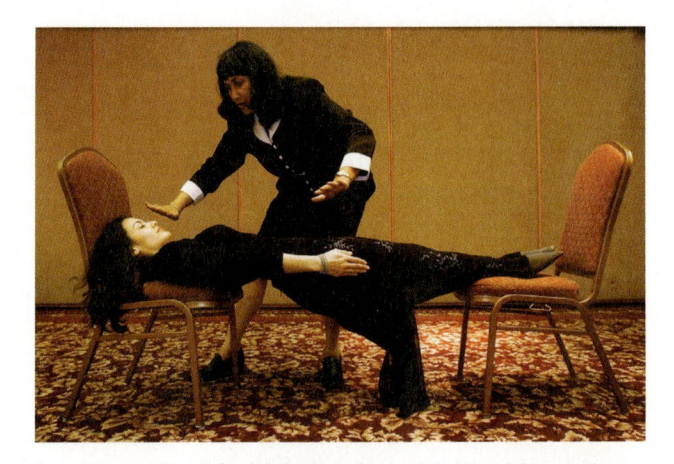

Hypnosis is commonly applied in clinical settings where psychologists can help treat patients. Knowing how hypnotism works can be as helpful for the patient as it can for the hypnotist.

David McNew / Staff/Getty

Coercion

As noted earlier, people cannot be hypnotized against their will. But can subjects, once under hypnosis, be coerced into acts that violate the conscience? Are they completely at the mercy of a skilled hypnotist? For the sake of those who may benefit from the therapeutic uses of hypnosis, one would hope not. In response to the notion that the subject is under the hypnotist's control, Karen Olness (1993), a pediatrician and hypnotherapist, says, "Nonsense. All hypnosis is self-hypnosis" (p. 280). Most psychologists similarly reject the view that hypnosis renders us helpless. And as a general rule, hypnotized subjects reject immoral commands, knowing full well that they are in control (Känd, 2020).

But evidence suggests that hypnotic coercion can lead people to shed inhibitions and perform hurtful or antisocial acts—such as stealing, picking up a dangerous snake, selling an illicit drug, and mutilating the Bible. In one experiment, Martin Orne and Frederick Evans (1965) convinced hypnotized subjects to throw what they thought to be nitric acid into a research assistant's face. To determine if this result proved that hypnosis can overpower the will, Orne and Evans told a second group of subjects only to pretend they were hypnotized, issued the same command, and found that they too threw the "acid." Additional studies also suggest that subjects in hypnosis experiments are aware of what they are doing—and are confident that they would not be asked to harm themselves or someone else (Gibson, 1991). As we'll explore later, these results may say more about obedience to authority than about hypnosis.

Pain Relief

"On the operating table, I put myself into a deeply relaxed state. I then concentrated on a favorite memory: living on a farm as a child. In my mind, I felt what it was like to lie on the grass, gaze up at the heavens, and see a bit of the barn out of the corner of my eye. As the surgeon cut into the base of my thumb, I reassured him that I felt no pain.... Although I was perfectly aware that I was undergoing surgery, I just wasn't very interested in it." This story, as described by Olness (1993, p. 277), embodies a real benefit of hypnosis: to serve as a psychological anesthetic.

In the classic test of this hypothesis, Hilgard, Morgan, and MacDonald (1975) instructed two groups of subjects to immerse one hand in a tank of ice water for almost a minute. Every 10 seconds, they rated how much pain they felt on a 10-point scale. In one group, subjects were hypnotized and given the suggestion that they would feel no pain. In the second group, there was no hypnosis and no suggestion. The result was that the hypnotized subjects reported less pain than did the control subjects. We'll return to this study shortly to find out what it implies about consciousness. What it implies about pain, however, is clear. Today, studies show that for people high in hypnotic responsiveness, hypnosis can be used to reduce pain—and that this effect can be achieved with or without the use of counter-pain images, such as suggestions that the hand is made of wood or is encased in a heavy protective glove (Hargadon, Bowers, & Woody, 1995). Not everyone can be hypnotized, and not all who are hypnotized will gain relief from pain. But the benefits are common enough that hypnosis is used today in medical settings, and for some, hypnosis can help in coping with dental work, childbirth, and the chronic pain of headaches, backaches, and arthritis (Häuser, Hagl, Schmierer, & Hansen, 2016).

Posthypnotic Suggestion

In the situations described thus far, the subject acts on the hypnotist's suggestions during the session. In a procedure known as **posthypnotic suggestion**, the subject carries out the hypnotist's suggestion *after* the session is terminated. You've probably seen this procedure depicted on TV shows. With a snap of the finger, the subject would emerge from his or her "trance" and reflexively do something odd in response to a preset cue. But does it really work? It can, but only with some individuals. To demonstrate the point, Amanda Barnier and Kevin McConkey (1998) gave 120 prepaid

---

posthypnotic suggestion. A suggestion made to a subject in hypnosis to be carried out after the induction session is over.

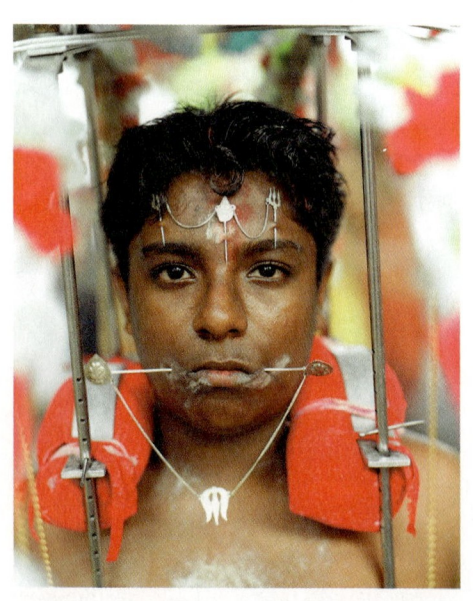

Many claims about the power of hypnosis are controversial, but research shows that it does enable some people to tolerate pain. At Thaipusam, a Hindu Festival that honors the god of power and virtue, devotees enter a hypnotic trance during which time they endure painful types of mutilation—like long silver needles that pierce the tongue, cheeks, and other body parts.

xPACIFICA/Getty

postcards to subjects who were high in hypnotic susceptibility and instructed them, during hypnosis, to mail one postcard every day for four months. Afterward, they counted the number of cards received and found that more than half of all the postcards were sent in accordance with the hypnotic suggestion.

In reality, posthypnotic suggestion lacks dramatic flair. But when it is coupled with psychological therapy, it has been used effectively to help people with insomnia, obesity, high blood pressure, and other behavior-related problems (Kirsch, Montgomery, & Sapirstein, 1995). It can also help speed the healing of warts and other skin conditions, and help in the medical treatment of asthma, nausea, and certain other conditions that have a psychological component (Pinnell & Covino, 2000).

Memory Enhancement

As in Hilgard's classroom demonstration, hypnosis subjects often exhibit **posthypnotic amnesia**, an inability to recall events that occurred during the session. However, these memories have not been permanently erased. In response to a prearranged signal ("When I snap my fingers, you'll recall everything that took place"), subjects can usually retrieve the lost events. Still, research suggests that hypnosis subjects do often exhibit temporary amnesia—and do so without effort or intention (Bowers & Woody, 1996).

At the other end of the hypnosis-memory spectrum, many hypnotists claim that the highly focused and relaxed state of mind produced by hypnosis enhances memory, a phenomenon known as **hypermnesia**. This claim has its roots in psychoanalysis—from Freud's reports that hypnotized patients sometimes relived repressed traumas from childhood—and has resurfaced in a rash of 1990s and early 21st century cases in which hypnosis was used to dredge up "memories" of child sex abuse.

In Chapter 6 on memory, we'll find that people cannot remember events from the first and second years of life. Yet research shows that people can be induced to report early childhood memories in hypnosis-like conditions. In one study, subjects asked for their earliest memories recounted events that occurred at about 3 and 4 years old. But after being induced to shut their eyes, visualize, and focus on the deep past, 78 percent "recalled" events that occurred before their second birthday and 33 percent even produced events from before their first birthday (Malinoski & Lynn, 1999). In a second study, 40 percent of those who were hypnotized and led to believe that hypnosis improves memory recounted events that took place before their first birthday (Green, 1999). Yet, what are the chances that these memories are false? How do we know that the "recalled" events truly happened to the participants? Questions like these are a big reason why the use of hypnosis as a memory aid has come under some close scrutiny within the legal system.

posthypnotic amnesia. A reported tendency for hypnosis subjects to forget events that occurred during the induction.

hypermnesia. A term referring to the unsubstantiated claim that hypnosis can be used to facilitate the retrieval of past memories.

Psychology Applied: Does Hypnosis Enhance Eyewitness Testimony?

It was an extraordinary case: A busload of California schoolchildren and their driver were abducted at gunpoint by three masked kidnappers and held for ransom in an underground tomb. Somehow, they managed to escape. The driver had tried to memorize the license plate number of the van the kidnappers used, but he could not later recall the number. He was then hypnotized by the police and was mentally transported back to the crime scene. All of a sudden, he blurted out all but one digit of the license plate—which led to the arrest and conviction of the abductors (Smith, 1983).

This story and others like it raise an intriguing question: Can hypnosis be used to refresh a witness's memory? Many police officers seem to think so and use hypnosis to help eyewitnesses recall details of violent crimes they seem to have forgotten. In one popular technique, devised by Martin Reiser (1980), subjects under hypnosis are asked to imagine that they are calmly watching a TV documentary about the event to be recalled and that they can rewind it, stop it, play it back, slow it down, speed it up, zoom in for close ups, and turn the sound volume up or down to improve hearing. Using this technique, police investigators have made some impressive claims about the memory-enhancing power of hypnosis (Hibbard & Worring, 1996).

When memory fades, this can be challenging for loved ones as well as the patients. Often the simple exercise of looking through childhood photos can bring back memories, even if only for a moment.

iStock.com/PeopleImages

The success stories are fascinating, but serious questions remain. When a hypnotized witness reports a memory, how do we know that the report is accurate? And if the recollection is later corroborated, how do we know that it was retrieved because of the hypnosis? To answer these questions, some researchers have studied actual cases. Others have conducted experiments in which subjects witness a staged event, report their memory, and then try to recall additional details—either under hypnosis or in a normal waking state. Consistently, the research has shown that although people report more information with repeated testing, they also inadvertently produce more distorted and false "memories" (Dinges et al., 1992; McConkey & Sheehan, 1995).

Another disturbing outcome of hypnosis is that it places witnesses in a state of heightened suggestibility. For example, Peter Sheehan and colleagues (1991) showed 168 subjects a videotape of a staged bank robbery. In it, a man entered a bank, waved a pistol, warned the tellers not to press an alarm, ordered them to put the money on the counter, put the money in a bag, and ran out. Subjects were immediately questioned about the incident. Half were then hypnotized; the others were not. Moments later, everyone was requestioned by an examiner who "suggested" that the robber wore a mask over his face, which he did not. All the hypnotized subjects were then dehypnotized, and everyone was questioned again, this time by a new examiner.

Did anyone "recall" the robber wearing a mask? If so, how often did this occur? As illustrated in Figure 4.10, the results were quite striking—and sobering. Subjects were more likely to incorporate the false suggestion into memory when they were under hypnosis, and this was particularly true of those who had high or medium scores on a test of hypnotic susceptibility. Among the most vulnerable subjects—those who were both highly susceptible and were exposed to a hypnotic suggestion—false memories were created 63 percent of the time. Other researchers have confirmed this finding, leading us to conclude that hypnosis adds to the risk that witnesses will make memory errors and be influenced by misleading questions (Scoboria, Mazzoni, Kirsch, & Milling, 2002).

Consider this evidence in light of the fact that eyewitness error is a leading cause of wrongful convictions (Wise, Sartori, Magnussen, & Safer, 2014). For example, eyewitness error or misidentification was evident in about 75 percent of 312 cases in which DNA exonerated a convicted person (The Innocence Project, 2021), and in about 76 percent of 873 cases reviewed in the National Registry of Exonerations (Gross & Shaffer, 2012). In an analysis of 1,198 cases of wrongful conviction, Smith and Cutler (2013) further concluded "that about 50% of the cases of conviction of the innocent involved mistaken identification" (p. 11), and the American Psychological Association (2016) estimates that about one of every three eyewitnesses makes an erroneous identification. It is therefore critical to be aware of this evidence, especially since hypnosis adds to the risk that witnesses will make memory errors.

Is Hypnosis an "Altered" State?

Since the time Mesmer first used hypnotism to treat medical ailments, there has been widespread interest in the phenomenon. Freud used hypnosis to unlock the unconscious. Others have used it to relieve pain, to treat psychological problems, to uncover repressed memories, and to entertain audiences around the world. Using hypnosis is easy. The tougher question is: What is it? Does hypnosis produce an out-of-the-ordinary, trancelike, "altered" state of consciousness?

Psychologists are not in agreement on this question. Some say yes, others say no. As a general rule, *special-process* theorists maintain that hypnosis induces a unique state of consciousness and that people are more responsive to suggestion while under hypnosis than in other states (Bowers, 1992; Yeh, Schnur, & Montgomery, 2014). In contrast, a growing number of *social-cognitive* theorists maintain that hypnosis is not a distinct physiological state and that the same phenomena can sometimes be produced through relaxation, role playing, positive expectations, or mere suggestion—without hypnotic induction (Lilienfeld & Arkowitz, 2008; Lynn, Rhue, & Weekcs, 1990; Nash & Benham, 2005).

FIGURE 4.10 ■ Hypnosis and the Suggestible Eyewitness

After observing a staged crime, subjects were questioned in a hypnotized or waking state by an examiner who suggested that the culprit had worn a mask. Under hypnosis, many subjects—particularly those high in responsiveness—later incorporated this false suggestion into memory.

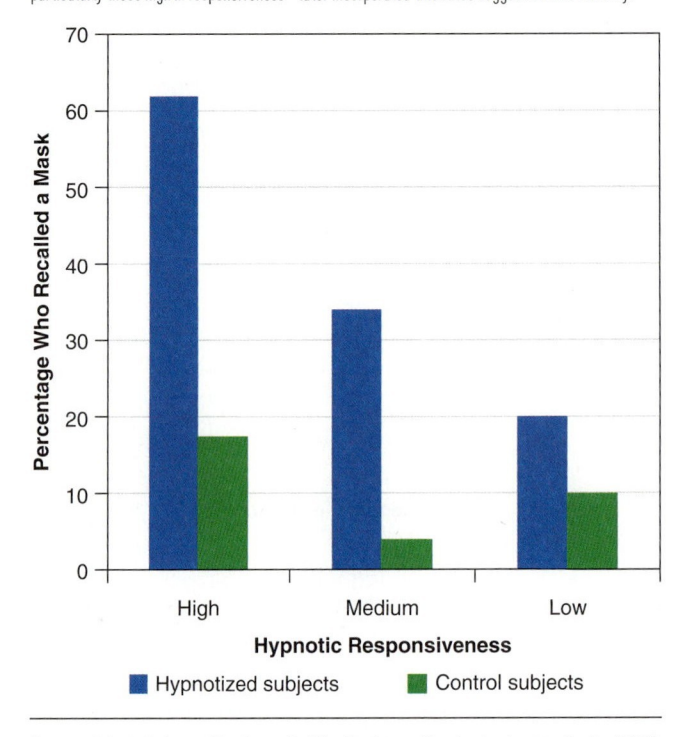

Source: Adapted from Sheehan, P. W., Statham, D., & Jamieson, G. A. (1991). Pseudomemory effects and their relationship to level of susceptibility to hypnosis and state instruction. Journal of Personality and Social Psychology, 60(1), 130–137. https://doi.org/10.1037/0022-3514.60.1.130

Special-Process Theories

According to Ernest Hilgard (1986), hypnosis can induce a state of **dissociation**—a division of consciousness into two or more parts that operate independently and are separated by an "amnesic barrier." In some ways, dissociation is a common experience—as when you drive somewhere, only to realize afterward that you "spaced out" and can't recall the route you took or the traffic signals you obeyed. One part of you drove, while another part of you daydreamed. In many people, says Hilgard, hypnosis produces a similar split in which one part of the mind goes along with hypnotic suggestions, while another part—a "hidden observer"—knows what's happening but does not participate.

To illustrate this concept, let's return to the pain-tolerance experiment described earlier, where subjects immersed a hand in ice water and periodically rated how much pain they were in (Hilgard et al., 1975). Figure 4.11 shows that subjects reported far less pain when they were hypnotized to "feel no pain" than when they were not. Compared to control subjects, who reached a pain level of 10 within 25 seconds, the average pain rating of hypnotized subjects never exceeded a 2 on the scale. In a fascinating variation on this study, hypnotized subjects were told to press a key with their free hand if "some part" of them was in pain. Figure 4.11 also illustrates the results of this variation. Even though the hypnotized subjects reported low pain levels, their hidden observer was passively aware of the pain. Because these subjects reported two very different experiences at once, reasoned Hilgard, the hypnosis must have induced a state of dissociation. Well, perhaps.

Social-Cognitive Theories

The skeptics differ in their emphases, but all agree that the impressive effects of hypnosis stem from the power of social influence, not from any special process or trancelike state of altered consciousness.

dissociation. A division of consciousness that permits one part of the mind to operate independently of another part.

FIGURE 4.11 ■ Hypnosis, Pain, and the "Hidden Observer"

Subjects immersed a hand in ice water and rated the pain they felt. Those under hypnosis reported less pain than did control subjects. But by pressing a key, they also indicated that a part of them—a "hidden observer"—was aware of the pain.

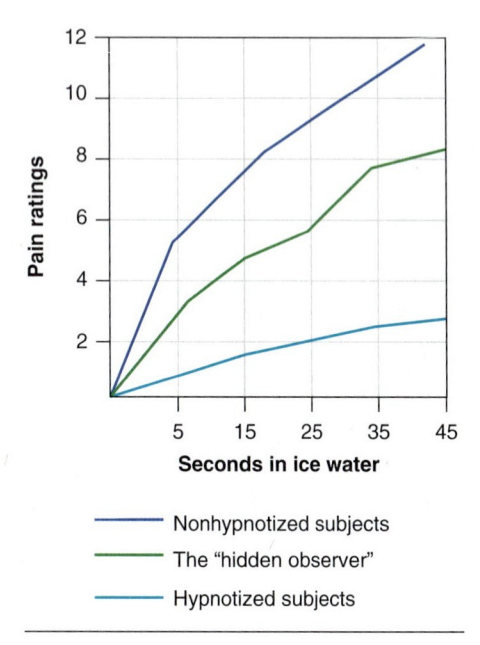

— Nonhypnotized subjects
— The "hidden observer"
— Hypnotized subjects

Source: Adapted from Hilgard, E. R., Morgan, A. H., & Macdonald, H. (1975). Pain and dissociation in the cold pressor test: A study of hypnotic analgesia with "hidden reports" through automatic key pressing and automatic talking. Journal of Abnormal Psychology, 84(3), 280–289. https://doi.org/10.1037/h0076654

Perhaps highly responsive subjects are motivated to comply. Or perhaps they simply become so absorbed by the situation that they get caught up in their role the way dramatic actors often do. In support of this view, research shows that control subjects in the waking state often exhibit the same remarkable behaviors—when they are sufficiently motivated and believe they can succeed. Thus, pain tolerance in the ice-water test can be increased without a hypnotic induction (Hay, Okkerse, van Amerongen, & Groeneveld, 2016).

Although there are exceptions, most social-cognitive theorists do not believe that hypnosis subjects consciously fake their compliance with the hypnotist's suggestions (Jensen et al., 2015; Kirsch & Lynn, 1995). Is it possible to test this hypothesis? Yes. If subjects are merely playing along, they might respond to suggestions in the hypnotist's presence—but certainly not in his or her absence. In fact, however, the hypnotic effects carry over. Eve Marie Perugini and others (1998) hypnotized highly responsive subjects but instructed low-responsive subjects to simulate the hypnosis. The hypnotic test was twice administered over a tape recorder—once in front of the examiner and once when the subject was left alone. The results were clear: In front of the examiner, both the hypnotized subjects and simulators complied equally with suggestions. But in the alone condition, a hidden camera revealed that highly responsive hypnosis subjects continued to pet imaginary cats, nod their heads to imaginary music, and respond to other suggestions even while the simulators did not. Additional studies too have shown that hypnotized subjects are not just deceiving the experimenter (Jensen et al., 2015; Kinnunen, Zamanksi, & Block, 1994). Hypnosis may not trigger a "special" process, but the behavior it produces reflects more than mere compliance.

At this point, hypnosis can be viewed in many ways. For example, highly responsive individuals in hypnosis may become so highly focused in their attention and so absorbed that the process feels "special." When college students were interviewed about their behavior in a campuswide hypnotism show, 28 percent of those who took part thought the hypnotist had complete control over their actions and that they could not resist the suggestions (Crawford, Kitner-Triolo, Clarke, & Otesko, 1992). In addition, EEG recordings show that alpha-wave activity—which typically accompanies a drowsy, presleep state—increases during hypnosis, particularly among subjects high in hypnotic responsiveness (Graffin, Ray, & Lundy, 1995). PET scan studies also reveal that hypnosis activates certain areas of the cerebral cortex (Graham, 2005; Rainville et al., 1999). At the same time, some people succumb to hypnosis and comply with suggestions through normal channels of social influence, without a change in the state of their consciousness—which explains why our expectations, motivations, and rapport with the hypnotist play an important role (Jensen et al., 2015; Kirsch & Lynn, 1999). In short, there may be two roads, both leading to the same state.

LEARNING CHECK

Consciousness Raising

Match each phenomenon of consciousness in the left column with its closest description from the right.

1.	Hypermnesia	a.	The tendency for a recently repeated word to facilitate responses in a subsequent situation.
2.	Priming	b.	Any regular, periodic fluctuation in an organism.
3.	Dissociation	c.	Sudden, irresistible attacks of REM sleep during the day.
4.	Biological rhythm	d.	Term referring to the unsubstantiated claim that hypnosis can facilitate retrieval of memories.
5.	Circadian rhythm	e.	A disorder in which a person repeatedly stops breathing during sleep.
6.	Sleep apnea	f.	A biological cycle that occurs about every 24 hours.
7.	Narcolepsy	g.	A division of consciousness that permits one part of the mind to operate independently of another part.

(Answers: 1.d; 2.a; 3.g; 4.b; 5.f; 6.e; 7.c)

CONSCIOUSNESS-ALTERING DRUGS

LEARNING OBJECTIVES

Identify psychoactive and addictive drugs and the effects of drug use on consciousness and long-term health.

- Identify drugs that are considered psychoactive and addictive, and explain their mechanism of action.
- Describe the effects on consciousness of alcohol and tobacco.
- Relate the long-term health effects of illicit drugs.
- Discuss whether people can control what is in the spotlight of consciousness.

Throughout history, people all over the world have sought new ways to achieve altered states of consciousness. Dancing, chanting, twirling in circles, repetitive prayer, yoga, ritualized fasting, meditation, sensory isolation, and intoxicants such as opium, alcohol, marijuana, and cocaine are a few examples (illustrated in Figure 4.12). The historical and cross-cultural consistency of these behaviors is so compelling that some researchers believe that humans have an inborn need to experience altered states of mind (Leotti, Iyengar, & Ochsner, 2010; Weil & Rosen, 1993; Rudgley, 1999).

Alcohol, possibly the first "mind-altering" substance used by humans, goes back about 10,000 years. According to Bert Vallee (1998), alcoholic beverages were the mother's milk of Western civilization before clean, pure water became available. He notes, for example, that the Bible contains many references to wine but little mention of water as a beverage. Other mind-altering drugs also have a long history, as opium was used 6,000 years ago and hallucinogenic mushrooms and weeds go back about 4,000 years (Palfai & Jankiewicz, 1991). More recently, Native Americans smoked tobacco as a goodwill offering. South Pacific islanders drank kava, a calming drink that is made from dried roots. Europeans celebrated special occasions with wine and champagne. Instances of drug use have even been observed in animals. Baboons eat tobacco, rabbits eat intoxicating mushrooms, and elephants seek out fermented fruit.

A quick but often dangerous way to alter consciousness is to use a **psychoactive drug**, a chemical that influences perceptions, moods, thoughts, or behavior. Depending on where in the world you are, a psychoactive substance may be legal or illegal. In most countries, caffeine, tobacco, alcohol, tranquilizers, and sleeping pills are legal. Cocaine, crack, heroin, and LSD (lysergic acid diethylamide) are illegal

psychoactive drug.
A chemical that alters perceptions, thoughts, moods, or behavior.

FIGURE 4.12 ■ Altered States of Consciousness

People all over the world behave in ways that alter states of consciousness. As shown, an enactment of a Zulu death ritual in Johannesburg, South Africa; a Mayan woman performs a ritual in front of the Santo Tomás church in Chichicastenango, Guatemala; and a large gathering of Hindu pilgrims pass a bridge during Kumbh Mela in Rishikesh, India.

iStock.com/ManoAfrica; iStock.com/Tiago_Fernandez; iStockphoto.com/ozgurdonmaz

and are referred to as illicit drugs. As in our ancient past, humans are also in hot pursuit of the perfect aphrodisiac—a drug that is supposed to enhance sexual desire, pleasure, and performance (Crowley, Kirschner, Dunn, & Bornstein, 2017; Korcha, Polcin, Bond, Lapp, & Galloway, 2011).

Psychoactive drugs can become physically or psychologically addictive. **Physical dependence** is a physiological state in which continued drug use is needed to satisfy an intense craving and to prevent the dreaded onset of *withdrawal* symptoms such as shaking, sweating, and vomiting. Continued use of psychoactive drugs also produces *tolerance*, a condition in which larger and larger doses are needed to induce the same effect. Even without a physical addiction, people can also develop a **psychological dependence**, in which continued drug use is needed to maintain a sense of well-being.

There are four major classes of psychoactive drugs: sedatives, stimulants, hallucinogens, and opiates (summarized in Table 4.1).

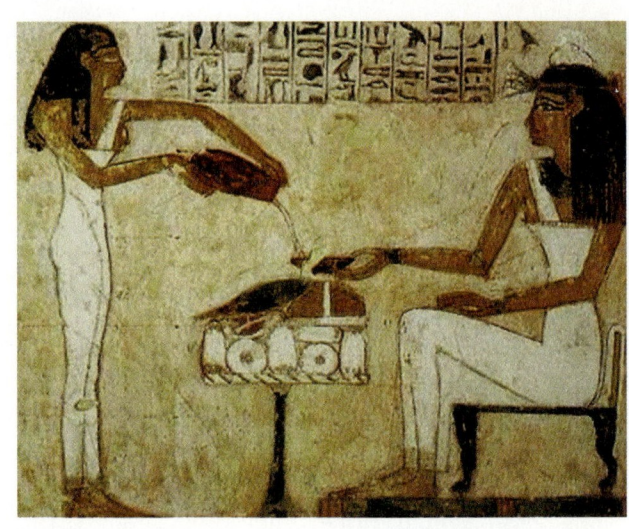

Drug use is a problem in general but is of greatest concern among youths. Drugs commonly used by youths in the United States are presented in Figure 4.13.

People have used psychoactive drugs throughout history. In this Egyptian painting, the woman on the left is pouring beer from a jug.
Historic Images / Alamy Stock Photo

Sedatives

Sedatives, or depressants, slow down activity in the central nervous system and produce calmness, drowsiness, and, in large doses, a loss of consciousness. The most commonly used sedatives are barbiturates, benzodiazepines, and, of course, alcohol. The first two are used for anesthetic purposes and in the treatment of anxiety and insomnia. As a rule, these drugs are highly addictive (Weaver, 2015).

Barbiturates are sedatives that have been used in the treatment of epilepsy, anxiety, and insomnia (Lickey & Gordon, 1991). The behavioral effects of barbiturates are similar to those of alcohol—such as drowsiness, slowness, and decreased performance on perceptual and cognitive tasks. In large doses, barbiturates also serve as an anesthetic, providing significant relief from pain. However, they tend to cause hangovers after the effects wear off. Barbiturates are among the most abused of all drugs. They are also addictive. Tolerance to barbiturates develops rapidly, and withdrawal symptoms are unpleasant. Mixing alcohol with barbiturates is especially dangerous.

physical dependence. A physiological addiction in which a drug is needed to prevent symptoms of withdrawal.

psychological dependence. A condition in which drugs are needed to maintain a sense of well-being or relief from negative emotions.

sedatives. A class of depressant drugs that slow down activity in the central nervous system.

TABLE 4.1 ■ Consciousness-Altering Drugs		
Type	**Substance**	**Range of Effects**
Sedatives	Alcohol, barbiturates, benzodiazepines	Slowdown of body functions, relaxation, drowsiness, possibly depression and loss of consciousness
Stimulants	Caffeine, nicotine, amphetamines, cocaine	Speed up of body functions, alertness, energy, elation, jitteriness, loss of appetite
Hallucinogens	LSD, marijuana	Heightened sensory awareness, distorted perceptions of time and space, hallucinations
Opiates	Heroin, morphine, codeine	Suppressed pain, depressed neural activity, relaxation, drowsiness, euphoria

FIGURE 4.13 ■ Commonly Used Drugs of Abuse

Past month substance use among people aged 12 or older, 2018.

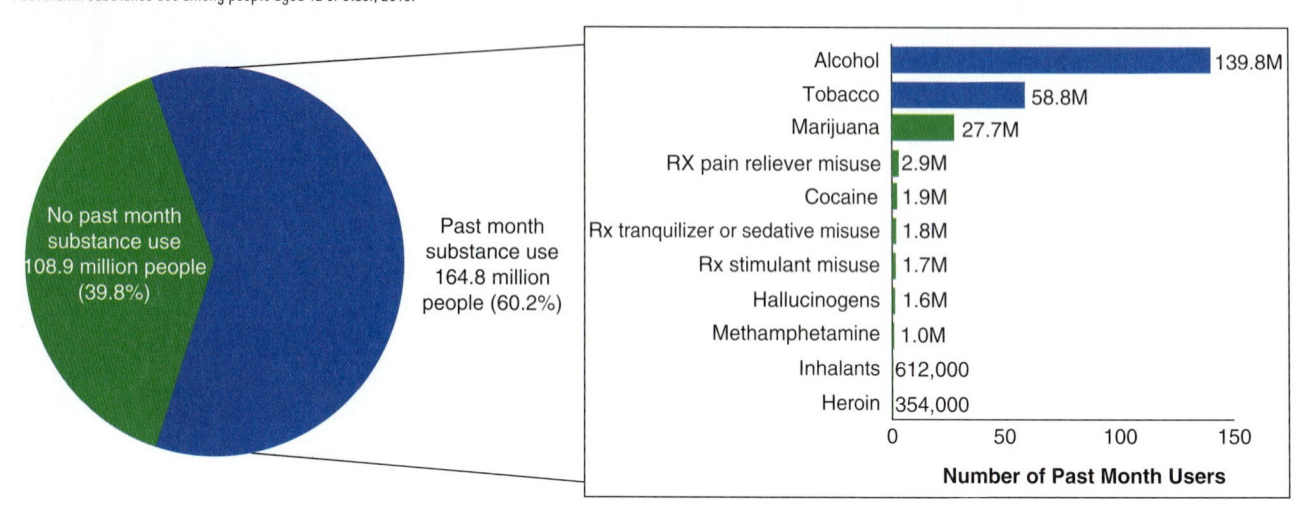

No past month substance use 108.9 million people (39.8%)

Past month substance use 164.8 million people (60.2%)

Substance	Number of Past Month Users
Alcohol	139.8M
Tobacco	58.8M
Marijuana	27.7M
RX pain reliever misuse	2.9M
Cocaine	1.9M
Rx tranquilizer or sedative misuse	1.8M
Rx stimulant misuse	1.7M
Hallucinogens	1.6M
Methamphetamine	1.0M
Inhalants	612,000
Heroin	354,000

RX = prescription.
Note: The estimated numbers of current users of different substances are not mutually exclusive because people could have used more than one type of substance in the past month.

Source: Key Substance Use and Mental Health Indicators in the United States: Results from the 2018 National Survey on Drug Use and Health. Substance Abuse and Mental Health Services Administration (SAMHSA), U.S. Department of Health and Human Services (HHS)

Benzodiazepines, or minor tranquilizers, are another class of drugs often used in the treatment of anxiety and insomnia. Valium, Librium, and, more recently, Xanax are the most common "downers." Taken in pill form, they have a calming and relaxing effect and put people to sleep—usually for the entire night. Benzodiazepines are safer than barbiturates—except when mixed with alcohol. They have become the sedatives of choice for many people, though they can be quite addictive with prolonged use.

Alcohol is one of the most widely used drugs in the world. The 2015 National Survey on Drug Use and Health (U.S. Department of Health and Human Services, 2017) revealed that, among college students (ages 18–22), 58 percent drank alcohol in the past month (compared to 48 percent of same-age peers), 38 percent reported binge drinking (five or more drinks in one sitting) in the past month (compared to 33 percent of same-age peers), and 12.5 percent reported heavy alcohol use in the past month (compared to 8.5 percent of same-age peers). The question is, what are the effects?

Regardless of whether it comes from a six pack, a bottle of wine, or a glass of whiskey, gin, or vodka, alcohol is something of a paradox. It's known as a party drug that lifts spirits and lowers inhibitions, yet it has a sedative, depressant effect on the body. The symptoms include decreased visual acuity; diminished attention; lowered sensitivity to taste, smell, and pain; slowed reaction times; a loss of balance; slurred speech; and lowered performance on intelligence tests. Alcohol hastens the onset of sleep (as do most depressants) but does not increase the overall amount of time one sleeps in a night. In fact, it suppresses REM sleep—which has a disruptive effect once the alcohol wears off.

Anyone who has had a few too many drinks knows that alcohol alters awareness and behavior. As we'll explore later in this book, alcohol has two effects in this regard. First, people often drown their sorrows in a bottle in order to escape from failure and its harsh implications for their self-esteem. Many of us expect alcohol to provide this type of "relief" (Leigh & Stacy, 1993) and to help us manage our emotional highs and lows (Cooper, Bloom, & Roth, 1995). By getting 100 adult men and women to keep a daily diary, and keep track of their alcohol consumption, Cynthia Mohr and her colleagues (2001) found that there are two distinct types of drinking: *social drinking*, out of the house and with others, which people do when they've had good days, and *solitary drinking*, at home and alone, which they tend to do on bad days. Apparently, alcohol consumption comes in two forms: "Crying in your beer and toasting good times" (p. 489).

A second effect is that people take more risks when they're drunk than when sober, in part because alcohol reduces anxiety, which leads us to shed social inhibitions (Ito, Miller, & Pollock, 1996), and in part because it leads us to become shortsighted about the consequences of our actions, evoking a state of "drunken excess" (Steele & Josephs, 1990). Put all these pieces together, and it's hardly surprising that drinking is statistically linked to highway fatalities, murders, assaults, child abuse, and other acts of recklessness and violence. Even in laboratory experiments, subjects are more aggressive after they're given alcohol to drink than when given a nonalcoholic beverage (Harris & Koob, 2017).

Stimulants

Stimulants excite the central nervous system and stimulate behavior. Caffeine and nicotine are common mild stimulants. Amphetamines and cocaine have much stronger effects. These drugs speed up bodily functions (that's why amphetamines are known as speed or uppers), increase breathing and heart rates, heighten alertness, suppress appetite, and produce feelings of excitement, self-confidence, and even elation. For these reasons, people use stimulants to stay awake, lose weight, and elevate mood. In large amounts, they can make a person anxious, jittery, and hyperalert. As is often the case with psychoactive drugs, the user may come down from the high in a "crash" and feel tired, downbeat, and irritable. Like the sedatives, stimulants, including coffee, can be addictive (Meredith, Juliano, Hughes, & Griffiths, 2013).

stimulants. A class of drugs that excite the central nervous system and energize behavior.

Amphetamines are synthetic drugs, often taken in pill form, for the treatment of asthma, narcolepsy, depression, attention-deficit/hyperactivity disorder, and obesity. In low doses, amphetamines increase alertness and arousal, boost energy, relieve fatigue, and suppress appetite. In higher doses, these drugs can cause confusion, manic behavior, and aggression. Chronic amphetamine use can even trigger schizophrenia-like symptoms. Recently, amphetamine modifications have been synthesized in the pharmaceutical laboratory. One of these "designer drugs" is methylenedioxymethamphetamine (MDMA), or Ecstasy. In addition to its stimulant properties, MDMA is said to evoke a sense of well-being, particularly in relation to others (Bershad et al., 2019). One powerful methamphetamine, commonly known as "speed," comes in a smokable form ("ice") that is highly addictive and can be fatal.

Cocaine ("coke") is a natural drug derived from the leaves of the coca plant, a shrub native to South America. Its use as a stimulant was discovered hundreds of years ago by Peruvian Indians, who chewed coca leaves to overcome fatigue and increase stamina. Taken in this manner, small amounts of cocaine gradually enter the bloodstream. Today, cocaine in white powder form is usually inhaled through the nose ("snorted"), resulting in a quick and intense rush of euphoria. Its consciousness-altering effects, which last up to 30 minutes, are predictably followed by a crash caused by a temporary depletion in the supplies of dopamine and norepinephrine. A highly potent form of cocaine known as "crack" is smoked in a pipe or injected directly into the bloodstream. Crack gives a higher high but is followed by a lower low—and a craving for another "hit." It is dangerous and highly addictive (Platt, 2000).

Hallucinogens

Hallucinogens are the psychoactive drugs that cause the most dramatic alterations in consciousness. These drugs (which are also called *psychedelics*, from the Greek words meaning "mind expanding") distort perceptions of time and space and cause hallucinations—sensations without sensory input. The best-known hallucinogens are psilocybin ("shrooms"), LSD, and PCP. The latter (also called "angel dust") is a potent but dangerous painkiller. Marijuana, which has mixed sedative and stimulant effects, also acts as a mild hallucinogen.

hallucinogens. Psychedelic drugs that distort perceptions and cause hallucinations.

LSD is a synthetic drug that was first discovered in 1938 by Albert Hofmann, a Swiss chemist. At one point, Hofmann experimented on himself. He took what he thought to be a small dose of LSD and found himself for 14 hours in a world he would never forget: "Everything in my field of vision was distorted as if seen in a curved mirror.... Familiar objects and furniture assumed grotesque, threatening forms... opening and closing themselves in circles and spirals, exploding in colored fountains" (Hofmann, 1980). Drug companies, researchers, and intelligence agencies in search of a truth serum soon went on to experiment with LSD. Even when they take small doses, acid "trippers" report that objects shimmer, colors become more vivid, their perception of time is slowed, old memories surface, and emotions range from euphoria to panic. Effects of LSD also include increased emotional responsiveness to music and the meaning of music, in addition to feelings of closeness to others, openness, trust, and suggestibility (Carhart-Harris et al., 2015). Many researchers believe that LSD and the other hallucinogens produce these effects largely by blocking activity of the neurotransmitter serotonin (Liechti, 2017).

A milder and less potent hallucinogen is cannabis, which is derived from the cannabis plant (*cannabis sativa*). It has two major active ingredients: THC (delta-9-tetrahydrocannabinol), which is the primary psychoactive component of marijuana, and CBD, which does not cause intoxication or euphoria (the "high") and has therapeutic effects used to treat Alzheimer's disease, inflammation, and certain seizure disorders (Maroon & Bost, 2018). Cannabis is used in three main forms: marijuana, hashish, and hash oil. Marijuana, the least potent of all the cannabis products, is made from dried flowers and leaves of the cannabis plant and is usually smoked in hand-rolled "joints" or vaporizers, or made into edibles like cookies or brownies. Hashish, often dried and pressed into small blocks and smoked, is made from the resin (a secreted gum) of the cannabis plant and can also be made into edibles and eaten. Hash oil, the most potent cannabis product, is a thick oil obtained from hashish and is also smoked. At low doses, cannabis may act like a sedative, producing a relaxed state and possibly a mild euphoria. It may also heighten awareness of colors, sounds, tastes, smells, and other sensations. At higher doses, it may distort perceptions of time and space. According to a 2017 Marist Poll, an estimated 52 percent of Americans age 18 years or older have used marijuana at least on one occasion, making it the most commonly used illicit drug in the United States. Today, marijuana has been a subject of a popular movement to legalize the drug, now being legalized for use for medical and recreational purposes in many U.S. states.

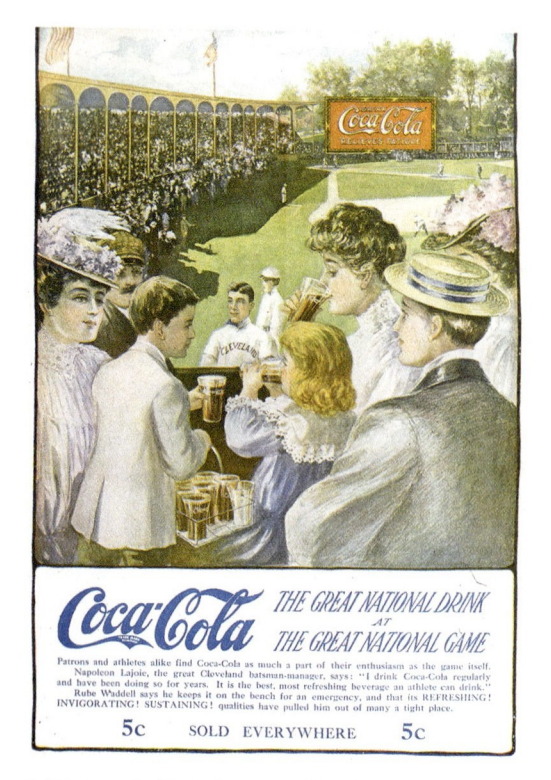

In 1886, pharmacist John Pemberton created Coca-Cola and sold it, at first, as a headache remedy and stimulant. The drink contained cocaine, which was later replaced by caffeine. This 1914 ad highlights Coca-Cola's stimulating effects.

Transcendental Graphics / Contributor

Opiates

opiates. A class of highly addictive drugs that depress neural activity and provide temporary relief from pain and anxiety.

Opiates are a class of drugs that are related to opium (an extract of the poppy plant), and they include morphine, codeine, and heroin. Their most prominent effect is to produce euphoria and analgesia (they also cause constipation). Because opiates depress neural activity, they are prescribed widely for the alleviation of pain—and have been used for this medical purpose for thousands of years. The user becomes drowsy and lethargic, yet happy and euphoric. Changes in consciousness are not particularly striking. These drugs are highly addictive, as the user quickly develops an insatiable need for more and larger doses. Heroin can be injected, smoked, or inhaled. Heroin users risk death through overdose, contaminated drugs, and AIDS contracted by sharing drug-injection needles.

People all over the world have sought to alter their states of consciousness, often by the consumption of psychoactive substances. Whatever the reasons for this desire, it is clear that drug use often turns to abuse and that social factors—like poverty, peer pressure, work stress, and a lack of personal fulfillment—play a role. In the United States, the number of people who use psychoactive drugs, which had declined over the past few years, is now on the rise for the first time in well over a decade. It is not clear, as a matter of public policy, how the problem can be solved. Thus, as policy makers debate the perennial question of whether to legalize the illicit drugs, many psychologists concede that there are risks and that they cannot confidently predict the impact of such a policy (Jones et al., 2018).

LEARNING CHECK

Random Drug Testing

Hallucinogens, opiates, sedatives and stimulants are four categories of consciousness-altering drugs. Identify the appropriate category for the substances below.

	Hallucinogens	Opiates	Sedatives	Stimulants
a. Benzodiazepines				
b. Amphetamines				
c. Nicotine				
d. Morphine				
e. Marijuana				
f. Valium				
g. Librium				
h. Heroin				
i. MDMA (Ecstasy)				
j. Codeine				
k. Cocaine				
l. Caffeine				
m. Xanax				
n. LSD				
o. PCP (angel dust)				
p. Barbiturates				
q. Alcohol				

(Answers: Hallucinogens—e, n, o; opiates—d, h, j; sedatives—a, f, g, m, p, q; stimulants—b, c, i, k, l.)

Consciousness and Control

Our ability to exert control over the contents of awareness is, at times, impressive. We saw earlier, for example, that lucid dreamers can sometimes control their dreams—and that almost anyone who is motivated can be trained to become a lucid dreamer. And we saw that although some of us can be hypnotized easily (a trait that requires the ability to focus attention and become absorbed), people cannot be hypnotized against their will—and those who are normally low in hypnotic susceptibility can learn to become more responsive to induction. Of course, when it comes to drug-induced altered states of consciousness, the choice is yours.

One particularly important way to control consciousness—meditation—first attracted great interest in the West in the 1950s when "beat generation" heroes like Jack Kerouac and Allen Ginsberg embraced Zen Buddhism. The interest broadened in the 1960s when the Beatles went to India to learn to meditate. In the 1990s, the number of people turning to meditation grew so dramatically that some meditation centers had to establish lotteries as a way to accommodate the applicants for retreats. Many are drawn by the promise of stress reduction, calm, equanimity, and even euphoria. But for experienced meditators, while they acknowledge these "side effects," the rewards are based on the analogy—more than 3,000 years old—that disciplining the mind is like taming an elephant to make it useful. For them, the value of meditation lies not in some kind of bliss trip but rather in the heightened awareness of their everyday lives.

Despite these impressive abilities, there are times when the control of consciousness seems out of reach. The mind may wander, you may slip into a daydream, and you may become distracted despite your efforts at concentration. People who become dependent on a psychoactive drug may lose the ability to control their states of consciousness. And those who suffer from various anxiety-related disorders may become literally obsessed with certain thoughts (refer to Chapter 13).

Studying what he calls "ironic processes" in mental control, Daniel Wegner (1994) has found that, at times, the harder you try to control your own thoughts, the less likely you are to succeed. Try not to think about a white bear for the next 30 seconds, and chances are that very image will intrude on your consciousness with remarkable frequency. Tell a jury to disregard an item of inadmissible testimony, and that censored material is sure to pop to mind as they deliberate on a verdict. Try not to worry about how long it's taking to fall asleep, and you'll stay awake. Try not to laugh in class or to think about the chocolate cake in the fridge or the itch on your nose—well, you get the idea.

According to Wegner, every conscious effort at control is met by a concern about failing to do so. This concern automatically triggers an "ironic operating process" as the person, trying *not* to fail, searches his or her mind for the unwanted thought. The ironic process will not necessarily prevail, says Wegner. Sometimes we can put the imaginary white bear out of mind. But if we're busy, distracted, tired, hurried, or under stress, then the ironic process, because it "just happens," will prevail over the intentional process—which requires conscious attention and effort. So, Wegner (1997) notes, "any attempt at mental control contains the seeds of its own undoing" (p. 148).

TRY THIS!

Beat the Clock

According to Daniel Wegner, "any attempt at mental control contains the seeds of its own undoing"—as demonstrated when one tries not to think about a white bear for 30 seconds.

To determine how irresistible Wegner's "ironic operating process" can be, **TRY THIS:** Go to one of your classes determined not to look at the time for the whole period (that means not looking at a clock on the wall or your watch—and no fair not wearing it—and not peeking at the time on your cellphone or your computer if you use it for note-taking). Can you make it all the way through without checking the time?

As a variation, attend the same class resolved to keep both feet on the floor throughout the entire lecture. You might ask a classmate to keep an eye on you to see if you cross your legs.

How did you do? Did you find yourself yearning to look at the clock or cross your legs? What does this tell you about "ironic processes" in mental control?

Ironic processes have been observed in a wide range of behaviors. In an intriguing study of this effect on the control of motor behavior, Wegner, Ansfield, and Pilloff (1998) had subjects hold a pendulum (a crystalline pendant suspended from a nylon fishing line) over the center of two intersecting axes on a glass grid, which formed a "+". Some subjects were instructed simply to keep the pendulum steady, while others were more specifically told not to allow it to swing back and forth along the horizontal axis. Try this yourself and you'll find that it's not easy to prevent at least some movement. In this experiment, however, the pendulum swung horizontally more when this direction was specifically forbidden. To further examine the role of mental distraction, some subjects were also required to count backward from a thousand by sevens while controlling the pendulum. In this situation, the ironic effect was even greater. Among subjects who specifically tried to prevent horizontal movement but could not concentrate fully on the task, the pendulum swayed freely back and forth—in the forbidden direction. Using a similar method, these researchers found that people were most likely to overshoot a golf putt when they specifically tried not to overshoot but were distracted while putting. It may seem both comic and tragic, but at times our efforts at self-control backfire, thwarting even our best intentions. For psychologists, and everyone else for that matter, the key is to learn how to minimize these ironic effects.

Thinking Like a Psychologist About Consciousness

"A penny for your thoughts?" Over the years, psychologists have equated consciousness with attention and have examined varying states of awareness, ranging from sleep and dreams to hypnosis and the effects of mind-altering drugs. We have found in this chapter that people can sometimes control the contents of consciousness. Research on selective attention shows that as we focus the spotlight of awareness on one stimulus, we can screen out irrelevant competing information. At times, we can divide our attention, simultaneously engage in two or more activities, and process information without awareness. Yet there are also times when we cannot control what we think about—and trying to do so can backfire.

Illustrating Wegner's proposition that "any attempt at mental control contains the seeds of its own undoing," research shows that people are most likely to overshoot a golf putt when they are specifically trying not to overshoot but are distracted while putting.
iStock.com/PhotoTalk

For researchers, it is crucial to consider what is underlying consciousness. In other words, it is critical to keep in mind that neural networks are the construction of our mind. Understanding consciousness, then, is a multidisciplinary endeavor. It requires an understanding of not just our neurology but also what we attend to (sensation and perception), our experiences (learning and memory), our development (lifespan development), our health, and so much more. Consciousness represents just the tip of the iceberg. It represents what we know we are attending to and what we can recall. As we will explore in Chapter 6 regarding memory, so much of our experiences occur beyond our awareness. Understanding consciousness, then, is a valuable endeavor for psychologists, not only because of its implications for so many other fields of science but also because it provides a gateway into our own awareness of ourselves, the world around us, and our very being.

SUMMARY

ATTENTIONAL PROCESSES

Psychologists generally define **consciousness** in terms of **attention**—an awareness of the sensations, thoughts, and feelings that one is attending to at a given moment.

SELECTIVE ATTENTION
Studies of the **cocktail party phenomenon** demonstrate that people can use **selective attention** to focus on one stimulus and virtually exclude other stimuli from consciousness. Many of these studies use a dichotic listening task in which subjects hear competing messages over headphones and must follow what is said in one ear while ignoring the other.

DIVIDED ATTENTION
Other listening experiments show that **divided attention** is possible: Some stimuli penetrate consciousness even when we are focused on something else. Moreover, if we are so experienced at a particular process that it becomes automatic, we can do other things at the same time. The **Stroop test** demonstrates that experienced readers process word meanings automatically, without effort or awareness.

INFLUENCE WITHOUT AWARENESS
Research shows that people can be influenced by **subliminal messages**—information that is presented "below" our threshold of awareness. Mere exposure to a stimulus increases liking, even when

the exposure is subliminal. This is shown in studies on **priming**, where subliminally presented concepts appear to facilitate, or "prime," responses in a subsequent situation.

SLEEP AND DREAMS

Until recently, there were many myths about sleep and dreams, but little was actually known about these processes.

THE SLEEP-WAKE CYCLE

As biological organisms, humans experience regular fluctuations known as **biological rhythms.** Our daylong **circadian rhythm**, such as the sleep-wake cycle, is controlled by the suprachiasmatic nucleus of the hypothalamus, which detects light via the retina. Cut off from sunlight, humans tend to drift toward longer daily cycles. When our rhythms are disrupted, we may experience reactions such as jet lag.

NIGHT WORK, SLEEPING, AND HEALTH

Both biological and social clocks set the body for activity during the daytime and sleep at night, so shift workers struggle to stay alert and experience problems on the job. Many traffic accidents occur at night, as drivers sometimes take brief **microsleeps** while driving. A brief nap or a cup of coffee can help drivers stay awake.

THE STAGES OF SLEEP

Sleep follows a cycle of distinct stages: presleep; stages 1 to 4 of deepening sleep, as the body relaxes and brain waves become larger and slower; and **REM sleep**, characterized by rapid eye movements, increased pulse rate, brain waves like those of presleep, and totally relaxed muscles. It is during REM sleep that vivid dreams occur. Each night, as we pass through several cycles, we gradually spend more time in REM sleep and less time in non-REM, or **NREM, sleep.**

WHY DO WE SLEEP?

Sleep is so necessary that when people try to stay awake for long periods, they fall into short microsleeps, a few seconds at a time. According to restoration theory, sleep helps us recover from the day's demands. Circadian theory offers an evolutionary explanation: Sleep helps animals conserve energy and avoid predators when not searching for food or seeking a mate. Individuals differ in the amount of sleep they require.

DREAMS

Dreams, too, serve an adaptive function. As shown by studies that measure REM sleep, people do most of their dreaming early in life when the brain is still developing. Common themes include falling and being chased or attacked. Both daily concerns and external stimuli also influence dream content. Some people experience **lucid dreaming**, a semiconscious state in which they are aware of—and can control—their own dreams.

Freud accounted for the bizarreness of dreams by theorizing that they are disguised expressions of unconscious wishes. To interpret dreams, he said, one has to go beyond the **manifest content** to uncover the unconscious meaning, or **latent content**. A more recent hypothesis, the **activation-synthesis theory**, contends that dreams begin with random neural signals in the brainstem. These signals spread up to the cortex, and the brain tries to make sense of them by constructing images and stories.

SLEEP DISTURBANCES

Sleep disturbances are common. **Insomnia**—the inability to fall asleep, stay asleep, or get enough sleep—has many causes and can be cured through behavioral means. Hypersomnia (sleeping too much) is less frequent but more dangerous, particularly among those with **narcolepsy**, a disorder that causes sudden attacks of REM sleep during the day. There are other serious sleep disturbances, or parasomnias. People with **sleep apnea** snore loudly and repeatedly stop breathing during sleep and awaken gasping for air. **REM sleep behavior disorder (RBD)** is a condition in which the skeletal muscles are not paralyzed during REM sleep, enabling sleepers to act on their nightmares, often violently. Other problems include night terrors and sleepwalking.

HYPNOSIS

THE SEEDS OF CONTROVERSY
Hypnosis is a set of attention-focusing procedures in which changes in a subject's behavior or mental state are suggested. It has a long and controversial history in psychology.

THE HYPNOTIC INDUCTION
In the first stage of hypnosis, induction, the subject's attention is focused. In the second stage, suggestion, the subject responds to the hypnotist's cues.

HYPNOTIC RESPONSIVENESS
People differ in their degree of **hypnotic susceptibility**, or responsiveness. Those who are most responsive tend to have vivid imaginations and long attention spans.

THE MYTHS AND REALITIES
Contrary to myth, people cannot be hypnotized against their will or be coerced into violating their consciences. Evidence suggests, however, that hypnotized subjects may shed their inhibitions. Hypnosis can reduce pain. Through **posthypnotic suggestion**, the hypnotist can influence a subject's behavior even after the session ends. **Posthypnotic amnesia** is also common, though not permanent. But **hypermnesia**, the supposed enhancement of a witness's memory by hypnosis, has not been confirmed in experiments. Rather, hypnosis makes witnesses more vulnerable to false memories.

IS HYPNOSIS AN "ALTERED" STATE?
Special-process theories maintain that hypnosis induces a unique state of suggestibility. According to one theory, the hypnosis subject experiences **dissociation**, a division of consciousness in which one part of the mind operates independent of another. Social-psychological theories see hypnosis as an ordinary state in which changes are produced by conscious faking or by processes of social influence. To some extent, both theories may be true.

CONSCIOUSNESS-ALTERING DRUGS

Throughout history, people have sought altered states of consciousness, often by using consciousness-altering **psychoactive drugs**, chemicals that change perceptions, moods, thoughts, or behavior. Such drugs are addictive, creating either **physical dependence** or **psychological dependence.**

SEDATIVES
Among psychoactive drugs, **sedatives** such as alcohol, barbiturates, and benzodiazepines slow activity in the central nervous system. Alcohol was the first and is one of the most widely used drugs in the world.

STIMULANTS
Stimulants, including caffeine, nicotine, amphetamines, and cocaine, excite the central nervous system and energize behavior. They can be addictive.

HALLUCINOGENS
Hallucinogens, or psychedelic drugs, such as LSD and marijuana, distort perceptions and can cause hallucinations.

OPIATES
The highly addictive **opiates**, such as heroin, morphine, and codeine, depress neural activity, relieve pain, and produce euphoria.

CONSCIOUSNESS AND CONTROL
As studies of attention and hypnosis illustrate, people have a great deal of command over their own consciousness. Yet there are times when our minds wander and we cannot control the distractions. Often we must contend with an irony: The harder we try to manage our thoughts, the less likely we are to succeed.

CRITICAL THINKING

Thinking Critically About Consciousness

1. Is hypnosis an altered state of consciousness? Compare the special-process and social-psychological answers to this question. Which do you find more compelling?

2. In what ways are we influenced by subliminal stimuli (i.e., stimuli presented below the level of conscious awareness)? Why might people continue to believe in the power of subliminal advertising?

3. Consider your cultural identity. Try to recall dreams that you've had, whether recently or in the past. How might your culture influence the nature of your dreams and what you dream about?

4. How can we use the concept of lucid dreaming to help people effectively deal with nightmares?

CAREER CONNECTION: RESEARCH

Psychological Technician

A psychological technician administers routine tests, helping patients under the supervision of a psychologist. They may work with populations such as the elderly, patients who have been psychiatrically hospitalized, and individuals with developmental disabilities, often in hospitals or group residential settings. Daily responsibilities include observing patients and helping them with daily activities, providing updates to physicians and other providers, and documenting patients' conditions in their medical records. Psychiatric technicians may also be responsible for administering therapeutic aid and medications. The understanding of psychology and human behavior developed during undergraduate study is directly applicable in this role, which may also require certification courses or continuing education while employed.

Key skills for this role that psychology students learn to develop:

- Effective communication in presentations and written works
- Self-efficacy and self-regulation
- Ethical standards and multicultural value application

KEY TERMS

activation-synthesis theory (p. 148)
attention (p. 133)
biological rhythms (p. 137)
circadian rhythm (p. 137)
cocktail party phenomenon (p. 133)
consciousness (p. 133)
dissociation (p. 159)
divided attention (p. 135)
hallucinogens (p. 165)
hypermnesia (p. 157)
hypnosis (p. 154)
hypnotic susceptibility (p. 155)
insomnia (p. 149)
latent content (p. 148)
lucid dreaming (p. 148)
manifest content (p. 148)
microsleeps (p. 140)

narcolepsy (p. 151)
NREM sleep (p. 143)
opiates (p. 166)
physical dependence (p. 163)
posthypnotic amnesia (p. 157)
posthypnotic suggestion (p. 156)
priming (p. 136)
psychoactive drug (p. 162)
psychological dependence (p. 163)
REM sleep (p. 143)
REM sleep behavior disorder (RBD) (p. 152)
sedatives (p. 163)
selective attention (p. 134)
sleep apnea (p. 152)
stimulants (p. 165)
Stroop test (p. 135)
subliminal messages (p. 136)

5 LEARNING

iStock.com/Prostock-Studio

LEARNING OBJECTIVES

Define and explain the nature of nonassociative learning.

Describe how Pavlov's work on classical conditioning influenced how we understand learning.

Describe the principles of operant conditioning and how this type of conditioning is applied today.

Summarize the process of observational learning and how this type of learning is applied today.

WHAT'S YOUR PREDICTION: CAN PEOPLE LEARN WITHOUT REALIZING IT?

The Situation

As you enter the laboratory reception area, you are met by an experimenter, taken to a small room, and told that you will be taking part in a study of human memory. Next you're told that you'll have 7 minutes to examine the following strings of letters and that you should simply try to "learn and remember as much as you can." Ready, begin:

PVV	TSSSXXVV	TSXXTVPS	PVPXTVPS	TSSXXVV
TSXS	PTVPXVV	TXXTVPS	TXXTTTVV	PVPXXVV
TSSXXVPS	TXXVPXVV	PTVPS	PTTTVPS	PTVPXV

173

You look at these meaningless items one by one, trying to memorize. *P-V-V. T-S-X-S*. You just keep repeating them under your breath. After 7 minutes, the experimenter stops you. Time's up. You can't wait to write down what you remember before you lose it—but the experimenter has other plans. The experimenter reveals that the items were formed according to a set of rules, an "artificial grammar" if you will, and wants to know whether you know what the rules are. As the experimenter explains the test you're about to take, you get a sinking feeling in the pit of your stomach. "Uh-oh. There were rules? I wasn't looking for rules!"

The test is straightforward. On slides, you'll view 100 new items made up of the same letters as before, one item per slide. Half the items will be grammatical (according to the rules); half will not. For each one, you are to press a button marked *YES* if you think the item is grammatical or *NO* if you think it's not. You should also rate your confidence in each judgment on a scale marked from 1 to 5. Oh, one more thing: Your responses will be timed.

The presentation is turned on, the overhead lights are shut off, and you've got your fingers on the buttons ready to go. First item: *PTTTVPVS*. It looks okay, as it contains the usual letters, and all. But are these letters ordered in a way that fits the grammar? "If I don't know," you ask, "should I just guess?" Instructed to respond to every item, you press a button and state your confidence. The next one is *PVTW*. Same routine. *PVPS. SVPXTW. SXXVPS*. Sometimes you answer quickly; at other times, you stare at the screen for a while before making a response. By the 100th slide, you're ready for a cool drink and a nap.

Make a Prediction

How well do you think people fare in this task? What you are likely to find is that many subjects shrug their shoulders in confusion. Based on what you've read, what do you think is the average test score? If all you did was guess, you would get roughly a 50 percent accuracy rate. If you came up with rules that were wrong, your score could be lower. If you knew the right rules, you would do better. So, what is your estimate, 10 percent? 30? 55? 90? What's your prediction:

0   5   10   15   20   25   30   35   40   45   50   55   60   65   70   75   80   85   90   95   100%

The Results

For decades, cognitive psychologist Arthur Reber (1993) used experiments like this one to study "implicit learning"—the tendency for people to acquire complex, abstract concepts without awareness or intention. Consistently, Reber has found that subjects cannot describe the grammar that they use to form the letter strings, nor can they explain the reasons for their *YES* and *NO* judgments. Yet in the study just described, subjects made the correct response 77 percent of the time—and usually did so quickly. How well do you think you would perform in this experiment?

What Does It All Mean?

Implicit learning, which occurs without our awareness, is a primitive but powerful form of adaptation. Indeed, people learn this grammar not by actively searching for rules or by receiving explicit instruction but simply through exposure to properly formed letter strings. Without really trying, subjects learn the grammar the way we learn to speak in our native tongue, figure out how to behave properly in a new setting, or "calculate" the trajectory of a ball in flight in order to make the catch. Implicit mental processes such as these are common (Cleeremans, Allakhverdov, & Kuvaldina, 2019; Reber, 2013). To learn from experience, as the subjects did in this study, people must be attuned to associations between stimuli in their environment and between behavior and its consequences. As we'll learn in this chapter, association is the basic building block for all learning.

In many ways, learning is the foundation on which we adapt, change, grow, advance, create, innovate, and at the most basic level, survive. We can learn in a moment in time (such as what you are learning now by reading these words), over the course of time (such as what you will have learned once you've finished this book), at different points in time (such as what you learn in each term or college semester), and even over evolutionary time (such as humans' formulation of written and spoken language as a species). Consider your own life, for example. Have your experiences changed the emotions you feel for someone (such as feelings of love)? The habits you developed (such as when you choose to go to sleep)? The foods you prefer (such as foods common in your culture)? Your personality (such as your tendencies to trust others or experience new things)? Possibly even the major you chose in college (maybe influenced by your caregivers, what you got excited about in school, or inspired by a teacher)? In this spirit, learning is not only a lifelong endeavor; it is a process. In this chapter, we introduce two foundational processes for how we learn: nonassociative and associative learning.

NONASSOCIATIVE LEARNING

LEARNING OBJECTIVES

Define and explain the nature of nonassociative learning.

- Explain what fixed action patterns are, and identify some examples.
- Relate some examples of fixed action patterns, and discuss whether humans display them.
- Define habituation, and explain how it is relevant to human behavior.

Every spring, a tiny freshwater fish called the stickleback performs an intriguing reproductive ritual. As the male's belly turns from dull gray to a bright red, he builds a nest and does a zigzag courtship "dance" to attract a female stickleback, sometimes brushing her belly with his stickles. He then escorts her to the nest, prods her tail to induce spawning, fertilizes her eggs, aerates the eggs by fanning the water, and vigorously attacks all red-bellied male intruders. Once the eggs hatch a week later, he guards the young and keeps them close by until they are ready to leave the nest.

Many land animals also exhibit adaptive, complex forms of behavior. When the herring-gull mother returns to the nest with food, newly hatched chicks peck at a red spot on the mother's bright yellow bill, causing her to regurgitate the food for their consumption. The honeybee uses a wax it secretes to build hives in which each comb consists of hexagonal cells that form a mathematically efficient, perfect design. The indigo bunting, a small bird, navigates south every winter, using as a guide the bright North Star, the only star in the Northern Hemisphere that maintains a fixed compass position through the night. Similarly prepared by instinct, the canary sings, the spider weaves its web, the beaver builds dams, and the newly hatched duckling follows the first moving object it sees, usually its mother. How do the stickleback and others know what to do? Simple. In many animal species, certain behaviors are programmed by instinct.

Programmed by instinct, indigo buntings navigate south each winter, guided by the light of the North Star.
iStock.com/SteveByland

Fixed Action Patterns

Inspired by Darwin's theory of evolution and led by Nobel Prize winners Konrad Lorenz and Nikolaas Tinbergen, **ethologists** study the behavior of animals in their natural habitats (Alcock, 1997; Cate, 2009; Cate et al., 2009). Based on their observations, these researchers refer to the instinctual behaviors as **fixed action patterns**. A fixed action pattern is a species-wide sequence of movements that is built into the nervous system and triggered or "released" by a specific stimulus. The response to the stimulus is automatic, like a reflex—no ifs, ands, or buts. Thus, the stickleback male attacks all red-bellied forms, even those that do not resemble a fish (illustrated in Figure 5.1). Similarly, the herring-gull chick pecks at all moving red dots (a begging response to the red spot on the parental bill for feeding), even if the dot is not on another bird.

ethologists. Scientists who study the behavior of animals in their natural habitats.

fixed action pattern. A species-specific behavior that is built into an animal's nervous system and triggered by a specific stimulus.

FIGURE 5.1 ■ Stickleback Models

Research shows that various red-bellied objects trigger male attack, yet a replica of another male stickleback without a red belly does not. The red belly is the stimulus that releases this fixed action pattern.

Republished with permission of Oxford Unviersity Press, from The Study of Instinct. N. Tinbergen. New York:1951; permission conveyed through Copyright Clearance Center, Inc.

You may notice that fixed action patterns are a bit unusual in that a fixed response is, well, fixed; it cannot change, whereas a flexible response is generally more adaptive to change. In essence, these behaviors tend to be essential to an animal's survival. Behaviors that are essential to survival are those such as courting or mating (e.g., the stickleback male attacks all red-bellied forms of fish that enter his territory while a sexually receptive female is present), and maternal behavior (e.g., the greylag goose's egg-rolling behavior is essential to the survival of its chicks). Certainly these responses can be exploited, such as when the herring-gull chick pecks at all moving red dots. Such behavior is essential to survival—in terms of feeding behavior in the herring-gull's case.

Do people exhibit fixed action patterns? Are we instinctual creatures? We'll find later that human newborns are equipped with adaptive, instinctlike behaviors in the form of reflexes. Upon birth, an infant will clutch anything that touches the palm of the hand, turn with an open mouth toward any object that grazes the cheek, start sucking when the lips are touched, and swallow when the back of the mouth is stimulated. These reflexes are not within the infant's control, and some disappear within a few months, never to return. Why are we humans less equipped with inborn, reflexlike rituals than the stickleback? Because we adapt to life's demands not by instinct but through learning.

Habituation

learning. A relatively permanent change in knowledge or behavior that results from experience.

When psychologists talk about **learning**, they are referring to a relatively permanent change in knowledge or behavior that comes about as a result of *experience*. Experience is necessary for us to speak, read, write, add and subtract, ride a bicycle, swim, play a saxophone or trumpet, or know how to charm a romantic partner. The topic of learning is near and dear to the hearts of all psychologists—regardless of whether they study biological, cognitive, developmental, social, or clinical processes. Often what we learn makes us happier, healthier, and more successful; sometimes it does not. The beauty of adaptation by learning is that it is flexible, not rigidly preset like a stickleback's dance-and-attack ritual. In principle, this means that each of us can learn to behave in ways that benefit rather than harm ourselves and others. The question is: How does this learning take place?

The simplest form of learning is **habituation**—a tendency to become familiar with a stimulus merely as a result of repeated exposure. The first time it happens, a sudden loud noise or a blast of cold air has a startling effect on us and triggers an "orienting reflex." Among humans, the eyes widen, the eyebrows rise, muscles tighten, the heart beats faster, skin resistance drops, and brain-wave patterns indicate a heightened level of physiological arousal (Sokolov, 1963). On the second and third exposures to the stimulus, the effect is weakened. Then as we become acclimated or "habituated" to the stimulus, the novelty wears off, the startle reaction disappears, and boredom sets in.

Habituation is a primitive form of learning and is found among mammals, birds, fish, insects, and all other organisms. For example, sea snails reflexively withdraw their gills at the slightest touch. Then after repeated tactile stimulation, the response disappears (Kandel, 1979). Animals may also habituate to objects that naturally evoke fear after repeated and harmless exposure. When lab rats were presented with a cat collar smeared with a cat's odor, they ran from it and hid. Figure 5.2, however, shows that after several presentations the rats hid for decreasing amounts of time, eventually resembling control group rats exposed to an odorless collar (Dielenberg & McGregor, 1999).

Habituation also occurs in human infants (Leader, 2016). In one classic study, for example, if a picture or sound is presented over and over again, an infant will eventually get bored, lose interest, look away, and exhibit a lower heart rate (Bornstein, 1989). Think about everyday life, and numerous examples of habituation will come to mind. People who move from a large city to the country or from a region of the world that is hot to one that is cold often need time to adjust to the sudden change in stimulation. Once they do, the new environment seems less noisy, quiet, hot, or cold. In a series of experiments, adults were subliminally exposed to words that arouse emotional reactions that are extremely positive (*free, beach, baby*) and negative (*cancer, war, hell*). Later, they rated these same words as less positive and negative than they did other, equally extreme, words that were not previously presented (Dijksterhuis & Smith, 2002). Habituation also has important implications for the power of rewards to motivate us. Regardless of whether the rewarding stimulus is food, water, or an opportunity to explore a new environment, it tends to lose impact, at least temporarily, with repeated use (Domjan, 2018a; McSweeney & Swindell, 1999).

habituation. The tendency of an organism to become familiar with a stimulus as a result of repeated exposure.

FIGURE 5.2 ■ Habituation of Fear

Rats were exposed to a cat collar that contained or did not contain a cat's odor, causing them to run and hide. After several presentations, the odor-exposed rats hid for less and less time, eventually resembling the odorless control rats.

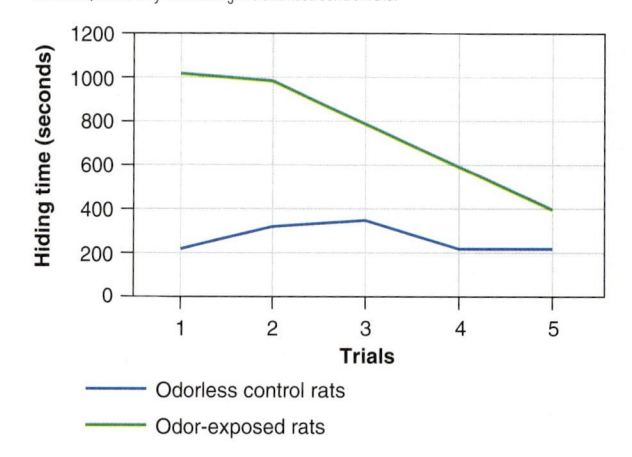

Adapted from Dielenberg, R. A., & McGregor, I. S. (1999). Habituation of the hiding response to cat odor in rats (Rattus norvegicus). *Journal of Comparative Psychology, 113*(4), 376–387. https://doi.org/10.1037/0735-7036.113.4.376

In habituation, an organism learns from exposure that a certain stimulus is familiar. Over the years, however, psychologists have focused more on the ways in which we learn relationships between events. In this chapter, three such processes are discussed: classical conditioning, operant conditioning, and observational learning.

CLASSICAL CONDITIONING

LEARNING OBJECTIVES

Explain what Pavlov learned from his experiments with salivating dogs.

- Describe how Pavlov's work on classical conditioning influenced how we understand learning.
- Describe how classical conditioning works and its relevance to human behavior.
- Discuss whether it is possible to condition new fears or preferences and whether bodily functions can be conditioned similarly.

There are certainly moments in your life that stand out, ones that you will always remember. Maybe it was your first kiss, the championship game you won, or even a moment as simple as your first day of college—meeting your classmates and feeling like an adult, ready to earn a degree and achieve your goals. To this day, these memories may flood to your mind in certain settings.

In stark contrast, the moments in our lives are not always pleasant. It could be something as simple as the first time you were pulled over for a minor traffic violation, or it could be something more serious, such as a car accident—as you vividly recall the red lights flashing on the dashboard, the smell of burned rubber, and the blast of cold air that hit your face when you climbed out through the door. Parts of the incident, such as the song playing in the car, may come to memory at other times. For years, you might flinch whenever you hear it.

Following Aristotle, modern philosophers and psychologists have long believed that the key to learning is *association*, a tendency to connect events that occur together in space or time. Can learning by association be studied in a scientific manner? Yes. In fact, many theories of associative learning have been proposed and tested over the years (Pearce & Bouton, 2001). With the arrival of the 20th century, psychology was poised and ready for one of its most important discoveries.

Pavlov's Discovery

Enter Ivan Pavlov, a Russian physiologist. After receiving his medical degree in 1882, he spent 20 years studying the digestive system and won a Nobel Prize for that research in 1904. Pavlov was the complete dedicated scientist. Rumor has it that he once reprimanded a lab assistant who was 10 minutes late for an experiment because of street riots stemming from the Russian Revolution: "Next time there's a revolution," he said, "get up earlier!" (Hothersall, 1990).

Ironically, Pavlov's most important contribution was the result of an incidental discovery. In studying the digestive system, he strapped dogs in a harness, placed different types of food in their mouths, and measured the flow of saliva through a tube surgically inserted in the cheek (illustrated in Figure 5.3). But there was a "problem": After repeated sessions, the dogs would begin to salivate *before* the food was put in their mouths. In fact, they would drool at the mere sight of food, the dish it was placed in, the assistant who brought it, or even the sound of the assistant's approaching

Ivan Pavlov and some of the 200 other scientists and a dog who worked with him during his illustrious career.
Bettmann / Contributor/Getty

> **FIGURE 5.3** ■ **Pavlov's Classical-Conditioning Apparatus**
>
> Strapped into an apparatus like the one shown here, Pavlov's dogs were conditioned to salivate. Through a tube surgically inserted into each dog's cheek, salivation was recorded by a rising and falling pen attached to a slowly rotating cylinder of paper.

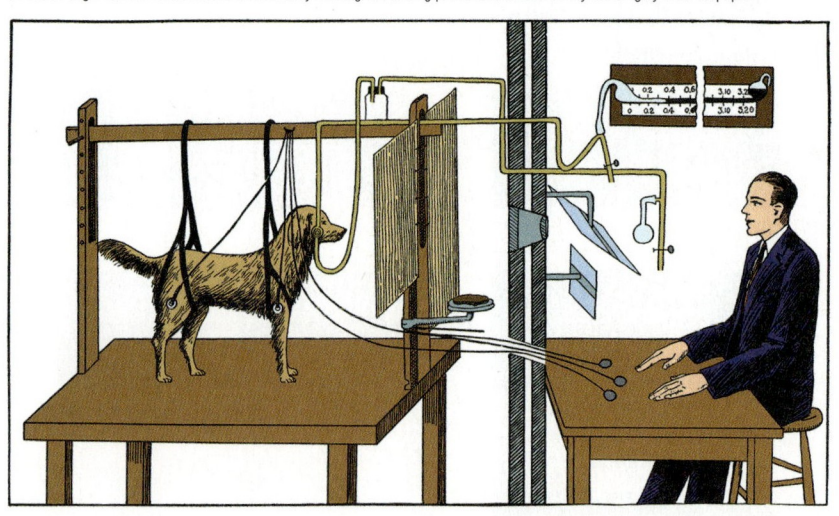

Science Source

footsteps. Pavlov saw these "psychic secretions" as a nuisance, so he tried to eliminate the problem by sneaking up on the dogs without warning. He soon realized, however, that he had stumbled on a very basic form of learning. This phenomenon was **classical conditioning**, and Pavlov devoted the rest of his life to studying it.

To examine the classical conditioning systematically, Pavlov needed to control the delivery of food, often a dry meat powder, as well as the events that preceded it. The animals did not have to be trained or "conditioned" to salivate. The salivary reflex is an innate **unconditioned response (UR)** that is naturally set off by food in the mouth, an **unconditioned stimulus (US)**. There are numerous unconditioned stimulus-response connections. Tap your knee with a rubber mallet (US) and your leg will jerk (UR). Blow a puff of air into your eye (US) and you'll blink (UR). Turn the volume up on an alarm clock (US) and, when it rings, your muscles will tighten (UR). In each case, the US automatically elicits the UR. No experience is necessary—just a reflex.

Using the salivary reflex as a starting point, Pavlov (1927) sought to determine whether dogs could be trained by association to respond to a "neutral" stimulus—one that does not naturally elicit a response. To find out, he conducted a series of experiments in which he repeatedly paired noises—such as the clicking of a metronome or the ringing of a bell—before placing food in the dog's mouth. Bell, food. Bell, food. After a series of these paired events, the dog started to salivate to the sound alone. Because the bell, which was initially a neutral stimulus, came to elicit the response through its association with food, it became a **conditioned stimulus (CS)**, and salivation, a **conditioned response (CR)**. With his initial experiment as a model, Pavlov and others trained dogs to salivate in response to a range of stimuli, not just noises. Odors, lights, colored objects, and a touch on the leg also elicited the salivation response.

Following the basic classical-conditioning procedure diagrammed in Figure 5.4, researchers have trained animals to react to a host of neutral stimuli that have been paired with an unpleasant or pleasant US. In one study, rats froze and did not move whenever they were put into a cage in which they had previously been exposed to high concentrations of carbon dioxide (Mongeluzi, Rosellini, Caldarone, Stock, & Abrahamson, 1996). In a second study, male quails became sexually aroused when they were placed into a chamber in which they had previously copulated with female birds (Domjan, Blesbois, & Williams, 1998). In a third study, human couples had a neutral odor paired with a sexual interaction (CS+) and another neutral odor paired with nonsexual coupled interaction, such as just watching a movie (CS−). Results showed increased genital responding to the CS+ and decreased responding to the CS− (Hoffmann, Peterson, & Garner, 2012).

---

classical conditioning. A type of learning in which an organism comes to associate one stimulus with another (also called Pavlovian conditioning).

unconditioned response (UR). An unlearned response (salivation) to an unconditioned stimulus (food).

unconditioned stimulus (US). A stimulus (food) that triggers an unconditioned response (salivation).

conditioned stimulus (CS). A neutral stimulus (bell) that comes to evoke a classically conditioned response (salivation).

conditioned response (CR). A learned response (salivation) to a classically conditioned stimulus (bell).

FIGURE 5.4 ■ Classical Conditioning

Note the sequence of events before, during, and after Pavlov's study. At first, only the US (meat) elicits an UR (salivation). After a neutral stimulus (bell) repeatedly precedes the US, however, it becomes a CS and can elicit a CR (salivation) on its own.

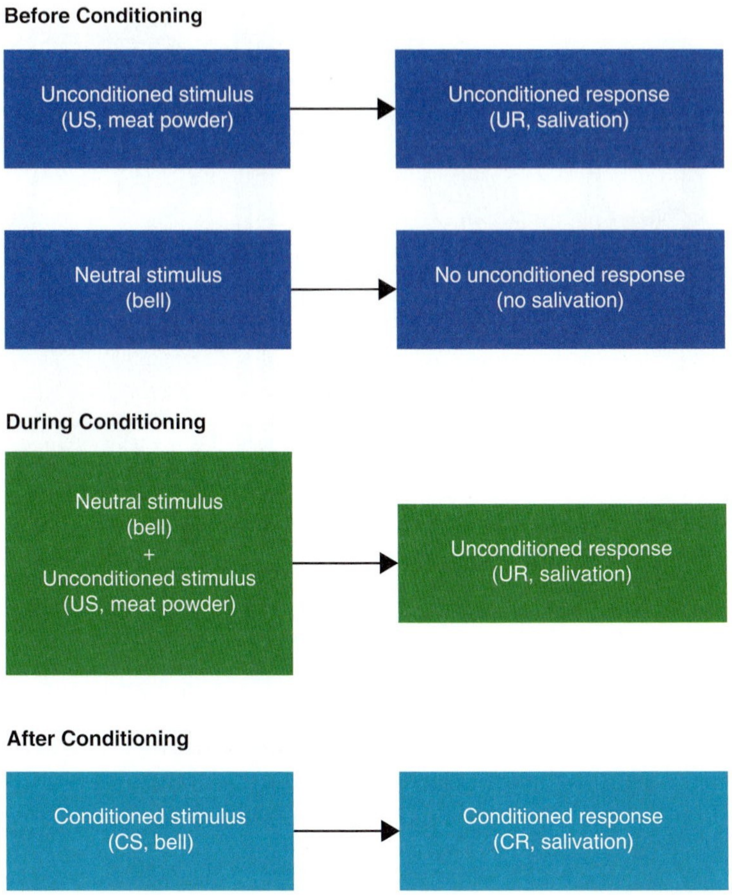

Before Conditioning

Unconditioned stimulus (US, meat powder) → Unconditioned response (UR, salivation)

Neutral stimulus (bell) → No unconditioned response (no salivation)

During Conditioning

Neutral stimulus (bell) + Unconditioned stimulus (US, meat powder) → Unconditioned response (UR, salivation)

After Conditioning

Conditioned stimulus (CS, bell) → Conditioned response (CR, salivation)

As we'll learn, classical conditioning affects us all in ways that we're often not aware of. We learn to salivate (CR) to lunch bells, menus, the smell of food cooking, and the sight of a refrigerator (CS) because these stimuli are often followed by eating (US). Similarly, we may cringe when seeing a needle in the doctor's office because of past associations between that sight and pain. And we tremble at the sight of flashing blue and red lights in the rearview mirror because of its past association with speeding tickets.

Basic Principles

Inspired by his initial discovery, Pavlov spent more than 30 years examining the factors that influence classical conditioning. Other researchers throughout the world also became involved. As a result, we now know that various species can be conditioned to blink when they hear a click that is paired with a puff of air to the eye, to fear colored lights that signal the onset of painful electric shocks, and to develop a dislike for foods they ate before becoming sick to the stomach (McSweeney & Murphy, 2014). We also know that there are four basic principles of learning: acquisition, extinction, generalization, and discrimination.

Acquisition

Classical conditioning seldom springs full blown after a single pairing of the CS and US. Usually, it takes some number of paired trials for the initial learning, or **acquisition**, of a CR. In Pavlov's experiments, the dogs did not salivate the first time they heard the bell or felt a touch on their leg. As shown in the left panel of Figure 5.5, however, the CR increases rapidly over the next few pairings—until the "learning curve" peaks and levels off.

acquisition. The formation of a learned response to a stimulus through the presentation of an unconditioned stimulus (classical conditioning) or reinforcement (operant conditioning).

FIGURE 5.5 ■ The Rise and Fall of a Conditioned Response

In classical conditioning, the CS does not evoke a CR on the first trial, but over time the CR increases rapidly until leveling off (acquisition). During extinction, the CR declines gradually. After a brief delay, however, there is usually a spontaneous recovery, or "rebounding," of the CR—until it is extinguished completely.

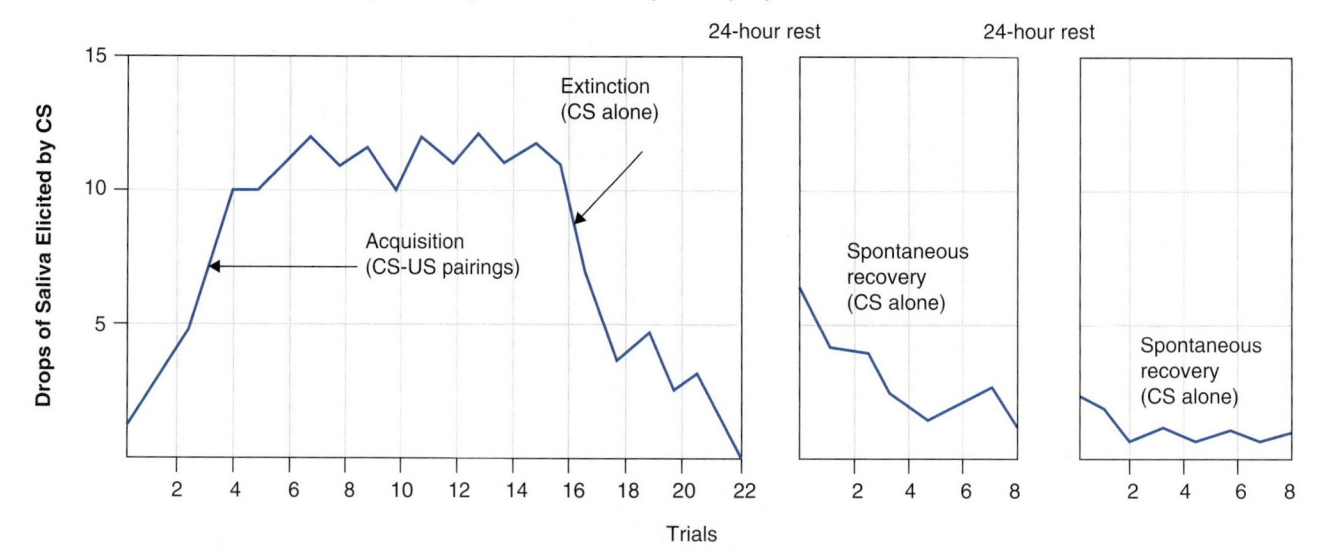

The acquisition of a classically conditioned response is influenced by various factors. The most critical are the order and timing of the presentation. In general, conditioning is quickest when the CS (the bell) precedes the onset of the US (food)—a procedure called *forward* conditioning. Ideally, the CS should precede the US by about half a second and the two should overlap somewhat in time. When the onset of the US is delayed, conditioning takes longer and the conditioned response is weaker. When the CS and US are *simultaneous*, it takes even longer. And when the US is presented before the CS (a procedure referred to as *backward* conditioning), learning often does not occur at all.

Once a buzzer, light, or other neutral stimulus gains the power to elicit a conditioned response, it becomes a CS—and can serve as though it were the US for yet another neutral stimulus. In one experiment, for example, Pavlov trained a dog to salivate to the sound of a bell, using meat powder as the US. After the CS-US link was established, he presented a second neutral stimulus, a black square, followed by the bell—but no food. The result: After repeated pairings, the black square on its own elicited small amounts of salivation. Through a process of higher-order conditioning, as shown in Figure 5.6, one CS was used to create another CS. In effect, the black square came to signal the bell, which, in turn, signaled the appearance of food (Rescorla, 1980).

Extinction

In the acquisition phase of classical conditioning, a CR is elicited by a neutral stimulus that is paired with a US. But what happens to the CR when the US is removed? Would a dog continue to salivate to a bell if the bell is no longer followed by food? Would the screeching dentist's drill continue to send chills up the spine if it is no longer followed by pain? No. If the CS is presented often enough without the US, it eventually loses its response-eliciting power. This apparent reversal of learning is called **extinction** (look again at the right side of the left panel in Figure 5.5).

Extinction is a gradual process. Pavlov found that when the same dog was returned for testing a day or two after extinction, it again salivated to the bell—a rebound effect known as **spontaneous recovery** (depicted in the middle and right panels of Figure 5.5). Often the dogs were easily retrained after just one repairing of the CS and US. As confirmed across multiple studies, extinction does not erase what was initially learned during acquisition—and retraining does not erase the effects of extinction. Rather, it appears that each learning experience suppresses, but does not destroy, those that preceded it (Rescorla, 1996, 2001).

extinction. The elimination of a learned response by removal of the unconditioned stimulus (classical conditioning) or reinforcement (operant conditioning).

spontaneous recovery. The reemergence of an extinguished conditioned response after a rest period.

FIGURE 5.6 ■ Higher-Order Conditioning

After Pavlov trained a dog to salivate (CR) to a bell (CS₁), he preceded the bell with another neutral stimulus, a black square (CS₂). After repeated pairings, the dog would salivate to the square itself. In effect, one CS was used to create another CS.

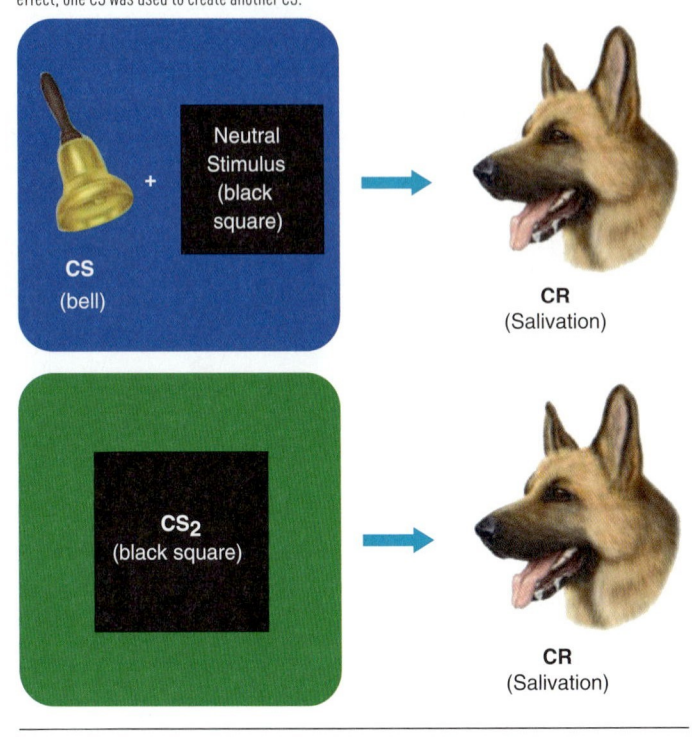

Monica Wierzbicki/Body Scientific Intl.

Generalization

After an animal is conditioned to respond to a particular CS, other similar stimuli will often evoke the same response. In Pavlov's experiments, the dogs salivated not only to the original tone but also to other tones that were similar but not identical to the CS. Other researchers have made the same observation. In one study, for example, rabbits were conditioned to blink to a tone of 1,200 Hz (a pitch that is roughly two octaves higher than middle C) that was followed by a puff of air to the eye. Later, they blinked to other tones ranging from 400 Hz to 2,000 Hz. The result: The more similar the tone was to the CS, the more likely it was to evoke a conditioned response. This tendency to respond to stimuli other than the original CS is called **stimulus generalization** (Pearce, 1987).

stimulus generalization. The tendency to respond to a stimulus that is similar to the conditioned stimulus.

Discrimination

Stimulus generalization can be useful because it enables us to apply what we learn to new, similar situations. But there are drawbacks. As illustrated by the child who is terrified of all animals because of one bad encounter with a barking dog, generalization is not always adaptive. Sometimes we need to distinguish between objects that are similar—a process of **discrimination**. Again, Pavlov was the first to demonstrate this process. He conditioned a dog to salivate in the presence of a black square (a CS) and then noticed that the response generalized to a gray-colored square. Next, he conducted a series of conditioning trials in which the black square was followed by food while the gray one was not. The result: The dog continued to salivate only to the original CS. In a similar manner, the dog eventually learned to discriminate between the color black and darker shades of gray.

discrimination. Behavior directed against persons because of their affiliation with a social group.

Pavlov's Legacy

Classical conditioning is so powerful and so basic that it occurs in animals as primitive as the sea slug, the fruit fly, and even the flatworm (the body of the flatworm contracts in response to electric shock; if the shock is paired repeatedly with light, the flatworm's body eventually contracts to the light alone) and in animals as sophisticated as us humans (Krasne & Glanzman, 1995; Turkkan, 1989). Recently, psychologists have taken classical conditioning in two directions: Some want to better *understand* the phenomenon—how, when, and why it works—while others are eager to *apply* it to different aspects of the human experience.

Theoretical Advances

Inspired by their initial success and by the Darwinian assumption that all animals share a common evolutionary past, Pavlov and other early behaviorists made this bold claim: Any organism can be conditioned to any stimulus. It does not matter if the subject is a dog, cat, rat, pigeon, or person. Nor does it matter if the conditioned stimulus is a bell, light, buzzer, or odor. Whenever an initially neutral stimulus is paired with an unconditioned stimulus, the result is classical conditioning.

The early behaviorists also insisted that a science of human behavior must focus only on external, objective, quantifiable events. A *stimulus* can be observed and measured. So can its effect on an overt *response*. Together, these form the basis for what is known as S-R psychology. As far as the organism itself is concerned—its instincts, drives, perceptions, thoughts, and feelings—the behaviorists would not speculate. In fact, Pavlov was said to have fined laboratory assistants who slipped into using "mentalistic" language. So where does the *organism* (O) fit in? In recent years, researchers have come to appreciate some of the ways in which the O bridges the S and R—giving rise to a more flexible S-O-R brand of behaviorism. Two factors within the organism are particularly important: biological preparedness and cognitive representations.

Biological Preparedness. For survival purposes, all animals are biologically programmed by evolution to learn some associations more easily than others. This phenomenon was first discovered by John Garcia and Robert Koelling (1966). While studying the effects of radiation exposure on laboratory rats, they noticed that the animals would not drink from the plastic water bottles inside the radiation chambers. Since the radiation (US) was causing nausea (UR), they reasoned, perhaps the rats had acquired an aversion (CR) to the "plastic" taste of the water (CS).

To test this hypothesis, these investigators rigged an apparatus that worked as follows: When a rat licked a plastic drinking tube, it tasted sweetened water, saw a flash of light, and heard a loud clicking noise—all at the same time. The rats were then exposed to a high dose of X-rays, which caused poisoning and nausea. The result: The rats later came to avoid the sweetened water after radiation poisoning, but they did not also learn to avoid the light or noise. The link between taste (CS) and poison (US) was so easily learned that it took only one pairing—even though the rats did not get sick until hours later (a far cry from the split-second CS-US interval that is usually necessary). Garcia and Koelling (1966) next found that when the US was a painful electric shock to the feet instead of X-ray poisoning, the rats continued to drink the water, but this time they avoided the audiovisual stimuli instead. In other words, although the rats were exposed to all stimuli, they proceeded to avoid only the flavored water after X-ray poisoning and only the light and noise after shock. Why was taste such a powerful CS when it was paired with poison but not with shock? And why were light and noise conditioned to shock but not to poison? Think about these associations for a moment, and one word will pop to mind: *adaptiveness*. In nature, food is more likely to produce stomach poisoning than a pain in the foot, and an external stimulus is more likely to cause a pain in the foot than stomach illness. If you get sick after eating in a new restaurant, you are likely to blame your illness on something you ate, not on the decor or the

In animal studies, rodents are often fed using drinking tubes, such as the one shown here.
iStock.com/felixmizioznikov

music that played. Clearly, we are "prepared" by nature to learn some CS-US associations more easily than others. More than this, when associated with dangerous outcomes, such as illness, we acquire these associations quickly, with aversion learning being demonstrated consistently in a single trial (Lin, Arthurs, & Reilly, 2017).

People acquire taste aversions, too—often with important practical implications. Consider, for example, an unfortunate side effect of chemotherapy treatments for cancer. These drugs tend to cause nausea and vomiting. As a result, patients often become conditioned to react with disgust and a loss of appetite to foods they had eaten hours before the treatment (Bovbjerg et al., 1992). Thankfully, the principles of classical conditioning offer a solution to this problem. When cancer patients are fed a distinctive maple-flavored ice cream before each treatment, they acquire a taste aversion to that ice cream—which becomes a "scapegoat" and protects the other foods in the patient's diet (Bernstein & Borson, 1986). Still, many cancer patients who had undergone chemotherapy and survived report that they continue to feel nauseous, and sometimes vomit, in response to the sights, smells, and tastes that remind them of treatment—as much as 20 years later (Bernstein, 1985; National Cancer Institute, 2017).

Cognitive Representations. How or what we think about stimuli can also influence our response. Research on the classical conditioning of fear reactions illustrates that organisms are biologically predisposed to learn certain stimulus–response connections more than others. As we'll explore in Chapter 13, people all over the world share many of the same fears. Particularly common are fears of darkness, height, snakes, and insects—relatively harmless objects, some of which we may never encounter. Yet very few of us are as terrified of automobiles, electrical outlets, appliances, and other objects that can be dangerous. Why? Martin Seligman (1971) speculated that the reason for this disparity is that humans are predisposed by evolution to be wary of stimuli and situations that posed a threat to our prehistoric ancestors.

Not everyone agrees with this evolutionary analysis (Davey, 1995). However, it is supported by various strands of research. When laboratory-raised rhesus monkeys saw a wild-reared monkey of the same species exhibit fear in the presence of a toy snake, they acquired an intense fear of snakes. But when they saw the other monkey show fear in the presence of a toy rabbit, they did not similarly acquire a fear of rabbits (Cook & Mineka, 1990; Mineka & Cook, 1993). Similar results are found in humans. When people are conditioned to fear an object that is paired with electric shock, their reaction—as measured by physiological arousal—is acquired faster and lasts longer when the object is a snake, a spider, or an angry face than when it is a neutral stimulus such as a flower, a house, or a happy face (McNally, 1987). This differential response to fear-relevant objects is so basic that it occurs even when the stimuli are presented subliminally, without awareness (Ohman & Soares, 1998).

After reviewing the research, Arne Ohman and Susan Mineka (2001) proposed that human beings are equipped by evolution with *fear modules* designed to help us defend against potentially life-threatening situations in the ecology of our distant ancestors. According to Ohman and Mineka, these fear modules have four characteristics: (a) They are highly selective, making us sensitive to some objects—such as heights, thunder, and snakes—but not others; (b) they elicit fear responses that are "automatic," requiring very little attention, thought, or effort; (c) the responses are hard to consciously control or avoid; and (d) the modules are controlled by neural circuits in the amygdala and hippocampus—primitive, subcortical limbic structures shared by all mammals (Adolphs, 2013; Maren, 2001).

Studies evaluating these fear modules indicate that humans' responsiveness to fear stimuli is similar across cultures (Landová et al., 2018), although cultural differences are evident. For example, Joan Chiao and her colleagues evaluated responsiveness in the amygdala among participants who were native Japanese in Japan and Caucasian Americans living in the United States. They found responsiveness was culture specific: The amygdala showed greater activation when participants viewed fear (versus nonfear) faces of their own cultural group (Chiao et al., 2008). Our experiences certainly play a significant role, but many studies today are focused on how our culture influences our fears, our preferences, and possibly our genetic evolution (Chiao & Immordino-Yang, 2013; Janovcová et al., 2019).

LEARNING CHECK

Going to the Dogs

You are one of Pavlov's dogs. To get some delicious meat powder, you must match each classical conditioning term in the right column with its closest example in the left.

1.	When Pavlov rings the bell after feeding you.	a.	Conditioned stimulus
2.	When Pavlov rings the bell before feeding you.	b.	Conditioned response
3.	Why you'll stop salivating at the sound of the bell if food does not accompany it.	c.	Unconditioned stimulus
4.	Why you salivate in the presence of food.	d.	Unconditioned response
5.	The food that makes you salivate.	e.	Forward conditioning
6.	How Pavlov might get you to salivate in the presence of a black square, but not a gray one.	f.	Backward conditioning
7.	Why you salivate when Pavlov rings the bell.	g.	Discrimination
8.	The bell Pavlov rings	h.	Extinction

(Answers: 1. f; 2. e; 3. h; 4. d; 5. c; 6. g; 7. b; 8. a.)

Practical Applications of Classical Conditioning

When Pavlov first found that he could train Russian dogs to drool to the sound of a dinner bell, nobody cared. In fact, E. B. Twitmyer, an American graduate student, had reported similar results at a psychology conference in 1904—the same year that Pavlov won the Nobel Prize. At the time, Twitmyer was studying the knee-jerk reflex in humans. Before each trial, he would ring a bell to warn subjects that a hammer was about to strike the knee. Like Pavlov, he found that the subject's leg would soon twitch in response to the bell—even before the knee was hit. Was this a profound development? You might think so, but Twitmyer's presentation attracted little interest.

Conditioned Fears

Psychologists finally took notice of classical conditioning in 1914, when behaviorist John Watson described Pavlov's work to a group of American psychologists. To demonstrate the relevance of the phenomenon to humans, Watson and his assistant Rosalie Rayner (1920) conditioned a 9-month-old infant boy named Albert to fear a white laboratory rat. "Little Albert" was a normal, healthy, well-developed infant. Like others his age, he was scared by loud noises but enjoyed playing with furry little animals. Enter John Watson. Modeled after Pavlov's research, Watson presented Albert with a harmless white rat. Then just as the boy reached for the animal, Watson made a loud, crashing sound by banging a steel bar with a hammer, which caused the startled boy to jump and fall forward, burying his head in the mattress he was lying on. After seven repetitions of this event, the boy was terrified of the animal. What's worse, his fear generalized, leading him to burst into tears at the sight of a rabbit, a dog, a Santa Claus mask, and even a white fur coat (illustrated in Figure 5.7).

From an ethical standpoint, Watson and Rayner's study was shameful. They conditioned an innocent baby with a fear that seemed to spread like it was a contagious disease from one white and furry stimulus to the next—and they did not "decondition" him (in case you're wondering, ethics committees would not approve this study today). Watson said that the boy was taken away before he had a chance to do so, but others believe he may have known in advance that Albert's mother was going to remove her son from the research project (Harris, 1979). That said, although Albert was not deconditioned, it is worth noting the possibility that the fear would extinguish anyway, over time, as he encountered many things that were white and fluffy but that did not elicit the same frightening clanging sound. On the positive side, Little Albert's fear is a legend in the history of psychology because it established for

FIGURE 5.7 ■ The Conditioning of Little Albert and Generalization

By linking a harmless white rat to an aversive loud noise, Watson conditioned a baby boy to react with terror to the rat. In fact, the fear spread, or generalized, to other, superficially similar objects.

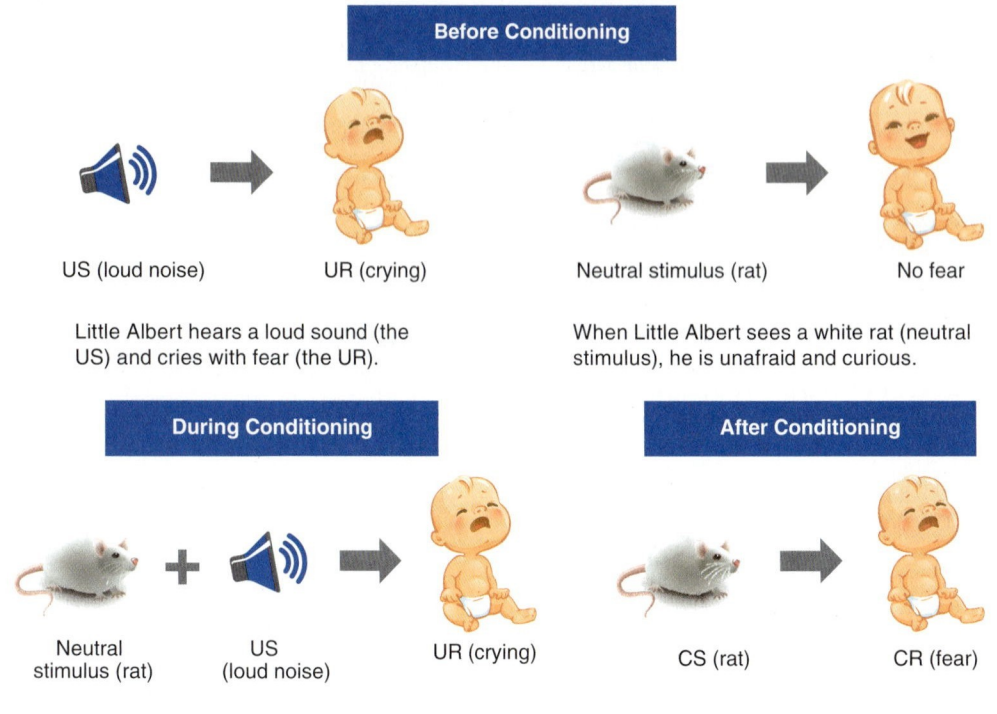

Before Conditioning

US (loud noise) → UR (crying)

Little Albert hears a loud sound (the US) and cries with fear (the UR).

Neutral stimulus (rat) → No fear

When Little Albert sees a white rat (neutral stimulus), he is unafraid and curious.

During Conditioning

Neutral stimulus (rat) + US (loud noise) → UR (crying)

Every time Little Albert is shown a white rat (neutral stimulus), he hears the loud sound (US) and cries with fear (UR).

After Conditioning

CS (rat) → CR (fear)

After several pairings of rat and loud sound, there is no loud sound but when Little Albert sees the white rat (CS), he cries with fear (CR).

---

the first time a link between Pavlov's dogs and an important aspect of the human experience. We now know that people can come to fear objects or places because they happened to be associated with aversive experiences. As we'll explore in Chapter 14, classical conditioning spawned a revolutionary and effective method of treating these irrational fears and other anxiety-related disorders. In a development with particularly profound implications, researchers are also finding links between classical conditioning and the immune system.

Naturally, babies can be conditioned to form positive *preferences* as well—for example, toward stimuli associated with maternal care. In one study, Regina Sullivan and her colleagues (1991) exposed newborns to a neutral odor. After each presentation, some newborns were touched gently, an inherently pleasurable experience, while others were not. The next day, all the infants were returned to the lab and tested. As predicted, those for whom the odor was paired with the tactile stimulation were more likely to turn their heads toward that odor rather than away from it. This effect occurs not only in human infants but also in young rats, mice, hamsters, deer, guinea pigs, squirrel monkeys, and other species (Leon, 1992). Even human adults can be classically conditioned to form new preferences. For example, work from Julie Mennella (2014) shows that the flavors of the foods that mothers consume during pregnancy and breastfeeding are transmitted from the maternal diet to amniotic fluid and mother's milk, which leads to breastfed infants liking these flavors more than novel flavors. In contrast, infants fed formula do not get this experience, learning

Now he fears even Santa Claus

Rosalie Raynor with Little Albert, a 9-month-old boy conditioned to fear objects.
John B. Watson via Wikimedia Commons

instead to prefer the unique flavor profile of the formula, which leads to more difficulty initially getting infants to accept flavors not found in formula, such as those of fruits and vegetables.

Social Attitudes and Behavior

Not everyone was happy about the possible uses of classical conditioning. In *Brave New World*, novelist Aldous Huxley (1932) warned readers of a future in which diabolical world leaders use Pavlov's methods to control their followers. These concerns are unfounded. However, classical conditioning does affect our lives in many ways. Think about the classic movie *Jaws*. Early in the film, pulsating bass music is followed by the sight of a shark's fin and the bloody underwater mutilation of a young swimmer. Then it happens again and again. Before you know it, the music alone (CS)—even without the shark (US)—has the audience trembling and ducking for cover. Other examples illustrate this point in American debate. As one example, the Confederate flag has close associations with racism. It was flown by the Confederate States of America (the "Confederacy") during the Civil War as part of a rebellion by Southern slave owners to defend their right to own slaves. While some claim the flag has been repurposed to represent Southern pride, its association with racism is too powerful, and even led to banning the Confederate flag at all NASCAR events and properties in 2020 (Romo, 2020).

These examples suggest that people form strong positive and negative *attitudes* toward neutral objects by virtue of their links to emotionally charged stimuli. In one classic study, college students were presented with a list of national names (German, Swedish, Dutch, Italian, French, and Greek), each repeatedly paired with words that had very pleasant (*happy, gift, sacred*) or unpleasant (*bitter, ugly, failure*) connotations. When the participants later evaluated the nationalities by name, they were more positive in their ratings of those that had been paired with pleasant words than those with unpleasant words (Staats & Staats, 1958). Indeed, we can be classically conditioned to form likes and dislikes of neutral people, situations, and objects, even when we are unaware of the cues associated with conditioning (De Houwer, Thomas, & Baeyen, 2001; Pine, Mendelsohn, & Dudai, 2014).

As another example, what do you think about when you hear your national anthem? As one person put it, "It makes people feel united. It makes you feel like you're thinking what everyone else is thinking" (Lausevic, cited by Gilboa & Bodner, 2009). A study that evaluated what is on people's minds while they listen to their respective national anthems found that participants had stronger associations with nationality, such as pride and patriotism, than they did when listening to three other nonnational songs (Gilboa & Bodner, 2009). Thus, due to associations between experiences resulting from country of citizenship and the anthem, a national anthem is more than just a song to a country's citizens. It can be associated with nostalgic images, family, culture, memories of times of service to country, and other emotion-eliciting symbols.

It's also possible to influence social behavior through classical conditioning. Consider the logos that popular companies and advertisers use. Have you ever considered the meaning or associations that companies want you to connect with their logos? For example, the logo for Beats by Dre has the letter *b* enclosed in a circle followed by the brand name. The circle actually "represents a human's head, and the 'b' letterform represents the brand's headphones. This gives the brand a personal element, allowing a customer to see themselves in the headphones" (Jordan, 2018, p. 1). Can you see yourself in the headphones? As another example, Amazon is by far the world's largest online retailer. In the company's logo, the yellow arrow starts at the letter *a* and ends at the letter *z*, implying that they "sell everything from a to z." The arrow also "represents a smile, with the arrowhead being a stylized dimple or smile line. The smile indicates the happiness people feel when they shop with Amazon" (Jordan, 2018, p. 1). In this way, attempts at classical conditioning can be seen everywhere, even in the logos of companies that you buy from, both in store and online.

Through classical conditioning, people often react with strong emotions to once-neutral objects such as national flags and other symbols.

iStock.com/ricochet64

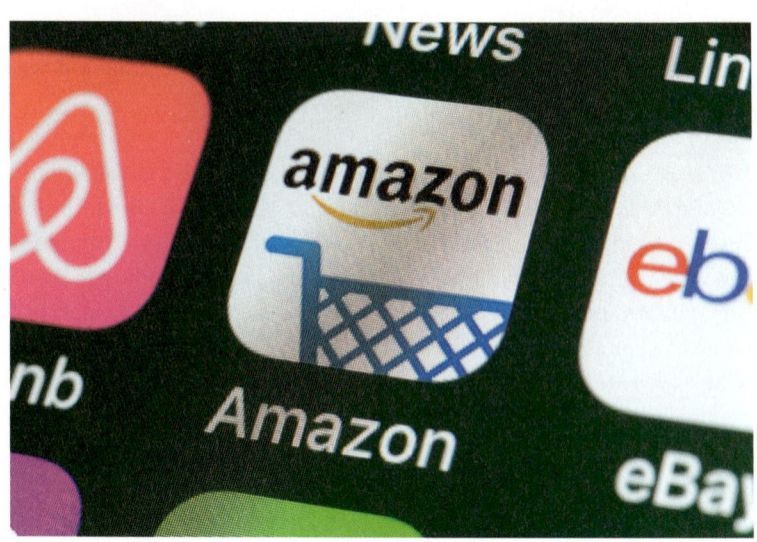

Popular brands like Beats by Dre and Amazon cleverly use imagery to connect meaning to their brands for their customers.
Ethan Miller / Staff / Getty
iStock.com/stockcam

Psychology Applied: Can the Immune System Be Classically Conditioned?

Ever since the work of Ivan Pavlov, psychologists have known that reflexes and emotional reactions can be classically conditioned. But what about the human immune system—can it also be trained to respond to neutral stimuli? Thanks to research developments beginning near the turn of the 21st century, we now know that it is also possible to train the body's immune system—and, as a result, certain aspects of our physical health and well-being (Ader & Cohen, 1993; Tekampe et al., 2017). Indeed, the pages of medical history are filled with stories that seem to indicate the effects of classical conditioning. Consider the case of a hay fever patient whose allergy was so severe that just looking at a picture of a hay field would trigger an attack (Martin, 1998) or studies showing that women are sexually responsive to neutral pictures when these images are associated with sexual stimulation (Both, Brauer, & Laan, 2011).

Consisting of more than a trillion white blood cells, the immune system guards our health by warding off bacteria, viruses, and other foreign substances that invade the body. When this system fails, as it does, for example, when it's ravaged by the AIDS virus, disease and death are the certain outcome. With that in mind, you can appreciate the following striking discovery. Psychologist Robert Ader had been using classical-conditioning procedures with rats in which he paired sweetened water with a drug that causes nausea—cyclophosphamide. Water, drug. Water, drug. As expected, the rats developed a taste aversion to the sweetened water. Unexpectedly, however, many of the animals died because the drug Ader used weakened the immune system by destroying certain types of white blood cells. To explore this phenomenon further, Ader joined with immunologist Nicholas Cohen (Ader & Cohen, 1985) in a series of landmark experiments. They repeatedly fed the rats sweetened water, which is harmless, followed by cyclophosphamide (US), which weakens the immune response (UR). The result: After several pairings, the sweetened water on its own (CS) caused a weakening of the immune response, followed by sickness and sometimes death (CR).

In light of this result, Dana Bovbjerg and others (1990) wondered about cancer patients who take chemotherapy drugs. These drugs are designed to inhibit the growth of

This color-enhanced microscopic image shows multiple "natural killer" immune cells engulfing and destroying a cancer cell. The immune system contains more than a trillion specialized white blood cells.

iStock.com/frentusha

new cancer cells, but they also inhibit the growth of immune cells. With chemotherapy drugs always being given in the same room in the same hospital, is it possible, over time, that a patient's immune system is conditioned to react in advance to cues in the surrounding environment? Yes. In a study of women who had undergone several chemotherapy treatments for ovarian cancer, these researchers found that the women's immune systems were weakened as soon as they entered the hospital—before they received treatment. Like Pavlov's bell, the hospital setting had become a conditioned stimulus, thus triggering a maladaptive change in cellular activity.

These discoveries raise an exciting question: If the immune system can be weakened by conditioning, can it similarly be strengthened and activity levels increased? The growing consensus for research on this question is yes, with positive results in animals and humans showing that it can be done (Madden et al., 2001; Tekampe et al., 2017). In early studies with human participants, for example, researchers found that after repeatedly pairing sweet sherbet or other neutral stimuli with shots of adrenaline (which has the unconditioned effect of increasing activity in certain types of immune cells), the sherbet flavor alone later triggered an increase in the immune response (Buske-Kirschbaum, Kirschbaum, Stierle, Jabaij, & Hellhammer, 1994; Buske-Kirschbaum, Kirschbaum, Stierle, Lehnert, & Hellhammer, 1992). Might it one day be possible for medical doctors to use classical conditioning to help people fight immune-related diseases, such as AIDS? Stay tuned. Pavlov's simple discovery may well prove useful in this battle (Ader & Cohen, 2001; Tekampe et al., 2017).

OPERANT CONDITIONING

LEARNING OBJECTIVES

Distinguish between operant conditioning and classical conditioning.

- Describe the principles of operant conditioning and how this type of conditioning is applied today.
- Explain the principles of reinforcement and punishment and distinguish between the two.
- Discuss how behaviorists explain the persistence of maladaptive behaviors like gambling.
- Identify the biological and cognitive perspectives on operant conditioning.

Classical conditioning may explain why people salivate at the smell of food, cringe at the sound of a dentist's drill, or tremble at the sight of flashing red and blue lights in the rearview mirror. But it cannot explain how we learn to solve equations, make people laugh, or behave in ways that earn love, praise, sympathy, or the respect of others. As we will learn, the acquisition of voluntary, complex, and goal-directed behaviors involves a second form of learning.

What's Your Prediction?

Through classical conditioning, we come to like or dislike (CR) unknown others (CS) because of their association to positive and negative events (US). How far does this power of association spread? Would you dislike someone you never met merely because of his or her link to *others* associated with bad events? Eva Walther (2002) had subjects rate their first impressions of people in face photographs, from −100 to +100. Neutral faces, not liked or disliked, were then shown in pairs. Next, one face from each pair was shown alongside a disliked face. Finally, all faces were rerated. Make a prediction: If neutral Faces 1 and 2 are paired, and if Face 2 is then linked to disliked Face 3, will people come to dislike Face 1 as well as Face 2? Yes, there is guilt by preassociation. What's worse, subjects did not know why they disliked innocent Faces 1 and 2. Even without awareness, we are influenced by layers of classical conditioning. These types of conditioning effects have been observed throughout the literature for other associations as well, such as our likes and dislikes toward students in a classroom, patients in a hospital, the products we shop for, and even chocolate (Appleton, Hemingway, Rajska, & Hartwell, 2018; De Ruddere et al., 2011; Domjan, 2018b; Wang et al., 2017).

The Law of Effect

Before Pavlov had begun his research, an American psychology student named Edward L. Thorndike (1898) was blazing another trail. Interested in animal intelligence, Thorndike built a "puzzle box" from wooden shipping crates so that he could observe how different animals learn to solve problems. In one study, he put hungry cats into a cage, one at a time, with a door that could be lifted by stepping on a lever. He then placed a tantalizing chunk of raw fish outside the cage—and beyond reach. You can imagine what happened next. After sniffing around the box, the cat tried to escape by reaching with its paws, scratching the bars, and pushing at the ceiling. At one point, the cat accidentally banged on the lever. The door opened and the cat scampered out to devour the food. Thorndike repeated the procedure again. The cat went through its previous sequence of movements and eventually found the one that caused the latch to open. After a series of trials, Thorndike's cats became more efficient: They went straight to the latch, stepped on the lever, and ate the food.

Based on studies like this one, Thorndike (1911) proposed the **law of effect**: Behaviors that are followed closely in time by a satisfying outcome are "stamped in" or repeated, whereas those followed by an undesired outcome or none at all are extinguished. In the puzzle box, cats spent progressively more time stepping on the latch and less time poking at the bars and ceiling. In the case of humans, Thorndike's law of effect was used to describe the process of socialization. By using rewards and punishments, caregivers train their children to eat with a utensil and not to fling their mashed potatoes across the table. To the extent that we learn how to produce desirable outcomes, the process is adaptive.

The Principles of Reinforcement

Following in Thorndike's footsteps, behaviorist B. F. Skinner transformed the landscape of modern psychology. But first things first. To study learning systematically, Skinner knew that he had to design an environment in which he controlled the organism's response-outcome contingencies. So as a graduate student in 1930, he used an old ice chest to build a soundproof chamber equipped with a stimulus light, a response bar (for rats) or pecking key (for pigeons), a device that dispenses dry food pellets or water, metal floor grids for the delivery of electric shock, and an instrument outside the chamber that automatically records and tabulates the responses. This apparatus came to be known as the **Skinner box** (illustrated in Figure 5.8).

Next, Skinner introduced a new vocabulary. To distinguish between the active type of learning that Thorndike had studied (whereby the organism operates on the environment) and Pavlov's classical conditioning (whereby the organism is a more passive respondent), Skinner coined the term *operant*

---

law of effect. A law stating that responses followed by positive outcomes are repeated, whereas those followed by negative outcomes are not.

Skinner box. An apparatus, invented by B. F. Skinner, used to study the effects of reinforcement on the behavior of laboratory animals.

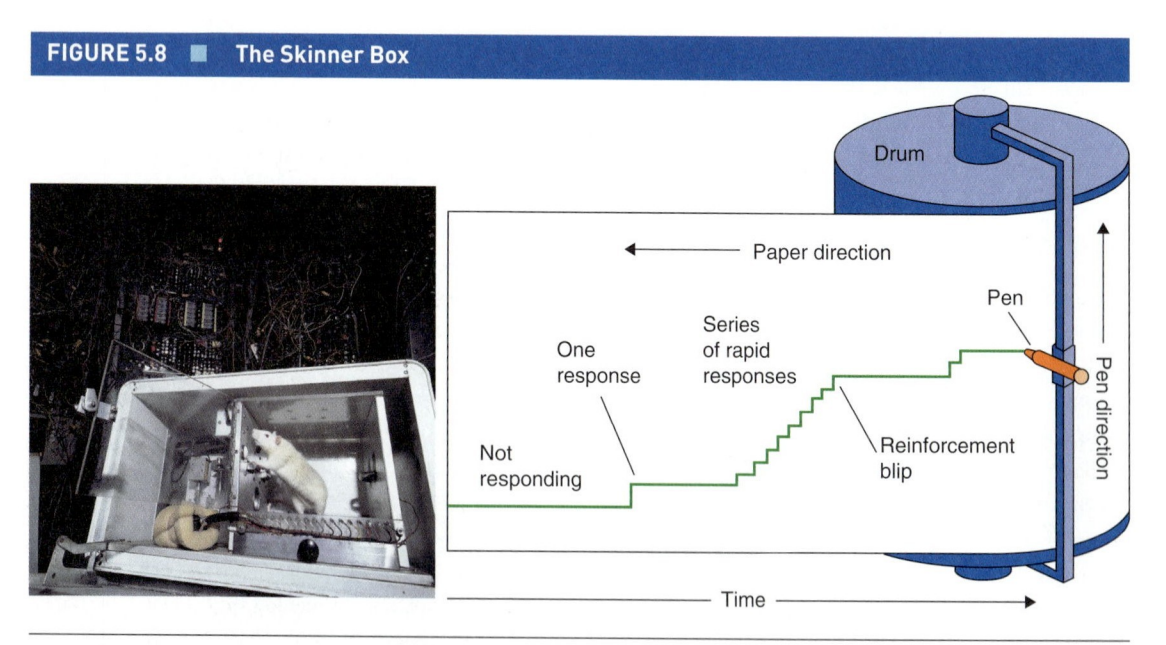

FIGURE 5.8 ■ The Skinner Box

Walter Dawn / Science Source

conditioning. **Operant conditioning** is the process by which organisms learn to behave in ways that produce desirable outcomes. The behavior itself is called an "operant" because it is designed to operate on the environment. In other words, in contrast to classical conditioning—which involves the learning of associations between stimuli, resulting in a passive response—operant conditioning involves the learning of an association between a spontaneously emitted action and its consequences (Rescorla, 1987).

To avoid speculating about an organism's internal state, Skinner also used the term **reinforcement** instead of *reward* or *satisfaction.* Objectively defined, a reinforcer is any stimulus that increases the likelihood of a prior response. There are two types of reinforcers: positive and negative. A *positive reinforcer* strengthens a prior response through the presentation of a positive stimulus—adding something desired. In the Skinner box, the food that follows a bar press is a positive reinforcer. For humans, it's food, money, grades, hugs, kisses, or a pat on the back. Even mild electrical stimulation to certain "pleasure centers" of the brain, which releases the chemical neurotransmitter dopamine, has a satisfying effect and serves as a positive reinforcer (Olds & Milner, 1954; Schultz, 2017; Wise, 2006). In contrast, a *negative reinforcer* strengthens a prior response through the removal of an aversive stimulus—subtracting something that is undesired. In a Skinner box, the termination of a painful electric shock is a negative reinforcer. Similarly, we learn to take aspirin to soften a headache, fasten our seatbelts to turn off the seatbelt buzzer, and rock babies to sleep to stop them from crying.

It is important to keep straight the fact that positive and negative reinforcers both have the same effect: to strengthen a prior response. Skinner was quick to point out that punishment is not a form of negative reinforcement. Although the two are often confused, **punishment** has the opposite effect: It decreases, not increases, the likelihood of a prior response. There are two types of punishment. A *positive punisher* weakens a prior response through the presentation of an aversive stimulus—subtracting something that is undesired. Shocking a lab rat for pressing the response lever, scolding a child, and boycotting a product all illustrate this form of punishment designed to weaken specific behaviors. In contrast, a *negative punisher* weakens a prior response through the removal of a stimulus typically characterized as positive—subtracting something that is desired. Taking food away from a hungry rat and grounding a teenager by suspending driving privileges are two examples.

To summarize, a reinforcement is a stimulus that strengthens a prior response through the presentation of a positive stimulus or the removal of a negative stimulus. In contrast, punishment is a stimulus that weakens a response through the presentation of a negative stimulus or the removal of a positive stimulus. The different types of reinforcement and punishment are summarized in Table 5.1.

Reinforcers and Punishers

A reinforcer or a punisher is specifically related to the outcome. In other words, anything that increases the likelihood of behavior (that is, anything that strengthens a prior response) is a reinforcer. Likewise, anything that decreases the likelihood of behavior (that is, anything that weakens a prior response) is a punisher. In this light, the terms *positive* and *negative* refer to whether a reinforcer or a punisher is added or removed—not to the pleasantness or aversiveness of a stimulus. For example, the annoying sound your car makes when you do not buckle your seat belt—a negative reinforcer—is designed to *increase* the likelihood that you will buckle your seat belt; likewise, getting a traffic ticket for speeding—a positive punisher—is designed to *decrease* the likelihood that you will speed again. Thus, negative reinforcers and positive reinforcers cause behavior to increase, and negative punishers and positive punishers cause behavior to decrease.

operant conditioning. The process by which organisms learn to behave in ways that produce reinforcement.

reinforcement. In operant conditioning, any stimulus that increases the likelihood of a prior response.

punishment. In operant conditioning, any stimulus that decreases the likelihood of a prior response.

TABLE 5.1 ■ Types of Reinforcement and Punishment

Procedure	Effect on Behavior: Increases	Effect on Behavior: Decreases
Presentation of stimulus after a behavior	Positive reinforcement (feed the rat)	Positive punishment (shock the rat)
Removal of stimulus after a behavior	Negative reinforcement (stop the shock)	Negative punishment (stop the food)

Let's look at three additional features of reinforcers and punishers, each of which highlights the fact that not all consequences lead to the same outcome:

Whether a consequence is a punisher or a reinforcer depends on the outcome. Again, the ultimate determination is whether the consequence causes an increase or a decrease in behavior. For example, if you spank your child because they are misbehaving, the child may have been seeking your attention, any type of attention, and thus may misbehave again. By definition, then, spanking—which is perceived by the child as attention—is a now positive reinforcer—it causes misbehaving to increase.

Intent is not relevant. The intent of a person delivering the reinforcer or punisher is not what matters. The key issue is whether the consequence causes an increase or a decrease in behavior. For example, a manager may set up rewards for meeting certain goals to increase productivity—the goals are a positive reinforcer. Yet, for low-performing employees, the goals may be seen as unattainable; thus, they may give up, and their productivity decreases—now the goals are a positive punisher.

"Effects" depend on circumstances. Reinforcers and punishers are defined by the effect they produce in a specific circumstance; they do not necessarily produce the same effect under all circumstances. For example, a stimulus (e.g., time with family) may be seen as a reinforcer to some individuals, but to others, it may be a punisher. Likewise, a stimulus that was once reinforcing (e.g., drinking alcohol) may lose its reinforcing capability at a different time (e.g., when a person has the flu).

It is important to note the complexity and yet the basic simplicity of reinforcers and punishers. Whether a stimulus is a reinforcer or a punisher can vary depending on a variety of factors, yet both are ultimately simply defined: reinforcers *increase* the likelihood of behavior (that is, they strengthen a prior response); punishers *decrease* the likelihood of behavior (that is, they weaken a prior response).

Shaping and Extinction

Modeled after the law of effect, Skinner's basic principle seemed straightforward. Responses that produce reinforcement are repeated. But wait. If organisms learn by the consequences of their behavior, where does the very first response come from? Before the first food pellet, how does the animal come to press the bar? As Thorndike had demonstrated, one possibility is that the response occurs naturally as the animal explores the cage. Skinner pointed to a second possibility: that **shaping** occurs. In other words, the behavior is gradually shaped, or guided, by the reinforcement of responses that come closer and closer to the desired behavior.

shaping. A procedure in which reinforcements are used to gradually guide an animal or a person toward a specific behavior.

Operant conditioning—with positive reinforcement and operant learning techniques—can be used to train animals.

picture alliance / Contributor / Getty

Imagine that you are trying to get a hungry white rat to press the bar in a Skinner box. Where do you begin? The rat has never been in this situation before, so it sniffs around, pokes its nose through the air holes, grooms itself, rears on its hind legs, and so on. At this point, you can wait for the target behavior to appear on its own, or you can speed up the process. If the rat turns toward the bar, you drop a food pellet into the cage. Reinforcement. If it steps toward the bar, you deliver another pellet. Reinforcement. If the rat moves closer or touches the bar, you deliver yet another one. Once the rat is hovering near the bar and pawing at it, you withhold the next pellet until it presses down, which triggers the feeder. Before long, your subject is pressing the bar at a rapid pace. By reinforcing "successive approximations" of the target response, you will have shaped a whole new behavior.

Shaping is the procedure that animal trainers use to get circus elephants to walk on their hind legs, bears to ride bicycles, chickens to play a piano, squirrels to water ski, and dolphins to jump through hoops. The dolphin trainer begins by throwing the dolphin a fish for turning toward a hoop, then for swimming toward it, swimming through it underwater, and finally jumping through a hoop that is held many feet up in the air. The process applies to people as well. Young children are toilet trained, socialized to behave properly, and taught to read through step-by-step reinforcement. Similarly, political candidates repeat statements that draw loud applause and abandon those that are met with silence—thereby creating messages that are shaped by what voters want to hear. Rumor has it that a group of college students once conspired to shape the behavior of their good-natured psychology professor. Using eye contact as a reinforcer, the students trained this professor to lecture from a certain corner of the room. Whenever he moved in that direction, they looked up at him; otherwise, they looked down. Before long, he was lecturing from the corner of the classroom, not quite realizing that he had been "shaped."

In classical conditioning, repeated presentation of the CS without the US causes the CR to gradually weaken and disappear. Extinction also occurs in operant conditioning. If you return your newly shaped rat to the Skinner box but disconnect the feeder from the response bar, you'll find that after the rat presses the bar some number of times without reinforcement, the behavior will fade and become extinguished. By the same token, people stop smiling at those who don't smile back, stop helping those who never reciprocate, and stop working when their efforts meet with continued failure.

Schedules of Reinforcement

Every now and then, scientists stumble into their greatest discoveries. Pavlov was a classic example. So was Skinner. Early in his research career, Skinner would reinforce his animals on a continuous basis: Every bar press produced a food pellet. Then something happened. At the time, Skinner had to make his own pellets by squeezing food paste through a pill machine and then waiting for them to dry. The process was time consuming. "One pleasant Saturday afternoon," Skinner recalled, "I surveyed my supply of dry pellets and, appealing to certain elemental theorems in arithmetic, deduced that unless I spent the rest of the afternoon and evening at the pill machine, the supply would be exhausted by 10:30 Monday morning" (Koch, 1959, p. 368). Not wanting to spend the weekend in the lab, Skinner rationalized to himself that not *every* response had to be reinforced. He adjusted his apparatus so that the bar-press response would be reinforced on a partial basis—only once per minute. Upon his return the next week, however, he found rolls of graph paper with response patterns that were different from anything he had seen before. From this experience, Skinner came to appreciate the powerful effects of "partial reinforcement." Indeed, he and others went on to identify four schedules of reinforcement (illustrated in Figure 5.9), each having different effects on behavior (Ferster & Skinner, 1957).

Fixed-Interval (FI) Schedule. In the situation just described, a reinforcer is followed by the first response made after a fixed interval of *time* has elapsed. In an FI-1 schedule, the response produces food after each new minute; or it may be made available only after every 2 (FI-2), 10 (FI-10), or 15 (FI-15) minutes. The schedule is fixed by time, and it tends to produce a slow, "scalloped" response pattern. After the animal learns that a certain amount of time must elapse, it pauses after each reinforcer and then responds at an accelerating rate until it nears the end of the cycle—which signals that the next reinforcement is available. The student whose rate of studying starts slow, increases before midterms, trails off after midterms, and picks up again before finals illustrates this reaction to an FI schedule. This schedule tends to be the weakest schedule of reinforcement (that is, it is the easiest to extinguish).

Variable-Interval (VI) Schedule. Once animals learn what the fixed pattern is, they press the bar only as they near the end of each interval. To counter this lazy response pattern, Skinner tried varying the interval around an average. In other words, an interval may average 1 minute in length (a VI-1 schedule), but the actual timing of a reinforcement is unpredictable from one interval to the next—say, after 50 seconds, then 2 minutes, 10 seconds, and 1 minute. The result is a slow but steady, not scalloped, pattern of responses. In effect, teachers who give pop quizzes are using a VI schedule to ensure that their students keep up with the reading rather than cram at the last minute.

FIGURE 5.9 ■ Schedules of Reinforcement

These curves show the response patterns typically produced by different schedules of reinforcement. The steeper the curve, the higher the response rate (the slash marks on each curve indicate the delivery of a reinforcement). As illustrated, the rate of responding is higher under ratio than interval schedules.

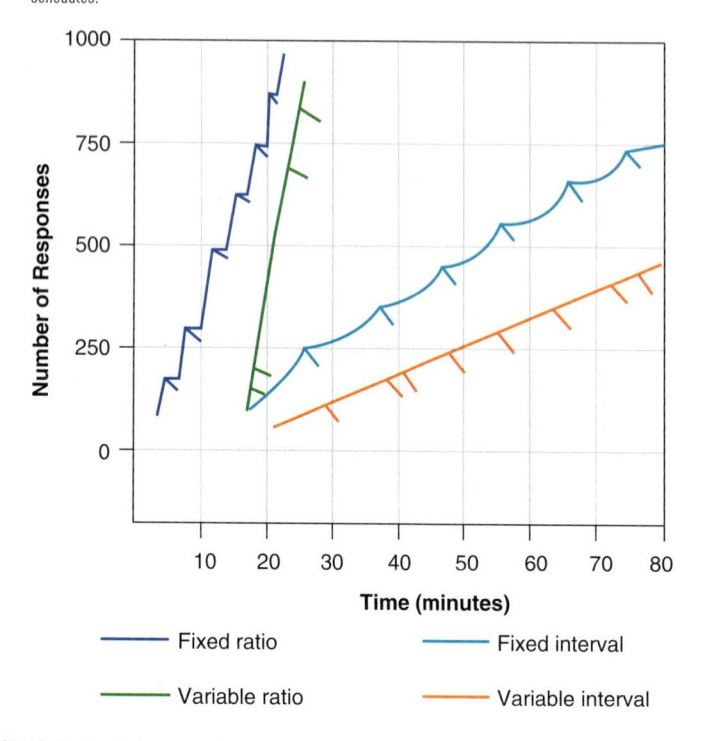

— Fixed ratio — Fixed interval
— Variable ratio — Variable interval

Fixed-Ratio (FR) Schedule. In this situation, a reinforcer is administered after a fixed number of *responses*—say, every 3rd response, or every 5th, 10th, or 50th. In an FR-10 schedule, it takes 10 bar presses to get food. If 30 responses are needed, it is an FR-30 schedule. The response-to-reinforcement ratio thus remains constant. In a Skinner box, animals on an FR schedule exhibit a burst of bar presses until the food appears, pause briefly, then produce another burst. The result is a fast, steplike response pattern. Frequent-flier programs where you can earn a free flight after 25,000 miles of air travel, credit card rewards where you earn 3 percent cash back for every dollar spent, and the employer who pays workers after they produce a certain number of products all operate on a fixed-ratio schedule.

Variable-Ratio (VR) Schedule. In this situation, the reinforcement appears after some average number of responses is made—a number that varies randomly from one reinforcement to the next. On a VR-15 schedule, a rat would have to press the bar an average of 15 times, but the food may appear on the 5th response, then on the 20th, 14th, and 21st responses, and so on. Unable to predict which response will produce a food pellet, animals on a VR schedule respond at a constant high rate. In one case, Skinner trained pigeons to peck a disk 10,000 times for a single food pellet! Slot machines and lotteries are rigged to pay off on a VR schedule, leading gamblers to deposit coins and purchase tickets at a furious, addictive pace. If you ever tried to purchase online tickets to a concert or sporting event only for the website to fail to load—chances are you too kept hitting refresh, trying to get the site to load with dogged persistence. The reason: When it comes to getting through, our efforts are reinforced, as with slot machines, on a variable-ratio schedule. As you may expect, this schedule tends to be the strongest schedule of reinforcement (that is, it is the most difficult to extinguish). Table 5.2 summarizes the four schedules of reinforcement.

Reinforcement schedules affect extinction rates as well as learning. Specifically, the operant response is more enduring and, later, more resistant to extinction when the organism is reinforced on a partial basis rather than on a continuous, 100 percent schedule. This phenomenon is called the **partial-reinforcement effect**. The rat that is fed after every bar press is quick to realize, once the feeder

---

partial-reinforcement effect. The tendency for a schedule of partial reinforcement to strengthen later resistance to extinction.

TABLE 5.2	Schedules of Reinforcement	
	Ratio	**Interval**
Fixed	A reinforcer is administered after a fixed number of responses	A reinforcer is followed by the first response made after a fixed interval of time had elapsed ***Easiest to extinguish**
Variable	A reinforcer is administered after a variable number of responses ***Most difficult to extinguish**	A reinforcer is followed by the first response made after a variable interval of time had elapsed

is disconnected, that the contingency has changed. But the rat that is fed on only an occasional basis persists more before realizing that reinforcement is no longer forthcoming. If you put money into a vending machine and do not get the drink you ordered, you walk away. Because vending machines are supposed to operate on a continuous-reinforcement basis, it would be quickly apparent that this one is out of order. Deposit money into a broken slot machine, however, and you may go on to lose hundreds more. After all, you expect slot machines to pay off on an irregular basis. The partial-reinforcement effect has some ironic implications. For example, caregivers who sometimes give in to (reinforce) a child's temper tantrums and at other times try to tough it out can create "little monsters" with more tenacious, harder-to-eliminate outbursts than do caregivers who always (or never) give in (Duncombe, Havighurst, Holland, & Frankling, 2012; Feehan, McGee, Stanton, & Silva, 1991).

Punishment

In 1948, Skinner wrote *Walden Two*, a novel about a fictional society in which socially adaptive behaviors were maintained by various schedules of reinforcement. The book was a blueprint for the use of "behavioral engineering" to design a happy, healthy, and productive community. Skinner never hesitated to preach the use of reinforcement. Yet he just as adamantly opposed the use of punishment, even though it is a common form of behavior control. Think about it. Caregivers scold their children, police officers fine motorists for speeding, referees penalize athletes for committing fouls, and employers fire workers who are lazy. So what's the problem? Aren't these forms of punishment effective?

Research shows that punishment has mixed effects (Axelrod & Apsche, 1983; Domjan, 2018c; Masui, Nomura, & Ura, 2012). When it's strong, immediate, consistent, and inescapable, punishment does suppress unwanted behaviors. Shock a rat for pressing the response bar and it will quickly stop making the response. Yell, "No!" at the top of your lungs to a child playing with matches, and it is unlikely to happen again. Clearly, punishment can be an effective deterrent.

To test punishment, Rebecca Bennett (1998) had 263 college students play the role of a corporate executive faced with an ethical dilemma. Those who selected an unethical path in order to maximize profits were then assessed a large or small fine and told that a competitor who had made the same choice was or was not similarly fined. Indicating the benefits of punishment, Bennett found that the large fine deterred subjects from later making another unethical choice. She also found that when the fine was administered even-handedly, the participants did not become resentful, angry, or aggressive.

While potentially effective, punishment can have unwanted side effects. There are four specific problems in this regard. First, a behavior that is met with punishment may be temporarily inhibited or hidden from

B. F. Skinner was born in 1904 and received his psychology degree from Harvard in 1931. He published his first paper in 1930, his last in 1990. He wrote 19 books and hundreds of journal articles.

On August 10, 1990, Skinner made his final public appearance in Boston at the American Psychological Association's convention. He was there to receive an award for Outstanding Lifetime Contribution to Psychology. Upon his introduction, Skinner was greeted with a thunderous standing ovation. Everyone in the audience knew they were watching a living legend. They also knew he was dying. The talk itself was vintage Skinner. For 20 minutes, he insisted, as always, that psychology could never be a science of the mind, only a science of behavior.

On August 17, 1990, one week after his Boston appearance, Skinner completed his last article, for the *American Psychologist*. He died the next day.

Nina Leen / Contributor / Getty

the punishing agent—but it is not necessarily extinguished. The child who lights matches and the teenager who smokes cigarettes may both continue to do so at school, at a friend's house, or at home when the parent is at work. Second, even when punishment does suppress an unwanted behavior, it does not always replace that behavior with one that is more adaptive. It's okay to lock up convicted criminals, but to change their future behavior, some form of rehabilitation program is necessary. Third, punishment can sometimes backfire because a stimulus thought to be aversive may, in fact, prove rewarding. The neglected child who acts up and is scolded by busy caregivers may "enjoy" the attention and make trouble again in the future. Fourth, punishment can arouse fear, anger, frustration, and other negative emotions—leading the person to strike back, retaliate, tune out, or run away.

A particularly contentious debate concerns the use of *corporal punishment* by caregivers who use spanking to discipline their children. Defined as the use of reasonable physical force, which causes a child pain but not injury, corporal punishment is more common in some parts of the world than others. Some countries prohibit corporal punishment by law; yet many American caregivers support it. So, what are the effects? Elizabeth Gershoff (2002) meta-analyzed 88 studies spanning 62 years and involving 36,309 children whose caregivers varied in their use of corporal punishment. Overall, she found that children who were spanked were more likely to stop misbehaving immediately afterward. However, they also had poorer relationships with their caregivers, were more aggressive and more antisocial, and were more likely as adults to have psychological problems and abuse their own spouses and children. In a later study, Gershoff (2013) concluded that "spanking is a form of violence against children that should no longer be a part of American childrearing" (p. 133). Others agree with Gershoff's conclusions. In 2014, Minnesota Vikings athlete Adrian Peterson was arrested and charged with injury to a child after using a wooden switch to discipline his son. As a result, the child suffered from cuts and bruises. Peterson's case went viral and thus "revived a debate about corporal punishment" (CBS News, 2014). Across the United States, corporal punishment is legal. Texas, where Peterson's case took place, allows a guardian to use nondeadly force for child disciplinary purposes as long as said guardian "reasonably believes the force is necessary to discipline the child or to safeguard or promote his welfare" (CBS News, 2014).

Interestingly, more recent studies also show that many caregivers simply do not equate their physical disciplinary strategies—such as spanking, or slapping of the hand, arm, or leg—to corporal punishment (Fréchette & Romano, 2017). Although beliefs about spanking can vary by culture (Lansford et al., 2017), many caregivers will report being against corporal punishment and yet use corporal punishment strategies to punish their own children. In many cases, caregivers are apparently unaware that they are using corporal punishment. Still, critics of studies like these are quick to note that the correlations do not prove that spanking itself *causes* the negative effects, that spanking is too often accompanied by abusive rearing, and that the results do not speak to the effects of nonphysical forms of punishment (Baumrind, Larzelere, & Cowan, 2002), such a public shaming, which can likewise be associated with negative outcomes, including suicide (Panagopoulou-Koutnatzi, 2014).

Properly administered, punishment can be used to suppress unwanted behavior. Improperly administered, however, it can create more problems than it solves. Thus, advised Skinner, it is better to use a combination of reinforcement (to bring out alternative desirable behaviors) and extinction (to extinguish the undesirable behaviors) in order to shape a new, more adaptive way of life.

Stimulus Control

In operant conditioning, organisms learn to respond in ways that are reinforced. But there is more to the story. A pigeon trained in a Skinner box learns to peck a key for food, but it may also learn that the response produces reinforcement only in the presence of certain cues. Because reinforcements are often available in some situations but not others, it is adaptive to learn not only *what* response to make but *when* to make it. If pecking a key produces food only when a green disk is lit, a pigeon may learn to discriminate and to respond on a selective basis. The green light is a **discriminative stimulus** that "sets the occasion" for the behavior to be reinforced (Ross & LoLordo, 1987).

When people learn to respond in some situations and not others, their behavior is said to be under *stimulus control*. In human terms, this is often important for treating behavioral disorders. Consider the problem of insomnia. Studies show that people with insomnia too often use the bed for nonsleeping

---

discriminative stimulus. A stimulus that signals the availability of reinforcement.

activities such as watching TV, gaming, listening to music on their phones, reading, and worrying about personal problems. In other words, the bed has become a discriminative stimulus for so many activities that it becomes a source of arousal, not relaxation. To counter this problem, people with insomnia are advised, frequently with successful results, to lie in bed only for the purpose of sleeping (Bullis & Sauer-Zavala, 2018).

An operant response may spread from one situation to another through the process of stimulus generalization. As in classical conditioning, the more similar a new stimulus is to the original discriminative stimulus, the more likely it is to trigger the response. In one study, pigeons were reinforced for pecking a key that was illuminated with yellow light. They were then tested with lights of different colors. The more similar the test lights were to the yellow discriminative stimulus—for example, green and orange as opposed to red and blue—the more likely the pigeons were to peck at it (Guttman & Kalish, 1956).

It now appears that even more subtle forms of discrimination are possible. In one clever study, eight pigeons were reinforced with birdseed to peck a key whenever a slide was projected into their cage. Half the pigeons were reinforced for the key press only in the presence of a painting by Monet, the French impressionist. The others were reinforced only in the presence of a painting by Picasso, the Spanish cubist. Showing an ability to both generalize and make fine discriminations, the pigeons in each condition later pecked when shown new paintings by the same artist (stimulus generalization) but not when shown new paintings by the other artist (discrimination). Remarkably, the pigeons even went on to generalize from Monet to other French impressionists, such as Renoir—and from Picasso to other cubists, such as Matisse (Watanabe, Sakamoto, & Wakita, 1995).

Discrimination and generalization are important aspects of human operant conditioning. From experience, a child may learn that temper tantrums bring results from busy caregivers but not from teachers, that studying increases grades in social studies but not math, that lewd remarks elicit laughter in the locker room but not in the classroom, and that aggression wins praise on the football field but not in other settings. As adults, we routinely regulate our behavior according to situational cues.

Self-Control

For many years, psychologists interested in operant behavior have studied the ways in which our life choices—for example, the economic decisions we make—are guided by our learned expectations for reinforcement (Mazur, 1998). In fact, the field of *behavioral economics* continues to grow and brings together various aspects of psychology and economics (Brocas & Carrillo, 2003; Earl, 2017).

Some psychologists have theorized that people (and animals too, for that matter) make behavioral choices according to how reinforcing these choices have been. Simply put, the more reinforcement we receive for a particular type of response, relative to others that are possible, the more likely we are to make that response in a future situation (Herrnstein, 1970). This principle suggests that people tend to behave in ways that maximize the value of their own return. This makes sense, but are people always so rational? Don't we often behave in ways that detract from our own long-term interests—as when we smoke, gamble, drink too much, eat too much, blow the paycheck without saving for tomorrow, and engage in other bad habits? To reconcile the notion that people seek to maximize reinforcements in their lives with the fact that they often behave in ways that are not personally adaptive, researchers have studied *self-control*—the extent to which people pass up small but immediate rewards in exchange for more valuable future gains (Beames, Schofield, & Denson, 2018; Rachlin, 1995).

Research shows that we often do not exhibit self-control, and hence we do not maximize our own gains, because rewards seem less valuable to us when we have to wait to get them than when they are immediately available. What's more, the longer people have to wait for a given reward, the less valuable it seems (Kirby, 1997). Consider this choice: Would you

By electrically stimulating a pleasure center in the brain for reinforcement, researchers can shape rats to move in various directions. Perhaps some day, remote-controlled rodents will be trained to search through piles of rubble for disaster survivors.

Ian Allen / Contributor / Getty

rather have $5 today or $6 in a week? What about $50 today or $75 in six months? When presented with these types of choices, subjects often make the "myopic" (which means near-sighted) decision to select the smaller but immediate reward. As you might expect, some people are more impulsive, or more present oriented, than others. For example, Kirby, Petry, and Bickel (1999) presented a series of monetary choices to groups of participants addicted to heroin and found that they discounted the value of the delayed-but-larger sum of money more than college students and others did. Similarly, Suzanne Mitchell (1999) found that smokers are more likely than nonsmokers to choose a smaller but more immediate sum of money. These classic findings have been extended beyond drug use to include how we make decisions about money and what to eat, and even our use of disposable surgical masks during the COVID-19 pandemic (Amlung, Gray, & MacKillop, 2016; Cannito et al., 2021).

Practical Applications of Operant Conditioning

From the start, Skinner was interested in the practical, everyday applications of operant conditioning. In World War II, he worked for the U.S. government on a top-secret project in which he shaped pigeons to guide missiles toward enemy ships. Based on this work, the U.S. Navy trained dolphins and sea lions to locate explosive mines in the Persian Gulf and to perform other dangerous underwater missions (Morrison, 1988). Similarly, the Coast Guard used pigeons to search for people lost at sea. The birds were strapped under the belly of a rescue helicopter and trained to spot floating orange objects (orange is the international color of life jackets). In response to this stimulus, the birds were conditioned to peck a key that buzzes the pilot (Simmons, 1981). In a provocative form of operant conditioning, researchers fitted five rats with electrodes and battery-powered backpacks and delivered reinforcement in the form of mild electrical stimulation to a pleasure center in the brain. In this way, they shaped the rats to climb up, and move forward, left, and right. Some day, they speculated, we'll be able to navigate remote-controlled rodents through piles of rubble to search for and rescue disaster survivors (Talwar et al., 2002).

Skinner was eager to use operant conditioning in other ways as well, but his efforts were sometimes misunderstood. In 1945, he constructed an "air crib" for his infant daughter, Deborah. This crib, which he called a "baby tender," was a temperature-controlled enclosed space equipped with an air filter, sound-absorbing walls, a stretched canvas floor, a safety glass window with a curtain, and a roll of diapers. The goal was to place the infant in an environment that was comfortable, safe, and stimulating. Skinner tried to market his new invention and wrote about it for *Ladies' Home Journal* in an article he titled "Baby Care Can Be Modernized." Unfortunately, the *Journal* editor changed the title to "Baby in a Box"—which led the public to think that he was experimenting on his daughter the way he did with rats and pigeons. Rumors later spread about his daughter's mental health. For years, many people believed that she had suffered a nervous breakdown and committed suicide. In fact, she remained very much alive and was actually quite close to her father (Bjork, 1997).

Over the years, Skinner advised caregivers to raise children with the use of reinforcement rather than punishment. He also invented a "teaching machine" that would enable students to learn at their own individualized pace by solving a graded series of problems and receiving immediate feedback on their answers. Today, computer-assisted instruction in schools is based on this early work (Benjamin, 1988). In fact, personal computers are being used just as Skinner had envisioned to train students to type, play the piano, or practice their academic skills. Inspired by Skinner, other behaviorists have applied the principles of operant conditioning to get people to use safety belts, recycle wastes, conserve energy, or simply help themselves (Lattal & Perone, 1998; Sigafoos et al., 2014).

Skinner's daughter in the air crib he invented. Contrary to popular misconceptions, he did not put her in a Skinner box to shape her behavior.

Sam Falk / Science Source

The use of operant conditioning is now commonplace in the health clinic, the workplace, the classroom, and other settings. For clinical purposes, it laid an important foundation for the techniques of behavior modification, in which reinforcement is used to change maladaptive thoughts, feelings, and behaviors (refer to Chapter 14). It also forms the basis for biofeedback—an operant procedure in which electronic instruments are used to provide people with continuous information, or "feedback," about their own physiological states. With the aid of electronic sensors on the body and an instrument that amplifies the signals, people can monitor—and then learn to regulate—their own heart rate, blood pressure, and muscular tension. Biofeedback can thus be used in the treatment of migraine headaches, sports injuries, chronic back pain, and other health problems (Blumenstein & Hung, 2016).

Operant conditioning has also been used extensively in the workplace. For example, many companies toil over the best ways to motivate employees. In a study conducted with 1,469 employees, Norberg (2017) compared employee motivation across a variety of reward strategies using cash, points, and gift card rewards. In this survey study, employees who received points and gift cards were more likely than those who received cash to talk to others about their rewards and to use their rewards (that is, the rewards were more rewarding). Interestingly, you may think that cash would be rewarding, but many participants who received cash paid bills with the money. While the flexibility of receiving cash can be rewarding, paying bills is not necessarily something people like to do. As Norberg observed, "one might even suggest that paying bills reduces negative emotions but does not necessarily increase positive emotions.... [I]ndividuals who receive cash are far less likely to treat themselves" (p. 384). The very nature of understanding rewards to motivate employees highlights the value of operant conditioning in workplace settings.

Finally, operant conditioning is used regularly in the classroom. Skinner's teaching machine was one application, but there are others as well. For example, many teachers establish large-scale reinforcement programs in which children earn gold stars, ribbons, or "tokens" for engaging in desired behaviors—tokens that can be exchanged for toys, extra recess time, and other privileges. Skinner (1988) himself described how a sixth-grade teacher gave her students a card every time they handed in an assignment. The students put their cards into a jar and, at the end of the week, one card was drawn randomly, with the winner receiving a prize, like a portable radio. The result was a dramatic improvement in the number of assignments completed. Another use of operant techniques is the "flipped classroom." In this approach, the teacher serves as a moderator, organizing material for students to complete and review ahead of class, and thus can use class time to identify student progress and provide students with immediate feedback. Students are thus trained to teach themselves and each other (Lin & Hwang, 2018).

Developments in Operant Conditioning

Believing that a science of behavior must restrict its focus to observable stimulus-response relationships, Pavlov did not account for aspects of the organism that influenced classical conditioning. In the realm of operant behavior, Skinner took the same narrow view, leaving others to study the impact of inborn biological predispositions and cognitive processes.

Biological Constraints

Behaviorists used to think that animals and humans alike could be trained to emit any response that they were physically capable of making. However, it is now clear that there are biological limits to what an animal can learn. In 1947, Keller and Marian Breland, former students of Skinner, founded Animal Behavior Enterprises in Hot Springs, Arkansas. The Brelands were in the business of training animals to do tricks in county fairs, zoos, circuses, movies, and TV commercials. Indeed, they trained thousands of animals belonging to 38 different species—including bears, whales, chickens, pigs, goats, and reindeer.

Despite their professional successes, the Brelands had to concede that biological predispositions often interfered with the shaping of a new behavior. At one point, for example, they tried to train a raccoon to pick up a wooden coin and deposit it into a piggy bank. But instead, the raccoon would clutch the coin or rub two coins together, dip them into the container, pull them out, and rub them again—rather than make the deposit that was reinforced with food. The Brelands also sought to train a pig in the same routine, but after a while the pig would drop the coin, push it with its snout, toss it in the air, and drop it again. What was the problem? In an article entitled "The Misbehavior of Organisms," Breland and Breland (1961) concluded that animals revert to species-specific behavior

Biological predispositions can lead to many fun behaviors, such as when a dog catches a frisbee using its predisposition to fetch, particularly for hunting breeds.
iStock.com/Capuski

patterns, a powerful tendency they called *instinctive drift*. In the wild, raccoons manipulate food objects and dunk, or "wash," them, and pigs "root" for food in the ground—foraging instincts that inhibit the learning of new operant responses.

Biological predispositions may also constrain an animal's ability to learn how to escape from danger. For example, rats are easily conditioned to freeze, run from one place to another, or attack another rat—if these responses are reinforced by the termination of a painful electric shock. Yet they are slow to learn to escape by pressing a lever, a response they easily learn to make for food and water. According to Robert Bolles (1970), an animal's innate defensive reactions compete with the learning of a new escape response. All this serves to remind us that behavior is guided not just by personal experience but also by an organism's evolutionary past. Like classical conditioning, in which some associations are learned more easily than others, operant learning is limited by an organism's own adaptive ways (Chance, 2013; Skora et al., 2021).

Cognitive Perspectives

Up to the day he died, Skinner (1990) steadfastly refused to speculate about internal mental processes. Although this radical position still has its share of proponents (Poling, Schlinger, Starin, & Blakely, 1990), most psychologists now believe that it is important to understand internal cognitive processes—not only in humans but in animals as well (Bekoff, Allen, & Burghardt, 2002; Vonk, 2016).

Latent Learning. The first prominent theorist to adopt a cognitive position was Edward Tolman. According to Tolman (1948), animals in their natural habitat learn more than just a series of stimulus-and-response connections. They also acquire a *cognitive map*, which is a mental spatial model of the layout—and they do so regardless of whether their explorations are reinforced. Thus, when Tolman trained rats to run a maze but then changed the starting place or blocked the most direct routes, the animals behaved as if they were using a street map of their surroundings: They rerouted themselves to take the best available detours (illustrated in Figure 5.10).

To examine whether spatial learning required that the rats be reinforced for their exploratory behavior, Tolman and Honzik (1930) conducted a classic experiment. Once a day for two weeks, they put three groups of rats into a complex maze and measured their speed in reaching the goal box. One group was rewarded with food and improved considerably over time. A second group was not rewarded and did not improve much over time. From an operant standpoint, neither of these results is surprising. The third group, however, was the key to this experiment. In this group, the rats were not rewarded during the first 10 days, but they received food beginning on the 11th. The result: They showed immediate and dramatic improvement. On the 11th day, before realizing that there was food in the goal box, they were just as slow as the no-reward group. But on the 12th day, after one reinforcement, they were just as fast as the group that had been rewarded all along (illustrated in Figure 5.11).

This result was significant because it demonstrated what Tolman called **latent learning**, learning that lies dormant and is not exhibited in overt performance until there is an incentive to do so. By making this distinction between "learning" and "performance," Tolman was able to demonstrate that animals learn from experience—with or without reinforcement. More recent research provides additional support for this phenomenon and is now being applied to or adapted for e-learning systems (Capuano, Gaeta, Ritrovato, & Salerno, 2014).

latent learning. Learning that occurs but is not exhibited in performance until there is an incentive to do so.

| FIGURE 5.10 | Rats in a Maze: Evidence for a Cognitive Map |

Tolman trained rats to run a maze like the one shown here. But after their training, he blocked the most direct routes to the goal box (Block A and Block B). Operating as if they had a cognitive map, the animals rerouted themselves around the blocked routes and took the best available detours.

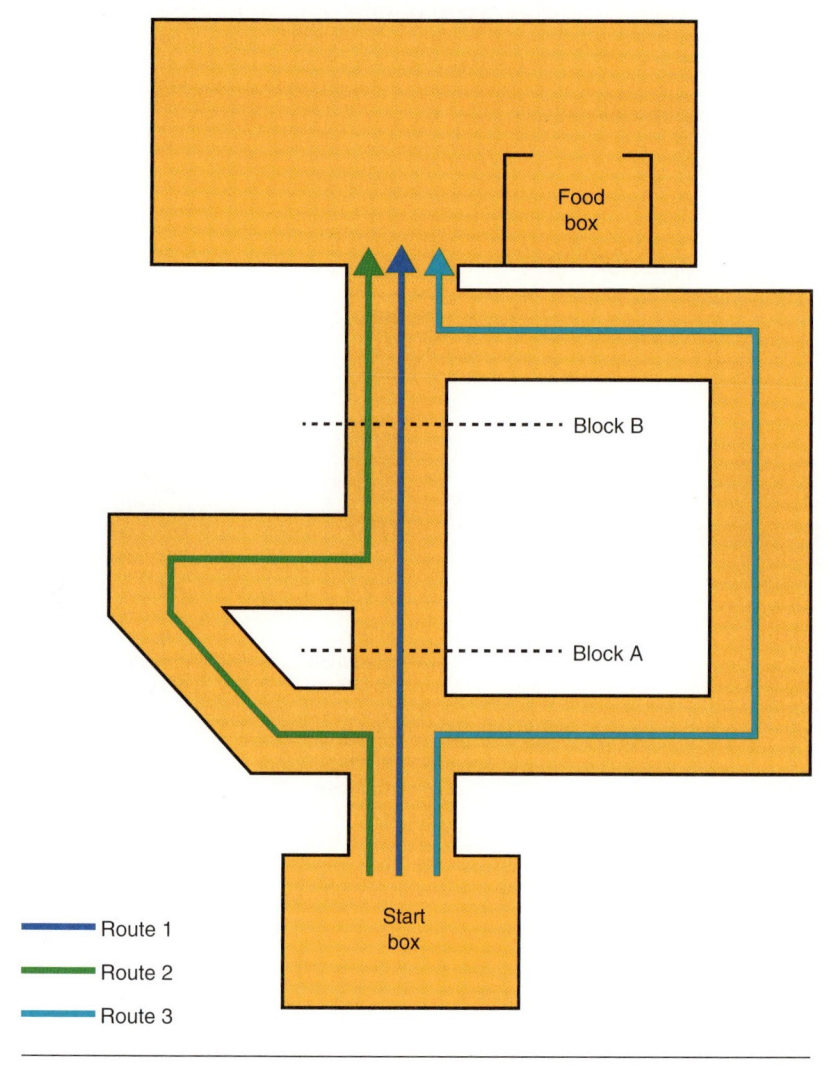

Adapted from Tolman, E. C. (1948). Cognitive maps in rats and men. Psychological Review, 55, 189-208.

Locus of Control. Strict behaviorists claim that people are controlled by objective reinforcement contingencies. In contrast, a cognitive perspective holds that behavior is influenced more by our subjective interpretations of reinforcement. To illustrate the point, consider two incidents. The first was a demonstration by Skinner (1948), in which he dropped food pellets into a pigeon's cage on a random basis, leading the animal to repeat whatever it happened to be doing at the time. Soon this "superstitious" pigeon was busy turning, hopping on one leg, bowing, scraping, and raising its head. This pigeon—like most humans, says Skinner—was under the illusion that it had control, even though it did not. The second incident concerns a young psychotherapy patient named Karl S. who was depressed because he felt incompetent to find a job, friends, or a woman. E. Jerry Phares (1976), Karl's therapist, tried to raise his expectancy for success through a series of small achievements—applying for a job, striking up a conversation with a woman, and so on. Karl succeeded in these efforts but remained passive and pessimistic. The problem? He did not see the link between his actions and successful outcomes. In contrast

FIGURE 5.11 ■ Latent Learning

Tolman and Honzik (1930) put rats into a maze and measured how quickly they reached the goal box. Those rewarded with food improved; those without reward did not. A third group received no food until the 11th day. As the rats in this third group explored the maze, they developed a cognitive map or mental picture of the layout of the maze. In this way, as soon as the rats in this last group became aware of the food, they used this cognitive map to run their way through the maze just as quickly as the group of rats that had been rewarded with food all along. These animals had exhibited latent learning, learning that is not observable until there is a reason to demonstrate it (e.g., food was placed in the maze).

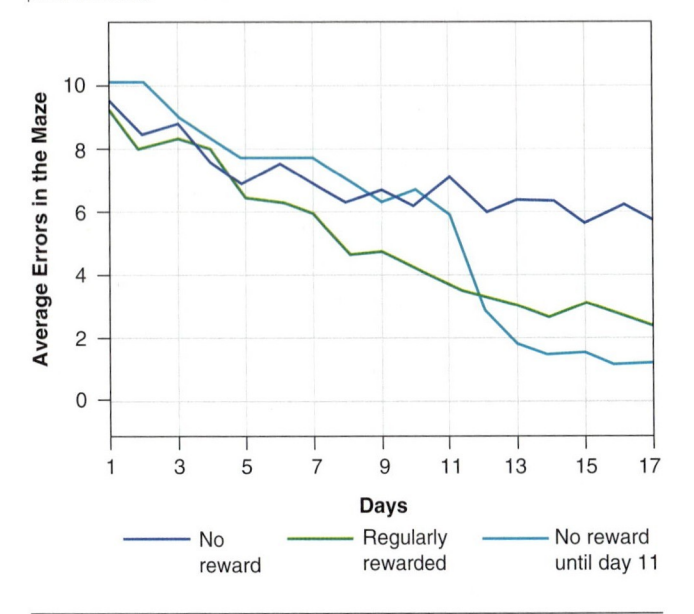

Adapted from Tolman, E. C., & Honzik, C. H. (1930). Introduction and removal of reward, and maze performance in rats. *University of California Publications in Psychology, 4*, 257–275.

Our locus of control can influence our behavior, such as how tempting a cupcake can be if we simply can't resist.

iStock.com/PeopleImages

to the superstitious pigeon, Karl had control but didn't realize it. So he didn't try.

According to Julian Rotter (1966), reinforcement influences behavior only if we perceive the two as causally connected. For students who believe that studying increases their grades, for workers who think that hard work will be rewarded, and for citizens who believe that they can influence government policy, reinforcement strengthens behavior. But for students who see grades as arbitrarily determined, for workers who think that getting ahead requires more luck than effort, and for citizens who feel that they're at the mercy of powerful leaders, reinforcement does not strengthen behavior. Research shows that people differ in their "generalized expectancies" for personal control and in their responsiveness to reinforcement. Those who have a relatively *internal* locus of control tend to believe that they determine their own destiny. Those with an *external* locus of control believe that luck, fate, and powerful others determine their reinforcements. Compared to those with an external locus of control, people with an internal locus of control tend to persist longer at laboratory tasks, get higher grades in school, and play a more active role in political and social affairs (Nowicki, 2016; Rotter, 1990). And as we'll explore in Chapter 13, behaviorists like Seligman also link our perceptions of control to psychological disorders.

> ## TRY THIS!
>
> ### Locus of Control
>
> Human behavior may be influenced not by reinforcements, but by our perceptions of control. People who have an internal locus of control believe they are in charge of their own destiny. People who have an external locus of control believe they are at the mercy of luck, fate, and powerful others. To determine whether you are an internal or an external, **TRY THIS:** For each item below, identify the letter (a or b) that you agree with more. Give yourself one point for each of your responses that matches the answers provided. Add up your total number of points (from 0 to 6). The higher your score, the more external you are.
>
> 1. **a.** No matter how hard you try, some people just don't like you.
>   **b.** People who can't get others to like them don't understand how to get along with others.
> 2. **a.** One of the major reasons we have wars is because people don't take enough interest in politics.
>   **b.** There will always be wars, no matter how hard people try to prevent them.
> 3. **a.** Sometimes I can't understand how teachers arrive at the grades they give.
>   **b.** There is a direct connection between how hard I study and the grades I get.
> 4. **a.** The average citizen can have an influence in government decisions.
>   **b.** This world is run by a few people in power, and there is not much the little guy can do about it.
> 5. **a.** Becoming a success is a matter of hard work; luck has little or nothing to do with it.
>   **b.** Getting a good job depends mainly on being in the right place at the right time.
> 6. **a.** Most people don't realize the extent to which their lives are controlled by accidental happenings.
>   **b.** There really is no such thing as "luck."
>
> *Source:* J. B. Rotter (1966). Generalized expectancies for internal versus external control of reinforcement. *Psychological Monographs, 80* (No. 609).
>
> (Answers: 1. a; 2. b; 3. a; 4. b; 5. b; 6. a.)

Hidden Costs of Reward. By focusing on how people interpret reinforcement, the cognitive perspective raises a second issue. After someone is rewarded for an enjoyable task, what happens to his or her interest and motivation once that reward is no longer available? Does reinforcement enhance motivation or detract from it? To explore how reinforcement can affect motivation, let's consider the implications for education, a topic close to Skinner's heart.

In a classic study conducted at a preschool, Lepper, Greene, and Nisbett (1973) gave children a chance to play with colorful felt-tipped markers—a chance most could not resist. By observing how much time the children spent on the activity, the researchers were able to measure their initial level of interest in it. Two weeks later, the children were randomly divided into three groups. In one, they were simply asked if they would draw some pictures with the markers. In the second, they were told that if they used the markers they would receive a "Good Player Award," a certificate with a gold star and a red ribbon. In the third group, the children were not offered a reward for drawing pictures, but then—like those in the second group—they received a reward when they were finished.

About a week later, the teachers placed the markers and paper on a table in the classroom while the experimenters hid behind a one-way mirror. The amount of free time the children spent playing with the markers, this time without a hint of reward, was once again recorded. Children who had previously drawn pictures for the promise of a reward were now less interested in the markers. Yet children who were not rewarded or had received a surprise reward (so they did not feel as if they had played with the markers in order to get it) were not adversely affected. In follow-up research, Teresa Amabile (1996) found that people who are offered payment for drawing pictures, writing poems, making paper collages, and coming up with solutions to business problems also tend to produce less creative work. This was also observed in business settings, in which a monetary reward was attributed with making people *less motivated* to be creative (Pink, 2011).

> ### LEARNING CHECK
>
> **Boxed In**
>
> You are a laboratory rat in a Skinner box. To get your food pellet, you must match each of the operant conditioning terms in the left column with its closest example in the right.
>
> | | | | |
> |---|---|---|---|
> | 1. | Shaping | a. | The tasty food pellet you get if you press the bar Professor Skinner wants you to press. |
> | 2. | Discriminative stimulus | b. | Getting food for pressing the bar only after a specific amount of time has elapsed. |
> | 3. | Fixed-ratio schedule | c. | Getting food after pressing the bar an unpredictable number of times. |
> | 4. | Variable-interval schedule | d. | Getting food for pressing the bar only when a certain light is on. |
> | 5. | Positive reinforcer | e. | Getting food for pressing the bar only after an unpredictable length of time has passed. |
> | 6. | Negative reinforcer | f. | Being guided gradually toward a behavior Professor Skinner wants. |
> | 7. | Variable-ratio schedule | g. | Getting food for pressing the bar a specific number of times. |
> | 8. | Fixed-interval schedule | h. | When you do something Professor Skinner wants and he stops shocking you. |
>
> (Answers: 1. f; 2. d; 3. g; 4. e; 5. a; 6. h; 7. c; 8. b.)

This hidden cost of reward can have serious implications in the classroom. Take a child who loves to read and a teacher who awards gold stars for books completed. During the year, the child continues to read at a lively pace. But what will happen later on, when there are no gold stars? Will the child then begin to wonder if it is still worth the effort? And does this mean that reinforcement should never be used? No, not at all. If a child does not engage in the wanted behavior to start with, offering a reward can help. For the child who doesn't normally read, gold stars provide a necessary incentive in much the same way food pellets increase bar pressing in the Skinner box. Also, rewards can be used to send different messages. When presented as a bonus (for superior performance) rather than as a bribe (for just doing it), a reward will enhance rather than diminish a child's future motivation (Eisenberger & Cameron, 1996; Eisenberger & Rhoades, 2001). The same is true of praise, a form of verbal reinforcement. When people are praised for their work, and see that praise as sincere, they become increasingly motivated (Henderlong & Lepper, 2002).

To summarize, the lessons of a cognitive perspective are clear: People do not mindlessly repeat behaviors that happen to be followed by reinforcement but instead are influenced by their perceptions, beliefs, and expectations.

OBSERVATIONAL LEARNING

> ### LEARNING OBJECTIVES
>
> Summarize the process of observational learning and how this type of learning is applied today.
>
> - Define observational learning.
> - Discuss whether learning by imitation is a uniquely human form of learning.
> - Identify the kinds of behaviors that are learned by observation, and explain how the process works.

One way of learning is simply to observe others, that is, by watching and imitating them. This form of learning occurs not only among humans but also in many types of animals (Bandura, 2016; Heyes & Galef, 1996). In one classic experiment, for example, golden hamster pups were put in a cage with their mothers. Some of the mothers, but not others, had been specifically pretrained to use their teeth and front paws to get sunflower seeds that dangled from a chain. The question was whether the young hamster pups would learn to do the same just by watching—and the answer was yes. Although fewer than 20 percent were able to retrieve seeds in the presence of the untrained mother, that proportion was up to 73 percent in the trained-mother group (Previde & Poli, 1996). In a second experiment, naive pigeons watched through a window other pigeons that were trained to get food from a feeder either by stepping on a bar or by pecking at it. When later given access to the same bar and feeder, the pigeons were more likely to use the technique they previously had seen used (Zentall, Sutton, & Sherburne, 1996). There is even evidence to suggest that "cultures" are transmitted through imitation in groups of whales and dolphins—as when humpback whales off the coast of Maine devised "lobtail feeding," a technique in which they slam their tail flukes onto the water, then dive and exhale, forming clouds of bubbles that envelope schools of prey fish. This behavior was first observed in 1981; by 1989 it was adopted by 50 percent of the whale population in that area (Rendell & Whitehead, 2001).

We often learning from observing others, such as when children learn how to brush their teeth by observing a parent or loved one.
iStock.com/CasarsaGuru

Human infants also exhibit rudimentary forms of imitation (Bremner, 2002). Research shows that they copy adults who stick out their tongues (Anisfeld, 1991; Meltzoff & Moore, 1983); use a certain hand to reach, point, wave, and make other gestures (Harkins & Uzgiris, 1991); utter sounds such as *meh* and *bee* (Poulson, Kymissis, Reeve, Andreatos, & Reeve, 1991); or imitate narrative cues in picture books and from television (Simcock, Garrity, & Barr, 2011). Similarly, toddlers imitate others of their own age grasping, pulling, pushing, and poking at various toys (Hanna & Meltzoff, 1993). It is clear that imitation is adaptive: By observing their peers and elders, young members of a species learn to interact and develop the skills of past generations.

Studies of Modeling

According to Albert Bandura (1986), people learn by watching others. These others are called models, and the process is known as **observational learning**. In a classic experiment to demonstrate the point, preschool-age children were exposed to a live adult model who behaved aggressively (Bandura, Ross, & Ross 1961). In a typical session, the child would be sitting quietly, drawing a picture. From another part of the room, an adult approached a Bobo doll, an inflatable clownlike toy that is weighted on the bottom so that it pops back up whenever it is knocked down. For 10 minutes, the adult repeatedly abused the doll—sitting on it, pounding it with a hammer, kicking it, throwing balls at it, and yelling, "Sock him in the nose! Kick him!"

After the outburst, the child was taken to a room filled with attractive toys but told that these toys were being saved "for the other children." Frustrated, the child was then taken to a third room containing additional toys, including—you guessed it—a Bobo doll. At that point, the child was left alone and observed through a one-way mirror. What happened? Compared to children exposed to a nonviolent model or to no model at all, those who had witnessed the aggressive display were far more likely to assault the doll. In fact, they often copied the model's attack, action for action, and repeated the same abusive remarks, word for word. The children had acquired a whole new repertoire of aggressive behavior. More recent research confirms the point: Among children and adolescents, exposure to aggressive models on TV, in video games, and in movies can

observational learning. Learning that takes place when one observes and models the behavior of others.

Animals as well as humans learn by observation. In early morning, the English titmouse breaks into containers of milk delivered to the porches of many homes in England and skims the cream from the top. This clever behavior has been passed by observation from one generation to the next.

Tucker / Stringer / Getty

trigger aggression—not just in the laboratory but also in the classroom, on the playground, and in other settings (Kimmig, Andringa, & Derntl, 2018; Wood, Wong, & Chachere, 1991).

Observational learning can also have beneficial effects. In one study, participants with a phobia of snakes gained the courage to approach a live snake by first watching someone else do so—which is why models are often used in the treatment of phobias (Bandura, Blanchard, & Ritter, 1969). In a second study, bystanders were more likely to help a stranded motorist or donate money to charity, two acts of generosity, if they had earlier observed someone else do the same (Bryan & Test, 1967). In a third study, young adolescents learned by watching others how to sharpen their argumentative writing skills—particularly when they observed models who were similarly strong or weak in their skill level (Braaksma, Rijlaarsdam, & van den Bergh, 2002).

The Process of Modeling

According to Bandura (1977, 1986), observational learning is not a simple, automatic, reflexlike reaction to models. Rather, it consists of two stages: acquisition and performance. You may recall that Edward Tolman had earlier made this distinction by noting that a newly acquired response often remains "latent" until the organism is motivated to perform it. Building on Tolman's work, Bandura described observational learning as a chain of events that involves four steps: attention, retention, reproduction, and motivation:

Attention. To learn by observation, one must pay attention to the model's behavior and to the consequences of that behavior. Due to their ability to command our attention, caregivers, teachers, political leaders, and TV celebrities are potentially effective models.

Retention. To model someone else's behavior minutes, days, weeks, months, or even years later, one must recall what was observed. Accordingly, modeling is likely to occur when the behavior is memorable or when the observer thinks about or rehearses the behavior.

Reproduction. Attention and memory are necessary conditions, but observers must also have the motor ability to reproduce the modeled behavior. As closely as we watch, and as hard as we try, most of us will never be able to imitate LeBron James's graceful flight to the basket.

Motivation. People may pay attention to a model, recall the behavior, and have the ability to reproduce it—all laying a necessary foundation for modeling. Whether an observer acts, however, is determined by his or her expectations for reinforcement—expectations that are based not only on personal experience but also on the experiences of others. This last point is important because it illustrates "vicarious" reinforcement: that people are more likely to imitate models who are rewarded for their behavior and less likely to imitate those who are punished. Apparently, learning can occur without direct, firsthand experience.

> **LEARNING CHECK**
>
> **Learning Curve**
>
> According to Bandura, observational learning has four steps: attention, retention, reproduction, and motivation. Match each step to the behavior on the right that best typifies it.
>
> | | | | |
> |---|---|---|---|
> | 1. | Attention | a. | Using the excuse that worked for your roommate. |
> | 2. | Retention | b. | Remembering what your mother told you about being careful. |
> | 3. | Reproduction | c. | Listening to your teacher in class. |
> | 4. | Motivation | d. | Shooting a basketball the way the coach showed you. |
>
> (Answers: 1. c; 2. b; 3. d; 4. a.)

Thinking Like a Psychologist About Learning

For about a century now, psychologists have studied with remarkable intensity the basic laws of classical conditioning, operant conditioning, and observational learning. To a large extent, the knowledge gained from this research has had far-reaching implications for a wide range of animal and human behaviors. Inspired by Pavlov and Skinner, the psychology of learning is grounded in hard-nosed S-R behaviorism. Today, however, the vast majority of researchers recognize that biological dispositions, cognitive processes, and other factors residing within the person play a critical role. Thus, we now know that all organisms are genetically prepared to learn some associations more easily than others, that beliefs about reinforcement can have a greater impact on behavior than the reinforcement itself, and that learning is also achieved by observing others.

In upcoming chapters, we'll find that many psychologists today are systematically exploring the inner workings of the human mind. Some are exploring the ways in which we can bolster our body's immune systems through classical conditioning procedures (Ader, Felten, & Cohen, 1991; Tekampe et al., 2017). Others are focused on how learning experiences can alter the neural connections in the brain (Rosenzweig, 1996; Kolb & Whishaw, 1998; Lin & Honey, 2016). Clearly, there is great interest in the "O" part of S-O-R psychology. Learning theorists are also studying the acquisition of complex human skills—such as how we learn to read, speak, understand stories, solve math problems, recognize music, play chess, use computers, and drive cars (Holding, 1989; Northoff, 2016). And they're interested in the way people learn complex material without really trying—through the kinds of unconscious or "implicit" processes described at the start of this chapter (Kihlstrom, 2013; Kirsner et al., 1998). Finally, as we'll learn, there's great interest in applications of learning theory to child development, instructional issues, education, and the acquisition of knowledge (Capuano et al., 2014; Glaser, 1990).

SUMMARY

NONASSOCIATIVE LEARNING

As in the case of the stickleback, **ethologists** have found that many aspects of animal behavior demonstrate nonassociative learning. Two types of nonassociative learning are fixed action patterns and habituation.

Fixed Action Patterns

Many aspects of animal behavior are programmed by inborn **fixed action patterns**. In contrast, human beings adapt primarily through **learning**, a relatively permanent change in knowledge or behavior that comes from experience.

Habituation

The simplest form of learning, found in lower organisms, is **habituation**, the tendency for an organism to become familiar with a stimulus as a result of repeated exposure.

CLASSICAL CONDITIONING

The key to learning is association, a tendency to connect events that occur together in space or time.

Pavlov's Discovery

Studying the digestive system in dogs, Pavlov stumbled upon **classical conditioning**. In his experiments, the salivary reflex was the **unconditioned response (UR)**, and it was elicited by food, an **unconditioned stimulus (US)**. Through pairing of a bell with the food, the bell became a **conditioned stimulus (CS)** that on its own could elicit salivation, a **conditioned response (CR)**. This experiment serves as a model of classical conditioning in humans.

Basic Principles

After Pavlov's initial experiment, he and others discovered four basic principles of learning: The **acquisition** of a CR is influenced by the order and timing of the CS-US pairing; in **extinction**, repeated presentation of the CS without the US causes the CR to lose its power, though there is an occasional rebound effect known as **spontaneous recovery**; after an organism is conditioned to a CS, similar stimuli will often evoke the CR through **stimulus generalization**; and **discrimination** is the opposite process, one of learning to distinguish between stimuli.

Pavlov's Legacy

As demonstrated by taste-aversion studies, research shows that animals are biologically prepared to learn some associations more easily than others. The process involves learning that one event (CS) predicts another event (US). There are many applications of classical conditioning. For example, people can be conditioned to develop fears or preferences and positive or negative social attitudes. Studies show that the body's immune cells can be classically conditioned as well.

OPERANT CONDITIONING

The learning of voluntary, complex, goal-directed behaviors is achieved by a different form of learning, one that involves the link between an action and its consequences.

The Law of Effect

Using animals, Thorndike studied the **law of effect**: that actions followed by a positive outcome are repeated, whereas those followed by a negative outcome or no outcome are not.

The Principles of Reinforcement

By testing animals in a controlled environment called a **Skinner box**, Skinner systematically examined **operant conditioning**, the process by which we learn to behave in ways that produce reinforcement. A **reinforcement** is any stimulus that strengthens a prior response. There are two types of reinforcers: positive (the presentation of a desirable stimulus) and negative (the withdrawal of an aversive stimulus). In contrast, **punishment** has the opposite effect of weakening, not strengthening, a prior response. Punishers may be positive (presentation of an aversive stimulus) or negative (withdrawal of a desirable stimulus).

Skinner found that **shaping** occurs in the learning of complex new behaviors, through reinforcement of successive responses that come closer and closer to the target behavior. Skinner discovered the

partial-reinforcement effect, that partial reinforcement increases resistance to extinction. He and others went on to identify four types of reinforcement schedules (fixed interval, variable interval, fixed ratio, and variable ratio), each having different effects on learning and extinction. In addition, animals can be trained to respond only in the presence of a **discriminative stimulus** that signals the availability of reinforcement. Although punishment can often be used to suppress unwanted behavior, it has unwanted side effects and should be used cautiously. As in classical conditioning, generalization and discrimination are key aspects of operant learning. In addition, research shows that people tend to behave in ways that maximize their reinforcements—but they often prefer small immediate rewards over those that are larger but delayed, a problem of self-control.

PRACTICAL APPLICATIONS OF OPERANT CONDITIONING
Skinner was interested in practical applications. Following in his footsteps, many behaviorists use the principles of operant conditioning to solve practical problems in clinical settings, the workplace, and the classroom.

DEVELOPMENTS IN OPERANT CONDITIONING
Although operant conditioning is broadly applicable, animal studies have shown that species-specific biological dispositions often interfere with the shaping of a new behavior. And although Skinner refused to speculate about mental processes, others have not. Thus, researchers have found that animals exhibit **latent learning** (learning without reinforcement), that people are more influenced by the perception of control over reinforcement than by objective contingencies, and that rewards sometimes undermine our intrinsic motivation.

OBSERVATIONAL LEARNING

Complex new behaviors are often learned not through direct experience but through the observation and imitation of others.

STUDIES OF MODELING
According to Bandura, we learn by watching others. These others are called models, and the process is called **observational learning**. Studies indicate that both desirable (helping) and undesirable (aggressive) behaviors may be learned in this manner.

THE PROCESS OF MODELING
Observational learning involves not simple, reflexlike imitation but a four-step process that requires attention, retention, reproduction, and motivation. Through a process of vicarious reinforcement, people are most likely to imitate models who are rewarded for their behavior.

CRITICAL THINKING

Thinking Critically About Learning

1. There has been some public discussion about lengthening jail sentences for certain types of criminal offenses. Given the evidence on the effectiveness of punishment as a means of behavior change, do you think this is a good idea? Why or why not? Can you offer any alternative strategies that would reduce criminal behavior?

2. In Anthony Burgess's novel *A Clockwork Orange*, the main protagonist (Alex), a sadistic young man, was classically conditioned to become horribly ill at the sight of violence. During the conditioning sessions, a chemical substance that induced severe nausea was injected into his bloodstream as he was forced to view violent films. Identify the conditioned and unconditioned stimuli and responses involved in these conditioning sessions. Following the conditioning, Alex also became sick whenever he heard classical music, which had accompanied the films. What learning principle can explain this outcome? Classical music had previously been Alex's favorite. If you wanted to restore Alex's ability to enjoy his favorite music, how would you go about it?

3. A child has developed a fear of dogs. Suggest three different strategies—one based on classical conditioning, one based on operant conditioning, and one based on observational learning—that could help eliminate this fear. Which strategy do you think would be most effective and long lasting? Why?

4. Would you expect there to be cultural differences with respect to locus of control? If so, what factors might contribute to such differences?

5. We have often heard caregivers tell their children, "Do as I say, not as I do." How likely are children to heed such advice? Why?

CAREER CONNECTION: EDUCATION

Career Counselor

A job as a career counselor involves helping people select a career, assisting those in the process of changing careers, or providing vocational training to individuals returning to the workforce. They may guide clients both on finding a new career path, often through self-assessments and one-on-one discussions, and in developing the job search, application, and interview skills needed to actually get a job on that path.

Some career counselors work with disabled adults who may need skills training, job search help, on-the-job training, or regular workplace supervision. Their goal is to help career-oriented students and job seekers discover their potential and match that potential to a career. Psychology graduates, with their understanding of human behavior and the routes to self-awareness and self-discovery, are uniquely qualified to help individuals in this discovery process.

A career counselor may be employed by a college or university or a specialized consulting firm, or may be self-employed. Others flip the role and work as recruiters or headhunters, trying to find the right person for a specific job.

Key skills for this role that psychology students learn to develop:
- Interpersonal relationship development
- Incorporation of sociocultural factors in scientific inquiry
- Application of scientific reasoning to interpret psychological phenomena

KEY TERMS

acquisition (p. 180)
classical conditioning (p. 179)
conditioned response (CR) (p. 179)
conditioned stimulus (CS) (p. 179)
discrimination (p. 182)
discriminative stimulus (p. 196)
ethologists (p. 175)
extinction (p. 181)
fixed action patterns (p. 175)
habituation (p. 177)
latent learning (p. 200)
law of effect (p. 190)

learning (p. 176)
observational learning (p. 205)
operant conditioning (p. 191)
partial-reinforcement effect (p. 194)
punishment (p. 191)
reinforcement (p. 191)
shaping (p. 192)
Skinner box (p. 190)
spontaneous recovery (p. 181)
stimulus generalization (p. 182)
unconditioned response (UR) (p. 179)
unconditioned stimulus (US) (p. 179)

6 MEMORY

Reeldeal Images / Alamy Stock Photo

LEARNING OBJECTIVES

Relate your own memory successes and failures to the successes and failures of your favorite technology; in what ways can you blame the technology, and in what ways can you blame the user for failures?

Connect sensation to memory; determine the importance of iconic and echoic memory.

Examine scientifically supported methods to enlarge the capacity of short-term memory.

Juxtapose the belief that memories are forever with the belief that memories eventually become extinct.

Consider the research on autobiographical memory and apply it to your own life.

WHAT'S YOUR PREDICTION: CAN A FALSE MEMORY BE CREATED?

The Situation

You sign up for a study of memory, and when you appear for the session, the experimenter says that you'll hear several lists of words via an audio recording. Listen carefully. After each list, you will hear either a tone or a knocking sound to signal whether you should spend the next 2 minutes writing down the words in that list or working on some arithmetic problems. After the first list, you'll hear a second list, a third list, and so on, until you're finished. You have no questions, so the session begins.

The experimenter turns on the recording and you hear a male voice reciting a word every 1.5 seconds. Try it: *bed, rest, awake, tired, dream, wake, night, blanket, doze, slumber, snore, pillow, peace, yawn, drowsy*. Got it? Now look away, take out a sheet of paper, and take 2 minutes to write down as many of these words as you can. Okay, time's up. Here's the next list: *note, sound, piano, sing, radio, band, melody, horn, concert, instrument, jazz, symphony, orchestra, art, rhythm*. Again, try to recall as many words as you can.

After completing all the lists, you are told that your ability to recognize the original words will now be tested. You'll receive a set of 96 words, some of which appeared earlier. For each word, you should indicate whether it is *new* (never presented before) or *old* (presented earlier). Next, for each word you recognize as old, you're asked: Are you sure you vividly recall hearing the speaker say that word on the recording? Try it. Cover the preceding paragraph and circle each of the following words that you recognize from before: *tooth, beach, sleep, art, traffic, pillow, kitten, music*.

As a participant in this experiment, you know that some of the test items are new, others old. What you don't know is that some of the new items were meaningfully related to words that did appear in the original lists. The experimenters referred to these as "lures." The question is, how easy was it to tell the difference?

Make a Prediction

Think about the recognition test. Participants were reshown some of the same words they had been presented with just minutes earlier. So how well could they recognize these items? And will they ever "remember" hearing the lure words *not* on the list? To get you started, the percentage of old items correctly identified as old is presented below. As you can see, participants recognized 79 percent of these words—57 percent of which they were absolutely sure about. Using these numbers as a guideline and the table below, predict how often (0–100 percent) the participants falsely recognized and were sure about the lures that were never actually presented.

RECOGNIZE?	OLD WORDS	NEW "LURES"
Yes	79%	-----%
Sure	57%	-----%

The Results

In this study, Henry Roediger and Kathleen McDermott (1995) were curious to determine whether they could get people to create "false memories" of words not previously heard. So, what did you predict? How often did participants "recognize" lure words compared to the percentage of old items correctly and confidently recognized? The results were striking. As shown below, participants could not tell the difference between words that were on the list and those that were not.

RECOGNIZE?	OLD WORDS	NEW "LURES"
Yes	79%	81%
Sure	57%	58%

> ### What Does It All Mean?
>
> To appreciate what happened in this experiment, take another look at the test materials and your own responses. After hearing (or reading) sleep-related words such as *bed* and *yawn* and music-related words such as *jazz* and *instrument*, didn't you think that you had also heard (read) *sleep* and *music*—words that fit but were not actually on the list? Most people do. During a talk that Henry Roediger gave a few years after the study, titled "Creating False Memories in the Classroom," he reproduced this result with an audience of psychology professors. Many other researchers have obtained this same result, with some investigating the role that even culture can play in constructing false memories (Wang, Otgarr, Santtila, Shen, & Zhou, 2021).
>
> Psychologists liken human memory to a computer that faithfully records information for later use. This study reveals, however, that there is much more to the story. As we'll see in this chapter, remembering is an active process, and we sometimes *construct* memories in light of our own beliefs, wishes, needs, contextual factors, and information received from outside sources.

"Indelible in the hippocampus is the laughter." Christine Blasey Ford said this during her Senate Judiciary Committee testimony about her remembered experiences with Supreme Court nominee Judge Brett Kavanaugh when they were high school students in suburban Maryland. Blasey Ford remembered many details of an attempted sexual assault by Kavanaugh. Kavanaugh remembered nothing of the sort. To corroborate his account, Kavanaugh produced a detailed calendar of his daily activities from the presumed year in question—1982. Blasey Ford had no calendar, just the lasting traumatic memory of that night, albeit she could not remember the exact date the incident happened, how she got to the house party where the alleged sexual assault occurred, or how she got home. Their testimonies reflected divisiveness not only between the two accounts, but also between political parties, opinions about binge drinking, and current thinking about how memories are (and are not) formed during trauma and why victims don't immediately report their assaults and accused assailants to police. Blasey Ford supporters tweeted #IBelieveChristine. Kavanaugh supporters wrote letters emphatically praising his character and respectful treatment of women.

Christine Blasey Ford is sworn in prior to giving testimony before the U.S. Senate Judiciary Committee on Capitol Hill, September 27, 2018, in Washington, D.C. Blasey Ford, a professor at Palo Alto University and a research psychologist at the Stanford University School of Medicine, had accused Supreme Court nominee Brett Kavanaugh of sexually assaulting her during a party in 1982, when they were high school students.

Pool / Pool/Getty Images News/Getty Images

The American people will never know what happened between Blasey Ford and Kavanaugh, but their testimony raised some important questions. One question was, why do some people believe Blasey Ford yet others believe Kavanaugh? Research on registered psychologists demonstrates that these differences in trusting the accuser can be influenced by the psychologist's sex and traumatic history (Page & Morrison, 2018). Even among 292 mental health professionals, "female psychologists believed disclosures regardless of their personal trauma history, while male psychologists with a personal history of trauma believed disclosures significantly more than male psychologists without personal trauma history" (p. 1). Furthermore, women and persons with higher "rape empathy" and lower "rape myth acceptance" have more belief in accusers than men and persons with lower rape empathy and higher rape myth acceptance (Nason et al., 2018).

A second question was, is it possible that both people are telling their truth? The short answer is yes. Human memory is often the subject of controversy. Sometimes we seem able to recall a face, a voice, the contents of a lecture, a foreign language, a news event, a first date, graduation, or the death of a loved one with precision and certainty. Yet, at other times, memory is limited, flawed, and biased—as when we forget an address we just looked up, the items on the grocery list we left at home, coursework from last semester, or the name of someone we met recently. We could swear we remember an important event like it was yesterday, and recall that event, but unbeknownst to us, our recollection of the event's details is imprecise and sometimes fabricated. How are experiences stored in the brain and then later retrieved? What causes us to preserve some events but not others? How accurate are our recollections of the past? To answer these questions, cognitive psychologists study **memory**, the process by which information is retained for later use (Baddeley, 1999; Schacter, 2001).

memory. The process by which information is retained for later use.

AN INFORMATION-PROCESSING MODEL

LEARNING OBJECTIVES

Relate your own memory successes and failures to the successes and failures of your favorite technology; in what ways can you blame the technology, and in what ways can you blame the user for failures?

- Compare human memory to the workings of a computer.
- Determine the differences among sensory, short-term, and long-term memory.

Aristotle and Plato likened memory to the stamping of an impression into a block of wax. Others, more recently, have compared memory to a switchboard, storage box, workbench, library, layered stack, and videorecorder. Today, cognitive psychologists like to compare the human mind to a computer and memory to an information-processing system. Your computer *receives* input from a keyboard, touchscreen, or mouse; it *converts* the symbols and clicks into a special numeric code; it *saves* the information on a hard drive or in the cloud; it then *retrieves* the data to be displayed on a screen. If the computer crashes, if there's not enough storage space on the hard drive or in the cloud, if the file was deleted, or if you enter the wrong retrieval command, the information becomes inaccessible, or "forgotten."

Using the computer as a model, memory researchers seek to trace the flow of information as it is mentally processed. In this **information-processing model**, a stimulus that registers on our senses can be remembered only if it (a) *draws attention*, which brings it into consciousness; (b) *is encoded*, or transferred to *storage* sites in the brain; and (c) *is retrieved* for use at a later time (Atkinson & Shiffrin, 1968). How might this model relate to your favorite photo app? First, you direct your camera to the stimulus of interest, say a group of you and your friends at a concert. This is the *draws attention* phase. You take six different pictures, because the first five weren't very good. Second, you save the sixth photo. This is the *encoding/storage* phase. Third, you pull up the photo up a few hours later to post it on social media—*retrieval*.

information-processing model. A model of memory in which information must pass through discrete stages via the processes of attention, encoding, storage, and retrieval.

Within this information-processing approach, three types of memory have been distinguished: sensory, short term, and long term. **Sensory memory** stores all stimuli that register on the senses, holding literal copies for a brief moment ranging from a fraction of a second to 3 seconds. Sensations that do not draw attention tend to vanish. Those things we "pay attention to" are transferred to **short-term memory (STM)**, another temporary storage system that can hold seven—plus or minus two—items of information for about 20 seconds. Although STM fades quickly, information can be held for a longer period of time through repetition and rehearsal. When people talk about attention span, they are referring to short-term memory. Finally, **long-term memory (LTM)** is a somewhat permanent storage system that can hold vast quantities of information for many years. Science writer Isaac Asimov once estimated that LTM takes in a quadrillion separate bits of information in the course of a lifetime. When people talk about memory, long-term memory is typically what they have in mind.

sensory memory. A memory storage system that records information from the senses for up to three seconds.

short-term memory (STM). A memory storage system that holds about seven items for up to 20 seconds before the material is transferred to long-term memory or is forgotten.

long-term memory (LTM). A relatively permanent memory storage system that can hold vast amounts of information for many years.

As you read this chapter, you'll see that memory researchers ask two types of questions. First, how are memories stored? Is there a single unitary system, as some believe, or are there multiple memory systems, each uniquely dedicated to storing certain types of information? Second, to what extent are our memories of the past faithful to reality? We will see that researchers have exposed some serious flaws and biases in human memory—what Daniel Schacter (2001) has called the "sins" of memory. Thus, you'll notice this recurring theme: Human beings are both competent and incompetent, and both objective and subjective, in their processing of information.

THE SENSORY REGISTER

> **LEARNING OBJECTIVES**
>
> Connect sensation to memory; determine the importance of iconic and echoic memory.
>
> - Create an argument for whether or not fleeting traces of sensation linger in the mind even after the removal of a stimulus.
> - Compare and contrast iconic and echoic memory.

Take a flashlight into a dark room, turn it on, shine it on a wall, and wave it quickly in a circular motion. What do you see? If you twirl it fast enough, the light will appear to leave a glowing trail, and you'll see a continuous circle. The reason: Even though the light illuminates only one point in the circle at a time, your visual system stores a "snapshot" of each point as you watch the next point. The visual image is called an icon, and the snapshot it stores is called **iconic memory** (Neisser, 1967).

iconic memory. A fleeting sensory memory for visual images that lasts only a fraction of a second.

Iconic Memory

People typically don't realize that a fleeting mental trace lingers after a stimulus is removed from view. Nor did cognitive psychologists realize it until George Sperling's (1960) ingenious series of experiments. Sperling instructed subjects to stare at the center of a blank screen. Then he flashed an array of letters for one-twentieth of a second and asked subjects to name as many of the letters as possible. Take a quick glance at Figure 6.1, and try it for yourself. You'll probably recall about a handful of letters. In fact, Sperling found that no matter how large the array was, subjects could name only four or five items. Why? One possibility is that people can register just so much visual input in a single glance—that 12 letters is too much to see in so little time. A second possibility is that all letters registered, but the image faded before subjects could report them all. Indeed, many subjects insisted they were able to "see" the whole array but then forgot some of the letters before they could name them.

Did the information that was lost leave a momentary trace, as subjects had claimed, or did it never register in the first place? To test these alternative hypotheses, Sperling devised the "partial-report technique." Instead of asking subjects to list all the letters, he asked them to name only one row in each array—a row that was not determined until *after* the array was shown. In this procedure, each presentation was immediately followed by a tone signaling which letters to name: A high-pitched tone indicated the top line; a medium pitch, the middle line; a low pitch, the bottom line. If they saw the entire array, subjects should have been able to report all the letters in a prompted row correctly—regardless of which row was prompted. Sperling was right: Subjects correctly recalled 3.3 letters per row. In other words, 10 letters (9.9), not 4 or 5, were instantly registered in consciousness before fading, held briefly in iconic memory. To determine how long this type of memory lasts, Sperling next varied the time between the letters and the tone that signaled the row to be recalled. As depicted in Figure 6.2, the visual image started to fade as the interval was increased to one-third of a second and had vanished almost completely two-thirds of a second later. Since this study, researchers have found that, when it comes to pictures of objects or scenes, words, sentences, and other visual stimuli presented briefly, people form "fleeting memories" that last for just a fraction of a second (Coltheart, 1999).

FIGURE 6.1 ■ Testing for Iconic Memory

Here is an array of letters like that used by Sperling. When subjects viewed this array for one-twentieth of a second and tried to name all the letters, they could recall only four or five. But when signaled after the items to recall only one row, they were able to recall three or four letters per line—for an average of ten letters.

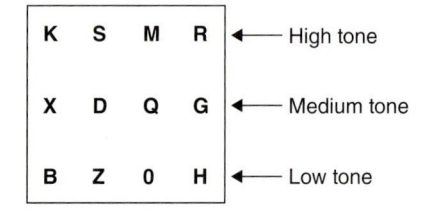

K	S	M	R	← High tone
X	D	Q	G	← Medium tone
B	Z	0	H	← Low tone

Source: Adapted from Sperling, G. (1960). The information available in brief visual presentations. Psychological Monographs: General and Applied, 74(11), 1–29. https://doi.org/10.1037/h0093759

FIGURE 6.2 ■ Duration of Iconic Memory

How long does an iconic memory last? Sperling varied the time between the letters and the tone signaling the row to be recalled. The iconic image started to fade after one-third of a second and vanished completely after one full second.

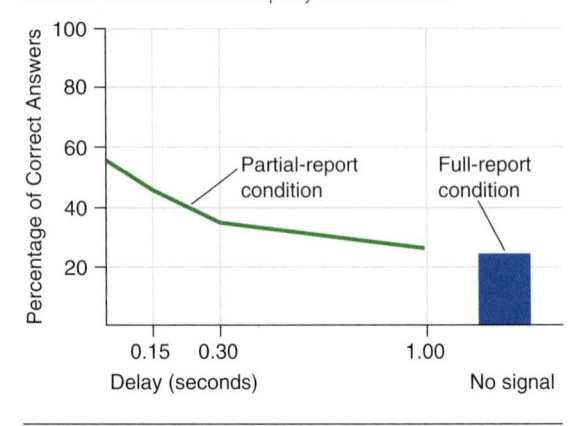

Source: Adapted from Sperling, G. (1960). The information available in brief visual presentations. Psychological Monographs: General and Applied, 74(11), 1–29. https://doi.org/10.1037/h0093759

Echoic Memory

A similar phenomenon exists for auditory stimuli. The next time you listen to music, notice after you turn it off how an "echo" of the sound seems to reverberate inside your head. This auditory sensory register is called **echoic memory**. Just how much auditory input is stored in echoic memory, and for how long? In a study modeled after Sperling's, Christopher Darwin and colleagues (1972) put headphones on subjects and all at once played three sets of spoken letters—in the right ear, in the left ear, and in both ears at once. Subjects then received a visual signal indicating which set to report. Using this study and others, researchers have found that echoic memory holds only a few items but lasts for 2 or 3 seconds, and perhaps even longer, before activation in the auditory cortex fades (Cowan, 1988; Lu, Williamson, & Kaufman, 1992; Sams, Hari, Rif, & Knuutila, 1993).

Whether a sensory memory system stores information for one-third of a second or for 3 seconds, you might wonder: What's the point of having a "memory" that is so quick to decay? To answer this question, try to imagine what your perceptions of the world would be like without sensory memories. Without the visual icon, for instance, you would lose track of what you see with every blink of the eye—as if you were viewing the world through a series of snapshots rather than on a continuous film. Similarly, it would be hard to understand spoken language without the persistent traces of echoic memory. Speech would be heard as a series of staccato sounds rather than as connected words and phrases. One case study that features a person with stroke demonstrates the importance of echoic memory. Without his echoic memory intact, the person could not "recall a single syllable he had heard one second before" (Kojima, Karino, Yumoto, & Funayama, 2012, p. 133).

echoic memory. A brief sensory memory for auditory input that lasts only 2 or 3 seconds.

SHORT-TERM MEMORY

LEARNING OBJECTIVES

Examine scientifically supported methods to enlarge the capacity of short-term memory.

- Identify the limits of our short-term memory.
- List the functions that are served by short-term memory.
- Explain the serial-position curve and why it occurs.

Try to imagine yourself behind the steering wheel of a car. As you drive, with the window down, your body is bombarded by sensations: the vibration under your feet from the terrain beneath the tires; the sound of your music overshadowed by horns honking; a siren blaring, and vehicles screeching to a stop; a faint aroma of freshly brewed coffee being overwhelmed by the smell of exhaust fumes; and the sight of skyscrapers, traffic lights, street vendors, delivery trucks bouncing over bumps in the road, while pedestrians scramble to reach the other side.

Those are just the sensations you register all while keeping track of speed, balance, turn signals, and safety. Most stimuli surrounding your journey will never reach consciousness and, instead, will be "forgotten" immediately. You might even wonder if you stopped at the stop sign a few streets back. The key is *attention*. As noted earlier, sensations that do not capture our attention tend to evaporate quickly, whereas those we notice are transferred to short-term memory—a somewhat more lasting but limited storage facility. People are selective in their perceptions and can instantly direct their attention to stimuli that are interesting, adaptive, or important. While driving the car, you are so busy avoiding pedestrians and other vehicles that you focus on those objects to the exclusion of everything else.

The information-processing model of memory regards attention as a necessary first step. In tennis and other tasks, people selectively tune in to stimuli that are adaptive, interesting, and important. Here, Naomi Osaka of Japan plays a shot during practice.

Scott Barbour / Stringer/Getty Images Sport/Getty Images

From the sensory register, the brain encodes information—that is, it converts the information into a form that can be stored in short-term memory. A stimulus may be encoded in different ways. After you read this sentence, for example, you might recall a picture of the letters and their placement on the page (visual encoding), the sounds of the words themselves (acoustic encoding), or the meaning of the sentence as a whole (semantic encoding). Research shows that people typically encode this type of information in acoustic terms. Thus, when subjects are presented with a string of letters and immediately asked to recall them, they make more "sound-alike" errors than "look-alike" errors. For example, subjects mis-recall an F as an S or X, but not as an E or B (Conrad, 1964). Subjects are also more likely to confuse words that sound alike (*man, can*) than words that are similar in meaning (*big, huge*)—further indicating that we tend to encode verbal information in acoustic terms rather than in semantic terms (Baddeley, 1966).

Capacity

Attention limits what information comes under the spotlight of short-term memory at any given time. To the extent that one stimulus captures our attention, others may be ignored—sometimes with startling effects on memory. For example, research on eyewitness testimony shows that when a criminal displays a weapon, witnesses are less able to identify the culprit than if no weapon is present (Hope & Wright, 2007; Kocab & Sporer, 2016; Steblay, 1992). Why? One reason is that the witness's eyes fixate on the weapon, particularly when it comes as a surprise, thereby drawing attention away from the face (Pickel, 1999, 2009). To demonstrate, Elizabeth Loftus and colleagues (1987) showed subjects slides of a customer who walked up to a bank teller and pulled out either a gun or a checkbook. By recording eye movements, these researchers found that subjects spent more time looking at the gun than at the checkbook. The result: impairment in their ability to identify the criminal in a lineup.

Limited by attentional resources, short-term memory can hold only a small number of items. How small a number? The accompanying "Try This!" activity illustrates the limited capacity of short-term memory. By presenting increasingly long lists of items, researchers seek to identify the point at which subjects can no longer recall without error. In tasks like this one, the average person can store seven or so list items (usually between five and nine)—regardless of whether the items are numbers, letters, words, or names. This limit seemed so consistent that George Miller (1956) described the human STM capacity by the phrase "the magical number seven, plus or minus two." Over the years, other studies have shown that our short-term storage capacity is more limited than Miller had suggested—and that the magical number is more like *four* plus or minus two (Cowan, 2000, 2010).

TRY THIS!

Memory-Span Task

To appreciate the limited capacity of short-term memory, **TRY THIS:** Read the top row of digits in Figure 6.3, one per second, then look away and repeat them back in order. Next, try the second row, the third row, and so on, until you make a mistake. The average person's memory span can hold seven items of information.

FIGURE 6.3 ■ Memory Span Test

5	7	3							
9	0	7	6						
8	5	4	0	2					
0	9	1	3	5	6				
8	6	0	4	8	7	2			
1	7	5	4	2	4	1	9		
9	6	5	8	3	0	8	0	1	
5	7	3	5	1	2	0	2	8	5
3	1	7	9	2	1	5	0	6	4	2
2	1	0	1	6	7	4	1	9	8	3	5

Once short-term memory is filled to capacity, whatever that number may be, the storage of new information requires that existing contents be discarded or "displaced." Thus, if you're trying to memorize historical dates, chemical elements, or a list of vocabulary words, you may find that the fifth or sixth item pushes out those earlier on the list. It's like the view you get on a computer screen. As you fill the screen with more and more new information, old material scrolls out of view. This limited capacity seems awfully disabling. But is it absolutely fixed, or can we overcome it?

According to Miller, short-term memory can accommodate only seven items, and that number may be smaller, but there's a hitch: Although an item may consist of one letter or digit, these items can be grouped into chunks of words, sentences, and large numbers—thus enabling us to use our storage capacity more efficiently. To see the effects of chunking on short-term memory, read the following letters, pausing at each space; then look up and name as many of the letters as you can in correct order: *CN NIB MMT VU SA*. Since this list contains 12 discrete letters, you probably found the task quite frustrating. Now try this next list, again pausing between spaces: *CNN IBM MTV USA*. Better, right? This list contains the same 12 letters. But because the letters are "repackaged" into familiar groups, you had to store only 4 chunks, not 12—well within our "magical" capacity (Bower, 1970).

Chunking enables us to improve our STM span by using our capacity more efficiently. We may be limited to seven or so chunks, but we can learn to increase the size of those chunks. To demonstrate, a group of researchers trained two male university students, both long-distance runners and of average intelligence, for several months. For an hour a day, three or four days a week, these students were asked to recall random strings of numbers. If they recalled a sequence correctly, another digit was added to the next sequence and the task was repeated. If they made a mistake, the number of digits in the next sequence was reduced by one. Their improvement was astonishing. Before practicing, their memory span was four to seven digits. After six months, they were up to 80 items (Ericsson & Chase, 1982; Ericsson, Chase, & Faloon, 1980). In one session, for example, the experimenter read the following numbers in order:

8931944349250215784166850612094888856877273
1418610546297480129497496599228

After 2 minutes of concentration, the subject repeated all 73 digits, in groups of three and four. How did he do it? Given no special instruction, the subject developed his own elaborate strategy: He converted the random numbers into ages ("89.3 years, a very old person"), dates (1944 was "near the end of World War II"), and cross-country racing times for various distances (3492 was "3 minutes and 49.2 seconds, nearly a world's record for the mile").

---

chunking. The process of grouping distinct bits of information into larger wholes, or chunks, to increase short-term-memory capacity.

The value of chunking is also evidenced by the way people retain information in their areas of expertise. Study the arrangement of pieces on the chessboard shown in Figure 6.4, and in 5 seconds memorize as much of it as you can. Chances are, you'll be able to reproduce approximately seven items. Yet after looking at the same arrangement for 5 seconds, chess masters can reproduce all the pieces and their row-and-column positions almost without error. It's not that chess masters are born with computer-like minds. When chess pieces are placed randomly on the board, chess masters are no more proficient than the rest of us. But when the arrangement is taken from an actual game between good players, masters naturally chunk the configurations of individual pieces into familiar patterns such as the "Romanian Pawn Defense" and "Casablanca Bishop's Gambit" (Chase & Simon, 1973; De Groot, 1965; Gobet, 2016). Researchers estimate that chess masters can store up to 50,000 such chunks in memory (Gobet & Simon, 1996).

From years of experience, experts in all domains—including computer programmers, figure skaters, servers, bridge players, ballet dancers, gamers, and professional actors—exhibit these advantages in their STM performance (Sala & Gobet, 2017; Vicente & Wang, 1998). Similarly, research demonstrates that in a comparison of musician and nonmusician memory performance, musicians highly outperform nonmusicians on tonal stimuli and moderately outperform nonmusicians on verbal stimuli (Talamini, Altoè, Carretti, & Grassi, 2017). Furthermore, there are hippocampal differences between musicians and nonmusicians, as illustrated in Figure 6.5. Specifically, musicians have denser hippocampi than do nonmusicians.

In a neighborhood park in London, a family plays a giant outdoor game of chess. Do you think chess masters could recall the configurations on this giant board as easily as they can from their perspective on a table? This question has never been put to test.

Julio Etchart / Alamy Stock Photo

FIGURE 6.4 ■ The Value of Chunking

Study this arrangement of chess pieces for 5 seconds. Then try to reproduce the arrangement as best you can on the empty board in Figure 6.10. Unless you are a highly experienced chess player, the number of pieces you can place in the correct squares should approximate the magical number seven.

FIGURE 6.5 ■ Functional and Structural Differences in Musicians' vs. Nonmusicians' Hippocampi

Musicians and nonmusicians were presented music familiarity tasks. During the tasks, they were scanned with an fMRI to collect brain activation data. The fMRI data demonstrated that musicians had more gray matter density in their hippocampi than did nonmusicians. The data also demonstrated that the hippocampus was more involved in the task for musicians than for nonmusicians.

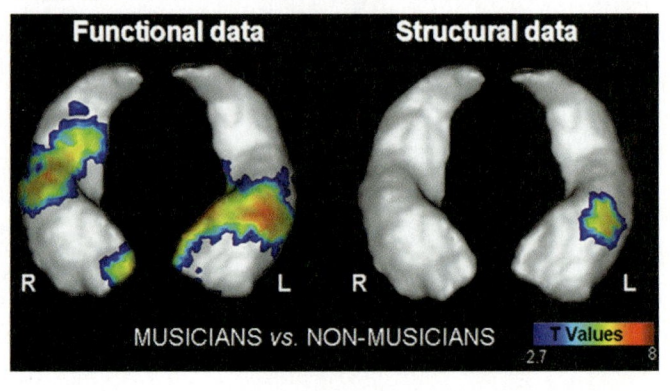

Source: Groussard M, La Joie R, Rauchs G, Landeau B, Chételat G, Viader F, et al. (2010) When Music and Long-Term Memory Interact: Effects of Musical Expertise on Functional and Structural Plasticity in the Hippocampus. PLoS ONE 5(10): e13225.

Duration

Memory is an important function of the brain, not just for knowledge and directions but also for socialization. Unfortunately, most people experience moments when memory limitations hinder their ability to perform. Imagine, for example, having the job of a short order cook on a busy night. Servers are lined up, yelling food orders into the air as fast as popping popcorn. Flames are rising from the grill, timers are ringing, water is boiling, music is playing in the background, everyone is yelling, and you are supposed to be able to tune all of that out and keep the orders straight. What happens if you forget to leave off the onions? What happens if you forget the name of the new server who walked off after saying, "I need this on the fly"? And if you use the wheat noodles by accident when someone has requested a gluten-free substitution, the consequences could be dire. Many strategies can help, but those who work in the food service industry have to juggle a lot of information at once—ingredients and steps for making a variety of menu items, food and workplace safety rules, charges for each table, names of patrons and coworkers, and cues from customers that they're getting impatient. Have you ever been on the other side, receiving the wrong order for your meal? It may be an inconvenience, but perhaps this chapter will give you a reason to be a bit more forgiving.

Experiences with forgetting are common because short-term memory is limited not only in the *amount* of information it can store—the cook brings in tons of sensory information when an order is called out—but also in the length of *time* it can hold that information. What is the duration of short-term memory? That is, how long does a memory trace last if a person does not actively rehearse or repeat it? To measure how rapidly information is forgotten, Lloyd Peterson and Margaret Peterson (1959) asked subjects to recall a set of unrelated consonants such as MJK. So that subjects could not rehearse the material, they were given a number and instructed to count backward from that number by 3s: 564, 561, 558, 555, and so on. After varying lengths of time, subjects were cued to recall the consonants. After 18 seconds, performance plummeted to below 10 percent (illustrated in Figure 6.6). So, from the time the server sends the order to the cook, to the time the cook is able to collect the ingredients, it is quite possible that 18 seconds have passed and what you ordered to accompany your steak is forgotten.

Knowing the fleeting nature of short-term memory, we can prevent forgetting by repeating information silently or aloud. A short order cook can silently repeat the order while collecting the ingredients. Repetition extends the 20-second duration of short-term memory in the same way that chunking expands its four- to seven-item capacity.

The retention benefits of sheer repetition, also called **maintenance rehearsal**, were first demonstrated by Hermann Ebbinghaus (1885/1913), a German philosopher who was a pioneer in memory research. Using himself as a subject, Ebbinghaus created a list of all possible nonsense syllables consisting of a vowel inserted between two consonants. Syllables that formed words were then eliminated—which left a list of unfamiliar items (e.g., *RUX, VOM, QEL, MIF*), each written on a separate card. To study the effects of rehearsal, Ebbinghaus would turn over the cards, one at a time, and say each syllable aloud to the ticking rhythm of a metronome. Then, after reading the items once, he would start again and go through the cards in the same order. This procedure was repeated until he could anticipate each syllable before turning over the card. Ebbinghaus found that he could recall a list of seven syllables after a single reading (there's that magical number again) but that he needed more practice for longer lists. The more often he repeated the items, the more

maintenance rehearsal. The use of sheer repetition to keep information in short-term memory.

FIGURE 6.6 ■ Duration of Short-Term Memory

What is the duration of short-term memory? When subjects are kept from rehearsing material they are trying to recall, items stored in short-term memory vanish within 20 seconds.

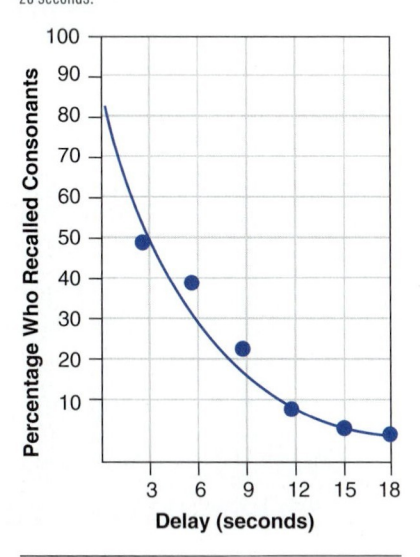

Source: Peterson, L., & Peterson, M. J. (1959). Short-term retention of individual verbal items. Journal of Experimental Psychology, 58(3), 193–198. https://doi.org/10.1037/h0049234

he could recall. Other studies have confirmed the point: "Rehearsal" can be used to "maintain" an item in short-term memory for an indefinite period of time.

Functions of Short-Term Memory

The limitations of short-term memory may seem to be a handicap, but in fact they are economic and adaptive. As with clearing outdated papers off a desk or purging old images from your phone, it helps to forget what is no longer useful. Otherwise, your mind would be cluttered with every sensation, every name, address, and morsel of trivia that ever entered the stream of your consciousness. If short-term memory had unlimited capacity, you would constantly be distracted—possibly with devastating results. When we discuss psychological disorders, for example, we'll learn that people who suffer from schizophrenia are often incoherent, jumping from one topic to the next as they speak, in part because they cannot filter out distractions.

Working Memory

In the computer we call the human mind, short-term memory is a mental workspace, like the screen. On a computer, material displayed on the screen may be entered on a keyboard, downloaded, or retrieved from previously saved files. Similarly, STM contains both new sensory input and material that is pulled from long-term storage. All cognitive psychologists agree that people have fleeting memories that are limited in their capacity and duration (Coltheart, 1999; Gathercole, 2001). However, many researchers are critical of the traditional view that STM is a passive storage depot that merely holds information until it fades or is transferred to a permanent warehouse (Crowder, 1993).

To conceptualize short-term memory as an active mental workspace where information is processed, Alan Baddeley (1992) and others prefer to use the term **working memory**. According to Baddeley, our working memory consists of a "central executive" processor and two specialized storage-and-rehearsal systems—one for auditory input, the other for visual and spatial images. However, according to Nelson Cowan (2016), this is just one of nine definitions for working memory. Cowan argues that Baddeley has provided the storage and processing definition of working memory. Within this definition, the working memory system is critical for intelligent functioning because a person must store the information while simultaneously processing said information. This requires attention. To interpret spoken or written language, for example, you have to remember the early part of a statement after it has receded into the past. Similarly, to solve an arithmetic problem, you have to keep track of the different steps you take—as in remembering to carry the 1 when adding 45 and 55. Now, think about all of the processes you require of your brain during a routine drive to class. What can you really pay attention to? The traffic signs? A text message that just came in? The new song on the radio? Chances are that if your attention is focused on the new song, and then refocused on the text message alert, you aren't able to remember whether or not you stopped at that last stop sign. But at least you do remember some of the new song and that a text message just came in, right? Figure 6.7 illustrates how Cowan (2016) believes information moves from sensory to activation in short-term memory.

Unsworth and Spillers (2010) also investigated the contribution of working memory to intelligence and concluded that the ability to retrieve information from long-term memory is also important. For example, to interpret a language we aren't fluent in, we must search our long-term memory for the words as they are read or spoken, and then connect those words with their meaning. This view of working memory is what Cowan calls the inclusive working memory definition. Regardless of the various definitions for working memory, research supports the notion that working memory contains separate systems for auditory and visual input—and that the system as a whole is highly adaptive (Andrade, Baddeley, & Hitch, 2002; Cowan, 2016; Miyake & Shah, 1999).

working memory. Term used to describe short-term memory as an active workspace where information is accessible for current use.

The Serial-Position Effect

Research also suggests that it may be useful to distinguish between short-term and long-term memory. Whenever people try to memorize a list, they inevitably recall items from the beginning and end of the list better than those sandwiched in the middle. The enhanced recall of early items in a sequence is called *primacy*, the advantage for the later items is called *recency*, and the combined pattern is known as

FIGURE 6.7 ■ Cowan's Model of Memory

According to Cowan, the central executive processor directs attention either inward toward long-term memory or outward toward the world. While driving, many stimuli are presented at once in the world. If a novel stimulus is sensed, like a new song you have never heard, then your attention helps direct that new song from sensory memory onward to LTM. There, short-term memory is activated so that you can "focus" on the information. Finally comes action. You might try to sing along and repeat the chorus over and over again—what is technically called maintenance rehearsal. Notice that the text message alert is also processed in STM. Cowan believes that some information still gets coded and stored in LTM, even if we don't pay much attention to it. But if we want to retrieve the information later, like the new song, attention is key. The stop sign you may or may not have obeyed is completely forgotten because it never made its way into LTM.

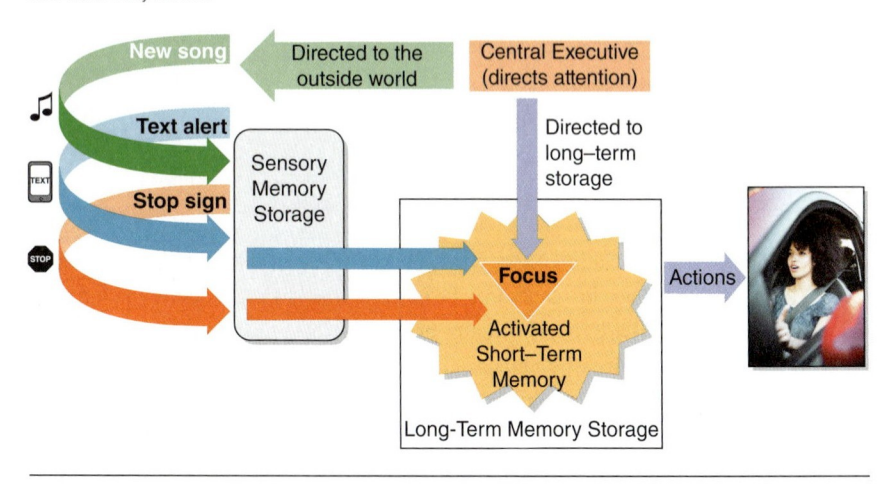

iStock.com/LeoPatrizi

---

serial-position curve. A U-shape pattern indicating the tendency to recall more items from the beginning and end of a list than from the middle.

the serial-position curve. This result was discovered in the 1890s by Mary Whiton Calkins, the first female president of the American Psychological Association (Madigan & O'Hara, 1992). Since that time, researchers have consistently observed the same effect.

What explains the serial-position effect? It appears that different factors are responsible for primacy and recency. Primacy is easy to understand. Imagine receiving a list of words and trying to recall them for a test: *chair, artichoke, bicycle, frame, teacher*, and so on. Chances are, you'll later recall the first word because you repeated it to yourself over and over again. You must divide your attention in half for the second word as you try to hold two in memory, divide your attention into thirds for the third item, and so on, through the list. In other words, primacy occurs because the first few words receive more attention and rehearsal than later ones—and are more likely to be transferred into long-term memory.

Explaining the recency effect is trickier. On the basis of the information-processing model described earlier, researchers argued that the last items in a list are easier to recall because they are still fresh in short-term working memory when the test begins. Initially, studies supported this explanation. For example, Murray Glanzer and Anita Cunitz (1966) presented two groups of subjects with 15 words to memorize. One group was tested right after the presentation; the second was distracted for 30 seconds and then tested. Figure 6.8 shows that subjects who were tested immediately after the presentation exhibited the usual effect: The first items were recalled by rehearsal, the last ones had not yet faded, and those in the middle slipped through the cracks. But there was no recency effect in the delayed-testing group—only primacy. After 30 seconds and no opportunity for rehearsal, the last few items vanished from working memory.

This explanation of the serial-position curve seems convincing, but there's a problem with it: Mack and colleagues (2017) argue that research in support of the serial-position effect tends to present items at one every 5 to 20 seconds. This presentation doesn't generalize to all circumstances. The researchers believed that the primacy and recency findings would be stronger if replicated under different conditions—specifically, more time between item presentation and outside of a controlled lab. Therefore, Mack and colleagues (2017) decided to use an iPhone recall app titled RECAPP, which allowed the experimenter to control the items and their rate of presentation in a setting closer to the real world. Across three experiments, and a span of several consecutive days, participants were presented with a list

FIGURE 6.8 ■ The Serial-Position Effect

Subjects trying to memorize a list of words were tested immediately or after 30 seconds of distraction. In the first group, subjects recalled the first and last few items the best, yielding the U-shape serial-position curve. In the delay group, however, there was no recency effect. After 30 seconds without rehearsal, subjects forgot the later items.

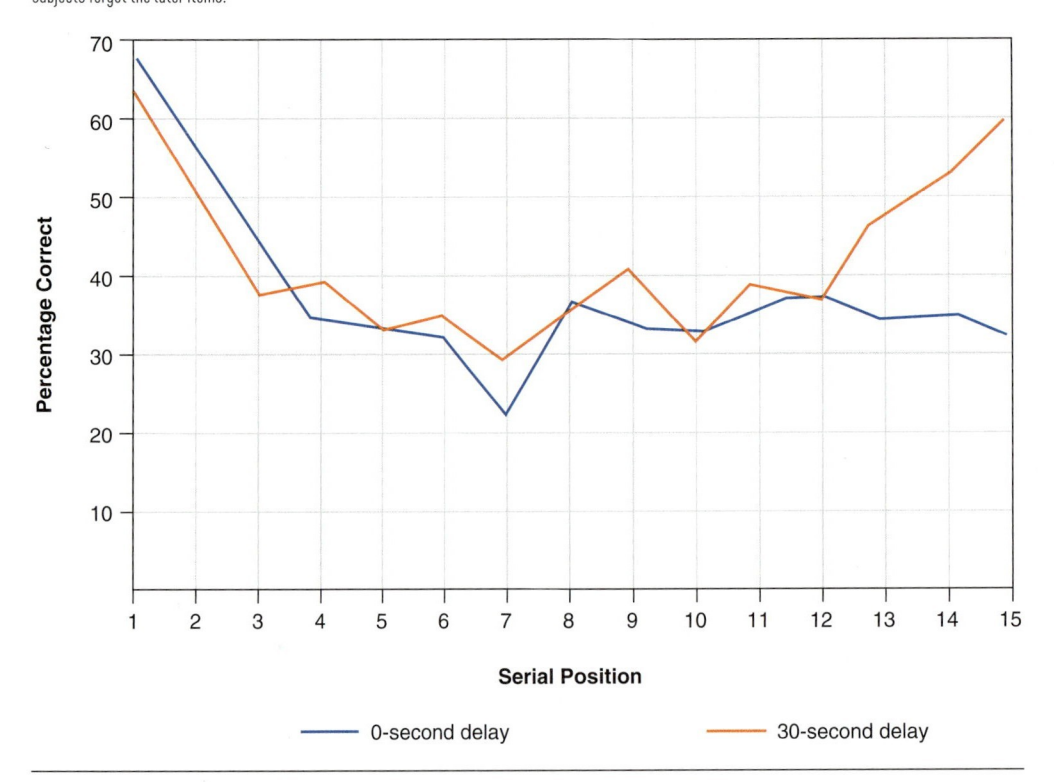

Source: Glanzer, M., & Cunitz, A. R. (1966). Two storage mechanisms in free recall. *Journal of Verbal Learning & Verbal Behavior, 5*(4), 351–360. https://doi.org/10.1016/S0022-5371(66)80044-0

of words at the rate of one word per hour via RECAPP. An hour after the last word was presented, participants were given a **free recall** test—a measure of memory performance absent cues to help retrieval. The results demonstrated a weak serial-position effect. Items presented first or last were not much more or less likely to be recalled. While this study did not strongly support the serial-position effect, it does not debunk it, either. According to Mack and colleagues (2017), participants used different strategies to help cue their recall of items, and these strategies might have depended on the length of the lists and time between exposure and recall. Some strategies may have been better than others. In the next section, we discuss some strategies participants may have used—elaborative rehearsal, for example—to increase their memory performance.

free recall. A type of explicit-memory task in which a person must reproduce information without the benefit of external cues (e.g., an essay exam).

LONG-TERM MEMORY

LEARNING OBJECTIVES

Juxtapose the belief that memories are forever with the belief that memories eventually become extinct.

- Describe the transfer of information from short-term memory into long-term memory.
- Explain memory retrieval, forgetting, and retrieval failure.
- Tell the story of H.M., and include why his story is so important.
- Create an argument for why people claim that "memory is reconstructive."

Do you remember your fourth birthday, the name of your first-grade teacher, or the smell of floor wax in the corridors of your elementary school? Can you describe a dream you had last night or recite the words of the national anthem? To answer these questions, you would have to retrieve information from the mental warehouse of long-term memory. Like the hard drive on a computer, LTM is a relatively enduring storage system that has the capacity to retain vast amounts of information for long periods of time. This section examines long-term memories of the recent and remote past—how they are encoded, stored, retrieved, forgotten, and even reconstructed in the course of a lifetime.

Encoding

Information can be kept alive in short-term working memory by rote repetition, or maintenance rehearsal. But to transfer something into long-term memory, you would find it much more effective to use **elaborative rehearsal**—a strategy that involves thinking about the material in a more meaningful way and associating it with other knowledge that is already in LTM. The more deeply you process something, the more likely you are to recall it at a later time.

To demonstrate this process, Fergus Craik and Endel Tulving (1975) showed subjects a list of words, one at a time, and for each asked them for (a) a simple visual judgment that required no thought about the words themselves ("Is—printed in capital letters?"); (b) an acoustic judgment that required subjects to at least pronounce the letters as words ("Does—rhyme with *small?*"); or (c) a more complex semantic judgment that compelled subjects to think about the meaning of the words ("Does the word fit the sentence 'I saw a—in the pond'?"). Subjects did not realize that their memory would be tested later. Yet words that were processed at a "deep" level, in terms of meaning, were more easily recognized than those processed at a "shallow" level (illustrated in Figure 6.9). This strategy could have been used in the RECAPP experiment discussed earlier. When presented with a word to remember, participants could have used the word in a sentence or looked up the definition. So, when you are studying, try to

> **elaborative rehearsal.** A technique for transferring information into long-term memory by thinking about it in a deeper way.

FIGURE 6.9 ■ Elaborative Rehearsal

Subjects read a long list of words and for each word judged how it was printed (visual), how it sounded (acoustic), or what it meant (semantic). The more thought required to process the words, the easier they were to recognize later.

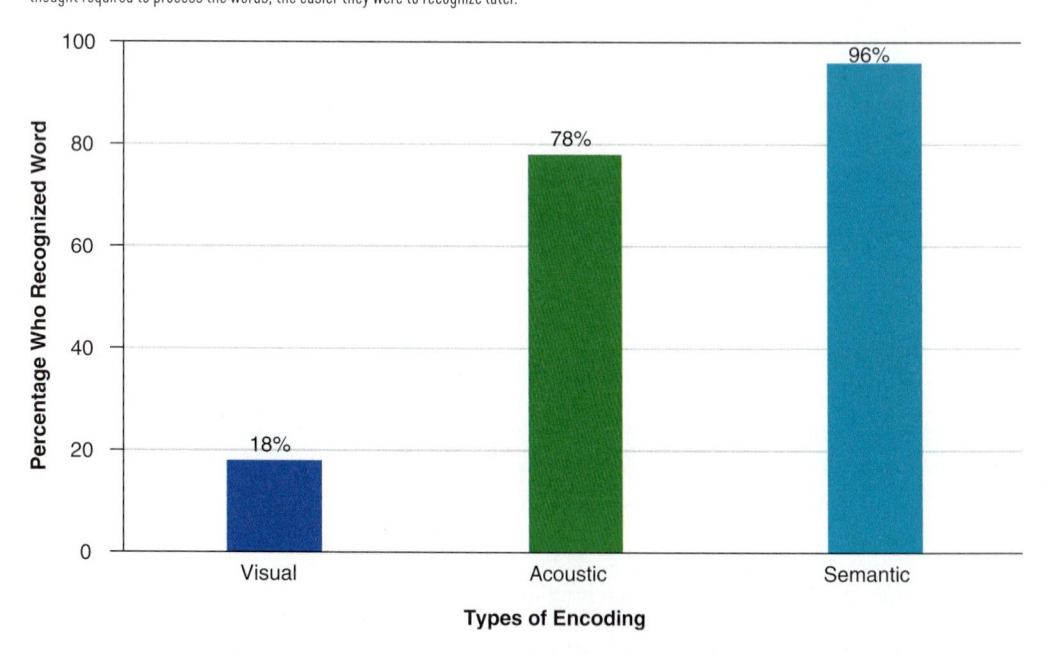

Type of Encoding	Percentage Who Recognized Word
Visual	18%
Acoustic	78%
Semantic	96%

Source: Adapted from Craik, F. I. M., & Tulving, E. (1975). Depth of processing and the retention of words in episodic memory. Journal of Experimental Psychology: General, 104(3), 268–294. https://doi.org/10.1037/0096-3445.104.3.268

process the information at a deeper level by focusing on its true meaning and how it applies to the real world.

Does making complex semantic judgments, compared to simple visual judgments, activate different regions of the brain? Is it possible to see physical traces of deep processing? Using fMRI technology, John Gabrieli et al. (1996) devised a study similar to Craik and Tulving's in which subjects were shown stimulus words on a computer and were instructed to determine whether the words were concrete or abstract (a semantic judgment) or simply whether they were printed in uppercase or lowercase letters (a visual judgment). As in past research, subjects later recalled more words for which they had made semantic rather than visual judgments. In addition, however, the brain-imaging measures showed that processing the words in semantic terms triggered more activity in a part of the frontal cortex of the language-dominant left hemisphere.

Memorizing—definitions, math formulas, poems, or historical dates—usually requires conscious effort and practice. In 1885, Ebbinghaus read through a list of nonsense syllables 0, 8, 16, 24, 32, 42, 53, or 64 times and checked his memory for the items 24 hours later. As predicted, the more learning time he spent the first day, the better his memory was on the second day.

But there's more. Ebbinghaus and others found that retention is increased through "overlearning"—that is, continued rehearsal even after the material seems to have been mastered (Driskell, Willis, & Copper, 1992; Semb, Ellis, & Araujo, 1993; Shibata et al., 2017). In fact, Shibata and colleagues (2017) discovered that overlearning solidifies connections in the brain, which protects the newly mastered material from interference. When we master new information, it is at risk of being overshadowed by the next set of information we must learn. Overlearning prevents this overshadowing. Shibata and colleagues' work demonstrates how this happens in the brain with neuronal adjustments to stabilize mastered materials when overlearning is implemented.

FIGURE 6.10 ■ The Value of Chunking (Blank Board)

Use this blank board to try to reproduce the chess board arrangement that you studied in Figure 6.4.

Long-term memory is also better when the practice is spread over a long period of time than when it is crammed in all at once, a phenomenon known as the "spacing effect" (Dempster, 1988). Harry Bahrick and Lynda Hall (1991) thus found that adults retained more of their high school math skills when they had later practiced the math in college—and when that practice was extended over semesters rather than condensed into a single year. When you think about it, this spacing effect makes adaptive sense. Names, faces, and events that recur over long intervals of time rather than in concentrated brief periods are probably, in real life, more important to remember (Anderson & Schooler, 1991). Therefore, another technique you can use to help you study is to revisit the material often. Take note of the items you missed, and read the material again. Try to figure out why you provided an incorrect answer. Next, talk to your instructor about why you missed it and ask for help. Then, take the practice quiz a second time. Repeat the process until it's time for your exam.

Storage

Whether the encoding process is effortful or automatic, cognitive psychologists have long been interested in the *format*, the *content*, and the *neural bases* of long-term memory as it is represented in the brain.

Formats of Long-Term Memory

In long-term memory, information is stored in two forms or "codes": semantic and visual. Semantic coding is easy to demonstrate. When we process verbal information—such as a spoken phrase, a speech, a written sentence, or a story—what we store is the meaning of the information, not specific words. For example, Jacqueline Sachs (1967) had subjects listen to a voice-recorded passage. She then presented a series of sentences (e.g., "He sent a letter about it to Galileo, the great Italian scientist") and asked if they were the same as or different from those of the original passage. Subjects correctly rejected sentences that changed the meaning ("Galileo, the great Italian scientist, sent him a letter about it"), but they did not reject sentences with the same meaning that were worded differently ("A letter about it was sent by him to Galileo, the great Italian scientist"). The reason: They had stored the semantic content of the passage—not an exact, word-for-word representation. In fact, people often read "between the lines" and recall hearing not just what was said but what was *implied*. For example, subjects who heard that a paratrooper "leaped out the door" often recalled later that he "jumped out of the plane." And mock jurors who heard a witness testify that "I ran up to the alarm" later assumed the witness had said, "I rang the alarm" (Harris & Monaco, 1978).

Although verbal information is stored in a semantic form, visual inputs and many long-term memories (including some of our most cherished childhood recollections) are stored as visual images. In visual coding, a mental picture of an object or a scene is generated—a process that has implications for how people retrieve the information. To demonstrate, Stephen Kosslyn (1980) showed subjects drawings like the boat in Figure 6.11. Later, he asked the subjects to visualize each drawing, to focus on the right or left side of it, and then, as quickly as possible, to indicate whether a specific object was present by pressing a YES or NO button that stopped a clock. If the drawing is stored in a visual manner, reasoned Kosslyn, then it should take longer for subjects to "scan" their image for an answer when the object is located away from the subject's focus of attention. That is exactly what happened. When subjects were mentally focused on the left rather than the right side of the drawing, for example, it took them longer to determine that a flag was present on the right side of the boat. In more recent experiments using PET scans, Kosslyn and others (1999) found that when subjects shut their eyes and tried to visualize patterns of stripes, parts of the visual cortex were activated—the same as when they actually viewed the stripes. Moulton and Kosslyn (2009) argue that mental imagery is a simulation that allows humans to "generate specific predictions based upon past experience" (p. 1273).

FIGURE 6.11 ■ Visual Coding

When subjects visualized the left rather than right side of this drawing, it took them longer to recall the flag. This result suggests that subjects "scanned" a mental image for the answer.

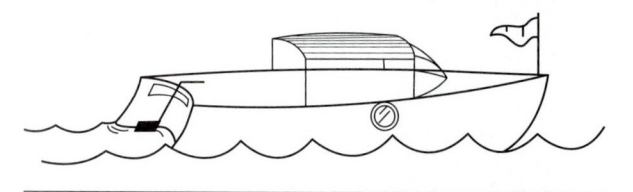

Source: Stephen M. Kosslyn. (2005). Mental images and the Brain, Cognitive Neuropsychology, 22:3-4, 333-347, DOI: 10.1080/02643290442000130

Mental images play an important role in long-term memory. Popular books on how to improve your memory advise people to use imagery, and research shows that this advice is well founded. As an illustration, try to memorize the following list of word pairs so that the first word triggers your memory of the second: *lawyer-chair, snowflake-mountain, shoes-milk, dog-bicycle, chef-pickle, student-sandwich, boy-flag.* You might try to master the list by silently repeating the items over and over—maintenance rehearsal. But now take a different approach: For each item, form an image in your "mind's eye" that contains the two words of each pair interacting in some way. For example, imagine a brown *dog* chasing a *bicycle* or a *student* eating a foot-long *sandwich*. This method should improve performance (Bower & Winzenz, 1970; Paivio, 1969). Consistent with the notion that imagery facilitates memory, concrete words that are easy to visualize (*fire, tent, statue, zebra*) are recalled more easily than abstract words that are difficult to represent in a picture (*infinite, freedom, process, future*). To remember something, it's better to encode it in both semantic and visual forms than in either alone (Paivio, 1986).

LEARNING CHECK

Numbers Game

How good is your memory for numbers? When you check your answers, you may have a better idea!

1. Short-term memory stores _____ for about 20 seconds.
   a. one item
   b. seven items, give or take two
   c. millions of items
   d. billions of items

2. Long-term memory stores _____ for many years.
   a. one item
   b. seven items, give or take two
   c. millions of items
   d. billions of items

3. Iconic memory stores visual images for _____.
   a. a fraction of a second
   b. 2 or 3 seconds
   c. 1 year
   d. 20 years

4. Echoic memory stores auditory images for _____.
   a. a fraction of a second
   b. 2 or 3 seconds
   c. 1 year
   d. 20 years

(Answers: 1. b; 2. c; 3. a; 4. b.)

Contents of Long-Term Memory

Increasingly it seems that we have more than one type of long-term memory (Kesner & Rolls, 2015; Rolls, 2000). Following Endel Tulving (1985), researchers now commonly distinguish two types, as illustrated in Figure 6.12. One is **procedural memory**, a "know how" memory that consists of our stored knowledge of well-learned habits and skills—such as how to drive, swim, type, ride a bike, and tie shoelaces. The second type is **declarative memory**, which consists of both *semantic* memories for facts about the world—such as who LeBron James is, what a dollar is worth, what you need to access the iCloud, and what the word *gravity* means—and *episodic* memories that we have about ourselves—such as who our parents are, where we went to school, and what our favorite movie is (Tulving, 2002). This distinction is important, as we'll see later, because people with amnesia are often unable to recall declarative memories of facts and events (Kensinger & Giovanello, 2006), yet they still retain many of the skills they had learned and committed to procedural memory.

procedural memory. Stored long-term knowledge of learned habits and skills.

declarative memory. Stored long-term knowledge of facts about ourselves and the world.

FIGURE 6.12 ■ Types of Long-Term Memory

There are two types of long-term memory. Procedural memory contains our knowledge of various skills—such as how to ride a bike. Declarative memory contains our knowledge of facts—for example, what a pyramid is or where one can be found.

iStock.com/vgajic; iStock.com/Gargolas

FIGURE 6.13 ■ Semantic Networks

According to semantic-network theories, memories are linked in a complex web of associations. The shorter the link between items, the more likely it is that the retrieval of one item will trigger that of the other.

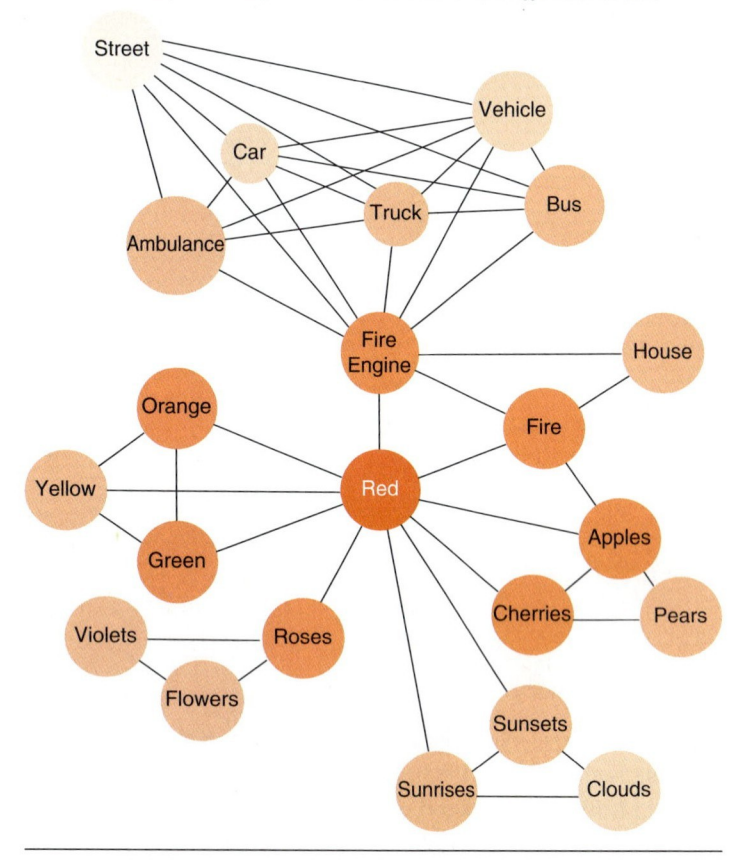

Source: Collins, A. M., & Loftus, E. F. (1975). A spreading-activation theory of semantic processing. Psychological Review, 82(6), 407–428. https://doi.org/10.1037/0033-295X.82.6.407

With all that's stored in long-term memory—habits; skills; verbal information; and knowledge of words, names, dates, faces, pictures, personal experiences, and the like—it's amazing that anything can ever be retrieved from this vast warehouse. Surely our knowledge must be organized in memory, perhaps the way books are filed in a library. One popular view is that memories are stored in a complex web of associations, or **semantic networks**. According to proponents of this view, items in memory are linked together by semantic relationships, as illustrated in Figure 6.13. When one item is brought to mind, the pathways leading to meaningfully related items are *primed*—thus increasing the likelihood that they too will be retrieved (Anderson, 1983; Collins & Loftus, 1975; Jones, Willits, & Dennis, 2015).

semantic network. A complex web of semantic associations that link items in memory such that retrieving one item triggers the retrieval of others as well.

A good deal of research supports the notion that memories are stored in semantic networks. When subjects are given a list of 60 words that fall into four categories (animals, professions, names, fruits)—even if the words are presented in a mixed order—subjects later tend to recall them in clusters. In other words, retrieving *tiger* is more likely to trigger one's memory for *baboon* than for *dentist, Jason*, or *banana* (Bousfield, 1953; Pacheco & Verschure, 2017; Romney, Brewer, & Batchelder, 1993).

Neural Bases of Long-Term Memory

Is it possible to pinpoint a site in the brain that houses these associations? Do memories leave a physical trace that can actually be "seen"? Are there drugs that we can take to improve our memory? Although led astray, at times, by exciting developments, neuroscientists have long been intrigued by such possibilities (Josselyn, Kohler, & Frankland, 2017; Squire & Schacter, 2002).

In one promising development, neurosurgeon Wilder Penfield reported that he had triggered long-forgotten memories in humans through brain stimulation. In the 1940s, Penfield was treating epileptic patients by removing portions of their brains. To locate the damage, he stimulated different cortical areas with a painless electrical current. Sometimes, his patients—who were awake during the procedure—would "relive" long-lost events from the past. For example, one woman said she heard a mother calling her child when a certain spot was stimulated. From reports like this, Penfield concluded that experience leaves a permanent "imprint" that can be played back years later as though there was a tape recorder in the brain (Penfield & Perot, 1963). This observation sparked a great deal of excitement until cognitive psychologists scrutinized the data and made two sobering discoveries. First, the phenomenon itself was very rare, reported by only a handful of Penfield's 1,100 patients. Second, the "flashbacks" were explained by some researchers as dreamlike illusions, not actual memories (Loftus & Loftus, 1980; Neisser, 1967). However, nine rodent experiments conducted between 2012 and 2016 (as reviewed by Josselyn et al., 2017) have demonstrated that electrical "stimulation is sufficient to induce behavioral memory expression" (p. 4652).

Penfield's work is said to have inspired today's researchers' hot pursuit of the *engram*—a term used to describe a physical memory trace. There are two objectives in this endeavor: (a) to locate the anatomical structures in the brain where memories are stored and (b) to understand the neural and biochemical changes that accompany memories. Let's now examine some recent developments along these lines.

Where is the "Engram"? Karl Lashley (1950) pioneered the search for memory traces in the brain. For 30 years, Lashley trained rats to run a maze, removed different structures from their brains, and then returned the rats to the maze to test their memory. No matter what structures he removed, however, the rats recalled at least some of what they had learned. Eventually, Lashley was forced to conclude that memories do not reside in any specific location.

In 1953, a 27-year-old man, Henry Molaison (referred to as H.M.), underwent brain surgery for severe epileptic seizures. Two holes were drilled into the patient's skull above the eyes, and through a silver straw the surgeon removed parts of both temporal lobes and sucked out the entire **hippocampus**—a curved pinkish-gray structure in the limbic system (illustrated in Figure 6.14). The operation succeeded in controlling the man's seizures. But something was terribly wrong. What made H.M. one of the most famous neurology cases of all time is that the surgery had an unexpected side effect: It produced **anterograde amnesia**, an inability to form new long-term memories. (This should not be confused with **retrograde amnesia**, which is an inability to retrieve long-term memories from the past.)

H.M. still recalled the people, places, and events from before the surgery. He also performed as well as before on IQ tests and could still read, write, and solve problems so long as he stayed focused on the task. But he could not retain new information. He would meet someone new but then forget the person; or he would read an article without realizing that he had read it before; or he would not know what he ate for his last meal. One year after his family moved, H.M. still did not know their new address. It was as if new information "went in one ear, out the next" (Milner, Corkin, & Teuber, 1968; Scoville & Milner, 1957). In his 70s, H.M. was the subject of *Memory's Ghost*, a book by Philip Hilts (1995). Hilts, who spent a great deal of time with H.M., tells of a remarkable experience. For H.M., he says, "Each moment is a surprise, a new puzzle to be worked out from a quick glance at the paltry evidence at hand as it comes rapidly upon him" (p. 139).

---

hippocampus. A portion of the brain in the limbic system that plays a key role in encoding and transferring new information into long-term memory.

anterograde amnesia. A memory disorder characterized by an inability to store new information in long-term memory.

retrograde amnesia. A memory disorder characterized by an inability to retrieve long-term memories from the past.

FIGURE 6.14 ■ The Hippocampal Region

As shown here, the hippocampus is located under the temporal lobe of the cerebral cortex and behind the amygdala. This structure is necessary for encoding and transferring new information into long-term memory.

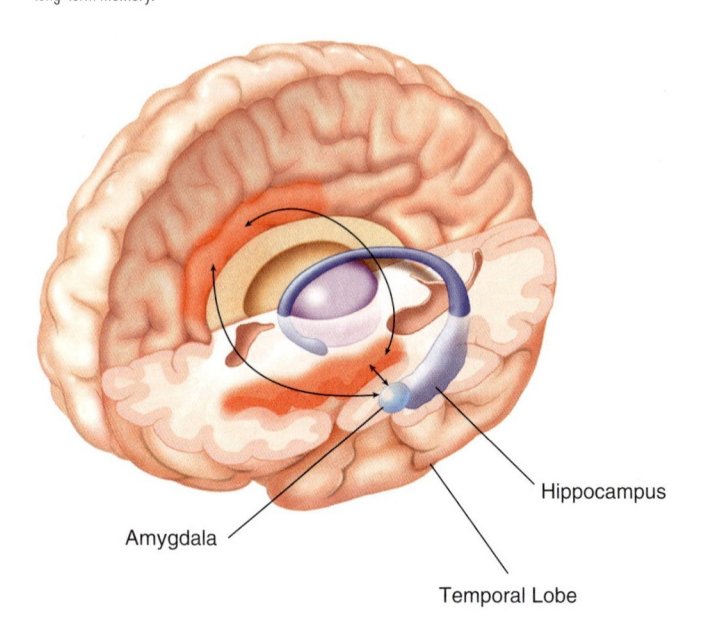

H.M.'s case is important for two reasons. First, he exhibited a very specific information-processing deficit. He could bring new material into short-term memory and he could retrieve long-term memories that were previously stored. But he could not form new long-term memories.

The second reason H.M.'s case is important is that it was the first to prove what Lashley could not—that localized lesions in the brain have disruptive effects on memory. Specifically, H.M.'s case and the work of Brenda Milner revealed that the hippocampus (and perhaps structures such as the amygdala and thalamus) plays a pivotal role (Josselyn et al., 2017). Recent studies in animals and humans have since confirmed the point: The hippocampus is essential for the explicit recollection of newly acquired information. Hippocampal lesions that mimic H.M.'s surgery produce a similar impairment in rats (Zhou, Zhou, & Xu, 2016), monkeys (Blue, Kazama, & Bachevalier, 2013), and other animals (Gafford, Parsons, & Helmstetter, 2011; Hampton & Shettleworth, 1996; Sherry, 1992; Squire & Schacter, 2002).

Is all of memory stored in the hippocampus? No. When this structure is surgically removed from monkeys, they lose most of their recall for events of the preceding month, but their more distant memories remain intact (Squire & Zola-Morgan, 1991). And among humans, older adults with a shrunken hippocampus are impaired in their ability to recall new words and pictures, but they can still revisit past events (Golomb et al., 1993). For example, persons with Alzheimer's disease, a progressive memory disorder, experience extreme deterioration of their hippocampus (Adler et al., 2018). One result is that they suffer from a striking loss of memory for new information. However, in a study where they were placed in an apartment—called the reminiscence apartment—fully decorated and stocked with items from the 1950s, persons with Alzheimer's recalled more of their past events and with increased detail than when in their everyday setting (Miles, Fischer-Mogensen, Nielsen, Hermansen, & Berntsen, 2013). Together, the various strands of evidence point to the conclusion that the hippocampus plays a role in the initial

In Aarhus, Denmark, a museum has created a special place called the reminiscence apartment. All of the rooms are decorated and stocked with items from the 1950s, similar to this cluttered kitchen from the same era. Only persons with dementia and Alzheimer's disease are allowed to tour and interact with the apartment, as it is used to help them remember, socialize, and improve their mood.

iStock.com/JodiJacobson

FIGURE 6.15 ■ The Mirror-Tracing Task

The most notable aspect of H.M.'s pattern of memory impairment was that his performance was intact on tasks that required only memories retrieved without conscious awareness. For example, the mirror-tracing task has participants trace a star by looking only at their drawing hand in a mirror. This might seem easy, but it isn't. While looking at your drawing hand in the mirror, your brain has to translate a traced line toward the left into the motion of moving your hand to the right, and vice versa. With practice, participants can learn how to do this task well. H.M. also became good at this task after a few rounds of practice. However, when asked if he remembered completing the mirror-tracing task before, he never remembered having practiced it.

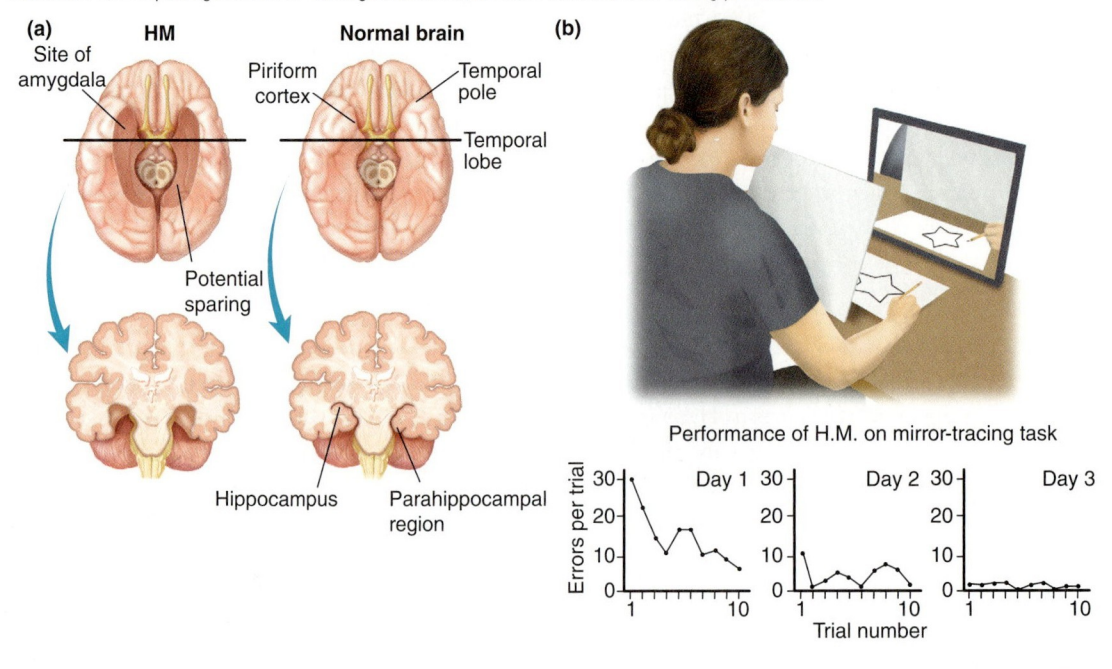

Adapted from Openstax Psychology text by Kathryn Dumper, William Jenkins, Arlene Lacombe, Marilyn Lovett and Marion Perlmutter licensed under CC BY v4.0. https://openstax.org/details/books/psychology

encoding of information and serves as a way station from which information is sent for long-term storage to neural circuits in the cerebral cortex. The hippocampus is especially involved in our memories of places, providing us with something of a "cognitive map" (Best, White, & Minai, 2001; Redish, 1999).

Clearly, not all aspects of memory require the hippocampus. As we'll see later, amnesics like H.M. do exhibit memory, but in indirect ways. They can be conditioned to blink to a tone that has been paired with a puff of air to the eye, and they can remember how to work a maze they have practiced (as illustrated in Figure 6.15)—but they cannot recall the training sessions. Similarly, they form preferences for new music they hear but do not recognize the melodies in a test situation. And they retain their procedural memories of how to read, write, and use other previously learned skills. For these types of memory tasks, different structures are involved. For example, David McCormick and Richard Thompson (1984) located a microscopic spot in the *cerebellum* that controls the classical conditioning of the eyeblink reflex. Certain areas of the brain specialize in certain types of input, but for something as complex as memory, many areas are needed.

The Biochemistry of Memory. As some researchers try to locate where memories are stored, others seek to identify the accompanying biochemical changes that take place in the neural circuits. Most of these changes are likely to be found at the synapses, the tiny gaps between neurons that are linked together by the release of neurotransmitters.

One neurotransmitter that seems to play an important role in memory is *acetylcholine*. (Review Chapter 2 on behavioral neuroscience for more on the functions of acetylcholine.) Research shows that people with Alzheimer's disease not only lose hippocampal density but also have lowered levels of acetylcholine and fewer acetylcholine receptors in the brain (Oz, Petroianu, & Lorke, 2016). Research with animal models has demonstrated that activation of acetylcholine receptors prevents memory impairments and, thus, can be a promising treatment for humans (Lebois et al., 2017). Currently, Alzheimer's disease has no cure, but pharmacotherapies have somewhat improved quality of life and shown moderate effectiveness (Folch et al., 2016).

Certain hormones are also involved in memory. Glucocorticoids—such as cortisol—are a group of hormones released during stress (Joëls & Krugers, 2007). Stress, in turn, can help or hinder memory (Joëls & Krugers, 2007; Schwabe, Joëls, Roozendaal, Wolf, & Oitzl, 2012). For example, some people perform well under pressure, while others choke. Researchers propose that when glucocorticoids are combined with catecholamines—epinephrine, norepinephrine, and dopamine—an organism can effectively encode new information during stressful events (Schwabe et al., 2012). Developmental studies argue that early life stress prepares organisms for better memory performance in stressful conditions later in life, which could also explain why some people succeed and others fail under pressure (Oitzl, Champagne, van der Veen, & de Kloet, 2010; Oomen et al., 2010). However, correlational studies with humans contradict these findings. In studies by Gutteling et al. (2006) and Laplante et al. (2008), mothers who experienced a natural disaster while pregnant had offspring who showed cognitive impairment when tested at the ages of 5 to 7 years. As you have probably guessed, many questions about hormones, stress, and memory remain (Schwabe et al., 2012).

Retrieval

Once information is stored, how do you know it exists? Because people can openly report their recollections, this seems like a silly question. In fact, however, this is one of the thorniest questions confronting cognitive psychologists. Hermann Ebbinghaus (1885/1913) was not only the first person to study memory systematically but also the first to realize that a memory may exist without awareness. In his words, "These experiences remain concealed from consciousness and yet produce an effect which is significant and which authenticates their previous experience" (p. 2).

Memory without awareness illustrates how human beings can be both competent and incompetent at the same time, and it poses a profound challenge to the researcher: If people have memories they cannot report, how can we ever know these memories exist? To his credit, Ebbinghaus devised a simple but clever technique. He tested memory by its effect on performance. Acting as his own subject, he would learn a set of nonsense syllables and then count the number of trials it later took him to *relearn* the same list. If it took fewer trials the second time around than the first, then he must have retained some of the material—even if he could not consciously recite it.

In recent years, other techniques have been devised. Basically, there are two types of tests, and each assesses a different type of memory: one explicit, the other implicit. **Explicit memory** is a term used to describe the recollections of facts and events that people try to retrieve in response to *direct* questions. In contrast, **implicit memory** is a term used to describe the retention of information without awareness, as measured by its *indirect* effects on performance (Jacoby, Toth, & Yonelinas, 1993; Roediger, 1990; Schacter, 1992). Why is this distinction important? The reason, as we'll see, is that people often exhibit dissociations between the two types of tasks. That is, people will consciously forget (have no explicit memory of) an experience but at the same time show the effects (have an implicit memory) of that experience. There are different ways to interpret this pattern. Some scientists believe that explicit and implicit memory are separate systems that are controlled by different parts of the brain (Kandel, Dudai, & Mayford, 2014). On the contrary, others believe that the dissociations merely indicate differences in the way information is encoded and retrieved (Belleville, Caza, & Peretz, 2003; Foster & Jelicic, 1999; Perrin, 2018). Either way, it's useful to consider these two aspects of memory separately (as summarized in Table 6.1).

explicit memory. The types of memory elicited through the conscious retrieval of recollections in response to direct questions.

implicit memory. A nonconscious recollection of a prior experience that is revealed indirectly, by its effects on performance.

TABLE 6.1 ■ Differences Between Explicit and Implicit Memory	
Explicit Memory	**Implicit Memory**
Conscious retention	Nonconscious retention
Direct tests	Indirect tests
Disrupted by amnesia	Intact with amnesia
Encoded in the hippocampus	Encoded elsewhere

Explicit Memory

Have you even taken a multiple-choice test? This task, which requires you to select a remembered item from a list of alternatives, is a **recognition** test—so are playing the popular game show *Beat Shazam*, picking a criminal from a lineup, or identifying photographs from a family album.

Research shows that recall and recognition are both forms of explicit memory in that people are consciously trying to retrieve the information (Haist, Shimamura, & Squire, 1992). There is, however, a key difference: People tend to perform better at recognition. Bahrick and colleagues (1975) reported this difference in a study of long-term memory. They showed people pictures of classmates taken from their high school yearbooks. Seven years after graduating, subjects were able to correctly *recall* only 60 percent of the names belonging to each face. But those who only had to *recognize* the right names from a list of possible alternatives were 90 percent accurate—even when tested 14 years after graduation.

The fact that recognition is easier than recall tells us that forgetting sometimes occurs not because memory has decayed but because the information is difficult to reclaim from storage. Retrieval failure is a common experience. Have you ever felt as though a word or a name you were trying to recall was just out of reach—on the tip of your tongue? In a classic study of the tip-of-the-tongue phenomenon, Roger Brown and David McNeill (1966) prompted this experience by giving students definitions of uncommon words and asking them to produce the words themselves. For example, what is "the green-colored matter found in plants"? And what is "the art of speaking in such a way that the voice seems to come from another place"? Most often, subjects either knew the word right away or were certain that they did not know it. But at times, subjects knew they knew the word but could not recall it—a frustrating state that Brown and McNeill likened to being on the brink of a sneeze.

The experience is an interesting one. When a word is on the tip of the tongue, subjects often come up with other words that are similar in sound or meaning. Searching their memory for *chlorophyll*, subjects might say *chlorine* or *cholesterol*. For *ventriloquism*, they produce words such as *ventilate* and *vernacular*. In fact, a surprising number of people will guess the correct first letter, last letter, and number of syllables contained in the missing word. These cases reveal that the information is in memory but that people need "hints" to dislodge it (Brown, 1991). Thus, while people in their 70s and 80s have more tip-of-the-tongue experiences than do younger adults, they too can bring the words to mind when given the right prompting (Heine, Ober, & Shenaut, 1999). The tip-of-the-tongue experience is common, frustrating, and effortful, and it tells us something about why stored memories are sometimes "lost" and how they can be retrieved (Schwartz, 2002).

Recognition is often easier than recall because recognition tasks contain retrieval cues, or reminders. A retrieval cue is a stimulus that helps us to access information in long-term memory. According to Tulving's (1983) principle of **encoding specificity**, any stimulus that is encoded along with an experience can later trigger one's memory of that experience. For mock jurors, a simple trial-ordered-notebook containing headings to outline the trial proceedings served as a successful retrieval enhancement (Thorley, Baxter, & Lorek, 2015). Retrieval cues can be anything from a picture, a location, a word, or a song, to another person, a fragrance, or the mood we're in.

Context-Dependent Memory. Tulving's principle gave rise to the interesting notion that memory is "context dependent"—that people find it easier to retrieve information from memory when they're in the same situation in which the information was obtained in the first place. In an unusual initial test of this hypothesis, researchers presented scuba divers with a list of words in one of two settings: 15 feet underwater or on the beach. Then they tested the divers in the same setting or in the other setting. Illustrating context-dependent memory, the divers recalled 40 percent more words when the material

recognition. A form of explicit-memory retrieval in which items are presented to a person who must determine if they were previously encountered.

encoding specificity. The principle that any stimulus encoded along with an experience can later jog one's memory of that experience.

The premise? To hear as few notes as possible before you are able to name the tune. Your competition? The Shazam app. The game show *Beat Shazam* is a test of recognition memory where notes from a wide range of songs act as retrieval cues. Think you can beat Shazam? Download the app, then listen to a streaming music service and test how quickly you can name the tunes. Players on the game show can win up to $1 million.

FOX / Contributor/FOX Image Collection/Getty Images

was learned and retrieved in the same context (Godden & Baddeley, 1975). This is why the "retrace your steps" method is helpful when you have lost an item. Standing in the places where you last had the item helps you to remember where you might have last placed it, since the environmental cues can serve as a prime to activate information located in your implicit memory. For example, you might haphazardly lay down your keys when in a hurry and, thus, not pay attention to their placement. When it comes time to leave, your keys are nowhere to be found until you move through the space the same way you did when you remembered having them in hand. You see your backpack, and that acts as a prime. Suddenly, your implicit memory becomes vivid and you lift your backpack to find the keys underneath.

Context seems to activate memory even in 3-month-old infants. In a series of studies, Carolyn Rovee-Collier and colleagues (1992) trained infants to shake an overhead mobile equipped with colorful blocks and bells by kicking a leg that was attached to the mobile by a ribbon. The infants were later more likely to recall what they learned—which they demonstrated by kicking—when tested in the same crib containing the same visual cues than when there were differences.

Cai and colleagues (2016) believe that a set of findings using animal models demonstrate the biological reason for contextual retrieval of memories. When learning occurs, an ensemble of overlapping neurons fire. These neurons are called CA 1, and they "serve to link and strengthen memories, thus facilitating integrated recall of experiences encoded close in time while separating those encoded further in time" (p. 118). With age, the excitability of CA 1 neurons decreases. Thus, a context-dependent fear response in mice happens for those that are younger but not for those that are older. In an attempt to repair the loss of CA 1 neuron excitability—and, as a result, reinvigorate context-dependent memory—Cai and colleagues (2016) injected aged mice with a specialized drug or saline. Aged mice that received the drug had the same context-dependent fear response as young mice, whereas aged mice that received the saline did not.

State-Dependent Memory. Internal cues that become associated with an event may also spark the retrieval of explicit memories. Illustrating the phenomenon of "state-dependent" memory, studies reveal that it is often easier to recall something when our state of mind is the same at testing as it was during encoding. If you have an experience when you are happy or sad, calm or aroused, that experience—unless your emotional state is intensely distracting—is more likely to pop to mind or be free-recalled when your internal state later is the same than when it's different (Bower, 1981; Kenealy, 1997).

Whether a person is drunk or sober during the experience has yielded mixed results in state-dependent memory experiments (Compo et al., 2017). Thus, Compo and colleagues (2017) decided to randomly assign participants to a control, placebo, or alcohol encoding condition. The memory that participants were tasked to encode was of a simulated crime. Participants witnessed the simulated crime and, after a delay, were placed in the same state during retrieval. Intoxicated participants were less accurate than those in the control and placebo conditions. Intoxicated participants' memory performance was best when they were able to immediately provide information about what they witnessed. In lieu of these findings, Compo and colleagues (2017) suggest that intoxicated witnesses be interviewed immediately instead of after a delay—providing time to sober up could harm memory retrieval.

What about state-dependent retrieval that relies on environment? Eric Eich (1995) has found that the reason it helps to be memory-tested in the same place where you learned the material is that the environment is likely to transport you back to the same mood state—and it's this mood state that serves as a retrieval cue. When it comes to mood as an internal state and memory, there is a complicating factor: The mood we're in often leads us to evoke memories that are congruent with that mood. When people are happy, the good times are easiest to recall. But when people are sad, depressed, or anxious, their minds become flooded with negative events of the past. Currently depressed people thus report having more intrusive memories of death and other bad experiences, compared to non-depressed control subjects (Brewin, Reynolds, & Tata, 1999). Furthermore, vocabulary acquisition can be harmed by the presentation of negative stimuli. Miller and colleagues (2017) discovered that English speakers who were exposed to negative stimuli while trying to learn a foreign language had poor recall performance. Their explanation was that negative stimuli impeded the brain's ability to connect new words with meaning.

Implicit Memory

In 1911, physician Édouard Claparède described an encounter he had with a young woman who suffered from Korsakoff syndrome—a brain disorder, common among those with chronic alcoholism, that impairs the transfer of information into long-term memory. When Claparède was introduced to the woman, he hid in his right palm a pin that pricked her painfully as the two shook hands. The next day, he returned to the hospital. Due to her memory disorder, the patient did not recognize the doctor and could not answer questions about their prior interaction. Yet when he reached out to shake her hand, she pulled back abruptly. Why did she refuse? After some confusion, all she could say was, "Sometimes pins are hidden in people's hands" (Schwartz & Reisberg, 1991).

Researchers have demonstrated that people find it easier to remember information when they are in the same environment where the information was first learned.

iStock.com/fizkes

Implicit Memory in Amnesia Patients. Did Claparède's patient remember him or not? On the one hand, she knew enough to be afraid. On the other hand, she did not know why. It was as if she had a memory but didn't know it. As unusual as this story may seem, we now know that there are many others like it. As in the case of H.M., cognitive psychologists are keenly interested in people with amnesia. Earlier, researchers believed that amnesics lacked the ability to encode or store information in long-term memory. They could still perform "skills"—but could not keep new "information" in memory.

Or could they? Elizabeth Warrington and Lawrence Weiskrantz (1970) published an article in *Nature* that challenged the prevailing view. These researchers gave a list of words to 4 amnesics and 16 normal control subjects. Four memory tests were then administered. Two were standard measures of explicit memory—one a recall task, the second involving recognition. The other tests were indirect measures of implicit memory in which the subjects were asked merely to complete word fragments (such as *k---ht, c-l---e,* and *t---v-s-on*) and stems (e.g., *kni---, col----,* and *tele------*) with the first "guess" that came to mind. The results are shown in Figure 6.16. As was expected, the control subjects scored higher than the amnesics on the explicit-memory tests. But on the incomplete-word tasks, the amnesics were just as likely to form words that appeared on the original list. Like Claparède's Korsakoff syndrome patient, they retained the information enough to use it. They just didn't realize it.

FIGURE 6.16 ■ Retention Without Awareness

Amnesic patients and normal control subjects were tested for their memory of words previously learned. The amnesics performed poorly on the measures of explicit memory (recall and recognition) but not on indirect measures of implicit memory (word-fragment and word-stem completion tasks). The amnesics retained the information but didn't know it.

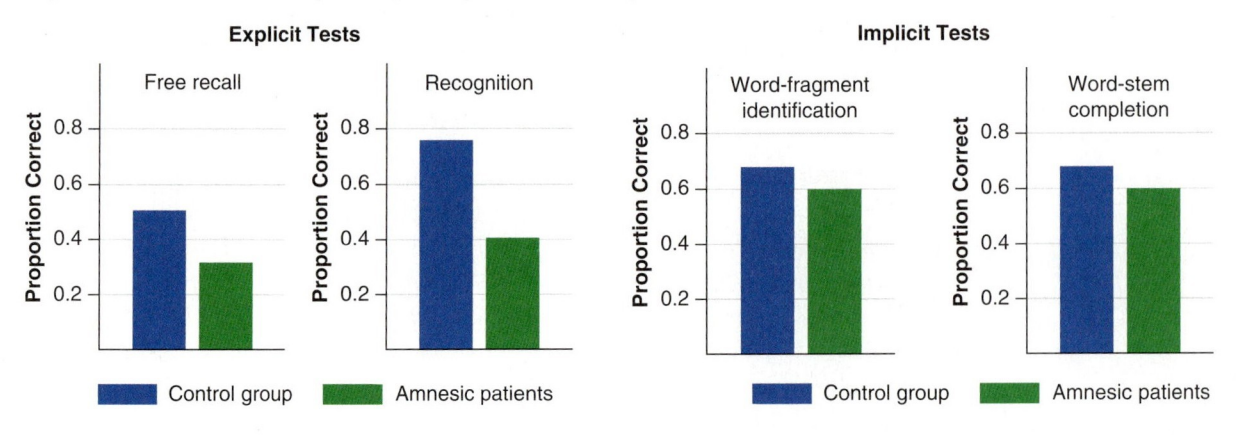

Source: Warrington, E. K., & Weiskrantz, L. (1970). Amnesic syndrome: Consolidation or retrieval? Nature, 228(5272), 628–630. https://doi.org/10.1038/228628a0

Today, many case studies indicate that amnesics know more than they realize. Consider the case of Clive Wearing, a musicologist, conductor, and pianist whose central nervous system was attacked by the herpes virus. According to a Radiolab interview with Clive's wife and Oliver Sacks, the virus damaged Clive's hippocampus, which resulted in a sense of "waking up"—from what he believed to be an incredibly long sleep—every 20 seconds (Abumrad & Krulwich, 2007). His diary has the following statement written in it over and over:

~~8:31 AM: Now I am really, completely awake.~~

~~9:06 AM: Now I am perfectly, overwhelmingly awake.~~

9:34 AM: Now I am superlatively, actually awake.

When asked who wrote the previous statements that are crossed out, Clive claimed that the statements were in his handwriting, but he had no idea who put the statements there.

Can Clive remember anything? Yes, he can. Take his wife, Deborah. When he sees her, it is like he is seeing Deborah for the first time in years. His face lights up, he begins to hum a love song, and he grabs Deborah in a romantic embrace. Clive can also play the piano and direct a choir without complication since his procedural memory was left intact. As for learning new information, repeated presentation of a video clip has revealed that Clive can anticipate what will happen next, regardless of his firm belief that the video is completely novel.

This dissociation—the tendency for amnesics to show signs of long-term retention of information without awareness—has now been amply observed in studies involving different types of amnesia and different implicit-memory tests. For example, researchers tried to classically condition a patient who had anterograde amnesia by pairing a harmless tone with electric shock. Although the patient could not later recall these sessions, he reacted with greater arousal whenever the tone was presented (Bechara, Tranel, Damasio, Adolphs, & Damasio, 1995). This classical conditioning is likely what led Claparède's patient to refuse to shake hands. In another study, elderly patients with Alzheimer's disease played a weather prediction game on a computer. They had to guess *rain* or *shine* after learning, through trial and error, what clues signaled the correct prediction. Compared to healthy elderly control subjects, the Alzheimer's patients could not later recall the clues, the test, or the layout of the computer display. But they were accurate in their weather predictions—indicating that they had an implicit memory of what they had learned, a form of retention without awareness (Eldridge, Masterman, & Knowlton, 2002).

Implicit Memory in Everyday Life. You don't have to suffer from brain damage or drug-induced amnesia to exhibit a dissociation between memory and awareness. Have you ever had the eerie feeling that you've been in a situation before, even though you had not? This is called *déjà vu*, and it is defined as the illusion that a new situation is familiar (the term is French for "already seen"). In a way, déjà vu is the opposite of amnesia. Whereas amnesics have memories without awareness or familiarity, the person with déjà vu has a sense of familiarity but no real memory. Estimates vary, but *Psychology Today* reports that between 60 and 70 percent of people report having had such an episode (Lewis, 2012).

Déjà vu is not the only type of dissociation that is commonly experienced. Retention without awareness occurs in all of us—sometimes with interesting consequences. Let's now consider two consequences: eyewitness transference and unintentional plagiarism:

Eyewitness Transference. False fame may seem amusing, but retention without awareness can also have serious consequences. Several years ago, psychologist Donald Thompson was falsely accused of rape on the basis of the victim's recollection. Remarkably for Thompson, he was being interviewed live on television as the rape occurred—an interview, ironically, on the subject of human memory. Apparently, the victim was watching Thompson's show just before being attacked and then mistook him for the rapist. Was Thompson familiar to her? Yes, he was—but from the TV show, not from the crime scene. Thanks to his airtight alibi, Thompson was vindicated instantly. Perhaps others have not been so fortunate.

The problem illustrated by this story is that sometimes witnesses remember a face but forget the circumstances in which they saw it. In one study, subjects witnessed a staged crime and then looked through mug shots (Brown, Deffenbacher, & Sturgill, 1977). A few days later, they were asked to view a lineup. The result was startling: Subjects were as likely to identify an innocent person whose photograph was in the mug shots as they were to pick the actual criminal. This familiarity effect gives rise to the phenomenon of eyewitness transference, whereby a person seen in one situation is later confused in memory, or "transferred," to another situation—often with tragic consequences (Dysart, Lindsay, Hammond, & Dupuis, 2001; Ross, Ceci, Dunning, & Toglia, 1994; Steblay & Dysart, 2016).

Unintentional Plagiarism. False fame and unconscious transference occur when we are aware that something is familiar but we cannot pinpoint the correct source of that familiarity (Johnson, Hashtroudi, & Lindsay, 1993; Mandler, 1980). In other words, the experience has an impact on behavior but without our conscious awareness. There is another possible repercussion of implicit memory: unintentional plagiarism. Unintentional plagiarism happens in music quite frequently. The song "My Sweet Lord" by former Beatles member George Harrison is almost identical to the song "He's So Fine" by the Chiffons. The latter song's author, Ronnie Mack, filed a lawsuit in 1971. Harrison was taken to court and found guilty of subconscious plagiarism, what we call unintentional plagiarism. This resulted in a $1,599,987 fine that was then reduced to $587,000 after Harrison's manager purchased the rights to "He's So Fine." The legal battle did not end officially until 1998, but it set a precedent for stricter copyright standards in the music industry (Runtagh, 2016). Musicians such as Robin Thicke, Pharrell Williams, Justin Bieber, Madonna, Lana Del Ray, and Ed Sheeran have all been sued for plagiarism in recent years.

Have you ever had an insight you thought was original, only to realize or be told later that it was "borrowed" from another source? Are people who write, compose music, solve problems, tell jokes, or think up creative ideas vulnerable to unintentional plagiarism? Alan Brown and Dana Murphy (1989) had subjects in groups take turns generating items that fit a particular category (sports, four-legged animals, musical instruments, and clothing). After four rounds, they asked subjects individually to recall the items that they personally had generated and to come up with new ones from the same categories. As it turned out, 75 percent of the subjects took credit for at least one item of someone else's, and 71 percent came up with a "new" item that was given earlier. Some subjects inadvertently plagiarized their own ideas, but most often they "stole" from others in the group.

Additional research has shown that people are vulnerable to unintentional plagiarism in some situations more than others. Predictably, the problem is more likely to occur when the ideas taken are highly memorable; when the person who gave the original ideas has status; when the original ideas were shared in anonymous group situations; when subjects were distracted, in a hurry, or not

FIGURE 6.17 ■ Inspiration and Plagiarism

Robin Thicke teamed with Pharrell Williams (a) to write the song "Blurred Lines," which became a hit despite the song's controversial lyrics. The song's studio arrangement was inspired by Marvin Gaye's (b) "Got to Give it Up" and wove in the sounds of a party, cowbell, and walking bass. The Marvin Gaye family sued Thicke and Williams because of said studio arrangement and were awarded. 3 million plus 50 percent of future earnings from "Blurred Lines." It is one of the largest payouts in music history and illustrates how the lines between inspiration and plagiarism can be blurred (pun intended).

Kevin Mazur / Contributor/WireImage/Getty Images; Afro Newspaper/Gado / Contributor/Archive Photos/Getty Images

overly concerned about the origin of their ideas; and after a long period of time has elapsed (Macrae, Bodenhausen, & Calvini, 1999; Marsh & Bower, 1993; Marsh, Landau, & Hicks, 1997; Tenpenny, Keriazakos, Lew-Gavin, & Phelan, 1998). As in other research on implicit memory, these studies show that there is a bit of amnesia in all of us. Commenting on the amount of unconscious plagiarism exhibited by research participants in his laboratory, Richard Marsh speculates that the problem is "a heck of a lot more common than anybody would realize" (Carpenter, 2002). One strategy to help avoid unintentional plagiarism is to keep track of ideas gathered from sources as you work. The free software Zotero and Evernote can assist with this. If you try to connect the sources with the ideas after the work is done, you risk forgetting which source goes with what idea, or if there was even a source at all. This is what happened to Harvard journalism lecturer, writer, and former *New York Times* executive editor Jill Abramson. Abramson's work *Merchants of Truth* reportedly plagiarized several different sources (Malooley, 2019). One of her plagiarized sources, Jake Malooley, interviewed her about why she plagiarized his work. Abramson admitted to not keeping track of citations and sources, stating simply, "I mistook it for mine" (Malooley, 2019). In other words, Abramson thought Malooley's work was really hers. Another strategy is to connect the source with the information always, even if you are putting that source's information into your own words. An explanation for an idea can be interpreted in many ways, but the idea itself—no matter how it is phrased—still has to be connected to its originator. Abramson also admitted to not giving credit to the proper sources when she rephrased their original ideas (Malooley, 2019). She gave Malooley a personal apology, but the damage had already been done. So, if a highly skilled writer can use these simple strategies to avoid plagiarism, you can too.

LEARNING CHECK

Partial Recall

It's harder to recall information without external cues than it is to select a remembered item from a list of alternatives. Bear that in mind as you ponder these questions about long-term memory.

1. The type of explicit-memory task that requires you to reproduce information without the benefit of external cues is called _____.

2. The type of explicit-memory task that requires you to select a remembered item from a list of alternatives is called _____.

   a. recollection
   b. recognition
   c. reconfirmation
   d. reconnaissance

3. _____ memory refers to the idea that people have a better memory for information when placed in the same environment where the information was first presented.

4. The portion of the brain that plays a key role in encoding and transferring new information into long-term memory is called the _____.

   a. hippodrome
   b. hippopotamus
   c. hippocampus
   d. hypochondriac

5. Transferring information into long-term memory by thinking about it in a deeper way is called _____.

(Answers: 1. free recall; 2. b; 3. context-dependent; 4. c; 5. elaborative rehearsal.)

Forgetting

Before we celebrate the virtues of memory and outline the techniques we can use to improve it, let's stop and ponder the wisdom of William James (1890), who said, "If we remembered everything, we should on most occasions be as ill off as if we remembered nothing" (p. 680). James was right. Many years ago, Russian psychologist Alexander Luria (1968) described his observations of Solomon Shereshevskii, a man he called S., who had a truly exceptional memory. After one presentation, S. would remember lists containing dozens of items, recite them forward or backward, and still retain the information 15 years later. But there was a drawback: No matter how hard S. tried, he could not forget. Images of letters, numbers, and other items of trivia were so distracting that he had to quit his job and support himself by entertaining audiences with his feats of memory. Sometimes it is better to forget—which is why some psychologists have suggested, and neuroscience supports, the paradoxical conclusion that forgetting is an adaptive, economical aspect of human memory (Bjork & Bjork, 1996; Schacter, 1999; Wimber, Alink, Charest, Kriegeskorte, & Anderson, 2015).

The Forgetting Curve

Memory failure is a common experience in everyday life (see Table 6.2). If we could all get paid $1 for each item we forgot, we would be wealthy. To measure the rate at which information is forgotten, Ebbinghaus (1885/1913) tested his own memory for nonsense syllables after intervals ranging from 20 minutes to 31 days. As shown in the **forgetting curve** plotted in Figure 6.18, Ebbinghaus found that there was a steep loss of retention within the first hour, that he forgot more than 60 percent of the items within 9 hours, and that the rate of forgetting leveled off after that. How quickly we forget.

The Ebbinghaus forgetting curve shows a rapid loss of memory for meaningless nonsense syllables. Does it apply to real-life memories as well? Bahrick (1984) tested nearly 800 English-speaking adults who took Spanish in high school. Depending on the subject, the interval between learning and being tested ranged from 0 to 50 years. Compared to students who had just taken the course, those who were tested two to three years later had forgotten much of what they learned. After that, however, scores on vocabulary, grammar, and reading-comprehension tests stabilized—even among people who had not used Spanish for 40 or 50 years (illustrated in Figure 6.19). A similar pattern was also found for the retention, for up to 12 years, of material learned in a college psychology course (Conway, Cohen, & Stanhope, 1991). In one study, Dutch researchers found that people remembered the street names from their elementary school neighborhoods up to 71 years later (Schmidt, Peeck, Paas, & van Breukelen, 2000). These kinds of impressive results have led Bahrick to argue that such knowledge may enter a *permastore*—a term he coined to describe permanent, very-long-term memory for well-learned material.

It's interesting that although this very-long-term curve is not identical to that reported by Ebbinghaus, there are similarities. Based on a summary analysis of 210 post-Ebbinghaus studies, David Rubin and Amy Wenzel (1996) concluded that his classic forgetting curve describes a consistent

forgetting curve. A consistent pattern in which the rate of memory loss for input is steepest right after input is received and levels off over time.

TABLE 6.2 ■ Forgetting in Everyday Life

How's your memory? Read the statements below and think about how often you've had each experience.

The numbers in parentheses are the ratings given by the average person.

___ 1. Forgetting where you have put something; losing things around the house (5)

___ 2. Having to go back to check whether you have done something that you meant to do (4)

___ 3. Failing to recognize, by sight, close relatives or friends that you meet frequently (1)

___ 4. Telling friends a story or joke that you have told them once already (2)

___ 5. Forgetting where things are normally kept, or looking for them in the wrong place (2)

___ 6. Finding that a word is on the "tip of your tongue"; you know what it is but cannot quite find it (4)

___ 7. Forgetting important details of what you did or what happened to you the day before (1)

___ 8. Forgetting important details about yourself, such as your birthday or where you live (1)

___ 9. Completely forgetting to take things with you, or leaving things behind and having to go back and fetch them (3)

___ 10. Finding that the faces of famous people, seen on TV or in photographs, look unfamiliar (2)

Note: Subjects responded on the following scale: 1 = never in the last six months, 2 = once in six months, 4 = once a month, 5 = more than once a month,... 9 = more than once a day.

FIGURE 6.18 ■ The Ebbinghaus Forgetting Curve

Ebbinghaus's forgetting curve indicates the rate at which nonsense syllables were forgotten. You can see that there was a steep decline in performance within the first day and that the rate of forgetting leveled off over time.

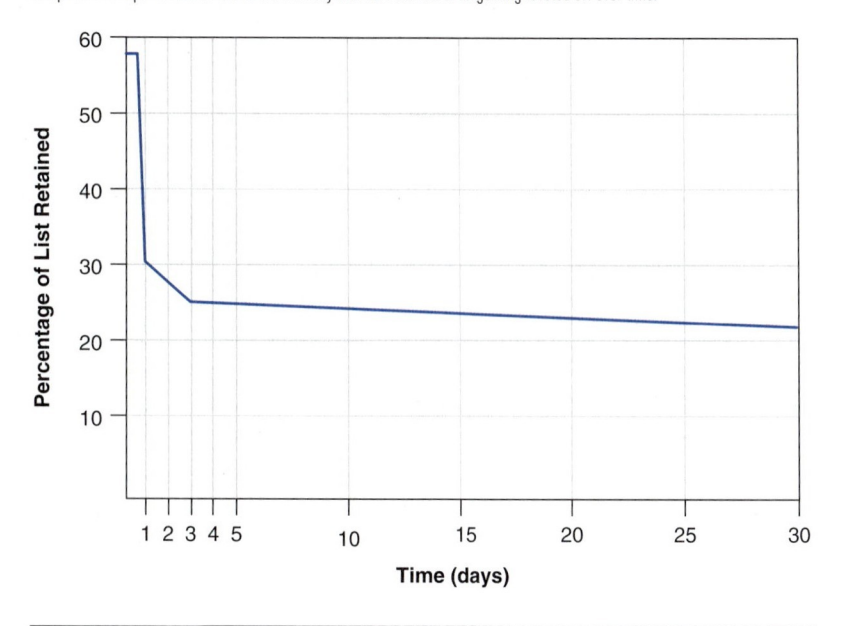

Sources: Adapted from Ebbinghaus (1897, 1908).

FIGURE 6.19 ■ Long-Term Forgetting Curve

This forgetting curve indicates the rate at which adults forgot the Spanish they took in high school. Compared to new graduates, those tested two to three years later forgot much of what they learned. After that, however, test scores stabilized.

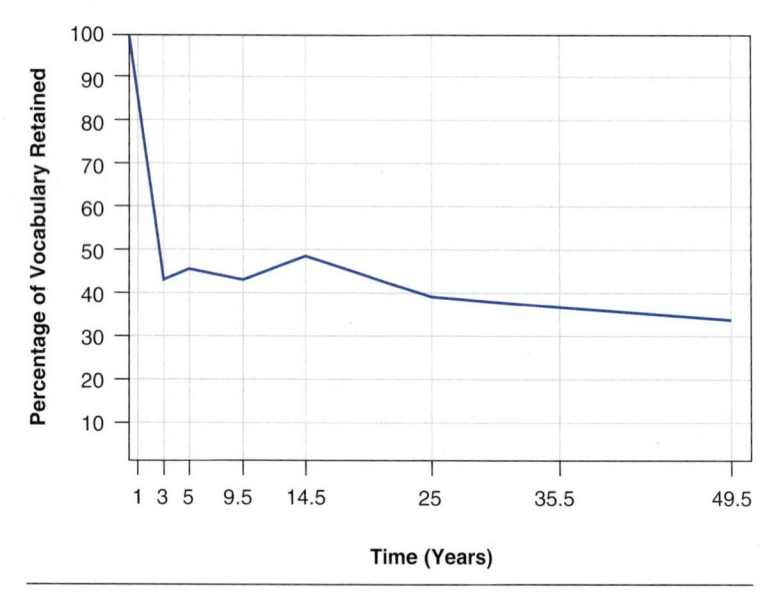

Source: Bahrick, H. P. (1984). Semantic memory content in permastore: Fifty years of memory for Spanish learned in school. *Journal of Experimental Psychology: General, 113*(1), 1–29.

and lawful pattern of human retention and forgetting. They also raise the possibility that we may have several long-term memory stores corresponding to different periods of time (Rubin, Hinton, & Wenzel, 1999).

What's Your Prediction?

Do you remember the study discussed earlier about the college students who used encoding strategies to increase their recalled digit span from 7 items to 80? Dario Donatelli was one of the students in this famous experiment, and 30 years later, Donatelli was assessed again for how many digits he could remember (Yoon, Ericsson, & Donatelli, 2018). Make a prediction about how many digits Donatelli could remember on the first try. Now, reflect on why you chose that number. Next, make a prediction about how many digits he could recall after three days of practice. Again, reflect on why you chose that number. The results? On the first day of testing, he could recall 10 digits but on the third day of testing, Donatelli could recall 19 digits. Not bad, considering that the typical number of items we can retain in working memory is seven plus or minus two! What encoding strategies did he use as a 50-something-year-old participant? Donatelli used chunking and rehearsal, just as he was taught to use as a 20-something-year-old participant. Donatelli demonstrated "retention of different aspects of exceptional memory skill" (Yoon et al., 2018, p. 895) but wasn't even close to his former glory of 80 digits. The published study, which included Donatelli as an author (Yoon et al., 2018), paid homage to Ebbinghaus by stating that Donatelli's results support the learning curve: as expected, "acquired memory associations decrease[d] over the time of disuse" (p. 898). Without consistent practice, the exceptional memory skills that Donatelli learned 30 years earlier were no longer refined.

Why Do People Forget?

Knowing the rate at which information is lost is just the first step. The next important question is: Why? Do memory traces fade with time? Are they displaced by newer memories? Or do memories get buried, perhaps blocked by unconscious forces? As we'll see, forgetting can result from one of four processes: a lack of encoding, decay, interference, or repression. In the first two, the forgotten information is simply not in long-term-memory storage. In the second two, the memory may exist, but it is difficult, if not impossible, to retrieve.

FIGURE 6.20 ■ Can You Recognize a Penny?

Which of these pennies is the real thing? The answer appears later in the chapter.

Source: Raymond S. Nickerson, Marilyn Jager Adams, Long-term memory for a common object, Cognitive Psychology, Volume 11, Issue 3, 1979, Pages 287-307.

Lack of Encoding. Do you know what an American penny looks like? Would you recognize one if you saw it? If you were born in the United States, you have looked at, held, and counted thousands of pennies in your life. Yet many people cannot accurately draw one from memory, name its features, or distinguish between a real penny and a fake. Look at the coins in Figure 6.20. Do you know which is the real one? Raymond Nickerson and Marilyn Adams (1979) presented this task to college students and found that 58 percent did *not* identify the right coin. The reason for this result is not that the subjects forgot what a penny looks like—it's that the features were never encoded into long-term memory in the first place. And why should they be? So long as you can tell the difference between pennies and other coins, there is no need to attend to the fine details. The penny is not the only common, everyday object whose features we fail to notice. People also have difficulty recalling the features of a dollar bill, a computer keyboard, and the letters associated with each number on a phone keypad—objects we look at and use all the time (Rinck, 1999).

When it comes to encoding information, people can be so profoundly absent-minded that they exhibit "change blindness," a failure to detect changes that take place in their presence. In an astonishing demonstration of this phenomenon, Daniel Simons and Daniel Levin (1998) had a research assistant approach people on a college campus and ask for directions. While they were talking, two men walked between them holding a door that concealed a second assistant. With the subject screened from view, the two assistants switched places so that when the men carrying the door passed, subjects found themselves talking to a different person. Did subjects notice the switch? Would *you* have noticed it? Remarkably, out of 15 subjects who were tested, only 7 noticed the change. Other studies, too, have shown this type of visual forgetting from a lack of attention (Simons, 2000), which is why some researchers refer to this phenomenon as "inattentional blindness."

Decay. The oldest theory of forgetting is that memory traces erode with the passage of time. But there are two problems with this simple explanation. One is that there is no physiological evidence of decay that corresponds to the fading of memory. The second is that time alone is not the most critical factor. As we saw earlier, memory for newly learned nonsense syllables fades in a matter of hours, but a foreign language learned in high school is retained for many years.

The key blow to the decay theory of forgetting was landed in 1924 by John Jenkins and Karl Dallenbach. Day after day, these researchers presented nonsense syllables to two subjects and then tested their memory after 1, 2, 4, or 8 hours. On some days, the subjects went to sleep between learning and testing; on other days, they stayed awake and kept busy. The subjects recalled more items after they had slept than when they were awake and involved in other activities. Jenkins and Dallenbach (1924) concluded that "forgetting is not so much a matter of the decay of old impressions and associations as it is a matter of interference, inhibition, or obliteration of the old by the new" (p. 612). To minimize forgetting, students may find it helpful to go to sleep shortly after studying, thus avoiding "new information" (Fowler, Sullivan, & Ekstrand, 1973).

The correctly drawn penny is shown in (A).

Interference. By showing that memory loss may be caused by mental activity that takes place when we are awake, Jenkins and Dallenbach's study suggested a third explanation of forgetting—that something learned may be forgotten due to interference from other information. As summarized in Figure 6.21, there are two kinds of interference. In **proactive interference**, prior information inhibits our ability to recall something new. If you try to learn a set of names, formulas, phone numbers, or glossary terms, you will find it more difficult if you had earlier studied a similar set of items. Many years ago, Underwood (1957) found that the more nonsense-syllable experiments subjects had taken part in, the more forgetting they exhibited in a brand new study.

A related problem is **retroactive interference**, whereby new material disrupts memory for previously learned information. Thus, subjects in various experiments are at least temporarily less likely to recognize previously seen pictures of nature scenes, faces, and common objects if they are then exposed to similar photographs before being tested (Chandler, 1991; Wheeler, 1995; Windschitl, 1996). One learning experience can displace—or at least inhibit—the retrieval of another. That is why Mercer (2014) and Schlichting and Bäuml (2017) suggest people take a break before participating in a task that could interfere with newly learned material. In Mercer's (2014) study, English-speaking individuals trying to learn

---

proactive interference. The tendency for previously learned material to disrupt the recall of new information.

retroactive interference. The tendency for new information to disrupt the memory of previously learned material.

FIGURE 6.21 ■ Interference and Forgetting

Filling out forms can reveal real-world interference issues. As shown in this student loan application example, proactive interference occurs when older information—your previous address—inhibits memory for newer information—your new address. You might forget your new address where you live now but remember your old address with ease. Retroactive interference occurs when newer information inhibits memory for older information. This would prevent you from remembering your past address of five years, but remembering your new address is effortless. The more similar the two sets of items are, the greater is the interference.

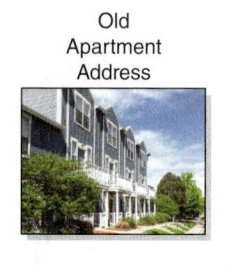

iStock.com/YinYang; iStock.com/georgeclerk

Icelandic words were given or not given the opportunity to take such a break. Those who did take a break had a reduced chance of forgetting the words, compared to those who did not. Schlichting and Bäuml (2017) found similar results in memory performance for people who spent some "passive" time with neutral stimuli—music and pictures—after learning. This type of forgetting is biologically supported in animal models by the previously discussed Cai and colleagues (2016) research on CA 1 neurons.

Repression. More than 100 years ago, Sigmund Freud, the founder of psychoanalysis, observed that his patients often could not recall unpleasant past events from their own lives. In fact, he observed, they would sometimes stop, pull back, and lose their train of thought just as they seemed on the brink of an insight. Freud called this repression, and he said it was an unconscious defense mechanism that keeps painful personal memories under lock and key—and out of awareness. When we discuss psychological disorders, we will learn that people who suffer childhood traumas such as war, abuse, and rape sometimes develop *dissociative disorders* characterized by apparent gaps in explicit memory. Repression has never been demonstrated in a laboratory setting, but psychotherapy case studies suggest that memories can be repressed for long periods of time and recovered in therapy. As we'll learn later in this chapter, however, it is difficult in actual cases to distinguish between dormant memories of true events and falsely constructed memories of experiences that never occurred (Baioui, Ambach,

Walter, & Vaitl, 2012; Loftus, 1993a; Read & Lindsay, 1997). Although Baioui and colleagues (2012) found that false memories can be detected with physiological feedback via skin conductance recordings, the findings should be considered with caution, especially given that similar physiological measurements to help differentiate between true and false statements—such as a lie detector test—have failed in the past.

> **LEARNING CHECK**
>
> **Forget Me Knots**
>
> Let's see what you remember about forgetting. Match each phenomenon in the left column with the cause or description most closely associated with it.
>
> 1. The tendency for previously learned material to disrupt the recall of new information.
> 2. The reason we often cannot accurately recall an object we see all the time.
> 3. The inability to retrieve long-term memories from the past.
> 4. The steep loss of retention of input shortly after the input is received.
> 5. The inability to recall traumatic past events from one's own life.
> 6. The inability to store new information in long-term memory.
> 7. The tendency for new information to disrupt one's memory of previously learned material.
>
> a. forgetting curve
> b. lack of encoding
> c. retroactive interference
> d. proactive interference
> e. retrograde amnesia
> f. anterograde amnesia
> g. repression
>
> (Answers: 1. d; 2. b; 3. e; 4. a; 5. g; 6. f; 7. c.)

schemas. In Piaget's theory, mental representations of the world that guide the processes of assimilation and accommodation.

Yanjaa Wintersoul is a Mongolian-Swedish memory athlete. As one of the world's best, Yanjaa has frequently demonstrated her memory prowess for large audiences. One demonstration was for the furniture company Ikea. In the span of one week, Yanjaa memorized all 328 pages of the Ikea catalogue, down to the color of the model's glasses and names of the books on the shelves!
AP Photo/Albin Lohr-Jones

Reconstruction

Up to now, we have likened human memory to a computer that faithfully encodes, stores, and retrieves information from the recent and distant past. Clearly, however, there is more to the story. As we'll see, remembering is an active process in which we reconstruct memories according to our beliefs, wishes, needs, and information received from outside sources.

In 1932, Frederick Bartlett asked British college students to recall a story taken from the folklore of a Native American culture. He found that although they correctly recalled the gist of this story, they changed, exaggerated, added, and omitted certain details—resulting in a narrative that was more coherent to them. Without realizing it, subjects reconstructed the material to fit their own **schemas**, a term that Bartlett used to describe the preconceptions that people have about persons and situations. Other researchers have replicated this result more recently using the same Native American story (Bergman & Roediger, 1999) and lists of words (Roediger, Meade, Gallo, & Olson, 2014).

It's now clear that schemas distort memory, often by leading us to fill in missing pieces. Research by Helene Intraub and others (1998) illustrates the point. In a series of studies, they showed people close-up photographs of various scenes—such as a telephone booth on a street corner, a basketball on a gym floor, and a lawn chair on a grassy field. Consistently, subjects who were later asked to recall these scenes mentally extended the borders by reporting or drawing details that were not in the pictures but might plausibly have existed outside the camera's field of view (illustrated in Figure 6.22). Why? It appears that the scenes activated perceptual schemas that led subjects over time to insert new details into memory.

FIGURE 6.22 ■ Perceptual Schemas

If you showed this image to a participant, what would they draw when you asked them to recreate it? According to Intraub and others, scenes like this one activate perceptual schemas into which people fill in missing details.

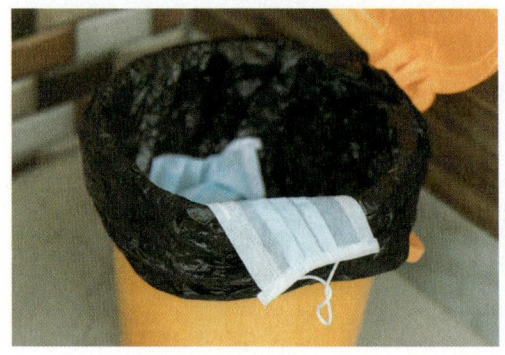

Source: Intraub, H., Gottesman, C. V., & Bills, A. J. (1998). Effects of perceiving and imagining scenes on memory for pictures. Journal of Experimental Psychology: Learning, Memory, and Cognition, 24(1), 186–201. https://doi.org/10.1037/0278-7393.24.1.186

iStock.com/lakshmiprasad S

There are many other examples of how schemas influence memory. In one study, subjects were left waiting alone in a small cluttered room that the experimenter called an "office." After 35 seconds, subjects were taken out and asked to recall what was in the room. What happened? Nearly everyone remembered the desk, chair, and shelves, objects typically found in an office. But many of the subjects also mistakenly recalled seeing books—items that fit the setting but were not actually present (Brewer & Treyens, 1981). Our schemas are sometimes so strong that an object that does not belong becomes particularly memorable. After spending time in an office, people are more likely to remember the presence of toy trucks, blocks, and finger paints than of textbooks, a laptop, and a coffee mug. But they are also more likely to imagine the existence of office objects that fit the setting but were not present (Lampinen, Copeland, & Neuschatz, 2001; Pezdek, Whetstone, Reynolds, Askari, & Dougherty, 1989). Neuroscientists have wondered what parts of the brain are activated when people are tasked to reconstruct a memory using schemas (Kurkela & Dennis, 2016). Webb and colleagues (2016) found that the visual cortex and hippocampus were more active during schematic recollection.

The Misinformation Effect

Memory is an active construction of the past—a construction that alters reality in ways that are consistent not only with prior expectations but also with postevent information. Consider the plight of those who witness crimes. Afterward, they talk to each other, read about it on Twitter, and sometimes even watch coverage via social media. By the time these witnesses are questioned by authorities, one wonders if their original memory is still "pure," uncontaminated by postevent information. How good are people at preventing postevent contamination? How can a person be a good eyewitness to a crime?

According to Elizabeth Loftus (1979), for most eyewitnesses, their memories are probably contaminated. Using her studies of eyewitness testimony, Loftus proposed a theory of reconstructive memory. After people observe an event, she said, later information about the event—whether it's true or not—becomes integrated into the fabric of their memory.

A classic study by Loftus and colleagues (1978) illustrates what has been called the **misinformation effect**. In that study, they presented subjects with a slide show in which a red car hits a pedestrian after turning at an intersection. Subjects saw either a STOP sign or a YIELD sign in the slides (illustrated in Figure 6.23), but then embedded in a series of questions they were asked was one that implied the presence of the other sign ("Did another car pass the Datsun as it reached the ___ sign?"). The result: The number of subjects who later "recognized" the slide with the wrong traffic sign increased from 25 percent to 59 percent. Other studies soon confirmed the effect. Researchers thus misled subjects into

misinformation effect. The tendency to incorporate false postevent information into one's memory of the event itself.

FIGURE 6.23 ■ Misinformation Effect

Subjects saw a slide show in which a car turns at a corner that has either a STOP sign or a YIELD sign. Illustrating the misinformation effect, subjects who were later asked questions that implied the presence of the other sign were more likely to "recognize" the wrong slide.

iStock.com/Brilt; iStock.com/Brilt

recalling hammers as screwdrivers, Coke cans as cans of peanuts, breakfast cereal as eggs, green objects as yellow, a clean-shaven man as having a mustache, and a bare-handed man as wearing gloves. To make matters worse, these subjects are often quick to respond and confident in the accuracy of these false memories (Loftus, Donders, Hoffman, & Schooler, 1989).

This provocative theory has aroused controversy. Does misinformation permanently impair a witness's real memory, never to be retrieved again (Belli, Lindsay, Gales, & McCarthy, 1994; Weingardt, Loftus, & Lindsay, 1995)? Or do subjects merely follow the experimenter's "suggestion," leaving a true memory intact for retrieval under other conditions (Dodson & Reisberg, 1991; McCloskey & Zaragoza, 1985)? Either way, an important practical lesson remains: Whether witnesses' memories are truly altered or not, their reports of what they remember are at risk for bias by postevent information. But research by Hoscheidt and colleagues (2014) gives us hope. This group of psychologists randomly assigned participants to either a stressful and negative situation, or a control and negative situation, and then measured their memory performance. Participants under stress had significantly better memory performance than control subjects. Specifically, participants who reported high arousal during the stressful condition were less likely to endorse false information.

Does this mean that if you are subjected to high levels of stress during an aversive event, your memory is protected from misinformation? Not necessarily. Other research on stress and the misinformation effect has produced findings in the opposite direction (Moran, Southwick, Steffian, Hazlett, & Loftus, 2013). Why the inconsistencies? Shields and colleagues (2017) desired to complete a thorough review to provide an answer. Their conclusion was that the timing and context of the lab-induced stress affected whether or not memory was helped or hindered. For example, in studies where stress occurred during retrieval, memory was hindered. If the study tasks were directly related to the stressor, and there was not much of a delay between the stressor and encoding, memory was helped. Furthermore, hormonal contraceptives seemed to play a protective role in women's memory performance when under stress.

This review by Shields and colleagues (2017) suggests that many factors influence the role stress plays in encoding and retrieval. Mind you, these participants were stressed and exposed to negative stimuli in a laboratory setting. They were not victims of a crime. Cases like that of Ronald Cotton and Jennifer Thompson provide clear examples of memory gone awry due to postevent information. Jennifer falsely identified Ronald as her rapist from a series of photographs and a lineup, even though she purposefully focused her attention on her rapist's face and characteristics during the assault (Innocence Project, 2017). When presented in court with the face of her actual rapist, Bobby Poole, Jennifer still misidentified Ronald as her rapist. She also believed she had never seen Bobby before. DNA evidence exonerated Ronald Cotton 10 years later, and Bobby Poole was convicted of the rape, demonstrating that the misinformation effect is real, is not perfectly protected by stress, and can have devastating results.

The Creation of Illusory Memories

The misinformation effect led cognitive psychologists to discover that people sometimes create memories that are completely false. At the start of this chapter, we learned that people who heard a list of sleep-related words (e.g., *bed, yawn*) or music-related words (e.g., *jazz, instrument*) were often convinced just minutes later that they had also heard *sleep* and *music*—words that fit their schemas but were not actually on the lists (Roediger & McDermott, 1995). But recalling words from a list is a low-stakes issue. What about planting false memories like one can plant false evidence? Strange and colleagues (2008), Wade and colleagues (2002), and Conway (2013) presented experimental evidence of how easy it can be to mislead adults about their own childhood experiences. In almost 40 percent of participants in the Strange and colleagues (2008) study, false childhood memories were successfully implanted.

This result is easy to find—for studies using false personal events before age 10 (Brewin & Andrews, 2017). Brewin and Andrews argue that experiments on the implantation of false personal memories are therefore somewhat problematic. Overall, the experiments are homogeneous, tend to be about personal experiences (e.g., your eighth birthday), and rest on plausibility (such as the likelihood of the event), who says the event occurred (an experimenter, or your mother), or proof of the event (some experiments have provided a photo of the false memory). Is it fair to argue that illusory memories are easy to implant when the phenomenon has not been thoroughly studied for nonpersonal events across a wider range of ages and when fake evidence in support of the false memory is provided? We know that presenting people with fake evidence can even mislead people to confess to a crime they know they did not commit. Thus, is fake evidence from a deeply trusted source a fair addition to illusory memory studies? Brewin and Andrews (2017) review suggests that even with such compelling evidence, only a minority of participants seem to be fooled into believing the false childhood memories are true, and the size of the effects is small. Regardless, we'll learn that these studies are unsettling for what they imply about the memories of childhood abuse that adults sometimes "recover" while in therapy.

Even as adults, our childhood memories aren't immune to false implants.
iStock.com/michellegibson

AUTOBIOGRAPHICAL MEMORY

> ### LEARNING OBJECTIVES
>
> Consider the research on autobiographical memory and apply it to your own life.
>
> - Determine why our memories for even the most personal events are at risk.
> - Describe the variables that makes some experiences particularly vivid and enduring.
> - Define childhood amnesia, and tell why it occurs.

Personal experience memories aren't just at risk when fake evidence is presented. Suppose you were to sit down to write about your personal experiences. What would you say? What stands out in your mind? Would your reports of the past be accurate or distorted in some way? To answer these kinds of questions, psychologist Marigold Linton (1982) kept an extensive diary and later used it to test her memory for the events of her life. Every day for six years, she wrote the date on one side of an index card and a description of something that happened to her. In all, the diary contained 5,000 entries—some important, others trivial. Once a month, Linton pulled 150 cards at random from her file and tried to recall the events and date them correctly. Like Ebbinghaus, she found that as time passed, her personal memories took longer to recall, were harder to date, and were less detailed—but that, right from the start, this fading occurred at a slower rate. More recently, two psychologists kept personal diaries for seven months and were then tested by colleagues who asked about events that were in the diaries and nonevents that seemed plausible

autobiographical memory. The recollections people have of their own personal experiences and observations.

but did not occur. The subjects knew in advance that items would be fabricated for the test, yet they still made several false recollections (Conway, Collins, Gatheicole, & Anderson, 1996).

Many cognitive psychologists have recently traded in their nonsense syllables to study **autobiographical memory**—the recollections people have of the events and experiences that have touched their lives (Koppel & Bernsten, 2014; Lemesle, Planton, Pagès, & Pariente, 2017; Söderlund et al., 2014). There are two key questions about these memories: (a) What aspects of our own past do we tend to preserve—and what are we likely to forget? (b) Are we generally accurate in our mental time travel, or does memory alter as we age or experience neurological changes?

What Events Do People Remember?

When people are prompted to recall their own experiences, they typically report more events that are recent than are from the distant past. There are two consistent exceptions to this rule. The first is that older adults retrieve an unusually large number of personal memories from their adolescence and early adulthood years (Fitzgerald, 1988; Jansari & Parkin, 1996; Steiner, Pillemer, Thomsen, & Minigan, 2013; Westerhof & Bohlmeijer, 2014). This "reminiscence peak" may occur because these early years are busy and formative in one's life. William Mackavey et al. (1991) analyzed the autobiographies written by 49 eminent psychologists and found that their most important life experiences tended to be concentrated between the ages of 18 and 35.

A second exception to the recency rule is that people are quick to remember transitional "firsts." Think about your college career. What events immediately pop to mind—and when did these events occur? Did you come up with the day you arrived on campus or the first time you met your closest friend? What about notable classes, exams, parties, or sports events? When David Pillemer and his colleagues (1996) asked college juniors and seniors to recount the most memorable experiences of their first year, 32 percent of all recollections were from the transitional month of September. And when graduated college alumni were given the same task, they too cited a disproportionate number of events from the opening two months of their first year—followed, interestingly, by the next major transitional period, the last month of their senior year (illustrated in Figure 6.24).

Obviously, not all experiences leave the same impression, and some dates are etched in memory for a lifetime. What information will most likely be remembered is influenced by a number of factors. One factor is gender (Grysman, Fivush, Merrill, & Graci, 2016; Grysman & Hudson, 2013; Nahari & Pazuelo, 2015). For example, women use more details when describing events (Grysman et al., 2016; Nahari & Pazuelo, 2015), remember more basic facts (Grysman et al., 2016), and have a better memory for emotional content (Bohanek & Fivush, 2010) than men. Why does this difference exist? The socialization hypothesis emphasizes that the gender roles and stereotypes one is raised with contributes to how autobiographical memory skills develop. The female role accentuates relationships, and the male role accentuates personal success and strength (Grysman & Hudson, 2013). With such an emphasis on others, it is possible that those who identify as females—and those who score high on feminine gender identity—simply learn to better encode information that seems to be relevant to the interaction and not just themselves. Compère and colleagues (2018) tested this hypothesis and found that gender identity—not biological sex—was the better predictor of autobiographical memory performance. This supports Grysman and Hudson's (2013) suggestion that using the male and female binary variable when measuring memory performance is not the best practice.

Another factor in memory longevity is the uniqueness of the event. Linton (1982) found that unique events were easy to recall but that routines were quickly forgotten. Among college students, Rubin and Kozin (1986) found that some of the clearest memories were births, deaths, weddings, accidents, injuries, sports events, romantic encounters, vacations, and graduations. Schrauf and Rubin (2001) had older Latinx adults narrate their life stories and found that they produced the most recollections from the ages at which they left home and immigrated to the United States. Clearly, special events serve as autobiographical landmarks—reference points that we use to organize our personal memories (Shum, 1998).

Some events in our lives are so vivid that they seem to occupy a particularly special status in memory. For instance, think about where you were when the announcement was made that Donald

FIGURE 6.24 ■ Memorable Transitions

College graduates of varying ages were asked to recount their most memorable experiences while in college. You can see that among the memories that could be pinpointed in time, there was a large number from the first two months of their first year and a large number from the other major transitional period—the last month of their senior year.

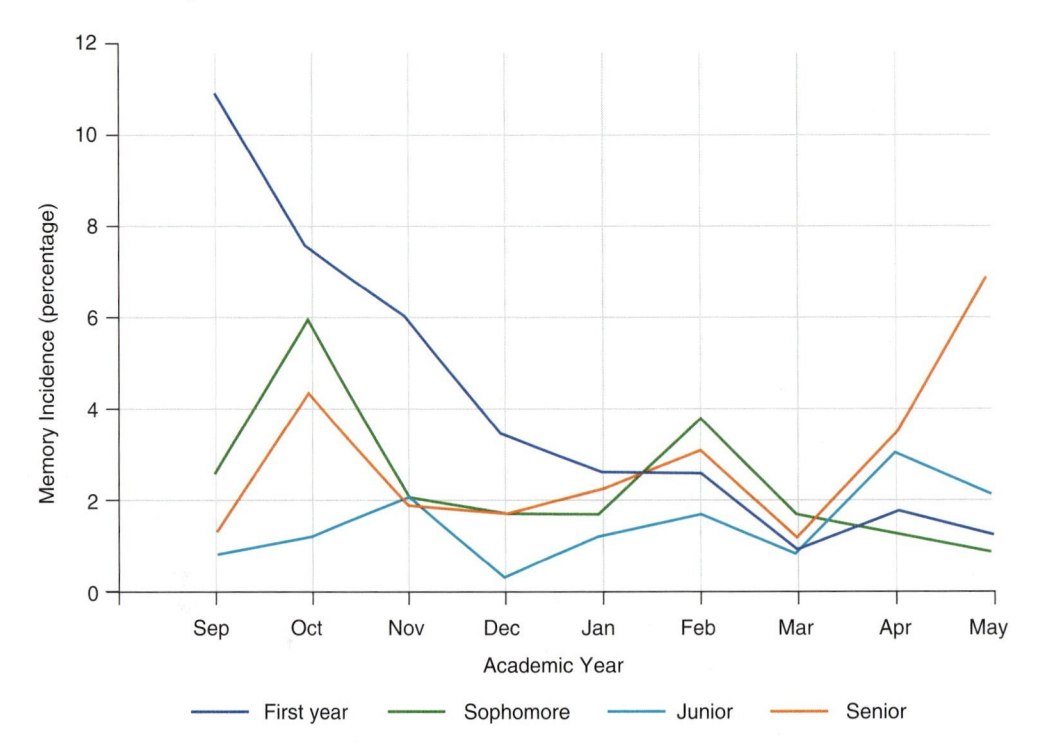

Source: Adapted from Pillemer, D., Picariello, M., Law, A., & Reichman, J. (1996). Memories of college: The importance of specific educational episodes. In D. Rubin (Ed.), Remembering our Past: Studies in Autobiographical Memory (pp. 318-338). Cambridge: Cambridge University Press. https://doi.org/10.1017/CBO9780511527913.013

Trump was elected president. Hirst (2016) believes that no matter your political leanings, the Trump election most likely resulted in a flashbulb memory. Brown and Kulik (1977) coined the term **flashbulb memories** to describe enduring, detailed, "high-resolution" recollections and speculated that humans are biologically equipped for survival purposes to "print" the most dramatic events in memory (as you may recall, physiological arousal releases hormones that can enhance memory). Since the coining of the term, research has demonstrated that flashbulb memories are not as perfect as once believed. In 2009, a group of 17 memory researchers published a study about those who had flashbulb memories of 9/11 (Hirst et al., 2009). The participants were tested for their recollection of events on three separate occasions—one week, 11 months, or 35 months after the attack. The results demonstrated that memories were not consistently clear, as a decline in accuracy occurred. Memory for emotional reactions suffered the most. However, the decline in memory accuracy began to stabilize after one year. What did remain fairly consistent between recollection assessments were confidence levels. This finding supported work completed by Talarico and Rubin (2007) that argues that flashbulb memories are not incredibly accurate, but those who have them report incredible confidence in those memories, nonetheless.

Although flashbulb memories aren't perfect, those events aren't completely lost to us. On the contrary, there is a period of life that does seem entirely lost. Think back to your earliest memory. It probably was not the sight of the doctor's hands in the delivery room, or the first time you waved, or even the first step you took as a toddler. An intriguing aspect of autobiographical memory is that most people generally cannot recall anything that happened before the age of 3 years (Dudycha & Dudycha, 1941; Rubin, 1996). In one study, for example, Pillemer and others (1994) interviewed preadolescent children about a fire drill evacuation they had experienced in preschool. Those who were 4 and 5 years old when

flashbulb memories. Highly vivid and enduring memories, typically for events that are dramatic and emotional.

childhood amnesia. The inability of most people to recall events from before the age of 3 or 4.

the incident occurred were able to recall it 7 years later; those who were 3 at the time could not. This memory gap, which is common, is known as **childhood amnesia**.

Why should this be? One possibility is that the forgetting is caused by the passage of time and by interference from later experiences. The problem with this explanation is that a college student may be unable to recall events from 18 years ago, but 35-year-olds can easily recall their college days after the same amount of time. Other explanations include the notions that young children lack the conceptual framework or self-concept for organizing information to be stored (Howe & Courage, 1993); that young children aren't good at correctly reporting how long ago a memory occurred, which thus biases the data (Wang & Peterson, 2014); and that the development of autobiographical memory is influenced by social factors—such as the extent to which parents reminisce about the past with their young children (Bauer & Larkina, 2014).

Do early memories exist? It's hard to say. Some researchers have found that adults can recall certain critical events—moving, the birth of a sibling, being hospitalized, and the death of a family member—from the age of 2 years, suggesting that there are exceptions to the rule (Usher & Neisser, 1993). Others caution that these reports may not be based on firsthand memories but, rather, on stories told by parents, photographs, and other external sources (Eacott & Crawley, 1998; Loftus, 1993b). Still others maintain that people may have partial, implicit memories of the early years. One way to trigger these implicit memories is through music (Janata, Tomic, & Rakowski, 2007; Krumhansl & Zupnick, 2013). Janata and colleagues (2007) exposed college students to top Billboard hits that were popular from 1955 to 2009, to cover both the songs their parents most likely played and the songs the college students heard during their own lifetimes. Songs that were recognizable, liked, and ignited happy and energetic feelings were correlated with autobiographical memory recall (illustrated in Figure 6.25).

FIGURE 6.25 ■ Classic Song Recognition

Do you recognize, or have fondness for, classic songs from your caregivers' era that bring back thoughts of home? Interestingly, for college-age listeners, there are two eras—the late 1960s and the early 1980s—for songs that are recognizable, liked, and autobiographical.

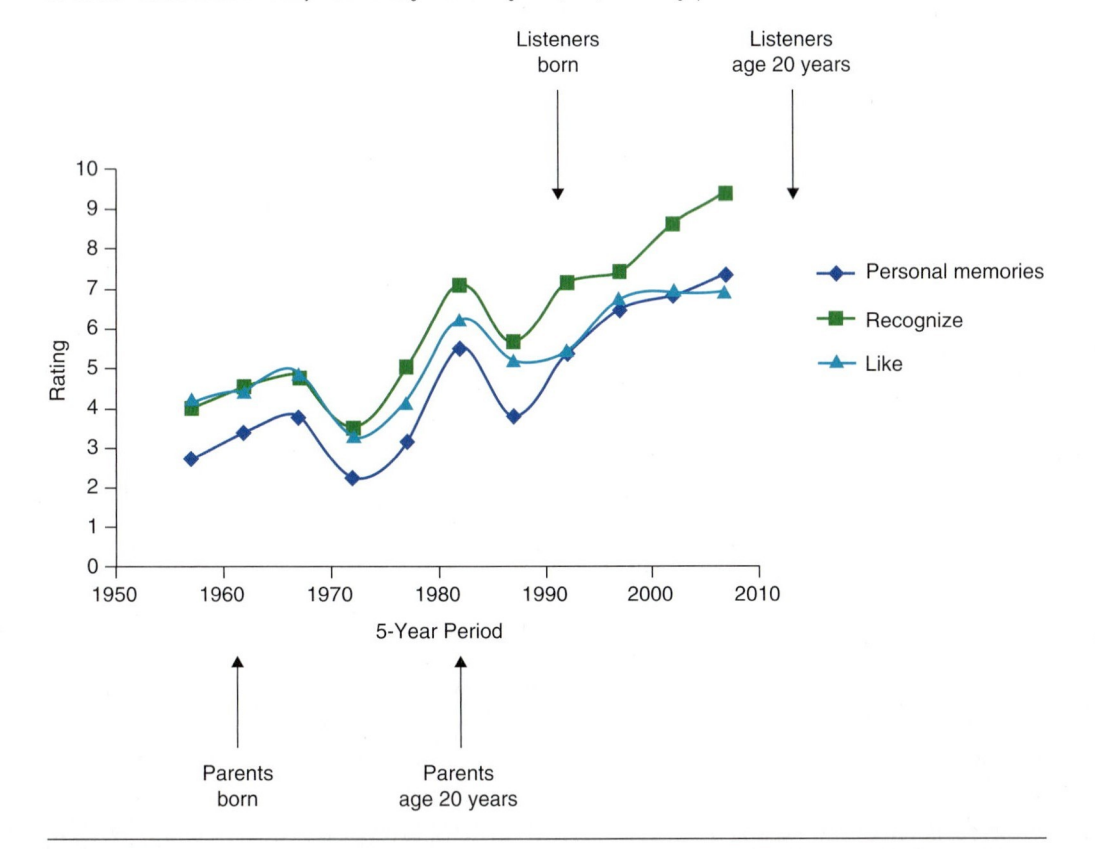

Source: Krumhansl CL, Zupnick JA. Cascading Reminiscence Bumps in Popular Music. Psychological Science. 2013;24(10):2057-2068. doi:10.1177/0956797613486486

Older songs had a tendency to spark nostalgia. As stated by Krumhansl and Zupnick (2013), "music heard during childhood, likely reflecting the tastes of previous generations, would make a lasting impression on children's autobiographical memories, preferences and emotional responses" (p. 2067). The next time you are in the car, turn your radio to the classic rock station and see if any of the notes or lyrics you hear light up a fond childhood memory.

Thinking Like a Psychologist About Memory

Human memory is often a subject of controversy. In this chapter, we've seen that people can accurately recall faces, names, music lyrics, skills such as riding a bike, high-impact world events, and personal experiences that stretch deep into their past. Cognitive psychologists have thus likened the human mind to a computer in which information is encoded, stored, and retrieved faithfully on demand. Within this model, researchers have sought to trace the flow of information as it is processed, and in doing so they have distinguished among fleeting sensory memory, short-term working memory, and the somewhat permanent storage systems of long-term memory.

At the same time that cognitive psychologists marveled at our information-processing capacities, they also found that our memory is limited, flawed, and biased—as when we forget a phone number we just looked up or misidentify an innocent person as the criminal in a lineup. What's more, it's now clear that memory is an active and constructive process—and that we sometimes unwittingly develop "memories" that are completely false, often to feel better or boost our self-esteem. Our gender identity also contributes to what we do and do not remember. Those who identify as female—and those who score high on feminine gender identity—are better at encoding information that is important to their interactions with others. Individual differences affect our attention. Therefore, we must keep in mind that human memory is not perfect. Commenting on this two-headed portrait of human memory as simultaneously competent and flawed, Schacter (1996) reminds us that "the computer is a retriever of information but not a rememberer of experiences" (p. 37).

SUMMARY

AN INFORMATION-PROCESSING MODEL

Cognitive psychologists view **memory** as an **information-processing** system. **Sensory memory** stores sensations for a brief moment. Those that draw attention are transferred to **short-term memory (STM)**, and those that are further encoded are stored in **long-term memory (LTM)**.

THE SENSORY REGISTER

The sensory register is the first step in the information-processing system.

Iconic Memory
The visual system stores images called icons in **iconic memory**. Using the partial-report technique, Sperling found that many items initially register in consciousness but that most last for only a fraction of a second before fading.

Echoic Memory
The auditory system stores sounds in **echoic memory**. Echoic memory holds only a few items but lasts 2 or 3 seconds, sometimes longer.

SHORT-TERM MEMORY

Sensations that do not capture attention fade quickly, but those we notice are encoded (in visual, acoustic, or semantic terms) and transferred to short-term memory. People usually encode information in acoustic terms.

Capacity

Using a memory-span task, researchers found that short-term memory has a limited capacity. People can store seven items, plus or minus two. STM can be used more efficiently, however, if we group items into larger chunks, called **chunking**.

Duration

STM is also limited in the length of time it can hold information. Studies show that items are held in STM for up to 20 seconds. Through repetition or **maintenance rehearsal**, however, input can be held for an indefinite period of time.

Functions of Short-Term Memory

STM contains new sensory input and material from long-term memory. The limits of STM are adaptive, enabling us to discard information that is no longer useful. STM is not just a passive storage depot but an active workspace referred to as **working memory**. When people memorize a list of items, they exhibit the **serial-position curve**, whereby items from the beginning and end are recalled better than those in the middle.

LONG-TERM MEMORY

LTM is a relatively enduring storage system that can hold vast amounts of information for long periods of time.

Encoding

To transfer input to LTM, it is best to use **elaborative rehearsal**—specifically, engaging in "deep" processing and associating the input with information already in LTM. Retention is also increased through overlearning (continued rehearsal after the material is mastered) and through practice spaced over time rather than crammed in all at once.

Storage

In LTM, information may be stored in semantic or visual form. In semantic coding, people store the meaning of verbal information, not just specific words. In fact, memories are stored in complex webs of association called **semantic networks**. In visual coding, people store input as mental pictures. Thus, the use of imagery, particularly when it is interactive and bizarre, improves memory.

There is more than one type of long-term memory. **Procedural memory** consists of learned habits and skills, whereas **declarative memory** consists of memories for facts about the world and about ourselves. Neuroscientists have sought to identify the physical traces of memory. In the case of H.M., the **hippocampus** was removed, producing **anterograde amnesia**, the inability to form new long-term memories (not **retrograde amnesia**, the inability to retrieve old memories from the past). Studies confirm that the hippocampus is involved in the encoding of information into long-term memory. Biochemically, the neurotransmitter acetylcholine plays a key role.

Retrieval

There are two basic techniques by which retrieval can be tested, and each assesses a different aspect of memory: explicit and implicit. **Explicit memories** are recollections consciously retrieved in response to direct questions. **Implicit memories** are nonconscious recollections that are indirectly measured by their effects on performance. This distinction is important because people may "forget" (have no explicit memory of) an experience and yet show the effects (have an implicit memory) of that experience.

In tests of explicit memory, people find it more difficult to produce a recollection in the form of **free recall** than **recognition**. Apparently, forgetting often occurs not because memory has faded but because the information is difficult to retrieve. Retrieval failure is indicated by the tip-of-the-tongue phenomenon and by the fact that memory is aided by retrieval cues. Research on **encoding specificity** indicates that any stimulus that is encoded along with an experience—including locations (which accounts for context-dependent memory) and internal states (which accounts for state-dependent memory)—can later jog memory of that experience.

Implicit tests uncover memories of which people are not aware by measuring their effects on performance. Many amnesia patients use material they cannot explicitly recall. As shown by the illusion of truth, unconscious transference in eyewitness testimony, and unconscious plagiarism, implicit memory is also common in everyday life.

FORGETTING

Beginning with Ebbinghaus, researchers have found evidence for a specific **forgetting curve** in which there is an initial steep loss of retention, with the loss rate leveling off over time. Forgetting can result from a lack of encoding, physical decay, interference, or repression. There are two kinds of interference. In **proactive interference**, prior information inhibits one's ability to recall something new. In **retroactive interference**, new material disrupts memory for previously learned information.

RECONSTRUCTION

Remembering is an active process in which people construct memories based on **schemas**, or preconceptions, and information from outside sources. Experiments by Loftus and others reveal that memory is also "reconstructive"—that after one observes an event, postevent input becomes integrated into the memory. When that information is false, the result is known as the **misinformation effect**. In other ways as well, false or illusory memories can be created.

AUTOBIOGRAPHICAL MEMORY

Autobiographical memory consists of the recollections people have of their own personal experiences. What aspects of our own past do we preserve? Are these memories accurate?

WHAT EVENTS DO PEOPLE REMEMBER?

People can best recall events from the recent rather than the distant past, though older adults report many memories from adolescence and early adulthood and people in general tend to recall transitional periods in their lives. For events that are particularly dramatic, people form **flashbulb memories** that are highly vivid and enduring—though accuracy tends to suffer as time passes. Most people report the inability to recall events from before the age of 3 or 4 years, a memory gap called **childhood amnesia**.

CRITICAL THINKING

Thinking Critically About Memory

1. Given what you have learned about memory, what strategies would you use to help you remember the information from this chapter? Why would those strategies be effective?

2. What do psychologists mean when they say that memory is an active process?

3. Suppose you meet a person with damage to the hippocampus. What types of deficits, if any, would you expect this person to exhibit? Why?

4. Distinguish between explicit and implicit memory. How could one study implicit memory if people cannot report having such memories? Design a study that would allow you to assess implicit memory.

5. Speculate as to how you might determine the veracity of an allegedly "recovered" memory.

6. Hypothesize about the relative capacity and duration of tactile, olfactory, and gustatory memories. How could you go about testing these memory abilities?

CAREER CONNECTION: BUSINESS

Human Resources Specialist

Human resources (HR) specialists are responsible for tasks related to employee relations, training, compensation, and benefits and are employed at all mid-sized and larger businesses and organizations. They're involved in recruiting, screening, interviewing, and hiring new employees while also helping to guide existing employees through all HR-related procedures and policies.

Professionals in this role are often also tasked with some basic administrative duties, such as creating and managing benefit plans, processing payroll, and keeping employment records up to date. HR specialists are also responsible for ensuring every HR function is compliant with federal, state, and local regulations. Many companies require HR certification or continuing education, but the skills learned in psychology coursework will provide a valuable foundation for the field.

Key skills for this role that psychology students learn to develop:

- Enhanced teamwork capacity
- Incorporation of sociocultural factors in scientific inquiry
- Interpersonal relationship development

KEY TERMS

anterograde amnesia (p. 229)
autobiographical memory (p. 248)
childhood amnesia (p. 250)
chunking (p. 218)
declarative memory (p. 227)
echoic memory (p. 216)
elaborative rehearsal (p. 224)
encoding specificity (p. 233)
explicit memory (p. 232)
flashbulb memories (p. 249)
forgetting curve (p. 239)
free recall (p. 223)
hippocampus (p. 229)
iconic memory (p. 215)
implicit memory (p. 232)
information-processing model (p. 214)

long-term memory (LTM) (p. 214)
maintenance rehearsal (p. 220)
memory (p. 214)
misinformation effect (p. 245)
proactive interference (p. 242)
procedural memory (p. 227)
recognition (p. 233)
retroactive interference (p. 242)
retrograde amnesia (p. 229)
schemas (p. 244)
semantic network (p. 228)
sensory memory (p. 214)
serial-position curve (p. 222)
short-term memory (STM) (p. 214)
working memory (p. 221)

7 THOUGHT, LANGUAGE, AND INTELLIGENCE

iStock.com/baona

LEARNING OBJECTIVES

Distinguish the difference between a prototype and a concept.

Recognize the methods humans use to solve problems and how humans are also hindered by those same problem-solving methods.

Define language, and recognize its properties.

Explain how the words we use influence our ideas about others, ourselves, and the world.

Critique the theoretical types of intelligence for accuracy and bias.

Appreciate the range of intelligences proposed by the field of psychology.

Apply the nature versus nurture debate to group variations in intelligence.

WHAT'S YOUR PREDICTION: ARE PEOPLE GETTING SMARTER?

The Situation

Just about everyone is curious about intelligence and the tests that are used to measure it. Most of the tests were created early in the 20th century, and since then IQ (intelligence quotient) scores have been used to determine academic potential in schools throughout the world. Hmm. The fact that people have been taking IQ tests for many years—and that you may have taken a test very similar to one taken by your parents and grandparents—raises a fascinating question: Have scores changed over time? Do people today have a lower or higher IQ than a few years ago, or is IQ a fairly stable trait that undergoes little change over time?

Being trained in psychology, you're accustomed to conducting experiments, often in the laboratory. To answer the question about IQ trends across generations, however, you'll need to use different methods. You'll need to gather old scores from IQ tests that were taken at different times by comparable groups of people. So, you contact researchers all over the world and ask if they would send you test scores that have been compiled over the years. In particular, you want scores from tests that were never altered over time and were given to large groups of adults of different generations. You receive the data you need from a number of developed countries, including Australia, Austria, Belgium, Brazil, Canada, China, France, Germany, Great Britain, Israel, Japan, the Netherlands, New Zealand, Norway, Switzerland, and the United States. Now it's time to analyze the results.

Make a Prediction

As we'll learn shortly, IQ tests are set so that the average score in the population is always 100. This means that if raw scores were to rise or fall over time, the scale would have to be readjusted like a thermostat in order to keep that average. The question is, what tends to happen to *raw scores* over the passage of time? Based on 1920 standards, which set the average IQ at 100, what do you think the raw, nonadjusted scores were in 1930, 1940, and other decades up to 1990? Did IQ steadily increase or decrease over time, fluctuate in response to historical events, or stay essentially the same? Think carefully about the problem. Then, modeling Figure 7.1, plot your predicted trend for each decade before looking at the actual results.

The Results

When James Flynn (1987) first compiled the IQ scores in 14 developed nations (he then added 6 more), the worldwide trend was unmistakable. Figure 7.2 shows that, from one generation to the next, steady and massive gains in IQ scores were observed—so much so that today's average adult scores 24 points higher than in 1920. Named after its discoverer, this phenomenon is now known as the Flynn effect.

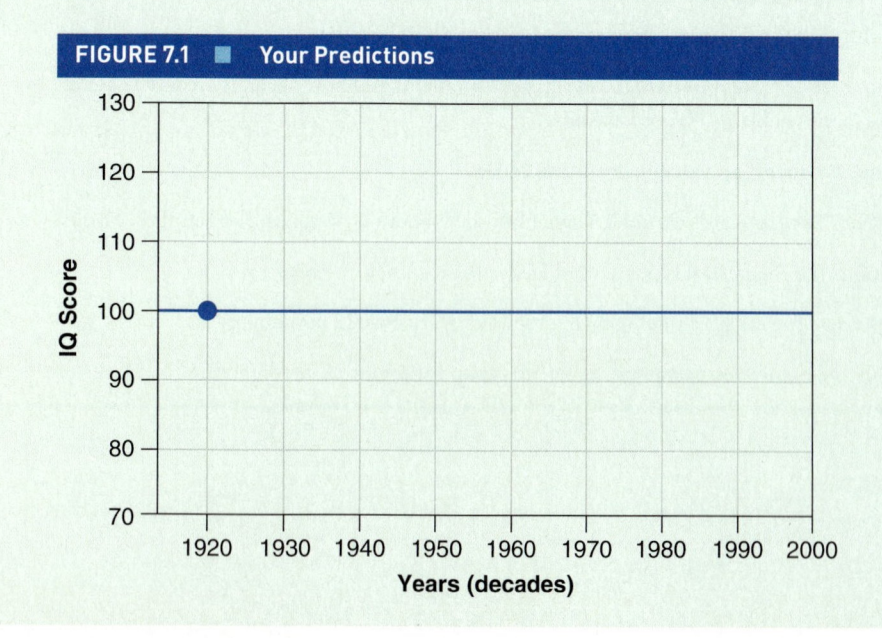

FIGURE 7.1 ■ Your Predictions

FIGURE 7.2 ■ The Actual Results

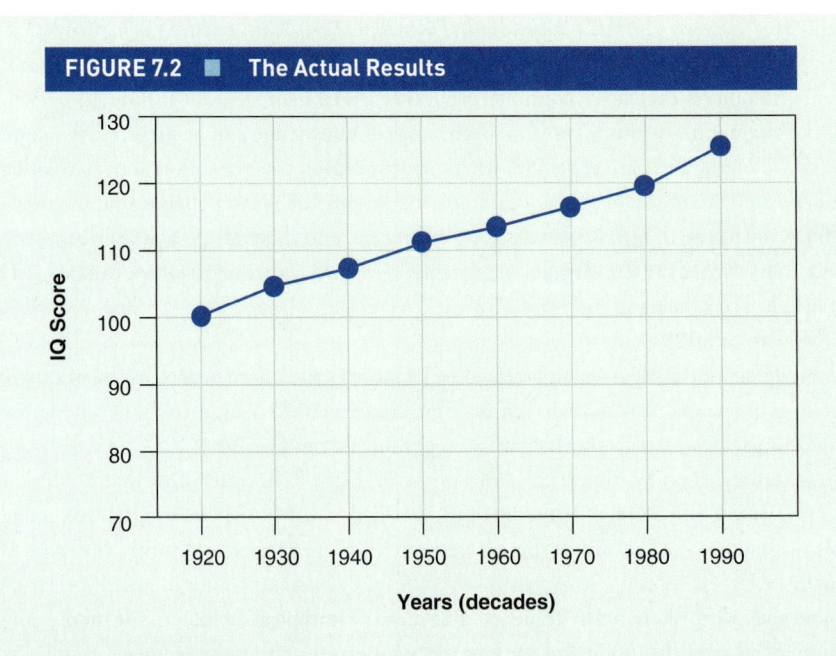

What Does It All Mean?

For years, psychologists have hotly debated the nature of intelligence, the validity of standard IQ tests, and the extent to which being smart is the product of nature, nurture, or both (Rindermann, Becker, & Coyle, 2017; Weber, Dekhtyar, & Herlitz, 2017). Flynn's discovery that IQ scores have risen steadily provoked new discussion of, and research into, these core issues. Is it possible that while IQ has risen, "intelligence" has not? Just what is intelligence, and how is it related to our ability to shape thoughts and express them? As we'll learn in this chapter, thought, language, and intelligence are interconnected.

We humans are a funny species. As a civilization, we have invented the wheel, kept historical records to guide present and future generations, landed space ships on the moon, unlocked the atom, cracked the genetic code, and revolutionized all we do using computers that connect us to the global Internet. When you stop to think about it, our list of triumphs is long and impressive. Yet at the same time, we massacre each other in war, wreak havoc on the environment, discriminate against racial and ethnic groups different from our own, mistreat our partners, throw hard-earned money away in games of chance, take drugs that make us sick, and deceive ourselves into believing in conspiracy theories. After all that, how can we refer to ourselves as "intelligent" life?

What is it about the way we humans think that leads us to be both rational and irrational? How do we use our intelligence to solve difficult problems and then evaluate the solutions, and what kinds of errors are we prone to make along the way? Are we logical in our reasoning, or are the judgments and decisions we make infected with bias? And what role does language have to play in the way we think? What is language, and is it this capacity that most clearly defines humans as more intelligent than other animal species? In the coming sections, we will examine some of the basic processes of thought, language, and intelligence. But first, let's examine *concepts*—the basic building blocks of abstract thought and language.

CONCEPTS

LEARNING OBJECTIVES

Distinguish the difference between a prototype and a concept.

- Explain how concepts are stored in memory.
- Create an argument for why a robin is considered "birdier" than a chicken.

concept. A mental grouping of persons, ideas, events, or objects that share common properties.

Freedom. Sports. Cancer. Animals. Education. Furniture. Sex. War. Peace. Music. Heroes. Triangles. Happiness. Each of these words represents a distinct **concept**—a mental grouping of persons, places, ideas, events, or objects that share common properties (Markman, 1999; Van Loocke, 1999). As discussed in the chapter on memory, our long-term store of knowledge can be pictured as a complex but orderly network of semantic concepts. So, when one concept in the network is activated, other closely related concepts pop to mind, or are *primed*. Look at the semantic network depicted in Figure 7.3. Note that a robin being a type of bird is illustrated by its linkage, and this linkage in itself is a concept that is stored in memory. What's interesting about semantic networks is that one concept can be used to bring others to mind. Thus, hearing the word *bird* makes it easier to pull *robin, chicken,* and *animal* from memory (McNamara, 1994).

Some members of a category are perceived to be more typical than others, as illustrated in Figure 7.4. Thus, to most people, a robin is a "birdier" bird than a chicken, an ostrich, or a penguin—all of which have wings and feathers and hatch from eggs but do not fly. What makes a category member more or less typical? Review Figure 7.3 and notice the lists of characteristics that are linked to the concepts *bird, robin,* and *chicken*. When people are asked to list properties of different concepts, the most typical members, called **prototypes**, have more of these properties (Smith, Shoben, & Ripps, 1974; Rosch, 1975).

prototype. A "typical" member of a category, one that has most of the defining features of that category.

Consider the categories listed in Table 7.1. The more prototypical an item is, the more easily we recognize it as a member of the group and use it to make judgments about the group as a whole (Whitney, 1986).

The use of prototypes is illustrated in many studies. For example, Lance Rips (1975) had subjects read a story about an island that was inhabited by sparrows, robins, eagles, hawks, ducks, geese, and ostriches. Some subjects were informed that a disease had infected the robins, whereas others were told that the disease had infected the ducks. Subjects were then asked, "What other species would be infected?" Remembering what you just read about prototypes, can you anticipate the result? Subjects in the robin-infected group predicted that the disease would spread to all other bird species on the island. In contrast, the duck group predicted that only the geese, a "related" species, would be infected. Evidently, robins serve as a prototype for birds, but ducks do not. It's also interesting that the first words children use to describe objects within various categories usually pertain to prototypic

FIGURE 7.3 ■ A Semantic Network

Long-term memory can be pictured as a complex web of concepts, some of which are cognitively closer than others. When one concept is "activated," others nearby in the network are primed.

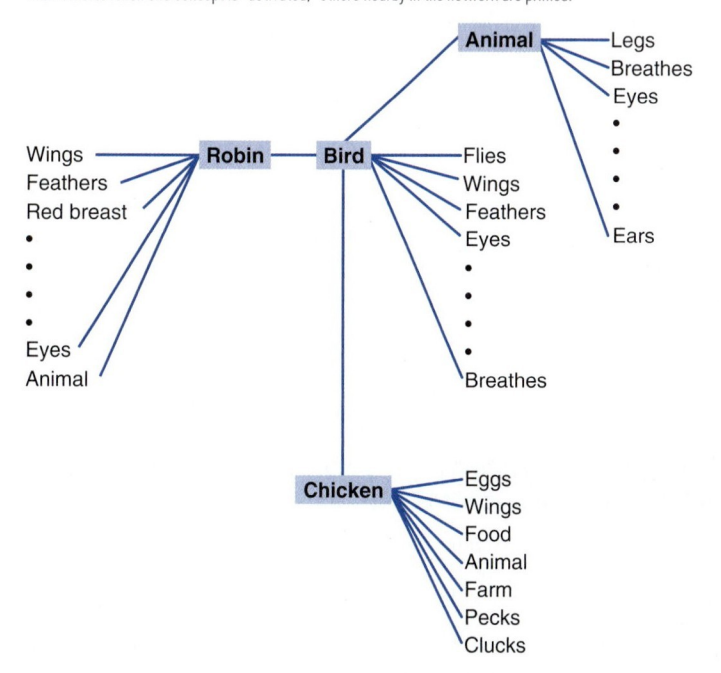

FIGURE 7.4 ■ Pet Prototypes

When you hear the word pet, what image comes to mind? For this particular concept, some animals (terrier) are more prototypical of the category than others (rabbits or iguanas).

iStock.com/Capuski; iStock.com/David-Prado; iStock.com/fotografixx

TABLE 7.1 ■ Typicality of Members in Three Categories

Category	Typicality		
	High	Moderate	Low
Furniture	Chair	Lamp	Vase
Fruit	Apple	Lemon	Coconut
Vehicle	Car	Boat	Blimp

members of those categories—apples rather than lemons, chairs rather than lamps, and so on (Poulin-DuBois, 1995).

Although many human concepts consist of taxonomies that are based on similarities among members such as dogs, foods, furniture, or rock bands, others bring items together according to what we know about their "thematic relations." In other words, you might sort a list of foods into such taxonomic categories as meats, fruits, vegetables, and dairy products; or you might sort them according to how or when they are eaten—such as breakfast foods, main dishes, fast foods, and desserts. In a series of studies, Emilie Lin and Gregory Murphy (2001) presented people with triads of words. Each triad contained a target word and two related words—one taxonomically related, the other thematically related. The subject's task was to pick the related word that goes best with the target. Table 7.2 lists 10 triads. How would you pair each one to form categories? What goes best with *French fries: baked potato* or *ketchup?* What about *movie theater: opera house* or *popcorn?* Across five studies, subjects selected the thematic choice 61 percent of the time. This result suggests that there is more than one way to conceptualize the world, and that people often construct categories according to thematic relations, not taxonomic similarity.

TABLE 7.2	Do People Categorize by Taxonomic or Thematic Relatedness?		
Triad	Target Word	Taxonomic	Thematic
1	French fries	baked potato	ketchup
2	camel	antelope	desert
3	Hawaii	Missouri	beach
4	beer	juice	party
5	movie theater	opera house	popcorn
6	pig	dog	barn
7	igloo	cabin	Inuit
8	pepperoni	pork chops	pizza
9	saxophone	harp	jazz
10	diamond ring	bracelet	engagement

SOLVING PROBLEMS

LEARNING OBJECTIVES

Recognize the methods humans use to solve problems and how humans are also hindered by those same problem-solving methods.

- Determine if heuristics are more efficient problem-solving methods than trial and error.
- Examine why some psychologists believe in problem solving by insight—and why others think insight is just an illusion.
- Identify some of the "blind spots" that impair our ability to solve problems.

When you lock your keys in the car, play Candy Crush Saga, mediate a dispute between friends, or struggle to learn a new app, the solution you're looking for requires that you combine and manipulate concepts, often in new ways, to solve the problem or to make the necessary judgment. When a solution cannot simply be pulled from memory, it takes effort to obtain. As we'll learn, it helps to view problem solving as a process that involves defining the problem, representing it in some way, and then generating and evaluating possible solutions. These steps are not a fixed series of stages but, rather, are mental activities that we use in cycles. So, if you're stuck on a problem and realize that you have not represented it correctly in the first place, you might start the process over again.

Representing the Problem

Many problems we encounter come to us in the form of words and concepts activated from semantic networks. Playing the TV game *Jeopardy!*, trying to recite the lyrics of an old song, and working on a crossword puzzle are some examples. But there are other ways as well to depict problems.

Mental Images

image. A mental representation of visual information.

Often, people represent information through **images**, or mental pictures. To run cold water from the faucet in your kitchen sink, which way do you move the handle? Which way do you twist a screw to tighten it? And if you can picture a map of the world, which city is farther north, London or New York? To answer these questions, people generate visual images.

In the past, psychologists had to take people at their word when they said they had formed mental pictures. Today, there are more objective ways to study the "mind's eye"—and these methods have confirmed that imagery is a pervasive aspect of human thought. Consider some specific examples. In one study, Margaret Intons-Peterson (1993) gave people verbal descriptions of simple line drawings, like the one in Figure 7.5, and found that the more rotations that were involved, the longer it took subjects to generate the image. This result suggests that people solve this problem by manipulating mental pictures of the described forms. Other research also suggests that if mental rotation is needed to solve a spatial problem, people take longer to make the judgment (Shepard & Cooper, 1982). Some people are better at mental rotation than others.

FIGURE 7.5 ■ Mental-Rotation Tasks

Imagine a capital letter T. Rotate it 90 degrees to the right. Put a triangle directly to the left of the figure so that it is pointing to the right. Now rotate the figure 90 degrees to the right. Got it? Now look at the images below and pick the correct one. You can check your answer by drawing the figure on paper. The solution can be found in Figure 7.6.

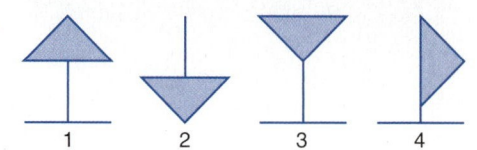

Mental Models

Do you understand how a virus spreads from one computer to another? Can you describe how a car engine works? What about the economy: Do you know how the inflation and unemployment rates interact? At times, the problems that confront us can be best represented in the form of **mental models**, which are intuitive theories of the way things work. When accurate, these theories can be powerful tools for reasoning. By having specific mental models of how human beings, organizations, machines, and other things work, we can diagnose problems and adapt accordingly (Gentner & Stevens 1983; Johnson-Laird, 1983, 2001).

Unfortunately, our mental models are often in error. Before reading on, try the problems in Figure 7.6. These problems are used to study *intuitive physics*—the mental models people have about the laws of motion. Research shows that people are poor intuitive physicists (Kubricht, Holyoak, & Lu, 2017). Consider three common errors. First, many people wrongly believe in the "impetus principle" that an object set in motion acquires its own internal force, which keeps it in motion. So when asked to predict the path of a metal ball rolling through a spiral tube, a majority of subjects predicted that the ball would follow a curved path even after it exits the tube (McCloskey & Kuhl, 1983). A second error is the "straight-down belief" that something dropped from a moving object will fall in a straight vertical line. So when asked to predict the path of a ball dropped at shoulder height by a walking adult, most subjects wrongly assumed that the ball would fall straight down rather than in a forward trajectory (McCloskey & Kuhl, 1983). A third error is made in the "water-level task" shown in Figure 7.6. When shown a tilted glass or a container filled with liquid, some subjects—including many bartenders and waitresses—harbor the belief that the water surface tilts as well rather than remains parallel to the ground (Hecht & Proffitt, 1995). It's interesting that physics students don't always perform better than others on these types of problems, which suggests that mental models can be difficult to change (Donley & Ashcraft, 1992; Kozhevnikov & Hegarty, 2001).

mental models. Intuitive theories about the way things work.

trial and error. A problem-solving strategy in which several solutions are attempted until one is found that works.

Generating Solutions

Once a problem is represented through words, static images, or mental models, we try out possible solutions and test to determine if they work. If the problem is solved, life goes on. If not, we return to the proverbial drawing board to come up with new ideas. There are many different ways to find solutions, but there are four basic problem-solving processes: trial and error, algorithms, heuristics, and insight.

Trial and Error

Trial and error is the simplest problem-solving strategy there is, and it's often effective. As discussed in the chapter on learning, Edward Thorndike, in 1898, studied animal intelligence by putting cats in a "puzzle box," placing food outside a door, and timing how long it took for them to figure out how to escape. At first, the cats tried various ineffective behaviors. They tried reaching with their paws, but the food was too far away. They scratched at the bars, but that did not work. They pushed at the ceiling,

FIGURE 7.6 ■ Intuitive Physics

(a) Subjects were asked to draw the path that a marble would take as it exited this curved tube. Most subjects incorrectly drew a curved path (dotted line) rather than the correct straight path (dashed line). Our mental models of motion are often wrong. (b) In this task, subjects were asked to draw a line to illustrate the surface of water in the tilted container. Although the line should be depicted as perfectly horizontal to the ground, as shown by the dotted line, many people placed it at the tilted angle shown above as the solid line.

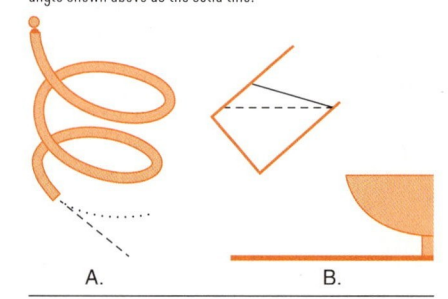

A.   B.

Solution to Figure 7.5: The answer is drawing number 3.

Source: Hecht, H., & Proffitt, D. R. (1995). The Price of Expertise: Effects of Experience on the Water-Level Task. *Psychological Science, 6*(2), 90–95. https://doi.org/10.1111/j.1467-9280.1995.tb00312.x

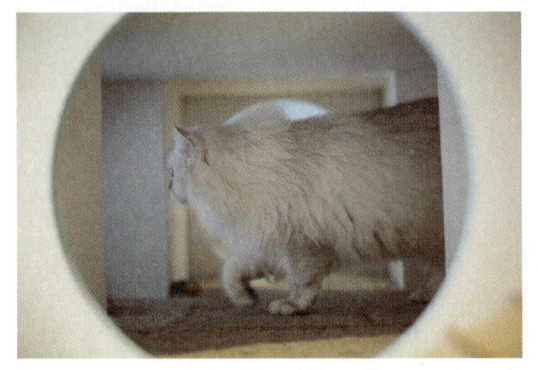

To study how cats learn, Edward Thorndike created puzzle boxes. In these puzzle boxes, cats would perform a series of behaviors until a behavior was successful. This demonstrated that cats understood trial and error.

iStock.com/iunderhill

algorithm. A systematic, step-by-step problem-solving strategy that is guaranteed to produce a solution.

heuristic. A rule of thumb that allows one to make judgments that are quick but often in error.

means-end analysis. A problem-solving heuristic that involves breaking down a larger problem into a series of subgoals.

analogy. A problem-solving heuristic that involves using an old solution as a model for a new, similar problem.

but that did not work either. Then they would literally stumble upon the solution (which was to step on a lever that opened the door) and repeat that solution whenever they were in the box. The cats solved the problem by trial and error.

As you can imagine, this aimless, hit-or-miss approach is not the most efficient way to proceed. Think about the last time your smartphone crashed. Did you start furiously tapping various areas of the screen, get no result, and resort to shutting it down in the hopes that a restart would correct the problem? Sometimes, strategies such as this prove enlightening. For example, Thomas Edison—the most prolific inventor in American history—tested thousands of light bulb filaments before stumbling on the one that worked. The problem is that this strategy often takes too long or fails completely. If possible, it's better to take a more systematic, planned approach.

Algorithms and Heuristics

An **algorithm** is a step-by-step procedure that is guaranteed, eventually, to produce a solution. When you were taught in school how to solve two-digit addition problems or long division, you learned an algorithm. An alternative is to use **heuristics**, mental shortcuts, or rules of thumb, which may or may not lead to the correct solution. The "*I* before *E*" heuristic for spelling *I–E* words is a good example. To appreciate the difference between algorithms and heuristics, consider the following anagram problem: Unscramble the letters *L K C C O* to make a word. One strategy is to use an algorithm—to try all possible combinations by systematically varying the letters in each position. Eventually, you will form the correct word. An alternative is to use a heuristic. For example, you could try the most familiar letter combinations. A common ending for English words is *CK*, so you might start with this combination and arrive quickly at the solution: *CLOCK*.

If algorithms are guaranteed to produce solutions, why not use them all the time? The reason is that algorithms are not always available—and sometimes they take too much time to be practical. Thus, chess experts do not consider all the possible moves on the board, because there are simply too many of them. This strategy is fine for computer chess programs made to evaluate millions of positions and moves per second. But great players must rely instead on heuristics, such as "Get control of the center of the board."

Some heuristics are general, in that they can be used to solve a wide range of problems. One important general heuristic is the **means-end analysis** (Newell & Simon, 1972). This involves breaking a larger problem into a series of subgoals. For example, let's say you are starting a new job Monday and have to get to work on time. You could solve this problem by driving your car to work, but your car needs repair. So, you set a subgoal of getting your car repaired. But this might require other subgoals, such as finding a mechanic. For some problems, the nested subgoals can get quite complex and involved. In fact, unless people carefully evaluate whether each step brings them closer to the endpoint, it is possible to lose track of what part of the problem is actually being solved (Simon, 1975).

Another powerful problem-solving heuristic consists of the use of **analogies**. If you have previously solved some problem that seems similar to a new one, you can use the old solution as a model. The trick is to recognize that the second problem resembles the first. Analogical thinking plays a central role in science, where the heart has been likened to a pump, the brain to a computer, the eye to a camera, molecules to billiard balls, the phone to an ear, and the spinning earth to a slowing toy top. Research shows that people are quicker to grasp and use new scientific concepts when these concepts are taught by analogy than when they are explained in literal terms (Donnelly & McDaniel, 1993)—and that the shorter the "mental leap" is between two problems, because they are similar in obvious ways, the more effective is the analogy for teaching said concepts (Chen, 2002; Holyoak & Thagard, 1997). Diagrams and animated displays may be particularly useful for getting people to notice the analogical link between problems.

Creativity is also associated with analogical thinking when participants are tasked with making connections that require a longer "mental leap" (Barnett & Ceci, 2002; Bowdle & Gentner, 2005).

For example, try solving the problem of connecting furnace:coal with stomach:food. Did you find the connection? A furnace burns coal, whereas a stomach "burns" (i.e., metabolizes) food. Another connection you might have thought of is fuel. Food and coal are both referred to as fuel, whereas a furnace and stomach both use fuel to create energy. Green and colleagues (2012) presented problems such as this while imaging the brain. They argued that connecting distant items reflects creative thinking and seems to be associated with activity in the frontopolar cortex of the brain.

Insight

When people struggle with a problem, they usually try to monitor their progress to evaluate whether they're closing in on a solution (Kotovsky, Hayes, & Simon, 1985). But have you ever puzzled over something, felt as if you were stumped, and then come up with the answer abruptly, out of the blue, as if a light bulb flashed inside your head? Aha! If so, then you have experienced problem solving by **insight**, a process in which the solution pops to mind all of a sudden—and in which the problem solver doesn't realize the solution is coming and cannot describe what he or she was thinking at the time (Sternberg & Davidson, 1999).

Insight is an experience that seems to arise whenever people at an impasse relax the way they approach a problem, reframe it, switch from one strategy to another, remove a mental block, or identify an analogy from a prior experience (Knoblich & Ohlsson, 1999; Ohlsson, 2011; Simon, 1989). Some researchers claim that these apparent flashes of insight actually result from a gradual, step-by-step process—but that sometimes we're just not aware of the progress we are making (Weisberg, 1992). Others find that certain types of tasks seem to promote a special form of problem solving that has a sudden, all-or-none quality (Smith & Kounios, 1996). Is insight gradual but nonconscious, or is it truly sudden? It's hard to know for sure. Weisberg (2015) argues that both claims should be combined to understand how insight works. But that understanding cannot come from participant reports alone. Consider research by Janet Metcalfe and David Wiebe (1987), for example. They had subjects work on different types of problems and periodically rate how "warm" they were getting on a seven-point scale. On multistep algebra problems, the ratings increased steadily as subjects neared a solution. On insight problems, however, the warmth ratings remained flat and low, then rose all at once, the moment subjects encountered a solution. It's interesting that when people working on insight problems are asked to describe their thinking along the way, which brings the process into consciousness, their problem-solving performance deteriorates (Schooler, Ohlsson, & Brooks, 1993).

People often report that they tried unsuccessfully for hours to solve a problem and then, after taking a break, came back and it "clicked": An insight quickly converted into a solution. The improved ability to solve a problem after taking a break from it is called the **incubation effect**. One puzzle that psychologists have used to investigate incubation effects in the laboratory is the "cheap-necklace problem," shown in Figure 7.7. Try it for 5 minutes before reading on. Using this problem, Silveira (1971) tested three groups of subjects. All groups worked on the same task for a total of 30 minutes. One group worked without a break. After 15 minutes, however, the second group took a half-hour break and the third group took a 4-hour break. During these rest periods, subjects were kept busy with other activities that prevented them from continuing to work on the necklace problem. The results provided strong evidence for incubation: Subjects who took a break were more likely to solve the problem than those who did not. In fact, the longer the interlude, the better the performance. The implication of this effect is clear. Sometimes it helps to take a break while trying to solve problems that require a critical insight—as in the cheap-necklace problem, where the key is to realize that you can't link all four chains (Anderson, 1990).

Insight is something we cannot reproduce since it is impossible to describe how the sudden solution was developed.
iStock.com/Igor Vershinsky

insight. A form of problem solving in which the solution seems to pop to mind all of a sudden.

incubation effect. Forming a solution to a problem as a result of taking a mental break from it.

FIGURE 7.7 ■ The Cheap-Necklace Problem

Make a necklace out of the separate chains. It costs 2 cents to open a link and 3 cents to close a link. You must make your necklace for 15 cents or less. The solution can be found in Figure 7.10.

Chain A

Chain B

Chain C

Chain D

Given state

> ## LEARNING CHECK
>
> ### Crash Project
>
> Here's the problem: Your computer has crashed, and you've lost the extremely important psychology paper you were just finishing. Each of the following approaches to recovering it falls under one of the four basic methods for solving problems: trial and error (T), algorithm (A), heuristic (H), or insight (I). Identify the appropriate letter for each.
>
> 1. Start by just trying to get the computer back on, and worry about how to recover the paper later.
> 2. Follow a diagnostic procedure the manufacturer says will always recover documents.
> 3. Think about how you fixed your smartphone when it froze.
> 4. Take a walk to clear your head.
> 5. Keep pushing buttons and hope something happens.
> 6. Use every possible recovery procedure until you find the one that works.
>
> (Answers: 1. H; 2. A; 3. H; 4. I; 5. T; 6. A.)

The history of science is filled with stories of discovery by flashes of insight. But is insight necessarily the product of a great mind? Many psychologists believe that other animals too are capable of insight, not just of trial-and-error problem solving. Many years ago, Wolfgang Köhler (1925) claimed that a chimpanzee named Sultan displayed insight in problem solving. Köhler put bananas and a long stick outside the chimp's cage, both out of reach, and put a short stick inside the cage. Sultan poked at the banana with the short stick, but it was too short to reach the fruit. After trying repeatedly, he gave up, dropped the stick, and walked away. Then all of a sudden, Sultan jumped up, picked up the short stick, and used it to get the longer stick—which he used to get the banana. Did this episode reveal insight? Many researchers are skeptical of such a claim and suggest that the apparent insight may be no more than an accumulation of learned behaviors (Epstein, Kirshnit, Lanza, & Rubin, 1984). Yet others agree with Köhler. Sociobiologist Edward O. Wilson tells a Sultan-like story of a chimp trying to reach some leaves: "He sat and looked at the tree for a long time, and went over to a log. He dragged it over to the tree, propped it against the trunk, then stood back and charged his ramp. It's extremely difficult to explain that, other than to say the chimp was consciously thinking" (Begley & Ramo, 1993).

"Blind Spots" in Problem Solving

Using trial and error, algorithms, heuristics, and insight, people often display a remarkable capacity to solve problems. As we have experienced time and again, however, our competencies are often compromised by certain "blind spots." To appreciate some of these shortcomings, try the problems in Figures 7.8 and 7.9 before reading on. The solutions are revealed later on in the section.

Representation Failures

For many years, problem-solving researchers have used the "nine-dot problem" presented in Figure 7.8 (Burnham & Davis, 1969; MacGregor, Ormerod, & Chronicle, 2001; Öllinger, Jones, & Knoblich, 2014). This problem is notoriously difficult, and it seems to illustrate that failure often results from an incorrect problem representation. Even though the instructions say nothing about staying inside an imaginary square formed from the dots, almost everyone behaves as though the outside dots form a boundary that cannot be crossed (to understand why, review the Gestalt principles of perceptual grouping discussed in the chapter on sensation and perception and think about your typical way of solving

FIGURE 7.8 ■ The Nine-Dot Problem

Connect all nine dots with four straight lines without lifting your pencil from the paper. The solution is revealed in Figure 7.11.

FIGURE 7.9 ■ Duncker's Candle Problem

Using just the objects shown, how could you mount the candle on a wall? The solution appears in Figure 7.12.

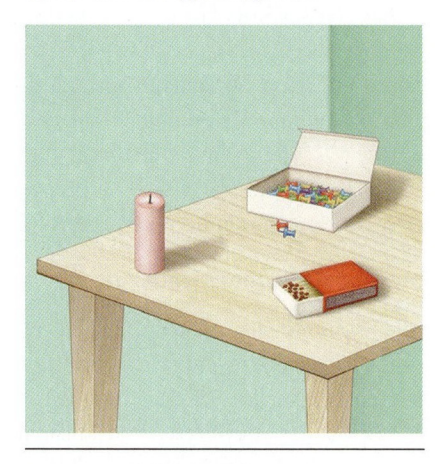

Monica Wierzbicki/Body Scientific Intl.

problems that required you to connect the dots). If you don't mentally handicap yourself in this way, the solution is simple. But people do, which is what makes the problem so difficult. Is this tendency to represent problems narrowly limited to clever laboratory puzzles and brainteasers? Sadly, no. As we'll learn in the Treatment and Interventions chapter, cognitively oriented clinical psychologists find that people often suffer needlessly because they conceptualize problems in ways that make them seem insurmountable.

Mental Set

The nine-dot problem can also illustrate a **mental set**, the desire to use strategies that have worked in the past to solve a current problem. When trying to solve the nine-dot problem, our minds can easily go back to a time when we were given problems that required us to connect the dots. Do you remember the last time you had to draw a straight line between two points? You were probably in elementary school. When connecting the dots, you learned that connecting lines were never drawn outside of the dots. You were also taught that when you color a picture with crayons, you are supposed to stay in the lines. Thus, your mental set from elementary school may have been the reason it never occurred to you to drag the line beyond the dot.

Functional Fixedness

The "candle problem" in Figure 7.9 illustrates a more specific type of representation failure. The difficulty in this case is one of **functional fixedness**, a tendency to think of objects only in terms of their usual functions. In a way, our brains almost become locked into how they view an object and its use. In the candle problem, for example, you'd struggle for as long as you recognized the thumbtack box as only a container, not as a possible shelf. A brick is a brick, but it can also be used as a paperweight. Finding creative new solutions to practical problems often requires that we think open-mindedly—or, as they say, "outside the box"—in order to imagine unusual uses for common objects (Sternberg & Lubart, 1991; Weisberg, 1986).

The Confirmation Bias

The nine-dot and candle problems are tricky not because they are intellectually demanding but because people tend to be overly rigid in their thinking. But there's more. Once we think we have a solution, we fall prey to **confirmation bias**, a tendency to look only for evidence that will verify our beliefs—which can prevent us from realizing that we are in error. This bias is pervasive and has a negative influence on the way people approach the problems in their daily lives (Nickerson, 1998).

mental set. Incorporating a strategy that worked in the past.

functional fixedness. The tendency to think of objects only in terms of their usual functions, a limitation that disrupts problem solving.

confirmation bias. The inclination to search only for evidence that will verify one's beliefs.

To demonstrate, Peter Wason (1960) gave students a three-number sequence, *2-4-6*, and challenged them to figure out the rule he had used to generate this set. How should they proceed? By making up their own sequences and asking the experimenter to indicate whether or not they fit the rule. Subjects were told they could test as many sequences as they wanted and to state the rule only if they felt certain that they knew it. The task was straightforward and the rule behind *2-4-6* was easy: any three increasing numbers. Yet out of 29 subjects, only 6 discovered the correct rule without first seizing on one that was incorrect. What happened was this: Subjects would start with an initial hypothesis (adding by 2s, even numbers, skipping numbers) and then search only for confirming evidence. Thinking that the rule was "adding by 2s," a subject might test *6-8-10, 50-52-54, 21-23-25*, and so on, yet never try disconfirming sets such as *6-8-4* or *3-2-1*. When all the sequences fit, the subject would proudly and with confidence announce the wrong rule.

The Representativeness Heuristic

One rule of thumb that people use to make probability estimates is the **representativeness heuristic**—the tendency to judge the likelihood of an event's occurring by how typical it seems (Kahneman & Tversky, 1973). Like other heuristics, this one enables us to make quick judgments. With speed, however, comes bias and a possible loss of accuracy. For example, which sequence of boys (B) and girls (G) would you say is more likely to occur in a family with six children: (1) B,G,B,G,B,G; (2) B,B,B,G,G,G; or (3) G,B,B,G,G,B? These sequences are all equally likely. Yet most people say that the third is more likely than the others because it looks typical of a random sequence.

The problem with this heuristic is that it often leads us to ignore numerical probabilities, or "base rates." Now that you've considered the boy-girl sequence example, contemplate this scenario. Suppose there's a group of 30 engineers and 70 lawyers. In that group, a random selection of one person results in a discussion with a conservative man named Jack, who enjoys mathematical puzzles and has no interest in social or political issues. Question: Is Jack a lawyer or an engineer? When Kahneman and Tversky (1973) presented this item to subjects, most guessed that Jack was an engineer (because he seemed to fit the stereotyped image of an engineer)—even though he came from a group containing a 70 percent majority of lawyers. In this instance, representativeness overwhelmed the more predictive base rate. Do you think your consideration of the boy-girl sequence example made you more aware of this flaw in thinking and, as a result, helped you to avoid the flaw that Kahneman and Tversky's participants made?

representativeness heuristic. A tendency to estimate the likelihood of an event in terms of how typical it seems.

FIGURE 7.10 ■ Solution to the Cheap-Necklace Problem

The key is to realize that you can't link all four chains. To solve the problem, open all three links on one of the four chains (this costs 6 cents), and then use these open links to join together the three remaining chains (which costs 9 cents).

Chain A
Chain B
Chain C
Chain D

Step 1: Open links to one set of chains. This costs $0.06.

Step 2: Use each open link to connect Chains B, C, and D.

GOAL STATE

Step 3: Close each open link to complete the necklace. This step costs $0.09.

FIGURE 7.11 ■ Solution to the Nine-Dot Problem

To solve this problem, you need to realize that all four lines must extend beyond the square of dots.

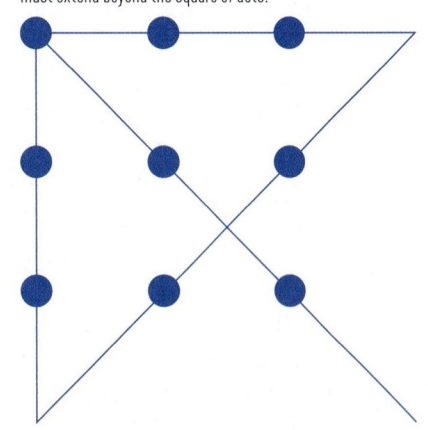

FIGURE 7.12 ■ Solution to Duncker's Candle Problem

To solve this problem, you need to realize that the box can be used not only as a container but also as a shelf.

Monica Wierzbicki/Body Scientific Intl.

The Availability Heuristic

Another mental shortcut that people use is the **availability heuristic**, the tendency to estimate the likelihood of an event based on how easily instances of that event come to mind. To demonstrate, Tversky and Kahneman (1973) asked subjects to judge whether there are more words in English that begin with the letter *K* or the letter *T*. To answer this question, subjects tried to think of words that started with each letter. More words came to mind that started with *T*, so most subjects correctly chose *T* as the answer. In this case, the availability heuristic was useful. It sure beat counting up all the relevant words in the dictionary.

As demonstrated, the availability heuristic enables us to make judgments that are quick and easy. But often, these judgments are in error. For example, Tversky and Kahneman asked some subjects the following question: Which is more common, words that start with the letter *K* or words that contain *K* as the third letter? It turns out the English language contains many more words with *K* as the third letter than as the first. Yet out of 152 subjects, 105 guessed it to be the other way around. The reason for this disparity is that it's easier to bring to mind words that start with *K*, so these are judged more common.

The letter-estimation bias is harmless, but the availability heuristic can lead us astray in important ways—as when uncommon events pop easily to mind because they are very recent or highly emotional. One possible consequence concerns the perception of risk. Which is a more likely cause of death in the United States: drowning in a pool or fatal injury due to a cataclysmic storm such as a tornado or hurricane? The truth is that swimming pools are much riskier—with the odds at 1 in 5,271—than cataclysmic storms—with the odds at 1 in 62,288 (Insurance Information Institute, 2016). However, the media posts more stories about storm fatalities than swimming pool drownings. Thus, people who are asked to guess the major causes of death tend to overestimate the number of those who die as a result of events that are highly publicized such as shootings, fires, floods, terrorist bombings, accidents, and other dramatic events—and to underestimate the number of deaths caused by heart attacks, diabetes, and other mundane and less memorable events (Slovic, Fischoff, & Lichtenstein, 1982). Made relevant by current fears of terrorism, research shows that people's perceptions of risk are affected more by fear, anxiety, and other emotions than by cold probabilities (Slovic, 2000; Tannenbaum et al., 2015).

Dramatic airline disasters are so memorable that people overestimate the risks of flying. In fact, mile for mile, travelers are far more likely to die in a car crash than on a commercial flight.
iStock.com/porpeller

availability heuristic. A tendency to estimate the likelihood of an event in terms of how easily instances of it can be recalled.

Anchoring Effects

Using the availability heuristic, people are influenced in their judgments by the facts that are most available in memory—and they fail to make adjustments to compensate for that bias. A related phenomenon is the **anchoring effect**, the tendency to use one stimulus as an "anchor," or reference point, in judging a second stimulus.

Imagine being asked, "What proportion of African nations are in the United Nations?" Think about it. What would be your estimate? Now suppose that before answering this question, the experimenter spun a roulette wheel marked with numbers from 1 to 100. You think the outcome of the spin is random, but actually the wheel is rigged to stop either at 10 or at 65. At that point, the experimenter asks, "Is the proportion of African nations in the United Nations above or below the wheel number? Then what, specifically, is your estimate?" As a result of this procedure, subjects vary their estimates according to the numerical reference point provided by the wheel number. Those for whom 10 was the initial anchor estimated that 25 percent of African nations were in the U.N. Among those given 65 as an anchor, the estimate was 45 percent. Even though subjects assumed the wheel number to be arbitrary, it served as a starting point for their numerical estimates (Kahneman et al., 1982). Additional studies have confirmed that anchoring effects are common and powerful—even with our own judgments about memory performance (Yang, Sun, & Shanks, 2017). Thus, numerical reference points bias judgments of events even among people who are offered prizes to be accurate and among those who say afterward that they were not influenced by the anchor (Wilson, Houston, Brekke, & Etling, 1996).

anchoring effect. The tendency to use an initial value as an "anchor," or reference point, in making a new numerical estimate.

LEARNING CHECK

Blind Spots and Biases

Don't let blind spots in problem solving or biases in judgment prevent you from seeing which description best matches each term in the left column.

1.	Confirmation bias	a.	Using one stimulus as a reference point in judging a second stimulus.
2.	Representation failure	b.	Judging the likelihood of an event based on how easily other instances of it come to mind.
3.	Availability heuristic	c.	Thinking about a problem in a way that makes it seem unsolvable.
4.	Representativeness heuristic	d.	Overlooking evidence that doesn't support your beliefs.
5.	Functional fixedness	e.	Letting past experience get in the way of thinking about a problem from a new perspective.
6.	Mental set	f.	Thinking of objects only in terms of their usual functions.
7.	Anchoring effect	g.	Judging the likelihood of an event based on how typical it seems.

(Answers: 1. d; 2. c; 3. b; 4. g; 5. f; 6. e; 7. a.)

What's Your Prediction?

If anchoring leads us to set high or low reference points, what are the implications? Can trial lawyers raise or lower the amount of money that juries award by stating large or small amounts? Would juries deem lawyers as greedy, and react against it? Or, are juries so focused on evidence that they disregard what lawyers ask for?

Mollie Marti and Roselle Wissler (2000) presented mock jurors with a case of a dock worker who fell and was badly injured, and who sued the trucking company responsible for the accident. There was no dispute that the company was at fault; jurors only had to decide how much money to award the worker for pain and suffering. In one version of the case, the plaintiff's lawyer did not state a figure. In other versions, he asked for $750,000, $1.5 million, or $5 million. Make a prediction: What effect do you think the requests had?

When no request was made, jurors gave an average of $680,000. Did the larger requests lead jurors to award more, less, or the same? Demonstrating an anchoring effect, Figure 7.13 shows that the more the lawyer asked for, the more he got. In fact, one follow-up study showed that jurors awarded even more when the lawyer sought $15 million. Bennett (2014) argues that the anchoring effect occurs "even when the anchor is incomplete, inaccurate, irrelevant, implausible, or even random" (p. 489). Bennett also reviews anchoring research across a wide range of fields such as medicine, real estate, psychology, and finances. In this way, the anchoring effect can have quite the impact on things such as the punishment given to a guilty party, the amount of money a home sells for, and investments. Thanks to anchoring effects, you can sometimes get what you ask for.

FIGURE 7.13 ■ Anchoring Effects

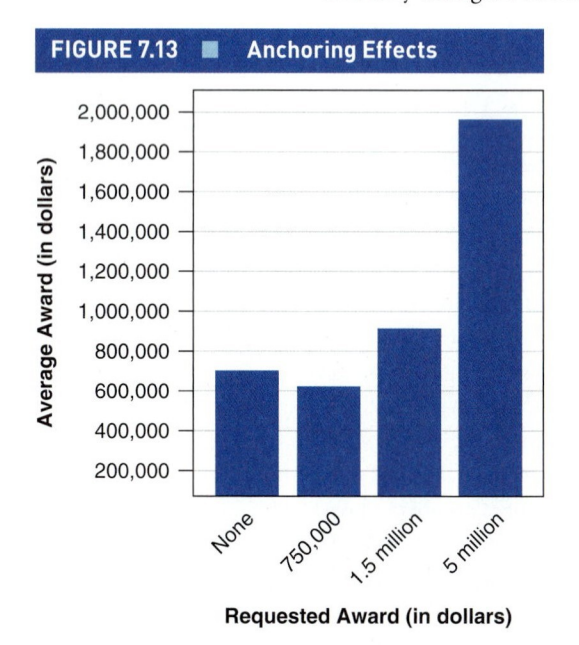

Source: Marti, M. W., & Wissler, R. L. (2000). Be careful what you ask for: The effect of anchors on personal-injury damages awards. Journal of Experimental Psychology: Applied, 6(2), 91–103. https://doi.org/10.1037/1076-898X.6.2.91

LANGUAGE

LEARNING OBJECTIVES

Define language, and recognize its properties.

- Determine if you agree with the saying, "All humans speak in the same tongue."
- Identify the universal properties of all languages.
- Describe how language emerges.

Language is a form of communication consisting of a system of sounds, words, meanings, and rules for their combination. Language is also a defining and adaptive milestone in human evolution. Linguist Noam Chomsky (1972) argued that the human brain is biologically hardwired for the acquisition of language. Thus, all cultures have language, all languages have certain structural properties (such as nouns and verbs) in common, and children all over the world learn to fluently speak the language they hear, at about the same age, and without much effort or instruction.

When it comes to language, it's clear that some form of learning occurs—but it's also clear that humans are born with a unique *sensitivity* to the sounds and structures of speech (MacWhinney, 1998). Terrence Deacon (1998) has argued that the human brain and language have coevolved over millions of years. Steven Pinker (1994) believes that the ability to learn, speak, and understand language is a powerful instinct, tightly woven into the human experience. "All over the world," he notes, "members of our species fashion their breath into hisses and hums and squeaks and pops and listen to others do the same.... We humans are fitted with a means of sharing our ideas, in all their unfathomable vastness" (Pinker, 1999, p. 1). In the coming sections, we will consider the unique properties of "language" and, finally, the relationship between thought and language.

language. A form of communication consisting of sounds, words, meanings, and rules for their combination.

Characteristics of Human Language

According to Ethnologue (2018), there are roughly 7,097 spoken languages worldwide, to say nothing of the different dialects within each language. When all the dialects are taken into account, tens of thousands of variations can be distinguished further. It's amazing how different many languages seem on the surface. To appreciate this point, consider the top 10 most spoken languages in the world (Babbel, 2018): Mandarin Chinese, Spanish, English, Hindi, Arabic, Portuguese, Bengali, Russian, Japanese, and Punjabi/Lahnda. Despite the differences, however, linguists are quick to note that from a Martian's perspective, all humans speak with a single tongue. The reason is that all languages share certain universal properties: **semanticity**, generativity, and displacement.

semanticity. The property of language that accounts for the communication of meaning.

phonemes. The basic, distinct sounds of a spoken language.

Semanticity

The smallest units of speech are **phonemes**, the basic *sounds*, or building blocks, of all spoken languages. Each separate sound you hear when you pronounce the word *unthinkable* is one phoneme. English has 26 letters, but 40 to 45 phonemes. The word *tip* has three phonemes: *t, i*, and *p*; so do the words *ship* (*sh, i*, and *p*) and *chip* (*ch, i*, and *p*). Linguists estimate that human beings are physiologically capable of producing 100 basic sounds. No one language uses all of them, however. Most contain between 28 and 80 phonemes. English speakers say *s* and *z* differently. In Spanish, they're one and the same. As a result of such differences in vocal experience, people sometimes struggle to pronounce the phonemes of other languages. For example, many Americans struggle to roll the German *r* or cough up the guttural *ch* sound of Arabic.

A string of randomly connected phonemes does not convey sound that is meaningful. The smallest unit that carries meaning

At a produce market in Hong Kong, shoppers converse in Chinese—the most widely spoken language in the world.

iStock.com/danielvfung

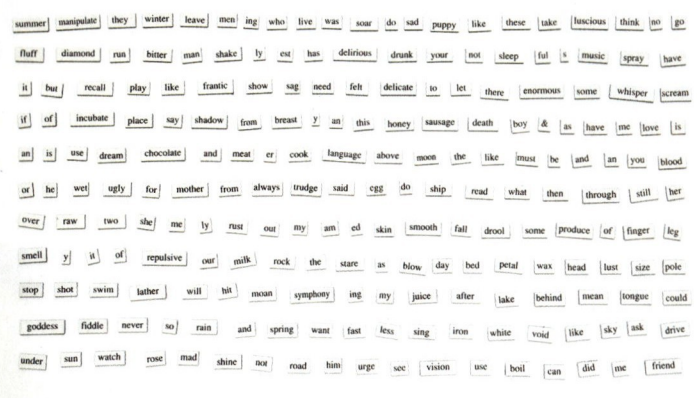

Each of these units can be combined to form meaning. To create a sentence, the units must complete words that are organized sequentially.

iStock.com/THPStock

morphemes. In language, the smallest units that carry meaning (e.g., prefixes, root words, suffixes).

phrase. A group of words that act as a unit to convey meaning. Phrases are formed from combinations of morphemes.

sentence. An organized sequence of words that expresses a thought, a statement of fact, a proposition, an intention, a request, or a question.

generativity. The property of language that accounts for the capacity to use a limited number of words to produce an infinite variety of expressions.

syntax. Rules of grammar that govern the arrangement of words in a sentence.

displacement. The property of language that accounts for the capacity to communicate about matters that are not in the here-and-now.

is called a **morpheme**. Words, prefixes, and suffixes are all morphemes. Every word has one or more morphemes. Simple words like *dog*, *run*, and *think* contain one. The word *unthinkable* has three morphemes—the prefix *un-*, the root word *think*, and the suffix *-able*—and each adds to the total meaning of the word. The average American high school graduate knows about 45,000 different words, and the average college graduate has a vocabulary that is nearly twice that size (Miller, 1991). It is quite remarkable that human beings are able to master a full language vocabulary so well, and so quickly, given that most word sounds are unrelated to meaning. There is no reason why a cat is called a *c-a-t* as opposed to a *d-o-g*. It just happens to be that way. There are exceptions to this rule, as some words do resemble the sounds they signify (such as *bang*, *crack*, and *oink*).

Combinations of morphemes become the building blocks for **phrases**, groups of words that act as a unit to convey meaning. Take this quote by author Joseph Heller, "When I grow up, I want to be a little boy." In this quote, the words "When I grow up" and "I want to be a little boy" are both phrases. Morphemes and phrases are then combined into larger units we call sentences. A **sentence** is an organized sequence of words that expresses a thought, a statement of fact, a proposition, an intention, a request, or a question. Most English sentences contain 20 words or fewer. When English sentences exceed that number of words, we often refer to it as a "run-on sentence." However, that doesn't mean a hard rule exists for sentence length. Jonathan Coe's book *Rotter's Club* contains a sentence that comprises 13,955 words.

Generativity

A second property of language is **generativity**, the capacity it offers to use a finite number of words and rules for combining words to produce an infinite variety of novel expressions. Generativity gives language virtually unlimited flexibility as a system of communication. Two features of human language enable this flexibility. The first is that a phrase can always be added to the end of a sentence in order to form an entirely new sentence. Thus, you could go from the sentence "I like psychology" to "I like psychology this semester" to "I like psychology this semester, thanks to the professor," and so on. A second aspect of language that makes it flexible is that one expression can always be inserted inside another. This makes possible the construction of long, embedded sentences.

If language is so generative that we can produce limitless numbers of novel sentences, how are we able to comprehend each other as competently as we do? The key to managing generativity is **syntax**, rules of grammar that govern how words can be arranged in a sentence. Expressions are not random strings of unrelated sounds but, rather, words that are combined in familiar and orderly ways. Every language has its own unique syntax. For example, adjectives usually come *before* the noun in English (*white wine*) but *after* the noun in Spanish (*vino blanco*). We'll learn later on in this chapter that children learn most of the rules of their language by the age of 5, and they do so without explicit instruction. Hardly anyone can explain the rules of grammar, yet most of us can instantly spot a statement that violates these rules.

Displacement

A third property of language is **displacement**. Displacement refers to the fact that language can be used to communicate about things that are not in our immediate surroundings, matters that extend beyond the limits of the here-and-now. Thus, we reminisce about the good old days, we talk about our hopes and dreams for the future, we gossip about others behind their backs, and we discuss abstract ideas concerning religion, politics, social justice, and love.

Emergence of Language

Paralleling the changes that take place in the way children think is their development of language, as summarized in Table 7.3. Between the ages of 1 and 6 years, children acquire a vocabulary that consists of an estimated 14,000 words, an average of 9 words per day. They also learn to combine words in ways that fit grammatical rules too complex for most of us to explain. What's amazing about these achievements is that children of all cultures absorb the words and grammar of language without formal instruction. It just happens. As in cognitive development, some children may speak sooner than others, but the sequence of achievements is the same for all (Brown, 1973; McNeill, 1970; Rice, 1989).

TABLE 7.3 ■ Milestones in the Emergence of Language

Ages	Stages
1–2 months	Cooing (*oh, ah*)
4 months	Babbling (*ah boo*)
8–16 months	First words
24 months	Two- and three-word telegraphic speech
2–3 years	Multiword sentences
4 years	Adultlike, mostly grammatical speech

Developmental Sequence

Newborns communicate their needs by crying. In their second month, they also use the tongue to make more articulated *cooing* sounds such as *oh* and *ah*. At about 4 months, babies begin playful **babbling**, vocalizing for the first time in ways that sound like human speech—*ah boo, da da*, and *ah gee*. As with crying and cooing, babbling is inborn. Regardless of whether the native language is English, French, Spanish, German, Hebrew, or Swahili, babies all over the world initially make the same sounds, including some they never hear at home (for example, the German *ch* and the rolled *r*). Even babies who are born deaf and cannot hear speech babble right on schedule.

Sometime near the first birthday, give or take 4 months, babies utter their first real *words*. The sounds are brief and not clearly pronounced, but they communicate meaning in the native tongue—for example, *ba* for *bottle*. For the next few months, babies speak one-word utterances, and the number of words in their vocabulary increases sharply (Woodward, Markman, & Fitzsimmons, 1994)—from 4 or 5 at 12 months, to 30 at 18 months, to 250 at 2 years. These utterances are not random. Babies tend to name objects and actions that they desire (a bottle, favorite toys, "more"), especially those that involve motion (cars, a pet dog)—an outcome that Piaget would predict of a sensorimotor child (Nelson, 1973), as discussed in the chapter on life span development.

At about 2 years of age, there is a vocabulary explosion, as children accumulate hundreds of new words a year. At this point, children will pick up a new word they encounter in conversation—even when they hear it only once or twice. For building a vocabulary, it helps for young children to be spoken to. Observational research has shown that toddlers whose mothers were more talkative, compared to those whose mothers were less talkative, had 131 more words in their vocabularies at 20 months and 295 more words at 2 years (Huttenlocher, Levine, & Vevea, 1998).

Another important development in language occurs when children begin to form two- and three-word phrases. These early word combinations illustrate what is called **telegraphic speech** because—as in telegrams, kept short for cost reasons—they include only nouns, verbs, and some essential modifiers, yet make sense to the listener ("More juice" for "I want more juice," or "No sit chair" for "I don't want to sit in a chair"). It's interesting that these primitive sentence forms contain the seeds of grammar—"more juice" rather than "juice more," for example. It's also interesting that the statements are often *overextensions*. For example, until different animals can be distinguished, the 2-year-old who uses the word *doggie* to call the family pet will use the same word about a cat, a horse, or a circus elephant.

babbling. Spontaneous vocalizations of basic speech sounds, which infants begin at about 4 months of age.

telegraphic speech. The early short form of speech in which the child omits unnecessary words—as telegrams once did ("More milk").

When children are building a vocabulary, it is helpful to frequently speak to and with them.
iStock.com/NicolasMcComber

Language tells us a lot about a child's developing knowledge of the world.

By the age of 3 to 5 years, a child's mind contains a small dictionary of words ready to be used correctly. Although new words are learned without any explicit thought or instruction, an enriched linguistic environment can accelerate the process. For example, preschoolers who watch the educational TV show *Sesame Street* have larger vocabularies than those who do not (Rice, Huston, Truglio, & Wright, 1990). With increasing age, children construct longer and more complex sentences; learn to use plurals, pronouns, past tense, and other rules of grammar; and begin to appreciate puns and words with double meanings. At puberty, corresponding to the onset of Piaget's formal operational stage, children even come to appreciate abstract metaphors—"like two ships passing in the night."

Developmental Theories

No one disputes the stages of language development in children or the sequence of those stages. But there are differences of opinion as to what it all means. One issue in particular has been whether language develops as a result of nature, nurture, or both. In 1957, behaviorist B. F. Skinner wrote a book entitled *Verbal Behavior*, in which he argued that children learn to speak the way animals learn to run mazes. They associate objects and words, imitate adults, and repeat phrases that are met by social reinforcement. Through trial and error, for example, a baby of English-speaking parents learns to repeat the babbling sounds that excite mom and dad but not foreign sounds that leave them cold.

Certainly, environmental experiences play a role in language acquisition, with enriched experiences associated with not only stronger language or conversation complexity but also greater school achievement in general (Huttenlocher, Waterfall, Vasilyeva, Vevea, & Hedges, 2010; Rowe, 2012). In response to Skinner, linguist Noam Chomsky (1959, 1972) argued forcefully that the human brain is hardwired for the acquisition of language. Specifically, he argued that children are endowed from birth with a "universal grammar," core rules common to all human languages, and the ability to apply these rules to the language they hear spoken. The evidence for this biological position is impressive: Language grows at a rate that exceeds all other kinds of learning. For example, 2-year-olds construct telegraphic statements they couldn't possibly have heard from adults, and children learn to speak properly even though nobody really stops to correct their grammar. Furthermore, the rate at which language grows appears to favor females, whose language performance during the first 30 months of life exceeds that of males in vocabulary growth (Bauer, Goldfield, & Reznick, 2002; Eriksson et al., 2012), communicative gestures (Ozçalişkan & Goldin-Meadow, 2010), and vocabulary size (Westerlund & Lagerberg, 2008). But be mindful that these findings do not necessarily prove that nature or nurture is at play. In fact, it is quite possible that we raise females in such a way that they are exposed to vocabulary with a higher frequency, given more attention, or receive additional encouragement in comparison to males during language development.

To some extent, it is clear that human beings are genetically prepared for language the way that computers are prewired for programming (Pinker, 1994). The environment we live in may provide the software that determines *what* language we learn to speak, but biology provides the hardware that controls when and *how* we learn it. It's also clear that in the acquisition of language, there is a critical, or at least sensitive, period during the first few years of life when humans are most receptive to language learning (Lenneberg, 1967). That is why adolescents and adults who learn a second language speak it with an accent, while children who acquire a new language before puberty speak it without an accent. It is also why linguists suggest that parents of deaf children teach their child sign language as early as possible (Humphries et al., 2014). Research investigating deaf children who are exposed to sign language after the critical period—because of cochlear implant failure—struggle to master both sign language and speech (Humphries et al., 2014). The same pattern is true in the acquisition of grammar. In a study of Asian immigrants to the United States, the younger they were as children when they moved, the higher was their score on a test of grammar (Johnson & Newport, 1989).

THE RELATIONSHIP BETWEEN THOUGHT AND LANGUAGE

> **LEARNING OBJECTIVES**
>
> Explain how the words we use influence our ideas about others, ourselves, and the world.
> - Relate the words we speak to the way we conceptualize the world.
> - Discuss how culture affects language.

This chapter has shown that thought and language are interrelated cognitive activities. Having now examined them separately, we are faced with the question "What is the nature of their interrelationship?"

The Linguistic-Relativity Hypothesis

Common sense tells us that language is a useful tool for expressing thought, but that it is not necessary. Thus, child development researchers have found that young children understand concepts before they have words to explain them (Flavell, Miller, & Miller, 1993) and that they can assign objects to categories even when they do not have the relevant vocabulary (Gershkoff-Stowe, Thal, Smith, & Namy, 1997).

In the fifth century BCE, Herodotus, a Greek historian, argued that the Greeks and Egyptians thought differently because the Greeks wrote from left to right and Egyptians from right to left. Many years later, inspired by anthropologist Edward Sapir, Benjamin Lee Whorf (1956) theorized that the language we speak—the words, rules, and so on—determines the way we conceptualize the world. This notion, that our thoughts are "relative" to our linguistic heritage, is called the **linguistic-relativity hypothesis**. This hypothesis gave rise to a profound prediction: that people of different cultures who speak different languages must think in different ways (Gumperz & Levinson, 1996; Lucy, 1992). As we'll learn shortly, this hypothesis led researchers to span the globe in search of cross-cultural comparisons.

Does language have the power to shape the way people think? As a result of many years of research, nobody believes that language *determines* thought the way genes determine a person's height. But most psychologists do agree with a less radical claim: that language *influences* thinking (Bloom, 1981; Goodman & Lassiter, 2014; Hardin & Banaji, 1993; Hunt & Agnoli, 1991; Lucy, 1992). In one study, researchers showed subjects line drawings and varied the label that accompanied each one, as illustrated in Figure 7.14. Afterward, subjects redrew these figures from memory in ways that were distorted by the labels (Carmichael, Hogan, & Walter, 1932). In a second study, subjects were presented with pictures of faces or color chips, and half were asked to describe them. Those who had put what they saw into words later had more difficulty recognizing the original faces and colors. Did language in this case disrupt thought? Yes, according to the investigators, "some things are better left unsaid" (Schooler & Engstler-Schooler, 1990).

If language can influence thought, then words are tools that can be used to socialize our children, sell products, mold public opinion, and stir the masses. People in power are aware of this connection and choose their words carefully. As colorfully documented by William Lutz (1996), the result is

linguistic-relativity hypothesis. The hypothesis that language determines, or at least influences, the way we think.

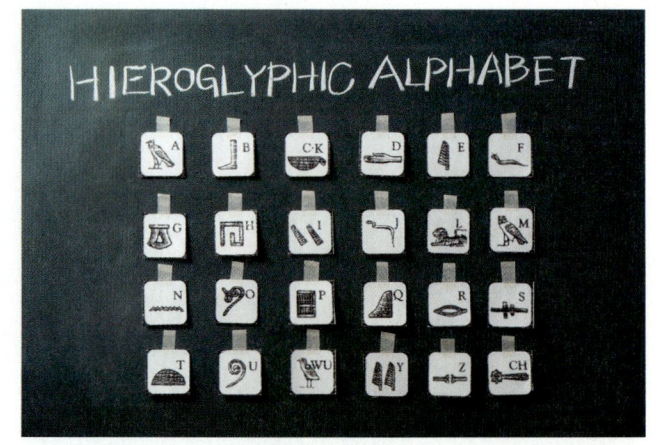

Hieroglyphs are read from the right to the left—the opposite of how we read the English language. Alphabets are different, too. Hieroglyphic letters are in the form of objects, such as a viper for the letter F.

iStock.com/kyoshino

FIGURE 7.14 ■ Words That Distort Memory for Images

Subjects who saw figures like those shown (*left*) later redrew these figures from memory in ways that fit the different labels they had been given (*right*).

Original figures	Labels	Sample drawings
◆	Curtains in a window	◆
	Diamond in a rectangle	◆
🌙	Crescent moon	🌙
	Letter "C"	🌙
○–○	Eyeglasses	○–○
	Dumbbell	○–○
☼	Ship's wheel	☼
	Sun	●
🫘	Kidney bean	🫘
	Canoe	🫘

"doublespeak"—language that is designed to mislead, conceal, inflate, confuse, and distort meaning. Thus, we are told that a new tax is a "user's fee," that companies that fire employees are merely "downsizing," that recession is "negative economic growth," that civilian war deaths are "collateral damage," and that plastic handbags are made of "genuine imitation leather." Even more common are the euphemisms we all use to talk about touchy subjects. Thus, we say that people who died "passed away," that being unemployed is being "between jobs," and that we need to use the toilet in a "restroom" (Allan & Burridge, 1991; Holder, 2002).

Culture, Language, and the Way We Think

According to Whorf's linguistic-relativity hypothesis, people who speak different languages think about the world in different ways. To illustrate, Whorf (1956) pointed to cultural variations in the use of words to represent reality. He noted, for example, the Hanunoo people of the Philippines have 92 names for rice—in contrast to the crude distinction North Americans make between "white rice" and "brown rice." Similarly, although English has only one word for snow, the Inuit have several words—which, Whorf argued, enables them to make distinctions that others may miss between "falling snow, snow on the ground, snow packed hard like ice, slushy snow, wind-driven flying snow—whatever the situation may be" (p. 216). Even grammar shapes thought, claimed Whorf. For example, he compared English to the language of the Hopis. In English, you can use the same numerical modifier for units of time ("five days") as for concrete objects ("five pebbles"). In the Hopi language, by contrast, different numerical modifiers are used in each case. Whorf argued that this feature causes the speakers of each language to perceive time differently.

Evaluating the linguistic-relativity hypothesis is not easy because people who speak different languages differ in other ways as well. Many bilingual people say that Whorf is right, citing as

In 2013, David Robson, a scientific journalist for the *Washington Post*, interviewed Igor Krupnik, a researcher at Smithsonian Institution's Arctic Studies Center. Krupnik believes there are around 50 words for snow in the Inuit dialect.

AGF / Contributor/Universal Images Group/Getty Images

personal evidence the odd sense that they think differently in each language—and sometimes get "lost in translation" (Hoffman, 1989). However, there are flaws in both the theory and the research. First, even if members of two cultures did think differently, who's to say that the difference in their language came first? Second, the Inuit may have several words for snow, but does that mean they think about snow differently? After all, people in other regions of North America distinguish between slush, fresh powder, packed powder, hail, wet snow, and the "loose granular" substance often found on ski slopes.

INTELLIGENCE

> ### LEARNING OBJECTIVES
>
> Critique the theoretical types of intelligence for accuracy and bias.
> - Examine the reasons why intelligence is measured.
> - Describe how IQ tests are constructed.
> - Recognize what it means to create an accurate IQ test.

The term **intelligence** means different things to different people, as illustrated in Figure 7.15. In fact, it's important to realize that your definition is influenced by the culture and generation in which you live. Many students are impressed by the combination of speed and general knowledge that enables contestants on TV game shows like *Jeopardy!* to win large sums of money. For some South Pacific islanders, however, intelligence is defined by your ability to navigate the ocean from one island to the next. For the San people in Africa, it means having the skills needed for productive hunting and gathering. For gang members in an inner city, "street smarts" is what matters most. To accommodate the many ways in which people all over the world exhibit their intelligence, many psychologists prefer to define the concept in general terms, as a capacity to learn from experience and adapt successfully to one's environment.

intelligence. The capacity to learn from experience and adapt successfully to one's environment.

Intelligence Tests

The study of intelligence began with the instruments used to measure it. Like much of psychology, intelligence testing is long on tradition but short on history. About 4,000 years ago, the Chinese used civil service exams to measure aptitude. But it was not until the end of the 19th century that modern forms of assessment were born. The first psychologist to devise such "mental tests" was Francis Galton (1883), Charles Darwin's cousin. Noticing that great achievements run in families like his own, Galton

FIGURE 7.15 ■ Concepts of Intelligence

There are many conceptions of intelligence. One is to associate it with the kind of general knowledge that is needed to play and win on *Jeopardy!* Intelligence can also be the capacity to adapt to one's environment and complete ritual challenges, like the Maori of New Zealand.

Handout / Handout/Getty Images; iStock.com/Uwe Moser

Galton's laboratory at the London Health Exhibition in 1884.
Science & Society Picture Library / Contributor/SSPL/Getty Images

believed that intelligence was inherited. Like it or not, he said, all men and women are *not* created equal. Taking a page from Darwin's book on evolution, Galton went on to suggest that if intelligence could be measured objectively, then the typically slow processes of "natural selection" and "survival of the fittest" could be hastened through *eugenics*, selective-breeding policies that encourage only the brightest of adults to reproduce.

How did Galton measure intelligence? If you had visited the Chicago World's Fair in 1883 or London's International Health Exhibition in 1884, you could have been one of thousands to find out. For a small fee, a technician using Galton's state-of-the-art equipment would measure biologically rooted abilities such as your muscular strength; the size of your head; your speed at reacting to signals; and, most importantly, your ability to detect slight differences between two weights, lights, and tones. Afterward, you would receive an intelligence score printed on a card (Johnson et al., 1985).

By today's standards, these measures are crude and inaccurate. Indeed, even Galton found that bright, highly accomplished adults did *not* get higher-than-average scores. Galton's elitist proposal for increasing the native intelligence of the human species through selective breeding laid the groundwork for what would become a bumpy road for the intelligence-testing movement that followed (Weinberg, 1989). What's worse, he founded a eugenics movement that spawned involuntary sterilization laws in a number of American states and later provided justification for the Holocaust in Nazi Germany—a development that would have distressed Galton (Gillham, 2001). The story is told in more detail by Adam Cohen (2016) in a book titled *Imbeciles: The Supreme Court, American Eugenics, and the Sterilization of Carrie Buck* and in his interview with Terry Gross on National Public Radio's *Fresh Air* (Gross, 2017).

The Stanford-Binet

Across the English Channel, French psychologist Alfred Binet sought to measure intelligence for humane reasons: to enhance the education of children needing special assistance. In 1904, a few years after a law was passed requiring all French children to attend school, the minister of public instruction hired Binet to develop an objective means of identifying children who would have difficulty with normal class work. With the help of Théophile Binet and Simon (1905) developed a test that contained questions on problem solving, numbers, vocabulary, logical reasoning, general knowledge, and memory—the kinds of skills that are necessary in an academic setting. Binet and Simon wrote hundreds of questions, administered them to students in Paris, and recorded the average performance of children at different ages. Questions for the test were retained if answered correctly by an increasing number of children from one grade level to the next.

Once the test was complete, questions were arranged in order of increasing difficulty and administered by someone trained to score and interpret the results. Assuming that children develop in similar ways but at different rates, Binet and Simon used their test to determine a student's **mental age**, the average age of children who pass the same number of items. In other words, the average 10-year-old would have a mental age of 10. Those who are exceptionally bright would have a mental age that is higher (like an average older child), whereas those who are slow to develop would have one that is lower (like an average younger child). Practically speaking, mental age was a convenient way to score a child's intelligence because it suggested an appropriate grade placement in school.

After Binet died in 1911, the scale was translated into English and imported to the United States by Stanford University psychologist Lewis Terman (1916). The age norms in California were different from those in Paris, so Terman revised many of the questions, added items suitable for adults, published a set of American norms, and gave the test a new name, the **Stanford-Binet**. This test has since been revised four more times (in 1937, 1960, 1986, and 2003). The most recent, the Stanford-Binet V, contains a number of subtests for use between the ages of 2 and 23, and takes about an hour to administer. Ironically, Binet's work was barely known in France until the Stanford-Binet caught on in the United

mental age. The average age of children who passed the same number of items on the Stanford-Binet intelligence test.

Stanford-Binet. An individually administered test designed to measure intelligence.

States. In 1971, 60 years after Binet's death, he and Simon were honored by a commemorative plaque installed at the school in Paris where it all began.

Back at Stanford, Terman was busy developing tests that could be administered in groups (including the popular Stanford Achievement Test), theorizing about the roots of intelligence (he favored nature over nurture as an explanation), and initiating a massive longitudinal study of gifted children. Yet his most notable contribution was the concept of IQ, or **intelligence quotient**. Basing his concept on an idea first offered by German psychologist William Stern, Terman proposed that performance on the Stanford-Binet test be converted to a single score—a ratio derived by dividing mental age (MA) by the person's chronological age (CA), and then multiplying the result by 100 to eliminate the decimal point. The concept is elegantly simple, yet powerful: IQ = (MA/CA) × 100. Using this formula, you can calculate that people who are average (that is, those whose MA and CA are exactly the same) have an IQ of 100. A 10-year-old child with an MA of 12 has an IQ of 120, and a 12-year-old with an MA of 10 has an IQ of 83.

Materials used in the 1937 version of the Stanford-Binet Intelligence Test.
Science & Society Picture Library / Contributor/SSPL/Getty Images

Although IQ is a convenient way to represent a child's intelligence, it makes little sense for adults. The problem is that mental age does not continue to increase with chronological age but levels off as we get older. An average 10-year-old may be two mental-age years ahead of the average 8-year-old, but you can't really say the same for someone who is 20 rather than 18, or 30 rather than 28. When you consider specific examples, the results are ludicrous: If at 18 you get the same score as the average 36-year-old, your IQ would be 200; but if at 36 you had the same score as an average 18-year-old, your IQ would be 50. The solution was to drop Terman's quotient and assign IQ-like scores based instead on a person's performance relative to the average of their same-age peers.

intelligence quotient (IQ). A metric used to represent a child's intelligence, calculated by dividing mental age by chronological age.

The Wechsler Scales

Galton, Binet, and Terman all developed tests that reduced intelligence to a single score. But is that necessarily the most informative approach? David Wechsler (1939) believed it was not, so he constructed a test for adults that considers different aspects of intelligence. The most current version of Wechsler's test has 14 subtests grouped within two major scales—one yielding a *verbal* score, and the other a nonverbal *performance* score useful for people who have language problems. He improved the test in 1955 and called it the **Wechsler Adult Intelligence Scale**, or WAIS (the test was revised in 1981, 1997, 2008, and is abbreviated WAIS–IV). He also created similar tests that have since been revised for different age groups. For children 6 to 16 years old, there is the *Wechsler Intelligence Scale for Children* (WISC–IV), and for preschoolers there is the *Wechsler Preschool and Primary Scale of Intelligence-Revised* (WPPSI–IV).

Wechsler Adult Intelligence Scale (WAIS). The most widely used IQ test for adults, it yields separate scores for verbal and performance subtests.

Because the IQ scale was so deeply ingrained in public consciousness, Wechsler kept the same scoring system, setting the average at 100. Keep in mind, however, that if you took the WAIS-IV, you would get three separate scores—one verbal, one performance, and the total (the most recent version of the Stanford-Binet also yields more than one score). The verbal items call for comprehension, arithmetic, vocabulary, general information, analogies, and the ability to recall strings of digits. In contrast, the items in the nonverbal performance scale ask you to find missing picture parts, arrange cartoons in a logical sequence, reproduce block designs, assemble pieces of a jigsaw-like puzzle, and copy symbols onto paper. The Wechsler scales are relatively easy to administer and score, and they are used in

In the early 1900s, hopeful American immigrants were subjected to examinations, including intelligence tests. Those who failed to pass the test were labeled "feebleminded" and not allowed to enter the country.
SeM / Contributor/Universal Images Group/Getty Images

many schools and clinics (Kaufman & Lichtenberger, 1999). In fact, Weiss and colleagues (2010) refer to the WAIS-IV as the most widely used intelligence test for adults in the world.

Group Aptitude Tests

The Stanford-Binet and the Wechsler scales are used to test one person at a time and take about an hour to administer. This procedure enables the examiner to interact with the test taker and observe whether he or she has trouble with instructions, loses attention, gets frustrated, or gives up too quickly. The disadvantage is that individualized tests are not practical for quick, large-scale assessment. During World War I, for example, the U.S. military needed an efficient way to screen recruits for service. With help from psychologists, two group tests were developed and administered to 1.7 million men—the Army Alpha Test, given in writing to those who could read English; and the Army Beta Test, given orally to those who could not (Lennon, 1985).

Today, group testing is a regular part of our lives. You are no doubt familiar with the Scholastic Assessment Test (SAT), a national rite of passage that many students have learned to fear. Sponsored by the College Board and administered by the Educational Testing Service (ETS), the SAT is a grueling two-and-a-half-hour college entrance exam taken by more than a million college-bound high school juniors and seniors every year. The test, which was developed in 1926, was designed to measure both verbal and mathematical reasoning in a multiple-choice format. As a historical matter, it's ironic that the SAT first came into use as a college admissions tool in the 1930s. At the time, Harvard president James Conant was unhappy that Harvard was a regional college, easy to get into, and filled with privileged young men from New England boarding schools. Looking to identify and recruit outstanding students from diverse regions and modest backgrounds, and needing a way to make comparisons across a national pool of high school seniors, he turned to the SAT. In light of criticisms today that these tests favor some segments of society over others, the irony lies in the fact that the SAT was first used for a noble purpose: to level the playing field for bright students from modest backgrounds (Lemann, 1999).

The newest version of the SAT was launched in 2016. According to David Coleman, the president and CEO of the College Board, the revisions were created with the purpose of measuring college readiness instead of how well students can use "tricks and [try] to eliminate answers" (Gumbrecht, 2014). The SAT is designed to supplement school grades as an objective predictor of academic performance. Instead of or in addition to the SAT, many students take the ACT, a rival exam developed by American College Testing in 1939 that tests abilities in English, math, reading, and science reasoning. Comparable tests are also used to screen applicants for advanced education. If you choose to go on to graduate school, you'll have to take the Graduate Record Examination, or GRE. For other more specialized professions, you would take the Medical College Admission Test (MCAT), the Law School Admission Test (LSAT), or the Graduate Management Admission Test (GMAT).

Are Intelligence Tests Accurate?

Every year, millions of dollars are spent on intelligence testing. But what is the bottom line? Are the tests "accurate"? To answer this question fully, it's important to know that all psychological tests—including those that are designed to measure intelligence—must have three ingredients: standardization, reliability, and validity (Anastasi & Urbina, 1997; Groth-Marnat, 2003).

Standardization means that a test provides a standard of existing norms that can be used to interpret an individual's score. Suppose you took a 150-item SAT and then received a letter indicating that you had correctly answered 115 of the questions. How would you feel? Would you celebrate your success or lament your failure? As you can surmise, a raw score does not provide you with enough information. To interpret the number, you would need to compare it to the performance of others. Standardization is achieved by administering a test to thousands of people similar to those for whom the test is designed. For the Wechsler scales,

---

standardization. The procedure by which existing norms are used to interpret an individual's test score.

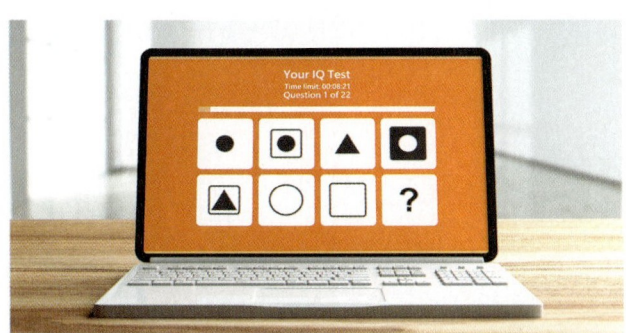

Intelligence tests can be administered online. However, not all intelligence tests are created equal. It's important to know which tests are scientifically valid and reliable.

iStock.com/Rawf8

the average was arbitrarily set at 100, with test scores distributed in a normal, bell-shaped curve where roughly 68 percent of all scores fall between 85 and 115, 95 percent fall between 70 and 130, and 99 percent fall between 55 and 145. The SAT was first standardized in 1941, using a sample of more than 10,000 college-bound students. The verbal and math scores were each put on a scale ranging from 200 to 800, with their averages set at 500. In any case, regardless of whether a test's average is set at 100, 500, or 12 million, your *raw score*—the sheer number of correct answers—must be converted into a standardized *test score* that reflects the distance between your performance and the norm, as illustrated in Figure 7.16.

The second ingredient is **reliability**, which refers to the consistency of a test's results. Two types of consistency are sought. One is **test-retest reliability**, the extent to which a test yields similar results on different occasions. Just as you would not trust a scale that shows moment-to-moment fluctuations in your weight, psychologists would not trust an IQ test that shows radical changes from one session to the next. Intelligence is thought to be a relatively stable trait, not one that varies much over a short period. To ensure that a scale has test-retest reliability, researchers test the same subjects on two occasions—say, a month or two apart—and calculate the correlation between their test and retest scores: the higher the correlation, the more reliable the scale.

The second kind of consistency is **split-half reliability**, the extent to which different forms of a test produce similar results. If you had two scales of the same brand and model, you would expect them to provide identical estimates of your weight. Likewise, alternate forms of an IQ test (often created by dividing it into odd and even items) should produce similar results. Using the test-retest and split-half methods, it's clear that the Stanford-Binet, WAIS, and SAT are reliable measures, all yielding correlations of about +.90. In fact, a study of 23,000 college seniors applying for graduate school showed a very high correlation of +.86 between their scores on the GRE (an exam much like the SAT) and their SAT performances four or more years earlier (Angoff, 1988).

reliability. The extent to which a test yields consistent results over time or using alternate forms.

test-retest reliability. The degree to which a test yields consistent results when readministered at a later time.

split-half reliability. The degree to which alternate forms of a test yield consistent results.

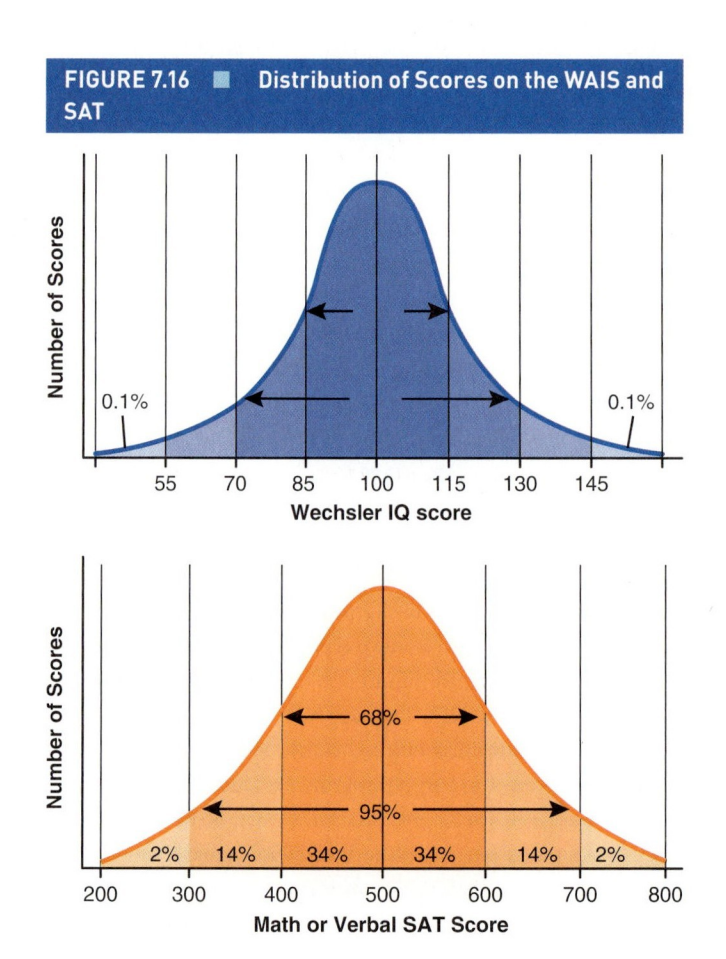

FIGURE 7.16 ■ Distribution of Scores on the WAIS and SAT

Americans differ across cultural heritage, language, and socioeconomic status. Critics of intelligence tests argue that IQ scores are reflective of the dominant White middle class and thus are inherently biased.

iStock.com/hyejin kang

validity. The extent to which a test measures or predicts what it is designed to.

The third essential ingredient is **validity**, a test's ability to measure or predict what it's supposed to. IQ tests may yield consistent scores, but do they indicate intelligence? Do college entrance exams measure aptitude? Better yet, are these tests able to predict academic performance?

If the goal is to assess academic performance, then the tests receive a passing grade, particularly in the earlier school years. In elementary school, there is a high correlation among IQ, class grades, and achievement-test scores. There is a somewhat lower correlation between SAT scores and performance in college, but the combination of high school grades and SAT scores is highly predictive of a student's grade point average (Jensen, 1980; Linn, 1982). As for the GRE, at best it is predictive of the student's first-year performance in graduate school, but the correlation is weak (Miller & Stassun, 2014). Among doctoral candidates in physics between the years 2000 to 2010, Miller and colleagues (2019) found that GRE and undergraduate GPA did "not predict completion as effectively as admissions committees presume" (p. 1). What if the goal is to predict achievement in nonacademic walks of life? If that is the case, then IQ tests are limited in their validity. Hence, many psychologists believe that although these tests assess academic performance, they do not adequately measure the ability to adapt to life outside the classroom (McClelland, 1998; Sedlacek, 2004; Sternberg, 2000).

Are Intelligence Tests Biased?

Critics charge that intelligence tests are culturally biased, in that they favor some social groups over others. To the extent that a test calls for specific cultural knowledge, it *is* biased. That's why Terman had to "Americanize" Binet's French test. But what about IQ testing in the United States, where Americans don't all share a common cultural heritage? Consider an issue that has deeply troubled many psychologists. Ever since cognitive ability tests were first administered, African Americans as a group have averaged 15 points lower than Whites on IQ tests, 200 points lower than Whites on the GRE, and 100 points lower on the SAT verbal and math tests (Miele, 2002; Miller & Stassun, 2014). Nobody disputes the fact that the difference exists. However, disagreements arise as to what it means and what the social implications are.

Later, we'll learn that there are many possible reasons for this difference. But for now, we'll examine one criticism in particular: that the question content within the tests favors the cultural and educational experiences of the White middle class (Garcia, 1981; Miller-Jones, 1989; Saklofske, van de Vijver, Oakland, Mpofu, & Suzuki, 2015). If you take the Stanford-Binet or Wechsler test, for example, you may be asked: What is the color of rubies? What does C.O.D. mean? Who was Thomas Jefferson? To answer these questions, one needs to have knowledge about the dominant culture. It's also important to realize that a person's racial and ethnic background may also guide his or her perception of the testing situation, understanding of the task instructions, motivation to succeed, trust in the examiner, and other aspects of the experience (Helms, 1992). There are many subtle ways in which test scores can be influenced by a person's background—independent of their intelligence.

Advocates of IQ testing have replied to this criticism in two ways. The first is that group differences are found even on test items that are deemed "culture-fair" (illustrated in Figure 7.17)—namely, nonverbal items that do not require extensive knowledge of a particular culture, tasks such as reciting a series of letters or digits, classifying objects, forming a pattern with blocks, or putting together the pieces of a picture puzzle (Cattell, 1949; Raven, Court, & Raven, 1985). One IQ test that is free from language barriers is the Test of Nonverbal Intelligence (TONI-4; Johnsen, 2017). The TONI-4 refrains from reliance on written questions and, according to Susan Johnsen, is "characterized as reliable, valid, relatively free of bias with regard

FIGURE 7.17 ■ Sample Item From Raven's "Culture-Fair" Intelligence Test

In this test, the person is given a series of matrices and must complete each one by selecting the appropriate symbol from the accompanying choices.

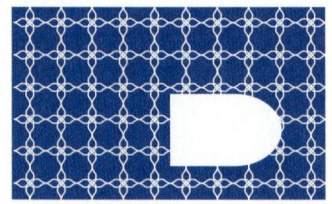

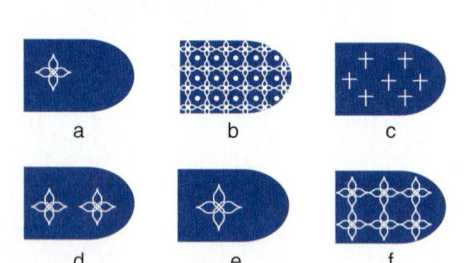

to gender, race, ethnicity, and other relevant variables" (p. 185). Second, intelligence and aptitude tests are statistically valid predictors of performance within the schools of a particular culture, the purpose for which they were designed—regardless of whether students are African American, White, Latinx, or Asian (Kaplan, 1985).

THE NATURE OF INTELLIGENCE

> **LEARNING OBJECTIVES**
>
> Appreciate the range of intelligences proposed by the field of psychology.
>
> - Examine why some psychologists believe intelligence to be one general ability.
> - Determine if we can predict a child's IQ in infancy.
> - Understand the arguments posed by psychologists who believe that there are multiple human intelligences.

From the beginning, intelligence tests were constructed for strictly practical purposes—to identify slow learners in school, assign new military recruits, and select strong college applicants from modest backgrounds. Unfortunately, the initial emphasis on tests and measurements may have stunted the growth of theories concerning the very nature of intelligence—what it is, where it comes from, and how it is developed. As one psychologist put it, "Intelligence is whatever an intelligence test measures" (Boring, 1923).

One of the most unsatisfying aspects of IQ tests is that they reduce intelligence to a single uncomplicated number. But does that number tell a rich enough story about any one person's intellect? Think about yourself for a minute. Here you are, taking a course in psychology, which means you have a desire and capacity to learn complex material. You can operate your smartphone, learn how to manage and apply a new app with ease, and live in a world that is constantly demanding adaptation. But can you solve a Rubik's Cube, find your way around without GPS, or correctly assemble a piece of furniture without using the instructions? It's amazing how a person can feel so smart and yet so dense all at once. The point is that you have to wonder whether a person's intelligence can really be summarized by a single IQ score or even by two scores, as in the WAIS and SAT.

Crystallized and Fluid Intelligence

For a moment, ponder how much information you have learned across the range of subjects you have studied throughout your education. Now, how important is it that you can use that information in various ways to solve problems? **Fluid intelligence** is the ability to reason quickly and abstractly, solve problems of logic, detect letter or number sequences, or learn new information. In contrast, **crystallized intelligence** reflects an accumulation of factual knowledge, skill, or expertise—as measured, for example, by the sheer size of one's vocabulary or the ability to add and subtract. Raymond Cattell (1963) and, later, John Horn (1982) distinguished between fluid and crystallized intelligence. More and more, psychologists find that this distinction helps us to understand why some intellectual abilities are vulnerable to decline with age, whereas others are maintained (Baltes, Staudinger, & Lindenberger, 1999; Kaufman, 2001; Zaval, Li, Johnson, & Weber, 2015).

The distinction between fluid and crystallized intelligence is important because, when both are tested separately, two different developmental patterns are found. In one large-scale study, for example, K. Warner Schaie and Sherry Willis (1993) tested more than 1,600 adults in age groups that ranged from 29 to 88 years old. As predicted, the fluid-intelligence test scores started to decline steadily through middle and late adulthood, but the measures of crystallized intelligence remained relatively stable—at least until subjects were in their 70s and 80s.

fluid intelligence. A form of intelligence that involves the ability to reason logically and abstractly.

crystallized intelligence. A form of intelligence that reflects the accumulation of verbal skills and factual knowledge.

The distinction between fluid and crystallized intelligence is related to another developmental change: that people lose mental *speed* as they get older. Whether a task involves folding paper, recognizing pictures, solving arithmetic problems or verbal analogies, proofreading, assembling cubes, or reading a story, we get slower and slower over the life span (Birren & Fisher, 1995; Salthouse, 1996; Frieske & Park, 1999). Unfortunately, no one is immune, not even senior university professors and others who are intellectually active and stimulated (Salthouse, Berish, & Miles, 2002; Shimamura, Berry, Mangels, Rusting, & Jurica, 1995; Zaval et al., 2015).

General Intelligence

Psychologists have long disagreed about whether there is one intelligence or many. Some theorists can be called "lumpers," in that they view different aspects of intelligence as part of a general underlying capacity. Others are "splitters" who divide intelligence into two or more specific abilities (Weinberg, 1989). Following in Binet's footsteps, all test developers make it a point to include many tasks and derive an IQ score by averaging a subject's performance on the different items. But is it then meaningful to calculate an average level of intelligence? Yes, according to the lumpers, some people are generally smarter and more capable than others, regardless of whether they are trying to design a web page, memorize a poem, learn a foreign language, solve a complex equation, or fix a car.

Charles Spearman (1904) was the first to propose that **general intelligence** (abbreviated as **g**) underlies all mental abilities. Spearman noticed that people who excel at one task—say, verbal analogies—also tend to perform well on mazes, block designs, and other seemingly unrelated tasks. His administration of different kinds of tests to subjects led to the discovery that although individuals may be more skilled in some areas than in others, the intellectual abilities are highly correlated. This pattern suggests that there is a general intelligence factor, g, which underlies our more specific abilities. As far as Spearman was concerned—and many others as well—a person's intelligence can, at least in a general way, be summarized by a single IQ score (Eysenck, 1982; Jensen, 1998).

Shortly after Spearman uncovered g, Louis Thurstone (1938) administered 56 different tests to college students and concluded that human intelligence consists of seven factors, which he called primary mental abilities. For Thurstone, a person's intellectual profile cannot be captured fully by a single number. Other psychologists agree with this emphasis on specific abilities but disagree on how many. John Horn and Raymond Cattell (1966) and Paul Kline (1991) said there are two types of intelligence. J. P. Guilford (1967) believed that intelligence consists of 120 different factors—a number he later increased to 150 (Guilford, 1985).

At this point, research provides evidence for both a general intelligence and specific abilities. Scores on the 14 WAIS subscales are correlated (those who do well on one subscale tend to do well on others)—evidence for a general intelligence. At the same time, it's not unusual for someone to score high on some of the subscales and low on some others, as correlations are far from perfect (usually in the .30 to .70 range)—evidence of separate mental abilities. So, what does an IQ score tell us about the nature of intelligence? Think about a few well-known geniuses such as Omar Khayyam, Albert Einstein, Jane Austen, Mae Jemison, and Nikola Tesla. Now, consider the intelligence of patented inventors that have transformed our lives, like Dean Kamen and Hedy Lamarr (both featured in Figure 7.18). Are these people similarly-abled individuals, or is that like comparing apples, oranges, bananas, and cherries? Many psychologists now believe that there's more to intelligence than IQ scores derived from paper-and-pencil tests. Two theories offer a broader view.

Gardner's "Frames of Mind"

In his 1983 book, *Frames of Mind*, Howard Gardner presents provocative evidence for the existence of **multiple intelligences**, each linked to a separate and independent system within the human brain, as illustrated in Figure 7.19. Gardner's main point is simple but revolutionary: The word *intelligence* is too narrowly used to describe cognitive abilities and does not adequately encompass the kinds of genius found in great musicians, poets, orators, dancers, athletes, artists, and inspirational leaders all

---

general intelligence (g). A broad intellectual-ability factor used to explain why performances on different intelligence-test items are often correlated.

multiple intelligences. Gardner's theory that there are seven types of intelligence (linguistic, logical-mathematical, spatial, musical, bodily-kinesthetic, interpersonal, intrapersonal).

Chapter 7 • Thought, Language, and Intelligence   283

FIGURE 7.18 ■ Invention

Hedy Lamarr was an actress and inventor of the frequency-hopping technology that is the foundation for Wi-Fi, Bluetooth, and GPS. Dean Kamen is a modern-day Thomas Edison. Among his more than 1,000 patents is an invention you probably recognize as the Segway—a self-balancing, battery-powered scooter that has changed the way individuals transport themselves over short distances.

Donaldson Collection / Contributor/Michael Ochs Archives/Getty Images; Kris Connor / Contributor/WireImage/Getty Images

FIGURE 7.19 ■ Types of Intelligence

Landscape artist Georgia O'Keeffe used visual-spatial intelligence (a), best-selling author Margaret Atwood exhibits linguistic intelligence in her writing (b), basketball great LeBron James exhibits extraordinary bodily-kinesthetic intelligence (c), and nuclear physicist Albert Einstein combined mathematical and spatial intelligences (d).

(a) Tony Vaccaro / Contributor/Archive Photos/Getty Images; (b) Dia Dipasupil / Staff/Getty Images Entertainment/Getty Images; (c) Michael Reaves / Stringer/Getty; (d) Bettmann / Contributor/Bettmann/ Getty Images;

On the game show *Are You Smarter Than a Fifth Grader*, an adult contestant answers questions taken from elementary school textbooks. Along the way, contestants can get assistance from "classmates" who are school-aged cast members.

FOX Image Collection/Contributor/Getty Images

prodigy. Someone who is highly precocious in a specific domain of endeavor.

savant syndrome. A term used to describe a developmental condition in which a person is neurodiverse but extraordinarily talented in some ways.

over the world. When basketball star LeBron James soars gracefully toward a hoop, evading blockers and shooting with laserlike precision, doesn't he exhibit a form of intelligence? Can't the same be said of Margaret Atwood, the author of *The Handmaid's Tale*, who with her masterful use of language and creativity started a cultural phenomenon? And what about Martin Luther King, Jr., the civil rights leader who stirred millions of Americans with his speeches and inspired massive social change?

Like a detective searching for fingerprints, smoking guns, and other clues, Gardner used converging lines of evidence to marshal support for his theory. He studied brain structures, diverse cultures, evolution, child development, and individuals with exceptional abilities—in other words, not just IQ tests. For example, the existence of **prodigies** (children who are typical in general but are highly precocious in a specific domain) and persons with **savant syndrome** (applied to those who are neurodiverse and extraordinarily talented in some way) tells us that it's possible to have one kind of intelligence and lack another. Similarly, that patients with brain damage can lose certain abilities but retain others tells us that different intelligences can be traced to autonomous systems in the brain. In all, Gardner initially proposed that there are seven types of intelligence: linguistic, logical-mathematical, spatial, musical, bodily-kinesthetic, interpersonal, and intrapersonal. The first three fit easily within existing conceptions of intelligence. The last four represent a radical departure from tradition. Gardner (2000) has also proposed that the list be expanded to include naturalistic intelligence, and perhaps spiritual and existential intelligences as well.

- **Linguistic intelligence.** A verbal aptitude that is rooted in the auditory and speech centers of the brain and consists of the skills involved in speaking, listening, reading, and writing. Storytellers and poets who are sensitive to shades of meaning, syntax, sounds, inflections, and rhythm are linguistic geniuses. So are politicians, evangelists, and successful trial lawyers who know how to use language for persuasive purposes.

- **Logical-mathematical intelligence.** The abstract reasoning skill necessary for solving puzzles and equations and programming computers. This form of intelligence blossoms early in childhood and is often displayed by "human calculators" who can perform rapid-fire mental arithmetic.

- **Spatial intelligence.** Rooted in the right hemisphere of the brain and consisting of the ability to visualize objects, find one's orientation in space, and navigate from one location to another (if you ever tried to find your way through a fun-house maze, you'll know the skill it takes). Great pilots, architects, chess masters, mechanics, and visual artists exhibit spatial intelligence.

- **Musical intelligence.** An intelligence that is found in all cultures, has existed throughout history, flowers early in childhood, and involves an ability to appreciate the tonal qualities of sound, compose music, and play an instrument. The concept of a "musical IQ" is supported by numerous case studies. The most prolific musical prodigy of all was Wolfgang Amadeus Mozart, who learned to play a harpsichord at the age of 3, composed at age 4, and performed in public at age 5.

- **Bodily-kinesthetic intelligence.** The ability to control gross and fine movements of the body. This kind of ability is rooted in the motor cortex and probably evolved in humans for running, climbing, swimming, hunting, and fighting. This form of intelligence can be seen in the figure skater who varies the timing and speed of her jumps, flips, and spins with clocklike precision, and lands softly on the blade of her skate. It can also be seen in skilled dancers, athletes, and surgeons.

- **Interpersonal intelligence.** The ability to understand other people—how they feel, what motivates them, what they like, and what they don't like. A person with these abilities can predict how others will act and, in turn, can interact smoothly with them. This form of intelligence can be found in successful politicians, salespersons, psychotherapists, and others with keen social skills.

- **Intrapersonal intelligence.** The ability to have insight into one's own thoughts and feelings, to understand the causes and consequences of one's own actions, and, as a result, to make effective decisions. Self-insight is a highly adaptive form of intelligence.

Gardner's theory is controversial. Some psychologists agree that intelligence should be defined broadly enough to encompass musical genius, exquisite use of the body, and personal insight. Others feel that the theory stretches the concept too far. To his critics, Gardner says that there is nothing magical about the word *intelligence*—that to define it narrowly is to place cognitive and academic endeavors on a pedestal. The point is that all kinds of intelligence should be valued—on tests, in school, and elsewhere in life.

LEARNING CHECK

Intelligences Testing Test

Now that you have learned about intelligence and how to test it, it is time to test yourself. Match each term in the left column with the best description in the right column.

1.	General intelligence	a.	The average age of children who pass the same number of items on the Stanford-Binet.
2.	Validity	b.	The consistency of a test's results.
3.	WAIS	c.	Gardner's theory that there are seven types of intelligence.
4.	Reliability	d.	Children who are typical in most areas but highly advanced in a specific domain.
5.	IQ	e.	Existing norms that can be used to interpret an individual's score.
6.	Mental age	f.	A broad measure of intelligence referred to as *g*.
7.	Standardization	g.	An adult intelligence scale developed by Wechsler.
8.	Prodigies	h.	The ability to visualize objects and navigate from place to place.
9.	Multiple intelligences	i.	A test's ability to predict what it's supposed to.
10.	Spatial intelligence	j.	Mental age divided by chronological age, multiplied by 100.

(Answers: 1. f; 2. i; 3. g; 4. b; 5. j; 6. a; 7. e; 8. d; 9. c; 10. h.)

THE GREAT INTELLIGENCE DEBATES

LEARNING OBJECTIVES

Apply the nature versus nurture debate to group variations in intelligence.
- Recognize the social impact that intelligence has on resources and opportunities.
- Summarize what research tell us about genetic and environmental influences.
- List some group differences researchers have found in test scores.

Intelligence testing is a "numbers game" with profound consequences for real people. IQ and aptitude scores help to determine which young children in need of parents are adopted first and which students are accepted into prestigious private schools. They determine whether a child is labeled as intellectually disabled or intellectually gifted, whether placed in the "developmental" courses or "advanced" courses at school. Later, these scores help to determine which students are admitted into elite colleges, are offered scholarships, and then have the best job prospects. As Richard Weinberg (1989) put it, "IQ tests play a pivotal role in allocating society's resources and opportunities" (p. 100). With the stakes so high, it's easy to understand why psychologists who study and measure intelligence find themselves in one emotional debate after another. In this section, we consider four heated issues: nature and nurture, racial differences, gender differences, and education.

Nature and Nurture

To what extent is intelligence determined by the forces of nature (genetics) and nurture (the environment)? How much does each factor contribute, and in what ways do they interact?

After many years of debate, most experts now agree that intelligence is strongly influenced—but not entirely determined—by genetic factors (Plomin, Shakeshaft, Mcmillan, & Trzaskowski, 2014). In support of this conclusion, Figure 7.20 summarizes the results of a meta-analysis that analyzed 11,000 pairs of twins (Haworth et al., 2010). While increases in intelligence are significant across development, how much of the similarity within twin pairs is rooted in nature?

To estimate the role of genetic factors, let's compare people who share a similar environment but differ in genetic relatedness. Three comparisons are worth noting: (a) Identical twins who are reared together (in fact, even those reared apart) are more similar than fraternal twins also reared together; (b) siblings who grow up together are more similar than unrelated individuals who grow up in the same home (even biological siblings reared apart show some degree of similarity); and (c) children are more similar to their biological parents than to adoptive parents. Additional research ties the genetic knot around IQ even tighter. Longitudinal studies show that the similarities do not diminish as blood relatives grow older but, rather, get stronger (Haworth & Plomin, 2011)—and that the similarities exist in verbal, mathematical, and spatial abilities; school grades; and vocational interests (McCartney, Harris, & Bernieri, 1990; Plomin, 1988). There is also far more similarity among biological twins than among "virtual twins"—unrelated siblings of the same age who grew up together as a result of adoption (Segal, 2000).

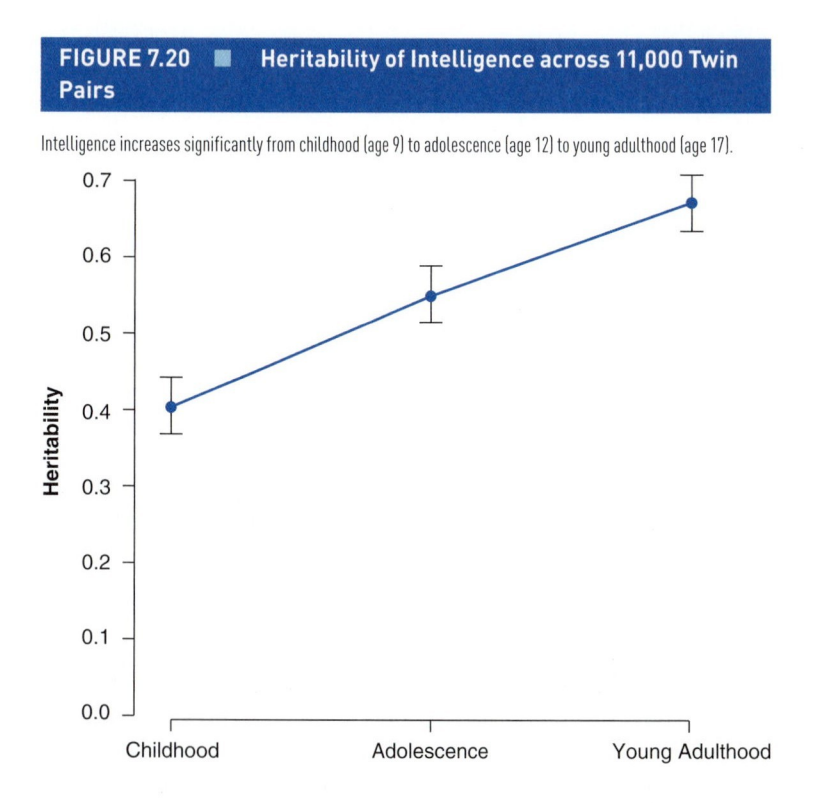

FIGURE 7.20 ■ Heritability of Intelligence across 11,000 Twin Pairs

Intelligence increases significantly from childhood (age 9) to adolescence (age 12) to young adulthood (age 17).

However, as Plomin and Deary (2015) put it, "all traits show substantial environmental influence, in that heritability is not 100% for any trait" (p. 98). This pro-nurture conclusion is based on comparisons of people who have the same genetic relatedness but who live in different environments.

Wait. Don't these results, which suggest a primary influence of heredity, contradict the finding described at the start of this chapter, that IQ scores all over the world have risen sharply and consistently since 1920? Human genes cannot change from one decade to the next, so the increased IQ presumably reflects changes in the environment—such as better nutrition, more schooling, and advances in technology that increase access to information.

William Dickens and James Flynn (2001) proposed a theory that helps to reconcile the apparent discrepancy in the powers of nature and nurture. Dickens and Flynn argue that genetic dispositions and environments are not independent, as illustrated in Figure 7.21. According to their theory, children who are brighter than average at birth will have initial success in school, which will bring praise from caregivers and teachers, motivate them to work hard, draw them to peers who are studious, and encourage them to prepare for college, all of which breeds intellectual success. In contrast, children who are not as bright at birth will have less initial success, receive less praise, care less about schoolwork, and affiliate with other weak students, all of which breeds failure. In other words, genes create environments, which in turn multiply the influence of genes. This theory explains how identical twins separated at birth can live in different homes but experience similar environments. It also explains the consistent but puzzling finding that genetic influences on intelligence seem to increase, not decrease, with age.

Clearly, environments influence intelligence. So, what environmental factors in particular are important? The possibilities are numerous: prenatal care, exposure to alcohol and other toxins, birth complications, malnutrition in the first few months of life, intellectual stimulation at home, stress, high-quality education, reliable Internet access, sufficient technology for online learning, and so on. Even the sheer amount of time spent in school is important (Ceci, 1991; Liu, Lee, & Gershenson, 2020), raising serious concerns during the coronavirus pandemic. Julie Frazier and Frederick Morrison (1998) compared kindergarten children at two closely matched schools, one of which was experimenting with an extended-year program consisting of 210 school days instead of the usual 180 (in other words, a shortened summer vacation). All the children were tested in the fall of their kindergarten year, again in the spring, and a third time in the fall of the first grade. The result: By first grade, children coming off the extended school year outpaced the others on all measures. Simply put, more time in school produced better students.

As mentioned previously, parents can also influence intelligence. One example that has been popular to discuss (*The Economist, 2017*; Vedantam, 2017) is the parental expectations in Chinese culture. In Chinese culture, it is believed that children born during the Dragon year have the highest chances of success (Goodkind, 1991; Vere, 2008). Therefore, parents strive to have their children during Dragon years. This belief is of interest to economists like Naci Mocan and Han Yu. In their research, Mocan and Yu (2017) look at trends in birth rate, financial success, education, and test scores among Dragon-year children. They have found that marriage rates increase two years *prior* to Dragon years and, in turn, that birth rates increase *during* Dragon years. With such a boom in childbirth, it

FIGURE 7.21 ■ How Environments Magnify Genetic Influences

Dickens and Flynn theorize that genes predispose young children toward varying degrees of initial success in school. These early experiences then steer the children into environments that later constrain or facilitate intellectual development, which increases the differences by adulthood.

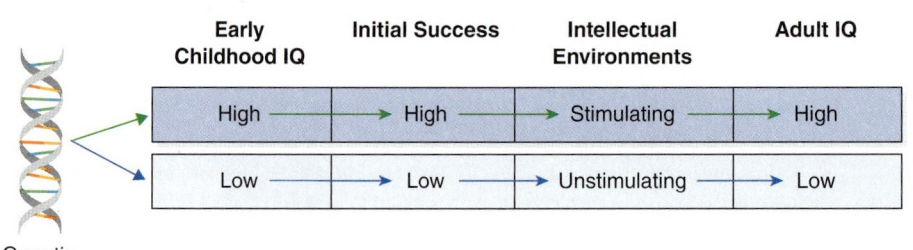

Genetic Predisposition	Early Childhood IQ	Initial Success	Intellectual Environments	Adult IQ
→	High	High	Stimulating	High
→	Low	Low	Unstimulating	Low

could be postulated that increased demand on resources would have a negative impact on success due to greater competition (Sim, 2015). However, Mocan and Yu's initial work has demonstrated that the Dragon offspring have higher university entrance examination scores and are more likely to earn a college education than offspring not born during Dragon years. Does this mean that the cultural belief is actually a fact? Not quite.

For a moment, think about how this cultural belief would influence parents' behavior toward their Dragon-year children. Mocan and Yu (2017) also thought about parental expectations and thus looked at parental contributions to, and perceptions of, their children's potential. Mocan and Yu found that parents of Dragon-year children have higher expectations than parents of non-Dragon-year children. They also found that Dragon children receive more pocket money and are required to do significantly fewer chores than non-Dragon children. What happens when parental contribution and perceptions are removed? Mocan and Yu used statistics to mathematically subtract the impact parents have on Dragon children's performance to determine if their scores would decrease. Sure enough, Dragon children's performance advantage disappeared. Mocan and Yu's research suggests that the belief our parents have in our success and the environments our parents surround us with really can influence our educational pursuits and performance.

The Racial Gap

One reason the nature versus nurture debate is so filled with emotion is that certain racial and cultural groups score higher than others on measures of ability and achievement, and these differences ignite blunt claims concerning genetic superiority and inferiority. Let's start with an empirical fact based on nationwide math SAT data from 2015. Black Americans and Latinx Americans had average math SAT scores of 428 and 457, respectively; and White Americans and Asian Americans had average scores of 534 and 598, respectively, as illustrated in Figure 7.22.

Why has this gap occurred? If heredity contributes to variations among individuals, does it also account for differences found among groups? No, not necessarily. To be sure, a few psychologists

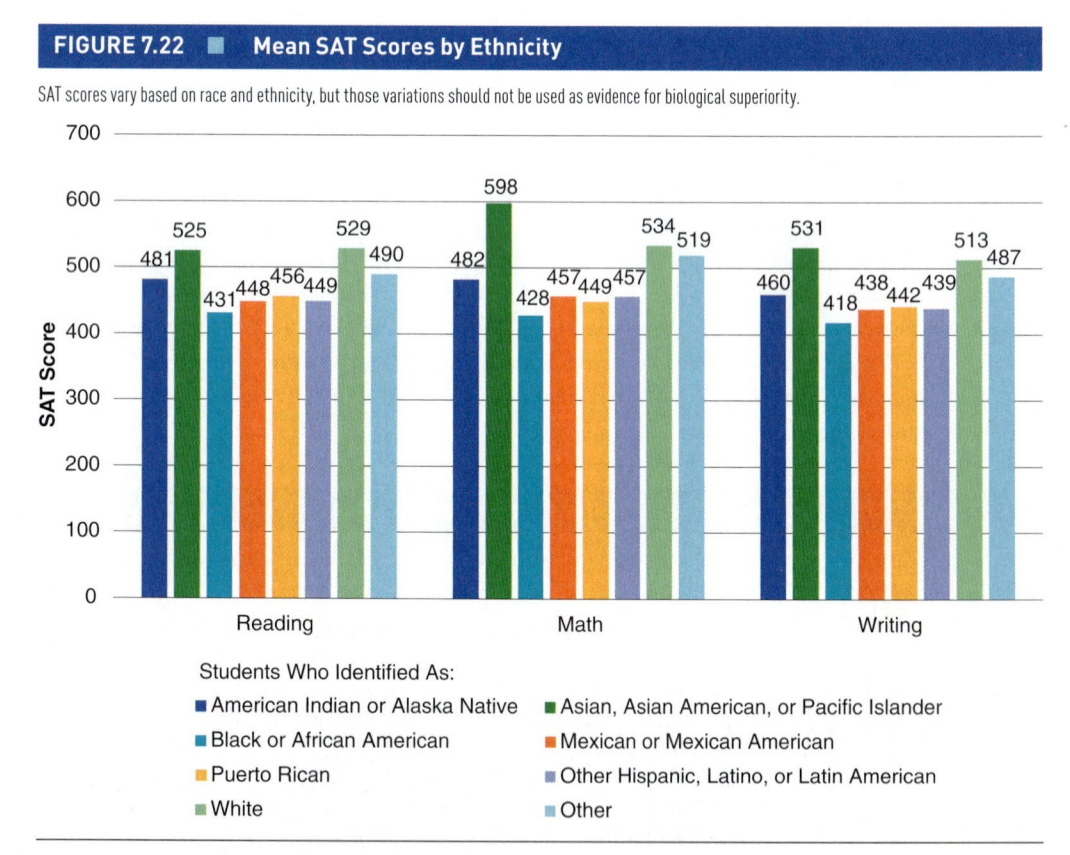

FIGURE 7.22 ■ Mean SAT Scores by Ethnicity

SAT scores vary based on race and ethnicity, but those variations should not be used as evidence for biological superiority.

Source: Data from National Center for Education Statistics

have speculated that differing evolutionary pressures in Europe, Asia, and Africa have, over time, produced measurable differences among humans in brain size and intelligence (Rushton & Ankney, 1996). But as critics of *The Bell Curve* (Herrnstein & Murray, 1994) were correct to note, genetic variation among *individuals* within a group does not mean that differences among *groups* are genetically based. Compared to the average Black American, White Americans grow up in more affluent homes and with better educational opportunities. Attending and graduating college is one such educational opportunity that can account for the IQ gap, as illustrated in Figure 7.23.

Three sets of research findings support this point. The first is from a study that asked what would happen to the IQ scores of Black American children adopted into White American middle-class homes. Sandra Scarr and Richard Weinberg (1976) studied 99 such cases in Minneapolis and found that the average IQ score was 110—well above the Black American average and comparable to that of White American children from similar families. When the adoptees were retested 10 years later, similar results were found (Weinberg, Scarr, & Waldman, 1992).

The second set of findings involves cross-cultural comparisons and historical trends. The cultural perspective reveals that the racial gap in IQ within the United States is not unique. Low scores in disadvantaged groups are found all over the world, including the Maori of New Zealand, the "untouchables" in India, non-European Jews in Israel, and the Burakumin in Japan (Ogbu, 1978). From a historical perspective, it's clear that as a result of school desegregation and social programs such as Head Start, Black Americans have had more educational doors opened in recent years than in the past. Paralleling these new opportunities, the racial gap is closing. Dickens and Flynn (2006) determined that Black Americans have gained 4 to 7 IQ points on White Americans across a span of 30 years.

A third, and particularly important, research finding concerns the effect of a college education on the racial gap in IQ. Joel Myerson and others (1998) examined data from a longitudinal study that tracked thousands of young men and women from the ages of 14 to 21. Specifically focusing on Black American and White American college graduates, these researchers analyzed the scores these students had received on tests taken after the 8th (pre–high school) through 12th (post–high school) and "16th" (post–college) grades. If the racial gap in IQ was immutable, as Herrnstein and Murray suggested in *The Bell Curve*, then the difference in standardized test scores would be little affected by a level educational playing field. Yet it was. Review Figure 7.23, and you'll notice that although the racial gap remained through high school, and even widened somewhat, it was substantially narrowed by the time the students were finished with college. Everyone gained from the experience, but the Black students gained more—and cut the gap in half.

FIGURE 7.23 ■ Education: The Great Equalizer

These are the cognitive test scores of future college graduates as they moved from grades 8 through "16" (the later referring to college graduation). Indicating the vital equalizing role of education, the initial gap between Black and White students was narrowed by the time they completed college.

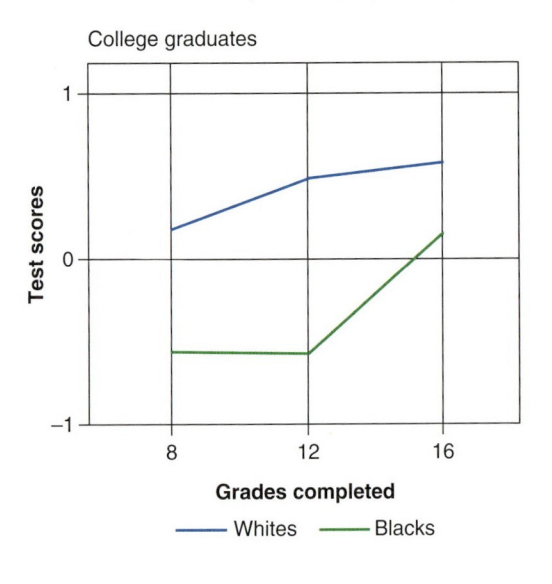

Gender Differences

When intelligence tests are constructed, a concerted effort is made to remove questions that prove more difficult for one sex than for the other—or at least to balance items favoring one sex with items favoring the other. The result is that total IQ scores are comparable for females and males. But what about specific abilities? Is there any truth to traditional gender stereotypes that depict math and spatial relations as

Math may be an intimidating subject to some, but not to Lenny Ng. Lenny, a son of Chinese immigrants, scored 800 on the math SAT at age 10. At age 16, he entered Harvard University. Julian Stanley, who founded the Center for Talented Youth at Johns Hopkins University, called him "the most brilliant math prodigy I've ever met." Lenny is now a highly successful mathematician, who is a full professor at Duke University.

iStock.com/ridvan_celik

masculine enterprises and language as the art of women? Several years ago, Eleanor Maccoby and Carol Jacklin (1974) reviewed the research and found that it supported the stereotype. According to Kurtzleben (2014), among high school students who take Advanced Placement exams, males outnumber female test-takers 4 to 1 in computer science, more than 2.5 to 1 in physics, and 1.5 to 1 on calculus, whereas females outnumber male test-takers in languages, English literature, and related fields.

Because the issue of gender differences has profound implications for how parents treat their sons and daughters—and for how teachers treat male and female students—psychologists have been eager to understand the nature and extent of these differences. Here is what we know at this point:

- **Verbal abilities.** On verbal aptitude tests, Janet Hyde and Marcia Linn (1988) analyzed data from millions of students tested between 1947 and 1980 and found that girls outscored boys but that the gender gap had narrowed. As of 2015, males had higher verbal SAT scores by 4 points but lower writing SAT scores by 10 points (College Board, 2015). Reed and colleagues (2017) performed neuroimaging studies on young adults and found that males had higher verbal working memory performance than females. However, as depicted in Figure 7.24 (Guiso, Monte, Sapienza, & Zingales, 2008), girls score slightly higher than boys on tests of reading comprehension and foreign languages (Hedges & Nowell, 1995; Stumpf & Stanley, 1996).

FIGURE 7.24 ■ Math and Reading Gender Gaps

In more gender-equal cultures, the math gender gap disappears and the reading gender gap becomes larger. (Top) Gender gaps in mathematics (blue) and reading (orange) are calculated as the difference between the average girls' score and the average boys' score. A subset of countries is shown here. In many countries, on average, girls perform more poorly than boys in mathematics. In all countries, girls perform better than boys in reading. The gender gap in mathematics and reading correlates with country measure of gender status within the culture, one of which measures is the GGI (bottom). Larger values of GGI point to a better average position of women in society. Besides USA, the countries are abbreviated as their first three letters, except for PRT, Portugal, and ISL, Iceland.

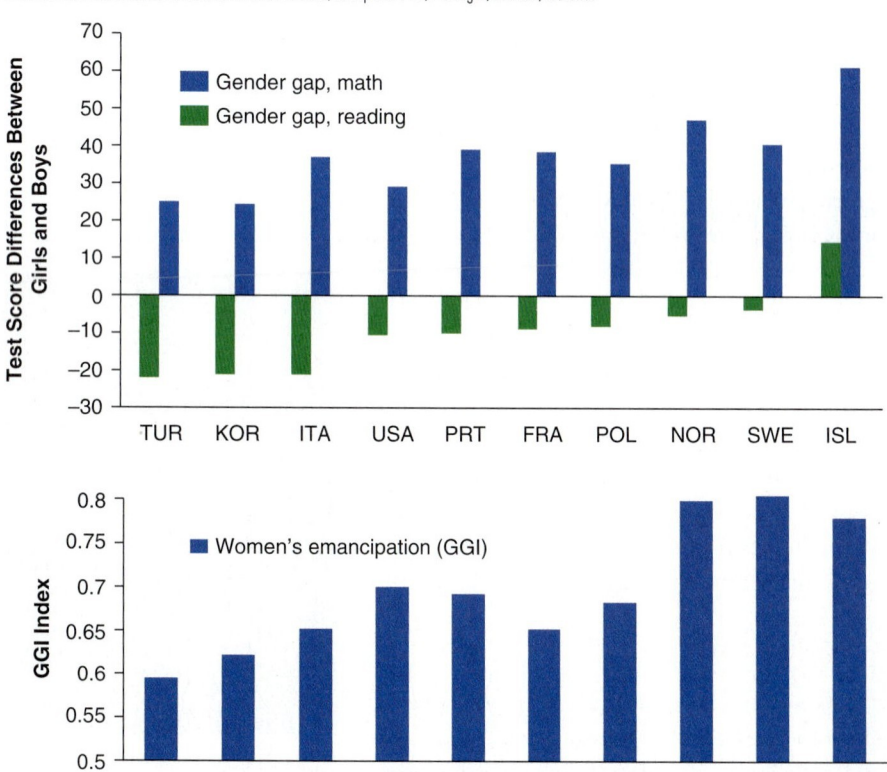

Republished with permission of American Association for the Advancement of Science, from Guiso, Luigi & Monte, Ferdinando & Sapienza, Paola & Zingales, Luigi. (2008). Culture, Gender, and Math. Science 30 May 2008:Vol. 320, Issue 5880, pp. 1164-1165; permission conveyed through Copyright Clearance Center, Inc.

- **Mathematical abilities.** Girls are better at arithmetic in elementary school, but boys surpass them in junior high school—a difference that continues past college except those in more gender-equal cultures (review Figure 7.24; Guiso, Monte, Sapienza, & Zingales, 2008). According to Mark Perry (2016), males had a 31-point edge on the math SAT in 2016 (the male and female averages were 527 and 469, respectively). This gap is most evident among the highest-level math students (Benbow, 1988; Hyde, Fennema, & Lamon, 1990) and on unconventional problems that require flexible problem-solving strategies (Gallagher et al., 2000). This difference may underlie the fact that males score higher on high school achievement tests in physics, chemistry, and computer science (Stumpf & Stanley, 1996).

- **Spatial abilities.** It has been argued that males outperform females on spatial tasks such as mentally rotating objects to determine what they look like from another perspective (as illustrated in the accompanying Try This! activity) and tracking moving objects in space (Linn & Petersen, 1985; Master, 1998). Sanchis-Segura and colleagues (2018) argue "that the common statement 'males have superior mental rotation abilities' simplifies a much more complex reality and might promote stereotypes which, in turn, might induce artefactual performance differences between females and males in such tasks" (p. 1). Hoffman and colleagues' (2011) research supports this complex reality. They wondered if these differences in spatial ability were not simply due to biological differences and, thus, investigated nurture's role. Across 1,300 participants who completed a spatial-ability task, gender differences disappeared when the participants were divided not just by male or female, but also by their society—patrilineal or matrilineal. For those raised and living in a matrilineal society, spatial task performance had no male or female advantage.

In games meant to challenge and develop mental rotation skills, players use spatial intelligence to predict degrees of rotation needed to orient different shapes. Studies show that as little as 10 hours of experience with these types of games increases spatial test scores—for girls as well as boys.

iStock.com/akinbostanci

TRY THIS!

Spatial Effects

Rooted in the right hemisphere of the brain, *spatial intelligence* is one of the seven multiple intelligences theorized by Howard Gardner. Spatial skills, such as the ability to visualize objects from a different perspective, are particularly useful in occupations such as airplane pilot or mechanical engineer.

To challenge your own spatial abilities, **TRY THIS:** Which of the pairs of geometric shapes in Figure 7.25 depict the same or different shapes. (Answers are below the figure.) How did you do? Are you more or less likely to pursue an occupation that uses spatial skills as a result of this exercise? What tests can you suggest to test levels of Gardner's six other multiple intelligences?

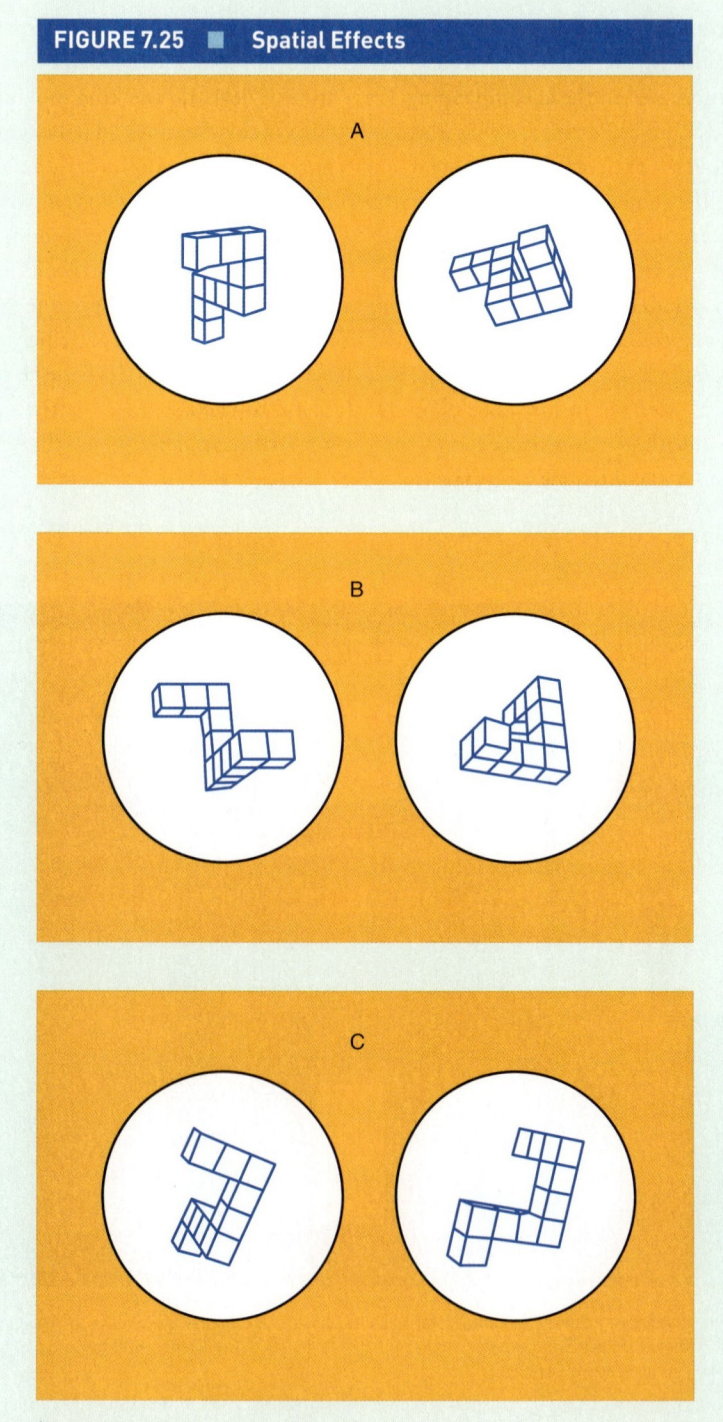

FIGURE 7.25 ■ Spatial Effects

(Answers: a. same; b. same; c. different.)

Education

Ever since Binet's work in the schools of Paris, many psychologists have had uneasy feelings about the link between their conceptions of intelligence and education. There are two principal questions. First, by focusing on the prediction of academic performance, have we adopted too narrow a conception of intelligence? Many influential theorists think so. Gardner complains that IQ tests completely ignore and devalue the musical, bodily-kinesthetic, and personal intelligences. The second question concerns the impact of IQ testing on the quality of education. Once a child is identified as a fast, slow, or average learner, what next? Do those with unusually high or low IQ scores benefit from being identified as "special"? What are the educational implications? Because schools rely heavily on IQ tests to sort children into academic categories, it's important to raise these kinds of critical questions.

The Self-Fulfilling Prophecy

In 1948, sociologist Robert Merton told a story about Cartwright Millingville, president of the Last National Bank during the Depression. Although the bank was solvent, a rumor began to spread that it was floundering. Within hours, hundreds of depositors lined up to withdraw their savings, until there was no money left. The rumor was false, but the bank eventually failed. Using stories such as this, Merton proposed that a person's expectation can actually lead to its own fulfillment—a phenomenon known as the **self-fulfilling prophecy**. As we'll learn, this can influence the educational process in two ways.

self-fulfilling prophecy. The idea that a person's expectation can lead to its own fulfillment (as in the effect of teacher expectations on student performance).

Teacher Expectancies

Using Merton's hypothesis, Robert Rosenthal and Lenore Jacobson (1968) wondered about the possible harmful effects of IQ testing. What happens to the educational experience of the child who receives a low score? Would it leave a permanent mark on his or her record, arouse negative expectations on the part of the teacher, and impair future performance? To examine the possible outcomes, Rosenthal and Jacobson told teachers in a San Francisco elementary school that certain pupils were on the verge of an intellectual growth spurt. The results of an IQ test were cited, but in fact the pupils were randomly selected. Rosenthal and Jacobson administered real tests eight months later and found that the so-called late bloomers (but not children assigned to a control group) had actually improved their scores and were evaluated more favorably by their classroom teachers.

When this study was published, it was greeted with chagrin. If high teacher expectations can increase student performance, can low expectations have the opposite effect? Could it be that children who get high scores are destined for success, whereas those who get low scores are doomed to failure, in part because educators hold different expectations of them? To this day, many researchers have been critical of the study and skeptical about the generality of the results (Spitz, 1999). But the phenomenon is potentially too important to be swept under the proverbial rug. After reviewing other tests of the hypothesis, Rosenthal (1985) concluded that teacher expectations significantly predicted student performance 36 percent of the time. Mercifully, the predictive value of teacher expectancies seems to wear off, not accumulate, as children advance from one grade to the next (Smith, Thompson, Raczynski, & Hilner, 1999).

How might teacher expectations be transformed into reality? There are two points of view. According to Rosenthal, the self-fulfilling prophecy can be viewed as a three-step process. First, the teacher forms an impression of the student early in the school year. This impression may be based on IQ-test scores or other information. Second, the teacher behaves in ways that are consistent with that first impression. If the expectations are high rather than low, the teacher gives the student more praise, attention, and challenging homework. Third, the student unwittingly adjusts their own behavior according to the teacher's actions. If the signals are positive,

Teacher expectations can affect student performance.
iStock.com/Marco VDM

FIGURE 7.26 ■ Three-Step Model of a Self-Fulfilling Prophecy

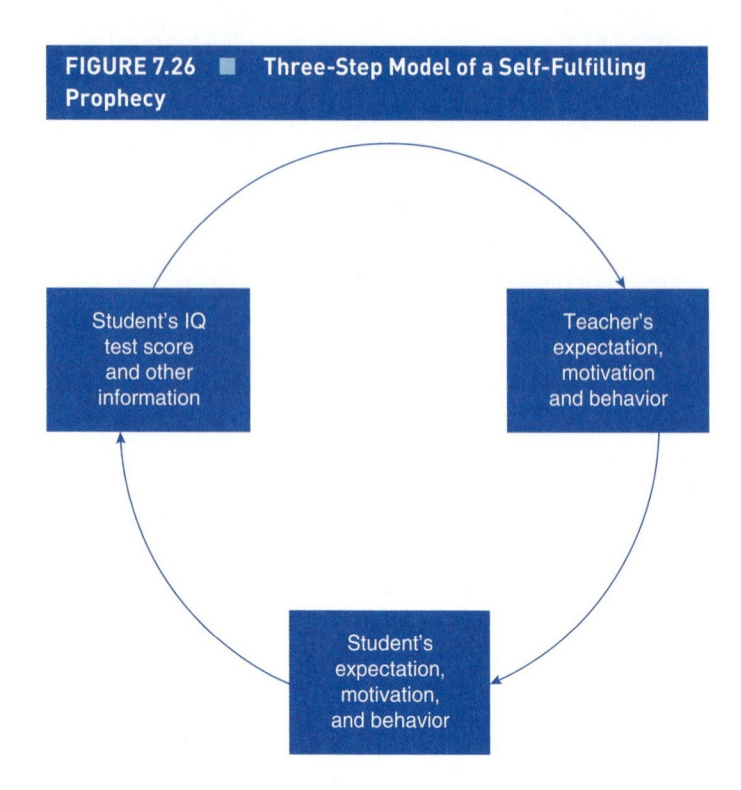

- Student's IQ test score and other information
- Teacher's expectation, motivation and behavior
- Student's expectation, motivation, and behavior

the student may become energized. If negative, they may lose interest and self-confidence. As depicted in Figure 7.26, the cycle is thus complete and the teacher's expectations confirmed. Importantly, self-fulfilling prophecies like this are at work in many settings—not only in schools but in a range of organizational settings, including the military (McNatt, 2000).

Stereotype Threat

There's a second way in which expectations can set in motion a self-fulfilling prophecy, which is known as **stereotype threat**. According to Claude Steele (1997), African Americans are painfully aware of the negative stereotypes people hold regarding their intelligence. As a result, scholastic test situations make African American students feel threatened by the stereotype and anxious about performance. To make matters worse, notes Steele, this threat can eventually become chronic, causing African American students to tune out and "disidentify" from academic pursuits.

Steele and Aronson (1995) administered a 30-item verbal test to African American and White college students. Half the subjects were told that the items were merely a device that psychologists use to study the way people solve problems—a "nondiagnostic" instruction that was given to underplay the testlike nature of the task. The other half were told that the same items measured verbal-reasoning ability—a "diagnostic" instruction designed to make stereotype-threatened subjects anxious. As shown in Figure 7.27, African American and White subjects did not differ much when given the low-key nondiagnostic instruction (their scores were statistically adjusted according to each subject's past verbal SAT score in order to equalize initial differences in their abilities). In the diagnostic condition, however, the African American subjects exhibited a decrease in their own performance. With the task defined as an ability test, those feeling vulnerable to the stereotype, sadly, helped to confirm it. How can this happen?

One possibility is suggested by a psychophysiological study showing that African Americans in the "diagnostic" condition exhibit an increase in blood pressure during and after the test (Blascovich, Spencer, Quinn, & Steele, 2001). However, as previously mentioned, and apparent in Figure 7.27, scores were adjusted based on verbal SAT scores. Therefore, many researchers argue that the scores do not truly depict the real average test scores for subjects (Jussim, Crawford, Anglin, Stevens, & Duarte, 2016; Sackett, Hardison, & Cullen, 2004). Knowing what you know now about SAT score differences and race, do you think that adjusting test scores was necessary, and as a result, more reflective of African American and White test performance? Flore and Wicherts (2015) were interested

---

stereotype threat. The tendency for positive and negative performance stereotypes about a group to influence its members when they are tested in the stereotyped domain.

FIGURE 7.27 ■ Stereotype Threat Effect on Test Performance

Steele and Aronson compared the performances (adjusted for their own ability) of African American and White students on a 30-item verbal-reasoning test. When the significance of the test was underplayed, there were no differences (*left*). When the test was presented as diagnostic of verbal ability, the African American students performed worse (*right*). This result is consistent with the stereotype-threat hypothesis.

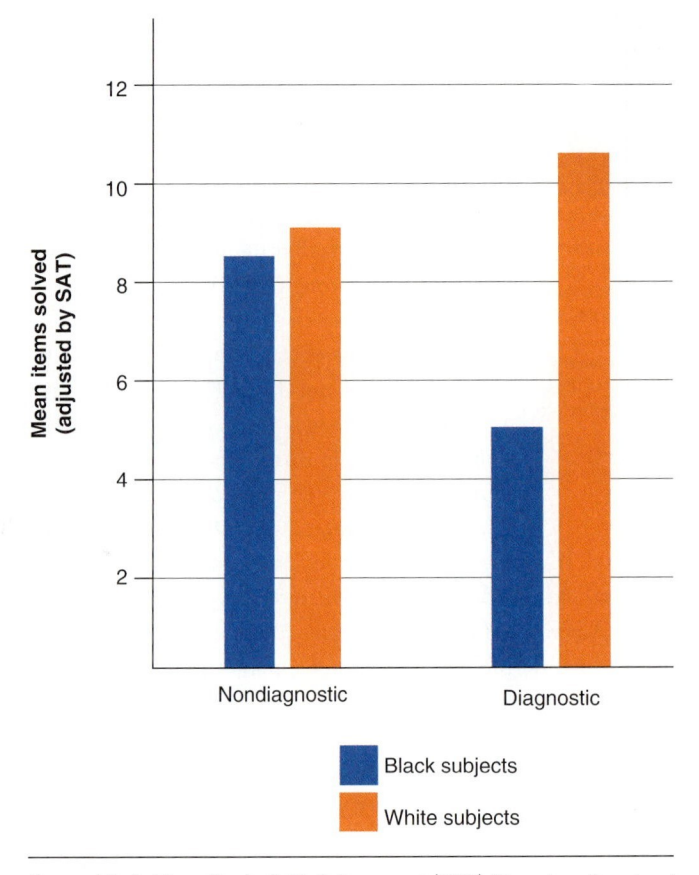

Source: Adapted from Steele, C. M., & Aronson, J. (1995). Stereotype threat and the intellectual test performance of African Americans. Journal of Personality and Social Psychology, 69(5), 797–811.

in uncovering whether stereotype threat research demonstrated actual female performance changes across stereotyped domains. They conducted a review of stereotype threat research with female adolescents and children. They found that, across several studies, stereotype threat among school-aged girls was not evident. Why did stereotype threat disappear? Amy Wax (2009) believes that stereotype threat might exist but only for a select set of people in unique settings.

Other research indicates that stereotype threat effects do exist, are general, and can interfere with other groups and other domains of ability. Imagine the following scenario: You walk into class and your teacher tells you that a new genetic researcher has discovered a marker for intelligence, and that marker demonstrates itself via eye color—the darker the eyes, the greater the intelligence. You sit there, stunned, and look around the room at others like you who have light eyes. You think, How is this possible? This science has to be flawed! But you keep your mouth shut, and snap out of your disbelief as your teacher, Dr. Elliott, announces she is going to demonstrate the validity of the science in the classroom today with the use of collars. The light-eyed students—including you—walk up, grab a collar, and fasten the button to hold it in place. Already you feel singled-out. The dark-eyed students, by contrast, look smug and confident. Will this classroom simulation have an impact on your performance? The answer is, yes, it will.

Claude Steele's work on stereotype threat shows that "invisible" sociocultural factors are at work in the classroom. When asked how he discovered this effect, Steele said, "My students and I had been struggling to understand the immeasurable processes that seemed to undermine the academic performance of certain groups in society.... Gradually, we were able to describe how people can become intimidated by the prospect of being reduced to a group stereotype in a domain where a stereotype about one's group could apply. When the stereotype is about something important—like intelligence or, for some, athletic ability— it can put a great deal of pressure on the person."

Claude Steele - TeachAIDS Interview via Wikimedia Commons confirmed to be licensed under the terms of the cc-by-sa-2.0.

Jane Elliot, a public school teacher from Riceville, Iowa, demonstrated this in a powerful way when she decided to expose her students to the impact that negative stereotypes could have on classroom performance. She divided her students into categories based on eye color—blue eyes and brown eyes. On the first day of her experiment, Elliott placed collars on the blue-eyed students and told them that they were less intelligent and motivated than brown-eyed people. Elliott crafted a biological reason for the differences, stating that melanin was a marker for intelligence, and darker eyes demonstrated more melanin. Students believed her explanation, and the experiment moved on. It did not take long for the blue-eyed children to act inferior to brown-eyed children, or for them to drop dramatically in scholastic performance on things such as spelling and math. One blue-eyed girl in particular, a math whiz, struggled with her multiplication tables (Bloom, 2005). The evidence is so strong that PBS documented it in *A Class Divided*, which you can watch on PBS.org.

But can this effect be found in the lab? In one classic study, Steven Spencer and others (1999) found that women performed poorly relative to men in a math test when led to believe that it was the type of test in which there were sex differences favoring men. Importantly, women performed better, and the male-female difference disappeared, when they were simply told beforehand that the test was gender neutral. In another classic study, Jeff Stone and others (1999) tested the hypothesis that, in the domain of athletic performance, White students would feel threatened by the popular stereotype that African American athletes are superior. Black and White college students were told they'd be putting on a miniature golf course as part of a sports aptitude test. Some students were told that performance required natural athletic ability, whereas others were told it required intelligence. Performance was measured by the number of strokes subjects needed to complete the course. Can you predict the result? When the task was presented as a test of natural athletic ability, Black students performed better—and White students performed worse. It seems that everyone is vulnerable. When a stereotype is "in the air," it is possible that people fear they will fail, which can make them more likely to do just that (Steele, Spencer, & Aronson, 2002).

Thinking Like a Psychologist About Thought, Language, and Intelligence

Psychologists who study thought and language—like those who study learning and memory—have come to realize that people are complex, "two-headed" creatures, competent in some ways, flawed in others. Often, we solve difficult problems through trial and error, algorithms, heuristics, and a great capacity for creative insight. Yet often we get stuck mentally and fail to find obvious solutions because of functional fixedness, mental sets, and confirmation biases that keep us from fully testing our ideas.

Then there's language. Despite recent successes in teaching apes to communicate, it is clear that the human capacity for language—whether measured by semanticity, generativity, or displacement—is impressive and unmatched. Yet it is also clear that words can be used to shape, and sometimes distort, the way we think. People are complicated creatures, both competent and flawed at the same time.

The good news is that we have the capacity to improve on the way we think and, therefore, on our ability to adapt to changing circumstances. Earlier, we saw that even when we feel stumped on a problem, it is possible to find the insight we need by representing it in a different way, opening our minds to alternative approaches, or perhaps just taking a break. There are many ways for us to maximize the use of our cognitive abilities.

For about a century now, psychologists have been trying to define, measure, understand, and enhance intelligence, an elusive concept. You can tell by the frequent use of the Stanford-Binet, Wechsler scales, SAT, and other instruments that ability testing is a booming enterprise. It's also one that should be viewed with a critical eye to safeguard against possible abuses. Intelligence is a many-splendored concept—more than just IQ, a magical number used to predict school performance. Intelligence shows up in one person's flair for writing, in a second person's ability to wheel-and-deal in business, and a third person's fluent mastery of five languages. It's the ability to process information with efficiency, generate creative ideas, and use one's skills to succeed.

Underlying much of the tension that surrounds the study of intelligence is the nature versus nurture debate. It is clear that both genetic and environmental factors contribute to an individual's intelligence. It's also clear that because racial and cultural groups have distinct life experiences, intellectual differences at the group level are hard to interpret. The same is true of the small differences that exist between males and females. Finally, it's important to consider the educational implications of using IQ tests for identification and placement purposes. On the one hand, objective measures of intelligence help us to predict academic potential and develop programs suitable for individual students. On the other hand, IQ tests can set in motion a self-fulfilling prophecy. Either way, it's important to keep in mind that *intelligence* is not a tangible object but a word that describes the skills that enable you to make a better life for yourself and others.

SUMMARY

People are rational and irrational at the same time. Why is this so? Is our thought, language and intelligence shaped by nature, nurture, or both?

CONCEPTS

Research shows that when a **concept** is activated in a person's mind, other related concepts in the semantic network are primed and emerge more readily from memory. **Prototypes**, concepts that seem "typical" of a particular category because they have most of its defining properties, come most readily to mind and have the strongest influence on our judgments.

SOLVING PROBLEMS

When we cannot find a solution by retrieving the answer from memory, we go through three steps: representing the problem, generating possible solutions, and evaluating those solutions.

REPRESENTING THE PROBLEM
Representing the problem often involves activating concepts from our semantic memory. It can also involve mental **images** of visual information and intuitive **mental models** of how things work. Our mental models, though useful, are sometimes inaccurate.

GENERATING SOLUTIONS
Once we have represented a problem, we generally choose from four basic problem-solving strategies: trial and error, algorithms, heuristics, and insight. **Trial and error** entails trying various solutions until one works. In contrast, an **algorithm** is a step-by-step procedure guaranteed to produce a solution eventually. **Heuristics** are rules of thumb that lead to quicker but not always accurate solutions. One general heuristic is **means-end analysis**, the breaking down of a problem into subgoals. Another is the use of **analogies**, which involve taking an old solution as a model for a new problem. Sometimes, in a flash of **insight**, a solution pops to mind. In long problem-solving sessions, people often exhibit the **incubation effect**, whereby sudden insight occurs after they take a break.

"BLIND SPOTS" IN PROBLEM SOLVING
Our "blind spots" in problem solving can result from a number of factors. A problem may be represented incorrectly. Or we may fall into **functional fixedness**, thinking of objects only in terms of their

usual functions. A **mental set**, taking us back to a strategy that worked in the past, can also be a hindrance. And **confirmation biases** dispose us to look only for evidence that supports our initial beliefs. In making everyday decisions, we consistently rely on judgmental heuristics. The **representativeness heuristic** leads us to judge an event's likelihood by its apparent typicality, so that we ignore numerical probabilities. The **availability heuristic** is the tendency for estimates of event likelihood to be influenced by how easily instances come to mind. The **anchoring effect** is the tendency for an initial value to serve as a reference point in making a new judgment. Despite the various biases, people are consistently overconfident about their judgment abilities.

LANGUAGE

Language is a form of communication consisting of a system of sounds, words, meanings, and rules for their combination.

CHARACTERISTICS OF HUMAN LANGUAGE
All languages share the properties of semanticity, generativity, and displacement. **Semanticity** refers to the fact that language has separate units of meaning. The smallest meaningful units are **morphemes**. In all spoken languages, morphemes are made up of basic sounds called **phonemes**.

Through the property of **generativity**, language can turn a finite number of words into an infinite variety of expressions. **Syntax**, the formal grammar, provides the rules for transforming the deep structure of a statement into various possible surface structures. Finally, all languages are capable of **displacement**, or communication about things beyond the here-and-now.

EMERGENCE OF LANGUAGE
Language development proceeds in a regular sequence: from cooing to **babbling**, single words, **telegraphic speech**, and full sentences. Evidence supports the view that humans are specially "wired" for language, and that there is a critical period for learning it.

THE RELATIONSHIP BETWEEN THOUGHT AND LANGUAGE

It is assumed that thought gives rise to language, but does language also shape thought? What is the relationship between these cognitive activities?

THE LINGUISTIC-RELATIVITY HYPOTHESIS
Going beyond the traditional view that thought shapes language, Whorf's **linguistic-relativity hypothesis** predicts that language can shape the way we think.

CULTURE, LANGUAGE, AND THE WAY WE THINK
Some research indicates that people from different cultures think differently, but investigators disagree about the interpretation. Today, research suggests that language influences but does not completely determine thought.

INTELLIGENCE

Many psychologists define **intelligence** as a capacity to learn from experience and adapt successfully to one's environment. This capacity can be tested with different measurements.

INTELLIGENCE TESTS
In the early 1900s, Binet and Simon developed a test to determine a student's **mental age**—the average age of children who achieve a given level of performance. Terman revised the test and renamed it the **Stanford-Binet**. He also scored the test by means of an **intelligence quotient (IQ)**: mental age

divided by chronological age and multiplied by 100. Today, an IQ represents a person's performance relative to the average of same-age peers.

To distinguish between different aspects of intelligence, the **Wechsler Adult Intelligence Scale (WAIS)** yields separate verbal and performance scores. There are also Wechsler scales for children.

In contrast to the Stanford-Binet and Wechsler measures, which are individually administered, aptitude tests like the SAT and ACT are given in groups.

ARE INTELLIGENCE TESTS ACCURATE?

To be accurate, a test must be standardized, reliable, and valid. **Standardization** means that the test provides a standard of norms that can be used to interpret a given score. **Reliability** means that the results are consistent. **Test-retest reliability** ensures that a test will yield similar results at different times; **split-half reliability** ensures that different forms of the test will produce similar results. **Validity** is the extent to which the test measures or predicts what it is supposed to.

ARE INTELLIGENCE TESTS BIASED?

Some say that intelligence tests are culturally biased because scores are influenced by such background factors as the test taker's racial or ethnic group. Advocates of testing note that race differences occur even on "culture-fair" items and that intelligence tests do predict academic performance.

THE NATURE OF INTELLIGENCE

There are theories concerning the very nature of intelligence—what it is, where it comes from, and how it is developed. Three theories have been discussed.

CRYSTALLIZED AND FLUID INTELLIGENCE

Crystallized intelligence is a person's factual knowledge, whereas **fluid intelligence** is a person's ability to reason, learn new information, and think flexibly to solve problems. Cattell believed that fluid intelligence helped facilitate crystallized intelligence, in that the more new information a person sought and understood, the more factual knowledge was gained.

GENERAL INTELLIGENCE

Spearman was the first to speak of **general intelligence (g)**, a broad factor underlying all mental abilities. Spearman found that all intellectual abilities are linked to g. Other researchers have divided intelligence into various components.

GARDNER'S "FRAMES OF MIND"

Partly because of the existence of **prodigies** and persons with **savant syndrome**, Gardner proposed a theory of **multiple intelligences**. According to Gardner, different systems in the brain produce seven different types of intelligence: linguistic, logical-mathematical, spatial, musical, bodily-kinesthetic, interpersonal, and intrapersonal. The last four types stretch the concept of intelligence beyond traditional notions.

THE GREAT INTELLIGENCE DEBATES

Because test scores affect so many aspects of our lives, debates about intelligence testing have been heated.

NATURE AND NURTURE

People have long disputed the extent to which intelligence is determined by nature (genetics) and by nurture (environment). Studies of twins and other family members appear to show that heredity accounts for 60 to 75 percent of the population variation in intelligence. Others now suggest that environmental factors multiply the effects of genes. The publication of *The Bell Curve* brought this issue into the limelight.

THE RACIAL GAP
Are group differences in average IQ and SAT scores brought about by nature or by nurture? This is debatable. But research suggests that environmental factors can help to explain the relatively low scores by African Americans and the relatively high scores by Asian Americans.

GENDER DIFFERENCES
Whereas girls score somewhat higher on tests involving language, boys on average perform better in mathematical and visual-spatial tasks. However, research has found that in matrilineal societies, these visual-spatial performance differences between females and males disappear. Furthermore, a global study revealed that countries with smaller gaps in equality have smaller gender gaps in math and larger gender gaps in reading. Such research makes a strong argument that the environment, and not so much biology, influences language, mathematical, and visual-spatial performance. Thus, beliefs in hardwired gender differences have profound implications for parents and teachers.

EDUCATION
According to studies of the **self-fulfilling prophecy**, teacher expectations influence student performance. If teachers expect little of a child because of a low IQ score, that child will likely perform accordingly.

Recent studies of **stereotype threat** also show that social and cultural groups feel threatened by negative stereotypes about them, which can make them anxious and impairs performance. However, the effects of stereotype threat are not consistently replicable.

CRITICAL THINKING

Thinking Critically About Thought, Language, and Intelligence

1. Imagine that you are developing a workshop to teach people to become better problem solvers. What specific strategies would you include? What suggestions would you give to promote the use of insight? What specific tactics would you recommend to eliminate the blind spots?

2. Suppose scientists invented a pill that would allow you to make all your decisions in a completely rational manner. Would you choose to take such a pill? Why or why not?

3. Do computers think? Do they have language capability? Why or why not?

4. Discuss the debate concerning one intelligence versus multiple intelligences. Which view do you believe?

5. Discuss the controversy surrounding the use of IQ and other standardized tests of intelligence. Explain how IQ tests might be both biased and accurate. In what ways might IQ scores influence intelligence rather than simply reflect it?

6. In what ways do genetic and environmental forces interact to determine intelligence? What practical implications does this have for the way we educate our children?

CAREER CONNECTION: EDUCATION

Teacher
Students who also earn a teaching certificate along with their bachelor's degree in psychology can become teachers. Psychology undergraduates can find jobs teaching nearly any subject matter, including psychology at all levels of the U.S. education system, from kindergarten to high school, and even occasionally in colleges and universities. These schools may be public or private, but the

responsibilities of teachers in all environments are largely the same. A background in psychology can allow a teacher to better understand human development and communication, improving the effectiveness of their teaching in preparing students for life and lifelong learning.

Key skills for this role that psychology students learn to develop:

- Effective communication in presentations and written works

- Self-regulation and collaboration

- Innovative and integrative thinking and problem solving

KEY TERMS

algorithm (p. 262)
analogies (p. 262)
anchoring effect (p. 267)
availability heuristic (p. 267)
babbling (p. 271)
concept (p. 258)
confirmation bias (p. 265)
crystallized intelligence (p. 281)
displacement (p. 270)
fluid intelligence (p. 281)
functional fixedness (p. 265)
general intelligence (p. 282)
generativity (p. 270)
heuristics (p. 262)
images (p. 260)
incubation effect (p. 263)
insight (p. 263)
intelligence (p. 275)
intelligence quotient (p. 277)
language (p. 269)
linguistic-relativity hypothesis (p. 273)
means-end analysis (p. 262)
mental age (p. 276)
mental models (p. 261)

mental set (p. 265)
morpheme (p. 270)
multiple intelligences (p. 282)
phonemes (p. 269)
phrases (p. 270)
prodigies (p. 284)
prototypes (p. 258)
reliability (p. 279)
representativeness heuristic (p. 266)
savant syndrome (p. 284)
self-fulfilling prophecy (p. 293)
semanticity (p. 269)
sentence (p. 270)
split-half reliability (p. 279)
standardization (p. 278)
Stanford-Binet (p. 276)
stereotype threat (p. 294)
syntax (p. 270)
telegraphic speech (p. 271)
test-retest reliability (p. 279)
trial and error (p. 261)
validity (p. 280)
Wechsler Adult Intelligence Scale (WAIS) (p. 277)

8 PERSONALITY

Sylvie Bouchard / Alamy Stock Photo

LEARNING OBJECTIVES

Examine the contributions Freud, Jung, and Adler made to psychology and the study of personality as we know it today.

Contrast psychoanalysis with the cognitive social-learning approach.

Investigate whether or not an interaction exists between self-actualization and unconditional positive regard.

Identify the roles that nature and nurture are believed to play in trait development.

WHAT'S YOUR PREDICTION: HOW STABLE IS PERSONALITY?

The Situation

From research you've read, you know that an individual's personality consists of various, presumably enduring traits. You also know that many psychologists find it useful to describe personality by comparing people along five broad dimensions: *neuroticism* (a proneness to anxiety and distress), *extraversion* (a desire for social interaction, stimulation, and activity), *openness* (a receptiveness to new experiences), *agreeableness* (a selfless concern for others), and *conscientiousness* (a tendency to be reliable, disciplined, and ambitious). Does one's relative standing on these traits stay basically the same over time, or does personality change with age, life experience, and other factors? If you're generally calm, outgoing, and open minded now, will that be your profile later in life? What about the fact that people's behavior differs from one situation to another?

To determine the stability of personality, you decide to contact a large group of adults who had completed a personality test six years ago as part of another study. The test they had taken was designed to measure the top three of the five major traits (neuroticism, extraversion, openness). Overall, 635 people had taken the test—365 men and 270 women, ranging in age from 25 to 91. In the original experiment, each person was given the test two times, with a six-month interval. Your goal now is to retest these same people on a newer version of the same scale. Most agree to take part in your study. But others, you come to learn, have died, moved, become disabled, or lost interest. In the end, you are able to recruit 398 of the original subjects. To each one, you mail the questionnaire, the instructions, and a stamped self-addressed envelope.

The questionnaire you use is called the Neuroticism-Extraversion-Openness Personality Inventory, or NEO-PI. This test is the one most often used in research (Costa & McCrae, 1992). The NEO-PI contains 181 statements (e.g., "I am usually cheerful," "I really like most people I meet," "I have a very active imagination"). Next to each statement, subjects rate on a five-point scale how much they agree or disagree. The items measuring neuroticism, extraversion, and openness are dispersed throughout the test, but afterward you total the scores separately for each "subscale"—a procedure that yields three scores per subject. Once all tests are scored, the data are ready to be analyzed.

So what next? To determine the stability of the traits you measured, you need to take a longitudinal approach by comparing each subject's scores in the first and second tests. What is the *correlation* between the two sets of scores? If personality, like mood, were to fluctuate wildly from one moment to the next or if you were to pair the scores of one subject with those of another, randomly selected subject, the correlation would be 0 (remember, a correlation coefficient ranges from 0 to +1 or −1). At the other extreme, if personality were completely set in stone or if the same subjects were retested only six days, weeks, or months apart, the two sets of scores should be strongly and positively correlated, in the .90 range. The question is: How strongly correlated would the two sets of scores be after six *years*?

Make a Prediction

Six years ago, your 398 subjects took the test, which yielded three trait scores: one for neuroticism, another for extraversion, and a third for openness to experience. Now you have tested them again. How high do you think the correlations are between the two sets of scores? To give you a basis of comparison, the correlation coefficients found in earlier research when the test was readministered after only six months appear in the table below. On a scale ranging from 0 (no correlation, no stability) to +1 (a perfect correlation, total stability), and using the six-month numbers as a guideline, predict the correlations that are found after six full years:

TRAIT	SIX MONTHS	SIX YEARS
Neuroticism	.87	
Extraversion	.91	
Openness	.86	

The Results

The research just described is based on studies of adult personality that were conducted by Robert McCrae and Paul Costa (1990). So, what did you predict? Does one's personality stay basically the same, or does it change over time? As shown below, the results revealed an extraordinary degree of stability—comparable, in fact, to that found after only six months.

TRAIT	SIX MONTHS	SIX YEARS
Neuroticism	.87	.83
Extraversion	.91	.82
Openness	.86	.83

What Does It All Mean?

Think for a moment about your own personality—your basic feelings, attitudes, and ways of relating to others. Have you changed at all or stayed pretty much the same? When McCrae and Costa (1990) asked their subjects this question, 51 percent said they had stayed the same, 35 percent said they had changed a little, and 14 percent said they had changed a good deal. Were the self-perceptions of those who said they had changed accurate? Not according to the test scores. Costa and McCrae recalculated the test-retest correlations for only those subjects who said they had changed a lot—and the numbers were just as high.

As much research suggests, personality is quite stable over time. Indeed, if it were not, you could not predict the kind of person you would be tomorrow, set a future career goal, or commit yourself to a marriage partner. This is not to say that our personalities stay completely the same as we get older. As described in the chapter on life span development, the aging process itself is accompanied by physical, sensory, and cognitive changes. As a result of life experiences, we may also change certain habits, attitudes, and behaviors. Even subtle shifts in personality are possible. When adults of different age groups are tested, for example, those who are older tend to score slightly lower on neuroticism, extraversion, and openness. Harris and Brett (2016) discovered that older adults in their study also demonstrated personality shifts, with the exception of conscientiousness. Furthermore, cognitive functioning contributes to personality stability. For example, Caselli and colleagues (2018) found that older adults with Alzheimer's disease demonstrate personality shifts while they transition from preclinical Alzheimer's disease to mild cognitive impairment. The shifts were an increase in neuroticism and a decrease in openness, in comparison to control subjects. Terracciano and colleagues (2018) also found personality shifts in adults with dementia, which led them to suggest "lower personality stability in older adults is not due to age but cognitive impairment and dementia" (p. 336).

For clinical psychologists who work at helping people in distress, this research in personality addressed a particularly critical question: Can people who suffer from psychological disorders be helped? In the chapter on treatment and interventions, we'll learn that they can. But as to the question of how much change is possible—and how difficult it is to facilitate that change—we'll learn in this chapter that the answer you come up with will depend, in part, on your theoretical orientation.

Search the American Psychological Association's website for the definition of **personality**. The organization defines it as "individual differences in characteristic patterns of thinking, feeling and behaving. The study of personality focuses on two broad areas: One is understanding individual differences in particular personality characteristics, such as sociability or irritability. The other is understanding how the various parts of a person come together as a whole" (American Psychological Association, n.d.). Now search the Internet for "personality tests." The likelihood that the Myers-Briggs Type Indicator (MBTI) is on the list of top results is quite high. It is estimated that the MBTI is taken by millions of people each year—at least 50 million people since 1962—and makes the company that produces it more than $20 million a year (Cunningham, 2012). The assessment can help people determine which of the 16 possible personality combinations they fit. The personality combinations can be

personality. An individual's distinct and relatively enduring pattern of thoughts, feelings, motives, and behaviors.

applied to leadership, conflict management, career planning, and more (Myers & Briggs Foundation, 2019). Some educational institutions even use it to help students discover the job that is right for them (Cunningham, 2012). With so much success, the MBTI can be said to be a gold standard in personality assessment…or can it?

Stein and Swan (2019) wanted to address whether the MBTI is a valid psychological assessment and, if not, the reason for its popularity. They began their argument with a discussion about Carl Jung, a man who believed in psychological types. These types, based on Jung's observations, were extraversion/introversion, sensing/intuition, and feeling/thinking. Later, Katharine Cook Briggs and Isabel Briggs Myers added the final dimension, judging/perceiving (Quenk, 2009, as cited by Stein & Swan, 2019). The mother-daughter team argued that one's personality type was determined by the individual's preference for either side of the dichotomy. For example, you could prefer extraversion, intuition, thinking, and perceiving over introversion, sensing, feeling, and judging. Thus, your type would be EITP.

This sounds good, but the first problem is testability. As explained in the chapter on psychology and its methods, scientific theories are testable. Jung did not develop his ideas about personality types from experimentation. Jung was a protégé of Freud and, thus, based much of his theories on observations and philosophical exercises. Like Freud's theories, as you will learn later, Jung's ideas about types cannot be tested. Without testability, the theory cannot be improved or debunked with new knowledge. This might be why the *Washington Post* reported that no major peer-reviewed journal has published research on the MBTI (Cunningham, 2012). The second problem is a claim made by MBTI marketing materials that it measures a "true type," which can be summed up by a quote from Isabel Briggs Myers: "It is up to each person to recognize his or her true preferences" (Myers & Briggs Foundation, 2019). Think for a minute about what your "true" self is. Will it be the same tomorrow as it is today? Will it be the same in five years as it is now? You can imagine from these questions how volatile a person's true self can be. Furthermore, the Briggses developed the assessment using friends and family as participants (Stein & Swan, 2019). Do you believe that an assessment of preferences based on the developers' acquaintances can likely tell you what *your* true self is?

This marketing may be questionable, but it is successful nonetheless. One strength is that it claims all types are equal—no one type is better than the others (Myers & Briggs Foundation, 2019). Another strength is ownership. Because of ownership, the assessment's distribution is limited. This makes it a scarce commodity. As a result, it can be seen as more worthy than something that is free (for a discussion of persuasion and scarcity, read the chapter on social and cultural influences). Plus, the people who deliver this commodity are not required to have any formal training in psychology. For $2,495, you too can become an MBTI administrator and tell people their "true type" in exchange for a fee.

Not all personality assessments are created equal. Only a few meet scientific standards.

iStock.com/sinseeho

The MBTI may not meet scientific standards, but there are personality assessments that do. One such assessment, the Big Five, has undergone decades of testing and is discussed later in this chapter. The truth is that humans are fascinated with figuring out who they are and who others are. This is probably why personality tests are so popular and the scientific study of personality is so intriguing. To study personality is to seek ways to describe individuals, the ways in which they are similar to one another, and the ways in which each is unique (Funder, 2001). At times you will wonder, "Do I act that way? Am I an introvert sometimes and an extravert at other times?" In this chapter, we introduce four major perspectives on personality—psychoanalysis, the cognitive social-learning approach, the humanistic approach, and the trait approach—as well as personality testing and its clinical implications. It all begins with Freud.

PSYCHOANALYSIS

> **LEARNING OBJECTIVES**
>
> Examine the contributions Freud, Jung, and Adler made to psychology and the study of personality as we know it today.
>
> - Discuss the experiences that inspired Freud to formulate psychoanalysis.
> - Determine what dreams, jokes, and slips of the tongue have in common.
> - Compare Jung and Adler's theories to Freud's psychoanalysis.
> - Describe how projective tests are used.
> - Create an argument for Freud's greatest legacy.

By his own admission, Freud was a driven young man who sorely wanted to make his mark on the world. He enrolled at the University of Vienna at the age of 17, received a medical degree eight years later, and became a practicing neurologist. Freud's future was bright. In 1884, however, his desire for fame took a downward turn. He had heard about a "magic drug" with anesthetic powers, tried it, and enjoyed the uplifting effects it had on his mood and work. Thinking he was on the verge of a medical breakthrough, Freud prescribed the drug to a friend, who became hopelessly addicted and died of an overdose. The drug was cocaine. Having lost a friend, a patient, and a measure of respect in the medical community, Freud abandoned the drug and pursued other interests—unconscious forces.

The Birth of Psychoanalysis

In 1885, Freud moved to Paris to study with Jean Charcot, an eminent French neurologist. Charcot was studying *hysteria*, a "conversion disorder" in which the patient experiences symptoms such as paralysis of the limbs, blindness, deafness, convulsions, and the like—without an organic basis. What is fascinating about hysteria is that there appears to be nothing physically wrong with the patient, who is not faking symptoms. Charcot found that hysterical disorders often started with a traumatic event in the patient's childhood and that he could make the symptoms vanish by putting the patient under hypnosis. You can imagine how dazzled Freud was by the sight of "paralyzed" patients suddenly able to walk and of those who were "blind" suddenly able to see. Demonstrations like these filled Freud with a profound regard for the power of unconscious forces.

Back in Vienna, Freud became intrigued by the case of Anna O., a patient who suffered from hysterical paralysis of three limbs, impaired vision and speech, and a nervous cough. With the help of her physician, Josef Breuer, Anna was able to recall the events that precipitated her symptoms. As if a large block had been removed from her mind, Anna's symptoms slowly disappeared. Breuer had invented a *talking cure*. But something else happened that would also prove significant. After many sessions, Anna had become emotionally attached to Breuer. Freud was puzzled by the intensity of Anna's feelings, until one day when he had the same experience. Without provocation, a female patient lovingly threw her arms around Freud's neck. Freud had not sought the patient's affection, he said, and assumed he was not the real target of her passion. He thought that this patient, without realizing it, must have transferred her feelings for someone else (maybe her father) onto him, a phenomenon Freud called *transference*.

Sigmund Freud and his daughter Anna—who went on to become a psychoanalyst in her own right.

Chronicle / Alamy Stock Photo

Freud went into private practice but did not have much luck using hypnosis. He realized that not everyone could be hypnotized and that the so-called cures produced in hypnosis often did not last. To help patients recall and talk freely about their past, Freud came up with his first technique of psychotherapy, *free association*. The procedure is simple: The patient lies on a couch, relaxes, and says whatever comes to mind, no matter how trivial, embarrassing, or illogical it may seem. After many sessions, Freud noticed something curious. Although patients would produce streams of ideas leading to the unconscious, many seemed unable to talk or even think about painful and unpleasant memories. In fact, once on the brink of an important insight, they would often stop, go blank, lose their train of thought, or change the subject. Freud called this phenomenon *resistance* and concluded that it was part of an unconscious defensive process designed to keep unwanted thoughts under lock and key—and out of awareness.

Freud's Theory of Personality

Freud's clinical experiences laid a foundation for the theory he later developed. As his work slowly progressed, Freud was convinced that the traumas and conflicts of early childhood can have lasting effects, that we are ruled by unconscious forces, that what's unconscious can be brought out through free association, that we resist painful self-insights, and that we often transfer our feelings for one object onto another. In 1896, Freud used the term **psychoanalysis** for the first time. Then in 1900, he published *The Interpretation of Dreams*, the first of his 24 books and the one that marked the birth of what would become one of the broadest, most influential theories in modern history. The theory is summarized in Freud's (1940) last book, *An Outline of Psychoanalysis*, published one year after his death.

psychoanalysis. Freud's theory of personality and method of psychotherapy, both of which assume that our motives are largely unconscious.

The Unconscious

Underlying psychoanalysis is the assumption that personality is shaped largely by forces that act within a person's *unconscious*. To illustrate, Freud compared the human mind to an iceberg. Like the small tip of the iceberg that can be seen above the water, the conscious part of the mind consists of all that a person is aware of at a given moment. Below the surface is the vast region of the unconscious, which contains thoughts, feelings, and memories that are hidden from view. Part of this region lies just beneath the surface, in an area Freud called the *preconscious*. Preconscious material is not threatening, just temporarily out of awareness and easy to bring to mind. The rest of the unconscious, however, is a deep, dark sea of secret urges, wishes, and drives. According to Freud, the mind keeps these unacceptable impulses out of awareness. Still, they rumble, make waves, and surface for air—in our dreams, our slips of the tongue, the jokes we tell, the people we're attracted to, and the anxieties we feel. Only through psychoanalysis, Freud thought, can we achieve meaningful insight into our personality.

What's in the unconscious? According to Freud, two major instincts motivate all of human behavior. The first is collectively referred to as the *life instincts*, which include the need for food, water, air, and sex. At the time of Freud's writing, the sex part raised eyebrows. But Freud felt it was critical because many of the childhood stories that his patients described were sexual in nature. Years later, after living through the stark destruction of World War I, Freud also proposed that there is a second, darker side of human nature—that buried in the unconscious is a *death instinct*, a need to reduce all tensions by returning to a calm lifeless state. Because these self-destructive impulses conflict with the more powerful life forces, reasoned Freud, they are turned away from the self and directed instead toward others. The fated result of the death instinct, then, is aggression—a problem that has plagued humans throughout history.

Traditional psychoanalysis is a lengthy process focused on bringing unconscious urges to awareness. This process can be psychologically uncomfortable for the client.

iStock.com/stefanamer

The Structure of Personality

Have you ever had a burning urge to kiss or embrace someone you're attracted to or to hit someone who has angered you, only to be stopped by the haunting voice of your conscience? If so, how do you resolve these dilemmas? Based on his clinical experiences, Freud believed that people are perpetually driven by inner conflicts (conscious vs. unconscious, free association vs. resistance, life vs. death)—and that compromise is a necessary solution. Freud thus divided the human personality into three interacting parts: the id, ego, and superego. These parts are not presumed to be actual structures in the brain. Rather, they are concepts that Freud used to represent the different aspects of personality.

The **id** is the most primitive part of personality. Present at birth, it is a reservoir of instincts and biological drives that energize us. According to Freud, the id operates according to the **pleasure principle**, motivating us to seek immediate and total gratification of all desires. When a person is deprived of food, water, air, or sex, a state of tension builds until the need is satisfied. Thus, the id is a blind, pleasure-seeking part of us that aims for the reduction of all tension. If the impulsive, id-dominated infant could speak, it would scream: "I want it, and I want it *now*!"

The **superego** is a socially developed aspect of personality that motivates us to behave in ways that are moral, ideal, even perfect. Whereas the id pushes people to seek immediate gratification, the superego is a prude, a moralist, a part of us that shuns sex and other innate sources of pleasure. Where does the superego come from? According to Freud, children learn society's values from their parents. Through repeated experiences with reward for good behavior and punishment for bad, children eventually develop their own internal standards of what's right and wrong.

The superego has two components. One is the *ego-ideal*, an image of the ideals we should strive for. The other is the *conscience*, a set of prohibitions that define how we should not behave. Once the superego is developed, people reward themselves internally for moral acts by feeling pride, and they punish themselves for immoral acts by suffering pangs of guilt.

The third aspect of personality is the **ego**, which mediates the conflict between the "wants" of the id and the "shoulds" of the superego. According to Freud, the ego is a pragmatic offshoot of the id, the part of personality that helps us achieve realistic forms of gratification. In contrast to the id (which strives for immediate gratification) and the superego (which seeks to inhibit the same impulses), the ego operates according to the **reality principle**—the goal being to reduce one's tensions, but only at the right time, in the right place, and in a socially appropriate manner. The ego is thus a master of compromise, a part of us that tries to satisfy our needs without offending our morals. The ego, said Freud, is the executive officer of the personality, the part that controls our behavior. Freud's model is illustrated in Figure 8.1.

Psychosexual Development

According to Freud, his clinical work led him to draw two conclusions about human development: that personality is shaped in the first few years of life, and that the resolution of "psychosexual" conflicts is the key contributor. He went on to propose that all children pass through an odyssey of **psychosexual stages** of development, with each stage defined by a different "erogenous zone," a part of the body that's most sensitive to erotic stimulation, as illustrated in Figure 8.2.

First in this theory comes the *oral stage*, which occurs in the first year of life, a time when the baby's mouth is the pleasure-seeking center of attention. Oral activity begins with the sucking of nipples, thumbs, and pacifiers, then moves on to biting, chewing, cooing, and other oral activities. In this stage, the infant is totally dependent on caregivers, feeding is a key activity, and weaning (the transition away from the breast or bottle) is a major source of conflict. Next comes the *anal stage*, which occurs during the second and third years of life, when the baby derives pleasure in the sensation of holding in and letting go of feces. In this stage, there is a regular and enjoyable cycle of tension buildup and release. However, toilet training brings the parent ("Wait!") and child ("I don't want to!") into sharp conflict. Between the ages of 4 and 6 years, the child then enters the *phallic stage*, a time when pleasure is felt in the genital area. In this stage, children become fascinated with the body and can often be seen playing with their own sex organs in public, a habit that once again brings them into conflict with parents. To Freud, the single most dramatic conflict in psychosexual development takes place at this point.

---

id. A primitive and unconscious part of personality that contains basic drives and operates according to the pleasure principle.

pleasure principle. The id's boundless drive for immediate gratification.

superego. The part of personality that consists of one's moral ideals and conscience.

ego. The part of personality that operates according to the reality principle and mediates the conflict between the id and superego.

reality principle. The ego's capacity to delay gratification.

psychosexual stages. Freud's stages of personality development during which pleasure is derived from different parts of the body (oral, anal, phallic, and genital).

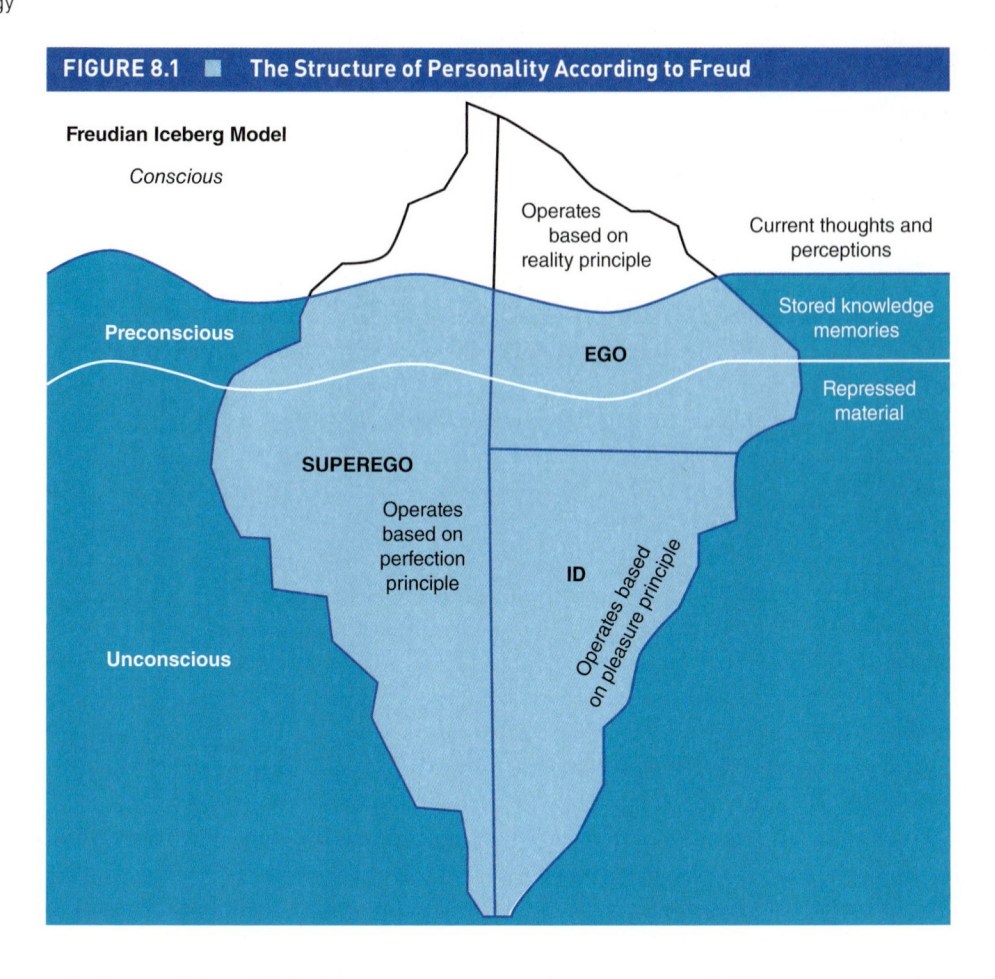

FIGURE 8.1 ■ The Structure of Personality According to Freud

Freudian Iceberg Model

- Conscious
- Preconscious
- Unconscious

- Operates based on reality principle
- Current thoughts and perceptions
- Stored knowledge memories
- Repressed material
- EGO
- SUPEREGO — Operates based on perfection principle
- ID — Operates based on pleasure principle

Ask a 4-year-old boy, "Who do you want to marry when you grow up?" The chances are quite good that he will say, "Mommy!" Society tends to find this response heartwarming, as it is demonstrative of the boy's innocent love for his caregiver. Freud and Greek mythology didn't have the same sentiment.

A famous Greek tragedy features an abandoned infant, who goes on to become King Oedipus. As a young man, he kills his father and marries his mother, without realizing who they are. According to Freud, this legend exposes an unconscious human wish he called the **Oedipus complex**—a tendency for children to become sexually attracted to the parent of the opposite sex and to develop feelings of jealousy and rage toward the rival parent of the same sex. Freud did not take non-heterosexual humans into account when creating this theory. Thus, Freud's theory focuses on heterosexual male development, and for this population the theory is clear: The young boy wants his mother and hates his father for standing in the way. Because the father is bigger and more powerful, however, the boy develops *castration anxiety*, a fear that the father will retaliate by cutting off his son's prized genitals. For defensive reasons, the boy represses his sexual urge for the mother and tries to emulate the father, in a process known as **identification**. As a result, the boy becomes less anxious, derives partial satisfaction from his repressed wish for his mother, and adopts his father's moral values.

If he grows up to be like his father, then he should be able to attract a woman quite similar to his mother. A man who marries someone like his mother? Never! Well, actually, it's not that far-fetched, is it? Research by Geher (2000) says it isn't far-fetched at all. Geher asked heterosexual participants to describe their parents and romantic partners across several personality traits. In addition, Geher had participants' parents and romantic partners describe themselves. Geher found that out of eight personality traits, participants' opposite-sex parents had scores similar to those of their romantic partners. In addition, participants found their romantic partners to be similar to their parents across all traits. Is this a bad thing? It depends. Relationship satisfaction and parental similarity in romantic partners were positively correlated for good traits—the higher the similarity for good traits, the higher the relationship satisfaction. On the contrary, relationship satisfaction and parental similarity in romantic partners were negatively correlated for bad traits—the higher the similarity for bad traits, the lower the relationship satisfaction.

Oedipus complex. A tendency for young children to become sexually attracted to the parent of the opposite sex and hostile toward the parent of the same sex.

identification. The process by which children internalize their parents' values and form a superego.

Chapter 8 • Personality 311

FIGURE 8.2 ■ Psychosexual Stages of Development

According to Freud, psychosexual development progresses through stages, each one of which is defined by a part of the body that is most sensitive. In the oral stage (a), everything is put into the mouth. During the anal stage (b), toilet training brings the child and parents into conflict. Middle childhood is considered a calm latency period (c) when sexual urges lie dormant. Beginning at puberty, the genital stage (d) is marked by the emergence of adultlike sexual desires.

iStock.com/bradleyhebdon; iStock.com/CareyHope; iStock.com/Yobro10; iStock.com/Sam Edwards

Do girls also fantasize about marrying their fathers? Freud admitted that his theory of female development is less clear. At some point, he says, the girl notices that her father has a penis but that she and her mother do not. Unconsciously, the girl blames and resents her mother for this deficiency, develops *penis envy*, and seeks to become daddy's little girl. Eventually, realizing the futility of these feelings, she represses her envy and identifies with her mother. For both boys and girls, then, the identification part of the process means that the superego springs full blown from the Oedipus complex.

Once Oedipal conflicts are resolved, the child enters a long *latency period*, which lasts roughly between the ages of 7 and 12. In these middle years of childhood, sexual impulses lie dormant, as boys and girls concentrate on friends of the same sex and schoolwork. This stage precedes the fourth and final stage of psychosexual development—the *genital stage*. Starting at puberty, boys and girls emerge from their latency shells and feel the stirring of adultlike sexual urges for the first time. Once again, the ego must cope with an undeclared state of war between biological drives and social prohibitions.

According to Freud, one must pass successfully through all psychosexual stages in order to form a healthy personality and enjoy mature adult relationships. If children receive *too much* or *too little* gratification at an earlier stage, they will become stuck or "fixated" at that stage. **Fixation** is thus responsible for the development of the following personality types:

- **Oral.** If you were weaned too early or too late as an infant, you would become fixated at the oral stage and feel the need to smoke, drink, bite your nails, chew on pencils, or spend hours talking on the phone. You might also seek symbolic forms of oral gratification by becoming passive, dependent, and demanding—like a nursing infant.

fixation. In psychoanalysis, a tendency to get "locked in" at early, immature stages of psychosexual development.

FIGURE 8.3 ■ The Psychodynamics of Personality

In psychoanalysis, unconscious sexual and aggressive impulses find acceptable forms of expression.

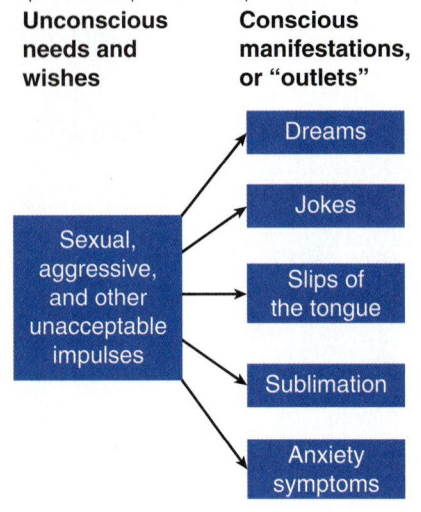

Unconscious needs and wishes: Sexual, aggressive, and other unacceptable impulses

Conscious manifestations, or "outlets": Dreams; Jokes; Slips of the tongue; Sublimation; Anxiety symptoms

defense mechanisms. Unconscious methods of minimizing anxiety by denying and distorting reality.

repression. A defense mechanism in which personally threatening thoughts, memories, and impulses are banned from awareness.

denial. A primitive form of repression in which anxiety-filled external events are barred from awareness.

- **Anal.** If, as a toddler, you were toilet trained in a harsh and rigid manner, you would become anally fixated and react in one of two ways—either by becoming tight, stubborn, punctual, and overcontrolled (the holding-on, "anal-retentive" type) or by becoming rebellious, messy, and disorganized (the letting-go, "anal-expulsive" type).

- **Phallic.** If you masturbated freely during the preschool years or if all genital contact was prohibited, resulting in frustration, you would develop a phallic personality—one that is entirely self-centered, vain, arrogant, and in constant need of attention. The man who seems obsessed with building his wealth, is power hungry, must wear expensive clothing and drive a fancy car, and is constantly trying to conquer women is a classic example.

The Dynamics of Personality

Influenced by the science of physics, Freud believed that the human mind has a constant, finite amount of "psychic energy"—energy that cannot be created or destroyed, only transformed from one state to another. What this means for personality is that even though the id's instinctual impulses can be suppressed temporarily, its energy must find an outlet, a way to leak out. According to Freud, the ego searches for safe and normal outlets for these needs.

In Freud's theory, the dreams you remember in the morning are a disguised, nonthreatening expression of your unconscious wishes. Pent-up energy is released while you're asleep, but in ways that are confusing and, therefore, nonthreatening. The same is true of the so-called Freudian slips of the tongue and, as we'll read later, a defense mechanism known as sublimation. Even humor can serve as an outlet, as when people tell ethnic jokes to relieve hostile impulses and erotic jokes to ease their sexual tension. Disguised wish fulfillment is the compromise we strike with ourselves, as illustrated in Figure 8.3.

To help minimize the anxiety that results from the clash between our wishes, morals, and reality, the ego uses powerful weapons: unconscious **defense mechanisms** that deny and distort our self-perceptions. Here are some common defense mechanisms described by Freud. Can you recognize any of them?

- **Repression** occurs when anxiety-provoking thoughts and memories are "forgotten" and pushed out of awareness. Freud believed that people repress unacceptable sexual and aggressive urges, traumas, and guilt feelings. Nicole Kluemper (formerly Taus) became a famous case of trauma-induced repression. As a child, Nicole received treatment from a psychologist, Dr. David Corwin. He filmed the treatment and found it to be educational. Thus, Corwin asked 17-year-old Nicole if he could use the films for training purposes. Nicole gave her permission, but for personal reasons requested she see the footage—and it would be her first time seeing it. Before proceeding, Corwin asked Nicole what she remembered. At first, she remembered nothing. When Corwin mentioned allegations of sexual abuse, Nicole described an incident with her mother in a bathtub. Nicole's filmed childhood testimony to Corwin corroborated her recalled memory. Corwin and Olafson (1997) published the case study in an academic journal, which later was scrutinized by Elizabeth Loftus and Melvin Guyer (2002). Their scrutiny made its way to the Supreme Court of California and has been the subject of an ethical debate ever since (Cheit, 2014; Dalenberg, 2014; Olafson, 2014).

- **Denial** is a primitive form of repression in which anxiety-filled external events not only are forgotten but also are barred from awareness in the first place (see no evil, hear no evil). Denial is common among terminally ill patients and in families that sometimes refuse to admit that a loved one is dying. It is also characteristic of smokers who refuse to recognize the health risks of their habit, partners who ignore signs of conflict, and politicians who manage to overlook corruption that takes place right under their noses.

- **Projection** occurs when people attribute or "project" their own unacceptable impulses onto others. In Freud's view, a person who is sexually attracted to a friend's spouse, or to anyone else who is "off limits," might repress those feelings and consciously come to believe that the friend's spouse is attracted to them. In this way, "I lust for this person" is transformed into "This person lusts after me." Similarly, people who are prejudiced against certain racial or ethnic groups are quick to attribute their own hostile impulses to "them."

- **Reaction formation** involves converting an unacceptable feeling into its opposite. Someone who brags may be masking feelings of inadequacy. Similarly, hatred can be transformed into love, and sadness into joy. Compared to true feelings, reaction formations often appear exaggerated. Examples include the father who smothers with affection a child he privately resents, the administrator who goes out of his way to prevent sexual harassment in the workplace but secretly has an affair with his subordinate, and the vocal antigay activist who fights to cover up his own homosexual impulses.

- **Rationalization** involves making excuses for one's failures and shortcomings. The fox in Aesop's fable who refused the grapes he could not reach "because they were sour" used rationalization. So do failing students who say they don't really care about their grades, gamblers who justify their massive losses as entertainment costs, and deceptive lovers who find fault with their partner as an excuse to cheat.

- **Sublimation** is the channeling of the id's repressed urges into socially acceptable substitute outlets. Freud saw this as the healthiest defense mechanism because it represents a genuine compromise among the id, ego, and superego. Thus, a person with pent-up hostile impulses may derive satisfaction by becoming a surgeon, football player, or critic. Similarly, a person may sublimate sexual needs by listening to others talk about sex or through music, art, dance, and other activities. Freud believed that civilization's greatest achievements spring from the wells of sexual and aggressive energies.

projection. A defense mechanism in which people attribute or "project" their own unacceptable impulses onto others.

reaction formation. A defense mechanism in which one converts an unacceptable feeling into its opposite.

rationalization. A defense mechanism that involves making excuses for one's failures and shortcomings.

sublimation. The channeling of repressed sexual and aggressive urges into socially acceptable substitute outlets.

Freud's Legacy

Freud was born and raised in the prudish Victorian era, so his theory was met with skepticism. Unconscious conflicts, dreams, jokes, and slips of the tongue that hold hidden meaning; erotic impulses churning in the innocent newborn baby; repression and other defense mechanisms that keep us from falling apart—it all seemed pretty wild at the time. Still, Freud's legacy is remarkable. As we'll learn, his ideas gave rise to other psychoanalytic theories and a whole class of personality tests. He also provided something for psychologists of other theoretical persuasions to aim at—and build upon.

Neo-Freudian Theorists

Despite the controversy, Freud's emerging theory immediately attracted a group of followers, many of whom went on to propose competing theories. But these dissenters were psychoanalytically oriented nonetheless. Following Freud, they assumed that unconscious factors play a critical role, that people need to resolve inner conflicts, and that personality is formed early in

Nicole Kluemper's case study spurred an ethical debate. As a patient who believed in her claims of sexual abuse, Nicole felt slandered when psychologists openly criticized her repressed memory. Now, inspired by Dr. David Corwin and her own experiences, Nicole works with children who have mental health issues and experience trauma (Watt, 2017).

iStock.com/Eshma

Carl Jung
World History Archive / Alamy Stock Photo

Alfred Adler
Lebrecht Music & Arts / Alamy Stock Photo

childhood. The main sticking point was—and still is, for many—Freud's emphasis on sex as a driving force.

Carl Jung, heir apparent to the throne of psychoanalysis, was a favorite within Freud's inner circle. However, Jung (1928) complained that Freud viewed the brain "as an appendage to the genital glands," and he sought to change the theory in two ways. First, Jung maintained that the unconscious consists not only of repressed material from one's personal life but also of universal symbols and memories from our ancestral past—an inherited **collective unconscious**. That's why, said Jung, so many humans are born with an irrational fear of snakes; why we're drawn like magnets to fire, water, wind, and other natural elements; and why certain common themes appear in cultural myths and legends around the world. Jung's second shift in emphasis concerned the subject of personality development. He agreed that people strive for the satisfaction of biological drives. But he also felt that at the age of 40 or so, we undergo a midlife transition, a time during which the youthful and vigorous pursuit of biological needs is replaced by deeper, more cerebral, even spiritual concerns. As far as Jung was concerned, personality development continues into adulthood.

Alfred Adler was another major theorist within Freud's inner circle. Like the others, Adler was trained in medicine. He broke with Freud, however, because he felt that personality was formed more from social conflicts than from sexual tension. According to Adler (1927), all humans feel small, helpless, and weak in the first few years of life, symptoms of what he termed an *inferiority complex*. As a result, we grow up trying unconsciously to compensate for these feelings and strive for superiority, while at the same time taking an interest in the welfare of others. Adler felt that Freud was so focused on the triangle of relationships among mother, father, and child that he neglected other family influences. Adler wrote, for example, about the impact of being first-, middle-, or later-born within the family, and he coined the term *sibling rivalry*.

Later generations of psychoanalytic theorists either viewed themselves as classical Freudians (Brenner, 1982) or extended the theory in two directions. One group followed in Adler's path by emphasizing that humans are inherently social animals. Erich Fromm (1941) maintained that as Western civilization abandoned the caste system, people felt freer and more independent but also more alone and isolated. Fromm argued that we unconsciously seek to "escape from freedom" by falling in love, getting married, having children, joining religious groups, and rallying behind powerful leaders. What distinguishes individuals from one another, he proposed, are the ways in which they resolve the

> **collective unconscious.** As proposed by Jung, a kind of memory bank that stores images and ideas that humans have accumulated over the course of evolution.

conflict between freedom and unity. Karen Horney (1945) similarly claimed that all humans need love and security and become highly anxious when they feel isolated and alone. She was one of the first to recognize the impact culture had on mental health (1936), and gave a voice to women in psychology (Horney, 1935; Horney, 1967; O'Connell, 1980). According to Horney, people have different ways of coping with this anxiety: Some are unconsciously driven to be loved, others to be feared, and still others to be admired. Again, the goal is to satisfy needs that are social, not biological. Horney was outspoken about her critiques of Freud—so outspoken she was forced to resign from the New York Psychoanalytic Institute in 1941.

A second group of psychoanalysts known as ego psychologists enlarged the role of the ego in personality. For Freud, the ego existed in order to accommodate the id and yet operate within the boundaries of reality, appease the superego, and ward off anxiety through the use of defense mechanisms. But according to daughter Anna Freud, Heinz Hartmann, David Rapaport, Erik Erikson, and other theorists, the ego is more than simply the id's brainy assistant. In their view, the ego is present at birth, is as basic as the id, and is the reason why people are thoughtful as well as passionate. This ego helps to organize our thoughts, feelings, and memories, and it leads us to grow and pursue creative activities for the sake of enjoyment, not simply the reduction of tension. As ego psychologist Robert White (1975) put it, "Human beings have intrinsic urges which make them want to grow up."

Karen Horney, unlike Freud, believed in life's ability to act as a therapist. She is quoted as saying, "Fortunately, analysis is not the only way to resolve inner conflicts. Life itself still remains a very effective therapist."

Bettmann / Contributor/Bettmann/Getty Images

Projective Personality Tests

Psychoanalysis is founded on the assumption that meaningful parts of one's personality are locked away in an unconscious part of the mind. This means that one cannot truly get to know someone by asking direct questions. Searching for the key to this warehouse of personal secrets, Freud tried hypnosis, free association, and the interpretation of dreams—the "royal road to the unconscious." Is it possible to explore the mind without psychotherapy? Seeking a shortcut to the unconscious, psychoanalytic researchers and practitioners devised what's known as **projective tests**. A projective test asks people to respond to an ambiguous stimulus—a word out of context, an incomplete sentence, an inkblot, a fuzzy picture. The assumption they make is that if a stimulus has no inherent meaning and can accommodate a multitude of interpretations, then whatever people see must be a *projection* of their own needs, wishes, hopes, fears, and conflicts.

The most popular of the projective tests is the **Rorschach**, introduced in 1921 by Swiss psychiatrist Hermann Rorschach, which consists of a set of 10 symmetrical inkblots—some in color, others in black and white. Figure 8.4 presents an example of a colored inkblot. In it you might see a bouquet of flowers. Or two green seahorses. Or a butterfly. You might see a single large image, or you might dissect the inkblot into many smaller images. In fact, the examiner is interested not only in what you see but also in how you approach the task—whether you take 2 seconds per card or 5 minutes; whether you're sensitive to form or to color; and whether the images you report are common or uncommon.

Over the years, many elaborate systems have been developed for scoring the Rorschach, which is still widely used in clinical practice. Critics cite two

projective tests. Psychoanalytic personality tests that allow people to "project" unconscious needs, wishes, and conflicts onto ambiguous stimuli.

rorschach. A projective personality test in which people are asked to report what they see in a set of inkblots.

FIGURE 8.4 ■ Sample Rorschach Card

According to psychoanalytically oriented psychologists, what you see in this inkblot—and how you see it—can be used to assess your personality.

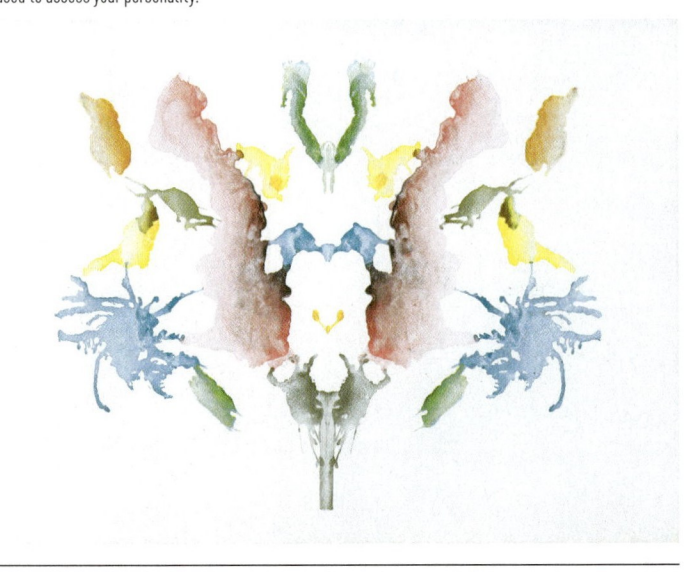

Science & Society Picture Library / Contributor/SSPL/Getty Images

Hermann Rorschach's background in art helped him develop his famous set of inkblots. Rorschach's career was shortened by his death at age 37.

Heritage Images / Contributor/Hulton Archive/Getty Images

Thematic Apperception Test (TAT). A projective personality test in which people are asked to make up stories from a set of ambiguous pictures.

problems with this test. The first is that it lacks reliability, which means that two examiners often reach different conclusions from the same set of responses. The second is that the test lacks validity, which means that it does not discriminate well among groups known to have different personalities. In a scathing critique, Robyn Dawes (1994) called the Rorschach a "shoddy" instrument and suggested that it "is not a valid test of anything" (p. 146).

Despite these criticisms, Rorschach users are now becoming more sophisticated. Using past research, John Exner, Jr. (1993) developed a computerized scoring system. Studies have shown that, as a general rule, higher levels of reliability and validity are reached now than in the past (Czopp & Zeligman, 2016)—but that these levels are not ideal (Garb, Florio, & Grove, 1998; Mihura, Meyer, Dumitrascu, & Bombel, 2013). According to many Rorschach users, however, skillful examiners can employ the test to understand how people think and to explore depths of personality that do not otherwise surface in questionnaires, interviews, or observations of behavior (Exner, 1996). In fact, one group of researchers has used the Rorschach and Exner's Rorschach Comprehensive System in a successful attempt to predict posttraumatic stress disorder (Arnon, Maoz, Gazit, & Klein, 2011). Another group of researchers argues that narcissism can be assessed using the Rorschach (Gritti, Marino, Lang, & Meyer, 2017). To this day, researchers are split in their opinions and continue to debate the value of this inkblot test as a measure of personality (Gacono, Gacono, & Evans, 2008; Hunsley & Bailey, 2001; Wood et al., 2010).

A second popular projective instrument is the **Thematic Apperception Test (TAT)**, introduced by Henry Murray. In 1938, Murray formulated a personality theory that distinguishes people by the kinds of psychological needs that motivate their behavior—such as the needs for power, achievement, nurturance, and affiliation. To measure these needs, Murray (1943) developed a set of drawings of characters in ambiguous situations (plus one blank card, the ultimate projective test!) and asked subjects to tell a story about the "hero." Figure 8.5 offers an example.

FIGURE 8.5 ■ Sample TAT picture

This ambiguous picture is used in the Thematic Apperception Test.

Science Source/Science Source

What's going on in the drawing? Who are the characters, and what's their relationship? What led up to this situation, and how will it all turn out? The possibilities are limitless—like a blank page awaiting your personal signature.

The TAT is based on the assumption that people identify with the heroes and project their own needs into their responses. If someone tells one story after another about the loss of a loved one, resistance to authority, the struggle to achieve success, or fear of rejection, chances are that the particular theme is an important one for the person. As with the Rorschach, the TAT has been criticized for lacking high levels of reliability and validity (Anastasi & Urbina, 1997; Jenkins, 2017). At the same time, TAT pictures have been reliably used to identify specific motives (Gruber, 2017), personality dispositions (Cramer, 2017), the realities of cancer treatment (Venturini & Roques, 2016), and to predict behavior. People whose TAT stories reveal a high rather than low *need for intimacy* think more often about their social relationships and spend more time talking, smiling, and making eye contact when engaged in conversation (McAdams, Jackson, & Kirshnit, 1984). In contrast, people whose stories reveal a high rather than low *need for achievement* set realistic goals, persist more in the face of failure, are more likely to succeed at work, and derive more pride from their accomplishments (Atkinson, 1957; McClelland, 1985; Spangler, 1992). Not all TAT cards will activate a person's need state, but when they do, the fantasy stories people tell, and the themes they emphasize, reveal their personalities (Cramer, 1996; Gieser & Stein, 1999; Tuerlinckx, De Boeck, & Lens, 2002).

Current Perspectives on Psychoanalysis

In 1993, *Time* magazine had a picture of Sigmund Freud on the cover, accompanied by three words: "Is Freud Dead?" It has now been more than 100 years since Freud started putting together the pieces of psychoanalysis, a theory that would alter the course of psychology as a discipline. Needless to say, Freud and other psychoanalysts have always attracted their share of critics, as new research developments within psychology lead us to modify or reject some propositions and to accept others. To this day, Freud remains a subject of biography, analysis, and controversy (Frosh, 2016; Razinsky, 2014; Rizzolo, 2016). His life, work, and relationship conflicts even inspired a 2011 film, *A Dangerous Game,* that was analyzed (the irony!) by Ferrell and Silverman (2014).

There are three major criticisms of psychoanalysis. One is that as a theory of personality it paints too bleak a portrait of human nature. It was bad enough when Copernicus exposed the myth that Earth is at the center of the universe and when Darwin said that human beings were descended from apes. But when Freud claimed that we are driven, even as infants, by lustful, incestuous desires and antisocial, aggressive impulses and that we are all at the mercy of unconscious forces beyond our control, some people felt he went too far. The theory was simply too pessimistic for many people to accept.

The second criticism of psychoanalysis is that it does not meet acceptable standards of science. From the start, Freud based his whole theory on observations he made of his Vienna patients during a time of sexual repression (Starr & Aron, 2011), hardly a representative group of human beings. He then proceeded to use the theory to explain family dynamics, mental illness, love and attraction, homosexuality, war, religion, suicide, crime and punishment, and the course of human history. Plus, Freud considered women to be less moral than men, was phallocentric, and saw libido as a masculine force (Hsieh, 2012). Of course, after-the-fact explanations are easy, very much like betting on a horse after the race has been run. But can Freud's theory predict these kinds of events in advance?

The critics say no, which leads to the third major criticism of psychoanalysis: Carefully controlled research fails to support many of its propositions, as the great scientific philosopher Karl Popper (1963) argued. One important example concerns the assumption that personality is completely formed in the first few years of life. In light of recent

David Cerny's sculpture of Sigmund Freud signifies the psychologist's constant struggle with death. The sculpture is on display in Prague, Czech Republic.

AP Photo/Alex Milan Tracy

research, we now know that although early childhood experiences are formative, and can have a lasting impact on us, development is a lifelong process. Freud's theory that childhood conflicts cause people to become fixated at certain psychosexual stages has also not stood the test of time. Research has shown that although oral, anal, and phallic personality types can be identified, they don't necessarily arise from difficulties experienced in weaning, toilet training, masturbation, or other psychosexual experiences. Even the Oedipus complex, the centerpiece of Freud's development theory, receives little support. Young boys and girls often do favor the opposite-sex parent and identify with the same-sex parent. Research by Fraley and Marks (2010) demonstrated that subliminally priming participants with a photo of their opposite-sex parents increases participants' perceived attractiveness of others. However, gender socialization and cultural norms contribute to which parent one identifies with—variables that Freud did not include. Finally, there's little evidence for castration anxiety, penis envy, or other sex-related motives (Daly & Wilson, 1990; Fisher & Greenberg, 1977).

So is Freud dead? The man is, but his influence clearly is not. In its classic form, psychoanalysis has shortcomings and relatively few adherents (Eysenck, 2002). But many of its concepts have become so absorbed into mainstream psychology—not to mention popular culture—that it is very much alive and continues to inspire new theories and research (Hobson, 2013; Hunyady, Josephs & Jost, 2008; Thompson & Keable, 2016). In fact, Kandel (1999) believed that advances in neuroscience in the late 1990s might make it possible to uncover the biological bases for some of Freud's ideas. Ceylan and colleagues (2016), Ruby (2011), and Guénolé and colleagues (2013) all agree with Kandel.

Perhaps the most enduring of Freud's ideas is his view of the mind as an iceberg. Today, virtually everyone agrees that the unconscious is vast and important—and that people have a limited awareness of why they think, feel, and behave as they do (Charles et al., 2017; Sandberg, Timmermans, Overgaard, & Cleeremans, 2010; Volz & Gazzaniga, 2017). Psychologists disagree, however, about the nature of the human unconscious. Some maintain that it contains thoughts, wishes, impulses, memories, and other information actively blocked from awareness for self-protective reasons (Bowers & Farvolden, 1996; Erdelyi, 1992) or due to lack of neural synchronization (Ceylan et al., 2016). Others maintain that the unconscious consists of material that is not brought to awareness, or else is forgotten, for strictly cognitive reasons (Barbosa, Vlassova, & Kouider, 2017; Greenwald, 1992; Kihlstrom, Barnhardt, & Tataryn, 1992).

As discussed throughout this book, psychologists today are busily studying a wide range of unconscious processes such as perception without awareness, implicit learning and memory, subliminal influences, and implicit social stereotypes. Throughout the course of several experiments, Pyszczynski and colleagues (2015) have found that when people are confronted with fleeting thoughts of death—a source of anxiety that Freud wrote about—they engage in a host of defensive processes, desperately trying to suppress thoughts about their own mortality. According to their provocative *terror-management theory*, this deeply rooted fear of death highly motivates people to consider themselves as valuable members of society, to believe their own cultural worldviews as good and correct, and to harbor contempt and prejudice for others who are different. Major and colleagues (2016) suggested that terror-management-theory be integrated into psychotherapy.

This leads us to a second enduring legacy of Freud's theory: his analysis of defense mechanisms. Based on the resistance shown by so many of his patients, Freud argued that people distort reality to ward off anxiety. Research shows that he was absolutely right. Some of us may be more defensive than others, but everyone harbors illusions about the self. We perceive ourselves in inflated terms, we have an exaggerated sense of control over uncontrollable events, we compare ourselves to others who are less fortunate, and we think more optimistically than we should about our own future—and these illusions may help us cope with adversity (Taylor & Armor, 1996). These forms of coping are defense mechanisms much like those Freud had described (Baumeister, Dale, & Sommer, 1998; Cramer, 1998). Indeed, Phebe Cramer (2000, 2015) notes that Freud's view of unconscious defense mechanisms is now supported throughout psychology in various studies of attention, thinking, feeling, memory, psychopathology, denial, and coping without awareness.

> ## LEARNING CHECK
>
> ### Mixed Sigmund
>
> Try to repress any slips as you match each Freudian term in the left column to its closest description in the right column.
>
> | | | | |
> |---|---|---|---|
> | 1. | Denial | a. | Pushing threatening thoughts out of consciousness. |
> | 2. | Identification | b. | A child's tendency to become attracted to the parent of the opposite sex and hostile to the parent of the same sex. |
> | 3. | Pleasure principle | c. | Barring anxiety-provoking thoughts from consciousness. |
> | 4. | Reality principle | d. | Making excuses for failures and shortcomings. |
> | 5. | Rationalization | e. | One's moral ideals and conscience. |
> | 6. | Oedipus complex | f. | A primitive, unconscious reservoir of basic drives. |
> | 7. | Repression | g. | The capacity to delay gratification. |
> | 8. | Projection | h. | Channeling repressed urges into socially acceptable outlets. |
> | 9. | Reaction formation | i. | Attributing unacceptable impulses to others. |
> | 10. | Sublimation | j. | The drive for immediate gratification. |
> | 11. | Superego | k. | The process by which children internalize parents' values. |
> | 12. | Id | l. | Converting an unacceptable feeling into its opposite. |
>
> (Answers: 1. c; 2. k; 3. j; 4. g; 5. d; 6. b; 7. a; 8. i; 9. l; 10. h; 11. e; 12. f.)

THE COGNITIVE SOCIAL-LEARNING APPROACH

> ### LEARNING OBJECTIVES
>
> Contrast psychoanalysis with the cognitive social-learning approach.
>
> - Describe the principles of learning that laid the foundation for an alternative approach to personality.
> - Determine if you have an internal or external locus of control.
> - Connect self-efficacy to wellness.

In contrast to psychoanalysis, **cognitive social-learning theory** is an approach that views personality as the product of a continuous interaction between persons and their environments. This theory has its roots in the behavioral principles of classical and operant conditioning, social-learning theory, and cognitive psychology. Let's trace the evolution of this important approach.

cognitive social-learning theory. An approach to personality that focuses on social learning (modeling), acquired cognitive factors (expectancies, values), and the person-situation interaction.

Principles of Learning and Behavior

As psychoanalysis was emerging in Europe, a second movement was being conceived in animal laboratories in the United States and Russia. At the time, animal researchers were discovering some very powerful principles of learning and were spreading the new word of *behaviorism*—a scientific approach to psychology that focuses on environmental determinants of observable behavior. To the hard-core behaviorist, personality was a nonscientific figment of the Freudian imagination. After all, behaviorists had refused to muddy the scientific study of behavior by speculating about inner states of "mind." The first spokesperson for this countermovement was John Watson (1925), whose message was loud and clear:

> Give me a dozen healthy infants, well-formed, and my own specified world to bring them up in, and I'll guarantee to take any one at random and train him to become any type of specialist I might select—doctor, lawyer, artist, merchant-chief and, yes, even beggarman and thief, regardless of his talents, penchants, tendencies, abilities, vocations, and race of his ancestors. (p. 104)

At the same time that Freud was writing his classic book on dreams, animal researchers were discovering five simple but very powerful principles of learning: classical conditioning, operant conditioning, stimulus generalization, discrimination, and extinction (these are described more fully in the chapter on learning).

The first, classical conditioning, was based on Ivan Pavlov's finding that the dogs in his laboratory would start to salivate before they were fed, in anticipation of the meal they were about to eat. By repeatedly pairing a sound with the presentation of food, Pavlov found that eventually the dogs would salivate as soon as they heard the noise even if food was not present. Thus, the animals were trained to react to a neutral stimulus that was associated with food, which is an unconditioned stimulus that naturally elicits the reaction. The second major principle was operant conditioning, first shown by Edward Thorndike's finding that organisms repeat behaviors that are rewarded. Working with cats and, later, with humans, Thorndike found that whatever solution succeeded for a subject on one puzzle was later tried on other puzzles as well. A few years later, B. F. Skinner tested the effects of reinforcement schedules on behavior by training rats to press bars and pigeons to peck at keys for food.

Both classical- and operant-conditioning researchers made parallel discoveries not yet relevant to the study of personality. The first was stimulus generalization, the principle that once a response is learned in one situation, it may also be evoked in other, similar situations—as when Pavlov's dogs learned to salivate to tones that were similar but not identical to the conditioned stimulus. The second, opposite principle is discrimination: the learned tendency to distinguish between a conditioned stimulus and other stimuli—as when a child learns that having tantrums works on parents but not on teachers and friends. The third principle is extinction, the tendency for a conditioned response to diminish if not reinforced. Pavlov's dogs eventually stopped salivating to the buzzer if it was no longer followed by meat, and Skinner's animals stopped pressing bars when food pellets were no longer forthcoming.

These principles of learning and behavior were momentous discoveries in psychology, the new science of behavior. But what did drooling dogs, puzzled cats, and key-pecking pigeons have to do with personality? In a crude first attempt to answer this question, John Watson and Rosalie Rayner (1920) conducted a well-known but ethically questionable demonstration. As described in the chapter on learning, Watson and Rayner brought a 9-month-old boy named Albert into contact with a harmless white rat, then repeatedly made a loud sound every time the boy reached for the animal. Soon poor Albert was terrified not only of the rat but of rabbits, dogs, and a white furry coat. Watson published this groundbreaking study at the age of 42, and it launched his career (Benjamin, Whitaker, Ramsey, & Zeve, 2007).

What was the point? Poking fun at Freud and his followers, Watson declared that one day a psychoanalyst would meet a man named Albert with a fur-coat phobia, analyze his dreams, and conclude that his fear is related to a scolding

Even though this dog has not tasted the treat, it cannot help but salivate in anticipation. Pavlov used this natural response to his advantage when developing his theory of classical conditioning.

iStock.com/stevecoleimages

he received from his white-haired mother. Such were the pitfalls of a nonscientific approach to personality, said Watson. Looking back, Mark Rilling (2000) notes an interesting paradox: Despite Watson's anti-Freudian bias, Watson popularized psychoanalysis and pioneered the scientific study of its concepts.

Picking up where Watson's behavior experiments left off, B. F. Skinner emerged as behaviorism's most forceful and dedicated proponent. He coined the term *operant conditioning*, studied different schedules of reinforcement, and wrote about how these principles could be used to socialize children, increase worker productivity, extinguish behavioral disorders, and build a better society. As far as Skinner was concerned, personality is nothing more than a collection of behavior patterns acquired, maintained, and—if necessary—modified by one's unique history of reinforcement. As a child, were you reinforced for staying quiet and keeping to yourself? If so, according to Skinner, that explains why you are introverted. Nothing more. Nothing less.

Social-Learning Theory

Although behaviorists offered a change of pace from psychoanalysis, many psychologists found their pointed focus on behavior too narrow and rejected their unwillingness to explore thoughts, feelings, motivations, and the richness and texture of the human personality. At the very least, it seemed that behaviorism had to be extended in two ways. Enter social-learning theory, an approach that examines the social and cognitive factors involved in learning and the development of personality. Leading the way were Albert Bandura, Julian Rotter, and Walter Mischel.

John Watson
JHU Sheridan Libraries/Gado / Contributor/Archive Photos/ Getty Images

The first important extension was to account for the fact that people often acquire new behavior patterns without personal experience with reward and punishment. According to Bandura (1977), people learn by observing and imitating others, a process called **modeling**. Children, for example, absorb what their parents say and how they act, pay close attention to TV characters and sports heroes, and emulate peers whom they admire. Research shows that modeling is a multistep process: We observe, we learn, and we store in memory (learning). Then, if we are capable and motivated, and if the time is right, we imitate (performance). Bandura thus reminded us that learning takes place in a social context and that people can learn to become aggressive, helpful, fearful, moral, and so on by observing others.

modeling. The social-learning process by which behavior is observed and imitated.

The second important extension of behaviorism was to examine how our thoughts can influence the effects of reinforcement on behavior. Skinner had insisted that behavior is determined by actual reinforcement contingencies, but Julian Rotter (1954) argued that what matters is how we perceive, interpret, and value the rewards in our lives. According to Rotter, human behavior in any given situation is determined by two broad factors: our subjective *expectancy* that a specific act will be reinforced, and the *value* to us of that reinforcement, as illustrated in Figure 8.6. If you expect that reading the rest of this text will help you learn psychology and earn a high grade for the course—and if these outcomes strike you as desirable—you'll probably read on. If you don't expect to learn from this text, or if you don't really care, this may be the last paragraph you read. As far as personality is concerned, Rotter and colleagues (1972) found that individuals differ both in the amount of control they expect to have over outcomes in their lives and in the kinds of outcomes they value.

Expanding on Rotter's model, Walter Mischel (1973) proposed a *cognitive* social-learning theory. According to Mischel, it is important to consider five "person variables" to understand how individuals interact with their environment:

- **Competencies.** Our mental and physical abilities, social skills, and creative talents, all of which influence what we strive for and what we can do.
- **Encoding strategies.** How we process information about other people and situations (for example, whether we tend to evaluate others in terms of their intelligence, friendliness, power, or physical appearance).

FIGURE 8.6 ■ Driven by Reinforcement

Can pigeons be taught to read? When will this person stop spending money on an unpredictable game? According to Skinner, both organisms are driven by the same force—reinforcement. As long as the rewards keep coming as expected, and those rewards are valued, the pigeon will learn how to read and the gambler will keep pressing SPIN.

iStock.com/tracielouise; iStock.com/Instants

- **Expectancies.** Our beliefs about the causes of success and failure and other possible consequences of our actions (there are two types of expectancies: whether we can perform a particular behavior, and whether it will be reinforced).

- **Subjective values.** The kinds of outcomes we find more or less rewarding (for example, whether we strive for love, security, respect, or dominance).

- **Self-regulatory systems.** Our ability to set goals, monitor and evaluate our progress, delay our short-term needs for gratification, and plan for the future.

Self-regulation is an important, highly adaptive person variable. In many years of research, Mischel and others (1989) have found that preschoolers who show they can defer their gratification in the laboratory—say, by waiting for a larger but delayed reward—grow up to become more competent, attentive, and deliberate; less likely to abuse substances or commit a crime; and better able to cope with real frustrations later in life (Moffitt et al., 2011; Moffitt, Poulton, & Caspi, 2013). In fact, the number of seconds a preschool child is willing to wait for two marshmallows—rather than settling for the one that is available immediately—is predictive of the child's SAT scores in high school and body mass index as a 30-something-year-old adult (Schlam, Wilson, Shoda, Mischel, & Ayduk, 2013). Metcalfe and Mischel (1999) and Mischel (2014) have suggested that to exercise such self-control, or willpower, we must learn to use various cognitive strategies that enable us to override the "go" impulses that can lure us away from our long-term goals. One way to do this is by working on some task rather than waiting passively for a future reward. Other research has supported the implementation of a strategy to delay gratification but demonstrates that additional variables—impulsivity, planning, emotion regulation, cognitive ability, home environment, and family background—also play a role (Neuenschwander & Blair, 2017; Watts, Duncan, & Quan, 2018). This is why the ability to delay gratification isn't necessarily a stable trait (Watts et al., 2018).

Locus of Control

According to cognitive social-learning theory, human behavior is influenced not by actual reinforcements, as Skinner had maintained, but by our perceptions of control. Think about it. Does getting ahead require hard work and persistence, or is it simply a matter of being in the right place at the right time? Can individuals influence government policies or global conflicts, or are we at the mercy of powerful leaders? And what about the quality of your health, friendships, and financial well-being—are you in control?

According to Rotter (1966), individuals differ in their **locus of control**, defined as a generalized expectancy for the control of reinforcement. People who have an *internal* locus of control believe they are in charge of their own destinies. Those who have an *external* locus of control feel they are at the mercy of luck, fate, and powerful others. To assess these contrasting orientations, Rotter constructed the I-E Scale. Immediately, psychologists grasped the implications of having an internal or external locus of control. Over the years, many hundreds of studies using the I-E Scale were published. Studying people of different ages, cultures, and ethnic backgrounds, researchers found that internals, compared to externals, are more inquisitive, active, hardworking, and persistent. They are also more likely to take preventive health measures, play an active role in social and political affairs, get high grades in school, and cope actively with stressful life events (Lefcourt, 1982; Rotter, 1990; Strickland, 1989) such as marginalization and the transition into college (Llamas, Consoli, Hendricks, & Nguyen, 2018), psychological distress following bariatric surgery (Peterhänsel, Linde, Wagner, Dietrich, & Kersting, 2017), or a cancer diagnosis (Lima, Moret-Tatay, & Irigaray, 2021), shifts in social status (Becker & Birkelbach, 2018), and raising a child who has an intellectual disability (Rajan, Srikrishna, & Romate, 2018).

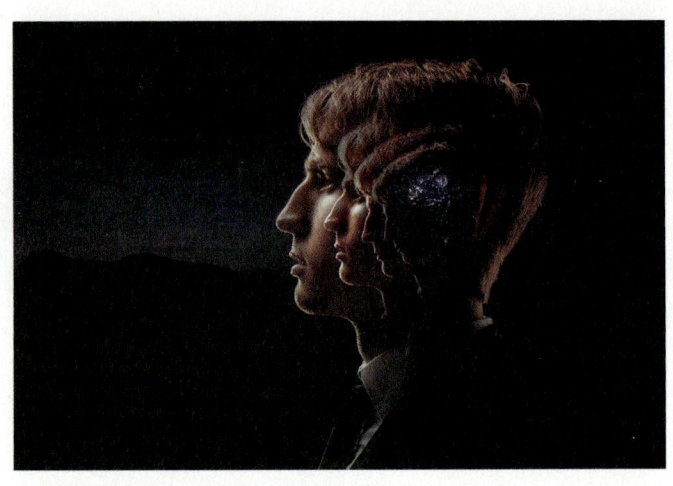

People who believe they have control over their own destinies tend to be more persistent, play an active role in politics, and use better coping mechanisms than those who don't believe they have control over their own destinies.
iStock.com/KrisCole

locus of control. The expectancy that one's reinforcements are generally controlled by internal or external factors.

Although people differ in their locus of control, there are two important qualifications. The first is that it is entirely possible to have an internal orientation in some life situations but an external orientation in others. The I-E Scale asks about control expectancies for a wide range of domains—including health, academics, career pursuits, friendships, and remote political and social events. The second is that individuals also differ in the extent to which they *want* control. Some of us care more deeply than others about making our own decisions or having an influence over others. People with a strong desire for control—regardless of whether they are internal or external in their expectancies—are more likely to become stressed and upset in situations that make them feel helpless (Burger, 1991). However, when given even the illusion of control, those with a strong desire for it can have improved treatment outcomes (Geers et al., 2013).

Is an expectation for control adaptive? At first glance, it seems that an internal orientation is the key to health, success, and emotional well-being—and a great deal of research supports this point (e.g., Mallers, Claver, & Lares, 2013; Marshall, 1991). In a classic study of nursing home patients, for example, 93 percent of those who by random assignment were given more control over minor daily affairs were happier, more active, and more alert when tested 18 months later (Rodin, 1986). But wait. Is an internal orientation *always* adaptive, or are there times when it's better to perceive life's reinforcements as beyond our command?

This is a tough question because there are two exceptions to the rule that it's better to be internal than external. First, an internal orientation can cause problems when we don't carefully distinguish between truly controllable and uncontrollable events. For example, people with an inflated sense of control are at risk of losing money gambling on games of pure chance (Langer, 1975). This inflated sense of control is an outcome that sports betting advertisements have seemed to rely on (Lopez-Gonzalez, Estévez, & Griffiths, 2017). And victims of sexual assault and other crimes suffer more distress when they blame themselves for having been careless or done something to provoke their attack (Donde & Ragsdale, 2017; Perilloux, Duntley, & Buss, 2014; Peter-Hagene & Ullman, 2016). Second, an internal orientation can cause problems if it leads us to develop an overcontrolling, stress-inducing style of behavior—whether that means always having the last word in an argument, driving from the back seat of a car, or planning every detail of a leisurely vacation. Sometimes it is better to practice acceptance and be in the moment, even when life's stressors and your lack of control seem overwhelming. Relinquishing control and practicing mindfulness has been a helpful stress reducer for oil company executives (Mulla, Govindaraj, Polisetti, George, & More, 2017), persons with chronic illness (Rush & Sharma, 2016; Simpson, Byrne, Wood, Mair, & Mercer, 2017) and posttraumatic stress disorder (Woidneck, Morrison, & Twohig, 2013), and prison inmates (Samuelson, Carmody, Kabat-Zinn, & Bratt, 2007). On this point, Japanese psychologist Hiroshi Azuma (1984) offers these Japanese proverbs: "Willow trees do not get broken by piled-up snow" and "The true tolerance is to tolerate the intolerable."

> ### TRY THIS!
>
> #### The Raisin Task: A Simple Exercise in Mindfulness
>
> Can something as simple as focusing on a single bite of food be an exercise in mindfulness? We are pleased to tell you that it can (Hopthrow, Hooper, Mahmood, Meier, & Weger, 2017). The Raisin Task is centered on attending to your senses—sight, touch, taste, smell, and sound—for a total of at least 5 minutes. You have 5 minutes before your next commitment, right? To observe what it's like to be present in the moment, TRY THIS: Set a timer to 5 minutes. Take a raisin (or any other small piece of food) and examine its texture. Look at how the skin folds. What color is it? Give the raisin a little pinch. How does it feel between your fingers? Smell the raisin. Does it smell sweet, tart, or slightly fermented? Now, put the raisin in your mouth and roll it around with your tongue. Allow the raisin to sit in your mouth for 1 minute before you place it between your teeth and bite into it. Chew slowly.
>
> Next, prepare to swallow the raisin by focusing on what the muscles in your mouth and neck are doing. Put your hand gently on your neck, underneath your chin, and as you swallow, take notice of how your neck and areas underneath your jaw react. Finally, focus on the journey the raisin takes down your esophagus.
>
> Write down a quick note that summarizes how you feel after the Raisin Task. Did you calm down a little bit? Were you more aware of how the raisin tasted than usual? Would you try this exercise again? Why or why not?

Self-Efficacy

As noted, locus of control refers to the expectation that our behaviors can produce satisfying outcomes. But people also differ in the extent to which they think they can perform these reinforced behaviors in the first place. These concepts seem related, but in fact they refer to different beliefs, both of which are necessary for us to feel that we control the outcomes in our lives (Skinner, 1996). According to Bandura (1997, 2011), the latter expectations are based on feelings of competence, or **self-efficacy**. Although some people are generally more confident than others, Bandura believes that self-efficacy is a state of mind that varies from one task and situation to another. In other words, you may have a high self-efficacy about meeting new people but not about raising your grades. Or you may have a high self-efficacy about speaking in public but not about writing a paper.

Bandura (1997, 2011) believes the following: Since life is filled with impediments, adversities, setbacks, and frustrations, a personal sense of self-efficacy is essential for success. How do we gain a belief in our own efficacy? Bandura cites four sources: our own experiences successfully overcoming obstacles and failures; our observations of similar others who overcome obstacles to succeed; words of encouragement from family, friends, and others in our lives who urge us forward; and feelings of relaxation and calm rather than tension during performance.

Numerous studies of self-efficacy indicate that the more of it you have at a particular task, the more likely you are to take on an activity, try hard, persist in the face of failure, and succeed. The implications for health are particularly interesting (Sheeran et al., 2016)—self-efficacy matters. Research shows that college students' locus of control over their health isn't enough. They also need self-efficacy and social support to achieve healthy behaviors (Marr & Wilcox, 2015). Roddenberry and Renk (2010) also measured college students' self-efficacy and analyzed how it related to stress and illness. They found a negative relationship between self-efficacy and physical symptoms—the lower the self-efficacy, the higher the level of physical symptoms. Roddenberry and Renk (2010) also found that general stress was positively

self-efficacy. The belief that one is capable of performing the behaviors required to produce a desired outcome.

related to reports of illness—the higher the student's stress level, the more often the student reported days of being sick. Even law students who were optimistic about their abilities to be successful in earning their juris doctorate degrees had better immunity than those who were less optimistic about their success (Segerstrom & Sephton, 2010). People with a high self-efficacy on health-related matters are more likely to succeed—if they want, and temptations are not too great—to stop smoking (Pinsker et al., 2018; Simon et al., 2015), abstain from alcohol (Noyes et al., 2018; Shaw & DiClemente, 2016), or overcome other forms of substance abuse (Bandura, 1999; Litt & Kadden, 2015; Maddux, 1991). However, the value of high self-efficacy is not universal. The reason is because different cultures may emphasize others more than self (Klassen, 2004).

FIGURE 8.7 ■ Reciprocal Determinism

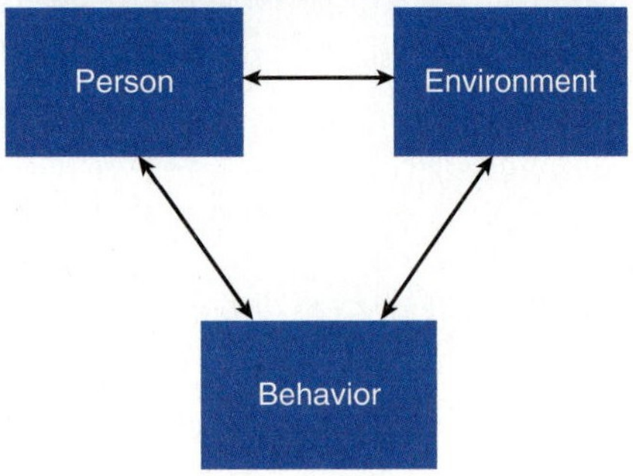

Perspectives on Cognitive Social-Learning Theory

Cognitive social-learning theorists believe that personality is rooted in the basic principles of learning. In contrast to psychoanalysis, this approach rests on the assumption that human behavior is derived more from external factors than from instincts and that personality is shaped by reinforcement, observation, and the development of learned abilities, expectancies, values, and information-processing strategies.

Although all learning-based theories of personality share this assumption, the more recent approach has come a long way from that taken by the hard-core behaviorists. In his facetious call for a dozen healthy infants, Watson claimed that he could mold people like clay through the use of reward and punishment. Years later, Skinner similarly argued that human behavior is shaped by external forces, by reinforcement contingencies beyond our awareness and control. Yet cognitive social-learning theorists maintain that personality emerges from an ongoing mutual interaction among persons, their actions, and their environments, a concept that Bandura calls **reciprocal determinism**, as illustrated in Figure 8.7. The point is that environmental forces may help shape personalities, but we can also choose and alter the situations we encounter and we can interpret these situations in light of our own points of view. In fact, Bandura (2001) sees human beings as not just reactive to outside forces, but as generative, creative, proactive, and reflective agents of change. "The capacity to exercise control over the nature and quality of one's life," he states, "is the essence of humanness" (p. 1).

reciprocal determinism. The view that personality emerges from a mutual interaction of individuals, their actions, and their environments.

To measure personality, cognitive social-learning theorists use fairly direct forms of assessment. One method is behavioral observation, in which subjects are studied either in real-life settings or in the laboratory. Another involves asking subjects to report on their own expectancies, values, and past behaviors using standardized interviews or questionnaires like the I-E Scale. Whatever the specific technique may be, information about an individual is measured in ways that are direct and to the point. No inkblots, no fuzzy pictures. To those in hot pursuit of the unconscious, the cognitive social-learning approach is doomed to shed light on only the tip of the iceberg. To others, this approach permits the study of personality in a more straightforward manner.

THE HUMANISTIC APPROACH

LEARNING OBJECTIVES

Investigate whether or not an interaction exists between self-actualization and unconditional positive regard.

- List the tenets of a humanistic approach to personality.
- Connect Carl Rogers's clinical observations to his theories about the self.
- Understand how self-discrepancies affect our emotional well-being.
- Describe how it feels to be self-actualized.

Faced with a choice between psychoanalysis and behaviorism, many personality psychologists in the 1940s and 1950s had the uneasy feeling that something was missing, something vital about human nature. Freud had drawn attention to the darker forces of the unconscious, and Skinner was interested only in the effects of reinforcement on observable behavior. But what about the conscious mind, free will, subjective experiences, and the capacity for self-reflection? If we want to know about someone, can't we just ask? Are people really that mechanical? And isn't there a brighter side to human nature? In short, where's the *person* as we know it in personality? To fill the void, a "third force" was born—the **humanistic theory** of personality. Inspired by Carl Rogers and Abraham Maslow, a group of psychologists founded the Association for Humanistic Psychology and adopted four basic principles: (a) The experiencing person is of primary interest; (b) human choice, creativity, and self-actualization are the preferred topics of investigation; (c) meaningfulness must precede objectivity in the selection of research problems; and (d) ultimate value is placed on the dignity of the person.

humanistic theory. An approach to personality that focuses on the self, subjective experience, and the capacity for fulfillment.

Carl Rogers

Carl Rogers was the first self-proclaimed humanistic theorist. He received his degree in 1931, the same year that B. F. Skinner got his. Like Freud, Rogers spent his early years as a therapist treating emotionally troubled "clients." Yet unlike Freud, who was impressed by his patients' efforts to resist their own cures, Rogers was struck by how often his clients reflected on who they were ("I'd like to be more independent, but that just isn't me," "I just haven't been myself lately") and by their natural will to get better and reach their full potential. True, Rogers saw signs of temporary resistance and other ego defense mechanisms. But he was much more impressed by the self-concept—and by the underlying will to improve. If therapists provide warmth, a gentle, guiding hand, and a climate of uncritical acceptance, he said, clients will ultimately solve their own problems and find the road to health, happiness, and fulfillment. As far as Rogers was concerned, there is in each of us an inner wisdom.

self-actualization. In humanistic personality theories, the need to realize and fulfill one's unique potential.

unconditional positive regard. A situation in which the acceptance and love one receives from significant others is unqualified.

conditional positive regard. A situation in which the acceptance and love one receives from significant others is contingent on one's behavior.

Rogers's Theory

The seeds of a new and different approach to personality were planted in fertile ground. From a humanist's standpoint, Rogers went on to develop client-centered therapy (1942) and a theory of personality, as described in his book *On Becoming a Person (1961)*. According to Rogers, all living organisms are innately endowed with an actualizing tendency, a forward drive not only to survive but also to grow and reach their full genetic capacity. For thinking and feeling humans, there is also a natural need for **self-actualization**—a drive to behave in ways that are consistent with one's conscious identity, inherent capabilities, or self-concept. So far, so good. But problems arise because we are social animals, born helpless and dependent on others for approval, support, and love. And therein lies the potential for conflict in the development of personality.

Because humans are driven by the need for self-actualization *and* the need for positive regard, one of two general outcomes is possible. If you're fortunate enough to get **unconditional positive regard** from parents and significant others—that is, if the important people in your life are loving and respectful despite your failures and setbacks, no ifs, ands, or buts—then life is rosy. Your need for positive regard is met, giving you the green light to pursue the all-important need for self-actualization. However, if you are subject to **conditional positive regard**—that is, if your parents, spouse, and close friends withdraw their love when your actions and life choices don't meet with their approval—then you get hung up trying to strike a balance between your true self and the kind of person others want you to

Rogers believed that although humans are dependent on others for support, approval, and love, we are driven to grow.

iStock.com/Ridofranz

become. The result: frustration, anxiety, and feelings of incongruence or "discrepancy" within the self. This theory is illustrated in Figure 8.8.

Self-Esteem

From the start, Rogers sought empirical verification for his newly formulated theory. To evaluate the importance of the self-concept, he taped, transcribed, and analyzed many of his therapy sessions and found that, as treatment progressed, clients made more and more positive statements about themselves. Whatever self-discrepancies that existed tended to diminish. More recent research confirms that people have clear, often complex beliefs about the self. According to Hazel Markus (1977), these beliefs are a collection of **self-schemas**, which are specific beliefs about the self that influence how we interpret self-relevant information. It also appears that we think about—and are guided by—images of what we might become, would like to become, and are afraid of becoming in the future (Bocage-Barthélémy, Selimbegović, & Chatard, 2018; Davidai & Gilovich, 2018; Ruvolo & Markus, 1992).

When it comes to the self, we are not mere cool and dispassionate observers. Rather, we evaluate ourselves in positive and negative terms, opinions that comprise a person's **self-esteem** (Coopersmith, 1967). Some individuals have higher opinions of themselves than others do. However, self-esteem is not a single trait etched permanently in stone. Rather, it is a state of mind that varies in response to success, failure, changes in fortune, social interactions, and other life experiences (Heatherton & Polivy, 1991; Orth & Robins, 2014; von Soest, Wichstrøm, & Kvalem, 2016). Also, because self-concepts are made up of many self-schemas, people may have higher self-esteem in some life domains than others (Pelham, 1995; Pelham & Swann, 1989; Ruiter, Geert, & Kunnen, 2017). In fact, some people consistently have high or low regard for themselves (Marigold, Cavallo, Holmes, & Wood, 2014; Robinson & Cameron, 2012), but others seem to fluctuate up and down as a result of daily experiences—which makes them highly responsive to praise and overly sensitive to criticism (Baldwin & Sinclair, 1996; Schimel, Arndt, Pyszczynski, & Greenberg, 2001; Zeigler-Hill et al., 2013).

In many ways, satisfying the need for self-esteem is critical to our entire outlook on life (Brown, 1998; Wagner, Hoppmann, Ram, & Gerstorf, 2015). People with positive rather than negative self-images tend to be happy, healthy, productive, and successful. They are also confident, bringing to new challenges a winning and motivating attitude—which leads them to persist longer at difficult tasks, sleep better at night, maintain independence in the face of peer pressure, and suffer fewer ulcers. In contrast, people with negative self-images tend to be more depressed, pessimistic about the future, and prone to failure. Lacking confidence, they bring to new tasks a losing attitude that traps them in a self-defeating cycle. Expecting to fail, and fearing the worst, they become anxious, exert less effort, disregard positive feedback (Josephs, Bosson, & Jacobs, 2003), and "tune out" on important challenges. Then when they do fail, people with low self-esteem blame themselves, which makes them feel even worse (Brockner, 1983; Brown & Dutton, 1995).

self-schemas. Specific beliefs about the self that influence how we interpret self-relevant information.

self-esteem. A positive or negative evaluation of the self.

FIGURE 8.8 ■ The Personality Theory of Carl Rogers

According to Rogers, the needs for self-actualization and positive regard present a potential for conflict. Unconditional positive regard permits self-actualization, but conditional positive regard can result in self-discrepancies.

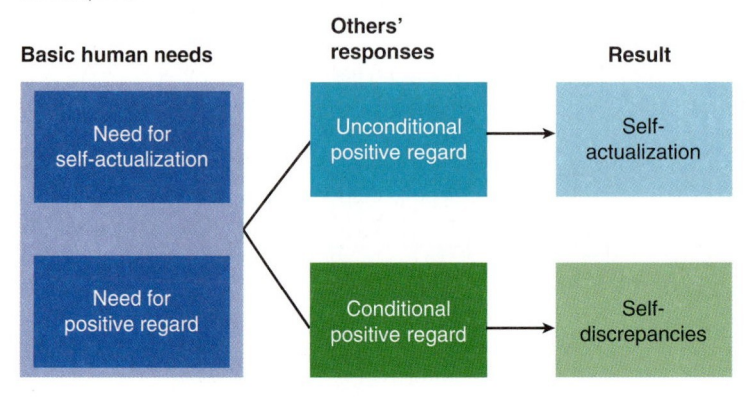

Basic human needs	Others' responses	Result
Need for self-actualization	Unconditional positive regard	Self-actualization
Need for positive regard	Conditional positive regard	Self-discrepancies

If we were meeting this woman for the first time, we would likely assume that she is confident. More senior women are making these types of fashion statements on social media to promote positive self-esteem at any age.

iStock.com/Diamond Dogs

Just as individuals differ in their self-esteem, so too do social and cultural groups. If you were to administer a self-esteem test to thousands of people all over the world, would you find that some segments of the population score higher than others? Believing that self-esteem promotes health, happiness, and success, and concerned that some social groups are disadvantaged in this regard, researchers have made these types of comparisons. Consider the possibility of a gender gap. Over the years, much has been written in the popular press about the inflated but fragile "male ego" and the low self-regard among adolescent girls and women. Does research support this assumption? To find out, Bleidorn and others (2016) collected data across 48 nations from 985,937 participants. The result: Males reported a consistently higher level of self-esteem than females. Zuckerman and colleagues (2016) investigated this same gender difference and discovered interesting trends. When comparing the results of numerous studies, Zuckerman and colleagues determined that while a difference in self-esteem between males and females exists, the difference is small. Reasons for this difference could be a number of factors: body dissatisfaction, gender roles, how either is valued by society, age, culture, and susceptibility to depression and anxiety.

Researchers have also wondered if low self-esteem is a problem for stigmatized minority groups, historical victims of prejudice and discrimination. Does being part of a minority group—such as being African American—deflate one's sense of self-worth? Based on the combined results of studies involving more than half a million respondents, Bernadette Gray-Little and Adam Hafdahl (2000 reported that Black American children, adolescents, and young adults tend to score higher, not lower, than their white counterparts on measures of self-esteem. In a meta-analysis of hundreds of studies that compared all age groups and other American minorities, Jean Twenge and Jennifer Crocker (2002) confirmed the African American advantage in self-esteem relative to whites but found that Latinx, Asian, and Native American minorities have lower self-esteem scores. As illustrated in Figure 8.9, a longitudinal study on self-esteem among Black, white, and Hispanic Americans revealed a different pattern that was dependent on age (Erol & Orth, 2011). At age 14, white and Black adolescents had similar levels

FIGURE 8.9 ■ Longitudinal Self-Esteem in U.S. Minorities

Through a longitudinal study, Erol and Orth (2011) found that Hispanic American adolescents score lower on self-esteem than white Americans and Black Americans, but score higher on self-esteem tests relative to white Americans by age 30. By age 30, Black Americans scored the highest.

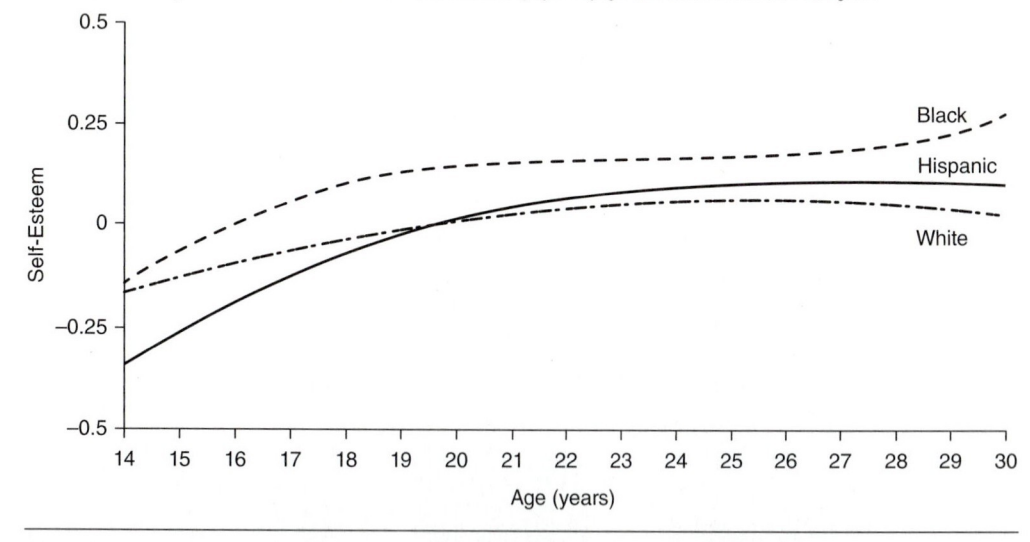

Adapted from Erol, R. Y., & Orth, U. (2011). Self-esteem development from age 14 to 30 years: A longitudinal study. *Journal of Personality and Social Psychology, 101*(3), 607–619. https://doi.org/10.1037/a0024299

of self-esteem, but Hispanics had the lowest level. By age 30, whites had the lowest level of self-esteem, Hispanics were in the middle, and Black Americans had the highest level. Some researchers have suggested that perhaps Black Americans protect their self-esteem in the face of adversity through a shared sense of identity. This shared sense of identity might be the reason Zuckerman and colleagues (2016) found a greater gender difference in self-esteem among whites than Black Americans. When we investigate the impact of sexual orientation on self-esteem, the results demonstrate a different trend. It is important to note that self-esteem of persons who identify as a sexual minority does tend to be lower than persons who identify as heterosexual (Bridge, Smith, & Rimes, 2019).

Variations in self-esteem have also been observed among people from different parts of the world. As described in the chapter on social and cultural influences, inhabitants of individualistic cultures tend to view themselves as distinct and autonomous, whereas those in collectivist cultures view the self as part of a larger, interdependent social network. Do these different orientations have implications for self-esteem? Steven Heine and others (1999) believe that they do. They compared the distribution of self-esteem scores in Canada and Japan and found that whereas most Canadians' scores clustered in the high-end range, the average Japanese respondent scored in the center of that same range. This result has led researchers to wonder: Do the Japanese truly have less inflated self-esteem than do North Americans, which can be seen in their tendency to speak in self-effacing terms? Or do Japanese respondents, high in self-esteem, simply feel compelled by the collectivist need to "fit in" rather than "stand out" to present themselves modestly to others? To answer this question, researchers have tried to develop indirect, "implicit" tests that would measure a person's self-esteem without his or her awareness. In a timed word-association study, for example, Anthony Greenwald and Shelly Farnham (2001) found that despite their noninflated scores on self-esteem tests, Asian Americans—like their European American counterparts—were quicker to associate themselves with positive words such as *happy* and *sunshine* than with negative words such as *vomit* and *poison*.

Does this mean that collectivists think highly of themselves but don't admit it? Not necessarily. Trafimow and colleagues (1991) and others have demonstrated that we can see ourselves in more individualistic or collectivistic terms based on environmental cues. Hannover and colleagues (2006) decided to apply Trafimow and colleagues' finding to self-esteem. They defined self-esteem as the outcome of a comparison between how you truly consider yourself to be versus the ideals that have been ingrained into your definition of self. To test this definition, they divided German participants into two groups—those who were more collectivistic and those who were more individualistic. When collectivists were environmentally cued with individualistic prompts, their self-esteem decreased. When individualists were environmentally cued with collectivistic prompts, their self-esteem decreased. Debrosse and colleagues (2017) found a similar result in their research. Within participants who were collectivistic and minorities, differences between their group identity and personal identity negatively correlated with anxiety and depression. These findings suggest that self-esteem is related to how close or how far we are from our ideal self, and that closeness can depend on environmental cues.

Environmental cues can include social media. Each time you flip through your social media feed, do you wonder why other people look so perfect? It is common to ask this question. Photo after photo features white teeth, flawless makeup, salon-groomed hair, smooth figures, and lighting that appears to come from the heavens. What you see in your social media feed, you might not see in yourself. As a result, you might feel out of shape and frumpy. These feelings could then lead to a decline in mood and self-esteem. Facebook, and other social media, are environmental cues that have been well studied in this domain (Ahadzadeh, Sharif, & Ong, 2017; Kim & Chock, 2015; Tiggemann & Slater, 2013).

Influencers are known for their fashionable personas, ability to set trends, and flawless looks. But these media posts require a lot of effort, such as special lighting, carefully selected décor, and professional makeup techniques.

iStock.com/Brothers91

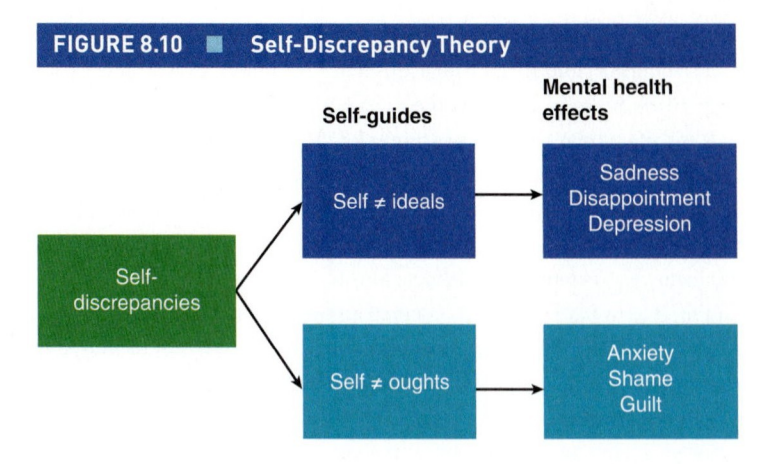

FIGURE 8.10 ■ Self-Discrepancy Theory

Self-discrepancies branches into two self-guides with their mental health effects:
- Self ≠ ideals → Sadness, Disappointment, Depression
- Self ≠ oughts → Anxiety, Shame, Guilt

self-discrepancy theory. The notion that discrepancies between one's self-concept and "ideal" and "ought" selves have negative emotional consequences.

One such explanation for the reaction described above is self-discrepancy theory. According to E. Tory Higgins's (1989) **self-discrepancy theory**, our self-esteem *is* defined by the match between how we see ourselves and how we want to see ourselves, as illustrated in Figure 8.10. It is possible that you do not see yourself the way you want to—like the perfectly posed and styled people of Instagram. Fardouly and colleagues (2015) found scientific evidence that demonstrates many people feel this way. Fardouly and colleagues exposed 112 females, scored for an appearance comparison tendency, to 10 minutes of browsing their Facebook account, a magazine website, or a control website. All females were randomly assigned to one of the three conditions, so they did not get to pick what they had to browse. When the 10 minutes were over, the participants completed surveys that measured mood, body dissatisfaction, and weight, face, hair, and skin-related appearance discrepancies. Participants who were randomly assigned to the Facebook condition were in a worse mood than the other participants. Those who scored high in appearance comparison tendency who were in the Facebook condition reported more discrepancies between theirs and others' weight, face, hair, and skin, in comparison to participants in the control and magazine conditions.

What's Your Prediction?

In exercising the scientific method, Popper (1963) has suggested that scientists pit theories or hypotheses against one another so that the best one can win. It's like playing king of the hill. The strong theory remains on the top of the hill and the weak theory is pushed off the hill. Steiger and colleagues (2015) decided to play this scientific game with two models for self-esteem: the vulnerability model and the scar model. Research using the vulnerability model argues that self-esteem is quite stable and can serve as a predictor of future depressive symptoms (Steiger, Fend, & Allemand, 2015). Competing research using the scar model argues that depressive episodes wound individuals and, thus, deteriorate the sufferer's self-esteem, leaving permanent scars in its wake. Which model do you think is correct?

To answer this question, Steiger and colleagues (2015) annually followed participants beginning at age 12 until age 16. Two additional measurements were taken when the participants were in early adulthood (approximately 35 years old) and then middle adulthood (approximately 45 years old). Children who were born to their original set of participants were also included in the study to see if intergenerational effects existed. The original set of participants' self-esteem and depressive symptoms were compared between ages 16 and 45. Results demonstrated that individuals suffer from the consequences of low self-esteem and depressive symptoms as they move through stages of their life. Adolescence was a developmental marker for self-esteem in that it prospectively predicted early adult depressive symptoms. Low adolescent self-esteem was substantially related to adult depressive symptoms.

Now, the researchers also compared the children's depressive symptoms with their parent's depressive symptoms. Do you predict a connection? The researchers found that parental and child depressive symptoms were related. They referred to this as "intergenerational transmission" (p. 244). The researchers offered possible explanations such as the passing on of depressive symptoms via genetics or environmental factors such a parent-child discord or a negative family atmosphere. While more research is necessary to determine the cause, this study is evidence that self-esteem is quite stable and that self-esteem in adolescence is a good predictor of depressive symptoms in adulthood. Thus, the vulnerability model is the winner.

Abraham Maslow

Abraham Maslow was the second influential spokesperson for the humanistic approach to personality. Oddly enough, Maslow started out as a behaviorist conducting learning experiments with monkeys. Then came the birth of his first child. As most parents would agree, this was an eye-opening experience. Said Maslow, "I was stunned by the mystery and by the sense of not really being in control. I felt small and weak and feeble before all this. I'd say anyone who had a baby couldn't be a behaviorist." Over the years, Maslow (1954, 1968) went on to formulate a motivational theory of personality, focusing on how people strive to fulfill their utmost potential.

Maslow's Theory

Have you ever met someone who seems to have it all—great looks, good financial status, successful career, nice home and car, loving partner, and wonderful wit—and yet seems unsatisfied, searching for more? If so, then you'll appreciate the essence of Maslow's theory. As described in the chapter on motivation and emotion, Maslow (1954) theorized that all people are motivated to fulfill a hierarchy of needs, from the physiological needs basic to survival to the needs for safety and security, belongingness and love, and esteem-related needs for achievement, status, and recognition. In short, said Maslow, each of us strives in our own way to be biologically content, safe, loved, and respected. Only when these needs are met are we ready, willing, and able to strive for self-actualization.

Maslow's primary interest was in self-actualization, which he considered the ultimate state. Thus, he went out of his way to study happy, healthy, and productive individuals who embody the best that human nature has to offer. He interviewed a select group of acquaintances, and he used biographies to examine the lives of great historical figures such as Ludwig van Beethoven, Abraham Lincoln, Albert Einstein, and Eleanor Roosevelt. What did these self-actualized people have in common? Maslow (1968) saw self-actualization as a rare state of being in which a person is open to new experiences, spontaneous, playful, loving, realistic, accepting of others, creative, energetic, independent rather than conforming, and problem-focused rather than self-centered. If you think that this set of traits sounds almost too good to be true, you're right. Maslow estimated that less than 1 percent of the world's adults are truly self-actualized. The rest of us are too busy trying to overcome obstacles in order to satisfy lower, more basic needs.

The State of Self-Actualization

Is it possible to determine how self-actualized one is? Based on Maslow's theory, Shostrom (1965) developed the Personal Orientation Inventory, a lengthy questionnaire designed to assess various aspects of self-actualization—such as the capacity for intimate contact, spontaneity, and self-acceptance. This scale was endorsed by Maslow and used in clinical settings. Research shows that people with high scores are psychologically healthier than those who receive low scores (Campbell, Amerikaner, Swank, & Vincent, 1989; Knapp, 1976). A sample of 10 statements from the Personal Orientation Inventory is given in Table 8.1. How many of the values thought to be associated with self-actualization do you possess?

If you're wondering what it feels like to be self-actualized, at least temporarily, try this: "Think about the most wonderful experiences of your life; happiest

Self-actualization is a state of mind that we achieve on a temporary basis—during peak experiences.

iStock.com/South_agency

TABLE 8.1	How Self-Actualized Are You?
1.	I live in terms of my wants, likes, dislikes, and values.
2.	I believe that man is essentially good and can be trusted.
3.	I don't feel guilty when I'm selfish.
4.	I believe it is important to accept others as they are.
5.	I am not afraid of making mistakes.
6.	I believe in saying what I feel in dealing with others.
7.	I often make decisions spontaneously.
8.	I welcome criticism as an opportunity for growth.
9.	I enjoy detachment and privacy.
10.	For me, work and play are the same.

Adapted from E. Shostrom (1965)

peak experience. A fleeting but intense moment of self-actualization in which people feel happy, absorbed, and extraordinarily capable.

moments, ecstatic moments, moments of rapture, perhaps from being in love, or from listening to music or suddenly 'being hit' by a book or a painting, or from some great creative moment" (Maslow, 1968, p. 71). Maslow claimed that self-actualized individuals have more moments like these than other people do. Still, each of us enjoys an occasional **peak experience**, defined as a fleeting but intense moment of self-actualization in which we feel happy, absorbed, and capable of extraordinary performance. In a classic experiment by Privette (1983), music, sexual love, religion, nature, running, sports, creative pursuits, childbirth, and reminiscing are the most common situations people cited when asked about their peak experiences.

CNN journalist David Allan (2018) revisited peak experiences in "The Wisdom Project." He recollected a moment when he had a peak experience and reflected on how to make such experiences more accessible. Allan found that jotting down any perfect moment in a journal on a daily basis made these peak moments tangible and his attention to them more frequent. At the end of his first year of journaling peak experiences, Allan had 125 moments. He then placed them in categories and learned something about himself. The most prevalent experiences in his life were categorized as "Family," "Nature," and "Music." Take a moment now to jot down any perfect moment you had this week. Then, we urge you to do what Allan did: Keep a journal of daily perfect moments. When things seem overwhelming, or you find a moment when you wish to reflect, read your journal. You might be surprised at the number of perfect moments you have been lucky enough to experience.

Working from Maslow's writings, Mihaly Csikszentmihalyi (1990) has studied a pleasant state of engagement he calls *flow*, an "optimal experience." Under what conditions, Csikszentmihalyi asks, do we tend to become so fully immersed in an activity that we lose all track of time and all awareness of the self, forget our worries, and concentrate our energy on what we're doing, much to our benefit and enjoyment? We sometimes have this exquisite experience when we write, play a sport, cook, have an intellectual conversation, or listen to music. Csikszentmihalyi interviewed athletes, dancers, rock climbers, artists, factory workers, chess masters, surgeons, sailors, elderly Korean women, Japanese motorcyclists, Navajo shepherds, and farmers in the Italian Alps. He found that people from all parts of the world and all walks of life describe a similar kind of experience—when what they're doing seems effortless and perfect, when they're so completely tuned in that nothing else seems to matter. In a demonstration of this point, Regina Conti (2001) found that college students who scored high rather than low on a measure of their intrinsic motivation checked time less often during the day, lost track of time more often, and perceived time as passing more quickly. Additionally, Wittmann (2015) argues that a decreased awareness of the self is associated with a diminished awareness of time. Apparently, time does fly when you're having fun—and "in the zone."

What precipitates flow? From his research, Csikszentmihalyi theorizes that this state arises when people engage in activities at which they are skilled and at levels that are challenging in relation to their ability. As depicted in Figure 8.11, tasks that are too easy result in boredom, whereas those that are too difficult cause anxiety. For students who are intrinsically motivated, checking and thinking about the time happens less often (Conti, 2001). These types of students also feel as if time flies by and are more susceptible to losing track of time. Those who were not intrinsically motivated felt that time moved slowly, overestimated the amount of time that had passed, and reported more negativity.

Also important is the capacity of these activities to present clear goals and immediate feedback. The desire to strike up a conversation presents such a goal that, by nature, provides immediate feedback. Imagine you are striking up a conversation with a stranger. They smile at you, quickly respond to your prompt with feedback, but follow up their feedback with an intellectual question. If this question is challenging, but not too difficult, and the conversation that ensues is enjoyable, how quickly does time fly? Now, it's time to make a prediction. Does time fly by faster, and do you perceive the conversation as more enjoyable, if the conversation is with an attractive person? Or do looks not matter?

FIGURE 8.11 ■ Flow, the Optimal Experience

A state of "flow" arises when we engage in activities that we are skilled at and at levels that are challenging but not too difficult (Csikszentmihalyi 1990).

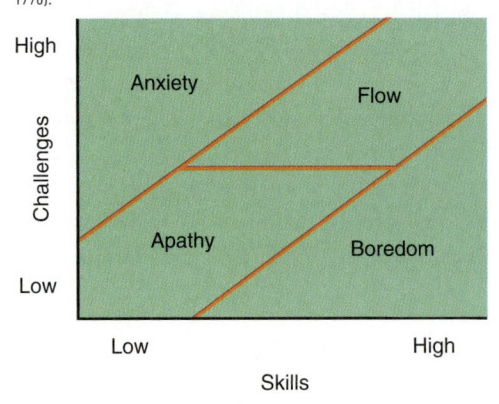

In a study by Dong and Wyer (2013), participants were partnered up to have an acquaintance meeting via Skype. The partners were strangers and never saw one another's real face. However, pictures of the partners were provided. The picture provided was deceptive; the photos were of either an attractive face or an unattractive face. The photos were not representative of the real conversation partner. All conversations were limited to 8 minutes. When the time was up, participants rated their conversation partner on attractiveness, the enjoyableness of the conversation, and how long they thought the conversation lasted. Participants who rated their partner as attractive estimated their conversation shorter and more enjoyable than those who rated their partner as unattractive. So, enjoying a conversation with an attractive partner can make time fly.

The feeling that time has flown by and you're entrenched in the moment can be applied to many domains, including sports. In all sports, it seems, athletes who are hot and playing at the top of their game often talk about being focused in mind and body, and "in the zone." In studies of amateur tennis players, basketball players, and golfers, for example, researchers found that this state occurs in all sports ("My attention was focused entirely on what I was doing," "I felt in control of my game," "My performance felt effortless," "Everything clicked") and that the conditions that produce it vary—depending on the competitive nature of the activity and the importance of winning. When good athletes are motivated but relaxed, their performance is fluid, almost without conscious thought or effort (Beilock, Carr, MacMahon, & Starkes, 2002). Research by Jackman and colleagues (2016) added mental toughness to the equation. The athletes interviewed described a need for toughness to control flow ("Don't dwell on the mistakes," "Overcome the fatigue and see the big picture," "Have confidence in my abilities"). Thus, people may be able to create for themselves the conditions that will unleash this optimal state of performance (Jackson & Csikszentmihalyi, 1999).

When we enjoy what we are doing or are incredibly focused, it can feel as if time is flying by. You might have experienced this when studying for your favorite class.

iStock.com/Sisoje

Perspectives on the Humanistic Approach

When Carl Rogers (1974) looked back on his career and on his impact on psychology, counseling, and education, he concluded that "[he] expressed an idea whose time had come." The idea he referred to was that people are inherently good, that conscious mental experience is important, and that the self-concept lies at the heart of personality.

Humanistic psychologists have received praise for drawing our attention to this idea, for providing an alternative perspective on personality, and for sparking interest among researchers in previously neglected topics related to the self. At the same time, they have been severely criticized for naively taking people's self-report statements at face value and for painting too rosy a picture of human nature while ignoring our demonstrated capacity for evil. Focused on the quest for self-actualization, humanistic psychologists have also been accused of inadvertently promoting a self-indulgent, "be true to yourself" approach to life. Sure, the self is important, say the critics, but where does the rest of the world fit in?

THE TRAIT APPROACH

> **LEARNING OBJECTIVES**
>
> Identify the roles that nature and nurture are believed to play in trait development.
>
> - List the main goals in a trait approach to personality.
> - Define the Big Five.
> - Compare the strengths and weaknesses of personality tests.
> - Create an argument that supports the role of genetic factors in personality.
> - Juxtapose introverts with extraverts.

In 1919, a 22-year-old psychology student from Indiana handwrote a letter to Sigmund Freud to say he'd be traveling in Europe and would like to meet. Freud was the master, known worldwide, and the student, a fan, wanted to meet him. A time was arranged, so the student took a train to Vienna, arrived on schedule, and entered the master's inner office. But Freud just sat there in silence, staring, waiting for his young, wide-eyed admirer to state his mission. Desperate to break the awkward stalemate, the student told about an incident he witnessed on the train that day involving a young boy who appeared to have a "dirt phobia." The boy complained that the seats were soiled and pleaded with his mother to keep dirty passengers from sitting nearby. The mother, it turned out, was a dominant, "well-starched" woman. When the student finished telling his story, Freud paused, then leaned over and said in a soft voice, "And was that little boy *you*?"

Freud's young admirer was terribly embarrassed. Wishing he could disappear, he nervously changed the subject, babbled a bit, then excused himself and left. It turns out that the student was Gordon Allport, who went on to become one of the most important personality psychologists of all time. In an autobiography published the year he died, Allport (1967) reflected on his interaction with Freud, and the fallacy of jumping to conclusions. Allport said that this experience convinced him that before personality theorists search for deep and analytical explanations, as Freud had done in their encounter, they should start by trying to *describe* and *measure* the basic units of personality. In other words, first things first. This rule now guides what is known as the trait approach.

The Building Blocks of Personality

Working from the ground up, Allport and Odbert (1936) combed through an unabridged English dictionary and came up with a list of 18,000 words that could be used to describe people. By eliminating synonyms, obscure words, and words referring to moods and other temporary states, they brought the list down to 4,500 words, and then grouped words that were similar into about 200 clusters of related traits. For Allport, these **traits** were the building blocks of personality (though he was quick to point out that not all traits are relevant to all people, nor do they all have an influence on behavior).

To reduce Allport's list to a more manageable size and construct a science of personality, Cattell (1965) used *factor analysis*, a statistical technique designed to identify clusters of items that correlate with one another. Cattell, who majored in chemistry in college, wanted to uncover the basic units of personality, much like chemistry's periodic table of elements. Are individuals who are passive also thoughtful, calm, and even-tempered? Do those who describe themselves as sociable also say they're easygoing, lively, and talkative? How many trait clusters are needed to fully describe personality? To answer these questions, Cattell collected people's ratings of themselves and others on various attributes, crunched the numbers through factor analysis, and found that personality consists of 16 distinct units, which he called *source traits*. What distinguishes one individual from another, said Cattell, is that each of us has a unique combination of traits—high levels of some, and low levels of others—a pattern that is summarized by a personality "profile." To derive this profile, Cattell devised the Sixteen Personality Factors Questionnaire (16 PF), a 187-item scale that yields 16 separate scores, one for each factor.

As factor analysis became more sophisticated, researchers began to notice that Cattell's model (and other models as well) could be simplified even further—and that five major factors often seemed to emerge from self-ratings, ratings of others, and an assortment of personality questionnaires. This **five-factor model** of personality (summarized in Table 8.2) has emerged consistently in studies of children, college students, and older adults; in men and women; in different languages; and in testing conducted in the United States, Canada, Finland, Germany, Japan, Poland, China, the Philippines, and other countries. Hence, these factors have been nicknamed the Big Five (De Raad, 2000; McCrae & Costa, 1997; Wiggins, 1996).

trait. A relatively stable predisposition to behave in a certain way.

five-factor model. A model of personality that consists of five basic traits: neuroticism, extraversion, openness, agreeableness, and conscientiousness.

TABLE 8.2 ■ The Big Five Personality Factors	
Factor	**Description of Traits**
Neuroticism	Anxious vs. relaxed
	Insecure vs. secure
	Emotional vs. calm
	Self-pitying vs. content
Extraversion	Sociable vs. withdrawn
	Fun-loving vs. sober
	Friendly vs. aloof
	Adventurous vs. cautious
Openness	Original vs. conventional
	Imaginative vs. down-to-earth
	Broad interests vs. narrow interests
	Receptive vs. closed to new ideas
Agreeableness	Good-natured vs. irritable
	Soft-hearted vs. ruthless
	Courteous vs. rude
	Sympathetic vs. tough-minded
Conscientiousness	Well-organized vs. disorganized
	Dependable vs. undependable
	Hardworking vs. lazy
	Ambitious vs. easygoing

Not everyone agrees with the five-factor model. Cattell thought five factors were too few. Eysenck, whom we will hear more about shortly, thought five was too many. Others believe that five is the right number but disagree about how the factors should be described. For the most part, however, evidence in support of the five-factor model is extensive. Maybe the most convincing evidence is that found by geneticists (Vukasović & Bratko, 2015) who have discovered genetic variations responsible for personality traits (Lo et al., 2016). Lo and colleagues (2016) found genetic variations associated with extroversion and neuroticism. Other researchers have found genetic variations associated with neuroticism (Genetics of Personality Consortium, 2015; Okbay et al., 2016; Smith et al., 2016). Another genetic contributor to personality is that pesky little X or Y chromosome that determines sex (Kajonius & Johnson, 2018). In a large study of 320,128 Americans, Kajonius and Johnson (2018) found that across age groups (19–69 years old), males had lower scores in agreeableness and neuroticism than females. Males were higher in excitement-seeking and openness to intellect. However, personality is not strictly determined by genes. Kandler and colleagues (2011) argue that, although there is plenty of support for biologically driven personalities, the environment also contributes to who we become, what we are like, and our interests. Vukasović and Bratko (2015) agree, as their large meta-analysis on heritability, environment, and personality revealed an average genetic contribution to individual personality at 40 percent.

Construction of Multitrait Inventories

As Allport had noted, the study of personality must begin not only with description but also with measurement. And so it did. One of the important contributions of trait psychology is the construction of personality inventories, questionnaires designed to assess a whole multitude of traits. Cattell's 16 PF is one such instrument. There are many others. The most widely used is the **Minnesota Multiphasic Personality Inventory**-Revised, or MMPI-2, a 567-item questionnaire originally developed in the 1940s as the **MMPI**, and since revised, to help in the diagnosis of psychological disorders (Hathaway & McKinley, 1983).

The MMPI is to personality measurement what the Stanford-Binet was to intelligence testing. Taking an empirical approach, Alfred Binet developed his test by generating a large number of problems, testing

Minnesota Multiphasic Personality Inventory (MMPI). A large-scale test designed to measure a multitude of psychological disorders and personality traits.

Identical twins Jim Springer and Jim Lewis were separated after birth and raised by different families. When reunited 39 years after their initial separation, they discovered that they were both raised in Ohio, both married women named Betty, both had sons named James Allen, worked as sheriffs, and had the same interests: woodwork, drinking beer, chainsmoking, and driving their Chevrolets. Even their personality tests were eerily similar!

iStock.com/leungchopan

schoolchildren, and retaining those problems that were solved differently by fast and slow learners. The MMPI developers used a similar strategy. They wrote hundreds of true-false statements, gave them to both normal adults and clinical patients with varying psychiatric diagnoses (depressed, paranoid, and so on), and then included in the final test only those items that were answered differently by the two groups—even if the content made little sense. The MMPI is filled with discriminating but odd items (for example, hysterical patients are more likely than others to answer "true" to the statement "My fingers sometimes feel numb").

These MMPI scales have been used for more than 70 years. Many of the original items became dated, however, and the norms had been based on a predominantly White, rural, middle-class group of subjects. To update the test, new items were written and a more diverse cross-section of the United States was sampled. The result was a newer 567-item version known as MMPI-2 (Butcher & Williams, 2000; Graham, 2000). Like the original MMPI, the MMPI-2 contains the *clinical scales* shown in Table 8.3. Eight of these is designed to distinguish between "normal" subjects and diagnostic groups.

TABLE 8.3 ■ Clinical and Validity Scales of the MMPI

Clinical Subscales	Descriptions	Sample Items
1. Hypochondriasis (Hs)	Excessive concern about self and physical health, fatigue, a pattern of complaining	"I have a great deal of stomach trouble."
2. Depression (D)	Low morale, pessimistic about the future, passive, hopeless, unhappy, and sluggish	"I wish I could be as happy as others seem to be."
3. Hysteria (Hy)	Use of physical symptoms to gain attention from others or avoid social responsibility	"I have had fainting spells."
4. Psychopathic Deviate (Pd)	Disregard for social rules and authority, impulsive, unreliable, self-centered, has shallow relationships	"In school I was sometimes sent to the principal for cutting up."
5. Masculinity/Femininity (Mf)	Identification with masculine and/or feminine sex roles	"I enjoy reading love stories."
6. Paranoia (Pa)	Feelings of persecution and/or grandeur, suspiciousness, hypersensitivity, use of blame and projection	"I am sure I get a raw deal from life."
7. Psychasthenia (Pt)	Anxiousness as exhibited in fears, self-doubt, worries, guilt, obsessions, and compulsions	"I feel anxiety about something or someone almost all of the time."
8. Schizophrenia (Sc)	Feelings of social alienation, aloofness, confusion and disorientation, bizarre thoughts and sensations	"I often feel as if things were not real."
9. Hypomania (Ma)	Hyperactivity, excitement, flakiness, elation, euphoria, and excessive optimism	"At times my thoughts race ahead faster than I could speak them."
10. Social Introversion (Si)	Withdrawal from social contact, isolation, shyness, a reserved, inhibited, self-effacing style	"Whenever possible I avoid being in a crowd."
Validity Scales	Descriptions	Sample Items
F scale	Intended to detect abnormal patterns of test item answers	"There is something wrong with my mind."
Lie scale (L)	Tendency to present oneself favorably, not honestly, to fake a good impression	"I always tell the truth."
Back F scale (F[b])	Measures the same issues as the F scale, but items are located only in the last half of the test	"My teachers have it in for me."
K scale	Self-control, interpersonal relationships, defensiveness	"At times I feel like smashing things."

Two other scales are used to measure masculinity-femininity and social introversion. The MMPI-2 also contains 15 *content scales* that measure work attitudes, family problems, and other characteristics. In addition, the MMPI and MMPI-2 contain a set of *validity scales* designed to expose test takers who are evasive, confused, lying to make a good impression, or defensive. Someone who answers "true" to many socially desirable but implausible statements such as "I never get angry" is assumed to be trying too hard to project a healthy image.

LEARNING CHECK

Schools of Thought

Sort these psychologists according to their respective approaches to personality. After each name, write a P for psychoanalytic, C for cognitive social-learning, H for humanistic, or T for trait.

1. Gordon Allport	6. E. Tory Higgins
2. Carl Jung	7. Walter Mischel
3. Sigmund Freud	8. Carl Rogers
4. Albert Bandura	9. Julian Rotter
5. Alfred Adler	10. Abraham Maslow

(Answers: 1. T; 2. P; 3. P; 4. C; 5. P; 6. H; 7. C; 8. H; 9. C; 10. H.)

The MMPI-2 is easy to administer, and in contrast to the Rorschach and TAT, in which two examiners may reach different conclusions, MMPI scoring is perfectly objective. Thus, a test taker's responses can be converted into a personality profile by computer. That's one reason why the test has been translated into more than 100 languages and is popular in both clinical and research settings. Test administrators must be cautious, however, about how to use the test and how to interpret the results. In spite of its reliability and validity, the test is far from perfect. Psychologists need to be particularly careful in interpreting the responses of test takers from cultural and subcultural groups that share different beliefs, values, ideals, and experiences. A pattern of responses may be considered normal in one culture and deviant in another (Butcher, Hass, Greene, & Nelson, 2015; Church, 2001; Dana, 2013).

Introversion and Extraversion

Psychologists may disagree over whether personality consists of 2, 5, 16, or 200 traits, but they all agree that one of the most powerful dimensions—one that can be seen in infants as well as adults, in cultures all over the world, and in written questionnaires as well as behavior—is introversion-extraversion, one of the Big Five traits. The ancient Greeks and Romans noticed it, as have philosophers, physicians, and creative writers through the ages. Jung wrote about individual differences on this dimension. So did Allport and Cattell. Even Pavlov said that some of the dogs in his classical-conditioning laboratory were more outgoing than other dogs. But it was British psychologist Eysenck who most clearly defined the trait, constructed a test to measure it, and proposed a provocative theory to explain its origin.

As described by Eysenck (1967), the typical **extravert** is someone who has many friends, likes parties, craves excitement, seeks adventure, takes chances, acts on the spur of the moment, and is uninhibited. In contrast, the typical **introvert** is low keyed, has just a few close friends, shies away from stimulation, acts cautiously, and distrusts the impulse of the moment. Based on past writings, personal observations, and factor analyses of trait questionnaires, Eysenck developed a test that includes a measure of introversion and extraversion, as summarized in Table 8.4. Using this instrument, and others, researchers have found that extraverts are generally more talkative, prefer occupations that involve social contact, take greater risks (Eysenck & Eysenck, 1985), and have larger social networks (Pollet, Roberts, & Dunbar, 2011). The question is, what accounts for this broad and pervasive aspect

extravert. A kind of person who seeks stimulation and is sociable and impulsive.

introvert. A kind of person who avoids stimulation and is low key and cautious.

TABLE 8.4 ■ Are You an Introvert or an Extravert?
1. Are you usually carefree?
2. Do you generally prefer reading to meeting people?
3. Do you often long for excitement?
4. Are you mostly quiet when you're with others?
5. Do you often do things on the spur of the moment?
6. Are you slow and unhurried in the way you move?

Source: Adapted from Eysenck and Eysenck (1964).

of personality? To determine whether you are an introvert or an extravert, answer the questions in Table 8.4 for yourself. If you said yes on most odd-numbered questions and no on the even-numbered ones, you are relatively extraverted. If you answered the other way around, then you're more introverted. Many people fall somewhere in the middle of the continuum.

Eysenck argues that individual differences are biologically rooted and that introverts have central nervous systems that are more sensitive to stimulation. According to Eysenck, people seek a moderate, comfortable level of CNS arousal. Introverts are easily aroused, so they avoid intense sources of excitement. In contrast, extraverts are not easily aroused, which leads them to approach high levels of excitement. Thus, it takes a more potent stimulus for the extravert to feel the "buzz." Research generally supports this hypothesis (Aron, Aron, & Jagiellowicz, 2012; Bullock & Gilliland, 1993; Eysenck, 1990). For example, one study (Dobbs, Furnham, & McClelland, 2011) put introverts and extraverts—quite literally—to the test in either noisy or quiet environments. In quiet environments, extraverts and introverts had similar test scores. On the contrary, in noisy environments, extraverts outperformed introverts. Deary and colleagues (1988) showed that when drops of natural lemon juice are placed on the tongue, most introverts salivate more than most extraverts. Von Gehlen and Sachse (2015) found corroborating evidence. Their extraverted participants outperformed introverted participants on an attention test when in the presence of an arousing auditory stimulus. As illustrated in Figure 8.12, others have shown that extraverts get more working memory benefit from caffeine than introverts (Smillie & Gokcen, 2010; Smith, 2012). A recent sleep-deprivation and learning experiment by Heinrich and colleagues (2018) found that high extraverts had better performance than others. When participants were not sleep deprived, no differences in performance were present. In short, says Eysenck, each of us is born with a nervous system that predisposes us to either love or hate large crowds, bright lights, blaring music, fast cars, roller coasters, suspenseful movies, spicy foods, and other, more social stimulants.

Interestingly, the rudiments of adult introversion and extraversion can be seen in the predispositions of infants shortly after birth. Over the years, Kagan (1994, 2018) and others have studied children who are *inhibited* and *uninhibited* in their temperament (most fall between these two extremes). At 16 weeks old, inhibited infants—compared to those who are uninhibited—are more easily distressed and cry more in response to hanging mobiles, human speech, intense odors, and other types of stimulation. At 2 years old, inhibited children are fearful, wary of strangers, and avoidant of novel situations, whereas their uninhibited peers are adventurous, outgoing, and quick to approach new people and situations. At 5 years old, socially inhibited children are shy and more easily aroused by mildly stressful tasks—as measured by increases in heart rate, dilation of the pupils, and a rise in

FIGURE 8.12 ■ Interaction Between Caffeine and Extraversion

In a recall task by Smith (2012), extraverted participants performed best with caffeine, whereas introverted participants performed best without caffeine.

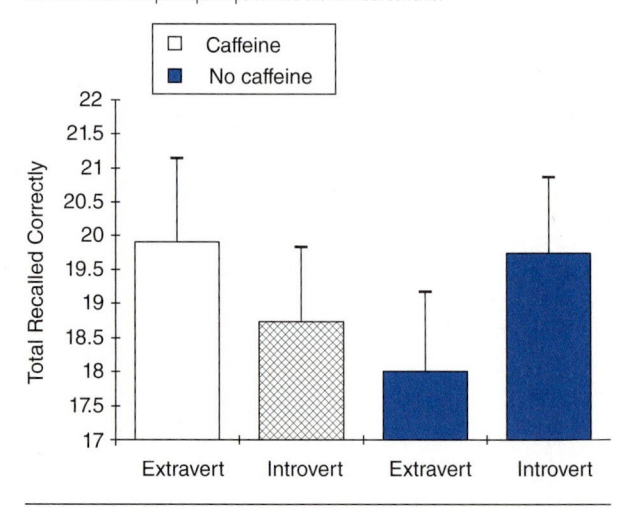

Smith AP. Caffeine, extraversion and working memory. *Journal of Psychopharmacology.* 2012;27(1):71-76. doi:10.1177/0269881112460111

Reprinted by Permission of SAGE Publications, Ltd.

norepinephrine. They often have more tension in the face muscles and are more likely to have higher-than-average levels of cortisol, a hormone associated with physiological arousal during stress. Even at 10 to 12 years of age, they are more excitable and sensitive to stimulation (Woodward et al., 2001).

Not all inhibited infants grow up to become inhibited adults. But longitudinal research indicates that there is continuity—that some aspects of personality later in life are predictable from temperament and behavior as infants and toddlers (Beekman et al., 2015; Casalin, Luyten, Vliegen, & Meurs, 2012). For example, toddlers who were observed to be highly irritable, impulsive, and hard to control at age 3 were more likely to have drug problems, problems at work, and relationship conflicts by the time they were 21. In contrast, those who were highly inhibited, fearful, and shy at age 3 were more likely to become socially isolated and depressed at age 21 (Caspi, 2000).

Psychology Applied: Use of Personality Tests and Social Media Sites in Hiring

Anyone who has applied for a desirable job knows that you sometimes have to climb hurdles and jump through hoops to get hired. One hurdle might be to take a personality test (Guion, 1965). A second hurdle might be to provide access to your social media accounts (McFarland, 2012; Ouirdi, Segers, Ouirdi, & Pais, 2015). Social media can tell us a lot about who a person is and their attitudes. But, as you can imagine, personality testing and social media access as requirements for employment spark a debate about ethics, violation of privacy, and validity.

As motivated test takers and savvy managers of their presentation of self, job candidates can fake their responses and selectively choose what posts, comments, and photos to make public in order to present themselves in a positive light. This is a serious possible drawback. Imagine having applied for a job you really wanted, and all that stands in your way are the results of a personality questionnaire and your professionalism on the Internet. Isn't it possible that you would cover up your flaws, consciously or not, according to what you think is desirable? And wouldn't this render your test results and social media information invalid? The answer is yes to the first question, but no to the second.

Industrial/organizational psychologists have found that people do bias their responses in a socially desirable direction—but this does not diminish the value of the tests. Employers tend to be confident in personality test results, maybe due to their frequency and history of use in the workforce (Christiansen, Tozek, & Burns, 2010). As for social media sites, the risk of losing a job opportunity or getting fired over a post in bad taste can have serious ramifications. Famous persons like Roseanne Barr, Kathy Griffin, and Antony Weiner have been public examples of what some people refer to as "Facebook fired" (Drouin, O'Connor, Schmidt, & Miller, 2015; Schmidt & O'Connor, 2015). Thus, most of us know what is at stake when we make something public. This segues nicely into traits that employers probably want—thinking twice before making a post, or keeping specific things private versus public.

Sure enough, people who are willing to be open with their social media information—even sharing passwords—scored higher on agreeableness, impression management, and conscientiousness (Schneider, Goffin, & Daljeet, 2015). As guessed, these are all desired traits in the workplace, both for predictive success (Barrick & Mount, 1991; Ones, Viswesvaran, & Reiss, 1996; Woods, Patterson, Koczwara, & Sofat, 2016) and for career commitment (Arora & Rangnekar, 2016). However, there is a fine line. If your impression management is too high, and employers know it, they might determine you are insincere. How would they know you are trying too hard to impress? Well, they could give you yet another test for social desirability. Christiansen and colleagues (2010) provided hiring professionals with job candidate information, some with scores on social desirability and some without. When social desirability scores were high, candidates were perceived as less sincere and candid. The outcome? Their hirability ratings declined. So, the moral of the story is to be likable, but not excessively so. None of us wants to work with someone who we think is just faking it.

LEARNING CHECK

Approach With Caution

Match the following psychological terms and tools with the approaches to which they relate: Psychoanalytic Approach, Cognitive Social-Learning Approach, Humanistic Approach, or Trait Approach.

a. Self-actualization

b. Reciprocal altruism

c. Rorschach test

d. Five-factor model

e. Locus of control

f. Minnesota Multiphasic Personality Inventory (MMPI)

g. Psychosexual stages

h. Thematic Apperception Test (TAT)

i. I-E Scale

j. Peak experiences

k. Modeling

l. Unconditional positive regard

(Answers: Psychoanalysis: c, g, h; Cognitive Social-Learning: b, e, k; Humanistic: a, j, l; Trait: d, f, i.)

Perspectives: Do Traits Exist?

Pause a moment and think about the last time you were on social media. Did you find yourself in the infamous social media rabbit hole? Clicking on one friend's profile leads you to another friend's profile, to a stranger's profile, and so on. As you looked at others' social media pages, you most likely studied their photos. Photos can tell us a lot about a person. For example, if you come across a social media profile of a person who is photographed while bungee jumping, at Times Square in New York City on New Year's Eve, and with his fraternity brothers at a tailgate party, you might assume that person is an extravert. In making that assumption, you have hypothesized about a person you don't even know. You have behaved like a trait psychologist.

We are all trait psychologists. We all use trait terms to describe ourselves and others, and we have preconceptions about how various characteristics relate to one another and to behavior. Social media is a great repository of information that can lead us to a conclusion about those we know and those we don't. Darbyshire and colleagues (2016) presented people with Facebook screenshots of an unknown target and asked for statements about their impression of said target. Some statements about the unknown target's photos were, "Pictures—more often than not in a large social group—most of which are at a nightclub drinking/socializing" and

Think about how people describe you. Now, think about how you describe yourself. The two perspectives might not be similar. Traits are dependent on many factors and, thus, are not 100 percent accurate. However, they are informative nonetheless.

iStock.com/Olivier Le Moal

"Pictures of slacking and doodling in college" (p. 384). When reading comments and verbal posts, some participants said, "seems easily offended," "appears to be very intelligent, talk about books," and "has lots of friends that care about her" (p. 384). The Big Five traits that were judged accurately were openness and conscientiousness. Other studies support the accurate judgement of these traits using online information (Stopfer, Egloff, Nestler, & Back, 2014; Wall, Taylor, Dixon, Conchie, & Ellis, 2013). However, the self—ideal, ought, or actual—that people choose to present online is debatable (Zhao, Grasmuch, & Martin, 2008).

Although it seems natural to think about people and their behavior in terms of traits, some critics complain that the approach is limited. Psychoanalysts say it's superficial, cognitive social-learning theorists say it neglects situational factors, and humanists say it's cold and impersonal. By far the most serious attack, however, was Mischel's (1968) startling claim that traits simply do not exist. After reviewing years of research, Mischel concluded that personality test scores are not predictive of behavior and that people do not act with trait-like consistency from one situation to the next. To illustrate, he cited a classic study by Hartshorne and May (1928) in which they observed the moral conduct of thousands of children in school, at home, at parties, and so on. Seeking evidence of a trait for honesty, Hartshorne and May found that the children exhibited strikingly little cross-situational consistency in behavior. A child might pass up a chance to cheat in class or steal money from a dropped wallet but then be quick to cheat in an athletic event or lie to parents. Thus, said Mischel (1968), traits—as measured by personality tests—cannot reliably predict behavior.

Mischel's critique whipped up a tremendous controversy among personality psychologists wondering whether traits were a mere figment of the imagination. After many years of debate and additional research, two main conclusions can be drawn. First, as noted by Epstein (1979), traits are highly informative—but only when they're used to predict an *aggregation* of behaviors. To measure personality, psychologists derive test scores by combining answers to several related questions. Similarly, says Epstein, behavior should be measured by combining several trait-related acts. Just as an IQ score is not expected to predict a grade in a particular class during a particular semester, your score on an introversion-extraversion scale cannot be expected to predict whether you will tell jokes at your next party. By the same token, just as an IQ score can predict grade point *averages*, a personality test can predict general behavior tendencies (Huang, Ryan, Zabel, & Palmer, 2014; Kluemper, Mclarty, & Bing, 2015).

The second important conclusion is that behavior springs from complex *interactions* between persons and situations (Ajzen & Fishbein, 1980; Cervone & Shoda, 1999; Sherman, Rauthmann & Brown, 2015). This interaction can take many forms. First, personality traits are expressed only in relevant situations. If you're the anxious type, you may break out in a cold sweat before a first date or public presentation but not when at home watching TV. Second, traits are expressed only in situations that do not constrain our behavior. Just about everyone is quiet and reserved in churches, libraries, and crowded elevators, but our unique personalities are free to emerge at home, at a party, or in the street. Third, people influence the situations they are in. The way we treat our friends, family, and others, for example, steers the treatment we receive in turn. Thus, child development researchers who used to write about how parents shape their children now realize that children, even infants, shape their parents as well. Fourth, people choose settings that are compatible with their own personalities. Extraverts craving excitement are likely to visit amusement parks and casinos, but introverts seek out quiet restaurants, hiking trails, and other out-of-the-way places. Fifth, our personalities color the way we interpret and react to situations. Optimists perceive the proverbial glass as half-full, whereas pessimists perceive the same glass as half-empty. As Allport (1961) said, "The same fire that melts the butter hardens the egg" (p. 102).

Thinking Like a Psychologist About Personality

Now that you are familiar with the four major approaches to personality, you are in a position to evaluate each perspective for yourself. If you were to stop and think about your own life—say, to write your autobiography—which of the four approaches would best describe your personality and explain how you got that way?

To summarize, psychoanalysis emphasizes unconscious conflicts, sex and aggression, defensive behavior, anxiety, and early childhood influences. Cognitive social-learning theory views personality as a socially acquired pattern of behavior, a learned response to how people perceive, interpret, and value the external reinforcements in their lives. Humanists believe that people are inherently good, that we have self-insight, and that personality springs from the desire and struggle to reach our full potential. The trait approach makes few value judgments about human nature, but it assumes that everyone can be compared on a standard set of dispositions that are consistent over time and, at least to some extent, genetically determined.

The four approaches also differ in their perspectives on change and in their approaches to the treatment of psychological disorders. Beginning with Freud, most psychoanalysts perceive the early years of childhood as formative, if not critical, to the development of personality—with relatively little room for change in adulthood. In fact, psychoanalytic therapists say that patients unconsciously resist the recovery process. The trait approach, with its emphasis on genetic factors and the stability of core dispositions, also takes a relatively dim view of change. In the trait approach, people are biologically introverted or extraverted, and calm or anxious—thus leaving little room for variation. In contrast, the behavioral and cognitive social-learning theorists perceive people as flexible and influenced by environmental factors. According to this view, psychological disorders are learned—and can be unlearned just as well. The humanistic approach is equally clear in its view that people have not only the capacity but also the will to change and, specifically, to strive toward self-actualization.

Although we have discussed the four approaches as distinct, you don't necessarily have to choose a favorite or accept any one approach completely. Many personality psychologists are *eclectic*, which means that they accept bits and pieces of different theories. It is also instructive to consider the possibility that each approach may better account for some aspects of personality than for others. Psychoanalysis may shed light on why we feel inexplicably troubled and anxious, cognitive social-learning theory may explain why having control is often so important to us, humanism may capture the experience of pursuing and catching lifelong dreams, and the trait approach may offer the best way to measure our unique predispositions. The human personality is so complex and multifaceted that all perspectives are necessary.

SUMMARY

The study of **personality**—an individual's distinct and relatively enduring pattern of thoughts, feelings, motives, and behaviors—shows that personality characteristics are quite stable over time unless cognitive decline occurs. There are four major approaches to personality.

PSYCHOANALYSIS

The Birth of Psychoanalysis

Just before the turn of the 20th century, Freud used his clinical experience with hysteria to formulate **psychoanalysis**.

Freud's Theory of Personality

Psychoanalysis assumes that unconscious conflicts play a large part in shaping personality. Freud divided personality into three parts. The **id**—a primitive, unconscious reservoir of basic drives—operates according to the **pleasure principle**. The personality's moral part, the **superego**, consists of the **ego**-ideal and the conscience. The ego mediates between the id's "wants" and the superego's "shoulds" and follows a **reality principle** that allows for gratification of needs in a socially appropriate manner.

Freud believed that personality is shaped by conflicts that arise during the **psychosexual stages** of development. Young children pass through the oral, anal, and phallic stages. During the phallic stage (ages 4 to 6 years), children experience the **Oedipus complex**, a tendency to become attracted to the parent of the opposite sex and hostile to the parent of the same sex. Children resolve this complex, however, and form an **identification** with the same-sex parent, internalizing the parent's values. At puberty, the genital stage begins. Too much or too little gratification in any of the first three stages can result in **fixation** at that stage and a distinct type of personality.

According to Freud, we feel anxiety when our impulses clash with morals, so the ego uses unconscious **defense mechanisms** that deny and distort reality. **Repression** helps us "forget" threatening thoughts, memories, and impulses by pushing them out of awareness. In **denial**, we bar anxiety-provoking thoughts from awareness in the first place. Through **projection**, we attribute our own unacceptable impulses to others. Through **reaction formation**, we convert an unacceptable feeling into its opposite. **Rationalization** involves making excuses for failures and shortcomings. And in **sublimation**, the healthiest defense mechanism, we channel repressed urges into socially acceptable substitute outlets.

FREUD'S LEGACY

Freud's followers continued to focus on unconscious factors, inner conflicts, and early-childhood influences. Jung proposed that people are influenced by a **collective unconscious** consisting of memories from our ancestral past, and he argued that personality development continues into adulthood. Adler stressed social conflicts and developed the notions of sibling rivalry and the inferiority complex. More recent theorists have emphasized social needs or the role of the ego.

Psychoanalytic researchers also developed **projective tests** to reveal the unconscious through responses to ambiguous stimuli. The **Rorschach** uses inkblots. The **Thematic Apperception Test (TAT)** asks people to make up stories from a set of pictures.

Critics say that psychoanalysis takes too bleak a view of human nature and that its propositions are not supported by controlled research. Yet Freud's ideas, particularly those about the unconscious and defense mechanisms, have become an integral part of psychology.

THE COGNITIVE SOCIAL-LEARNING APPROACH

Unlike psychoanalysis, **cognitive social-learning theory** sees personality as the result of a continuous interaction between persons and environments.

PRINCIPLES OF LEARNING AND BEHAVIOR

Early behaviorists investigated classical conditioning, operant conditioning, and other key principles of learning. Watson and Skinner applied these principles to the study of personality.

SOCIAL-LEARNING THEORY

Social-learning theory extended behaviorism to include social and cognitive factors. Through **modeling**, people can learn behavior by observing and imitating. Rotter and Mischel further showed that thoughts influence the link between reinforcement and behavior.

According to cognitive social-learning theory, people differ in **locus of control**—expectations about the control of reinforcement. Internals, who believe they can control their own fate, tend to be healthier and more successful. People also differ in **self-efficacy**, the belief that they can perform the behaviors needed for a desired outcome. The more self-efficacy people have for a task, the more likely they are to succeed.

PERSPECTIVES ON COGNITIVE SOCIAL-LEARNING THEORY

Cognitive social-learning theory emphasizes **reciprocal determinism**, the notion that personality emerges from an ongoing interaction among individuals, their actions, and environments. Environmental forces shape our personalities, but we can choose, alter, and interpret the situations we encounter. To assess personality, cognitive social-learning theorists use direct methods such as behavioral observations and self-reports.

THE HUMANISTIC APPROACH

By the 1940s, some psychologists began to develop a **humanistic theory** of personality.

CARL ROGERS

Impressed by his patients' self-insight and will to improve, Rogers theorized that we all have a natural need for self-actualization—that is, a drive to behave in ways consistent with our self-concepts. The self-concept is made up of various **self-schemas**, specific beliefs about the self. As social beings, however, we also have a competing need for positive regard. **Unconditional positive regard** from significant others frees us to pursue self-actualization. But if we receive **conditional positive regard**, we experience frustration, anxiety, and **self-discrepancie**s. Studies have shown that individuals as well as social and cultural groups differ in their **self-esteem**, the extent to which they evaluate themselves favorably.

ABRAHAM MASLOW

Maslow believed that people are motivated to fulfill a hierarchy of needs en route to **self-actualization**, the distinctly human need to become everything one is capable of becoming. Few people reach this state, though it is common to have momentary **peak experiences**.

PERSPECTIVES ON THE HUMANISTIC APPROACH

Humanistic psychologists have been praised for focusing on the good in human beings, the self-concept, and conscious experience. They have been criticized for ignoring the darker side of human nature and relying too heavily on people's self-reports.

THE TRAIT APPROACH

THE BUILDING BLOCKS OF PERSONALITY

To start with what he felt was a critical foundation, Gordon Allport decided to study the basic units of personality and compiled a list of 200 personality **traits**. With factor analysis, Raymond Cattell reduced these to 16 source traits. Now, researchers have condensed the list to a **five-factor model** consisting of five traits: neuroticism, extraversion, openness, agreeableness, and conscientiousness (juggle them and think OCEAN).

CONSTRUCTION OF MULTITRAIT INVENTORIES

The trait approach gave rise to the construction of personality inventories such as the **Minnesota Multiphasic Personality Inventory (MMPI)**.

INTROVERSION AND EXTRAVERSION

One of the most powerful trait dimensions is introversion and extraversion. An **extravert** is sociable and impulsive and seeks stimulation. An **introvert** is low keyed, cautious, and avoidant of stimulation. Research suggests that extraverts are sensation seekers, whereas introverts are overly sensitive to stimulation. Recent studies reveal similar differences in temperament between inhibited and uninhibited infants and children.

PERSPECTIVES: DO TRAITS EXIST?

Debates about trait theory lead to two major conclusions. First, traits can predict an aggregation of behaviors but not specific acts. Second, behavior springs from an interaction between traits and situations.

CRITICAL THINKING

Thinking Critically About Personality

1. Compare the four approaches to personality (psychoanalytic, cognitive social-learning, humanistic, and trait). What are the implications of these differences for the way in which personality is measured? Give examples of the different measurement instruments advocated by each approach.

2. Take a few moments to write down a description of your own personality, and then use each of the four approaches to explain it. Which of the four approaches do you think best accounts for your personality?

3. What are the major criticisms of Freudian theory? What Freudian concepts continue to endure? What would you say is Freud's most enduring legacy?

4. Csikszentmihalyi's research seems to suggest that anyone can have "optimal experiences." Identify a domain in which you have experienced, or would like to experience, flow. What did this experience feel like (or what do you think it would feel like)? Suggest some ways that you would increase the likelihood of experiencing flow.

5. Discuss the evidence that introversion is biologically based. What are the implications of this work for personality change? That is, can an introvert become more extraverted, or vice versa? If so, how might this be accomplished?

CAREER CONNECTION: BUSINESS

Sales

Undergraduate psychology programs help students acquire a wide range of interpersonal skills, which can be put to use in sales and marketing positions across the business world. Employers value skills developed in psychology coursework, such as the ability to speak well and communicate effectively. Specific understanding of people and human behavior, acquired in courses in social psychology, personality, and communications, can be especially helpful. Those engaged in market research may also find their knowledge of the scientific method and data analysis to be invaluable.

Key skills for this role that psychology students learn to develop:

- Enhanced teamwork capacity
- Effective communication in presentations and written works
- Self-efficacy and self-regulation

KEY TERMS

cognitive social-learning theory (p. 319)
collective unconscious (p. 314)
conditional positive regard (p. 326)
defense mechanisms (p. 312)
denial (p. 312)
ego (p. 309)
extravert (p. 338)
five-factor model (p. 335)
fixation (p. 311)
humanistic theory (p. 326)
id (p. 309)
identification (p. 310)
introvert (p. 338)
locus of control (p. 323)
Minnesota Multiphasic Personality Inventory (MMPI) (p. 336)
modeling (p. 321)
Oedipus complex (p. 310)
peak experience (p. 332)
personality (p. 305)
pleasure principle (p. 309)

projection (p. 313)
projective tests (p. 315)
psychoanalysis (p. 308)
psychosexual stages (p. 309)
rationalization (p. 313)
reaction formation (p. 313)
reality principle (p. 309)
reciprocal determinism (p. 325)
repression (p. 312)
Rorschach (p. 315)
self-actualization (p. 326)
self-discrepancy theory (p. 330)
self-efficacy (p. 324)
self-esteem (p. 327)
self-schemas (p. 327)
sublimation (p. 313)
superego (p. 309)
Thematic Apperception Test (TAT) (p. 316)
traits (p. 335)
unconditional positive regard (p. 326)

9 LIFE SPAN DEVELOPMENT AND ITS CONTEXTS

iStock.com/monkeybusinessimages

LEARNING OBJECTIVES

Describe genes and the role they play in behavior.

Identify the three stages of prenatal development and describe the complexities of fertility.

Describe the abilities that a newborn infant can demonstrate and the adaptive significance of their preferences.

Describe biological, cognitive, and social development during childhood.

Explain the importance and challenges of making the transition to adolescence.

Describe the physical and cognitive changes that are evident in adulthood and old age.

WHAT'S YOUR PREDICTION: HOW OLD DO PEOPLE FEEL?

The Situation

You know that people change as they get older, for better and for worse, and that development is a lifelong process. At the same time, you've heard it said that "age is a state of mind" and that "you're only as old as you feel." Hmm, you wonder. To what extent do people feel their chronological age? As children, did we tend to feel older than we were, or younger? How do we feel in relation to our age as adults?

Imagine that you are a developmental psychologist. To answer this question, you need to ask people to tell you how old they feel. So you devise a questionnaire in which you ask respondents to write down their actual age and then to specify how old they feel, how old they look, how old they behave, and so on. You realize that you need to survey people of different ages, so you recruit high school and college students, faculty members from your university, adults taking part in an educational workshop, and local senior citizen centers. You send out 298 questionnaires, and 188 are completed and returned. Those who participate range in age from 14 to 83.

Make a Prediction

By averaging each respondent's answers to various "how old do you feel" questions, you can calculate the person's "subjective-age identity." So what do you think you'd find? How old do *you* feel? Review Figure 9.1. Using a separate document, create a similar graph to plot your predictions. The diagonal line in the figure illustrates the pattern you would expect if subjective ages were identical to chronological ages—in other words, if people felt exactly as young or old as they truly were. If you think that this is what happened, then all you have to do is trace over that existing line. Otherwise, use it as a guide and (without looking at Figure 9.2) put an X at the age felt by the average 15-year-old, and then do the same for those at the ages of 25, 35, 45, 55, 65, 75, and 85. If you think that people in a particular age group feel younger than they are, place the X below the existing line. If you think they feel older, put the X above the line. Connect the Xs and you'll have your predicted subjective-age line.

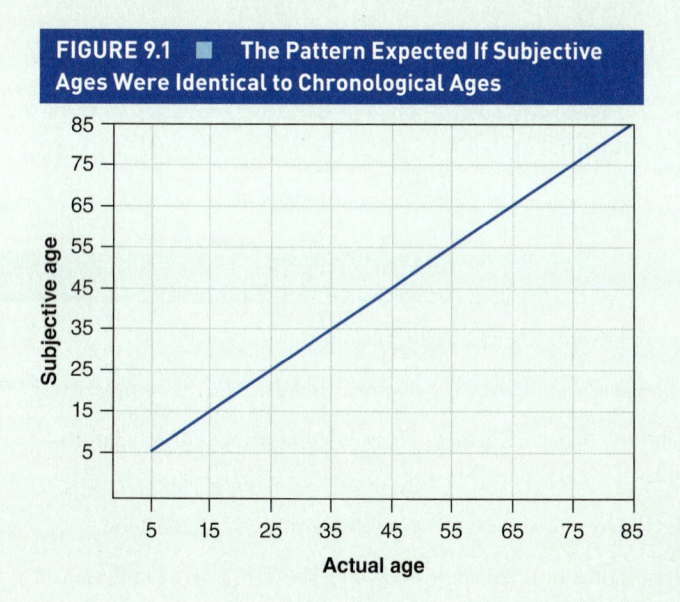

FIGURE 9.1 ■ The Pattern Expected If Subjective Ages Were Identical to Chronological Ages

The Results

Based on research suggesting that life satisfaction has more to do with subjective age than with chronological age, Joann Montepare and Margie Lachman (1989) conducted the study just described. As shown, the results are plotted alongside the comparison line in Figure 9.2. So how did you do? The figure illustrates three interesting findings: (a) Teenagers in general feel older than they are; (b) adults feel younger; and (c) the tendency for adults to feel younger becomes more pronounced with advancing age; and this is still just as true today (Westerhof et al., 2014).

What Does It All Mean?

One of the most important and recurring questions in developmental psychology concerns the extent to which people change over the course of a lifetime, particularly during the adult years. We'll learn in this chapter that development is a lifelong process in which we change—physically, cognitively, and socially—as we get older. We'll also learn, however, that in other respects each of us is the same person today that we were five years ago and will remain that person five years from now. In this context, Montepare and Lachman's (1989) study and others since then (Westerhof et al., 2014) show, at least to some extent, that we age less in our minds than we do on the clock.

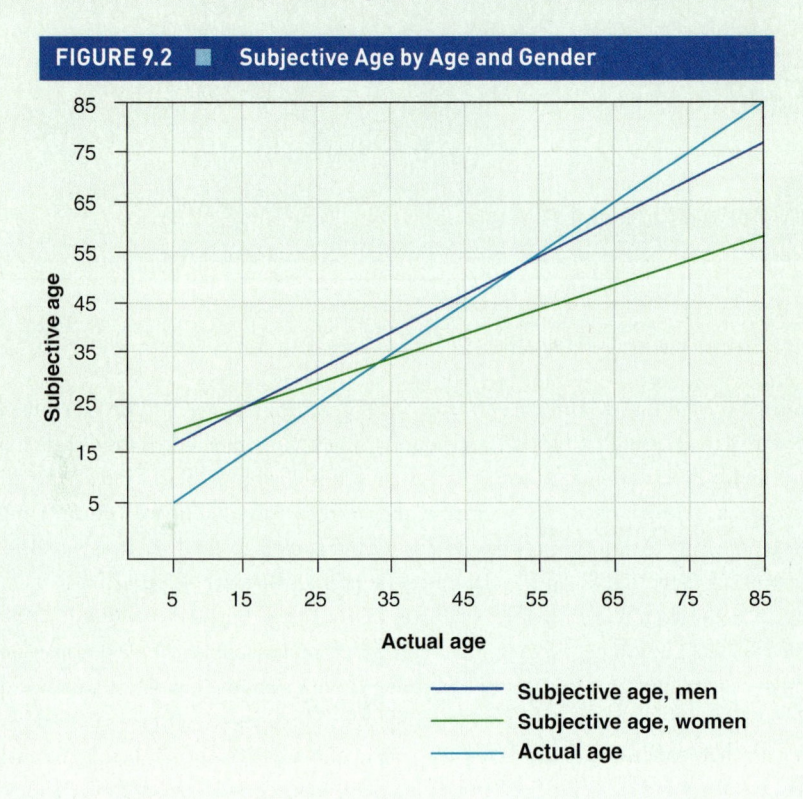

FIGURE 9.2 ■ Subjective Age by Age and Gender

— Subjective age, men
— Subjective age, women
— Actual age

When it comes to understanding people, it often seems that playwrights, philosophers, poets, and artists are a step ahead of the rest of us. In the seventh century BCE, the Greek poet Solon described nine stages in human development, beginning in the cradle and ending in the grave. Then, in roughly 500 BCE, the Chinese philosopher Confucius described six life phases spanning the ages of 15 to 70. At the end of the 16th century, William Shakespeare immortalized his vision of seven life stages. And in Sweden, an unnamed artist depicted the ages of man and woman in 10-decade pyramids that peak at the age of 50. In some cultures, the human life span is pictured as a straight line. In others, it is thought of as a circle, spiral, square, or change of seasons (Kotre & Hall, 1990).

To begin understanding human development, it is important first to look at our very nature, and how it is nurtured. Consider, for example, Laila Amaria Ali—a former professional boxer, and the daughter of legendary boxing champion Muhammad Ali (refer to Figure 9.3). She became a boxing legend of her own, defeating some of the most prominent names in women's boxing. In a little over eight years she amassed a 24–0 record, including 21 knockouts; winning four super middleweight titles and one light heavyweight title before retiring in 2007. Why was she so successful? Is it so simple as who her father was? Many great athletes have children who never become great athletes themselves. These are the types of presumptions that do not capture the complexities of development and all the diversity and richness of our experiences.

The Alis are not the only example. Many examples can be found in and out of sports. Award-winning actress Gwyneth Paltrow is the daughter of award-winning actress Blythe Danner. Football legend Archie Manning, who played 13 years in the NFL, is father to two football greats: Hall of Famer Peyton Manning

FIGURE 9.3 ■ Muhammad and Laila Ali

Laila Amaria Ali with her father, Muhammad Ali, as a child and as a champion. Laila became a legendary boxer—like father, like daughter.

The Stanley Weston Archive / Contributor/Archive Photos/Getty Images; Ed Mulholland / Contributor/WireImage/Getty Images

and his brother Eli Manning—both are two-time Super Bowl champions. Wallflowers musician Jakob Dylan is the son of rock legend Bob Dylan, and country singer Wynonna Judd is the daughter of country singer Naomi Judd. Even in politics, there is former president George W. Bush, son of former president George H. W. Bush. Think for just a few moments, and you're sure to come up with other examples. With all of these examples of talent seemingly passed down from parents to children, it seems there is quite a promising career ahead for, say, Blue Ivy—daughter of superstars Beyoncé and Jay Z.

At first glance, the resemblances in these examples seem striking. But do they illustrate a rule or exceptions to a rule? What, if anything, do they tell us about human development? One possible conclusion is that the similarities are built into nature and that these famous sons and daughters are chips off the old blocks because of genetic similarity to their parents. But, wait. These famous offspring also likely share lived experiences with their parents, such as where they were raised, many aspects of their home environment, the foods they were exposed to, seeing firsthand their parents' careers, and learning from these experiences. In this chapter, we look at the complexities of development across the life span—from your genetic makeup (nature) to your lived social, psychological, and physical experiences (nurture) that make you, well, you.

GENES

LEARNING OBJECTIVES

Describe genes and the role they play in behavior.

- Discuss the areas included in the study of developmental psychology and genetics.
- Explain what genes are and how they work.
- Summarize how genes are passed from parent to offspring.

developmental psychology. The study of how people grow, mature, and change over the life span.

Inheriting the wisdom of past generations, psychologists view human development as a lifelong process. The study of **developmental psychology** thus examines the kinds of questions that parents ask about their offspring and that all of us ask about ourselves: How do individuals *change* as they get older? Will an infant with a precocious smile become a sociable adult? Is the early-walking toddler a future athlete? Is the preschooler who clings to mom fated to become a dependent spouse? And is the overly anxious college student doomed to a life of anxiety? Focusing on the extent to which development is characterized by stability or change, in this chapter we explore the genetic—and then the biological, cognitive, and social—aspects of development across the life span, from conception through infancy, childhood, adolescence, adulthood, and old age.

Ultimately, the recipe for our existence is coded in our genes. **Genes** are the biological units of heredity. They copy themselves, they pass from parent to offspring, and they play a key role in the development of individuals and species. The study of **genetics** is in the news a lot lately—in part because, now that scientists have mapped the entire sequence of human genes, they can identify genetic markers of disease; in part because crime investigators are using "DNA prints" to identify criminals and exonerate the innocent; in part because of cloning and the intense ethical controversies that swirl around this technology; and in part because of companies like 23andMe, which can provide DNA sequencing to anyone to inform them not only about their ancestry but also about their genetically based health risks. So, what are genes, how do they work, and how do they make us both similar to each other and different?

genes. The biochemical units of heredity that govern the development of an individual life.

genetics. The branch of biology that deals with the mechanisms of heredity.

What Genes Are and How They Work

On this planet at least, cells are the basic working units of every organism. There are trillions of cells within the body of a human or other animal. Within the nucleus of every cell, except for red blood cells, is a copy of the organism's genetic blueprint. Each human nucleus contains 46 tiny rodlike structures called **chromosomes**, arranged in 23 pairs. For purposes of communication, geneticists have numbered these chromosomes 1, 2, 3, and so on, from the largest to the smallest. Thus, we each have two versions, or paired members, of chromosome 1, two versions of chromosome 2, and on down the line. The two members of a chromosome pair are not identical because one was donated by your biological mother, the other by your biological father (illustrated in Figure 9.4).

chromosomes. Rodlike structures, found in all biological cells, that contain DNA molecules in the form of genes

Each chromosome consists of tightly coiled strands of large molecules of the substance **deoxyribonucleic acid**, or **DNA**. These molecules can be found in the sperm and egg cells that join to form a new being, and they replicate themselves over the course of development. Within each DNA molecule are segments called *genes*—long, stringy, self-replicating molecules that contain instructions to synthesize proteins, the building blocks of life, and thereby provide the biochemical basis for heredity. To the extent that a characteristic is biologically inherited, it is inherited through genes. The normal human

deoxyribonucleic acid (DNA). The complex molecular structure of a chromosome that carries genetic information.

FIGURE 9.4 ■ Human Chromosomes

Geneticists have numbered the human chromosome pairs from 1 (the largest) to 22 (the smallest), followed by the two sex chromosomes, X and Y.

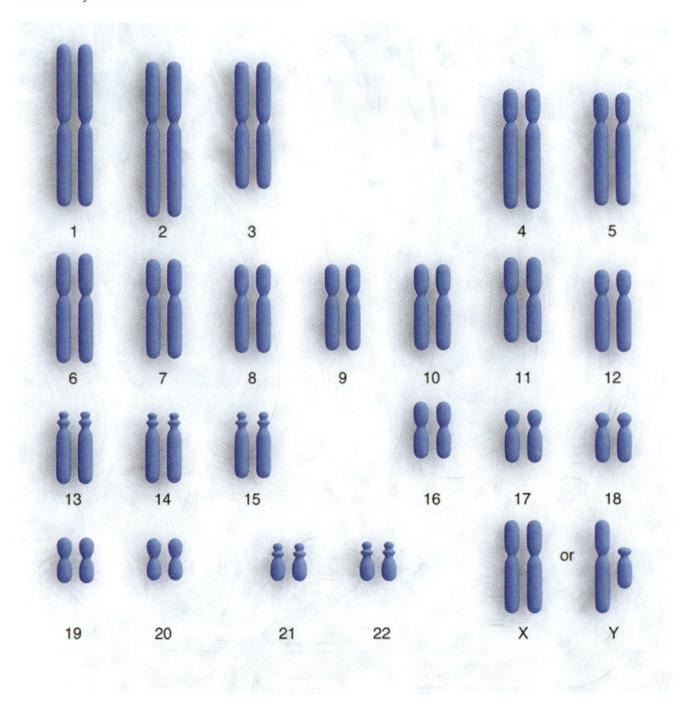

iStock.com/somersault18:24

complement of some tens of thousands of genes is thus grouped into 46 chromosomes. Remember that your chromosomes come in 23 pairs, so your genes are represented in 35,000 pairs.

One of the crowning achievements of 20th century science was the discovery by James Watson and Francis Crick (1953) of what genes are and how they work. Thanks in part to their pioneering work, we now know that genes contain a biochemical recipe written in code. We also know that genes perform two essential tasks: They make copies of themselves that are transmitted over the course of generations, in principle, forever; and they direct the assembly of organisms, like us.

Genes are composed of subunits of DNA. In total, there are four DNA bases, or nucleotides: adenine, guanine, thymine, and cytosine, typically referred to by their initial letters A, G, T, and C. As you'll learn shortly, these four "letters" of the genetic alphabet come together in various combinations, producing a twisted DNA ladder that looks like a spiral staircase. These genetic building blocks are summarized in Figure 9.5.

Genetic Building Blocks

Life begins when a male *sperm* cell—one of the hundreds of millions released into the Fallopian tube during intercourse—is united with a female's ovum, or egg cell. The fertilized *ovum* then forms a barrier that blocks the entry of other sperm. In the meantime, the nuclei of the male and female cells move toward each other, fusing within hours into a single, brand new cell. This fusion marks the beginning of a new life, genetically endowed by a mother and a father. Right from the start, this single cell has a full genetic heritage contained within the 23 pairs of chromosomes—half carried in the mother's ovum, and half in the father's sperm. As we saw earlier, each of the 46 chromosomes contains strands of DNA. In turn, each DNA molecule is made up of thousands of genes, the biochemical building blocks of an individual life.

Like a photograph that has already been taken but not yet developed, genes determine our skin color, height, weight, blood type, certain behavioral dispositions, as well as medical and psychological disorders. All humans have certain genes in common, which is why we all can walk and talk—but not fly, bark, or breathe underwater. At the same time, unless you are one of two identical twins or one of three triplets, you have a distinct combination of genes that makes you unique among all past, present, and future human beings. The 23rd pair of chromosomes determines your sex. Whereas everyone receives an X chromosome from the mother, there is an equal chance that the father will contribute an X or Y chromosome to the pair. If it is X, the offspring will be female (XX); if it is Y, it will be male (XY). Assuming no anomalies occur, which are rare, the biological sex of a child thus depends on the father's contribution.

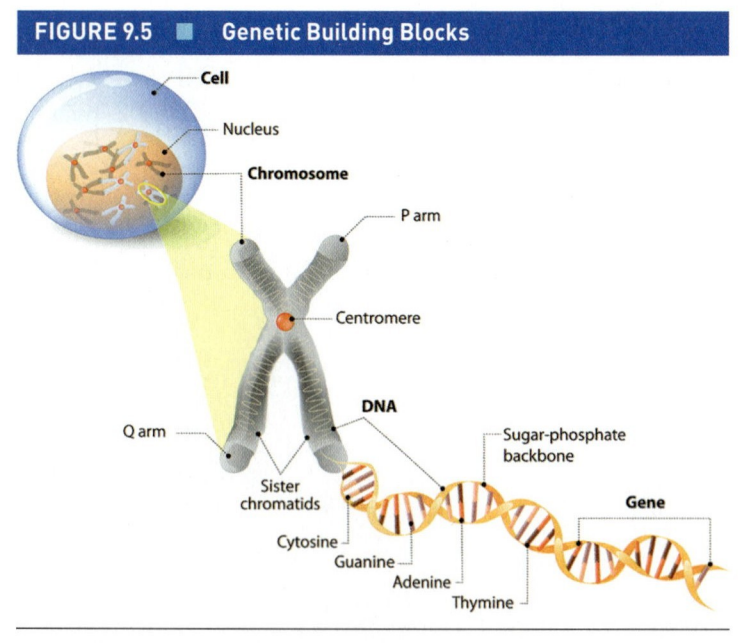

FIGURE 9.5 ■ Genetic Building Blocks

iStock.com/ttsz

Chapter 9 • Life Span Development and Its Contexts   353

PRENATAL DEVELOPMENT

> **LEARNING OBJECTIVES**
>
> Identify the three stages of prenatal development and describe the complexities of fertility.
>
> - Summarize the three stages of prenatal development.
> - Identify the stage of prenatal development in which sexual differentiation occurs, and explain what it determines.
> - Define fertility and elaborate on how it changes over the life span.

Recognizing that the passage from the womb into the outside world is a profound one, Westerners celebrate the birthday as the starting point in a person's development. In fact, birth is not so much a beginning as it is a transition. The real beginning occurs nine months earlier, at the moment of conception. That is why the Chinese calculate age from that moment and consider the baby to be a 1-year-old at birth. In cross-sectional studies, subjects of different ages are examined at the same time and compared for differences. In longitudinal studies, the same subjects are tested at different times in order to measure change.

The Growing Fetus

Prenatal development during the nine months of pregnancy is divided into three stages. From one stage to the next, dramatic biological and behavioral changes take place—and environmental influences are plentiful. These developments are illustrated in Figure 9.6. The three stage of prenatal development are as follows:

- Germinal stage (conception to approximately two weeks)
- Embryonic stage (approximately two weeks to eight weeks)
- Fetal stage (approximately eight weeks to birth).

Germinal Stage

First, there is the germinal stage. Thanks to **conception**, life begins with one remarkable new cell called a **zygote**—about the size of the period at the end of this sentence, yet fully equipped with a rich genetic heritage. To set the stage for conception to occur, toward the end of a female's menstrual cycle, a follicle in the female's ovary matures and releases an egg cell, called an **ovum**, in a process called **ovulation**. The mature egg takes an excursion traveling down the Fallopian tube toward the uterus. Unless the ovum is fertilized by a sperm cell while in the Fallopian tube, within about two weeks the egg will dry up and leave the body; this process is called *menstruation*.

Immediately upon fertilization, the outside of a zygote thickens to block other sperm cells from penetrating the egg. Very quickly following conception, a process of cell division takes place: The first cell splits into two, four, eight, and so on. After two and a half days, there are 12 to 16 cells. By the fourth day, there are more than 100 cells clustered together in a ball, traveling from the Fallopian tube into the uterus and increasing in both their number and their diversity. Some cells will form muscles and bone; others will form the stomach, liver, and so on. At two weeks, the ball of cells attaches to the uterine wall, braced and ready for eight and a half months in a new home. By the time this zygote is born, it will consist of hundreds of trillions of cells.

conception. The fertilization of an egg cell by a sperm cell.

zygote. A fertilized egg that undergoes a two-week period of rapid cell division and develops into an embryo.

ovum. An unfertilized egg cell.

ovulation. The release of a mature egg cell from a woman's ovary.

FIGURE 9.6 ■ Prenatal Development

Just prior to conception, a sperm penetrates the ovum wall. After 30 hours, the fertilized ovum divides for the first time and each cell contains genes from both the mother and the father. After six weeks, parts of the embryo's body have formed and the heart beats. At four months, the fetus is 2 to 4 inches long and has a conspicuously human appearance.

24 HOURS AFTER FERTILIZATION: 2 CELLS

3 WEEKS AFTER FERTILIZATION: 3-LAYERED EMBRYO

8-WEEK-OLD EMBRYO

10-WEEK-OLD FETUS

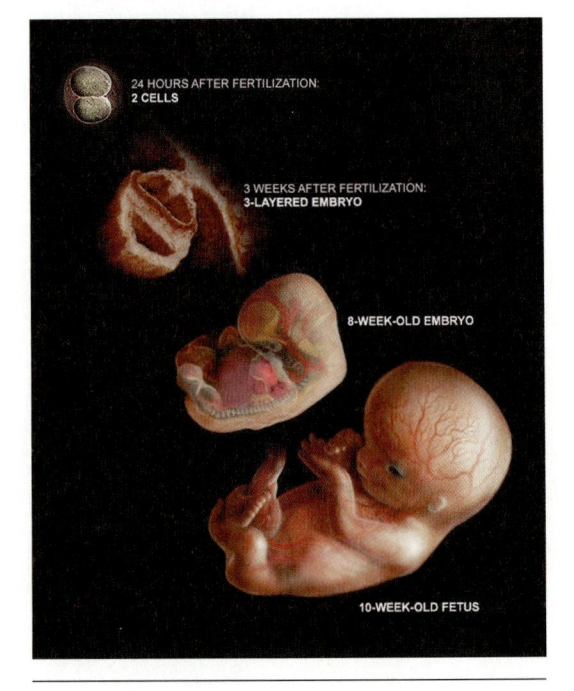

TheVisualMD / Science Source

embryo. The developing human organism, from two weeks to two months after conception.

fetus. The developing human organism, from nine weeks after conception to birth.

teratogens. Toxic substances that can harm the embryo or fetus during prenatal development.

fetal alcohol syndrome (FAS). A specific pattern of birth defects (stunted growth, facial deformity, and intellectual disability) often found in the offspring of mothers who have alcoholism.

Embryonic Stage

Once the zygote is firmly attached to the uterine wall, called *implantation*, the germinal stage is over, and the zygote is called an **embryo**. Surprisingly, it is estimated that about 30 to 50 percent of conceptions fail to implant and do not survive (Moore, Persaud, & Tochia, 2013). If implantation fails, the zygote will pass out of the female's body, and the female will likely never know conception had ever occurred.

At this point, when implantation occurs, all parts of the body begin to form—an oversize head with a primitive brain and central nervous system, eyes, ears, a nose, and a mouth with lips and teeth, a heart and circulatory system, arms, legs, fingers, toes, and a tail. During this stage, organs start to function, including a heart that pumps blood and beats, quickly, for the first time. Also during this stage *sexual differentiation* occurs: The male hormone testosterone is secreted in embryos that are genetically male, but not in those destined to become female. All the pieces of an individual are in place in an embryo, yet at eight weeks of age it is only an inch long and weighs a tenth of an ounce. You could hold one in the palm of your hand.

Fetal Stage

From the ninth week on, the embryo becomes a conspicuously human **fetus**. At first, the cartilage in the bones starts to harden and there is rapid growth of the brain, heart, lungs, genitals, and other internal organs and body parts. Depending on its age, the fetus can squirm, open its eyes, suck its thumb, kick its legs, and turn somersaults. By the seventh month, the key life-support systems are sufficiently developed so that the fetus can breathe, circulate blood, digest nutrients, and dispose of wastes. At this point, the 2-pound fetus has a fighting chance to survive if born prematurely. If born on schedule, it will weigh an average of 7 pounds.

Although fetal development follows a biological clock, it is also influenced by external factors. Depending on the stage of development, for example, exposure to harmful substances called **teratogens** (from the Greek *teras*, meaning "monster") can have devastating effects. Babies of mothers who have alcoholism, for example, often show a pattern of birth defects known as **fetal alcohol syndrome (FAS)**. Obstetricians warn expectant mothers that malnutrition, X-rays, AIDS, German measles and other viral infections, certain antibiotics, painkillers, large doses of aspirin, heavy exposure to paint fumes, and a long list of drugs can all prove dangerous (summarized in Table 9.1). Some teratogens

TABLE 9.1 ■ Some Hazards to the Developing Embryo and Fetus

Substance/Disease	Possible Danger
Alcohol	Excessive use can produce fetal alcohol syndrome. Even one or two drinks a day can cause problems, especially in the early stages of pregnancy.
Cigarettes	Smoking is linked to miscarriages, premature births, and low birth weight. Effects on later behavior and cognitive functioning are harder to pinpoint.
Cocaine	Cocaine use results in lower birth weight and later cognitive and social learning deficits.
Aspirin	Taken in large quantities, aspirin can cause prenatal bleeding, intestinal discomfort, respiratory problems, and low birth weight.
Marijuana	Heavy use can lead to premature birth and to babies with abnormal reactions to stimulation.
AIDS	AIDS can be transmitted to the fetus (or to the newborn during birth). AIDS babies are often born small and with facial deformities.
Rubella	Before the 11th week, rubella, or German measles, can cause heart problems, mental health issues, cataracts, and deafness.
X-rays	Heavy exposure can cause malformation of organs.

cannot be avoided—and some problems will arise without exposure to toxic substances. There are no guarantees. Even a mother's emotional state can affect the fetus. For example, women who are depressed during the last trimester of pregnancy pass on stress hormones to the fetus and give birth to infants that are initially passive and slow to react to stimulation (Lundy et al., 1999). Expectant mothers cannot easily control inner turmoil, but they can limit their intake of certain foods and drugs.

Psychology Applied: How Does Alcohol Affect the Fetus?

Legally and illegally, people have used drugs throughout history. The psychoactive effects of various substances on the user are described in the chapter on consciousness. But are there health risks to a fetus when the user is an expectant mother? Is the fetus more vulnerable in some stages of pregnancy than others? In the emerging area of "behavioral toxicology," researchers examine the effects of substances such as alcohol, tobacco, and cocaine. In animal studies, pregnant mothers are randomly injected with a toxic substance and the effects on their offspring are later measured. In human studies, researchers look for correlations between substances that mothers consumed while pregnant and the later behavior of their offspring. Because women who take drugs differ in other ways from those who do not, and because the long-term effects of exposure can be subtle, it is important to realize that the effects may be overestimated in some cases and underestimated in others (Popova, Lange, Probst, Gmel, & Rehm, 2017).

Does alcohol, a universally popular drug, affect the fetus? In 1899, English doctor William Sullivan studied the babies born to women in prison. He compared the children of heavy-drinking mothers with those of nondrinkers and discovered that the rate of stillbirths and infant mortality was two and a half times higher among the children of drinking mothers. This discovery lay dormant for many years. Then in 1973, Kenneth Jones and others noticed that 11 babies of mothers with alcoholism were born with a pattern of defects that included stunted growth, intellectual disability, and facial deformities (widely spaced eyes, a flattened nose, and a thin upper lip). They called this pattern fetal alcohol syndrome.

The devastating impact of alcohol is not that surprising in light of the immediate effects it has on the fetus. Soon after a mother drinks—whether it's beer, wine, or hard liquor—the alcohol enters her bloodstream, passes through the placenta and into the fetus's blood, flows to the brain, and impairs breathing. Using ultrasound, researchers observed that fetuses breathed less often after their mothers drank a "screwdriver"—a mixture of orange juice and vodka—than when they had a glass of orange juice (Lewis & Boylan, 1979). When an expectant mother drinks, to some extent so does the fetus.

From animal experiments, and from studies with humans, the evidence is clear: Mothers who have alcoholism are at risk of having a child who suffers from brain damage, cognitive impairments, attention disorders, speech problems, hyperactivity, and motor problems (Streissguth et al., 2004). What about social drinking during pregnancy? Does an occasional glass of wine over dinner or bubbly champagne on New Year's Eve damage the fetus? For social drinking, too, the evidence suggests that expectant mothers should exercise restraint (Lubbe, van Walbeek, & Vellios, 2017).

Sandra Jacobson and others (1993) tested infants born to females who drank varying degrees of alcohol while pregnant. Infants whose mothers had two drinks a day were slower to process information and less likely to engage in playful imitation. In other research, Ann Streissguth and others (1993, 1999) interviewed hundreds of pregnant women about their consumption of alcohol and other substances before and after they knew they were pregnant. For 14 years, these women's children were tested periodically. The more alcohol the mother consumed, the more serious the child's problems were. Three findings gave cause for alarm. First, even small doses were harmful. At 4 years old, the children of mothers who had only one drink a day while pregnant lacked balance, manual dexterity, and a steady hand. At three drinks a day, IQ scores were five points lower, and the damage was greatest when mothers drank during the early weeks of pregnancy—before realizing they were pregnant. Thus there seemed to be no safe level of drinking—and the timing couldn't be worse. Third, the effects were lasting. When the children were retested at 14 years old, those prenatally exposed to alcohol still performed poorly on various cognitive tests and had more trouble in school.

Fertility

While most pregnancies result in a single birth, multiple births are more common today due to a variety of factors, such as women conceiving later in age and the increased use of fertility drugs in developed countries (Diergaarde & Kurta, 2014). Twins account for more than 90 percent of multiple births and can be identical (monozygotic) or fraternal (dizygotic). Identical twins form when one fertilized egg (ovum) splits, thus creating two ova with identical genetic information. By contrast, fraternal twins form when two distinct eggs (ova) are each fertilized by a different sperm; each ovum therefore contains distinctive genetic information that is no more similar than would be found in individual siblings, although fraternal twins will uniquely share the same *amnion* (the innermost membrane that surrounds the embryo) until birth. About 3.4 percent of pregnancies result in the birth of twins, and pregnancies that result in higher-order births, such as triplets or quadruplets, are much rarer; only about 113 in every 100,000 births are higher-order births (Hamilton, Martin, Osterman, Curtin, & Mathews, 2015).

For couples who engage in unprotected *intercourse*, or sex, with the intent to conceive, conception should occur within one year (Greil, Slauson-Blevins, & McQuillan, 2010). If conception does not occur, then one or both individuals may have a medical condition called *infertility*. About 7 percent of males and about 11 percent of females of reproductive age in the United States have experienced fertility problems (Chandra, Copen, & Stephen, 2014), which not only can be frustrating but also can lead to psychological distress due to the "psychological rollercoaster" (Read et al., 2014, p. 390) of trying to conceive. In both males and females, fertility declines with age, although the decline is much greater in females. Females are about half as fertile in their 30s as they are in their early 20s, and their chances of conception decline substantially after age 35 (Practice Committee of the American Society for Reproductive Medicine, 2013). Male fertility also declines with age but more gradually, with substantial declines in the quality of a male's sperm generally starting after age 40. Infertility treatment has advanced due to the development of fertility drugs starting in the 1950s and with the more recent development of assisted reproductive technologies (ARTs) such as in vitro fertilization (IVF) and intracytoplasmic sperm injection. While generally effective, these options are often expensive, costing thousands of dollars, typically out of pocket. It is estimated that approximately 1.6 percent of all infants born in the United States every year are conceived using ART (Centers for Disease Control and Prevention, 2017).

LEARNING CHECK

A Developing Situation

Imagine you are developing from zygote to embryo to fetus to infant. For each of the events below, identify the order in which they occur. Answer Z for Zygote, E for Embryo, or F for Fetus.

Zygote	Embryo	Fetus
a. You can distinguish sounds from the outside.		
b. You split from one cell into two.		
c. You've attached to the uterine wall.		
d. You travel down the Fallopian tube.		
e. You're developing body parts.		

(Answers: Zygote: b, d; Embryo: c; Fetus: a, e.)

THE REMARKABLE NEWBORN

LEARNING OBJECTIVES

Describe the abilities that a newborn infant can demonstrate and the adaptive significance of their preferences.

- Outline how newborn infants can "communicate" what they know to researchers.
- Define reflexes and explain how they are adaptive for the newborn.
- Identify the kinds of sights and sounds that most attract the newborn.

In 1890, William James described the newborn's experience of the world as "one great booming, buzzing confusion." Some 80 later, Lewis Lipsitt (1971) signaled the dawn of a new era in an article entitled "Babies: They're a Lot Smarter Than They Look." Why is there such a discrepancy between James and Lipsitt? Babies are not more capable today than in the past—they still sleep 16 to 20 hours a day, wet their diapers, and cry a lot. The difference is that developmental psychologists now have high-tech equipment and more sophisticated methods to measure what the newborn cannot tell us in words.

Observing Infants

In *The Scientist in the Crib*, Alison Gopnik, Andrew Meltzoff, and Patricia Kuhl (1999) first describe this exciting research and conclude that "babies and young children know and learn more about the world than we could ever have imagined" (p. viii). As they put it, the human infant is "the most powerful learning machine in the universe" (p. 1). In an interview regarding her most recent book, *The Gardener and the Carpenter*, Alison Gopnik (2016) captures the takeaway from her decades of research: "Children learn much more from using their own brains to just observe and play than they do by having someone sit down and teach them."

One valuable research technique is based on the measurement of **habituation**, the tendency for attention to a novel stimulus to wane over time. If a picture or a sound is presented over and over again, an infant will eventually get bored, lose interest, look away, and exhibit a change in heart rate—a sure sign that it has "learned" the stimulus and "remembered" the previous exposures (Bornstein, 1989). If the infant then perks up, regains interest, and spends more time looking when a new stimulus is presented, this **recovery** response suggests that it has noticed a difference between the old and new. Using this technique, researchers can determine the age at which infants begin to distinguish among faces, voices, musical notes, speech sounds, geometric shapes, and rudimentary concepts. In one experiment, for example, Russell Adams and Mary Courage (1998) habituated 173 newborn infants to white light and then flashed green, red, and yellow lights to determine how sensitive they were to changes in color (compared to adults, they were not).

Other techniques are also used. To determine what infants find interesting or surprising, researchers put different objects in front of them—dots, lines, balls, whatever—and use an eye-tracking device to record the amount of time spent looking at each object. There are many

habituation. The tendency for attention to a stimulus to wane over time (often used to determine whether an infant has "learned" a stimulus).

recovery. Following habituation to one stimulus, the tendency for a second stimulus to arouse new interest (often used to test whether infants can discriminate between stimuli).

Children learn at least as much from simply observing and playing as they do from having someone sit down and teach them.
iStock.com/SanyaSM

Owing to the grasping reflex, an infant grips a parent's thumb.
iStock.com/damircudic

subtle ways for newborns to communicate to researchers. Head movements, facial expressions, and measured changes in brain waves, heart rate, and respiration are just a few of the possibilities. Some researchers worry that it's too easy to *over*interpret what infants know from indirect measures. Marshall Haith (1998) asks, "How much of cognition is in the head of the infant and how much in the mind of the theoretician?" (p. 167). That's why Carolyn Rovee-Collier (2001) observes whether infants *act upon* objects and events they have observed. Other researchers note that it's easy to *under*interpret what infants know. As Mark Strauss put it, "You can tell the wheels are turning. They're paying attention to the world in incredibly subtle ways" (cited in Grunwald & Goldberg, 1993).

Reflexes

In light of recent research, developmental psychologists now have a profound respect for the newborn's capacities. To begin with, babies are prepared at birth with many adaptive reflexes—automatic, unlearned reactions to certain types of stimulation. Press into a newborn's palm, and you will stimulate a **grasping reflex** that causes the baby to clutch your hand so hard that it can support its own weight. Touch the newborn's right or left cheek with a nipple, or even a finger, and you will stimulate a **rooting reflex**, causing the baby automatically to turn in that direction and open its mouth. Touch the newborn's lips, and it will try to squeeze your finger between its tongue and palate, breathe through the nose, and begin to *suck*. Move your finger to the back of the baby's mouth, and it will try to *swallow*. None of these reflexes is within an infant's control, and most disappear within three or four months, never to return. But while they last, grasping, turning, opening the mouth, sucking, and swallowing are important parts of the newborn's adaptive machinery.

Sensory Capacities

Contrary to what maternity doctors and nurses used to tell new mothers, the newborn can see, hear, taste, smell, and feel pain. The question is not whether they have these senses, but what their limitations are and what kinds of stimulation they prefer. Researchers have used various techniques to study the development of perception in infancy.

Vision and Visual Preferences

At birth, parts of the eye and the visual cortex are not fully developed, and the newborn is nearsighted. In fact, to see an object as would an adult with 20/20 vision, the newborn needs to be 20 to 30 times closer—with the best distance being about 8 inches (Banks & Salapatek, 1983). The problem is that the newborn's lenses do not focus on objects at a distance and cannot detect subtle differences in light, shading, or color. For that reason, soft pastel colors in the crib do not arouse as much interest as a newspaper with bold print or a checkerboard that has stark black-on-white contrast (Adams & Maurer, 1984). What would it be like to see through the eyes of a newborn baby? According to Daphne Maurer and Charles Maurer (1988), the world would look like "a badly focused snapshot that has been fading in the sun for so many years that you can barely identify the subject" (p. 127).

Newborns may be limited in their vision, but their sensory abilities develop quickly and they have marked preferences for certain kinds of stimulation. Just hours after birth, for example, infants distinguish between light and dark, stare at objects that show contrast, and can track slow movement with their eyes. In an especially intriguing study, Robert Fantz (1961) recorded the amount of time that 2- to 5-day-old infants spent gazing at each of the six disks illustrated in Figure 9.7—a human face, a bull's-eye, newsprint, and three solids colored red, white, and yellow. As shown, the infants preferred to look at the patterns over solids. Lo and behold, their favorite pattern was the human face. This finding

grasping reflex. In infants, an automatic tendency to grasp an object that stimulates the palm.

rooting reflex. In response to contact on the cheek, an infant's tendency to turn toward the stimulus and open its mouth.

FIGURE 9.7 ■ Visual Preferences in Newborns

Fantz recorded the amount of time newborns spent gazing at various disks. They looked more at the patterns than at solids, and they looked most of all at the human face.

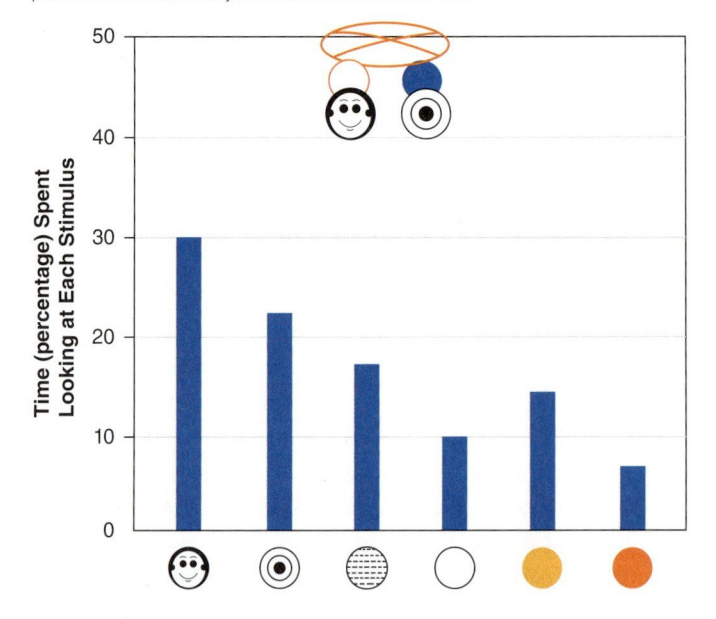

raised an intriguing question: Do faces just happen to provide the right kind of visual stimulation, or is the human nervous system primed to pay special attention to social stimuli? Is the attraction a mere happy coincidence or the clever design of evolution?

Research supports the evolutionary interpretation. To be sure, newborns look at any object that has complexity, contrast, and a symmetrical pattern of eyelike dots in an outline—whether that object resembles a face or not (Kleiner, 1987). But infants tested within an hour or two of birth exhibit a unique level of interest in facelike stimuli. Mark Johnson and others (1991) presented newborns with head-shaped forms that depict a properly featured face, a scrambled face, or a blank, featureless face. The experimenter moved each pattern slowly across each infant's field of view and recorded the extent to which the infants rotated their heads and eyes to follow the visual stimulus. The infants tracked the facelike pattern more than they did the scrambled and blank patterns. It appears that humans are born with a special orientation toward the face (Mondloch et al., 1999; Morton & Johnson, 1991; Valenza, Simion, Cassia, & Umilta, 1996). They can even distinguish between the faces of their own mothers and those of female strangers (Pascalis, de Schonen, Morton, DeRuelle, & Fabre-Grenet, 1995; Walton, Bower, & Bower, 1992).

Other lines of research also indicate that newborns are "tuned in" to the face as a social object. Andrew Meltzoff and Keith Moore (1983) found that within 72 hours of birth, babies not only look at faces but also often mimic gestures such as moving the head, pursing the lips, or sticking out the tongue. This rudimentary form of imitation occurs even when the model is a stranger (Meltzoff & Moore, 1992). In another study, newborns were recorded as they watched an adult wear a happy, sad, or surprised expression. Observers who later saw only the tape were able to guess the adult's expression from changes in the baby's face (Field, Woodson, Greenberg, & Cohen, 1982). What do these findings mean? It's not clear that newborns are capable of deliberate and coordinated imitation. But they do react automatically to certain facial cues—almost as if babies were born with a "social reflex," to the delight of parents all over the world.

Facial recognition among infants helps them recognize familiar faces, such as the faces of their parents or loved ones.

iStock.com/monkeybusinessimages

Hearing and Auditory Preferences

Slam the nursery door while a newborn is asleep, and they will open their eyes wide and fling out their arms. Clearly, the newborn can hear. But what does it hear, and how well? As with vision, the human auditory system is not completely developed at birth. The baby's outer ear is small, its eardrum does not vibrate effectively, and the auditory cortex is still immature. For the first week or so, the baby's ears are also clogged with amniotic fluid, which muffles sound. The result of all this is that the newborn baby is hard of hearing, compared to adults.

Though not in perfect form, the newborn reacts to life's sounds in consistent ways. If you stand on the baby's right or left side and shake a rattle, you'll notice that they slowly turns their head in your direction, as if trying to locate the source of the sound. Newborns cannot easily detect low-pitch sounds, but they are particularly sensitive to high-pitch sounds, melodies, and the human voice (Aslin, 1989). They can tell the difference between tones that are one note apart on the musical scale, between the mother's voice and that of another female, and between speech sounds that are as similar as *pa* and *ba*. As measured by changes in sucking rate, newborn infants can distinguish among multisyllable words that vary in stress patterns or rhythm (Sansavini, Bertoncini, & Giovanelli, 1997). By 20 weeks old, they're more likely to turn toward the sound of their own names than to similar other names (Mandel, Jusczyk, & Pisoni, 1995). They also seem to enjoy music. By recording the amount of time spent looking at stereo speakers as they deliver sound, researchers have found that infants show a measurable preference for Mozart and European folk songs over sounds that are "dissonant" or unpleasant to most adults (Trainor & Heinmiller, 1998; Zentner & Kagan, 1998).

In light of these various findings, it's interesting to consider the way adults talk to babies. In cultures all over the world, men, women, and children use baby talk, or "motherese"—a form of speech that is slow, clear, simple, high in pitch, rhythmic, songlike, and practically giddy, just the kinds of sounds that seize a newborn's attention. Infants like listening to higher-pitched voices (Trainor & Zacharias, 1998). They also prefer to hear baby talk than ordinary adult conversation. So when babies listen to recordings of women talking, they turn their head more toward the sound when the female is talking to a baby than to another adult (Fernald, 1985; Fernald et al., 1989).

Sensitivity to Number

Of all the discoveries about infants and what they know, perhaps the most startling come from classic experiments suggesting that babies are mini mathematicians. Karen Wynn (1992) showed 5-month-old

FIGURE 9.8 ■ Can Infants Add and Subtract?

Infants show a fundamental awareness of counting, as well as correct and incorrect answers.

iStock.com/lostinbids

infants one or two Mickey Mouse dolls being put on a puppet stage and covered by a screen. Next, they saw her add a doll to the one behind the screen (1 + 1) or take one away (2 − 1). The screen was then lowered so the babies could see how many dolls were now on stage. Sometimes the number was correct (2 in addition, 1 in subtraction); at other times, it was incorrect (1 in addition, 2 in subtraction). Can infants add and subtract? If they could, reasoned Wynn, they would "expect" correct outcomes and be surprised by incorrect outcomes. That is what happened. By recording their looking time, Wynn found that the babies looked longer at the incorrect—and apparently unexpected—outcomes. Using similar methods, Wynn and others have discovered that 5-month-olds have a rudimentary ability not only to add and subtract but also to tell the difference between two objects or event sequences and three (Canfield & Smith, 1996; Wynn, 1996).

This research has sparked a controversy over whether infants are born with an innate sensitivity to numbers. Studies have shown that when infants are habituated to a certain number of objects, say two blocks or rubber ducks, they look longer at a new display containing one or three objects than another two-object display. In other words, they seem to notice the difference in number. Or do they? Melissa Clearfield and Kelly Mix (1999) argue that these infants may have responded to a change in the overall amount of material in the display, not in the discrete number of objects present. To test this hypothesis, they habituated infants, 6 to 8 months old, to two black squares on a white board. Then they showed either three small squares that combined to produce the same amount of black space or two large squares that produced a larger combined black space. The result: The babies looked longer at the total change in space, or surface area (the two large squares) than at the change in number (the three small squares). Other studies have found similar results (Feigenson, Carey, & Spelke, 2002; Mix, Huttenlocher, & Levine, 2002; vanMarle & Wynn, 2011).

The human newborn is not a miniature adult and is obviously too helpless to survive on its own. Thanks to recent research, however, we are in a better position to appreciate a newborn's capacities. From the moment of birth, babies are equipped with primitive but adaptive reflexes. They're also prepared to experience certain forms of stimulation, especially those provided by human contact—faces, voices, and mother's scent. And they are capable of rudimentary forms of learning and memory. In a particularly intriguing program of research, Carolyn Rovee-Collier (1988) hung a mobile over the crib of 6-week-olds, attaching the mobile by a ribbon to one of their legs so they could move it. When these infants were brought back two weeks later, they remembered which leg to kick. Newborn capacities like these have existed for generations, but only now are we beginning to appreciate them.

THE INFANT AND THE GROWING CHILD

LEARNING OBJECTIVES

Describe biological, cognitive, and social development during childhood.

- Outline how the brain and body develop in the first few years of life.
- Describe the developmental changes that take place in the way children think, reason, and speak.
- Distinguish among the four stages of development that Jean Piaget identified.

The newborn has come a long way—both in our understanding and in its own short history of development. But there is much more to come. First, there is an *infant*, from the Latin word meaning "without language." The infant grows into a walking and talking toddler, who then graduates on the first day of school to the category of *child*. Puberty spurs the *adolescent*, though what it means to be an *adult* is anybody's guess. Throughout the rest of this chapter, we look at biological, cognitive, and social aspects of development and consider the interplay among them.

Biological Development

During the first year or so, babies grow at a pace never to be equaled again. On average, babies double their birth weight in five months and triple it by their first birthday. They grow 10 inches in height during the first year, and another 4 to 6 inches the year after. To the distress of caregivers without hand-me-downs, a baby's clothing size changes almost every month. Though it is not always accurate, there's a general rule of thumb you might find remarkable: By their second birthday, most toddlers have reached half of their adult height.

Physical Growth

Matching the observable changes in body size, other aspects of growth also proceed at a fast pace. Cartilage turns to bone, muscle fibers thicken, and teeth break through the gums. Most impressive are the changes that occur in the brain and nervous system—and what these changes mean for cognitive and social development. At birth, an infant's brain weighs close to a pound and is fully equipped with all of the 100 to 200 billion neurons it will have in its lifetime. But the brain and nervous system are immature, and relatively few synaptic connections have formed. Starting in the first year, the neural axons grow longer, the dendrites increase in number, and a surplus of new synaptic connections are carved into the brain—trillions, more than can possibly be used. Then in childhood, the brain undergoes a pruning process in which often-used synaptic connections survive while unused connections are eliminated. The neurons also become more tightly wrapped in myelin sheath, the fatty substance that enhances the speed of neural transmission. This process of myelination continues to early adolescence.

The brain's maturation is closely linked to psychological development. For example, natural increases in the number of synaptic connections, or "pathways," in the brain are often accompanied by advances in cognitive ability (Gage & Baars, 2018; Gazzaniga, 1984). The same is true of myelination. At birth, the brainstem and spinal cord—which govern simple reflexes—are well myelinated and in working order. The visual cortex is less developed, as is the newborn's vision. Those parts of the cortex that control attention and information processing are not fully myelinated until the ages of 4 to 7 years, which is when children become capable of reading and simple arithmetic (Parmelee & Sigman, 1983). In short, growth spurts in the brain correspond nicely to developments of the mind.

Motor Skills

From infancy to childhood, physical growth—as measured by gains in height and weight—is the most predictable change that takes place. The second most predictable is the coordination of *motor skills*. On average, babies can lift their heads at 2 months, sit without support at 5.5 months, crawl at 10 months, and walk at 12 months. Children differ somewhat in their *rate* of motor development, but the *sequence* of events is usually the same: Lifting the head precedes sitting, which precedes crawling, standing, and walking. Infants differ in the way they learn to crawl and then walk. For example, some begin by inching along on their bellies before crawling on hands and knees; others do not (Adolph, Vereijken, & Denny, 1998). More advanced activities like running, jumping, climbing stairs, and throwing a ball develop later and are less rigid in their sequence. So are fine motor skills like gripping a pencil, tying a shoelace, and using a fork (Wade & Whiting, 1986).

The development of motor skills can be a fun experience for children and their parents.
iStock.com/mapodile

Cognitive Development

You don't have to be a psychologist to notice physical growth or the development of motor skills. The real challenge is to unravel the mystery of how children of different ages think—not just what they know but *how* they come to know it and the mistakes they make along the way (Siegler, 1998). To understand this aspect of development, we turn to Jean Piaget (1896–1980), the most influential figure in the study of cognitive development.

Piaget's Theory

Born in Switzerland, Jean Piaget was a precocious boy interested in seashells, birds, and mechanics. He published his first article at the age of 10 and was offered a curator-ship at a natural history museum in Geneva while in high school. At 21, Piaget earned a doctorate in biology. Then he studied psychology in Paris and took a job administering intelligence tests to schoolchildren. As luck would have it, this experience proved to be a turning point—for Piaget and for psychology.

While testing, Piaget became intrigued by the mistakes children made. Far from being random or idiosyncratic, he realized, these errors signaled that young children use a logic that is foreign to adults. To understand this logic, Piaget had children explain their answers, a simple but informative method. From these interviews, Piaget published a series of articles, and in 1921 he was named director of a child development institute in Geneva. The seed was planted. In the years that followed, Piaget studied thousands of children, including his own. By the time he died in 1980, he had written more than 40 books on how children think about people, nature, time, morality, and other aspects of the world (Ginsburg & Opper, 1988; Piaget & Inhelder, 1969). Today, anyone interested in cognitive development—parents, educators, or philosophers—begins with Piaget.

Piaget's theory rests on the assumption that children are curious, active, and constructive thinkers who want to understand the world around them. According to Piaget, infants and children form **schemas**, or mental representations of the world, in order to make sense of it. Through a process of **assimilation**, he said, children try to fit new information into their existing schemas. Through the process of **accommodation**, they modify existing schemas to fit new information. Viewed in this way, development is not a process by which children merely "copy and paste" what they are told. Rather, the creation of knowledge occurs "through a complex interplay between preexisting knowledge and new information gathered through interaction with the external world" (Siegler & Ellis, 1996, p. 212).

In a study that illustrates how children form and revise their conceptions in light of new information, Stella Vosniadou and William Brewer (1992) asked children of varying ages about the shape of the earth. Seeing that the ground they walk on is flat, preschoolers believe the earth as a whole is flat—either rectangular or disk-shaped. What happens when they're told that the earth is spherical? Rather than shed their incorrect schemas for an accurate representation, they incorporate the sphere into their beliefs that the earth is flat by constructing the synthetic models shown in Figure 9.9. Many first-graders adopt the "dual earth" notion that the earth is round but that humans live on a flat surface. By the third grade, many children see the world as a "flattened sphere" or as a "hollow sphere"—like a fishbowl with people living on the bottom. By fifth grade, most have adopted the correct "sphere" model. Gradually, then, through a dynamic interplay of assimilation and accommodation, children form new and accurate conceptions of, quite literally, the world.

Another assumption made by Piaget is that as children get older, they advance through a series of chronological *cognitive stages*, each distinguished by a specific kind of thinking. For Piaget, cognitive development is like climbing a staircase, one step at a time. This view has two implications. First, even though some children advance more quickly than others, the sequence is universally the same: The first stage must precede the second, which must precede the third, and so on. In this way, each stage holds both the fruits of the past and the seeds of the future. Second, even though the cognitive stages build on one another, the increments are seen as qualitative and abrupt, not quantitative and gradual—in other words, like climbing stairs, not a ramp. As shown in Figure 9.10, Piaget described four stages in cognitive development: sensorimotor, preoperational, concrete operational, and formal operational.

Sensorimotor Stage. Beginning at birth and lasting about two years, infants come to know the world by touching, grasping, smelling, sucking, chewing, poking, prodding, banging, shaking, and manipulating objects. Piaget called this the **sensorimotor stage** of development. As far as infants are concerned,

Jean Piaget
Staff/AFP/Getty Images

schemas. In Piaget's theory, mental representations of the world that guide the processes of assimilation and accommodation.

assimilation. In Piaget's theory, the process of incorporating and, if necessary, changing new information to fit existing cognitive structures.

accommodation. In Piaget's theory, the process of modifying existing cognitive structures in response to new information.

sensorimotor stage. Piaget's first stage of cognitive development, from birth to 2 years old, when infants come to know the world through their own actions.

FIGURE 9.9 ■ Changing Schemas of the Earth

Compared to preschoolers, who think the world is flat, school-age children at first assimilate the spherical model into their schemas, then accommodate their schemas to form an accurate representation.

Sphere

Flattened sphere

Hollow sphere

Dual earth

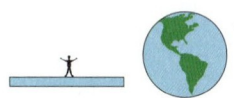

Disc earth

Rectangular earth

object permanence. Developing at 6 to 8 months of age, an awareness that objects continue to exist after they disappear from view.

separation anxiety. Among infants with object permanence, a fear reaction to the absence of their primary caregiver.

By uncovering the hidden toy, this baby is demonstrating object permanence.

Doug Goodman / Science Source

FIGURE 9.10 ■ Piaget's Stages of Cognitive Development

Piaget portrayed development as a staircase in which the different steps, or stages, are distinguished by specific kinds of thinking.

- **Formal operational (12 years–adult):** The adolescent can reason abstractly and think in hypothetical terms.
- **Concrete operational (7–12 years):** The child can think logically about concrete objects and can thus add and subtract. The child also understands conservation.
- **Preoperational (2–6 years):** The child uses symbols (words and images) to represent objects but does not reason logically. The child also has the ability to pretend. During this stage, the child is egocentric.
- **Sensorimotor (0–2 years):** The infant explores the world through direct sensory and motor contact. Object permanence and separation anxiety develop during this stage.

an object exists only for the moment and only when it is in direct sensory contact. In fact, research shows that the way infants explore objects changes predictably with age. Beginning at 1 month old, they learn about the shape, texture, and substance of objects with the mouth (Gibson & Walker, 1984). At 5 months, they also acquire information with their hands (Streri & Pecheux, 1986) or by coordinating movement of the hands, eyes, and mouth together (Rochat, 1989). This sensorimotor mode can be seen in the way young babies try to stuff crayons, toys, and limbs into the mouth—and in the way they pull, push, shake, squeeze, and bang everything they can get their fingers on.

According to Piaget, the crowning cognitive achievement of the sensorimotor stage is the development of **object permanence**, an awareness that objects continue to exist even after they disappear from view. This may not seem to be much of an accomplishment, but Piaget (1936) noticed that whenever he covered a toy with his beret or a handkerchief, babies younger than 8 months old did not protest, made no effort to retrieve it, and were unaware of its absence—even when the toy made noise. Quite literally, out of sight means out of mind. Given this lack of object permanence, it is no wonder that until babies approach their first birthday, they never seem to tire of playing peek-a-boo, a game in which each round is met with a fresh look of surprise.

Object permanence may be linked to important aspects of social development. It is probably not a coincidence that just as babies become capable of recalling objects that are out of view, they also begin to experience **separation anxiety**, a fear reaction to the absence of their primary caregiver. The baby who is not aware of its mother when she isn't perceptible will not seem distressed by her absence. However, the baby who has achieved object permanence is capable of missing its mother and cries frantically the moment she slips out of sight. As with other aspects of sensorimotor development, this pattern—of object permanence accompanied by several months of separation anxiety—can be seen in cultures all over the world (Moore & Meltzoff, 1999; Whiting & Edwards, 1988).

Preoperational Stage. Sometime during the second year, developments in memory lend permanence to people no longer in view, and peek-a-boo games give way to hide-and-seek. At 8 months old, a delay of 2 or 3 seconds is enough for babies to become distracted from the location of a hidden object. At 10 months, they can wait 8 seconds, and at 16 months, 20 to 30 seconds (Kail, 1990). At 20 months old, babies who watched an adult hide a Big Bird doll in a desk drawer or behind a pillow were able to find the toy even on the next day (DeLoache & Brown, 1983). The second year is also a time when children become more verbal and more abstract in their thinking. For the first time, words and images are used to symbolize objects. And one object may be used as a symbol for another. Thus, children pretend that the spoon is an airplane and their mouth a runway, and they understand that when an adult pretends to pour tea over a toy monkey, the monkey becomes "wet" (Harris & Kavanaugh, 1993; Kavanaugh, Eizenman, & Harris, 1997).

Despite enormous cognitive gains, the 2-year-old does not think like an adult or even like a school-age child. According to Piaget, preschoolers are in a **preoperational stage**, during which they reason in an intuitive, prelogical manner, unable to perform mental operations. Preoperational thought has two key features. The first is that the child is **egocentric**, or self-centered—unable to adopt the perspective of another person. At this stage of development, children tend to assume that you can tell what they are thinking, that you know all the people in their lives, or that you can see a picture in a book they are reading. Play a hiding game with 3-year-olds, and they'll stand in full view and cover their eyes—assuming that if they cannot see, then they cannot be seen. Or eavesdrop on a conversation between 4-year-olds and you will hear each of them jabbering away and taking turns—oblivious to what the other is saying. These "collective monologues" are also evidence of egocentrism.

A second limitation at this stage is that the preoperational child does not understand **conservation**, the idea that physical properties of an object stay the same despite superficial changes in appearance. To illustrate, take a tall, thin 8-ounce glass of lemonade and pour it into an 8-ounce cup that is shorter and wider. You and I know that the quantity of liquid stays the same regardless of changes in the container's shape, but to the preschooler the tall, thin glass holds more to drink. Figure 9.11 illustrates additional examples. Flatten a ball of clay and the preoperational child will think there is less. Roll the clay into a long thin snake, and the child will think there is more. Or if you use a handful of pennies, the child will think there are more if you spread them out than if you push them close together. What these demonstrations show is that, until the age of 7, children can't seem to *center* on two object features at a time (height and width, for example) or mentally reverse such operations as pouring, rolling, flattening, or spreading. Very simply, "What you see is what you get."

Concrete Operational Stage. At about the age of 7, children advance to what Piaget called the **concrete operational stage**, becoming capable of logical reasoning. By their first few years of schooling, children are able to take the perspective of another person and understand that various object properties can stay the same despite surface changes in their appearance. They can now group similar objects into categories, order the objects according to size or number, and appreciate the logic that if A is greater than B, and B is greater than C, then A is greater than C. Capable of performing concrete operations, the first-grader can also be taught to add and subtract without counting (Resnick, 1989).

Piaget believed that conservation marks the beginning of a major advance in cognitive development, one that lasts to the age of 11 or 12. However, even though concrete operational children appear to reason like adults do in response to specific problems, they do not think on an abstract level. Children may know that 2 is an even number and that 2 + 1 is an odd number, and they may well realize the same for 4 + 1, 6 + 1, and 100 + 1—but they will not necessarily put the pieces together to form the more general principle that any even number plus one yields an odd

preoperational stage. Piaget's second stage of cognitive development, when 2- to 6-year-olds become capable of reasoning in an intuitive, prelogical manner.

egocentric. Self-centered, unable to adopt the perspective of another person.

conservation. The concept that physical properties of an object remain the same despite superficial changes in appearance.

concrete operational stage. Piaget's third stage of cognitive development, when children become capable of logical reasoning.

In the concrete operational stage, a child can be taught to add and subtract without counting.

iStock.com/FlamingoImages

FIGURE 9.11 ■ Tasks Used to Test Conservation

According to Piaget, the ability to conserve marks the transition from the preoperational to the concrete operational stages of cognitive development.

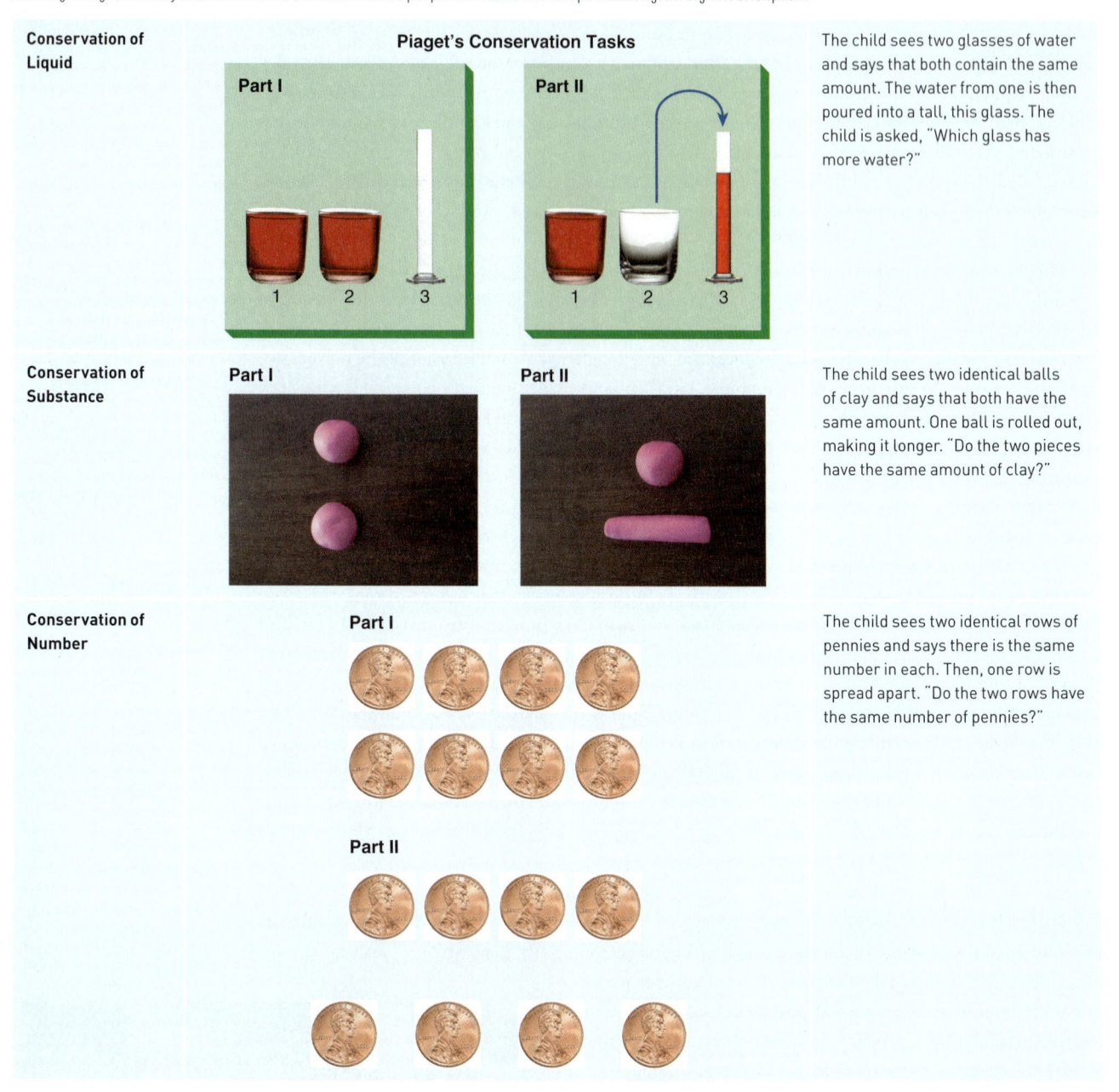

Piaget's Conservation Tasks

Conservation of Liquid

The child sees two glasses of water and says that both contain the same amount. The water from one is then poured into a tall, this glass. The child is asked, "Which glass has more water?"

Conservation of Substance

The child sees two identical balls of clay and says that both have the same amount. One ball is rolled out, making it longer. "Do the two pieces have the same amount of clay?"

Conservation of Number

The child sees two identical rows of pennies and says there is the same number in each. Then, one row is spread apart. "Do the two rows have the same number of pennies?"

number. The ability to use methods of logic—inductive reasoning, deductive reasoning, and systematic hypothesis testing—is the hallmark of Piaget's next stage, the formal operational stage of cognitive development.

Formal Operational Stage. What distinguishes Piaget's third and fourth levels of development is the ability to formulate solutions in advance and to reason on a logical, hypothetical level. To illustrate, imagine how you might approach the following test. You have four beakers, each containing a colorless chemical, and a dropper filled with potassium iodide. You are then told that when the potassium iodide is mixed with one or more of the four chemicals, it produces a bright yellow solution. Your task is to determine which chemicals to mix. Faced with this problem, the typical 9- or 10-year-old child will arbitrarily begin to mix chemicals, trying one combination after another until stumbling upon the solution. In contrast, the typical 13-year-old will plan a systematic course of action, first adding potassium iodide to each beaker, then trying other combinations of chemicals and keeping track of outcomes until the problem is solved (Inhelder & Piaget, 1958).

Unlike Piaget's first three stages, which appear roughly on schedule in different cultures, the **formal operational stage** does not characterize all adults. Many Western adults are not necessarily formal operational in their problem solving, often falling back on rules of thumb known as heuristics. Piaget's point, however, is that adolescents and adults are cognitively *capable* of formal operations, whereas children are not. It's interesting that, in France, adolescents tested in the 1990s scored higher on measures of formal operational thought than those tested 20 to 30 years earlier—when fewer teenagers attended secondary school. Piaget may have been right about the age at which children first become capable of formal operational thought, but performance is also influenced by schooling, culture, and other variable experiences (Flieller, 1999).

formal operational stage. Piaget's fourth stage of cognitive development, when adolescents become capable of logic and abstract thought.

Piaget's Legacy

Piaget was an astute observer of children, and his writings brought the study of cognitive development to life (Beilin, 1992; Flavell, 1996; Piaget, 1976). Important practical lessons also stem from his theory—like the idea that a child may not be developmentally "ready" for reading, writing, arithmetic, taking turns, and other cognitive and social tasks. Today, many caregivers try to "jump-start" their children by enrolling them in academically rigorous preschools or by training them for athletics and other types of competition. Thanks to Piaget, however, many child development experts are quick to warn that children should not be pushed too early—before they have matured to the necessary stage of development (Elkind, 1989; Zigler, 1987).

Many of Piaget's writings have stirred both criticisms and vigorous defenses of his theory (Hammond, 2014; Lourenco & Machado, 1996) Neo-Piagetian researchers are revising and extending his work in important ways. One criticism is that Piaget's interview method was crude by today's standards. As a result, he underestimated young children's cognitive abilities and taxed their capacity to process task-relevant information (Case, 1992). Some studies have shown that babies even have an intuitive grasp of simple laws of physics. For example, they look longer at a ball that appears to roll through a solid object or at one that appears to stop in midair than at one that does *not* produce an unexpected physical outcome (Baillargeon, 1994; Spelke, Breinlinger, Macomber, & Jacobson, 1992).

Other examples illustrate the point. Piaget said that object permanence did not develop until 8 months of age, when babies first try to retrieve toys that have been hidden from view. But what if a more sensitive measure were used? Renee Baillargeon (1986) recorded eye movements and found that 6-month-olds reacted with surprise when an object temporarily hidden from view seemed to disappear. This experiment, and others like it, suggests that an out-of-sight object may not be out of mind at this age (Meltzoff & Moore, 1998). Similarly, Piaget thought that 3- and 4-year-olds are egocentric, unable to take the perspective of another person. Yet children at these ages speak more simply to babies than to adults and show pictures to others with the front side facing the viewer (Gelman, 1979). They also understand that someone else will see a visible object only if that person's eyes are open and aimed in the right direction—and only if there are no vision-blocking obstacles in the way (Flavell, 1999).

Were Piaget's timetables wrong? Yes and no. Yes, it's clear that young children are more precocious than Piaget had realized. But no, his developmental sequences—for example, the hypothesis that object permanence precedes conservation, which in turn precedes formal logic—have stood up well. Piaget may have underestimated the overall *rate* of development, but he was right about the *sequence* of achievements.

A second question is often raised that goes right to the heart of Piaget's theory: Does cognitive development progress through distinct stages, like a staircase, or is it more gradual,

Although Piaget estimated the ages at which certain cognitive skills develop, experience plays an important role. For example, teaching children about measurement, such as needed with baking, can help to develop their understanding of the concept of conservation.

iStock.com/FatCamera

like a ramp? Or, as Robert Siegler (1996) has suggested, should cognitive development be depicted in waves, with the flow of new strategies overlapping with the ebb of old strategies? Robert Thatcher and others (1986) measured electrical brain activity in 577 humans ranging from 2 months old to young adulthood and spotted distinct growth spurts that corresponded roughly to the emergence of Piaget's stages. Yet Piaget's all-or-none view of development has been challenged inasmuch as children often master a concept in some tasks but not in others. Four-year-olds can order colors from light to dark, but they can't order sticks by length. Six-year-olds understand conservation in the pennies problem before they can solve the liquid and clay problems. These kinds of inconsistencies tell us that cognitive concepts don't burst into mind all at once but, instead, are used for one task at a time. What, then, are we to conclude? Once again, Piaget was only partly correct. The pace of development is more rapid at some ages and in some cultures than others. But within these periods of rapid growth, it takes time for new skills to reach their full maturity.

LEARNING CHECK

Stage Managing

Now that you've been born, you are ready to go through Jean Piaget's theoretical four stages of cognitive development. But at which stage does each of the developments below occur? Answer S for Sensorimotor, P for Preoperational, C for Concrete Operational, or F for Formal Operational.

1. You can group similar objects into categories.
2. You can formulate solutions in advance.
3. You understand that objects continue to exist even after they disappear from view.
4. You know that words and images can symbolize objects, but you don't understand that objects retain their physical properties despite superficial changes in appearance.
5. You can be taught to add and subtract without counting, but you can't think in abstract terms.
6. You can reason intuitively but you can't adopt the perspective of another person.
7. You can reason on a logical, hypothetical level.
8. You become afraid when your primary caregiver is absent.

(Answers: 1. C; 2. F; 3. S; 4. P; 5. C; 6. P; 7. F; 8. S.)

Social Development

Born completely helpless, equipped with reflexes that orient them toward people, responsive to human faces and voices, and prepared to mimic facial expressions on cue, the newborn is an inherently social animal. For eager parents, the baby's first smile is the warmest sign of all. It's funny sometimes how nature finds ways to lubricate a parent-newborn bond. If you gently stroke or blow on a newborn baby's face, it reacts to this stimulation by contracting its muscles and pulling back its mouth into what looks like—you guessed it—a smile (Emde, Gaensbauer, & Harmon, 1976). Like adults, infants exhibit different types of smiles—some that last longer than others, and some with the mouth open rather than closed (Messinger, Fogel, & Dickson, 1999; Mireault, 2017). In fact, babies don't crinkle up their eyes and flash "social smiles" at people until they are at least six weeks old (Bower, 1982).

Social-Cultural Influences on Cognitive Development

When we consider the work of Piaget, we find a largely internal process of maturation and development. Piaget proposed, in part, that cognitive development was a process of maturation largely within the child. In this light, Piaget tended to focus more so on the child than on the environment within which the child lives. However, as with many aspects of psychology, it is difficult to define behavior outside the context of the environment within which behavior occurs, and this includes our cognitions.

Contemporary researchers therefore also identify the need to focus on social and cultural factors that can influence cognitive development.

The origins of this social-cultural focus on cognitive development can be traced, in part, to Russian psychologist Lev Vygotsky, who proposed that children develop though a process of **internalization**. Through this process of internalization, children absorb knowledge from the social-cultural context within which they live, and this can impact their cognitive development. Indeed, there is good evidence from cross-cultural studies on development to support the notion that cognitive development may not be as biologically predetermined as Piaget initially proposed. Cross-cultural studies on development evaluated the cognitive abilities of children from diverse backgrounds and revealed that the universality of Piaget's claims should be called into question; for example, showing that people from many cultures failed to show evidence that they had attained formal operations (Rogoff, 2002; Rogoff & Morelli, 1989). Piaget himself eventually acknowledged that achieving the abilities characterized as formal operations may rely more on the type of children assessed than on the unfolding of biologically predetermined cognitive stages of development (Lourenco & Machado, 1996).

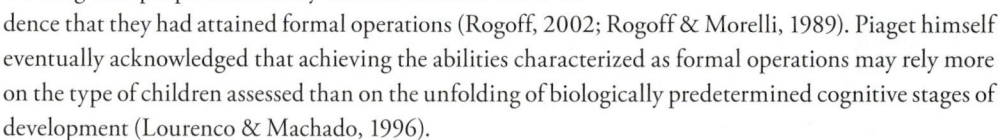

The process of internalization helps to explain the effect culture can have on cognitive development. Specifically, cross-cultural studies reveal that cognition is dynamic in that children show evidence that their cognition develops to perform culturally valued abilities (Serpell & Boykin, 1994). For example, the tasks that Piaget invented for his studies were based on preconceived notions for what constituted appropriate cognitive abilities. In other words, the tasks Piaget constructed were biased toward his own conceptions for what abilities should be valued, particularly in the latter stages he proposed. However, cross-cultural studies reveal that performance on the tasks that Piaget invented are quite dependent on the type of schooling that the children receive (Rogoff & Chavajay, 1995). If Piaget had evaluated abilities to weave, for example, his children may have appeared to underperform in their development compared to, say, Mayan children from Guatemala (Rogoff, 1990). Psychologists today use these types of social-cultural findings to balance their perspectives regarding the nature and nurture of cognitive development.

The Parent-Child Relationship

Many developmental psychologists believe that a baby's first relationship to the mother or another caregiver sets the stage for social development. Clearly, it is critical in certain species of animals. Newly hatched ducks and geese, for example, will follow their mother automatically—an instinctive form of attachment called **imprinting**, which serves the purpose of keeping the young birds in proximity to each other and to their mother. Intrigued by how automatic the process is, Konrad Lorenz (1937) suspected that any moving, honking stimulus (whether it is the mother or not) will trigger this response. So he squatted, clucked, and moved about in front of birds hatched in an incubator, and it worked like a charm. One of Lorenz's favorite pictures shows him strolling through high grass trailed by a line of geese imprinted by his actions. In fact, geese will follow all sorts of first-seen moving objects—decoys, rubber balls, wooden blocks, and even a striped metal pipe (Hess, 1959).

If baby birds are to follow the mother, they must be exposed to her within the first day or so, during a **critical period** for the development of imprinting. In humans, attachment is less automatic, the mother plays a more active role, and there is no "critical" period. Still, the infant does form a very deep and affectionate emotional bond called an **attachment**.

The First Attachment.
Beginning in the second half of the first year, accompanying the development of object permanence, infants all over the world form an intense, exclusive bond with their primary caregiver. This first relationship is highly charged with emotion and emerges with consistency from

Soon after hatching, ducklings will follow the first moving object they see. In this photograph, the imprinted object was ethologist Konrad Lorenz.
Nina Leen / Contributor/The LIFE Picture Collection/Getty Images

internalization. A process proposed by Vygotsky through which children absorb knowledge from the social-cultural context within which they live that can impact cognitive development.

imprinting. Among newly hatched ducks and geese, an instinctive tendency to follow the mother.

critical period. A period of time during which an organism must be exposed to a certain stimulus for proper development to occur.

attachment. A deep emotional bond that an infant develops with its primary caregiver.

one culture to the next. What motivates the infant? Some years ago, psychologists assumed that infants would become attached to anyone who feeds them and satisfies their basic physiological needs. That assumption was then put to rest by a classic series of dramatic experiments by Harry Harlow (1958, 1971).

In the 1950s, Harlow was breeding rhesus monkeys to study learning. Infant monkeys were separated from their mothers, fed regularly, and housed in cages equipped with a blanket. At one point, Harlow noticed that the infants had become passionately attached to their blankets—as they would be to their mothers. It is interesting that, like Linus of the old comic strip *Peanuts*, many normal children in the United States, Sweden, New Zealand, and elsewhere clutch security blankets (Passman, 1987). At any rate, this observation sparked in Harlow an interest in the origins of attachment: Are infants drawn to mother for the comfort of her warm and cuddly body or for the food and nourishment she provides? To answer this question, Harlow placed newborn monkeys into a cage that contained two substitute mothers—one was a wire-mesh cylinder with a wooden head; the other was covered with soft terrycloth. Both provided a bottle of milk with a nipple. It was no contest. The infant monkeys spent almost all of their time with the terrycloth doll. In fact, they clung to the cloth substitute even when it did not contain a bottle for feeding. Given the choice, the infant monkeys preferred "contact comfort" over food. In later variations of this study, Harlow found that warmth and rocking motions further intensified the contact comfort provided by a cloth mother. Infants need more from parents than milk and a clean diaper.

Sadly, Harlow found that the infant monkeys raised with inanimate cloth substitutes grew into unhealthy adults, fearful in new settings, socially awkward, and sexually unable to function. But the discovery that contact comfort has therapeutic benefits for the isolated infant has proved useful. For example, consider the predicament of a typical premature baby—kept in an incubator without physical contact and at risk for a host of problems later in life. Working in the maternity ward of a hospital, Saul Schanberg and Tiffany Field (1987) treated premature babies with 45 minutes of body massage for 10 days and then compared their progress to others not receiving massage. The two groups drank the same amount of formula, but the massaged infants gained 47 percent more weight; were more alert, active, and coordinated; and left the hospital an average of six days earlier—for a savings of $10,000 per infant in expenses. Similar interventions show that massage therapy has beneficial effects on premature infants, cocaine-exposed infants, and full-term infants born to depressed mothers. According to Field (2001), touch is a valuable therapeutic tool—not only for premature infants but also for children and adults, many of whom are "touch-deprived."

Styles of Attachment. Watch different parents and infants, and you'll notice that some attachments seem more intense than others. Is it possible to measure the intensity of this first relationship? How much of it depends on the parent and how much on the child? And does an infant's first attachment foreshadow their social relationships later in life? Developmental psychologists are actively researching questions such as these about the attachment process (Cassidy, Shaver, & Main, 1999; Lai & Carr, 2018).

Drawing on evolutionary theory and on Harlow's studies with primates, psychiatrist John Bowlby (1969) theorized that infants are born with a repertoire of behaviors (like sucking, gazing, clinging, and crying) designed to elicit nurturance from parents and lay a foundation for a strong relationship. Bowlby (1988) further argued that this attachment provides a secure base from which children can explore their surroundings and develop their cognitive and social skills. The impact of this first relationship, he said, influences future relationships and lasts a lifetime.

Is it possible to measure the quality of the infant-parent attachment? To study the process systematically, Mary Ainsworth and her colleagues (1978) created the **strange-situation test** in which the caregiver (usually the mother) brings the baby into an unfamiliar laboratory playroom and proceeds through a routine whereby the caregiver and a stranger come and go according to a set script. Based on how the infants react to the separations and reunions with the caregiver, they are classified as having either a secure or an insecure attachment. Infants with a **secure attachment** wander and explore

In his classic studies with rhesus monkeys, Harlow found that the babies clung to soft cloth "mothers"—and preferred this contact comfort to wire-mesh mothers that provided milk.

Nina Leen/The LIFE Picture Collection /Getty Images

strange-situation test. A parent-infant "separation and reunion" procedure that is staged in a laboratory to test the security of a child's attachment.

when the caregiver is present, react with distress when they leave, and beam with sheer delight when they return. These babies shower the returning caregiver with smiles, laughter, hugs, and kisses. Infants having an **insecure attachment** are classified into two types. Some are *anxious* and resistant, clinging to the caregiver, crying when they leave, and reacting with anger or indifference when they return. These babies often push the returning caregiver away, stiffen up, squirm, or even cry when picked up. Others are more detached and *avoidant*, not caring if the caregiver leaves and ignoring them when they return. In the United States, about two-thirds of infants tested are securely attached (Lamb, Sternberg, & Prodromidis, 1992)—and the classifications are generally the same whether the caregiver and child are tested in an unfamiliar setting or at home (Moullin, Waldfogel, & Washbrook, 2014; Pederson & Moran, 1996).

It's hard to know for sure what causes a secure or insecure attachment. Clearly, parenting style is important. Caregivers of securely attached babies are more sensitive to their needs, more affectionate, and more playful (Isabella & Belsky, 1991; Moullin et al., 2014). The infant's temperament also plays a role, though, as securely attached babies are by nature less fussy and more easygoing than those who are not securely attached (Benoit, 2004; Kagan, Snidman, & Arcus, 1992). After several months, as you can imagine, the personalities of the caregivers and child become so tangled up that trying to separate the effects of one on the other is like trying to untie a twisted knot.

How important is this first relationship? Does a secure and trusting attachment provide a foundation for close friendships later in life? What is the long-term fate of an insecurely attached infant? According to Bowlby, secure and insecure infants form "internal working models" of attachment figures—and these models influence their perceptions of others and their relationships later in life. Indeed, research shows that infants classified as securely attached at 12 months are later more positive in their outlook toward others (Cassidy, Kirsh, Scolton, & Parke, 1996)—and have somewhat better peer relations in school (Schneider, Atkinson, & Tardif, 2001). Some researchers are further exploring the possibility that our attachments in infancy exert long-term effects on our romantic relationships as adults (Gleeson & Fitzgerald, 2014). It's important, however, not to overstate the case by concluding that our future relationships are predetermined in the first year of life. The infant-to-child-to-adult correlation is far from perfect, and early attachments per se may not *cause* the differences that appear later in life. Responsive parents and easygoing infants may well continue in their positive ways long after the first-year attachment period has ended. These later interactions may prove to be just as important in a multitude of family settings, whether children are raised by their biological parents, relatives, LGBTQ+ parents, or by adoptive parents (Kuppens & Ceulemans, 2019; McConnachie et al., 2020).

The Day-Care Controversy. If you've seen black-and-white reruns of *Leave It to Beaver, Father Knows Best*, or other TV shows produced in the 1950s, you are no doubt familiar with the image of the "traditional" all-American family: a working father and a mother who stays home to take care of the house and kids. The typical 21st-century American child grows up in a vastly different environment, consisting of either a single caregiver or two or more caregivers who both work outside the home. As a result, many infants in the United States spend much of their "attachment time" with babysitters, in day-care centers, or at home with other relatives. This scenario is not true of all societies. In China and Russia, mothers are encouraged to work full time while their children are cared for in state-supported institutions. In Israel, mothers who live on rural collective settlements called *kibbutzim* work on the farm while childcare specialists raise the children in groups. Does nonmaternal or nonpaternal child care for infants disrupt the security of attachment? Should new parents—starting careers or struggling to make ends meet—worry about harmful long-term effects? As the research evidence mounts, professional opinion is divided.

In homes where children are raised by two parents or caregivers, some psychologists suggest that dual employment where both parents work full time puts infants at risk for

secure attachment. A parent-infant relationship in which the baby is secure when the parent is present, distressed by separation, and delighted by reunion.

insecure attachment. A parent-infant relationship in which the baby clings to the parent, cries at separation, and reacts with anger or apathy to reunion.

Attachment is a critical bond that can have a big impact on a child's development.
iStock.com/fizkes

insecure attachments and minor adjustment problems. Studies using the strange-situation test show that day-care infants whose caregivers both work full time are somewhat more likely than home-raised infants to be insecurely attached (36 percent to 29 percent). However, although infant-caregiver attachment is closely related to the time a caregiver and child spend bonding, many additional factors need to be considered (Friedman & Boyle, 2008). It is largely a matter of understanding the role of child care in the context of broader sociocultural factors that include the quality of care a child receives, the type of family unit (e.g., single parent, same- or different-sex parents), the degree of extended family involvement (e.g., grandparents, uncles, aunts), and more.

To summarize, there is no "bottom line." Day care and home care seem to foster different personal styles, though neither is necessarily better for healthy development. If one, both, or many caregivers work outside the home, day care is a viable option that does not necessarily have harmful effects. What matters is not the *quantity* of time spent in one setting or the other but the *quality* of that time (Golombok et al., 2021; Ruzek, Burchinal, Farkas, & Duncan, 2014). Just as some caregivers are more attentive, loving, and stimulating than others, so too are some other childcare situations. Those that are spacious, well equipped, and adequately staffed to provide warm, individual attention and stimulating activities offer an excellent alternative to caregivers who work outside the home.

Peer Relationships

The mother-child attachment is only one factor in social development, as children form key relationships with grandparents, siblings, teachers, classmates, and neighbors. The older the child is, the more important are *horizontal relationships*—friendships among peers, or equals.

The growth of friendships may not pass through stages, but certain patterns are evident. At 1-year-old, infants show little interest in each other and come together only if drawn to the same person or toy. At first, these interactions breed friction, but with experience infants learn to take turns and minimize conflict. By age 2, children play near each other rather than alone. By 4 or 5, they begin to prefer some playmates over others. Although these relationships are quickly formed, quickly broken, and based on convenience, they mark the beginning of what can be called friendship (Hartup & Stevens, 1999; Kochendorfer & Kerns, 2020).

It is interesting that most child relationships are between members of the same sex—not only in American culture but in others as well. Watch children on a school playground, and you will find that 4-year-olds spend three times as much time with playmates of the same sex as with those of the opposite sex. By the age of 6, this ratio can be as large as 11 to 1 (Maccoby & Jacklin, 1987). Why is gender segregation common? According to Eleanor Maccoby (1998), it's because boys and girls prefer different kinds of activities. Boys stereotypically like competitive, rough-and-tumble play that takes up lots of space and involves large groups; girls stereotypically like to congregate at home with one or two close friends. These differences may have a socializing impact on children: The more boys and girls play with same-sex peers, the more "boyish" and "girlish" their behavior becomes over time (Martin & Fabes, 2001). However, other factors also impact play behavior. For example, boys tend to behave more stereotypically of their gender than girls do, and this behavior is more stereotyped when playing with adults. While children rarely play exclusively with same-sex children, about one-fourth of interactions involve at least one different-sex peer. These mixed-sex interactions tend to occur closer to adults and tend to be stereotypes for each gender (Fabes, Martin, & Hanish, 2003).

Just as attachments inside the home are important to healthy social development, so is the formation of friendships outside the home. To study this aspect of development, researchers ask schoolchildren to rate themselves and to nominate the classmates they like the most and the least. They may also get ratings from teachers and parents, observe behavior firsthand, and combine the results for each child. Using these methods, researchers have identified four types of school-age children—compared to those in the average majority—based on their "sociometric" status among peers. As described by Andrew Newcomb and others (1993), children can be classified as *popular* (sociable, skilled, and liked), *rejected* (aggressive or withdrawn, lacking in social skills, and disliked), *controversial* (sociable but often aggressive, both liked and disliked), or *neglected* (less sociable and less aggressive than average, and seldom mentioned by peers).

As you might expect, popular children have the most friends (George & Hartmann, 1996) and derive social and emotional benefits from these friendships (Newcomb & Bagwell, 1995). In contrast, children who are rejected by classmates are the most "at risk." Longitudinal studies show that they are lonely and are more likely to drop out of school, have academic and drug problems, and have social-adjustment problems as adults regardless of whether they are raised by their biological parents, relatives, LGBTQ+ parents, or by adoptive parents (McConnachie et al., 2020; Wolke & Lereya, 2015). It's hard to know from these correlations if peer rejection is just part of a deeper problem or if it's the problem itself. And it's hard to know how possible it is to escape the peer rejection trap once caught in it. Some children, once rejected, are always rejected, but others manage over time to gain acceptance from peers. So what distinguishes the two groups? Marlene Sandstrom and John Coie (1999) studied 44 rejected schoolchildren over a two-year period. They found that those who believed they were partly to blame for their social difficulties, who took part in extracurricular social activities, and who had concerned parents who played an active role in their social lives were ultimately the most likely to gain acceptance.

Importantly, a growing concern today is cyberbullying, which occurs when someone uses electronic devices or media—such as mobile phones, text messaging, instant messaging, blogs, websites (e.g., Instagram, YouTube), or emails—to upset or harm another person. Examples of cyberbullying include having private emails or text messages posted where others can see them, such as on social media, having rumors spread about a person online, and having embarrassing pictures posted online without a person's permission. Rates of cyberbullying are around 4.5 percent for victims of bullying and 2.8 percent for perpetrators of bullying, with upwards of 90 percent of the cyberbullying victims also experiencing face-to-face bulling (Olweus, 2012). Many bullied children suffer in silence, reluctant to tell their parents, teachers, or other adults about their experiences, in part, out of fear of reprisals or because they experience shame (Benton, Golden, Chamberlain, George, & Walker, 2010). It is especially important for health practitioners to address bullying and reduce mental health problems related to it, particularly for cyberbullying, which disproportionately affects minority youths (Wolke & Lereya, 2015, Zhu et al., 2021).

ADOLESCENCE

LEARNING OBJECTIVES

Explain the importance and challenges of making the transition to adolescence.

- Explain why the timing of puberty is important in the transition to adolescence.
- Define moral reasoning, and outline how the levels of moral thought differ according to Kohlberg.
- Analyze why adolescence has been described as a period of "storm and stress" and summarize the evidence that supports this description.
- Discuss why adolescents tend to engage in risky behaviors, compared to adults.

Many cultures have initiation rites to celebrate the passage from childhood to adulthood. Among the African Thongas, boys who reach puberty are beaten with clubs, shaved, stripped, exposed to cold, forced to eat unsavory foods, circumcised, and secluded for three months. Among certain Native American groups of North America, girls who menstruate for the first time are bathed, their bodies are painted red by older women, and they are isolated for four days. The ritual may vary, but most cultures have ways of marking adolescence. While these practices differ from many of those in the United States, they emphasize the universality of this transition from childhood to adulthood as a significant milestone cross-culturally. As illustrated in Figure 9.12, confirmation, bar mitzvah, and the shift from

adolescence. The period of life from puberty to adulthood, corresponding roughly to the ages of 13 to 20.

middle school to high school are some of the ways that Westerners recognize this transitional time of life (Cohen, 1964).

Adolescence is to adulthood what infancy is to childhood: the dawn of a new era, like a second birth. Beginning with a biological event (puberty) and culminating in a social event (independence from parents), adolescence in the United States corresponds roughly to the teen years, 13 to 20. No longer a child but not yet an adult, the adolescent is in an important transitional phase of life—a time characterized by biological, cognitive, and social changes (Sawyer, Azzopardi, Wickremarathne, & Patton, 2018).

Puberty

puberty. The onset of adolescence, as evidenced by rapid growth, rising levels of sex hormones, and sexual maturity.

The biological motor of adolescence is **puberty**, the gradual onset of sexual maturation brought on by rising hormone levels—estrogen and progesterone in females, and testosterone in males. Plus or minus two years, females reach puberty between the ages of 11 and 13, and males between the ages of 13 and 15. This sex difference can be seen in the rapid growth that propels children to almost their full adult height. Review Figure 9.13, and you will find that the growth spurt begins a bit earlier for girls but lasts longer for males, eventually leaving adult men an average of 5 inches taller than women. For females, puberty is highlighted by the first menstrual period, called **menarche**. A female's development during puberty is a continuous process, and her first period is only a single event in a continuum of hormonal and psychological changes that take place (Hoyt, Niu, Pachucki, & Chaku, 2020). Still, it is often a memorable event in a female's life, one that she experiences with a mixture of pride, nervousness, and embarrassment (Greif & Ulman, 1982).

menarche. A girl's first menstrual period.

A female's reaction to puberty is influenced in part by her age. When Anne Petersen (1984) interviewed hundreds of adolescents, she found that females who mature early tend to be dissatisfied with their size, weight, and figure. A mature seventh-grade female may tower over classmates and get teased about her appearance. In general, females who reach puberty early rather than "on time" or late are the most negative about their own body image and are more likely to diet and develop eating disorders (Graber, Brooks-Gunn, Paikoff, & Warren, 1994).

It's interesting that the timing of menarche is highly influenced by environmental factors (Chaudhuri, Bhattacharya, & Sengupta, 2016). In the 1800s, the average American female didn't begin to menstruate until the age of 17. As a likely result of improved nutrition, the average female now menstruates at a much younger age. In fact, pediatric studies in the United States show that today's females are starting puberty even younger, typically at around 12 years (Chumlea et al., 2003; Khadilkar,

---

FIGURE 9.12 ■ Passage To Adulthood

Many cultures celebrate the passage from childhood to adulthood. A Hispanic girl poses with her proud parents to celebrate her 15th birthday, marking her passage from girlhood to womanhood (a). At age 13, Jewish boys achieve their manhood in a religious ceremony known as a bar mitzvah (b).

Sollina Images/Getty Images/; edelmar/Getty Images

FIGURE 9.13 ■ Adolescent Growth Spurts in Height

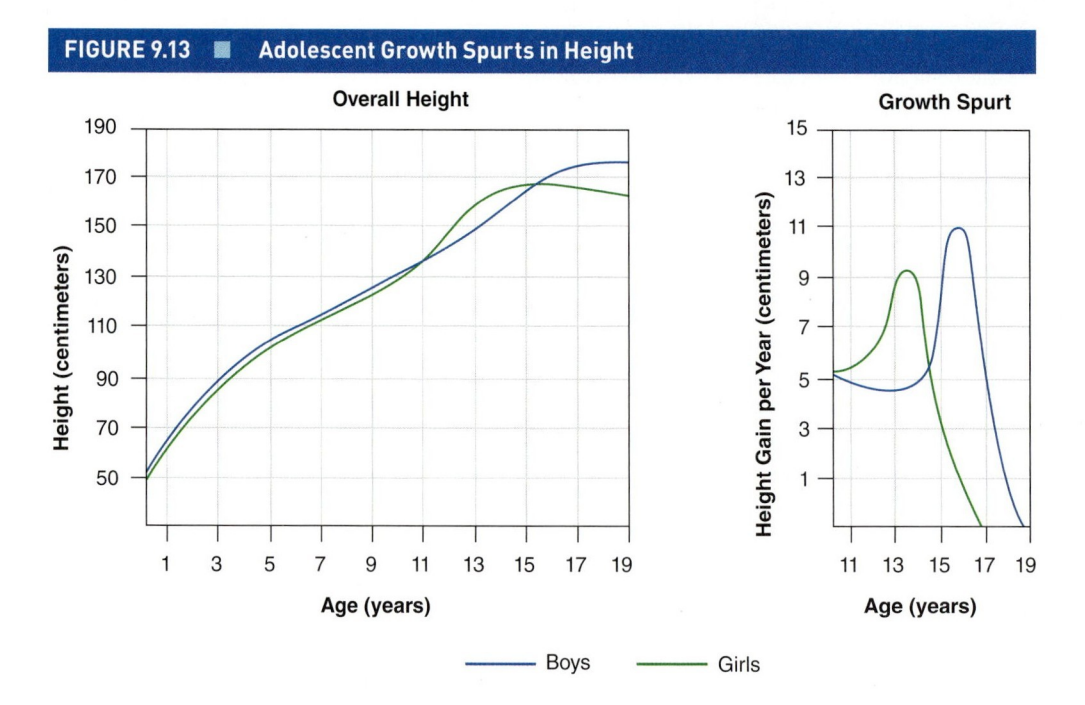

Overall Height / **Growth Spurt**

— Boys   — Girls

Stanhope, & Khadilkar, 2006)—a trend that concerns parents and pediatricians. There are, however, vast individual differences. Models, gymnasts, and ballet dancers who exercise hard, diet, and have low body fat tend to reach menarche later in their teens (Brooks-Gunn & Warren, 1985). At the other extreme, an alarming number of females are reaching puberty as young as 8 or 9 years old—particularly if they are overweight (Li et al., 2017; Wang, 2002).

For males, puberty is marked by the growth of the penis and testes, accompanied by facial hair, pubic hair, increased muscle mass, a lowered voice, and broadened shoulders. Akin to menarche, the high point of male puberty is a male's first ejaculation, which occurs at about the age of 14 (although it is not until a year later that the semen holds live sperm cells ready for reproduction). As with females, males are reaching puberty at a younger age than in the past (Brix et al., 2019; Herman-Giddens, Wang, & Koch, 2001)—with some maturing earlier than others. Among males, however, this is a generally positive experience, and early maturation—which means being taller and stronger than peers at younger ages—tends to be a social asset (Brix et al., 2019; Stein & Reiser, 1994).

Cognition and Moral Reasoning

Paralleling the physical growth spurt brought on by puberty is what might be called a cognitive growth spurt. You may recall Piaget's observation that adolescents are capable of logic and abstract reasoning—hallmarks of the *formal operational stage* of cognitive development. This capacity for abstraction spurs teenagers to think critically and to challenge parents and societal norms. Eliot Turiel (1983) found that at the age of 12 or 13, adolescents begin to see various social conventions—for example, appropriate clothing, hairstyle, or the proper way to address a teacher—as arbitrary and unreasonable.

According to Piaget (1932), the adolescent's capacity for abstraction gives rise to a more mature form of **moral reasoning**. Building on the idea that moral reasoning requires cognitive sophistication, Lawrence Kohlberg (1981, 1984) argued that adolescence is a particularly rich time of life for moral development. Kohlberg presented stories containing moral dilemmas to children, adolescents, and adults and asked them how these dilemmas should be resolved. To illustrate, consider the following classic story:

> In Europe, a woman was near death from cancer. One drug might save her, a form of radium that a druggist in the same town had recently discovered. The druggist was charging $2,000—10 times what the drug cost him to make. The sick woman's husband, Heinz, went to everyone

moral reasoning. The way people think about and try to solve moral dilemmas.

he knew to borrow the money, but he could only get together about half of what it cost. He told the druggist that his wife was dying and asked him to sell it cheaper or let him pay later. But the druggist said, "No." The husband got desperate and broke into the man's store to steal the drug for his wife. (Kohlberg, 1969, p. 379)

What do you think: Should Heinz have stolen the drug? Were his actions morally right or wrong, and why? Based on responses to stories like this one, Kohlberg proposed that people advance through three levels of moral thought, further divided into six stages. First, there is a *preconventional level*, in which moral dilemmas are resolved in ways that satisfy self-serving motives—so an act is moral if it enables someone to avoid punishment or obtain reward. Second is a *conventional level*, in which moral dilemmas are resolved in ways that reflect the laws of the land or norms set by parents and other sources of authority. Thus, an act is moral if it meets with social approval or maintains the social order. Third, adolescents and adults who attain Piaget's formal operational stage of cognitive development may also reach a *postconventional level* of moral thought, one that is based on abstract principles such as equality, justice, and the value of life. At this level, an act is moral if it affirms one's own conscience—even if it violates the law.

Is this theory of moral development valid? Over the years, it has drawn an enormous amount of attention, support, and criticism. To Kohlberg's credit, he and others have found that as children and adolescents mature, they climb his moral ladder in the predicted order, step by step, with periods of transition in between steps (Colby, Kohlberg, Gibbs, & Lieberman, 1983; Mathes, 2019). Research shows that although most 7- to 10-year-olds are preconventional in their moral thinking, many 13- to 16-year-olds reason in conventional terms, and few adolescents—or even mature adults, for that matter—resolve moral issues on a postconventional level (illustrated in Figure 9.14).

There are three criticisms of Kohlberg's theory. The first is that it cannot be applied equally across all cultures. This is partly true. John Snarey (1985) reviewed studies in 28 countries and found that most children and adolescents advanced at the same rate and in the same sequence through the first two levels. He also found, however, that only educated middle-class adults from urban societies consistently exhibited postconventional forms of morality. In Kohlberg's dilemmas, many non-Westerners—including Tibetan Buddhist monks and respected village leaders from Papua New Guinea—do not reason at this third level. Why? In cultures that value traditions, rules, and authority over individualism and personal rights, conventional moral reasoning is common and desirable.

A second criticism is that the model is gender biased. When Kohlberg first constructed his dilemmas, he tested only males and used their responses as a moral yardstick. Yet according to Carol Gilligan (1982), women address moral issues "in a different voice." Concerned more about compassion for

FIGURE 9.14 ■ Levels of Moral Reasoning

On standard moral dilemmas, most 7- to 10-year-olds are preconventional in their reasoning, whereas most 13- to 16-year-olds are conventional. Very few participants resolved these dilemmas on a postconventional level.

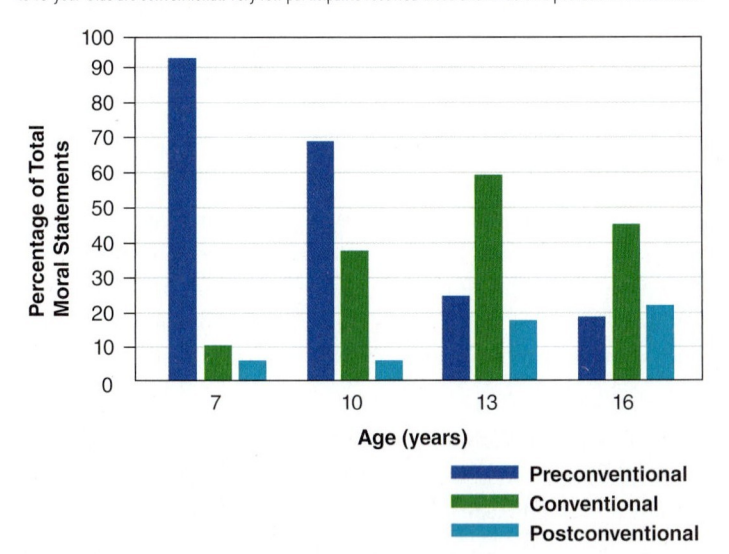

others than about abstract rules, the female voice may be different—but not morally inferior. Gilligan's point has some intuitive appeal, but it lacks empirical support. Public opinion pollsters do find that women care more than men about social issues and relations. But moral development researchers find that women and men obtain similar scores on Kohlberg's dilemmas (Rest, 1986; Walker, 1984). Also contradicting the assumption that people resolve moral dilemmas in set ways, as defined either by Kohlberg or Gilligan, is that men and women are flexible in their reasoning. The kinds of moral judgments we make in real life depend on the situations we're in and the kinds of dilemmas we face (Krebs, Denton, Vermeulen, Carpendale, & Bush, 1991; Wark & Krebs, 1996).

Finally, many developmental psychologists have argued that Kohlberg's model is limited because morality consists of more than just an ability to think about hypothetical dilemmas in ways that are intellectually sophisticated. There are two criticisms of Kohlberg's model in this regard. John Haidt (2001) argues that people make moral judgments intuitively, in a process that is fast, effortless, and without awareness, like a learned reflex—not through slow, hard, and conscious process of cognitive reasoning. A second criticism concerns the assumption that moral reasoning breeds moral conduct. But are postconventional thinkers kinder, more caring, or more virtuous in their daily affairs than those lower on the cognitive ladder? Moral actions speak louder than words, which is why William Damon (1999) asks, "Regardless of how children develop their initial system of values, the key question is: What makes them live up to their ideals?" (p. 75).

It's a sad and ironic postscript that Kohlberg—who had a chronic parasitic infection that caused him excruciating stomach pain—died by suicide in 1987, before his 60th birthday. He had discussed his predicament with a close friend and concluded that someone with social responsibilities to others ought morally to go on. But overcome with pain and deeply depressed, he drowned himself in Boston Harbor (Doorey, 2020).

Social and Personal Development

To many people, the word *teenager* is synonymous with ripped jeans, loud music, pierced body parts, long phone conversations, and sleeping past noon. The teen years are a curious time of life. Absorbed in closer-than-ever friendships, newly aroused by sexual urges, needing to fit in and yet wanting to stand out, feeling caught between parents and peers, and anxious about the future, the teen years are fraught with mixed emotions. The highs are high, the lows are low, and the changes are frequent.

According to Erik Erikson (1963), all people pass through a series of life stages, each marked by a "crisis" that has to be resolved in order for healthy development to occur. During the transitional period of adolescence, the central task is to form an *identity*, or self-concept—hence, the term **identity crisis**. Some teenagers pass through this stage easily—clear about who they are, what values they hold, and what they want out of life. Others drift in confusion as they struggle to break from their parents, find the right friends, establish their sexual orientation, and set career goals for the future. For Erikson (1959), this identity crisis is best described by a sign he once saw in a cowboy bar: "I ain't what I ought to be, I ain't what I'm going to be, but I ain't what I was" (p. 93).

Whatever identity issues adolescents have, there are three aspects of social and personal development that all must come to grips with: parent relationships, peer influences, and sexuality.

identity crisis. An adolescent's struggle to establish a personal identity, or self-concept.

Parent Relationships

For the parents of a cuddly new baby, it's hard to imagine that the intense emotional bond could ever be broken, or even cracked. To the parent or caregiver of a teenager, it's no longer so hard to imagine. Whether the topic is a blaring speaker, school grades, money, or dirty laundry, it seems that parents and adolescents engage in a power struggle, involved in one squabble after another. As described by the mother of an 11-year-old daughter, "It's like being bitten to death by ducks" (Steinberg, 1987, p. 36).

As children mature, what happens to their relationship with parents and caregivers, and what is the effect? Through questionnaires and interviews, and by observing interactions in the laboratory and in the home, researchers are coming to answer these questions. What emerges from these studies is a portrait of parents and teenagers characterized by two changes. First, coinciding with the onset of puberty and physical maturation, there is a rise in tension between 12- and 13-year-olds asserting their independence and parents, especially the mother. Young adolescents and parents argue about twice a week—but over routine household matters such as taking out the garbage, not about explosive issues such as sex, religion, or politics (Smetana, 1988). Despite cultural differences, similar interaction patterns have been observed between Chinese parents and adolescents in Hong Kong (Yau & Smetana, 1996).

A second change is that adolescents undergo a period marked by both *disengagement* and *transformation* in their family relationships. Reed Larson and his colleagues (1996) studied more than 200 Chicago-area boys and girls from fifth to eighth grades and then returned four years later when they were in high school. For one week at a time, each subject carried an electronic pager and was signaled several times a day during normal waking hours. Whenever they were signaled, the subjects had to indicate where they were, whom they were with, what they were doing, and how they felt. Together, the students provided a total of 16,477 reports. There were two key results. First, there was a steady decline in the sheer amount of waking time spent with family members—from 35 percent in the 5th grade to 14 percent in the 12th grade. Interestingly, the students spent the same number of hours alone with mothers and fathers but "disengaged" from family group situations, siblings, and other relatives (illustrated in Figure 9.15). Second, there were marked changes in the way the students felt during family interactions. Most felt worse during the early adolescent years. But boys then became positively "transformed" within the family setting during the 9th and 10th grades, and girls followed suit in the 11th and 12th grades. This process of both *disengagement* and *transformation* in family relationships can foster more positive health outcomes such as alleviating stress (Chen, Brody, & Miller, 2017).

A unique generational characteristic of adolescents today is that they have access to modern technology, spending many hours a day using their devices. Whereas generations born even as late as the 1990s learned to use technology at later ages, generations born in the 2000s have had unprecedented access to technology, with the invention of Wi-Fi in 1991 (first accessible in homes in 1997) and the invention of the iPhone in 2007 (smartphones were invented in 1992 and the term *smartphone* was first used in 1995). This generational gap is of great interest in understanding the dynamics of parent-teen relationships in the technology age. The more time children spend on television, computers, devices, and gaming, the lower the quality of attachment teens have with their parents. The

FIGURE 9.15 ■ Patterns of Adolescent "Disengagement" From the Family

This study revealed that over the course of adolescent development, the amount of time spent with the family decreased by an average of 2.74 percent per year. As shown, there was not a similar decline in time spent alone with parents.

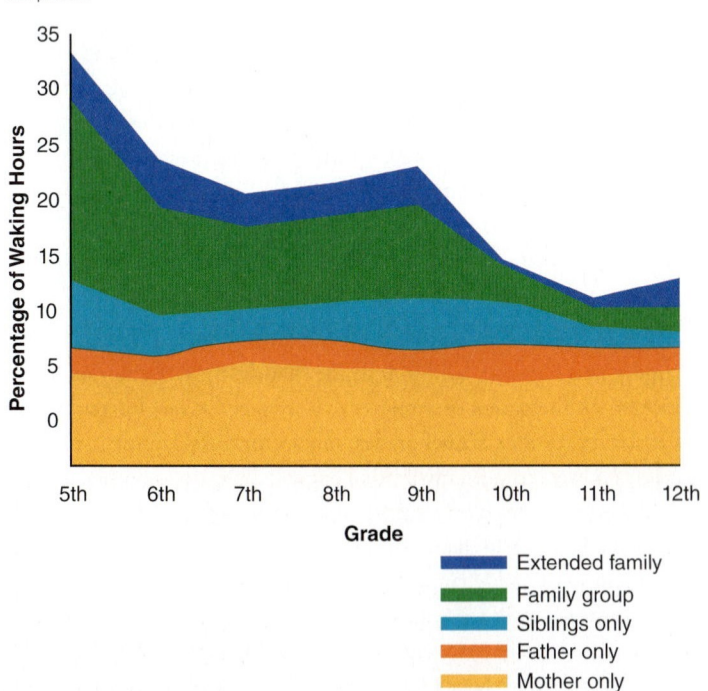

more time teens spend on technology, the less they interact socially with their parents and the less close they feel with their parents (Khan, 2011; Nabawy, Moawad, & Ebrahem, 2016). The overarching implication tends to suggest that communication is key. Parents should communicate with their children about their technology use to foster understanding and reduce risky online behaviors. The takeaway is that "parents need to educate themselves about social media and the ways their teens may use it, as well as the common risks, to help them understand and navigate the technologies" (Nabawy et al., 2016, p. 168).

Peer Influences

Another important aspect of adolescent social development is the heightened significance of peer groups and relations outside the home—long phone conversations, flirtation, and dating. For the first time, the child becomes primarily oriented to the outside world and may not even want to be seen with parents or other caregivers. Compared to childhood friendships, adolescent relationships are highly intimate. It's not unusual for best friends to talk freely about their thoughts and feelings and to reveal some of their deepest secrets (Berndt, 1996).

Compared to the gender segregation found in childhood friendships, adolescents often explore friendships with peers of the opposite sex. In the electronic pager study described earlier, the children exhibited a steady increase—from grades 5 through 8 to grades 9 through 12—in the amount of time they spent thinking about, and then being alone with, members of the opposite sex (Garcia, Reiber, Massey, & Merriwether, 2012). They even make the distinction that adults do, between opposite-sex friends and romantic heterosexual "boyfriends" and "girlfriends" (Fraley & Roisman, 2015).

For the LGBTQ+ community, there is much less research. (There is no consensus on the scope of the abbreviation LGBTQ+: Here, we use it to be inclusive of those who identify as lesbian, gay, bisexual, trans, queer, intersex, asexual, ally, pansexual, gender nonconforming, and others.) However, research conducted over the past 20 years clearly shows that sexual identity is formed early in life, with children having their first same- or opposite-sex "crush" similarly around the age of 10 years; identifying as LGBTQ+ on average around the age of 13 years; and expressing their gender identity as young as 2 to 3 years of age (Ryan, 2009). Coming out as LGBTQ+ can be difficult (Town, Hayes, Fonagy, & Stapley, 2021). While the culture today is generally more open than in previous generations, many members of the LGBTQ+ community still wait until their mid-teens to be open about their sexuality and gender identity. Researchers have identified more than 100 behaviors that families and caregivers use to react to their children's identity, with about half of them being accepting and half rejecting—both reaction types can affect a young person's health and well-being.

Adolescents often feel that their parents do not love them or, worse, hate them when they think their parents want to change who they are. The key implication for parents or caregivers of LGBTQ+ children is to listen (Town et al., 2021). Communication is key to reduce conflict and to avoid misunderstandings. For LGBTQ+ children, in particular, increased fighting and family conflict can result in an adolescent being removed from or forced out of the home—often placed in foster care, in juvenile detention, or even on the streets, thereby increasing their risk for abuse and mental health problems later in life (Carone, Bos, Shenkman, & Tasker, 2021; Moagi et al., 2021). When children feel they must hide their gender or sexual identity, this can lead to increased risky behaviors and even suicide (Garcia et al., 2020). The best advice for parents and caregivers is to be advocates for their children. When children feel valued by their parents, family, and schools, they learn to value and care about themselves (Glazzard & Stones, 2021).

Although most adolescents retain the fundamental values of their parents, they look to peers for guidance on how to dress or wear their hair, what music to listen to, how to speak, and how to behave in ways that are acceptable. As social beings, we all have a tendency to conform. Is this tendency more pronounced in adolescence? The answer is yes, especially in the early stages. In a classic experiment, Thomas Berndt (1979) asked students in grades 3, 6, 9, and 12 how they'd react if their friends tried to influence them to see a certain movie, go bowling, help a new kid on the block, or cheat on a test. The result: Conformity rose steadily with age, peaked in the ninth grade, and then declined. The tendency to conform is much weaker for actions that are immoral or illegal, but younger adolescents are the most likely followers, wanting more desperately to fit in (Brown, Clasen, & Eicher, 1986; Gavin & Furman, 1989).

As children reach adolescence, peer relationships become more important and developmentally influential, relative to parents.

Maskot/Getty Images

Sexuality

Triggered by rising hormone levels and physical maturation, adolescent males and females are sexual beings, curious and readily aroused. Whether teenagers act on these impulses, however, depends, in part, on social factors. National surveys of sexual practices—beginning with those conducted by Kinsey and his associates (1948, 1953)—have shown that there has been a constant 50 to 70 percent rate of sexual activity among males but that the proportion of sexually active females climbed from a low of 10 percent in the 1940s to a high of more than 50 percent in the 1980s. Since that time, however, rates of sexual activity have somewhat declined. In more recent years, 38 percent of teenagers in high school reported having had sexual intercourse (Abma & Martinez, 2020).

Even with American teenagers being less sexually active today than at the time of Kinsey's survey, they are also not always better informed about the health risks or more diligent in the use of contraceptives. In the United States, the teen birth rate (births per 1,000 females ages 15–19 in a given year) in the United States was 18.8—down 10 percent from 2015, and down an astonishing 70 percent from 1991 when it was at a record high of 61.8. Teen birth rates show disparities by race (lowest rates among non-Hispanic groups), socioeconomic status (SES; lower SES associated with higher rates), marital status (nearly 9 in every 10 teen births are outside of marriage), and more, but the teen birth rate today is at the lowest level ever recorded (Centers for Disease Control and Prevention, 2019a; Martin, Hamilton, Osterman, Driscoll, & Drake, 2018).

Teenage pregnancies may be part of a bigger problem: that adolescents are risk takers. Across a range of problem behaviors—such as smoking, drinking, abusing drugs, driving too fast, or having unsafe and unprotected sex—it seems that teenagers are more reckless in health-related matters than adults (Jessor, 1998; Lightfoot, 1999; Steinberg, 2010). Why does adolescence bring risk taking? Why, for example, do only 57 percent of high school students report using a condom at their most recent sexual intercourse, down from 63 percent in 2003 (Child Trends Data Bank, 2016)? One theory is that recklessness and delinquency stems from the fact that the early onset of puberty makes adolescents biological adults before they are accepted into the adult world. As such, they engage in sex, alcohol, and other "adult" activities available to them (Moffitt, 1993). An alternative theory is that adolescents engage in risk-taking behaviors not to join the adult world but to set themselves apart from it, as a form of rebellion (Harris, 1995). A third explanation looks to the brain with evidence that humans are "wired" to be risky in adolescence because the prefrontal cortex (the region of the brain largely responsible for decision making, problem solving, and more) is not yet fully developed (Reniers, Murphy, Lin, Bartolomé, & Wood, 2016).

Offering an important perspective, Frederick Gibbons and colleagues (1998) found that a key to understanding adolescents' risk taking is to realize that they often do not intend or plan these behaviors but, rather, find themselves having to react to social situations that call for risk. The party where cigarettes are passed around, the friend who wants to drive home after too many beers, and the date who is eager to have sex are the kinds of situations that often lead adolescents to engage in behaviors they did not plan. As one 16-year-old girl put it about her first sexual experience, "The first time, it was like totally out of the blue... I mean, you don't know it's coming, so how are you to be prepared?" (Stark, 1986, p. 28). When it comes to sex, of course, it's possible that teenagers do not make the necessary arrangements because they feel guilty about their desires. After all, if you're ambivalent, it's easier to justify getting "swept off your feet" and "carried away" than it is to have premeditated sex (Byrne, Kelley, & Fisher, 1993; Gerrard, 1987).

ADULTHOOD AND OLD AGE

LEARNING OBJECTIVES

Describe the physical and cognitive changes that are evident in adulthood and old age.

- Distinguish between the human life span and life expectancy.
- Summarize the physical changes that mark adult development.
- Discuss how capabilities related to memory and intelligence change with age.

For many years, it was assumed that our individual life scripts were written in infancy and childhood, waiting only to be acted out during our adult years. Freud felt that personality is largely formed by the sixth birthday, whereas Piaget claimed that the ultimate stage of cognitive development typically blossoms with puberty. These narrow views of the early years of life as critical may well describe changes in height, whereby early growth spurts are followed by a leveling off in adulthood. But such views do not yield an accurate picture when it comes to the full range of biological, cognitive, and social development. In this section, we will learn that even though the early years are in some ways formative, each of us continues to change in important ways when we mature in our adulthood and old age. As our ancestors told us, development is a lifelong process.

In all species of animals, there is a maximum **life span** that sets an upper limit on the oldest possible age of an organism under ideal conditions. Scientists have long held that just as a time clock has 24 hours in a day, our biological clocks contain a finite number of years in a life—about 120 among humans. Although this assumption still prevails, it is becoming a subject of controversy. In recent years, some biologists have managed to extend the life span of fruit flies, roundworms, and mice through selective breeding, genetic manipulation, and alterations in diet (Fontana & Partridge, 2015; Medina, 1996).

In most species, the **life expectancy**—the actual number of years lived by an average member—is shorter than the maximum life span. On average, guinea pigs live to the tender age of 3 years; dogs, 10 to 15 years; chimpanzees, 15 to 20 years; elephants, 30 to 40 years; and eagles, 105 years (Lansing, 1959). Among humans, the life expectancy is influenced not only by genetics but also by personality, nutrition, health practices, the environment, health care, and other factors. The average Roman in the year 1 CE lived to the age of 22. In the United States, the life expectancy rose from 36 in the 19th century to 47 in the year 1900 and to 78.7 in 2018. Women outlive men by an average of five to six years.

life span. The maximum age possible for members of a given species.

life expectancy. The number of years that an average member of a species is expected to live.

Physical Changes in Adulthood

At birth, a human infant has more than 100 billion brain cells. From that point, however, there is a steady process of attrition: Most neurons that die are not replaced, and those that survive tend to thin out. However, not all parts of the brain experience these changes at the same rate. In the brainstem, which controls many simple reflexes, there is little or no cell loss over time. Yet in the motor cortex and frontal lobes, which control motor and cognitive activity, thousands of neurons a day are lost, especially after the age of 50. By the time people are 80, the brain weighs 8 percent less than it did during the peak of adulthood. What's fascinating about

Betty Reid Soskin (born on September 22, 1921) became the oldest National Park Ranger serving the United States at age 99. In February 2018, she released a memoir, *Sign My Name to Freedom.*

AP Photo/Eric Risberg

this aspect of development is that the aging brain is simultaneously in a process of growth and decline. A newborn has a surplus of brain cells, so maturation involves the death of cells that are not used, coupled with the formation of new synaptic connections among those that remain. As we saw in the chapter on behavioral neuroscience, the human brain has great plasticity, a capacity to change as a result of experience. In the mature adult, then, more can be accomplished with less (Fuchs & Flügge, 2014; Scheibel, 1995).

The Adult Years

In addition to changes within the brain and nervous system, aging brings other physical changes to adults. Muscle strength, heart and lung capacity, speed of reflexes, and vision increase during the 20s, peak at about the age of 30, and then gradually start to decline. Also at that time, metabolism slows down, leading men and women to lose their youthful physique and to gain weight. Does this mean that young adults who rely on physical skills are over the hill by the age of 30? No, it depends on one's diet, health, and exercise habits and on the physical demands of a particular activity.

Baseball statisticians have analyzed thousands of career records of major league ballplayers and found that batters and pitchers peaked at the age of 29 (Bradbury, 2010). Football, basketball, and tennis players follow a similar age pattern. Yet world-class sprinters and swimmers peak in their teens and early 20s, and professional bowlers and golfers reach the top of their game in their 30s. It all depends on whether a sport requires speed and agility, endurance, or power—which decline at different rates. Age sets limits on what the body can do, but adults who keep in shape can minimize the effects of aging and stretch performance beyond the average.

One inevitable biological event for females is **menopause**, the end of menstruation, which signals the end of fertility. At about the age of 50, a female's ovaries stop producing estrogen. The most common symptoms of this change are "hot flashes" (sudden feelings of warmth usually in the upper body) and sometimes profuse sweating, dizziness, nausea, and headaches. Some females get moody, depressed, or anxious, but most are not terribly bothered by menopause. While attitudes toward menopause can vary—some females having negative reactions, and other females having positive reactions—data suggest that females with more optimistic attitudes toward menopause will tend to have a more positive overall body image and their depression levels tend to be lower (Erbil, 2018).

For males, there is no biological equivalent to menopause. Testosterone levels (which peak during adolescence) diminish only gradually, and even though the sperm count may drop, there is little loss of fertility. As with some females, some males pass through a difficult midlife period in which they question their marriage and career, worry about their health and sexual vigor, and feel frustrated about goals they did not achieve. For males and females alike, aging is not just a biological process but a psychological one as well. For example, how we think about our age is illustrated by a Marist Poll (2016) showing that as we age we view "middle-aged" differently:

> A majority of Americans, 55%, say 65 is middle-aged. 34% consider it old, and more than one in ten, 11%, thinks age 65 is young.... Not surprisingly, perceptions differ based on age. Americans 45 years old and older, 63%, are more likely than younger residents to consider 65 to be middle-aged. Those under 45 divide. 49% think 65 years of age is old while 47% say it is middle-aged. This is driven by Americans under 30, among whom 60% call 65 "old."

Old Age

As people enter their 60s and 70s, the cumulative effects of age begin to show, and the process seems to accelerate. Inside the body, brain cells die at a faster rate, the reflexes continue to slow, muscles continue to lose strength, the

menopause. The end of menstruation and fertility.

Jeanne Calment of Arles, France, is purportedly the oldest living human ever recorded. Biologists consider 120 as the upper limit of the human life span. In February 1997, six months before her death, Calment celebrated her 122nd birthday.

AP Photo/GEORGES GOBET

immune system begins to fail, bones become more brittle, joints stiffen, and the sense of taste and smell is reduced. Resulting from a steady loss of visual acuity, many older people are farsighted—and some have difficulty adapting to brightness or darkness. There are also noticeable auditory losses, as many older people report having trouble hearing high-pitched sounds and normal speech amid background noise. Perhaps most obvious are the effects of chronological age on appearance—including the wrinkles, stooped posture, thinned white hair, and shrinkage, as the average male loses about 1 inch in height and the average female loses 2 inches (Schaie & Willis, 2016; Whitbourne, 2002).

When Ponce de León left Spain in 1513 and landed in what is now the state of Florida, he was looking for the legendary and mythical fountain of youth. Biologists say that it's impossible to reverse the aging process, but can it be slowed? Can longevity be increased? According to current estimates, only one in a thousand people reading this will live to celebrate a 100th birthday—and there's no secret formula for the rest of us. Osborn Segerberg (1982) interviewed 1,200 centenarians and found that many of them cited peculiar reasons for their longevity ("because I sleep with my head to the north," "because I don't believe in germs"). In fact, what you need is a mixture of healthy genes, a healthy lifestyle, and luck (Palmore, 1982). Having a good attitude about aging may help too. In a study of 660 adults, Becca Levy and her colleagues (2002) found that men and women who had positive views of aging, when measured up to 23 years earlier, lived seven and a half years longer than those with less positive views of aging. Apparently a positive attitude about aging—which is accompanied by a strong will to live—is more predictive of longevity than gender, wealth, cholesterol level, blood pressure, weight, smoking, and exercise.

Aging and Intellectual Functions

The human body peaks at 30 and then declines gradually. What about the trajectory of *cognitive* development through adulthood? Does a weakened body signal a feeble mind, or are the two paths separate? At what age do "growth" and "maturity" turn to "aging" when it comes to memory, intelligence, and the ability to be productive at one's work?

Memory and Forgetting

Many people believe that as we age we inevitably begin to forget names, numbers, the car keys, and whatever else is important. According to this stereotype, people who are ready to retire are forgetful and absentminded. A deterioration of cognitive abilities is not, however, a necessary part of aging. Listen to the nostalgic remembrances of a grandparent and you will marvel at the ease with which he or she can vividly describe the details of an experience that took place a half-century earlier. Certain experiences leave an imprint on a person's memory, never to be erased. Sports, politics, wars, disasters, entertainment, and crime are topics that leave clear traces of newsprint on the mind (Howes & Katz, 1988). So do friends from earlier in life. Studies show that although elderly adults often cannot free-recall the names of high school classmates, they have an uncanny ability to recognize names, recognize faces, and match them up (Bahrick, Bahrick, & Wittlinger, 1975).

Clearly, there is much about our past that we tend not to forget, even as we get older. But studies have shown that although the elderly are as capable as younger adults of recognizing stimuli they have seen before, there is a decline in the ability to free-recall nonsense syllables, word lists, written prose, series of numbers, map directions, names of people just introduced, geometric forms, faces, and other newly learned material (Craik, 1992; Light, 1991).

With regard to memory, there are two neurocognitive bases for the age-related decline in memory. The first is related to sensory acuity—that as people age, their eyesight and hearing become impaired. When people who are very old are tested on cognitive tasks, their performance depends largely on their sensory acuity (Baltes & Lindenberger, 1997; Frieske & Park, 1999). The second change has to do with neural speed. In tightly controlled experiments, Timothy Salthouse (1996) and others have discovered that as people get older they process information and react more slowly—and that this loss of neural speed impairs performance on a range of cognitive tasks, including those used to test memory. The reason that slowness in the nervous system creates problems is that the more time it takes to process information, the less time people have to rehearse the material or attend to items that appear later in the sequence—like getting "backed up" on an assembly line.

Alzheimer's Disease

Although the brain and nervous system slow gradually as a natural part of aging, there are, sadly, many bright adults with brain damage that causes dementia—a mental disorder that causes severe cognitive impairments. Dementia can occur at any time during adulthood, but it is most likely to happen after age 65, striking about 10 percent of the elderly population. It is not a normal part of the aging process but, rather, stems from brain damage, a tumor, the cumulative effects of alcohol, or certain diseases (Alzheimer's Association, 2019; Parks, Zee, & Wilson, 1993).

The most common cause of dementia is **Alzheimer's disease**, a progressive and irreversible brain disorder that afflicts mostly the elderly and kills brain cells at a terrifying pace. When the German psychiatrist Alois Alzheimer first described the disease in 1906, it was rare because most people died young enough to avoid it. As the human life expectancy has increased, however, so has the prevalence of the disease, which also show disparities by race and ethnicity (illustrated in Figure 9.16). Today, the statistics on it are staggering. Worldwide, the Alzheimer's Association estimates that Alzheimer's disease claims as victims about 5 percent of adults by age 65, 10 to 15 percent by age 75, 20 to 40 percent by age 85, and nearly half of those over 85. At present, about 5.7 million Americans have Alzheimer's, accounting for nearly half of all nursing home admissions (Centers for Disease Control and Prevention, 2019b). As of 2012, the estimated annual cost of Alzheimer's disease in the United States exceeded $277 billion (Alzheimer's Association, 2019).

In patients with Alzheimer's disease, the brain tissue contains wads of sticky debris, called plaques, which exterminate brain cells. Although researchers do not know what sets the process in motion, they are in hot pursuit of clues (Terry, Katzman, Sisodia, & Bick, 1999), and have now even developed a vaccine for the disorder that they feel has promising potential (Bachmann, Jennings, & Vogel, 2019; Lambracht-Washington & Rosenberg, 2013). Whatever the root causes of Alzheimer's, the effects are devastating. It begins with simple lapses in memory and is soon followed by attention problems and an overall loss of cognitive functions. As the disease worsens over time, there are periods of disorientation, bursts of anger, depression, changes in mood and personality, and a deterioration of physical functions. Alzheimer's patients may lose track of a conversation, neglect to turn off a faucet or the stove, forget where they parked the car, or forget the name of a loved one. To make matters worse, they sometimes do not realize the extent of their problem (Kumar & Ekavali, 2015; McGlynn & Kaszniak, 1991). Once diagnosed, people with Alzheimer's live an average of eight more years.

There is no means of prevention and no cure for Alzheimer's disease, although treatments are on the horizon to help those with the disease live meaningful lives. For patients still in the early stages of Alzheimer's disease, there are memory-retraining programs to teach them how to use mnemonic devices and external memory aids. Treatments for Alzheimer's disease boost the actions of chemicals in the brain that carry information from one cell to another, although these treatments do not stop the

> **Alzheimer's disease.** A progressive brain disorder that strikes older people, causing a failure to retrieve memory and other symptoms.

FIGURE 9.16 ■ The Alzheimer's Problem

As the U.S. population ages, so does the projected number of Alzheimer's patients—from 5 million in 2014 to an estimated 14 million in 2060, and these projections show disparities by race and ethnicity.

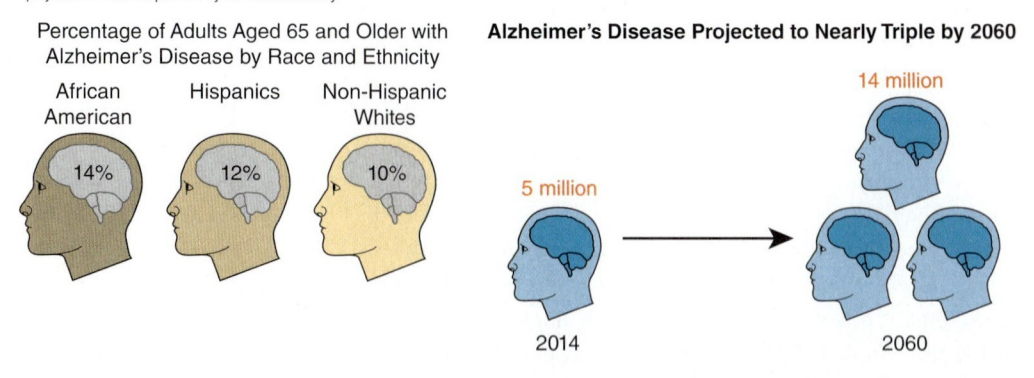

Percentage of Adults Aged 65 and Older with Alzheimer's Disease by Race and Ethnicity

- African American: 14%
- Hispanics: 12%
- Non-Hispanic Whites: 10%

Alzheimer's Disease Projected to Nearly Triple by 2060

- 2014: 5 million
- 2060: 14 million

Source: Centers for Disease Control

underlying cause of the disease: As more cells die, the disease will continue to progress. While for doctors, patients, and family members alike, managing this disease is not easy, researchers are optimistic that more effective treatments will emerge (Mayo Clinic, 2019).

Social and Personal Development

Psychologists who study infants and young children are impressed by how accurately chronological age can be used to mark the milestones of social development. The first social smile is seen at 6 weeks of age and is followed predictably by attachment behaviors, separation anxiety, crawling, walking, first words, and so on. Do adults similarly pass through an orderly succession of stages? Can chronological age be used to predict changes in self-concept, social relationships, or life satisfaction? Some say yes, others no.

What's Your Prediction?

What makes you happy? Happiness or, specifically, what makes us happy is not the same for all of us. For example, eating a yummy cake may make one person excited and another feel regret; having "just enough money to get by" may make one person stressed and another feel resilient. Psychologists have long struggled to define happiness (Paulson, Azzarelli, McMahon, & Schwartz, 2016). Can being *happy* actually lead to a better life? In short, the answer appears to be a cautious yes. Health and happiness generally go hand in hand, although the extent to which happiness leads to a longer life expectancy can vary based on many factors, including income, marital status, educational achievement, physical health, sexual activity, race, gender, age, and more (Lawrence, Rogers, & Wadsworth, 2015; Yang, 2008).

With this in mind, let's take an international perspective. Which nation is the healthiest? Are they also happy? Given what you know about biological, cognitive, and social development, what do you think? Table 9.2 lists the 10 healthiest nations according to the Bloomberg Healthiest Country Index (left column), and the 10 happiest nations according to the World Happiness Index (right column), as of 2019. How many of the top 10 healthiest nations do you think also cracked the top 10 in happiness? Before looking at Table 9.2, what's your prediction?

The answer is somewhat surprising. Only 4 of the top 10 healthiest nations (40 percent) cracked the top 10 for happiness. Most notably, the two healthiest nations, Spain (ranked 30th for happiness) and Italy (ranked 36th for happiness) ranked outside the top 25 for happiness. By comparison, the United States ranked 35th on the Bloomberg Healthiest Country Index and 19th for happiness—happier than

TABLE 9.2 ■ The Top 10 Healthiest and Happiest Nations in the World, 2019

Healthiest Nations	Happiest Nations
Spain	Finland
Italy	Denmark
Iceland	Norway
Japan	Iceland
Switzerland	Netherlands
Sweden	Switzerland
Australia	Sweden
Singapore	New Zealand
Norway	Canada
Israel	Austria

Source: Adapted from National Institutes of Health; World Happiest Report; Bloomberg Healthiest Country.

three of the top five healthiest nations: ahead of Spain, Italy, and Japan (ranked 58th for happiness). Tracking metrics like these can be important to strengthen our understanding of how health and happiness may be related (Institute of Medicine, 2011; Steptoe, 2019).

Ages and Stages of Adulthood

In contrast to the once-prevailing view that life patterns are set in early childhood, Erik Erikson (1963) proposed a life-span theory of development. According to Erikson, people mature through eight psychosocial stages, each marked by a crisis that has to be resolved. Stages 1 to 4 unfold in infancy and childhood; stage 5, in adolescence; and stages 6 to 8 in the years of adulthood.

In Erikson's view, those who emerge from adolescence with a sense of identity enter young adulthood, a time when it's critical to fuse with someone else, to find *intimacy* through meaningful close friendships or marriage. The next stage is middle adulthood, a time when people feel the need to achieve *generativity*, by contributing to the welfare of a new generation—at work, at home, or in the community. Research shows that most middle-age adults are more generative in their orientation than college students and young adults—and that generativity can be expressed in different ways (McAdams & de St. Aubin, 1998). The final stage is late adulthood, a time when it's important to gain a sense of *integrity*, a feeling that one's life has been worthwhile. Those fortunate enough to resolve their early crises enjoy a sense of serenity and self-fulfillment. Those not so fortunate live their final years in regret and despair. The final transition to late adulthood begins at age 60 to 65. Psychologist and theorist Daniel Levinson (Levinson, 1996; Levinson, Darrow, Klein, Levinson, & McKee, 1978) only speculated about this era, but others have found that this time can prove gratifying to those who are healthy and active. Studies show that, in this final transition, people who have more positive attitudes toward aging are predicted to have a better quality of life (Korkmaz, Kulakçı, Özen, & Veren, 2019).

LEARNING CHECK

Marking Milestones

Identify each of these milestones in human development with its closest description.

Menarche	Menopause	Identity Crisis	Critical Period
Life Expectancy	Life Span	Adolescence	Puberty

1. The onset of sexual maturation.
2. Time during which an organism must be exposed to a certain stimulus to develop properly.
3. The transition from childhood to adulthood.
4. The number of years that an average member of a species is expected to live.
5. A teenager's struggle to establish a self-concept.
6. A girl's first menstrual period.
7. The maximum age possible for members of a given species.
8. The end of menstruation and fertility.

(Answers: Menarche, 6; Menopause, 8; Identity Crisis, 5; Critical Period, 2; Life Expectancy, 4; Life Span, 7; Adolescence, 3; Puberty, 1.)

Critical Events of Adulthood

Erikson, Levinson, and other age-and-stage theorists believe that adults change in predictable ways and that these changes are linked to chronological age. But in light of the diversity of lifestyles across cultures and within a culture, which often lead people to take different developmental paths, others believe that the course of adult development follows critical events—regardless of the age at which they occur. What are these events? Ask people about turning points in their lives, and they inevitably mention starting school, graduation, their first job, getting married, having children, moving from one home to another, the death of a loved one, health changes, and world events (Ryff, 1989).

For certain milestones, timing seems critical. According to Bernice Neugarten (1979), people are sensitive to the ticking of a **social clock**—the set of culturally shared expectations, known to us all, concerning the best age for men and women to leave home, marry, start a career, have children, retire, and complete other life tasks. Social clocks differ from one culture to the next and from one generation to the next. In the 1950s, for example, most Americans believed that people should marry between the the ages of 19 and 24 and start a career between the ages of 24 and 26. Yet today, it seems more appropriate to attend college first and then marry and settle down later or, as is becoming increasingly common in recent years, for adults to cohabitate and engage in long-term romantic relationships after graduating from college without immediately (or even ever) getting married. In Neugarten's view, social clocks give us a developmental guideline, and people who are "out of sync" (e.g., leaving home too late or marrying too young) feel more stress than those who are "on time."

Not only are expected transitions important, but the fickle finger of fate can alter the course of development in unanticipated ways. Writing on the psychology of chance encounters, Albert Bandura (1982) noted that life paths are often twisted and turned by fortuitous events—as when a student is inspired to choose a career by a professor whose class happened to meet at a convenient hour or when a talented young athlete is permanently injured and sidelined by a hit-and-run driver. Such events cannot be anticipated, but autobiographers who reflect on their own lives are often struck by the powerful influence of these chance encounters (Handel, 1987).

Graduating college is a celebratory experience that can have a great impact on the developmental paths we pursue.
iStock.com/Motortion

social clock. A set of cultural expectations concerning the most appropriate ages for men and women to leave home, marry, start a career, have children, and retire.

TRY THIS!

Social Clock-Watching

A social clock is a set of culturally shared expectations about the best age to complete critical life tasks, such as getting married. But social clocks differ from generation to generation. To estimate how fast your own social clock is ticking, **TRY THIS:** Think about what which age you think each task should be completed. Then ask a few friends of your gender and approximate age to also answer, without showing them your answers.

| Leave home_____ | Finish school_____ | Start a career_____ | Get married_____ |
| Have a child_____ | Earn the most_____ | Have a grandchild_____ | Retire_____ |

How do your friends' answers compare to yours? Is your social clock fast, slow, or about the same? As a variation, ask some friends of the opposite sex to fill in the blanks. How do their answers compare? Another variation would be to ask people of your parents' generation. Is the social clock speeding up or slowing down?

Changing Perspectives on Time

As people get older, something happens to the way they perceive and manage time. In an article on "taking time seriously," Laura Carstensen and her colleagues (1999) theorized that people have an underlying sense about the amount of future that awaits them. As people age—and view their time as limited—they become more motivated to enjoy the present and less concerned with building bridges to the distant future. Compared to young adults on the lookout for new friends, social contacts, educational and job opportunities, and acquisitions, older adults are less willing to sacrifice the precious moments of the present for the future. Indicating this orientation toward time, research has shown that older people become narrower and more selective about whom they choose to spend time with, preferring an inner circle of family and close friends to all others (Lang & Carstensen, 2002).

It's interesting what changes with one's orientation to the present relative to the future. Among newly married couples, the initial honeymoon period is often followed by a decline in satisfaction for four years. Yet long-married couples—those who survive the post-honeymoon blues, the children, the empty nest, and other strains—grow closer. Over time, spouses and lifelong partners come to enjoy each other more, being less concerned with impressing, dominating, or molding one another (Levenson, Carstensen, & Gottman, 1993). At work, too, people who have spent many years on a job are most satisfied with it as they get older and more experienced. As with long-term romantic relationships, older workers care less about climbing the organizational ladder and focus on enjoying the job itself and their coworkers (Hoyer, Rybash, & Roodin, 1999).

Dying and Death

Humans are probably the only animals who know they are going to die or think about what it means. Many Westerners view death as a transition point in which the body ceases to exist but a soul lives on. Hindus and Buddhists believe in reincarnation. Still others view death as a final parting period. The ways in which death is viewed, the intense emotions it elicits, the ways dying people are treated, and how the dead are mourned all vary from one person, time, and culture to the next.

Whatever their beliefs, people must cope with the experience of dying and the terrifying prospect of their own demise. After interviewing hundreds of terminally ill patients, psychiatrist Elisabeth Kübler-Ross (1969) proposed that when people know they're dying, they pass through five stages in the coping process: (a) *denial* of their terminal condition ("It's not possible, it must be a mistake"); (b) *anger* and resentment, often directed at physicians and family members ("Why me? It isn't fair!"); (c) *bargaining* for more time ("God, let me live longer, and I'll be virtuous"); (d) *depression* accompanied by crying and refusal to see visitors ("Now I've lost everything I ever cared for"); and, finally, (e) *acceptance* of one's fate, often marked by a sense of peace and calm ("Oh well, what has to be, has to be").

Kübler-Ross's observations offer a glimpse at some of the ways that people cope with dying. Of course, people can die at all ages and not everyone passes in sequence through all the stages, which means that the experience can be different from one person to the next. Some patients struggle to the bitter end, whereas others accept death with quiet resignation (Kalish, 1981; Shneidman, 1984). For that reason, Kübler-Ross's stages should not be taken too literally. It may be reassuring for family members and friends to know that irrational denial and anger are common reactions, but it's also important to respect the uniqueness of the process. When a dying patient lashes out or bursts into tears of depression, these feelings should be treated with sensitivity, not dismissed as signs of a person "just going through a stage."

Thinking Like a Psychologist About Life Span Development

For the sake of convenience, developmental psychologists tend to separate the biological, cognitive, and social aspects of development. It's important to realize, however, that the way human beings mature, how they think, and how they interact socially with others are intertwined. For example, only when the brain is sufficiently developed for infants to be capable of object permanence do they experience separation anxiety. A baby must have a capacity to be conscious of its absent mother and father in order to be distressed by their absence. Similarly, as suggested by Piaget, social

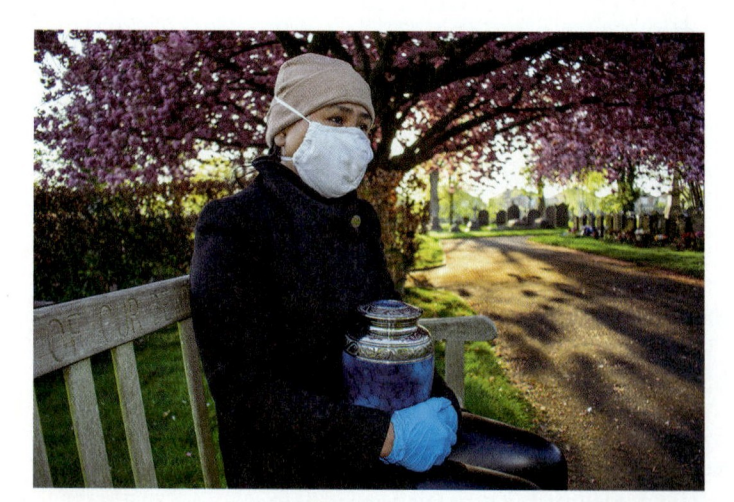

In the midst of a pandemic, a female mourner reflects on a bench as she holds a loved one's cremation ashes in a funeral urn.

iStock.com/Des Green

relations inspire cognitive growth. By talking, sharing, playing, arguing, and watching one another, young children learn from peer interactions to shed their egocentric ways and acquire logical skills such as conservation. In short, the various aspects of development are intimately linked.

Long past infancy and childhood, development continues across the entire life span. Adolescence is not a mere extension of childhood but a time of rapid change. Then there are the various stages of adulthood and old age. Physically, humans are in their prime at age 30, and then lose speed, power, sensory acuity, strength, and endurance. Cognitively, there are two courses of development. A small but steady decline occurs in mental speed, the ability to recall new information, and fluid intelligence. Yet autobiographical memories do not fade, and both crystallized intelligence and wisdom are relatively stable, if not incremental, with age. (Review the chapter on thought, language, and intelligence for more on these topics.) On the social and personal front, the trajectories of development are more difficult to plot because they are influenced more by critical life events. The one pattern that remains clear is that life satisfaction peaks in late adulthood and doesn't diminish until we are very old, nearing death.

There's one last point worth making about continuity and its relationship to how old we feel. I know someone in his 50s going on 60, and someone else who is in his 40s going on 18. It's often said that age is a state of mind. There is some truth to this statement. There is no denying chronology, which provides a rough measure of adult development. But as we saw in the study that opened this chapter, *subjective age*—that is, how old each of feels—is, in some ways, as psychologically important as how old we really are.

SUMMARY

GENES

Genetics is the branch of biology that deals with heredity. **Genes** are the biological units of heredity.

WHAT GENES ARE AND HOW THEY WORK
Each of the trillions of cells in your body contains in its nucleus 23 pairs of **chromosomes** consisting of strands of **DNA** made up of segments called genes. When an egg and a sperm cell unite to form a **zygote**, each passes along 23 chromosomes. The biochemical recipe they contain determines the unique characteristics of the offspring, including its sex. In 2001, scientists announced that they had completed sequencing the human genome—and today anyone can now have their DNA sequence read and decoded to reveal ancestry and even health indicators.

GENETIC BUILDING BLOCKS
All humans have certain genes in common, and with the exception of identical twins or triplets, we all have a distinct combination of genes that makes us unique. The 23rd pair of chromosomes determines your sex. Whereas everyone receives an X chromosome from the mother, there is an equal chance that the father will contribute an X or Y chromosome to the pair. If it is X, the offspring will be female (XX); if it is Y, it will be male (XY). Assuming no anomalies occur, which are rare, the biological sex of a child thus depends on the father's contribution.

PRENATAL DEVELOPMENT

The three stages of prenatal development help to explain the sensory and perceptual environment of a fetus in the womb during these stages.

THE GROWING FETUS
In the germinal stage (the first two weeks after **conception**), the fertilized **ovum**, or zygote, divides into a cluster of cells that pass out of the Fallopian tube and attach to the uterine wall. At this point, the zygote becomes an **embryo**. During the embryonic stage (third to ninth weeks), body parts form and organs start to function. After the ninth week, the embryo becomes a **fetus,** which develops movement, circulation, and even the ability to recognize its mother's voice.

Teratogens are toxic substances that can harm the embryo or fetus. Babies of mothers who are alcoholic often show a pattern of birth defects known as **fetal alcohol syndrome (FAS).** Even small doses of teratogens may be harmful.

FERTILITY

While most pregnancies result in a single birth, multiple births are more common today due to a variety of factors, including women conceiving later in age and the increased use of fertility drugs in developed countries.

THE REMARKABLE NEWBORN

Newborns experience many milestones, often very quickly, as they age.

OBSERVING INFANTS

To investigate how infants distinguish among stimuli, researchers often measure **habituation**, the tendency for attention to a novel stimulus to wane over time, and **recovery**, the tendency for a different stimulus to arouse new interest. These studies and others reveal that infants have remarkable abilities.

REFLEXES

Babies are born with many adaptive reflexes, such as the **grasping reflex**, the **rooting reflex**, sucking, and swallowing.

SENSORY CAPACITIES

Though nearsighted, newborns can distinguish between light and dark, follow movements, notice facelike patterns, and mimic adult gestures. Though hard of hearing, they respond to the human voice, especially high pitches and melodic patterns.

SENSITIVITY TO NUMBER

Using the habituation and recovery method, studies show that 5-month-old infants have a rudimentary sense of numbers, including the concepts of addition and subtraction.

THE INFANT AND GROWING CHILD

An infant experiences substantial biological, cognitive, and social development. The brain and body develop during childhood, and attachment has a critical role during this stage.

BIOLOGICAL DEVELOPMENT

Babies grow rapidly in the first year. The brain and nervous system develop more synaptic connections and increased myelination. Motor skills also advance in a predictable sequence. Yet these biological aspects of development are influenced by environmental factors.

COGNITIVE DEVELOPMENT

According to Piaget, infants and children form **schemas** in order to make sense of the world. Through **assimilation**, they try to fit new information into their existing schemas. Through **accommodation**, they modify existing schemas to fit new information.

Piaget described four stages in cognitive development. In the **sensorimotor stage** (birth to 2 years), infants learn through sensory and motor contact. They develop **object permanence**, an awareness that objects continue to exist after they disappear from view, and **separation anxiety**, a fear reaction to the absence of a caregiver. In the **preoperational stage** (2 to 6 years), children begin to reason in an intuitive, prelogical way. They are still **egocentric**, however, and they do not understand **conservation**—the concept that an object's physical properties stay the same despite superficial changes in appearance. The **concrete operational stage** (6 to 12 years) brings logical reasoning but not abstract thought. Finally, at the **formal operational stage** (12 years to adulthood), people learn to reason at an abstract level.

Piaget may have underestimated the rates of development, but he was right about the sequence. Likewise, he was only partly right about the sharp distinctions between stages. Researchers who study age-related changes in information processing have found that short-term memory and processing speed increase as children grow older.

Social Development

Some animals exhibit **imprinting**, an instinctive tendency to follow the mother during a **critical period** just after birth. In humans, the process is less automatic, but infants form an **attachment**, a deep emotional bond, with the primary caregiver. Studies of humans and monkeys show that "contact comfort" is an important source of attachment. The **strange-situation test** is used to distinguish between **secure attachment** and **insecure attachment**, a difference that results from both parenting style and the infant's own temperament. Although securely attached infants are later more independent and socially skilled, it isn't clear that the early attachment causes these results. In addition, through this process of **internalization**, children can absorb knowledge from the social-cultural context within which they live, and this can further impact their cognitive development.

On the effects of day care, recent evidence shows that enriched high-quality day care has more benefits than drawbacks. Horizontal (peer) relationships—mostly between children of the same sex—become more important as the child grows older. Popular children enjoy the social and cognitive benefits of many friendships, while children rejected by their peers are most at risk for later adjustment problems.

ADOLESCENCE

Adolescence is a transition from childhood to adulthood that corresponds roughly to ages 13 to 20 in our society.

Puberty

Adolescence begins with **puberty**, the onset of sexual maturation marked by rising levels of sex hormones and rapid growth. For girls, puberty brings **menarche**, the first menstrual period. Cultural practices and the timing of menarche influence a girl's reaction. Those who reach puberty early face embarrassment, adjustment problems, and a poor body image. For boys, puberty brings the first ejaculation, as well as growth of the sexual organs and other physical changes. For boys, early maturation is a positive experience.

Cognition and Moral Reasoning

Adolescence is also a time of rapid cognitive growth. Entering what Piaget called the formal operational stage, teenagers begin to think critically and abstractly. In **moral reasoning**, they show more flexibility in interpreting rules than they did as children.

According to Kohlberg, moral reasoning develops in three stages: preconventional, conventional, and postconventional. But some critics identify both cultural and gender bias in this theory, and others question how moral reasoning relates to behavior. Scores on Kohlberg's reasoning tasks correlate only modestly with prosocial behavior, and young children can act morally without sophisticated reasoning.

Social and Personal Development

An adolescent's struggle to establish a personal identity, or self-concept, is called an **identity crisis**. Young adolescents typically experience a rise in tension with parents characterized by bickering and disengagement from family activities. At the same time, peer relationships become more important. In early adolescence, peer pressure brings conformity, especially in the early stages. Sexuality is a natural part of adolescent development, but it can sometimes bring confusion and harmful consequences. American adolescents are more sexually active today than two generations ago, though rates of sexual activity among teens have declined recently.

ADULTHOOD AND OLD AGE

Biologists agree that each species has a maximum possible **life span**, which is greater than its average **life expectancy**. Among humans, the life expectancy is influenced by personality, nutrition, health practices, the environment, health care, and other factors. In addition, women consistently outlive men.

PHYSICAL CHANGES IN ADULTHOOD

The number of brain cells diminishes steadily after birth. Muscle strength and reflexes peak at about age 30 and then decline; also at that age, metabolism begins to slow, so that people tend to gain weight. For women, middle age brings **menopause**, the end of menstruation and fertility but without psychological effects. For men, there's only a gradual decline in fertility after adolescence, but no abrupt end.

When people are in their 60s and 70s, the aging process accelerates. The senses decline sharply, and the bones, joints, and immune system begin to deteriorate.

AGING AND INTELLECTUAL FUNCTIONS

Aging need not mean cognitive decline. Autobiographical memories, for instance, survive into old age. Although experiments show an age-related decline in ability to free-recall new material, there is no comparable decline in recognition performance. The memory problems that do exist are largely due to a general slowing of neural processes.

Dementia, a disorder resulting in severe cognitive damage, strikes 10 percent of the elderly population. The most common cause is **Alzheimer's disease**, which progressively destroys brain cells, causing memory loss and other symptoms.

SOCIAL AND PERSONAL DEVELOPMENT

Theorists such as Erikson and Levinson have described adulthood in terms of distinct stages. In this view, the stages are linked to chronological age, and the transitions produce stress. Other theorists believe that social development has less to do with age than with critical events such as marriage and having children. The **social clock** sets the expected times when major life events should occur. People are also influenced by fate in the form of chance encounters that change a person's life.

DYING AND DEATH

Kübler-Ross proposed five stages that people go through in coping with the knowledge of impending death: denial, anger, bargaining, depression, and acceptance. However, not everyone experiences these stages.

CRITICAL THINKING

Thinking Critically About Life Span Development

1. What is heritability, and how is it studied? Is it possible to separate the effects of genes and environment?

2. In what ways have your peers and your parents helped shape you?

3. Why do people often help nonrelated friends, acquaintances, and even strangers? Do animals do this too? How might this be adaptive in terms of evolution?

4. Given what you now know about the limitations of early sensory experience and the developmental changes that occur early in life, what kinds of toys would you select (or design) for an infant to foster biological, cognitive, and social development? Why would these be effective?

5. Research suggests that child witnesses are especially susceptible to bias. Describe the kinds of biases that children are likely to exhibit. Use what you have learned about development to explain why these biases might occur.

CAREER CONNECTION: HEALTH CARE

Medical and Health Services Manager

Medical and health services managers are responsible for planning, directing, and coordinating health care services. This could mean managing an entire hospital, a specific clinical area, a department, or a medical practice for one or more physicians. They focus on improving efficiency and quality of services and ensuring their facility is compliant with all federal, state, and local laws and regulations. Medical and health services managers often work closely with a range of different professionals in the health care setting. They may collaborate with medical providers, patients, and support providers such as insurance claims agents.

To obtain a position in this realm, candidates need at least a bachelor's degree, but these are not typically entry-level jobs. Prior experience in a health care setting—either as a care provider or in administration—is desired and a master's degree may be required depending on the facility. That said, studying psychology can help hone the skills needed for this role and for related entry-level positions. Key skills for this role that psychology students learn to develop:

- Enhanced teamwork capacity
- Project management
- Innovative and integrative thinking and problem solving

KEY TERMS

accommodation (p. 363)
adolescence (p. 374)
Alzheimer's disease (p. 384)
assimilation (p. 363)
attachment (p. 369)
chromosomes (p. 351)
conception (p. 353)
concrete operational stage (p. 365)
conservation (p. 365)
critical period (p. 369)
deoxyribonucleic acid (DNA) (p. 351)
developmental psychology (p. 350)
egocentric (p. 365)
embryo (p. 354)
fetal alcohol syndrome (FAS) (p. 354)
fetus (p. 354)
formal operational stage (p. 367)
genes (p. 351)
genetics (p. 351)
grasping reflex (p. 358)
habituation (p. 357)
identity crisis (p. 377)
imprinting (p. 369)

insecure attachment (p. 371)
internalization (p. 369)
life expectancy (p. 381)
life span (p. 381)
menarche (p. 374)
menopause (p. 382)
moral reasoning (p. 375)
object permanence (p. 364)
ovulation (p. 353)
ovum (p. 353)
preoperational stage (p. 365)
puberty (p. 374)
recovery (p. 357)
rooting reflex (p. 358)
schemas (p. 363)
secure attachment (p. 370)
sensorimotor stage (p. 363)
separation anxiety (p. 364)
social clock (p. 387)
strange-situation test (p. 370)
teratogens (p. 354)
zygote (p. 353)

10 SOCIAL AND CULTURAL INFLUENCES

Monkey Business Images / Shutterstock

LEARNING OBJECTIVES

Identify how we can make errors in judgments about others and how to reduce those incorrect judgments using psychological tools.

Estimate which situations can have the greatest impact on behavioral change.

Contrast variables that increase helping and aggressive behavior.

Appraise the contribution of culture to our perceptions of the world and others.

Recognize the variables that contribute to prejudice, and assess the brain's role in stereotype development.

WHAT'S YOUR PREDICTION: HOW FAR CAN PEOPLE BE PUSHED?

The Situation

You read a newspaper ad for a psychology experiment that pays well, so you sign up. As you arrive at the laboratory, located at Yale University, you meet two men. One is the experimenter, a young man dressed in a white lab coat. The other is a pleasant middle-age man named Mr. Wallace. After introductions, the experimenter explains that you will be taking part in a study on the effects of punishment on learning. By a drawing of lots, it is determined that you'll serve as the "teacher" and Mr. Wallace as the "learner." So far, so good.

Before you know it, however, the situation takes on a more ominous tone. You find out that your job is to test the learner's memory and administer electric shocks of increasing intensity whenever he makes a mistake. While in another room, you watch the experimenter strap Mr. Wallace into a chair, roll up his sleeve, tape electrodes onto his arm, and apply "electrode paste" to prevent blisters and burns. You overhear Mr. Wallace say that he has a heart problem and the experimenter reply, "although the shocks are painful, they will not cause permanent damage." You then go back to the main room, where you're seated in front of a shock generator—a machine with thirty switches that range from 15 volts (labeled "slight shock") to 450 volts (labeled "XXX").

Your task is easy. First, you read a list of word pairs to Mr. Wallace through a microphone. Blue—phone. Girl—hat. Fish—spoon. Then, you test his memory with a series of multiple-choice questions. If his answer is correct, you go to the next question. If it's incorrect, you announce the correct answer and shock him. As you press the shock switch, you can hear a buzzer go off in the learner's room. After each wrong answer, you're told to increase the shock intensity by 15 volts.

You don't realize it, but the experiment is rigged, and Mr. Wallace—who works for the experimenter—is not receiving any shocks. As the session proceeds, the learner makes more and more errors, leading you to work your way up the shock scale. As you reach 75 volts, you hear the learner grunt in pain. At 120 volts, he shouts. If you're still in it at 150 volts, he complains about his heart and cries out, "Experimenter! That's all. Get me out of here. I refuse to go on!" Screams of agony and protest follow. If you reach 300 volts, he absolutely refuses to go on. By the time you surpass 330 volts, the learner falls silent. 360 volts. Zap. Not a peep. 420, 435, 450. Zap. Still no response. At some point, you turn to the experimenter. What should I do? Shouldn't we check on him? But in answer to your inquiries, the experimenter calmly repeats his commands: "Please continue." "The experiment requires that you continue." "You have no other choice, you must go on."

Make a Prediction

What do you do? Feeling caught between a rock and a hard place, do you follow your conscience or obey the experimenter? At what voltage do you stop? How would other participants react? Would anyone in their right mind keep shocking the hapless Mr. Wallace all the way to 450 volts? Based on what you know about people, try to predict the point at which most participants stopped and defied the experimenter. Make your prediction by identifying a voltage level.

15	45	75	105	135	165	195	225
255	285	315	345	375	405	435	450

The Results

Almost 60 years ago, social psychologist Stanley Milgram (1963) staged this situation to examine obedience to authority. When Milgram described the study to college students, adults, and a group of psychiatrists, they predicted that, on average, they would stop at 135 volts—and that almost nobody would go all the way. They were wrong. In Milgram's initial study, 26 out of 40 men—that's 65 percent—delivered the ultimate punishment of 450 volts.

What Does It All Mean?

Why did so many participants obey, even while thinking they were hurting a fellow human being? One possible explanation for these scary results is that Milgram's participants—all of whom were male—were unusually cruel and sadistic. Who were these guys? Or maybe the result says something about men in general. What if the participants were women instead? How far up the shock scale would they go? In a follow-up study, Milgram examined this question by putting 40 women in the same situation. The result: 65 percent of the women tested administered 450 volts, identical to the number of men.

Perhaps people in general will harm a fellow human being. As a sad commentary on human nature, perhaps Milgram's study says more about aggression than obedience. But how far would participants go if not ordered to do so? What if the experimenter did not constantly prod the participants to raise the voltage level? In this situation, Milgram found that only 1 participant out of 40 (2.5 percent) pressed the last switch. Most stopped at 75 volts.

Milgram's participants had acted out of obedience, not cruelty. In fact, most were visibly tormented by the experience. Many of those who administered 450 volts perspired, stuttered, trembled, bit their lips, and even burst into fits of nervous laughter. It was as if they wanted to stop but felt powerless to do so. What does it mean? When Nazis were on trial for their war crimes, their defense was, "I just followed orders." Intrigued by the power of authority implied by this statement, Milgram devised a laboratory situation to mimic the forces that operate in real-life crimes of obedience. As we'll learn throughout this chapter, this classic research cries out the message of social psychology loud and clear: Other people can have a profound impact on our behavior.

On September 11, 2001, in New York City, the morning was sunny, bright, and clear. While it started like a typical Fall day in the city, it altered the social fabric of the United States forever. On this day, which might have been before you were born, the American sense of safety, air travel norms, and the American stereotype of terrorism changed forever. At 8:46 AM, a Boeing 767 that had been hijacked by Middle Eastern terrorists, crashed into the North Tower of the World Trade Center. Seventeen minutes later, a second hijacked jumbo jet plunged into the South Tower. Nobody knew it at the time, but both towers would soon collapse, forever altering the skyline of lower Manhattan. Moments later, a third hijacked jet slammed into the Pentagon outside of Washington, D.C. A fourth jet, which may have been headed for the White House, then crashed into a wooded area in Pennsylvania after passengers—hearing of the other attacks—battled their hijackers and forced the plane down. Overall, nearly 3,000 people from more than 90 countries were killed.

In downtown Manhattan, gray smoke billowed up into a blue city sky as glass, metal, and paper rained onto the ground below. Inside the twin towers, where thousands of people were at work, the upper floors filled with fire, heat, smoke, and fumes. People made last-minute cell phone calls to helpless loved ones. Remarkably, fleeing workers said that they had crossed paths with firefighters and police

FIGURE 10.1 ■ September 11, 2001

Tragic scenes from 9/11 illustrate the range of human social behavior. That day, a jumbo jet hijacked by terrorists slammed into the South Tower of the World Trade Center in New York City, the second attack of the morning. As workers fled the building, heroic firefighters climbed up the stairs, many to their own deaths, looking for survivors. On the streets below, dazed people were covered in soot and ash. Nearby, families of missing victims posted fliers of their loved ones on walls that would later become memorials.

Mario Tama / Staff / Getty Images; Richard Levine / Alamy Stock Photo; Louis Lanzano / Associated Press

officers who climbed up the stairs, many to their own deaths, looking for survivors. Mohammad Salman Hamdani, was one such emergency responder. As a Muslim, Salman believed deeply that life was sacred. As an emergency responder, Salman believed that his life was worth risking to save the lives of others. And his life is what he gave.

On the street, sirens blared everywhere. When the buildings collapsed, daylight turned to night. Chased by an avalanche of powder and rubble, people dropped everything, covered their mouths, and ran as fast as they could.

Away from this site, which would later be dubbed "Ground Zero," worried friends and relatives flooded phone lines and tried desperately to communicate via email. Thousands of New Yorkers rallied to offer a helping hand. They brought towels, aspirins, T-shirts, bandages, ice, water bottles, and other necessities to Ground Zero. Over the next few weeks, crowds gathered to cheer police, firefighters, and rescue workers. All over the country, people donated thousands of pints of blood and more than a billion dollars in relief funds. In an outburst of patriotism, millions of Americans hung flags from their houses and cars. At the same time, some people experienced such paranoia that they saw the potential for terrorism in every airplane, van, briefcase, and person with olive-toned skin and dark hair. Some even targeted Arab and Muslim citizens in retaliation, but most showed restraint. And although some segments of the world population celebrated the attack, the vast majority expressed sadness, sympathy, outrage, and support.

The entire episode raises profound questions about human social behavior. What could possibly have triggered the attack? Were the terrorists intensely frustrated and enraged, or did they blindly follow orders from a leader in whom they believed? In the chaos that ensued, what inspired heroic firefighters, rescue workers, and the passengers who took down the plane in Pennsylvania to sacrifice their lives? Why, afterward, did Americans come together rather than break apart, gathering in groups at candlelight vigils and patriotic ceremonies, and displaying the Stars and Stripes wherever they went? In this chapter, we address questions like these—about aggression, altruism, group pride, intergroup conflict, and perceptions of others—as we look at **social psychology**: the study of how individuals think, feel, and behave in social situations.

Mohammad Salman Hamdani, a biochemist with dreams of medical school, was mentioned in the 2001 USA Patriot Act as an example of Muslim Americans who acted heroically on 9/11. His heroism also earned him a memorial in Bayside, Queens, where an intersection was renamed "Salman Hamdani Way." Scholarship awards were established in his name at Rockefeller University and Queens College in New York. Here, his mother continues his legacy.

David McNew/ Staff/ Getty Images

social psychology. The study of how individuals think, feel, and behave in social situations.

SOCIAL PERCEPTION

LEARNING OBJECTIVES

Identify how we can make errors in judgments about others and how to reduce those incorrect judgments using psychological tools.

- Define the fundamental attribution error—and discuss whether it is really "fundamental."
- Identify the reasons we are slow to revise our first impressions in the light of new evidence.
- Explain the variables that contribute to attraction.

As social beings, humans are drawn to each other. We work together, play together, live together, and often make lifetime commitments to grow old together. In all of our interactions, we engage in **social perception**, the process of knowing and evaluating other persons. People are complex, so it's not easy to form accurate impressions of them. So how do we do it? What kinds of evidence do we use? We cannot actually "see" inner dispositions or states of mind. Therefore, like the detective who tries to reconstruct events from physical traces, witnesses, and other clues, we observe the way people behave, try to explain that behavior, and then put all the pieces together to form an impression.

social perception. The processes by which we come to know and evaluate other persons.

Making Attributions

Why did the 9/11 terrorists commit such a vicious act? Many people assumed that their religion—Islam—was the motivator. This assumption fueled a fear or hatred of all Muslims among some people—what is labeled as Islamophobia (Kaplan, 2006; Sheridan, 2006). But, of course, such a fear is contradicted by heroes like Salman—a Muslim American who risked his own life to save American strangers. How, then, could Islam be the motivator? What makes the 9/11 terrorists different from Muslim Americans like Salman? In trying to make sense of people from their actions, we must understand what caused their behavior. Fritz Heider (1958) proposed that we are all "intuitive scientists." We are collecting data about others in an attempt to explain why people behave the way they do. The explanations we develop are called **attributions**, and the process humans experience when making attributions is explained by **attribution theory**.

attribution. An explanation we create to explain a person's behavior.

Attribution Theory

Psychology can explain human behavior in many ways. Think about Salman. Why did he help? Well, he believed his purpose was to save lives; Salman was self-sacrificing. That is a personal reason for why Salman helped—what Harold Kelley (1967) refers to as a disposition. Another explanation could be that Salman was ordered by his lieutenant to go into the burning tower. That is a situational reason for why Salman helped. Heider (1958) believed that most explanations for behavior fell into one of these two categories: personal or situational. However, attribution theorists aren't necessarily trying to determine which category provides the best explanation. Instead, attributional theorists are trying to determine *our* social perceptions of why people behave the way they do (Kelley, 1967). Do you think Salman helped because of situational or personal reasons?

attribution theory. A set of theories that describe how people explain the causes of behavior.

fundamental attribution error. A tendency to overestimate the impact of personal causes of behavior and to overlook the role of situations.

The Fundamental Attribution Error

Social psychologists devote much research to the role situations play in our behaviors, thoughts, and feelings. However, the typical person does not, especially if that typical person is from an individualistic culture. An individualistic person is raised in a culture that discounts the situation and, instead, emphasizes the individual as unique and autonomous (Kuhnen, Hannover, & Schubert, 2001; Lee, Beckert, & Goodrich, 2010; Santos, Varnum, & Grossman, 2017). American culture is individualistic. Therefore, when we try to explain the behavior of others, we typically overestimate the role of personal factors and underestimate the role of the situation. You might be thinking, "There's no way I have this bias!" This bias, called the **fundamental attribution error** (Ross, 1977) is quite pervasive and, thus, can mislead even the best of us—psychology training or not.

To illustrate the fundamental attribution error, imagine you are parking your car at the grocery store and happen to notice a White, blonde, and tall woman exit her Mercedes. You admire her car and then go about your business. After a few forgetful moments (Cereal…Do I need cereal?), you complete your shopping and make your way to the cashier. As fate would have it, you end up in line behind the blonde,

An activist holds a sign that says "Islamophobia is Unamerican" during a 2016 event in Cleveland, Ohio, which was organized to protest various forms of discrimination.

vichinterlang / istock

female Mercedes owner. Like most of us, you look at what is in her shopping cart. She has three cases of infant formula at $15 per can, two cases of root beer, diapers, organic chicken, vegetables, and other random foods.

Now, stop for a minute. Predict what the woman uses to pay for her items by identifying her most likely payment method:

   a. Credit card
   b. Check
   c. Cash
   d. Debit card
   e. Coupons
   f. Other (fill in the blank) _____

What did she use to pay for her items? She used food stamps. Wait. Food stamps?

What are you thinking at this very moment? Did your mind dart back to the fact that she was driving a Mercedes? Are you wondering why she hasn't sold the Mercedes? Do you think she is selfish and "working the system"? Well, we know why this woman was driving a Mercedes although she was on food stamps. The scenario you just considered is based on the experiences of Darlene Cunha, a successful television producer who lost her job in 2008 as a result of the market crash (Cunha, 2014). Darlene and her husband had bought a home just before the crash, and after Darlene lost her job, she found herself pregnant with twins. Then her husband lost his job a few weeks before the twins were born. The Mercedes had been purchased years earlier and was paid in full. Now unemployed and with twins, the couple had only one reliable vehicle: the Mercedes. It started every time and had excellent brakes and advanced airbag technology, so the twins would be kept safe on the road. Now that we know more about Darlene, might we still judge her for driving a Mercedes? This quick judgment about Darlene and her "working the system" is a fundamental attribution error. We overestimated Darlene's personal attributions—selfish and "working the system"—and underestimated situational attributions—sudden job loss, home loan debt, and dependence on a safe and reliable car that was paid for.

What's going on here? Why do we fail to appreciate the impact of situations? According to Daniel Gilbert and Patrick Malone (1995), the problem stems from *how* attributions are made. Theorists used to assume that people survey all the evidence and then decide on either a personal or a situational attribution. Instead, claims Gilbert, there is a two-step process: First, we identify the behavior and make a quick personal attribution. Then we try to correct or adjust that inference to account for situational influences. The first step is simple, natural, and effortless—like a reflex. It happens with such automaticity, you are most likely unaware of the conclusions you have drawn about that person (Uleman, Saribay, & Gonzalez, 2008). When you pictured a White, blonde, well-dressed woman who drove a Mercedes in the checkout line with food stamps, you probably experienced an instant response. The second step requires attention, thought, and effort.

Here, a store displays a sign indicating that it accepts SNAP (Supplemental Nutrition Assistance Program) benefits in the form of EBT (electronic benefits transfer). What assumptions might you make about a person who you observed using government assistance to buy items in the store?

Jonathan Weiss/ Shutterstock

Attributions as Cultural Constructions

Why is it natural to attribute behavior to persons rather than to the situations they are in? Earlier, you learned that this bias is quite common among individualistic cultures. However, does that mean it is specific to those types of persons? What about non-individualistic cultures? Many non-individualistic cultures—specifically, collectivistic cultures—take a more holistic view that focuses on the relationship between persons and their social roles (Cousins, 1989; Kanagawa, Cross, & Markus, 2001). Miller (1984) compared and contrasted Euro-American and Indian explanations for certain positive and negative behaviors that happen in their lives. As the age of participants increased, so did differences in responses. Americans made more personal attributions, whereas Indian participants made more situational attributions. Zárate, Uleman, and Voils (2001) compared Latinxs (collectivistic culture) with Anglo-Americans (individualistic culture) and found that Anglo-Americans are more likely than Latinxs to ascribe an actor's behavior to their traits. With the help of neurological feedback, Na and Kitayama (2011) found a similar attribution disparity in collectivists and individualists. Finally, Lee, Shimizu, and Uleman (2015) found that Americans formed more associations between speakers and traits than did Japanese. These findings suggest that individualistic people may be more susceptible to the fundamental attribution error. (For more on individualistic versus collectivistic cultures, see the section on cross-cultural perspectives.)

There are many settings, including job interviews, where first impressions may seem like they have particularly high stakes.
fizkes/ Shutterstock

Forming Impressions

In forming an impression of a person, making attributions is only the first step. A second step is to combine and integrate all the evidence into a coherent picture. Studies show that people's impressions of others are generally based on a "weighted average" of all the evidence (Anderson, 1981; Kashima & Kerekes, 1994). This same research also shows, however, that once we do form an impression of someone, we become less and less likely to revise our opinion in light of new evidence, even if it's contradictory. Thus, first impressions are powerful.

Cognitive-Confirmation Biases

It's often said that first impressions stick, and social psychologists are inclined to agree. In a classic demonstration, Solomon Asch (1946) told a group of research participants that a hypothetical person was "intelligent, industrious, impulsive, critical, stubborn, and envious." He then presented a second group with exactly the same list, but in reverse order. Logically, the two groups should have formed the same impression. Instead, however, participants who heard the first list—in which the positive traits came first—were more favorable in their evaluations than those who heard the second list. A cognitive explanation: Review the chapter on memory and apply the serial-position effect. Is there a high likelihood of remembering items presented first? The answer is yes. This segues nicely into a social explanation: People are influenced more by information they receive early in an interaction than by information that appears later. Think about how often the lasting impression one makes is often the first impression. This finding is known as the **primacy effect**.

primacy effect. The tendency for impressions of others to be influenced heavily by information appearing early in an interaction.

TRY THIS!

Primacy Effect: The Power of First Impressions

Are first impressions lasting impressions? Even when first impressions turn out to be wrong, do they still stick? TRY THIS variation on Asch's (1946) experiment to find out.

Ask a handful of friends to rate on a scale from 1 to 10 how much they like Angela, who you describe as "intelligent, industrious, critical, stubborn, and envious."

Then ask a handful of different friends to rate on the same scale how much they like Sarah, who you describe as "envious, stubborn, critical, industrious, and intelligent."

Average the two sets of ratings. If the primacy effect is operating, which woman do you think would be seen in a more positive light, Angela or Sarah? What are the results?

The primacy effect occurs for two reasons. The first is that we become somewhat less attentive to later behavioral evidence once we have already formed an impression. We can apply this effect to job interviews. When a job candidate is introduced to the hiring committee, a dynamic between the parties ensues. This dynamic can be positive and result in rapport between the job candidate and hiring committee (Barrick et al., 2012; Swider, Barrick, & Harris, 2016). Why does this matter? Highly qualified job candidates who are not good at building rapport might get passed over for a job. One way to combat this could be to use structured interviews so that all job candidates are asked the exact same questions and scored on their performance.

To test this, Swider and colleagues (2016) conducted mock interviews in a controlled setting with 163 undergraduate students in need of career preparation and 54 human resources graduate students who were highly trained in delivering structured interviews. Before each structured interview began, mock candidates were given 2 to 3 minutes to introduce themselves. Interviewers scored job candidates on their initial impression of the introductions. Immediately after, the structured interview began. Questions that were not part of the structured interview were strictly prohibited. Swider and colleagues found that scores on the introductions portion were highly correlated with scores on the structured interview portion. First impressions matter. The better it is, the higher your interview score.

Does this mean that even a plan won't stop us from a life of primacy? Not necessarily. If we are tired or unstimulated, our attention may wane. Donna Webster and others (1996) found that college students "leaped to conclusions" about a person on the basis of preliminary information when they were mentally fatigued from having just taken a 2-hour exam. But when the students were alert and sufficiently motivated to keep from tuning out, this bias was diminished. Another way to combat first impressions is through mindfulness (Hopthrow et al., 2016). One tested mindfulness exercise is the raisin task, described in the "Try This!" activity in the chapter on personality (Jordan, Wang, Donatoni, & Meier, 2014; Ostafin & Kassman, 2012; Weger, Hooper, Meier, & Hopthrow, 2012). The full experience of eating two raisins requires the person to slow down and focus attention on the smell, taste, texture, and appearance of each raisin before and during consumption. Participants who completed the raisin task before making a judgment were less likely to engage in bias toward a writer's attitude compared to those who did not complete the raisin task (Hopthrow et al., 2016).

More unsettling is the second reason for primacy, known as the change-of-meaning hypothesis. Once people form an impression, they later interpret inconsistent information in light of that impression. Asch's research shows how malleable the meaning of a trait can be. When people are told that a kind person is *calm*, they assume that the person is gentle, peaceful, and serene. When a cruel person is said to be *calm*, however, the same word is interpreted to mean cool, shrewd, and calculating. There are many examples to illustrate the point. Depending on your first impression, the word *proud* can mean self-respecting or conceited; *critical* can mean astute or picky; and *impulsive* can mean spontaneous or reckless (Hamilton & Zanna, 1974; Watkins & Peynircioglu, 1984).

Behavioral-Confirmation Biases

As social perceivers, we interpret new information in light of our existing beliefs and preferences. At times, we may even unwittingly *create* support for these beliefs and preferences. A classic study by Rosenthal and Jacobson showed that teachers who are given positive or negative expectations of a student, perhaps based on an IQ score, alter their behavior toward that student, setting into motion a self-fulfilling prophecy (discussed in the chapter on thought, language, and intelligence). This teacher expectations study inspired—and continues to inspire—a great deal of research (Egalite & Kisida, 2018; Tobisch & Dresel, 2017; Urdan & Bruchmann, 2018).

This process is at work not only in schools but in other settings, too, including the military (McNatt, 2000), sports (Siekanska, Blecharz, & Wojtowicz, 2013), job interviews (Dougherty, Turban, & Callender, 1994; Phillips & Dipboye, 1989), and interrogations (Kassin, Goldstein, & Savitsky, 2003; Minhas, Walsh, & Bull, 2016; Villalobos & Davis, 2016). According to research cited by Minhas and colleagues (2016), dangerous biases in law enforcement are negative stereotypes and prejudices toward a person simply based on the individual's group membership. Take juveniles, for instance. Meyer and Reppucci (2007) discovered that police have a certain perception of juveniles in general and a contradictory perception of juveniles in an interrogation setting. Reppucci and colleagues

(2010) replicated these findings. According to their results, police generally believe juveniles can be treated like adults during interrogations, suggesting that once under investigation, a suspected juvenile has an adult-level of reasoning and/or maturity. A plethora of psychological research demonstrates this is not true. This false belief can possibly explain why Feld (2012) found that interrogations conducted on 16- and 17-year-old juveniles in Minnesota frequently included tactics such as presenting false evidence, accusing the juvenile of lying, and urging the juvenile to tell the truth in an attempt to increase fear or anxiety. What can be the result? A false confession (Perillo & Kassin, 2011).

How do social perceivers transform beliefs into reality? As shown by research on teacher expectations, the process involves a three-step chain of events, as illustrated in Figure 10.2. First, a perceiver forms an opinion of a target person—based on the target's physical appearance, reputation, gender, race, or initial interactions. Research demonstrates that, in policing, interrogators more often than not presume suspects to be guilty, even before the interview is conducted (Mortimer & Shepherd, 1999; Moston, Stephenson, & Williamson, 1992). Second, the perceiver behaves in a manner that is consistent with that first impression. Thus, suspects seem to demonstrate their guilt by smirking, shifting their gaze, and squirming in their chair. Third, the target unwittingly adjusts his or her behavior in response to the perceiver's actions. Suspects could easily become defensive or shut down after hours of receiving false accusations from police officers. By steering interactions with others along a path narrowed by our beliefs, we engage in a behavioral-confirmation bias that keeps us from judging others objectively.

Attraction

When you meet someone for the first time, what are you drawn to? Common sense is filled with contradiction: Does familiarity breed fondness or contempt? Do birds of a feather flock together, or do opposites attract? And is beauty the object of our desire, or do we think appearances are deceiving? Over the years, researchers have identified various determinants of attraction (Berscheid & Reis, 1998; Birnbaum, 2018; Brehm, Miller, Perlman, & Campbell, 2001; Lamm, Wiesmann, & Keller, 1997). Two of the most powerful are similarity and physical attractiveness.

Similarity and Liking

Time and again, studies have revealed a basic principle of attraction: The more exposure we have to a stimulus, and the more familiar it becomes—whether it's a face, a foreign word, a melody, or a geometric form—the more we like it (Bornstein, 1989; Harmon-Jones & Allen, 2001; Zajonc, 1968). As described in the chapter on consciousness, this **mere exposure effect** occurs even when stimuli are presented without a participant's awareness. Mere exposure can also influence our self-evaluations. Imagine, for example, that you are Abraham Lincoln. You are asked to choose one of two photographs for display in the White House. Which photograph would you choose? Review the photos in Figure 10.3 and choose either a or b (Abumrad & Krulwich, 2011).

Now, imagine you are a close friend of Abraham Lincoln. Using the same two photographs, choose the photograph you prefer as Lincoln's friend. Did you choose photo *a* both times? Theodore Mita and others (1977) tried this experiment with female college students and found that most preferred their own mirror images (long live the selfie!), whereas their friends liked the actual photos. In both cases,

mere exposure effect. The attraction to a stimulus that results from increased exposure to it.

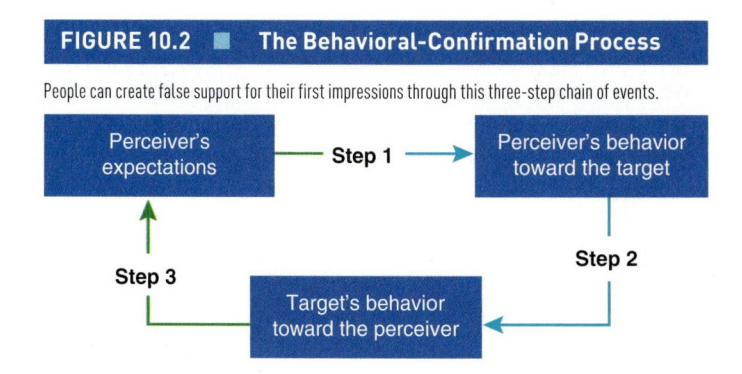

FIGURE 10.2 ■ The Behavioral-Confirmation Process

People can create false support for their first impressions through this three-step chain of events.

FIGURE 10.3 ■ Mirror, Mirror

WNYC's Radiolab posted these images of Abraham Lincoln to accompany their podcast about our mirror selves. The story is titled "Mirror, Mirror."

pictor/iStock

the preference was for the view of the face that was most familiar. For our Abraham Lincoln example, you most likely chose photo *a* because it is the one that presents Lincoln as you know him. However, Lincoln would have been most familiar with his mirror image—photo *b*.

Familiarity preference does not stop with our own images. As a general rule, people prefer to associate with others who are similar to themselves. According to Byrne and others (1986), this effect on attraction is a two-step process: First, we avoid others who are very different, and then, among those who are left, we seek out those people who are the most similar to us. As a result, friends and couples are more likely than are randomly paired persons to share common attitudes and interests. They are also more likely to be similar in their age, race, religion, education level, intelligence, height, and economic status. Genetic research supports these findings. A study by Domingue and colleagues (2018) demonstrated genetic similarities among pairs of friends, while other studies have demonstrated genetic similarities among spouses (Domingue, Fletcher, Conley, & Boardman, 2014; Guo, Wang, Liu, & Randall, 2014; Robinson et al., 2017; Zou et al., 2015). The more similar two individuals are, the better the chances that the relationship will last (Byrne, 1971, 1997). Commenting on the magnet-like appeal of similarity, even in diverse multicultural societies, sociologist John Macionis (2001) notes, "Cupid's arrow is aimed by society more than we think." And society isn't all that's involved. Genetics also play a role. One unfortunate result is that by associating only with similar others, people form social niches that are homogeneous, divided along the lines of race, ethnic background, age, religion, level of education, and occupation (McPherson, Smith-Lovin, & Cook, 2001). This limited association can prevent us from developing relationships with people of different cultures and belief systems, and in turn, decrease our concerns for all humanity (Sparkman & Hamer, 2020). When our concerns for all humanity are low, negative intergroup attitudes can result (Sparkman & Hamer, 2020).

Physical Attractiveness

When we first encounter people, our perceptions are influenced in subtle ways by their height, weight, skin color, hair color, clothing, and other aspects of outward appearance. The most influential aspect of appearance is physical attractiveness; as children, we were told that "beauty is only skin deep." Yet as adults, we like others who are good looking. Studies have shown that in the affairs of our social world, attractive people fare better in the way they are treated by teachers, employers, judges, juries,

FIGURE 10.4 ■ Attractiveness Halo Effect

Zebrowitz and Franklin found that the attractiveness halo effect occurred across the lifespan when both the participants and target faces were younger and older. Can you guess how this finding, specifically on untrustworthiness, applies to the criminal justice system?

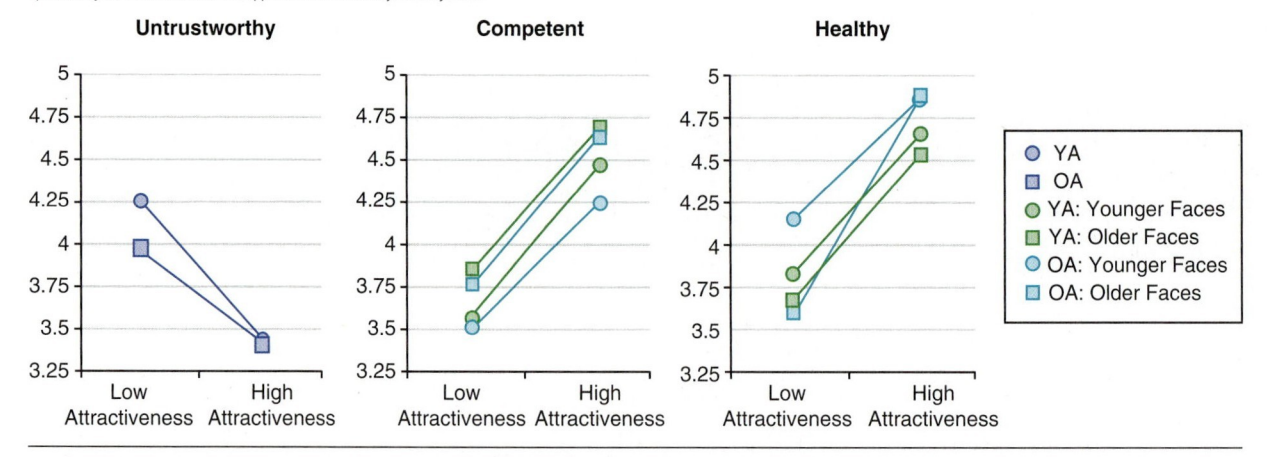

- YA
- OA
- YA: Younger Faces
- YA: Older Faces
- OA: Younger Faces
- OA: Older Faces

Leslie A. Zebrowitz & Robert G. Franklin Jr. (2014) The Attractiveness Halo Effect and the Babyface Stereotype in Older and Younger Adults: Similarities, Own-Age Accentuation, and Older Adult Positivity Effects, Experimental Aging Research, 40:3, 375-393, DOI: 10.1080/0361073X.2014.897151

and others (Langlois et al., 2000). In fact, a study on mock job interviews demonstrated that ratings of physical appearance were positively correlated with initial impressions (Swider et al., 2016). Through interviews conducted in the United States and Canada, for example, economists discovered that across occupational groups, good-looking men and women earned more money than others who were comparable—except less attractive (Hamermesh & Biddle, 1994). This can be explained by the attractiveness halo effect—what is seen as beautiful is assumed to be good. Many studies have replicated this effect, including one by Zebrowitz and Franklin (2014) that included younger and older adult raters. Their study demonstrated that faces considered attractive were also rated as healthier, more competent, and less untrustworthy than faces considered less attractive. You can review their findings in Figure 10.4.

How do we define *attractiveness*? Is beauty an objective and measurable quality, like height and weight? Or is beauty subjective, existing in the eye of the beholder? Some psychologists believe that some faces are inherently more attractive than others (Rhodes & Zebrowitz, 2001). This "objective" view of beauty has two sources of evidence. First, when people rate faces on a 10-point scale, there are typically high levels of agreement over which are more or less attractive (Langlois et al., 2000). It appears that people prefer faces with eyes, noses, lips, and other features that are not too different from the average. Langlois and Roggman (1990) showed actual yearbook photographs to college students as well as computerized facial composites that "averaged" the features in these photos. Time and again, participants preferred the averaged composites to the actual faces. Other studies have since confirmed this effect (Langlois, Roggman, & Musselman, 1994; Rhodes, Sumich, & Byatt, 1999). Still other studies have shown that people are attracted to faces that are symmetrical—in other words, faces in which the right and left sides closely mirror each other (Grammer & Thornhill, 1994; Little, DeBruine, & Jones, 2011; Mealey, Bridgstock, & Townsend, 1999). The more symmetrical, like the face of Iman (pictured in Figure 10.5d), the higher the attractiveness rating.

A second source of evidence comes from the infant research laboratory, which shows that even babies who are too young to have learned their culture's standards of beauty exhibit a measurable preference for faces seen as attractive by adults. Judging from their eye movements, young infants spend more time gazing at attractive faces than at unattractive ones—regardless of whether the faces are young or old, male or female, or Black or White (Langlois, Ritter, Roggman, & Vaughn, 1991). Other studies have similarly revealed that infants look longer at faces that are "averaged" in their features (Rubenstein, Kalakanis, & Langlois, 1999). "These kids don't read *Vogue* or watch TV," notes Langlois, "yet they make the same judgments as adults" (Cowley, 1996, p. 66).

Other researchers argue that beauty is relative. People from different cultures enhance their appearance with face painting, makeup, plastic surgery, hairstyling, scarring, tattooing, the molding of bones, the filing of teeth, braces, and the piercing of body parts—all contributing to "the enigma of beauty" (Newman, 2000). Body structure also contributes to attractiveness. The waist-to-hip ratio (WHR;

FIGURE 10.5 ■ Global Beauty

People from different cultures enhance their appearance in different ways. Pictured here are a Yanomami woman from the Amazon rainforest, Venezuela (a), a Tuareg woman from Niger (b), a woman from the state of Gujarat in India (c), and model Iman (d). While beauty may be subjective, Julian De Silva, a face mapping specialist, proposed a scientific approach to measuring beauty. With face mapping, we can evaluate facial symmetry by looking at the distances between nose and mouth, mouth and chin, pupils, and forehead and brow. Our own eyes make these distance and symmetry judgments almost in an instant, without us even knowing that we are looking for these calculations.

DEA / G. SIOEN / Contributor / Getty Images; frans lemmens / Alamy Stock Photo; Ajit Solanki/ Associated Press; Dimitrios Kambouris/Getty Images

Singh, 1993) has become one highly researched indicator in various cultures. Studies have found that men's preferred WHR in women varies depending on culture. For example, New Zealand prefers women with a 0.7 WHR (Dixson, Dixson, Bishop, & Parish, 2009), women from Cameroon get more preference with a 0.8 WHR (Dixson, Dixson, Morgan, & Anderson, 2007), and Tanzanian men prefer women with a 0.9 WHR (Marlowe & Wetsman, 2001). However, these cultural preferences are not set in stone. Men who lived on a reserve in Peru changed their WHR preferences for female bodies after spending 30 years living away from the reserve where they were exposed to Western media (Yu & Shepard, 1998). However, it doesn't take 30 years for attractiveness judgments to change. Participants who viewed nude *Playboy* models later lowered their ratings of the attractiveness of average-looking women—the result of a contrast effect (Kenrick, Gutierres, & Goldberg, 1989), and we evaluate others as more attractive after we have grown to like them (Gross & Crofton, 1977).

SOCIAL INFLUENCE

> **LEARNING OBJECTIVES**
>
> Estimate which situations can have the greatest impact on behavioral change.
>
> - Differentiate between informational and normative influence.
> - List the conditions for persuasive communication.
> - Explain why a change in behavior can elicit a change in attitude.
> - Identify when groups arouse us, relax us, and sometimes make bad decisions.

Advertisers hire celebrities and supermodels to sell soft drinks, sneakers, and other products. Sports fans spread the "wave" and chant "defense" in a spectacular show of unison. Performers with stage fright tremble, turn pale, and freeze before appearing in front of an audience. These examples illustrate that people influence one another in various ways. As you'll learn, the source of influence may be a person or a group, its effect may be on behavior or attitude, and the change may be socially hurtful or helpful to others. In all the forms that it takes, social influence is pervasive (Cialdini & Trost, 1998).

Social Influence as "Automatic"

As social animals, human beings are vulnerable to a host of subtle, almost reflex-like influences. Without realizing it, we yawn when we see someone else yawn and laugh when we hear others laughing. Knowing that people imitate others, TV producers infuse their situation comedies with canned laughter to make viewers think the shows are funny, political candidates trumpet their own inflated poll results to attract new voters, and bartenders stuff dollar bills into empty tip jars to draw more money from customers.

Research demonstrates the compelling nature of this automatic and nonconscious social response (Dijksterhuis & Bargh, 2001). In one study, Milgram and others (1969) had research confederates stop on a busy street in New York City, look up, and gawk at a sixth-floor window of a nearby building. Films shot from behind the window showed that 80 percent of passersby stopped and gazed up when they saw the confederates. In another study, Chartrand and Bargh (1999) set up participants to work with a partner, a confederate who exhibited a habit of rubbing his face or shaking his foot. Hidden cameras revealed that, without realizing it, the participants mimicked these motor behaviors, rubbing their face or shaking a foot to match their partner's behavior. Chartrand and Bargh called this finding "the chameleon effect," after the lizard that changes colors according to its physical environment, as illustrated in Figure 10.6.

Sometimes, the automatic social influences on us are not funny but potentially hazardous to our health—as when people die of suicide while under the influence of certain fanatic cults (Galanter, 1999) or information featured in mass media (Etzersdorfer & Sonneck, 1998; Phillips, 1982; Phillips, & Lesyna, 1995). The Netflix series *13 Reasons Why*, based on the book by Jay Asher, sparked controversy because of its possible suicide contagion (Devitt, 2018). Consider the less extreme but still unusual events that occurred in a Tennessee high school. It all started when a teacher noticed a gas-like smell in her classroom and then came down with a headache, nausea, shortness of breath, and dizziness. Word spread, others reported the same symptoms, and soon the school was evacuated, with 80 students and 19 staff members taken to a local emergency room. Nothing showed up in blood tests, urine tests, or other medical procedures; nor were gases, pesticides, or other toxins detected in or near the

FIGURE 10.6 ■ The Chameleon Effect

This study shows the number of times per minute participants rubbed their faces and shook their feet when with a confederate who was rubbing his face or shaking his foot.

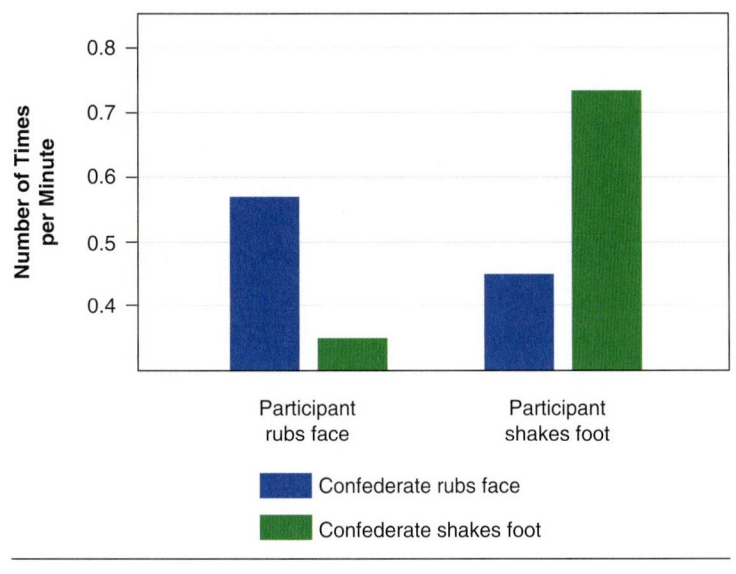

Chartrand & Bargh, 1999.

building. What the investigation did turn up was that students who reported feeling ill that day were more likely than others to have seen someone with symptoms, heard about someone with symptoms, or knew a classmate who was ill. The researchers, who reported the findings in the *New England Journal of Medicine*, concluded that the problems were the product of "mass psychogenic illness"—a profound form of social influence (Jones et al., 2000).

Conformity

conformity. A tendency to alter one's opinion or behavior in ways that are consistent with group norms.

Conformity, defined as the tendency for people to bring their behavior in line with group norms, is a fact of social life. Cast in a positive light, it promotes harmony, group solidarity, and peaceful coexistence—as when people assume their places in a waiting line. Cast in a negative light, conformity has harmful effects—as when people drink too much at parties or tell offensive ethnic or sexually explicit jokes because others are doing the same. For social psychologists, the goal is not to make moral judgments, but to determine the factors that promote conformity and the reasons for it.

The Early Classics

In 1936, Muzafer Sherif published a classic laboratory experiment on how norms develop in small groups. The participants in his study, thinking their visual perception was being tested, sat in a dark room, saw a beam of light, and then estimated the distance the light had moved. This procedure was repeated several times. The participants didn't realize it, but the light never moved. The movement they thought they saw was merely an optical illusion. At first, each participant sat alone and reported his or her perceptions only to the experimenter (most estimates stabilized in the range of 1 to 10 inches). During the next few days, they returned to work in three-person groups. Each time a beam of light flashed, participants stated their estimates one by one. As shown in Figure 10.7, initial estimates varied considerably, but the individuals eventually converged on a common perception, each group establishing its own set of norms.

Fifteen years after Sherif's experiment, Asch (1951) constructed a different situation. Imagine yourself in the following study. You sign up for a psychology experiment, and when you arrive you find six other students waiting around a table. You take an empty seat, and the experimenter explains that he is measuring people's ability to make visual discriminations. As a warm-up, he asks you and the others to indicate which of three comparison lines is identical in length to a standard line, as illustrated in Figure 10.8. That seems easy enough. The experimenter then asks you all to take turns in order of your seating position. Starting on his left, he asks the first person for a judgment. Noticing that you are in the next-to-last position, you patiently await your turn. The opening moments pass uneventfully. The task is clear and everyone agrees on the answers. On the third set of lines, however, the first participant selects the wrong line. Huh? What is wrong with this guy? Before you know it, the next four participants choose the same wrong line. Now it's your turn. What do you think? Better yet, what do you do? As you may have guessed by now, the other "participants" were actually confederates trained to make incorrect judgments on certain trials. The right answers were clear. In a control group, where participants made their judgments alone, performance was virtually errorless. Yet those in the experimental group went along with the incorrect majority 37 percent of the time. This result may seem surprising, but other studies have shown that people conform to others on a variety of cognitive tasks (Larsen, 1990; Schneider & Watkins, 1996).

Social influence and conformity extend to many areas of life, including what we decide to wear in various settings. We may conform to explicit or implicit clothing choices such as wearing suits in a business setting if our colleagues do.
iStock.com/qingwa

Both Sherif and Asch found that people are influenced by the behavior of others. But there is an important difference in the types of conformity exhibited in these studies. In short, Sherif's participants experienced informational influence whereas Asch's participants experienced normative influence (Deutsch & Gerard, 1955; Campbell & Fairey, 1989). **Informational influence** leads people to

informational influence. Conformity motivated by the belief that others are correct.

FIGURE 10.7 ■ A Classic Case of Suggestibility

This group in Sherif's study illustrates how participants' estimates of the apparent movement of light converged over time. Gradually, the group established its own set of norms.

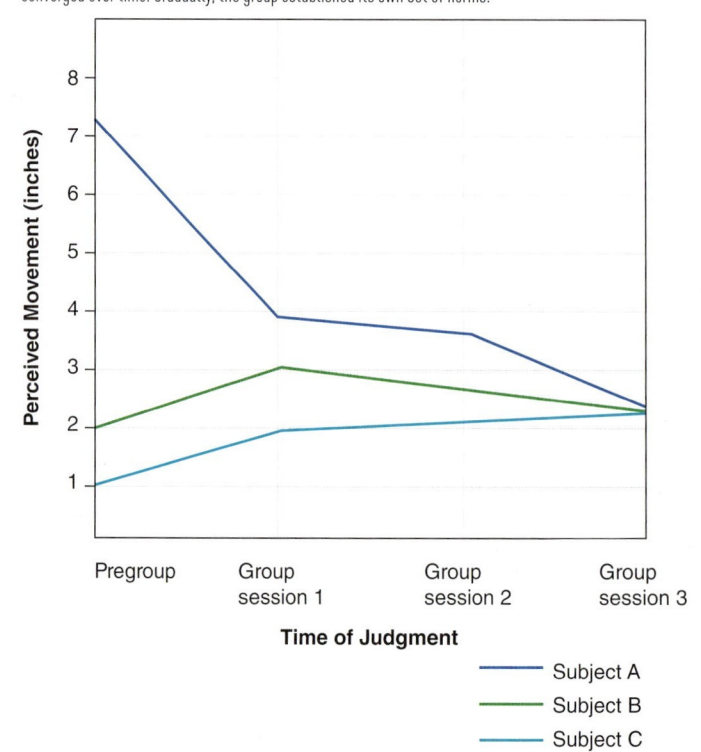

Muzafer Sherif, 1936

FIGURE 10.8 ■ Line-Judgment Task in Asch's Study

Which comparison line—A, B, or C—is the same length as the standard line?

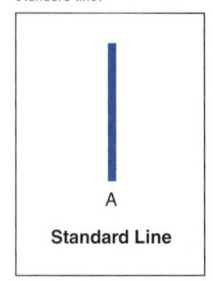

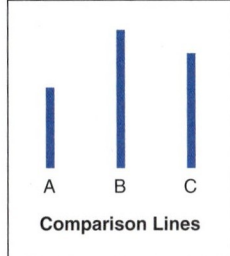

A
Standard Line

A   B   C
Comparison Lines

Source: Asch (1956)

normative influence. Conformity motivated by a fear of social rejection.

conform because they assume that the majority is correct. For example, imagine that your instructor has asked the class, "With a show of hands, who thinks that the answer is 'True'?" You didn't complete the reading, so you aren't quite sure what the answer is. You look around the room and see that the majority of students have their hand up. So, you think to yourself, "All of these students think the answer is 'True,' so I will raise my hand." You believe the other students in class have more knowledge than you do, so you answer the same way to appear as if you also have that knowledge. In **normative influence**, people conform because they fear the social rejection that accompanies deviance. Now, imagine that your instructor is talking about cultural differences in food choices and asks, "With a show of hands, who here has ever eaten a tarantula?" Your heart races a little bit as you hear the class vocalize a long, disgusted, "eeeeewwwwwwwwwww!" Immediately, you recognize that you, in fact, HAVE eaten a tarantula thanks to your study abroad experience in Cambodia…and it was actually quite delicious. Do you raise your hand? No. Way.

This decision is made for good reason. People who stray from the norm are disliked and often are ridiculed and laughed at (Levine, 1989; Levine & Tindale, 2015). These types of negative social reactions are hard to take. In fact, Williams and his colleagues (2002) conducted a series of controlled experiments in which they found that when people are socially *ostracized*—that is, neglected, ignored, and excluded in a live or Internet chat room conversation—they react by feeling hurt, angry, alone, and, in some cases, helpless. The reactions of those ostracized at school (Saylor et al., 2012; Saylor et al., 2013) and in the workplace (O'Reilly, Robinson, Berdahl, & Banki, 2014) have been described by researchers as more severe than if they were bullied.

Majority Influence

Communication often takes place over the Internet and via text messaging, so you may wonder: Do the social forces that influence people in face-to-face groups also operate in virtual groups, where the members are anonymous? Yes. McKenna and Bargh (1998) observed behavior in a number of social media groups in which people with common interests post and respond to messages on a range of topics such as obesity, sexual orientation, and the stock market. The groups in this situation consisted of people who chose to hide their true identities from people in their lives (e.g., people who have concealed their sexual orientation and/or identity from known others). However, in this context, the group members did not stay silent or avoid conversation. Instead, they were highly responsive to social feedback from other members. Here we learn that the majority is powerful in a positive way—it can empower members to share their feelings because those feelings result in encouragement from the masses.

This responsiveness and togetherness has been replicated in research investigating online support groups for persons who identify as transgender (Cipolletta, Votadoro, & Faccio, 2017), identify as bisexual (Maliepaard, 2017), or have an intellectual disability (Shpigelman, 2018). Furthermore, people often choose to share more positive than negative traits about themselves in the hopes of gaining majority approval from online communities (Bargh, McKenna, & Fitzsimons, 2002; Marriott & Buchanan, 2014). Messages and information expected to garner approval are posted more readily than messages and information expected to garner disapproval. Even the response medium for

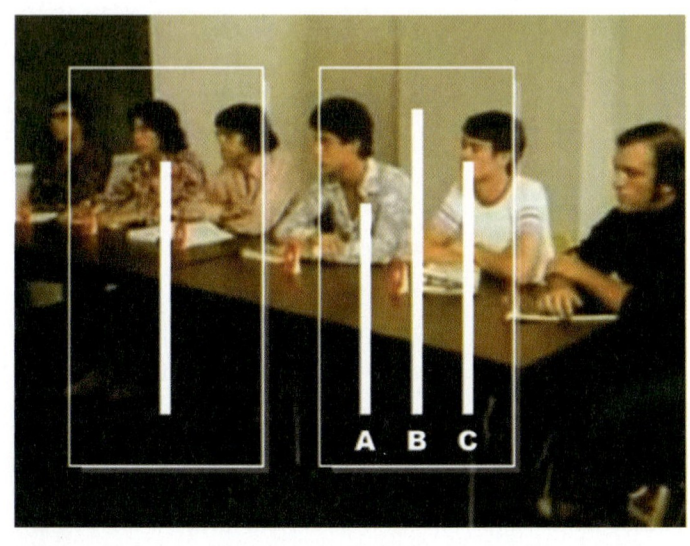

After two uneventful rounds in Asch's line-judgment study, the subject faces a dilemma. Confederates 1 through 5 all gave the same wrong answer. Should he give his own or conform?

D-janous via Wikimedia Commons, licensed under CC BY-SA 4.0

Facebook, Instagram, and Twitter fosters this with the "Like" button. Have you ever wondered why a "thumbs down" option does not exist? When it comes to social support and rejection, even virtual groups have the power to shape our behavior (Bargh et al., 2002; Tosun & Lajunen, 2009; Williams, Cheung, & Choi, 2000).

Realizing that people can be pressured by others is only the first step in understanding the process of social influence. The next step is to identify the situational factors that make us more or less likely to conform. One obvious factor is the size of a group. Common sense suggests that as a majority increases in size, so does its impact. But it is not that simple. Asch (1956) varied the size of his groups by using 1, 2, 3, 4, 8, or 15 confederates, and he found that conformity rose only up to a point. After four confederates, the amount of *additional* influence was negligible, subject to the law of diminishing returns. Latané (1981) likened this impact on an individual to the way lightbulbs illuminate a surface. Add a second bulb in a room, and the effect is dramatic. Add a tenth bulb, and its impact is barely noticed, as illustrated in Figure 10.9.

In Asch's initial study, participants were pitted against a unanimous majority. But what if they had an ally, a partner in dissent? Put yourself in this situation: How do you think having an ally would affect *you?* Varying this aspect of his experiment, Asch found that the presence of just one confederate who gave the correct answer reduced conformity by almost 80 percent. In fact, any dissenter—even one whose competence is questionable—can break the spell cast by a unanimous majority and reduce the pressure to conform (Allen & Levine, 1971).

Finally, cultural factors play an invisible but certain role in conformity to tasks similar to that developed by Asch. In many Western cultures—notably, the United States, Australia, Great Britain, Canada, and the Netherlands—independence and autonomy are highly valued. In contrast, many cultures of Asia, Africa, and Latin America place a value on social harmony and "fitting in" for the sake of the community. Among the Bantu of Zimbabwe, for example, an African people who scorn deviance, 51 percent of those placed in an Asch-like study conformed to the majority's wrong answer, which is more than the proportion typically obtained in the West (Bond & Smith, 1996; Triandis, 1994). Not surprisingly, many anthropologists—interested in how cultures shape individuals—study the processes of conformity and conflict (Spradley, Spradley, & McCurdy, 2000). So do those interested in management techniques. Rink and colleagues (2013) conducted a review on a 50-year span of research on team acceptance for newcomer knowledge. They found that newcomer knowledge was rarely utilized, even when that knowledge was helpful.

FIGURE 10.9 ■ Group Size and Conformity

By varying the number of confederates, Asch found that conformity increased with the size of the majority, but only up to a point. Fifteen confederates had no more impact than did four.

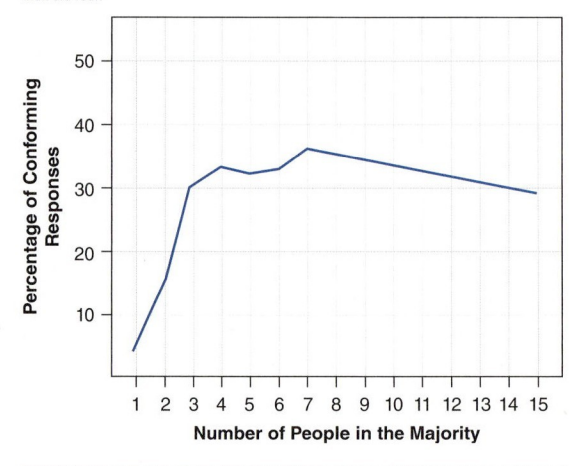

Source: Asch, S. E. (1955)

Taken to the extreme, blind obedience can have tragic results. In World War II, Nazi officials killed millions of Jews in the Holocaust. Were these Germans willing participants, as suggested by Daniel Goldhagen in his 1996 book *Hitler's Willing Executioners*? Or were they just following orders, as subjects did in Milgram's research?

Topical Press Agency / Stringer/Hulton Archive/Getty Images

Obedience to Authority

In World War II, Nazi officials participated in the deaths of millions of Jewish men, women, and children. When they came to trial for these crimes, their defense was always the same: "I was just following orders." Was this episode a fluke, or a historical aberration? In *Hitler's Willing Executioners*, historian Daniel Goldhagen (1996) argues that many ordinary German people were willing accomplices in the Holocaust—not just following orders. At the same time, human crimes of obedience are not unique to Nazi Germany and are committed all over the world (Kelman & Hamilton, 1989). On one most extraordinary occasion, such obedience was carried to its limit: In 1978, 912 men and women of the Peoples Temple cult obeyed an order from the Reverend Jim Jones to kill themselves and their children.

To study the power of authority, Milgram conducted the dramatic experiments described at the beginning of this chapter. In his 1974 book, *Obedience to Authority*, Milgram reported on the results of having put 1,000 participants into a situation in which they were ordered by an experimenter to administer painful electric shocks to a confederate, as illustrated in Figure 10.10. Recall that participants thought they were "teachers" testing the effects of punishment on learning and that each time the "learner" made a mistake, they were to deliver a shock of increasing intensity. The participants could not see the learner, but they could hear grunts of pain, objections, loud screams, and eventual silence. Yet at each step, participants were ordered to continue up the shock scale. Despite the pain participants thought they were inflicting, and despite the guilt and anguish they were experiencing, 65 percent of participants in Milgram's initial study delivered the ultimate punishment of 450 volts.

Similar to the questions we pondered after 9/11, people pondered if Milgram's participants were simply just evil. On the contrary, most participants were tormented by the experience—they demonstrated uncomfortable body language, pleaded with the experimenter, and paused numerous times throughout the study. Regardless of the internal struggle, comparable levels of obedience were found among men, women, and college students all over the world, leading one author to ask, "Are we all Nazis?" (Askenasy, 1978). Indeed, high levels of obedience were found just a few years ago in studies much like Milgram's that were conducted in Poland (Doliński et al., 2017).

But wait…what if we change things up a bit? What if we take the white coat off the experimenter? What if the learner is in the room with the participant? Do those manipulations make a difference in the numbers of participants who continuously obey? The short answer is this: By changing things up a bit, we can reduce or increase the numbers of participants who obey the experimenter. Many systematic variations of Milgram's study have occurred over the years, with variations in the authority figure, victim proximity, and situation. For example, some of these replications have made manipulations such as replacing the experimenter with an average person (authority figure), placing the learner and the teacher in the same room (victim proximity), and carrying out the study in a run-down office building (situation). The closer the learner is to the teacher, the lower the obedience levels. The opposite goes for experimenter to teacher proximity; the farther the experimenter is from the teacher, the lower the obedience. Also, how the situation is staged and what language is used when the order is given to the participant can reduce or increase obedience. The less professional the setting, the lower the percentage of obedient participants.

FIGURE 10.10 ■ Milgram

Milgram's subjects used the shock generator shown here to seemingly deliver up to 450 volts to a confederate who was strapped into his chair.

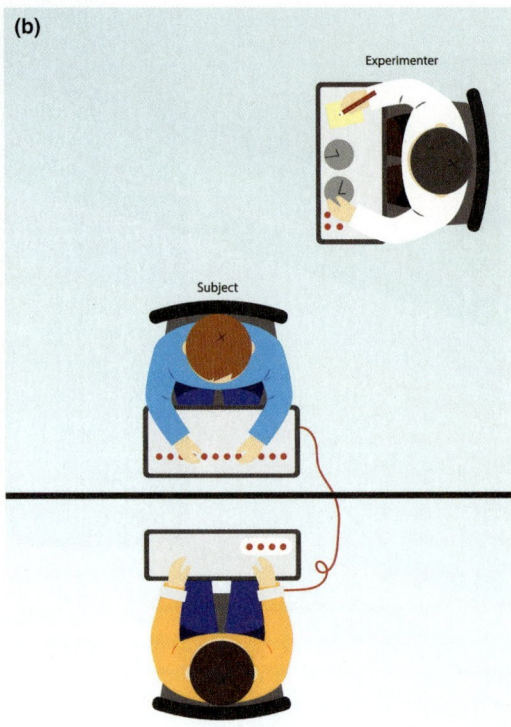

Photo 12/ Alamy Stock Photo/ployy/ Shutterstock

However, there are still those few participants who obey regardless of authority proximity, victim, or situation. Take the real story of a McDonald's in Kentucky where an employee was wrongfully strip searched by her assistant manager and her assistant manager's fiancé (ABC News, 2005). A hoax gone terribly awry began with a phone call from a man pretending to be a police officer (authority figure). The caller told the assistant manager who he was and his purpose for the call. He claimed an employee, Louise Ogborn, was a thief (victim). From there, the caller instructed the assistant manager to make innocent Louise strip, dance around the office, and do jumping jacks. Regardless of Louise's pleas, tears, and strong words of innocence, the assistant manager continued to do as the caller instructed. Eventually, the caller instructed the assistant manager to get her fiancé to watch Louise so that the store would run as needed until the officer could officially detain Louise.

During that time, Louise was sexually harassed and abused. After a 3-hour ordeal, another employee refused to participate in the abuse and called an area manager, who put a stop to it all. During interviews, the assistant manager claimed, "I honestly thought he [the caller] was a police officer." Several other fast food restaurant managers in the U.S. fell for the same hoax. Obedience is real. It is the reason why Louise did as she was told. In fact, Louise stated, "My parents taught me when an adult tells you to do something, that's what you do." Can you think of a time when you did something you didn't want to, but did it anyway because an authority figure told you to do it? Clearly, authority is a social issue of such massive importance that social psychologists all over the world continue to ponder and debate the ramifications of Milgram's studies (Blass, 2000).

Louise Ogborn was not supposed to be at work during the dreadful phone call hoax that changed her life. Louise had offered to stay at work late after her shift officially ended. The call led to Louise's being strip searched by her manager and sexually assaulted and abused by the manager's fiancé. As a result, a jury awarded Louise $6.1 million in total damages and expenses. The manager's fiancé, Walter Nix, was sentenced to five years in prison. David Stewart, the man charged with making the call and impersonating a police officer, was acquitted.

Brian Bohannon/ Associated Press

LEARNING CHECK

Social Study

The left column contains terms related to social influences. Match each term to its closest description.

1.	Social perception	a.	The processes by which we come to know and evaluate other persons
2.	Attribution theory	b.	A tendency to alter one's opinion or behavior in ways consistent with group norms
3.	Fundamental attribution error	c.	A set of theories that describe how people explain the causes of behavior
4.	Primacy effect	d.	The tendency for impressions of others to be heavily influenced by information appearing early in an interaction
5.	Conformity	e.	Conformity motivated by the belief that others are correct
6.	Informational influence	f.	Conformity motivated by a fear of social rejection
7.	Normative influence	g.	A tendency to overestimate the impact of personal causes of behavior and to overlook the role of situations

(Answers: 1. a; 2. c; 3. g; 4. d; 5. b; 6. e; 7. f.)

Attitude Change

People often change their behavior in response to social pressure from a group or figure of authority. These changes, however, are typically limited to one act in one situation at one fleeting moment in time. For the effects to endure, it is necessary to change attitudes, not just behaviors. An **attitude** is

attitude. A positive, negative, or mixed reaction to any person, object, or idea.

a positive, negative, mixed, or indifferent reaction toward a person, object, or idea. People hold quite passionate attitudes about a whole range of issues—from abortion rights, political correctness, and the way to approach the war on terrorism to whether they prefer Google or DuckDuckGo as an Internet search engine. Thus, whether the goal is to win votes on Election Day, get consumers to buy a product, raise funds for a worthy cause, or combat sexual harassment in the military, attitude change is the key to a deeper, more lasting form of social influence (Ajzen, 2001; Eagly & Chaiken, 1998; Glaser et al., 2015; Petty & Cacioppo, 2019; Petty, Wegener, & Fabrigar, 1997; Wood, 2000).

Persuasive Communications

Persuasion, which is the process of changing attitudes, is a part of everyday life. The most common approach is to make a persuasive communication. A familiar example can be found in American politics: Every four years, presidential candidates launch extensive campaigns for office. In a way, if you've seen one election, you've seen them all. The names and dates change, but the action is typically the same: Opposing candidates accuse each other of ducking the issues and turning the election into a popularity contest. Whether or not the accusations are true, they show that politicians are keenly aware that they can win votes by two very different methods. They can stick to the issues, or they can base their appeals on slogans, jingles, images of flag-waving crowds, and other grounds.

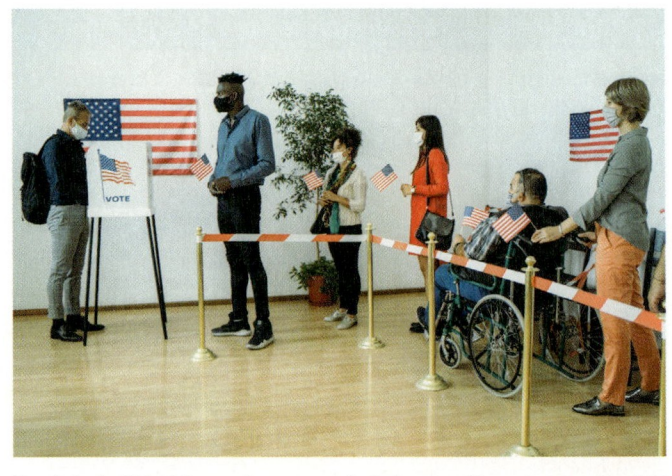

People in the United States place a great deal of personal importance on the right to vote. When asked about the importance of five rights and freedoms, the right to vote ranks about as high as any item on the list. Approximately 155.5 million Americans voted in the 2020 presidential election.

iStock.com/Vladimir Vladimirov

To account for these varying approaches, Petty and Cacioppo (1986) proposed a two-track model of persuasion. When people have the ability and motivation to think critically about the contents of a message, they take the **central route to persuasion**. In these instances, people are influenced by the strength and quality of the arguments. When people do not have the ability or motivation to pay close attention to the issues, however, they take mental shortcuts along the **peripheral route to persuasion**, as illustrated in Figure 10.11 (Rahman, 2018). In this case, people may be influenced by a speaker's appearance, slogans, one-liners, emotions, audience reactions, and other superficial cues (Kergoat, Meyer, & Merot, 2017).

central route to persuasion. A process in which people think carefully about a message and are influenced by its arguments.

peripheral route to persuasion. A process in which people do not think carefully about a message and are influenced by superficial cues.

One way to look at these routes is to think of persuasion as the vehicle. The vehicle gets you to the destination—say, voting for president of the United States. A vehicle can get you to this destination of voting for president in one of two ways—as the driver (central route) or as the passenger (the peripheral route). The driver is thinking critically about the route, how much pressure to put on the brake, when to turn, and if the traffic lights are green. The passenger is along for the ride, looking at scenery, watching people walking into shops, and playing with the radio. Both the driver and the passenger get to the same destination—voting for Katya—but in different ways. So, when we are being persuaded to vote, the central route aims for the engaged "driver" with things like statistics and facts, whereas the peripheral route aims for the passive "passenger" with things like emotional appeals and attractive speakers. This two-track model helps to explain how voters, consumers, juries, and other targets of persuasion can seem so logical on some occasions yet so illogical on other occasions (Petty & Wegener, 1999; Sanjosé-Cabezudo, Gutiérrez-Arranz, & Gutiérrez-Cillán, 2009).

To understand the conditions that produce change using one route or the other, it's helpful to view persuasion as the outcome of three factors: a *source* (who), a *message* (says what), and an *audience* (to whom). If a speaker is clear, if the message is relevant and important, and if there is a bright and captive audience that cares deeply about the issues, then that audience will take the effortful central route. But if the source speaks too fast to comprehend, if the message is trivial, or if the audience is distracted, pressed for time, or just not interested, then the less strenuous peripheral route is taken. Particularly important is whether the target audience is personally involved in the issue under consideration, such as parents who are contemplating their child's vaccination (Goh & Chi, 2017). High involvement leads

FIGURE 10.11 ■ Social Influencing

Can attractive sources help sell products and events? Targeting the peripheral route to persuasion, the advertising industry seems to think so. And after a massive 2017 music festival—Fyre Festival—was discovered to be fraudulently advertised, influencers and celebrities have been highly encouraged to include #ad when they are promoting products and experiences. Kendall Jenner and Bella Hadid were two of the celebrities who promoted the failed Fyre Festival and faced extreme backlash as a result (Cerullo, 2019). This backlash prompted Hadid to release an apology tweet.

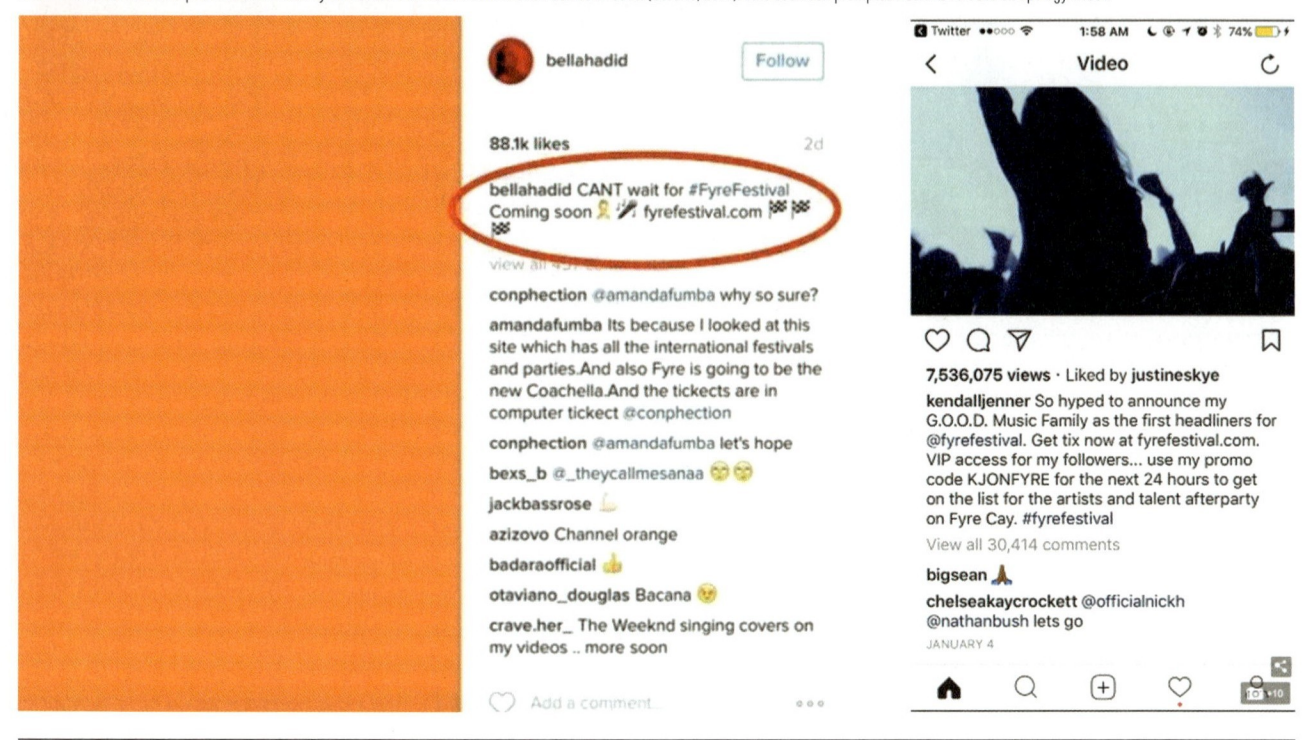

Atstock Productions/ Shutterstock/

us to take the central route; low involvement, the peripheral route (Johnson & Eagly, 1989; Petty & Cacioppo, 1990). This model is illustrated in Figure 10.12.

Cognitive Dissonance Theory

Anyone who has ever acted on stage knows how easy it is to become so absorbed in a role that the experience seems real. Forced laughter can make an actor feel happy, and fake tears can turn to sadness. Even in real life, the effect can be dramatic. In 1974, Patty Hearst—a sheltered young college student from a wealthy family—was kidnapped by a revolutionary group. When arrested months later, she was carrying a gun and calling herself Tania. How could someone be so totally converted? In Hearst's own words, "I had thought I was humoring [my captors] by parroting their clichés and buzzwords without believing in them. In trying to convince them I convinced myself."

The Patty Hearst case reveals the powerful effects of role-playing. Nonetheless, you don't have to be terrorized to be coaxed into doing something that contradicts your inner convictions. People often engage in attitude-discrepant behavior—as part of a job, for example, or to please others. This raises a profound question: What happens when people behave in ways that do not follow from their attitudes? We know that attitudes influence behavior. But can the causal arrow be reversed? That is, can a forced change in behavior spark a change in attitude?

cognitive dissonance. An unpleasant psychological state often aroused when people behave in ways that are discrepant with their attitudes.

The answer to this question was provided by Festinger's (1957) **cognitive dissonance** theory. According to Festinger, people hold numerous cognitions about themselves and the world around them—and sometimes these cognitions clash. For example, you say you're on a budget, but all of those products endorsed by celebrities keep popping up in your Instagram feed and suddenly you've spent $200. Or you waited in the rain for hours to see a concert, but when the rain stopped and the band finally took the stage, the entire experience was disappointing. Or you baked under the hot summer sun, even though you knew of the health risks. In each case, there is inconsistency and conflict. You committed yourself to a course of action, but you realize that your behavior contradicts your attitude.

FIGURE 10.12 ■ Two Routes to Persuasion

Based on aspects of the source, message, and audience, people take either a central or a peripheral route to persuasion. On the central route, we are influenced by strong arguments and evidence. On the peripheral route, we are influenced more by superficial cues.

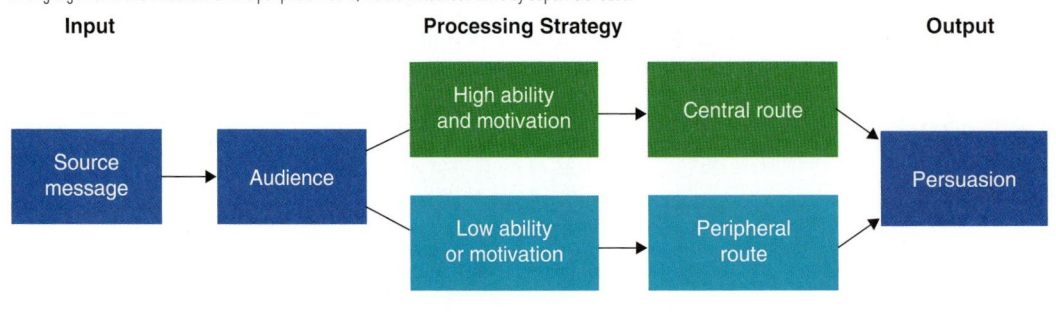

Input → Source message → **Processing Strategy** → Audience → High ability and motivation → Central route / Low ability or motivation → Peripheral route → **Output** → Persuasion

Source: Adapted from Kassin, Fein and Markus (2017).

According to Festinger, these kinds of discrepancies often produce an unpleasant state of tension that he called cognitive dissonance. Attitude-discrepant behavior doesn't always arouse dissonance. If you broke a diet for a holiday dinner or if you thought that the mousse you ate was low in calories, you would be relatively free of tension. Attitude-discrepant behavior that is performed freely and with knowledge of the consequences, however, does arouse dissonance—and the motivation to reduce it. There are different ways to cope with this unpleasant state. Often the easiest is to change your attitude so that it becomes consistent with your behavior.

To understand dissonance theory, imagine for a moment that you are a participant in the classic study by Festinger and Carlsmith (1959). The experimenter tells you that he is interested in various measures of performance. He hands you a wooden board containing 48 pegs in square holes and asks you to turn each peg to the left, then to the right, then back to the left, and again to the right. The routine seems endless. After 30 minutes, the experimenter comes to your rescue. Or does he? Just when you think things are looking up, he hands you another board, another assignment. For the next half-hour, you are to take 12 spools of thread off the board, put them back on, take them off, and so on. By now, you're just about ready to tear your hair out. As you think back over better times, even the first task begins to look good.

Finally, you've finished. After one of the longest hours of your life, the experimenter lets you in on a secret: There's more to this study than meets the eye. You were in the control group. To test the effects of motivation on performance, the experimenter will tell other participants that the experiment is fun. You don't realize it, but you're being set up for a critical part of the study. Would you tell the next participant that the experiment is enjoyable? Just as you hem and haw, the experimenter offers to pay for your lie. Some participants, like you, are offered $1; others, $20. Before you know it, you're in the waiting room trying to dupe an unsuspecting fellow student.

By means of this staged presentation, participants were goaded into an attitude-discrepant behavior, an act that contradicted their private attitudes. They knew the experiment was dull, but they raved. Was cognitive dissonance aroused? It depended on how much participants were paid. Suppose you were one of the lucky ones offered $20. Even by today's standards, that amount provides sufficient justification for telling a little white lie. Being well compensated, these participants did not feel dissonance. Now imagine you were offered only $1. Surely your integrity is worth more than that, don't you think? In this case, you do not have sufficient justification for lying. So you cope by changing your view of the task. If you can convince yourself that the experiment was interesting, then there is no conflict.

When the experiment was presumably over, participants were asked to rate the peg-board tasks. Control-group participants who did not mislead a confederate admitted the tasks were boring. So did those in the $20 condition who had ample justification for what they did. Those paid only $1, however, rated the tasks as more enjoyable. After engaging in an attitude-discrepant behavior without sufficient justification, these participants felt internally pressured to change their attitudes in order to reduce cognitive dissonance, as illustrated in Figure 10.13. In an interesting replication of this provocative study, Eddie Harmon-Jones and others (1996) found that participants who were asked to lie about

FIGURE 10.13 ■ Festinger and Carlsmith's Classic Dissonance Study

How interesting is a boring task? Compared to participants who did not have to lie and those paid to do so, those paid only later rated the task as more enjoyable. Having engaged in an attitude-discrepant behavior, these latter participants reduced dissonance by changing their attitudes.

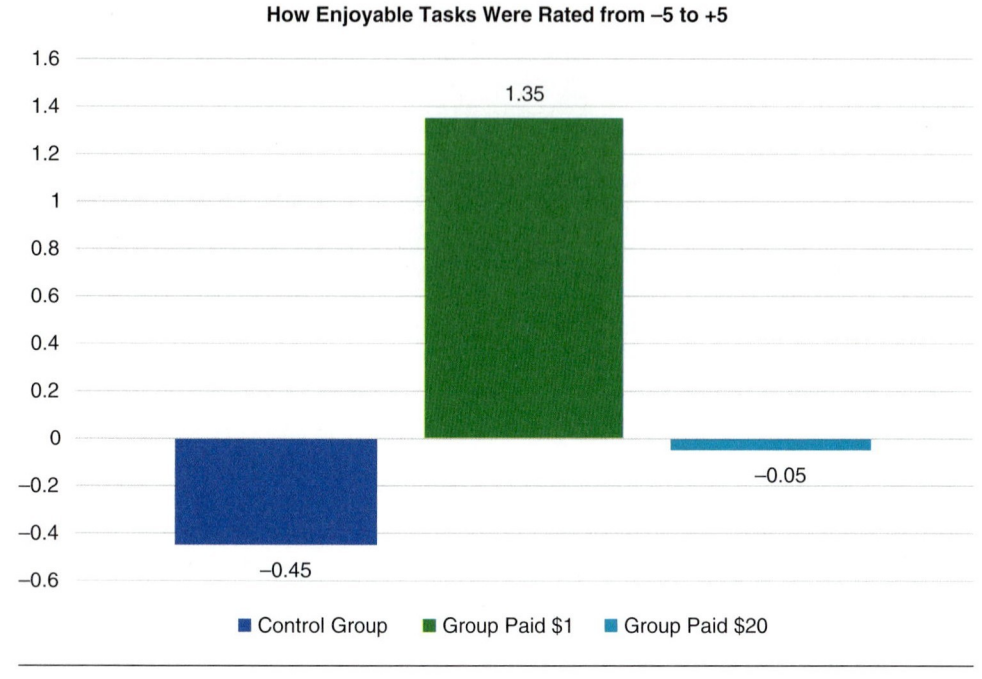

How Enjoyable Tasks Were Rated from −5 to +5

- Control Group: −0.45
- Group Paid $1: 1.35
- Group Paid $20: −0.05

Festinger, L., & Carlsmith, J. M. (1959)

the good taste of a Kool-Aid beverage laced with vinegar later rated that drink as more pleasing to the palette than it actually was.

What's Your Prediction?

Cognitive dissonance theory makes another interesting prediction: that we will change our attitudes to justify our effort, money spent, time, or suffering. In a classic study, Eliot Aronson and Judson Mills (1959) invited female students to join a discussion group about sex. But first they had to pass an "embarrassment test." Some underwent a severe test (they had to read obscene passages out loud), others underwent a mild test (they read only mildly erotic words), and still others were admitted without initiation. All passed, only to find that the discussion group was dreadfully boring. Afterward, the women were asked to rate how interesting they found the group. Make a prediction: Who rated the group most interesting: those who were put through a *severe initiation* (and had to justify their suffering), *mild initiation* (creating positive feelings for the group), or *no initiation* (it was all new to them)? As predicted by dissonance theory, women who endured a severe initiation rated the group as most interesting. Apparently, we have to justify our efforts—leading us to like what we suffer for.

Psychology Applied: How Persuasion Fueled Fyre Festival

#FyreFestival. The exclusive music festival, tailored to millennials, was backed by a gorgeous island, public appearances by Ja Rule, and an entrepreneurial genius named Billy McFarland. Behind him was a team of software engineers, stacks of credit cards, the world's most beautiful supermodels, and a team of approximately 400 influencers whose posts reached an audience of at least 300 million (Talbot, 2019). The media storm was so successful that tickets sold out within hours. It was destined to be the most incredible and luxurious music festival there ever was. Until it wasn't.

Unbeknownst to ticket-holders, the island could not sustain thousands of people. Luxury housing became hurricane relief tents, soaked by the rain, and furnished with inflatable mattresses. Catered meals became two pieces of bread with cheese and a salad. In a matter of hours, Fyre Festival evolved into the joke of the year. Those who actually arrived at the festival site went into a panic and began looting whatever they could get their hands on. Billy and his team, out of fear for their lives, had to flee the Bahamas, leaving behind thousands of angry patrons and unpaid workers.

How could so many people be persuaded to invest their resources and careers in an unknown music festival? Cialdini's (2009) theory of persuasion explains this phenomenon quite well. In summary, if we are to be persuaded, we look for certain traits. These traits include authority, likeability, reciprocity, consistency, consensus, and scarcity. Billy and the team that built Fyre Festival had all of these traits. One trait in particular is consensus. Fyre Festival became so popular that it lent itself to what is now called FoMO, or fear of missing out. "FoMO is characterized by the desire to stay continually connected with what others are doing" (Przybylski, Murayama, Dehaan, & Gladwell, 2013, p. 1841). We want to make choices that others support and are a part of. The principle of scarcity also connects with FoMO. We don't want to miss out on something that might be a once-in-a-lifetime opportunity. You can imagine the desire of a young professional at Fyre Media to be a part of something rare that could easily make your career. And you can imagine the desire of a ticket-holder to be at the exclusive Fyre Festival with your friends, making memories that will last a lifetime. Last, think about the knowledge of having something that everybody wants, but only you get. The harder it is to own, the more it is worth. With so few tickets and housing options available, purchasers surely felt they had to get what they could while they could. Unfortunately, Fyre Festival investments did not pay off. In some instances, people were left in debt. Will ticket-holders ever be reimbursed? Will Billy's former employees receive wages for their work? What about the Bahamians who went into debt to feed and shelter Billy's employees? These answers are uncertain, but important lessons have been learned about social media and persuasion. In future posts made by celebrities and influencers, look for #ad and remember that sometimes missing out is a good thing. The people who were stranded at Fyre Festival and never saw a return on their investment would probably agree.

In the Netflix documentary, *FYRE: The Greatest Party That Never Happened* (Jerry Media & Smith, 2019), an employee of Billy McFarland talks about the irony that 400 influencers and a team of bikini-clad supermodels made the unknown music festival an overnight success. It went on to become a laughingstock and punch line for jokes after it failed to live up to the hype.

Ollie Millington / Contributor / Getty Images

Group Processes

When individuals assemble in groups, profound changes sometimes take place. Examples include the random violence and vandalism of street gangs, avid sports fans who scream at the top of their lungs and sometimes riot after victory, high-powered corporate groups that make unusually risky decisions, and angry and militant mobs seeking revenge. It's as if the group casts a spell over the individuals who compose it.

Fyre Festival was not Billy McFarland's only attempt at fraud. In total, investors and customers lost $26 million as a result of his various schemes. He was convicted of fraud in 2018 and sentenced to 6 years, a lenient sentence requested by his attorneys due to his "mental health issues" (Madani, 2018).

Mark Lennihan / Associated Press

social facilitation. The tendency for the presence of others to enhance performance on simple tasks and impair performance on complex tasks.

Social Facilitation

How does the mere presence of others affect behavior? Appropriately, this most basic question in social psychology was also the first to be tested. In 1898, Triplett studied bicycle-racing records and discovered that the cyclists were faster when they competed alongside others than when they pedaled alone against the clock. Intrigued by this finding, Triplett had 40 children simply wind a fishing reel—sometimes alone, other times in pairs. Again, performance was faster among those who worked together than alone. Triplett's conclusion: The presence of others triggers "nervous energy," thereby enhancing performance.

Subsequently, many researchers confirmed that the presence of others speeds up performance on various cognitive and motor tasks (even ants excavate more and chickens eat more when they are in the company of other members of their species). At the same time, however, other researchers were observing performance declines. Why did the presence of others have such different effects on task performance? In 1965, Zajonc solved the problem. He noted that the presence of others increases arousal and that arousal enhances the "dominant" response—that is, whatever response is most likely to occur. Zajonc reasoned that the dominant response is more likely to be the correct one when a task is easy (such as adding two numbers) but to be incorrect when the task is more difficult (such as solving a complex equation). The presence of other people should thus improve our performance on simple tasks but impair performance on tasks that are difficult. To demonstrate, Zajonc found that participants who tried to memorize simple word associations *(mother-father)* performed better in the presence of others than alone, but those who tried to learn difficult associations *(mother-algebra)* did worse. This phenomenon is called social facilitation, as illustrated in Figure 10.14.

Social Loafing

Social facilitation effects are found for *individual* tasks such as running a race, solving a problem, or memorizing a word list. In these types of activities, one's own performance is easy to identify. What about cooperative *joint* activities where individual contributions are pooled? In a tug-of-war, say, or in a cooperative class project, does each person exert more effort when participating as part of a team or alone? To find out, Ingham and others (1974) asked blindfolded participants to pull on a rope "as hard

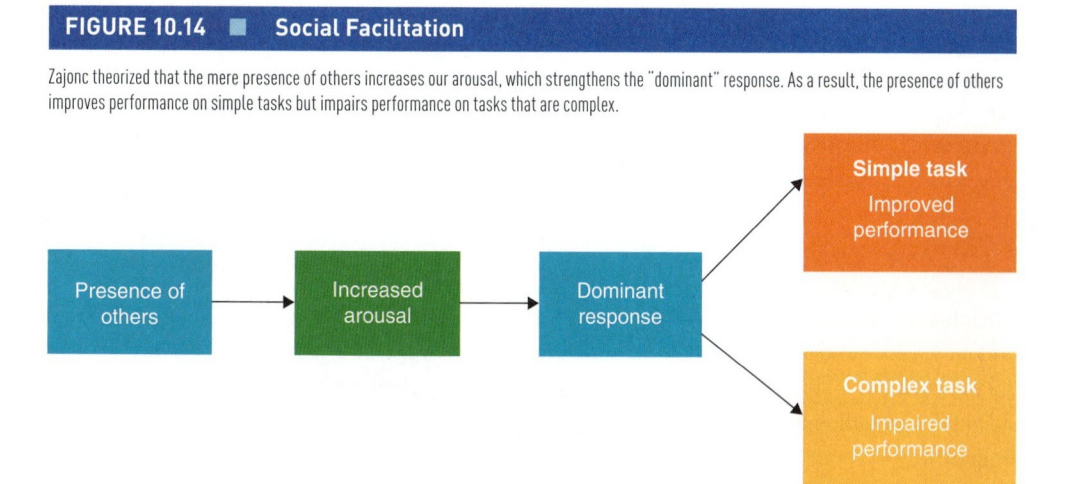

FIGURE 10.14 ■ Social Facilitation

Zajonc theorized that the mere presence of others increases our arousal, which strengthens the "dominant" response. As a result, the presence of others improves performance on simple tasks but impairs performance on tasks that are complex.

Presence of others → Increased arousal → Dominant response → Simple task: Improved performance / Complex task: Impaired performance

as you can" and found that participants pulled 18 percent harder when they knew they were alone than when they thought that three other participants were pulling with them. Latané and others (1979) then asked participants to clap or cheer "as loud as you can"—either alone or in groups of two, four, or six. The result: As individuals, participants produced less noise when they thought they were part of a group than when they thought they were alone.

The Latané and others (1979) coined the term **social loafing** to describe this group-produced reduction in individual effort. As illustrated in Figure 10.15, social loafing increases with group size: The more others there are, the less effort each individual participant exerts. In the clapping and cheering study, for example, two-person groups performed at only 71 percent of their individual capacity, four-person groups at 51 percent, and six-person groups at 40 percent. Why do people slack off when others are there to pick up the slack? There are a few reasons. One is that people see their own contribution as unessential to the group's success. A second is that people are less concerned about being personally evaluated—in part because individual performance standards within a group are unclear. A third possibility is that people slack off in order to guard against looking like the "sucker" who works harder than everyone else. Putting all the pieces together, researchers have concluded that social loafing occurs because individuals often do not see the connection between their own effort and the desired outcome (Sheppard, 1993). Remember this the next time you have a group assignment!

FIGURE 10.15 ■ Social Loafing

Participants were told to clap or cheer "as loud as you can"—either alone or in groups of two, four, or six. The more others there were, the less effort each individual participant exerted.

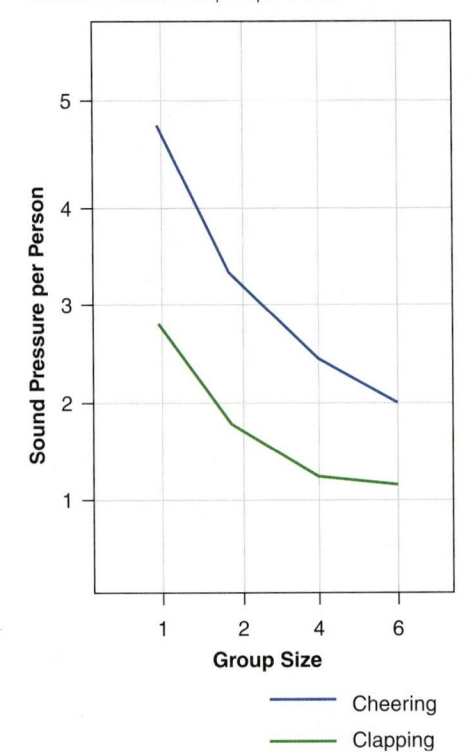

Latané, B., Williams, K., & Harkins, S. (1979). Many hands make light the work: The causes and consequences of social loafing. Journal of Personality and Social Psychology, 37(6), 822–832. https://doi.org/10.1037/0022-3514.37.6.822

social loafing. The tendency for people to exert less effort in group tasks for which individual contributions are pooled.

SOCIAL RELATIONS

LEARNING OBJECTIVES

Contrast variables that increase helping and aggressive behavior.

- Determine the types of aversive events that predispose people to behave aggressively.
- Contrast aggression with altruism.
- List situational factors that influence helping behavior.

People relate to one another in different ways. Sometimes our interactions and the decisions we make are negative, hostile, and antisocial. At other times, we are helpful, charitable, and prosocial in our behavior. Let's examine these two contrasting tendencies and the situations that bring them out in us.

Aggression

On a Portland MAX train in May 2017, Jeremy Joseph Christian verbally attacked two women with ethnic and religious slurs (Haag & Fortin, 2017). Three innocent witnesses intervened—Ricky John

Best, Taliesin Myrddin Namkai-Meche, and Micah David-Cole Fletcher. In a violent response, Jeremy attacked these three men with a knife. Sadly, Ricky and Taliesin died from their stab wounds. Then there was the tragic killing of Ahmaud Arbery—a Black man who was jogging through a neighborhood in Georgia when he was chased down and fatally shot by a White father and son (Romo, 2020). At YouTube headquarters in April 2018, a popular animal rights activist and vlogger, Nasim Najafi Aghdam, opened fire on employees (Thanawala & Nakashima, 2018). According to sources, she was furious that YouTube had censored her videos. That same month, another woman, Jordan Worth, made history. An honors graduate from the University of Hertfordshire, Jordan volunteered to raise funds for sheltered pets and neglected children in Africa. But her petite frame, loving Facebook posts, and charity work cleverly disguised a horrendous secret. For years she had tortured her boyfriend and the father of her children, Alex Skeel. The torture was so brutal, police found Alex with seriously infected burns, fluid buildup in his skull from head trauma, stab wounds, and severe malnutrition. Alex was days away from death when police intervened. In April 2018, Jordan became the first woman in the United Kingdom prosecuted for coercive control, and she was sentenced to serve 7.5 years in prison (BBC News, 2018). These examples serve as a sad reminder that human aggression is everywhere. From domestic terrorism, to violent episodes of road rage that flare up on highways, to cyberbullying, the list of violent incidents seems endless.

In some ways, these acts are so deviant that they shed little light on "normal" human nature. After all, if you think about the number of opportunities we have every day to inflict harm, we more often than not choose to keep the peace. We sit in idle cars when crosswalks are occupied, hold doors open so that others can easily pass, and move to the right on escalators so that those in a hurry can safely hustle to their destination. However, these examples of violence serve to remind us that **aggression**—behavior that is intended to inflict harm on someone motivated to avoid it—is a common and contagious social disease. Every day, people all over the world are victims of wars between nations, conflicts between ethnic and religious groups, racism, street gangs, drug dealers, sexual assaults, intimate violence, and police brutality. Some argue that aggression is programmed into human nature by instincts, genes, hormones, and other biological factors. Others emphasize the role of culture, social learning, and environmental stressors. As always, human behavior is not the product of either nature or nurture but the interaction of many factors (Anderson & Bushman, 2002; Berkowitz, 1993).

aggression. Behavior intended to inflict harm on someone who is motivated to avoid it.

Biological Roots

Human aggression is subject to biological influences (Ball et al., 2008; Renfrew, 1997; Silberg et al., 2016; Zhang et al, 2018). Twin and adoption studies have suggested that genetic factors play a role, though it's not clear how large that role is (Coccaro et al., 2018; DiLalla & Gottesman, 1991; Mann, Tackett, Tucker-Drob, & Harden, 2017; Miles & Carey, 1997). There are also consistent sex differences in aggression. Among children and adolescents, males are more physically aggressive than females in the way they play and fight (Loeber & Hay, 1997), with these differences appearing in early childhood (Alink et al., 2006; Baillargeon et al., 2007). Similarly, among adults, males behave more aggressively than females in laboratory experiments (Bettencourt & Miller, 1996; Eagly & Steffen, 1986). In every country that has kept criminal records, males commit more violent crimes than females. According to the FBI, the ratio of male to female murderers in the United States is about 10 to 1.

What explains the sex difference in direct physical aggression? One possibility is that aggression is linked to the male sex hormone testosterone. Although both males and females have testosterone, males have higher levels on average than females do. What is the effect? In rats, mice, cattle (Needham, Lambrechts, & Hoffman, 2017), and other animals, injections of testosterone increase levels of aggression, whereas castration, which lowers testosterone, has the opposite effect (Breuer, McGinnis, Lumia, & Possidente, 2001). In humans, correlational studies show that people with high levels of testosterone tend to be bold, courageous, energetic, competitive, rambunctious, and yes—aggressive (Dabbs, 2000).

Contrary to the stereotype, women can be physically abusive. Men, too, can be victims of intimate partner abuse. Gender does not protect anyone from victimization.

iStock.com/LightFieldStudios

Aversive Stimulation

Aggression may have biological roots, but it is also learned from experience and then is triggered by factors in the environment. Put two rats in a cage together; subject them to painful shocks, loud noise, or intense heat; and a fight is likely to break out. Put people together in unpleasant conditions—overcrowded living quarters, intense shifts in climate (Hsiang, Burke, & Miguel, 2013; Mares, 2013) the stench of body odor, or the company of an obnoxious coworker—and they too become more likely to lash out. As a general rule, aversive stimulation sparks aggression (Berkowitz, 1983).

frustration-aggression hypothesis. The theory that frustration causes aggression.

One type of aversive event that we all experience is frustration. In 1939, John Dollard and others proposed the hypothesis that frustration leads to aggression either against the source of frustration or against an innocent but vulnerable substitute, or scapegoat. According to the U.S. Department of Transportation, this frequently occurs on highways and city streets, where motorists obstructed by traffic scream, honk, tailgate, and hurl obscene gestures at other drivers, as they erupt in fits of "road rage." The effects of frustration are exhibited by passengers in the not-so-friendly skies of commercial airlines, where long lines, cramped spaces, schedule delays, overbooked planes, stale air, and battles for the armrest have frayed nerves and increased incidents of "air rage," often directed at flight attendants (Morgan & Nickson, 2001; Zoroya, 1999).

Testing the implications of this **frustration-aggression hypothesis**, Hovland and Sears (1940) examined the link between economic hard times and racial violence. They analyzed records from 14 southern states during the years 1882 to 1930 and discovered a strong negative correlation between the value of cotton and lynchings: As the price of cotton fell, the number of lynchings increased. Although this correlation cannot be interpreted in causal terms, experiments have confirmed that frustration sparks aggression by arousing anger, fear, and other negative emotions (Berkowitz, 1989). Staub (1996) believes that historical acts of genocide—as in the Holocaust of World War II—often stem from societal frustration, poor economic conditions, and the need to find a scapegoat. A meta-analysis of 49 studies showed that people who are frustrated do, at times, *displace* their aggression by lashing out against innocent others (Marcus-Newhall, Pedersen, Carlson, & Miller, 2000). For example, Twenge and others (2001) found that college students who experienced social exclusion from a research group later reacted more aggressively toward a critical fellow student. Another study on exclusion by Chow and colleagues (2008) experimentally manipulated rejection in a virtual dodge ball game. The researchers found that those participants who felt angry as a result of exclusion were more likely to engage in antisocial behaviors.

Situational Cues

Frustration, extreme heat, and other aversive events predispose us to aggression by arousing negative affect. Once we are in this state of readiness, the presence of people and objects associated with aggression may then prompt us to act on this predisposition. Aversive events "load the gun," so to speak, but situational cues get us to "pull the trigger." What situational cues have this effect?

Weapons. The sights and sounds of violence are everywhere. In the United States, millions of adults own handguns. Daily TV news reports flood us not only with graphic images of street violence but also with talk of nuclear, chemical, and biological weapons of mass destruction. Does any of this matter? Yes. According to Berkowitz, the mere sight of an aggressive stimulus can influence behavior. In a classic demonstration of this point, Berkowitz and LePage (1967) had male participants administer electric shocks to a confederate who had insulted half the participants right before the session. In one condition, only the shock-generating apparatus was present in the lab. In a second condition, a .38-caliber pistol and a 12-gauge shotgun were on the table near the shock button—supposedly left from an earlier previous experiment. As measured by the number of shocks given, aggression was increased by the sight of these guns. Participants who were angered and primed to be aggressive retaliated more in the presence of the weapons than in their absence.

This provocative "weapons effect" has been observed across 56 experiments (Benjamin, Kepes, & Bushman, 2017). For example, Anderson and colleagues (1998) presented participants with pictures of weapons or plants and then recorded the amount of time it took those participants to read aloud as quickly as possible various words flashed on a screen. The result: After seeing images of weapons as opposed to plants, participants were quicker to read aggression-related words such as *punch, choke, butcher,* and *shoot.*

Studies have linked engaging in virtual aggressive behaviors with exhibiting aggression in real life.

iStock.com/EvgeniyShkolenko

Why do images of weapons have this impact on reading speed? Weapons are commonly associated with violence, so the mere sight of a pistol, a club, or a sword automatically brings aggression-related thoughts to mind. Anderson and Bushman's (2002) General Aggression Model (GAM) provides a way for us to understand the progression of events. The GAM has two types of input—personal (gender, age, genetics, values) and situational (media exposure, frustration, provocation, climate, alcohol). One type of input is not necessarily more important than the other. Say there are two people, a hunter and a nonhunter, in the exact same situation—they are standing in a room and there is an assault gun on the table. Would their perceptions of the gun differ because of personal traits? Bartholow and colleagues (2005) looked at differences in reactions to images of weapons between hunters and nonhunters. Sure enough, hunters' and nonhunters' reactions differed depending on the type of gun. Assault guns were more likely to cue aggression in hunters, and hunting guns were more likely to cue aggression in nonhunters. Personal factors can make a difference.

Personal and situational factors then have an impact on the person's internal state. The internal state includes emotions, thought processes, and arousal. Next, the person appraises the situation and makes decisions. Finally, there is a behavioral outcome. The behavioral outcome brings us to the question, do guns kill, or are people the problem? After all, a person has to pull the trigger.

Media Violence. As if reality did not provide enough of a stimulus, the entertainment industry adds fuel to the fire. Estimates suggest that there are 2.3 television sets per American household (U.S. Energy Information Administration, 2015). Add that to cell phones, computers, and tablets and you have several opportunities to observe violence. Over the years, analyses of television shows have revealed what you might have suspected: Depictions of violence are common in media, entertainment, commercials, and, worst of all, children's cartoons—where heroes, villains, and other creatures fight dozens of battles an hour. Research has shown that roughly 60 percent of all programs contain some violence. What's worse, the perpetrators are often "good guys," the context is often humorous, the violence is almost never punished, and it is seldom depicted as bloody, painful, or harmful in the long run (Seawell, 1998).

Does exposure to TV violence promote aggression? Literally hundreds of studies have addressed this important question, with alarming results (Bushman, 2016). Correlational studies reveal a link between the amount of TV violence watched by young boys and their subsequent levels of aggression—a link commonly observed in the United States and Europe (Geen & Donnerstein, 1998; Huesmann & Eron, 1986). In a longitudinal development study, for example, Eron (1987) found that a boy's exposure to TV violence at 8 years of age predicted criminal activity 22 years later. Violent video games have also been connected with delinquent behaviors (Exelmans, Custers, & Bulck, 2015). Critics are quick to note that these correlations cannot be used to draw conclusions about cause and effect (Bender, Plante, & Gentile, 2018). Perhaps exposure to violent media causes aggression, as it seems; or perhaps aggressiveness causes children to seek out violent media; or perhaps poverty and other external conditions cause the tendency both to watch and to commit acts of aggression (Freedman, 1988). A meta-analysis of 37 studies on violent media and hostile appraisals found significant connections between violent media consumption and how hostile the participants viewed the world (Bushman, 2016). In turn, those who view the world as hostile are more prone to behave aggressively (Bushman, 2016). Whatever the explanation, the link between TV violence exposure and aggressive behavior is almost as strong as the correlation between cigarette smoking and lung cancer (Bushman & Huesmann, 2001).

To pin down cause and effect, researchers have observed participants who are randomly assigned to watch violent or nonviolent events. Controlled laboratory studies of this sort show that exposure to aggressive models, either live or on film, has negative effects. In the first of these experiments, Bandura and others (1961) found that preschool children

Observing violent models, whether in video games or on screen, may increase aggression in children. This image of a child striking a toy is reflective of the aggressive modeling behavior that Bandura investigated in his classic study.

WATFORD/Mirrorpix/Mirrorpix via Getty Images

were more likely to attack an inflated doll after watching an aggressive adult model than after watching a nonaggressive adult model. In a similar experiment, Dillon and Bushman (2017) randomly assigned children to one of two film-viewing conditions—a PG-rated film clip where characters can be seen with guns or without guns. After viewing the film clip, the children played in a room for 20 minutes. A real, but disabled, gun with a trigger sensor was available in the room for the children to handle. The median number of trigger pulls for children who saw the film clip with guns was 2.8 compared to 0.01 for children who did not see the gun-containing film clip. Children who watched the gun-containing film clip spent 53.1 seconds holding the gun, whereas children who did not watch the gun-containing film clip held the gun for 11.1 seconds. Dillon and Bushman (2017) concluded that children who observe movie characters use guns have a higher probability of using guns themselves. The common finding for these studies is that among children and adolescents, exposure to violent models increases aggression—not just in laboratories but also in classrooms, playgrounds, and other settings (Wood, Wong, & Chachere, 1991).

Altruism

While situations like climate can increase aggression, they can also reveal humans behaving at their best. The United States has experienced many tragic natural disasters, and according to climate change experts, these natural disasters won't be happening with less frequency. In August 2017, Hurricane Harvey hit Houston with no mercy. The vicious downpour and high winds drowned areas of the highly populated city, resulting in the displacement of tens of thousands of residents. People were floating on pool toys, sitting on roofs, and swimming in debris-laden waters desperate to be rescued. One man, Dr. Stephen Kimmel, watched helplessly as his home flooded…until he received a call about Jacob Terrazes.

Jacob Terrazes was a teenager in great need of immediate surgery (Squitieri, 2017). But on this day, getting to the hospital for such a procedure seemed nearly impossible to both the surgeon and his patient. In waist-high floodwater, Kimmel set his mind to making the impossible possible. A volunteer fire department assisted Kimmel via canoe and pickup truck on an hour-long journey to the hospital. Meanwhile, Jacob and his family required rescue by another team of firefighters to get there. Once Jacob arrived safely, Kimmel performed the surgery. In an interview with CNN about his heroism, the surgeon humbly responded, "It's great to take care of kids and see them get better" (Squitieri, 2017).

Stories of raw heroism are everywhere. During the tragic collapse of the World Trade Center towers, firefighters climbed *up* the twin buildings' stairs without hesitation—many to their own deaths—to rescue their fellow humans who were trapped (Smith, 2002). From the horrors of Nazi Germany came a number of heroic stories about German citizens who risked their lives to hide their Jewish friends and neighbors (Schneider, 2000). Why did all these heroes try to rescue those in need? Why do some people faced with a crisis not intervene?

Focusing on prosocial aspects of human interaction, many social psychologists study **altruism**, helping behavior that is motivated primarily by a desire to benefit a person other than oneself. When people are asked to list instances of helping in their own lives, they cite helping a classmate with homework, listening to a friend's problems, giving moral support, giving rides, and so on (McGuire, 1994). Everyday examples are not hard to find. Take Patrick Hutchinson, a man who carried an injured far-right activist out of a crowd of Black Lives Matter protestors (Vera, Abdelaziz, & Mahmood, 2020). Yet psychologists ask: Does altruism really exist, or is helping always selfishly motivated? And why do we sometimes fail to come to the aid of someone who needs it? These are just some of the puzzling questions asked about helping and the factors that

altruism. Helping behavior that is motivated primarily by a desire to benefit others, not oneself.

Climate change has led to an increase in wildfires due to abnormally dry conditions. After fireworks at a gender-reveal party triggered a California wildfire in September 2020, thousands of acres and many homes were destroyed. Here, a firefighter works to slow down the wildfire's movement toward homes in Madera County. Firefighting is a heroic yet dangerous job.

JOSH EDELSON / Contributor/AFP/Getty Images

influence it (Barclay, 2010; Batson, 1998; Farrelly, Clemson, & Guthrie, 2016; Farrelly, Lazarus, & Roberts, 2007; Schroeder, Dovidio, Sibicky, Matthews, & Allen, 1995).

Bystander Intervention

The debate about altruism and human nature is fascinating. What inspired social psychologists to study helping in the first place? It was hair-raising news stories about bystanders who failed to take action even when someone's life was in danger. The problem first made headlines in March 1964. The March 27, 1964 *New York Times* headline read "37 Who Saw Murder Didn't Call Police" (Gansberg, 1964). It was the sensationalized story of Kitty Genovese. Kitty was walking home from work in Queens, New York, at 3:20 in the morning. As she crossed the street from her car to her apartment, a man with a knife appeared. She ran, but he caught up and stabbed her. She cried frantically for help and screamed, "Oh my God, he stabbed me!... I'm dying, I'm dying!"—but to no avail. The

Patrick Hutchinson was participating in a Black Lives Matter protest in London when a far-right activist was injured. Hutchinson carried the man to police, where he could get assistance for his wounds. When interviewed about his altruism, Hutchinson stated that he wanted to demonstrate equality for everyone.

Luke Dray / Stringer/Getty Images News/Getty Images

man fled but then returned, raped her, and stabbed her eight more times, until she was dead. Reporters claimed that regardless of the number of people within earshot of Kitty's screams, no one attempted to help her. We now know that is not entirely true (Manning, Levine, & Collins, 2007). There were attempts to help Kitty, and people did call the police. However, the sensationalism of the story grabbed readers' attention, and rightfully so. Bibb Latané and John Darley were two of those readers, and they decided to do something about it. They demonstrated that this type of nonhelping response, as reported in the *New York Times*, should—and could—be studied.

Unlike the newspaper article, Latané and Darley (1970) refrained from blaming the bystanders and, instead, focused on the social factors at work in these types of situations. In a series of important experiments, they staged emergencies, varied the conditions, and observed what happened. In one study, Darley and Latané (1968) took participants to a cubicle and asked them to discuss the kinds of adjustment problems that college students face. For confidentiality purposes, they were told, participants would communicate over an intercom system and the experimenter would not be listening. The participants were also told to speak one at a time and to take turns. Some were assigned to two-person discussions, others to larger groups. Although the opening moments were uneventful, one participant (an accomplice) mentioned in passing that he had a seizure disorder that was triggered by pressure. Sure enough, when it came his turn to speak again, this participant struggled and pleaded for help:

> I could really-er-use some help so if somebody would-er-give me a little . . . h-help-uh-er-er-er . . . c-could . . . somebody-er-er-help-er-uh-uh-uh (choking sounds) . . . I'm gonna die-er-er-I'm . . . gonna die-er-help-er-er-seizure-er.

If you were in this situation, how would you react? Would you stop the experiment, dash out of your cubicle, and seek out the experimenter? As it turned out, the response was strongly influenced by the size of the group. Although all participants participated alone, they were led to believe that others were present and that there was a real crisis. Almost all participants who thought they were in a two-person discussion left the room for help immediately. In the larger "groups," however, participants were less likely to intervene and were slower to do so when they did. In fact, the larger the group was supposed to be, the less helping occurred, as illustrated in Figure 10.16. This pattern of results was labeled the **bystander effect**: The more bystanders there are, the less likely a victim is to get help. In an emergency, the presence of others paradoxically inhibits helping.

bystander effect. The finding that the presence of others inhibits helping in an emergency.

At first, this pioneering research seemed to defy all common sense. Isn't there safety in numbers? Don't we feel more secure rushing in to help when others are there for support? To understand fully what went wrong, Latané and Darley (1970) provided a careful, step-by-step analysis of the decision-making process in emergency situations. According to their scheme, bystanders help only when they

FIGURE 10.16 ■ The Bystander Effect

When participants thought that they alone heard a seizure victim in need, the vast majority sought help. As the number of bystanders increased, however, they became less likely to intervene.

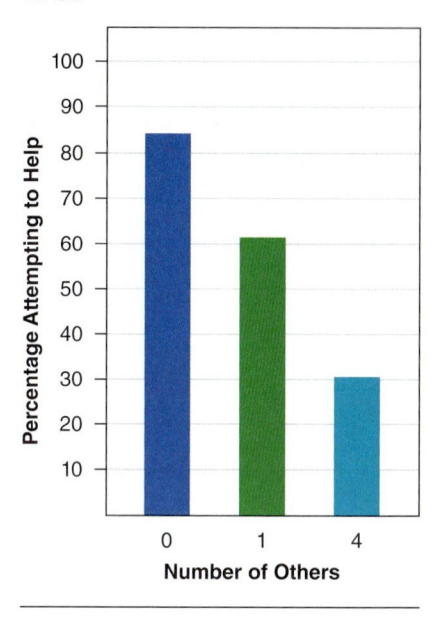

Adapted from Darley, J. M., & Latané, B. (1968). Bystander intervention in emergencies: Diffusion of responsibility. Journal of Personality and Social Psychology, 8(4, Pt.1), 377–383. https://doi.org/10.1037/h0025589

diffusion of responsibility. In groups, a tendency for bystanders to assume that someone else will help.

notice the event, *interpret* it as an emergency, *take responsibility* for helping, *decide* to intervene, and then *act* on that decision, as illustrated in Figure 10.17.

This analysis of the intervention process sheds light on the bystander effect, in that the presence of others can inhibit helping at each of the five steps. Consider, for example, the second requirement, that bystanders interpret an event as an emergency. Have you ever heard screaming from a nearby house and the sound of crashing objects, only to wonder if you were overhearing an assault or just a family quarrel? Cries of pain may sound like shrieks of laughter, and heart-attack victims may be mistaken for drunk. How do other bystanders influence our interpretation? Faced with a sudden, possibly dangerous event, everyone pretends to stay calm. As each person sees that others seem indifferent, they shrug it off. As a result, the event no longer feels like an emergency.

Latané and Darley (1970) observed this process in their study, which had participants fill out questionnaires alone or in groups of three. After the experimenter left, white smoke was pumped into the room through a vent. Alone, most participants worried that there was a fire and quickly reported the smoke to the experimenter. Yet in the company of others, most participants did not seek help. In some groups, the smoke was so thick that participants rubbed their eyes and waved fumes away from their face as they worked on the questionnaires, but they did not call for help. Why not? In postexperiment interviews, they said they assumed the smoke was harmless steam, air-conditioning vapor, or even "truth gas"—but not a fire.

The presence of others also inhibits helping by causing a **diffusion of responsibility**, a belief that others will intervene. This is what most likely happened in the case of Hugo Alfredo Tale-Yax, a story eerily similar to the one published about Kitty. But this story, unlike Kitty's, was caught on video surveillance. Hugo's story begins with heroism and ends in an avoidable tragedy. Hugo was a homeless man living in Queens, New York, who witnessed a mugging. Hugo, an unsuspected hero, jumped

FIGURE 10.17 ■ A Model of Bystander Intervention

This step-by-step analysis suggests several reasons for the fact that bystanders often do not help in emergencies.

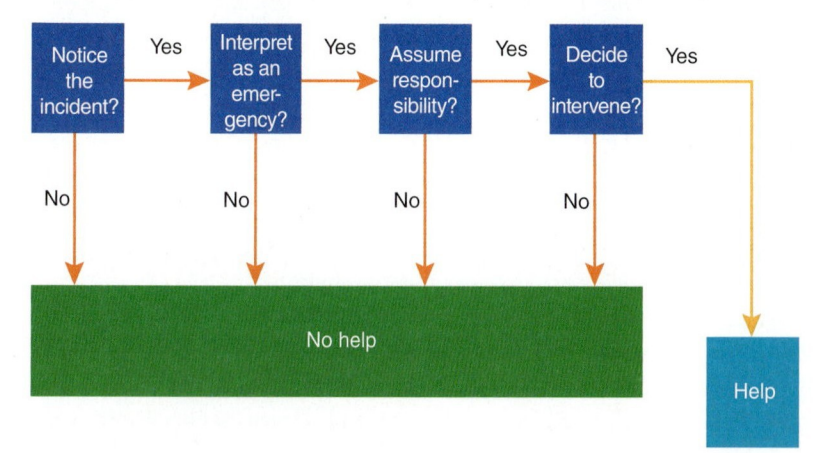

into the fray to rescue the female victim. During the struggle with the mugger, the woman ran away but Hugo was stabbed multiple times (Hutchinson, 2010). As he lay on the street dying from his wounds, 20 people walked by without calling police or attempting to get Hugo help. In fact, camera footage shows one man taking a picture of the dying Hugo, while another rolls him over and then walks away.

Person after person walked by Hugo, and the number of people who passed him by increased as the morning matured. You would think that with so many people in the area, Hugo would get the help he desperately needed. Sadly, this was not the case. By the time emergency responders finally came to Hugo's aid, he was already dead. As predicted by laboratory research, psychologists have confirmed that individuals working in groups diffuse the responsibility for their collective performance, with each member assuming less responsibility as the number of others present increases from two to eight (Forsyth, Zyzniewski, & Giammanco, 2002). The people who continued to pass by Hugo probably thought that surely someone else had done something to help.

The bystander effect is powerful and scary. Over the years, researchers have observed behavior in different kinds of staged crises. Would participants stop for a stranded motorist, help a person who faints or sprains an ankle, or try to break up a fight? Would they rush to the aid of a seizure victim, a subway passenger who staggers and falls to the ground, or an experimenter having an asthma attack? What are the odds that a person in need will actually receive help? Clearly, helping depends in complex ways on various characteristics of the victim, the bystanders, and the situation (as summarized in Table 10.1). The fact remains, however, that a person is less likely to intervene in a group than when alone. Even more remarkable is that victims are more likely to get help from someone when their welfare rests on the shoulders of a single potential helper than when many others are present (Latané & Nida, 1981).

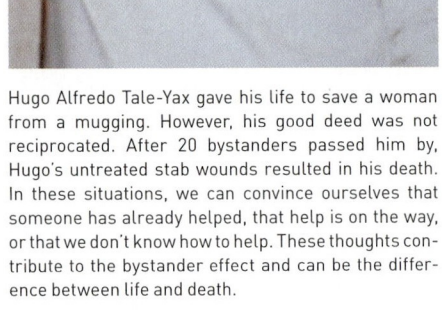

If ever you are in need of help in public, is there anything you can do to get someone to step out from the shadow of the crowd? Consider the necessary steps to intervention, and you will see that a person in need should draw attention to himself or herself, make it clear that help is needed, and single out an individual bystander—through eye contact, by pointing, or even by making a direct request.

What if you need help in cyberspace? In the first extension of Latané and Darley's research to "cyberhelping," a plea for help was made to nearly 5,000 participants in some 400 Internet chat rooms. As shown in Figure 10.18, the more others that were assumed to be online, the slower the participants were to help. When the person in need addressed participants by name, however, the bystander effect was eliminated. In this case, the helping response was quick—regardless of how many others were supposedly in the chat room (Markey, 2000).

Hugo Alfredo Tale-Yax gave his life to save a woman from a mugging. However, his good deed was not reciprocated. After 20 bystanders passed him by, Hugo's untreated stab wounds resulted in his death. In these situations, we can convince ourselves that someone has already helped, that help is on the way, or that we don't know how to help. These thoughts contribute to the bystander effect and can be the difference between life and death.

Christopher Sadowski/Splash News/Newscom

TABLE 10.1 ■ When Helping Is Most Likely to Occur
1. When the bystander is in a good mood
2. When the bystander feels guilty or needs a self-esteem boost
3. When the bystander observes someone else helping
4. When the bystander is not pressed for time
5. When the bystander is male and the victim female
6. When the victim makes a direct request for help
7. When the victim is physically attractive
8. When the victim appears to deserve help
9. When the victim is similar in some way to the bystander
10. In a small town or rural area, not a large city

FIGURE 10.18 ■ Cyberhelping

In this study, individuals participating in an online chat room saw a plea for help. Illustrating the bystander effect, the more others thought to be present, the slower people were to respond. If the individual's name was identified in the request for help, however, the inhibiting effect of other bystanders on helping was eliminated.

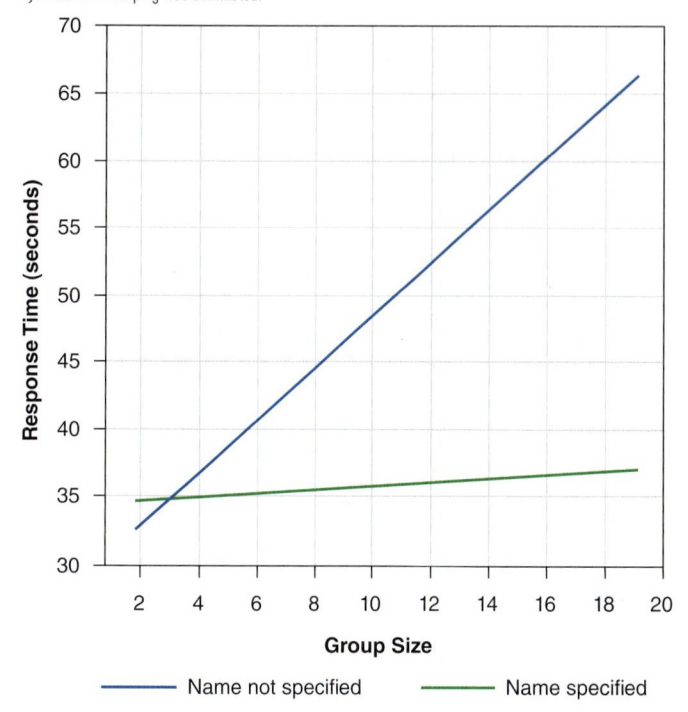

Similar results have been found in other cyber media such as private email requests (Barron & Yechiam, 2002) and public discussion forums (Voelpel, Eckhoff, & Förster, 2008). Interestingly, Barron and Yechiam's study found that private emails sent to one recipient were more likely to initiate assistance in comparison to private emails sent to five recipients. Furthermore, Voelpel and colleagues discovered the same diffusion-of-responsibility trend: Smaller discussion forums increased the likelihood of helping, whereas larger discussion forums decreased it.

However, research on altruism in cyberspace has its limits. Not every attempt at replicating diffusion of responsibility has worked perfectly (Fischer et al., 2011). Some critics argue that by the time we encounter a request for help on the Internet, the help may no longer be needed. For example, when scrolling through your Twitter feed, you may notice a comment from someone asking for advice or the location of a particular resource, but that comment was posted 3 hours earlier. Others point out that the number of bystanders might be ignored, unknown, or too high (Allison & Bussey, 2016). Regardless, people on the Internet do need help and often are ignored, which can have devastating effects in the case of cyberbullying (Cassidy, Faucher, & Jackson, 2013).

LEARNING CHECK

Social Relations

Identify the best fits for each sentence from the accompanying list of words. (Note: There are more choices than there are answers.)

less	testosterone	aggression instinct	full moon
size	increases	frustration	more
summer	decreases	theft	winter

1. _____, a hormone more prominent in males, has been correlated with aggression.
2. _____ is one type of aversive event experienced by most people.
3. More violent crimes occur during the _____.
4. Aggression _____ when guns are in the room.
5. The more bystanders there are, the _____ likely a victim is to get help.

(Answers: 1. testosterone; 2. frustration; 3. summer; 4. increases; 5. less.)

CROSS-CULTURAL PERSPECTIVES

LEARNING OBJECTIVES

Appraise the contribution of culture to our perceptions of the world and others.

- Evaluate how cultures influence the way people see themselves in relation to others.
- Define individualism and collectivism, and discuss how cultures differ on this dimension.
- Explain the role of the environment in our self-conceptions.

The similarities among us are so self-evident that they are invisible, taken for granted. For example, people all over the world seem to enjoy McDonald's, as illustrated in Figure 10.19. Despite the "universals" of human behavior, there are some differences—both *among* cultures and between racial and ethnic groups *within* cultures. Immersed in our own ways of life, we can all too easily overlook an important fact: There is no dominant world culture. The most populous country is China at 1,397,897,720 people, followed by India at 1,339,330,514 people, and then the United States at 332,475,723 (U.S. Census Bureau, 2021). Although the United States is referred to as a "melting pot," the nation isn't even close to being called home by a billion people, whereas China and India surpass that number of citizens by millions.

FIGURE 10.19 ■ Global Expansion

Americans love their fast food, and so do other cultures. McDonald's serves its food in over 100 countries at approximately 40,000 restaurants all over the world.

Education & Exploration 1 / Alamy Stock Photo; iStockPhoto.com/raisbeckfoto

Cultural Diversity: A Fact of Life

We humans are a heterogeneous lot. As a matter of *geography*, some of us live in large, heavily populated cities, whereas others live in small towns, fishing communities, expansive deserts, high-altitude mountains, tropical islands, or icy arctic plains. According to Ethnologue.com (2018), there are more than 7,000 spoken languages—including Chinese, Hindi, Spanish, Russian, Arabic, Portuguese, French, German, and Japanese. There are also hundreds of *religions* that people identify with (illustrated in Figure 10.20)—the most popular being Christianity (31.2 percent), Islam (24.1 percent), Hinduism (15.1 percent), and Buddhism (6.9 percent), with Judaism (0.2 percent) and others claiming fewer adherents (Hackett & McClendon, 2017). Roughly 15 to 20 percent of the world's population is not affiliated with a religion. In light of the many ways in which cultures differ, psychologists make cross-cultural comparisons in order to fully understand the commonalities and boundaries of human behavior (Berry, Segall, & Poortinga, 2002; Shiraev & Levy, 2001).

Linked together by space, language, religion, and historical bonds, each cultural group has its own ideology, folklore, music, political system, family structure, sexual mores, fashions, and foods. As governments and world travelers come to learn, sometimes the hard way, local customs and laws also vary in significant ways. In the affairs of day-to-day living, each culture operates by its own implicit rules of conduct, or social norms. **Social norms** can be so different from one country to the next that people who travel for business or for pleasure should be armed with an awareness of local customs.

Just as cultures differ in their social norms, so too do they differ in the extent to which people are expected to adhere to those norms. As an example, compare the United States and China. In the United States, people value self-reliance, independence, and assertiveness. In China, by contrast, people value conformity, loyalty, and political harmony (Oyserman & Lee, 2008; Zhai, 2017; Zhang, Lin, Nonaka, & Beom, 2005). As we'll see, this comparison indicates that there are two very different cultural orientations toward persons and the groups to which they belong. One orientation centers on the individual, the other on the group.

Individualism and Collectivism: A Tale of Two Cultural Worldviews

During the coronavirus pandemic, researchers investigated individual differences that mitigated the decline of well-being (Ahuja, Banerjee, Chaudhary, & Gidwani, 2020) and increased the likelihood that a person would practice social distancing (Biddlestone, Green, & Douglas, 2020). One of those individual differences was **collectivism**. In collectivist cultures, the person values cooperation and

social norms. Implicit rules of conduct according to which each culture operates.

collectivism. A cultural orientation in which cooperation and group harmony take priority over the self.

FIGURE 10.20 ■ Religious Groups by Population

Psychologists are ethically obliged to be respectful of and attentive to their clients' cultural diversity, and religion and spirituality contribute to our personal and social identities.

Christians are the largest religious group in 2015

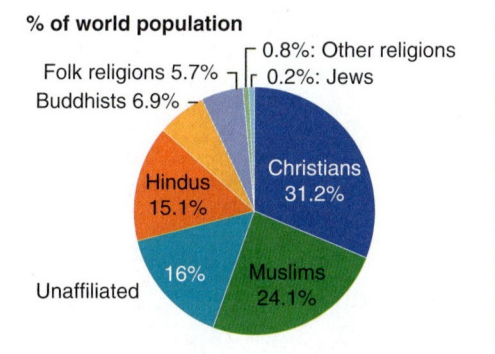

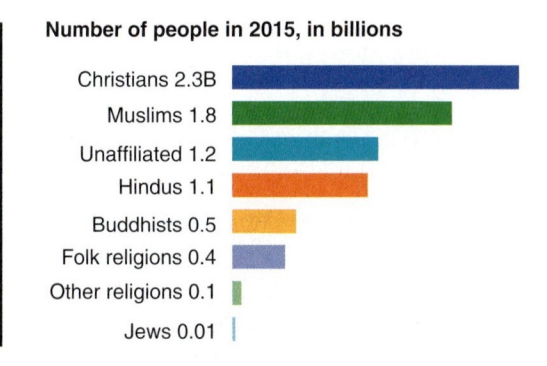

% of world population
- Christians 31.2%
- Muslims 24.1%
- Unaffiliated 16%
- Hindus 15.1%
- Buddhists 6.9%
- Folk religions 5.7%
- Other religions 0.8%
- Jews 0.2%

Number of people in 2015, in billions
- Christians 2.3B
- Muslims 1.8
- Unaffiliated 1.2
- Hindus 1.1
- Buddhists 0.5
- Folk religions 0.4
- Other religions 0.1
- Jews 0.01

Hackett, Conrad, and David McClendon. "Christians remain world's largest religious group, but they are declining in Europe." Pew Research Center, Washington, DC (April 5, 2017) https://www.pewresearch.org/fact-tank/2017/04/05/christians-remain-worlds-largest-religious-group-but-they-are-declining-in-europe/

social harmony and is, first and foremost, a loyal member of a family, team, company, church, state, or another group. Under the banner of **individualism**, by contrast, personal goals and independence take priority over group allegiances. In what countries are these differing orientations most extreme? Geert Hofstede (1980, 2013) reported that the most fiercely individualistic people were from the United States, Australia, Great Britain, Canada, and the Netherlands, in that order. The most collectivist people were from Venezuela, Colombia, Pakistan, Peru, Taiwan, and China. Other researchers have argued that Hofstede's inferences are flawed, since important variables that could contribute to collectivism and individualism were not measured (Brewer & Venaik, 2010; Minkov et al., 2017; Taras, Steel, & Kirkman, 2010). In fact, Minkov and colleagues (2017) developed a revised measure of Hofstede's individualism-collectivism measure to include some of these important variables and determined that the most individualistic people were from the Netherlands, and the most collectivistic from Nigeria. U.S. citizens were ranked 20th in individualism. What is *your* orientation? Read the statements in Table 10.2 and see whether you agree or disagree with them. People from collectivist cultures tend to agree more with the C statements; those from individualistic cultures tend to agree more with the *I* statements.

Cultures differ in their unique norms. Here, a man representing the devil leaps over newborns during the Baby Jumping Festival of Castrillo du Murcia in Spain. The yearly festival, known locally as "El Colacho," takes place during the village's religious feast of Corpus Christi. This ritual represents the devil absorbing the sins of the babies, affording them protection from disease and misfortune. Afterward, the babies are sprinkled with rose petals and returned to their parents.

Samuel de Roman / Contributor / Getty Images

individualism. A cultural orientation in which personal goals and preferences take priority over group allegiances.

Why are some cultures individualistic and others collectivistic? Speculating about the origins of these orientations, Triandis (1995) suggests that there are three key factors. The first is the *complexity* of a society. As people live in more complex industrialized societies—for example, compared to a life of hunting and food gathering among desert nomads—they have more groups to identify with (family, hometown, alma mater, church, place of employment, political party, sports teams, social clubs, and so on), which means less loyalty to any one group and a greater focus on personal rather than collective goals. Second is the *affluence* of a society. As people prosper, they gain financial independence from one another, a condition that promotes social independence, mobility, and, again, a focus on personal rather than collective goals. Something as simple as the number of toothbrushes a family has can demonstrate the impact of affluence on independence, as depicted in Figure 10.21. The third factor is *heterogeneity*. Societies that are homogeneous or "tight" (where members share the same language, religion, and social customs) tend to be rigid and intolerant of those who veer from the norm.

TABLE 10.2 ■ Individualistic and Collectivist Orientations

1. If the group is slowing me down, it is better to leave it and work alone. (I)
2. I like my privacy. (I)
3. I can count on my relatives for help if I find myself in any kind of trouble. (C)
4. If you want something done right, you've got to do it yourself. (I)
5. It is reasonable for a son to continue his father's business. (C)
6. In the long run, the only person you can count on is yourself. (I)
7. I enjoy meeting and talking to my neighbors every day. (C)
8. I like to live close to my good friends. (C)
9. The bigger the family, the more family problems there are. (I)
10. There is everything to gain and nothing to lose for classmates to group themselves for study and discussion. (C)

Adapted from H. C. Triandis, 1995.

FIGURE 10.21 — Disparities

These photographs are featured on Dollar Street, a collection of 264 family photos from 50 countries. Even something as simple as tooth brushing can be taken for granted and demonstrate vast differences in affluence and culture. The electronic toothbrushes belong to a family in the Netherlands, where each person has their own designated toothbrush. Contrast that with the single toothbrush on the wooden board, which belongs to a Rwandan family who shares one toothbrush for the entire group.

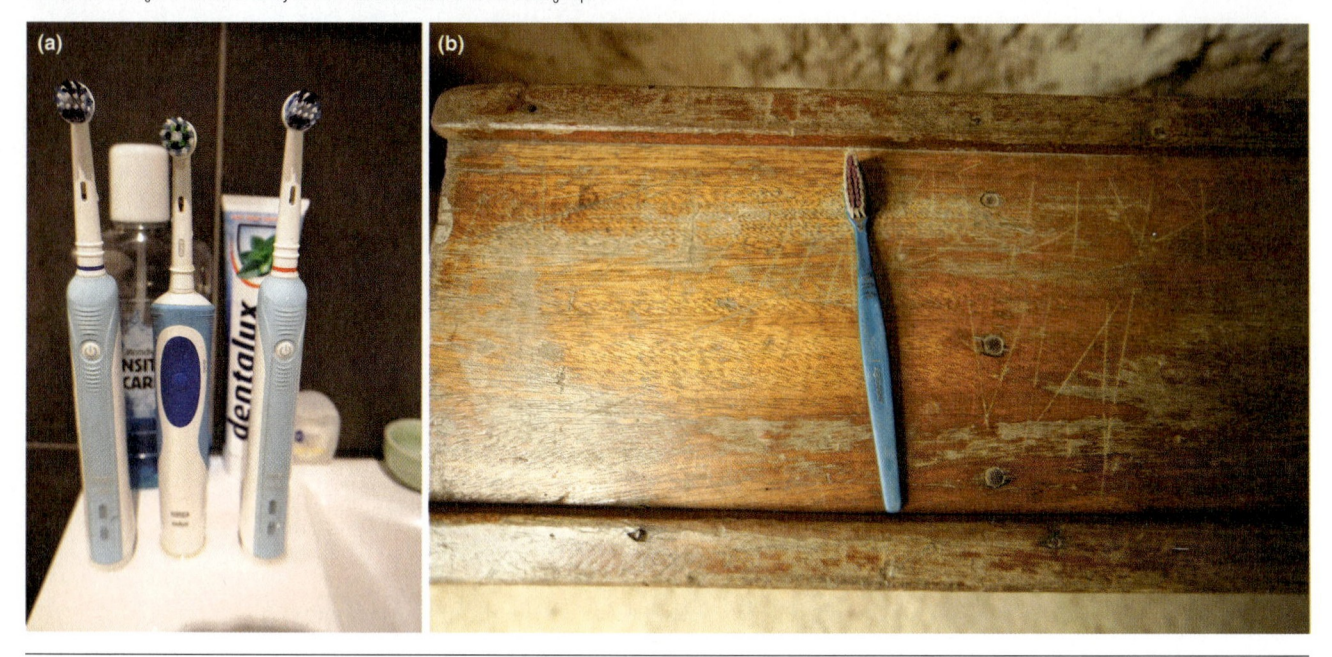

Dollarstreet, licensed under CC BY 4.0 / Dollarstreet, licensed under CC BY 4.0

In contrast, societies that are culturally diverse or "loose" (where two or more cultures coexist) tend to be more permissive of dissent—thus allowing for greater individual expression. Other psychologists have speculated that these cultural orientations are rooted in religious ideologies—as in the link between Christianity and individualism (Sampson, 2000).

Conceptions of the Self

Individualism and collectivism can be so deeply ingrained in a culture that they mold our very self-conceptions and identities. According to Hazel Markus and Shinobu Kitayama (1991, 2010), people who grow up in individualistic countries see themselves as entities that are *independent*—distinct, autonomous, and endowed with unique dispositions. By contrast, people from more collectivist countries hold *interdependent* views of the self as part of a larger social network that includes family, coworkers, friends, and others with whom they are socially connected. People with independent views say things like "The only person you can count on is yourself" and "I enjoy being unique and different from others." Those with interdependent views are more likely to agree that "I'm partly to blame if one of my family members or coworkers fails" and "My happiness depends on the happiness of those around me" (Rhee, Uleman, Lee, & Roman, 1995; Singelis, 1994; Triandis, Chen, & Chan, 1998). These contrasting orientations—one focused on the personal self, the other on the collective self—are depicted in Figure 10.22 (Heine, 2008; Markus & Kitayama, 1991).

But as Americans, do we only think individualistically? Research by Trafimow and others (1991) pondered this same question. They primed college students with a story about a warrior who made military decisions based on either what was good for the family (collectivistic) or what was good for his personal glory (individualistic). After reading the story, participants completed 20 "I am _____" statements (Kuhn & McPartland, 1954). Trafimow found that the people who read the individualistic warrior story were more likely to fill in the blank with personal trait descriptions (e.g., "I am shy") than were people who read the collectivistic warrior story. Trafimow concluded that people aren't just collectivistic or individualistic. Information in our environment—like the story participants read—can

FIGURE 10.22 ■ Self-Conceptions

People from individualistic cultures perceive themselves as independent and distinct from others (left). In contrast, people in collectivist cultures perceive themselves as interdependent, as part of a larger social network (right).

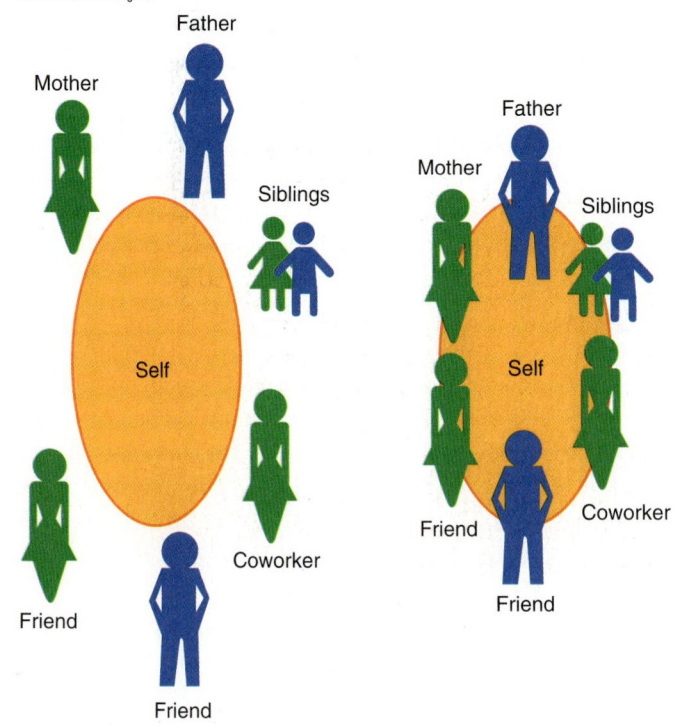

bring to the surface one trait or the other. Additional research has also demonstrated that the collectivistic and individualistic selves can be activated with the environment (Grossman & Jowhari, 2017; Mandel, 2003; Orehek, Sasota, Kruglanski, Dechesne, & Ridgeway, 2014; Trafimow, Silverman, Fan, & Law, 1997). It's no wonder that the environment in the United States is ripe with slogans such as, "Have it your way," "May the best car win," and "I'm lovin' it."

INTERGROUP DISCRIMINATION

LEARNING OBJECTIVES

Recognize the variables that contribute to prejudice, and assess the brain's role in stereotype development.

- Explain how discrimination is a by-product of our thinking.
- Discuss whether we can control stereotyping.
- Identify the motives that fuel prejudice.
- Create an intervention for treating implicit racial bias.

Minority groups of the world face unique challenges in their formation of an identity—and may need to cope in different ways. Of the many obstacles that confront minorities in many cultures, the most disheartening is **discrimination**: behavior directed against persons because of their affiliation with a "different" social, racial, ethnic, or religious group. Instances of discrimination happen all over the world, causing its victims to be avoided, excluded, rejected, belittled, and attacked. The victims

discrimination. In classical and operant conditioning, the ability to distinguish between different stimuli.

Stereotypes

To some extent, discrimination is a by-product of the beliefs we hold and the way we think. The beliefs are called stereotypes, and the cognitive processes that promote stereotyping are social categorization and the outgroup-homogeneity bias (Hilton & von Hippel, 1996).

A **stereotype** is a belief that associates a whole group of people with certain traits. When you stop to think about it, the list of common, well-known stereotypes seems endless. Consider some examples: Women are nurturers, Asians excel at school, Italians are pasta experts, Jews are materialistic, the elderly cannot use technology, college professors are absent-minded, Black people have rhythm, White men are power-hungry, and used-car salespeople cannot be trusted. Now, truthfully, how many of these images ring a bell? More important, how do they influence our evaluations of each other? Some of these stereotypes are positive, and others are negative—depending on your perspective and the context. Labeled as nurturing because you are a woman could result in various outcomes. For one, a woman might get immediate acceptance at the playground. At the same time, her gender might misguide police. It is a fact that women are not immune to behaving badly. However, when police respond to an intimate partner abuse call, they may readily make false assumptions about who is at fault simply due to gender stereotypes (Russell, 2018). There are many theories on how such stereotypes are born within a culture. But social psychologists ask a different question: How do stereotypes operate in the minds of individuals, and how do they affect our judgments of others?

From a cognitive perspective, the formation of stereotypes involves two related processes. The first is that people naturally divide each other into groups based on sex, race, age, nationality, religion, and other attributes. This process is called **social categorization**. In some ways, social categorization is natural and adaptive. For example, what do limes, oranges, and grapefruits all have in common? They are all acidic fruits that grow on trees. By grouping human beings the way we group fruits, furniture, and other objects, we make judgments quickly and easily (Keller, 2005) and use past experience to guide interactions with people we've never met (Macrae & Bodenhausen, 2000). Some researchers argue that social categorization is innate and, thus, can be seen in infancy (Liberman, Woodward, & Kinzler, 2017). So how could something the brain does naturally be bad? The problem is that categorization may lead us to magnify the differences *between* groups and overlook the differences among individuals *within* groups (Stangor & Lange, 1994; Wilder, 1986; Zhang, 2015).

The second process that promotes stereotyping follows from the first. Although grouping people is like grouping objects, there's a key difference: In social categorization, the perceivers themselves are members or nonmembers of the categories they employ. Groups that you identify with—your country, religion, political party, or even your hometown sports team—are called *ingroups*, whereas groups other than your own are called *outgroups*. The tendency to carve up the world into "us" and "them" has important psychological and social consequences, such as the pervasive tendency to assume that "they" are all alike—a phenomenon known as the **outgroup-homogeneity bias** (Linville & Jones, 1980). These effects are common—and there are many real-life examples. Asians who arrive from Korea, China, Vietnam, Taiwan, and the Philippines perceive themselves as quite different from one another, but to the Western eye they are all Asian. Likewise, the people of Mexico, Puerto Rico, Central America, and Cuba distinguish among themselves, but others refer to them all as Hispanic. Conservatives perceive liberals as all peas from the same pod, and although natives of New York City proclaim their cultural and ethnic diversity, outsiders talk of the typical New Yorker. This phenomenon is also seen in

---

stereotype. A belief that associates a group of people with certain traits.

social categorization. The classification of persons into groups based on common attributes.

outgroup-homogeneity bias. The tendency to assume that "they" (members of groups other than our own) are all alike.

Stereotypes are one way we simplify our social world. By stereotyping, we infer that a person has a whole range of characteristics and abilities that we assume all members of that group have.

fizkes / Shutterstock

studies of visual memory, which show that eyewitnesses find it relatively difficult to recognize members of a racial or ethnic group other than their own (Havard, Memon, & Humphries, 2017; Meissner & Brigham, 2001).

Clearly, we can bring stereotypes to mind automatically, without trying, and without awareness, and they can color our judgments of others. But this does not mean that each of us is inevitably trapped into evaluating people on the basis of social categories. Studies have shown that people are most likely to form a quick impression based on simple stereotypes when they're busy or distracted (Cralley & Ruscher, 2005; Gilbert & Hixon, 1991; Reich & Mather, 2008) or are pressed for time (Pratto & Bargh, 1991); if they are superior pattern detectors (Lick, Alter, & Freeman, 2018); when they are mentally tired (Bodenhausen, 1990) or under the influence of alcohol (Bartholow, Dickter, & Sestir, 2006; von Hippel, Sekaquaptewa, & Vargas, 1995); or if they are elderly and set in their ways (Henry, Hippel, & Baynes, 2009; Stewart, Hippel, & Radvansky, 2009; von Hippel, Silver, & Lynch, 2000). Thankfully, recent studies have also shown that we can stop ourselves from judging others in stereotyped ways just as we can learn to break other bad habits—as long as we are informed, alert, and motivated to do so (Blair, Ma, & Lenton, 2001; Galinsky & Moskowitz, 2000; Johns, Cullum, Smith, & Freng, 2008; Moskowitz & Li, 2011; Kung et al., 2017).

Prejudice: The Motivational Roots

As people interact with others who are different in their culture, social class, or ethnic and religious background, tolerance of diversity becomes a social necessity. Too often, however, people evaluate others negatively because they are members of a particular group. This problem was illustrated by a viral video that captured Manhattan attorney Aaron Schlossberg saying to a group of Spanish speakers, "I pay for their welfare, I pay for their ability to be here—the least they can do is speak English" (Brito, 2018). This statement—which reveals a dislike of others because they are members of a particular group—is an expression of **prejudice**.

The streets of America are no stranger to prejudice. In Philadelphia in February 2017, a man visiting his deceased loved ones at a Jewish cemetery came upon a disheartening scene. More than 100 headstones had been vandalized. The coronavirus pandemic sparked increased incidents of aggression against Asian-Americans, including physical harm, extreme physical distancing, racial slurs, and wrongful workplace termination (Croucher, Nguyen, & Rahmani, 2020). Unfortunately, in the workplace, people are often on the receiving end of harassment because of their gender identity, sexual orientation, race, religion, ethnicity, age, or disability (U.S. Equal Employment Opportunity Commission, 2016). In the case of Laudente Montoya, a mechanic, his first few days at work set the stage for the rampant prejudicial remarks yet to come. Laudente's supervisor called Laudente, who was new to the job, and a co-worker "stupid Mexicans" and claimed that Mexicans caused the swine flu epidemic in the United States (U.S. Equal Employment Opportunity Commission, 2016). Laudente's supervisor had no need or reason to use such hate speech. People often dislike and resent others simply because they are different. Throughout history, and in all parts of the world, prejudice is one of the most tenacious social problems of modern times.

prejudice. Negative feelings toward others based solely on their membership in a certain group.

realistic-conflict theory. The theory that prejudice stems from intergroup competition for limited resources.

Realistic-Conflict Theory

There are two major motivational theories of prejudice. The first is **realistic-conflict theory**, which begins with a simple observation: Many intergroup conflicts in the world today stem from direct competition for valuable but limited resources (Levine & Campbell, 1972). As a matter of economics, one group may fare better than a neighboring group in a struggle for land, jobs, or power. The losers become frustrated, the winners feel threatened, and before long the conflict heats to a rapid boil. Chances are that a

Prejudice is one of the most tenacious social afflictions of our time. The problem, as shown by these children of members of the Westboro Baptist Church, is that the hatred is passed from one generation to the next.

ZUMA Press, Inc. / Alamy Stock Photo

good deal of prejudice in the world—such as the hostility often directed at immigrants—is driven by the realities of competition (Binggeli, Krings, & Sczesny, 2014; Hellwig & Sinno, 2016; Stephan, Ybarra, & Bachman, 1999; Taylor & Moghaddam, 1994; Tsukamoto & Fiske, 2017).

The premise of realistic-conflict theory in the study of prejudice seems compelling, but there's more to the story—much more. Research has shown that people are often prejudiced even when the quality of their lives is *not* directly threatened by the outgroup they despise, and that people are sensitive about the status of their ingroups relative to rival outgroups even when personal interests are *not* at stake. Is it possible that personal interests really *are* at stake, that our protectiveness of ingroups is nourished by a concern for the self? If so, might that explain why people all over the world seem to think that their own nation, culture, and religion are better and more deserving than others?

Social-Identity Theory

Questions about ingroups and outgroups were initially raised in a series of laboratory studies. In the first of these, Henri Tajfel and his colleagues (1971) showed participants a sequence of dotted slides and asked them to estimate the number of dots on each. The slides were flashed in rapid-fire succession, so the dots could not be counted. The experimenter then told participants that some people are chronic "overestimators" and others are "underestimators." As part of a second, separate task, participants were then divided, supposedly for the sake of convenience, into groups of overestimators and underestimators (in fact, the assignments were random). Knowing who was in their group, the participants allocated points to each other for various tasks, points that reflected favorable judgments and could be cashed in for money. This procedure was designed to create *minimal groups* of persons categorized by trivial similarities. The overestimators and underestimators were not bitter rivals, they had no history of antagonism, and they did not compete for a limited resource. Yet they allocated more points to members of their own group than to those of the outgroup. This pattern of discrimination, which is known as **ingroup favoritism**, has been observed in experiments conducted all over the world (Capozza & Brown, 2000).

To explain ingroup favoritism in the absence of realistic conflict, Tajfel (1982) and John Turner (1987) proposed **social-identity theory**. According to this theory, each of us strives to enhance our self-esteem, which has two components: a *personal* identity and various collective or *social* identities that are based on the groups to which we belong. In other words, people can boost their self-esteem through their personal achievements or by affiliating with successful groups. What's nice about the need for social identity is that it leads us to derive pride from our connections with others. What's sad, however, is that often we feel the need to belittle "them" in order to feel secure about "us." Religious fervor, racial and ethnic conceit, and patriotism may all fulfill this darker side of our social identity. In this way, prejudice is nourished by a concern for oneself. The theory is summarized in Figure 10.23.

Social-identity theory makes two predictions: First, threats to self-esteem should heighten the need to exhibit prejudice, and second, expressions of prejudice should, in turn, restore one's self-esteem. Research generally supports these predictions (Brewer & Brown, 1998; Capozza & Brown, 2000; Hogg & Abrams, 1990; Turner, Oakes, Haslam, & McGarty, 1994). People differ in the extent to which they want their social ingroups to dominate others. In studies conducted in the United States and Canada, people who are motivated by a need for social dominance exhibit more ingroup favoritism and endorse more cultural values that favor "us" over "them" (Pratto et al., 2000; Sidanius, Levin, Liu, & Pratto, 2000; Whitley, 1999). However, other research does not support the aforementioned predictions. Turner and Reynolds (2003) argue that social dominance is a flawed theory. Mainly, its claim that humans have a

---

ingroup favoritism. The tendency to discriminate in favor of ingroups over outgroups.

social-identity theory. The theory that people favor ingroups and discriminate against outgroups in order to enhance their own self-esteem.

In one of the world's most volatile areas of conflict, the Gaza Strip, the Israeli military fires tear gas at Palestinian protesters along the barrier between Gaza and Israel on June 8, 2018.

Xinhua / Alamy Stock Photo

FIGURE 10.23 Social-Identity Theory

According to social-identity theory, people strive to enhance self-esteem, which has two components: a personal identity and various social identities derived from the groups to which we belong. Thus, people can boost their self-image by viewing and treating ingroups more favorably than outgroups.

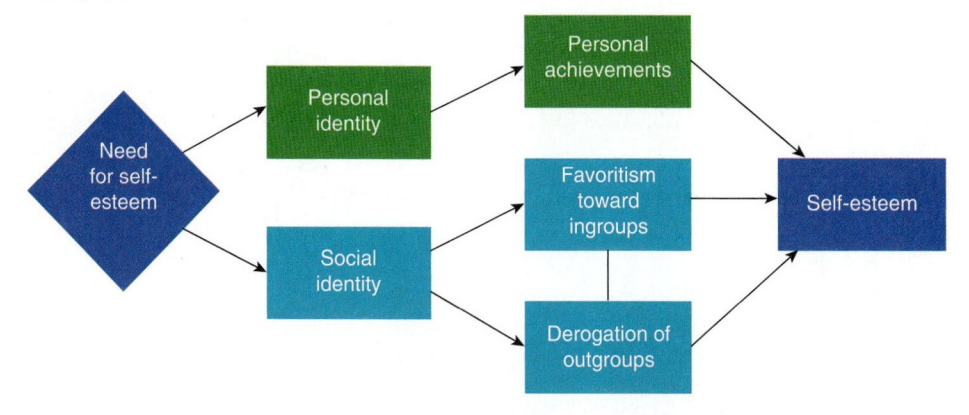

"ubiquitous drive for social hierarchy irrespective of group position, has been disconfirmed" (Turner & Reynolds, 2003, p. 205). Not everyone has such a motivation, which might be why findings on social dominance are inconsistent.

Racism in America

The slave trade. The Deep South. Abolitionists. The Civil War. Lynch mobs. Separate but equal. The Ku Klux Klan. Jackie Robinson. Sitting in the back of the bus. Martin Luther King Jr. Civil rights. Malcolm X. Ruby Bridges. *Roots*. Muhammad Ali. Affirmative action. The Reverend Jesse Jackson. The Confederate flag. Rodney King. O. J. Simpson. *12 Years a Slave*. Trayvon Martin. The removal of Confederate monuments. Unite the Right Rally. George Floyd. Black Lives Matter. #SayTheirNames. Race relations in the United States have had a checkered, troubled, and emotional history—a history marked by both hatred and guilt, riots and peace marches, tolerance and intolerance, advances and setbacks, as illustrated in Figure 10.24. At the heart of it all is **racism**: a deep-seated form of prejudice based on the color of a person's skin. In the United States, this conflict is multidirectional, with all groups exhibiting prejudice in one form or another.

racism. A deep-seated form of prejudice that is based on the color of a person's skin.

The Problem

It has been said that if a person is White, then that person will never really understand what it feels like to be a Black person living in the United States—and what it felt like many years ago, in the segregated South. In a powerful and revealing book, *Remembering Jim Crow*, historian William Chafe and others (2002) interviewed 1,200 elderly Black Americans who lived in 10 states of the segregated South during the first half of the 20th century. These witnesses to history recalled separate drinking fountains and restrooms, backdoor entries to public facilities, and separate platforms at the train station. Some recalled rapes, beatings, and harrowing escapes from lynch mobs in the middle of the night. All recalled how carefully they had to move about in an unpredictable land—where some Whites were friendly and helpful, others hostile and prejudiced.

The Symptoms

Racism in the 21st century is a problem that poisons social relations between Black and White people. Detecting racism is not as easy as it may seem. In 1958, only 4 percent of Americans polled approved of biracial Black-White marriages (Newport, 2013). By 2013, the approval rate for biracial Black-White marriages had leaped to 87 percent. These data might lead us to assume that racism would continue to decline. However, a Gallup poll in 2017 demonstrated that 42 percent of Americans worry a "great deal" about race relations, up from 17 percent in 2014—a staggering increase of 25 percentage points (Swift, 2020).

440 Essentials of Psychology

FIGURE 10.24 ■ Advancements

Although racism is still a serious and pervasive problem in the United States, it is from a historical perspective on the decline. Looking back, America has come a long way from the forced segregation common in the first half of the 20th century (a) to a historic day, on January 20, 2009, when Barack Obama was inaugurated as the 44th president of the United States (b) and to 2020, when Kamala Harris became the first female and Black Asian American elected vice president (c).

Bettmann/ Contributor/ Getty Images; Bart Stupak via Wikimedia Commons; OLIVIER DOULIERY / Contributor/AFP/Getty Images

Whether or not we judge people because of their race is still a controversial topic. An interview with political influencer Tomi Lahren on *The Daily Show with Trevor Noah* stirred the controversy when Lahren claimed she didn't see color in matters of race (Comedy Central, 2016). Other celebrities, such as Jennifer Lopez (Woog, 2008), have claimed the same. Is the United States becoming "color-blind," or are we fooling ourselves? Consider several incidents that happened in 2018 where White women called the police on innocent Black men and women. None of the Black men and women in question was behaving illegally: Two Black men at a Philadelphia Starbucks simply wanted to use the restroom while waiting for a business associate (Siegel, 2018). A Black woman at Yale University was a student who happened to fall asleep while studying in the dorm common room (Reilly, 2018). And a Black man was accused of trespassing in Memphis, Tennessee, after he took photos of a home for sale because he was contemplating buying it (Criss, 2018). A collection of sociological research reviewed by Shams (2015) argues that color-blindness is a flawed concept. Shams claims that racism persists; it is simply subtler than it was during the pre–civil rights era.

In an old and classic demonstration of subtle racism, Allport and Postman (1947) showed White participants a picture of a subway train filled with passengers. In the picture were a Black man dressed in a suit and a White man holding a razor, illustrated in Figure 10.25. One participant viewed the scene briefly and described it to a second person who had not seen it. The second participant communicated the description to a third person and so on, through six rounds of communication. The result: The final participant's report often indicated that the Black man, not the White man, had held the razor. Some participants even reported that he was waving the weapon in a threatening manner.

Needing to measure prejudice in order to study it, social psychologists sought to develop indirect tests that can detect negative feelings that people are not willing or able to admit to a pollster. Several years ago, researchers found that reaction time—the speed it takes to answer a question—can be used to uncover hidden prejudices (Dovidio, Kawakami, Johnson, Johnson, & Howard, 1997; Gaertner & McLaughlin, 1983). It takes less time to react to information that fits into existing beliefs, and more time to react to information that contradicts existing beliefs.

Picking up on the use of reaction time to betray a person's unconscious feelings, Anthony Greenwald, Mahzarin Banaji, and their colleagues developed the **Implicit Association Test**, or **IAT**. The IAT measures how readily people can associate pairs of concepts (Greenwald, McGhee, & Schwartz, 1998). As people work through it, they often find that some pairings are harder—and take longer to respond to—than others. In general, people are quicker to respond when liked faces pair with positive words and disliked faces pair with negative words than the other way around. The IAT intends to detect implicit attitudes about concepts by the speed it takes a person to respond to pairings such as *Black-bad/White-good* relative to *Black-good/White-bad* pairings.

Reaction-time tests may seem like they don't tell us much about how we behave or think in the real world. Couldn't we simply fake our responses? Interestingly, one IAT study asked participants to do exactly that (Banse, Seise, & Zerbes, 2001). However, participants who identified as heterosexual could only fake their explicit attitudes. When they tried to fake positive attitudes toward persons who identified as homosexual during the IAT, they failed. Do all IAT findings predict behavioral outcomes? Oswald and colleagues (2013) argue that the IAT is in need of improvement, since IAT research doesn't

Implicit Association Test (IAT). A measure of stereotyping that is derived from the speed at which people respond to pairings of concepts (such as Blacks or Whites with good or bad).

FIGURE 10.25 ■ How Racist Beliefs Distort Perceptions

After looking at this drawing, one participant described it to a second, who described it to a third, and so on. After six rounds of communication, the final report often placed the razor blade held by the White man into the Black man's hand.

Allport and Postman (1947).

consistently predict behavioral outcomes. On the contrary, a collection of results from various IAT studies demonstrates that for socially sensitive subjects, the IAT does a good job of predicting behavior (Greenwald, Poehlman, Uhlmann, & Banaji, 2009). A study on obesity and hiring practices found that employers who chose to interview fewer obese persons than nonobese persons had significantly more negative implicit associations toward obesity than employers who interviewed more obese persons (Agerström & Rooth, 2011). In a study by Richetin and colleagues (2010), participants completed the IAT for aggression and found that it significantly predicted whether or not a person would respond aggressively if provoked. Cooper and colleagues (2012) had clinicians complete the IAT and then surveyed the clinicians' patients about the clinicians' communication and quality of care. The researchers found that clinician implicit bias was associated with poorer ratings of care and visit communication.

Other medical research has focused on the ramifications of racial bias on patients. One research group studied the health records for 300,000 senior citizens enrolled in Medicare-managed health care plans. Figure 10.26 shows that Black patients were less likely than White patients to receive breast cancer screening, beta-blocker medications after heart attacks, follow-up visits after hospitalization for a psychological disorder, and eye examinations for those with diabetes. These disparities in medical care were significant even after socioeconomic differences were accounted for (Schneider, Zaslavsky, & Epstein, 2002). Hoffman and colleagues (2016) discovered that half of a sample of White medical students and White medical residents held false beliefs about biological differences between White and Black patients and, thus, rated Black patients' pain as lower. Hoffman and colleagues (2016) argue that these false beliefs could explain why doctors systematically undertreat pain in Black Americans.

This racial disparity in medical treatment garnered much-deserved attention during COVID-19 (Qeadan et al., 2021). Compared with white patients, Black patients had "longer hospital stays, higher rates of ventilator dependence, and a higher mortality rate" (Qeadan et al., 2021). Racial disparities in medical treatment can also be exacerbated when intersectionality is taken into account. One such famous case of how being female and Black had an impact on medical care is that of after Serena Williams. Serena gave birth via C-section. She knew she had a history of blood clots, and when her symptoms appeared, she quickly grabbed a nurse but was ignored. Serena persisted, told the doctors she needed a CT scan, but they chose another procedure that revealed nothing. Finally, the medical team performed the CT she requested and found several small blood clots in her lungs (Haskell, 2018). Serena's story is not isolated. The United

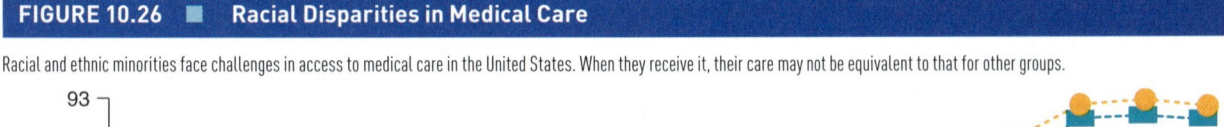

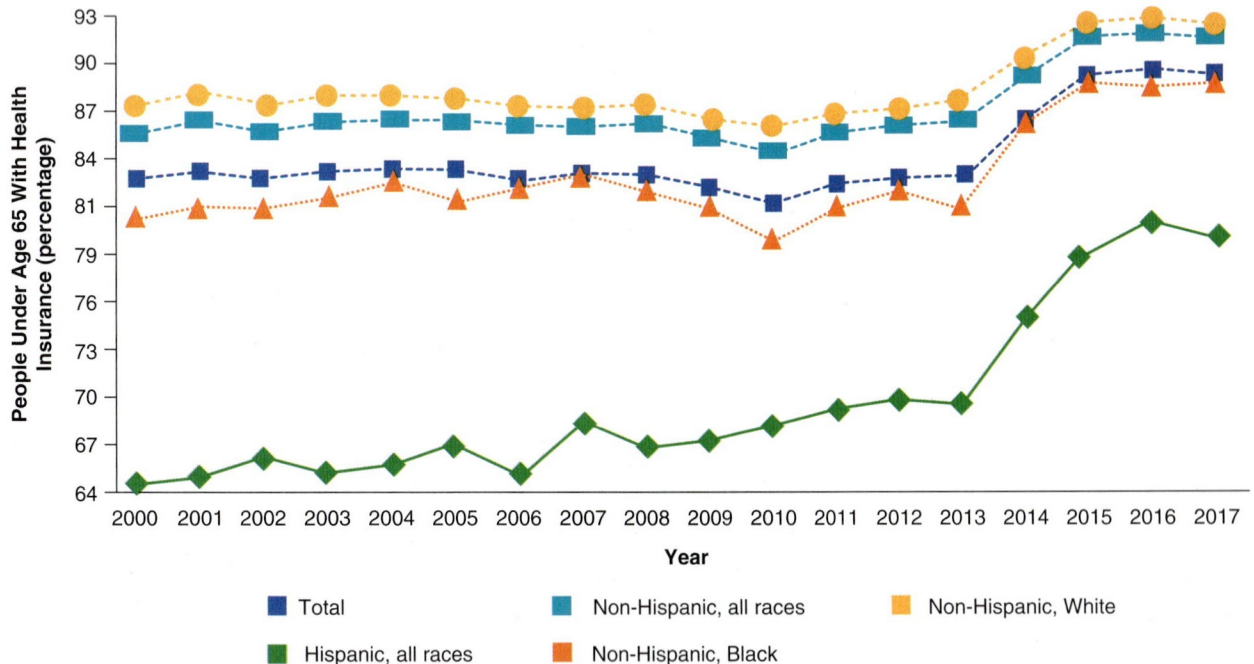

FIGURE 10.26 ■ Racial Disparities in Medical Care

Racial and ethnic minorities face challenges in access to medical care in the United States. When they receive it, their care may not be equivalent to that for other groups.

Legend: Total; Non-Hispanic, all races; Non-Hispanic, White; Hispanic, all races; Non-Hispanic, Black

States has the industrialized world's mortality rate for women due to childbirth complications (Ellison & Martin, 2019). In terms of racial differences, the Centers for Disease Control and Prevention (2018) notes that in 2013, 43.5 percent of women who died due to pregnancy complications were Black; by comparison, 12.7 percent of the women were white and 14.4 percent were of other races. No matter how subtle, innocent, or unintended the racism, the effect can mean the difference between life and death.

The Intervention

Racism is a social disease transmitted from one generation to the next. This transmission can arguably be seen within US law enforcement. Researchers at Yale and the University of Pennsylvania utilized a database of police-involved shootings from The Washington Post. They discovered that over the last five years, persons killed in police-involved shootings, who identified as "Black, Indigenous, or People of Color, whether armed or unarmed, had significantly higher death rates compared to whites. And those numbers remained relatively unchanged from 2015-2020" (Belli, 2020). With so many lives damaged and lost, one wonders if an intervention can reduce racism whatsoever. Law enforcement, for example, is investigating methods to decrease bias and racism. These include civilian review boards (Ajilore, 2018), early Intervention systems (Gullion, Orrick & Bishopp, 2021), and programs that attempt to address and correct implicit bias among officers. Two of the better known programs are called The Fair and Impartial Policing Program and the Counter Bias Training Simulation Program. Corporations, in response to incidents like the one previously mentioned at Starbucks, are also implementing anti-bias programs. While these methods seem like a great start, as a budding psychologist, you have to wonder if there is any scientific support for anti-bias interventions?

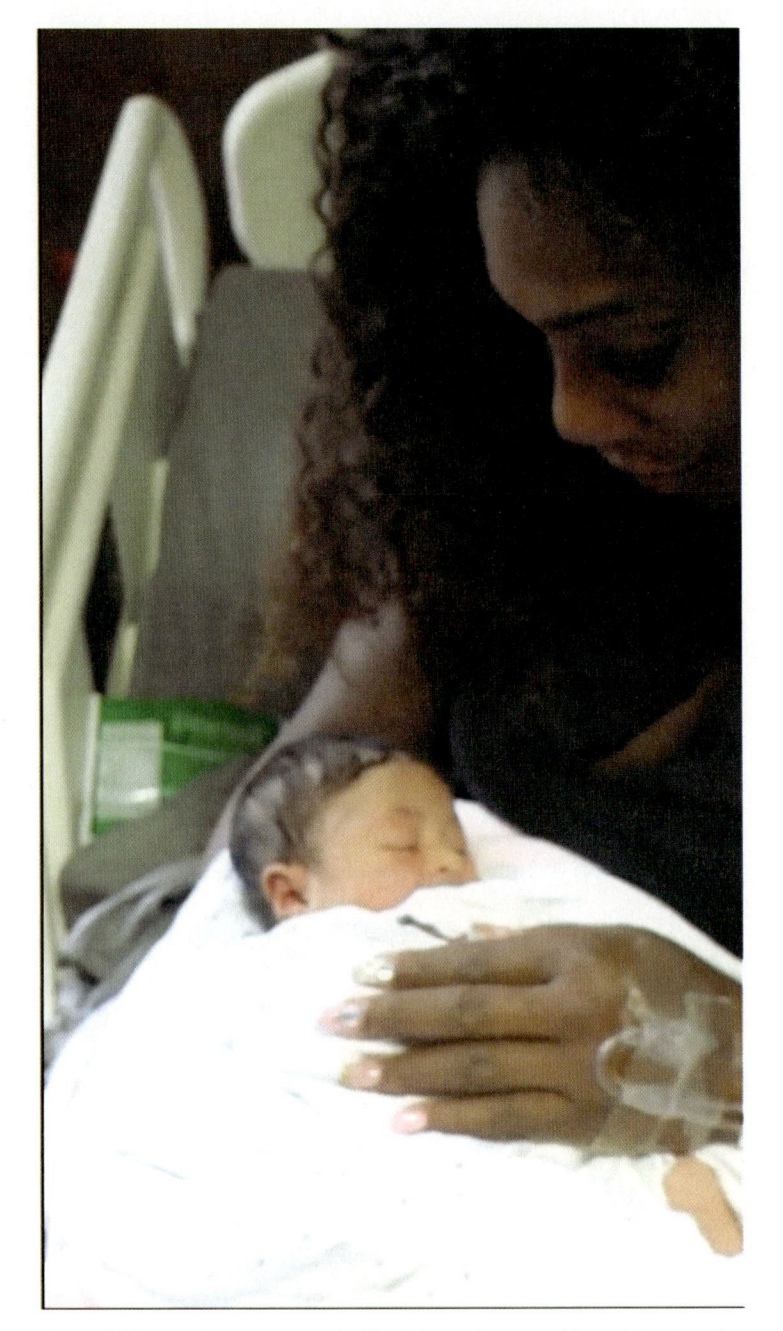

Serena Williams underwent surgery for blood clots and a ruptured C-section suture after childbirth complications. Her complications were so serious that her doctor ordered 6 weeks of bed rest after treatment. Serena shared her story to bring more attention to the matter.

SOCIAL MEDIA/REUTERS/Newscom

In a laboratory study, Devine and colleagues (2012) developed an intervention intended to reduce implicit racial bias. They divided non-Black college students into two groups—intervention and control. All students completed the IAT and measures of explicit bias and then returned to complete those same measures across a span of several weeks. Control subjects were dismissed after the first measurements were taken, but the intervention group was educated on the idea of prejudice as a habit, implicit bias, and the perpetuation of discrimination. Next, the intervention group was taught five strategies for reducing prejudice and racial bias: stereotype replacement, counterstereotype imaging, individuation, perspective taking, and increasing opportunities for contact. Results demonstrated that the intervention group had lower IAT scores, more concern about discrimination, and more awareness about their personal biases than control subjects. This habit-breaking intervention was replicated by Forscher and colleagues (2017) when a larger group of intervention participants demonstrated long-term effects in increased sensitivity to biases and were more likely than control subjects to object to online endorsements of racial stereotyping. Another study on training-away bias demonstrated that participants who practiced counterstereotype training scored lower on measures of implicit bias than did those who did not practice the training (Burns, Monteith, & Parker, 2017). Results like these have inspired Starbucks to be one of the first major corporations to implement antibias training (Nordell, 2018).

Two of the better known programs are called The Fair and Impartial Policing Program and the Counter Bias Training Simulation Program. Corporations, in response to incidents like the one previously mentioned at Starbucks, are also implementing anti-bias programs. While these methods seem like a great start, as a budding psychologist, you have to wonder if there is any scientific support for anti-bias interventions?

This transmission can arguably be seen within US law enforcement. Researchers at Yale and the University of Pennsylvania utilized a database of police-involved shootings from The Washington Post. They discovered that over the last five years, persons killed in police-involved shootings, who identified as "Black, Indigenous, or People of Color, whether armed or unarmed, had significantly higher death rates compared to whites. And those numbers remained relatively unchanged from 2015-2020" (Belli, 2020). With so many lives damaged and lost, one wonders if an intervention can reduce racism whatsoever. Law enforcement, for example, is investigating methods to decrease bias and racism. These include civilian review boards (Ajilore, 2018), Early Intervention systems (Gullion et al., 2021), and programs that attempt to address and correct implicit bias among officers. Two of the better known programs are called The Fair and Impartial Policing Program and the Counter Bias Training Simulation Program. Corporations, in response to incidents like the one previously mentioned at Starbucks, are also implementing anti-bias programs. While these methods seem like a great start, as a budding psychologist, you have to wonder if there is any scientific support for anti-bias interventions?

> **LEARNING CHECK**
>
> ### Intergroup Hostility
>
> Match each term in the left column to the statement from the right column that most closely illustrates it.
>
> | | | | |
> |---|---|---|---|
> | 1. | Discrimination | a. | White men can't jump. |
> | 2. | Racism | b. | All Asians like sushi. |
> | 3. | Stereotype | c. | My team rules. |
> | 4. | Outgroup-homogeneity bias | d. | My dad's country club doesn't allow Jews. |
> | 5. | Realistic-conflict theory | e. | Everybody knows jocks are stupid. |
> | 6. | Ingroup favoritism | f. | Affirmative action keeps White people out of jobs they deserve. |
>
> (Answers: 1. d; 2. a; 3. b; 4. e; 5. f; 6. c.)

Thinking Like a Psychologist About Social and Cultural Influences

Let's step back for a moment and revisit Milgram's studies of obedience to authority. This counterintuitive, if not shocking, research cries out the message of social psychology: that people are influenced in profound ways by their social surroundings. At the core, human beings are highly social creatures. We need each other, sometimes desperately. This is precisely why we have the power to influence others—and why we are sometimes so vulnerable to manipulation by others.

Think about the material presented in this chapter—from Dr. Kimmel's heroism to the abuse of Louise Ogborn—and you'll recognize that human social behavior is filled with contradiction. From studies of social perception, interpersonal attraction, conformity, persuasion, group processes, aggression, and altruism, it's clear that each of us is influenced and even changed, for better and for worse, by the words and actions of other people.

When you stop to consider the ways in which all humans are similar and share a common fate, the differences seem small and unimportant. Yet as we come into more and more contact with people from other cultures, as our society becomes increasingly diverse, and as tensions between Black and White Americans persist, it seems clear that we must recognize the differences among us if we are to understand, communicate with, and be tolerant of—if not appreciative of—one another.

Should we ignore the differences among individuals and groups? If we ignore our differences, we could lose our ability to appreciate the beautiful diversity in the world. And based on what you have learned about social categorization, can the brain really ignore differences? If we use an alternative strategy—one that encourages people to derive pride and a sense of belonging from their social identities—that could result in equal treatment devoid of discrimination. Diversity should be celebrated, not ignored. Clearly, there are similarities among us, and there are differences. The trick is not to focus exclusively on one or the other but to strike a sensible balance.

SUMMARY

Social psychology is the study of how individuals think, feel, and behave in social situations. The principal message is that people can influence one another's behavior in profound ways.

SOCIAL PERCEPTION

Social perception refers to the processes of coming to know and evaluate other people. The impressions we form of others are based largely on our observations of their behavior.

MAKING ATTRIBUTIONS
People make **attributions** for other people's behavior. According to **attribution theory**, people analyze a person's behavior and its situational context in order to make a personal attribution or a situational attribution.

In explaining the behavior of others, we typically overestimate the role of personal factors, the **fundamental attribution error**. This tendency may be unique to cultures that value individualism.

FORMING IMPRESSIONS
In perceiving others, people are subject to a **primacy effect** by which first impressions weigh heavily and are highly resistant to change. Through various cognitive-confirmation biases, first impressions guide the way they interpret later contradictory evidence. Through behavioral-confirmation biases, we often alter our behavior and unwittingly shape others in ways that confirm our impressions.

ATTRACTION
There are several factors that spark a positive impression, or attraction. The first is familiarity. Through the **mere exposure effect**, exposure to a person increases liking. A second factor is physical attractiveness. People like others who are physically attractive and behave more warmly toward them.

SOCIAL INFLUENCE

SOCIAL INFLUENCE AS "AUTOMATIC"
As social animals, human beings are vulnerable to a host of subtle influences. This was demonstrated in studies showing that, in both social and nonsocial situations, people unconsciously mimic each other's behaviors.

CONFORMITY
Conformity is the tendency to change one's opinion or behavior in response to social norms. Classic studies by Sherif and Asch revealed two types of social influence. People demonstrating

informational influence go along with the group and change their opinions because they believe the others are correct. **Normative influence** leads people to conform only in their public behavior because they fear social rejection.

Conformity increases with group size (up to a point) and with the salience of social norms. When an ally who refuses to conform is present, conformity decreases. Cultural factors are also important, as more conformity is found in cultures that value social harmony.

Milgram's research showed that even decent people can violate their conscience on command. By varying characteristics of the authority, victim, and situation, he was able to determine what factors increase the likelihood of obedience.

ATTITUDE CHANGE

An **attitude** is a positive, negative, mixed, or indifferent reaction toward a person, object, or idea. Attitudes can be changed using the **central** or **peripheral route of persuasion**. The central route requires people's attention since it uses logic and facts, whereas the peripheral route uses emotions. Behaviors can also lead to attitude change. One method for such attitude change is through **cognitive dissonance**. For example, you might have once thought sushi was disgusting (attitude) and told your friends how gross you believe them to be for eating it. But then, after trying it (behavior), you discovered that sushi is delicious. To ensure that your attitude and behavior toward sushi align, you change your attitude about it from negative to positive. As a result, you now share with your friends how wrong you were about your disgust.

GROUP PROCESSES

People behave differently in groups than when alone. Through **social facilitation**, the presence of others enhances performance on simple tasks but impairs performance on complex tasks. Zajonc explained that the mere presence of others increases arousal and triggers our dominant response. Others have proposed different interpretations. In joint activities, people often exert less effort than they would alone. This **social loafing** increases with group size because people do not recognize the link between their own effort and the desired group outcome.

SOCIAL RELATIONS

AGGRESSION

Aggression is rooted in both human biology and social factors. Although instinct theories do not account for differences among cultures, there are biological influences, perhaps even a genetic component. Men are more physically aggressive than women, and aggression is also increased by alcohol.

In general, aversive stimulation sparks aggression. Studies of the **frustration-aggression hypothesis** show that frustration correlates with aggressive behavior. Climate is also linked to aggression. Once aversive stimulation arouses negative emotion, situational cues—such as the presence of weapons and exposure to violence—prompt us to turn the feeling into action.

ALTRUISM

Does **altruism**—helping behavior primarily motivated by a desire to benefit others—really exist, or is helping always selfishly motivated? Examples like that of Patrick Hutchinson and Germans who helped Jews escape Nazi persecution provide real-world evidence that helping others isn't always selfishly motivated. In fact, helping others can put our own reputation or safety at risk.

BYSTANDER INTERVENTION

Studies demonstrate a **bystander effect** in which the presence of others inhibits helping. The bystander effect can reduce our tendency to interpret an event as an emergency and create a **diffusion of responsibility**, a belief that others are providing the necessary help.

CROSS-CULTURAL PERSPECTIVES

Cultural Diversity: A Fact of Life
It's a small world, but there are still differences among cultures and ethnic groups. To understand the commonalities and differences among people around the world, psychologists make cross-cultural comparisons. Each culture operates according to its own implicit **social norms**.

Individualism and Collectivism: A Tale of Two Cultural Worldviews
Social psychologists have observed that cultures differ in the extent to which they value **individualism** or **collectivism**. One theory suggests that a society's complexity, affluence, and heterogeneity may be factors, while others point to religious ideologies.

Conceptions of the Self
Research shows that cultural individualism and collectivism mold our conceptions of ourselves as independent or interdependent. While we all have individualistic and collectivistic traits, environmental cues can make one trait or the other more accessible.

INTERGROUP DISCRIMINATION

Of the many obstacles that confront minorities, the most disheartening is **discrimination**: behavior directed against persons because of their affiliation with a social group.

Stereotypes
Discrimination is a by-product of **stereotypes**: beliefs that associate a group of people with certain traits. The process of **social categorization**, by which we divide persons into groups based on common attributes, is natural but can lead to **outgroup-homogeneity bias**—the tendency to assume that members of groups other than our own are all alike, causing us to overlook diversity within groups and misjudge individuals. Thankfully, we can overcome stereotypes if we are alert, informed, and motivated.

Prejudice: The Motivational Roots
Examples of **prejudice**—negative feelings toward others based solely on their membership in a certain group—are all too common. **Realistic-conflict theory** attributes prejudice to intergroup competition for limited resources, but **social-identity theory** holds that people practice **ingroup favoritism** even in the absence of realistic conflict because their self-esteem is based on the groups to which they belong as well as on their personal identity.

Racism in America
Racism, a deep-seated form of prejudice based on the color of a person's skin, poisons social relations between people who are Black and White. While many of the obvious negative stereotypes of Black people may have faded, the **Implicit Association Test (IAT)** was first developed to determine if such a preference for White over Black may be deeply ingrained in our culture. The bias still exists, but research suggests it can be overcome when people are made aware, have the motivation to change, and are brought together in a common cause.

CRITICAL THINKING

Thinking Critically About Social and Cultural Influences
1. Most students, at one time or another, have experienced social loafing firsthand when working in groups for a class project. What policies could a professor implement to reduce the incidence of social loafing on group projects?

2. Is aggression innate, learned, or both? Support your position with empirical evidence. What does this imply about the most effective method(s) of reducing violence?

3. Discuss some of the strengths and weaknesses of collectivistic and individualistic cultural orientations. In what ways might the formation of an ethnic identity be influenced by a conflict of cultural orientations?

4. Are discrimination, stereotyping, racism, and prejudice inevitable? Why or why not?

5. Suppose you are in charge of student relations at a diverse university. What specific things can you do to foster positive interactions for diversity among all students?

CAREER CONNECTION: PUBLIC SERVICE

Community Relations Officer

A community relations officer (CRO) uses messaging, media and public events, and group activities to create a positive public image of their organization. Businesses, nonprofit organizations, health care institutions, and even the government may employ CROs to promote positive relations with local officials, activists, businesses, and the community at large. Psychology graduates' understanding of human behavior will inform their strategies and campaigns at a fundamental level, and their critical-thinking and problem-solving skills will allow them to enact those strategies efficiently and effectively. Job duties include ensuring that outreach missions are meeting stated objectives and remaining on budget. Qualifications for a CRO may include advanced training in community psychology and experience designing programs that meet the goals of the respective programs.

Key skills for this role that psychology students learn to develop:

- Understanding of local, national, and global values
- Effective communication in presentations and written works
- Innovative and integrative thinking and problem solving

KEY TERMS

aggression (p. 422)
altruism (p. 426)
attitude (p. 414)
attribution theory (p. 399)
attributions (p. 399)
bystander effect (p. 427)
central route to persuasion (p. 415)
cognitive dissonance (p. 416)
collectivism (p. 432)
conformity (p. 408)
diffusion of responsibility (p. 428)
discrimination (p. 435)
frustration-aggression hypothesis (p. 424)
fundamental attribution error (p. 399)
Implicit Association Test (IAT) (p. 441)
individualism (p. 433)
informational influence (p. 409)

ingroup favoritism (p. 438)
mere exposure effect (p. 403)
normative influence (p. 410)
outgroup-homogeneity bias (p. 436)
peripheral route to persuasion (p. 415)
prejudice (p. 437)
primacy effect (p. 401)
racism (p. 439)
realistic-conflict theory (p. 437)
social categorization (p. 436)
social facilitation (p. 420)
social-identity theory (p. 438)
social loafing (p. 421)
social norms (p. 432)
social perception (p. 399)
social psychology (p. 398)
stereotype (p. 436)

11 MOTIVATION AND EMOTION

iStock.com/JM_Image_Factory

LEARNING OBJECTIVES

Explain the general theories of motivation and how these are applied to understanding motivation.

Explain the biological and social components of motivation related to hunger, obesity, and eating disorders.

Explain how emotion is a physiological experience.

Analyze the role of nonverbal communication and sensory feedback in emotion.

Explain the role that thoughts or cognitions play in our experience of emotion.

Examine how emotions, including happiness and motivation, are displayed across cultures.

WHAT'S YOUR PREDICTION: CAN CULTURE INFLUENCE EMOTION?

The Situation

Imagine that you are working as part of a research team that is studying cultural influences. The goal of the project is to examine the effects of culture on the way people interpret facial expressions. Do human beings all over the world show joy, sadness, and other emotions in the same way, or are there differences in facial expressions as there are in the languages we speak?

To answer this question, you collect portrait photographs of adult men and women smiling, frowning, pouting, and expressing other emotions on the face. Your goal is to get pictures of people experiencing, or pretending to experience, six emotional states: happiness, sadness, anger, fear, surprise, and disgust. Then you contact colleagues from other countries and arrange for them to translate the words and show the pictures to natives of their culture. In all, you're able to test more than 500 people from Estonia, Germany, Greece, Hong Kong, Italy, Japan, Scotland, Sumatra, Turkey, and the United States.

The testing procedure is straightforward. Your experimenters schedule "observers" for group sessions. In total, 18 pictures are shown on slides, for 10 seconds each and in random order, and each slide depicts one of the six emotions. Participants are given a response sheet on which they are asked to check off the emotion being displayed in each picture.

Make a Prediction

The first question raised from the data you collect in this study is: Are emotions universally recognized, or are there cultural differences? In other words, to what extent do people in general (as represented in the 10 cultures) *agree* on the emotions displayed by various facial expressions? The second question is: Do some expressions elicit a higher agreement rate across cultures than others? As you prepare to analyze the results, what are your hypotheses? The table below lists the six emotions represented in this study. On a scale from 0 to 100 percent, what percentage of the participants, across all 10 cultures, do you think recognized each type of emotion?

| Happiness | ____% | Sadness | ____% | Anger | ____% |
| Fear | ____% | Surprise | ____% | Disgust | ____% |

The Results

You receive a total of 547 response forms in the mail, tally the results, and notice two key findings. Look at the table below and you'll find, first, that a majority of observers in *all* cultures interpreted facial expressions in the same way. The total agreement rate was far from perfect, but, over all cultures and emotions, it was quite high, at 82 percent. The second finding is that some emotions elicited more agreement than others. As shown, people in general were most likely to agree on expressions of happiness and surprise and least likely to agree on anger and disgust.

Happiness	90%
Sadness	85%
Anger	74%
Fear	80%
Surprise	90%
Disgust	73%

What Does It All Mean?

When Paul Ekman and his colleagues (1987) conducted the study just described, they were addressing a recurring debate in psychology concerning the "universality" of emotional states. On the one hand, emotion is so basic to the human experience that one would expect people all over the world to express their feelings in similar ways. On the other hand, there are cultural differences in the way people think about and interpret each other's behavior. Both positions are partly correct. Ekman's cross-cultural study showed that certain facial expressions are similarly interpreted by people all over the world. But what about other aspects of emotion? There is no simple answer. We'll learn in this chapter that emotions are a product of physiological, behavioral, and cognitive factors and that they are deeply involved in the motivations that underlie human behavior.

Michael is the son of James Jordan, an Air Force veteran and mechanic, and Marilyn Walker, a bank teller. When Michael was a sophomore in high school, he tried out for his school's varsity basketball team but was rejected because he was too short and inexperienced. He didn't give up. He grew a few inches and practiced every chance he could. By his senior year, he not only played for his varsity team but also was selected as an All-American. In college, as a freshman, he played on the University of North Carolina Tar Heels' 1982 national championship team. In 1984, at the age of 21, Michael was drafted into the NBA. That same year, his sneakers, Nike's Air Jordan, were introduced, and they're still popular today. Michael "MJ" Jordan went on to win many accolades in his career, including six NBA titles, all as Most Valuable Player, or MVP. The young man who at first could not make his high school basketball team became one of the greatest basketball players of all time. Certainly, his success has come with challenges, but he persisted. As MJ states,

I've missed more than 9,000 shots in my career. I've lost almost 300 games. 26 times, I've been trusted to take the game winning shot and missed. I've failed over and over again in my life. And that is why I succeed.

Consider also the true stories of seemingly ordinary people doing extraordinary things. Tricia Seaman, an oncology nurse in Harrisburg, Pennsylvania, took in the son of her patient, Tricia Somers, a terminally ill single mom, after knowing her for only 10 days. Somers passed away in 2014. How about the incredible feat of 9-year-old Milla Bizzotto, who completed a BattleFrog Xtreme 24-hour obstacle course designed for Navy SEALs: a course that included a 36-mile run, an 8-kilometer swim, and 25 obstacles. She is the youngest competitor ever to complete the course. Then there is Bethany Hamilton, a Hawaii native who at the age of 13 lost her entire left arm after being attacked by a tiger shark while surfing just off the coast of Kauai. Not deterred, she was back in the water and on her surf board less than a month after the incident. Bethany has gone to have a successful pro surfer career and is an inspiration to millions.

When we think of the incredible feats and resilience of individuals, and about other human endeavors that result in triumph or defeat, we need to understand the psychology of human *motivation*. In this chapter, we'll explore various domains of motivation, including hunger and eating, and the social needs for affiliation, intimacy, achievement, and power. As we'll learn, words such as *want, try, wish, urge, intent, desire, drive, goal, energy,* and *ambition* provide the language used to describe motivation.

Michael Jordan came from humble beginnings to become one of the greatest basketball players in NBA history.
JEFF HAYNES/AFP via Getty Images

WHAT MOTIVATES US?

> ### LEARNING OBJECTIVES
>
> Explain the general theories of motivation and how these are applied to understanding motivation.
>
> - Distinguish among the general theories that explain what motivates us.
> - Explain whether people are driven by instincts, a need to achieve a certain level of bodily tension, or a desire for attractive rewards.
> - Elaborate on Maslow's hierarchy of needs and whether all people want to satisfy the same basic needs.

Motivation is an inner state that energizes an individual toward fulfillment of a *goal*. Over the years, psychologists have approached the subject of motivation in two ways. Some have proposed general theories to explain what all human motives have in common. Others have focused on specific motives such as hunger, affiliation and belonging, and achievement.

motivation. An inner state that energizes people toward the fulfilment of a goal.

General Theories of Motivation

Early in the 20th century, as Darwin's theory of evolution gained prominence, many psychologists believed that human behavior, like the behavior of other animals, was biologically rooted in instincts. As discussed in the chapter on learning, an **instinct** is a fixed pattern of behavior that is unlearned, universal within a species, and "released" by a specific set of conditions. Thus, canaries sing, spiders weave webs, and beavers build dams—specific acts that are "hard-wired" by evolution. But is complex human behavior similarly programmed? In 1908, motivation theorist William McDougall argued that a whole range of human behaviors is instinctually based. He went on to compile a long list of instincts—including those for acquisition, jealousy, mating, parenting, pugnacity, greed, curiosity, cleanliness, and self-assertion.

Instinct theories of human motivation were soon rejected. One problem was that they explained human behavior through a flawed process of circular reasoning: "Why are people aggressive? Because human beings possess a powerful instinct to aggress. How do we know humans have this instinct? Because there is so much aggression." Notice the circularity in the logic: Behavior is attributed to an instinct that, in turn, is inferred from the behavior. A second problem with instinct theory is that many so-called instinctual behaviors (such as hunger and fullness) are learned, shaped by experience, subject to individual differences, and influenced by culture.

Drive Theory

With the demise of instinct-based accounts, psychologists turned to a **drive theory** of human motivation. According to drive theory, physiological needs that arise within the body create an unpleasant state of tension, which motivates or *drives* the organism to behave in ways that reduce the need and return the body to a balanced, less tense state (Hull, 1943). In its original form, drive theory was used to explain various biological functions such as eating, drinking, sleeping, and having sex. The hunger-eating cycle illustrates a presumed chain of events: food deprivation → hunger (drive) → seeking food and eating → drive reduction.

Clearly, drive theory can be used to explain certain biologically driven behaviors. But today, psychologists agree that it cannot explain what motivates the adolescent who has an eating disorder, the person who works excessively every night, or the greedy corporate executive. In particular, drive theory cannot explain why people often engage in activities that increase rather than reduce tension, as when we explore new surroundings just to satisfy our curiosity, skip a snack to save our appetite for dinner, or run miles with our hearts pounding in order to stay in shape. Nor can drive theory explain the behavior of high-risk activities such as ice climbing, extreme skiing, and skydiving.

---

instinct. A fixed pattern of behavior that is unlearned, universal in a species, and "released" by specific stimuli.

drive theory. The notion that physiological needs arouse tension that motivates people to satisfy the need.

FIGURE 11.1 ■ Having Fun in the Snow

When snow falls, children in all parts of the world make snowballs. Instinct theorists of the past would attribute this universal behavior to an instinct for play. Young Japanese macaque primates also make snowballs, carry them around as play objects, and even roll them along the ground. But here's where the similarity ends: No one has ever seen a macaque throw a snowball.

Imaginechina Limited / Alamy Stock Photo; istock.com/lmgorthand

Arousal Theory

To account for the fact that people often seek to increase rather than reduce tension, many psychologists turned to the **arousal theory** of motivation. According to arousal theory, all human beings are motivated to achieve and maintain an *optimum* level of bodily arousal—not too little, not too much (Fiske & Maddi, 1961). Studies show that people who are put into a state of sensory restriction (blindfolded, ears plugged, and unable to move) or into a highly monotonous situation quickly become bored and crave stimulation. Studies also show that when people are bombarded with bright lights, blaring music, and other intense stimuli, they soon withdraw in an effort to lower their level of arousal. The chapter on health, stress, and wellness explains that individuals differ in the amount of stimulation they find "optimal" (Aron & Aron, 1997; Simpson & Balsam, 2016). It also explores the finding that people are generally happier and more motivated when they engage in activities that are challenging in relation to their ability—not too easy, which is boring, and not too difficult, which triggers anxiety (Csikszentmihalyi, 1997; Seligman & Csikszentmihalyi, 2000).

arousal theory. The notion that people are motivated to achieve and maintain an optimum level of bodily arousal.

Incentive Theory

In contrast to the notion that people are "pushed" into action by internal need states, many motivation psychologists believe that people are often "pulled" by external goals, or incentives. According to **incentive theory** of motivation, any stimulus object that people have learned to associate with positive or negative outcomes can serve as an incentive—grades, money, access to Wi-Fi, gaming, respect, ice cream, a romantic night out, a pat on the back, or relief from pain. People are motivated to behave in certain ways when they *expect* that they can gain the incentive through their efforts and when they *value* that incentive. Recognizing that human beings set goals, make plans, and think about the outcomes they produce, motivation theorists today believe that there is a strong cognitive component to many of our aspirations (Atkinson, 1964; Šimleša et al., 2018).

incentive theory. The notion that people are motivated to behave in ways that produce a valued inducement.

The Pyramid of Human Motivations

Let us now examine some of the specific motives that direct and energize our behavior. In other words, what is it that we want most in life? In response to this question, Abraham Maslow (1954) proposed that human beings are motivated to fulfill a **hierarchy of needs**, from those that are basic for survival up to those that promote growth and self-enhancement (illustrated in Figure 11.2).

hierarchy of needs. Maslow's list of basic needs that have to be satisfied before people can become self-actualized.

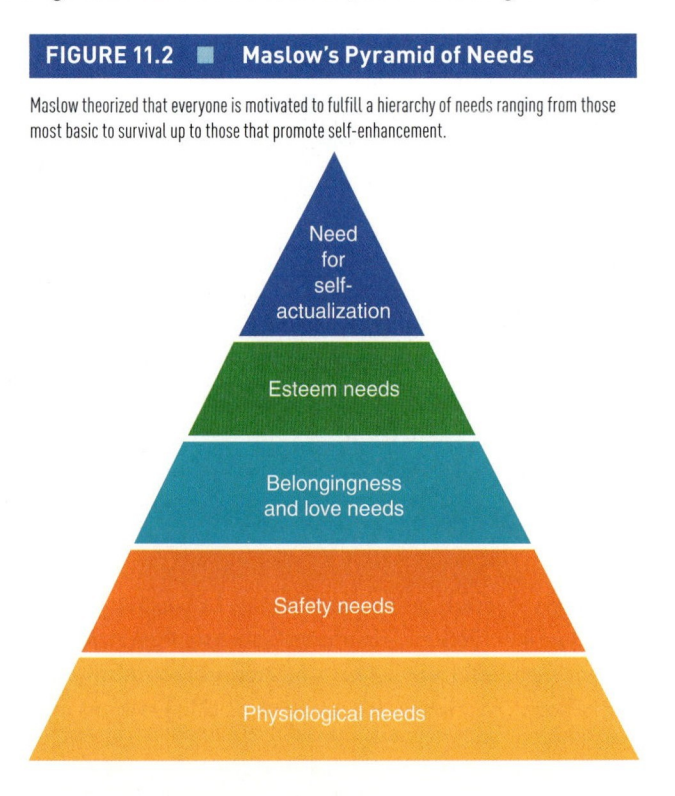

FIGURE 11.2 ■ Maslow's Pyramid of Needs

Maslow theorized that everyone is motivated to fulfill a hierarchy of needs ranging from those most basic to survival up to those that promote self-enhancement.

- Need for self-actualization
- Esteem needs
- Belongingness and love needs
- Safety needs
- Physiological needs

At the base of the hierarchy are the physiological needs for food, water, oxygen, sleep, and sex. Once these needs are met, people seek safety, steady work, financial security, stability at home, and a predictable environment. Next on the ladder are the social needs for affiliation, belongingness and love, affection, close relations, family ties, and group membership (if these needs are not met, we feel lonely and alienated). Next are the esteem needs, which include our desires for social status, respect, recognition, achievement, and power (failing to satisfy this need, we feel inferior and unimportant). In short, everyone strives in their own way to satisfy all the needs on the hierarchy. Once these needs are met, said Maslow, we become ready, willing, and able to strive for self-actualization—a distinctly human need to fulfill one's potential. As Maslow (1968) put it, "A musician must make music, an artist must paint, a poet must write, if he is ultimately to be at peace with himself. What a man *can* be, he *must* be" (p. 46).

By arranging human needs in the shape of a pyramid, Maslow claimed that the needs at the base take priority over those at the top. In other words, the higher needs become important to us only after more basic needs are satisfied. Thus, in countries where many citizens have their basic needs met, the search for meaning and fulfillment is more likely (Tay & Diener, 2011). Research generally confirms this prediction that motives lower in the pyramid take precedence, though there are occasional exceptions, as when people starve themselves to death in order to make a political statement. Research also shows that not everyone climbs Maslow's hierarchy in the same prescribed order. Some people seek love and romance before fulfilling their esteem motives, but others who are more achievement oriented may try to establish a career before a family (Goebel & Brown, 1981). In this regard, culture can also shape our motivational priorities. Shigehiro Oishi and others (1999) surveyed more than 6,000 people living in 39 countries and found that the fulfillment of esteem needs was more satisfying to people from "individualist" Western cultures that value independence and autonomy than to those from "collectivist" cultures that value interdependence and social connections.

Maslow's theory may not accurately describe the motivational path all people take. It does not, for example, account for our need to feel capable, autonomous, and socially secure in our endeavors (Harvath, 2008; Taormina & Gao, 2013). But his distinctions—and the notion that the various needs form a hierarchy—provide a convenient framework for the study of motivation. In the rest of this chapter, we'll begin at the base of Maslow's pyramid with physiological needs (focusing on hunger and eating), then we'll work our way up to the needs for affiliation, intimacy, achievement, and power. Finally, we'll put the psychology of motivation to work, literally, in a discussion of what motivates people on the job.

BASIC APPETITIVE AND SOCIAL MOTIVES

LEARNING OBJECTIVES

Explain the biological and social components of motivation related to hunger, obesity, and eating disorders.

- Outline how we biologically and physiologically regulate eating, and what happens when that regulation fails.
- Explain whether the desire for social relationships is a fundamental human motivation.
- Discuss what drives individuals who are highly motivated to achieve and whether the need for power promotes good leadership or bad.

Hunger and Eating

It has been said that "a hungry stomach has no ears" (Jean de La Fontaine), that "nobody wants a kiss when they are hungry" (Dorothea Dix), and that "even God cannot speak to a hungry man except in terms of bread" (Mahatma Gandhi). It seems that when it's time to eat, all other urges, desires, and ambitions fade into the background. Hunger is a powerful sensation that sets in motion the search for and consumption of food.

The Biological Component

The biological mechanisms underlying hunger are complex. Following common sense, early researchers believed that hunger was triggered by sensations in the stomach. In an initial experiment, A. L. Washburn, working with physiologist Walter Cannon, swallowed a long tube with a balloon that was then partially inflated and specially designed to rest in his stomach. Whenever the stomach contracted, the balloon compressed. At the same time, Washburn pressed a key each time he felt hungry. Using this device, and testing other participants, Cannon and Washburn (1912) observed a link between stomach contractions and reports of hunger. In fact, the participants reported feeling hungry at the height of a contraction, not at the beginning—thus suggesting that the contractions had caused the hunger and not the other way around (illustrated in Figure 11.3). Indeed, people begin to feel hungry when the stomach is about 60 percent empty (Sanger, Hellström, & Näslun, 2011; Sepple & Read, 1989).

A correlation between stomach contractions and hunger may exist, but additional observations soon discredited Cannon and Washburn's theory. The fatal blow came when studies revealed that even after people had had cancerous or ulcerated stomachs surgically removed, they continued to feel hungry. Clearly, if hunger can be felt without a stomach, then stomach contractions cannot be the cause of hunger. Another blow to the Cannon and Washburn theory comes from a clever study of two amnesia patients unable to form memories of new events. Within 30 minutes of eating a full lunch, these patients were offered a second meal, soon to be followed by a third. Their stomachs were full, but because they could not remember having eaten so recently, both patients consumed the meals that were offered (Rozin, Dow, Moscovitch, & Rajaram, 1998).

Confronted with the realization that stomach contractions are not the cause of hunger, researchers have focused on the brain and central nervous system. According to one theory, the brain monitors fluctuating levels of glucose (a simple sugar that provides energy) and other nutrients that circulate in the bloodstream. When glucose drops below a certain level, people become hungry and eat. When the glucose level in the blood exceeds a certain point, they feel satiated and stop eating (illustrated in Figure 11.4). A good deal of evidence supports this thermostat-like mechanism. In one study, for example, researchers continuously monitored the glucose levels of human participants and found that momentary decreases were accompanied by subjective reports of hunger and requests for food (Campfield, Arthur, Francoise, Rosenbaum, & Hirsch, 1996).

FIGURE 11.3 ■ Cannon and Washburn's Hunger Study

In this study, participants swallowed a balloon, which rested in the stomach. Recorded over time (A) is the volume of the balloon (B) in minutes (C). Participants pressed a key whenever they felt hungry (D). Participants reported feeling hungry at the height of their stomach contractions.; Carolina Hrejsa/Body Scientific Intl.

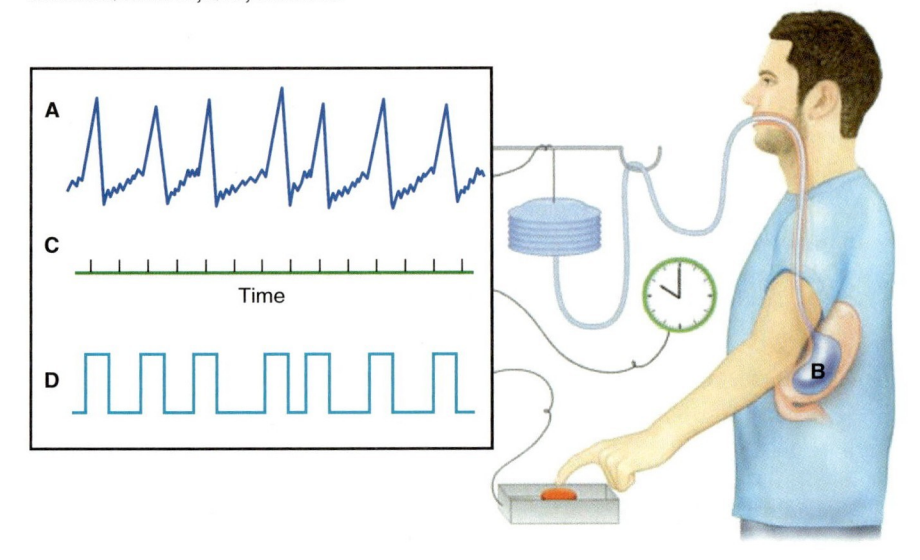

FIGURE 11.4 ■ The Hunger-Regulation Cycle

When blood glucose levels are low, people become hungry and eat. The food then raises glucose levels, which lessens hunger and eating. The "thermostat" that monitors glucose levels is in or near the hypothalamus. Other factors also control hunger and eating.

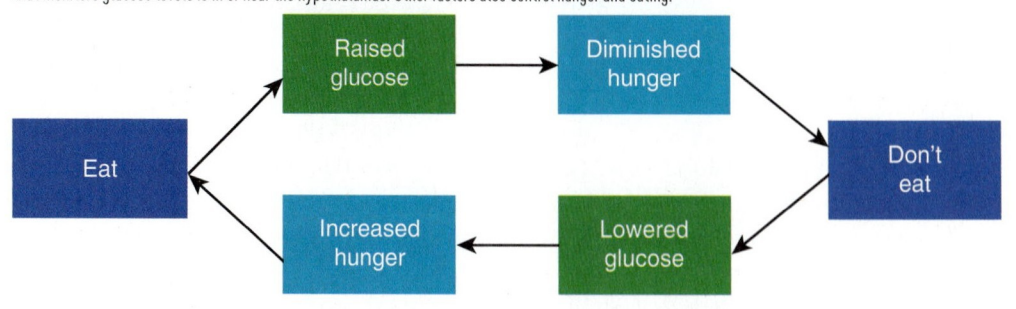

How and where in the body is blood glucose monitored? Although different regions of the brain may be involved in the process, two distinct areas of the *hypothalamus* play a key role (as described in the chapter on behavioral neuroscience, the hypothalamus is a tiny structure that regulates body temperature, the autonomic nervous system, and the release of hormones). Initially, researchers saw the *lateral hypothalamus* as the "hunger center": When its neurons are stimulated, an animal will eat, and eat, and eat—even after it's full. When the lateral hypothalamus is destroyed, the animal will not eat—and may even starve to death unless it is force-fed (Anand & Brobeck, 1951; Teitelbaum & Epstein, 1962). At about the same time, researchers identified the *ventromedial hypothalamus* as a "satiation center": When it is stimulated, an animal will not eat, even if it has been deprived of food. When this same area is destroyed, an animal will consume larger quantities than usual, eventually tripling its own body weight (Hetherington & Ranson, 1942; Wyrwicka & Dobrzecka, 1960).

At first, these findings suggested that the hypothalamus monitors blood glucose levels and has an on-off switch for eating (Stellar, 1954). But subsequent studies indicate that the mechanism is far more complicated. It turns out, for example, that certain nerves form a tract that runs up from the brainstem through the lateral hypothalamus—and these nerves are somehow involved. In fact, such areas may be part of a more general motor-activation system that, when stimulated, motivates an animal to "Do something!" This general command triggers eating if food is present, drinking if water is present, or running if neither food nor water is present (Kim, 2012). Research also shows that other factors control hunger and eating as well—including levels of protein, fat, and insulin and other hormonal activities associated with the liver, pancreas, and intestines. In short, the body is equipped with a complex biochemical system for the regulation of hunger and eating (MacLean, Blundell, Mennella, & Batterham, 2017).

Psychological Influences

Hunger may be biologically driven, but researchers have learned that other factors such as taste, smell, and visual cues also play an important role—and that eating patterns, which are learned, can also be unlearned (Logue, 2014; Privitera, 2008).

Among the influences on eating is taste. The chapter on sensation and perception explained that there are four primary tastes: sweet, sour, salty, and bitter, with umami being a fifth taste. It turns out that people all over the world seek out sweet-tasting foods such as cookies, ice cream, soda, ripe fruit, and candy, as well as salty foods such as pretzels and potato chips. Some of these preferences appear to be innate and universal. Thus, studies with newborns show that sugar-sweetened and artificially sweetened water, compared to unsweetened water, has a soothing effect and can stop infants from crying (Fidler Mis et al., 2017) and leads them to form a preference for the adult who fed them (Blass & Camp, 2001; Drewnowski, Mennella, Johnson, & Bellisle, 2012). A person's state of mind may also influence his or her preference for certain types of food. For example, American college students who were asked about their eating habits reported that during times of stress they eat more "snack-type" foods such as cake and chocolates and fewer "meal-type" foods such as meat, fish, fruit, and vegetables (Oliver & Wardle, 1999); these types of "snacking when stressed" responses are similarly observed in children and in socioeconomically diverse samples (Debeuf, Verbeken, Van Beveren, Michels, & Braet, 2018; Fanelli Kuczmarski et al., 2017).

For Americans, xternal food cues can also entice us into eating. If you've ever inhaled the yeasty aroma of pastries in a bakery, popcorn in a movie theater, or garlic in an Italian restaurant, or if you've ever had a sudden urge for soda and a hot dog while sitting in a ball park, you know that we're sometimes drawn into eating by external cues, or incentives. Research shows that people are naturally attracted to the tastes, smells, and textures of fatty foods such as hamburgers, French fries, mozzarella cheese pizzas, crispy bacon, and ice cream (Privitera et al., 2018; Schiffman, Graham, Sattely-Miller, & Warwick, 1998). In what is likely an adaptive preference, people also eat more when there is variety in the food supply, as in a multicourse meal (Keenan, Brunstrom, & Ferriday, 2015). Time of day can also be a powerful food cue. For example, in one classic study Stanley Schachter and Larry Gross (1968) brought participants into a laboratory, rigged the clock on the wall so that it ran fast or slow, and then offered crackers as a snack. Not wanting to spoil their appetite, most participants of average weight ate fewer crackers when they thought it was late than when they thought it was early in the afternoon.

Finally, it's important to realize that eating is a social activity and is often subject to social influences. At times, the presence of others can inhibit us from eating—as when young women consume less food in front of others than when alone in order to present themselves as appropriately "feminine" (Cavazza, Guidetti, & Butera, 2015). As a general rule, however, people eat more rather than less in the company of others. Eating diary studies show that the more people we're with, the longer time we spend at the table and the more food we consume (Bellisle, Dalix, & de Castro, 1999; de Castro & Brewer, 1992). This effect is especially pronounced when the people we're with are family and friends (de Castro, 1994) and when we're in a noticeably good or bad mood (Patel & Schlundt, 2001; Privitera, 2016). Similarly, whether we are alone or with others, we tend to eat more food (mostly snacks) when we binge-watch our favorite shows on TV or streaming on our devices (Flayelle et al., 2020; Umesh & Bose, 2019).

What's Your Prediction?

Eating can be such a social activity that you may wonder: What effect does the holiday season have on our eating habits and weight? If you were to recruit some research volunteers from three countries (United States, Japan, and Germany) and record their daily weight changes for a period of 12 months, would you observe weight gain, weight loss, or no change during the holiday seasons of their cultures? Make a prediction: Would people gain or lose 0, 1, 5, or 10 pounds? And what would their weight be one year later?

Elina Helander from Finland and other researchers from the United States and France (2016) gave wireless digital scales to 2,924 research volunteers from three countries and had them record their daily weight change for one full year from August 2012 to July 2013. The research team then used the electronic scale data to see how participant weights changed compared to their starting weights. Their results highlight the role of culture in weight gain, as illustrated in Figure 11.5. The average weights of participants increased around the national holidays of their countries. That said, one season seems closely linked to weight gain regardless of culture. All participants showed the largest average weight gains during winter and the New Year holidays.

Obesity

With all the talk that surrounds us about dieting and exercise, you'd think that Americans were obsessed with losing weight. In fact, they spend an estimated $60 billion a year on weight loss products and services. Yet estimates based on Americans' body mass index (BMI) scores—a standard measure derived from a formula that uses a person's height and weight, as illustrated in Figure 11.6—show that among American adults over age 25, a staggering 65 percent are now overweight, with about 33 percent being so overweight as to be considered obese (Kaiser Family Foundation, 2018). **Obesity** is defined as an excess of body fat, which normally accounts for about 25 percent of weight in women and 18 percent in men. This problem has worsened in recent years, as obesity rates rose from the 1980s to the present—among men and women, young and old, Black and White, college educated and uneducated, and smokers and nonsmokers. What's particularly puzzling about this trend is that it comes at a time when Americans are otherwise health conscious—for example, smoking less and using seat belts more than in the past. That's why the World Health Organization and others describe today's obesity problem, observed in many developed countries, as a global epidemic—termed "globesity" (Friedrich, 2002; World Health Organization, 2020).

obesity. The state of having a surplus of body fat that causes a person to exceed his or her optimum weight by 20 percent.

FIGURE 11.5 ■ Weight Gain Through the Holiday Seasons

Weight gain during the holidays tends to occur across cultures, particularly during winter and the New Year holidays.

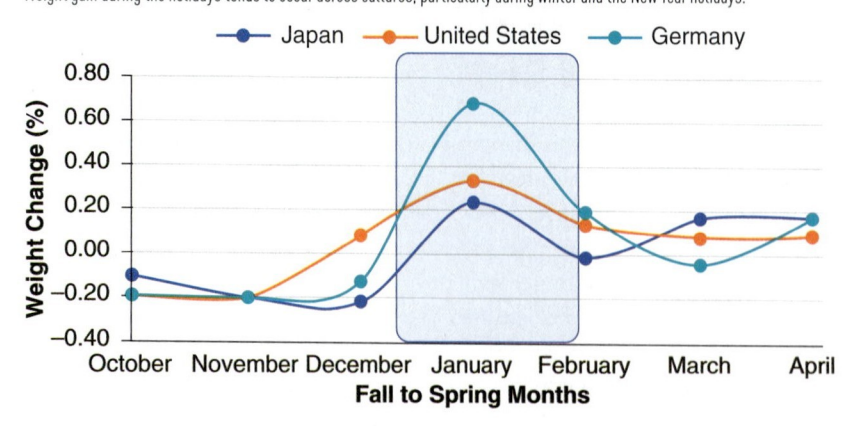

Source: Author adapted using minimal data from Helander, E. E., Wansink, B., & Chieh, A. (2016). Weight gain over the holidays in three countries. The New England Journal of Medicine, 375(12), p. 1201.

iStock.com/IrisImages

FIGURE 11.6 ■ Being Overweight: How Heavy Is Too Heavy?

The Body Mass Index Calculation Chart is a widely used tool for identifying individuals as being overweight or obese based on their height and weight. This photo was taken during the 2001 World Figure Skating Championships in Vancouver when Sale and Pelletier won a gold medal in front of their hometown crowd.

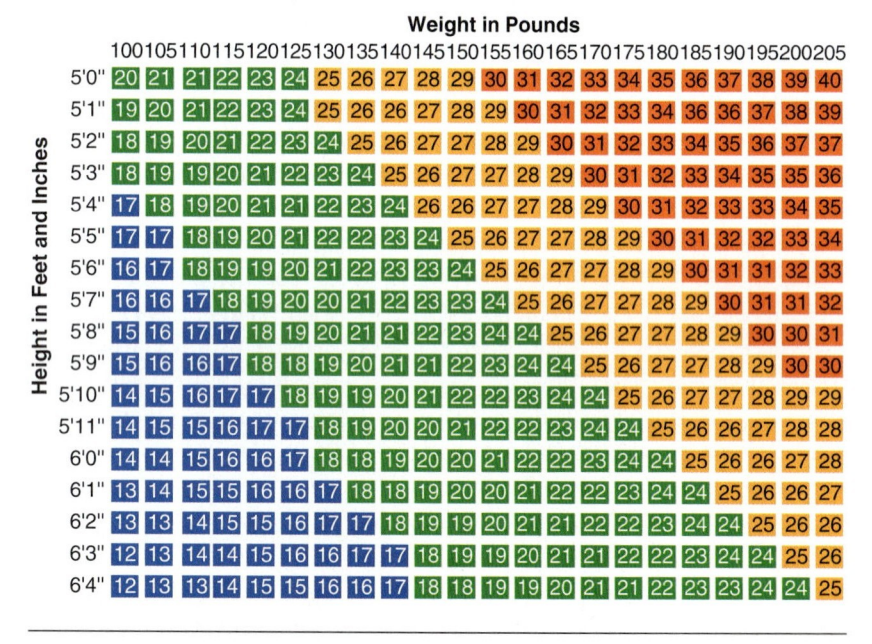

Source: Centers for Disease Control

Being slightly overweight does not pose a health risk. But statistically, people who are obese are also more likely to suffer from diabetes, heart disease, high blood pressure, high cholesterol, respiratory problems, arthritis, strokes, depression, pregnancy complications, sleep apnea, and certain forms of cancer. In fact, obesity is a risk factor for 6 of the top 10 leading causes of death in the United States, and these risks disproportionately affect people based on race, socioeconomic status, and more (CDC, 2019; National Center for Health Statistics, 2017).

What Causes Obesity? Why do some people but not others fight a chronic battle against gaining weight? As with other aspects of hunger and eating, both biological and psychological factors play a role. Physiologically speaking, getting fat is easy to explain. People gain weight when they *consume* more calories than their bodies *metabolize*, or burn up. The excess calories are stored as fat. Evidence for the role of biological factors begins with the fact that obesity runs in families and is influenced by genetics. In one study, Albert Stunkard and others (1990) compared the BMIs of genetically identical twins and fraternal twins who were raised together or apart. As illustrated in Figure 11.7, two results provided strong evidence for the role of genetics: (a) The identical twins were more similar in their BMI than were fraternal twins, and (b) identical twins were similar even when raised apart, in separate homes. The same conclusion emerges from adoption studies, which show that in body weight, adoptees resemble their biological parents more than their adoptive parents (Grilo & Pogue-Geile, 1991). Overall, researchers estimate that genes account for 40 to 75 percent of the BMI differences among people (Herrera & Lindgren, 2010; Herrera, Keildson, & Lindgren, 2011).

So, what, specifically, is inherited? Do obese people inherit a tendency to consume large quantities of food or a tendency toward physical *in*activity, or are they born with a particularly slow metabolism, making it difficult for them to burn up calories? These are all possibilities. According to one theory, each of us has a **set point**, a level of weight toward which our own bodies gravitate, and obese people are programmed to maintain a high set-point weight (Keesey, 1995). The set point itself may be genetic or it may stem from eating habits established early in life. Either way, set points are relatively stable—which explains why it's hard to lose massive quantities of weight and why, after dieting, it's challenging to maintain the loss over time (Privitera, 2008).

Not everyone agrees, however, that hunger and eating are driven by a precise set point—or that people who are too heavy are doomed to stay that way despite their best efforts to lose weight. Considering the research on hunger and weight regulation, John Pinel and others (2000) believe that the human body does not have a fixed set point but, rather, a loose *settling point* that drifts upward and downward over time in response to changes in behavior. According to this model, permanent changes in diet and activity level, or energy intake and output, can move a settling point—and keep it there.

Genetic predispositions may help to explain why some people battle the bulge more than others do, but they cannot explain why the world's population has gained dangerous amounts of weight in recent years. Most health experts agree that the global obesity epidemic reflects recent changes in our eating and activity habits, not in our gene pool (Gillespie & Privitera, 2018; Price, 2002). Some researchers blame the epidemic on a "toxic environment" filled with fatty fast foods, all-you-can-eat buffets, minimarkets in gasoline stations, vending machines stocked with sugar-filled soft drinks and snacks, sedentary office work, too little emphasis on physical education in schools, and too much time spent watching television or using devices (Gillespie & Privitera, 2018; Horgen & Brownell, 2002).

How Can Body Weight Be Managed? Search online for books about dieting, and you'll find that the weight loss industry is alive and well. There are many approaches to losing and managing weight, including

set point. A level of weight toward which a person's body gravitates.

FIGURE 11.7 ■ Body Weight of Identical and Fraternal Twins

Indicating the role of genetic factors in body weight, identical twins had more similar body weights than did fraternal twins. Note also that this same pattern was found regardless of whether the twins were

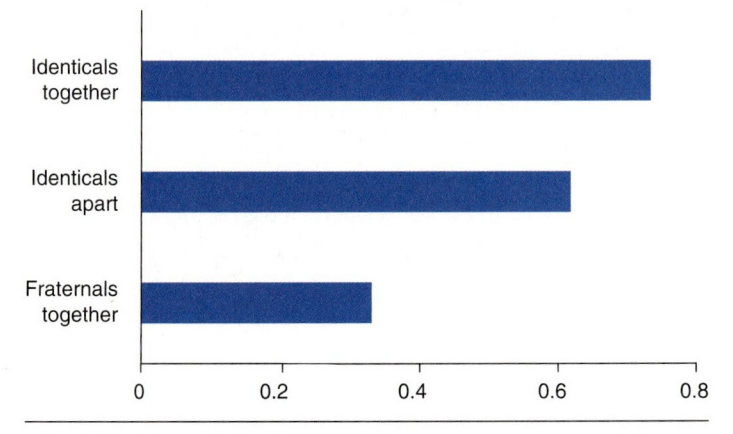

Identicals together	0.74
Identicals apart	0.62
Fraternals together	0.33

Grilo, C. M., & Pogue-Geile, M. F. (1991). The nature of environmental influences on weight and obesity: A behavior genetic analysis. Psychological Bulletin, 110(3), 520–537. https://doi.org/10.1037/0033-2909.110.3.520

behavioral changes in diet, exercise and activity, medication, and surgery (Soeliman & Azadbakht, 2014). Some people resort to higher-risk medical procedures such as gastric-restriction surgery to shrink the stomach and diet drugs that suppress appetite or increase energy expenditure. For most, however, weight reduction can be achieved through alterations in behavior. In this regard, the key to success is to realize that a change in diet must be sustained and permanent—and that it must be accompanied by a steady regimen of physical exercise (Swift et al., 2014).

Two factors must be present for someone to sustain the dieting effort: information and motivation. First, a person must have an accurate sense of his or her caloric intake and exercise. This sounds easy, but Steven Lichtman and his colleagues (1992) had a group of failed dieters keep a diary and discovered that they unwittingly underreported the amount of food they had consumed and overestimated their daily exercise. Second, a person's motivation for losing weight is critical. Research shows that people are generally more likely to succeed in a long-term weight-reduction program when motivated by their own desires than when motivated by external incentives such as the wishes of a partner (Mroz, Pullen, & Hageman, 2018; Teixeira, Silva, Mata, Palmeira, & Markland, 2012).

Eating Disorders

Psychological influences on hunger and eating are most evident when it comes to serious eating disorders. Eating disorders are highly prevalent (or widespread) worldwide, especially among women. Worldwide, the prevalence of eating disorders has risen sharply, increasing 3.5 percent from 2000 to 2006 and increasing at more than twice that rate (7.8 percent) from 2013 to 2018 (Galmiche, Déchelotte, Lambert, & Tavolacci, 2019). These rates highlight the need for interventions to address the devastating effects of eating disorders. In this section, we discuss three common eating disorders: anorexia nervosa, bulimia nervosa, and binge-eating disorder.

anorexia nervosa. An eating disorder in which the person limits eating and becomes emaciated.

Anorexia nervosa is a disorder in which a person becomes so fearful of gaining weight that the person ignores hunger pangs, limits eating, becomes emaciated, and sometimes even starves to death. Most people with anorexia die from heart failure. Anorexia has the highest fatality rate of any psychological disorder—including depression. Often, the heart failure happens suddenly, even when the patient is in "recovery" (Jáuregui-Garrido & Jáuregui-Lobera, 2012). Many become compulsive about running and exercising. The prevalence for anorexia nervosa is approximately five times higher among females (0.5 percent) than males (0.1 percent) in the United States (National Institute of Mental Health, 2017).

bulimia nervosa. An eating disorder marked by cycles of binge eating followed by purging.

Closely related is **bulimia nervosa**, an eating disorder that is marked by cycles of extreme binge eating followed by self-induced vomiting (purging) and the overuse of laxatives. A person with bulimia may eat a whole pizza, a box of cookies, a bucket of fried chicken, or a half-gallon of ice cream—all in one sitting—and then purge the food. These binge-and-purge episodes may occur 2 to 14 times a week. Bulimia nervosa is seldom life threatening (most sufferers are normal in weight, which makes it easy for them to hide their condition), but the repeated vomiting can cause erosion of tooth enamel, dehydration, damage to the intestines, nutritional imbalances, and other medical problems (National Eating Disorders Association, 2018). The prevalence of bulimia nervosa is approximately three times higher among females (1.6 percent) than males (0.8 percent) in the United States (National Institute of Mental Health, 2017).

binge-eating disorder. An eating disorder marked by binge eating without chronic purging.

Binge-eating disorder has been recognized as a distinct disorder from bulimia nervosa by the American Psychiatric Association (2013). A key difference between bulimia nervosa and binge-eating disorder is that a person with the latter binges without the chronic purging (vomiting or expulsions of food contents immediately after eating) that is characteristic of bulimia nervosa. As a result, those with binge-eating disorder are often overweight or obese, leading to the need for treatment that addresses both the binge eating and obesity-related risk factors, such as diabetes and metabolic disorders (Brownley et al., 2016). Binge-eating disorder is the most common eating disorder, affecting approximately 3 percent of U.S. adults in their lifetime. The prevalence for binge-eating disorder is more than two times higher among females (3.8 percent) than males (1.5 percent) in the United States (National Institute of Mental Health, 2017).

As to the possible causes of eating disorders, psychologists have speculated about genetics, hormone abnormalities, low set points, overly perfectionistic parents, and traumas such as sexual abuse.

Many contributing factors can be identified. One is cultural and/or peer pressure. Eating disorders, for example, are most prevalent in weight-conscious cultures in which food is abundant, diet centers and exercise videos are rampant, and people feel pressured to copy the appearance of shapely or muscular models (Nasser, 1988; Syurina, Bood, Ryman, & Muftugil-Yalcin, 2018). Media plays a powerful role, especially today—with greater use of social media being associated with greater concerns about weight (Sidani, Shensa, Hoffman, Hanmer, & Primack, 2016). Other factors associated with eating disorders include having a professional career that promotes being thin, such as ballet or modeling, and being an athlete in "lean" sports such as rowing, diving, gymnastics, wrestling, and cross country running (Privitera & Dickinson, 2015).

As for the role of cultural ideals, researchers have found that exposure to slender female models in the media leads women who are dissatisfied with their own bodies to become even more anxious about their own weight (Kim & Lee, 2018). Trying to measure up to the ultrathin multimillion-dollar supermodel can only prove frustrating to most women. The cultural ideal for thinness may even be set early in childhood. When Kevin Norton and others (1996) projected the life-size dimensions of the world-popular Ken and Barbie dolls, they found that both were unrealistically thin compared to the average young adult. In fact, the estimated odds of a young woman having Barbie's classic shape are about 1 in 100,000.

Ken and Barbie are the most popular-selling dolls in the world. Yet both are unrealistically thin compared to the average young adult.
JENS-ULRICH KOCH/DDP via Getty Images

Belongingness Motives

Although born dependent on others, human infants are equipped at birth with reflexes that orient them toward people. They are responsive to faces, turn their head toward voices, and are prepared to mimic certain facial gestures on cue. Much to the delight of caregivers, the newborn seems an inherently social animal. If you reflect on the amount of time you spend talking to, being with, pining for, or worrying about other people, you'll realize that we all are. People need people.

Recognizing the power of our social impulses, Maslow ranked love and belongingness needs third in his hierarchy. Being part of a family or community, playing on a sports team, joining a social or religious or professional group, making friends, falling in love, and having children—all service this important motive. So just how important is it? Do people really *need* other people?

Dan McAdams (1989) notes that Maslow's belongingness motive is composed of two distinct needs. The first is the **need for affiliation**, which is defined as a desire to establish and maintain social contacts. The second is a **need for intimacy**, defined as a further desire for close relationships characterized by an openness of communication.

need for affiliation. The desire to establish and maintain social contacts.

need for intimacy. The desire for close relationships characterized by open and intimate communication.

The Need for Affiliation

Do you ever crave the company of others? Do you ever enjoy being alone? Chances are that you answered *yes* to both questions. Research shows that individuals differ in the strength of their need for affiliation. As you might expect, people with a high need for affiliation are socially more active than those with a low need. They prefer to be in contact with others more often and are more likely to visit friends, stay connected via social media, and even engage in networking to get ahead in business (Wolff, Weikamp, & Batinic, 2018).

Although individuals differ, even the most gregarious among us wants to be alone at times. In fact, it seems that people are motivated to establish and maintain an *optimum* balance of social contact (not too much, not too little) the way the body maintains a certain level of caloric intake. In an interesting study, Bibb Latané and Carol

Our need for love and belongingness was never more evident than during the coronavirus pandemic, when many loved ones struggled to find ways to express their love during a time of social isolation.
iStock.com/FG Trade

Werner (1978) found that laboratory rats were more likely to approach others of their species after a period of isolation and were less likely after prolonged social contact. These researchers suggested that, like many other animals, rats have a built-in "sociostat" (a social thermostat) to regulate their affiliative tendencies. Is there any evidence of a similar mechanism in humans? Shawn O'Connor and Lome Rosenblood (1996) had college students carry portable beepers for four days. Whenever the beeper went off (on average, every hour), the students wrote down whether at the time they were *actually* alone or in the company of other people, and whether, at the time, they *wanted* to be alone or with others. The results showed that the students were in the state they desired two-thirds of the time—and that the situation they wished they were in on one occasion predicted their actual situation the next time they were signaled. Whether it was solitude or social contact that the students were craving, they successfully managed to regulate their own personal needs for affiliation.

People may differ in the strength of their affiliative needs and in the overall amount of social contact they find satisfying, but there are times when we would all rather be with other people. Affiliating can be satisfying for many reasons. From other people, we get energy, attention, stimulation, information, and emotional support (Cullum, O'Grady, & Tennen, 2011). One condition that strongly arouses our need for affiliation is stress. It's always amazing to see how neighbors who otherwise never stop to say hello come together in snowstorms, hurricanes, fires, power failures, and other major crises. People under stress may even seek out each other online—as when stock market investors jam into Internet message boards to talk and support each other after their stocks tumble. Many years ago, Stanley Schachter (1959) theorized that external threat triggers fear and motivates us to affiliate—particularly with others who are facing a similar threat. In a laboratory experiment, Schachter found that participants expecting to receive painful electric shocks chose to wait with other nervous participants rather than alone.

The Need for Intimacy

Affiliating with other people, even superficially, satisfies part of our need for social contact. But in varying degrees, people also have a need for close and intimate relationships. Research shows that individuals who score high rather than low on measures of the need for intimacy are seen by peers as warm, sincere, and loving. They also look at others more, smile more, laugh more, and confide more in their friends. People who score high rather than low on intimacy may also be happier and healthier (Gómez-López, Viejo, & Ortega-Ruiz, 2019).

self-disclosure. The sharing of intimate details about oneself with another person.

In looking at close relationships and the deep affection that grows between friends or lovers, psychologists have found that the key ingredient is **self-disclosure**, the sharing of intimate, often confidential details about oneself with another person, when such disclosure is perceived as appropriate from the other person (Lin & Utz, 2017). Self-disclosure tends to follow three predictable patterns. The first is that we typically reciprocate another person's self-disclosure with one of our own—and at a comparable level of intimacy. Bare your soul to someone and that person is likely to react by doing the same (Rotenberg & Chase, 1992). Second, there are sex differences in openness of communication. Compared to men, women tend to self-disclose more than men *to* others (both male and female), and, in turn, they elicit more self-disclosure *from* others (Dindia & Allen, 1992). Third, people reveal more and more to each other as relationships grow over time. In the early stages, people give relatively little of themselves to others and receive comparably little in return. If these encounters are rewarding, however, the communication often becomes more frequent and more intimate (Tamir & Mitchell, 2012). This increase in self-disclosure can be seen in the fact that the more intimate a relationship people have, the less likely they are to lie to each other. In a naturalistic study that illustrates this point, Bella DePaulo and Deborah Kashy (1998) asked people to keep a one-week diary of all social interactions and record every instance in which they tried to mislead someone, including white lies told to spare another person's feelings. They found that lying rates decreased according to the closeness of a relationship.

Esteem Motives

Have you ever met someone so single-mindedly driven to succeed that you couldn't help but wonder why? What fuels the drive we often have to succeed, excel, and advance in our work? For years, psychologists have examined the motive that plays a key role in this regard: the need for achievement.

The Need for Achievement

In a classic book entitled *The Achievement Motive*, David McClelland and his colleagues (1953) sought to identify people with high levels of **achievement motivation**—defined as a strong desire to accomplish difficult tasks, outperform others, and excel. There was no question that individuals differ in the intensity of their achievement strivings. The question was how this important and perhaps unconscious motive could be measured. Seeking what he would later call a "psychic X ray," McClelland believed that our motives are revealed in our fantasies. To bring these fantasies out, he asked participants to make up stories about a series of ambiguous pictures. Look at the image in Figure 11.8. What's your interpretation? Who is the child, what are they thinking about, and what will happen to them? Assuming that participants will naturally identify with the main character, researchers posited that pictures like this provide a screen on which people can project their own needs. If you used the scoring system devised by McClelland and his colleagues, you'd be classified as high in the need for achievement if you say that the boy in Figure 11.8 is recalling with pride an exam he aced, thinking about how to win a prize or scholarship, or dreaming of becoming a doctor—and if these types of concerns are a recurring theme in your stories.

From the start, this fantasy measure proved intriguing. For example, it proved to be a reasonably sensitive measure of the need for achievement. To demonstrate this, McClelland and his colleagues (1953) had participants solve word puzzles before responding to the pictures. Some participants were told that the puzzles were not that important; others were told that the puzzles tested intelligence and leadership ability—an instruction used to arouse performance concerns. Sure enough, participants who were induced into a heightened state of achievement need told more achievement-relevant stories. Yet research soon showed that scores from this fantasy measure of achievement do not correlate with the way participants described their own achievement needs on questionnaires. The reason: It appears that the story-based measure uncovers deeply ingrained, enduring, unconscious motives that predict a person's behavior over long periods of time, whereas questionnaires measure only conscious, self-attributed motives relevant to the way a person is likely to behave in the immediate situation (McClelland, Koestner, & Weinberger, 1989).

As you might expect, there are strong links among a person's motivation, behavior, and level of accomplishment. Those who score high rather than low in the need for achievement work harder and are more persistent, innovative, and future oriented. They also crave success more than they fear failure (Atkinson, 1964) and then credit success to their own abilities and efforts rather than to external factors (Weiner, 1989). One particularly interesting difference between the highs and lows concerns

> **achievement motivation.** A strong desire to accomplish difficult tasks, outperform others, and excel.

FIGURE 11.8 ■ Fantasy Measure of Achievement

Who is the child, what are they thinking about, and what will happen to them? Using ambiguous pictures like this one, researchers get people to tell stories and then code the stories for achievement imagery.

iStock.com/graphixel

their mindset, which can be fixed or growth oriented (Dweck, 2012). If you have a fixed mindset, you tend to be rigid, believing that traits that are often associated with success—such as intelligence and leadership ability—are fixed from birth and generally cannot be changed. With a growth mindset, you tend to be more malleable—to believe that these same traits can shift and develop with time and effort (Dweck, 2012). People with a high need for achievement tend to have a growth mindset; those with a low need for achievement tend to have a fixed mindset (Ng, 2018; Yeager et al., 2019). When it comes to our pursuits, having a growth mindset can even make us more adaptive when we experience setbacks (such as bad grades in school). For those with a growth mindset, challenges or setbacks are viewed as chances to learn and improve, which can lead to greater achievement (Yeager & Dweck, 2012).

People with a high need for achievement set high but realistic goals and then exert enough effort to reach those goals. But what about the *process* of achievement? How are people in pursuit of long-term goals affected by the successes and failures that they will invariably encounter along the way? Focused on children, developmental psychologist Carol Dweck notes that people can attribute their own positive and negative outcomes to intelligence, athleticism, or other natural abilities they see as fixed or immutable. Or, she notes, people can attribute outcomes to preparation, practice, persistence, and other factors within their power to control. Does it matter? Is one type of attribution more adaptive than the other? Yes. In a series of studies, Mueller and Dweck (1998) gave a test with some easy problems to elementary-school children. In giving positive feedback to the students, they told some, "You must be smart at these problems," and others, "You must have worked hard at these problems." In a second phase, the students were given tough problems to solve. Their reaction: Those earlier praised for their effort, compared to those praised for intelligence, stayed more focused, were willing to take on difficult problems, and persisted longer in the face of failure. When the "going gets tough," as they say, it helps to believe that you have the capacity to improve. The implication is: Be positive. A positive environment for learning can improve social competence, motivation and engagement, and academic achievement while reducing socioemotional distress for children from kindergarten to high school who come from many backgrounds and learning abilities (Bertills, Granlund, & Augustine, 2021; Wang et al., 2020).

Psychology Applied: Finding Your Work-Health Balance

We often think of our work ethic as reflecting our *need for achievement*, but what motivates us to work? Do we work to live, or do we live to work? Most people would agree that *we work to live*, and many countries are taking this idea seriously. In January 2017, France initiated the so-called "right to disconnect" law (Morris, 2017), which requires companies with more than 50 employees to disclose the hours when employees are paid to work. Outside this defined "paid" period, employees cannot be required to send or answer emails. That is, they must be allowed the right to "disconnect." The rationale for this law was about *fairness* (being

---

FIGURE 11.9 ■ Work Ethic and Bringing Home the Gold

Exhibiting work ethic at its best, Olympians Michael Phelps and Simone Biles are at the top of their sports. Phelps won an unprecedented 28 Olympic medals in his career (23 gold, 3 silver, and 2 bronze), which includes five Olympic appearances. Biles is America's most decorated gymnast, having earned the most world all-around titles, including all-around gold at the 2016 Olympic games in Rio de Janeiro. In 2019, Biles became the first female gymnast ever to land a double-double as part of a dismount on the balance beam. What motivates Phelps and Biles? "If you want to be the best, you have to do things that other people aren't willing to do," says Phelps. For Biles, it isn't about comparing herself to anyone but herself: "I'm not the next Usain Bolt or Michael Phelps, I'm the first Simone Biles."

Adam Pretty/Getty Images Sport via Getty Images; Alex Livesey/Getty Images Sport via Getty Images

paid when working), *allowing employees to have time with family* (being free to be with those you love outside of work), and *protecting employees' health* (risks due to work-related stress include burnout, sleeping problems, and even death).

Indeed, our quantity of work can often affect our health. In Japan, overworking is so common that the term *Karōshi* was coined, which translates to "death by overworking." Two factors contributing to the phenomenon of Karōshi are long commutes, with travel of two or more hours not uncommon in Japan—indeed, in Japan, the long commutes are called *tukin jigoku*, which translates to "commuting hell"; and working "off the clock" unpaid—while Japanese employees who work longer hours (at least 55 hours per week) report higher job satisfaction, they also show worse mental health outcomes (Kuroda & Yamamoto, 2018). A review of 46 Karōshi cases from 2013 to 2015 in China (Shan et al., 2017) showed that work-related fatigue and emotional stress were contributing risk factors for Karōshi.

iStock.com/wildpixel

In the United States, "getting ahead" is still a staple of business, and with advancements in technology, employees are more accessible to employers than ever before. There is a pressure to get ahead, yet at what cost? A large-scale analysis that included 24 groups or cohorts in Europe, the United States, and Australia evaluated 603,838 men and women who had not suffered from coronary heart disease at an initial baseline (Kivimäki et al., 2015). In a follow-up averaging about 8 years after baseline, 4,768 coronary heart disease events and 1,722 stroke events were recorded. Even after adjusting for age, sex, and socioeconomic status, results clearly showed that employees who worked longer hours (at least 55 hours per week) were at greater risk of coronary heart disease and stroke compared to employees who worked standard hours (35–40 hours per week).

In Japan, China, Europe, America, Australia, and across the globe, evidence overwhelmingly shows that working overtime hours is often associated with increased emotional and physical exhaustion, and even risks of vascular disease. In the case of Japan, this was despite findings that working overtime hours was associated with greater overall job satisfaction. Consider your own goals for your future: Do you want to work to live, or live to work? Your answer to this question could have grave consequences, literally. In this light, when you think of *work-life balance*, it may be better to think of it as *work-health balance*.

LEARNING CHECK

Motivational Speech

Satisfy your achievement motivation: Match each of the words or phrases related to motivation in the right column to its closest description in the left column.

1.	The notion that we are motivated to behave in ways that produce a valued inducement.	a.	need for intimacy
2.	The desire for close relationships.	b.	need for affiliation
3.	The desire to accomplish difficult tasks and excel.	c.	motivation
4.	The desire to establish and maintain social contacts.	d.	achievement motivation
5.	The notion that we are motivated to achieve and maintain an optimum level of bodily arousal.	e.	instinct
6.	A fixed pattern of behavior released by certain stimuli.	f.	incentive theory
7.	An inner state that energizes us to fulfill a goal.	g.	drive theory
8.	The notion that physiological needs arouse tension that motivates us to satisfy the need.	h.	arousal theory

(Answers: 1. f; 2. a; 3. d; 4. b; 5. h; 6. e; 7. c; 8. g.)

THE PHYSIOLOGICAL COMPONENT OF EMOTION

> **LEARNING OBJECTIVES**
>
> Explain how emotion is a physiological experience.
>
> - Why is emotion considered a physiological event, and what roles do the brain and nervous system play?
> - Are all emotions accompanied by a state of general arousal, or does each emotion have its own unique set of symptoms?

Bohemian Rhapsody. Moonlight. A Star Is Born. Black Panther. Crazy Rich Asians. Star Wars. Go to the movies or simply stay at home and stream a movie on a Saturday night, and you'll witness firsthand the power of human emotion. In darkened theaters all over the world, audiences laugh hysterically, cry in sorrow, gasp in fear, bite their fingernails in suspense, clench their jaws in anger, and tingle with delight. Cheers, tears, sweaty palms, tense muscles, and a pounding heart are a vital part of the entertainment experience.

When scientists compare human beings and other animals, they are quick to point to our superior intellect; to the cognitive processes of learning, memory, thought, and language; and to the ability to formulate plans in order to pursue our goals. However, we humans are also intensely emotional, warm-blooded creatures. Love, hate, joy, sadness, pride, shame, hope, fear, lust, boredom, surprise, embarrassment, guilt, jealousy, and disgust are among the powerful feelings that color and animate our daily lives.

Emotion is a difficult concept to define, in part because there are so many different emotions in the repertoire of human feelings. Some are universal; others are found only in certain cultures. Some are intense; others are mild. Some are positive; others are negative. Some move us to take action; others do not. Despite these vast differences, however, psychologists agree that emotions in general consist of three interacting components: (a) internal physiological arousal, (b) expressive behavior in the face, body, and voice, and (c) a cognitive appraisal (illustrated in Figure 11.10). In this section, we will focus on the physiological component.

emotion. A feeling state characterized by physiological arousal, expressive behaviors, and a cognitive interpretation.

A Historical Perspective

William James was the first psychologist to theorize about the role of bodily functions in emotion. Common sense tells us that we smile because we're happy, cry because we're sad, clench our fists because we're angry, and tremble because we're afraid. So, if you're crossing the street and see a car speeding toward you, that stimulus will trigger fear, which in turn will cause your heart to pound as you try to escape. This seems reasonable, but in 1884, James proposed what he thought was a radical new idea (philosopher René Descartes had made a similar proposal in the 17th century): that people feel happy because they smile, sad because they cry, angry because they clench their fists, and afraid because they tremble. In other words, the *perception* of danger causes your heart to pound as you run for cover—and it's this physiological and behavioral reaction that causes you to become afraid. This proposed chain of events, which was also suggested by a Danish physician named Carl Lange, is known as the **James-Lange theory** of emotion (illustrated in Figure 11.11).

James-Lange theory. The theory that emotion stems from the physiological arousal that is triggered by an emotion-eliciting stimulus.

In 1927, physiologist Walter Cannon challenged the James-Lange theory on three grounds. First, said Cannon, bodily sensations alone cannot produce emotion. Indeed, when people are injected with epinephrine—a hormone that energizes the body—they report feeling "pumped up" and aroused but do not experience any specific emotion. Second, said Cannon, we sometimes feel fear, anger, and other emotions instantly, before all the systems of the body have had time to react. Third, the physical changes that do occur are often too general for us to distinguish between different emotions. Fear may make the heart beat faster, but so do anger and love.

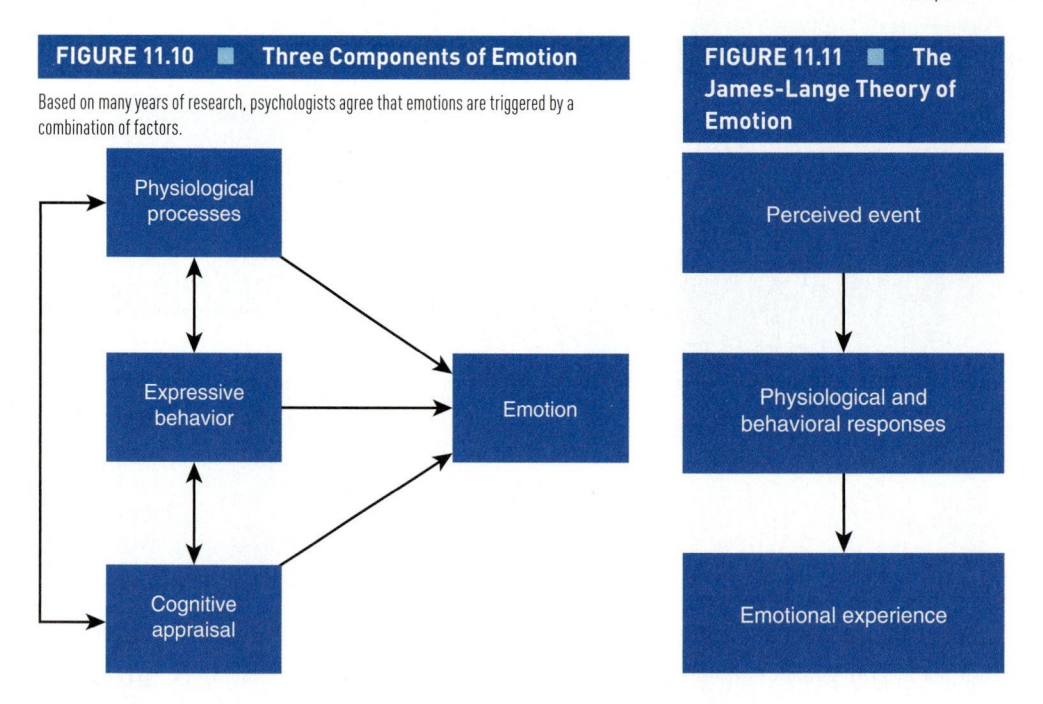

FIGURE 11.10 ■ Three Components of Emotion

Based on many years of research, psychologists agree that emotions are triggered by a combination of factors.

- Physiological processes
- Expressive behavior
- Cognitive appraisal
→ Emotion

FIGURE 11.11 ■ The James-Lange Theory of Emotion

Perceived event → Physiological and behavioral responses → Emotional experience

As an alternative to the James-Lange theory, Cannon and a colleague named Philip Bard proposed that emotion originates in the thalamus, the part of the brain that simultaneously relays messages from the sensory organs to the autonomic nervous system (arousal), skeletal muscles (motor behavior), and cerebral cortex (conscious thought). According to the **Cannon-Bard theory**, the body and "mind" are activated independently in the experience of emotion, as illustrated in Figure 11.12. Thus, if you see a car swerving in your direction, your heart will start to pound, you'll run, and you'll become afraid—all at the same time.

The debate between supporters of the James-Lange and Cannon-Bard theories of emotion was never resolved, and emotion researchers today are not quite as focused on the precise timing and sequence of the internal stream of events (Ellsworth, 1994). Equipped with sophisticated measurement devices, many physiologically oriented researchers seek instead to understand the role in emotion played by different brain structures, neural pathways, and autonomic arousal (Devonport et al., 2017; Rolls, 1999, 2008).

Cannon-Bard theory. The theory that an emotion-eliciting stimulus simultaneously triggers physiological arousal and the experience of emotion.

Brain Centers of Emotion

What role does the brain play in the experience of emotion? To begin with, research shows that some emotions are regulated by the *limbic system*—an evolutionarily primitive set of neural structures (including the thalamus, hypothalamus, hippocampus, and amygdala) that surrounds the brainstem and is found in lower mammals (illustrated in Figure 2.14 in the chapter on behavioral neuroscience). If you stimulate one part of the limbic system in a cat, the cat will pull back in fear; stimulate an adjacent area, and the cat will become enraged—snarling, hissing, and ready to pounce. Electronic stimulation of limbic structures in humans, as is sometimes used in the treatment of epilepsy, has similar effects (Panskepp, 1986).

Research points directly to the *amygdala* as a center for fear responses. For example, Ralph Adolphs and others (1999) encountered a patient who had a rare brain disorder in which excessive amounts of calcium were deposited in her amygdala. The structure was damaged, but other parts of her brain were unaffected. The deficits she exhibited were strikingly specific. When shown pictures of people with different facial expressions, she could identify most of their emotions, but not fear. She also had difficulty identifying emotions that were highly intense or arousing. This case study parallels findings in animal research. In experiments with rats, LeDoux (1996) found that when the amygdala was destroyed, the rats lost the ability to react to harmful stimuli with fear—which they typically do by freezing in place. In other experiments, LeDoux chemically traced the pathways in the brain that are activated in threatening situations and found that fear cut a path from the thalamus, where sensory input is sent,

FIGURE 11.12 ■ **The Cannon-Bard Theory of Emotion**

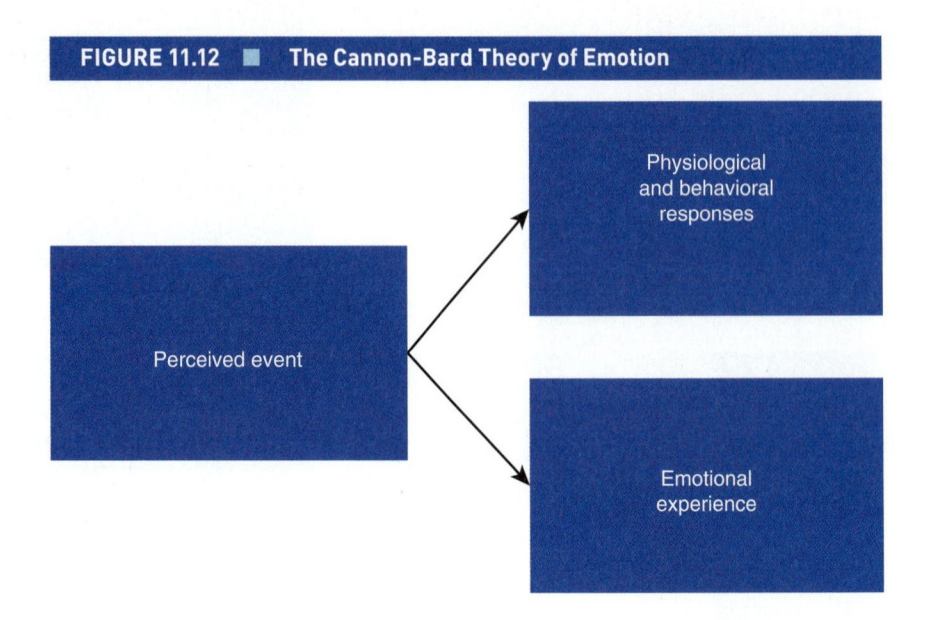

straight to the amygdala, without involvement of the "thinking" cerebral cortex. As we'll learn later, this research indicates that fear, and perhaps other raw emotions, too, are triggered instantly—before information reaches the cortex and before we have had time to appraise the situation and formulate a response.

Certain emotions may be quick and automatic, but others involve the *cerebral cortex*, the seat of human intellect. One cannot pinpoint a single region of the cortex that regulates all of our feelings because different emotions involve distinct patterns of neural activity. At the very least, research reveals two basic types of emotions: mostly positive feeling states such as joy, interest, and love, that motivate a tendency to *approach* people and situations (though anger, a negative emotion, also prompts approach), and negative feeling states such as sadness, fear, and disgust that motivate the tendency to *withdraw* from people and situations (Spielberg et al., 2008; Watson, Wiese, Vaidya, & Tellegen, 1999).

Generalized Autonomic Arousal

When an event prompts an emotional response, the human body prepares for action. To mobilize us for "fight" or "flight," the hypothalamus activates the **sympathetic nervous system**—the branch of the autonomic nervous system that controls involuntary activities of the heart, lungs, and other organs. Specifically, the adrenal glands secrete more of the hormones epinephrine and norepinephrine (commonly known as adrenaline and noradrenaline), which increase the heart rate and blood pressure and heighten physiological arousal. Then all at once, the liver pours extra sugar into the bloodstream for energy, the pupils dilate to let in more light, the breathing rate speeds up to take in more oxygen, perspiration increases to cool down the body, blood clots faster to heal wounds, saliva flow is inhibited, and digestion slows down to divert blood to the brain and skeletal muscles. Epinephrine and norepinephrine supply the physiological fuel for our many passions.

After an emotional event, the **parasympathetic nervous system** takes over and restores the body to its premobilized calm state. The heart stops racing, blood pressure is lowered, the pupils contract, breathing slows down, saliva flows again, the digestive system resumes its normal functions, and energy is conserved. As the levels of epinephrine and norepinephrine in the bloodstream slowly diminish, the intensity of our feelings gradually decreases, thereby enabling us to relax, cool down, and get on with our normal functions. This aspect of emotion is illustrated in Figure 11.13.

sympathetic nervous system. A branch of the autonomic nervous system that controls the involuntary activities of various organs and mobilizes the body for fight or flight.

parasympathetic nervous system. The division of the autonomic nervous system that reduces arousal and restores the body to its premobilized state.

Riding a roller-coaster activates the sympathetic nervous system. When the ride is over, the parasympathetic nervous system restores the body to its calm state.

iStock.com/colleenbradley

FIGURE 11.13 ■ The Autonomic Nervous System

Note the differing functions of the sympathetic (arousing) and parasympathetic (calming) divisions of the autonomic nervous system.

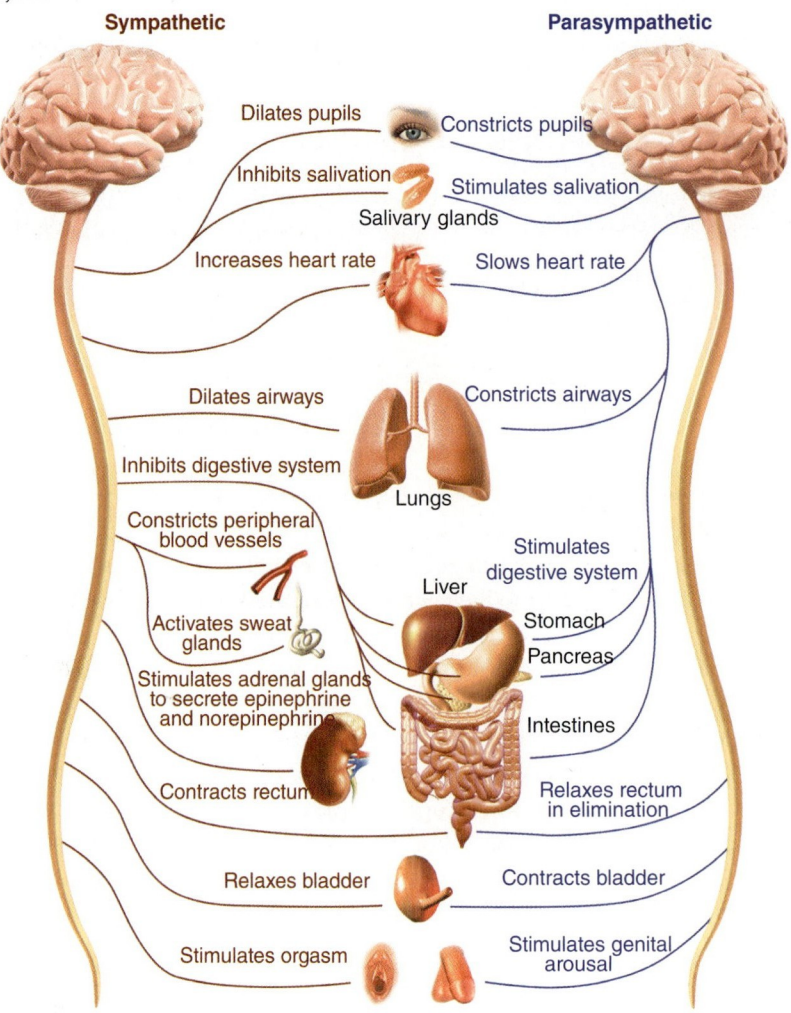

Sympathetic
- Dilates pupils
- Inhibits salivation
- Increases heart rate
- Dilates airways
- Inhibits digestive system
- Constricts peripheral blood vessels
- Activates sweat glands
- Stimulates adrenal glands to secrete epinephrine and norepinephrine
- Contracts rectum
- Relaxes bladder
- Stimulates orgasm

Parasympathetic
- Constricts pupils
- Stimulates salivation
- Slows heart rate
- Constricts airways
- Stimulates digestive system
- Relaxes rectum in elimination
- Contracts bladder
- Stimulates genital arousal

Specific Patterns of Arousal

Clearly, physiological arousal intensifies an emotional experience. But are all emotions accompanied by the same general state of arousal, or does each emotion have its own unique set of symptoms? Scholars have been debating this question for many years. William James (1884) and others have argued that each emotion feels different to us because each is associated with its own specific pattern of autonomic activity. Noting that love, rage, and fear all make the heart beat faster, however, Walter Cannon (1927) and, later, others have maintained that all emotions spark the same physiological arousal. Who is right? Does each emotion have its own autonomic "fingerprint," or do they all feel basically the same?

Research suggests there is a bit of truth to both positions. In one classic study, Paul Ekman and others (1983) trained participants (many of whom were actors) to tense up the facial muscles that express happiness, anger, surprise, fear, sadness, or disgust. Using a mirror, participants held each face for 10 seconds and the researchers took various measures of autonomic arousal. As it turned out, the posed expressions produced physiological differences. For example, heart rate increased for both anger and fear, but anger increased skin temperature, whereas fear had the opposite effect. Other studies have since confirmed this point (Paul, Sher, Tamietto, Winkielman, & Mendl, 2020; Résibois, 2017). Many emotions make the heart beat faster, but this similarity masks important differences—differences that are betrayed in the language we use to describe our feelings. Thus, in anger, we say that we're "hot under the collar," that our "blood is boiling," and that we need to "cool off" and "simmer down." In contrast, we describe fear as a "bone-chilling" emotion in which we "freeze" or get "cold feet" (Izard, 2009; Kovecses,

1990). Even more distinctive is the all-too-familiar pattern of arousal that signals embarrassment, a highly social emotion. When people feel ashamed or embarrassed in front of others, they blush, an involuntary reflex characterized by redness in the cheeks and ears and a rise in body temperature (Lindquist, Wager, Kober, Bliss-Moreau, & Barrett, 2012). How our bodies react when we lie also has serious implications for the legal system regarding the use of lie detector tests (Cook & Mitschow, 2019).

THE EXPRESSIVE COMPONENT OF EMOTION

> **LEARNING OBJECTIVES**
>
> Analyze the role of nonverbal communication and sensory feedback in emotion.
>
> - Identify which emotions are considered to be "basic."
> - Describe the evidence that facial expressions are inborn and universal.
> - Explain the facial-feedback hypothesis and identify what, according to the hypothesis, can make us happy.

Emotion may be an internal, purely subjective experience, but it also has an observable behavioral component. The links between inner feelings and outward expressions are numerous: We smile when we're happy, cry when we're sad, blush when we're embarrassed, stand tall when we feel proud, drag our feet when we're down, press our lips in anger, bow our heads in shame, and wrinkle our faces in disgust.

These behavioral expressions of emotion serve two functions. First, they provide us with a means of *nonverbal communication*. People often use words to tell others how they're feeling. But by smiling, frowning, turning bright red in the face, shrugging the shoulders, or winking an eye, we also communicate our feelings nonverbally—which encourages others to approach us, or stay away. Thus, Alan Fridlund (1994) has argued that our expressive behaviors serve more as *signals* to other people than as *symptoms* of how we feel, making the display of emotion an inherently social experience. The second effect of behavioral expression is to provide us with *sensory feedback*. In 1872, Darwin theorized that the expressions that we make clarify and intensify emotional experiences by providing us with bodily feedback about how we feel. In short, the expressive component of emotion has two audiences: other people and ourselves.

Nonverbal Communication

Knowing how another person is feeling can be tricky because people sometimes try to hide their true emotions. Think about it. Have you ever had to suppress your rage at someone, mask your disappointment after failure, feign surprise, or pretend to like something just to be polite? Sometimes we come right out and tell people how we feel. But often we actively try to conceal our true feelings. In instances like these, observers tune in to a silent language—the language of **nonverbal communication**.

What kinds of nonverbal cues do people use to judge how someone is feeling? In *The Expression of the Emotions in Man and Animals*, Charles Darwin (1872) argued that the *face* communicates emotion in ways that are innate and are understood by people all over the world. Contemporary research provides strong support for this proposition. In a groundbreaking study, Ekman and Friesen (1974) showed 30 photographs (like those in the accompanying Try This! feature) to participants from New York to New Guinea—including Argentina, Borneo, Brazil, and Japan—and asked them to guess the emotion being portrayed in each photo. The results of this study, and of many others like it, indicate that people can reliably identify six emotions: joy, fear, anger, sadness, surprise, and disgust. In the experiment described at the start of this chapter, people from 10 different countries exhibited high levels of agreement in their recognition of these same emotions (Ekman et al., 1987).

nonverbal communication. Conveying information without the use of spoken language, such as through gestures, facial expressions, and body posture.

Chapter 11 • Motivation and Emotion 471

TRY THIS!

Recognizing Emotions

People all over the world tend to agree on matching certain facial expressions with certain emotions. To explore for yourself, **TRY THIS:** Look at the photographs below and try to match each with one of the following emotions: surprise, anger, disgust, fear, joy, and sadness. How did you do? The norms for this type of task are presented in Figure 11.14.

FIGURE 11.14 ■ Faces of Emotion

(a) (b) (c) (d) (e) (f)

(Answers: a. joy; b. fear; c. anger; d. sadness; e. surprise; and f. disgust.)

(a) iStock.com/nazar_ab; (b) iStock.com/CiydemImages; (c) iStock.com/Inside Creative House; (d) iStock.com/azndc; (e) iStock.com/SensorSpot; (f) iStock.com/master1305

Not everyone agrees that the results are strong enough to support the claim that basic emotions are "universally" recognized in the face (Jack, Garrod, Yu, Caldara, & Schyns, 2012; Russell, 1994). In general, however, from one end of the world to the other, a smile is a smile and a frown is a frown, and just about everyone knows what they mean—even when the expressions are "put on" by actors and not genuinely felt (Gosselin, Kirouac, & Dore, 1995). Hillary Elfenbein and Nalini Ambady (2002) meta-analyzed 97 emotion recognition studies involving a total of 22,148 people from 42 countries. As shown in Figure 11.15, they confirmed the main result that people can generally identify certain basic emotions from facial expressions. By comparing performances across different studies, they also discovered that people are 9 percent more accurate when they judge members of their own national, ethnic, or regional groups than when they judge members of other less familiar groups. In other words, we enjoy an "in-group advantage" when it comes to knowing how those who are closest to us are feeling. We also react to some emotional displays more than others. From an evolutionary standpoint, it is more adaptive to beware of someone who is angry, and likely to lash out in violence, than someone who is happy, a nonthreatening emotion. Studies have shown that angry faces arouse us and cause us to frown even when presented subliminally—without our awareness (Dimberg & Ohman, 1996; Dimberg, Thunberg, & Elmehed, 2000). How good are you at identifying expressions of emotion?

Emotion is accompanied by changes in facial expression—even when these changes are subtle and cannot be seen with the naked eye. The human face has 80 muscles that can create more than 7,000 different expressions. (Figure 11.16 illustrates what can happen when those muscles don't work properly.)

To measure the spontaneous activity of these muscles and their links to emotion, many researchers use a physiological device known as the **facial electromyograph (EMG)**. In facial EMG studies, participants are shown images that evoke positive or negative emotions, while electrodes attached to the face record the activity of various muscles (illustrated in Figure 11.17). Images that elicit positive emotions such as joy, interest, and attraction increase activity in the cheek muscles; those that arouse negative emotions such as anger, distress, and fear spark activity in the forehead and brow area (Cacioppo & Petty, 1982). Evidently, the muscles in the human face reveal smiles, frowns, and other expressions that are otherwise hidden from view (Dimberg, 1990; Wingenbach, Brosnan, Pfaltz, Peyk, & Ashwin, 2020).

Sensory Feedback

Draw the corners of your mouth back and up and wrinkle your eye muscles. Relax. Now raise your eyebrows, open your eyes wide, and let your mouth drop open slightly. Relax. Now pull your brows down and together and clench your teeth. Relax. If you followed each of these directions, you would have

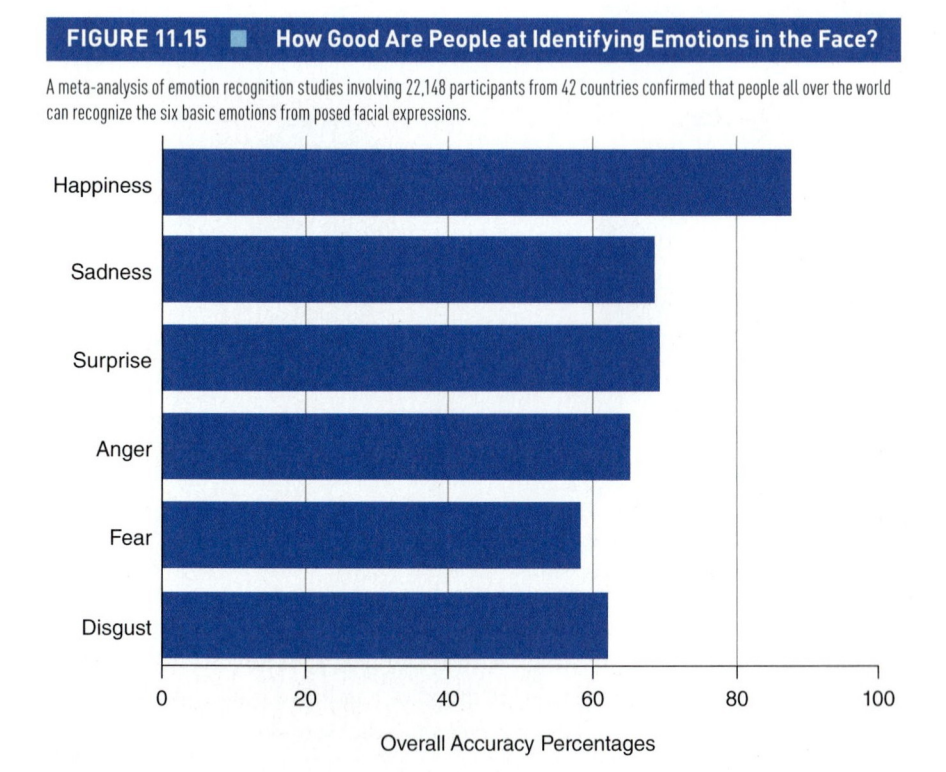

---

facial electromyograph (EMG). An electronic instrument used by emotion researchers to record activity in the facial muscles.

FIGURE 11.15 ■ How Good Are People at Identifying Emotions in the Face?

A meta-analysis of emotion recognition studies involving 22,148 participants from 42 countries confirmed that people all over the world can recognize the six basic emotions from posed facial expressions.

Overall Accuracy Percentages
- Happiness
- Sadness
- Surprise
- Anger
- Fear
- Disgust

FIGURE 11.16 ■ Expressing Emotions and Moebius Syndrome

Chelsey Thomas was known as the little girl who could not smile. She was born with Moebius syndrome, a rare neurological disorder that impairs activity in the facial muscles. "She always smiled, really, on the inside," said her mother. But with the face playing a vital role in communication, one can only imagine what a social price she paid for her outward blank expression. So, Chelsey had corrective surgery and then had to learn how—and when—to smile. At the age of seven, she smiled for the first time.

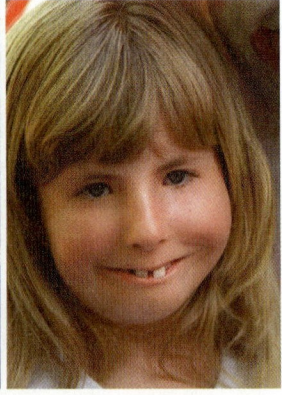

Associated Press / Nick Ut; Associated Press / Michael Tweed

FIGURE 11.17 ■ The Facial Electromyograph (EMG)

Electrodes placed on the face record activity in various muscles. These recordings reveal that positive emotions increase activity in the cheek muscles, and negative emotions increase activity in the forehead and brow areas.

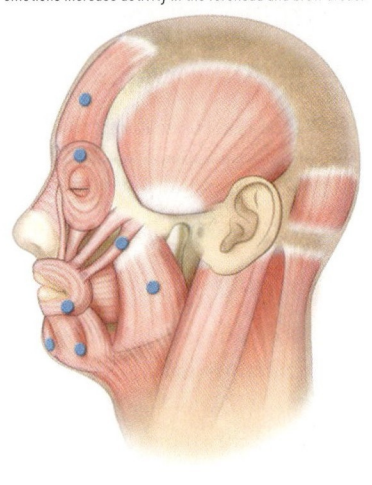

Carolina Hrejsa/Body Scientific Intl.

appeared to others to be feeling first happy, then fearful, and finally angry. The question is, do these expressions affect how you actually feel?

According to the **facial-feedback hypothesis**, an expression does more than simply reflect one's emotion—it actually triggers an emotional experience. In an interesting first test of this hypothesis, James Laird (1974) told college students that they would take part in an experiment on the activity of the facial muscles. After attaching electrodes to the face, he showed them a series of cartoons and asked them before each one to contract certain facial muscles in ways that made them smile or frown. The result: The students thought the material was funnier and reported feeling happier when they wore a smile than a frown. Similarly, other posed-expression studies show that people can also be induced to experience fear, anger, sadness, and disgust (Duclos et al., 1989). Together, this research suggests that facial expressions—though not *necessary* for the experience of emotion—can evoke and magnify certain emotional states (McIntosh, 1996), although these findings have been difficult to replicate, possibly due to the influence of being recorded during experimental sessions (Noah, Schul, & Mayo, 2018).

Why does this occur? Laird believes that facial expressions activate emotion through a process of self-perception: "If I'm smiling, I must be happy." To test this hypothesis, Chris Kleinke and his colleagues (1998) asked people to emulate either the happy or angry facial expressions that were depicted in a series of pictures. Half the participants saw themselves in a mirror during the task; the others did not. Did these manipulations affect mood states? Yes. Compared to participants in a no-expression control group, those who put on happy faces felt better—and those who put on angry faces felt worse. As Laird would predict, these effects were most pronounced among participants who saw themselves in a mirror.

Other researchers speculate that there is a second possible reason for this effect, that perhaps expressions trigger an emotional experience by causing physiological changes in the brain (Izard, 1990). For example, Robert Zajonc (1993) proposed that smiling causes facial muscles to increase the flow of air-cooled blood to the brain, which has a pleasant effect by lowering the brain's temperature. Conversely, frowning decreases blood flow, which produces an unpleasant state by raising brain temperature. To demonstrate this mechanism, Zajonc and his colleagues (1989) used the repetition of certain sounds to show a link between temperature and mood. The experiment showed that movement of the facial muscles influenced emotion even though participants didn't realize that they were wearing an expression. The lesson: If you want an emotional lift, just put on a happy face.

facial-feedback hypothesis. The hypothesis that changes in facial expression can produce corresponding changes in emotion.

THE COGNITIVE COMPONENT OF EMOTION

LEARNING OBJECTIVES

Explain the role that thoughts or cognitions play in our experience of emotion.

- Identify the two factors in the two-factor theory of emotion.
- Explain how counterfactual thinking affects our experience of emotion.
- Describe the evidence that suggests cognition is or is not a necessary component of emotion.

Emotion is much more than physiological sensations and expressive behaviors. After all, the heart pounds in fear, but it also pounds in anger. We cry out in grief over the death of a loved one, but we also shed tears of joy at weddings and other happy occasions. We laugh when we're amused, but sometimes we laugh out of nervousness. In other words, there has to be more to grief, joy, amusement, and nervousness than arousal and expression. The missing link is cognitive appraisal.

Psychologists have long been embroiled in debate over the role of cognitive factors in emotion. Are your feelings, like inborn reflexes, triggered by stimuli without conscious thought or awareness, or does the way you feel depend largely on how you perceive, interpret, and evaluate the situation you're in? Do you think first and feel second, or is it the other way around? Theories of emotion suggest different answers to these questions, as illustrated in Figure 11.18.

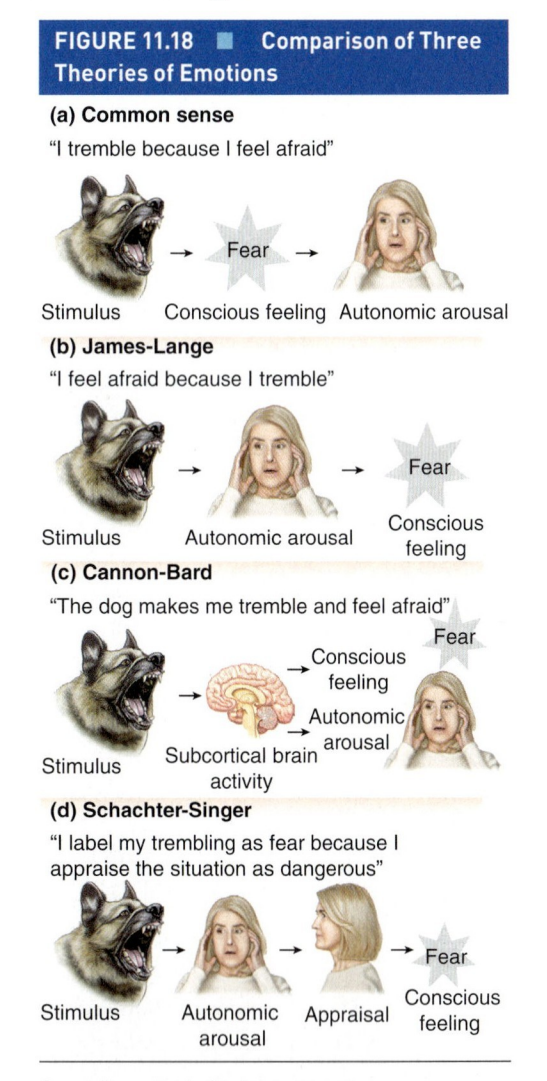

FIGURE 11.18 ■ Comparison of Three Theories of Emotions

(a) Common sense
"I tremble because I feel afraid"

Stimulus → Conscious feeling (Fear) → Autonomic arousal

(b) James-Lange
"I feel afraid because I tremble"

Stimulus → Autonomic arousal → Conscious feeling (Fear)

(c) Cannon-Bard
"The dog makes me tremble and feel afraid"

Stimulus → Subcortical brain activity → Conscious feeling (Fear) / Autonomic arousal

(d) Schachter-Singer
"I label my trembling as fear because I appraise the situation as dangerous"

Stimulus → Autonomic arousal → Appraisal → Conscious feeling (Fear)

Amanda Tomasikiewicz/ Body Scientific Int'l

Schachter's Two-Factor Theory of Emotion

Imagine you are in your apartment, upstairs, at home, late at night. Nobody else is there. Your phone is on the charger downstairs, and you are on the verge of falling asleep. Then suddenly you hear scraping, clicking, the front door opening, and footsteps downstairs. There is an intruder in the house. Your heart pounds so hard that you can feel your chest throb with every beat. Except for the trembling, you are frozen in place like a statue knowing that your phone is out of reach. You have no doubt the emotion you feel is raw fear, plain and simple. But how do you "know" that you are feeling afraid and not sad, angry, disgusted, or ill?

According to Stanley Schachter (1964), two factors are necessary to have a specific emotion. First, the person must experience a heightened state of *physiological arousal*, such as a racing heart, sweaty palms, tightening of the stomach, rapid breathing, and so on—the kind of jitteriness you might feel after drinking too much coffee. Second, the person must find a *cognitive label* or attribution to explain the source of that arousal. In the example where you hear an intruder, you likely would have such an obvious explanation for your symptoms that labeling the emotion as fear was easy. The same is true when people watch intensely emotional films. When millions of viewers saw *The Walking Dead*, they knew they were feeling disgusted rather than ashamed, angry, or sad, because the stimulus itself was unambiguous. At times, however, people become generally excited without knowing why—and must examine their surroundings in order to identify the emotion (illustrated in Figure 11.19).

To test this **two-factor theory of emotion**, Schachter and Jerome Singer (1962) injected male participants with epinephrine, the hormone that produces physiological arousal. The participants in one group were warned in advance about the side effects (they were drug-informed), but those in a second group were not (they were drug-uninformed). In a third group, the participants were injected with a harmless placebo (this was the placebo control group). Before the drug—which was described as a vitamin supplement—actually took effect, participants were left alone with a male confederate introduced as another subject who had received the same injection. In some cases, the confederate's behavior was euphoric: He bounced around happily, doodled on paper, sank jump shots into the waste basket, flew paper airplanes across the room, and swung his hips in a hula hoop. In the presence of other participants, the same confederate behaved angrily. At one point, for example, he ridiculed a questionnaire they were filling out and, in a fit of rage, ripped it up and hurled it into the wastebasket.

two-factor theory of emotion. The theory that emotion is based on both physiological arousal and a cognitive interpretation of that arousal.

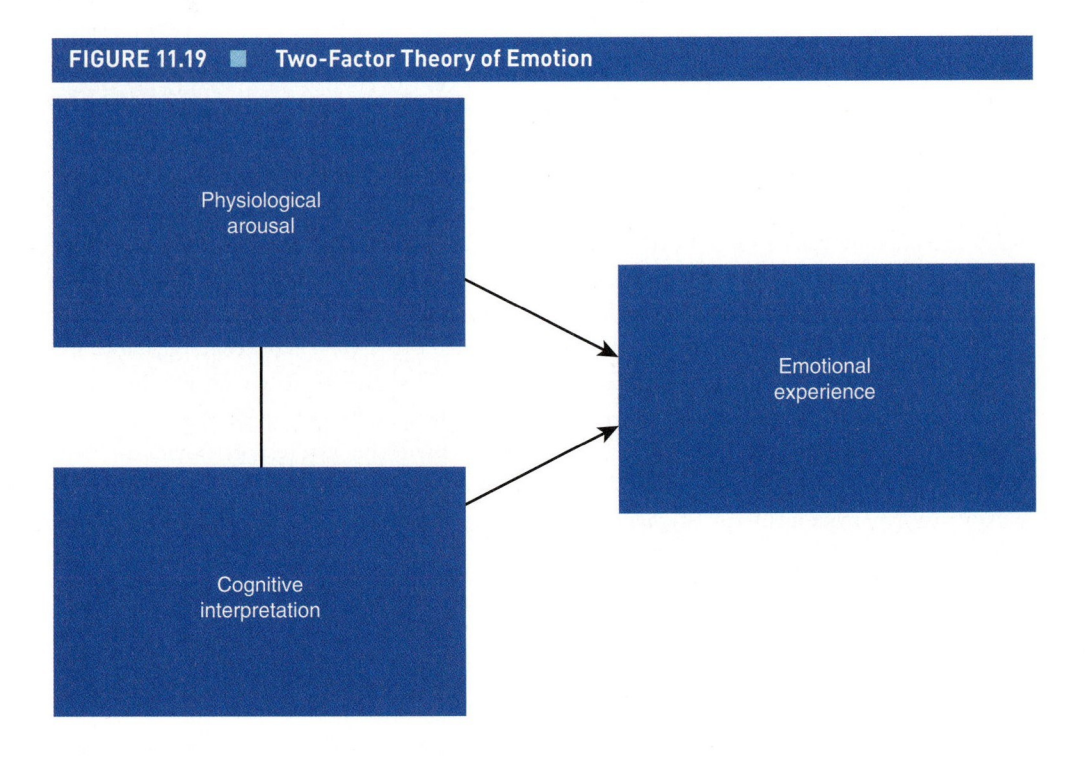

FIGURE 11.19 ■ Two-Factor Theory of Emotion

Physiological arousal → Emotional experience

Cognitive interpretation → Emotional experience

How happy are these athletes? When genuinely happy, our smiles raise the cheeks high enough to wrinkle up the eyes (when we wear false smiles, the muscle activity in the lips does not extend up to the eyes). During the 2002 Winter Olympics, Canadian figure skaters David Pelletier and Jamie Salé, shown here, were initially awarded the gold medal. However, in a judging reversal, they received the silver medal instead. This irregularity uncovered a judging scandal and ultimately the International Olympic Committee awarded these skaters a second gold medal.

Doug Pensinger/Getty Images Sport via Getty Images

counterfactual thinking. Imagining alternative scenarios and outcomes that might have happened but did not.

In the *drug-informed* group, participants began to feel their hearts pound, their hands shake, and their faces flush. Led to expect these side effects, however, they did not have to search very far for an explanation. In the *placebo* group, the participants did not become aroused in the first place, so they had no symptoms to explain. But now consider the predicament of the participants in the *drug-uninformed* group, who suddenly became aroused without knowing why. Trying to identify the sensations, these participants—according to the theory—would take their cues from others who are in the same situation, namely the confederate. The results generally supported this prediction. The drug-uninformed participants reported that they felt more happy or angry depending on the confederate's actions. In some cases, they even displayed similar behavior. For example, one subject "threw open the window and, laughing, hurled paper basketballs at passersby." Those in the drug-informed group, who attributed their arousal to the epinephrine, were not as influenced by these social cues. Neither were participants in the no-drug placebo group—who, after all, were not physiologically aroused.

Not all the research has confirmed Schachter's (1964) two-factor theory, but one general conclusion can be drawn: When people are aroused and do not know why, they try to identify their own emotions by observing the situation they're in and making an attribution for their arousal (Reisenzein, 1983). This conclusion has interesting implications. One is that if people attribute their arousal to a nonemotional source, they will experience less emotion (this is what happened in the drug-informed group, where participants blamed their autonomic symptoms on the epinephrine). Another is that if people attribute their arousal to an emotional source, they will experience more of that emotion (which was the experience of those in the drug-uninformed group). In short, once people are stimulated, they can cognitively intensify, diminish, and alter their own emotions.

Counterfactual Thinking

As thoughtful and curious beings, we often are not content to accept the outcomes in our lives without wondering, at least in private, "What if... ?" According to Daniel Kahneman and Dale Miller (1986), people's emotional reactions to events are colored by **counterfactual thinking**, the tendency to imagine alternative outcomes that might have occurred but did not. If the imagined result is better than the actual result, we're likely to suffer from feelings of disappointment, frustration, and regret. If the imagined result is worse, then we may react with emotions that range from mild relief to elation. True to the cognitive perspective, then, the emotional impact of positive and negative events depends on the way we think about "what might have been" (Roese, 1997; Roese & Olson, 1995). Importantly, the bridge that connects our cognitive and emotional states holds two-way traffic. Just as counterfactual thoughts can alter our mood, the mood we are in can influence the kind of counterfactual thinking we do. When people feel good, they imagine how much worse things could be; when down in the dumps, they imagine how much better they could be (Epstude & Roese, 2008).

People don't immerse themselves in counterfactual thought after every experience, obviously. But we do tend to wonder "what if"—often with feelings of regret—after negative outcomes that result from actions we take rather than inactions (Byrne & McEleney, 2000; Hoppen, Heinz-Fischer, & Morina, 2020). According to Victoria Medvec and Kenneth Savitsky (1997), certain situations—such as being on the verge of a better or worse outcome, just above or below some cutoff point—make it particularly easy to conjure up images of what might have been. The implications are intriguing. Imagine, for example, that you are an Olympic athlete and have just won a silver medal, a truly remarkable feat. Now imagine that you have just won the bronze medal. Which situation would make you feel better?

To examine this question, Medvec and others (1995) videotaped 41 athletes in the 1992 summer Olympic Games the moment they realized that they had won a silver or bronze medal and again later, during the medal ceremony. Then they showed these tapes, without sound, to participants who did not know the order of finish. The participants were asked to watch the medalists and rate their emotional states on a scale ranging from "agony" to "ecstasy." The intriguing result, as you might expect, was that the bronze medalist, on average, looked happier than the silver medalist. Was there any direct evidence of counterfactual thinking? In a second study, participants who watched interviews with many of these same athletes rated the silver medalist as more negatively focused on finishing second rather than first and the bronze medalist as more positively focused on finishing third rather than fourth. For these great athletes, feelings of satisfaction were based more on their thoughts of what might have been than on the reality of what was.

During the 1996 summer Olympics, Nike ran a counterfactual—and controversial—advertisement: "You don't win silver, you lose gold."

Drew Angerer/Getty Images News via Getty Images

Is Cognition Necessary?

Schachter and Singer's two-factor theory and the theory of cognitive appraisal are based on the assumption that emotion requires thought. Cognitive-emotion theorists would tell the intruder story as follows: You heard a noise (stimulus) and attributed that noise to someone in the house (cognition), which caused you to feel scared (emotion) and to freeze (behavior). Indeed, many psychologists claim that cognition plays a vital role in the experience of emotion. This claim is a source of controversy, however, and was the topic of a spirited exchange between Robert Zajonc (1984), who wrote an article on "the primacy of affect," and Richard Lazarus (1984), who countered with one on "the primacy of cognition."

According to Zajonc, people sometimes react with emotion instantly and without prior appraisal. In other words, sometimes we feel before we think. If you've ever banged your toe into a table, only to explode in anger and pound your fist, you know that the link between pain and rage seems automatic—that you reacted with an angry outburst before realizing just how ridiculous it is to be mad at a piece of furniture. If you've ever sipped milk that was old and curdled, only to gag and spit it out, you likewise know that the link between aversive tastes and disgust may also be automatic. This primacy of affect may help to explain why people develop intense, irrational, persistent fears of objects that are not inherently dangerous. It may also help to explain why infants make reflex-like facial expressions of pain, interest, joy, distress, disgust, and anger before they have the brain capacity to make the proposed cognitive appraisals (Izard, 1990). It may also help to explain the research finding that our affective states influence the way we process information (Ashby, Isen, & Turken, 1999), which reinforces the widespread assumption that rational thought "can be hijacked by the pirates of emotion" (Cacioppo & Gardner, 1999, p. 194).

Zajonc (1984) argued that human emotions and thoughts are controlled by separate anatomical structures within the brain. In support of this argument, animal research shows that certain emotions are triggered instantly—before it is even possible to appraise the situation and formulate a response. According to LeDoux (1996), a primitive, subcortical pathway within the limbic system—a pathway that connects the eyes and ears through the thalamus directly to the amygdala—serves as an early warning system, so that the amygdala is activated quickly. When we're confronted with pain, noxious food substances, and other threats, this direct pipeline between sensation and emotion enables us to make a rapid-fire defensive motor response without having to stop for a cognitive appraisal (illustrated in Figure 11.20).

Representing the cognitive approach, Richard Lazarus (1991) agrees that emotions can spring up quickly and without awareness, but he maintains that it's just not possible to have an emotion without some kind of thought—even a thought that is quick, effortless, and unconscious. "Without cognitive activity to guide us," says Lazarus, "we could not grasp the significance of what's happening in our adaptational encounters with the environment, nor could we choose among alternative values and courses of action" (p. 353). According to Lazarus (1993), emotion is an individual's response to the perceived harms and benefits of a given situation. Is cognition necessary to emotion? The debate rages on.

478 Essentials of Psychology

FIGURE 11.20 ■ Pathway of Fear Without "Thought"

According to LeDoux, the sensation of a threat can reach the amygdala by way of direct pathways from the thalamus (a quick route) or from the thalamus through the cerebral cortex (a slow route). The direct path permits an instantaneous reaction to danger, which can be critical in life and death situations, although this initial response may be overridden after the threat is more fully appraised in the cortex.

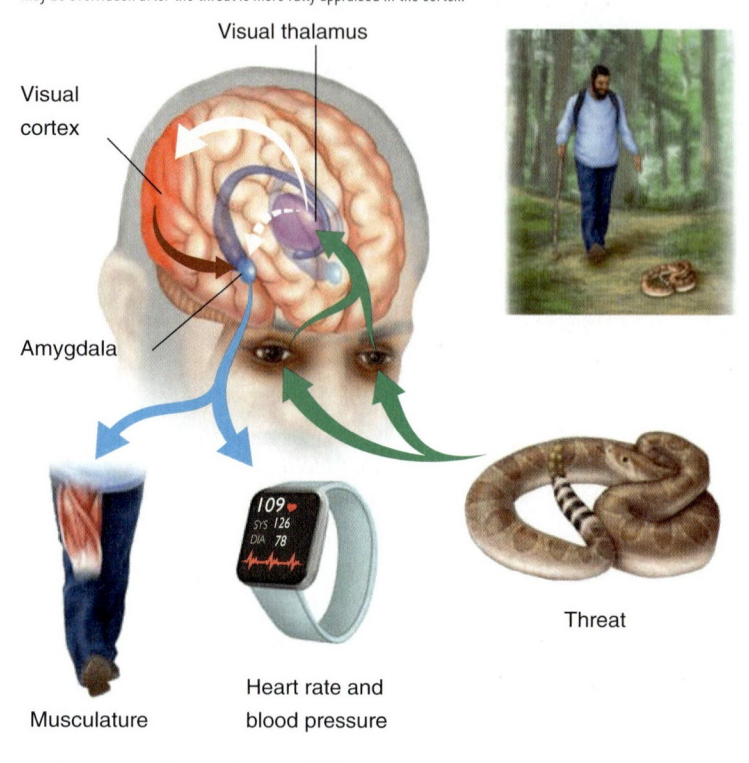

Visual thalamus
Visual cortex
Amygdala
Musculature
Heart rate and blood pressure
Threat

Monica Wierzbicki/Body Scientific Intl.

LEARNING CHECK

Feeling Formulas

From the following list of emotion-related terms, choose the one that is most closely related to each of the formulas below. (The arrow means "produces.")

A. emotion   B. two-factor theory of emotion   C. James-Lange theory
D. facial electromyograph (EMG)   E. facial-feedback hypothesis
F. Cannon-Bard theory   G. counterfactual thinking

1. perceived event → (physiological arousal + emotional experience) _____
2. (physiological arousal + cognitive interpretation) → emotional experience _____
3. change in facial expression → change in emotion _____
4. alternative scenario → alternative outcome _____
5. physiological arousal + expressive behaviors + cognitive interpretation → ? _____
6. perceived event → physiological arousal → emotional experience _____
7. emotion → change in facial expression that can be electronically recorded _____

(Answers: 1. F; 2. B; 3. E; 4. G; 5. A; 6. C; 7. D.)

HUMAN EMOTION: PUTTING THE PIECES TOGETHER

LEARNING OBJECTIVES

Examine how emotions, including happiness and motivation, are displayed across cultures.

- Can the range of human emotions be categorized into a small number of types?
- Are emotions, such as joy and anger, universally expressed across cultures?
- Who is happy—and why?

Knowing that emotions stem from physiological sensations, expressive behaviors, and cognitive activities is only a first step. The next step is to determine how the different pieces of this puzzle fit together to produce an emotional experience.

Types of Emotions

The English language contains more than 2,000 words for categories of emotions. Are some of these universal, felt by people in all cultures? Over the years, psychologists have tried to classify human emotions in various ways. Today, there is widespread agreement that fear, anger, joy, disgust, surprise, and sadness are "basic": Each is accompanied by a distinct facial expression, each is shown by infants and young children, and each is found in the words that people of diverse cultures and regions use to describe their feelings. Figure 11.21 illustrates two such emotions expressed similarly across cultures: joy and grief. Some researchers believe that interest, acceptance, contempt, pride, shame, and guilt should be added to the list.

If there are only a few basic emotions, what accounts for the vast array of other feelings we often experience? One possibility suggested by Robert Plutchik (1980) is that basic emotions provide the building blocks for more complex emotions in the way that the three primary colors combine to form the hues of the color wheel. According to Plutchik, the richness of human emotions is accounted for in three ways. First, there are eight basic types of emotions (he adds interest and acceptance to the original six). Second, each type comes in varying "shades," or levels of intensity (for example, intense disgust may be felt as hatred or loathing, and mild disgust as boredom). Third, new emotions are formed through mixtures of the eight basic ones (for example, love blends joy and acceptance, contempt blends disgust and anger, and nostalgia blends joy and sadness).

FIGURE 11.21 ■ The Intensity of Emotions

Certain emotions such as intense joy and grief are "basic" to the human experience. Here, members of the French soccer team celebrate after winning the 2018 World Cup, and the losing team, Croatia, reacts with sadness after failing to win the World Cup in 2018.

Matthias Hangst/Getty Images Sport via Getty Images; Laurence Griffiths/Getty Images Sport via Getty Images

It's easy to come up with a list of emotions. The trick is to classify and compare the emotions along a small number of common dimensions. Perhaps the most obvious way to classify emotions is according to whether they involve positive or negative affect. Most people assume that positive feelings are the opposite of negative feelings—that someone who is happy, for example, cannot at the same time be sad. Research confirms this intuitive assumption about the bipolarity of emotion. So, "Is a human being a pendulum betwixt a smile and a tear? Apparently so" (Russell & Carroll, 1999).

Using this positive-negative distinction as a starting point, James Russell (1980) proposed the *circumplex model*, a taxonomy that divides all human emotions along two independent dimensions: pleasantness and intensity. According to Russell, emotions are either (1) pleasant or unpleasant, and (2) mild or intense. As illustrated in Figure 11.22, the result is a fourfold circle of emotions that are pleasant and intense ("delighted"), pleasant and mild ("relaxed"), unpleasant and mild ("bored"), and unpleasant and intense ("alarmed"). Research shows that when people are asked to rate emotion words or sort them into piles, this circular ordering consistently appears—not only in English but also in Chinese, Croatian, Estonian, Greek, Hebrew, Japanese, Polish, Swedish, and German (Jonauskaite, Parraga, Quiblier, & Mohr, 2020; Larsen & Diener, 1992). People's ratings of the emotions triggered by images of other human beings, animals, nature, objects, scenes, and events can similarly be classified (Lang, 1995). Over the years, many psychologists have theorized about the structure of human emotions and have come up with similar two-dimensional models (Watson et al., 1999), although other psychologists have theorized models should be as large as four dimensional (Fontaine, Scherer, Roesch, & Ellsworth, 2007).

Are There Cultural Differences in Emotion?

Certain aspects of human emotion seem universal. We saw earlier that people from diverse cultures react to emotion-filled events with similar physiological symptoms and facial expressions. In fact, certain events trigger the same emotions everywhere in the world. In all cultures, for example, friendship and achievement elicit joy; insult and injustice elicit anger; novelty and risk taking elicit fear; death and separation from a loved one elicit sadness. Yet there are regional differences as well in the types of

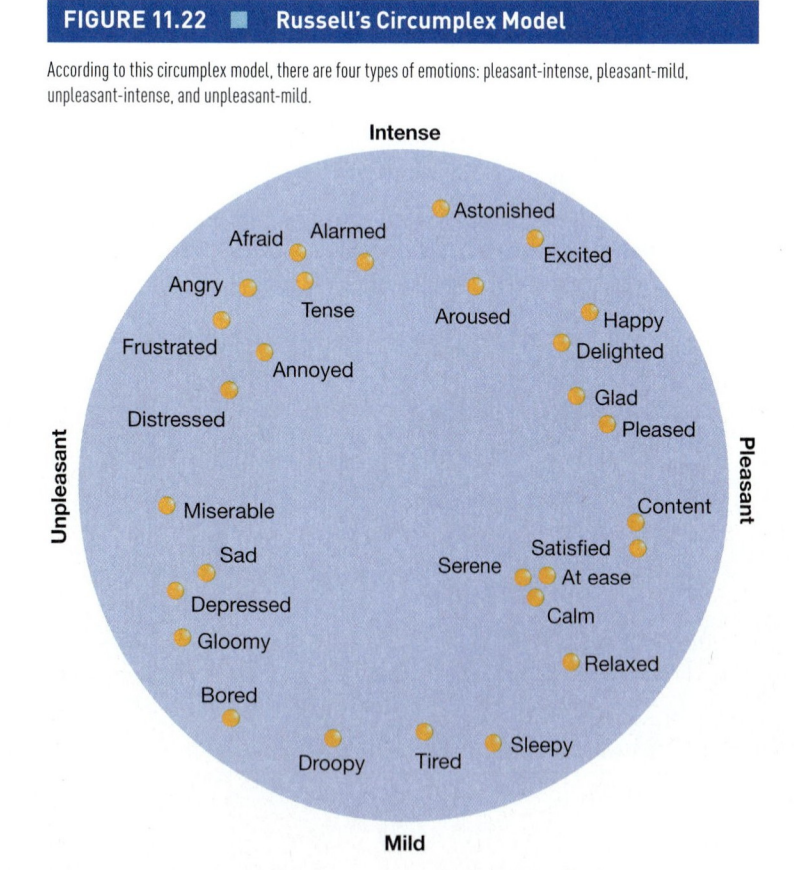

FIGURE 11.22 ■ Russell's Circumplex Model

According to this circumplex model, there are four types of emotions: pleasant-intense, pleasant-mild, unpleasant-intense, and unpleasant-mild.

antecedent events that stir our various passions. Among the Utku Eskimos, fear is triggered by thin ice, rough seas, dangerous animals, and evil spirits.

Culture also shapes the way people categorize their feelings. Consider the words we use to describe various emotions. Based on ethnographies and cross-cultural studies of language, James Russell (1991) uncovered some striking differences. For example, although the English language contains more than 2,000 words for categories of emotion, there are only 1,501 emotion words in Dutch, 750 in Taiwanese, 58 among the Ifalukian of Micronesia, and 7 among the Chewong of Malaysia. Among the Ilongot, a head-hunting people of the Philippines, the word *liget* is used to describe both anger and grief-intense feelings. Japanese does not have a word for "disappointed," Tahitian lacks a word for "sadness," and Gujarati, a language spoken in India, lacks a word for "excited."

Ralph Hupka and others (1999) combed through the dictionaries of 60 major languages from all regions of the world and found that certain basic emotions—such as joy, grief, affection, fear, anger, and disgust—are universally represented in words. Some languages, however, have precise emotion words that have no clear counterpart in English. For example, the German word *Schadenfreude* specifically refers to the pleasure derived from another person's suffering. In Indonesia, a distinction is made between *malu*, a feeling of shame brought on by one's own actions, and *dipermalukan*, a feeling of shame caused by someone else's deeds. Among the Baining of Papua New Guinea, *awumbuk* is an emotion that combines sadness, tiredness, and boredom that is brought on specifically by the departure of visiting friends or relatives. Among the Utku Eskimos, *naklik* refers to the love of babies, sick people, and others in need of protection, whereas *niviuq* is a form of love felt toward those who are charming or admired.

Finally, some striking cultural differences can be seen in the *display rules*, or the informal norms for how to express oneself in different contexts or cultures, that determine when it's appropriate for people to express certain feelings. The release of anger sparked by insult, frustration, or a physical attack is a prime example. People all over the world exhibit similar patterns of autonomic arousal, but cultures teach us whether to manage that arousal by exploding or by suppressing our rage. Among the !Kung Bushmen of the Kalahari Desert, nomadic hunters and gatherers who forage as a group and share food, people must control their fury in order to survive. In Japanese culture, people also practice restraint, often masking anger with a polite smile. In Japan, an angry outburst is seen as a shameful loss of control, so it is better to publicly "grin and bear it" (Akutsu, Yamaguchi, Kim, & Oshio, 2016). Yet among the Yanomamo of the Amazon jungle, public displays of anger are common. As anthropologists have observed, Yanomamo who are angry sometimes scream at the top of their lungs and launch into a barrage of personal and public insults: "You scaly ass, you bucktooth, you protruding fang, you caiman skin!" (Good & Chanoff, 1991, p. 71).

Pleasure and the Pursuit of Happiness

Long before psychology was born into science, philosophers regarded happiness to be the ultimate state of being. In the Declaration of Independence, Thomas Jefferson cited life, liberty, and "the pursuit of happiness" as the most cherished of human rights. But what is happiness, and how is it achieved? Aristotle said it was the reward of an active life. Freud pointed to both work and love. Others have focused on money, power, health and fitness, religion, beauty, the satisfaction of basic desires, and the achievement of goals. According to some, a sense of well-being springs from an ability to derive pleasure and avoid pain in the events of everyday life (Kahneman, Diener, & Schwarz, 1999). According to others, our well-being emerges from leading a life that enables us to realize our talents, values, potentialities, and sense of self (Kiefer, 2008).

To study happiness—or, as many psychologists now call it, "subjective well-being"—one must be able to measure it. How do researchers know if someone is happy? Simple: They ask. Better yet, they use brief questionnaires such as the Satisfaction With Life Scale, in which participants respond to statements such as "If I could live my life over, I would change almost nothing" (Diener, Emmons, Larsen, & Griffin, 1984; Pavot & Diener, 1993). As Marcus Aurelius said, "No man is happy who does not think himself so." In general, people who are happy also have cheerful moods, high self-esteem, physical and mental health, a sense of personal control, more memories for positive than negative events, and optimism about the future (Ford, Lappi, & Holden, 2016). It's no secret that our outlook on life becomes rosy right after we win a game, fall in love, land a great job, or make money. Nor is it a secret that the world seems gloomy right after we lose, fall out of love, or suffer a personal tragedy or financial setback. Predictably, the events of everyday life trigger fluctuations in mood. For example, people are most happy on Fridays and Saturdays and least happy on Mondays and Tuesdays (Helliwell & Wang, 2015). Even during the day, happiness levels fluctuate like clockwork. For example, David Watson and his colleagues (1999) asked college students to rate their mood states once a day for 45 days, always at a different hour. They found, on average, that the students felt best during the middle of the day (noon to 6 PM) and worst in the early morning and late evening hours.

The Roots of Happiness

What determines our long-term satisfaction, and why are some people happier in general than others? Seeking the roots of happiness, it is evident that what makes us happy is in the eye of the beholder. Peering at happiness through a diverse lens, we find that racial disparities in happiness are largely narrowing. In the United States, while white Americans (36 percent very happy) were happier than Black Americans (21 percent very happy) in the 1970s; today that gap has narrowed substantially, with happiness among white Americans declining slightly (34 percent very happy) and happiness among Black Americans increasing sharply (28 percent) within the past few years (Iceland & Ludwig-Dehm, 2019). Among racial and gender groups in the United States, Black women show a remarkably consistent pattern of improvement in happiness in recent decades, while whitewomen tend to show a consistent pattern of decline (Cummings, 2019). Explaining such patterns of change in happiness can be complex, although three key factors are considered here: (a) *social relationships* (people with an active social life, close friends, and a happy marriage are more satisfied than those who lack these intimate connections), (b) *employment status* (employed people are happier than those who are out of work—regardless of income), and (c) *physical health* (people who are healthy are happier than those who are not). Reflecting the impact of these and other factors, research shows that happiness levels vary, and remain relatively stable, from one culture to the next (Diener & Suh, 2000). According to the World Happiness Report in 2021, happiness is highest in Finland and lowest in Afghanistan; the United States ranks 19th in the world and Canada ranks 14th in the world (Helliwell, Huang, Wang, & Norton, 2021).

Does Money Buy Happiness?

Perhaps the most interesting relationship is between income and subjective well-being. Everyone knows the saying "Money can't buy happiness." But personally, very few people in general—particularly among those who are financially strapped—believe it. Is wealth a key to happiness? The evidence is mixed (Killingsworth, 2021; Miñarro et al., 2021).

Cross-national studies have revealed a positive association between a nation's prosperity and the subjective well-being of its people. There are some exceptions, but as a general rule the more prosperous a country is, the happier its citizens are. The reason for this association is not clear. It may be that affluence brings pleasure through the satisfaction of basic needs and material possessions—or by affording freedom, which makes life more enjoyable (Helliwell et al., 2020). Within a given country, however, the differences between wealthy and middle-income people are more modest. In one survey, a group of the wealthiest Americans said they were happy 77 percent of the time—which was only moderately higher than the 62 percent figure given by those of average income. And when we make comparisons within a single culture over time, there is no connection between affluence and happiness. Americans on average are more than twice as rich now as they were 50 years ago—before we had smartphones, personal computers, and social media. Yet over that time period, the number of respondents who said they were "very happy" increased little, from about 28 percent in the 1970s to about 31 percent today (Iceland & Ludwig-Dehm, 2019). That is not an impressive change overall. So, what are we to conclude? It looks as though having

Money may buy summer homes, convertible sports cars, boats, and other luxuries, but research suggests that among those whose basic needs are already satisfied, money does not buy long-term happiness.

iStock.com/AndresGarciaM

shelter, food, and safety are essential for subjective well-being, but once these basic needs are met, increased affluence does not appreciably raise levels of happiness. It seems that the adage is true: Money simply can't buy happiness.

Why doesn't money contribute more to subjective well-being? Perhaps each of us, as a result of biological and environmental factors, has a set baseline level of happiness toward which we gravitate. This notion is supported by three recent findings. One is that ratings of happiness are higher among pairs of identical twins raised together or apart than among fraternal twins (Lykken & Tellegen, 1996), a finding that led David Lykken (2000) to speculate that there may be a genetic basis for being happy and content. It appears that happiness levels, like personalities, are relatively stable over time and place, leading to the conclusion that some people, in general, are happier than others (Kaliterna-Lipovčan & Prizmić-Larsen, 2016).

LEARNING CHECK

Emotions by the Numbers

1. Name six basic emotions widely agreed upon by psychologists.
   a.   b.   c.   d.   e.   f.

2. Name the four types of emotions in James Russell's circumplex model.
   a.   b.   c.   d.

3. Name three predictive indicators of happiness according to Ed Diener and others.
   a.   b.   c.

(Answers: 1. fear, anger, joy, disgust, surprise, sadness; 2. pleasant-intense, pleasant-mild, unpleasant-intense, unpleasant-mild; 3. social relationships, employment status, physical health.)

Thinking Like a Psychologist About Motivation and Emotion

When we stop to reflect on our own motivations, we find just how varied they are. From the constant short-term need to stuff our face with food or satisfy the urge to have sex, to the desire to be with others or form close relationships, to the burning ambition to achieve excellence or gain power over others, it's clear that we are energized in many ways and toward many goal objects. Is there more that we want from life? Is achieving the "American Dream" of prosperity truly fulfilling? If not, is there some other "ultimate" motivation? Perhaps. If you've ever met someone who seems to have it all—money, a successful career, good friends, a loving partner, and wonderful children—and yet yearns for more, you will appreciate what's at the very peak of Maslow's pyramid. As we've learned in this chapter, Maslow theorized that once our biological and social needs are met, we strive to fulfill all of our potential—toward a state that he called self-actualization.

Now that we have explored the psychology of emotion, let us step back and reflect on what it contributes to our understanding of human competence and rationality. You will recall that many cognitive psychologists compare human beings to computers, noting the ease with which we are able to learn, recall, reason, and communicate our knowledge. At the same time, however, research shows that performance often falls short of competence. Sometimes people fail to learn (or, instead, learn to behave in maladaptive ways), forget or distort their memories of past events, and use cognitive heuristics that steer them into making poor judgments. This two-headed portrait characterizes our emotional lives as well. In this chapter, for example, we saw that although emotion often follows from a rational interpretation of events, it may also arise instantly and without conscious thought, perhaps leading us to feel before we think. In addition, we sometimes attribute our arousal sensations to the wrong source, causing us to mislabel our own emotions. In matters of the heart and mind, human beings are not entirely competent or incompetent but a complex and fascinating mixture of both.

SUMMARY

WHAT MOTIVATES US?

Motivation is an inner state that energizes people toward the fulfillment of a goal. The question psychologists ask is: What motivates us?

GENERAL THEORIES OF MOTIVATION

Instinct theories of motivation used to be common but were soon rejected. According to **drive theory**, physiological needs that arise within the body create tension, which motivates us toward its reduction. To account for the fact that people often seek to increase tension, **arousal theory** posits that people are driven to maintain an optimum level of arousal—not too low, not too high. And in **incentive theory**, people behave in ways that they expect will gain a valued external incentive.

THE PYRAMID OF HUMAN MOTIVATIONS

According to Maslow, all human beings are motivated to fulfill a **hierarchy of needs**. At the base are physiological needs for food, water, and so on. Next, in order, are safety and security needs, the need for belonging, and esteem needs. Once all needs are met, people strive for self-actualization.

BASIC APPETITIVE AND SOCIAL MOTIVES

Among the human motivations at the base of Maslow's pyramid are physiological motivations such as those that drive eating behavior. Further up the pyramid are social motivations such as those driven by the needs for belongingness and love and for esteem.

HUNGER AND EATING

Hunger is a sensation that motivates food search and consumption. The brain monitors glucose in the blood. When glucose drops below a certain level, people experience hunger. Eating then raises the glucose and reduces the motivation to eat. The glucose levels are monitored in or near the hypothalamus. Psychological factors such as personal taste, and external food cues such as time of day and the company of other people, also play a role in hunger and eating.

People are considered **obese** when they have a surplus of body fat that causes them to exceed their optimum weight by 20 percent. There is a strong genetic component to obesity, which may determine **set point**, a level of weight toward which the body gravitates. Most people can achieve long-term weight loss through changes in diet and exercise. Psychological influences on eating are most evident in **anorexia nervosa**, **bulimia nervosa**, and **binge-eating disorder**. All three eating disorders are most common among adolescent girls and young women, particularly in weight-conscious cultures and in women with negative body images.

BELONGINGNESS MOTIVES

Maslow's belongingness motives are composed of two distinct needs. To varying degrees, people enjoy being with others, a **need for affiliation**. Research shows that we seek an optimum balance of social contact. People also have a **need for intimacy**, for close relationships that are characterized by open and confidential communication known as **self-disclosure**.

ESTEEM MOTIVES

People differ in their level of **achievement motivation**, which is defined as the desire to accomplish difficult tasks and to excel. To assess the strength of this motive, researchers use a fantasy measure in which participants tell stories about the characters in ambiguous pictures and code these stories for achievement themes. Research has shown that people who score high rather than low on this measure work harder, set more realistic goals, and achieve more.

THE PHYSIOLOGICAL COMPONENT OF EMOTION

Although **emotion** is a difficult concept to define, most psychologists agree that emotions consist of three interacting components: physiological arousal, expressive behavior, and a cognitive appraisal. The body is intimately involved in feelings of joy, fear, anger, and other emotions. The question is, in what capacity?

A Historical Perspective
According to the **James-Lange theory**, emotion follows from one's reactions to an emotion-eliciting stimulus (you're afraid because you are trembling). In contrast, the **Cannon-Bard theory** states that a stimulus elicits various reactions and emotion at the same time (perceiving a danger causes you to tremble and feel afraid). Today, physiologically oriented emotion researchers seek to understand the role played by different brain structures, neural pathways, and autonomic arousal.

Brain Centers of Emotion
Many emotions are regulated by the limbic system—an evolutionarily primitive set of neural structures. Certain emotional reactions are automatic (triggered instantly by the amygdala); others involve the processing of information in the cerebral cortex. We cannot pinpoint a single region of the cortex that regulates all feelings because different emotions involve distinct patterns of neural activity.

Generalized Autonomic Arousal
When an event prompts an emotional response, the **sympathetic nervous system** mobilizes the body for an adaptive fight-or-flight response. Afterward, the **parasympathetic nervous system** restores the body to its premobilized calm state.

Specific Patterns of Arousal
Are all emotions associated with the same state of arousal, or does each emotion have unique symptoms? Research supports the latter alternative. For example, heart rate increases for both anger and fear, but anger increases skin temperature, whereas fear has the opposite effect.

THE EXPRESSIVE COMPONENT OF EMOTION

Behavioral expressions of emotion serve two functions. They provide us not only with a means of nonverbal communication to others but also with sensory feedback for the self.

Nonverbal Communication
Facial expressions represent a key component of **nonverbal communication**. The face communicates emotion in ways that are understood by people from different countries of the world. Further suggesting that these expressions are innate is the fact that even young infants make the faces that are associated with basic emotions. To measure the activity of facial muscles and their links to emotion, researchers use the **facial electromyograph (EMG)**.

Sensory Feedback
According to the **facial-feedback hypothesis**, an expression not only reflects one's emotion but also triggers an emotional state. Although psychologists disagree over the reason for this effect, research indicates that it does occur.

THE COGNITIVE COMPONENT OF EMOTION

Psychologists have long debated the role of cognitive factors in emotion. Different theories of emotion provide different points of view.

Schachter's Two-Factor Theory of Emotion

According to the **two-factor theory of emotion**, two factors are necessary to have a specific emotion: a heightened state of arousal and a cognitive label. When people are aroused and do not know why, they determine their emotions by scanning the situation and making an attribution.

Counterfactual Thinking

Sometimes our emotional reactions to outcomes are influenced by **counterfactual thinking**—as when bronze medalists feel better by imagining a fourth-place finish, whereas silver medalists feel worse by imagining a first-place finish.

Is Cognition Necessary?

Some psychologists argue that people sometimes react with emotion instantly and without cognitive appraisal and that our emotions and thoughts are controlled by separate anatomical structures within the brain. Others maintain that it is not possible to have emotion without thought, even thought that is quick, effortless, and unconscious. This debate remains unresolved.

HUMAN EMOTION: PUTTING THE PIECES TOGETHER

Knowing that emotions stem from physiological, expressive, and cognitive activities is only a first step. The next step is to determine how these elements combine to produce an emotional experience.

Types of Emotions

There is widespread agreement that fear, anger, disgust, joy, surprise, and sadness are basic human emotions. Some researchers speculate that other emotions are derived from mixtures of these or that all emotions can be classified along two independent dimensions: pleasantness and intensity.

Are There Cultural Differences In Emotion?

Certain aspects of human emotion seem universal, as when people from diverse cultures react to emotion-filled events with similar bodily reactions and facial expressions. Clearly, however, cultures shape the way people categorize their feelings as well as the display rules that determine when it's appropriate to express these feelings.

Pleasure and the Pursuit of Happiness

Most people report being relatively happy, but there are marked individual differences. Three important factors are having social relationships, being employed, and being healthy. Although more affluent nations are happier, the evidence for an association between income level and happiness is mixed. It has been suggested that people have a certain dispositional level of happiness toward which they gravitate over time.

CRITICAL THINKING

Thinking Critically About Motivation and Emotion

1. Have you ever "people-watched"? Say, watching children interact on a playground or maybe students on your college campus? Try this. What emotions do you see expressed? How do you know? In other words, what expressions did you observe that convinced you of the emotions you think you observed?

2. Psychologists have approached the study of human motivation in two ways. Compare and contrast these two approaches. Which approach do you believe is better?

3. In some cultures, being overweight does not have the same negative connotation that it does in American culture. In addition, the desire for extreme thinness is a relatively recent phenomenon. Do you think the incidence of eating disorders would change if the popular image of attractive men and women moved closer to normal American weight patterns?

4. Consider what life would be like with limited or no emotions (like Mr. Spock from *Star Trek* or Sheldon Cooper from *The Big Bang Theory*). What would be the advantages of not having emotions? What about the disadvantages?

5. Read the most recent rankings for the happiest countries in the world provided in the World Happiness Report. Considering the reasons for happiness described in this chapter, why do you believe many countries reach the top 10 in happiness. Why might some countries be happier than others?

CAREER CONNECTION: BUSINESS

Advertising Agent

Careers in advertising often involve researching a target audience to create product messaging and developing ad campaigns to reach that audience effectively. Psychology graduates are a good fit for many advertising roles as the science of persuasion and research are major topics in the field. Ad agencies are responsible for the television and radio commercials, billboards, magazine and newspapers ads, and even bus and subway posters that we see around us everywhere we go. They also create the broader strategy for an ad campaign based on conversations with their clients about the goals they seek to accomplish. An advertising agent may also solicit new clients, adding a sales component to the job description. Most entry-level positions in this field are advertising assistants, whose jobs include supporting the rest of the business, from the designers in the creative department to the buyers selecting ad space.

Key skills for this role that psychology students learn to develop:

- Effective communication in presentations and written works
- Goal setting and application of ethical standards
- Adoption of values that build community at local, national, and global levels

KEY TERMS

achievement motivation (p. 463)
anorexia nervosa (p. 460)
arousal theory (p. 453)
binge-eating disorder (p. 460)
bulimia nervosa (p. 460)
Cannon-Bard theory (p. 467)
counterfactual thinking (p. 476)
drive theory (p. 452)
emotion (p. 466)
facial electromyograph (EMG) (p. 472)
facial-feedback hypothesis (p. 473)
hierarchy of needs (p. 453)
incentive theory (p. 453)

instinct (p. 452)
James-Lange theory (p. 466)
motivation (p. 451)
need for affiliation (p. 461)
need for intimacy (p. 461)
nonverbal communication (p. 470)
obesity (p. 457)
parasympathetic nervous system (p. 468)
self-disclosure (p. 462)
set point (p. 459)
sympathetic nervous system (p. 468)
two-factor theory of emotion (p. 475)

12 HEALTH, STRESS, AND WELLNESS

iStock.com/Hiraman

LEARNING OBJECTIVES

Explain how psychologists study health and wellness.

Identify the main sources of stress and how it affects health.

Describe how our thoughts, emotions, physical activity, and social support influence stress, health, and wellness.

WHAT'S YOUR PREDICTION: DOES STRESS LOWER RESISTANCE?

The Situation

This time you really outdid yourself. You're one of 420 volunteers in a medical experiment for which you agreed to risk exposure to a common-cold virus. You'll be reimbursed for all travel expenses, and for nine days you'll receive free room and board in the clinic. So, you pack your bags, check in, and sign an informed-consent statement.

The first two days are hectic. First, you're given a complete medical examination that includes a blood test. Then you fill out a stack of questionnaires. You answer questions about your mood, personality, health practices, and recent stressful experiences (such as a death in the family, pressures at work, or the breakup of a relationship). Then it happens. To simulate the person-to-person transmission of a virus, an attendant drops a clear liquid solution into your nose. If you're lucky, you were randomly assigned to the control group and receive only saline. If not, then you're in an experimental group and receive a low dose of a cold virus—just what you need. These exposures tend to produce illness at rates of 20 to 60 percent.

You are now quarantined in a large apartment for seven days—alone or with one or two roommates. Every day, you're examined by a nurse who takes your temperature, extracts a mucus sample, and looks for signs of a cold: sneezing, watery eyes, stuffy nose, hoarseness, sore throat, and cough (you don't know it, but the nurse also keeps track of the number of tissues you use). Basically, the researchers are interested in two results: (a) Are you infected (is there a virus in your system)? (b) Do you have a cold (as judged by the various symptoms)? The researchers are trying to determine if there is a link between the recent stress in your life and your susceptibility to illness.

Make a Prediction

On the basis of the questionnaires initially filled out, you and others are classified as having a high or low level of stress in your life. Does this psychological factor make a person more or less vulnerable to viral infection? Among those who are infected, does recent life stress elevate the risk of catching a cold? All participants were healthy at the start of the project—and not a single saline control subject developed cold symptoms. Among those exposed to the virus, however, 82 percent became infected, and 46 percent developed cold symptoms. A virus is a virus, and there is no escape. But were the rates significantly different among the high- and low-stress groups? What do you think?

1. Were high stress participants more likely to become infected?	YES	NO
2. Were high stress participants more likely to catch a cold?	YES	NO

The Results

In 1985, the prestigious *New England Journal of Medicine* published a study that failed to find a link between psychological factors and medical outcomes. In an accompanying note, the journal's editor took the opportunity to scoff at the very notion that a person's mental state can affect physical health. Six years later, Sheldon Cohen and others (1991) published the study just described in the same *New England Journal of Medicine*—an event that marked a "turning point in medical acceptance of a mind/body connection" (Kiecolt-Glaser & Glaser, 1993).

The results of this study were convincing. Life stress was not correlated with the rate of infection. Among those exposed to a virus, 85 percent of the high-stress participants and 81 percent of the low-stress participants became infected. Among those who were infected, however, high-stress participants were more likely to catch a cold than were the low-stress participants—53 percent compared to 40 percent. In fact, when participants who had been housed with infected roommates were eliminated from the analysis (because of the risk that they had been reexposed), the high-stress participants were still more likely to catch a cold than their low-stress counterparts—45 percent to 28 percent. Thus, once infected, people whose lives are filled with stress are particularly vulnerable to illness.

What Does It All Mean?

This study reveals that there is a correlation between life stress and susceptibility to illness. Correlations do not prove causality, however, so we cannot conclude from this study alone that stress per se has this effect (it's theoretically possible, for example, that people are under stress because they are physically vulnerable). However, other researchers are finding that stress lowers resistance and compromises the immune system, the body's first line of defense against illness. Studies show that the activity of the immune system's white blood cells, which are part of that immune defense system, can be altered temporarily in participants who are exposed to even a mildly stressful laboratory experience—such as a difficult mental task, a gruesome film, the recollection of bad memories, loud noise, or a bad social interaction (Straub & Cutolo, 2018).

This research has profound implications. Until the last few decades of the 1900s, psychological and medical researchers believed that the human brain and immune system were separate and noninteracting. Not so! We now know that the organs of the immune system are richly endowed with nerve fibers, providing a direct pipeline to the brain—and that psychological factors such as stress can play an important role on our health. The result is a new field that focuses on the seamless interplay of mental and physical health. This new field is called **psychoneuroimmunology**: *psycho* for mind, *neuro* for the nervous system, and *immunology* for the immune system (Ader, Felton, & Cohen, 2001). Later in this chapter, we'll find that psychoneuroimmunology is generating a great deal of excitement in all areas of psychology.

psychoneuroimmunology. A subfield of psychology that examines the interactions among psychological factors, the nervous system, and the immune system.

We've explored throughout this textbook the remarkably diverse and dynamic discipline of psychology. Some psychologists define what they do as the study of the mind; others prefer to focus on behavior. Some are interested in the evolutionary and biological roots of human nature; others are interested more in cognitive and affective processes, growth and development, social and cultural factors, personality, or clinical disorders. Some of us build theories and conduct research to understand basic human processes; others want to apply what is known to improve health, education, law, life in the workplace, and other aspects of the human condition. It has all become so diversified that Sigmund Koch (1993)—a prominent psychology historian—believes the discipline should be renamed the Psychological Studies.

Koch may have a point. A more important point, however, is that although psychology appears fragmented on the surface, many researchers in different areas of specialization unite in sharing a common objective: *to help improve our health and wellness and to enhance the quality of our lives.* In this chapter, we'll aim at putting psychology's puzzle pieces together, beginning with the field of health psychology as a discipline and the foundational models for how we understand health and the mind-body relationship.

STUDYING HEALTH AND WELLNESS

LEARNING OBJECTIVES

Explain how psychologists study health and wellness.

- Define the illness-wellness continuum and describe how it is applied.
- Differentiate between the biomedical and biopsychosocial models of health and elaborate on how these models relate to the mind-body debate.
- Outline the health belief model and explain how it is related to health behavior.
- Outline the health onion and explain how it is applied to understand illness prevention and health promotion.
- Define the placebo effect and describe what it tells us.

Health and wellness are common topics in popular media and press, and in scientific research as well. However, how we conceptualize health and wellness has evolved over time. Increasingly, we are recognizing that illness is not purely physical. Even when an illness is physical, such as when a person has cancer, the psychology of how a person experiences that illness can play an important role in the progression of the illness. This is the psychosocial and behavioral component of health.

The World Health Organization defines **health** as "a complete state of physical, mental and social well-being, and not merely the absence of disease or infirmity" (World Health Organization [WHO], 1948, p. 100). At the time, this was quite a progressive definition for health, although we now understand that it falls short of being a comprehensive definition in that it misses key elements of health, such as psychological and sociocultural aspects, which together are often called *psychosocial* health factors.

health. A state of physical, mental, and social well-being that is also affected by various psychological and social/cultural factors.

To illustrate the influence of psychosocial factors on health, consider that it is very likely that you do not eat the recommended five servings of fruits and vegetables a day. Why? For many people, these foods are too expensive (an economic reason). For others, fruits and vegetables may not be a staple food,

health psychology. A subfield of psychology that examines psychosocial and behavioral processes related to health, illness, wellness, and health care in order to understand how such processes contribute to the landscape of health across the lifespan.

and thus cultural or familial customs make it unlikely that these foods will be eaten five times a day. Similarly, health can be related to religious practices (certain foods may be sacred), lifestyle factors (a busy work life leads to poorer dietary choices), bodily changes (pregnancy affects diet), or even personal experiences (divorce may lead to depression, which is related to weight gain). The interplay between psychology and society (or "the world we live in") is a crucial part of the definition of health.

Health psychology is a growing and increasingly important subfield of psychology that explores health-related behaviors. Health psychologists study health behaviors and are interested in the psychosocial and behavioral processes related to health, illness, and wellness so that they can understand how such processes contribute to health-related behaviors across the lifespan. Health, illness, and wellness are treated as part of a continuum in practice, so let's begin by introducing this foundational continuum for understanding health.

Illness-Wellness Continuum

illness-wellness continuum. A model for understanding health, ranging from illness and death to health and wellness.

illness. A disease or sickness over any length of time that can affect an individual.

wellness. A physical state or condition to the right of the illness-wellness continuum that involves being in good physical and mental health, typically characterized by overt efforts aimed at maintaining this state or condition.

Consider your state of health at this very moment. What behaviors are you engaging in so that you can be healthy? For example, if you are ill, are you taking medications, drinking lots of water, eating healthfully, and getting much needed rest? If you are healthy, aren't you still engaging in behaviors that contribute to your health—for better or worse? For example, eating a balanced diet and exercising regularly can positively impact your health (moving you toward wellness), whereas smoking and living a sedentary lifestyle can negatively impact your health (moving you toward illness). These two states of health—wellness and illness—follow a continuum called the **illness-wellness continuum**.

Figure 12.1 illustrates how the illness-wellness continuum reveals the state of our health at any given moment. For example, individuals are often thought of as "healthy" when they have no apparent **illness**—a disease or sickness over any length of time that can affect the individual. "Healthy" is the generic neutral point in the continuum. You are healthy if you are not sick. But do we not engage in many behaviors that help us avoid getting sick, even if we are healthy, such as watching our diet and exercising? In this light, **wellness** involves caring for the physical self while also attending to the psychosocial self. In medicine, a *treatment approach* begins with illness, with the goal of eradicating the illness. By contrast, a *wellness approach* can begin with illness or with health. In the latter case, individuals who are not necessarily ill make efforts to promote wellness or to become more than just "healthy" as a way to minimize their likelihood of illness.

The illness-wellness continuum is dynamic. It is not a static model; it varies over time from a progressively worsening to a progressively improving state of health. Throughout our lives, we will vary along this continuum. The treatment approach aims to alleviate symptoms of illness, meaning it can help return you to the center of the continuum, such as when doctors use drugs, surgery, or psychotherapy to treat illness (Gillespie & Privitera, 2018). To the right in the continuum is a progressively improving state of health or wellness. The wellness approach can be applied across the continuum to help people achieve optimal wellness beyond simply not being ill. It can also help them cope with and manage ongoing illness (Ryff, 2014; Shanafelt et al., 2019).

Notably, optimal wellness is more than just a physical state in this continuum. Even if individuals lack physical symptoms, they may still experience psychological symptoms, such as depression, anxiety, or a general dissatisfaction with life, which can often affect mental and physical health. For example,

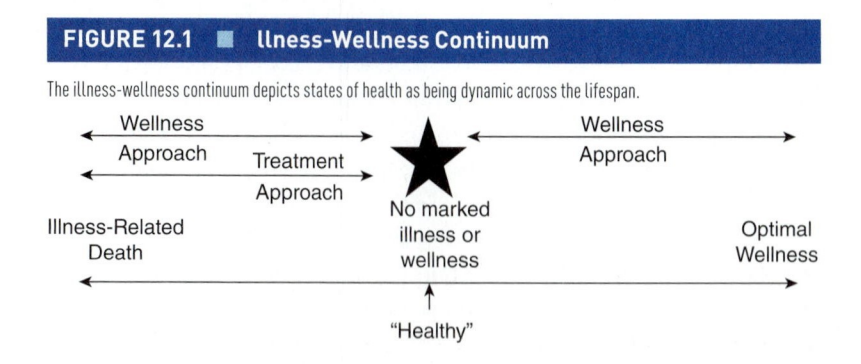

FIGURE 12.1 ■ Illness-Wellness Continuum

The illness-wellness continuum depicts states of health as being dynamic across the lifespan.

Illness-Related Death ← Wellness Approach ← Treatment Approach ← ★ No marked illness or wellness → Wellness Approach → Optimal Wellness

"Healthy"

excessive stress can weaken the immune system, leading to increased likelihood of diseases such as cancer (Corthay, 2014). Negative emotional states can also influence health behaviors, leading to smoking, alcohol consumption, overeating, or even suicide. Death may be a natural part of life, and an individual's place on the continuum often cannot be controlled. However, people can control which direction they are facing on this continuum—and facing to the right of this continuum points to wellness.

Wellness is an increasingly important focus in psychology. In the 1990s, American Hungarian psychologist Mihaly Csikszentmihalyi introduced the concept of *flow* in an effort to understand how people flourish and experience wellness (Csikszentmihalyi, 1990; Seligman & Csikszentmihalyi, 2000). Flow occurs when people become so engaged in an activity that they become engrossed, losing a sense of self and time. Csikszentmihalyi's work fundamentally focuses on wellness, specifically on what gives people enjoyment and happiness in their lives. He found that even those activities in which people experience discomfort (e.g., training for an athletic event or earning a degree) can be enjoyable and produce a strong sense of gratification if they contribute to feelings of happiness and well-being. Activities that can induce flow vary from engaging in exercise and sports to reading a book or making friends. Research in this area of positive psychology is leading the way to help practitioners understand how people can flourish and find happiness, thereby enhancing their experience of being well.

Biopsychosocial and Biomedical Models

Psychologists have varying perspectives on how to best understand health that generally fit within the traditional debate of the **mind-body relationship**. The philosophical debate asks whether the mind and body are one (part of the same system) or distinct (part of separate systems). The *mind* pertains to the mental "self," including mental processes, thoughts, and consciousness. The *body* is the physical "self," including the actions of neurons and the structure of the brain.

One of the central questions in psychology, and among philosophers, is whether the mind is part of the body, or vice versa. In other words, is the mind-body a synergistic whole, or are they distinct? And if they are distinct, which is in control? Humans consist of a mind and a body. From a **dualism** perspective, the mind and the body constitute separate systems; they are distinct. From a **monism** perspective, the mind and the body are synergistic; the mind and the body are part of the same system.

The most widely adopted viewpoint among psychologists is the **biopsychosocial model** of health, which is a holistic perspective in that it identifies illness, health, and wellness as being best explained by biological, psychological, and social interactions (Suls & Rothman, 2004). In this way, the biopsychosocial model fits best with a monistic viewpoint that the mind and the body are interconnected. The biopsychosocial model has the key advantage of incorporating all aspects of health, from the mind (psychological, cognitive, mental) to the body (biological, physical). To illustrate, consider how we can explain emotions (the mind) that induce physical ailments (the body), known as *psychosomatic symptoms* (e.g., emotional stress can induce physical ailments, such as ulcers). In this way, the biopsychosocial model is an understanding of illness, health, and wellness at a psychosocial level (e.g., the impact of social support, emotional well-being, or perceived anxiety on illness, health, and wellness) and at a physical level (e.g., the impact of cellular, chemical, or structural dysfunction on illness, health, and wellness).

An alternative viewpoint, called the **biomedical model**, identifies a perspective that health and illness can be explained almost entirely on the basis of biological factors. Thus,

mind-body relationship. The historical and philosophical debate over whether the mind and the body are one (part of the same system) or distinct (part of separate systems).

dualism. The assumption that the body and mind are separate, though perhaps interacting, entities.

monism. The assumption that the body and mind are the same; the mind and body are part of one synergistic entity.

biopsychosocial model. The holistic perspective that illness, health, and wellness can be best explained in the interactions of biological, psychological, and social factors.

biomedical model. The perspective that health and illness can be explained solely on the basis of biological dysfunction.

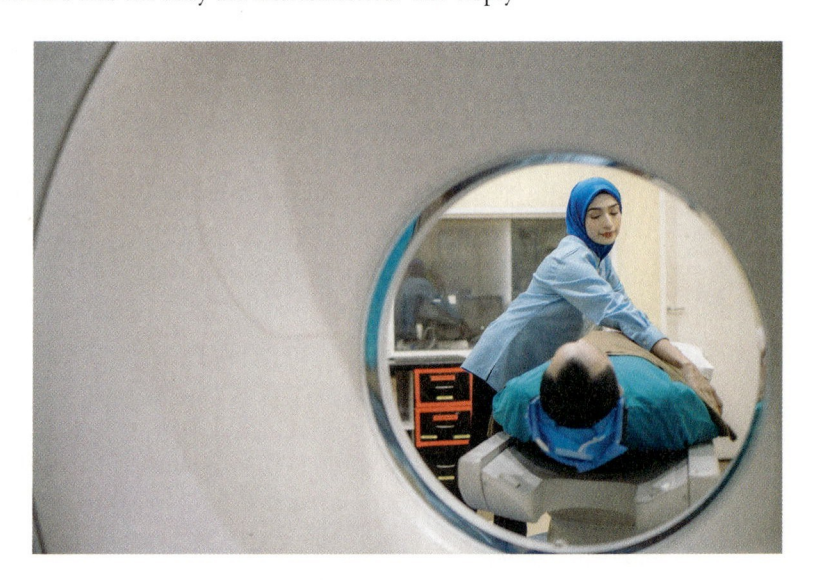

The balance between the mind and body is often reflected in medicine and psychology, particularly when treating the health of the brain.

iStock.com/chee gin tan

this perspective largely reduces the complexity of health to a single cause: the physical self. In this way, the biomedical model largely follows a dualistic view in that we can understand health and illness by studying the body (physical, biological factors) separate from the mind (psychosocial factors). The advantage of the biomedical model is its simplicity; however, this is also its key disadvantage. The biomedical model emphasizes an understanding of the physical causes of dysfunction or illness with little to no emphasis on factors that promote health and wellness. Also, wellness is largely a psychological endeavor to attain health even when healthy—largely driven by a need to "feel" healthy. This makes the biomedical model an incomplete model in that it is not well adapted to explain the wellness approach in the absence of illness.

Health Belief Model

As an individual, you probably have your own set of beliefs about your health, such as how healthy you feel, how likely you are to see a doctor, or how healthy your diet is. Our **health beliefs** or the knowledge, attitudes, and expectations that people have about their health, is critical to understanding **health behaviors**—the actions people take to achieve and maintain good health, promote wellness, and prevent illness. For example, beliefs about seeking help for depression can vary by gender (women tend to be more likely than men to seek help for depression), and such beliefs can guide a person's health behaviors (or their lack thereof). Similarly, the people providing care, such as a physician or family member, may experience frustration when a person misses scheduled appointments or does not fully disclose their symptoms, maybe due to the symptoms being too embarrassing. These expectations or beliefs about health can affect health behaviors.

Our health beliefs can influence our health behaviors, such as how much we exercise, how balanced our diet is, and the amount of sleep we get each day. This interplay between health behaviors and health beliefs can be understood in a multitude of ways that fit within the *health belief model* (Rosenstock, Strecher, & Becker, 1988). Let's consider a few health beliefs that can affect our health behaviors (Jones et al., 2015):

- **Locus of control.** With an internal locus of control, we believe we control our health (e.g., "I'm tired because I didn't get enough sleep"). With an external locus of control, we believe our health is out of our control (e.g., "I'm tired because it's a dreary day outside") or under the control of others (e.g., "I'm tired because my boss works me too hard"). A higher locus of control is associated with better health outcomes.

- **Health motivation or desire to be healthy.** The more motivated people are about their health, the more likely they are to engage in healthy behaviors.

- **Perception of susceptibility and risk.** If you perceive your risk of illness to be low, then you will be less likely to see a doctor, even if, in fact, your risk is high ("I don't feel well, but it will pass; I don't need to see a doctor"). This health belief can be based on valid information (e.g., "I have a high risk due to a family history") or invalid information (e.g., "I can't get lung cancer because I don't smoke").

- **Severity of illness or necessity of action.** The more severe an illness, the more motivated people will be to take immediate actions to improve their health. As an example, a young person who is obese and diabetic will be more likely to make dietary changes than will a young person who is obese but otherwise healthy.

- **Cost-benefit analysis of changing behavior.** This is related to a person's openness to changing their behavior ("If I stop smoking, I'll save money, but I'll probably gain weight"). The process by which a person changes their behavior can be described in part by the *stages of change model* (Prochaska & DiClemente, 1982). A person may go back and forth through the following stages: precontemplation ("I enjoy smoking"), contemplation ("Smoking is affecting my life; maybe I should think about stopping"), preparation ("I will stop buying cigarettes"), action ("I have stopped smoking"), and maintenance ("It has been 6 months since I last smoked").

---

health beliefs. The knowledge, attitudes, and expectations that people have about their personal health and how that health is cared for.

health behaviors. The actions people take to achieve and maintain good health, promote wellness, and prevent illness.

- **Cues to action.** Cues can trigger people to think about their health behaviors. Such cues could be internal, such as a physical symptom ("I feel shortness of breath") or external ("I read a pamphlet that said I may be at risk"). Cues to action are important inasmuch as they make people concerned. In terms of health behavior, the more that you believe that your actions can influence your health, the more likely you are to take action.

As you can appreciate, the interplay between health beliefs and health behaviors can be complex and can have a great impact on an individual's health. Extending our understanding of health to include the full spectrum from illness to wellness has helped guide the growth of health psychology and our understanding of health behaviors.

Illness Prevention and Health Promotion

When we think of health, psychologists focus on the **etiology**, or causes of a disease or illness, and are just as interested in health and wellness as they are in illness. A common model for understanding health behaviors is a "health onion" perspective (Dahlgren & Whitehead, 1991). The health onion is a multilayered framework that focuses on four layers of etiology (illustrated in Figure 12.2):

- Individual lifestyle factors
- Social and community networks
- Living and working conditions
- General socioeconomic, cultural, and environmental conditions

etiology. The origins or causes of disease or illness.

A central focus in health psychology is on both treatment (the left side of the illness-wellness continuum) and the prevention of disease (the continuum from left to right). When applied to health, **prevention** reflects the actions we take to stop a given disease from developing or to avoid a disease entirely, and it can be categorized into three types:

prevention. Efforts to avoid a disease entirely by taking actions that can stop a given disease from developing.

- *Primary prevention* is aimed at stopping disease before it occurs. For example, the immunization program has all but eradicated many diseases that were epidemic in the early 1900s.
- *Secondary prevention* is aimed at the early diagnosis and detection of treatable diseases aimed at identifying diseases early to make them easier to manage. For example, medical screening tests such as mammograms and colonoscopies are a secondary prevention action.

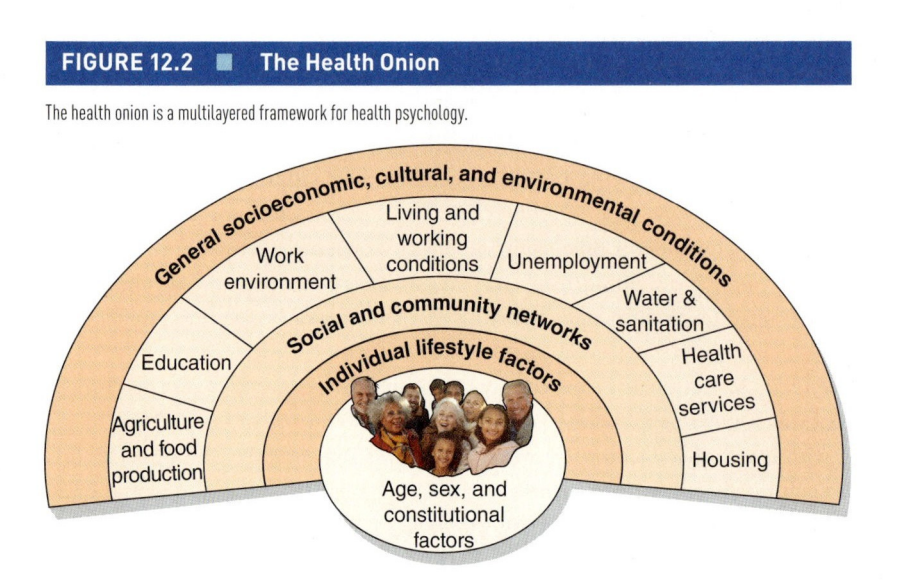

FIGURE 12.2 ■ The Health Onion

The health onion is a multilayered framework for health psychology.

- *Tertiary prevention* is aimed at wellness for those with chronic irreversible diseases. For example, providing physical therapy for those with arthritis can help individuals manage the disease in order to improve their quality of life or wellness.

While prevention of disease is an important step toward healthy living, psychologists focus also on the promotion and maintenance of good health, called **health promotion**. This is a critical effort in psychology in terms of its impact beyond individual behavior to include other factors. For example, health promotion activities include building community parks to increase activity in communities, opening grocery stores in "food deserts" to make fresh fruits and vegetables more available to those who might otherwise have difficulty obtaining them, and individual efforts such as lifestyle changes to increase exercise. Health promotion is critical for promoting health and wellness even among those who are not ill. The Centers for Disease Control and Prevention (2021) and HealthyPeople.gov (2021) promote specific aims to increase health promotion efforts specifically aimed at targeting social determinants of health. These efforts include the development of community gardens to increase access to affordable healthy food options in underserved communities and the implementation of taxing and zoning policies that encourage the expansion of full-service grocery stores into neighborhoods where they are needed.

health promotion. Efforts to enable people to have greater control over, and to improve, their health and wellness.

Psychology Applied: Growing Up Transgender: When Is It Appropriate to Transition?

A fundamental aspect of our health is our identity, and this issue can be instrumentally important for those in the LBGTQ+ community. For those who identify as transgender, transitioning can be challenging. *Transgender* (or *trans*) describes a person whose gender identity (the internal knowledge of one's gender) does not match their biological sex (male, female). The American Psychological Association (2015), in an effort "to be as broadly inclusive as possible" (p. 832), describes people who have a gender identity that is not fully aligned with their birth sex as "transgender and gender nonconforming" or TGNC. However, also keep in mind that not everyone whose behavior, appearance, or identify fits with gender nonconforming will identify as a transgender person.

Today, it is estimated that about 1 in every 250 adults (nearly 1 million Americans) identify as transgender (Meerwijk & Sevelius, 2017). The lived experience of being transgender can be quite challenging both personally and socially. According to a national survey by the American Foundation for Suicide Prevention (2014), the attempted suicide rate (that is, those who self-report a suicide attempt in their lifetime) among transgender people is an astonishing 41 percent—much higher than for the general population (4.6%) or for lesbian, gay, and bisexual adults (ranging between 10% and 20%). Attempted suicide rates among transgender people are highest among those who are men (46%), younger (45%), multiracial (54%), American Indian or Alaska Native (56%), or disabled (55% to 65%), and among those with no college education (48%) and an annual income below $10,000 (54%).

Socially, transgender people often have difficulty spending time and communicating with their families. They also experience harassment and discrimination. According to the same national survey, 50 to 54 percent experience bullying and harassment in school, 50 to 59 percent experience discrimination or harassment at work, and nearly 60 percent report harassment or disrespect by law enforcement—with many transgender people reporting physical or sexual violence at school (70 percent), at work (64 percent), and by law enforcement (65 percent). Discrimination is even evident in health care, with 60 percent of transgender people reporting that a doctor or health care provider refused them treatment.

These statistics reflect the lived experience of transgender people. It is not surprising at all, then, that for most transgender people, there is a genuine desire to transition—from their biological sex to the gender with which they identify. However, with transgender adults gaining wider acceptance in mainstream culture, many children are now transitioning too. Lia, a girl featured in the PBS *Frontline* feature "Growing Up Trans," described it this way:

I am transgender. I was born male and identify as female. But I like to say that I am a girl stuck in a boy's body. So I've changed my name, my clothes, my room, and my pronouns. And that's really all you need, except for the fifth one that I still need… surgery and medicine to help me look like a girl.

Lia's description highlights the desire of many transgender people—the desire to transition. However, Lia is not an adult but, rather, a prepubescent child who seeks surgery and medicine to make the final physiological change as a child—to "look like a girl." With the introduction of hormone blockers in 2007, new medical options exist to suspend puberty and change its course of action in children—to allow children more time to gain confidence in their gender identity. Although children must typically enter at least the initial stages of puberty to begin using the blockers, this medical option allows children to almost entirely avoid experiencing the puberty of their biological sex.

But this option does not come without controversy. When is it appropriate to make this transition? Can children really *know* their gender without at least first experiencing the puberty of their biological sex? Two physicians from the Lurie Children's Hospital of Chicago summarized the challenges:

The majority of children with gender dysphoria will not grow up to be transgender adolescents or adults… but I think the challenge is that we're not able to definitively predict for whom gender dysphoria will continue and for those that it may not continue.
—*Lisa Simons, M.D., Adolescent Medicine*

Our goal is to try to figure out which children are going to continue to identify as different than their natal sex, and we don't have any definitive test to do that right now…. I wish there was a test to say "oh yeah, of course, you're five and you think this now and you will when you're 15 and you will when you're 30".… We don't have it though, so it's a real challenge.
—*Courtney Finlayson, M.D., Pediatric Endocrinologist*

The challenge is that these are children—many of whom cannot even legally ride in the front seat of a car. Giving treatment to children who might later change their minds in adolescence or adulthood brings with it ethical concerns related to allowing such drastic procedures for these children—the long-term consequences of which are unknown. At the same time, many of these children will continue to identify as transgender as adults. For those children, such medical advances can be instrumental in shaping not only their development but also their outlook on life. Further advancements are needed to predict which children will continue to identify as different from their biological sex, so that treatments can be targeted toward the children who will benefit in the long term.

Mind Over Matter: The Placebo Effect

Although we often tend to focus on physical health, what we *think* about our health can have just as much of an impact on how healthy we feel. In *The Healing Brain*, Robert Ornstein and David Sobel (1987) contend that "the brain minds the body," for the brain's primary function is not perception, consciousness, learning, thought, language, memory, motivation, or emotion—but health maintenance. According to Ornstein and Sobel, "The brain is the largest organ of secretion in the body, and the neuron, far from being like a chip within a computer, is a flesh-and-blood little gland, one that produces hundreds of chemicals. These chemicals do not, for the most part, serve thought or reason. They serve keeping the body out of trouble" (p. 11). Taking the argument one step further, Howard Friedman (1991), author of *The Self-Healing Personality*, notes that although he never saw a death certificate marked "death due to unhealthy personality," there is a link to chronic conditions such as headaches, ulcers, asthma, arthritis, and even cancer. In *Mind-Body Deceptions*, Steven Dubovsky (1997) argues that in "the psychosomatics of everyday life," the mind can often be used to heal the body. It all sounds similar to the expression "Mind over matter."

A classic and profound illustration of the theme that people can use the mind to heal the body can be seen most clearly in the *placebo effect*, the observation that all sorts of interventions can improve a person's health through the powers of suggestion, faith, and reassurance (Harrington, 1997). For a wide range of ailments, people often feel better simply because they *think* they have received an effective treatment. Estimating that 30 to 40 percent of patients experience relief from symptoms after taking a placebo, psychiatrist Walter Brown (1998) asks, "Should doctors be prescribing sugar pills?"

It is common for people to think that placebo effects are all in the mind—that although inactive treatments can make us feel better, the physical improvements are imagined, not real. This is not true. In an early demonstration of the placebo effect, Robert Sternbach (1964) gave to volunteer participants a white sugar pill that contained no active ingredients. At first, participants were told that the pill contained a drug that would stimulate a strong churning sensation in the stomach. The next time they were told that it would reduce their stomach activity and make them feel full. On a third occasion, they were informed that the pill was only a placebo. The result: Participants always swallowed the same tablet, yet they exhibited measurable changes in stomach activity consistent with their expectations. Other research has shown that placebos can influence a wide range of physical changes, including changes in cholesterol levels and hair loss (Ernst & Abbot, 1999).

Over the years, placebos have been used to treat allergies, headaches, insomnia, constipation, skin rashes, upset stomachs, chronic pain, and other ailments. That is why, in order to test the effectiveness of a new drug or other form of treatment, researchers must demonstrate that the participants who received the treatment improved more than others who *believed* they had received it but did not. Only then can the actual effect of the treatment be separated from the power of suggestion. Somehow, in the seamless interplay of mind and body, beliefs transform reality.

Is the placebo effect real? Danish researchers Asbjorn Hrobjartsson and Peter Gotzsche (2001) reviewed 114 medical studies that compared patients who received placebos for various illnesses with those who received no treatment and concluded that the two groups did not differ much in their treatment outcomes. When this review was published in the *New England Journal of Medicine*, the *Boston Globe* wrote of the placebo effect, "It's a scam." And the *New York Times* called it "More myth than science." In fact, powerful placebo effects are found all the time—*for some conditions* (even the Danish researchers admitted that placebos have proved effective for pain-killing purposes). As Walter Brown put it, "If you tested penicillin on 40 different clinical conditions, you would get similar results: it works for some infections but it won't do anything for arthritis" (quoted in Gibbs, 2001). A study out of Harvard Medical School even found that the placebo effect persists, even when participants know they received a placebo (Kaptchuk et al., 2010).

The placebo effect is not a magical occurrence, or a miracle, or even a purely mental phenomenon (Koenig, 2012). And psychologists would not accept the claims made in the medical community solely on the basis of stories, anecdotes, and case studies. So is there a way to explain what Norman Cousins (1989) described as the biology of hope? The process is not entirely understood—probably because there is not one process, but many. Some have suggested that the positive expectations communicated by a confident and optimistic doctor can trigger the release of endorphins, naturally occurring morphine-like substances in the brain that provide temporary relief from pain (Levine, Gordon, & Fields, 1978). Others suggest that placebos reduce people's anxiety about being sick, which dampens the release of stress hormones that lower the body's resistance (Kirsch & Sapirstein, 1999). In a study of male patients with depression, for example, those given a placebo exhibited some of the same changes in glucose metabolism activity in the brain as those who received a common antidepressant (Mayberg et al., 2002). Knowing this, Irving Kirsch (2019) suggested that given the harmful side effects of many antidepressants (e.g., increased risk of relapse, suicidality), prescribing a placebo instead may be just as effective without any of the side effects, although such a suggestion raises ethical considerations associated with prescribing patients "fake" albeit effective medications (Miller, Colloca, & Kaptchuk, 2009). That said, depending on what a person is told, he or she can even have more symptoms or side effects after a placebo, called the *nocebo effect* (Colloca & Miller, 2011). When it comes to placebos and nocebos, the question is not *if* they work, but *when* and *how* they work.

Placebo and nocebo effects often result from expectancy effects, such that information about the effects of a given drug can shape a person's expectation about its efficacy (illustrated in Figure 12.3). Positive expectancies about the treatment can increase its efficacy (*placebo effect*); negative expectancies can reduce its efficacy (*nocebo effect*). For this reason, in clinical settings, it is strongly recommended that when a drug is prescribed, such as an analgesic, it is "useful to emphasize positive drug effects and to avoid overemphasizing side effects" (Klinger, Blasini, Schmitz, & Colloca, 2017, p. 2).

FIGURE 12.3 ■ Placebo and Nocebo Effects

Placebo effect

Placebo effect Instruction
- "This medication will decrease your pain"

→ Patient's Expectation
- "My pain is going to decrease soon"

→ Placebo effect
- Perceived reduction of pain

Nocebo effect

Nocebo effect Instruction
- "I can offer a medication with less side effects but it would not be as effective in decreasing your pain"

→ Patient's Expectation
- "My pain will stay the same or will get worse"

→ Nocebo effect
- Perceived increase of pain

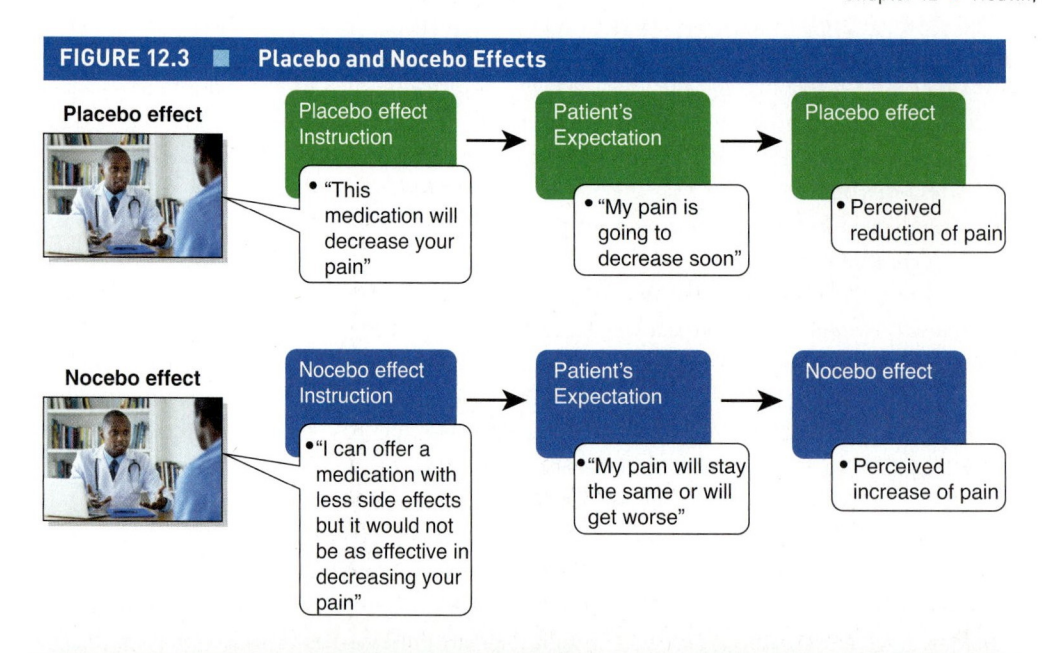

LEARNING CHECK

Understanding Health

For each of the following, identify which description in the right column best matches each term in the left column.

Health beliefs	1. A holistic perspective that illness, health, and wellness can be best explained in the interactions of biological, psychological, and social factors.
Illness-wellness continuum	2. The perspective that the mind and the body are distinct.
Monism	3. The knowledge, attitudes, and expectations that people have about their personal health and how that health is cared for.
Dualism	4. The origins or causes of disease or illness.
Biopsychosocial model	5. The perspective that the mind and the body are the same.
Etiology	6. A continuum for understanding states of health as being dynamic across the lifespan.

(Answers: 1. Biopsychosocial model; 2. Dualism; 3. Health beliefs; 4. Etiology; 5. Monism; 6. Illness-wellness continuum.)

STRESS AND HEALTH

LEARNING OBJECTIVES

Identify the main sources of stress and how it affects health.

- Enumerate the main sources of stress in our lives.
- Describe the effects of stress on the body.
- Explain how the immune system works and how it is affected by stress and other psychological states.

The field of psychology has had a long-standing interest not only in mental health but also in physical health—a domain typically associated with medicine. Influenced by psychoanalysis, clinical psychologists used to study *psychosomatic* ailments such as asthma, ulcers, headaches, and constipation—conditions thought to result from unconscious conflicts. Working from a behavioral perspective, others later referred to these same ailments as *psychophysiological* disorders. Either way, it's long been clear that psychological states can influence physical well-being.

The emerging area of health psychology—which has grown substantially since the turn of the century—is the application of psychology to promote physical health and wellness, and to prevent and treat illness (Privitera, 2016). You may wonder: What does psychology have to do with catching a cold, having a heart attack, or being afflicted with cancer? If you could turn the clock back a few years and ask your family doctor, the answer would be "very little." In the past, illness was considered a purely biological event. But this strict medical perspective has given way to a broader model that holds that health is a joint product of biological and psychological factors.

Part of the reason for this broadened view is that illness patterns over the years have changed in significant ways. In the year 1900, the principal causes of death were contagious diseases—polio, smallpox, tuberculosis, typhoid fever, malaria, influenza, pneumonia, and the like. Today, none of these infectious illnesses is currently a leading killer. Instead, Americans are most likely to die, in order of risk, from heart disease, cancer, accidents, chronic respiratory diseases, and strokes—problems that are often preventable through changes in lifestyle, outlook, and behavior (illustrated in Table 12.1).

Although it's not possible to quantify the extent of the problem, psychological stress is a known potent killer. Regardless of who you are, when you were born, or where you live, you have no doubt experienced stress. Sitting in a rush-hour traffic jam, getting married or divorced, losing hours of work to a computer crash, getting into an argument with a close friend, worrying about an unwanted pregnancy or the health of your child, being stranded at an airport, living in a noisy neighborhood, struggling to make financial ends meet, and caring for a loved one who is sick—these are the kinds of stresses and strains we all must learn to live with. Whether they are short term or long term, serious or mild, no one is immune and there is no escape. But there are ways to cope.

In this section, we examine three interrelated questions of relevance to your health and wellness: (a) What are some of the primary sources of stress? (b) What are the effects of stress on the body? and

TABLE 12.1 ■ Leading Causes of Death, 2019

The majority of the leading causes of death in the United States are preventable through changes in lifestyle, outlook, and behavior.

Top 10 Leading Causes of Death in U.S., 2019		
Rank	Disease	Number of Deaths per Year
1	Heart disease	659,041
2	Cancer	599,601
3	Accidents (unintentional injuries)	173,040
4	Chronic lower respiratory diseases	156,979
5	Stroke (cerebrovascular diseases)	150,005
6	Alzheimer's disease	121,499
7	Diabetes	87,647
8	Nephritis, nephrotic syndrome, and nephrosis	51,565
9	Influenza and pneumonia	49,783
10	Intentional self-harm (suicide)	47,511

Source: Centers for Disease Control and Prevention (2021).

FIGURE 12.4 ■ Stress and Coping

Advances in health psychology indicate that, although stressful events have effects on the body, the way we cope with stress can promote health or illness.

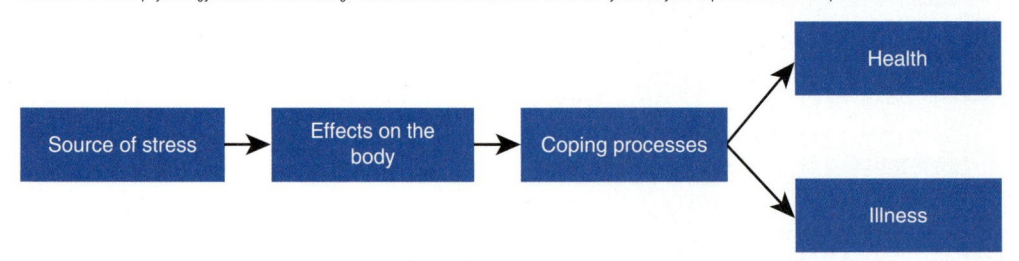

Source of stress → Effects on the body → Coping processes → Health / Illness

(c) How does stress affect the immune system? In the next section we examine an additional question: What are the most adaptive ways of coping with stress? Together, the answers to these questions provide a useful model for understanding the stress-and-coping process (illustrated in Figure 12.4).

Sources of Stress

Stress is an unpleasant state of arousal that arises when we perceive that an event threatens our ability to cope effectively. There are many different sources of stress, or *stressors*. Try writing down the stressors in your own life, and you'll probably find that the items in your list can be divided into three major categories: catastrophes, major life events, and daily hassles.

Sources of stress are not experienced equally by all people. What is stressful to one person is not necessarily stressful to another. For example, a worldwide health pandemic declared by the World Health Organization (WHO) should be stressful, such as the coronavirus pandemic. However, the pandemic created very different responses in the United States. Many Americans were appropriately stressed and cautious, whereas many others seemed to show no indication of stress at all as they congregated in large groups even in states where "shelter in place" mandates were in effect (Silverman & Moon, 2020). The health belief model can help us understand some of the reasons for such varied responses. For example, *perception of susceptibility and risk* (younger people were most likely to ignore mandates, as they were at least risk) and *cost-benefit analysis* (for many, the costs of changing their habits and routines was worse than the potential benefits of obeying mandates, particularly if doing so did not offer them an immediate benefit).

Likewise, what is stressful varies by racial and socioeconomic factors. For example, minority groups are more likely than nonminority groups to experience stress as the result of perceived discrimination, including that based on gender, race/ethnicity, and sexual orientation (Pinderhughes, Davis, & Williams, 2015; Williams & Sternthal, 2010). These stressors can lead to further disparities in health—including greater maternal stress; unhealthy behaviors such as cigarette smoking, increased alcohol use, and improper nutrition; and the development of mental health disorders (American Psychological Association, 2012). Other types of stress—such as *acculturative stress*, which is stress experienced in efforts to adapt to a dominant culture that is different from your own, and *socioeconomic stress*, which is often experienced most by those in lower social positions—can have equally traumatic effects, including physical and mental health disparities such as increased substance use, anxiety, and depression (American Psychological Association, 2012).

Other events—such as motor vehicle accidents, plane crashes, violent crimes, physical or sexual abuse, the death of a loved one, and natural disasters such as hurricanes, tornadoes, floods, earthquakes,

stress. An aversive state of arousal triggered by the perception that an event threatens our ability to cope effectively.

Being stuck in traffic is one of the most common microstressors in daily life.
iStock.com/Grafissimo

Amid the coronavirus outbreak, crowds gather near California's Newport Beach Pier in 2020.
MediaNews Group/Orange County Register via Getty Images

posttraumatic stress disorder (PTSD). A psychological disorder that develops as a result of exposure to a traumatic event.

Tornadoes have such devastating power that those who survive them often exhibit posttraumatic stress disorder.
Brett Carlsen/Getty Images News via Getty Images

and fires—can have quite similar traumatic effects on people (Sareen, 2014). The harmful effects of catastrophic stressors on physical health are well documented. Paul Adams and Gerald Adams (1984) examined the public records in Othello, Washington, before and after the 1980 eruption of the Mount St. Helens volcano, which spewed thick layers of ash all over the community. They discovered that there were posteruption increases in calls made to a mental health crisis line, police reports of domestic violence, referrals to the alcohol treatment center, and visits to the local hospital emergency room. However, more recent studies show evidence that traumatic effects are not necessarily all doom and gloom. In a systematic review of natural disasters and suicidal behavior, researchers discovered what they called a "honeymoon" phase immediately after a disaster, when nonfatal suicidal behaviors actually decreased, although some studies found a delayed increase in suicidal behaviors after the initial postdisaster period (Kõlves, Kõlves, & De Leo, 2013).

War, in particular, leaves deep and permanent psychological scars. Soldiers who experience combat see horrifying injuries, death, and destruction on a routine basis, leaving them with images and emotions that do not fade. In World War I, the problem was called shell shock. In World War II, it was called combat fatigue. It's now called **posttraumatic stress disorder (PTSD)** and is identified by symptoms such as recurring anxiety, sleeplessness, nightmares, vivid flashbacks, intrusive thoughts, attentional problems, and social withdrawal. To evaluate the extent of the problem, the Centers for Disease Control Vietnam Experience Study (1988) compared 7,000 Vietnam combat veterans with 7,000 noncombat veterans who served in the military at the same time (that is, more than 20 years before the study). They found that although the Vietnam War was a distant memory to most Americans, 15 percent of those who saw combat—twice as many as were in the comparison group—reported lingering symptoms of PTSD. Those who had the most traumatic of experiences (crossing enemy lines, being ambushed or shot at, handling dead bodies) were five times more likely to have nightmares, flashbacks, startle reactions, and other problems. Similar results have been found among older veterans of World War II and the Korean War (Palmer et al., 2019; Spiro, Schnurr, & Aldwin, 1994).

PTSD, a form of anxiety disorder, can be caused by traumas off the battlefield as well. In a report evaluating the prevalence of PTSD, Jonathan Bisson and his colleagues (2015) estimated that up to 3 percent of the adult population has PTSD in the course of a lifetime—with estimated lifetime prevalence rates of 1.9 to 8.8 percent. But among people who experience greater trauma, these rates can more than double—for example, prevalence rates reach more than 50 percent for survivors of rape. This research shows that such traumas can be caused by a range of experiences—such as life-threatening accidents, fires, natural disasters, combat, being raped or attacked, and witnessing an injury or murder. In a study of Miami residents caught in a major hurricane, Gail Ironson and others (1997) found that after a few months, one-third exhibited symptoms of PTSD and that the more injury, property damage, and loss they suffered from the storm, the more severe their symptoms were.

You may have viewed a questionnaire like the Social Readjustment Rating Scale (SRRS), more commonly known as the Holmes and Rahe Stress Scale (Holmes & Rahe, 1967). The claim made is that the number of stress points or "life-change units" you accumulate in a recent period of time indicates the amount of stress you are under. The simple notion that change is inherently stressful has an intuitive appeal to it. Indeed, research shows that people with high scores on the SRRS are more likely to come down with physical illnesses (Maddi, Bartone, & Puccetti, 1987; Roca et al., 2013). But is change per se necessarily harmful? There are two problems with this notion. First, although there is a statistical link between negative events and illness, research does not similarly support the claim that positive "stressors"—taking a vacation, graduating, winning a lottery, starting a new career, or getting married—are similarly harmful (McLeod, 2010). The second complicating factor is that the impact of any change depends on who the person is and how the change is interpreted. For example, moving to a new country is less stressful to immigrants who can speak the new language (Alegría, Álvarez, & DiMarzio, 2017); having an abortion is less stressful to women who have the support of family, partners, and friends (Reardon, 2018); and a diagnosis of infertility is less devastating to married men and women who want children when they confront the issue, emotionally, rather than avoid it (Berghuis & Stanton, 2002). The amount of change in a person's life may provide crude estimates of stress and future health, but the predictive equation is more complex.

It has long been recognized that combat leaves psychological scars and the symptoms of posttraumatic stress disorder.

Associated Press / Jeff Roberson

Think again about the sources of stress in your life. Although catastrophes or exceptional events may spring to mind, researchers have found that the most significant sources of stress arise from the hassles that irritate us on a daily basis. Environmental irritants such as population density, loud noise, extreme heat or cold, and cigarette smoke are all possible sources of stress. Car problems, waiting in lines, losing keys, arguments with friends, nosy neighbors, bad workdays, money troubles, and other "microstressors" also place a constant strain on us. Table 12.2 lists the events that most routinely stress children, college students, and adults (Kanner, Feldman, Weinberger, & Ford, 1991; Wolverton, 2019). However, there is nothing "micro" about the impact of these stressors on health and wellness. Studies show that the accumulation of daily hassles contributes more to illness than do major life events (Kohn, Lafreniere, & Gurevich, 1991; Salleh, 2008).

One source of stress that plagues many people in the workplace is *burnout*—a prolonged response to job stress characterized by emotional exhaustion, cynicism, disengagement, and a lack of personal accomplishment. Teachers, doctors, nurses, police officers, social workers, and others in human-service professions are particularly at risk for burnout. Under relentless job pressures, those who are burned out describe themselves as feeling drained, frustrated, hardened, apathetic, and lacking in energy and motivation (Maslach & Leiter, 2016; Reith, 2018). Burnout also impacts productivity, with more than 60 percent of workers saying that their mental health affects their productivity. This has led to a revolution of sorts, with about half of millennials and 75 percent of Gen-Zers saying that they have left a job for mental health reasons (Braverman, 2020; Stieg, 2019).

On the home front, economic pressure is another common source of stress. In a three-year study of more than 400 married couples, researchers found that those who are strained by a tight budget and have difficulty paying the bills experience more distress and conflict in their marriages (Conger, Reuter, & Elder, 1999). A follow-up study of Black families further showed that economic hardship spells emotional distress for parents—and adjustment problems for their children (Conger et al., 2002). For the largest growing demographic in the United States—Latinx immigrants—findings show that when economic hardship and sociocultural stressors are both high, detrimental effects on wellness are most evident (Mendoza, Dmitrieva, Perreira, Hurwich-Reiss, & Watamura, 2017).

Physiological Effects of Stress

The term *stress* was popularized by Hans Selye (1936, 1976), an endocrinologist. As a young medical student, Selye noticed that patients who were hospitalized for different illnesses often had similar

TABLE 12.2 ■ Common Daily Hassles

Children and Early Adolescents

Having to clean up your room

Being bored and having nothing to do

Seeing that another kid can do something better

Getting punished for doing something wrong

Having to go to bed when you don't want to

Being teased at school

College Students

Conflicts with a boyfriend or girlfriend

Dissatisfaction with your athletic skills

Having your trust betrayed by a friend

Struggling to meet your own academic standards

Not having enough leisure time

Concerns for career and future goals

Dissatisfaction with your physical appearance

Middle-Aged Adults

Concerns about weight

Health of a family member

Social obligations

Inconsiderate smokers

Concerns about money

Misplacing or losing things

Home maintenance

Job security

---

symptoms, such as muscle weakness, a loss of weight and appetite, and a lack of ambition. Maybe these symptoms were part of a generalized response to an attack on the body, he thought. In the 1930s, Selye tested this hypothesis by exposing laboratory rats to various stressors, including heat, cold, heavy exercise, toxic substances, food deprivation, and electric shock. As anticipated, the different stressors all produced a similar physiological response: enlarged adrenal glands, shrunken lymph nodes, and bleeding stomach ulcers. Selye borrowed a term from engineering and called the reaction "stress," a word that quickly became part of everyday language.

The Stress Process

According to Selye, the body naturally responds to stress in a three-stage process he called the **general adaptation syndrome** (illustrated in Figure 12.5). Sparked by the recognition of a threat, any threat—predator, enemy soldier, speeding automobile, or virus—the body has an initial alarm reaction. To meet the challenge, adrenaline and other hormones are poured into the bloodstream, thus heightening physiological arousal. Heart rate, blood pressure, and breathing rates increase, while slower, long-term functions such as growth, digestion, and the operation of the immune system are inhibited. At this stage, the body mobilizes all its resources to ward off the threat. Next comes a

general adaptation syndrome. A three-stage process (alarm, resistance, and exhaustion) by which the body responds to stress.

resistance stage, during which the body remains aroused and on the alert. There is a continued release of stress hormones, and local defenses are activated (if there is a virus, for example, immune-system antibodies are called into action). But if the stress persists for a prolonged time (as in a failing marriage, high-pressure job, or poverty), the body will fall into an exhaustion stage. According to Selye, the body's natural antistress resources are limited. Eventually, resistance breaks down, putting us at risk for illness and even death.

Types of Stressors

Research has since revealed that different types of stressors elicit somewhat different bodily responses—and that exhaustion occurs not because the body's stress-fighting resources are limited but because the overuse of these resources causes other systems in the body to break down. Still, Selye's basic model makes an important point: Stress may be an adaptive short-term reaction to threat, but over time it compromises our health and wellness.

FIGURE 12.5 ■ The General Adaptation Syndrome

According to Selye, the human body responds to threat in three phases: alarm, resistance, and exhaustion.

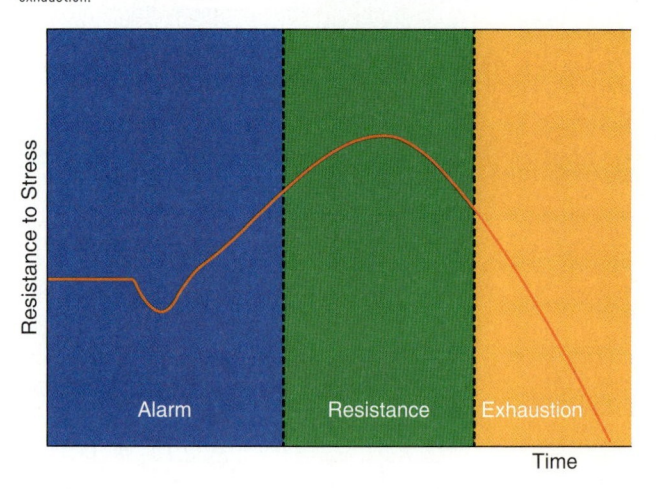

Stress that is negative is called **distress**. Examples of distress include a death of a loved one, financial strains, or divorce. These can lead to a stress response that can be harmful to our health over time. That said, stress is not always a bad thing. Stress that is positive is called **eustress**. Examples of eustress include the stress you experience earning a degree, working out to feel fit, and getting ready for a first date. These may be stressful events, but earning a degree is rewarding, working out makes you feel healthier, and, oh, the anticipation of whether or not your date will like you—how exciting!

distress. A stressor that one interprets as having harmful effects.

eustress. A stressor that one interprets as having beneficial effects.

A stress response is found in all mammals. So why, asks neuroscientist Robert Sapolsky (1994), don't zebras get ulcers? Sapolsky notes that the physiological stress response is superbly designed through evolution to help animals mobilize to fight or escape in an acute emergency. For the zebra, this occurs when a hungry lion leaps out from a bush and sprints at top speed across the savanna. For humans, it occurs in combat or in competitive sports—maybe even on first dates and job interviews. But make a mental list of the situations you find stressful, and you'll learn that people become anxious over things that would make no sense to a zebra. "We humans live well enough and long enough, and are smart enough, to generate all sorts of stressful events purely in our heads," notes Sapolsky. "From the perspective of the evolution of the animal kingdom, psychological stress is a recent invention" (p. 5). The reason that stress causes ulcers and other illnesses, then, is that the response is designed for acute physical emergencies, yet we turn it on often and for prolonged periods as we worry about taxes, rent or mortgages, family members, public speaking, career goals, and the inevitability of death.

Effects of Stress

All humans respond bodily to stress, which is what enables us to mount a defense. Physiologically, the sympathetic nervous system is activated and more adrenaline is secreted, which increases the heart rate and heightens arousal. Then all at once the liver pours extra sugar into the bloodstream for energy, the pupils dilate to let in more light, breathing speeds up to obtain more oxygen, perspiration increases to cool down the body, blood clots faster to heal wounds, saliva flow is

Many activities we engage in can be stressful yet enjoyable, such as exercise, which makes us feel and be healthier.

iStock.com/vgajic

inhibited, and digestion slows down to divert blood to the brain and skeletal muscles. In the face of threat, the body readies for action. But what, behaviorally, is the nature of the defense? Many years ago, Walter Cannon (1932) described the body as prepared for "fight or flight."

One common effect of stress is coronary heart disease (CHD), which is a narrowing of the blood vessels that carry oxygen and nutrients to the heart muscle. It is currently the leading cause of death in the United States (Virani et al., 2020). An estimated 18.2 million Americans age 20 or older have CHD. For many, the result is a heart attack, which occurs when the blood supply to the heart is blocked. This causes an uncomfortable feeling of pressure, fullness, squeezing, or pain in the center of the chest—and sometimes also sweating, dizziness, nausea, fainting, and shortness of breath. Every year, 805,000 Americans have heart attacks—that is, approximately one heart attack every 40 seconds. Nearly one in seven do not survive a heart attack (Centers for Disease Control and Prevention, 2019).

Several factors are known to increase the risk of CHD. The three most important are hypertension, or high blood pressure; cigarette smoking; and high cholesterol (others include a family history of CHD, obesity, and a lack of exercise). People with one of these three major risk factors are twice as likely to develop CHD, those with two risk factors are 3.5 times as likely, and those with all three are six times as likely. These statistics are compelling and should not be taken lightly. But combined, these factors account for fewer than half of the known cases of CHD. What's missing from the equation is the fourth major risk factor: stress.

Personality Types and Stress

In 1956, cardiologists Meyer Friedman and Ray Rosenman were studying the relationship between cholesterol and coronary heart disease. After noticing that husbands were more likely than their wives to have CHD, they speculated that work-related stress might be the reason (at the time, most women did not work outside the home). To test this hypothesis, Friedman and Rosenman interviewed 3,000 healthy middle-aged men. Those who seemed to be the most hard-driving, competitive, impatient, time conscious, and quick to anger were classified as having a **Type A personality**. Roughly an equal number of those who were easygoing, relaxed, and laid back were classified as having a **Type B personality**. Interestingly, out of 258 men who eventually had heart attacks over the following nine years, 69 percent had been classified as Type As and only 31 percent were Type Bs (Rosenman et al., 1975).

The Type A personality of the so-called workaholic is made up of many traits, including a competitive drive, a sense of always being in a hurry, and a mix of impatience, anger, cynicism, and hostility (Ekselius, 2018; Matthews, 1988). In interviews and questionnaires, people who are Type A say they tend to walk fast and talk fast, work late hours, interrupt other speakers in midsentence, get angry with people who are late, detest waiting in lines, race through yellow lights when they drive, lash out at others when frustrated, strive to win at all costs, and save time by doing many things at once. In contrast, "there are those who breeze through the day as pleased as park rangers—despite having deadlines and kids and a broken-down car and charity work and scowling Aunt Agnes living in the spare bedroom" (Carey, 1997, p. 75).

Over the years, researchers have found that being time-pressured, competitive, and driven to achieve do not put us at risk. However, the one trait that is toxic and is related to an individual's proneness to CHD is *hostility*—as seen in people who are constantly angry, cynical, and mistrustful of others (as assessed in Table 12.3). People who are often in a negative emotional state are besieged by stress. But because the heart is just a dumb pump and the blood vessels merely hoses, "the cardiovascular stress-response basically consists of making them work harder for a while, and if you do that on a regular basis, they will wear out, just like [a computer or phone charger]" (Sapolsky, 1994, p. 42). In the long run, a pattern of hostility and anger can be lethal (Miller, Smith, Turner, Guijarro, & Hallet, 1996; Vlachakis et al., 2018). In fact, it is suggested that providing people with a way to manage or handle stress properly can have substantial benefits for reducing stress and even increasing performance in the workplace for those with either Type A or Type B personality (Janjhua & Chandrakanta, 2012; Kheirkhah, Shayegan, Haghani, & Jafar Jalal, 2018).

Compared to people with a Type B personality, the strength of the link between Type A behavior and CHD depends on how people are diagnosed. What explains the connection between Type A

Type A personality. A personality characterized by an impatient, hard-driving, and hostile pattern of behavior.

Type B personality. A personality characterized by an easy-going, relaxed pattern of behavior.

TABLE 12.3 ■ How "Hostile" Is Your Pattern of Behavior?
• When in the express checkout line at the supermarket, do you often count the items in the baskets of the people ahead of you to be sure they aren't over the limit?
• When an elevator doesn't come as quickly as it should, do your thoughts quickly focus on the inconsiderate behavior of the person on another floor who's holding it up?
• When someone criticizes you, do you quickly begin to feel annoyed?
• Do you frequently find yourself muttering at the television during a news broadcast?
• When you are held up in a slow line in traffic, do you quickly sense your heart pounding and your breath quickening?

behavior and CHD? One explanation is that Type As are less health conscious than Type Bs. They tend to smoke more, consume more caffeine and alcohol, exercise less, sleep less, and eat less healthful foods, and they also are less likely to comply with health advice from doctors (Israel et al., 2014; Siegler, 1994). A second explanation is that people who are Type A are physiologically more reactive than Type Bs are. In tense social situations, they react with greater increases in pulse rate, blood pressure, and adrenaline—a hormone that accelerates the build-up of fatty plaques on the artery walls, causing a hardening of the arteries (Krantz & McCeney, 2002). In fact, research shows that people who are hostile exhibit more intense cardiovascular reactions not only during the event that makes them angry—say, being involved in a heated argument (Davis, Matthews, & McGrath, 2000)—but long afterward as well, when asked to relive the event (Frederickson et al., 2000; Suls, 2013).

The Immune System

When it comes to the interaction between mind and body, the link between stress and the heart is just the tip of the iceberg. It now appears that stress also increases the risk of chronic back pain, diabetes, arthritis, appendicitis, upper respiratory infections, herpes, gum disease, the common cold, and some forms of cancer. How can stress have this wide range of disabling effects? Answer: by compromising the body's immune system—the first line of defense against illness (Dhabhar, 2014; Yaribeygi, Panahi, Sahraei, Johnston, & Sahebkar, 2017).

The **immune system** is a complex surveillance system that fights bacteria, parasites, viruses, fungi, and other "nonself" substances that invade the body (Sompayrac, 1999). The system consists of more than a trillion specialized white blood cells called **lymphocytes** that originate in the bone marrow (*B cells*) and thymus (*T cells*), migrate to various organs, circulate through the bloodstream, and secrete chemical antibodies. These sharklike search-and-destroy cells protect us by patrolling the body 24 hours a day and attacking trespassers. Yet on occasion, they overreact and strike at benign material. This can result in autoimmune diseases such as multiple sclerosis, trigger allergic reactions to harmless pollen and ragweed, and cause the body to reject transplanted organs. The immune system is also equipped with large scavenger cells known as *macrophages* ("big eaters") and *natural killer cells* (NK cells) that zero in on viruses and cancerous tumors. Serving as a "sixth sense" for foreign invaders, the immune system continually renews itself. During the few seconds it takes to read this sentence, your body will have produced 10 million new lymphocytes (the immune system is illustrated in Figure 12.6).

It's clear that stress can adversely affect the immune system, at least temporarily, and that psychological interventions can help matters. The medical community used to reject the idea, but most among it are now convinced. What changed?

immune system. A biological surveillance system that detects and destroys "nonself" substances that invade the body.

lymphocytes. Specialized white blood cells that secrete chemical antibodies and facilitate the immune response.

The Link Between Stress and the Immune Response

At first, animal experiments showed that rats exposed to noise, overcrowding, or inescapable shocks, and that primates separated from their social companions, exhibit a drop in immune-cell activity compared to nonexposed animals (Coe, 1993; Moynihan & Ader, 1996). A link was also observed in human participants. Intrigued by the fact that people often become sick and die shortly after they are widowed,

FIGURE 12.6 ■ The Immune System

This is an illustration of a standard immune response in an organism infected with an allergen (here, the influenza virus) and the chain reaction that occurs, resulting in the production of antibodies that destroy the virus.

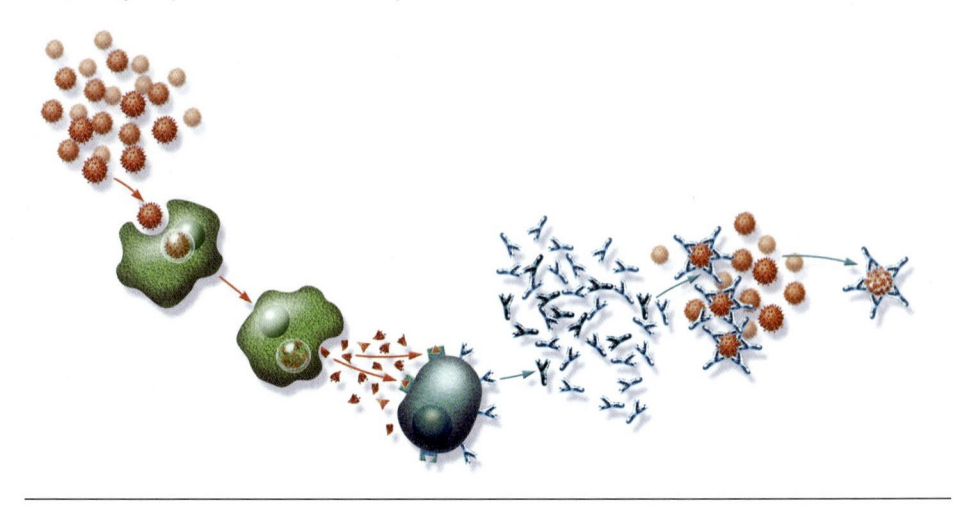

BSIP / Science Source

R. W. Barthrop and his colleagues (1977) took blood samples from 26 men and women whose spouses had just died. Compared to nonwidowed controls, these grief-stricken spouses exhibited a weakened immune response, as measured by T-cell activity. This was the first demonstration of its kind.

Many health psychologists—specializing in psychoneuroimmunology—are now studying connections among the brain, behavior, the immune system, health, and illness (Yaribeygi et al., 2017). Before we get into some of the fascinating results, let's pause for a moment and consider three of the methods that these researchers use to spy on the operations of the immune system. One method is to take blood samples from animal or human participants exposed to varying degrees of stress and simply count the numbers of lymphocytes and other white blood cells circulating in the bloodstream. A second is to extract blood, add cancerous tumor cells to the mix, and measure the extent to which the NK cells destroy the tumors. A third method is to "challenge" the living organism by injecting a foreign agent into the skin and measuring the amount of swelling that arises at the site of the injection. The more swelling there is, the more potent the immune reaction is assumed to be (Molgora, Cortez, & Colonna, 2021).

Additional studies soon revealed weakened immune responses in NASA astronauts after their reentry into the atmosphere and splashdown, in participants who were deprived of sleep for a prolonged period of time, in students in the midst of final exams, in men and women recently divorced or separated, in people caring for a family member with Alzheimer's disease, in people with a fear of snakes exposed to a live snake, and in workers who had lost their jobs (O'Leary, 1990). Even in the laboratory, participants who are given complex arithmetic problems to solve, or painful stimuli to tolerate, exhibit changes in immune-cell activity—and these changes last for one or more hours after the stress has subsided (Cohen & Herbert, 1996).

In a particularly intriguing study, Arthur Stone and others (1994) paid 48 adult volunteers to take a harmless but novel protein pill every day for 12 weeks—a substance that would lead the immune system to respond by producing an antibody. Every day, the participants completed a diary in which they reported on their moods and on experiences at work, at home, in financial matters, in leisure activities, and in relationships with their spouses, children, and friends. Participants also gave daily saliva samples that were later used to measure the amount of the antibody that was produced. The results were striking, as are their implications: The more positive events participants had in a given day, the more of the antibody that was produced. The more negative the events, the less of the antibody that was produced. In many ways, it's now clear that negative experiences—and the emotions they elicit—can weaken the immune system's ability to protect us from injuries, infections, and a wide range of illnesses (Kiecolt-Glaser, McGuire, Rubles, & Glaser, 2002). However, on the question of whether positive psychological interventions can be used to reinvigorate immune responses, more research is needed (Shields, Spahr, & Slavich, 2021).

How Stress Impacts the Immune System

We have learned that psychological states can "get into" the immune system. But how? To be sure, certain organs that play a key role in the immune system (the thymus, bone marrow, and lymph nodes) are richly endowed with nerve fibers, providing a direct pipeline to the brain.

But what explains the link between stress and the activity of lymphocytes? As illustrated in Figure 12.7, there are two possible ways this can happen. First, as described earlier, people who are stressed tend to smoke more, use more alcohol and drugs, sleep less, exercise less, and have poorer diets—behaviors that compromise the immune system. For example, one study showed that when healthy male adults were kept awake between 3:00 and 7:00 am, NK cell activity diminished but returned to normal only after a full night of uninterrupted sleep (Irwin et al., 1994). Second, stress triggers the release of adrenaline and other stress hormones into the bloodstream, and these hormones suppress lymphocyte activity (Dhabhar & McEwen, 1995). The result is a temporary lowering of the body's resistance and increased susceptibility to illness (Cohen & Williamson, 1991).

The link between stress and illness is evident. At the start of this chapter, we saw that participants who had reported high rather than low levels of everyday stress were more likely to catch a common cold after exposure to a cold virus. In one follow-up of this experiment, Sheldon Cohen and others (1998) interviewed 276 volunteers about recent life stressors, infected them with a cold virus, and then measured whether or not they developed a cold. These researchers found that some types of stress were more toxic than others. Specifically, people who had experienced *chronic* stress that lasted for more than a month (such as ongoing marital problems or unemployment) were more likely to develop a cold than those who had experienced acute short-term stress (such as having a fight with a spouse or being reprimanded at work). The longer a stressor had lasted, the more likely a person was to catch a cold. In a second follow-up, Cohen and his colleagues (2002) found that people who reacted to a stressful lab task with high levels of the stress-related hormone cortisol were more likely to get sick than those who did not react as strongly. What they discovered was that over time, stress breaks down the body's immune system.

The common-cold studies are important because they demonstrate not only that stress can weaken the immune system but also, as a result, that it can leave us vulnerable to illness. Does stress have similar effects on more serious illnesses? Can it, for example, hasten the spread of cancer? In an early test of this hypothesis, Madeline Visintainer and others (1982) implanted tumorous cancer cells into laboratory rats, some of whom were then repeatedly exposed to shocks they could not escape. After one month, 50 percent of the animals not shocked died of cancer. Yet relative to that baseline, the death rate climbed to 73 percent among those subjected to the inescapable shock. This study was among the first to show that psychological states—such as a feeling of helplessness—can influence the spread of cancer.

The growth of tumors in helpless white laboratory rats is noteworthy, but does the same principle apply to people? For obvious ethical reasons, researchers cannot fill human participants with despair or inject lethal tumors into their bodies to test the cause-and-effect chain directly. But they can examine the medical records of people whose lives are struck by tragedy. Studies of this sort have

FIGURE 12.7 ■ Pathways From Stress to Illness

Negative emotional states may cause illness in two ways: by promoting unhealthful behaviors (more alcohol, less sleep, and so on) and by triggering the release of hormones that weaken the immune system by suppressing activity of the lymphocytes.

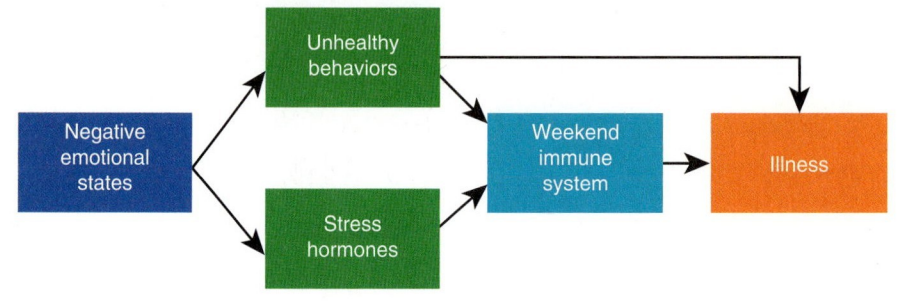

Negative emotional states → Unhealthy behaviors / Stress hormones → Weekend immune system → Illness

revealed that cancer appears more often than normal in people prone to being in a negative emotional state (Adikari et al., 2020; Sklar & Anisman, 1981). In one large-scale study, investigators looked up 2,000 male workers of the Western Electric Company in Chicago whose personalities had been assessed in 1958. At the time, test scores indicated that some of the men were low in self-esteem, unhappy, and depressed. The result? Some 20 years later, these men were more likely than their coworkers to have died of cancer (Persky, Kempthorne-Rawson, & Shekelle, 1987). Let's be clear about what these results mean. Nobody disputes the notion that cancer is caused by exposure to toxic substances and other biological factors. But individuals who are clinically depressed or under great stress have weakened immune systems—in some cases, this may result in a higher death rate from cancer and other killer diseases (Andersen, Kiecolt-Glaser, & Glaser, 1994; Pinquart & Duberstein, 2010).

Toward the end of his life, the philosopher-theologian-physician Albert Schweitzer was asked for his opinion of traditional African medicine and the witch doctors who practice it. His reply: "The witch doctor succeeds for the same reason all the rest of us succeed. Each patient carries his own doctor inside him." Robert Ornstein and David Sobel (1987) notably referred to the human brain as an "internal pharmacy dispensing a stream of powerful drugs" (p. 89). Whether it involves pharmacists or doctors, psychoneuroimmunology research suggests that the key to healthier immune function is to find ways for each of us to tap our own inner resources.

NASA astronauts work under extreme stress conditions. Given what is known about the link between stress and immunity, these astronauts' immune responses may have been in a weakened state when this photo was taken.

Eliot J. Schechter/Getty Images News via Getty Images

LEARNING CHECK

Stress Test

Don't stress as you match the terms in the left column to their closest descriptions in the right column.

1.	Type A personality	a.	A three-stage process (alarm, resistance, and exhaustion) by which the body responds to stress.
2.	Type B personality	b.	An anxiety disorder triggered by an extremely stressful event.
3.	Immune system	c.	An impatient, hard-driving, hostile pattern of behavior.
4.	General adaptation syndrome	d.	An easy-going, relaxed pattern of behavior.
5.	Posttraumatic stress disorder (PTSD)	e.	A specialized white blood cell that secretes chemical antibodies.
6.	Psychoneuroimmunology	f.	The study of the interactions among psychological factors, the nervous system, and the immune system.
7.	Lymphocyte	g.	A biological surveillance system that fights "nonself" substances that invade the body.

(Answers: 1. c; 2. d; 3. g; 4. a; 5. b; 6. f; 7. e.)

COPING WITH STRESS

> **LEARNING OBJECTIVES**
>
> Describe how our thoughts, emotions, physical activity, and social support influence stress, health, and wellness.
>
> - Discuss whether it is adaptive to block unwanted thoughts and emotions from awareness.
> - Explain whether relaxation and exercise are truly healthful.
> - Summarize the influence that feelings of control and optimism have on our health and wellness.
> - Elaborate on why friendships and other forms of social support are said to be vital to our health and wellness.

Stress is inevitable. No one can prevent it. But we can try to minimize its harmful effects on our health. To understand how some people keep their composure while others crumble under pressure, it is useful to examine the coping process and ask the question: What are some adaptive ways to cope with stress?

Coping Strategies

Leaving home. Taking exams. Working long nights. Seeking employment in a competitive job market. Living in unsafe neighborhoods. Having children. Raising children. Encountering racism, discrimination, or sexism. Facing pressures to be successful. Struggling to find love. We could cope with these sources of stress in any number of ways. In each case, we may focus on solving the problem (or ignoring it), talking to friends, inviting distractions to pass the time, having a few drinks—or we could just freak out.

Problem-Focused and Emotion-Focused Coping

Richard Lazarus and Susan Folkman (1984) distinguished two general types of coping strategies. The first is *problem-focused coping*, designed to reduce stress by overcoming the problem. Difficulties in school? Study harder, hire a tutor, or reduce your workload. Relationship on the rocks? Talk it out or see a counselor. Problems at work? Talk to your boss or look for another job. The goal is to attack the source of your stress. A second approach is *emotion-focused coping*, in which one tries to manage the emotional turmoil, perhaps by learning to live with the problem. If you're struggling at school, at work, or in a relationship, you can keep a stiff upper lip and ignore the situation or make the best of it. People probably take an active problem-focused approach when they think they can overcome a stressor but fall back on an emotion-focused approach when they see the problem as out of their control.

An emotion-focused strategy that people often use is to block stressful thoughts and feelings from awareness, called *thoughtful suppression*. This strategy can have a peculiar and paradoxical effect. Daniel Wegner (1994) conducted a series of experiments in which he had people say whatever came to mind into a microphone—and he told half of them not to think about a white bear. Wegner found that people could not keep the image from popping to mind. What's more, he found that when permitted later to think about a white bear, those who had earlier tried to suppress the image were unusually preoccupied with it, providing evidence of a "rebound" effect. It's difficult to follow the command "Don't think about it"—and the harder you try, the less likely you are to succeed. The solution: focused self-distraction. When people were told to imagine a tiny red Volkswagen whenever the forbidden white bear intruded into consciousness, the rebound effect vanished (Wenzlaff & Wegner, 2000).

What do white bears and red cars have to do with coping? Lots. When people try to force stressful thoughts or painful sensations out of awareness, they are doomed to fail. In fact, the problem may worsen. That's where focused self-distraction comes in. In a study of pain tolerance, Delia Cioffi and James Holloway (1993) had participants put a hand into a bucket of ice-cold water and keep it there until they could no longer bear the pain—a bit more challenging than the "Ice Bucket Challenge," which raised more than $155 million to raise awareness of amyotrophic lateral sclerosis, more commonly known as ALS. One group was instructed to avoid thinking about the sensation. A second group was told to form a mental picture of their room at home. Afterward, participants who had coped through suppression were slower to recover from the pain than were those who used focused self-distraction. To manage stress—whether it's caused by physical pain, a strained romance, final exams, or problems at work—distraction ("think about lying on the beach") is a better coping strategy than mere suppression ("don't think about the dentist's drill").

It may be particularly maladaptive to keep secrets and hold in strong emotions. More than a hundred years ago, Breuer and Freud (1895) theorized that emotional inhibition, or what they called *strangulated affect*, can cause mental illness. Current studies suggest it may be physically taxing as well. Phillip Quartana and John Burns (2010) randomly assigned 201 participants to conditions in which participants completed a mental arithmetic task and were instructed or not instructed (control) to suppress their emotion. Given that all participants completed the same arithmetic task, we may expect physiological responses to be the same across conditions. But physiological recordings using systolic blood pressure revealed that participants had a greater cardiovascular response when they tried to inhibit their feelings (emotional suppression) than when they did not. Physiologically, the effort to suppress the display of emotion backfired.

Relaxation

There are also ways to manage the physical symptoms of stress through relaxation. One popular technique is *relaxation*. Years ago, cardiologist Herbert Benson (1975) recruited experienced meditators for a study and fitted them with various physiological measurement devices—including catheters in the veins and arteries. Participants spent 20 minutes in a quiet resting state, then meditated, then returned to a normal state. There were no observable changes in participants' posture or level of physical activity. But the physiological results were striking. While meditating, participants consumed 17 percent less oxygen and produced less carbon dioxide. Breathing slowed from 14 or 15 breaths per minute to 10 or 11 breaths per minute. Blood tests showed there was a marked drop in the amount of lactate, a chemical typically associated with anxiety. Finally, brain-wave patterns were slower than those normally found in the waking state.

According to Benson, who went on to establish the Institute for Mind Body Medicine at Harvard Medical School, anyone can be taught this "relaxation response." Try it. Sit quietly and comfortably, close your eyes, and relax all the muscles from your feet to your face. Then breathe deeply through the nose, and each time you exhale, silently utter some word (such as "one... one... one..."). As you proceed, let your mind drift freely. If anxiety-provoking thoughts pop into mind, refocus your attention on the word you are chanting and stay calm. Repeat this exercise once or twice a day, for 10 to 20 minutes. Says Benson (1993), "By practicing two basic steps—the repetition of a sound, word, phrase, prayer, or muscular activity; and a passive return to the repetition whenever distracting thoughts recur—you can trigger a series of physiological changes that offer protection against stress" (p. 256).

Meditative relaxation can be powerfully effective to reduce stress. In one study, Friedman and Ulmer (1984) randomly assigned hundreds of heart attack patients to one of two treatment groups. In one group, they received standard medical advice on drugs, exercise, work, and diet. In the second

Try not to think of a white bear, and this image is likely to intrude on your consciousness with remarkable frequency.

Alain Pons/PhotoAlto Agency RF Collections via Getty Images

group, they were also counseled on how to relax, slow down their pace, smile more, and take time to enjoy the moment. After three years, the relaxation patients had suffered only half as many repeat heart attacks as did those in the control group. In another study, Deepak Chopra and his colleagues found that relaxation also fortifies the immune system. They evaluated meditation as a relaxation technique and found that it helped regulate the stress response by suppressing chronic inflammation and maintaining a healthy gut-barrier function (Househam, Peterson, Mills, & Chopra, 2017). This result offers hope that we can keep ourselves immunologically protected in the face of stress using relaxation techniques we could follow—techniques that are quite accessible and can be found on YouTube.

Physical Activity

Another way to manage stress is through *aerobic exercise*—sustained, vigorous physical activity designed to build heart and lung capacity and enhance the body's use of oxygen. Walking, running, swimming, bicycling, cross-country skiing, and dancing are ideal forms of aerobic exercise. The health benefits seem clear. One large-scale study showed that men who burned at least 2,000 calories a week through exercise lived longer than those who were less active (Paffenbarger, Hyde, Wing, & Hsieh, 1986). A more recent study of both men and women showed that even a moderate amount of exercise is associated with increased longevity (Rennemark et al., 2018).

Don't jump from these correlations to the causal conclusion that if you start running, you'll live longer. It is possible, for example, that people who exercise regularly are also more health conscious about what they eat, wearing seat belts, not smoking, and other factors that promote longevity. Still, the effects of exercise on physical health and wellness are extensive. Research shows that exercise strengthens the heart, lowers blood pressure, aids in the metabolism of carbohydrates and fats, boosts self-esteem, elevates mood, and improves cognitive functioning (Forbes, Fichera, Rogers, & Sutton, 2017; Warburton, Nicol, & Bredin, 2006). In a review of the research literature, Laura Mandolesi and colleagues (2018) showed that physical exercise has benefits that are more than just biological (e.g., increased cerebral blood flow, spatial and motor ability, and healthier cardiovascular functioning) but also psychological (greater well-being, emotional stability, positive body image, and sexual satisfaction; decreased anxiety, depression, tension, and even phobias). Other studies have shown that physical fitness can also soften the toxic effects of stress on health and wellness (Schultchen et al., 2019; Stults-Kolehmainen & Sinha, 2014).

The "Self-Healing Personality"

For years, psychologists have speculated about specific correlations between personality traits and illness. People who are anxious are doomed to get ulcers, we're told, just as "angry types" are prone to headaches, "depressives" are prone to cancer, "weak and dependent types" suffer from asthma, and "workaholics" die of heart attacks. In light of work on psychology and the immune system, others have considered the alternative possibility that there's a generic "disease-prone personality" consisting of a cluster of negative emotional states. According to this view, anger, anxiety, hostility, and depression all lead us to complain of bodily ailments (Watson & Pennebaker, 1989) and perhaps put us at risk for a whole range of illnesses (Friedman & Booth-Kewley, 1987). Whether the links are specific or general is a matter of dispute. However, most health researchers believe that certain traits are healthier and more adaptive than others (Bronchain, Raynal, & Chabrol, 2020)—that there is, in essence, a "self-healing personality" (Friedman, 1991).

Hardiness

Stress affects people differently, an observation that led Suzanne Kobasa (1979) to wonder why some of us are more resilient than others. Kobasa studied 200 business executives who were under stress. Many said they were frequently sick, affirming the link between stress and illness; others had managed to stay healthy. The two groups were similar in terms of age, education, job status, income, and ethnic and religious background. But from various tests, it was clear that they differed in their attitudes toward themselves, their jobs, and the people in their lives. On the basis of these differences, Kobasa identified a personality style that she called **hardiness** and concluded that hardy people have three characteristics: (a) *commitment*, a sense of purpose with regard to work, family, and other domains; (b) *challenge*, an

hardiness. A personality style that is characterized by commitment, challenge, and control. Hardiness acts as a buffer against stress.

Being optimistic or pessimistic can affect how you see the world.
iStock.com/NiseriN

openness to new experiences and a desire to embrace change; and (c) *control*, the belief that one has the power to influence important future outcomes.

In general, research supports the point that hardiness acts as a buffer against stress (Funk, 1992)—and that control is the active ingredient. Studies have shown that the harmful effects of noise, crowding, heat, and other stressors are reduced when people think they can exert control over these aspects of their environment. Thus, rats exposed to electric shock are less likely to develop ulcers if they are trained to know they can avoid it; children awaiting a doctor's injection cope better when they're prepared with a pain-reducing cognitive strategy; nursing home residents become healthier and more active when they're given more control over daily events; and patients with cancer, AIDS, and coronary heart disease are better adjusted, emotionally, when they think that they can influence the course of their illness (Abedi, Salimi, Feizi, & Safari, 2013; Farley, 2019).

Optimism and Pessimism

A second important trait in the self-healing personality is optimism, a generalized tendency to expect positive outcomes. Are you an optimist or a pessimist? Do you see the proverbial glass as half empty or as half full? Do you expect good things to happen, or do you tend to believe in Murphy's Law, that if something can go wrong, it will? By asking questions like these, Michael Scheier and Charles Carver (1985) categorized college students along this dimension and found that dispositional optimists reported fewer symptoms of illness during the semester than did pessimists. Correlations between optimism and health are common. Other studies have shown that optimists are more likely to take a problem-focused approach to coping with stress; complete a rehabilitation program for alcoholism; and make a quicker, fuller recovery from coronary artery bypass surgery (Scheier & Carver, 1992). In a study of 1,306 healthy adult men from the Boston area, those reporting high levels of optimism rather than pessimism were half as likely to have coronary heart disease 10 years later (Kubzansky, Sparrow, Vokonas, & Kawachi, 2001).

In the book *Learned Optimism*, Martin Seligman (1991) argues that optimism and pessimism are rooted in our "explanatory styles"—in the ways we explain good and bad events. Based on a large number of studies, Seligman described the typical pessimist as someone who attributes failure to factors that are internal ("It was my fault"), permanent ("I'm washed up"), and global ("I'm bad at everything")—and success to factors that are external ("I lucked out"), temporary ("The task was easy"), and specific ("It was my strength"). This explanatory style breeds despair and low self-esteem. In contrast, the typical optimist is someone who makes the opposite attributions. According to Seligman, the optimist blames failure on factors that are external, temporary, and specific, while crediting success to factors that are internal, permanent, and global—an explanatory style that fosters hope, effort, and a high regard for oneself. Do *you* interpret events as an optimist or a pessimist? See for yourself in this chapter's "Try This!" feature.

TRY THIS!

Optimist or Pessimist?

Do you interpret events as an optimist or a pessimist? To find out, **TRY THIS:** Imagine the situations described below and in each case identify cause A or B—whichever you think is the more likely. When you've finished, count the number of points you earned (in parentheses after each question). A score of 0 indicates a high degree of pessimism; a score of 8 indicates a high degree of optimism.

1. You forget your significant other's birthday:
   A. I'm not good at remembering birthdays. (0)
   B. I was preoccupied with other things. (1)

2. You stop a crime by calling the police:
   A. A strange noise caught my attention. (0)
   B. I was alert that day. (1)

3. You were extremely healthy all year:
   A. Few people around me were sick, so I wasn't exposed. (0)
   B. I made sure I ate well and got enough rest. (1)

4. You fail an important examination:
   A. I wasn't as smart as the others taking the exam. (0)
   B. I didn't prepare for it well. (1)

5. You ask someone to dance, and the person says no:
   A. I am not a good enough dancer. (0)
   B. The person I asked doesn't like to dance. (1)

6. You gain weight over the holidays and you can't lose it:
   A. Diets don't work in the long run. (0)
   B. The diet I tried didn't work. (1)

7. You win the lottery:
   A. It was pure chance. (0)
   B. I picked the right numbers. (1)

8. You do extremely well in a job interview:
   A. I felt extremely confident during the interview. (0)
   B. I interview well. (1)

In the course of a lifetime, everyone has setbacks. Do optimists weather the storms better? Are they happier, healthier, and more successful? Do they have, in the words of Alan McGinnis (1987), "the gift for turning stumbling blocks into stepping stones" (p. 16)? To find out, Christopher Peterson and others (1988) collected personal essays that were written in the 1940s by 99 men who had just graduated from Harvard, and they analyzed these materials to determine what each subject's explanatory style was in his youth. Were these men optimists or pessimists? What eventually happened to them? Their health at age 60 was predictable from their explanatory styles 35 years earlier. Young optimists were healthier than young pessimists later in life. How can this result be explained? There are two possibilities: One is biological, the other behavioral.

In studies that support a biological explanation, researchers have found that pessimists exhibit a weaker immune-system response to stress than optimists (Conversano et al., 2010; Dantzer, Cohen, Russo, & Dinan, 2018). In a study supporting a behavioral explanation, Peterson and his colleagues (1988) scored the explanatory styles of 1,528 healthy young adults from some questionnaires they had filled out between 1936 and 1940. After 50 years, the pessimists (specifically, those who made global rather than specific attributions for bad events) were more likely to have died an accidental or violent death.

There's an old saying "While there's life, there's hope." It's possible that the opposite is also true: "While there's hope, there's life." In a remarkable illustration of this point, Susan Everson and others (1996) studied 2,428 middle-aged men in Finland. Based on the extent to which they agreed with two simple statements ("I feel that it is impossible to reach the goals I would like to strive for" and "The future seems hopeless, and I can't believe that things are changing for the better"), the men were initially classified as having a high, medium, or low sense of hopelessness. When the investigators checked the death records roughly six years later, they found that the more hopeless the men were at the start, the more likely they were to have died of various causes—even when the men were otherwise equated for their age and prior health status. Compared to those who were low in hopelessness, the highs were more than twice as likely to die from cancer and four times more likely to die of cardiovascular disease (illustrated in Figure 12.8).

As usual, we should be cautious in interpreting correlations—in this case, between optimism, pessimism, and longevity. Assuming that optimism is adaptive, however, and that it's better to be safe than sorry, Seligman (1991) believes that pessimists can be retrained—not through "mindless devices like whistling a happy tune" but by learning a new set of cognitive skills. According to Seligman, people can train themselves to make optimistic explanations by following three steps:

1. Think about situations of adversity (losing in a sports competition, a friend's not returning your calls).

2. Consider the way you normally explain these events, and if it is pessimistic ("I always choke under pressure," "My friend does not really care about me"), then...

3. Dispute these explanations by looking closely at the facts ("My opponent played a great game," "My friend has been very busy").

Practice this exercise over and over again. You may find that changing a pessimistic outlook is like breaking a bad habit. Chances are, it will be worth the effort, as "positive expectations can be self-fulfilling" (Peterson, 2000).

FIGURE 12.8 ■ Hopelessness and the Risk of Death

Among middle-aged men in Finland, those who were initially high rather than low in hopelessness were more likely to die within six years—overall, from cancer, and from cardiovascular disease. On the same measures of mortality, those who were moderate in hopelessness fell between the two extremes.

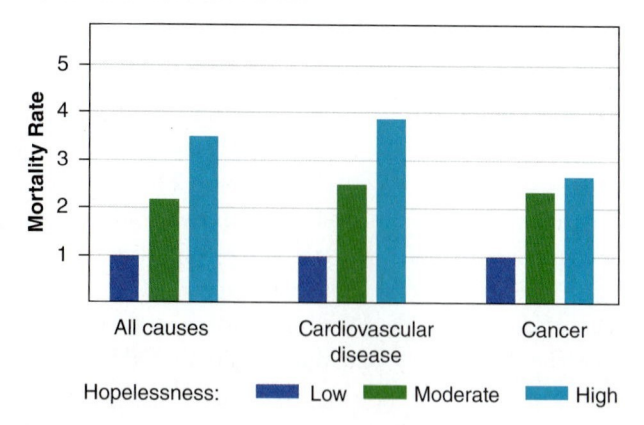

Social Support

We hear it all the time: No one is an island, human beings are social animals, people need people, and to get by you need a little help from your friends. Is all this true? Do close family ties, lovers, buddies, community support groups, and relationships at work serve as a buffer against stress? The truth is, yes. An overwhelming amount of evidence now shows that **social support** has therapeutic effects on our psychological and physical well-being (Reblin & Uchino, 2008; Zunic, Corcoran, & Spasic, 2020).

social support. The healthful coping resources provided by friends and other people.

The Health Benefits of Social Support

Psychiatrist David Spiegel, of the Stanford University School of Medicine, came to appreciate the value of social connections several years ago when he organized support groups for women with advanced breast cancer. The groups met weekly in 90-minute sessions to laugh, cry, share stories, and discuss ways of coping. Spiegel had fully expected the women to benefit, emotionally, from the experience. But he found something else he did not expect: These women lived an average of 18 months longer than did similar others who did not attend these groups. According to Spiegel (1993), "the added survival time was longer than any medication or other known medical treatment could be expected to provide for women with breast cancer so far advanced" (pp. 331–332).

Similar discoveries were also made by other researchers. In one study, Lisa Berkman and Leonard Syme (1979) surveyed 7,000 residents of Alameda County, California; conducted a nine-year follow-up of mortality rates, and found that the more social contacts people had, the longer they lived. In fact, those who lived alone, had very few close friends or relatives, and did not participate in community groups died at a rate two to five times greater than those with more extensive social networks. This was true of both men and women, young and old, rich and poor, and people from all racial and ethnic backgrounds. James House and his colleagues (1988) then studied 2,754 adults interviewed during visits to their doctors. He found that the most socially active men were two to three times less likely to die within 9 to 12 years than those of similar age who were more isolated. Socially active women were almost two times less likely to die. According to House, social isolation, statistically, is as predictive of early death as smoking or high cholesterol. A review of more recent findings substantiates such claims that social isolation can have harmful effects on our health (Rico-Uribe et al., 2018).

Research findings like these are now common. People who are married are generally more likely than people who are unmarried to survive cancer for five years (Aizer et al., 2013); people who have a heart attack are less likely to have a second one if they're living with someone than if they live alone (Dupre & Nelson, 2016). Social support can even act as a "buffer" to diminish the negative effects of racial discrimination among Black women (Paradies et al., 2015; Seawell, Cutrona, & Russell, 2014) and to enhance the connectedness of the LGBTQ+ and transgender or gender nonconforming (TGNC) communities by acting as a "buffer" against external stigmatization, prejudice, and discrimination (Pflum, Testa, Balsam, Goldblum, & Bongar, 2015; Trujillo, Perrin, Sutter, Tabaac, & Benotsch, 2017). Based on a review of 81 studies, Bert Uchino and others (1996) concluded that in times of stress, social support lowers blood pressure, suppresses the secretion of stress hormones, and strengthens immune responses.

Our interactions on social media have a powerful effect on our self-beliefs and health. Overall, the results are mixed (Pantic, 2014). In a study evaluating 100 Facebook users at York University, Soraya Mehdizadeh (2010) showed that "individuals with lower self-esteem are more active online in terms of having more self-promotional content (e.g., selfies, photos) on their [social media] profiles" (p. 357). Amy Gonzales and Jeffrey Hancock (2011), by contrast, found positive effects of Facebook use, with selective presentation of one's self on Facebook positively impacting self-esteem. Two competing theories seem to explain these mixed findings. According to the *objective self-awareness theory* (Duval & Wicklund, 1972), awareness of the self may lead to lower self-esteem. From this view, researchers warn that visiting one's own profile page to view posted photographs, biographical data, status updates, and so on may lead to lower self-esteem, either in the short term or the long term. However, according to the *hyperpersonal model*, presentation of oneself in a positive light may

Today, we are more connected than ever because of social media, extending the reach of our social groups and support networks.

iStock.com/ViewApart

have a positive effect on one's impressions of oneself. In this view, users of online platforms have more time to select, emphasize, and present only the most positive aspects of themselves, thereby leading to higher self-esteem. This pattern of findings is similar to findings for mental health, with positive interactions and connectedness on social media related to lower levels of depression and anxiety, whereas negative interactions and connectedness on social media are related to higher levels of depression and anxiety (Seabrook, Kern, & Rickard, 2016).

Our social connections can be therapeutic for many reasons. Friends encourage us to get out, exercise, eat regularly, or seek professional help. Emotionally, friends offer sympathy and reassurance in times of stress. Perhaps having a good friend around boosts our confidence, self-esteem, and sense of security. On an intellectual level, someone to talk to provides a sounding board, new perspectives, and advice as we struggle to solve problems. There is, however, a vital exception to this rule. Of all the social networks that support us, romantic partnerships, as in marriage, are the most powerful. But while those who are happily married tend to live longer than those who are single or divorced, marital conflict breeds stress, elevated blood pressure, ulcers, depression, alcohol and drug abuse, changes in immune function, and other unhealthy or undesired effects (Robles, Slatcher, Trombello, & McGinn, 2014; Yang & Schuler, 2009). Although it's important to talk about upsetting experiences as well, communicating, particularly in a positive or uplifting way, helps us sort things out in our own minds (Chichirez & Purcărea, 2018).

Finally, religion provides a deeply important source of social and emotional support for many people. Currently more than six billion people in the world belong to hundreds of religions—the most popular, in order, being Christianity, Islam, Hinduism, and Buddhism (Judaism and others have much fewer adherents). Only about 16 percent of the world's population is not affiliated with a religious group (Pew Research Center, 2012). Is there a link between religiosity and health? This is an intriguing question. On the one hand, population surveys suggest that people who regularly attend religious services live longer than those who do not (Gillum, King, Obisesan, & Koenig, 2008; Koenig, 2012). When you think about it, this correlation may make some sense. Religious faith may fill people with hope and optimism rather than despair, offer relaxation in prayer, provide a community of social support to prevent isolation, and promote a safe and healthy way of life by discouraging such toxic habits as drinking and smoking. In analyzing 30 years of health data from 2,600 California adults, for example, William Strawbridge and others (2001) found that men and women who regularly attend religious services drink less, smoke less, and exercise more. On the other hand, some researchers note that the correlations between religiosity and longevity are modest and can be interpreted in different ways. For example, it's possible that nonsmokers, teetotalers, and others who abstain from unhealthful behaviors are more likely to adopt religion as part of their lives than smokers, drinkers, and risk takers—that their survival comes from who they are, not from their attendance at religious services (Ten Kate, de Koster, & van der Waal, 2017).

What's Your Prediction?

The health benefits of social support show just how important it is to connect with people. Are there drawbacks to an active social life? Is it possible that the more people we interact with in a day—such as family, friends, classmates, teammates, coworkers, and neighbors—the more exposed we are to catch a cold or flu? Natalie Hamrick and others (2002) asked 18- to 30-year-old adults about recent stressful events and about their social lives and then had them keep a health diary for three months. Based on past research, they expected that participants who were under high stress would get sick more than those under low stress. But what about people with high versus low levels of social contact? Would their social connections make them vulnerable or protect them? Make a prediction. According to the

FIGURE 12.9 ■ Social Connections and Life Stress

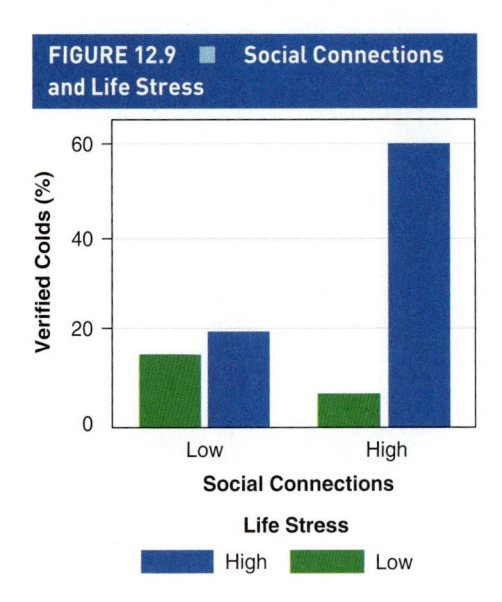

results, the answer is, it depends. Figure 12.9 shows that for people under low stress, social connections did not matter. For people under high stress, however, those with high levels of social contact were *more* likely to catch a cold or flu. It's healthy to be popular... except, perhaps, during flu season.

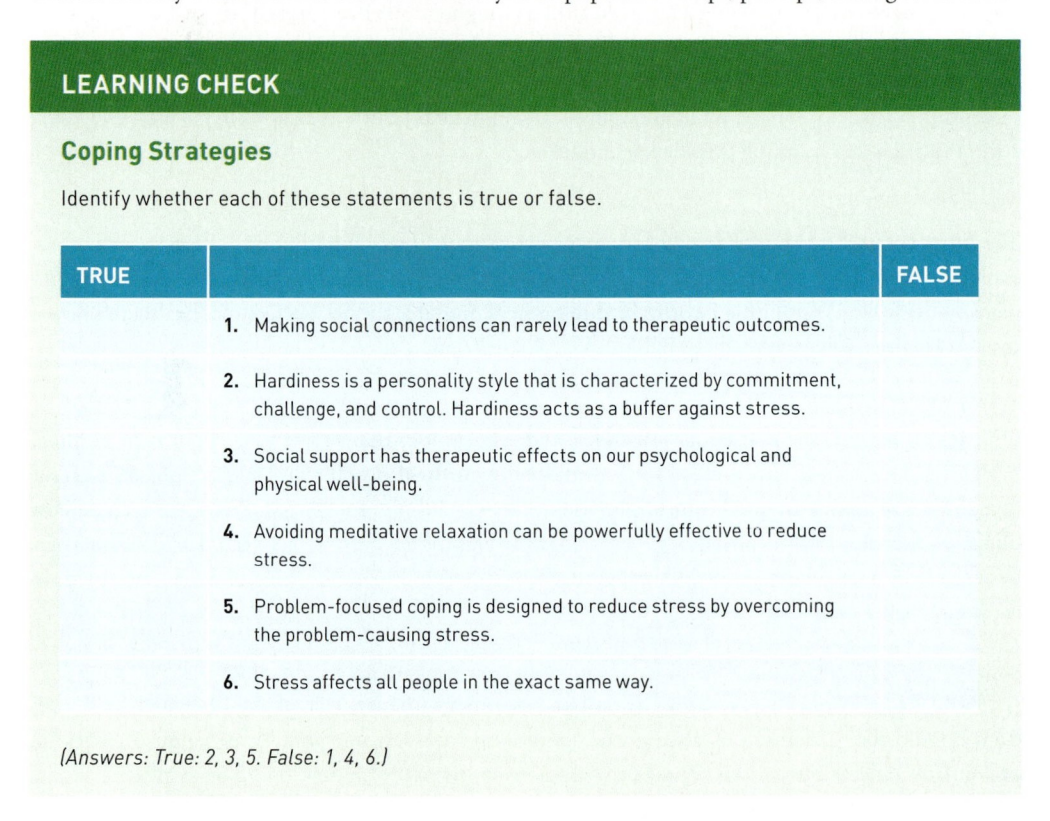

LEARNING CHECK

Coping Strategies

Identify whether each of these statements is true or false.

TRUE		FALSE
	1. Making social connections can rarely lead to therapeutic outcomes.	
	2. Hardiness is a personality style that is characterized by commitment, challenge, and control. Hardiness acts as a buffer against stress.	
	3. Social support has therapeutic effects on our psychological and physical well-being.	
	4. Avoiding meditative relaxation can be powerfully effective to reduce stress.	
	5. Problem-focused coping is designed to reduce stress by overcoming the problem-causing stress.	
	6. Stress affects all people in the exact same way.	

(Answers: True: 2, 3, 5. False: 1, 4, 6.)

Thinking Like a Psychologist About Health, Stress, and Wellness

Health is a concern for all of us. In medical settings, health psychologists are learning what leads people to become stressed, the effects of stress on health, and some effective ways for us to cope with problems. Particularly exciting developments in this area suggest that there are links among the brain, the mind, and the immune system, linking physical and mental health and bringing together psychology and medicine. Increasingly, we are also recognizing that our health and illness is not purely physical. Our health and the course of a disease are affected also by how we think, feel, and behave to stay healthy (wellness) and to manage disease (illness). Being healthy involves interactions across psychological, social, behavioral, and cultural contexts that affect our health and the health of others. The field of psychology, and in particular health psychology, is increasingly promoting a better understanding of how to manage stress, health and wellness across the lifespan in diverse settings—from schools, hospitals, and clinics to how we behave and interact in our daily lives.

This chapter has revealed just the tip of the iceberg in applying psychology for managing stress, health, and wellness. As we've learned, for a great deal of factors that affect our health, it is largely how we think of them that gives them power. How we think about stress or our beliefs about our health, for example, can have a large influence on our behavior to manage that stress or behave in healthy ways. The mind is a powerful tool. The more you know how to use it, the better off you'll be.

SUMMARY

STUDYING HEALTH AND WELLNESS

Health is state of physical, mental, and social well-being that is also affected by various psychological and sociocultural factors. Understanding health and wellness requires the conceptual framework provided by the illness-wellness continuum.

ILLNESS-WELLNESS CONTINUUM

The **illness-wellness continuum** is not a static model; it varies over time from a progressively worsening to a progressively improving state of health. Throughout our lives, we will move along this continuum. On one end of the continuum is **illness**, which is a disease or sickness over any length of time that can affect an individual. On the other end of the continuum is **wellness**, which is a physical state or condition that involves being in good physical and mental health, typically characterized by overt efforts aimed at maintaining this state or condition.

BIOPSYCHOSOCIAL AND BIOMEDICAL MODELS

The **biopsychosocial model** is a holistic perspective that illness, health, and wellness can be best explained in the interactions of biological, psychological, and social factors. This model is a more complete model for understanding health. The **biomedical model** is the perspective that health and illness can be explained solely on the basis of biological dysfunction.

HEALTH BELIEF MODEL

Our **health beliefs** (the knowledge, attitudes, and expectations that people have about their personal health and how that health is cared for) can influence our **health behaviors** (the actions people take to achieve and maintain good health, promote wellness, and prevent illness). Examples include how much we exercise, how balanced our diet is, and the amount of sleep we get each day. This interplay between health behaviors and health beliefs can be understood in a multitude of ways that fit within the health belief model.

ILLNESS PREVENTION AND HEALTH PROMOTION

A central focus in health psychology is on both treatment (the left side of the illness-wellness continuum) and the prevention of disease (the continuum from left to right). When applied to health, **prevention** reflects the actions we take to stop a given disease from developing or to avoid a disease entirely. While prevention of disease is an important step toward healthy living, psychologists focus also on the promotion and maintenance of good health, called **health promotion**.

MIND OVER MATTER: THE PLACEBO EFFECT

It is common for people to think that placebo effects are all in the mind, although research has shown that placebos can influence a wide range of physical changes. Placebos have been used to treat allergies, headaches, insomnia, constipation, skin rashes, upset stomachs, chronic pain, and other ailments.

STRESS AND HEALTH

Researchers have taken a growing interest in **health psychology**, which applies psychology to the promotion of physical health and the prevention and treatment of illness. Among the influences on health, stress is especially important.

THE SOURCES OF STRESS
Stress is an unpleasant state of arousal that occurs when we perceive that an event threatens our ability to cope. Catastrophes are one major type of stressor. **Posttraumatic stress disorder (PTSD)** among combat veterans and other trauma victims produces long-lasting symptoms ranging from sleeplessness to social withdrawal.

According to one view, major life events such as marriage, divorce, or promotion cause stress. Research shows a link between negative life events and health problems, but no such connection has been found for positive events. It's also important to recognize that people interpret events differently.

Daily hassles, or microstressors, can have even more impact than major life events. Job pressures may cause burnout. Environmental factors such as crowding also play a role.

THE PHYSIOLOGICAL EFFECTS OF STRESS
Selye saw the body's response to stress as a **general adaptation syndrome** marked by the stages of alarm, resistance, and exhaustion. This model suggests that stress may be adaptive in the short term but a threat to health in the long term. According to Sapolsky, the problem for humans is that although the stress response is designed for occasional emergencies, psychological stress occurs often and for prolonged periods of time.

Other researchers have linked stress to coronary heart disease (CHD). People with a hostile **Type A personality** make up a greater percentage of those with CHD than people with a more relaxed **Type B personality**.

THE IMMUNE SYSTEM
Stress also compromises the **immune system**, which relies on specialized white blood cells called **lymphocytes** and other types of cells to fight bacteria, viruses, and other invaders. Stress alters the activity of the various immune-system cells and can increase the likelihood of illness by weakening resistance. The new field of **psychoneuroimmunology** studies this interplay between the mind and the immune system.

COPING WITH STRESS

Although we cannot prevent stress, we can minimize its effects on our health by means of active coping strategies.

COPING STRATEGIES
Coping strategies can be divided broadly into problem-focused coping (overcoming the source of the problem) and emotion-focused coping (managing the emotional turmoil). Thought suppression, an emotion-focused strategy, doesn't usually work unless accompanied by focused self-distraction—deliberately thinking about something else. Relaxation techniques have been shown to boost the immune system. Aerobic exercise, which correlates with longevity and physical health, may also reduce the impact of stress.

THE "SELF-HEALING PERSONALITY"
The personality style known as **hardiness**, which includes a strong sense of control, seems to act as a buffer against stress. Another important trait is optimism, which has been linked with health and a

strong immune response. Optimism and pessimism are often related to explanatory style, and some researchers believe that people can train themselves to use optimistic explanations.

Social Support

Social support from friends and family members can reduce stress and promote health. Research shows that people with more social contacts survive illness better and live longer. Correlational research also suggests that people who are involved in religion live longer and healthier lives.

CRITICAL THINKING

Thinking Critically About Health, Stress, and Wellness

1. Discuss why it is important to understand health in terms of a continuum from illness to wellness. How might this conception of health help you to live a healthier, higher-quality life? Support your position with empirical evidence.

2. Distinguish between positive and negative stressors. If both types of life events can result in stress, then why are negative life events, but not positive ones, related to illness?

3. Identify several specific actions that you could implement in your life right now to help you reduce or cope with stress. Why would these actions work?

4. The Bloomberg Healthiest Country Index is published every year. Using a basic Google search, you can find the most recent rankings in this index. In 2019, Spain was ranked the healthiest country in the world; the U.S. ranked 35th. Consider the cultural context of health. What type of regional or cultural factors may help account for why some countries are regarded as healthier than others? Why do you think the U.S. ranks so low?

5. Discuss the implications of the research concerning the impact of stress on the immune system, as well as research concerning coping with stress, to current systems of health care. How could you apply this research to improve the quality of care in hospitals, nursing homes, and the like?

CAREER CONNECTION: PUBLIC SERVICE

Correctional Treatment Specialist

Correctional treatment specialists, also known as case managers or correctional counselors, with a degree in psychology will put their knowledge of human behavior to work with inmates, probationers, and parolees. These specialists may advise inmates directly and typically evaluate them using questionnaires and psychological tests. For inmates approaching probation or parole, they may participate in developing rehabilitation plans, which often includes facilitating education and training programs to help improve probationers' job skills. They monitor inmates, track behaviors, coordinate with other professionals or therapists, and make recommendations to the courts.

When inmates become eligible for parole, a review board uses the case reports written by correctional treatment specialists to evaluate their petitions. A parole officer will then keep detailed written accounts of each parolee's progress. They may also help connect released inmates and their families with counseling services, locate substance abuse or mental health treatment opportunities, find adequate housing, or assist with job placement.

Key skills for this role that psychology students learn to develop:

- Use of scientific reasoning to interpret psychological phenomena
- Adoption of values that build community at local, national, and global levels
- Self-efficacy and self-regulation

KEY TERMS

biomedical model (p. 493)
biopsychosocial model (p. 493)
distress (p. 505)
dualism (p. 493)
etiology (p. 495)
eustress (p. 505)
general adaptation syndrome (p. 504)
hardiness (p. 513)
health (p. 491)
health behaviors (p. 494)
health beliefs (p. 494)
health promotion (p. 496)
health psychology (p. 492)
illness (p. 492)

illness-wellness continuum (p. 492)
immune system (p. 507)
lymphocytes (p. 507)
mind-body relationship (p. 493)
monism (p. 493)
posttraumatic stress disorder (PTSD) (p. 502)
prevention (p. 495)
psychoneuroimmunology (p. 491)
social support (p. 517)
stress (p. 501)
Type A personality (p. 506)
Type B personality (p. 506)
wellness (p. 492)

13 PSYCHOLOGICAL DISORDERS

Artokoloro / Alamy Stock Photo

LEARNING OBJECTIVES

Distinguish among biological, social, and cultural factors that contribute to psychological disorders.

Synthesize the biological and psychological explanations of depressive disorder.

Understand the causes of an anxiety disorder.

Understand how exposure to a traumatic or stressful event can result in the development of post-traumatic stress disorder (PTSD).

Describe the purpose of a compulsive behavior for persons with obsessive-compulsive disorder.

Recognize the differences between a manic phase and a depressed phase.

Recognize the features that personality disorders have in common.

Understand the range of symptoms that persons with schizophrenia experience.

Define what it means to "dissociate," and connect that definition with the disorder; appreciate the perspectives of believers and skeptics.

WHAT'S YOUR PREDICTION: HOW COMMON ARE PSYCHOLOGICAL DISORDERS?

The Situation

For clinical psychologists, it's important to know the mental health status of the nation's population and the kinds of problems most in need of attention. This information helps clinicians determine, and plan for, resources. How common are psychological disorders? Are some segments of the population more "at risk" than others? And how can we make estimates that can be trusted?

Imagine that, as a person with extensive experience at conducting personal interviews, you get a call from the Substance Abuse and Mental Health Services Administration (SAMHSA). The center is planning a massive nationwide study to determine the prevalence of psychological disorders in the United States. SAMHSA recruits you to help conduct the interviews.

Using a standard set of questions, you and other interviewers collect data from a total of 17,109 adolescents aged 12–17 years (representing 25 percent of the total interviews) and 50,833 adults aged 18 and older (25 percent of the total interviews are of those aged 18–25 years and 50 percent are of those aged 26 or older) (SAMHSA, 2016). All participants have fixed addresses, so homeless persons, those on active-duty military service, those who are hospitalized, and those in assisted living facilities are excluded. You interview adolescents about substance abuse disorder and any episode of major depression in the past year. You interview adults about substance abuse disorder, any episode of major depression, and any mental illness in the past year. After you complete each interview, you send the results to your regional supervisor, who checks to make sure that all the necessary questions were asked and answered. If responses are incomplete or unclear, the forms are returned for you to go back and collect the missing information. If responses are complete, the interview data are sent to the national office, where all the results are compiled and analyzed.

Make a Prediction

Think carefully about the disorders listed above. How prevalent are they? Are men and women equally at risk? For each disorder below, predict the percentages of men and women (from 0 to 100) who have ever suffered from the disorder during their past year.

TYPES OF DISORDER	ADULTS	ADOLESCENTS
Any mental illness	____%	NA
Major depressive episode	____%	____%
Substance abuse disorder	____%	____%

The Results

When the responses were tallied, the results were consistent with previous research. Review the table below, and you'll find, first, that the prevalence rate for substance abuse is highest for adults, but the rate for a major depressive episode is highest for adolescents.

TYPES OF DISORDER	ADULTS	ADOLESCENTS
Any mental illness	18.3%	NA
Major depressive episode	6.7%	12.8%
Substance abuse disorder	21.7%	4.3%

What Does It All Mean?

In this 2106 study, SAMHSA conducted extensive interviews with a large national sample of respondents and provided much-needed information about the mental health status of American men and women that year. For now, three aspects of these results are worth noting.

First, the numbers for adolescents reflect a trend that clinicians have noted—depression among Gen-Z adolescents has increased since 2010, especially for females (Twenge, Joiner, Rogers, & Martin, 2017). Second, these numbers represent prevalence rates for the past year. Therefore, those who have

> suffered from a mental health issue in their lifetime might not have had a recent episode. In other words, someone might experience anxiety, depression, or substance abuse at one point in life but then recover. The third important point is that the proportion of Americans likely to have a major depressive episode in the past year is roughly 20 percent. This percentage does not include other mental health issues or substance abuse. Mental health is a greater concern than we often lead ourselves to believe or, in some cases, allow ourselves to discuss freely.
>
> In this chapter, we'll discuss these disorders, and others that are less common, in greater detail. We will look not only at their incidence in the population but also at the possible causes, symptoms, and likely outcomes.

Have you ever lost a loved one to death, only to be stricken by grief, despair, and the numb feeling that life is just not worth living? Have you ever been so nervous before making a speech or going on a date that your heart raced, your voice trembled, and your stomach tightened up? Have you ever been the victim of a car accident and blocked out the whole experience? Have you ever jumped out of bed in the middle of the night, startled by a terrifying nightmare you couldn't shake or by creaking noises you imagined were the sound of an intruder? Have you ever been haunted by a tune you kept humming and couldn't get out of your mind, no matter how hard you tried? And have you ever heard the sound of laughter as you entered a room, only to wonder for a moment if everyone was looking and laughing at *you*?

Chances are that one or more of these descriptions will ring a bell and provide you with a personal glimpse into the unhappy, disturbing, and sometimes frightening world of psychological disorders. You don't have to be "out of your mind" to have these kinds of episodes. The reality is that no one is invulnerable in times of great stress, a fact that was acutely evident in the large numbers of people who suffered anxiety, nightmares, depression, sleep loss, and other symptoms during the coronavirus pandemic (Abba-Aji et al., 2020; Ma et al., 2020; Mrklas et al., 2020; Quittkat et al., 2020). For some of us, episodes of anxiety and despair are frequent, prolonged, and intense. Based on surveys, the World Health Organization estimated that in the course of a lifetime, 47.4 percent of all Americans will suffer from one or more problems serious enough to be diagnosed as a psychological disorder (Kessler et al., 2007). In 2002, for any given one-year period, it was estimated that 19 percent would suffer from a disorder significant enough to interfere with their everyday lives or require professional help or medication (Narrow, Rae, Robins, & Regier, 2002). We now know that those percentages still hold true today, thanks to the SAMHSA (2016) results reported at the beginning of this chapter.

Surveys, such as the ones cited above, supplemented by clinical case studies, tell us that psychological disorders can be temporary. With the right normative support, "such as employment, education, and community life" (Drake & Whitley, 2014, p. 236) people can recover. In this chapter, we examine the contributing factors and effects of psychological disorders.

PSYCHOLOGICAL DISORDERS: A GENERAL OUTLOOK

LEARNING OBJECTIVES

Distinguish among biological, social, and cultural factors that contribute to psychological disorders.

- Juxtapose normal behavior with abnormal behavior.
- Discuss the medical perspective on psychological disorders.
- Determine the sociocultural connections to psychological disorders.
- Create an argument for why diagnoses are necessary.

To start, three general questions need to be considered. First, when does a person cross the invisible line between health and illness, psychology and *psychopathology*, normal and abnormal? Second, what biological and environmental factors put our psychological well-being at risk? Third, how can different problems be distinguished for the sake of providing treatment to those in need of assistance?

Defining Normal and Abnormal

Picture this. You are on a journey through a subway station in New York City. You pass by a middle-aged man in a neatly pressed blue suit who stands on a bench, arms waving, while loudly urging commuters to repent for their sins before the imminent end-of-days. On the opposite side of the dual bench, an older bearded man in a heavy wool coat lies all curled up, with his arms folded together and his eyes cast down to the ground. Standing against the black-and-white tiled wall is a woman who rocks back and forth. Simultaneously, she makes a swatting motion near her left ear, but you cannot see any evidence of a flying insect. Once on the train, you notice a man who switches his seat several times during the ride. You watch him quietly, your arms folded, headphones in your ears, taking internal notes. Based on your observations, you cannot help but wonder, are these people suffering from psychological disorders? Well, what about you? During your train ride, you focus intently on a man who—for whatever reason—could not be comfortable in any available seat. All of your resources were devoted to a stranger. Why must you spy on others? Are you paranoid?

People-watching experiences like this one demonstrate how tricky it can be to determine whether someone has a psychological disorder. To make that determination, clinicians need guidance in the form of criteria. Various criteria have been proposed over the years, and many are still being proposed—yet none has been accepted by all (Bergner & Bunford, 2017; Clark, 1999, Pierre, 2010). The criteria frequently used by clinicians is provided in the *Diagnostic and Statistical Manual of Mental Disorders*-5 (*DSM-5*; American Psychiatric Association, 2013). For a **psychological disorder**, the *DSM-5* criteria are as follows:

psychological disorder. A condition in which a person's thoughts, feelings, or behavior is judged to be dysfunctional.

1. The person experiences clinically significant disturbance in their thinking, emotional regulation, or behavior.

2. The clinically significant disturbance reflects a dysfunction in the psychological, biological, or developmental processes underlying mental functioning.

3. The clinically significant disturbance is most likely associated with significant distress in social, occupational, or other important activities.

4. The source of the disturbance resides within the person, and is not a culturally approved response to a common stressor or loss such as the death of a loved one.

5. The disturbance is not simply attributed to socially deviant behavior or conflicts that are primarily between the individual and society unless the deviance or conflict results from the clinically significant disturbance that resides within the person.

These criteria suggest some key points about a definition. One is that the term *abnormal* means more than just "different from the norm" in a statistical sense. Nobel Prize winners and Olympic gold medalists are also atypical, but most are not clinically troubled. Also, what's normative in one cultural or ethnic group may not be normative in another. This means that the definition of an abnormality is culturally dependent—consider, for example, the idea of exorcisms. A second point is that normal and abnormal are merely points along a continuum, not distinct conditions separated by a bright line. At what point should nervousness be called "anxiety," or sadness "depression"? How much pain, distress, or impairment is too much? And when it comes to people who are poverty stricken or homeless, how can we tell that their actions are not a normal response to a cruel and hostile environment? These difficult questions can be addressed only on a case-by-case basis. A third point is that certain behavior patterns are considered abnormal not because they are disabling to the individual but because they threaten the

David Blaine held his breath for 7 minutes and 8 seconds in an attempt to beat the record of 8 minutes and 58 seconds. Blaine has become famous for his extreme performances. What does this behavior reveal about him—is he normal or abnormal? What more information would you need to make such a judgment?

Astrid Stawiarz/Getty Images Entertainment via Getty Images

safety and welfare of others. The model citizen who has a well-paying job but is an abusive partner is an all-too-familiar example.

Finally, the criteria used to identify psychological disorders do not in themselves explain the source of those disorders or imply a certain form of treatment. As we'll learn, the unhealthy mind is sometimes the product of an unhealthy body, in which case the disorder may be treatable with nutrition, physical activity, and pharmaceuticals. Yet often the problem stems from deep-seated personal conflicts, bad habits, negative life experiences, daily stress, faulty processing of information, and sociocultural factors. Before describing the kinds of disorders from which so many of us suffer, let's examine these theoretical models.

Models of Abnormality

Egyptian, Chinese, Hebrew, and American historical writings have something in common—their explanations for psychological deviance are demonic possession. The Bible tells a story of King Saul who was possessed by an evil spirit. In the early beginnings of the United States, witchcraft was confused with psychological disturbance (Bartholomew & Wessely, 2002). In 1867, Paul Broca speculated that ancient skulls had holes drilled into them for the purpose of releasing evil spirits (Clower & Finger, 2001). Interestingly, it was in the 1930s that the lobotomy procedure—the insertion and sweeping motion of a sharp instrument into the frontal lobe (illustrated in Figure 13.1)—was developed and performed by Egaz Moniz to disrupt dysfunctional neural circuits (Swayze, 1995). Over 50,000 Americans had their frontal lobes stabbed and swept with a sharp instrument between 1949 and 1952 (National Public Radio, 2005). One of those patients was Rosemary Kennedy, the eldest sister of President John Kennedy. Lobotomies are no longer performed today, thanks to clinical observation, research, scientific advances, and more naturalistic perspectives—medical, psychological, and sociocultural—on abnormality.

Perspectives

Within the **medical model**, disordered thoughts, feelings, and behaviors are caused by physical disease. Today's researchers try to identify genetic links, damage to parts of the brain and nervous system, hormone

medical model. The perspective that mental disorders are caused by biological conditions and can be treated through medical intervention.

FIGURE 13.1 ■ The 10-Minute Lobotomy

The transorbital lobotomy procedure was created by Walter Freeman as a new and improved way to perform a lobotomy. The insertion of the sharp tool through the eye socket left no scars, took only 10 minutes, and could be performed as an outpatient procedure. Freeman performed his last lobotomy in 1967.

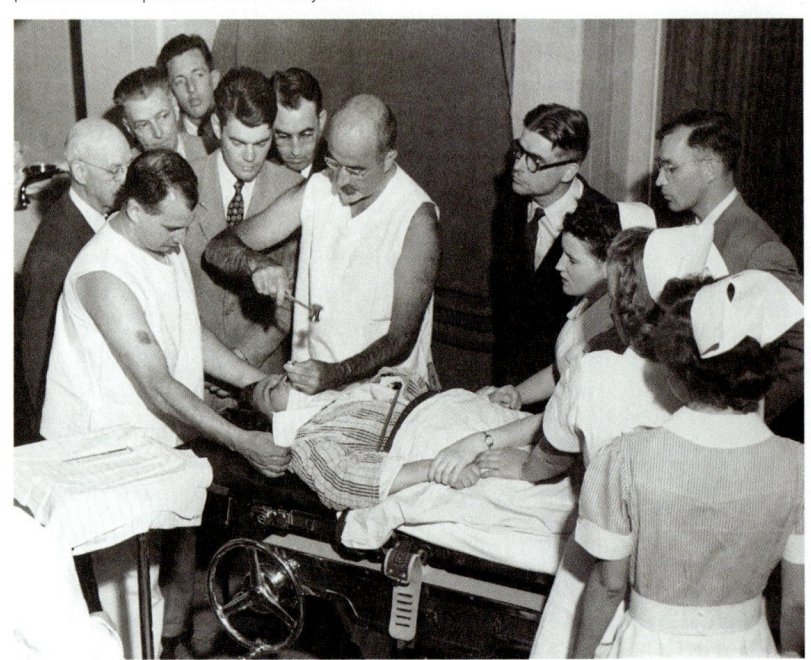

Bettmann via Getty Images

imbalances, and neurotransmitter activity that is associated with various problems. The medical approach is not without critics. In *The Myth of Mental Illness*, psychiatrist Thomas Szasz (1961) argued that mental illness is a socially defined, relative concept used to cast aside people who are deviant. Szasz (1987) charged that psychologists, psychiatrists, and other mental health experts are too quick to guard society's norms and values.

But recent advances in genetics demonstrate clearly that psychological disorders are *not* mythical—and it would be cruel to deny treatment to people whose psychological disorders have biological as well as environmental origins and consequences. Describing how a neurobiological approach helps to destigmatize psychological disorders, Nancy Andreasen (2001) says that "human sufferers should be accorded the same compassion and respect as we accord people with other illnesses such as cancer or diabetes" (p. ix).

psychological model. The perspective that mental disorders are caused and maintained by one's life experiences.

A second major approach to abnormal behavior is based on the **psychological model**. From this perspective, psychological disorders are caused and then maintained by a person's negative life experiences—in both the past and present. Examples of such experiences include prolonged illness, natural disasters, war, physical and sexual abuse, domestic violence, divorce, poverty, the death of a loved one, a lack of friendships, and persistent failure. This perspective was first born of Freud's interest in hysteria, a disorder in which the patient experiences bodily symptoms in the absence of physical damage. Today, three broad perspectives attempt to provide psychological models of abnormality. The first is psychoanalysis, which emphasizes the role of parental influences, unconscious conflicts, guilt, frustration, and an array of defense mechanisms used to ward off anxiety. According to this view, psychological disorders spring from inner conflicts so intense that they overwhelm our normal defenses. The second perspective is rooted in behaviorism and cognitive social-learning theories. In this view, abnormal behavior is a learned response to reward and punishment, further influenced by our perceptions, expectations, values, and role models. The third perspective is humanistic, which holds that mental disorders arise when we are blocked in our efforts to grow and achieve self-actualization. In this view, the self-concept is all-important.

sociocultural model. The perspective that psychological disorders are influenced by cultural factors.

The social and cultural context in which we live also affects the kinds of stresses we're exposed to, the kinds of disorders we're likely to have, and the treatment we're likely to get. Particularly impressive evidence for a **sociocultural model** comes from the fact that different disorders, or symptoms, appear in different cultures (Braveman & Gottlieb, 2014; Lopez & Guarnaccia, 2000). John Weisz and others (1993) studied behavioral and emotional problems among teenagers in the United States and Thailand. In the United States, they found that troubled teens tend to act out by bullying others, getting into fights, or running afoul of teachers. But in the predominantly Buddhist country of Thailand, troubled teens are more likely to sulk, go silent, sleep too much, or become constipated.

culture-bound syndromes. Recurring patterns of maladaptive behavior that are limited to a specific cultural group or location.

Additional evidence of sociocultural influence comes from the fact that some disorders are found almost exclusively in specific regional groups. The *DSM-5* argues that *anorexia nervosa* and *bulimia nervosa* strike primarily women of industrialized countries such as in the United States, Australia, and Japan. In these cultures, women are often bombarded with images of an impossible body ideal. This bombardment was brought to the attention of the fashion industry by women like Isabell Caro, a former French model and anti-anorexia crusader. Indeed, many women with eating disorders have negatively distorted images of their own bodies, often seeing themselves as overweight (Thompson, Heinberg, Altabe, & Tantleff-Dunn, 1999).

Medical anthropologists and psychologists have identified a number of **culture-bound syndromes** characterized by alterations in behavior. One that is particularly well known is *amok*, a brief period of brooding followed by a violent outburst, often resulting in murder. This disorder is frequently triggered by a perceived insult and is found only among men in Malaysia, Papua New Guinea, the Philippines, Polynesia, and Puerto Rico, and among the Navajo. Psychological disorders are a universal aspect of the human condition, but the forms they take may vary from one culture to the next (American Psychiatric Association, 2000; Lopez & Guarnaccia, 2000; Simons & Hughes, 1986; Tseng, 2001).

Some psychological disorders are connected to personal and developmental issues.
iStock.com/LumiNola

Combining Perspectives in a "Synthetic" Model

As you will learn in this chapter, no single perspective can fully explain the array of psychological disorders that people encounter. Whereas some problems are largely biological, and perhaps genetic, in origin, others are based more on personal and developmental experiences embedded within a context of time, place, and culture. Further complicating matters is that most mental disorders spring from a combination of factors, as when individuals who are genetically vulnerable suffer intense life stress. To understand psychological disorders, thinking in either-or terms about all the possible influences or treatment alternatives is limiting. Andreasen (2001) seeks to capture the complexity of the problem by offering a "synthetic" model of psychological disorders, one that recognizes the interaction of multiple biological, psychological, and sociocultural influences.

Diagnosis: A Necessary Step

In science, as in other pursuits, it often helps to group people, objects, and situations that share similar properties. Biologists classify animals into species and geographers split Earth into regions. Likewise, mental health professionals find it enormously useful—for the sake of prediction, understanding, and treatment—to categorize mental disorders that involve similar patterns of behavior, or syndromes. This process of grouping and naming mental disorders is referred to as **diagnosis**.

Today, the most widely used classification scheme in the United States is the American Psychiatric Association's **DSM-5** (American Psychiatric Association, 2013). Written for mental health professionals, this manual provides a comprehensive list of psychological disorders that are grouped into 19 broad categories. (Those discussed in this chapter are previewed in Table 13.1.) For each disorder, the key features and prominent symptoms are described in concrete behavioral terms. Also presented are the prevalence rates for men and women, cultural and gender factors, references used to describe the disorder, the normal age of onset, and the expected outcome. Accompanying the manual is a book with illustrative case studies and standardized interviews for use in making a diagnosis—all updated in light of recent research (Barnhill, 2014).

diagnosis. The process of identifying and grouping mental disorders with similar symptoms.

DSM-5. Acronym for the American Psychiatric Association's *Diagnostic and Statistical Manual of Mental Disorders* (5th edition).

TABLE 13.1 ■ DSM-5 Mental Disorders and Their Key Features Described in This Chapter

Depressive disorders	Disorders marked by sad, empty, or irritable mood accompanied with somatic and cognitive changes that impair functioning.
Anxiety disorders	Disorders marked by excessive fear and anxiety with related behavioral disturbances.
Trauma- and stressor-related disorders	Disorders that develop due to traumatic or stressful event exposure and/or experience. This category includes posttraumatic stress disorder.
Obsessive-compulsive and related disorders	Disorders characterized by preoccupations and repetitive behaviors or mental acts in response to said preoccupations.
Bipolar and related disorders	Disorders marked by an alternating or mixed pattern of depressive and manic mood disturbances.
Personality disorders	Long-term, inflexible, maladaptive patterns of behavior. This category includes the borderline and antisocial personality disorders.
Schizophrenia spectrum disorders	A group of psychotic disorders characterized by delusions, hallucinations, disorganized thinking, disorganized and/or diminished speech, grossly disorganized or abnormal motor behavior, reduction in emotional expression, and decreased ability to experience pleasure or participate in purposeful activities.
Dissociative disorders	Disorders in which part of one's experience is detached from consciousness. This category includes amnesia, fugue states, and dissociative identity disorder (formerly known as multiple personality disorder).

The *DSM-5*, released in 2013, is only one link in an evolving chain of diagnostic schemes and was preceded by five earlier versions. The *DSM* was first published in 1952 and was substantially revised in 1968 (*DSM-II*), 1980 (*DSM-III*), 1987 (*DSM-III-R*), 1994 (*DSM-IV*), 2000 (*DSM-IV TR*), and 2013 (*DSM-5*). The *DSM-I* listed 60 disorders, the *DSM-II* listed 145, and the *DSM-IV* had 410. Currently, the *DSM-5* lists 260 disorders. What do these shifts in the number of disorders mean? Some would say that psychologists and psychiatrists have become more sophisticated in their ability to detect and then treat problems. Others would argue that they have become overly sensitive to human frailties and imperfections—and that they "patholo-gize" everyday behaviors (Kutchins & Kirk, 1997). The proposition that teenagers who spend too much time on the Internet can be labeled "Internet addicts" may be a case in point (Griffiths, 1998).

Over the years, critics of psychiatric diagnosis have voiced three concerns. The first was that the system lacked reliability. If two mental health experts interview the same person, what are the chances that they will independently come up with the same diagnosis? Research on the earliest versions of the *DSM* revealed low levels of reliability. However, more recent versions, most notably the *DSM-5*, base classifications on observable behavior and thus provide a checklist of specific, objective items to guide the diagnosis. Furthermore, the *DSM-5* provides a discussion to help clinicians differentiate one disorder category from another. As in medicine, the system is still not perfect. But reliability estimates are higher now than in the past when proper methodology is used (Chmielewski, Clark, Bagby, & Watson, 2015; Nathan & Langenbucher, 1999; Stinchfield et al., 2015).

A second concern is that clinical judgments, like all other judgments that people make, may be biased by stereotypes about a person's gender, race, age, socioeconomic status, ethnic and cultural background, and other factors (Adeponle, Groleau, & Kirmayer, 2015; Dovidio & Fiske, 2012; Mezzich, Kleinman, Fabrega, & Parron, 1996). Gender provides a common example. In general, men and women suffer equally from mental disorders, but some specific problems are more common among men, others among women (Hartung & Widiger, 1998). Is it possible that these well-known differences influence a mental health expert's judgment?

To examine this possibility, Maureen Ford and Thomas Widiger (1989) mailed a case history of a fictitious male or female adult to 354 clinical psychologists and asked each for a diagnosis. For some, the case depicted a classic "antisocial personality," a mostly male disorder characterized by self-centered behavior and reckless disregard for rules. For other subjects, the case portrayed a "histrionic personality," a mostly female disorder characterized by excessive attention seeking, emotionality, and flirtatiousness. The result: The diagnoses that were made were clearly biased by gender. Regardless of which case history was read, the male patient was more likely to be labeled antisocial, and the female histrionic. Similar research suggests the possibility that African American patients are more often diagnosed—or misdiagnosed—as having schizophrenia than are White patients with the same general symptoms (DelBello, 2002).

Clinicians have recognized and attempted to correct for possible cultural bias in diagnosis by providing an Outline for Cultural Formulation (OCF) in the *DSM-IV* (American Psychiatric Association, 2000) and *DSM-5* (American Psychiatric Association, 2013). In addition to the OCF, the *DSM-5* provides the Cultural Formulation Interview—an outline that presents cultural context for diagnosis. Clinicians have commented that the interview is helpful in ethnic and immigrant patient assessment and diagnosis (Kirmayer, Jarvis, & Guzder, 2013; Rosso & Bäärnhielm, 2012). However, we have a long way to go before biases are completely removed from the diagnostic process.

A third concern is that diagnostic labels can adversely affect the way we perceive and provide treatment to people who suffer from mental disorders. In a review of media portrayals of psychological disorders, Stuart (2006) argued that these portrayals are negatively distorted. Stuart found that characters are often depicted as violent, criminal, and unpredictable; one in four characters with a psychologically disorder kills someone, and half harm someone. Consider films such as *Split*, where the main character kidnaps and tortures teenage girls under the influence of his dissociative identity disorder.

In the news, discussions about mass shooters are frequently connected to accusations of a psychological disorder at play (Gold & Simon, 2016). In reality, mass shootings by persons with a psychological disorder account for only 1 percent of gun-related homicides. Take, for example, Stephen

Paddock—the man responsible for the 2017 mass shooting in Las Vegas, Nevada. Early in the investigation, law enforcement made a statement to ABC News that the gunman had a "severe undiagnosed mental illness" (Thomas, 2017). After months of postmortem forensic autopsy, no such diagnosis was made, in spite of some interviewees feeling that Paddock was delusional, had symptoms of bipolar disorder, and was paranoid (Romo, 2018).

Clinical diagnosis is an imperfect human enterprise. As in medicine, mental health professionals sometimes disagree on a patient, their judgments may subtly be influenced by stereotypes, and there is the ever-present danger that labels will color the way people with disorders are perceived. Furthermore, although each disorder is presented separately in its own neat and tidy package, people diagnosed with one disorder often have symptoms of others as well, a common phenomenon known as **comorbidity** (Kendall & Clarkin, 1992; Kessler et al., 1994). It turns out, for example, that 57 percent of people diagnosed with an anxiety disorder and 81 percent of those with a mood disorder have at least one other diagnosable disorder (Brown, Campbell, Lehman, Grisham, & Mancill, 2001). Yet diagnosis is necessary. Just as physicians have to distinguish among heart disease, cancer, and pneumonia in order to prescribe an effective treatment, mental health professionals must distinguish among different psychological disorders. To ease the stigma associated with diagnostic categories, the American Psychiatric Association (2000) recommends that the labels be applied to *behaviors*, not to *individuals*. It's better to say that someone has schizophrenia or alcohol dependence than to call that person a schizophrenic or an alcoholic—terms that imply permanence. If a person had cancer, you wouldn't call them "a cancer," would you? Therefore, we should adjust our language accordingly and not refer to a person with a psychological disorder as "a schizophrenic" or "a bipolar," for example.

In the remainder of this chapter, we consider some of the most common as well as some of the most bewildering disorders identified in the *DSM-5*. But first, a word of caution: Watch out for "medical student's disease," the tendency to recognize in yourself the disorders described in this chapter. If you are troubled or find it hard to function on a day-to-day basis, see a trained and licensed clinician about your problems. Otherwise, don't be alarmed. Normal and abnormal are points on a continuum—and everyone experiences some of the symptoms some of the time.

"What exactly is crazy?" In *Girl, Interrupted*, Winona Ryder plays Susanna Kaysen, an 18-year-old girl described as depressed, lazy, and apathetic who is checked into a mental hospital after an aspirin overdose. While there, Susanna was surrounded by a pathological liar, someone with an addiction to laxatives, and someone who purposely burned herself with gasoline and a match—all of whom made her feel "normal" by comparison.
Allstar Picture Library Ltd. / Alamy Stock Photo

comorbidity. The tendency for people diagnosed with one mental disorder to exhibit symptoms of other disorders as well.

DEPRESSIVE DISORDERS

LEARNING OBJECTIVES

Synthesize the biological and psychological explanations of depressive disorder.

- Create an argument for why depression is often called the "common cold" of psychological disorders.
- List the biological and psychological causes of depression.
- Determine if persons who die by suicide leave clues of their intention.

Loss is a fact of life. We have all dealt with it, and will continue to deal with it. Whether it be the loss of a family member, beloved pet, personal health, or a scholarship, grieving that loss is a natural reaction. However, sometimes the grief can last so long and be so severe that it is debilitating. There is more than one form of a depressive disorder, but unlike bipolar disorder, depressive disorders do not have a cycle of highs and lows, nor is there a tendency to experience psychosis. Instead, the consistent internal state is sadness, emptiness, and irritation. In this section, we will focus on the depressive disorder people tend to be most familiar with—major depressive disorder.

Major Depressive Disorder

A chronic sufferer of depression, Winston Churchill referred to his condition as the "black dog" that followed him around. He was not alone. According to Our World in Data, 268 million people in the world are living with depression (Ritchie & Roser, 2018). An estimated 19 million Americans—12 percent of American males and 21 percent of females—will suffer a major depression at some point in life (Kessler et al., 1994). In a given year, 4 to 5 percent of Americans will experience depression that is bad enough to interfere with their daily lives and require treatment (Narrow et al., 2002). Figure 13.2 illustrates the prevalence of major depressive order in the United States.

Depression is so widespread that Churchill's black dog has been called the common cold of mental disorders. It appears that no one is immune from an occasional bout with depression—not even the rich and famous. Halle Berry, who won the 2002 Academy Award for Best Actress, was so depressed after a prior divorce that she contemplated suicide (Norman, 2007). Others notable figures who have suffered from depression include Lady Gaga, Anthony Bourdain, Kate Spade, Cara Delevingne, Kurt Cobain, Jim Carrey, Kristen Bell, Sheryl Crow, Ellen DeGeneres, Ashley Judd, Dwayne "The Rock" Johnson, Katy Perry, and Michael Phelps.

FIGURE 13.2 ■ Rates of Diagnosed Major Depressive Disorder, by State

A study conducted by Blue Cross Blue Shield demonstrates the prevalence of major depressive disorder by state in the year 2016. Hawaii has the lowest rate. The data do not reflect those persons who don't seek professional care and thus whose depressive disorders go undiagnosed.

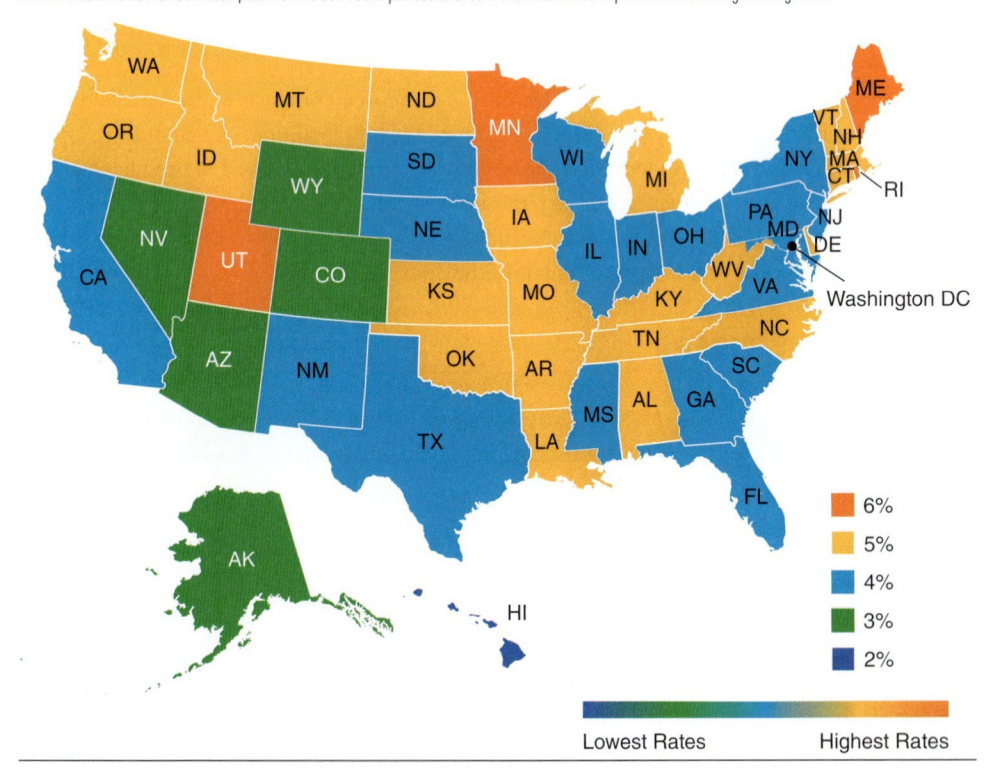

Source: National Center for Health Statistics/ Centers for Disease Control

Depression is a **mood disorder** characterized by deep sadness and despair. Because these feelings are sometimes an appropriate and normal reaction to tragedy, someone is considered clinically depressed only if the episode arises without a discernible cause and lasts for two or more weeks. In addition to the effects on mood, symptoms include (a) diminished pleasure or interest in food, sex, social banter, and other joys; (b) intense feelings of worthlessness, guilt, and self-blame; (c) restlessness and agitation, marked by difficulty sleeping, concentrating on work, and making decisions; (d) fatigue, slowness, and a lack of energy (in extreme cases, there is such a paralysis of the will that the person has to be pushed out of bed, washed, dressed, and fed by others); and (e) recurring thoughts of suicide and death. Indeed, up to 6 percent of people ever receiving treatment for depression will die by suicide (U.S. Department of Health and Human Services, 2018). For now, consider some quick facts and numbers related to this disorder:

depression. A mood disorder characterized by sadness, despair, feelings of worthlessness, and low self-esteem.

mood disorder. A condition characterized by prolonged emotional extremes ranging from mania to depression.

- Age is a relevant factor. Depression is seldom identified for the first time in someone's life before early adolescence. As demonstrated in Figure 13.3, the age of first onset rises sharply during the teen years, increases through adulthood, peaks at middle age, and then declines (Lewinsohn, Duncan, Stanton, & Hautzinger, 1986).

- People all over the world get depressed, though the form it takes may differ (Kleinman, 2004). For example, people with depression complain of headaches and "nerves" in Latinx cultures, of "imbalance" in Chinese and Asian cultures, and of problems of the "heart" in Middle Eastern cultures (American Psychiatric Association, 1994). As Western influences become more pervasive in countries like China, people are describing more cognitive characteristics of their depression (Matsumoto & Juang, 2008).

- The depression rate has been rising with each successive generation. Between 2013 and 2016, depression diagnoses surged among millennials and adolescents (Blue Cross Blue Shield Association, 2018).

- About twice as many women as men seek treatment for depression—a disparity that first appears in adolescence, at about the age of 13 (Cyranowski, Frank, Young, & Shear, 2000; Nolen-Hoeksema & Girgus, 1994). This may occur because adolescent females encounter more adversity than adolescent males do (as physical appearance, sexuality, and relationships become major sources of stress); they ruminate more about negative events (boys, and later men, tend to use physical activity, alcohol, and other distractions); and then they become needy when depressed, which causes friends to withdraw, further worsening the problem (Hankin & Abramson, 2001). In addition, Western societies are more accepting of female emotional expression and less accepting of male emotional expression (Chaplin, 2015).

- Regardless of one's sex, age, culture, or generation, it's reassuring to know that depressive episodes often last only a few weeks. Diagnosis with major depressive disorder requires a two-week period (American Psychiatric Association, 2013). However, 50 to 60 percent of those who suffer one episode of major depression later have a recurrence that is longer lasting and more severe (Maj, Veltro, Pirozzi, Lobrace, & Magliano, 1992; Winokur, Coryell, Keller, Endicott, & Akiskall, 1993).

Theories of Depression

Why, one wonders, does depression afflict so many millions of people in the world? From an evolutionary standpoint, shouldn't the processes of natural selection have lessened the survival odds of humans prone to depression? Randolph Nesse (2000) asked this very question and speculated that the deflated mood that blankets the body and mind in depression can be a useful form of adaptation. Nesse noted that depression-like symptoms are often seen in apes and monkeys who are doomed to stay in subordinate positions within their social groups. To survive, they withdraw rather than compete, and appear lonely and depressed, a strategy that helps them to survive within the group. In a similar manner, he suggests, human beings may have adapted depression—the low mood, the lack of energy, and the lack

FIGURE 13.3 ■ Depression: Ages of First Onset

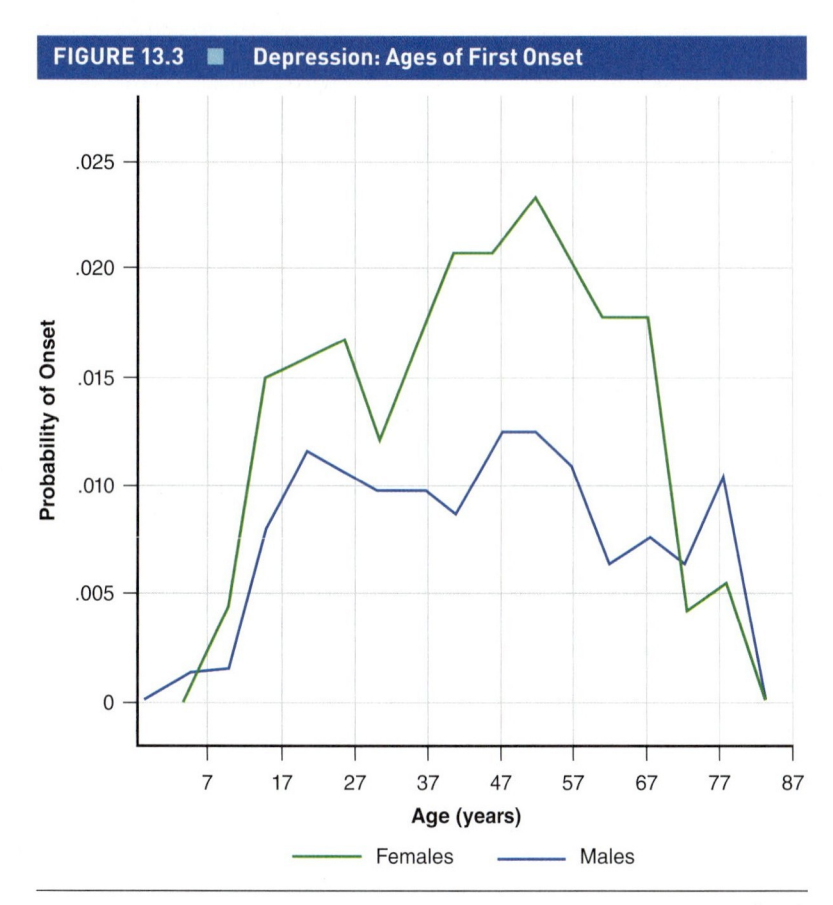

Source: Adapted from Lewinsohn, P. M., Duncan, E. M., Stanton, A. K., & Hautzinger, M. (1986). Age at first onset for nonbipolar depression. Journal of Abnormal Psychology, 95(4), 378–383. https://doi.org/10.1037/0021-843X.95.4.378

of initiative and activity—as a way to cope with life situations that are difficult, futile, or too dangerous to confront.

Psychologists have tried for many years to find a cure for this common cold of mental disorders. To treat and prevent depression, however, one must first understand where it comes from and what factors serve to maintain it.

Biological Factors

Is depression likely to be inherited? Or is it the product of shared environments? Research shows that if one fraternal twin suffers a major depression, there is a 20 percent chance that at some point the other will too. Yet the rate for identical twins is about 50 percent, a comparison that reveals a clear genetic linkage (Kendler, Neale, Kessler, Heath, & Eaves, 1993; McGuffin, Katz, Watkins, & Rutherford, 1996; Tsuang & Faraone, 1990). This finding suggests two compatible conclusions: (a) There is a genetic basis of depression, but (b) environmental factors also play a prominent role.

Researchers suspect that genes influence mood disorders by acting on neurotransmitters. In the 1950s, doctors noticed that drugs used to treat blood pressure and tuberculosis often had dramatic side effects on a patient's mood—sometimes causing depression, at other times euphoria. Researchers then found that the same drugs also increase the supply of norepinephrine and serotonin, neurotransmitters that regulate moods and emotions. So what does it all mean? When the two strands of evidence were combined, it became apparent

Vincent van Gogh's "Wheatfield with Crows" is an intense and haunting portrayal of the French countryside under troubled skies. This may have been Van Gogh's last painting before he died by suicide in 1890.

incamerastock / Alamy Stock Photo

that depression is associated with lower than normal levels of these neurotransmitters—and that mania is caused by an overabundance. As discussed in the chapter on treatment and interventions, the practical benefit of this discovery was the development of antidepressant drugs such as Prozac, Zoloft, and Paxil.

Psychological Factors

In a 1917 paper entitled "Mourning and Melancholia," Sigmund Freud noted similarities between depression and the kind of grief that accompanies the death of a loved one. According to Freud, melancholia, like mourning, is a reaction to *loss*. The loss may involve the breakup of a relationship, physical and mental impairment caused by neurological damage (Hughes & Cummings, 2020), or failure to reach an important goal. Not everyone overreacts to these kinds of events. Among those who were abandoned or neglected as children, however, even a minor setback may cause them to retreat into a passive, dependent, childlike state. It can also awaken intense anger that is turned inward, or "internalized"—which is why people who are depressed often punish themselves with self-blame, feelings of worthlessness, and suicide.

Behaviorally oriented psychologists trace depression to one's history of reinforcement and perception of control. According to Peter Lewinsohn (1974), people get depressed when they are unable to produce for themselves a high rate of positive reinforcement. Similarly, Martin Seligman (1975) argued that depression is a form of **learned helplessness**, an expectation that one cannot control important outcomes in life. In a series of experiments during the 1960s, Seligman found that dogs strapped into a harness and exposed to painful electric shocks soon became passive and gave up trying to escape—even in new situations where escape was possible. As applied to humans, this finding suggests that prolonged exposure to uncontrollable outcomes may similarly cause apathy, inactivity, a loss of motivation, and pessimism (Maier & Seligman, 2016). According to Dr. Christopher Palmer, a psychiatrist, the coronavirus pandemic created exactly that for many Americans—the repetition of stressful and life-threatening circumstances that are out of anyone's control (Tucker, 2020). Among those adversely affected by the pandemic, health care workers suffered considerable mood, anxiety, and sleep disturbances (Pappa et al., 2020).

learned helplessness. A learned expectation that one cannot control important life outcomes, resulting in apathy and depression.

Realizing that perception is more important than reality, most psychologists now focus on *social-cognitive* aspects of depression. Some years ago, psychiatrist Aaron Beck (1967) noticed that his depressed patients viewed themselves, their world, and the future through dark glasses. According to Beck, these patients distorted reality by focusing more attention on negative events than on positive ones—a pattern consistently found in research (Haaga, Dyck, & Ernst, 1991). This bleak, self-defeating outlook is pervasive. Research shows that depressed people are not only down on themselves but also down on their parents and romantic partners (Gara et al., 1993).

depressive explanatory style. The tendency for depressed people to attribute negative events to factors that are internal, stable, and global.

Lynn Abramson, Gerald Metalsky, and Lauren Alloy (1989) proposed that depression is a state of *hopelessness* brought on by the negative self-attributions that people make for failure. Specifically, they note, some people have a **depressive explanatory style**, a tendency to attribute bad events to factors that are internal rather than external ("It's my fault"), stable rather than unstable ("It will not change"), and global rather than specific ("It affects other parts of my life"). Many studies now provide support for this proposition. Whether people are trying to explain social rejection, a sports defeat, low grades, or inability to solve an experimenter's puzzle, those who are depressed are more likely than others to blame factors that are within the self, unlikely to change, and broad enough to impair other aspects of life. The result: pessimism, hopelessness, and despair (Maier & Seligman, 2016; Metalsky, Joiner, Hardin, & Abramson, 1993; Seligman, 1975).

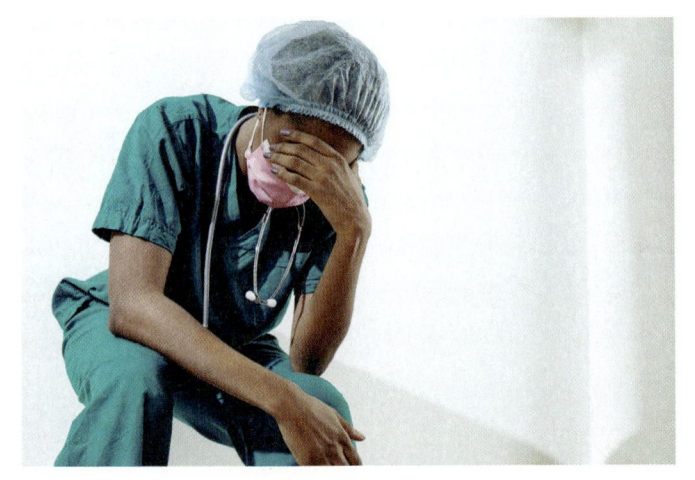

Medical professionals are not immune to learned helplessness. Repeated exposure to uncontrollable illness and death during the coronavirus pandemic took its toll on health care workers.

iStock.com/DragonImages

Does having a negative explanatory style signal a person's vulnerability to depression? Psychologists definitely think so (DeRubeis & Hollon, 2014). In a classic study, Alloy and her colleagues (1999) measured the explanatory styles of nondepressed first-year college students. They then followed up on these students in their junior year and found that those who had a negative explanatory style in their first year—compared to classmates who had a more positive style—were more likely to suffer their first major or minor depressive disorder (illustrated in Figure 13.4).

What's Your Prediction?

Concerned about the mental health of teenagers, Susan Furr and others (2001) surveyed 1,455 students at four American colleges and universities about whether they had felt depression while in school and whether they had thought about or attempted suicide. How prevalent are these problems? Think about yourself, your friends, and acquaintances, and make a prediction: What percentage of students, from 0 to 100, said that they had (a) experienced depression, (b) thought about suicide, and (c) actually attempted suicide? For mental health professionals, the results were sobering. Of the students surveyed, 53 percent said they had experienced depression at some point, 9 percent said they had thought about suicide, and 1 percent had actually attempted suicide. Why is depression so common? When asked, students most frequently cited grade problems, loneliness, money problems, and boyfriend or girlfriend problems.

The Vicious Cycle of Depression

It's one of the sad ironies for people with depression: They desperately need social support and a shoulder to cry on, yet they tend to behave in ways that drive away the most important people in their lives. As illustrated in Figure 13.5, the result is a vicious, self-perpetuating cycle: Depression elicits social rejection, which in turn worsens the depression (Joiner & Coyne, 1999).

Do people with depression really elicit negative reactions and rejection? Are we all so cold-hearted that we turn our backs on those in need of emotional support? Sometimes, yes. When people are severely depressed, friends do try to cheer them up and offer a sympathetic ear, a shoulder to lean on, and advice. As psychotherapists are the first to admit, however, these efforts usually fail and the depression persists. The suffering person is full of complaints, regrets, and expressions of self-pity, which

FIGURE 13.4 ■ Explanatory Styles and Depression

In this study, researchers measured explanatory styles among first-year college students. Two years later, those with a negative as opposed to positive style were more likely to experience a major or minor depressive disorder.

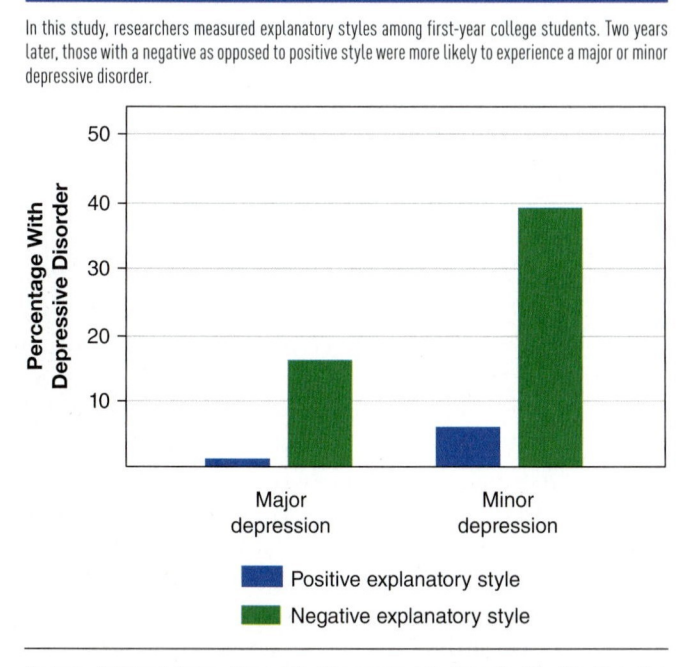

Source: Adapted from Alloy LB, Abramson LY, Francis EL. Do Negative Cognitive Styles Confer Vulnerability to Depression? Current Directions in Psychological Science. 1999;8(4):128–132. doi:10.1111/1467-8721.00030

FIGURE 13.5 ■ The Vicious Cycle of Depression

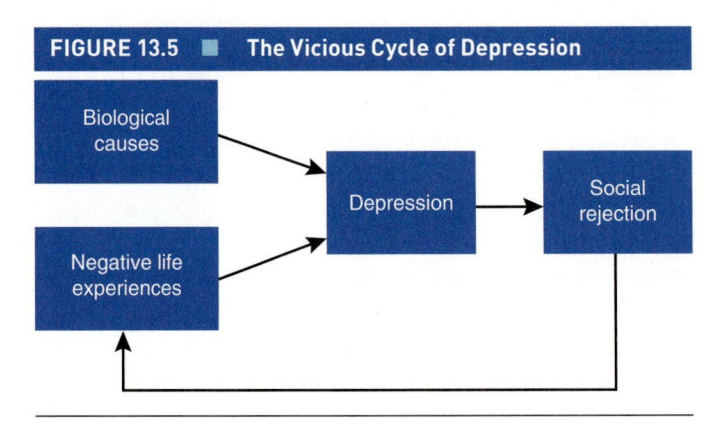

Source: Adapted from Joiner, T., Coyne, J. C., & Blalock, J. (1999). On the interpersonal nature of depression: Overview and synthesis. In T. Joiner & J. C. Coyne (Eds.), The interactional nature of depression: Advances in interpersonal approaches (p. 3–19). American Psychological Association. https://doi.org/10.1037/10311-013

makes social interaction unpleasant. What's worse, studies have shown that people who are depressed avoid eye contact, speak softly, are slow to respond, wear sad or blank facial expressions, and are negative in their demeanor—a pattern of behavior that is seen as rude, detached, and nonresponsive (Segrin & Abramson, 1994). The result is that people react to those who are depressed with mixed emotions—sorrow laced with frustration, anger, and a desire to avoid future contact (Coyne, 1976; Gurtman, 1987; Sacco & Dunn, 1990). Depression takes a toll on marriage, too. Studies show that in married heterosexual couples in which the wife is depressed, she and her husband have more conflict, more complaints, and less physical and emotional affection (Benazon & Coyne, 2000; Coyne et al., 2002).

Question: In the United States, what's more common: Suicide or homicide?

Answer: Suicide is twice as common (Morgan, Rowhani-Rahbar, Azrael, & Miller, 2018).

Suicide

"I don't believe it. I just saw them and they looked fine." "I knew she was depressed, but I had no idea it was this bad. Why didn't she call me?" These statements are typical of how people react when someone they know dies by suicide.

The World Health Organization (2019) estimates that, worldwide, roughly one million people a year die from suicide. In the United States, that number is 30,000, for an average of one suicide every half-hour. Remarkably, for every one person who actually dies by suicide, there are 10 to 20 others who try. Among persons who identify as transgender, several studies have determined that 40 percent have attempted suicide at least once (Dickey & Budge, 2020). To many of us, nothing about human behavior seems more puzzling, tragic, or senseless. Yet to those who are depressed and in a state of mental pain and anguish, it often seems like the only solution (Jamison, 1999; Maltsberger & Goldblatt, 1996).

Who tries to die by suicide, and why? Suicidology researchers are providing answers (Hawton & van Heeringen, 2000; Maris, Berman, & Silverman, 2001). In the United States, statistics show that females are three times more likely to attempt suicide, but males are four times more likely to complete it. This difference reflects the fact that most males use hanging, asphyxia, and firearms, whereas females are more likely to overdose on sleeping pills or attempt exsanguination (Tsirigotis, Gruszczynski, & Tsirigotis, 2011)—slower and less certain methods.

Does this mean that females don't use firearms when attempting to take their own lives? No, it does not. Take the case of Katie Stubblefield. An 18-year-old female in emotional turmoil, Katie was grappling with yet another relocation due to her father's job as a pastor, a devastating breakup, and health issues. It was too much for Katie to bear. She grabbed a .308 caliber hunting rifle, put the barrel to her chin, and pulled the trigger. But Katie didn't die. She was rushed to the emergency room, where a medical team stabilized her. Three years and countless surgical procedures later, Katie received a face transplant. To help others with their own mental health issues, Katie allowed her journey to be documented by *National Geographic*. She admits that she is thankful to be alive and desires to go to college so that she can have a career in helping others. Katie's case is unusual because she had never thought of suicide before that day. However, about 75 percent of completed suicides are by people who are depressed. In fact, the single best predictor of suicide potential is a sense of hopelessness. In one study, more than 2,000 psychiatric outpatients were tested and followed for up to seven years. Of the 17 who went on to die by suicide, 16 had initially gotten high scores on a "hopelessness scale" (Beck, Brown, Berchick, Stewart, & Steer, 1990).

Shocked friends and relatives always wonder: Should I have known? Could I have done something to prevent it? These are tough personal questions. Suicide is difficult to predict, and nobody should feel guilty about getting caught by surprise. But there are patterns to watch for (Shneidman, 1996). First, people who are depressed and who use drugs are particularly vulnerable—not while they are in the depths of despair, as you may think, but afterward, as they start to regain their energy and spirit. Second, about 90 percent of all suicides are preceded by remarks about one's death or departure—such as "Sometimes I wonder if life is worth living" or "You won't see me again" (note that only 2 or 3 percent of people who talk about suicide make the attempt, but of those who die by suicide, almost all have talked about it). Third, people preparing to die by suicide often leave telltale behavioral clues. They might start to put their papers in order, pull back from prior commitments, take unusual risks, or give away prized possessions. Fourth, it helps to know that people who attempt suicide once are at a higher-than-average risk to do so again, even much later in life.

Is there a way to prevent suicide? Edwin Shneidman (1996) recommends taking certain actions if you are concerned about someone you know. Stay close and communicate openly. If the person alludes to death, gives away valued possessions, or leaves other hints, it's best to inquire as to what's happening and, if necessary, ask directly, "Are you thinking about suicide?" Offer sympathy, suggest options, and most important of all—make sure the person gets professional help. In case of a crisis, call for help yourself.

ANXIETY DISORDERS

LEARNING OBJECTIVES

Understand the causes of an anxiety disorder.

- Connect cultural variables to anxiety disorders.
- Describe the biological origins of panic.
- Compare a simple phobia with a social phobia.

The yellow ribbon is a symbol for suicide awareness. An estimated 123 Americans die by suicide every day. Among the reasons most often cited in such are loneliness, depression, problems with boyfriends and girlfriends, grades, money, and feelings of helplessness.
iStock.com/Panuwat Dangsungnoen

Anyone who has faced military combat, the interview of a lifetime, a championship game, major surgery, or the menacing sound of a prowler in the house knows what anxiety feels like. On occasion, we all do. It's a nervous, jittery feeling of apprehension accompanied by a pounding heart, trembling hands, cold and sweaty palms, a quivering voice, a dry mouth, dizziness, light-headedness, fatigue, shortness of breath, an upset stomach, or diarrhea.

Generalized Anxiety Disorder

Anxiety is a normal response to threatening and stressful situations. As we saw earlier, however, about 25 percent of all Americans will at some time in life experience anxiety that is so intense, persistent, and disabling that it is considered to be a disorder (Kessler et al., 1994). Over the course of a lifetime, an estimated 5 percent of adults suffer what is known as **generalized** anxiety disorder—a persistent, gnawing undercurrent of anxiety that is "free floating" (not linked to an identifiable source). Feeling aroused and not knowing why, the person with a generalized anxiety disorder is highly sensitive to criticism, has difficulty making decisions, dwells on past mistakes, and worries constantly and excessively about money, work, family matters, and illness (Barlow, 2001). What is not clear, however, is whether these are effects or causes of the disorder. Research suggests that people with generalized anxiety disorder are hypersensitive and anxious before they seek treatment—and remain so after the disorder is in remission (Brown et al., 2001).

Many people have anxiety attacks that are more focused than generalized anxiety disorder. In particular, three such disorders are described in this section: panic disorder, phobias, and social anxiety disorder. Before you read on, however, two points are worth noting. First, although the different anxiety disorders are in some ways distinct, most people who have one type are likely to exhibit the symptoms of at least one other type as well (Brown & Barlow, 1992; Sanderson, DiNardo, Rapee, & Barlow, 1990). Second, although people all over the world suffer from intense anxiety, the specific symptoms they experience are molded by their cultural upbringing (Good & Kleinman, 1985).

People with generalized anxiety disorder can experience debilitating anxiety.
iStock.com/AntonioGuillem

generalized anxiety disorder. A psychological disorder characterized by a constant state of anxiety not linked to an identifiable source.

Panic Disorder

People who are diagnosed with **panic disorder** experience frequent, sudden, and intense rushes of anxiety, usually lasting for several minutes. The symptoms of a panic attack include chest pains and heart palpitations, hyperventilation, shortness of breath, choking and smothering sensations, and fainting. These symptoms are often accompanied by feelings of unreality and detachment from one's body and by a fear of going crazy, losing control, or dying. Table 13.2 presents the percentages of patients with panic disorder who experience various symptoms. An attack is considered "panic" if it includes four or more of these symptoms (Craske & Barlow, 2001).

Research shows that panic strikes most often during the day but that it also frequently occurs between the hours of 1:30 and 3:30 AM, while people are asleep; that heart rates increase an average of 39 beats per minute; and that the episodes last for approximately 16 minutes, followed by exhaustion (Taylor et al., 1986). What's worse, those who get frequent panic attacks worry so much about embarrassing themselves in front of others—by fainting, vomiting, gasping for air, or losing bladder control—that they very often develop **agoraphobia**, a fear of being in public places that are hard to escape. People with agoraphobia frequently become prisoners in their own homes, afraid to stray into shopping malls, restaurants, sports arenas, theaters, airports, or train stations. The word *agoraphobia* itself comes from a Greek term meaning "fear of the marketplace."

According to the National Institute of Mental Health (2017), approximately 2.7 percent of U.S. adults had panic disorder in 2016, and an estimated 4.7 percent of adults will experience panic disorder at one time in their lives. What causes panic disorder? There are two major perspectives—one biological, the other psychological (McNally, 1994). Supporting a biological point of view, research shows that panic attacks tend to strike without warning or provocation, that attacks are accompanied by changes in the prefrontal cortex, and that the experience can be induced and treated with drugs (Bremner et al., 2000; Gorman, Liebowitz, Fyer, & Stein, 1989).

The psychological approach is supported by three kinds of evidence. First, many patients report that their first attack struck shortly after an illness, a miscarriage, or another traumatic event. Through the processes of classical conditioning described in the chapter on learning, the individual may then become anxious in response to situational cues innocently associated with that first attack—such as the time, place, and people who were present (Bouton, Mineka, & Barlow, 2001). Second, people with

panic disorder. A disorder characterized by sudden and intense rushes of anxiety without an apparent reason.

agoraphobia. An anxiety disorder in which the main symptom is an intense fear of public places.

TABLE 13.2 ■ The Panic Button: Symptoms

Symptoms	Percentages
Heart palpitations	87
Dizziness or faintness	87
Trembling or shaking	86
Fear of losing control	76
Shortness of breath	75
Hot flashes or chills	74
Excessive sweating	70
Numbness or tingling sensations	58
Depersonalization	57
Nausea or abdominal distress	56
Fear of dying	52
Choking sensation	50
Chest pains	38

Source: Adapted from D. H. Barlow (2001). *Anxiety and its disorders.* New York, Guilford Press.

panic disorder are highly attuned to bodily sensations and are prone to misinterpret the signals in ways that are "catastrophic." Feeling aroused, for example, they are quick to fear that they are having a heart attack, stroke, or some other life-threatening ordeal—and this belief fuels the fire (Clark et al., 1997; Ehlers & Breuer, 1992; Schmidt & Trakowski, 1997). Among people prone to panic, for example, inhaling carbon dioxide—or air that contains a shortage of oxygen—sets off a false "suffocation-alarm" (Beck, Ohtake, & Shipherd, 1999; Klein, 1993). Even during sleep, people with panic disorder are quick to make catastrophic attributions for "normal" but unexpected sensations (Craske et al., 2002). Third, psychological forms of therapy—such as exposure and relaxation training, breathing exercises, and various behavioral and cognitive techniques—can help to alleviate panic attacks without the use of drugs (Craske & Barlow, 2001; McNally, 1994; Rachman & Maser, 1988). To sum up: The human panic button can be activated by biological or psychological means.

Specific Phobia

Five times a month, Kendra Wilkinson flies around the country to maintain her career as reality TV star and entrepreneur. As a woman who became famous for dating Hugh Hefner, you would surmise that Kendra is used to being on a plane. Hugh Hefner owned and frequently flew in his own jet, the Big Bunny. However, Kendra is terrified of flying. "Every time I fly, I grab on to the person next to me," she says (Wrenn, 2012). Kendra shares this fear with millions of others.

Whereas panic attacks strike suddenly and without warning, specific phobias are more focused and predictable. A **specific phobia** is an intense and irrational fear of a specific object or situation. The most common are fear of heights, airplanes, closed spaces, blood, snakes, and spiders, with some of these being reported as severe (Figure 13.6). But there are other, more idiosyncratic phobias as well. Some people grip their car seat, stiffen up, and break into a cold sweat whenever they drive over a drawbridge with a metal-grating surface. Table 13.3 presents a partial list of specific phobias that have been identified and named over the years. Some names may sound familiar; others you may be able to figure out from the prefix (Maser, 1985). The frequencies of the most prevalent phobias are provided in Figure 13.6.

What causes phobic disorders? Freud argued that people with phobias are anxious about hidden impulses and cope by displacing their anxiety onto substitute objects that are less threatening and easier to avoid. Consider the classic case of Little Hans, a 5-year-old boy who would not leave home

specific phobia. An intense, irrational fear of a specific object or situation.

TABLE 13.3 ■ Partial List of Specific Phobias

Phobia	Feared Object or Situation
Acrophobia	Heights
Aerophobia	Flying
Agoraphobia	Public places
Aichmophobia	Sharp pointed objects
Aquaphobia	Water
Arachnophobia	Spiders
Brontophobia	Thunderstorms
Claustrophobia	Closed spaces
Entomophobia	Insects
Hematophobia	Blood
Homilophobia	Sermons
Monophobia	Being alone
Mysophobia	Dirt and germs
Nyctophobia	Darkness
Ophidiophobia	Snakes
Parthenophobia	Virgins
Porphyrophobia	The color purple
Triskaidekaphobia	The number 13
Xenophobia	Strangers
Zoophobia	Animals

because he was terrified of being bitten by a horse. According to Freud (1909), Hans was in the midst of an Oedipal conflict and had converted an unconscious fear that his father would castrate him into a conscious fear of getting bitten by a horse. From a psychoanalytic perspective, then, the phobic object is merely a symbol for a deeper, more troubling problem.

In reaction to Freud's case study, behaviorist John Watson demonstrated with a baby named Little Albert that phobias can develop through conditioning (as described in the chapter on learning). Since that time, researchers have found that phobias may be learned by classical conditioning (Ost, 1992) or by the observation of someone else's fear reaction to an object. To the behaviorist, phobias originate in a personal experience or observation and then spread through a process of stimulus generalization. Thus, if a child is locked in a closet at a tender young age, they may acquire a specific fear of closets or a more general case of claustrophobia. In this view, the reason phobias last long after the precipitating experience is forgotten is that we tend to avoid phobic objects, denying ourselves an opportunity to unlearn the fear. Also consistent with this view, research shows that people whose phobias are extinguished in treatment are later less likely to suffer a relapse when reexposed to the phobic object in exactly the same situation (Mineka, Mystkowski, Hladek, & Rodriguez, 1999).

A third view is that humans are genetically programmed through evolution, or "prepared," to develop certain kinds of phobias (Ohman & Mineka, 2001). People all over the world fear darkness, heights, snakes, insects, and other harmless objects, some of which they may never encounter. The reason, according to Seligman (1971), is that human beings, like other animals, are prepared by evolution to fear and avoid objects and situations that were harmful to their prehistoric ancestors.

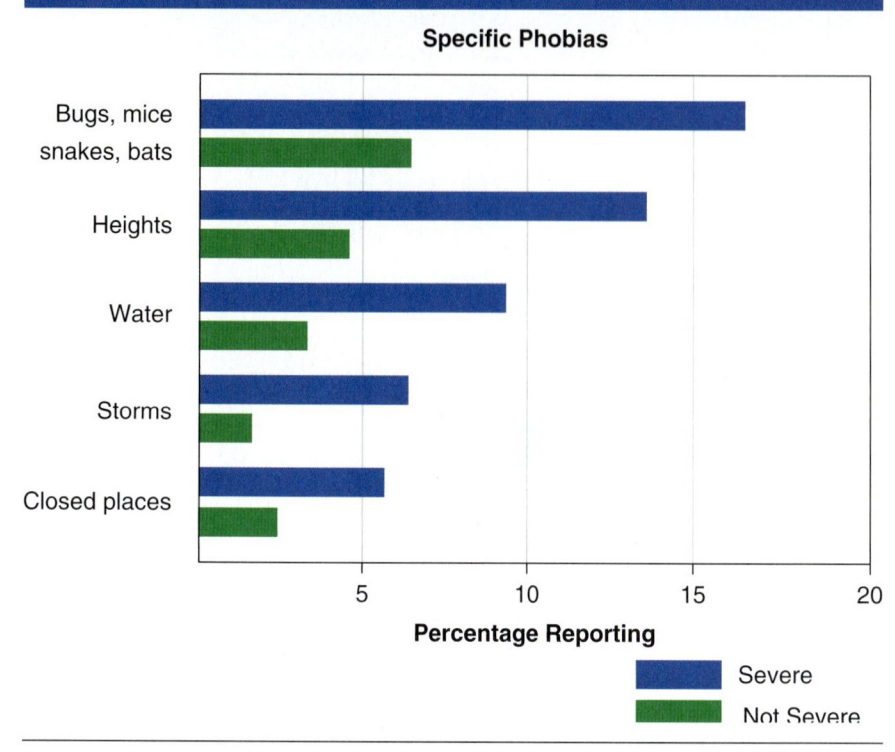

FIGURE 13.6 ■ Frequency of the Most Prevalent Specific Phobias

Specific Phobias

Phobia	
Bugs, mice, snakes, bats	~17 (Severe), ~6 (Not Severe)
Heights	~13 (Severe), ~5 (Not Severe)
Water	~9 (Severe), ~3 (Not Severe)
Storms	~6 (Severe), ~2 (Not Severe)
Closed places	~6 (Severe), ~3 (Not Severe)

Percentage Reporting

■ Severe
■ Not Severe

Sources: Adapted from Curtis et al. (1998).

FIGURE 13.7 ■ It's OK to Not Be OK

The "It's OK" mental health campaign tries to reduce the stigma that is sometimes associated with talking about feelings. In London, the campaign targets men of diverse backgrounds who might feel societal or cultural pressure to be stoic.

iStock.com/clubfoto

Social Anxiety Disorder

social anxiety disorder. An intense fear of situations that invite public scrutiny.

Once considered a phobia, **social anxiety disorder** is an exaggerated fear, in children or adults, of situations that invite public scrutiny (American Psychiatric Association, 2013; Beidel & Turner, 1998; Heimberg, Liebowitz, Hope, & Schneier, 1995; Leary & Kowalski, 1995; Turk, Heimberg, & Hope,

2001). Social anxiety disorder is among the most prevalent of psychological disorders. Probably the most familiar example is public-speaking anxiety, or stage fright—a performer's worst nightmare. If you've ever had to make a presentation, only to feel weak in the knees and hear your voice quiver, you will have endured at least a hint of this disorder. What is there to fear in public speaking? When people were asked this question, the most common responses were shaking and showing other signs of anxiety, going blank, saying something foolish, and being unable to continue (Stein, Walker, & Forde, 1996). For the social phobic, unbearable levels of self-consciousness may also be evoked by other situations. Examples include eating at a public lunch counter and, for males, urinating in a crowded men's room. In private, these behaviors pose no problem. In front of others, however, they arouse so much fear that the situations are avoided and escaped at all costs. In extreme cases, the reaction becomes so debilitating that the person just stays at home.

Certain phobic disorders occur with greater frequency than others. One of the most common is acrophobia (a fear of heights).
Simon Dack / Alamy Stock Photo

Cultural Influences on Anxiety Disorders

Anxiety is a universal human affliction, but the specific forms it takes may vary according to cultural beliefs (Hofmann, Asnaani, & Hinton, 2010; Hofmann & Hinton, 2014; Stein, 2009). In Mexico and certain Latin American cultures, people are sometimes afflicted with *susto*—an intense fear reaction, insomnia, and irritability, believed to be brought on by the "evil eye" of voodoo or black magic. In Japan, there is *shinkeishitsu*—an emotional disorder in which people become so self-conscious and perfectionistic that they feel too inadequate to interact with others. In Southeast Asia, *koro* is an intense fear that one's sexual organs will disappear into the body, causing death.

Three important lessons can be learned from these cross-cultural comparisons. First, anxiety is universal, and the *physiological* symptoms are the same from one culture to the next. Regardless of where you are born and raised, anxiety is a bodily reaction characterized by such symptoms as shortness of breath, a racing heart, trembling, sweating, dry mouth, and weak knees. Second, culture influences the *cognitive* component of anxiety, so the symptoms people worry about, how they interpret those symptoms, and their beliefs about the causes of anxiety all depend on the values and ideologies to which they are exposed (Barlow, 2001; Good & Kleinman, 1985; Hofmann & Hinton, 2014; Simons & Hughes, 1986; Tseng, 2001). The third lesson concerns treatment. Precisely because our cultural heritage can influence the source of our anxiety and the way it's expressed, mental health workers must self-consciously step outside the boundaries of their way of thinking in order to counsel those who are culturally different (Sue & Sue, 1999).

TRAUMA- AND STRESSOR-RELATED DISORDERS

LEARNING OBJECTIVES

Understand how exposure to a traumatic or stressful event can result in the development of posttraumatic stress disorder (PTSD).

- Determine if gender differences in PTSD exist.
- List the functional consequences of PTSD.

In a *Washington Post* interactive article discussing mass shootings in America (Berkowitz & Alcantara, 2020), readers could click on over 1,246 different icons—each representing an individual victim. An interactive reading experience such as this reminds us of the lives lost. However, individuals who were immensely affected, yet not featured in this article, were those who survived and are possibly suffering from a trauma- and stressor-related disorder. In these types of disorders, being exposed to a traumatic or stressful event is considered a direct contributor (American Psychiatric Association, 2013).

Posttraumatic Stress Disorder

It is estimated that half of the U.S. population has been exposed to trauma (U.S. Department of Veterans Affairs, 2019). Out of those exposed to trauma, roughly 7 to 8 percent develop **posttraumatic stress disorder**, commonly known as **PTSD** (Kessler & Wang, 2008; U.S. Department of Veterans Affairs, 2019). PTSD is a trauma- and stressor-related disorder that can result following exposure to a traumatic event. It is the only disorder in the *DSM-5* that requires exposure to a traumatic event for diagnosis. According to the *DSM-5* diagnostic criteria, a person must have been exposed to actual or threatened death, serious injury, or sexual violence (American Psychiatric Association, 2013). This can include directly experiencing the traumatic event, assisting in the damage control after the traumatic event (such as a first responder or emergency room medic), witnessing the event as it occurred to others, or learning that the traumatic event happened to a close friend or loved one. In other words, the person who develops PTSD does not have to be injured, nor does "exposure" mean the person has to be present at the actual event.

Imagine for a moment that you are a paramedic responding to a mass shooting. You are under tremendous pressure as you apply tourniquets, connect IVs, administer CPR, and load people onto stretchers. As you travel to the nearest hospital, the pressure continues since it is your job to get the person in your ambulance there as medically stable and as quickly as possible. Upon your arrival, dozens of other paramedics and their patients are being wheeled into the hospital. Everywhere you look, there are gruesome injuries. The moment you hand your patient over to the emergency room medics, you turn around and swiftly make your way back to the ambulance, only to return to the harrowing scene you just left. You will do this at least 20 more times before the day is through. A few weeks later, your thoughts are filled with the imagery, sounds, and smells that bombarded you while you were trying to save lives. You can't sleep or concentrate, since you often experience flashbacks. You begin to have recurring migraine headaches and painful stiffness in your neck and shoulders. Your stomach is frequently upset. You are so exhausted and numb that you use all of your sick and mental health days in an attempt to avoid going to work. Work is where all of the reminders are. This lasts for two months before you finally seek help from a psychiatrist who diagnoses PTSD.

This example describes both physiological and psychological symptoms. Physiological symptoms include irritable bowel syndrome (Ng et al., 2019), chronic pain (Sachs-Ericsson, Sheffler, Stanley, Piazza, & Preacher, 2017), and migraines (Friedman et al., 2017; Peterlin, Nijjar, & Tietjen, 2011). Adults with a history of adverse childhood experiences can also demonstrate a higher rate of disease than those with no such history (Felitti et al., 1998). Among females, one study found that pregnant women who had migraines were two times more likely to have PTSD than pregnant women without migraines (Friedman et al., 2017). Migraines can occur without warning and can be debilitating. Another thing that can occur without warning is an environmental cue that reminds people of the traumatic event. When PTSD sufferers are exposed to these environmental cues—for example, the sound of an ambulance, images of the event on social media, being around other people who were there that day—other physiological responses can result, such as increased heart rate (Gutner et al., 2010).

Psychological symptoms of PTSD are numerous, such as avoidance of things that remind you of the trauma; irritability; flashbacks; poor concentration; lack of sleep; an exaggerated startle response; and impairment in everyday functioning (American Psychiatric Association, 2013). Impairment in everyday functioning is more serious than you might surmise. Kataoka and colleagues (2012) noted that students with traumatic experiences have a higher risk for academic, social, and emotional problems. In particular, academic problems can result due to an inability to concentrate, intrusive thoughts (Kataoka et al., 2012; Swain, Pillay, & Kliewer, 2017), and suspension from school because of emotional outbursts, aggressiveness, and irritability (Rossen & Cowan, 2013). Suspensions of this nature have become problematic for Black public school students in Connecticut. That demographic receives the "emotional disturbance" label—an umbrella term that encompasses all psychological disorders including PTSD—twice as often as all other racial and ethnic groups (Skahill & DesRoches, 2019).

---

posttraumatic stress disorder (PTSD). A psychological disorder that develops as a result of exposure to a traumatic event.

posttraumatic stress disorder (PTSD). An anxiety disorder triggered by an extremely stressful event, such as combat.

This is concerning, especially when suspensions can result in poor academic performance or a failure to return to school. Furthermore, the number of suspensions might also suggest that students are not getting the support they need to achieve. This does not mean that educators aren't trying to support students who have a history of trauma; instead, it means that educators might not know *how* to support such students (Cole et al., 2005; Rodenbush, 2015; Wolpow, Johnson, Hertel, & Kincaid, 2009).

Thankfully, some educators are doing what they can to provide the proper support to trauma-exposed students. For example, Education Northwest (2017) provides a postsecondary education guide on trauma-informed practices. The guide provides principles for working with trauma-affected individuals, tips on deescalating a classroom situation, the power of mindfulness, and how educators can deal with their own wellness so that they have the mental and emotional capacity to assist students. According to Education Northwest, among the groups who are at a higher risk of trauma than other populations are students who have been or are in foster care; American Indian, Alaska Native, and refugee students; LGBTQ+ students; and nontraditional adult learners. The guide also suggests online resources such as the National Center on Safe Supportive Learning Environments and the National Child Traumatic Stress Network. Such resources for educators are not just beneficial; they're necessary. Poor academic performance and a failure to return to school can significantly decrease the chances that the student will secure and maintain employment (Bradley, Doolittle, & Bartolotta, 2008). In addition, Education Northwest (2017) notes that "education institutions are often regarded as an ideal entry point to mental health services for students" (p. 15). Universities often have counseling centers, support staff who can connect students to community resources, and groups of peers who gather to share their experiences.

PTSD includes various symptoms, from bad dreams to avoidance. Which symptoms are expressed depends on the person.
iStock.com/leremy

Although educational institutions can provide assistance, not all trauma-affected persons have such access. Therefore, the cost of PTSD treatment is concerning. Veterans are a good example. The Congressional Budget Office (2012) estimated that a four-year course of PTSD-specific care for a single combat veteran cost approximately $10,000. If you multiply that cost times the millions of veterans who have PTSD (Murdoch et al., 2017), the amount easily exceeds hundreds of billions of dollars. These costs could be so high in part because the veterans who received treatment during the congressional study may also have been suffering from other conditions. Treatment for multiple conditions is more expensive than treatment for a single condition. Yet, among all types of PTSD sufferers, comorbidities are not rare. In fact, the *DSM-5* (American Psychiatric Association, 2013) notes that "individuals with PTSD are 80% more likely than those without PTSD to have symptoms... for at least one other mental disorder" (p. 280). These mental disorders include depression, substance abuse, bipolar disorder, and anxiety (American Psychiatric Association, 2013).

Theories of Posttraumatic Stress Disorder

One such person who has made public her PTSD and anxiety diagnosis is performing artist Ariana Grande (Hattersley, 2018). Her traumatic experience occurred at her concert in Manchester, England, when a suicide bomber killed 22 people. Ariana is a famous figure and has graciously shared her story, but no one knows exactly why some people develop PTSD and others do not. Psychologists, however, have discovered some risk factors and predictors.

Psychological History Factors

Ariana's anxiety did not begin after the Manchester concert bombing. She admitted that she already had anxiety before the trauma (Hattersley, 2018). Does a prior experience with anxiety put one at a higher risk of developing PTSD? Researchers and clinicians suggest that, yes, a pre-trauma psychiatric history is predictive of PTSD development (Brewin, Andrews, & Valentine, 2000; Mayo Clinic, 2019). This includes not only the individual's past experiences with a psychological disorder such as

Traumatic experiences and heritability often overlap, as with the families who survived the devastating tornado that tore through Nashville, Tennessee, in 2020.
iStock.com/ZoccoPhoto

depression or anxiety but also the individual's family history of psychological disorders (Davidson, Hughes, Blazer, & George, 1991).

However, because trauma exposure and genetics tend to overlap, not all studies agree that a parental diagnosis of PTSD is predictive of a child's development of PTSD (Smoller, 2016). For example, when a parent is in an abusive relationship with an intimate partner, there is a significant chance that the child is exposed to that trauma (Wathen & Macmillan, 2013). How can a researcher identify the main contributor to that child's PTSD—genes, the intimate partner violence exposure, or both? Twin studies have been conducted in an attempt to answer this question (Jang, Taylor, Stein, & Yamagata, 2007; Stein, Jang, Taylor, Vernon, & Livesley, 2002). Stein and colleagues' (2002) twin study revealed that genetic factors contributed to the risk of exposure to trauma. This could be due to life events that result from choices, and those choices could be influenced by genetic predispositions. One such genetic predisposition could be that of neuroticism (as discussed in the chapter on personality; Docherty et al., 2016; Genetics of Personality Consortium et al., 2015; Power & Pluess, 2015), which has been frequently correlated with PTSD (Breslau & Schultz, 2013). In another twin study, Jang and colleagues (2007) determined that genetic contributors to PTSD development existed but became less important as the number of traumatic experiences increased. These findings suggest that environmental factors play an important role, one that might supersede genetics.

Environment and Severity Factors

Not all persons with PTSD have a history of pre-trauma or familial psychological disorders. Several studies have revealed environmental factors that contribute to poor psychological and physical health, including PTSD. People whose childhoods included exposure to a catastrophe (Osofsky, Osofsky, Kronenberg, Brennan, & Hansel, 2009), who were younger than 10 years old when their parents separated or divorced (Davidson et al., 1991), who had neglectful and maladaptive caregivers (Dorrington et al., 2019), and who experienced assault or abuse (Chivers-Wilson, 2006; Foa, Riggs, & Gershuny, 1995; Kuwert et al., 2014) are at higher risk for PTSD than those whose childhoods did not include such adversity. In addition, the severity and type of traumatic event play a role. Events that include serious physical injury, dismemberment, burns, and witnessing injuries or the deaths of others seem to increase the risk of developing a stress disorder (Koren, Norman, Cohen, Barman, & Klein, 2005; Sareen et al., 2013; Ursano, McCarroll, & Fullerton, 2003).

Gender and Cultural Factors

Following a traumatic event, females are more susceptible than males to developing PTSD (Bryant & Harvey, 2003; Inslicht et al., 2013; Tolin & Foa, 2006). Why might this be? Some researchers believe that higher rates of sexual assault, intimate partner violence, and abuse among females, as well as gender roles, are possibilities (Olff, 2017; Stein, Walker, & Forde, 2000; Street & Dardis, 2018; U.S. Department of Veterans Affairs, 2019). Other researchers note that females use coping mechanisms that are more emotionally involved, such as tend-and-befriend, rather than flight-or-fight and problem-solving mechanisms found more often in males (Olff, 2017). Furthermore, females seem to have a different learned fear response than males (Inslicht et al., 2013). If you think back to the description of classical conditioning in the chapter on learning, you might surmise that learning plays a role in PTSD. Many researchers believe this to be the case. Neutral stimuli present at the time of the traumatic event can pair with the fear response and, in turn, result in a triggering of the fear response in the future (Lissek & van Meurs, 2015). Inslicht and colleagues (2013) tested this stimulus and fear response pairing in males and females and found that females with PTSD had higher rates of fear conditioning than males. However, fear conditioning results like these have not been replicated consistently (Kornfield, Hantsoo, & Epperson, 2018). Inconsistencies in findings might be the result of fluctuations in hormones and how hormones impact males versus females brain (Kornfield et al., 2018; Olff, 2017).

Culture also plays a role among persons with PTSD. It is reported that Latinx individuals are at a higher risk for PTSD (Alcántara, Casement, & Lewis-Fernández, 2013) and experience more severe symptoms (Marshall, Schell, & Miles, 2009), compared to non-Latinx individuals. For example, Latinx police officers have been found to have more severe stress responses than non-Latinx police officers (Pole, Best, Metzler, & Marmar, 2005; Pole et al., 2001). Hispanic veterans of Vietnam also show more severe PTSD symptoms and are at higher risk of developing the disorder than their non-Hispanic counterparts (Ortega & Rosenheck, 2000). One explanation is that people from Latinx and Hispanic cultures are less likely to seek treatment and more likely to participate in avoidance behaviors (Pole et al., 2005)—both of which could result in an increased chance of developing PTSD (Perilla, Norris, & Lavizzo, 2002). Current research has demonstrated that these Latinx cultural influences begin at a young age, with parents of Latinx youth reporting difficulty with identifying mental distress, frequent reliance on familial support instead of professional support, and a desire to avoid stigma towards their children's mental health issues (Dixon De Silva et al., 2020). However, these same parents also report an openness to get their children the proper treatment and an interest in learning more about mental health (Dixon De Silva et al., 2020).

OBSESSIVE-COMPULSIVE AND RELATED DISORDERS

> **LEARNING OBJECTIVES**
>
> Describe the purpose of a compulsive behavior for persons with obsessive-compulsive disorder.
>
> - Provide examples of obsessive thoughts.
> - Discuss the biology underlying obsessive-compulsive disorder.

Howard Hughes had it all. He was a billionaire, a famous pilot, an entrepreneur, and a Hollywood producer. There was just one hitch: Howard was tormented by an uncontrollable preoccupation with germs, eventually causing him to live the life of a hermit. He sealed all windows and doors with tape and spent many hours each day washing himself. His aides had to open doors with their feet to avoid contaminating doorknobs, wear white cotton gloves before serving his food, and deliver newspapers in stacks of three so that he could slide the middle one out with a tissue. Toward the end of his life, Howard became so overwhelmed by his own routines that he could not take care of himself. When he died at the age of 69, his body was filthy and emaciated, his beard was scraggly, his teeth were rotted, and his fingernails were so long that they curled in on themselves—a sad and ironic ending for a man who had once said, "I want to live longer than my parents, so I avoid germs" (Fowler, 1986, p. 33).

Obsessive-Compulsive Disorder

Along with an estimated four million other Americans, Howard Hughes suffered from **obsessive-compulsive disorder (OCD)**—a crippling anxiety ailment characterized by constant *obsessions* (the intrusion into consciousness of persistent, often disturbing thoughts) and *compulsions* (behavior rituals performed in response to the obsessions). OCD usually begins in late adolescence and early adulthood; affects men and women equally; and is found in India, England, Norway, Egypt, Nigeria, Japan, Hong Kong, and other countries around the world (Insel, 1984). Most people with OCD know that their habits are irrational, but they just can't stop themselves. Fearing shame and humiliation, many of them try to keep their actions a secret and wait years before seeking treatment.

If left untreated, what happens to people with OCD? Gunnar Skoog and Ingmar Skoog (1999) conducted a long-term follow-up study of 144 patients who were diagnosed as having OCD in the 1950s and then reexamined by the same psychiatrist in the 1990s. Very few of these patients had received the treatments known today to be effective. The results were mixed. The good news was that two-thirds of the patients had improved within 10 years of the onset of OCD, and four-fifths had improved within

obsessive-compulsive disorder (OCD). An anxiety disorder defined by persistent thoughts (obsessions) and the need to perform repetitive acts (compulsions).

FIGURE 13.8 ■ What Happens to People With OCD

A long-term follow-up study of untreated OCD patients revealed that two-thirds improved after 10 years and four-fifths improved after 40 years. Unfortunately, very few fully recovered—and some even got worse.

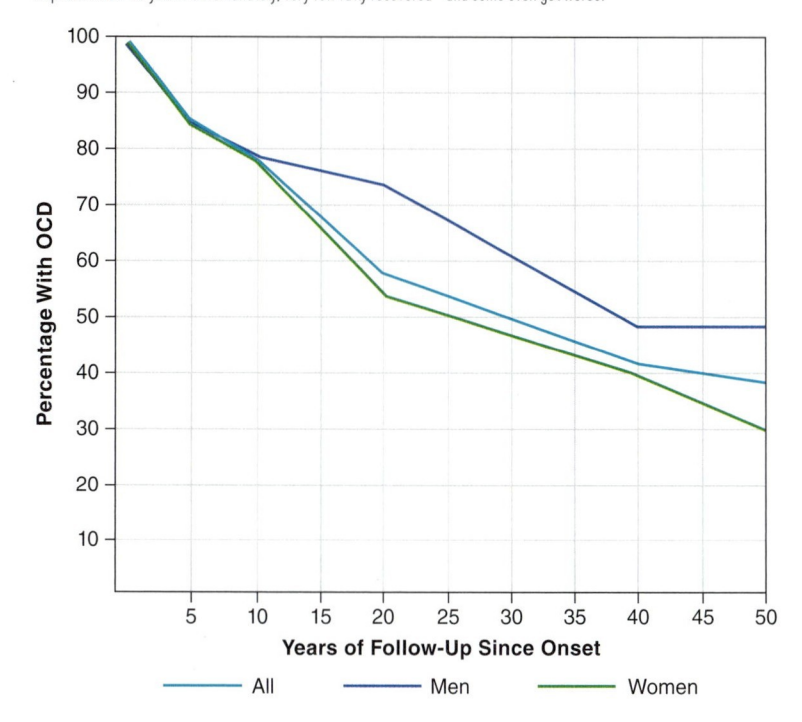

40 years. The bad news was that only one-fifth of the original patients were *fully* recovered, with two-thirds continuing to experience some of the symptoms. After 40 years, one-tenth of them showed no improvement—and another one-tenth got worse (illustrated in Figure 13.8).

What kinds of thoughts and behaviors haunt OCD patients? In *The Boy Who Couldn't Stop Washing,* psychiatrist Judith Rapoport (1989) described one boy who washed his hands so much they became raw and bloodied from all the scrubbing, another boy who ran up and down a flight of stairs exactly 63 times a day, and a woman who was so determined to keep her eyebrows symmetrical that she plucked out each and every hair. In fact, game show host Howie Mandel went public with his lifelong battle against OCD. Howie has a fear of germs and, as a result, uses his famous "fist bump" to avoid shaking hands. His humorous and candid autobiography, *Here's the Deal: Don't Touch Me,* provides an account of his journey. As bizarre as these stories seem, research shows that OCD sufferers constantly check, doubt, wash, hoard, order, obsess, and mentally neutralize their unacceptable thoughts and behaviors (Foa, Kozak, Salkovskis, Coles, & Amir, 1999).

Everyone has a few mild obsessions and compulsions. You may double- and triple-check your alarm clock at night, or try to avoid stepping on sidewalk cracks, or feel a burning need to straighten out crooked wall hangings. Professional athletes are especially well known for their compulsive rituals. Many baseball players, for example, adjust their caps, tug at their shirts, bang their shoes, and run through a complicated sequence of superstitious gestures before every pitch. If these examples don't apply to you, try this: Do not imagine a white bear. Seriously, put this book down, and try not to think about white bears. Recognize the problem described in the chapter on health, stress, and wellness? Daniel Wegner (1989) finds that when people actively try to suppress a thought, that thought intrudes into consciousness with remarkable frequency—like a newly developed obsession. What distinguishes these mild quirks from OCD is the intensity of the accompanying anxiety and the extent to which it interferes with one's life.

Theories of Obsessive-Compulsive Disorder

There are different theories about the causes of OCD. Psychoanalysts maintain that obsessive thoughts leak forbidden sexual and aggressive urges into consciousness, compelling the person to devise elaborate rituals as a countermeasure. In this view, compulsive washing symbolizes a person's need to cleanse the soul of dirty impulses. Behaviorally oriented theorists note that the compulsions endure because they help to reduce the anxiety aroused by obsessive thoughts. Indeed, many compulsions can be extinguished in a few weeks by exposing patients to the source of the obsession but preventing them from responding to it—for example, no washing allowed despite the buildup of anxiety (Foa & Franklin, 2001).

Biological factors also play a role, as indicated by the fact that antidepressant drugs help most sufferers of OCD to terminate their rituals (Rapoport, 1989; Williams, Mugno, Franklin, & Faber, 2013). Also, positron emission tomography (PET) scans of the brains of OCD patients have revealed abnormally high levels of activity in a group of nuclei that are involved in the control of habitual behaviors. In a PET study of 18 OCD patients, Jeffrey Schwartz and others (1996) found that this area became less active after behavioral and cognitive therapy. For about 10 weeks, patients were prevented from acting on their obsessions. Struck with the urge to wash for the umpteenth time of the day, for example, they were trained to label the urge a mere brain-triggered obsession and refocus their attention on a constructive activity such as gardening or golf. As Schwartz (1996) describes in his book *Brain Lock*, this refocusing procedure is designed to engage a new part of the brain, and this helps to "unlock" the area that had become stuck in its pattern. When it comes to OCD, it appears that the mind can change the brain. We discuss more treatments for OCD in the chapter on treatment and interventions.

Howie Mandel has gone public with his OCD diagnosis in an attempt to educate people about the disorder. He advocates for psychological treatment and admits that it is not a "magic pill" but, rather, a set of tools to help people with OCD cope and enjoy a better quality of life.
Associated Press / Evan Agostini

LEARNING CHECK

Order From Disorders

Each of the terms in the left column is related to psychological disorders. Bring order from disorders by identifying their closest descriptions in the right column.

1. Medical model
2. Psychological model
3. Panic disorder
4. Specific phobia
5. Sociocultural model
6. Obsessive-compulsive disorder (OCD)
7. Generalized anxiety disorder
8. Posttraumatic stress disorder

a. The perspective that psychological disorders are influenced by cultural factors.
b. A disorder that results from exposure to trauma.
c. An anxiety disorder characterized by an intense and irrational fear.
d. Sudden and intense rushes of anxiety without an apparent reason.
e. The perspective that mental disorders are caused by biological conditions.
f. The perspective that mental disorders are caused and maintained by one's life experiences.
g. An anxiety disorder characterized by persistent thoughts and the need to perform repetitive acts.
h. A constant state of anxiety not linked to an identifiable source.

(Answers: 1. e; 2. f; 3. d; 4. c; 5. a; 6. g; 7. h; 8. b.)

BIPOLAR AND RELATED DISORDERS

LEARNING OBJECTIVES

Recognize the differences between a manic phase and a depressed phase.

- Understand why the DSM-5 separated bipolar disorder from depressive disorders.
- Identify biological issues that might contribute to the progression of a manic phase.
- Explain the significance of public figures advocating for persons with bipolar disorder.

Personal experience tells us that mood can powerfully shade our view of ourselves, the world, and the future. On the roller-coaster of life, the range of feelings is familiar to all of us: The exhilarating highs are on one end of the continuum, and the depths of despair are on the other. Land the job of your dreams, fall head over heels in love, or win a lottery, and you fly elatedly "on cloud 9." Lose a job or money, break up with a lover, or struggle in school or at work, and you become sad, even depressed. These fluctuations are normal. Problems arise, however, when someone's mood state—whether high or low—is so intense that it profoundly impairs the ability to function.

Bipolar Disorder

bipolar disorder. A rare mood disorder characterized by wild fluctuations from mania (a euphoric, overactive state) to depression (a state of hopelessness and apathy).

Bipolar disorder produces wild fluctuations that range from *manic* (a euphoric, overactive state) to *depressed* (a state of hopelessness and apathy). Having what used to be called "manic depression," patients with bipolar disorder alternate uncontrollably between the two extremes, in cycles that last from a few days to several months. What does the manic phase of this disorder feel like? What are the symptoms? In its early stages, mania is an exhilarating state of mind that many of us have enjoyed from time to time. The mildly manic person is boundless in energy, filled with self-esteem, and confident that no challenge is too daunting. With the mind racing at full speed, the manic person is entertaining, witty, imaginative, quick to make connections between ideas, and filled with ambitious and creative schemes.

In *Touched with Fire*, Kay Redfield Jamison (1993) notes that among the many creative geniuses who had bipolar disorder were composers Robert Schumann and George Frideric Handel, artist Vincent van Gogh, and writers Edgar Allan Poe, Ernest Hemingway, Eugene O'Neill, Sylvia Plath, F. Scott Fitzgerald, Mark Twain, Walt Whitman, Tennessee Williams, and Virginia Woolf. In *The Price of Greatness*, Arnold Ludwig (1995) reported on a biographical survey of more than a thousand famous people of the 20th century. He discovered that writers, poets, and artists were two to three times more likely to have bipolar disorder than successful professionals in business, science, sports, and public life. In fact, many brave celebrities have advocated for those diagnosed with bipolar disorder. Carrie Fisher publicly advocated for better mental health treatment across a span of decades and frequently shared her own experiences with bipolar disorder. You may recognize her as Princess Leia Organa from *Star Wars*. In 2018, Mariah Carey, an award-winning vocal artist, went public with her bipolar disorder diagnosis. Another female vocalist diagnosed with bipolar disorder, Demi Lovato, chose to use her fame to advocate for mental health awareness.

Is there a connection between creativity and bipolar disorder? Murray and Johnson (2010) write that "there is a natural co-occurrence of creativity and bipolar disorder (BD), and clinicians who treat people with BD are therefore likely to work with highly creative individuals" (p. 721). Santosa and colleagues (2007) conducted a controlled study that compared persons with bipolar disorder to control subjects without a psychological disorder. They found that persons with

Actress Carrie Fisher may best be known for her role as Princess Leia Organa—a tough, independent, and witty character who fought relentlessly against the Dark Side. Interestingly, her real-life role as a person with bipolar disorder was not far from Princess Leia. Fisher publicly discussed her tremendously difficult battle with bipolar disorder and became one of psychology's strongest advocates for better mental health care and acceptance.

Associated Press / Chris Pizzello

bipolar disorder scored higher in creativity on the Barron-Welsh Art Scale compared to control subjects. MacCabe and colleagues (2018) discovered that students majoring in an artistic field had an increased risk of developing bipolar disorder in adulthood. Does this mean that bipolar disorder is something to be envied if you desperately desire to live a life of creativity?

Before jumping to the conclusion that bipolar disorder is worth having, you should know that there is a much darker side. As the disorder progresses, the mania accelerates out of control, and "high" becomes "too high." The person becomes easily distracted, moves from one project to another, stays awake at night, and is extremely sensitive to stimulation. People in an advanced state of mania also harbor delusions (false beliefs) of grandeur. They make promises they cannot keep, buy things they cannot afford, start new sexual relationships, and drag others into risky moneymaking schemes that are bound to fail.

Socially, the charm and wit give way to behavior that embarrasses others. Fitting the stereotype of the "raving maniac," the person becomes loud, fast-talking, frenzied, and explosive. Even mild criticism may trigger anger and hostility. As the mania progresses, psychotic features can also occur such as hallucinations or delusions of invincibility. It is this symptomology—combined with family history and genetics—that led researchers and clinicians to place bipolar disorder between schizophrenia and depression in the *DSM-5* (American Psychiatric Association, 2013). Inflated sense of self, excessive talking, flighty ideas, and psychotic features are also seen in schizophrenia. Where is bipolar disorder bridged with depression? Well, this manic phase is sometimes followed by a bout of major depression. Illustrating that what goes up must come down, persons with bipolar disorder either return to normal or hit the ground in a crash landing. This exhilarating high and devastating low can happen countless times for a person with bipolar disorder. Sometimes, the low can be so bottomless that the person cannot find a way out. A remarkable number of creative geniuses who reaped the benefits of their manic energy later killed themselves while depressed (Goodwin & Jamison, 1990; Ludwig, 1995).

Professor Kay Redfield Jamison (1995), who has bipolar disorder, describes the experience in a memoir, *An Unquiet Mind*: "When you're high it's tremendous. The ideas and feelings are fast and frequent like shooting stars.... But, somewhere, this changes. The fast ideas are far too fast, and there are far too many.... [Y]ou are irritable, angry, frightened, uncontrollable, and enmeshed totally in the blackest caves of the mind" (p. 67).

Leonardo Cendamo/Hulton Archive via Getty Images

Theories of Bipolar and Related Disorders

As you may have surmised, bipolar disorder is complex and its development is not completely understood. Like many scientific breakthroughs, some of psychology's breakthroughs in bipolar disorder have happened by accident. Those accidents have allowed researchers to work backward to develop theories about the causes of bipolar disorder. These theories include genetics, neurotransmitters, and cognition.

Biological Factors

Ernest Hemingway, a creative genius with bipolar disorder, killed himself with a shotgun. So did his father and brother. Then many years later, in June 1996, his granddaughter Margaux Hemingway died by suicide with a drug overdose. Clearly, say researchers, the depression that triggers suicide runs in families. But does this mean that bipolar disorder is inherited? Smoller and Finn (2003) completed genetic models and found that genes explain 60 to 80 percent of bipolar disorder development risk. Thus, bipolar disorder has been described as one of "the most heritable of medical disorders" (Barnett & Smoller, 2009, p. 331). Research shows that if one identical twin has bipolar disorder, there is a 40 percent chance that at some point the other will have it, too. However, in fraternal twins, the chance of developing bipolar disorder drops dramatically to an average of 5 percent (Kieseppa, Partonen, Haukka, Kaprio, & Lonnqvist, 2004; McGuffin et al., 2003). Yet the rate for first-degree relatives is 9 percent (Barnett & Smoller, 2009).

In all likelihood, genes influence mood disorders by acting on neurotransmitters, the biochemicals that relay impulses from one neuron to another. Post and colleagues (1980, 1978) found higher norepinephrine activity in persons with bipolar disorder than in those without. Telner and colleagues (1986) provided support to the norepinephrine and mania link when an interesting side effect of blood pressure medication occurred in persons with bipolar disorder; their manic symptoms lessened. Others have demonstrated that serotonin (Mahmood & Silverstone, 2001; Shastry, 2005) and dopamine play a role in mood disorders (Ashok et al., 2017).

The success of lithium as a treatment for bipolar disorder has also suggested that neurotransmitters are the culprit. But do we know exactly which neurotransmitters react to lithium? Not quite, and that might be because it isn't a specific neurotransmitter that interacts with lithium but, instead, is a physiological response. An international collaborative study led by Evan Snyder, discussed further in the chapter on treatment and interventions, recently discovered how lithium interacts with neurons (Tobe et al., 2017). In addition, Giakoumatos and colleagues (2015) demonstrated that lithium protected against the thinning of cortical tissue among brains affected by bipolar disorder (illustrated in Figure 13.9). These discoveries, however, still do not account for the percentage of bipolar disorder development that is not accounted for by biology.

Cognitive Factors

"When I am in a manic episode, I am full of wonderful ideas!" Clearly, this is a positive perspective of bipolar disorder. Compare that to, "When I am in a manic episode, I feel out of control and as if I cannot shut my mind off… it's overwhelming." You can imagine why a person experiencing a manic episode might describe it in this manner. Does the way we think about our circumstances and experiences have an impact on our psychological well-being? It most certainly does. The integrative cognitive model (Mansell, Morrison, Reid, Lowens, & Tai, 2007) argues that when persons with bipolar disorder are in either high or low internal states, how they appraise those states makes an impact on their severity. Take, for example, a person who dreads a manic episode and, thus, attempts to feverishly control how they feel. The constant worry about a future manic episode takes over their thoughts and, as a

FIGURE 13.9 ■ Bipolar Disorder and Brain Thinning

This MRI scan shows thinning of the cortex in adult patients with bipolar disorder. Gradations of cortical thickness loss are shown using the scale at right, with gray representing no significant cortical thinning

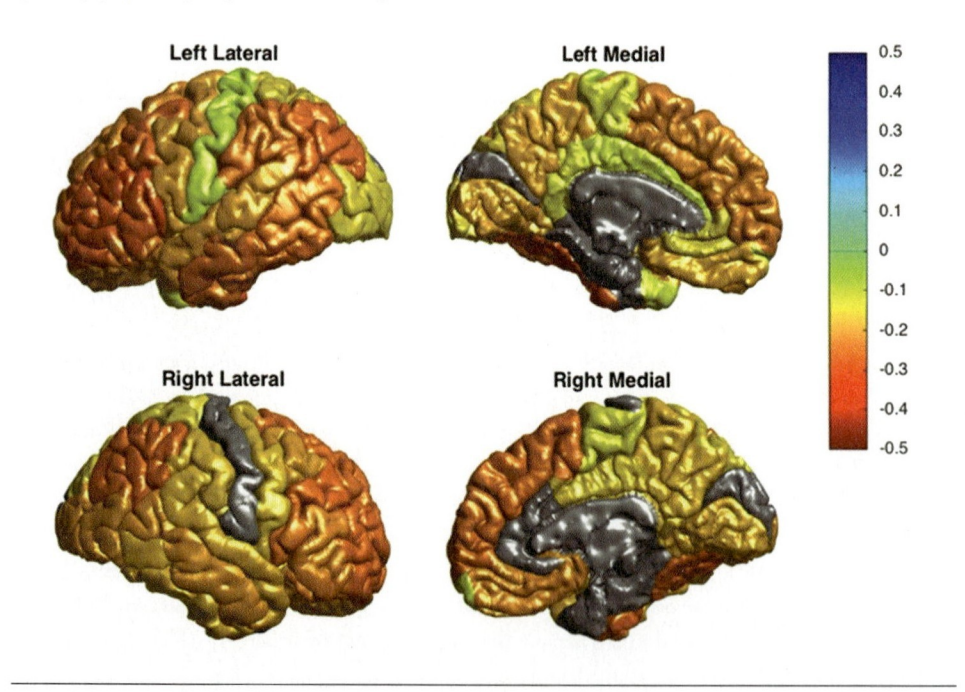

Source: Hibar, D., Westlye, L., Doan, N. et al. Cortical abnormalities in bipolar disorder: an MRI analysis of 6503 individuals from the ENIGMA Bipolar Disorder Working Group. Mol Psychiatry 23, 932–942 (2018). https://doi.org/10.1038/mp.2017.73

http://creativecommons.org/licenses/by-nc-nd/4.0/

result, becomes a self-fulfilling prophecy. Kelly and colleagues (2017) reviewed a collection of studies on this type of thinking to determine if, in fact, these types of appraisals were correlated with bipolar disorder. What they found was that persons with bipolar disorder did have a tendency to appraise their internal states in a more elevated manner than control subjects. These elevated appraisals—whether during highs or lows—also predicted bipolar-relevant symptoms. Whether or not they are a sign of risk for developing bipolar disorder or a vulnerability as a result of bipolar disorder development is not known, but how one thinks about their internal states is definitely an area worth further investigation. Research has connected negative appraisals with people who feel trapped in a cycle of uncontrollably bad factors (Metalsky et al., 1993; Seligman, 1991).

PERSONALITY DISORDERS

LEARNING OBJECTIVES

Recognize the features that personality disorders have in common.

- Define a personality disorder.
- Compare borderline personality disorder with antisocial personality disorder.
- Create an argument for why is there so much interest in antisocial personality disorder.

You have a unique personality. We all do. You may be sloppy or meticulous, calm or emotional, self-centered or altruistic, cautious or impulsive, a loner or a social butterfly. However, if someone's personality is highly inflexible and maladaptive, is abnormal in comparison to their culture, and causes distress, the person is diagnosed as having a **personality disorder** (American Psychiatric Association, 2013; Livesley, 2001; Millon, 1995).

Of the disorders classified in the *DSM-5*, personality disorders are among the most controversial. People diagnosed with personality disorders—an estimated 1 to 6 percent of the population (Tyrer, Reed, & Crawford, 2015)—are not swamped with anxiety, depression, or confusion, nor have they lost touch with reality. In fact, they are not particularly motivated to change. The problem is that they are trapped by their own rigid ways in self-defeating patterns of behavior, patterns that begin to form in adolescence and then harden like plaster for the rest of their lives.

Thirteen personality disorders are listed in the *DSM-5*, many of them quite colorful in their character. For example, there is the socially isolated and emotionally detached *schizoid personality*, the perfectionistic *obsessive-compulsive personality*, the overly sensitive and suspicious *paranoid personality*, the melodramatic and attention-seeking *histrionic personality*, the self-centered and ego-inflated *narcissistic personality*, and the *avoidant personality*, who so fears rejection that they do not start new relationships or make social commitments. Two others in particular have attracted widespread attention: the borderline personality, which is quite common; and the antisocial personality, which can be socially destructive.

personality disorder. One of a group of disorders characterized by a personality that is highly inflexible and maladaptive.

People diagnosed with personality disorders tend to behave in a maladaptive and rigid manner. The paranoid personality is highly sensitive and suspicious of others.

iStock.com/Siphotography

The Borderline Personality

Marilyn Monroe was famous for her beauty and her tremendous success in Hollywood. She was also known for being unpredictable, impulsive, insecure, impossible to live with, and yet desperately afraid to be alone. At the age of 36, she shocked the world when she died by suicide. From what is known about her life, Marilyn did not have a serious anxiety, somatoform, conversion, or dissociative disorder, nor did she have schizophrenia. At times, she was depressed. If she were alive today, however, she might well be diagnosed as having a **borderline personality disorder**.

Borderline personality disorder features a lack of identity and a pattern of instability in self-image, mood, and social relationships. People with this disorder (about two-thirds of whom are female) are uncertain of who they are in terms of their career goals, friends, and values. They complain of feeling empty and bored, can't stand to be left alone, and are desperate for the company of others. Unhappily, people with a borderline personality cling to others with such fierce dependence that their relationships are stormy and do not last. Persons with borderline personality disorder have an extreme fear of abandonment. They are impulsive and in the habit of running away, getting into fights, and jumping into bed with strangers. As a way to get attention, they are also notorious for committing acts of self-destruction or threatening suicide.

In a study of the lives of 57 patients with borderline personality disorder, there were 42 suicide threats, 40 overdoses, 38 cases of drug abuse, 36 acts of self-mutilation (slashing wrists, banging heads, burning skin with cigarettes, pulling out hair), 36 cases of sexual promiscuity, and 14 automobile accidents caused by reckless driving (Gunderson, 1984, 2001). As for what motivates these acts, females with borderline personality disorder say they had committed nonsuicidal self-injury to punish themselves, distract themselves, experience emotions, and vent anger—but that they had attempted suicide to benefit others whom they burden (Brown, Comtois, & Linhan, 2002). This disorder is somewhat prevalent among university students (Meaney, Hasking, & Reupert, 2016). While females are diagnosed with borderline personality disorder more often than males, the latter also suffer from this disorder. *Saturday Night Live* cast member Pete Davidson has gone public with his diagnosis (McCluskey, 2018). His social media posts provide examples of what it's like to be stereotyped and bullied as a result of having a psychological disorder. Pete was diagnosed with borderline personality disorder in 2016 and has since been candid about what it's like to date, be a public figure, and navigate treatment.

Actor and comedian Pete Davidson has openly discussed his diagnosis of borderline personality disorder. He is an example of how people with a psychological disorder can lead fulfilling and successful lives.
Dimitrios Kambouris/Getty Images Entertainment via Getty Images

borderline personality disorder. A type of personality characterized by instability in one's self-image, mood, and social relationships and a lack of clear identity.

The Antisocial Personality

The brutally cold, calculating, and callous individual is often depicted in books and in films such as *Silence of the Lambs*. Unfortunately, the characters depicted in art come from real life. Every now and then, a crime story appears on the news that is so horrible it give us chills. Three high school students pour gasoline on their teacher and set her on fire. A man slashes the face of a model with a razor blade in exchange for $200. What kind of person is capable of these atrocities? Who are these monstrous creatures? In the 19th century, they were described as morally insane. More recently, they were called psychopaths, then sociopaths. Today, the term **antisocial personality disorder** is used to describe people who have "ice in their veins" and who behave in ways that are self-centered, irresponsible, destructive, and completely without regard for the welfare of others.

According to the *DSM-5*, antisocial personality disorder (ASPD) applies to people who, as children, would cut school, run away from home, set fires, harm animals, steal, cheat, and get into fights—and who, as adults, drive recklessly, borrow money and do not return it, get into fights, behave irresponsibly as spouses or parents, abuse substances excessively, and engage in unlawful activities.

antisocial personality disorder. A personality disorder involving a chronic pattern of self-centered, manipulative, and destructive behavior toward others.

As you might expect, a person with ASPD has difficulty with close relationships. But the most striking feature is that he (80 percent are men) lacks a conscience and feels little to no guilt, remorse, or empathy for people he has harmed. He uses others for pleasure—or profit—and then discards them. Therefore, people are nothing but an object to be used. When intelligent, the person with ASPD is not a common street criminal but a cool, manipulative, charming, and clever con artist who can seduce romantic companions with empty words of love, lie to business partners with a straight face, and sweet-talk his way out of trouble (Cleckley, 1976; Hare, 1993; Lykken, 1995; Millon, Simonsen, Birket-Smith,

& Davis, 1998). Nathan Brooks (2017) has suggested a connection between antisocial personality traits and corporate executives. However, Landay and colleagues (2019) disagree with the findings and believe them to be overblown based on their deep and thorough review of the literature. Interestingly, though, they did find a disparity between antisocial personality traits and gender; females with these traits are labeled as ineffective in their organizations, whereas males with these traits are seen as effective. Think about how beneficial it would be to have no remorse when deciding what company to break apart, which corporation to lie to, or whom to fire. It comes as no surprise that surveys conducted across 12 countries revealed that 47 percent of male prisoners and 21 percent of female prisoners have ASPD—which is 10 times more than in the general population (Fazel & Danesh, 2002). These percentages are close to the one found by Black and colleagues (2010). They measured the frequency of ASPD among 320 newly incarcerated offenders and found that ASPD was present in 35 percent of them.

For many years, researchers have speculated about the causes of ASPD. Some have tried to trace the disorder in childhood to broken homes, neglectful parents, and faulty role models that impede the formation of a superego and moral development. Others have measured brain-wave patterns and heart rates, and they have found that people with antisocial personalities are less excitable than the average person and are not as easily startled. They remain physiologically calm in the face of electric shock, tense situations, and images of children screaming and crying, an attribute that makes them fearless (Blair, Jones, Clark, & Smith, 1997; Patrick, Bradley, & Lang, 1993). In fact, boys who are referred for their antisocial behavior have lower-than-average levels of cortisol, a stress hormone normally released in situations that arouse fear (McBurnett, Lahey, Rathouz, & Loeber, 2000).

James Fallon is a cousin of the infamous murderer Lizzie Borden and a researcher devoted to investigating the brains of psychopaths—people with ASPD who take pleasure in the torture, and even murder, of others. In Fallon's 2013 book, *The Psychopath Inside,* he shares his findings that were both troubling and surprising. He saw low activity in brain areas responsible for moral reasoning and impulse control. This supports findings from others who also observed a lack of impulse control in persons with ASPD—a problem that is worsened by their tendency to abuse alcohol and other disinhibiting drugs (Myers, Stewart, & Brown, 1998). Society can take some comfort in the fact that individuals with antisocial personalities who go on to become criminals tend to burn out and commit fewer crimes after age 40 (Hare, McPherson, & Forth, 1988). And not everyone with the brain of a psychopath or familial history of psychopathology will commit heinous crimes. How do we know? Because James Fallon himself has the brain of a psychopath but has never committed a crime.

Psychology Applied: The Insanity Defense

In Houston, Texas, 36-year-old Andrea Yates drowned her five children—Noah, 7, John, 5, Luke, 3, Paul, 2, and Mary, 6 months. One by one, she put and held them in a bathtub of water until they lay breathless and motionless. Her oldest boy pleaded with his mother and tried to escape but she chased him down, dragged him to the bathroom, and drowned him too. She then dialed 911, and when the police arrived, she confessed. In an emotionless, zombie-like manner, Yates said she killed her children to rid herself of Satan and save them from going to hell. As it turned out, Yates had suffered from severe postpartum depression, which worsened after the birth of her last child. She had been hospitalized in the past, and on antipsychotic medications, and had twice attempted suicide. Yates went to trial and pleaded not guilty by reason of insanity. The trial lasted for four weeks and included expert testimony on both sides from psychologists and psychiatrists. Then on March 12, 2002, a jury of four men and eight women voted that Yates was sane—and guilty. She was sentenced to life in prison. In 2006, her conviction was overturned, and Yates was found not guilty by reason of insanity (Newman, 2006). As a result, she was released from prison and placed in a psychiatric facility where she could remain for the rest of her life.

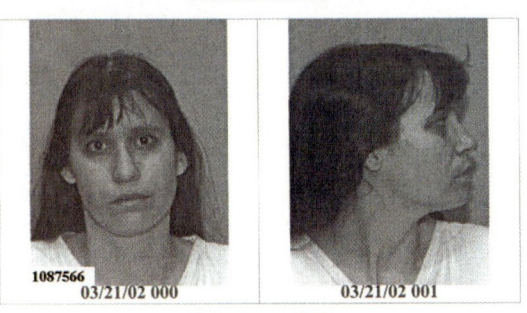

Andrea Yates.
Getty Images News via Getty Images

Understandably, many people fear that the insanity defense opens up a loophole through which massive numbers of criminals can use "designer defenses" to escape punishment for their crimes (Kirwin, 1997). But is that fear justified? Consider these three questions: (a) What percentage of criminal defendants enter a plea of insanity? (b) Of those who do, what percentage succeed? and (c) Of those who succeed, what percentage are set free? Eric Silver and others (1994) compared public opinions on these questions to the actual figures gathered from 49 counties in eight different states and found that respondents, on average, vastly overestimated the overall impact of the insanity defense in criminal justice. Specifically, the public estimated that 37 percent of all criminal defendants plead insane, that 44 percent are acquitted, and that 26 percent of those acquitted are set free. In actuality, less than 1 percent of all defendants plead insanity, 26 percent are acquitted, and 15 percent of those acquitted are set free (the others are committed to mental hospitals). Put these numbers together, and you'll recognize that public opinion is highly distorted. For every 1,000 cases, people estimate that 163 defendants are acquitted by reason of insanity and that 47 are set free. In actuality, two defendants in 1,000 are acquitted by reason of insanity, and only three in 10,000 are set free. In most cases, those who are found to be insane spend as much time confined to a hospital as they would have spent in prison. Other studies too have confirmed the point: The insanity defense is rarely used and seldom successful—despite what people think (Lymburner & Roesch, 1999).

Despite the moral underpinnings of the insanity defense and the reassuring odds concerning the frequency of its usage, there are problems in its implementation. One is that many defendants who are evaluated for insanity engage in some form of malingering, or faking. To overcome this problem, psychologists have developed tests and interview methods to try to detect such faking (Hall & Pritchard, 1996; Rogers, 1997; Wygant & Lareau, 2015). A second problem is that judges often turn for expert opinion to clinical psychologists and psychiatrists who are trained to diagnose psychological disorders—not to resolve disputes about criminal responsibility. Predictably, many insanity trials feature a battle of opposing experts who disagree in their opinions (Dawes, Faust, & Meehl, 1989; Hagen, 1997; Wool & Saragoza, 2012).

Is there a solution to the insanity dilemma? On the one hand, it seems inhumane to punish people who cannot be held responsible for their actions. On the other hand, it seems repugnant to provide a loophole for violent criminals. Many courts have reformed their laws to discourage acquittals by reason of insanity (Borum & Fulero, 1999). Although it remains to be determined what effect these changes will have on judges and juries, controversy will clearly continue to surround this awkward relationship between clinical psychology and the law.

LEARNING CHECK

Symptomology

Show your skills by identifying the sets of symptoms with the psychological disorders to which they most closely correspond.

| 1. Depression | 2. Personality disorder | 3. Borderline personality disorder | 4. Bipolar disorder | 5. Antisocial personality disorder |

a. Characterized by fear of abandonment, instability, and unclear identity.

b. Usually diagnosed in males; symptoms include treating people like objects, lack of empathy, and manipulation.

c. A disorder where the person experiences shifts from euphoria to hopelessness.

d. A mood disorder characterized by sadness, despair, feelings of worthlessness, and low self-esteem.

e. A cluster of disorders characterized by rigidity and the inability to adapt.

(Answers: 1. d; 2. e; 3. a; 4. c; 5. b.)

SCHIZOPHRENIA SPECTRUM DISORDERS

LEARNING OBJECTIVES

Understand the range of symptoms that persons with schizophrenia experience.

- Tell what the word schizophrenia means.
- List the five major symptoms of schizophrenia spectrum disorders.
- Compare a delusion with a hallucination.
- Explain the evidence for the genetic and environmental roots of schizophrenia.

When you stop to think about "madness" or "insanity," what comes to mind? For many of us, the words alone evoke stereotyped images of people who stare blankly into space, talk in gibberish to themselves, see imaginary pink animals, walk in circles, and erupt in fits of rage and violence. These images are not generally accurate, as we'll learn, but they come closest to describing schizophrenia—the most dreaded of psychological disorders (Lenzenweger & Dworkin, 1998). According to Ventriglio and colleagues (2016), suicide is a leading cause of death among persons with schizophrenia. Hor and Taylor (2010) estimate that risk of suicidal death among persons with schizophrenia is 5.6 percent.

Schizophrenia spectrum disorders are marked by gross distortions of thought and perception and by a loss of contact with reality. In some cases, the disorder strikes suddenly between the ages of 17 and 25 and is followed by a full recovery. In other cases, the disorder develops slowly, causes the person to deteriorate over a period of years and casts a life sentence on its victim—no parole, no time off for good behavior. Schizophrenia is found in all cultures of the world and affects males and females equally. It is estimated that slightly less than 1 percent of all Americans will exhibit a schizophrenia spectrum disorder—in the course of a lifetime (Regier, Boyd, & Burke, 1988) or within a given year (Narrow et al., 2002). The most likely age of first onset is 18 to 25 for males, 26 to 45 for females. This sex difference in the age of onset shows up all over the world and has researchers puzzled (Gottesman, 1991; Straube & Oades, 1992).

schizophrenia spectrum disorders. Disorders involving gross distortions of thoughts and perceptions coupled with the loss of contact with reality.

delusions. False beliefs that often accompany schizophrenia and other psychotic disorders.

FIGURE 13.10 ■ Painting by a Psychiatric Patient

"Mummy, its dark in here," writes the 25-year-old woman with schizophrenia who painted this picture. The woman's feelings were displayed as part of an exhibition of works by psychiatric patients in London in 1968.

Symptoms of Schizophrenia Spectrum Disorders

Translated from Greek, the word *schizophrenia* means "split brain." The so-called split is not between two or more inner selves, as in dissociative identity disorder, but rather between thoughts, beliefs, perceptions, emotions, motor behavior, and other brain functions. To people with schizophrenia, it's like being stuck in a "Twilight Zone" (Torrey, 1988), as depicted in Figure 13.10 by an artist who was diagnosed with schizophrenia.

Five major symptoms are found in people with a schizophrenia spectrum disorder. First and foremost, many of them exhibit **delusions**, or false beliefs. In persons with schizophrenia, certain delusional themes appear with great frequency (Appelbaum, Robbins, & Roth, 1999). Among the most common are delusions of *influence*—the belief that one's thoughts are being broadcast in public, stolen from one's mind, or controlled by evil forces. Thus, one patient was convinced that his thoughts were publicized to others on a "mental ticker-tape," another spoke of having her thoughts "sucked out of my mind by a phrenological vacuum extractor," and a third believed "a radio was implanted in my skull." Also common are delusions of *grandeur* (that one is famous or powerful, capable of controlling weather, planets, and other people), delusions of *reference* (that one is the primary recipient of other people's actions), and delusions of *persecution* (that one is a target of secret plots by others).

Bettman via Getty Images

A second symptom is the presence of **hallucinations**, sensory experiences that occur without actual stimulation. To hallucinate is to see, hear, smell, taste, or feel something that does not exist. The most common hallucinations are auditory. Many people with schizophrenia report that they "hear" the swishing or thumping sound of a heartbeat, musical choirs, or disembodied voices that comment on their lives, make accusations, and issue commands. "Son of Sam" David Berkowitz, who terrorized New York City in the 1970s by killing young women, claimed he was ordered to stalk and shoot his victims by the demonic voice of a barking dog. Sometimes, but less often, hallucinations occur in other sensory systems as well. People may "see" heavenly visions, "smell" foul body odors, "taste" poison in their food, or "feel" a tingling, burning, or pricking sensation on their skin. Other perceptual distortions are also evident. According to some reports, lights seem brighter, colors more vibrant, and sounds more intense. And people's bodies often appear longer, shorter, smaller, rounder, or otherwise deformed—like viewing the world through a funhouse mirror.

The third symptom is *disorganized speech*. Disorganized speech reflects mental confusion—a sign that the person is on a different wavelength than the rest of us. Listen to people with this symptom talk, and you may well hear them create new words and drift illogically from one topic to another, making their statements sound like something of a "word salad." Often, for example, they will string together utterances that are only loosely associated. Eugene Bleuler (1911), the Swiss psychiatrist who gave schizophrenia its name, cited an example from one of his patients: "I wish you a happy, joyful, healthy, and fruitful year, and many good wine years to come as well as a healthy and good apple-year, and sauerkraut and cabbage and squash and seed year." In this sample of speech, the word fruitful set off a chain of food-related associations. The reason is that patients with schizophrenia who exhibit disorganized thinking tend to have difficulty focusing attention on one stimulus and filtering out distractions (Freedman et al., 1987; McGhie & Chapman, 1961). In the autobiographies of 50 former patients, concentration problems were the most frequent thought-related complaint (Freedman, 1974).

The fourth symptom is *disorganized or catatonic behavior*. Absorbed in an inner world of stimulation, perhaps confused by distorted perceptions of the outer world, people with schizophrenia often withdraw, go into social exile, and cease to function effectively at work. They may talk to themselves, repeat like parrots what others say, spend hours in statue-like poses, walk backward or in circles, or take their clothes off in public.

The fifth symptom includes what are generally called *negative symptoms*. Negative symptoms include poverty of speech, flat affect, loss of volition, and social withdrawal. For example, some persons with schizophrenia sit still for hours, wear a blank expression on the face, speak in a low and monotonic voice, avoid eye contact, and show little interest or concern in anything. As one psychiatrist noted, "It is uncannily like interacting with a robot" (Torrey, 1988). Others express feelings that are highly animated and exaggerated or are inappropriate to the situation—crying at happy news, laughing at tragedy, or screaming in anger without external provocation. Remarkably, they also lack self-insight. People with schizophrenia often think that their word salads are coherent, their delusions and hallucinations real, and their emotions appropriate.

Theories of Schizophrenia Spectrum Disorders

Can anyone stressed by adverse life circumstances "catch" a schizophrenia spectrum disorder, or are some of us more prone than others? Can the outbreak of schizophrenia in a young adult be predicted in childhood? Indeed, are the causes biological, psychological, or a combination of both?

In the 2001 film *A Beautiful Mind*, Russell Crowe plays an eccentric mathematical genius, John Nash Jr., who won a Nobel Prize for work he did in the 1940s. Early in his career, Nash was diagnosed with paranoid schizophrenia and overwhelmed by delusions, hallucinations, and other incapacitating symptoms. Remarkably, after 30 years, the schizophrenia lifted in what some have called a "miraculous remission," enabling Nash to reengage with people and his work. Sylvia Nasar, the biographer of the late John Nash, often characterized the economist as having "aged out" of the devastating mental illness.

Universal Pictures/Moviepix via Getty Images

hallucinations. Sensory experiences that occur in the absence of actual stimulation.

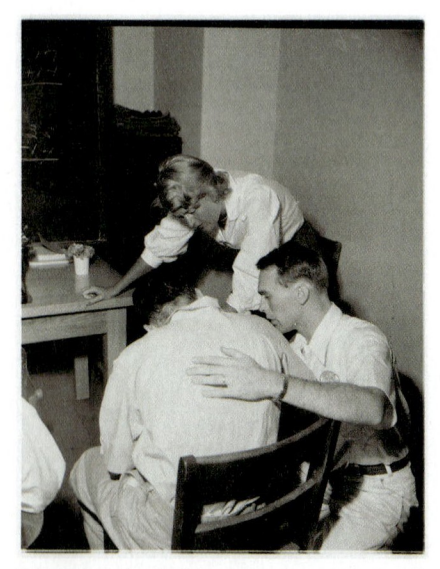

Here, a patient with catatonic schizophrenia is receiving treatment at Brentwood Veterans Hospital in 1951. While in a catatonic state, the person does not move or speak.

University of Southern California/Corbis Historical via Getty Images

Biological Factors

Family, twin, and adoption studies reveal a strong genetic basis for schizophrenia spectrum disorders (Holzman & Matthysse, 1990; Meltzer, 2000). You may recall that about 1 percent of the American population is diagnosed as having schizophrenia at some point in life. However, the more closely related you are to someone with schizophrenia, the greater the risk (illustrated in Figure 13.11). When one fraternal twin has it, the odds are 17 percent for the other. With an identical twin, however, the odds increase even further, to 48 percent—a number that remains high regardless of whether the twins are raised together or apart (Gottesman, 1991; Gottesman & Shields, 1982).

Searching for the biological origins of schizophrenia, many researchers have found that several symptoms are associated with overactivity of the neurotransmitter dopamine. Three kinds of evidence support this linkage. First, antipsychotic drugs that block the activity of dopamine in the brain also lessen hallucinations, delusions, and other behavioral excesses. Second, amphetamines both increase dopamine activity and intensify these same symptoms (long-term usage or overdoses can even trigger schizophrenia-like episodes in normal people). Third, autopsies on deceased patients' brains often reveal an excess of dopamine receptors (Seeman, Guan, & Van Tol, 1993; Wong et al., 1986).

Thanks to recent discoveries, it is evident that schizophrenia is a genetic disorder. A team of researchers believes that one particular gene affected is the C4 gene. A large research team led by Steven McCarroll and Aswin Sekar (2016) analyzed the DNA of more than 100,000 people and 700

FIGURE 13.11 ■ Genetic Relationships and Schizophrenia

As shown, the lifetime risk of schizophrenia increases as a function of how genetically related a person is to someone else who is known to have schizophrenia.

Relationship	Genetic relatedness	Risk
Identical twins	100%	48%
Offspring of two parents with schizophrenia	100%	46%
Fraternal twins	50%	17%
Offspring of one parent with schizophrenia	50%	17%
Sibling	50%	9%
Nephew or niece	25%	4%
Spouse	0%	2%
Unrelated person	0%	1%

Adapted from Gottesman, I. I. (1991). A series of books in psychology: Schizophrenia genesis: The origins of madness.

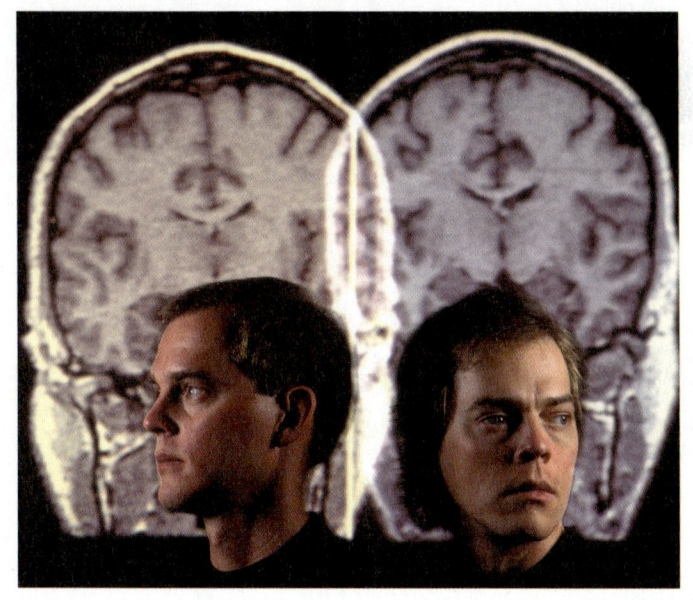

Identical twins David (left) and Steven Elmore (right) stand in front of their brain scans. The brain scans show that Steven has less brain tissue and larger ventricles than David. Steven has schizophrenia, but David does not.

Joe McNally/Hulton Archive via Getty Images

Studies into the biological underpinnings of schizophrenia have demonstrated that a person has a 48 percent likelihood of developing the disorder if their identical twin has been diagnosed.

iStock.com/MesquitaFMS

diathesis-stress model. The theory that certain mental disorders (such as schizophrenia) develop when people with a genetic or acquired vulnerability are exposed to high levels of stress.

postmortem brain samples. What they found was a strong correlation between certain structural forms of the C4 gene and schizophrenia development. The C4 gene plays a crucial role in adolescent synaptic pruning—a process by which "extra" neurons and synaptic connections are removed in order to increase the efficiency of neuronal activity. In brains with schizophrenia, the C4 gene is overactive. This overactivity could result in too much synaptic pruning. Too much synaptic pruning could be the reason for the cognitive symptoms of schizophrenia. It could also be the reason why the cerebral cortex of brains with schizophrenia are not as dense as brains without. But don't be fooled. The C4 gene doesn't seem to be the only culprit. The brain is very complex. Other researchers are studying people with a genetic issue called 22a11.2 deletion syndrome. People with this deletion syndrome are at a 25 percent higher risk of developing a psychotic disorder—including schizophrenia—than those without (National Institutes of Health, 2018).

Psychological Factors

Although there is a genetic basis for schizophrenia, 54 percent of those people born to two parents with schizophrenia do *not* themselves develop the disorder. In other words, heredity may increase the risk, but it does not by itself predetermine one's fate. For example, an article featured in *Science* (Couzin-Frankel, 2017) states that children who hear voices at age 11 are at a 16-fold increased risk of developing schizophrenia but, surprisingly, most of these children won't develop it. This notion has given rise to the **diathesis-stress model**, which states that people with a genetic or acquired vulnerability, or "diathesis," develop schizophrenia when exposed to high levels of stress (Fowles, 1992; Meehl, 1962; Pruessner, Cullen, Aas, & Walker, 2017; Walker & Diforio, 1997). What experiences act as triggering mechanisms?

To identify factors that predict the onset of schizophrenia, researchers on the North American Prodrome Longitudinal Study (Addington et al., 2015) and Personalized Prognostic Tools for Early Psychosis Management (PRONIA; Bonivento et al., 2018) followed youth at high clinical risk for psychosis. So far, the results show that high-risk subjects who developed psychosis had complications at birth and low birth weight. They were also more likely to have had mothers who were exposed to serious infection during their second trimester of pregnancy. Around 8 to 11 years of age, these youths were more likely to be victims of abuse, suffer from a head injury, or be the target of bullying. At 16 years of age, the abuse was also present. In addition, excess stress was present in combination with smoking marijuana. Can the future of a high-risk child be predicted? Perhaps. When psychology graduate students were shown old home movies of future schizophrenia patients and their healthy siblings—all of whom were normal while growing up—78 percent guessed correctly which of the children in the films went on to develop the disorder (Walker & Lewine, 1990). However, there were also children who exhibited all of these aforementioned risks but did not develop psychosis.

It is easier to identify factors that can *predict* the onset of a disorder than to pinpoint its psychological *causes*. To understand why, consider some classic findings that are intriguing but hard to interpret. First, differences in diagnostic frequency exist among racial and ethnic groups. In the African

American community, 2.1 percent receive a diagnosis of schizophrenia, compared to 1.4 percent of Caucasian Americans (Folsom, Fleisher, & Depp, 2006; Lawson, 2008). Similar research by Barnes (2013) discovered that out of 1,641 inpatient clients, Black clients were more likely to be diagnosed with schizophrenia than white clients. Hispanic Americans also are more likely to be diagnosed with schizophrenia than Caucasian Americans (Blow et al., 2004). Furthermore, persons with schizophrenia, compared to their counterparts without, have poorer physical health (Melamed et al., 2020) and during hospitalization for COVID-19, experienced decreased admittance to an intensive care unit (Fond et al., 2021). Combined, these factors put them at a high risk of severe COVID-19 infection, and in turn, in-hospital death (Fond et al., 2021). Such health care disparities could be due to schizophrenia's prevalencein the lowest socioeconomic classes of society. This pattern appears in studies all over the world and is sometimes taken to mean that poverty causes schizophrenia. Or is it the other way around? Perhaps schizophrenia—precisely because it is characterized by massive cognitive and social impairment—leads its sufferers to drop out of school, lose jobs, and drift downward into poverty.

However, in other developing countries, persons diagnosed with schizophrenia have better recovery rates than those who live in developed countries like the United States (Vahia & Vahia, 2008). Another example is the well-publicized observation that parents of children with schizophrenia communicate to their offspring in ways that are inconsistent and confusing. This finding is often taken to suggest that faulty communication patterns at home cause schizophrenia. Again, however, it is equally possible that the behavior of parents is not a cause but a *response* to the problem of communicating with children who have started to demonstrate disorganized symptoms. Which comes first, the chicken or the egg? It is not known. Either way, it seems that biological and environmental forces combine to produce this devastating disorder.

DISSOCIATIVE DISORDERS

> **LEARNING OBJECTIVES**
>
> Define what it means to "dissociate," and connect that definition with the disorder; appreciate the perspectives of believers and skeptics.
>
> - Recognize the symptoms of a dissociative disorder.
> - Develop an argument for the skepticism toward dissociative identity disorder.

Have you ever found yourself listening to someone talk, only to realize that you missed most of what was said? Were you ever in a place that was familiar but could not remember having been there before? Did you ever have trouble figuring out whether an experience that you had was real or just a dream? Many of us experience absentmindedness and other lapses of awareness. Some are common. In a survey of hundreds of adults for example, 94 percent said they had at least occasionally "spaced out" on chunks of a conversation and 52 percent said they had driven somewhere without later recalling details of the drive (Goldberg, 1999). In Japan, Belgium, the Netherlands, and the United States, studies have shown that people consistently report having such experiences (Ray, 1996; Ross, 1997). However, when these episodes of total memory loss are for an extended period of time, and lack of awareness of who and where we are in time impair everyday functioning and cause distress, then it is possible that something more serious is at play. In contrast to these normal episodes that we all experience, people diagnosed with a **dissociative disorder** have serious long-term memory gaps. In essence, it is believed, people with this diagnosis have learned to cope with intense trauma and stress by mentally erasing unwanted parts of life from their memory (Dalenberg et al., 2012; Selvi et al., 2012).

dissociative disorder. A condition marked by a temporary disruption in one's memory, consciousness, or self-identity.

Dissociative Amnesia

The most common dissociative disorder is **dissociative amnesia**, which involves a partial or complete loss of memory. Dissociative amnesia can last for varying periods of time and can be caused by physical trauma such as a hard blow to the head or alcohol intoxication. Alternatively, the problem can

dissociative amnesia. A dissociative disorder involving a partial or complete loss of memory.

People with a dissociative disorder experience memory lapses and might describe their lives as "blurry" or "disjointed."
iStock.com/KatarzynaBialasiewicz

dissociative fugue. A specifier of dissociative amnesia in which a person "forgets" his or her identity, wanders from home, and develops new autobiographical memories.

dissociative identity disorder (DID). Formerly known as multiple personality disorder, it is a condition in which an individual develops two or more distinct identities.

Based on a true story from the 1970s, Halle Berry plays a stripper with DID in *Frankie and Alice*. One of her personalities is a white racist.
AF archive / Alamy Stock Photo

sometimes be traced to a stressful event such as a car accident, a rape, or a physical beating. In these cases of dissociative amnesia, only self-relevant memories are blocked. Amnesia victims may forget who they are and where they live, but they remember clearly how to speak, read, drive a car, and recite information from general knowledge (Weingartner, Grafman, Boutelle, Kaye, & Martin, 1983). Dissociative amnesia can happen in combination with another psychological disorder. For example, persons with bipolar disorder who also have a history of childhood maltreatment report more dissociation than control participants (Hariri et al., 2015; Kefeli, Turow, Yıldırım, & Boysan, 2018).

Dissociative fugue (*fugue*, as in the word *fugitive*, means "flight") is an extension to the diagnosis of dissociative amnesia. In extreme cases, someone who has dissociative fugue not only forgets his or her name but also wanders from home, takes on a new identity, gets a new job, and starts a new life. Then, just as suddenly, the person will "wake up"—disoriented and confused, oblivious to what has transpired, and eager to return home as if no time has passed. Dissociative fugue may last for hours or for years. Sometimes, the victim's new life is more exciting and uninhibited than the old routine. At other times, it provides an escape from responsibility and harm. Either way, it is difficult, if not sometimes impossible, to tell whether a fugue victim has a genuine dissociative disorder or is faking (Schacter, 1986).

Dissociative Identity Disorder

The most dramatic instance of dissociation is **dissociative identity disorder (DID)**, an extremely rare condition in which a person displays two or more distinct identities (until the *DSM-IV* was published in 1994, this condition was called *multiple personality disorder*). Sometimes, two opposing identities battle for control, as in the classic tale of Dr. Jekyll and Mr. Hyde. Sometimes there are three personalities, as in *The Three Faces of Eve*, a film about a woman who alternated among Eve White, a timid housewife; Eve Black, a sexually promiscuous woman; and Jane, a balanced blend of the other two. In other cases, one dominant identity is accompanied by a host of subordinate personalities, as in the case of Sybil Dorsett, whose 16 personalities were portrayed in the film *Sybil*, or the fictitious film *Split*, in which the main character has 23 personalities.

Dissociative identity disorder is such a strange phenomenon that you might think it springs from the imaginative minds of playwrights and novelists. What are the facts and fictions about DID? According to the *DSM-5*, it is more prevalent among female adults than male adults. In child clinical settings, these sex differences in prevalence disappear. This might be due to the fact that DID is ordinarily preceded by repeated childhood abuse. Summarizing five major studies of 843 DID patients, for example, Colin Ross and his colleagues (1990a) found that more than 88 percent reported having been victims of sexual, physical, or emotional child abuse—a striking statistic that was confirmed in a later study in the Netherlands (Boon & Draijer, 1993). This finding suggests the hypothesis that children who are abused and are utterly defenseless learn early in life to cope by tuning out, divorcing a part of themselves from the pain and suffering, and constructing alternative persons within which to live. Ross (1977) thus described DID as "a little girl imagining that the abuse is happening to someone else" (p. 59).

In almost all cases, at least one personality is unable to recall what happens to the others (Putnam, Guroff, Silberman, Barban, & Post, 1986). Thus, nine DID patients who were presented with words to learn while in a particular identity were better able to recall those words within the same identity than while in an alternate identity state (Eich, Macaulay, Loewenstein, & Dihle, 1997). Clinical reports suggest that, at times, the differences among personalities can be extraordinary, as each may have its own voice, speech pattern, motor habits, memories, clothing, and handwriting. Some reports suggest that physical changes may also occur, as when two personalities coexisting within the patient exhibit different brain-wave patterns, blood pressure readings, eyeglass prescriptions, allergies, or reactions to medicine (Kluft, 1996). Table 13.4 presents the most common symptoms of DID, along with percentages of patients exhibiting each symptom, based on interviews with 102 people with DID (Ross et al., 1990b).

If you find the notion of multiple personalities hard to believe, you are not alone. Dorahy and colleagues (2014) and Sar and colleagues (2017) recognized the controversy underlying DID and conducted empirical reviews. Dorahy and colleagues (2014) found that DID was a "complex, valid, and not uncommon disorder, associated with developmental and cultural variables" (p. 417). Sar and colleagues (2017) supported that finding and determined DID to be a robust psychiatric disorder caused by tremendous stress. However, since the first case was reported in 1817, fewer than 200 appeared in psychiatric journals up to the year 1970. Since that time, however, thousands of new cases have been reported, virtually all in North America. To be sure, DID can be found in most societies, but the frequency of the disorder and the form it takes vary from one generation and culture to another (Dorahy et al., 2014; Lilienfeld et al., 1999; Spanos, 1996). All of this has skeptics wondering: Is the disorder really on the rise? There are three possible explanations. One is that many patients are faking DID for personal gain, and therapists are simply unable to distinguish between true and false cases (Pietkiewicz, Bańbura-Nowak, Tomalski, & Boon, 2021). A second is that therapists used to miss or misdiagnose the problem and are now more sensitive to the symptoms. A third possible explanation is that therapists are now overdiagnosing the disorder or, worse, are suggesting and reinforcing its presence in patients, thus producing a "psychiatric growth industry" (Pietkiewicz et al., 2021; Weissberg, 1993).

TABLE 13.4 ■ Symptoms of Dissociative Identity Disorder

Symptoms	Percentages
Another person existing inside	90
Voices talking	87
Amnesia for childhood	83
Referring to self as "we" or "us"	74
Blank spells	68
Being told by others of unremembered events	63
Feelings of unreality	57
Strangers know the patient	44
Noticing that objects are missing	42
Coming out of a blank spell in a strange place	36
Objects are present that cannot be accounted for	31
Different handwriting styles	28

Source: Adapted from C. A. Ross et al. (1990). Structured interview data on 102 cases of Multiple Personality Disorder from four centers. *American Journal of Psychiatry,* 147, p. 599.

> **LEARNING CHECK**
>
> ### Diagnostic Chart
>
> **Show your diagnostic skills by matching the sets of symptoms on the left with the categories to which they most closely correspond on the right.**
>
> 1. Related to dissociative amnesia but where a person also wanders from home to start a new life.
> 2. False beliefs, such as that one's thoughts are being stolen from their mind.
> 3. Blank facial expression; absence of emotion; little to no speech.
> 4. Perceiving a stimulus that isn't there, such as hearing voices when no speaker is present.
> 5. Chronically self-centered, manipulative, destructive behavior toward others.
> 6. Instability in self-image, mood, and social relationships; lack of clear identity.
> 7. A condition in which an individual develops two or more distinct personalities.
>
> a. Borderline personality disorder
> b. Dissociative fugue
> c. Delusions
> d. Hallucinations
> e. Negative symptoms
> f. Dissociative identity disorder
> g. Antisocial personality disorder
>
> (Answers: 1. b; 2. c; 3. e; 4. d; 5. g; 6. a; 7. f.)

Thinking Like a Psychologist About Psychological Disorders

Psychological disorders keep people from adapting in the most effective way to their environment. In this chapter, eight categories of disorders were described, each featuring different primary symptoms: intense anxiety, physical ailments and complaints, dissociation of the self from memory, extreme moods ranging from depression to euphoria, schizophrenic devastation of mental functions, and self-defeating patterns of behavior. Yet there are many more—such as disorders involving sleep, sex, impulse control, substance abuse, and development. Clearly, no aspect of our existence is immune to breakdown.

Now that you've learned about a range of psychological disorders, you should note two ways in which the picture is more complicated than it appears. First, a diagnosis of more than one psychological disorder is common. Thus, people with phobias often suffer too from obsessive-compulsive disorder, many of those with generalized anxiety disorder are also depressed, those who are depressed often have sleep disorders, and people with schizophrenia often abuse drugs. In a similar vein, psychological disorders do not exist in caricature-like terms. Depression may be considered a mood disorder, but it also has cognitive symptoms; schizophrenia is considered a thought disorder, but it has a marked impact on emotion.

The second complication is that "normal" and "abnormal" are not distinct, well-defined categories but, rather, points on a continuum. Hence, people who are otherwise happy, healthy, and well adjusted may experience some symptoms of psychological disorders. On occasion, most of us have felt panic, phobic anxiety, mania, or depression. Most of us know what it's like to lose sleep when we're nervous or to worry excessively about our health when a contagious disease or threat of terrorism begins to spread. Most of us know what it's like to tune out for short periods of time and dissociate mentally from our surroundings. Sometimes we even catch brief, mild glimpses of schizophrenia symptoms. For example, the new parent who "hears" his or her newborn cry, only to learn that the baby is fast asleep, is having an auditory hallucination. And the person who dines alone in a restaurant and self-consciously thinks everyone is watching is under some kind of delusion. In short, psychological order and disorder are not always clear cut categories but shades of gray. At times, diagnosis is a judgment call based on how intense, frequent, prolonged, and disabling the symptoms are.

Once psychological disorders are identified and diagnosed, and once we understand their causes, what next? At this point, we must return our attention to the underlying challenge of clinical psychology: the potential for positive *change*. Personality remains relatively stable throughout adulthood, as discussed in the chapter on that topic. But what about the problems that afflict so many people? What about episodes of anxiety or depression? For those needing professional help, the answer is to seek treatment through drugs, counseling and psychotherapy, and other forms of intervention. Reflecting the hope and the reality that people can help other people change, the next chapter addresses these topics.

SUMMARY

PSYCHOLOGICAL DISORDERS: A GENERAL OUTLOOK

Because psychological disorders are widespread, it's important to define them, make distinctions among different types of problems, and know what factors put us at risk.

Defining Normal and Abnormal

The term **psychological disorder** has been defined in various ways. The American Psychiatric Association definition stresses significant pain or dysfunctional behavior and an internal, involuntary source. Whatever definition is used, there is no strict line between normal and abnormal.

Models of Abnormality

The **medical model** attributes mental disorders to biological conditions. The **psychological model** locates the cause of disorder in past and present experiences. The **sociocultural model** stresses the importance of cultural context, as seen in **culture-bound syndromes,** recurring patterns of maladaptive behavior that are limited to a specific cultural group or location.

Diagnosis: A Necessary Step

Today, the process of **diagnosis**—the grouping and naming of mental disorders—is based on the **DSM-5**. Although diagnosis is more reliable than in the past, stereotypes can bias judgments, and diagnostic labels can then affect the way people are perceived and treated.

Although the disorders presented in this chapter are treated separately, people diagnosed with one disorder often have symptoms of other disorders too, a phenomenon known as **comorbidity**.

DEPRESSIVE DISORDERS

People normally have many fluctuations of mood. But prolonged emotional extremes that impair the ability to function is a **mood disorder** diagnosed as **depression**.

Major Depressive Disorder

Depression brings feelings of deep sadness and despair without a discernible cause and lasts for two weeks or more. Other symptoms include loss of sleep and appetite, feelings of worthlessness, hopelessness, and a lack of energy.

Theories of Depression

Twin studies show a genetic foundation for depression. Early research stressed the role of neurotransmitters.

Psychological factors have also been noted. Freud considered depression a reaction to loss. Behaviorists link it to **learned helplessness**, an expectation that we cannot control important life outcomes. Social-cognitive theorists say that depressed people have a **depressive explanatory style**, a tendency to attribute negative events to factors that are internal, stable, and global—and to assume that things will not change.

The Vicious Cycle of Depression

Depressed people often behave in ways that alienate others. Social rejection then intensifies the depression—a vicious cycle.

Suicide

Three-quarters of suicides are completed by depressed people. Clinically, scales of hopelessness are the best predictor. Signs of potential suicide include depression and drug use, remarks about death, and previous attempts.

ANXIETY DISORDERS

Anxiety is a nervous feeling of apprehension accompanied by physical symptoms, such as a pounding heart and trembling hands.

Generalized Anxiety Disorder

A constant state of anxiety not linked to an identifiable source is the mark of **generalized anxiety disorder**. Cross-cultural studies show that the physiological symptoms of anxiety are universal but that the cognitive component (the particular set of worries and interpretations) varies with the culture.

Panic Disorder

Panic disorder—characterized by frequent, sudden, intense rushes of anxiety for no apparent reason—is often accompanied by **agoraphobia**, a fear of public places. There is evidence for both biological and psychological causes.

Specific Phobia

A **specific phobia** involves a fear of a specific object or situation. Freud attributed phobias to anxiety over hidden impulses, behaviorists stress conditioning and learning, and others have linked common phobias to evolutionary programming or "preparedness."

Social Anxiety Disorder

A social anxiety disorder is a fear of a situation that invites public scrutiny such as dining with friends and public speaking.

Cultural Influences on Anxiety Disorders

Anxiety is a universal human affliction, but the specific forms it takes may vary according to cultural beliefs. Thus, certain anxiety disorders are found in some cultures but not others.

TRAUMA- AND STRESSOR-RELATED DISORDERS

This cluster of disorders includes those where being exposed to a traumatic or stressful event is considered to be a direct contributor.

Posttraumatic Stress Disorder

Posttraumatic stress disorder (PTSD) can result following exposure to a traumatic event. The exposure can be actual or threatened death, serious injury, or sexual violence. This can include directly experiencing the traumatic event, assisting in the damage control after the traumatic event (such as a first responder or emergency room medic), witnessing the event as it occurred to others, and learning that the traumatic event happened to a close friend or loved one.

Theories of Posttraumatic Stress Disorder

Research demonstrates that psychological history, genetics, and environment contribute to the development of PTSD. Furthermore, some people have more severe cases than others. Those with more severe cases tend to have childhood exposure to trauma such as a divorce, catastrophe, abuse, or maladaptive caregivers. Gender and culture also play a role. Females and Latinx persons are more susceptible to developing PTSD.

OBSESSIVE-COMPULSIVE AND RELATED DISORDERS

Obsessive-Compulsive Disorder
In **obsessive-compulsive disorder (OCD)**, the person is plagued by obsessions (persistent thoughts) and compulsions (the need to perform repetitive acts or rituals).

Theories of Obsessive-Compulsive Disorder
Psychoanalysts, behaviorists, and biological psychologists have all proposed different theories to explain why people develop OCD. The disorder can be treated with different therapies. For example, not allowing a person to act on the compulsion to wash hands reduces the frequency of that compulsive behavior over time. Medication, such as antidepressants, also reduces obsessive thoughts and compulsive behaviors.

BIPOLAR AND RELATED DISORDERS

Bipolar Disorder
People with **bipolar disorder** experience wild mood swings from depression at one extreme to mania (a euphoric, overactive state) at the other. Many famous artists had bipolar disorder, and their manic phases may have contributed to their brilliance. But mania may also spiral out of control, producing delusions and risky and embarrassing behavior. Though related to simple depression, bipolar disorder has a stronger genetic component.

Theories of Bipolar and Related Disorders
Biological and cognitive theories help explain why people develop bipolar disorder. Bipolar disorder has been described as one of the most heritable psychological disorders, and it can be treated with medication. Cognitive factors include elevated appraisals of internal states.

PERSONALITY DISORDERS

A person with a highly inflexible and maladaptive personality is said to have a **personality disorder**.

The Borderline Personality
People with **borderline personality disorder** lack identity, cling to others, act impulsively, and are prone to self-destruction.

The Antisocial Personality
Of those who have **antisocial personality disorder**, 80 percent are men. The condition produces a chronic pattern of self-centered, manipulative, and destructive behavior toward others. Its most notable feature is lack of conscience.

SCHIZOPHRENIA SPECTRUM DISORDERS

Marked by gross distortions of thought and perception and a loss of contact with reality, **schizophrenia spectrum disorders** are equally common in women and men all over the world, though they tend to strike women at a later age.

Symptoms of Schizophrenia Spectrum Disorders
Schizophrenia's major symptoms are **delusions** (false beliefs), **hallucinations** (sensory experiences without actual stimulation), disorganized speech, disorganized or catatonic behavior, and negative symptoms (flattened, exaggerated, or inappropriate emotion).

THEORIES OF SCHIZOPHRENIA SPECTRUM DISORDERS

Twin, family, and adoption studies reveal a genetic basis for schizophrenia, linked to the neurotransmitter dopamine or to structural brain defects. But psychological factors also play a role. Some evidence supports the **diathesis-stress model**, which holds that people with genetic or acquired vulnerability develop schizophrenia when exposed to a high level of stress.

DISSOCIATIVE DISORDERS

Many people have experiences in which they lose their memory for a portion of their lives or identity. A severe condition of this sort is known as a **dissociative disorder**.

DISSOCIATIVE AMNESIA

Dissociative amnesia is a partial or complete loss of memory. Causes include physical trauma, alcohol, and stressful events. In a rare specifier known as **dissociative fugue**, people forget their identity, wander away, and start a new life.

DISSOCIATIVE IDENTITY DISORDER

In **dissociative identity disorder (DID)**, which used to be called multiple personality disorder, the person develops two or more distinct personalities. Women exhibit this disorder more often than men and often have a history of abuse as children. Reported cases of DID are on the rise, a situation that has triggered controversy.

CRITICAL THINKING

Thinking Critically About Psychological Disorders

1. Discuss the major criticisms of psychiatric diagnosis. Why does the psychological community continue to use diagnosis? How can the problems be minimized?
2. Is the desire to take one's own life necessarily a sign of poor mental health? Should individuals be allowed to die by suicide if they so desire? Why or why not?
3. The majority of individuals with borderline personality disorder are women, whereas the vast majority of those with antisocial personality disorder are men. Why might this gender difference exist?
4. Use the three perspectives of abnormality to explain the high incidence of comorbidity.
5. Think back to the theories of personality that you learned about in the previous chapter. How would these theories account for dissociative identity disorder (DID)?
6. Discuss the controversy surrounding the use of the insanity defense. What is your position on this controversy?

CAREER CONNECTION: PUBLIC SERVICE

Social Worker

Social workers with a bachelor's degree will often work with groups, community organizations, and policymakers to develop programs, services, and policies. These positions might entail helping individuals locate resources in their community, providing counseling services directly to clients, and conducting other types of case management services. Government agencies, nonprofits, hospitals, and private mental health practices may employ social workers.

The understanding of human behavior and psychological practices gained through an undergraduate psychology degree will be of immediate value in social work, but prospective employers may expect professionals with a bachelor's degree in something other than social work to complete additional education and training over time and potentially to pursue a Master of Social Work (MSW) degree. Key skills for this role that psychology students learn to develop:

- Effective communication in presentations and written works
- Application of ethical standards
- Innovative and inclusive thinking

KEY TERMS

agoraphobia (p. 541)
antisocial personality disorder (p. 556)
bipolar disorder (p. 552)
borderline personality disorder (p. 556)
comorbidity (p. 533)
culture-bound syndromes (p. 530)
delusions (p. 559)
depression (p. 535)
depressive explanatory style (p. 537)
diagnosis (p. 531)
diathesis-stress model (p. 562)
dissociative amnesia (p. 563)
dissociative disorder (p. 563)
dissociative fugue (p. 564)
dissociative identity disorder (DID) (p. 564)
DSM-5 (p. 531)

generalized anxiety disorder (p. 540)
hallucinations (p. 560)
learned helplessness (p. 537)
medical model (p. 529)
mood disorder (p. 535)
obsessive-compulsive disorder (OCD) (p. 549)
panic disorder (p. 541)
personality disorder (p. 555)
posttraumatic stress disorder (p. 546)
psychological disorder (p. 528)
psychological model (p. 530)
PTSD (p. 546)
schizophrenia spectrum disorders (p. 559)
social anxiety disorder (p. 544)
sociocultural model (p. 530)
specific phobia (p. 542)

14 TREATMENT AND INTERVENTIONS

iStock.com/NoSystem images

LEARNING OBJECTIVES

Recognize different forms of psychotherapy and their corresponding goals for treatment.

Determine what types of psychotherapy are effective, and list the properties that various types of psychotherapy have in common.

Understand the different types and cost-benefit trade-offs of medical interventions for psychological disorders.

WHAT'S YOUR PREDICTION: IS PSYCHIATRIC DRUG USE COMMOM?

The Situation

People who have psychological problems—feeling anxious, depressed, or generally unhappy without knowing why—wonder where they can turn for help. Sometimes people turn to friends, relatives, clergy, mental health professionals, or family doctors; at other times, they seek help from pharmaceuticals. Why would people use pharmaceuticals to treat psychological issues? As you know, mental health is a topic surrounded by stigma. People rarely admit openly that they are getting psychological treatment. In spite of that, how prevalent are psychiatric drug prescriptions? And does prevalence differ depending on demographics such as age and race/ethnicity?

To answer these questions, Moore and Mattison (2017) reviewed prescription data to calculate the percentages of persons aged 18–85 who filled a prescription for three types of psychiatric pharmaceuticals: antidepressants; anxiolytics, sedatives, and hypnotics; and antipsychotics. They analyzed the prescription histories of approximately 36,940 people. As part of their analysis, they investigated differences in race/ethnicity and age.

Make a Prediction

How prevalent are psychiatric drug prescriptions across demographics? Does age or race/ethnicity matter? Which demographic do you believe will have the highest percentage of psychiatric drug prescriptions? The lowest? Make predictions for all sets of measures.

DEMOGRAPHIC	USE OF PSYCHIATRIC DRUGS
Aged 18–39	_____%
Aged 40–59	_____%
Aged 60–85	_____%
White	_____%
Black	_____%
Latinx	_____%
Asian American	_____%

The Results

Moore and Mattison (2017) found that plenty of people are indeed seeking psychiatric drug prescriptions and that, yes, demographics make a difference. As you can see in the table below, people who are white have the largest use of psychiatric drug prescriptions. Among age groups, those aged 60 years and older receive the most prescriptions for psychiatric drugs. Overall, more people are seeking a chemical treatment for psychological disorders than we might think.

DEMOGRAPHIC	USE OF PSYCHIATRIC DRUGS
Aged 18–39	9.0%
Aged 40–59	18.8%
Aged 60–85	25.1%
White	20.8%
Black	9.7%
Latinx	8.7%
Asian American	4.8%

What Does It All Mean?

Age is positively correlated with prescription percentage—the older the person, the more likely that individual is to be prescribed a psychiatric drug. In 2015, the Centers for Disease Control and Prevention found that among adults aged 18–64, those aged 50–64 were the most likely to talk to a mental health professional. One reason for this finding is that older people might be more comfortable speaking with a doctor about any issue regarding quality of life due to exposure. The more often you visit a doctor, the more chances you have to talk about what is wrong. In addition, the more often you visit a doctor, the better rapport the two of you might have.

Another thing to consider in light of these results is the differences found in race/ethnicity. In the United States, people who are white generally have greater access to a doctor's care and, thus, better chances of getting psychiatric treatment. In a study of health insurance, Sohn (2016) found that people who are white had the fewest expected years without insurance and the lowest probability of losing insurance within one year, compared to people who are Black, Latinx, or Asian. For people who are Black or Latinx, a reduction in mental health care and psychiatric drug disparities could save as much a $1 billion in medical expenditures nationwide (Cook, Liu, Lessios, Loder, & McGuire, 2015). In terms of the whole population, nearly 29 million people living in the United States are without insurance (Gaffney & McCormick, 2017).

However, even if all Americans had insurance, would this substantially reduce the number of people who live with untreated mental health problems? Not necessarily. Some people refuse to take psychiatric drugs and instead pursue psychotherapy. As we will learn, there isn't just one psychological treatment option, much like there isn't just one type of person who needs psychological treatment. However, some forms of treatment are better tested than others. We'll learn from more controlled studies that psychological therapies (as well as medical interventions) *are* generally effective—and that for people in distress, they offer hope, social support, and an opportunity to open up. This is especially important for you to learn, especially since students of all types are dealing with mental health problems at a high rate (Gulliver et al., 2018).

In *Love's Executioner and Other Tales of Psychotherapy*, Irvin Yalom (1989) tells the story of Betty, a 27-year-old female patient who was 5'2'' and weighed 250 pounds. A few moments into the first meeting, Yalom asked his standard opening question, "So what ails?" Betty's reply: "Everything." She worked 60 hours a week, had no friends, cried every night, had frequent headaches, and spent weekends at home eating in front of the TV. According to Betty, she was too heavy for people to accept yet too depressed to lose weight. Had she sought professional help before? Yes, but without much success.

Throughout the first few weeks of therapy, Betty did not really open up. Thus, Yalom decided to confront Betty about her avoidant tactics. Soon she began to open up (a frightening prospect, she said, "like jumping out of a plane without a parachute"). Betty became more engaged in the sessions, but she was also more anxious. To provide a supportive social network, Yalom then put Betty into a therapy group, which worked wonders. She gradually made a number of positive changes. One insight after another brought about by therapy resulted in a happier, healthier, more confident woman. After 15 months, Betty had a final session with Yalom.

Practicing clinical psychologists—like Yalom—help people cope with real-life problems. Sometimes the goal is to treat the symptoms of a specific disorder or to help people cope with a stressful life event; at other times, it is to foster growth in those of us who are without a psychological disorder but are not content with the state of our lives. Whatever the problem, this chapter addresses three questions: (a) What treatments are available to people in need of psychological help? (b) Are these treatments effective? (c) And if so, why?

The methods for treating psychological disorders are far from perfect, and they're not always successful, but they've come a long way in a few short years (Gamwell & Tomes, 1995; Stone, 1997). Our prehistoric ancestors believed that evil spirits inhabited people afflicted with psychological disorders—so they drilled holes in the skull large enough for these spirits to escape. In the 17th century, the same disorders were attributed to witchcraft and demonic possession and were "treated" with exorcism, noise making, bloodletting, beating, bitter potions, starvation, and torture. By the 18th century, people with mental disorders were considered ill but were hidden from public view—often chained to the walls of dark, dungeon-like hospitals called "asylums" (illustrated in Figure 14.1). Then during the 19th century, a spirit of humanitarian reform swept through many institutions in the United States and Europe. The inmates were unchained, housed in clean rooms with windows, and permitted to walk outside on hospital grounds.

At the turn of the 20th century, major advances were made on two fronts. One was the finding that the symptoms of *hysteria* (such as paralysis of a limb or blindness) could be treated with hypnosis. The other was the discovery that a schizophrenia-like disorder called *general paresis*—which is marked by hallucinations, delusions, personality changes, and death—was caused by syphilis, a sexually transmitted genital infection. These developments now stand as symbols for the two predominant models of treatment: one psychological, the other medical. Today, as we'll soon understand, these two models complement rather than compete with each other.

FIGURE 14.1 ■ Old Fashioned "Cures" for Mental Illness

In the 18th century, many crude devices were used to treat psychological disorders. A popular choice was the tranquilizing chair, designed by Dr. Benjamin Rush. It was used to calm those who were manic or violent.

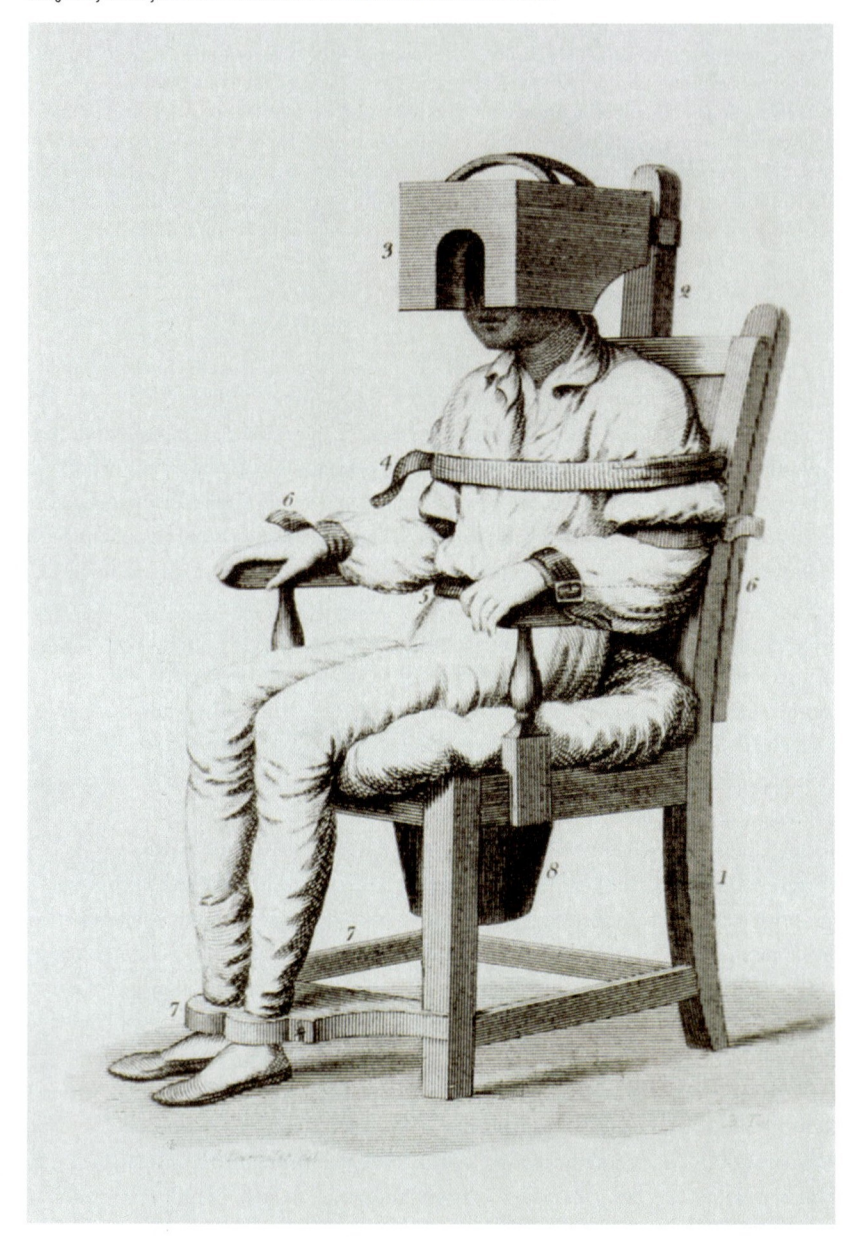

Everett Collection Inc / Alamy Stock Photo

PSYCHOLOGICAL THERAPIES

LEARNING OBJECTIVES

Recognize different forms of psychotherapy and their corresponding goals for treatment.

- Describe how a client would know if psychotherapy was successful.
- Discuss the principles that underlie behavioral therapy.
- List the main features of cognitive therapies.
- Explain the humanistic approach.

The term **psychotherapy** is used to describe all forms of treatment in which a trained professional uses psychological techniques to help persons in need of assistance. Psychotherapy can be provided by many different mental health professionals, from clinical psychologists and social workers to psychiatric nurses and psychiatrists (as outlined in Table 14.1). The person in need of assistance also varies. The individual may suffer from one of the psychological disorders listed in the *DSM-5* or may simply feel inadequate, lonely, unimportant, or unloved and may just want more from life.

Psychotherapists can choose from a vast array of techniques. A small number of therapists, who get too much attention from the media, use "the latest craze" techniques—for example, insulting patients to shake them up, having patients scream at the top of their lungs, or "regressing" them to infancy and into the womb. These techniques are available because psychotherapies do not undergo a formal approval process like medications do (National Institute of Mental Health, 2016). But the vast majority of therapists are professionals who work with individual children or adults, families, and groups—and who are trained in one of five major approaches: psychoanalytic, behavioral, cognitive, cognitive-behavioral, and humanistic. These approaches are described in the following pages.

> **psychotherapy.** A term used to describe any treatment in which a trained professional uses psychological techniques to help someone in need of assistance.

Psychoanalytic Therapies

Imagine you are lying outstretched on a couch, with a soft pillow tucked underneath your head. You stare at the walls and ceiling, noticing subtle streaks of white paint, shadows, hairline cracks in the plaster, and dust on the drapes. You fixate on a small, neatly drilled hole in the wall from which a picture must have been hung. As your eyes scan every nook and cranny, however, your mind is elsewhere, in another time and place. You recall the tantrum you had on your first day of school, the fight your parents had after putting you to bed one night, the moment you were told that your favorite grandfather died, the peculiar dream you had the night before, or the way the family used to get together on Thanksgiving to eat, drink, and watch the parade on TV. As an image comes to mind, you talk about it and relive the emotions you felt. You laugh, you cry, you clench your teeth in anger as you become reabsorbed in the events of your own life. But you're not alone. Sitting behind you—listening to every word you say, commenting from time to time, and passing the Kleenex—is your "analyst."

Orthodox Psychoanalysis

Ever since Josef Breuer and Sigmund Freud (1895) found that people often feel better after purging their minds of material buried in the unconscious, psychoanalysis has had a marked influence on the

TABLE 14.1 ■ Types of Mental Health Professionals and Their Educational Backgrounds

Professional	Educational Background
Clinical psychologist	Attends graduate school; earns a PhD in clinical psychology; and conducts testing, diagnosis, treatment, and research. Is able to prescribe psychiatric drugs in a few states with the proper psychopharmacology training.
Doctor of psychology	Attends graduate school; earns a PsyD in psychology; and conducts testing, diagnosis, and treatment.
Counseling psychologist	Attends graduate school; earns a PhD in counseling psychology to help people with marital, family, and minor adjustment problems.
Psychiatric social worker	Attends graduate school, earns a two-year master's degree in social work, and has had special training in therapy. Often works with other medical providers, the community, and family members to support the client.
Licensed clinical social worker	Attends graduate school, earns a two-year master's degree in social work and receives special training and supervision in a clinical setting to provide treatment to those with emotional and mental health issues.
Psychiatric nurse	Earns a bachelor's degree in nursing and specified certification to assist clients in crisis intervention, mental health assessments, and medication management.
Psychiatrist	Attends medical school, earns an MD, does a residency in psychiatry, and is the only mental health professional who can prescribe psychiatric drugs in all states.

treatment of mental disorders. Breuer treated a young patient named Anna O., who suffered from hysterical blindness, paralysis of an arm, a nervous cough, and other symptoms of conversion disorder. This case was important in three ways. First, Breuer found that when Anna talked about herself, she sometimes stumbled upon memories that had been repressed for many years. Second, these insights often brought about a relief of her symptoms. Third, Anna became intensely attached to Breuer, eventually causing him, a married man, to terminate their sessions.

Freud went on to use this case, and others like it, to develop psychoanalysis, the first systematic method of "talking cure." Psychoanalysis is designed to achieve two goals: *catharsis*, a release of bottled-up psychic tension, and *insight*, or self-understanding. These goals are achieved through the therapist's interpretation of three types of behavior: free association, resistance, and transference.

free association. A basic technique of psychoanalysis in which the patient says whatever comes to mind—freely and without censorship.

resistance. In psychoanalysis, the tendency for patients to actively block, or "resist," psychologically painful insights.

Free association For Freud, the principal technique of psychoanalysis was born in 1892 with a patient named Elisabeth. At first, Freud had her lie down, close her eyes, think hard about a symptom, and try to recall the moment it started. After many futile attempts, Elisabeth had an insight—but concerning a part of her life that was unrelated to the symptom she was trying to recall. Freud was taken by surprise. Why had she waited so long to reveal something so important? "I could have told you that the first time, but I didn't think that it was what you wanted," she said (quoted in Jones, 1953, p. 243). Humbled by this turn of events, Freud came up with a new set of rules. From now on, he said, follow your own train of thought. Elisabeth was agreeable but, in turn, asked Freud to stop asking so many irrelevant questions. This episode marked the first use of **free association**, where the patient lies back, relaxes, and talks about thoughts, wishes, memories, fantasies, and whatever else comes to mind—no matter how trivial, embarrassing, or crazy it may seem. No censorship. No interruption. In the meantime, the analyst listens attentively, trying to put together the pieces of an emerging puzzle.

Beginning with Freud's (1900) work on dreams, psychoanalysts have encouraged patients to free-associate about their dreams—the "royal road to the unconscious." As we saw in the chapter on personality, this emphasis is based on the theory that pent-up psychic energy from repressed sexual and aggressive impulses is released when we're asleep, but in ways that are confusing and hard to interpret. As patients describe the conscious *manifest content* of dreams, their analysts are busy trying to unmask the underlying *latent content*—what the dreams "really" mean.

Resistance Free association was only the beginning. Freud noticed his patients would not discuss unpleasant thoughts and memories. On the brink of an important but painful insight, patients would stop, go blank, lose their train of thought, change the subject, argue with the therapist, "forget" the next appointment, make jokes, call it quits, or seek another therapist. Freud called this pattern of avoidance **resistance** and concluded that it was part of an unconscious defensive process designed to keep threatening personal insights out of awareness.

In psychoanalysis, resistance slows down the course of therapy but also signals that the patient is on the verge of exposing a psychic raw nerve. Where there's resistance, there's emotional turmoil. The analyst's goal is to make the patient aware of the resistance by carefully interpreting what it means. "I notice you never want to talk about your mother" and "Why do you always make jokes when you discuss your illness?" are the kinds of interpretive statements analysts make in order to get at underlying problems and nudge patients toward difficult self-insights.

Treated by Breuer in the 1880s, Anna O. played a pivotal role in the birth of psychoanalysis. In relating her dreams and "fairy tales," she coined the term "talking cure" to describe the process. Her symptoms (which appeared when she was 21 years old and her father became terminally ill) were relieved only temporarily under Breuer's care, but she did eventually recover. Seventy years later, a biographer of Freud revealed Anna O.'s true identity for the first time. Her name was Bertha Pappenheim. When she died in 1936, she was an internationally renowned social activist, writer, and feminist (Guttmann, 2001).

The History Collection / Alamy Stock Photo

Transference Also critical to psychoanalysis is the therapist-patient relationship. Many of Freud's patients developed intense, unsolicited feelings toward him. Freud speculated that people have an unconscious tendency to transfer feelings for parents, siblings, lovers, and other significant persons onto the therapist—a phenomenon he called **transference**. Sometimes the patient reacts with passionate love and affection (positive transference) but at other times with hatred, anger, and hostility (negative transference). Either way, the therapist is merely a convenient substitute for the person for whom these feelings are really meant. In fact, said Freud, therapists need to beware of their own tendency to "countertransfer" feelings they have for others onto their patients.

Transference is a welcomed disruption in psychoanalysis. It may slow down and complicate matters, but it also provides a window to the unconscious. The goal is for people to gain insight into current relationships—to understand why they are attracted to certain kinds of people or why they shy away from commitments, need constant reassurance, or become fiercely possessive and jealous. Based on material that is provided by free association, resistance, and transference, psychoanalysts seek insight through a process of interpretation (as illustrated in Table 14.2). One key factor in this endeavor is timing. Someone who

To encourage patients to relax, Freud had them recline on the couch in his study while he sat out of view. You can see this couch if you visit Freud's historic home in London.

Tom Ferguson / Alamy Stock Photo

transference. In psychoanalysis, the tendency of patients to displace intense feelings for others onto the therapist.

TABLE 14.2 ■ Psychoanalysis in Action

Taken from an actual therapy session, this dialog illustrates one psychoanalyst's use of interpretation.

Patient:	I really didn't want to come today. (long silence) I'm just not really sure what to say; maybe you can suggest a topic.
Therapist:	You'd like for me to tell you what to talk about, to give you some structure?
Patient:	Sure. (pause) It seems that you just sit there all the time not saying anything. I'm not really sure this is helping very much.
Therapist:	Perhaps we should talk about your feeling that I'm not giving you what you want.
Patient:	You always just sit there; you never give me advice; you never tell me what to do. I thought therapy would be different from this.
Therapist:	You expected more?
Patient:	It's a little irritating to pay out good money and feel like you're not getting your money's worth.
Therapist:	So it feels as if I'm cheating or depriving you in some way. Perhaps that is why you're feeling so angry today.
Patient:	I'm not feeling angry, (pause) Well... I guess I am a little. In fact, I really didn't even want to come.
Therapist:	Perhaps there's a relationship between those feelings... feeling angry and then wanting to withdraw.
Patient:	I think I do that a lot. I feel uncomfortable being angry at you. It doesn't seem justified somehow. I just want to not come and not talk. I guess I do that a lot. I mean, when I get angry, I get quiet and I just don't talk.
Therapist:	Perhaps that is why you were so quiet at the beginning of the hour. It was a way of indirectly letting me know that you were angry, while at the same time protecting yourself and me from that anger and your fears of what it might do.
Patient:	I guess you are right. I am afraid of anger and I have a lot of difficulty letting people know directly when I feel they have done something bad or hurt me in some way. So I just... withdraw.

Source: Baker (1985), pp. 41–42.

is emotionally prepared to face painful ideas will feel relieved and enlightened by an interpretation. But for someone who is not, the technique will backfire, heightening anxiety and resistance. Psychoanalysis is thus a long, hard, and expensive process—typically requiring four or five 50-minute sessions a week and lasting for some number of years.

Brief Psychoanalytic Therapies

Inspired by neo-Freudian theorists such as Jung, Adler, Fromm, Horney, and Erikson (as described in the chapter on personality) and by a practical need for shorter-term, less costly methods of treatment, most psychoanalytic therapists today use modified, nonorthodox techniques such as psychodynamic therapy (Leichsenring & Schauenburg, 2014). They still share key aspects of Freud's approach—such as an appreciation for the importance of past experiences and unconscious processes. In general, however, these newer therapies are briefer, less intense, and more flexible. Sessions are usually scheduled once a week and for a limited period of time, usually just a few months rather than years. To accelerate the therapy process, many analysts now sit face-to-face with their patients and take a more active conversational role, often asking direct questions and prompting certain lines of inquiry. Unconscious resistance is still interpreted, and transference is still considered a useful vehicle for insight, but today's analyst tries to minimize these reactions or else to facilitate the process through role-playing exercises. Analysts also spend less time plunging into the past and more time addressing current life problems (Alexander & French, 1946; Crits-Christoph & Barber, 1991; Henry, Strupp, Schacht, & Gaston, 1994; Luborsky, 1984). Some have even suggested that analysts can facilitate the therapy process by occasionally self-disclosing personal experiences or feelings to their patients, a practice once regarded as off limits (Jacobs, 1999).

Controversies in Psychoanalysis

Psychoanalysis as a theory has been steeped in controversy. It is also controversial as a form of treatment. First, it takes too long and is too expensive, available only to those who are affluent. Second, psychoanalytic interpretations can never be disproved. Third, some argue that psychoanalysis is not truly therapeutic and that people are no better off after they come out than before they went in. We'll learn later that this claim is unfair. Studies show that psychoanalytic therapy, like other types of psychotherapy, is generally effective. But must people dive head first into the past and open old wounds in order to solve current life problems? Many psychologists and psychiatrists do not think so. Thus, psychoanalysis has been on the decline, leaving some people wondering, "Is psychoanalysis still relevant to psychiatry?" (Paris, 2017).

Despite the criticisms, therapists from all orientations agree that resistance is a typical behavior among psychotherapy patients (Mahoney, 1991; McAleavey & Castonguay, 2015). Indeed, research shows that defensiveness and self-deception are normal, if not adaptive, parts of human nature. Many practitioners also agree that transference and other aspects of the therapist-patient relationship are key to success (Kahn, 1991). In laboratory experiments, participants have been shown to react positively or negatively toward neutral strangers depending on whether they resembled liked or disliked others from their own lives (Berk & Andersen, 2000). Finally, many of us now take for granted the psychoanalytic assumptions that mental disorders are often rooted in childhood, that trauma triggers defensive mechanisms, that we often avoid thinking about deep-seated conflicts, and that insight has therapeutic value.

Psychology Applied: Putting Repressed Memories on Trial

While formulating his theory of psychoanalysis, Freud reported hearing his patients recount horrifying tales of early childhood abuse. One after another, they told of incest and other traumas, often sexual in nature. But Freud soon came to believe that at least some of the stories told were false, the figments of overactive imaginations. This notion seemed a terrible blow, but Freud later concluded that the patients were not really lying—that they truly believed the incidents they recounted had happened. To this day, psychologists debate the validity of Freud's reports and interpretations (Berger, 1995; Esterson, 2001; Gleaves & Hernandez, 1999).

In 1990 in Redwood City, California, 51-year-old George Franklin stood trial for the murder of an 8-year-old girl that had taken place more than 20 years earlier. For years, the crime was left unsolved. Then Eileen Franklin, the victim's friend—who was 8 years old at the time of the girl's death—came forward to implicate the defendant, her father. According to Eileen, she had forgotten the incident and just recently had started to have flashbacks. She now remembered seeing her father harm the girl and was able to recall the gruesome details. Solely on the basis of her testimony, Franklin was convicted of first-degree murder and sentenced to prison. It was the first time ever that someone was tried and convicted of murder on the basis of a newly recovered repressed memory.

The Franklin conviction was followed by a barrage of new charges. Alleged victims soon appeared in courtrooms and on daytime TV talk shows to tell horrifying tales of abuse, at times as part of satanic-cult rituals. Thousands of men and women filed multimillion-dollar lawsuits against family members and others in their distant past, leaving the courts to decide how to treat this evidence. These cases went on to trigger a backlash against the use of repressed memories. Accused mothers, fathers, grandparents, and others sought each other out and formed the False Memory Syndrome Foundation, a nationwide support group. These people, too, had stories to tell about having their families and reputations torn apart by false accusations. Many repressed-memory accusers later withdrew their claims—some even joined their families in suing the therapists who brought the so-called memories out in the first place (de Rivera, 1997).

Childhood sex abuse is a real crime, can have devastating and lasting consequences for mental health, and may be more common than was previously realized. Some psychotherapists point to cases in which patients had "forgotten" traumatic events until the memories surfaced years later, to be corroborated by independent evidence. But what should be done when there is no independent evidence? On one side of the debate are Ellen Bass and Laura Davis (1988), authors of *The Courage to Heal*, a book that has been described as the "bible" for the survivors of incest and childhood sex abuse. Though not trained in psychology, Bass and Davis provide readers with a list of symptoms to watch for—such as anxiety, depression, intimacy problems, dependence, and loss of appetite.

On the other side of the debate, Elizabeth Loftus (1993) warns that a person's memories for remote-past events are often not memories at all but images and ideas suggested by therapists eager to find the source of a patient's distress. Is it possible for one person to plant a false trauma memory into the mind of another? Loftus (1997) described some compelling demonstrations. In one, she and Jacqueline Pickrell arranged for a 14-year-old boy named Chris to be told by his older brother Jim that he got lost in a mall when he was 5 years old and that he was found crying by a tall older man wearing a flannel shirt. The story was false. Yet a few days later, Chris "recalled" being scared, being asked by an older man if he was lost, and being scolded afterward by his mother.

As judges and juries struggle to sort facts from fictions, it is important to balance our concerns for both the victims of abuse and the victims of false accusations. Research suggests that people often avoid certain thoughts and that events once forgotten can sometimes be recalled (Erdelyi, 1996). Richard McNally (2011) believes there is another explanation. When children are sexually abused, they might not understand that what is happening to them is wrong. Then, as an adult, they revisit the memories and suddenly recognize the events as abusive and traumatic. The American Psychological Association has also chimed in and assembled a task force to examine the issue. The group could agree on little, however, except the following:

- Sexual abuse is a pervasive problem.
- Most people abused as children remember all or part of what happened.
- It is possible to recall old memories that have been forgotten over time.
- It is possible to construct false memories of events that did not occur.
- There are many unanswered questions about what leads to accurate versus inaccurate childhood memories.

In November 1990, George Franklin was wrongfully convicted of murder solely based on his daughter's erroneous testimony. His conviction was finally overturned in July 1996.
Associated Press / Paul Sakuma

Finally, let's return to the case of George Franklin. After Franklin spent five years in prison, his conviction was overturned by an appeals court on a matter of evidence. Franklin was freed and granted a new trial. It was later revealed that Eileen had reported the event in therapy, that she had undergone hypnosis, that the details she recounted had been published in the newspaper, that her reports had changed during the investigation, and that she had falsely accused her father of another murder. The prosecutor was concerned enough about Eileen's credibility as a witness that he chose not to retry Franklin. Finally, in 2018, DNA evidence connected Rodney Lynn Halbower to the crime. He was convicted and sentenced to life in prison. As the debate rages on, it is clear that these questions can be answered only on a case-by-case basis—and with the help of independent evidence.

Behavioral Therapies

Armed with the principles of classical and operant conditioning, Pavlov, Watson, Skinner, and other behaviorists argued that psychological disorders consist of maladaptive behaviors that are learned by reinforcement and can be unlearned in the same manner. Afraid to fly? Depressed? Think everyone is out to get you? Well, said the behaviorists, forget the past, ignore your dreams, and stop waiting for pearls of wisdom to fall from the lips of your all-knowing analyst. Instead, tell me what it is you want to change about yourself. Then we'll make a list of concrete behavioral goals and try to achieve these goals as quickly as we can. Eliminate the symptom and you have solved the problem.

Whether people have a phobia, test anxiety, a sexual disorder, a child with autism spectrum disorder who has food selectivity (Peterson, Piazza, & Volkert, 2016), or an inability to stop smoking, classical and operant conditioning—in addition to other well-established principles of learning—can offer solutions. A book on behavioral techniques described 158 specific procedures, including "anger-control therapy," "verbal-satiation therapy," and "implosion therapy" (Bellack & Hersen, 1985). Together, these various techniques are known as **behavioral therapy** (Kazdin, 2001) or, in some forms, behavior modification.

Behavior modification can work for a range of needs. Here, a child is positively reinforced with play time after completing some physical therapy exercises.
iStock.com/FatCamera

behavioral therapy. Techniques used to modify disordered thoughts, feelings, and behaviors through the principles of learning.

Classical Conditioning Techniques

Classical conditioning is the Pavlovian process by which a once-neutral stimulus (a bell) comes to elicit an emotional or behavioral response (salivation) after being paired repeatedly with an unconditioned stimulus (food) that already has the power to elicit that reaction. In 1920, Watson and Rayner used this model to train a baby boy to react with fear to a white rat by pairing the rat with an aversive loud noise.

If phobias and other disorders develop through classical conditioning, suggested Watson, then perhaps they can be erased in the same manner.

Flooding If Watson was right, it should be possible to treat certain disorders through *extinction*. After repeated presentations of a bell without food, Pavlov's dogs eventually stopped salivating in response to the sound. Similarly, people who confront a fearful situation without a negative consequence should learn that the fear is unfounded. This idea gave rise to **flooding**—a technique in which a person is exposed to, or "flooded" with, an anxiety-provoking stimulus until the anxiety is extinguished. Sometimes the person is guided to imagine the dreaded stimulus; at other times, the experience is firsthand. Someone with agoraphobia (a fear of being in public places), for example, might be taken by a reassuring therapist into a crowded shopping mall and kept there for hours until the fear subsides. This procedure is repeated several times until the anxiety is completely diminished. Flooding is sometimes effective, but success is not guaranteed. Some people can't bring themselves to confront their feared situation; others agree to but then panic, escape, and become even more anxious; still others complete the program but later experience a relapse (Barlow, 1988; King, Graham, & Richardson, 2018).

flooding. A behavioral therapy technique in which the patient is saturated with a fear-provoking stimulus until the anxiety is extinguished.

Systematic desensitization Another powerful and more reliable antidote to anxiety is *counterconditioning*—a procedure in which a person is trained to react to a feared stimulus with a positive response that is incompatible with anxiety. Mary Cover Jones (1924), a student of Watson's, sought to demonstrate that anxiety could be erased by associating a feared stimulus with a pleasurable experience. Jones provided treatment to a 3-year-old boy named Peter, who had become intensely fearful of rabbits and other furry animals. One afternoon, Jones took Peter into a room with a caged rabbit, sat him at a table, and fed him milk and crackers. This routine was repeated several times, and each time the rabbit was moved closer as the boy devoured his snack. After a few weeks, Peter was holding the rabbit on his lap, stroking it with one hand, and eating with the other. Through the process of stimulus generalization, he shed his fear of other animals as well.

Thirty-four years after Jones reported on this case, Joseph Wolpe (1958) devised **systematic desensitization**, a technique that is now widely used in the treatment of specific phobias and other anxiety disorders. Based on the fact that a person cannot simultaneously feel anxious and relaxed, systematic desensitization is designed to condition people to respond to a feared stimulus with calm, not anxiety. There are three steps in this procedure: relaxation training, the construction of an anxiety hierarchy, and gradual exposure. To understand how systematic desensitization works, imagine that you are afraid to fly and that whenever you see an airplane on a runway, hear the thunderous noise of its engines, smell the fuel, or feel the vibrations, your heart races and you break into a cold sweat. You make an appointment with a behavior therapist, and during the first session, she teaches you how to relax in response to a cue. This is accomplished through *relaxation training*—a procedure in which you are taught to concentrate on what it feels like to tighten and then relax various muscle groups throughout the body. Next, you develop an *anxiety hierarchy*, a graduated sequence of fear-provoking situations that you rate on a 100-point scale, ranging from mild to terrifying. As illustrated in Table 14.3, your anxiety hierarchy might begin with "You see a social media ad for discount airfares" and progress to "You look out the window as the plane leaves the ground."

systematic desensitization. A behavioral therapy technique used to treat phobias and other anxiety disorders by pairing gradual exposure to an anxiety-provoking situation with relaxation.

Prepared with an ability to relax on cue and with a hierarchy of fear-provoking situations, you brace yourself for the third and final step. The therapist guides you through a gradual series of *exposures*. You're instructed to close your eyes and imagine the mildest fear-provoking situation in the hierarchy. If you keep your cool while visualizing this scene, you move on to the next item on the list. If you begin to get anxious, however, the therapist will instruct you to stop and relax. This same routine is repeated across several sessions and for all items in the hierarchy until you are "cured" of the fear. This technique, in which the person mentally confronts the anxiety-provoking stimulus, is known as *imaginal exposure*. To ensure long-term success, however, many therapists prefer to use *in vivo exposure*—in which the person confronts the feared situations in real life. In fact, a review of 33 studies demonstrated that in vivo exposure was significantly more effective than imaginal exposure (Wolitzky-Taylor, Horowitz,

TABLE 14.3 ■ A Sample Anxiety Hierarchy

The scenes in this hierarchy are typical of those used in the systematic desensitization of a fear of flying. The numbers to the left of each item represent one patient's subjective rating of how anxiety provoking a situation is, on a scale from 0 to 100.

5	You see a social media ad for discount airfares.
10	You see a TV commercial for an airline.
20	A group of friends talks about arranging a trip that requires flying.
30	You visit a travel agent to make plane reservations.
35	The week before the trip, you get your plane tickets in the mail.
40	The night before the trip, you pull out your suitcase to pack.
55	You park your car near the departure terminal.
60	You check in, and the agent asks if you want a window or an aisle seat.
65	The announcement is made that your flight is ready for passenger boarding.
70	You're in line, with ticket in hand, ready to board.
80	You're in your seat, and the flight attendant says, "Fasten your seatbelts for takeoff."
90	You feel the plane begin to roll down the runway.
95	You look out the window as the plane leaves the ground.

Some behavioral therapists now use virtual reality to expose patients to phobic objects and situations. As part of systematic desensitization, clients receive exposure to anxiety-provoking visual displays through a virtual reality headset.

iStock.com/PeopleImages

Powers, & Telch, 2008). The ultimate test is in your ability to board an airplane, stay calm during the flight, and make the return trip later on.

For a little over a decade, behavioral therapists have been experimenting with exposure through the use of virtual reality. In this type of therapy, patients wear a virtual reality apparatus and are exposed to a digitally created world where they can be safely exposed to their fears. For example, as part of systematic desensitization, patients can realistically experience what it feels like to stand on the roof of a virtual skyscraper, speak in front of a virtual audience, or fly in a virtual airplane, all without leaving the therapist's office. A review of 30 virtual reality exposure therapy (VRET) studies showed that this technique is successful—and that the gains made are lasting (Carl et al., 2019). Importantly, a 12-month follow-up to one airplane-specific phobia VRET study revealed that 92 percent of participants had flown on a real airplane, on their own, since their "graduation flight" (Rothbaum, Hodges, Anderson, Price, & Smith, 2002). This collection of results contributes to the belief that VRET will significantly improve outcomes in clinical contexts (Botella, Fernández-Álvarez, Guillén, García-Palacios, & Baños, 2017).

Systematic desensitization is a common and highly effective form of therapy (Tryon, 2014). According to Wolpe (1982), systematic desensitization works via counterconditioning, by associating a new response (relaxation) with the feared stimulus. However, others find that exposure alone is all that's needed, with or without the relaxation (Rachman, 1990). In a study on the therapeutic effects of *modeling*, Albert Bandura and others (1969) had persons with snake phobias observe a filmed or live model handling snakes and found that these exposures—especially to a live model—increased the extent to which subjects were able to approach a snake without anxiety.

FIGURE 14.2 ■ Aversion Therapy to Treat Alcoholism

In aversion therapy, the goal is to eliminate the urge to drink by pairing alcohol with a chemical that causes nausea and vomiting. When used, this conditioning-based technique is typically accompanied by other forms of treatment. CR = conditioned response; CS = conditioned stimulus; UCR = unconditioned response; UCS = unconditioned stimulus.

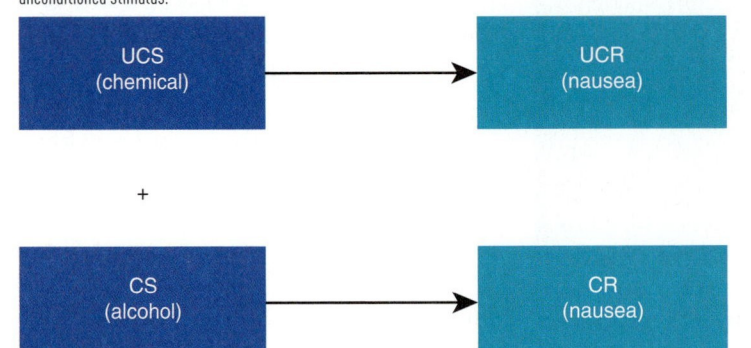

UCS (chemical) → UCR (nausea)

+

CS (alcohol) → CR (nausea)

aversion therapy. A behavioral therapy technique for classically conditioning people to react with aversion to alcohol and other harmful substances.

Aversive conditioning When people are attracted to activities that are harmful—such as smoking, drinking, overeating, and other destructive habits—behavioral therapists often use **aversion therapy**, a technique designed to elicit an aversive rather than pleasurable reaction to a harmful stimulus. In the treatment of alcoholism, the goal of aversion therapy is to cause heavy drinkers to feel sick to the stomach at the sight, smell, and taste of liquor (as illustrated in Figure 14.2). This objective can be achieved in a number of ways. In one technique, the person with alcoholism is given Antabuse (a drug that causes nausea when combined with certain other drugs, including alcohol) and then is taken to a darkened room (one designed to look much like a bar) and served beer, wine, gin, whiskey, or other favorite drinks. After a few minutes, the person vomits uncontrollably. In a study of 685 hospitalized patients treated with aversion therapy for alcoholism, 63 percent were still "dry" after one year, and 33 percent were still dry after three years (Wiens & Menustik, 1983). How does this type of treatment affect the brain? Elkins and colleagues (2017) asked the same question. They conducted an fMRI study of aversion therapy's impact on alcohol drinkers. Their study demonstrated that the craving centers of the brain were less active after aversion therapy (Elkins et al., 2017).

Illustrating aversive conditioning, behavioral therapists use the "rapid succession smoking technique" by forcing smokers who can't break the habit to puff continuously, every few seconds. For a period of time, this procedure is repeated over and over again until the urge to smoke is suppressed.

iStock.com/Rattankun Thongbun

By itself, aversion therapy is not a sufficient treatment for alcoholism. With people who are desperate and willing, however, this technique is sometimes used in conjunction with other forms of therapy. There are nonchemical aversion methods as well—such as having the problem drinker imagine unpleasant and disgusting scenes along with vivid images of drinking. As part of a larger treatment program, the goal of this conditioning technique is to suppress the urge to drink (Rimmele, Howard, & Hilfrink, 1995). However, keep in mind the principles of classical conditioning. If a person who abuses alcohol stops taking a pill that causes vomiting after alcohol consumption, eventually the person will eliminate the pairing (i.e., alcohol consumption will no longer be paired with vomiting) and, as a result, the individual will no longer vomit reflexively in response to alcohol.

Operant Conditioning Techniques

While some behaviorists were discovering the principles of reinforcement by training animals to peck keys, press bars, and jump over barriers for food, water, or the termination of electric shock, others began using the methods of operant conditioning for clinical purposes. On the assumption that all the world's a Skinner box, reinforcement can be used to promote behaviors that are desirable and to extinguish those that are not.

It isn't unusual for modern prison and jail cells to have flat screen TVs mounted on the walls. Television privileges can function as a reward for good behavior, and the removal of those privileges, as a punishment.

iStock.com/Vesnaandjic

token economy. A large-scale behavior-change program in which participants earn valuable tokens for engaging in desired target behaviors.

Reward and punishment It is sometimes necessary to establish clear reinforcement programs to treat people who are severely disordered. In one case, a female patient with schizophrenia wore 25 pounds of clothing, so the therapist in charge required this woman to weigh in at the door of the dining room before meals. Whether she was then allowed to enter and eat was contingent on a steadily decreasing clothing weight. After 13 weeks, the problem was solved (Ayllon, 1963). Sometimes, in an institutional setting, the staff establish a large-scale reinforcement program called a **token economy**. In a token economy, patients earn plastic chips or "tokens" for engaging in desirable behaviors (such as prompt attendance at group-therapy meetings). The tokens can then be used to purchase things like visitation privileges and commodities (Ayllon & Azrin, 1968). This is an effective way to shape behavior—not only in psychiatric hospitals but also in classrooms, homes for juvenile delinquents, and other settings (Kazdin, 1982, 2001).

Reward usually produces impressive changes, but punishment is sometimes necessary to temporarily eliminate dangerous or self-destructive behavior. One context where punishment is frequently used for such behaviors is the prison system. Have you ever wondered why incarcerated persons get access to cable TV? Well, cable TV is a commodity in prison that can easily be taken away if certain rules are broken. So, it is used as a negative punishment. But this type of negative punishment might not work for violent behaviors. Thus, many prisons use solitary confinement, also known as segregation or isolation.

Solitary confinement has been described as "the harshest mechanism of formal social control that prisons can employ" (Cochran, Toman, Mears, & Bales, 2017, p. 383). Typically, solitary confinement is the complete deprivation of meaningful contact with the purpose of deterring future misbehavior if used as a punishment (National Commission on Correctional Health Care, 2018). For instance, if an inmate lashes out against a guard, then the inmate's punishment is a number of days in solitary. The belief is that once released from solitary, the inmate will behave as desired to avoid ever being sent to solitary again. Some inmates refrain from repeating the bad behavior, but others do not. A bigger issue than the lack of consistent success with solitary confinement is the potential for adverse effects resulting from the practice. Clements and colleagues (2007) and Gendreau and Goggin (2014) claim that, under the right conditions, solitary confinement has little impact on mental and physical health. However, the World Health Organization, the United Nations, and the American Psychological Association—among others—disagree. Dr. Craig Haney testified to the Senate Judiciary Subcommittee on the Constitution, Civil Rights, and Human Rights that "conditions of confinement are far too severe to serve any kind of penological purpose" (Dingfelder, 2012). Anthony Graves, a wrongfully convicted inmate who spent 10 years in solitary confinement for a murder he did not commit, "still feels the effects... that cause emotional breakdowns" (Dingfelder, 2012). But when safety of the inmate and others is the overwhelming concern in that moment, solitary confinement is often the only available recourse. With people's mental health at risk, an alternative solution to solitary confinement is desperately needed.

Biofeedback Can people control their physiological behavior? Yes, absolutely. Yoga practitioner Swami Rama once astonished psychologists by proving in controlled laboratory tests that he could voluntarily slow down or speed up his pulse rate, stop his heart from pumping blood for 17 seconds, raise or lower the temperature in his hand, and alter his brain-wave patterns. But does one have to be a serious yoga practitioner to achieve such physiological control? The answer is no. In 1969, Neal Miller found that he could condition heart rates in animals to increase or decrease in response to rewarding, pleasurable brain stimulation.

biofeedback. An operant procedure in which people learn to control physiological responses with the help of "feedback" about their internal states.

As an outgrowth of this research, psychologists developed **biofeedback**, a procedure by which people learn to control their own autonomic processes by receiving continuous, moment-to-moment

FIGURE 14.3 ■ Biofeedback

Biofeedback as a part of therapy is becoming more common. Here, a teenager participates in a neurofeedback session with her therapist.

iStock.com/AndreaObzerova

information, or feedback, in the form of visual or auditory displays, as illustrated in Figure 14.3. With the aid of electronic sensors, people can monitor and eventually regulate not only their heart rate but also their blood pressure, skin temperature, gastric acidity, hormone secretions, and muscle tension. Today, behavior therapists use biofeedback to treat hypertension, chronic back pain, ulcers, bedwetting, headaches, anxiety, and other health problems (Blanchard et al., 1982; Frank, Khorshid, Kiffer, Moravec, & McKee, 2010; Hatch, Fisher, & Rugh, 1987). For people with sleep problems, attentional problems, migraine headaches, or certain types of seizures, some psychologists now use neurofeedback, a similar procedure that trains people to alter their brain waves through feedback about their own electroencephalogram (EEG) activity (Evans & Aberbanel, 1999). For example, Keith and colleagues (2015) used biofeedback to increase attention in persons with substance abuse. It's no wonder that these techniques have been referred to as the "Yoga of the West" and as "electronic Zen" (Schwartz et al., 1999).

Social skills training For people who are painfully shy, who struggle with social cues due to autism spectrum disorder, or who are unresponsive or socially awkward, there is **social skills training**—lessons on how to speak clearly, make eye contact, maintain a comfortable amount of social distance, and respond appropriately to questions (Curran & Monti, 1982; Guivarch et al., 2017). In some forms of social skills training, the therapist models the desired behaviors, the patient imitates and rehearses these behaviors in role-playing exercises, and the therapist responds with a combination of praise and constructive criticism. In other forms of social skills training, groups simulate situations so that patients can safely participate in socialization via group exercises. Simulated situations are conducted as a game to encourage participation and cooperation; thus, goal achievement is rewarded with something like snacks or points. These reinforcement-based therapies produce impressive results. One study on children with autism spectrum disorder showed that, in group simulations, social skills training improved participants' interpersonal skills (Guivarch et al., 2017).

A once-popular type of social skills training is *assertiveness training* (Alberti & Emmons, 1986). Imagine that you are a nurse and felt that your patient's safety was at risk if the doctor progressed as planned. How would you react in such a situation? For people who feel easily manipulated, assertiveness training—through the use of modeling and reinforcement—teaches them how to protect their

social skills training. A form of behavioral therapy used to teach interpersonal skills through modeling, rehearsal, and reinforcement (e.g., assertiveness training).

own self-interests and the interests of others, resulting in treatment gains that may be enduring (Baggs & Spence, 1990; Omura, Maguire, Levett-Jones, & Stone, 2017).

Eye Movement Desensitization and Reprocessing Therapy

Eye movement desensitization and reprocessing (EMDR) therapy was developed by Francine Shapiro, who argues that our traumatic experiences get "stored in the brain with the emotions and the physical sensations and the beliefs that were there at the time" (Wetherford, 2019). EMDR is a unique blend of psychotherapeutic techniques created to help the client process and cope with traumatic events. It does not fit perfectly under classical or operant conditioning, nor any other psychotherapeutic technique, but does include desensitization, physiological response awareness, and the replacement of negative reactions, feelings, and thoughts with positive ones.

The first of EMDR therapy's eight steps consists in a discussion about the client's history and the formation of a treatment plan (Shapiro, Kaslow, & Maxfield, 2007). Clients recall the images they saw, their thoughts, and how their body and emotions responded at the time of the traumatic event. Desensitization in EMDR is where eye movements are utilized. Clients are asked to focus their thoughts on the traumatic event and to follow the therapist's back-and-forth finger movements with their eyes. Physiological responses are also important to attend to during this exercise. Then, with the guidance of the therapist, clients process their mental, emotional, and physiological reactions and get assistance replacing negative associations with positive associations—a process called *installation*. Finally, the therapist helps clients wrap up the current session, and during the next appointment they revisit the same traumatic event. When revisiting the same traumatic event, clients go through the steps again until the traumatic event no longer causes high levels of anxiety, depression, stress, or other issues such as relationship difficulties.

EMDR is one of the forms of therapy the World Health Organization (2013) suggests for the treatment of posttraumatic stress disorder (PTSD). It has been argued that persons with PTSD are conditioned to have a fear response as the result of a traumatic event. A stimulus present at the event—sirens, uniforms, the color of the shirt worn by an injured bystander—is paired with the fear. Exposure to that stimulus can, in turn, reactivate the physiological and neurological arousal that happened during the trauma (Peri, Ben-Shakhar, Orr, & Shalev, 2000). Thus, EMDR therapy is meant to bring to the surface the traumatic memory, and responses to it, in a safe place. In classical conditioning terms, the fear response to the memory needs to undergo *extinction* or *counterconditioning* to help the person with PTSD recover. Research has demonstrated that persons who underwent EMDR therapy do experience decreased fear responses associated with PTSD symptoms in comparison to control subjects (Chen et al., 2018; Cusack et al., 2016; Rousseau et al., 2019; Woudenberg et al., 2018).

eye movement desensitization and reprocessing (EMDR). A blend of psychotherapeutic techniques that include desensitization, physiological response awareness, and the replacement of negative reactions, feelings, and thoughts with positive ones.

LEARNING CHECK

Matchmaker

From the list on the right, identify the type of program or therapy that best matches the described client's needs.

1.	Luis wants to be empowered to control his headaches in response to stress.	a.	Psychoanalysis
2.	Li has a terrible fear of the dentist and needs to extinguish his fear as soon as possible.	b.	Systematic desensitization
3.	Shala believes she has a repressed memory and wants to bring it to the level of her conscious.	c.	Social skills training
4.	Kathy is afraid of germs and wants to learn how to respond to unclean environments with calm instead of anxiety.	d.	Biofeedback
5.	Alex is very shy and struggles to understand the social cues of others. They want to learn how to interact in a social setting.	e.	Flooding

(Answers: 1. d; 2. e; 3. a; 4. b; 5. c.)

Cognitive Therapies

Behaviorists seek to modify maladaptive behavior through the use of classical or operant conditioning. But what matters most, stimulus-response connections and reinforcement per se, or the way we perceive these events? Reflecting psychology's interest in mental processes, many therapists use a more cognitive, rational approach. The result is **cognitive therapy**, a form of treatment designed to alter the maladaptive ways in which people interpret significant events in their lives. To the cognitive therapist, "As you think, so shall you feel" (McMullin, 2000).

Different brands of cognitive therapy and their many techniques all have certain features in common. Based on the assumption that anxiety, depression, and other emotional disorders spring from the way we think, cognitive therapists try to get people to open their minds, challenge their assumptions, and think about old problems in new ways. Sessions are centered on concrete problems, and the therapist maintains a brisk, businesslike pace. Among the most prominent pioneers of this approach are Albert Ellis and Aaron Beck.

cognitive therapy. A form of psychotherapy in which people are taught to think in more adaptive ways.

Rational-Emotive Behavior Therapy

Albert Ellis (1962) developed what is now called **rational-emotive behavior therapy, or (REBT)** (Ellis, 1999). His basic proposition is this: Mental distress is caused not by upsetting events per se but by the rigid and maladaptive ways in which we construe these events. In other words, A (activating events) gives rise to B (beliefs), which triggers C (emotional consequences). This A-B-C model is illustrated in Figure 14.4. The problem, said Ellis, is that too many of us hold beliefs that set us up for emotional turmoil.

rational-emotive behavior therapy (REBT). A form of cognitive therapy in which people are confronted with their irrational, maladaptive beliefs.

It's not easy for people to get rid of their lifelong assumptions or open their minds to new ways of thinking. To meet the task, REBT therapists use blunt, confrontational techniques: "Why do you always have to make mountains out of tiny molehills?" "Where is it written that life is supposed to be fair?" REBT therapists also encourage their clients to step out of character and try new behaviors. Another part of REBT is "psycho-education," in which clients are lectured on the ABCs of emotional distress and given tapes of their own therapy sessions to review at home, along with booklets and audio recordings that teach the cognitive approach. Ellis himself made a series of self-help tapes, with straight-shooting titles such as "How to Stubbornly Refuse to Be Ashamed of Anything" (Bernard & DiGiuseppe, 1989).

Ellis's approach has had substantial impact on the practice of psychotherapy. Studies designed to measure its effects on a patient's later adjustment and well-being have generally revealed positive results (Engels, Garnefski, & Diekstra, 1993; Lyons & Woods, 1991). In a randomized, controlled study comparing REBT to cognitive therapy and Prozac for major depressive disorder, Sava and colleagues (2009) found that patients treated with REBT did not fare better or worse than those treated with cognitive therapy or Prozac. All three therapies resulted in decreased depression scores. However, REBT and cognitive therapy were found to be "more cost-effective, and had better cost-utility, than pharmacotherapy" (p. 36).

Beck's Cognitive Therapy

Aaron Beck devised a cognitive therapy when he noticed that his patients were filled with self-defeating beliefs (Beck, 1991). People who are depressed, for example, view themselves, their world, and the future

---

FIGURE 14.4 ■ Ellis's A-B-C Theory of Emotional Distress

According to Ellis, emotional distress is caused by irrational thoughts and the assumptions people make. This distress, in turn, helps to sustain the

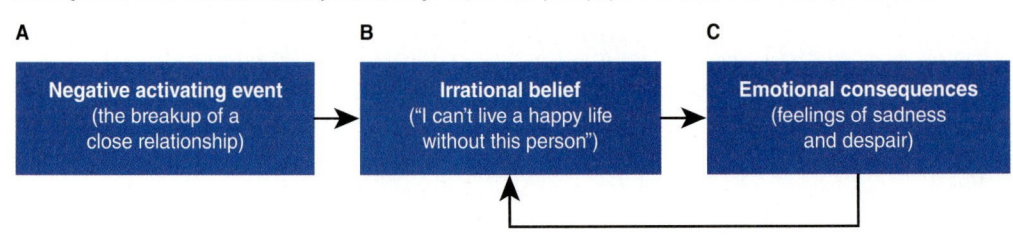

A
Negative activating event
(the breakup of a close relationship)
→
B
Irrational belief
("I can't live a happy life without this person")
→
C
Emotional consequences
(feelings of sadness and despair)

through dark-colored glasses and make statements like "It's my fault" or "I can't do anything right" (Beck, Rush, Shaw, & Emery, 1979). People with anxiety disorders also think in ways that are maladaptive. They exaggerate the likelihood that they will fall victim to fatal accidents or diseases, and they engage in catastrophic thinking about their own bodies. When those with panic disorder get aroused, for example, they often assume that they're having a heart attack or a stroke—beliefs that further heighten anxiety. Whether the problem is depression, an eating disorder, a sexual disorder, obsessive-compulsive disorder, drug abuse, schizophrenia, or a fear of speaking in public, there exists an element of irrational thinking that can and should be changed. Beck (1999) applied his cognitive approach to understanding and treating "prisoners of hate," people whose dysfunctional beliefs lead them to become angry, hostile, and violent.

All cognitive therapists share the same objectives, but they differ in style. Beck's therapeutic approach tends to be gentle and collaborative. The goal is to help people restructure the way they interpret events by means of a Socratic style of questioning. As illustrated in Table 14.4, Beckian cognitive therapists commonly ask questions such as "What's the evidence for this idea?" and "Are these facts, or your interpretation of the facts?"

Many techniques play an important role in Beck's cognitive therapy. One is to get clients to experience their distress in therapy. In one case, an 18-year-old woman who had frequent panic attacks was instructed to hyperventilate. Then, her therapist helped her to interpret her bodily sensations in noncatastrophic

TABLE 14.4 ■ Beck's Cognitive Therapy in Action

The following dialog between Beck and a client epitomizes his approach to therapy. When the client came in, he was upset over the poor job he did wallpapering a kitchen. Note how Beck gets the client to realize that he was exaggerating his negative appraisal.

Therapist:	Why didn't you rate wallpapering the kitchen as a mastery experience?
Patient:	Because the flowers didn't line up.
Therapist:	You did in fact complete the job?
Patient:	Yes.
Therapist:	Your kitchen?
Patient:	No, I helped a neighbor do his kitchen.
Therapist:	Did he do most of the work?
Patient:	No, I really did almost all of it. He hadn't wallpapered before.
Therapist:	Did anything else go wrong? Did you spill paste all over? Ruin the wallpaper? Leave a big mess?
Patient:	No, the only problem was that the flowers didn't line up.
Therapist:	Just how far off was this alignment of the flowers?
Patient:	(holding his fingers about an eighth of an inch apart) About this much.
Therapist:	On each strip of paper?
Patient:	No... on two or three pieces.
Therapist:	Out of how many?
Patient:	About 20 or 25.
Therapist:	Did anyone else notice it?
Patient:	No, in fact my neighbor thought it was great.
Therapist:	Could you see the defect when you stood back and looked at the whole wall?
Patient:	Well, not really.

Source: Beck et al. (1979), pp. 130–131.

terms. After four sessions, the woman's attacks subsided: "Every time my heart rate increased, I'd say, it's okay, it's no big deal" (Alford, Freeman, Beck, & Wright, 1990, p. 232). Keeping a diary is another important part of Beck's approach. Clients are encouraged to keep a daily log in which they describe the situation they were in, how they felt, what they were thinking, and how rational these thoughts were when they became upset. Assigned reading, or bibliotherapy, is a third important technique. Clients are given books that explain the cognitive basis of psychological distress. Indeed, research shows that people benefit from reading cognitive therapy self-help books that communicate the message "You feel the way you think" (Hedman, Axelsson, Andersson, Lekander, & Ljótsson, 2016; Jamison & Scogin, 1995).

Cognitive therapy is popular among clinical psychologists. As noted, Ellis and Beck are the pioneers of the approach, but there are others as well. For example, mindfulness-based cognitive therapy (MBCT) for persons with depression and anxiety combines meditation practices with cognitive theory (Abbott et al., 2014; Finucane & Mercer, 2006). Clients are taught how to have nonjudgmental awareness in the present moment so that they can practice mindfulness as needed. Breathing and stretching are part of the technique, to draw the mind's attention to the body and reach a state of calm. The mind and body connection is important, since emotions can influence how the body feels (Smith, Graham, & Senthinathan, 2007). This eight-week course of treatment is also combined with homework assignments, education about depression and anxiety, and in some cases, a retreat. As a result, clients can demonstrate decreases in anxiety, depression, and stress (Abbott et al., 2014; Nyklíček, Mommersteeg, Beugen, Ramakers, & Boxtel, 2013). MBCT clients have also demonstrated a decrease in relapse risk and, thus, have a lower probability of experiencing another depressive episode (Bondolfi et al., 2010; Segal et al., 2010). Whatever the specific technique may be, cognitive therapy is an effective form of treatment for a wide range of problems (McMullin, 2000) and can even be used as a preventive to help people safely taper off antidepressants (Bockting et al., 2018).

cognitive-behavioral therapy. Techniques used to modify disordered thoughts, feelings, and behaviors through the principles of learning and cognition.

Cognitive-Behavioral Therapies

As introduced earlier in this chapter, cognitive therapies and behavioral therapies are effective approaches for treating certain disorders. You may wonder if these therapies are mutually exclusive. In other words, is it possible to combine these types of therapy, or can they only be used separately? As the title of this section implies, these therapies can absolutely be used together, in an approach called **cognitive-behavioral therapy (CBT)**.

CBT is a popular form of therapy that focuses on the management of both thoughts and actions. It is regarded by many as "the most effective treatment approach, based on solid yet ever-evolving scientific models and methods" (van Emmerik, Jong, & Hofmann, 2018, p. 832). CBT has been used successfully to treat a variety of disorders, including bulimia, anger control problems, and stress (Hofmann, Asnaani, Vonk, Sawyer, & Fang, 2012). One CBT method used to treat stress is *stress-inoculation training*, developed by Donald Meichenbaum (1985). Using this form of therapy, people are taught to make optimistic, positive self-statements in combination with muscle relaxation training, deep breathing, and role playing—to insulate them from stress the way vaccines inoculate us against medical disease. Stress-inoculation training can significantly decrease perceived stress during pregnancy (Khorsandi, Vakilian, Salehi, Goudarzi, & Abdi, 2016) and prepare emergency medical professionals for performance under extreme pressure (McParland & Hicks, 2018). However, not all psychological distress is created equal. To give you a glimpse into what CBT might be like for a person diagnosed with a severe psychological disorder, in the next section we consider how a therapist might use CBT in the treatment of schizophrenia.

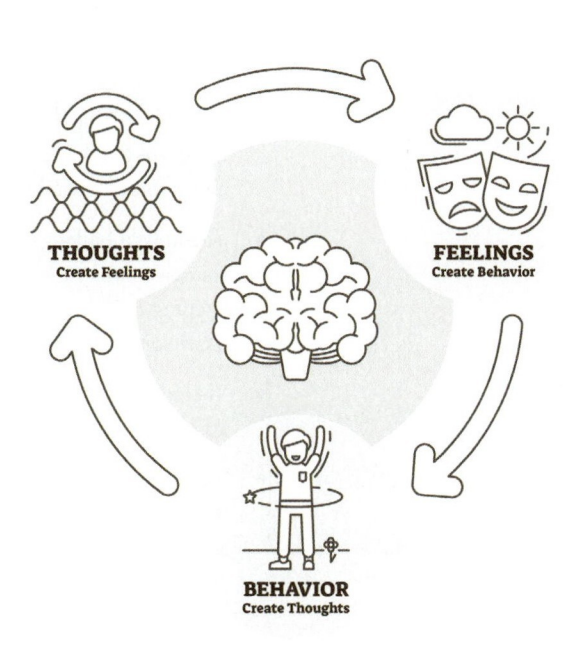

CBT focuses on the interconnectedness of thoughts, feelings, and behavior.
iStock.com/VectorMine

Schizophrenia and Cognitive-Behavioral Therapy

Cognition plays a major role in schizophrenia, mainly because people who have schizophrenia can experience hallucinations and delusions. Imagine you are attending your weekly university seminar, except this week is the last week of the semester. You hear someone say, "She is leaving the room." You look around and realize there is no one near you. Your heart rate speeds up as you rush out of the building, desperate to make it home to the place you feel safest. Fumbling with your keys, you finally unlock the deadbolt and turn the doorknob. "She is opening the door...." There it is again, a voice as clear as day.

Weeks and months go by, and the voice pops in and out randomly, acting as a narrator for your day. You learn to live with the voice but feel alone, so you confide in your closest friend and share your secret. Sadly, she acts appalled and immediately you regret your choice to share. Your friend convinces you to seek help, so you meet with a therapist at the university counseling center. Aware of your own issues, you express that you have low self-esteem, are afraid of failure, and are uncertain about the future. The therapist nods his head, throws you some softball questions, and doesn't seem too worried. But then you bring up the voice. Suddenly, the therapist drops his pen, jerks his head up, and begins asking questions with extreme interest and depth. Your therapist refers you to a psychiatrist. She hospitalizes you, and there you learn of your diagnosis—schizophrenia. While in the hospital, the voices become hostile. They are no longer commenting about your day. They are now calling you vile names and suggesting you harm yourself.

Can schizophrenia really progress in such a manner? Yes, it can. This story you were asked to imagine is a true story—that of Eleanor Longden (2013), as featured in her TED Talk, "The Voices in My Head." Eleanor is a psychologist featured by the Hearing Voices Network. In public forums, Eleanor discusses the auditory hallucinations of schizophrenia—voices in people's heads. In her TED Talk, Eleanor discusses her relationship with *the voices*. At one point, she was so desperate to silence them, she attempted to drill a hole into her own head. Thankfully, she was unsuccessful. Albeit a rare feat, she managed to conquer her schizophrenia. How did she do it? First, she started to recognize the voices in her head as a meaningful response. Eleanor learned how to deconstruct the message behind the words and to react differently to her hallucinations and delusions. Over time, she no longer needed medication and went from patient to practitioner.

Beck and other clinicians believe those diagnosed with schizophrenia can cognitively reappraise their symptoms and learn more appropriate actions when the symptoms appear (Beck, Rector, Stolar, & Grant, 2011; Hagen, Turkingon, Berge, & Gawe, 2011). If people can be taught to frame their delusions and hallucinations in a manner that is helpful and manageable, fear and confusion can diminish, resulting in a better treatment outcome and quality of life. The techniques look something like the following:

- Clients are taught about the chemical imbalances that can result in hallucinations and delusions.

- Clients are assigned homework, where they journal the dates, times, and contexts of their delusions and hallucinations to track their patterns. For example, "On February 5, 2019, I was about to drive to a job interview when my voices told me how dumb and worthless I am."

- Therapists challenge the messages relayed by the voices. Take the previous example. The therapist might ask, "How can a person with a 3.85 GPA be dumb?" If the voices command the client to do something, and threaten repercussions if disobeyed, the therapist can give the client a safe space to disobey and determine if that behavior really resulted in any repercussions.

- Therapists can provide clients with internal dialogue to use when hallucinations and delusions appear, such as, "These voices aren't real. They are just my inner thoughts reacting to my stress."

- Therapists can train clients to relax when uncomfortable, anxious, or fearful. This is like relaxation training, or the type of behavioral therapy that is often used to treat specific phobias, as discussed earlier. If clients feel distressed, they can start to breathe slowly and deeply, think about things that make them happy, and take a seat for a few minutes until the distress subsides.

The Hearing Voices Network is a collection of individuals and resources determined to help people deal with hallucinations in a manner similar to cognitive-behavioral therapy. They believe in recovery and, thus, have "serious concerns about the way we currently understand, categorize and respond to mental distress" (Hearing Voices Network, 2018). If you think about it, once people are labeled with a diagnosis such as schizophrenia, they are stigmatized. We learn to fear people who are diagnosed with psychological disorders, as we rarely are exposed to positive images of people whose mental functioning is unlike our own. Eleanor and other members of the Hearing Voices Network are trying to overcome that stigma by openly discussing their own experiences with hallucinations and delusions and the many cases that are in remission.

Hearing voices is a common symptom of schizophrenia. Although some of the messages may be menacing, people who have schizophrenia should not be stigmatized as harmful.
iStock.com/Siphotography

Humanistic Therapies

When Carl Rogers was a young therapist, he noticed that his clients had a strong sense of self and an inner drive to grow, improve, and fulfill their potential. All the therapist has to do, he said, is provide warmth, a gentle, guiding hand, and a climate of uncritical acceptance, and clients will find the way to happiness and personal fulfillment. With this simple advice, the humanistic approach to psychotherapy was born. This approach trusts a client's growth instincts; focuses on feelings, not cognitions or behavior; is oriented in the here-and-now, not in the distant past; and makes the client responsible for change. Over the years, two types of humanistic therapy have had a marked impact on clinical practice: person-centered therapy and Gestalt therapy.

Person-Centered Therapy

When 415 psychotherapists were asked to name the person who most influenced their work, Carl Rogers was cited more often than anyone else (Smith, 1982). The reason? In a profound way, Rogers redefined the role that a therapist should play: not detective, teacher, or adviser but a facilitator for the client. As Rogers (1942) put it, "Therapy is not a matter of doing something to the individual or inducing him to do something about himself. It is instead a matter of freeing him for normal growth and development" (p. 7). Believing that people know what's right for themselves, Rogers let his clients call the shots. At various times, he referred to this approach as *nondirective, client-centered,* and *person-centered* (Farber, Brink, & Raskin, 1996).

Person-centered therapy is designed to provide a safe haven for people to clarify their feelings, their sense of who they are, and their hopes for what they would like to become, without fear of punishment or disapproval. To foster this process, the therapist needs to exhibit *empathy* (an ability to take the client's perspective in order to understand how he or she feels) and to offer *unconditional positive regard* (an unwavering respect for the client as a person—and these qualities have to be genuine, not put on) for people to open up and reveal themselves. Person-centered therapists also use *reflection*, a nondirective, minimum-intervention technique in which the therapist actively listens to a client's statements, responding by paraphrasing what was said and seeking clarification. No interruption, no analysis, no evaluation. As illustrated in Table 14.5, if psychotherapy were a dance, the person-centered client would lead and the therapist would follow.

person-centered therapy. A humanistic psychotherapy in which a warm and accepting environment is created to foster self-insight and acceptance.

Gestalt Therapy

A therapist with a sympathetic ear and refusal to offer advice isn't for everyone. For those who prefer to be responsible for their own growth and development, but do not mind dramatic and confrontational techniques, there is Fritz Perls's Gestalt therapy. During this treatment, clients are put on the "hot

Gestalt therapy. A humanistic form of psychotherapy in which clients are aggressively prompted to express their feelings.

TABLE 14.5 ■ Person-Centered Therapy in Action

The following dialog between Carl Rogers and a young man who is upset over his relationship with his mother illustrates the technique of reflection. Note how skillfully Rogers helped his client clarify his feelings toward his stepfather. Without prompting, he moved from a blunt statement of mutual hatred, to one of unilateral hatred, to an expression of respect.

Client:	You see I have a stepfather.
Therapist:	I see.
Client:	Let's put it this way. My stepfather and I are not on the happiest terms in the world. And so, when he states something and, of course, she goes along, and I stand up and let her know that I don't like what he is telling me, well, she usually gives in to me.
Therapist:	I see.
Client:	Sometimes, and sometimes it's just the opposite.
Therapist:	But part of what really makes for difficulty is the fact that you and your stepfather, as you say, are not... the relationship isn't completely rosy.
Client:	Let's just put it this way, I hate him and he hates me. It's that way.
Therapist:	But you really hate him and you feel he really hates you.
Client:	Well, I don't know if he hates me or not, but I know one thing, I don't like him whatsoever.
Therapist:	You can't speak for sure about his feelings because only he knows exactly what those are, but as far as you are concerned...
Client	... he knows how I feel about it.
Therapist:	You don't have any use for him.
Client:	None whatsoever. And that's been for about eight years now.
Therapist:	So for about eight years you've lived with a person whom you have no respect for and really hate.
Client:	Oh, I respect him.
Therapist:	Ah. Excuse me. I got that wrong.
Client:	I have to respect him. I don't have to, but I do. But I don't love him, I hate him. I can't stand him.
Therapist:	There are certain things you respect him for, but that doesn't alter the fact that you definitely hate him and don't love him.
Client:	That's the truth. I respect anybody who has bravery and courage, and he does.
Therapist:	... You do give him credit for the fact that he is brave, he has guts or something.
Client:	Yeah. He shows that he can do a lot of things that, well, a lot of men can't.
Therapist:	M-hm, m-hm.
Client:	And also he has asthma, and the doctor hasn't given him very long to live. And he, even though he knows he is going to die, he keeps working and he works at a killing pace, so I respect him for that, too.
Therapist:	M-hm. So I guess you're saying he really has...
Client	... what it takes.

Source: Raskin (1985), pp. 167–168.

seat." When they speak in ways that are not brutally honest—by slipping into the past to avoid the present or by talking in general, abstract terms rather than in the first person—they should be challenged. "Do you really *need* to stay in this dysfunctional relationship, or do you *want* to?" "Do you *have* to work for seven days a week, or do you *choose* to?" (Perls, 1969; Perls, Heffertine, & Goodman, 1951).

To help clients confront unresolved issues, Perls developed some specific techniques—such as the *empty chair dialog*, in which the therapist guides the person through an imaginary conversation with a significant other. Typically, in this "dialog," clients air their complaints, venting, and blaming the significant other, often shifting roles to imagine and understand the other's likely response. A study of 26 clients who underwent Gestalt therapy for interpersonal problems revealed that those who expressed previously unmet needs in an empty chair dialog felt better and improved more than those who did not (Greenberg & Malcolm, 2002).

> **TRY THIS!**
>
> **Handle With Chair**
>
> *Empty chair dialog* is a technique developed by Gestalt therapist Fritz Perls, in which the client is guided through an imaginary conversation with a significant other. By addressing an empty chair, the client can often articulate feelings that are difficult to express to the real person.
>
> For a taste of how the empty chair technique works, **TRY THIS:** Think of someone with whom you have a minor issue—perhaps a friend with an annoying habit like playing music too loud. Set two chairs facing each other, sit in one, and visualize your friend sitting in the other. Speak out loud to your absent friend, describing the behavior you object to, how it makes you feel, and what you would like your friend to do about it.
>
> Next, switch chairs and pretend to be your friend. Imagine yourself in the facing chair and respond to your complaint as you think your friend would.
>
> How do you feel afterward? Did you get a sense of relief from complaining to the empty chair? And when you switched seats, did you gain any insight into your friend's point of view?

Group-Therapy Approaches

In the case study described at the beginning of this chapter, Yalom (1989) put Betty, his patient, into a therapy group. She felt isolated, craved companionship, and needed a fresh perspective. At one point, a young man named Carlos revealed to the group that he was dying of cancer, the disease that had terrified Betty ever since it took her father's life. At first, Betty became physically ill and obsessed with the fear that she too would get cancer, lose weight, and shrivel away; she was fighting the skin-and-bones image of her father before he died. This insight was a key to Betty's problems. Soon she began to change her eating habits, with her therapy group acting as a supportive community, rooting her on the healthier she became.

As this story illustrates, **group therapy** provides a valuable alternative to individual psychotherapy. Typically, one or two therapists work with 4 to 10 clients at a time, and often the clients have similar problems. The benefits are numerous, as groups furnish social support and encouragement, new outlooks on old problems, and interpersonal experience for those who are shy or socially awkward. There are different types of group therapy. The format and goals depend on the therapist's theoretical orientation (Brabender, 2002).

Specialized *self-help groups* represent a popular form of group therapy. In these groups, people who share a common problem come together for mutual help and social support. The best known is Alcoholics Anonymous, or AA. AA was founded in 1935 and now has 115,000 groups worldwide (American Addiction Centers, 2018). Many other groups are available for people with AIDS, survivors of intimate partner abuse, single caregivers, people with drug addiction, survivors of sexual assault, smokers, newly arrived immigrants, and so on. It's estimated that 25 million Americans will participate in thousands of self-help groups in the course of their lifetimes (Kessler, Mickelson, & Zhao, 1997). But are self-help groups effective? To date, not all of these programs have been evaluated extensively, so firm conclusions cannot be drawn (Christensen & Jacobson, 1994), although evidence suggests that AA has pretty good success rates, with nearly two times better abstinence rates at a 16-year follow-up for those who attended AA meetings compared to those who didn't (Moos & Moos, 2006).

People often enter therapy because of problems that arise at home, so many psychologists prefer to treat families, not individuals. There is no single approach, but **family therapies** in general treat

group therapy. The simultaneous treatment of several clients in a group setting.

family therapy. A form of psychotherapy that treats the members of a family as an interactive system.

Alcoholics Anonymous is a successful self-help group that ensures anonymity. Meetings held in community settings usually begin with a reading of the AA Preamble: "Alcoholics Anonymous is a fellowship of men and women who share their experience, strength, and hope with each other that they may solve their common problem and help others to recover from alcoholism. The only requirement for membership is a desire to stop drinking."

iStock.com/KatarzynaBialasiewicz

the family as an interdependent social "system" in which the whole is greater than the sum of its parts (Cox & Paley, 1997). The therapist observes family members together—how they relate, what roles they play, and what alliances they form. Problems within the family vary—a boy acts out to get attention from two busy working parents; estranged parents don't get along and use their daughter as a scapegoat. Whatever the problem, whole families are gathered in an effort to heal old wounds and prevent further conflict (Glick, Clarkin, Rait, & Berman, 2000; Hazelrigg, Cooper, & Borduin, 1987; Minuchin, 1974).

LEARNING CHECK

Thera-Ps & Qs

From the list on the right, identify the type of program or therapy in which you are likeliest to be involved if the situation described in the left column is happening.

1	With the help of journals, you are tasked to track your thoughts and behaviors.	a.	Gestalt
2.	Your therapist displays empathy and offers unconditional positive regard to foster your self-insight and acceptance.	b.	Self-help group
3.	You want to be responsible for your own change and react well to those who are willing to confront you with the truth, even if it is a dramatic confrontation.	c.	Person-centered therapy
4.	For mutual support, you meet with other people who share your problem.	d.	Cognitive-behavioral therapy
5.	You participate in psychoeducation and are challenged to get rid of your maladaptive assumptions.	e.	Rational-emotive behavior therapy

(Answers: 1. d; 2. c; 3. a; 4. b; 5. e.)

PERSPECTIVES ON PSYCHOTHERAPY

> **LEARNING OBJECTIVES**
>
> Determine what types of psychotherapy are effective, and list the properties that various types of psychotherapy have in common.
>
> - Create an argument that supports the effectiveness of psychotherapy.
> - List the properties that various types of psychotherapy share.
> - Define what it means to be "eclectic" in a therapeutic approach.

At the heart of psychotherapy is the assumption that people have a capacity for change. Thus, two questions loom over the entire enterprise: Can humans help humans to change? And are some forms of helping better than others (Mahoney, 1991)? For those interested in the answers to these questions, the American Psychological Association (2013) and the Canadian Psychological Association (2013) released empirically based statements supporting the efficacy of psychotherapy.

The Bottom Line: Does Psychotherapy Work?

Not everyone agrees that psychotherapy works. There are reasons for skepticism. One reason is that researchers are cautious when it comes to using personal endorsements from clients—or therapists, for that matter—to measure the effectiveness of psychotherapy. First, both therapists and clients are motivated to believe that their efforts were successful. Therapists want to affirm their professional value and integrity, and clients need to justify their investment of time and money. Researchers thus seek independent and objective measures of improvement—for example, pre- to posttreatment changes in test scores, behavior, or third-party evaluations. Second, people often get better on their own—without treatment. This improvement may occur as a result of support received from friends and family members or simply because "Time heals all wounds." If psychotherapy is to be judged effective, those who receive treatment should improve more than comparable others who do not. The question is whether they do.

In 1952, Hans Eysenck reviewed 24 psychotherapy studies and found that roughly two-thirds of all patients showed improvement. However, about two-thirds of people who were on waiting lists for therapy but never received treatment also improved in the same time frame, on their own. Eysenck's conclusion was that psychotherapy is worthless. His article stirred a major debate. Psychologists attacked the studies Eysenck had cited as well as his analysis of the results. It turned out, for example, that many of the control-group subjects were healthier initially than those who were received treatment, that some control subjects were taking drugs prescribed by physicians, and that they improved less than Eysenck believed (Bergin & Lambert, 1978).

Despite its shortcomings, Eysenck's article inspired an active, sophisticated generation of clinical researchers determined to evaluate psychotherapy outcomes. By 1980, when Mary Lee Smith and others reviewed the available research, there were 475 published studies involving literally thousands of patients. Using meta-analysis to statistically combine the results of these studies, they found that psychotherapy was effective for a whole range of problems—including anxiety disorders, low self-esteem, social problems, and addiction. As demonstrated in Figure 14.5, the average psychotherapy patient improved more than did 80 percent of no-treatment control subjects. Smith and her colleagues (1980) concluded that "psychotherapy benefits people of all ages as reliably as schooling educates them, medicine cures them, or business turns a profit" (p. 183).

Although some psychologists still question the benefits of psychotherapy (Chow, Wagner, Lüdtke, Trautwein, & Roberts, 2017), others have drawn positive conclusions from the research evidence (Chorpita et al., 2011; Cuijpers, Andersson, Donker, & Van Straten, 2011; Lipsey & Wilson, 1993; Rosa-Alcazar, Sanchez-Meca, Gomez-Conesa, & Marin-Martinez, 2008; Russell & Orlinsky, 1996; Shadish et al., 1997; Shedler, 2010). Many clinical researchers have explored the links between processes and outcomes (Bisson et al., 2007; Cuijpers et al., 2011; Kopta, Lueger, Saunders, & Howard, 1999). If a person started psychotherapy

FIGURE 14.5 ■ The Benefits of Psychotherapy

Summarizing the results of 475 studies, Smith and others found that the average psychotherapy client shows more

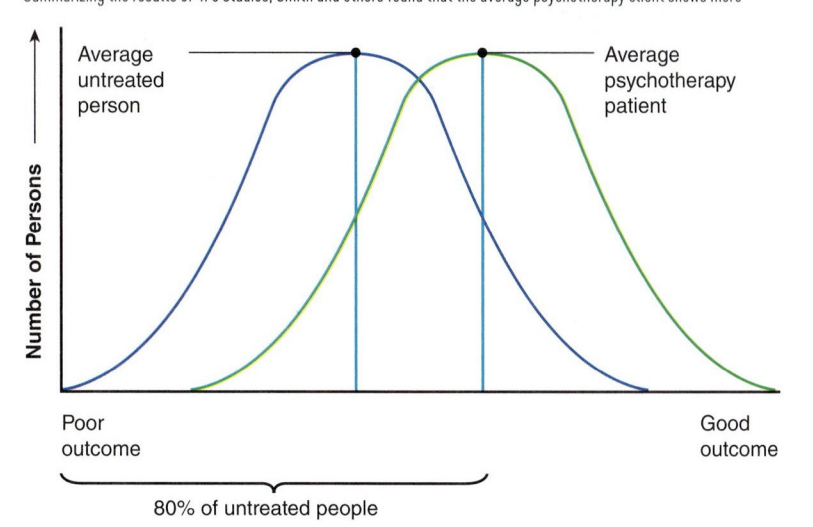

FIGURE 14.6 ■ Improvement in Psychotherapy: The More the Better?

A summary of 15 studies indicates that there is continued improvement over 26 sessions but that the rate of improvement then levels off. At one

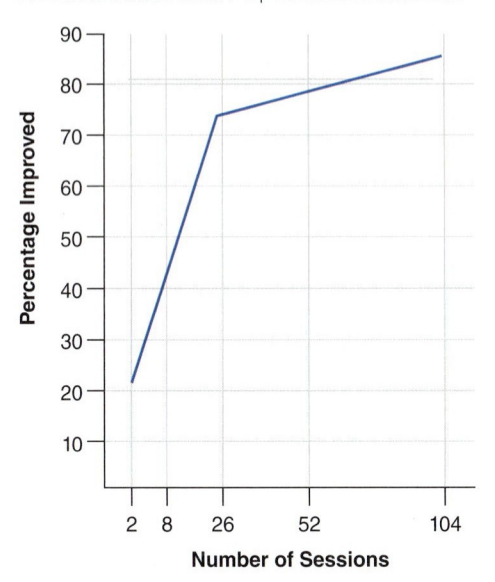

today, for example, how long would it take to feel better? Is there a timetable? A classic review by Howard and colleagues (1986) analyzed 15 studies involving more than 2,400 clients. The researchers found that the percentage of people who improved increased with the number of therapy sessions *up to a point*. After six months, or 26 sessions, 70 percent of the outcomes were successful. From then on, however, the improvement rate leveled off and additional sessions contributed little more to the final outcome (as illustrated in Figure 14.6). Short-term psychotherapies (eight sessions or less) have demonstrated desired effects, too, for those with depression who either cannot, or don't desire to, commit to six months of therapy (Nieuwsma et al., 2012).

Are Some Therapies Better Than Others?

Some 80 percent of all therapy patients improve more than no-treatment control subjects; and 70 percent of those who improve do so within six months. You may think, don't some people derive more or less benefit than the average? Aren't some problems more amenable to change than others? What about the differences among the psychoanalytic, behavioral, cognitive, cognitive-behavioral, and humanistic approaches? Smith and her colleagues (1980) compared the different types of therapies, and they found a surprising result: All approaches were effective, and all were *equivalent*—that is, despite radical differences in techniques, no single approach was consistently superior to another. The American Psychological Association (2013) corroborated this conclusion in its "Recognition of Psychotherapy Effectiveness" statement.

How can such different forms of treatment—ranging from a probing analysis of unconscious childhood conflicts, to a hard-nosed modification of behaviors or cognitions, to warm and nondirective reflection and acceptance—produce the same results? There are three answers to this question. First, specific techniques are less critical to the final outcome than are personal characteristics of the client and therapist (Hill, Spiegel, Hoffman, Kivlighan, & Gelso, 2017; Lambert & Bergin, 1994). Therapist expertise—much like for any type of clinician—can vary (Hill et al., 2017). Second, the different approaches may well be equivalent on average, but the value of any one technique depends on the problem. For example, cognitive therapy and cognitive-behavioral therapy are particularly potent in the battle against depression (Ablon & Jones, 2002; Canadian Psychological Association, 2013; Cuijpers et al., 2011; Dobson, 1989). A third explanation is that all psychological therapies are more similar in important ways than one might think. In other words, despite the surface differences, all psychotherapies have much in common at a deeper level—and these common factors, not the specific techniques, provide the active ingredients necessary for change (Stiles, Shapiro, & Elliott, 1986; Strupp, 1989).

What Are the Active Ingredients?

Regardless of differences in theoretical orientations and techniques, there are three common, "nonspecific" factors at work in all brands of psychotherapy.

A Supportive Relationship

First, all therapists provide a *supportive relationship* that contains warmth, trust, concern, encouragement, reassurance, acceptance, a shoulder to cry on, and agreement on treatment goals and processes. Indeed, the better the "working alliance" is between a therapist and client, the more favorable the outcome (Horvath & Luborsky, 1993; Horvath & Symonds, 1991; Stiles et al., 1998). Why is this one-on-one human relationship so important? Hans Strupp (1996) believes that people find it immensely gratifying to be listened to with concern, empathy, and respect.

Support is a key to a healthy alliance between psychotherapist and patient, but it's also important that the therapist understand that the patient belongs to a specific cultural group. In the United States, for example, African American, Asian American, Latinx, European American, and Native Americans bring to therapy different family backgrounds, religious beliefs, values, worldviews, and problems. Therefore, mental health workers must seek to become "multiculturally competent" when working with patients from cultural groups other than their own (American Psychological Association, 1990; Chu & Leino, 2017; Inman & Kreider, 2013; Sue & Sue, 1999, 2002).

Take, for example, American Indians and their concept of health. According to researchers (Stewart, Moodley, & Hyatt, 2016; Yurkovich & Lattergrass, 2008), their view is more holistic than that of white Americans. American Indians believe there are four inseparable dimensions of the self: physical, mental, emotional, and spiritual. The spiritual dimension is typically not included in Caucasian definitions of health. For American Indians, if one dimension is out of balance, then the person is not considered to be "well." Thus, these four dimensions create the Medicine Wheel, which is utilized by some—but not all—American Indian cultures. Yurkovich and Lattergrass (2008) suggest that mental health practitioners who work with American Indians be mindful of the four dimensions and incorporate them into treatment as appropriate. These researchers also note that "there is no uniform formula for the delivery of health care to individuals" (p. 457).

Can treatments be adapted to meet cultural needs, and is this adaptation important? As Beckstead and colleagues (2015) discovered, treatments can be adapted and still be effective. These clinicians incorporated cultural, spiritual, and traditional practices with psychotherapy when treating American Indian adolescents who had substance use disorders. Ninety-six percent of the adolescents receiving treatment demonstrated significantly positive outcomes. This

A positive rapport built on trust, acceptance, and cultural competency helps create an environment suitable for growth.
iStock.com/fizkes

On the island of Bali, people with mental disorders are often seen as victims of witchcraft and are sent for treatment to a shaman, like the one shown here. Using massage, healing smoke, holy water, and other rituals, the shaman would drive evil wind spirits from the patient's body. Like healers in other cultures, Balinese shamans are often successful. Perhaps nonspecific factors that contribute to psychotherapy—such as hope and social support—are also at work in these rituals.
Peter Treanor / Alamy Stock Photo

high success rate is possibly due to the clinicians' efforts to make the treatment culturally appropriate. As Novins and colleagues (2016) determined, the usefulness of substance abuse treatments for American Indians is likely limited when those treatments lack cultural appropriateness. To prevent cultural adaptation from being a barrier, traditional healing consultants and ceremonial providers can be collaborators when creating and providing treatment programs to American Indians (Rieckmann, Moore, Croy, Novins, & Aarons, 2016).

A Ray of Hope

Second, all therapies offer a ray of *hope* to people who are unhappy, demoralized, and down on themselves. In all aspects of life, we are motivated by positive expectations, faith, and optimism (Seligman, 1991). The same is true in psychotherapy. It's even been suggested that high expectations alone are sufficient to produce change even when they are not justified (Greenberg, Constantino, & Bruce, 2006; Prioleau, Murdock, & Brody, 1983). This suggestion is based on the **placebo effect**, an established medical phenomenon whereby patients will show more improvement when they are given an inactive drug, or placebo, than when they are not. Somehow, believing can help make it so, which raises the question, is psychotherapy just one big placebo effect? No, carefully controlled studies have shown that although people randomly assigned to receive a placebo therapy (bogus exercises, group discussions, self-help tapes, and sugar pills) are often better off than those who do not, they typically do not improve as much as those who undergo psychotherapy (Barker, Funk, & Houston, 1988; Peng, Huang, Chen, & Lu, 2009; Powers, Halpern, Ferenschak, Gillihan, & Foa, 2010). Hope may be necessary, but it's not sufficient.

> **placebo effect.** The curative effect of an inactive treatment that results simply from the patient's belief in its therapeutic value.

An Opportunity to Open Up

A third common ingredient is that all psychotherapies offer an ideal setting for *opening up*, a chance for people to confide in someone and talk freely about their troubles—maybe for the first time. Studies have shown that keeping secrets is stressful and that "letting it out" has therapeutic effects on our mental and physical health—effects that are especially strong when the events being described are highly traumatic (Pennebaker, 1997; Smyth, 1998).

Why does it help to open up? Why do *you* sometimes feel the need to talk out your problems? One possibility, recognized many years ago by Freud, is that the experience itself provides a much-needed *catharsis*, a discharge of psychic tension—like taking the lid off a boiling pot of water to slow the boiling. Another interpretation, favored by most therapists, is that talking about a problem helps you to sort out your thoughts, understand the problem better, and gain *insight*, in cognitive terms. Whatever the reason, it's clear that psychotherapy provides an ideal setting for self-disclosure: The listener is patient, caring, and nonjudgmental, and what's said is kept in confidence. This last point is critical because despite the potential for gain, opening up can also cause great distress when the people we choose to confide in react with rejection or unwanted advice or, worse, when they disclose to others what was said (Kelly & McKillop, 1996). Have you thought about opening up to someone else about your wellness?

What's Your Prediction?

People join social-support groups for hundreds of life problems. But do all problems trigger this need for social support, or are some problems "needier" than others? Kathryn Davison and her colleagues (2000) asked this question in a survey of thousands of social-support group members in New York, Los Angeles, Chicago, and Dallas. Look at the list below of eight support groups and make a prediction: Out of 20 health problem groups surveyed, adjusted for populations of sufferers, which four were the *most* heavily enrolled (M) and which were the *least* enrolled (L)?

AIDS	____	Migraines	____
Chronic pain	____	Anorexia	____
Alcoholism	____	Breast cancer	____
Ulcers	____	Hypertension	____

What kinds of illnesses lead people to seek each other out? In order, the top four illness groups were alcoholism, AIDS, breast cancer, and anorexia. In order, the least enrolled groups were for hypertension, migraine headaches, chronic pain, and ulcers. Do you notice a pattern in these results? What does it all mean? According to the researchers, people are most likely to affiliate for illnesses that are socially embarrassing or stigmatizing. Hence, AIDS patients are 250 times more likely to participate in a support group than are hypertension patients.

What's the Future of Psychotherapy?

The 21st century has placed urgent new demands on the practice of psychotherapy. The coronavirus pandemic, the terrorist attacks of 9/11 and thereafter, mass shootings, hate crimes, wildfires, floods, and the stress these traumatic events have unleashed leave no doubt of the need for mental health professionals to help those who are forever changed. Yet as health costs skyrocket, and as people turn for insurance reasons to managed health care programs, it's clear that consumers are in need of psychological therapies that are quick, inexpensive, and proven effective. Thus, three major trends have emerged—at least partly in response to consumer demand for quick, effective, cheap, and available treatment.

World Mental Health Day, an international day for education, awareness, and advocacy against the stigma of psychological disorders, is observed on October 10.

iStock.com/Vector Artist

Eclectic Approach

One trend is for therapists to be flexible in their approach and **eclectic**, borrowing ideas and techniques, as needed, from different orientations rather than identifying themselves with a single orientation (Beitman, Goldfried, & Norcross, 1989; Feixas & Botella, 2004; Watkins, Sprang, & Rothbaum, 2018). Today, psychoanalytic therapists are playing a more active and interpersonal role than in the past. Some cognitive-behavioral therapists are even called "new wave" or practitioners of *acceptance and commitment therapy*—an approach that recognizes the importance of mindfulness and the commitment to growth (Hayes, 2018).

eclectic. A therapeutic approach that uses a range of orientations instead of a single orientation.

According to this model, specific treatment techniques should be chosen on a case-by-case basis, depending on the client, the client's problem, and the desired outcome (Norcross, 1991). Others argue that combined treatment orientations should be labeled as "integrative" (Norcross, Karpiak, & Lister, 2005; Zarbo, Tasca, Cattafi, & Compare, 2016). In an examination of 187 eclectic psychologists, the majority preferred the term *integrative* to *eclectic*, and viewed the term as an "endorsement of a broader orientation" (Norcross et al., 2005, p. 1597), with the most frequent theoretical foundations stemming from cognitive therapy.

Empirical Support

A second trend born of economic necessity is to identify, through research, "empirically supported treatments" that therapists can choose from. There is reason to believe that some approaches are better than others—depending on the problem. For example, Gestalt therapy might not work well for those who have problems with assertiveness. This is why some researchers argue that the theoretical orientation used is not nearly as important as the therapists themselves (Hill et al., 2017) or clients' positive expectations (Greenberg et al., 2006). These arguments have led to the suggestion that therapists measure client expectations and outcomes before and after therapy, respectively (Angus, Watson, Elliott, Schneider, & Timulak, 2015).

There is also the issue of affordability. Many insurance providers limit the number of psychotherapy visits, resulting in more out-of-pocket costs for clients. Then, there are those who do not have insurance. When people cannot pay for more than a few sessions, treatment can be ineffective. To increase mental health treatment accessibility, the Obama administration made changes via the Affordable Care Act. Hockenberry and colleagues (2019) investigated whether these changes had an impact on depression treatment. After analyzing trends between 1998 and 2015, they found that treatment for depression, and the amount of money the United States spent on said treatment, increased. However, these increases did not meet expectations, which suggests that people in need continue to face barriers to treatment.

Treatment and Technology

With all the pressure on mental health workers to provide affordable and effective services, it is no wonder that technology is becoming more commonplace in treatment (Andersson & Titov, 2014). The use of technology to videoconference clients can remove many barriers to treatment. For example, it reduces costs across several domains for practitioners such as real estate payments, office maintenance, and transportation. These reduced costs, in turn, can lead to client savings. Furthermore, clients can save the costs of, and time needed for, transportation. Clients can also avoid the possible stigmatization of being seen at a therapist's office (Renn, Hoeft, Lee, Bauer, & Areán, 2019). Technology-delivered therapy is also beneficial because it can happen anywhere the client has access to the Internet and a device. Therefore, rural residents who have little to no therapist access, or persons unable to leave their homes, would not be without treatment options.

Telemental health and telepsychiatry are two types of mental health care delivered via technology. Both are forms of videoconferencing treatment where the client and practitioner hold a session using livestreaming video software. To understand how this might work, imagine you are the parent of a child who has autism spectrum disorder. According to the *DSM-5*, autism spectrum disorder symptoms include deficits in social communication and social interaction in many contexts (American Psychological Association, 2013). Because of this disorder, getting your child out of the house is somewhat difficult. She has problems adjusting to new environments and can react adversely to unexpected stimuli. Furthermore, the clinician cannot observe how your child behaves in her natural setting. So, a videoconference is scheduled. Through a Bluetooth headset connected to a laptop, your clinician is able to watch playtime between you and your child. The clinician can then give you instructions about how to interact with your child, like, "Flip her toy over." During this livestreamed therapy session, the clinician takes notes, provides feedback, and acts as a behavioral coach when your child has an adverse response.

Telemental health and telepsychiatry have demonstrated effectiveness in the treatment of psychological disorders (García-Lizana & Muñoz-Mayorga, 2010; Hubley, Lynch, Schneck, Thomas, & Shore, 2016; Norman, 2006; Reay, Looi, & Keightley, 2020). In addition, during the coronavirus pandemic, telemental health aided in delivering needed care without exposing practitioners or clients to the virus (Centers for Disease Control and Prevention, 2020). In addition, both methods have garnered support from the American Psychiatric Association and ATA (formerly the American Telemedicine Association). However, telemental health does pose a risk to confidentiality and is not available to persons without the necessary technology or Internet access (Madigan, Racine, Cooke, & Korczak, 2020). A guide written by the American Psychiatric Association and ATA (2018) offers empirically based best practices and an overview to providing such care for clinicians.

Granted, not all clients would benefit more from, or be motivated to try, videoconferenced treatment in comparison to traditional treatment. But some people desire assistance with their mental health that requires little to no practitioner involvement (Renn et al., 2019). For those people, there are digital treatment apps. Mental health apps for mobile devices, called *mHealth*, are increasing in popularity. They don't necessarily offer livestreamed therapy sessions from a licensed clinician, like telepsychiatry does; instead, they tend to offer things like cognitive-behavioral activities, journals, mood trackers, and materials to help people manage and monitor their thoughts and behaviors. Not all apps require the user to manually enter information. Some tracking apps passively collect information such as location, number of text messages sent and received, Internet searches, physical activity, and social engagement (Ameringen, Turna, Khalesi, Pullia, & Patterson, 2017). For example, a person with bipolar disorder might be able to better track mood shifts based on passively collected data. These data can show patterns in behaviors such as increases in social activities, spending, and physical activity, and a decrease in sleep, a few days before a manic phase. In turn, this pattern could be used to inform the person's clinician about necessary changes in medication and/or therapeutic sessions (Ameringen et al., 2017). Although these apps can be beneficial, clinicians are not typically trained in app development, use, or evaluation (American Psychiatric Association & ATA, 2018; Singh et al., 2016), nor do all apps require clinician approval or guidance for consumer access. Singh and colleagues (2016) argue that

---

telemental health and telepsychiatry. Types of mental health care delivered via technology such as video conferencing.

these self-directed apps don't always meet the needs of users, can fail to respond appropriately when the user enters health information that may signal an emergency, vary greatly in their usability, and are susceptible to data breaches. Therefore, before using an mHealth app, it is important to find an app that has been supported by research and that takes necessary precautions to protect users' privacy.

MEDICAL INTERVENTIONS

LEARNING OBJECTIVES

Understand the different types and cost-benefit trade-offs of medical interventions for psychological disorders.

- List the types of drugs used to treat psychological disorders.
- Compare the advantages and disadvantages of taking drugs for the treatment of psychological disorders.
- Describe the conditions that lead to the use of electroconvulsive therapy and psychosurgery.

For people who suffer from severe anxiety, mood disorders, and schizophrenia, medical interventions may provide an alternative or supplement to psychotherapy. Based on established links among the brain, the mind, and behavior, three types of medical treatment are available: drug therapy, electroshock therapy, and psychosurgery.

Drug Therapies

In 1952, French psychiatrists Jean Delay and Pierre Deniker used a wonder drug called *chlorpromazine* to eliminate the symptoms of schizophrenia in a patient. David Healy (2002) argues that this discovery is as important in the history of medicine as the discovery of penicillin. From then on, the use of medications in the treatment of psychological disorders has skyrocketed in popularity. As a result, pharmaceutical companies find themselves in a race against time—and against each other—to create, test, gain government approval for, and market newer and better drugs.

Today, in the booming area of **psychopharmacology**, a vast array of drugs is used for psychotherapeutic purposes (Schatzberg & Nemeroff, 1998). Most of them work by acting on neurotransmitters, the biochemicals that relay impulses between neurons. For the hundreds of thousands of people who used to languish in psychiatric wards and hospitals, these drugs opened doors to life in the community—for better and for worse (as illustrated in Figure 14.7). Robert M. Julien's book, *A Primer of Drug Action* (Advokat, Comaty, & Julien, 2014) describes these drugs in clear, nontechnical language—their trade names, purposes, dosage levels, effects on the brain and behavior, the benefits, potential side effects, and dangers. The main types are summarized in Table 14.6.

psychopharmacology. The study of the effects of drugs on psychological processes and disorders.

Antianxiety Drugs

Whether the cause is internal or external, and whether the condition is chronic or acute, there are many possible sources of anxiety and many people who at times suffer through it. Thus, it's no wonder there has always been a great demand for—and abuse of—**antianxiety drugs**, or tranquilizers. During the 1950s, many doctors prescribed *barbiturates* for anxious patients. Barbiturates combat anxiety by depressing central nervous system activity. They are effective but highly addictive. They help us to relax but also cause us to become clumsy and drowsy.

antianxiety drugs. Tranquilizing medications used in the treatment of anxiety.

In the 1960s, a new class of tranquilizers was developed. Called *benzodiazepines*, they include chlordiazepoxide (Librium), diazepam (Valium), and alprazolam (Xanax). These drugs have the same desired calming effect and are less likely than barbiturates to cause drowsiness or addiction. Their impact is almost immediate, and they are most effective in treating generalized anxiety disorder, if taken regularly. Benzodiazepines are often prescribed by family doctors, not psychiatrists, for people in the midst of a

FIGURE 14.7 ■ Antipsychotic Drugs and Hospitalization Trends

The inpatient population in U.S. mental hospitals has declined sharply since 1960, putting the treatment emphasis on outpatient community care. This trend resulted from the widespread use of antipsychotic drugs, which were introduced in the 1950s. Some

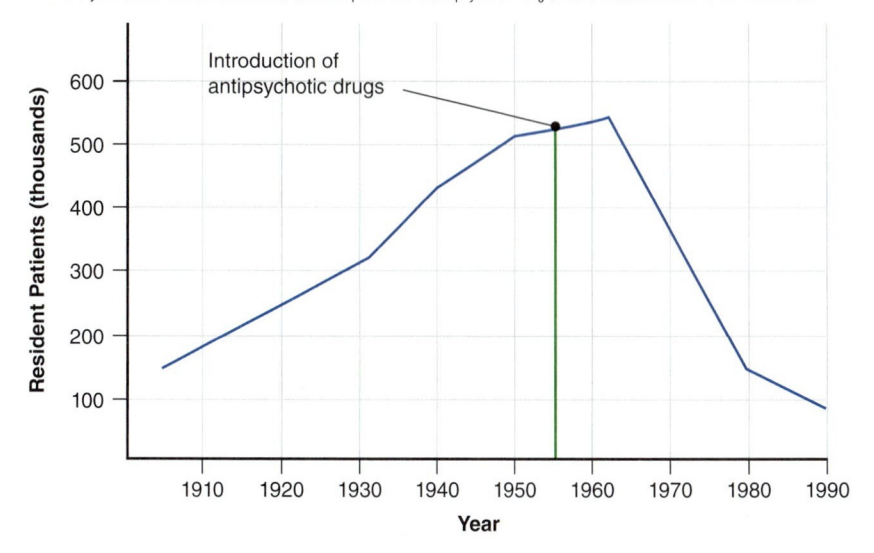

stressful time of life. These drugs are not as safe as once thought, however. They are dangerous when combined with alcohol, and they may produce temporary side effects such as slurred speech, dry mouth, lightheadedness, and diminished psychomotor control. When a regular user stops taking them, the result may be a two-week "rebound anxiety" more intense than ever (Julien, 1992). A drug called *buspirone*, which was first released in 1986, provides an alternative. It acts more slowly, usually taking a few days or weeks to have an effect, but it is also less likely to promote dependence or have unpleasant side effects.

TABLE 14.6 ■ Types of Drug Treatments

Drug Type	Trade Name	Beneficial Effects
Antianxiety Drugs		
chlordiazepoxide	Librium	Act as tranquilizers and, if taken regularly, can be used in the treatment of generalized anxiety disorder.
diazepam	Valium	
alprazolam	Xanax	
buspirone	BuSpar	
Antidepressants		
imipramine	Tofranil	Have mood-elevating effects and can relieve depression.
fluoxetine	Prozac	
Mood Stabilizer		
lithium	Lithium carbonate	Calms mania and, if taken continuously, may reduce bipolar mood swings.
Antipsychotic Drugs		
chlorpromazine	Thorazine	Reduce hallucinations, delusions, and other positive symptoms of schizophrenia.
clozapine	Clozaril	
risperidone	Risperdal	

FIGURE 14.8 ■ Antidepressant Consumption for Americans in the Past 30 Days

From 1988 to 2014, the percentage of Americans who reportedly took an antidepressant drug increased drastically, especially among those aged 45 years and older.

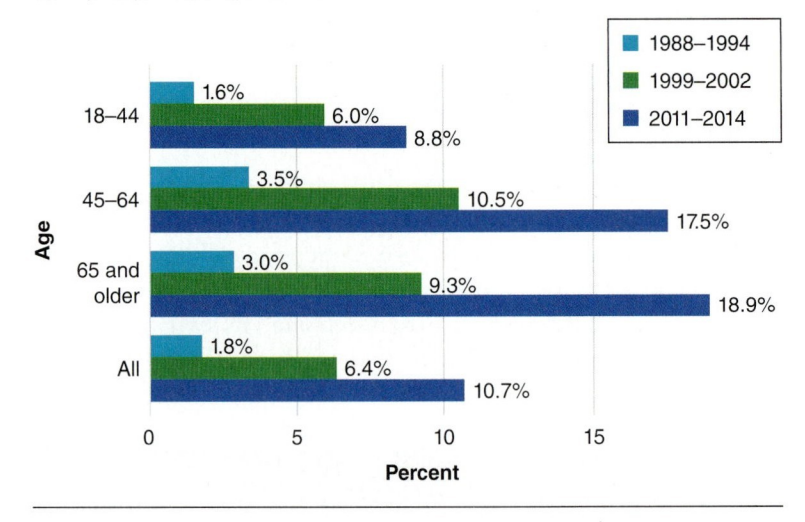

Age	1988–1994	1999–2002	2011–2014
18–44	1.6%	6.0%	8.8%
45–64	3.5%	10.5%	17.5%
65 and older	3.0%	9.3%	18.9%
All	1.8%	6.4%	10.7%

Centers for Disease Control

Antidepressants

In the 1950s, doctors noticed that drugs being used to treat high blood pressure and tuberculosis had dramatic side effects on mood—sometimes causing depression, other times euphoria. At about the same time, researchers found that these drugs also increased levels of the neurotransmitter norepinephrine, a chemical cousin of adrenaline found in a part of the brain that regulates mood and emotion. Together, these strands of evidence suggested that depression is associated with lower-than-needed norepinephrine levels. Later research also linked depression to serotonin. The practical result was the development of **antidepressants** such as imipramine (Tofranil), drugs that tend to increase the supply of norepinephrine or serotonin and elevate mood. Studies have shown that the antidepressants are effective. They are not addictive and cause only minor side effects such as dry mouth, constipation, blurred vision, and fatigue. As illustrated in Figure 14.8, the number of Americans who took at least one type of antidepressant in the past 30 days skyrocketed from 1988 to 2014 (Centers for Disease Control, 2019).

Today, psychiatrists are most likely to prescribe selective serotonin reuptake inhibitors (SSRIs). The best known of these drugs is fluoxetine—better known by its trade name, Prozac. By prolonging serotonin's presence in the synapse, Prozac can make serotonin release more efficient without affecting other neurotransmitters and, in turn, can be effective with only mild side effects. Prozac is the most widely used antidepressant in the world; however, a large-scale study demonstrated that it does not result in the best treatment outcomes (Cipriani et al., 2009). The antidepressant with the highest efficacy was mirtazapine (Remeron), followed by escitalopram (Lexapro), venlafaxine (Effexor), and sertraline (Zoloft). The antidepressant that was most acceptable to patients and, thus, continued for the duration of the study was Zoloft followed by Lexapro, bupropion (Wellbutrin), citalopram (Celexa), and Prozac.

In some patients, Prozac can relieve not only depression but also certain anxiety disorders and eating disorders. It also seems to transform the personality, making users happier, more self-confident and productive at work, and more engaged and relaxed in social situations. As a result, this "wonder drug" in a little green-and-white capsule is sometimes prescribed for people who are not clinically depressed. Its popularity raises hard ethical questions concerning the proper use of psychoactive drugs (Kramer, 1993). Some psychiatrists have also expressed concern that this breed of antidepressant is indiscriminately overprescribed and not without risk (Breggin, 2001).

Mood Stabilizers

For bipolar disorder—which is characterized by wild manic-depressive mood swings—different, mood-stabilizing drugs are used. The best known of these is **lithium**—an inexpensive mineral found

antidepressants. Drugs that relieve depression by increasing the supply of norepinephrine, serotonin, or dopamine.

lithium. A mineral prescribed as an effective treatment for bipolar disorder.

in rocks, water, plants, and animals. Taken on a continuous basis, lithium can usually prevent moods from reeling out of control and is considered the most effective treatment for bipolar disorder (Schou, 1997). Common side effects include dry mouth, thirst, weight gain, excessive urination, fatigue, and tremors. Taken in dosages that are too high, lithium can prove dangerous, even life-threatening. For persons with bipolar disorder who don't respond to lithium or who can't tolerate the side effects, other mood-stabilizing drugs can be used instead (Anderson, Haddad, & Scott, 2012; Rivas-Vazquez, Johnson, Rey, Blais, & Rivas-Vazquez, 2002).

Antipsychotic Drugs

In the past, people with schizophrenia who exhibited hallucinations, delusions, confused speech, exaggerated displays of emotion, paranoia, and utterly bizarre behavior were dismissed as lost causes. All that changed in the 1950s, however, with the discovery of **antipsychotic drugs**, which reduce the intensity of these positive "uncontrollable" symptoms. The first in this class of drugs was *chlorpromazine*, better known as Thorazine. By blocking the activity of dopamine, the neurotransmitter that has been linked to schizophrenia, antipsychotic drugs enable many people previously confined to hospital wards to live relatively normal lives.

antipsychotic drugs. Drugs that are used to control the positive symptoms of schizophrenia and other psychotic disorders.

LEARNING CHECK

Medicinal Purposes

Identify the medications below with their intended psychotherapeutic effects.

Antianxiety Drugs	Antidepressants	Mood Stabilizers	Antipsychotic Drugs
a. Librium			
b. Lithium			
c. Valium			
d. Thorazine			
e. Prozac			
f. Barbiturates			
g. Benzodiazepines			
h. Selective serotonin reuptake inhibitors (SSRIs)			

(Answers: Antianxiety Drugs: a, c, f, g; Antidepressants: e, h; Mood Stabilizers: b; Antipsychotic Drugs: d.)

Chlorpromazine has two drawbacks. First, it often does not relieve the negative symptoms of schizophrenia—symptoms such as flat affect, apathy, immobility, and social withdrawal, which may be linked to structural defects in the brain, not to dopamine (review the chapter on behavioral neuroscience). Second, it can have very unpleasant side effects. In the worst of cases, these include Parkinson's disease–like symptoms such as shaking and a loss of control over voluntary movements, stiff muscles, sluggishness, blunted affect, weight gain, and sexual impotence in men. These symptoms can often be treated with other drugs. Still, psychiatrists and patients must weigh the benefits of relief from the symptoms of schizophrenia against the costs of drug-induced side effects (Gitlin, 1996; Leucht et al., 2013).

Research suggests that clozapine (Clozaril), an antipsychotic medication first released in 1990, is an effective treatment for schizophrenia (DeFazio et al., 2015). Clozapine operates through a different mechanism. It is effective at controlling hallucinations and other psychotic symptoms (even in some patients who do not respond to Thorazine). Yet for about 2 percent of those who take it, clozapine has a toxic effect on the white blood cells and increases the risk of a rare but fatal blood disorder.

Its use has also been connected to gastroesophageal reflux disease, pulmonary thromboembolism, and other rare but adverse effects (DeFazio et al., 2015). Released in 1994, risperidone (Risperdal) is another frequently prescribed antipsychotic, but it is connected with side effects such as Parkinson's-like symptoms, headache, skin rash, and stomach pain. Regardless of the drug, side effects tend to be expected—with some more severe than others.

Perspectives on Drug Therapies

The debate over psychotherapy and drugs is as old as the split between psychology and medicine. But there is no winner, no right or wrong answer, no contest. In the spirit of taking an eclectic/integrative approach to the treatment of disorders, mental health professionals are advised to make their judgments on an individual case basis as to whether a medication, psychotherapy, or a combination of both would be best. In some people, the disorders do not respond as well to psychological forms of treatment as to medication. Drugs have helped hundreds of thousands of people once hidden away in psychiatric institutions, and they will continue to do so in years to come. There are reasons for caution, however. One is that some drugs produce side effects that are unpleasant or, at times, dangerous under high dosage levels. A second is that some drugs produce a physical or psychological dependence, relegating patients to play a passive role in their own healing process. The person who gets into the habit of popping a Valium at the first sign of tension learns how to control the aversive symptoms of anxiety but not how to cope with the source of the problem. A third reason for caution is that not all providers are trained to be culturally competent; this includes pharmacists (Rice & Harris, 2021). When the providers responsible for drug prescription and dissemination are either unable to ask or answer important questions due to cultural ignorance, then the person in need is at risk of receiving improper care (Rice & Harris, 2021). For example, ethnopsychiatry is a relatively new field of how culture and genetics impact responsiveness to a range of drugs (Silva, 2013). This research demonstrates that not all cultures respond equally to a pharmaceutical. Furthermore, racial and ethnic minorities are not equally represented in research on mental health. This contributes to the utilization of diagnostic assessments tested on white participants, which, in turn, can cause a misdiagnosis for non-white clients (Burgess, Ding, Hargreaves, van Ryn, & Phelan, 2008; Johnson & Cameron, 2001; Trinh, Bernard-Negron, & Ahmed, 2019).

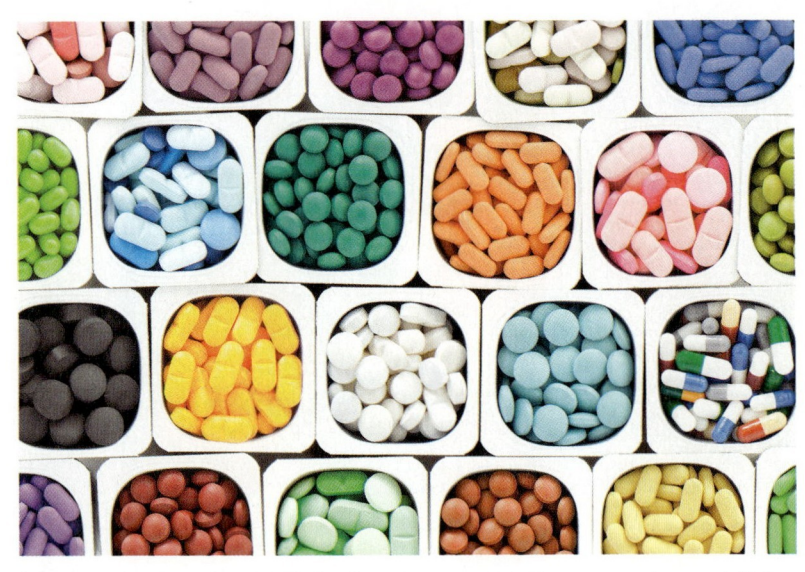

A variety of drug therapies exist. Finding the right one can take time, since each person's biology and needs are different.
iStock.com/FotografiaBasica

In an effort to match treatments to specific disorders, many researchers are currently evaluating the relative effectiveness of psychological and drug therapies. So far neither approach has emerged as uniformly more effective. In one large-scale and classic study, for example, the National Institute of Mental Health compared cognitive therapy, an interpersonal form of psychotherapy that focuses on social relations, an antidepressant, and a placebo control group in which the patients were given an inactive pill, attention, and encouragement. A total of 239 patients of 28 therapists in Oklahoma, Pennsylvania, and Washington, D.C., were randomly assigned to receive one form of treatment for a total of 16 weeks. Among those in the placebo group, 29 percent were no longer depressed when the "treatment" was ended. In the other groups, that proportion was near 50 percent—and the psychological and drug therapies were equally effective (Elkin, Shea, & Watkins, 1989). Other research shows that the outcome changes over time and that for those who are depressed, cognitive therapy may be slower than antidepressants to take effect but is then more likely to last (Dobson, 1989; Hollon, Shelton, & Loosen, 1991), although others have reported comparable short-term effects for these two treatment options (DeRubeis, Siegle, & Hollon, 2008).

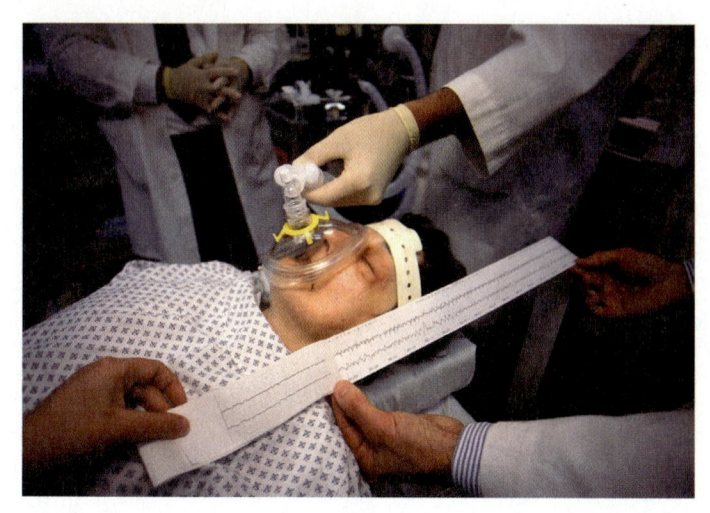

Doctors prepare a patient for a dose of electroconvulsive therapy.
Joe McNally/Hulton Archive via Getty Images

Electroconvulsive Therapy

It used to be a terrifying experience, a Frankenstein-like nightmare come to life. The patient would be dragged kicking and screaming to a hospital table and strapped down by the arms and legs, lying helpless as a white-coated physician leaned over to administer the pain. The patient would then be jolted by 100 volts of electricity to both sides of the skull, triggering seizures, unconsciousness, and muscle spasms so violent that they sometimes resulted in broken bones. The shock also had a mind-scrambling effect, causing confusion and amnesia for chunks of time before and after the treatment.

Electroconvulsive therapy (ECT) has a curious history. In the 19th century, an "electric machine" was used to stimulate the nerves. In 1938, an Italian doctor, Ugo Cerletti, introduced ECT—the notion that mental illness could be cured by quite literally shocking the system. From the start, it was clear that ECT provided relief from depression. It was widely used in the 1950s and 1960s but fell out of favor when antidepressant drugs became available. Eventually, it made a quiet comeback when procedures were made safer and more humane. Today, consenting ECT patients are given a general anesthetic and a muscle relaxant to prevent injury from convulsions. They then receive briefer, milder shock to the head, which sets off a brain seizure that lasts for a minute or so. As in surgery, patients regain consciousness within minutes, unable to remember what happened. The entire process consists of 10 or so sessions administered over a two-week period.

electroconvulsive therapy (ECT). Electric shock treatments that often relieve severe depression by triggering seizures in the brain.

Although ECT has always stirred controversy, and is often misunderstood, it is now a viable alternative for people who are deeply and chronically depressed, suicidal, and not responsive to psychological or drug therapies (Abrams, 2002; American Psychiatric Association Task Force, 2001; Fink, 1999). It has also been used with some success to treat mania in people with bipolar disorder and some of the symptoms of schizophrenia. The convulsions triggered by electrical current to the brain provide quick, sometimes permanent, relief. ECT is also safe, as it results in only two deaths per 100,000 treatments, a mortality rate lower than that for childbirth (Abrams, 1988; Endler & Persad, 1988). Brain scans of ECT patients show no signs of structural brain damage (Coffey, Weiner, & Djang, 1991; Devanand, Dwork, Hutchinson, Bolwig, & Sackeim, 1994). As far as side effects are concerned, however, patients undergo a temporary state of confusion and impairments in cognitive performance (Andrade, Arumugham, & Thirthalli, 2016; Eschweiler et al., 2007; Li et al., 2020). Some patients experience more severe memory loss than others.

ECT techniques continue to be refined for the more than 100,000 patients per year who receive it. For example, researchers recently found that better clinical results are produced when shocks are delivered to the forehead than to the temple (Bailine et al., 2000). It's still not clear why ECT is effective—that is, whether it works by stimulating seizures in inactive parts of the brain, inhibiting overactive parts, or triggering the release of scarce neurotransmitters. What is clear is that despite its therapeutic value, there is a stigma that follows those who use it. In the words of one patient who describes the treatment as lifesaving, "You should see the look in people's eyes when I tell them. They think I'm a freak, like Frankenstein, so I've learned to keep it a secret" (Fischer, 2000, p. 46).

Psychosurgery

psychosurgery. The surgical removal of portions of the brain for the purpose of treating psychological disorders.

The most controversial of interventions is **psychosurgery**, the removal of portions of the brain for the purpose of treating psychological disorders. In 1935, Portuguese neurologist Egas Moniz performed the first *lobotomy*, a surgical procedure in which he cut the nerves that connect the frontal lobes to the rest of the brain, in order to tame patients who were agitated, manic, and violent. Moniz based this procedure on his belief that pathological mental activity occurred in the frontal lobes, which needed to be

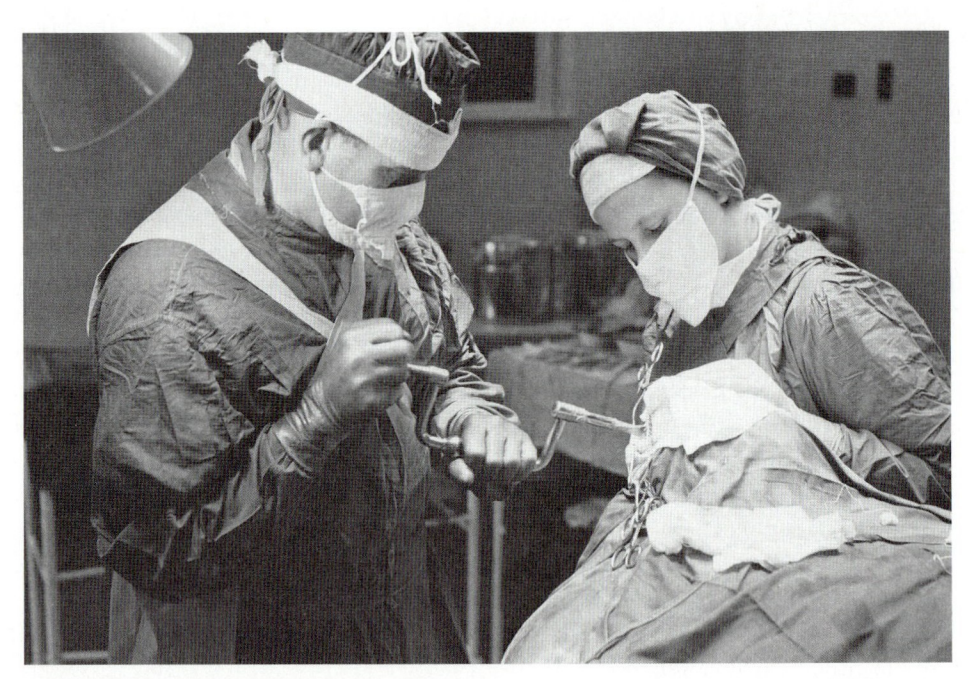

Like all surgical procedures, psychosurgery has vastly improved since this procedure was conducted in 1954.
Kurt Hutton / Picture Post via Getty Images

severed "to cut off the flow of morbid ideas." The operation was so highly regarded that in 1949 Moniz was awarded a Nobel Prize in medicine.

Was the lobotomy all that it was cracked up to be? In a book entitled *Great and Desperate Cures*, Elliot Valenstein (1986) described how thousands of mentally ill patients around the world were mutilated on the operating table: "After drilling two or more holes in a patient's skull, a surgeon inserted into the brain any of various instruments—some resembling an apple corer, a butter spreader, or an ice pick—and, often without being able to see what he was cutting, destroyed parts of the brain" (p. 3). The results were often tragic. The lobotomy was supposed to relieve patients of crippling emotions, but it also profoundly altered their core personalities, creating people who were like robots: lethargic, flat, emotionless, unmotivated, and without aim or purpose. Talking about her lobotomized husband, one woman said, "His soul appears to be destroyed; he is not the man I once knew." These lobotomies were not merely the work of incompetent or evil physicians but were practiced within the mainstream medical community (Pressman, 1998). Mercifully, the procedure was virtually extinguished when antipsychotic drugs came into use (Swayze, 1995).

Psychosurgery is more sophisticated today than in the past, enabling neurosurgeons to "damage the brain to save the mind" (Rodgers, 1992). Specific regions of the brain can now be destroyed with precision through ultrasonic irradiation or by sending electrical currents through fine wire electrodes. For people who are stricken with uncontrollable seizures, for example, the nerve fibers involved can be deactivated. Psychosurgery is also used sparingly, but with some success, on people incapacitated by chronic anxiety and depression or by severe obsessive-compulsive disorders or schizophrenia that are not responsive to other forms of treatment (Baer et al., 1995; Paiva et al., 2013). Still, there is debate over the science and ethics of psychosurgery, a treatment of last resort. After all, whether the outcome is positive or negative, the effect is irreversible.

Thinking Like a Psychologist About Treatment and Interventions

Over the years, the number of people seeking professional help for psychological problems has climbed dramatically. The helpers are psychiatrists, clinical psychologists, psychiatric nurses, social workers, and marital and family counselors. The kinds of help provided range from the most intensive one-on-one psychoanalysis to behavioral, cognitive, humanistic, and group therapies. In a growing number of cases, people are turning to nonprofessionals and apps, such as the many self-help books, support groups, and mental health apps that are widely available (Ameringen et al., 2017; Avramova, 2019; Christensen & Jacobson, 1994). And today, some people are seeking psychotherapy via videoconferencing. The research on the effectiveness of videoconferencing to deliver psychotherapy is promising.

Faced with an overwhelming array of treatment alternatives, people in the market for professional help have choices to make and problems to solve. One problem is that although someone must have a professional degree and supervised training to become licensed as a psychologist, anyone can hang up a shingle, offer a service, and call it therapy. From among those who are qualified, how do you select someone, and what kind of experience can you expect to have? Should you set your sights on psychotherapy or medical treatment?

If you need help and don't know where to turn, it's probably best to start with personal recommendations from a close friend, relative, family doctor, or teacher. Or you might check with the college counseling service, which is usually free or very low cost, or a local community mental health center. If you have a health insurance policy that covers psychological services, find out whether the policy covers what you want. If not, the hourly rates vary. Shop around and talk to two or three therapists until you are satisfied that you have found one you like, respect, and can work with. Talk openly about your goals and ask about fees, credentials, orientations, and values, to determine whether the two of you are on the same wavelength. Remember: The working relationship between therapist and client is an essential first step on the road to successful treatment.

All this brings us back to an important theme in the study of psychological disorders and treatment: the possibility of change. Under normal conditions, our personalities remain relatively stable throughout our adult lives. Individuals who are outgoing at one point in time are likely to remain that way later in life. But changes in behavior can be made, as when someone seeks to overcome shyness. When people suffer through a mental disorder, the need for change takes on an added dimension of importance. Some problems are relatively easy to overcome, others more difficult. Through psychological and medical forms of therapy, however, the possibilities for improvement are real. Whether the specific goal is to overcome a fear, lower anxiety, lift depression, or clear the mind of illogical thoughts and perceptions, there is reason for hope, which is necessary for change.

SUMMARY

Treatment raises the basic question of the possibilities and limits of human change. The two primary models of treatment are psychological and medical.

PSYCHOLOGICAL THERAPIES

The term **psychotherapy** refers to all forms of treatment in which a trained professional uses psychological techniques to help people who are distressed. The five major approaches are psychoanalytic, behavioral, cognitive, cognitive-behavioral, and humanistic.

Psychoanalytic Therapies

Orthodox psychoanalysis aims for catharsis and insight. Its key technique, pioneered by Freud, is **free association**, in which patients say whatever comes to mind without censoring it. Often, the patient free-associates about dreams while the therapist tries to get behind the manifest content to the latent content. **Resistance**—a patient's tendency to block painful thoughts—can be an obstacle but can also signal that therapy is heading in the right direction. The same is true of **transference**, whereby the patient displaces intense feelings for others onto the therapist. On the basis of these behaviors, the therapist offers interpretations to help the patient gain insight.

In briefer psychoanalytic therapies, the analyst plays a more active role, focuses less on the patient's past, and puts more emphasis on current life problems. The psychoanalytic approach has been criticized on various grounds. Yet despite the criticisms, it has left a strong mark on therapeutic practice.

Behavioral Therapies

Rather than search for deep problems, **behavioral therapies** use learning principles to modify the symptoms. Classical conditioning techniques include **flooding** the patient with an anxiety-provoking stimulus until the anxiety is extinguished. **Systematic desensitization**, a form of counterconditioning, pairs gradual exposure to an anxiety-provoking stimulus with relaxation training. **Aversion therapy** is designed to produce an aversive reaction to a harmful stimulus.

Other behavioral therapies use the principles of operant conditioning. **Token economies** reward patients for desirable behaviors; for dangerous behavior, punishment may be necessary. **Biofeedback**—learning to use feedback from the body to control physiological processes—is useful for health problems such as tension-related headaches. Assertiveness training and other types of **social skills training** use the techniques of modeling, rehearsal, and reinforcement.

Eye movement desensitization and reprocessing (EMDR) therapy is recommended by the World Health Organization, and is empirically supported by an array of research, for the treatment of post-traumatic stress disorder. EMDR is not a purely behavioral technique, but it does utilize desensitization, relaxation training, and replacing the fear response with a positive response when triggering stimuli are encountered.

Cognitive Therapies

Cognitive therapies focus on maladaptive perceptions and thoughts. Developed by Ellis, **rational-emotive behavior therapy (REBT)** bluntly confronts people with their irrational beliefs and provides "psychoeducation" on ways to change. Beck's cognitive therapy takes a more collaborative approach, giving clients homework assignments and role-playing exercises. These and other cognitive approaches are now the most common approaches to psychotherapy.

Cognitive-Behavioral Therapies

Cognitive-behavioral therapy (CBT) combines the cognitive and behavioral approaches to effectively treat thought mismanagement and distressing behaviors. Schizophrenia is one disorder that can be treated with CBT.

Humanistic Therapies

Acting as a facilitator, Rogers developed **person-centered therapy**, which creates a warm, caring environment to promote self-insight. Person-centered therapists offer empathy and unconditional positive regard. Through reflection, the therapist becomes an emotional mirror for the client. **Gestalt therapy**, developed by Perls, also makes clients responsible for their own change, but it focuses more on unconscious feelings and dreams, and it aggressively challenges clients to express their feelings.

Group-Therapy Approaches

An alternative to individual therapies, **group therapy** involves working with several clients simultaneously and together. Behavioral and cognitive therapies can also take place in groups. In **family therapies**, the members of a family are treated together as an interdependent social system.

PERSPECTIVES ON PSYCHOTHERAPY

Is psychotherapy effective? Are some approaches better than others? What are the active ingredients of effective psychotherapy? These are among the important questions raised over the years.

The Bottom Line: Does Psychotherapy Work?

As the American Psychological Association and the Canadian Psychological Association showed, psychologists have long argued about the effectiveness of psychotherapy. Meta-analysis has shown that psychotherapy patients experience more improvement, on average, than people who do not treatment. After about six months of therapy, however, improvement rates appear to level off.

Are Some Therapies Better Than Others?
Overall, the different forms of psychotherapy are about equally effective. Some work better on particular problems than others, but all share certain features in common that make them more similar than different in their effects.

What are the Active Ingredients?
There are three common attributes of all therapies that constitute the active ingredients for a successful outcome: a supportive relationship; hope, which, as the **placebo effect** demonstrates, can itself produce improvement; and an ideal setting in which the patient is able to open up and confide in another person.

What's the Future of Psychotherapy?
In need of speedy and effective forms of treatment, most therapists today use a pragmatic, flexible, **eclectic** strategy. Thus, they borrow ideas and techniques from the various approaches. There is also a trend toward standardization in the use of techniques shown empirically to be effective for certain disorders. **Telemental health** and **telepsychiatry** have demonstrated effectiveness in the treatment of psychological disorders. In addition, both have garnered support from the American Psychiatric Association and the ATA (formerly the American Telehealth Association). Best practices for the utilization of telemental health and telepsychiatry can be found in a guide written by these two organizations.

MEDICAL INTERVENTIONS

Medical interventions take three major forms: drug therapy; electroconvulsive, or shock, therapy; and psychosurgery.

Drug Therapies
Psychopharmacology is concerned with the effects of certain drugs on mental processes and disorders. **Antianxiety drugs** include buspirone and the widely used class of benzodiazepines. Research linking depression to neurotransmitters led to the development of **antidepressants**, such as the controversial drug fluoxetine (Prozac). The mood stabilizer **lithium**, a mineral found in nature, can control mood swings in bipolar disorder. For schizophrenia and other psychotic disorders, **antipsychotic drugs** often reduce the positive symptoms, though often with side effects.

Perspectives on Drug Therapies
In the debate about the relative merits of psychoactive drugs and psychotherapy, there is no one answer. On the one hand, drugs have helped hundreds of thousands of patients; on the other, they can have unpleasant or dangerous side effects, and some produce physical or psychological dependence.

Electroconvulsive Therapy
Though once a nightmare-like experience, **electroconvulsive therapy (ECT)** now provides milder electric shock that can relieve severe depression.

Psychosurgery
Psychosurgery, the most controversial medical intervention, involves removing portions of the brain to treat a psychological disorder. The technique of lobotomy, once popular, has fallen into disrepute. Today's psychosurgery is more sophisticated, targeting specific regions of the brain with ultrasonic irradiation or electrical currents. But safer methods are available, and the effects of psychosurgery are irreversible.

CRITICAL THINKING

Thinking Critically About Treatment and Interventions

1. Imagine yourself as a therapist. Which type of therapy do you think you would practice? Why? Now imagine yourself as a client. Which type of therapy would you prefer to experience? Why?

2. Browse your favorite online bookstore, and you will probably find a large section devoted to self-help books. What types of therapies are likely to be addressed in such books? Are particular disorders more amenable to self-treatment?

3. In many states, people with psychiatric diagnoses are required by law to receive drug therapy (often, but not always, antipsychotic drugs). Discuss the ethics of such court-ordered medication. Do people have the right to be psychotic?

4. Speculate as to the role of culture in the treatment of disorders. In what ways might cultural factors affect the therapeutic relationship? Are all therapies equally effective for all cultures?

CAREER CONNECTION: HEALTH CARE

Mental Health Counselor

Individuals with a variety of conditions, including anxiety, depression, grief, low self-esteem, stress, suicidal impulses, along with those with relationship issues, may seek help from a mental health counselor. Counselors may see individuals, couples, families, and other groups to discuss their lives and concerns. Some mental health counselors will work with specific populations, such as the elderly, college students, or children, or specialize in certain disorders or types of treatment. They are expected to keep careful records of their sessions with each client and to maintain a high standard of ethical conduct.

In addition to needing a bachelor's degree in psychology or a related field, these professionals are required to obtain licensure after completing a period of supervised clinical work. Depending on the setting and role, a master's degree or a PhD may be required.

Key skills for this role that psychology students learn to develop:
- Application of ethical standards
- Innovative and inclusive thinking
- Self-efficacy and self-regulation

KEY TERMS

antianxiety drugs (p. 603)
antidepressants (p. 605)
antipsychotic drugs (p. 606)
aversion therapy (p. 585)
behavioral therapy (p. 582)
biofeedback (p. 586)
cognitive therapy (p. 589)
cognitive-behavioral therapy (CBT) (p. 591)
eclectic (p. 601)
electroconvulsive therapy (ECT) (p. 608)
eye movement desensitization and reprocessing therapy (EMDR) (p. 588)
family therapies (p. 595)
flooding (p. 583)
free association (p. 578)
Gestalt therapy (p. 593)

group therapy (p. 595)
lithium (p. 605)
person-centered therapy (p. 593)
placebo effect (p. 600)
psychopharmacology (p. 603)
psychosurgery (p. 608)
psychotherapy (p. 577)
rational-emotive behavior therapy (REBT) (p. 589)
resistance (p. 578)
social skills training (p. 587)
systematic desensitization (p. 583)
telemental health and telepsychiatry (p. 602)
token economy (p. 586)
transference (p. 579)

APPENDIX: STATISTICS IN PSYCHOLOGY

Are you curious about the world around you? When a friend says something is true, are you critical of the claim? At any point while reading this textbook did you think to yourself, "How do they know that?" If you answered yes to these questions, then you are thinking like a psychologist. In a sense, scientists "crunch the numbers"—to make the numbers themselves more sensible or meaningful.

"Crunching the numbers" is a common phrase typically used to describe the large-scale processing or analysis of **data**, meaning a set of scores, measurements, or observations that are typically numeric. The implication is that by "crunching the numbers," the numbers themselves will become values that we can use to make decisions or gain a better understanding of the world. In the same way a sports analyst crunches the numbers to make sense of sports data (e.g., to determine which player has the best performance, or which team has the best chances of winning a game), a scientist crunches numbers to make sense of data collected in a research study—to answer questions about human behavior and the world we live in. To crunch the numbers, we use *descriptive statistics*, which are ways of summarizing data to make the data more meaningful to a general audience.

Throughout this book, you have been introduced to the foundations of knowledge and innovations in psychology. In this appendix, we introduce you to the statistical applications that allow psychologists to understand (*descriptive statistics*) and make decisions about (*inferential statistics*) the observations they make to advance knowledge. Understanding how this knowledge was obtained and learned can be valuable. After all, *science* is all around you—therefore, being a critical consumer of the information you come across each day can be useful and necessary across professions.

To begin, psychologists do not apply statistics in a vacuum. Instead, statistics are closely tied to the scientific process. Statistics help scientists acquire, modify, and integrate data or knowledge—to make sense of their observations and to make decisions about them. In this light, the application of statistics in this appendix is introduced in the context of science. Figure A.1 provides a broad overview of the scientific process. We will revisit Figure A.1 as we introduce statistical concepts to help you see how the application of statistics fits into the broader scope of psychology as a science.

DESCRIPTIVE STATISTICS

> **LEARNING OBJECTIVE**
>
> Explain what data is, why it is important, and how we summarize data graphically, in tabular form, and as summary statistics.

To describe data, we use **descriptive statistics**, which are procedures used to summarize, organize, and make sense of a set of scores. Descriptive statistics are typically presented graphically, in tabular form (in tables), or as summary statistics (single values). These procedures are most often used to quantify the behaviors researchers measure. Thus, we measure or record data (e.g., milliliters consumed) and then use descriptive statistics to summarize or make sense of those data, which describe the phenomenon of interest (e.g., intake of a healthy fruit juice). In our example, *consumption* is measured in milliliters of juice consumed. If we observe hundreds of participants, then the data in a spreadsheet will be overwhelming. For this reason, researchers use descriptive statistics to summarize sets of individual measurements so that they can be clearly presented and interpreted.

What We Know About Data and Why It Is Important

Throughout this book, we have shared the story of psychology and its impact and relevance to many disciplines and to your own lives. Many concepts in psychology were introduced

A-1

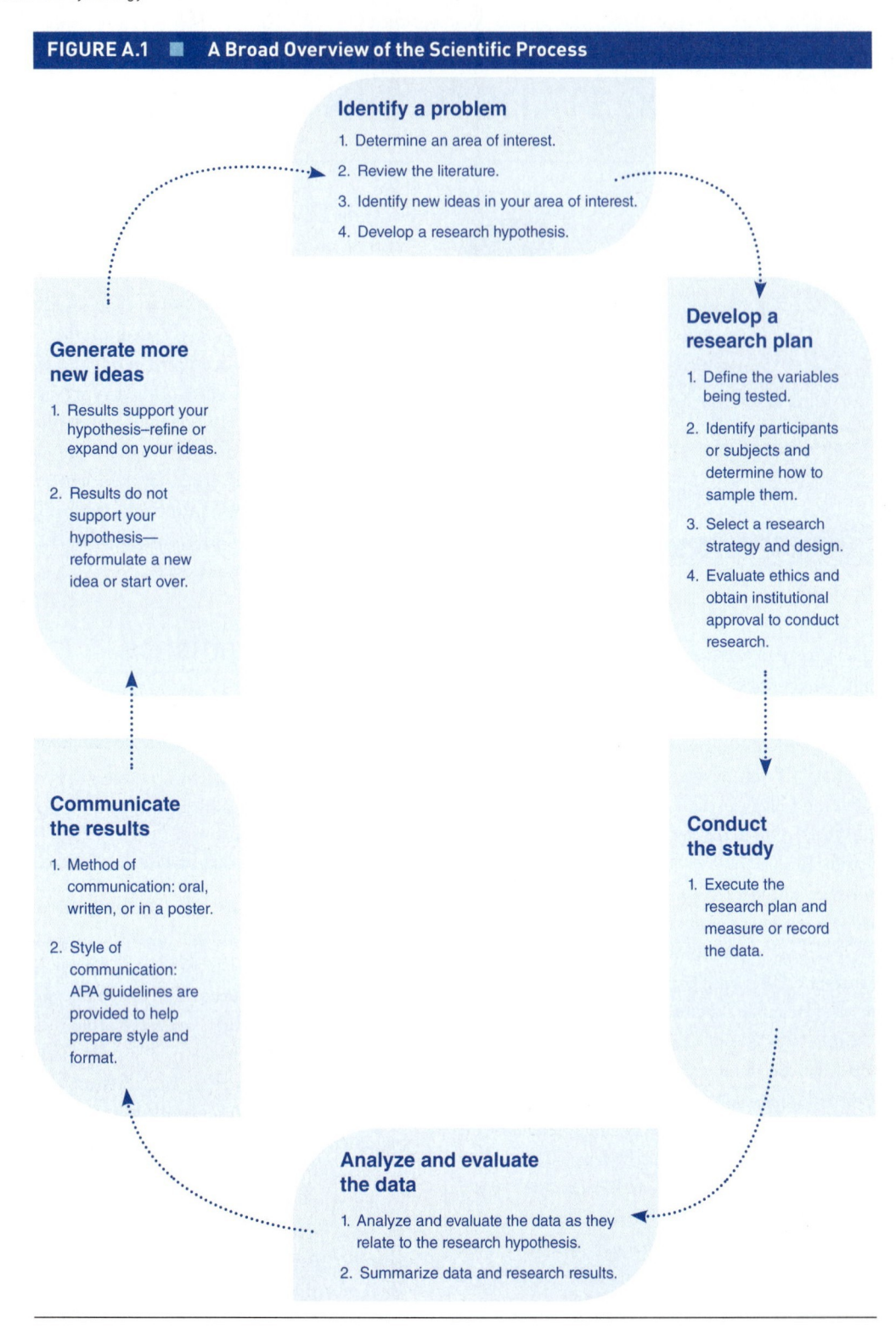

FIGURE A.1 ■ A Broad Overview of the Scientific Process

Identify a problem
1. Determine an area of interest.
2. Review the literature.
3. Identify new ideas in your area of interest.
4. Develop a research hypothesis.

Develop a research plan
1. Define the variables being tested.
2. Identify participants or subjects and determine how to sample them.
3. Select a research strategy and design.
4. Evaluate ethics and obtain institutional approval to conduct research.

Conduct the study
1. Execute the research plan and measure or record the data.

Analyze and evaluate the data
1. Analyze and evaluate the data as they relate to the research hypothesis.
2. Summarize data and research results.

Communicate the results
1. Method of communication: oral, written, or in a poster.
2. Style of communication: APA guidelines are provided to help prepare style and format.

Generate more new ideas
1. Results support your hypothesis—refine or expand on your ideas.
2. Results do not support your hypothesis—reformulate a new idea or start over.

Statistics play a critical role in supporting the scientific process to help scientists make sense of their observations and make decisions about them.

to show the *what* (the concept is), the *when* (it was founded or learned), the *why* (the concept is useful or important), and the *how* (to apply or make use of it). At the foundation of this knowledge is the realization that these concepts were derived from data—from the evidence that researchers identified to learn about the concepts taught in this book. We therefore cannot tell the story of psychology without at least acknowledging the importance of data in psychology. That said, as with any story, we start at the beginning... and in the beginning, there was *data*.

Scientists measure data to learn, typically by testing their hypotheses. What can be learned from data, however, depends on the nature of the data itself. In sum, data can be described by the following:

- How informative it is: scale of measurement (nominal, ordinal, interval, ratio)
- How it varies: by amount (quantitative) or by class (qualitative)
- How it is measured: in whole units or categories (discrete) or along a continuum (continuous)

Table A.1 summarizes each of the ways in which data can be described and provides examples. How data are measured, how they vary, and the informativeness of data are critical details that help researchers understand how to appropriately summarize and interpret the observations they make based on the data they collect.

Continuous and Discrete Data

The data that psychologists observe are defined in terms of how they are measured. The different types of data we can measure fall into two categories:

- Continuous or discrete
- Quantitative or qualitative

Continuous data are measured along a continuum, meaning that continuous data can be measured at any place beyond the decimal point. Consider, for example, that Olympic sprinters are timed to the nearest hundredths place (in seconds), but if the Olympic judges wanted to clock them to the nearest millionths place, they could.

Discrete data, by contrast, are measured in whole units or categories, meaning that discrete data are not measured along a continuum. For example, the number of brothers and sisters you have and your family's socioeconomic class (working class, middle class, upper class) are examples of discrete variables. Refer to Table A.1 for more examples of continuous and discrete data.

Quantitative and Qualitative Data

Quantitative data vary by amount or *quantity*—the base for the term, *quantit*ative. These data are measured in numeric units, so both continuous and discrete data can be quantitative. For example, we can measure food intake in calories (a continuous variable), or we can count the number of pieces of food consumed (a discrete variable). In both cases, the data are measured by amount (in numeric units).

Qualitative data, by contrast, vary by class. These data are often represented with a label that describes nonnumeric aspects of what researchers observe—so only discrete variables

TABLE A.1 ■ Types of Data

Type of Data	Definition	Description	Examples
How informative it is: scale of measurement (from least to most informative)			
Nominal	Measurements in which a number is assigned to represent something or someone	Can be qualitative or quantitative; discrete only	City/state, participant ID numbers, biological sex
Ordinal	Measurements where values convey order or rank alone	Can be qualitative or quantitative; discrete only	College rankings, grade level (freshman to senior)
Interval	Measurements that have no true zero and are distributed in equal units	Can be qualitative or quantitative; discrete or continuous	Likert-type rating scales, temperature (Fahrenheit)
Ratio	Measurements that have a true zero and are distributed in equal units	Ratio data can be qualitative or quantitative; discrete or continuous	Weight (g), height (cm), time (seconds)
How it varies: quantitative, qualitative			
Quantitative	Varies by amount; measured numerically; often collected by measuring or counting	Can be any scale of measurement; discrete or continuous	ID numbers, rankings, temperature, height (cm)
Qualitative	Varies by class; often represented as a label; describes nonnumeric aspects of phenomena	Can be nominal or ordinal scale of measurement; discrete only	Gender, city/state you live in, race, ethnicity
How it is measured: discrete, continuous			
Discrete	Measured in whole units or categories that are not distributed along a continuum	Can be any scale of measurement; qualitative or quantitative	Number of students in a class, college rankings
Continuous	Measured along a continuum at any place beyond the decimal point	Can be interval or ratio scale of measurement; quantitative only	Height (cm), weight (g), time (sec), distance (miles)

A summary of the three ways to describe data with a definition, description, and examples given for each data type.

can be qualitative. For example, class year (freshman, sophomore, junior, senior) is discrete and qualitative; so are many behavioral disorders, such as types of anxiety disorders (social anxiety and generalized anxiety) and depression (seasonal affective, postpartum, and major depression). Refer to Table A.1 for more examples of quantitative and qualitative variables.

Scales of Measurement

Researchers can measure data using one of four **scales of measurement**, or rules that describe the informativeness of measured data. In the early 1940s, Harvard psychologist S. S. Stevens (1946) coined the terms *nominal, ordinal, interval,* and *ratio* to classify the scales of measurement. In this section, we discuss the extent to which data are informative on each scale of measurement. In all, scales of measurement are characterized by three properties: order, differences, and ratios. Each property can be described by answering the following questions:

- *Order:* Does a larger number indicate a greater value than a smaller number?
- *Differences:* Does subtracting one set of numbers represent some meaningful value?
- *Ratio:* Does dividing, or taking the ratio of, one set of numbers represent some meaningful value?

Table A.2 gives the answers to the questions for each scale of measurement. In this section, we begin with the least informative scale (nominal) and finish with the most informative scale (ratio). Refer to Table A.1 for more examples of each of the scales of measurement introduced in this section.

Nominal scale. Numbers on a **nominal scale** identify something or someone; they provide no additional information. Common examples of nominal numbers include ZIP codes, license plate numbers, credit card numbers, country codes, telephone numbers, and Social Security numbers. These numbers identify locations, vehicles, or individuals and nothing more. One credit card number, for example, is not greater than another; it is simply different.

In science, numbers on a nominal scale are typically categorical variables that have undergone **coding**—conversion to numeric values. Examples of nominal variables include a person's race, gender, nationality, sexual orientation, hair and eye color, season of birth, marital status, or other demographic or personal information. Researchers may code cisgender men as 1 and cisgender women as 2. They may code the seasons of birth as 1, 2, 3, and 4 for spring, summer, fall, and winter, respectively. These numbers are used to identify gender or the seasons and nothing more. We often code words with numeric values when entering them into statistical programs. Because nominal data simply identify something or someone, they convey no meaning in terms of order, difference, and ratios.

Ordinal scale. An **ordinal scale** of measurement is one that conveys order alone. Examples of variables on an ordinal scale include finishing order in a competition, education level, and ranking. Ordinal scales indicate only that one value is greater than or less than another, so differences between ranks do not have meaning. Consider, for example, a race in which the top four finishers for a one-mile race are as follows: first place (4 minutes 20 seconds), second place (4 minutes 22 seconds), third place (4 minutes 30 seconds), and fourth place (4 minutes 50 seconds). Based on ranks alone, can we say that the difference between first place and second place is the same as the difference between third place and fourth place? After all, one rank separates each runner. Yet, if you look at the actual times for determining rank, you find that the difference between first place and second place (ranks 1 and 2) is only 2 seconds, whereas the difference between third place and fourth place (ranks 3 and 4) is 20 seconds. So the difference in times is not the same. Ranks alone do not convey this difference. They simply indicate that one rank is greater or less than another rank.

Interval scale. An **interval scale** of measurement can be understood readily by two defining principles: equidistant scales and no **true zero**. A common example for interval scales in behavioral science is the rating scale. Rating scales are taught here as an interval scale because most researchers report these as interval data in published research. This type of scale is a numeric response scale used to indicate a participant's level of agreement or opinion with some statement. Here we will look at each defining principle.

TABLE A.2 ■ The Informativeness of Data on Different Scales of Measurement

		Scale of Measurement			
		Nominal	Ordinal	Interval	Ratio
Property	Order	NO	YES	YES	YES
	Difference	NO	NO	YES	YES
	Ratio	NO	NO	NO	YES

The scales of measurement differ in terms of the information they provide concerning the order, difference, and ratio of numbers.

An equidistant scale is a scale distributed in units that are equal distance from one another. Many behavioral scientists assume that scores on a rating scale are distributed in equal intervals. For example, if you are asked to rate your satisfaction with a partner or job on a scale from 0 (*completely unsatisfied*) to 9 (*completely satisfied*), then you are using an interval scale. Because the distance between each point (0 to 9) is assumed to be the same or equal, it is appropriate to compute differences between scores on this scale. So a statement such as "The difference in job satisfaction among managers and supervisors was 2 points" is appropriate with interval scale measurements.

However, an interval scale does not have a *true zero*, meaning that 0 on the scale does not represent the absence of the phenomenon being measured. A common example of a scale with no true zero is temperature. A temperature equal to zero for most measures of temperature (e.g., Fahrenheit and Celsius) does not mean that there is no temperature; it is just an arbitrary zero point. Values on a rating scale also have no true zero. In the example for rating satisfaction, a 0 was used to indicate *no satisfaction*, but we could have used any number to represent the absence of satisfaction. Each value, including 0, is arbitrary. Measurements of latitude and longitude also fit this criterion for having no true zero. The implication is that without a true zero, there is no absolute value to indicate the absence of the phenomenon you are observing; so a zero proportion is not meaningful. For this reason, stating a ratio such as "Satisfaction ratings were 3 times greater among managers compared to supervisors" is not appropriate with interval-scale measurements.

Ratio scale. **Ratio scales** are similar to interval scales in that scores are distributed in equal units. Yet, unlike interval scales, a distribution of scores on a ratio scale has a true zero. That is, a ratio-scale value includes a value equal to 0 that indicates the absence of the phenomenon being observed. This is an ideal scale in behavioral research because ratio-scale measurements convey order, differences, and ratios. Common examples of ratio-scale measurements include length, height, weight, and time. For scores on a ratio scale, order is informative. For example, a person who is 25 years old is older than another who is 20 (i.e., 5 years older). Differences are also informative. For example, the difference between 70 and 60 seconds is the same as the difference between 30 and 20 seconds (i.e., 10 seconds). Ratios are also informative on this scale because a true zero is defined—it truly means nothing. Hence, it is meaningful to state that 60 pounds is twice as heavy as 30 pounds. Because a ratio scale can convey order, differences, and ratios, it is regarded as the most informative of the scales of measurement.

In science, researchers often go out of their way to measure variables on a ratio scale. For example, if they measure hunger, they may choose to measure the amount of time between meals, or the amount of food consumed (in ounces). If they measure memory, they may choose to measure the amount of time it takes to memorize some list, or the number of errors made. In these examples, hunger and memory were measured using ratio scales, thereby allowing researchers to draw conclusions in terms of the order, differences, and ratios of values on those scales—there are no restrictions for variables measured on a ratio scale.

Why Summarize Data?

In a research study, scientists report the data. To report the data, you typically do not disclose each individual score or measure. Instead, you summarize the data because this is a clearer way to present them. A clear presentation of the data is necessary because it allows the reader to critically evaluate the data you are reporting.

To illustrate the usefulness of summarizing data, Table A.3a shows the number of healthy foods chosen by each of 48 participants when these foods were made more or less accessible to reach in a buffet—the data are adapted from studies on the effects of the built food environment on healthy choices and behavior (Hunter, Hollands, & Couturier, 2018; Privitera & Zuraikat, 2014). The listing in Table A.3a is not particularly helpful because you cannot see at a glance how the number of healthy foods choices compares between the groups. A more meaningful arrangement of the data is to place them in a summary table that shows the total number of healthy food choices in each group. When the data are arranged in this way, as shown in Table A.3b, you can see at a glance that many more healthy foods were chosen when the foods were made more accessible (or easier to reach) in a buffet. In all, there are two common reasons why we summarize data using descriptive statistics:

- To clarify what patterns were observed in a data set at a glance. It is more meaningful to present data in a way that makes the interpretation of the data clearer.

- To be concise. When publishing an article, many journals have limited space, which requires that the description of data be concise. The presentation in Table A.3b takes up much less space to summarize the same data given in Table A.3a and is therefore more concise.

Before we summarize data in a figure or table, we often need to explore or review the data to identify possible omissions, errors, or other anomalies (Hoaglin, Mosteller, & Tukey, 1991; Privitera, 2019; Tukey, 1977). We can apply this step as we measure the data for each participant or after all data have been recorded. However, this step, if used, must be applied before the data are analyzed statistically or displayed in a figure or table. Figure A.2 illustrates where this step can be applied in the research process based on the steps of the scientific process first summarized in Figure A.1.

TABLE A.3 ■ Arranging Data in a Frequency Distribution

Accessibility of Healthy Foods

High Accessibility		Low Accessibility	
6	4	2	2
5	6	4	2
7	4	3	4
6	7	3	1
6	5	3	3
4	3	1	4
5	5	2	0
4	4	5	3
7	6	3	2
5	5	4	1
6	3	2	3
8	4	3	0

Groups	Total Number of Healthy Foods Chosen
High Accessibility	125
Low Accessibility	60

A list of the number of healthy foods chosen by 24 participants in each of two groups (a) and a summary table for the total number of health foods chosen in each group (b).

FIGURE A.2 ■ Arranging Data in a Frequency Distribution

Step 3: Conduct the study.

Execute the research plan and measure or record the data.

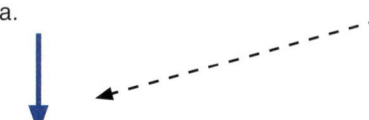

Explore or review the data to identify possible omissions, errors, or other anomalies.

Step 4: Analyze and evaluate the data.

Analyze and evaluate the data as they relate to the research hypothesis.

Step 5: Communicate the results.

1. Method of communication: oral, written, or in a poster.
2. Style of communication: APA guidelines are provided to help prepare style and format.

The box illustrates where data exploration fits in this process. All steps of the scientific method are illustrated in Figure A.1.

As an example for applying an exploratory analysis, consider data from a behavioral measure that is scored from 0 to 25. One criterion for exploring these data for errors is to identify entries that are larger than 25. If an entry is larger than 25 for this behavioral measure, then that entry must have been an error because scores above 25 on the measure are not possible. Thus we would remove these values—and, if possible, correct them—before further analysis. Likewise, we could review the data for missing values, and we could check that values for one group were not mistakenly recorded for another group. The advantage of exploring or reviewing data before reporting them is to make sure that all errors have been removed from the data before further analysis is conducted.

Frequency Distributions: Tables and Graphs

Suppose you scored 90 percent on your first statistics exam. How could you determine how well you did compared with the rest of the class? One meaningful arrangement to answer this question would be to place the data in a table that lists the ranges of exam scores in one column and the *frequency* of exam scores for each grade range in a second column. When scores are arranged in this way, as shown in Table A.4b, it is clear that an exam score of 90 percent is excellent—only two other students fared as well or better, and most students in the class had lower scores.

A **frequency** is the number of times or how often a category, score, or range of scores occurs. In this section, we will describe the types of tables and graphs used to summarize frequencies. Tables and graphs of frequency data can make the presentation and interpretation of data clearer. In all, this section will help you appropriately construct and accurately interpret many of the tables and graphs used to summarize frequency data in behavioral research.

TABLE A.4 ■ Arranging Data in a Frequency Distribution

Time (in seconds)	$f(x)$
50–59	4
40–49	9
30–39	9
20–29	13
10–19	7
0–9	5
Total Participants	50

Quiz Scores	$f(x)$
4	5
3	7
2	8
1	6
0	4
Total Participants	30

College Year	$f(x)$
Senior	12
Junior	15
Sophomore	28
Freshman	20
Total Participants	75

A list of 20 exam scores (a) and a summary of the frequency of scores from that list (b).

Frequency Distribution Tables

One way to describe frequency data is to count how often a particular score or range of scores occurs using a **frequency distribution table**. In a frequency distribution table, we list each score or range of scores in one column and list the corresponding frequencies for each score or range of scores in a second column. Table A.5 illustrates frequency distribution tables for three different types of variables.

We can summarize the frequency of a continuous variable, a discrete variable, or a categorical variable, and we can summarize the frequency of data that are grouped into intervals or listed as individual scores. To illustrate, Table A.5a lists continuous data in intervals by summarizing the time in seconds to complete a task (the continuous variable) among a sample of college students. Table A.5b lists the frequency of discrete data as individual scores by summarizing quiz scores (the discrete variable) for students in a college class. Table A.5c lists the frequency of categorical data by summarizing the number of students in each class year (the categorical variable) at a small school. In each display, the sum of all frequencies (in the right column) equals the total number of observations or counts made.

The type of data measured determines whether to group data into intervals or leave data as individual scores or categories. We group data when many different scores are recorded, as shown in Table A.5a for the time (in seconds) it took participants to complete a task. When grouping data, it is recommended that the number of intervals ranges from 5 to 20. Fewer than 5 intervals can provide too little information; more than 20 intervals can be too confusing.

We leave data as individual scores when only a few possible scores are recorded, as shown in Table A.5b for quiz scores ranging in whole units from 0 to 4. For data that are categorical, we also identify each individual category, as shown in Table A.5c for college year.

TABLE A.5 ■ Frequency Distribution Tables for Continuous, Discrete, and Categorical Variables

Time (in seconds)	$f(x)$
50–59	4
40–49	9
30–39	12
20–29	13
10–19	7
0–9	5
Total Participants	50

Quiz Scores	$f(x)$
4	5
3	7
2	8
1	6
0	4
Total Participants	30

College Year	$f(x)$
Senior	12
Junior	15
Sophomore	28
Freshman	20
Total Participants	75

Continuous data grouped into intervals (a), discrete data listed as individual scores (b), and categorical data given as individual categories (c).

Appendix: Statistics in Psychology   **A-9**

Frequency Distribution Graphs

The same information conveyed in a frequency distribution table can also be presented graphically. To present frequency data graphically, we list the categories, scores, or intervals of scores on the *x*-axis (the horizontal axis) and the frequency in each category, for each score, or in each interval on the *y*-axis (the vertical axis) of a graph. The type of graph we use to describe frequency data depends on whether the data are continuous or discrete.

Continuous data are often summarized graphically using a histogram. The **histogram** is a graph that lists continuous data that are grouped into intervals along the horizontal scale (*x*-axis) and lists the frequency of scores in each interval on the vertical scale (*y*-axis). To illustrate, Figure A.3 displays a frequency distribution table and a corresponding histogram for the number of traffic stops made over a period of time along a dangerous stretch of roadway. Notice that each bar in the histogram represents the frequency of traffic stops made in each interval.

Discrete data are often summarized using a bar chart or a pie chart. A **bar chart, or bar graph**, is like a histogram, except that the bars do not touch. The separation between bars reflects the separation or "break" between the whole numbers or categories being summarized. Figure A.4 displays a bar chart for the number or frequency of students who are majors in psychology, education, or biology at a small school. To summarize these same data as percentages, a **pie chart** can be a more effective display (Hollands & Spence, 1992, 1998; Privitera, 2019). Using a pie chart, we split the data into sectors that represent the relative proportion of counts in each category. The larger a sector, the larger the percentage of scores in a given category. To illustrate, Figure A.4 also displays a pie chart for the percentage of students in each of three academic majors. Notice in the pie chart that larger percentages take up a larger portion of the pie.

Measures of Central Tendency

Descriptive statistics often used to describe behavior are those that measure **central tendency**. Measures of central tendency are single

FIGURE A.3 ■ Summarizing Data in a Histogram

Traffic Stops	Frequency
0–2	3
3–5	6
6–8	4
9–11	3
12–14	2

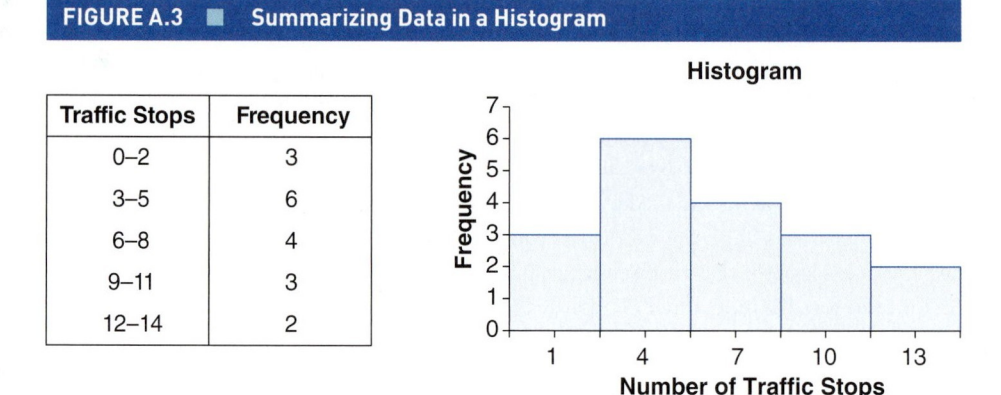

A grouped frequency distribution table (left) and a histogram (right) for the number of traffic stops along a dangerous stretch of roadway.

FIGURE A.4 ■ Summarizing Data in a Bar Chart and a Pie Chart

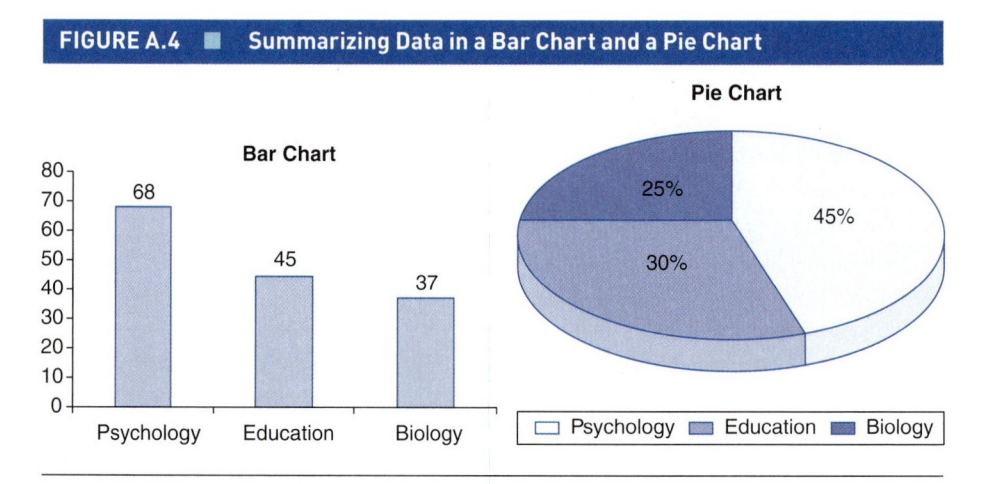

Bar Chart: Psychology 68, Education 45, Biology 37

Pie Chart: Psychology 45%, Education 30%, Biology 25%

A bar chart (left) giving the frequency of students in each of three academic majors at a small college, and a pie chart (right) giving the percentage of students in each major. The same data are summarized in each graphical display.

values that have a "tendency" to be at or near the "center" of a distribution. Although we lose some meaning anytime we reduce a set of data to a single score, statistical measures of central tendency ensure that the single score meaningfully represents a data set. In this section, we introduce three measures of central tendency:

- Mean
- Median
- Mode

Mean

One way to describe behavior is to compute the average score in a distribution, called the *mean*. Because researchers in the behavioral sciences rarely select data from an entire population, we will introduce the **sample mean**. To compute a sample mean, we sum all scores in a distribution and divide by the number of scores summed.

The sample mean is the balance point of a distribution. The balance point is not always at the exact center of a distribution, as this analogy will demonstrate. Pick up a pen with a cap and remove the cap. Then place the pen sideways on your index finger until it is balanced and parallel with the floor. Once you have steadied the pen, your finger represents the balance point of the distribution of the weight of that pen. In the same way, the mean is the balance point of a distribution of data. Now, put the cap back on the pen and balance it again on your index finger. To balance the pen, you must move your finger toward the side with the cap, right? Now your finger is not at the center of the pen but closer to the cap. In the same way, the mean is not necessarily the middle value; it is the value that balances an entire distribution of numbers.

Using the sample mean as an appropriate measure of central tendency depends largely on the type of distribution and the scale of measurement of the data. The sample mean is typically used to describe data that are normally distributed and measures on an interval or ratio scale. Each is described here:

- The **normal distribution** is a distribution in which scores are symmetrically distributed around the mean, median, and mode (note: the median and mode are introduced in the next two sections). Hence, the mean, median, and mode are all located at the center of a normal distribution, as illustrated in Figure A.5. In cases in which the mean is approximately equal to all other measures of central tendency, the mean is used to summarize the data. We could choose to summarize a normal distribution with the median or mode, but the mean is most often used because all scores are included in its calculation (i.e., its value is most reflective of all of the data).

- The mean is used for data that can be described in terms of the *distance* that scores deviate from it. After all, the mean balances a distribution of values. For this reason, data that are described by the mean should convey differences (or deviations) from the mean. Differences between two scores are conveyed for data on an interval or ratio scale only. Hence, the mean is an appropriate measure of central tendency used to describe interval- and ratio-scale data.

Median

Another measure of central tendency is the **median**, which is the middle value or midpoint of a distribution listed in numeric order in which half of all scores fall above and half fall below its value. To explain the need for another measure of central tendency, suppose you measure the following set of scores: 2, 3, 4, 5, 6, 6, and 100. The mean of these scores is 18 (add up the seven scores and divide by 7). Yet the score of 100 is an outlier in this data set, which causes the mean value to increase so much that the mean fails to reflect most of the data—its value ($M = 18$) is larger than the values of all scores, except one. For these data, the mean can actually be misleading because its value shifts toward the value of that outlier. In this case, the median will be more reflective of all data because it is the middle score of data listed in numeric order. For these data, the median is 5.

Using the median as an appropriate measure of central tendency also depends largely on the type of distribution and the scale of measurement of the data. The median is typically used to describe data that have a **skewed distribution** and measures on an ordinal scale. Each is described here:

- Some data can have outliers that skew or distort a data set. As an example, U.S. income is typically skewed, with very few people earning substantially higher incomes than

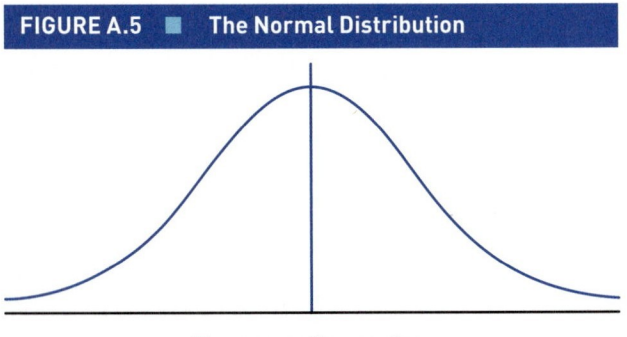

FIGURE A.5 ■ The Normal Distribution

The mean, the median, and the mode are located at the center of a normal distribution.

In a normal distribution, the mean, median, and mode are located at the center of the distribution.

most others in the population. Income, then, is skewed. Outliers in a data set will distort the value of a mean, making it a less meaningful measure for describing all data in a distribution. For example, the median (middle) income in the United States is approximately $61,000 (U.S. Census Bureau, 2019), whereas the mean (average) income would be much larger than this because the income of billionaires (the outliers) would be included in the calculation. Hence, the median is used to describe skewed data sets because it is most representative of all data for these types of distributions.

- The median is used to describe ranked or ordinal data that convey *direction* only. For example, the fifth person to finish a task took longer than the first person to finish a task; a child in first grade is in a lower grade than a child in fourth grade. In both examples, the ordinal data convey direction (greater than or less than) only. Because the *distance* (or deviation) of ordinal scale scores from their mean is not meaningful, the median is an appropriate measure used to describe ordinal-scale data.

Mode

Another measure of central tendency is the **mode**, which is the value that occurs most often. The mode is a count; no calculations or formulas are necessary to compute a mode. The mode can be used to describe data in any distribution, so long as one or more scores occur most often. However, the mode is rarely used as the sole way to describe data and is typically reported with other measures of central tendency, such as the mean and median. The mode is typically used to describe data in a distribution with a mode and measures on a nominal scale. Each is described here:

- So long as a distribution has a value that occurs most often—that is, a mode—the mode can be used as a measure of central tendency. Modal distributions can have a single mode, such as a normal distribution (the mode and the mean are reported together) or a skewed distribution (the mode and the median are reported together). A distribution can also have two or more modes, in which case each mode is reported either with the mean or with the median.

- The mode is used to describe nominal data that identify something or someone, nothing more. Because a nominal scale value is not a *quantity*, it does not make sense to use the mean or median to describe these data. The mode is used instead. For example, the mean or median season of birth for persons with schizophrenia is not very meaningful or sensible. However, describing these nominal data with the mode is meaningful by saying, for example, that most persons with schizophrenia are born in winter months. Anytime you see phrases such as *most often*, *typical*, or *common*, the mode is being used to describe these data.

Table A.6 summarizes the discussion presented here regarding when it is appropriate to use each measure of central tendency.

Measures of Variability

Measures of central tendency inform us only of scores that tend to be near the center of a distribution, but they do not inform us of all other scores in a distribution, as illustrated in Figure A.6. The most common procedure for locating all other scores is to identify the mean (a measure of central tendency) and then compute the **variability** of scores from the mean. By definition, variability can never be negative: Variability ranges from 0 to $+\infty$. If four students receive the same score of 8, 8, 8, and 8 on an assessment, then their scores do not vary because they are all the same value—the variability is 0. However, if the scores were 8, 8, 8, and 9, then they do vary because at least one score differs from the others. Thus, either scores do not vary (variability is 0), or scores do vary (variability is greater than 0). A negative variability is meaningless. In this section, we introduce three key measures of variability:

- Range
- Variance
- Standard deviation

Range

One measure of variability is the **range**. The range is the difference between the largest value (L) and smallest value (S) in a data set. The formula for the range can be stated as follows:

$$\text{Range} = L - S$$

The range is most informative for data sets without outliers. For example, suppose you measure five scores: 1, 2, 3, 4, and 5. The range of these data is $5 - 1 = 4$. In this example, the range gives a fair description of the variability of these data. Now suppose your friend also measures five scores: 2, 4, 6, 8, and 100. The range of these data is $100 - 2 = 98$ because the outlier is the largest value in the data set. In this example, a range of 98 is misleading because only one value is greater than 8.

Although the range provides a simple measure of variability, the range accounts for only two values (the largest value and the smallest value) in a distribution. Whether the data set has five scores or 5 million scores, calculations of the range consider only the largest value and the smallest value in that distribution. The

TABLE A.6 ■ Appropriate Use of Measures of Central Tendency

Measure of Central Tendency	Shape of Distribution	Measurement Scale
Mean	Normal	Interval, ratio
Median	Skewed	Ordinal
Mode	Modal	Nominal

The appropriate use of each measure of central tendency based on the shape of the distribution and the measurement scale of the data.

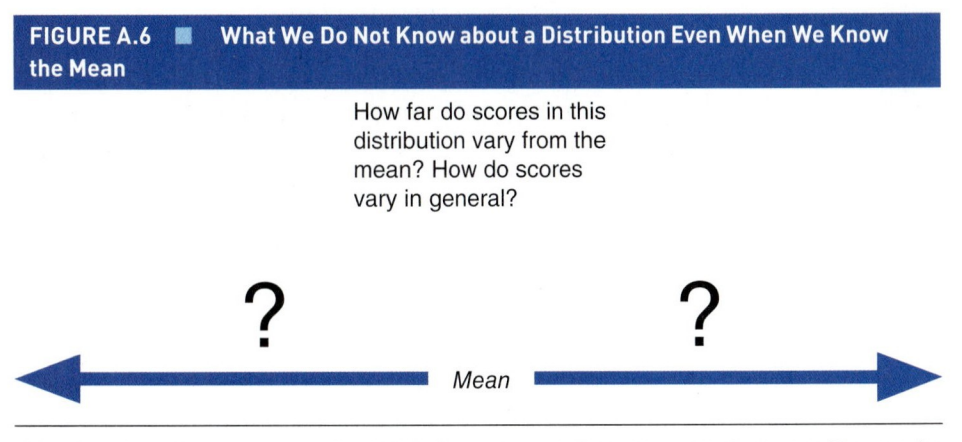

FIGURE A.6 ■ What We Do Not Know about a Distribution Even When We Know the Mean

How far do scores in this distribution vary from the mean? How do scores vary in general?

Although we know the mean score in this distribution, we know nothing of the remaining scores. By computing measures of variability, we can determine how scores vary around the mean and how scores vary in general.

range in a data set of $n = 3$ may be very informative, but a typical data set for human participant research can be in the hundreds or even thousands. For this reason, many researchers favor other measures of variability to describe data sets.

Variance

One measure of variability is the **sample variance**, represented as s^2. The variance is a measure of the average squared distance that scores deviate from the mean. A deviation is a measure of distance. For example, if the mean is 10 and you score 15, then your score is a deviation (or distance) of 5 points above the mean. To compute variance, we square this deviation, which would represent the distance of 15 from 10 as $5^2 = 25$ points. We could subtract all scores from the mean and sum the values in order to find the distance that all scores deviate from the mean. However, using this procedure will always result in a solution equal to 0. For this reason, we square each deviation, and then sum the squared deviations, which gives the smallest solution greater than 0 for determining the distance that scores deviate from the mean. To avoid a 0 solution, then, researchers square each deviation, and then sum them, which is represented by the **sum of squares (SS)**:

$$S = \sum ((x - M))^2$$

To find the average squared distance of scores from the mean, we then divide by the number of scores subtracted from the mean. However, dividing by the number of scores, or sample size, will underestimate the variance of scores in a population. The solution is to divide by one less than the number of scores or deviations summed. Doing so ensures that the sample variance will equal the variance in the population on average. When we subtract one from the sample size, the resulting value is called the **degrees of freedom (df) for sample variance**, which can be represented as follows:

$$df = n - 1$$

Hence, the formula for sample variance is the following:

$$s^2 = \frac{SS}{df}$$

An advantage of the sample variance is that its interpretation is clear: The larger the sample variance, the farther that scores deviate from the mean on average. However, one limitation of the sample variance is that the average distance of scores from the mean is squared. To find the distance (and not the squared distance) of scores from the mean, we need a new measure of variability called the standard deviation.

Standard Deviation

To find the average distance that scores deviate from the mean, called the standard deviation, we take the square root of the variance. Mathematically, square rooting is a correction for having squared each deviation to compute the variance. The formula for the **sample standard deviation (SD)** can be represented as follows:

$$SD = \sqrt{s^2} = \sqrt{\frac{SS}{df}}$$

The advantage of using standard deviation is that it provides detailed information about a distribution of scores, particularly for scores in a normal distribution. The standard deviation is most informative for scores in a normal distribution. For a normal distribution, more than 99 percent of all scores will fall within three standard deviations of the mean. We can use the **empirical rule** to identify the percentage of scores that fall within one, two, and three standard deviations of the mean. The name, *empirical rule*, comes from the word *empiricism*, meaning "to observe," because many of the behaviors that researchers observe are approximately normally distributed. The empirical rule, then, is an approximation—the percentages at each standard deviation are correct, give or take a few fractions of a standard deviation. Nevertheless, this rule is critical because of how specific it is for describing behavior. The empirical rule identifies the following:

- At least 68 percent of all scores fall within one standard deviation of the mean.
- At least 95 percent of all scores fall within two standard deviations of the mean.
- At least 99.7 percent of all scores fall within three standard deviations of the mean.

To illustrate how useful the empirical rule is, consider how we can apply it to a sample data set and can come to some immediate conclusions about the distribution of scores. Suppose we read about a sample of students whose creativity scores had a mean of 20 ($M = 20$) and a standard deviation of 4 (SD = 4). The data are normally distributed. Using this information, the data would be distributed as shown in Figure A.7, with at least 68 percent of scores falling between 16 and 24, at least 95 percent of scores falling between 12 and 28, and at least 99.7 percent of scores falling between 8 and 32. Hence, without knowing the scores for each individual in the sample, we still know a lot about this sample. When the data are normally distributed, we can use the sample mean and standard deviation to identify the distribution of almost all scores in a sample, which makes both measures (*M* and SD) very informative when used together.

Graphing Means and Correlations

Graphs can be used to display group means for one or more factors, which is particularly useful when differences in a dependent variable are compared between groups. Graphs also summarize correlations by plotting data points for two variables. This section introduces graphs for each type of data.

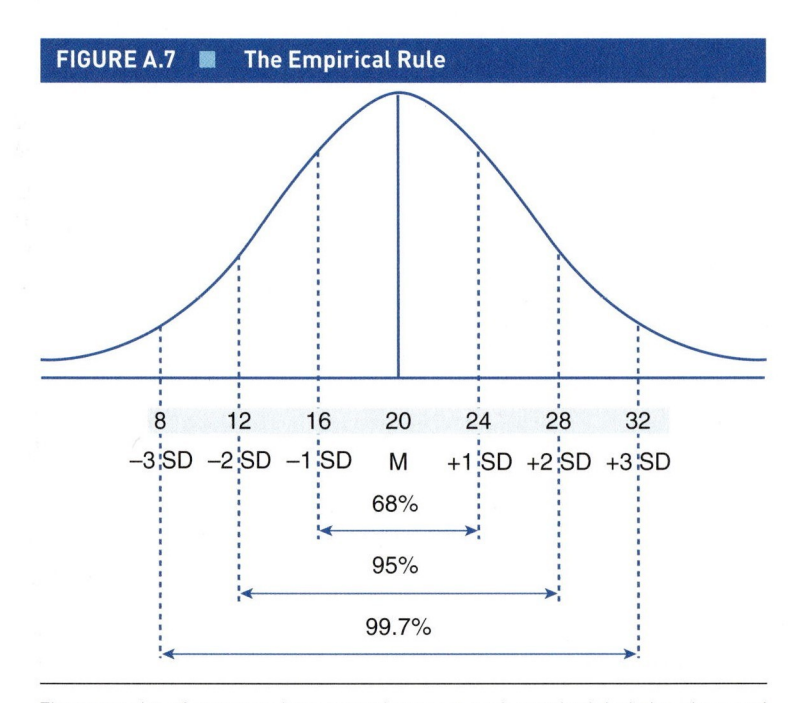

FIGURE A.7 ■ The Empirical Rule

8	12	16	20	24	28	32
−3 SD	−2 SD	−1 SD	M	+1 SD	+2 SD	+3 SD

68%
95%
99.7%

The proportion of scores under a normal curve at each standard deviation above and below the mean. The data are distributed as 20 ± 4 (*M* ± SD).

Graphing Group Means

We can graph a mean for one or more groups using a graph with lines or bars to represent the means. By convention, we use a bar graph when the groups on the *x*-axis (horizontal axis) are represented on a nominal or ordinal scale; we use a line graph when the groups on the *x*-axis are represented on an interval or ratio scale.

To use a bar graph, we list the groups on the *x*-axis and use bars to represent the means along the *y*-axis (vertical axis). As an example of a bar graph to display group means, Figure A.8a displays the mean time (in seconds) attending to a task among students chewing or not chewing gum. To use a line graph, we similarly list the groups on the *x*-axis and instead use dots connected by a single line to represent the means along the *y*-axis. As an example of a line graph to display group means, Figure A.8b displays the mean amount consumed (in milliliters) of a flavor mixed with a concentration of 2 percent, 5 percent, or 10 percent sucrose.

Graphing Correlations

We can graph a correlation using a **scatter plot**, which is a graphical display of discrete data points (*x, y*). To plot a data point, you first move across the *x*-axis, and then move up or down the *y*-axis to mark or plot each pair of (*x, y*) data points. A *correlation*, introduced in the chapter on psychology and its methods, is a statistic used to measure the strength and the direction of the linear relationship between two factors. The relationship between two factors can be evident by the pattern of data points plotted in a scatter plot.

When the values of two factors change in the same direction, the two factors have a positive correlation. To illustrate, Figure A.9a shows a scatter plot of a positive correlation between body image satisfaction and exercise. Notice that as the number of minutes of exercise increase, so do ratings of body image satisfaction; as the minutes of exercise decrease, so do ratings of body image satisfaction. In a scatter plot, the pattern of a positive correlation appears as an ascending line.

When the values of two factors change in the opposite direction, then the two factors have a negative correlation. To illustrate, Figure A.9b shows a scatter plot of a negative correlation between class absences and quiz grades. Notice that as the number of absences increase, quiz grades decrease; as the number of absences decrease, quiz grades increase. In a scatter plot, the pattern of a negative correlation appears as a descending line.

Ethics in Focus: Deception Due to the Distortion of Data

Mark Twain popularized the saying "There are lies, damned lies, and statistics." In other words, statistics can be deceiving—and difficult to interpret. Descriptive statistics are used to inform us. Therefore, being able to identify statistics and

FIGURE A.8 ■ Graphing Group Means

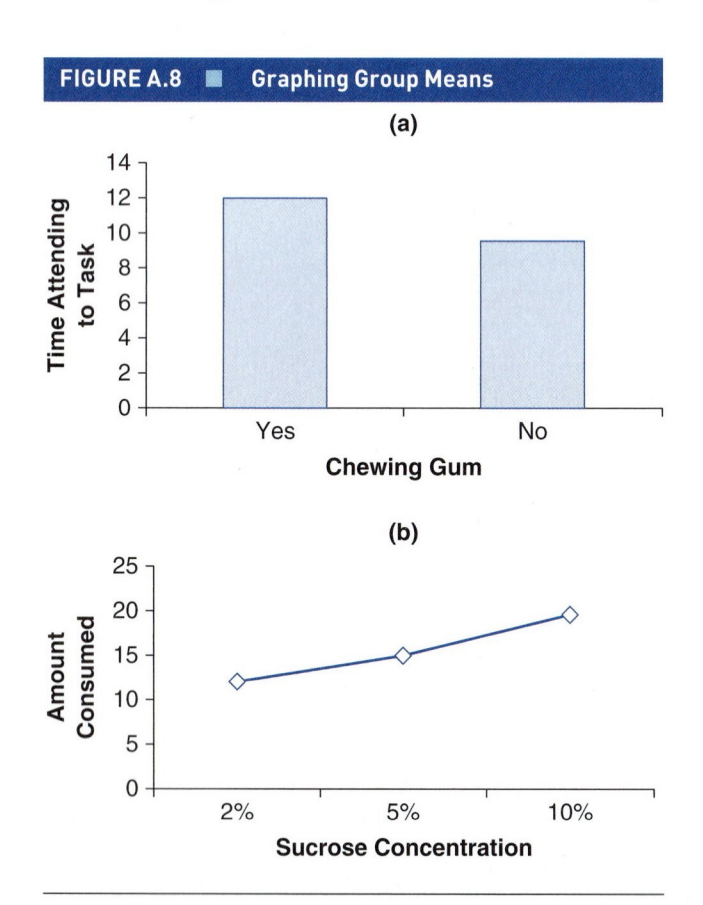

A bar graph (a) and a line graph (b) of group means obtained from two hypothetical studies.

FIGURE A.9 ■ Graphing Correlations

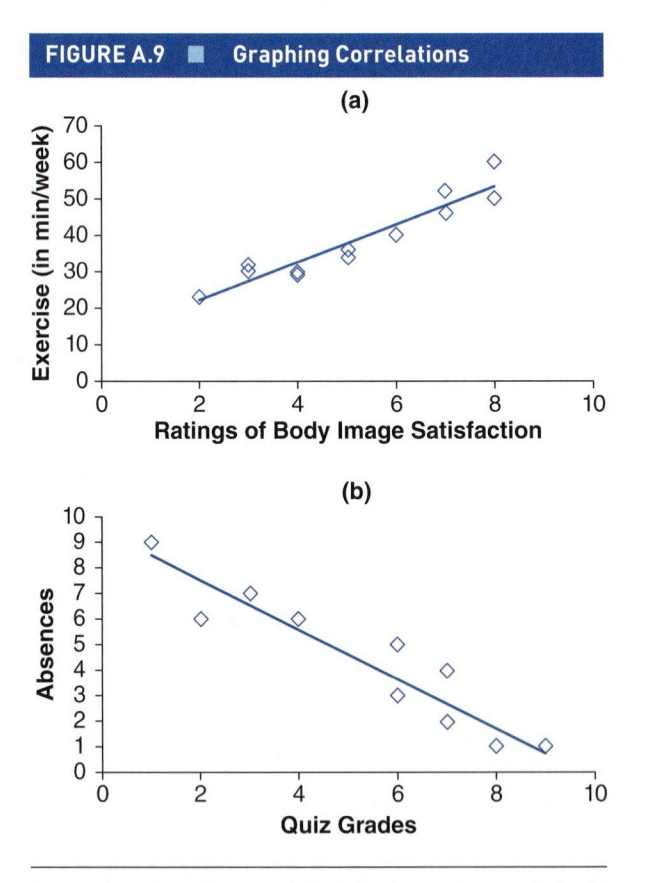

Scatter plots of a positive correlation (a) and a negative correlation (b) obtained from two hypothetical studies. The solid lines represent the regression lines.

correctly interpret what they mean is an important part of the research process. Presenting data can be an ethical concern when the data are distorted in any way, whether accidentally or intentionally. The distortion of data can occur for data presented graphically or as summary statistics. How the presentation of data can be distorted is described in this section.

When a graph is distorted, it can deceive the reader into thinking differences exist, when in truth differences are negligible (Good & Hardin, 2003; Privitera, 2019). Three common distortions to look for in graphs are (a) displays with an unlabeled axis, (b) displays with one axis altered in relation to the other axis, and (c) displays in which the vertical axis (y-axis) does not begin with 0. As an example of how a graphical display can be distorted, Figure A.10 displays a line graph for U.S. unemployment rates in 2019 (U.S. Bureau of Labor Statistics, 2020). Figure A.10a displays the data correctly with the y-axis starting at 0 percent; Figure A.10b displays the same data with the y-axis distorted and beginning at 3.2 percent. When the graph is distorted in this way, it can make the slope of the line appear steeper, as if unemployment rates are declining at a faster rate than is depicted in Figure A.10a. In fact, U.S. unemployment rates did decline in 2019, although this decline is depicted more accurately in Figure A.10a. To avoid misleading or deceiving readers, pay attention to how data are displayed in graphs so that the data are presented accurately and appropriately.

Distortion can also occur when presenting summary statistics. Two common distortions to look for with summary statistics are when data are omitted or differences are described in a way that gives the impression of larger differences than really are meaningful in the data. It can sometimes be difficult to determine if data are misleading or have been omitted, although some data should naturally be reported together. Means and standard deviations should be reported together; correlations and proportions should be reported with sample size; standard error should be reported anytime data are recorded in a sample. When these data are omitted or not reported together,

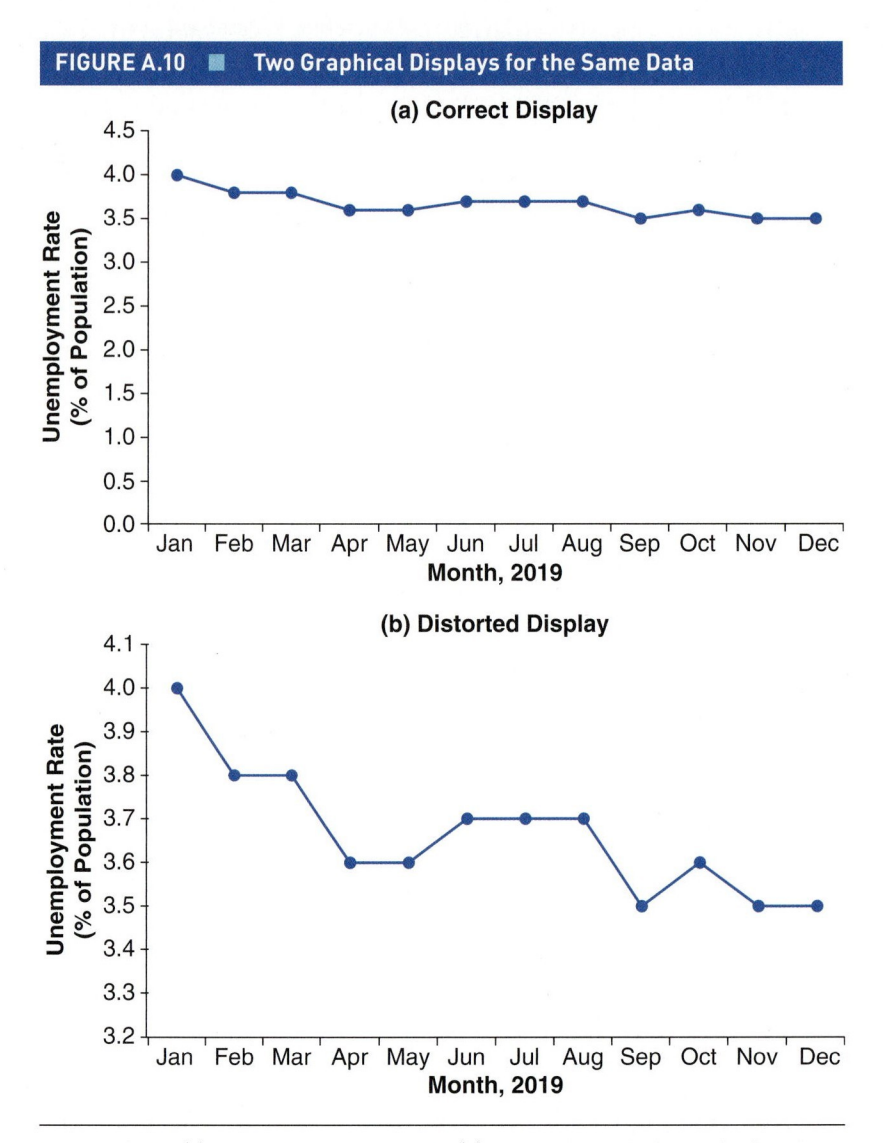

FIGURE A.10   Two Graphical Displays for the Same Data

A correct display (a) and a display that is distorted (b) because the y-axis does not begin at 0 percent. Data are of unemployment rates in the United States in 2019.

erroneous conclusions can result. For example, if we report that 75 percent of those surveyed preferred Product A to Product B, you may be inclined to conclude that Product A is a better product. However, if you were also informed that only four people were sampled, then 75 percent may not seem as convincing. Whenever you read a claim about results in a study, it is important to refer back to the data to confirm the extent to which the data support the claim the study's authors are making.

INFERENTIAL STATISTICS

> **LEARNING OBJECTIVE**
>
> Explain the foundation of inferential statistics and align the types of statistics utilized with the conclusions that can be drawn about data in psychology.

Most research studies include only a select group of participants, and not all participants who are members of a particular group of interest. In other words, most scientists have limited access to the phenomena they study. To accommodate this, researchers select a portion of all members of a group (the *sample*) when they do not have access to all members of a group (the *population*). Imagine, for example, observing every person who is attending college, or is serving in the military, or is taking a psychology class—each is an example of a population of interest. However, in most cases and for most phenomena, the population of interest is likely too large to observe. Because it is often not possible to identify all individuals in a population, researchers require statistical procedures, called **inferential statistics**, which allow them to infer or generalize observations made with samples to the larger population from which they were selected.

What Are We Making Inferences About?

Using inferential statistics, we infer that observations made with a sample are also likely to be observed in the larger population from which the sample was selected. To illustrate, suppose we test if sweetening a grapefruit juice will increasing liking for the juice among children who do not like plain grapefruit juice. If we are interested in all children who do not like plain grapefruit juice, then this group would constitute the population of interest. A **population** is the set of all individuals, items, or data of interest. This is the group about which scientists will generalize. In our example, we want to test if adding sugar increases liking for grapefruit juice in this population; this characteristic (liking for grapefruit juice) in the population is called a **population parameter**, which is a characteristic (usually numeric) that describes a population. Liking, then, is the characteristic we will measure, but not in the population. In practice, researchers will not have access to an entire population. They simply do not have the time,

money, or other resources to even consider studying all those who have a general dislike for sour-tasting grapefruit juice.

An alternative to selecting all members of a population is to select a portion or sample of individuals in the population. A **sample** is a set of individuals, items, or data selected from a population of interest. Selecting a sample is more practical, and most scientific research is based on findings in samples, not populations. In our example, we can select any portion of children who do not like plain grapefruit juice from the larger population; the portion of those we select will constitute our sample (see Step 2 in Figure A.11). A characteristic (usually numeric) that describes a sample, such as liking for a grapefruit juice, is called a **sample statistic**, which is a characteristic that describes a sample. A sample statistic is measured to estimate what this value may be for the corresponding population parameter. In this way, a sample is selected from a population to learn more about the characteristics in a population of interest. As illustrated in Figure A.11, we select a sampling method in Step 2 of the research process to select a portion of all members of a group of interest in a population.

Null Hypothesis Significance Testing

In Step 4 of the research process, we often use inferential statistics to analyze and evaluate the data because we are interested in describing the population of interest based on data measured in a sample. Inferential statistics include a diverse set of tests more formally known as **null hypothesis significance testing (NHST)**, which is a method of evaluating statistics in a sample to test hypotheses about parameters in a given population. NHST lets us use statistics to determine if our findings from a sample are likely to occur in a specific population. To use NHST, we begin by stating a **null hypothesis**. A null hypothesis is a statement we assume to be true about a population parameter. The word *null* means to have no value, effect, or significance. Therefore, a null hypothesis is a result in which we find no value, effect, or significance in our experiment.

The key reason we are testing the null hypothesis is because we think it is wrong. We state what we think is wrong about the null hypothesis in an **alternative hypothesis**. The alternative hypothesis is a statement that directly contradicts a null hypothesis by stating that the actual value of a population parameter is less than, greater than, or not equal to the value stated in the null hypothesis. In a courtroom, the defendant is assumed to be innocent (this is the null hypothesis, so to speak), so the burden is on a prosecutor to conduct a trial to show evidence that the defendant is not innocent. In a similar way, we assume the null hypothesis is true, placing the burden on the researcher to conduct a study to show evidence that the null hypothesis is unlikely to be true. Regardless, we always make a decision about the null hypothesis (that it is likely or unlikely to be true).

Appendix: Statistics in Psychology **A-17**

FIGURE A.11 ■ **Steps 2 to 4 of the Scientific Method and Why Inferential Statistics Are Needed in This Process**

All steps of the scientific method are illustrated in Figure A.1 in this appendix.

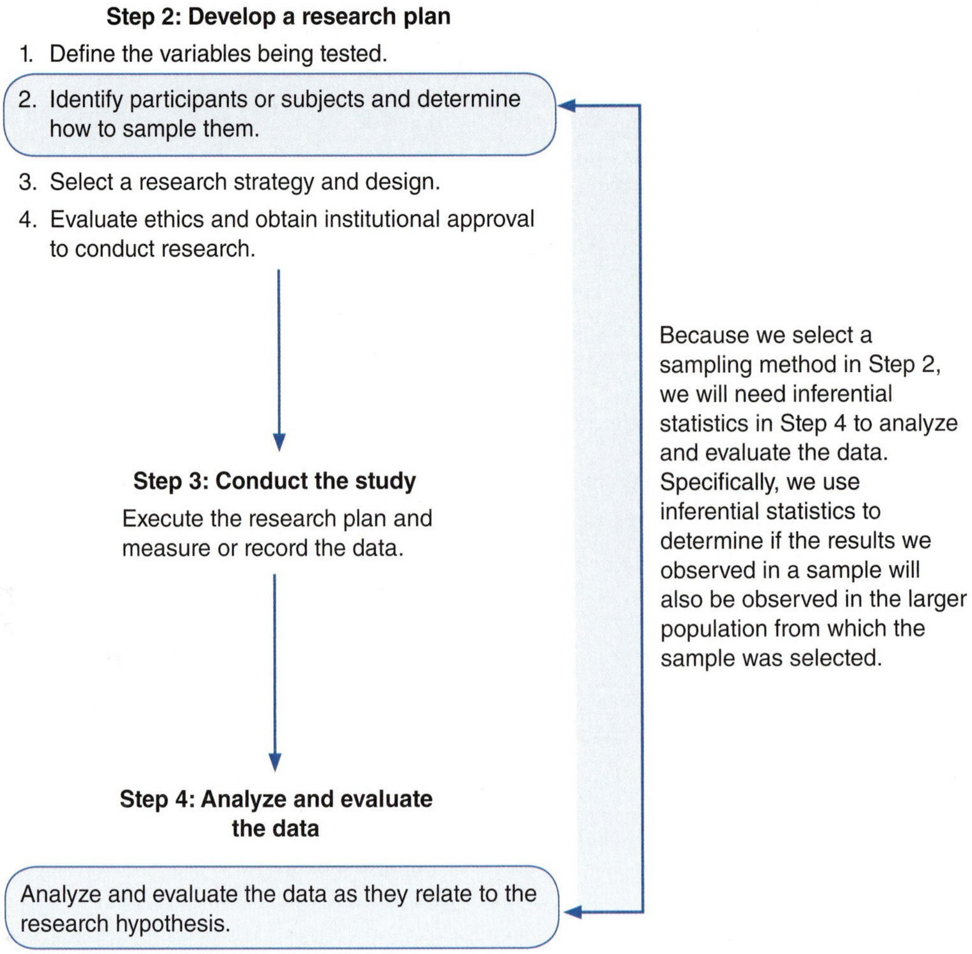

Step 2: Develop a research plan
1. Define the variables being tested.
2. Identify participants or subjects and determine how to sample them.
3. Select a research strategy and design.
4. Evaluate ethics and obtain institutional approval to conduct research.

Step 3: Conduct the study
Execute the research plan and measure or record the data.

Step 4: Analyze and evaluate the data
Analyze and evaluate the data as they relate to the research hypothesis.

Because we select a sampling method in Step 2, we will need inferential statistics in Step 4 to analyze and evaluate the data. Specifically, we use inferential statistics to determine if the results we observed in a sample will also be observed in the larger population from which the sample was selected.

Using the Criterion and Test Statistic to Make a Decision

If our goal is to describe the mean behavior in a population based on observations made in a sample, then it is important to know exactly how informative the sample mean is; in the behavioral sciences, we are most often testing hypotheses about mean changes or differences in behavior. In other words, what does the sample mean tell us about the population mean? Two important characteristics make the sample mean particularly informative and thus useful for NHST. First, it is an **unbiased estimator** of the population mean, meaning that if we select a sample at random from a population, on average, the sample mean will equal the population mean. Second, it is characterized by the **central limit theorem**, which states that all other possible sample means we could select from a given population will approach the shape of a normal distribution, as the number of samples in the sampling distribution increases. The advantage of knowing this is that we can identify the probability or likelihood of selecting any sample mean from a population by applying the empirical rule introduced earlier in this appendix.

To illustrate the informativeness of the sample mean, suppose we select all possible samples of two people from a population of three people (A, B, C) who scored an 8, 5, and 2, respectively, on some assessment—thus, the mean in the population is 5. If we select all possible samples of a certain size from this population, then we should find that the sample mean is equal to 5 on average (unbiased estimator) and all other possible sample means we could select from this population are normally distributed (central limit theorem). Notice in Figure A.12 that this is exactly what we find in our example: On average, the same mean equals the population mean (both equal 5) and the means for all other possible samples we could select are normally distributed. Knowing this, we can therefore use a sample mean selected at random to test the likelihood of selecting that sample mean, if what we think is the value of a population mean (stated in a null hypothesis) is true.

FIGURE A.12 ■ **Participants, Individual Scores, and Sample Mean for Each Possible Sample of Size 2 From This Population of Size 3**

Participants Sampled ($n = 2$)	Scores for Each Participant	Sample Mean for Each Sample (M)
A,A	8,8	8.0
A,B	8,5	6.5
A,C	8,2	5.0
B,A	5,8	6.5
B,B	5,5	5.0
B,C	5,2	3.5
C,A	2,8	5.0
C,B	2,5	3.5
C,C	2,2	2.0

Unbiased Estimator → Mean = 5.0

Central Limit Theorem: The distribution of possible sample means approximates a normal distribution.

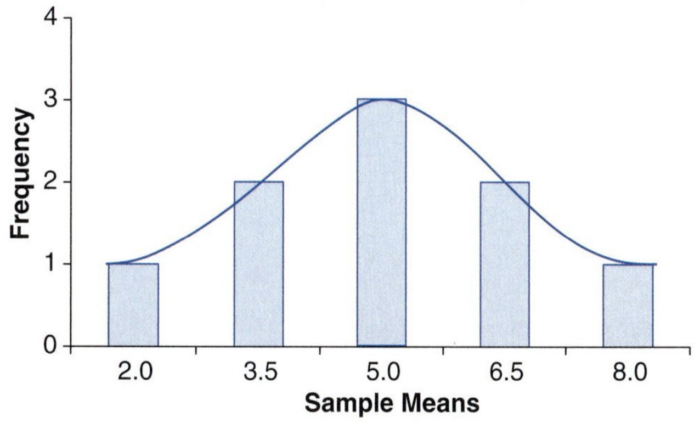

The example given here demonstrates that the sample mean is an *unbiased estimator* and follows the *central limit theorem*.

To establish a criterion for a decision (to choose whether or not to reject a null hypothesis), we state a **level of significance** for a test. The level of significance for most studies in behavioral science is .05 or 5 percent. When the likelihood of obtaining a sample outcome is less than 5 percent if the null hypothesis is true, we reject the null hypothesis because the sample outcome would be unlikely to occur (less than 5 percent likely) if the null hypothesis were true. When the likelihood of obtaining a sample outcome is greater than 5 percent if the null hypothesis were true, we retain the null hypothesis because the sample outcome would be likely to occur (greater than 5 percent likely) if the null hypothesis is true.

To determine the likelihood or probability of obtaining a sample outcome, if the value stated in the null hypothesis is true, we compute a **test statistic**. The test statistic is a mathematical formula used to determine how far a sample outcome deviates or varies from the outcome that is assumed to be true in the null hypothesis. A test statistic is used to find the *p* **value**, which is the actual probability of obtaining a sample outcome if the null hypothesis is true.

The *p* value is interpreted as error. When differences observed in a sample are attributed to error (or random variation in participant responding), error is large, and the *p* value is larger than .05 (the criterion). When $p > .05$, we retain the null hypothesis and state that an effect or difference failed to reach **significance**. When differences observed in a sample are attributed to a manipulation or treatment, error is low, and the *p* value is less than or equal to .05. When $p \leq .05$, we reject the null hypothesis and state that an effect or difference reached significance.

Illustrating NHST: The Courtroom Analogy

The process of NHST, in its purest form, aims to make the correct decision but also to bias the decision-making process so that if a mistake is made, the mistake is that we do nothing—meaning that if we do make a mistake, then we mistakenly decided to retain the null hypothesis. At all cost, we want to avoid incorrectly rejecting the null hypothesis. This approach is akin to the process of criminal trials, which in its purest form, aims to make the correct decision but also to bias the decision-making process so that if a mistake is made, the mistake is that we do nothing—meaning we mistakenly decide to let the guilty go free. At all cost, we want to avoid mistakenly putting the innocent in prison.

Figure A.13 illustrates how the process of a criminal trial and the process of NHST align. For Step 1, a trial begins with the assumption of innocence (i.e., state a null hypothesis) and an assertion of guilt by a prosecutor (i.e., state an alternative hypothesis). Step 1 is critical in that by beginning with the assumption of innocence (i.e., that the null hypothesis is true), the decision should be biased toward retaining this assumption. In Step 2, a criterion of "beyond reasonable doubt" is set for making a decision (i.e., the level of significance, α, is set), and a trial is conducted (i.e., research methods are implemented). Once all evidence has been presented (i.e., all data have been collected), then in Step 3, the evidence is weighed by a jury (i.e., a test statistic is computed), and in Step 4, a decision is made against the criterion set in Step 2 to decide guilty or not guilty (i.e., retain or reject the null hypothesis).

Types of Error and Power

Whenever we select a sample from a population, there is some probability of sampling error inasmuch as p is some value greater than 0. Because we are observing a sample and not an entire population, it is certainly possible that a decision made using

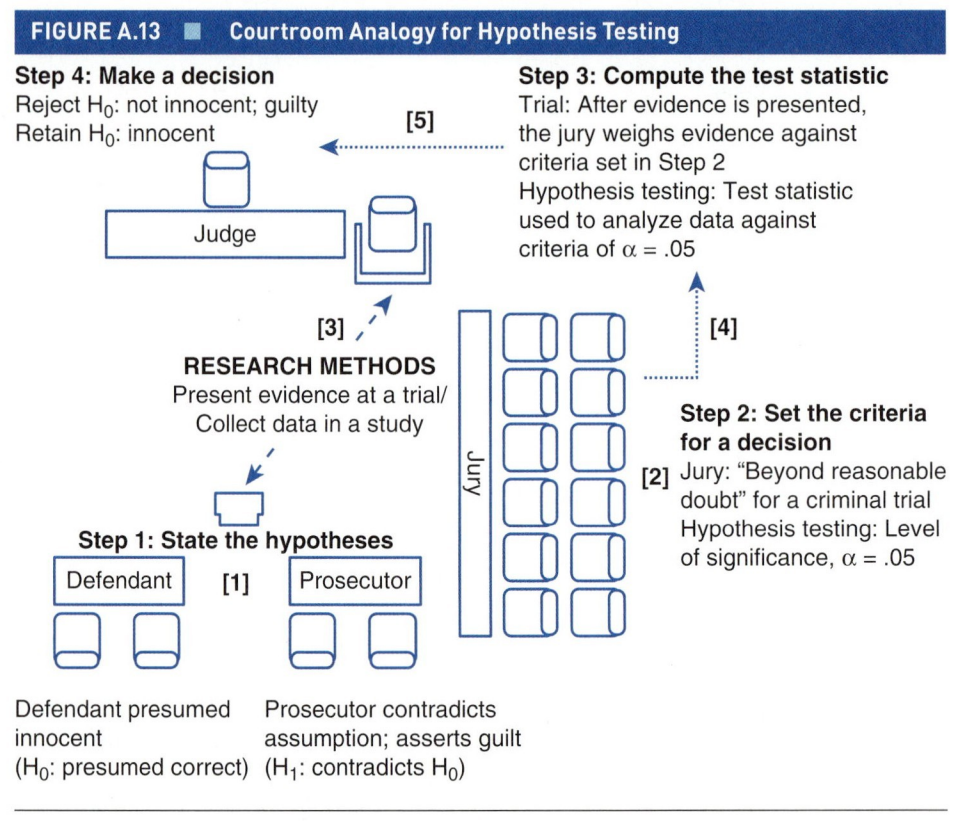

FIGURE A.13 ■ Courtroom Analogy for Hypothesis Testing

Step 4: Make a decision
Reject H_0: not innocent; guilty
Retain H_0: innocent

Step 3: Compute the test statistic
Trial: After evidence is presented, the jury weighs evidence against criteria set in Step 2
Hypothesis testing: Test statistic used to analyze data against criteria of $\alpha = .05$

RESEARCH METHODS
Present evidence at a trial/
Collect data in a study

Step 2: Set the criteria for a decision
Jury: "Beyond reasonable doubt" for a criminal trial
Hypothesis testing: Level of significance, $\alpha = .05$

Step 1: State the hypotheses
Defendant — Prosecutor

Defendant presumed innocent
(H_0: presumed correct)

Prosecutor contradicts assumption; asserts guilt
(H_1: contradicts H_0)

The process of hypothesis testing can be seen as analogous to that of a criminal trial.

TABLE A.7 ■ Four Decision Alternatives Using NHST

	Retain the Null	Reject the Null
True	CORRECT	TYPE I ERROR
False	TYPE II ERROR	CORRECT POWER

A decision can be either correct (correctly reject or retain null hypothesis) or incorrect (incorrectly reject or retain null hypothesis).

NHST is wrong. Table A.7 summarizes four decision alternatives regarding the truth and falsity of the decision we make about a null hypothesis:

- The decision to retain the null hypothesis could be correct.
- The decision to retain the null hypothesis could be incorrect.
- The decision to reject the null hypothesis could be correct.
- The decision to reject the null hypothesis could be incorrect.

We investigate each decision alternative in this section. Because we will observe a sample, and not a population, it is impossible to know for sure the truth in a population. So, for the sake of illustration, we will assume we know this. This assumption is labeled as "Truth in the Population" in Table A.7.

Decision: Retain the Null Hypothesis

When we decide to retain the null hypothesis, we can be correct or incorrect. The correct decision, called a *null result* or a *null finding*, is to retain a true null hypothesis. A null finding can be interesting, inasmuch as these findings can confirm what we would expect to see in a population, if the null hypothesis were true. This finding can also be practically meaningful. For example, suppose we tested a new intervention for a behavioral disorder and correctly obtained a null result. In this case, we identified that the intervention did not work, which could be potentially important for eventually discovering an intervention that will work. That said, in science, this decision is often termed "not *novel* (new) enough" because the decision is to retain what we already assumed. For this reason, a null result alone is rarely published in scientific journals for behavioral research.

The incorrect decision is to retain a false null hypothesis. This decision is an example of a **Type II error**, which equates to a "false negative" finding. With each test we make, there is always some probability that the decision could be a Type II error. In this decision, we decide to retain previous notions of truth that are in fact false. Although it is an error, we still changed nothing; we retained the null hypothesis. We can always go back and conduct more studies.

Decision: Reject the Null Hypothesis

When we decide to reject the null hypothesis, we can be correct or incorrect. The incorrect decision is to reject a true null hypothesis, which is a **Type I error**, which equates to a "false positive" finding. With each test we make, there is always some probability that our decision is a Type I error. A researcher who makes this error decides to reject previous notions of truth that are in fact true. The goal in NHST is to avoid this error by starting with the assumption that the null hypothesis is correct, thereby placing the burden on the researcher to show evidence that the null hypothesis is indeed false. To demonstrate evidence that leads to a decision to reject the null hypothesis, the research must reach significance ($p < .05$); that is, we must show that the likelihood of committing a Type I error by rejecting the null hypothesis is less than 5 percent.

The correct decision is to reject a false null hypothesis. In other words, we decide that the null hypothesis is false when it is indeed false. This decision is called the **power** of the decision-making process because it is the decision we aim for. Remember that we are testing the null hypothesis because we think it is wrong. The greater the power, the more likely it is that we will detect an effect, if it really exists. Deciding to reject a false null hypothesis, then, is the power, inasmuch as we learn the most about populations when we accurately reject false notions of truth. This decision is the most publishable outcome in behavioral research.

Parametric Tests: Applying the Decision Tree

We apply NHST to analyze a data set in Step 4 of the research process, as was illustrated in Figure A.11. The most common tests of significance are **parametric tests**, which are significance tests used to test hypotheses about parameters in a population in which each of the following is true:

- Data in the population are normally distributed.
- Data are measured on an interval or ratio scale of measurement.

Parametric tests are commonly applied to analyze behavioral data because most behavioral phenomena are approximately normally distributed and most behavioral data can be measured on an interval or ratio scale. Parametric tests are used with interval and ratio data because differences are meaningful on these scales. Therefore, analyzing mean differences between groups is also meaningful—this is the computation made by the test statistics for each parametric test listed in Figure A.14. Also, many of the physical and behavioral phenomena that researchers study are normally distributed, with few people at the extremes of behavior relative to the general population. For example, if we measure blood pressure or insulin levels in the body, we can identify that most people will fall within a normal or typical range, a few will have abnormally low levels, and a few will have abnormally high levels; if we measure activity levels, we will identify that most people are moderately active, a few are very active (such as Olympic athletes), and a few are sedentary.

If many groups are observed, then to use parametric tests we must also make the assumption that the variance in the population for each group is approximately the same or equal.

FIGURE A.14 ■ A Decision Tree for Choosing Parametric Tests for One and Two Factors

Parametric Tests for One and Two Factors With Interval/Ratio Data

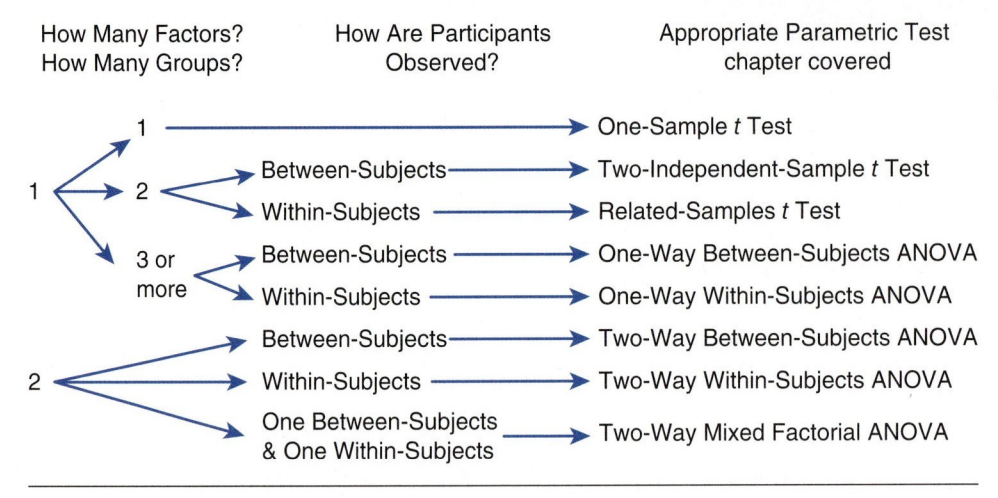

How Many Factors? How Many Groups?	How Are Participants Observed?	Appropriate Parametric Test chapter covered
1 → 1		One-Sample *t* Test
1 → 2	Between-Subjects	Two-Independent-Sample *t* Test
1 → 2	Within-Subjects	Related-Samples *t* Test
1 → 3 or more	Between-Subjects	One-Way Between-Subjects ANOVA
1 → 3 or more	Within-Subjects	One-Way Within-Subjects ANOVA
2	Between-Subjects	Two-Way Between-Subjects ANOVA
2	Within-Subjects	Two-Way Within-Subjects ANOVA
2	One Between-Subjects & One Within-Subjects	Two-Way Mixed Factorial ANOVA

Parametric tests are used to analyze data on a ratio or interval scale of measurement and for data that are normally distributed.

Hence, parametric tests require assumptions concerning mean differences between groups, assuming that the variances in each group are about the same. Note that while parametric testing is far and away the most commonly utilized analysis for testing hypotheses in the social and behavioral sciences, it can have many limitations for interpretation (for critical views, see Cohen, 1994; Nickerson, 2000; Wasserstein & Lazar, 2016), which is why it is critical to check that the assumptions for a given parametric test are met prior to conducting such a test.

In this section, we describe how to choose among the following parametric tests in various research situations: the *t* tests, analyses of variance (ANOVAs), correlation, and regression.

t Tests and ANOVAs

To use parametric tests, we must measure interval/ratio data from populations with data that are normally distributed and have similar variances. If these criteria are met, then parametric tests are appropriate for analyzing the data. Choosing an appropriate parametric test depends largely on how participants were observed (between subjects or within subjects) and how many factors and groups were included in a research design. Figure A.14 illustrates how to choose each parametric test for different research situations.

We use parametric tests for any case in which one or more groups or factors are observed, to include experiments, quasi-experiments, and nonexperiments. An advantage of using parametric tests to analyze data is that the test statistics provide statistical control of individual error variation that cannot be explained by the levels of a factor. However, keep in mind that we cannot draw causal conclusions without the methodological control that can be attained only in an experiment—that is, randomization (or control of order effects if the same participants are observed across groups), manipulation (of the levels of an independent variable), and the inclusion of a control or comparison group. Consequently, quasi-experiments and nonexperiments have research designs for which parametric tests can establish statistical control, but because these research designs lack methodological control, they fail to demonstrate cause and effect.

Correlation and Regression

For tests concerning the extent to which two factors are related (correlation) and the extent to which we can use known values of one factor to predict values of a second factor (linear regression), we treat each factor like a dependent variable and measure its value for each participant in a study. The correlation coefficient and linear regression do provide statistical control of individual error variation that cannot be explained by the two factors. However, research designs that require these statistics are typically not experimental and thus lack the methodological control needed to demonstrate cause and effect.

To choose a correlation, we need to know the scale of measurement of the data. For a parametric test, we use the *Pearson correlation coefficient* for data measured on an interval or ratio scale. Other coefficients have been derived from the Pearson correlation coefficient for situations in which at least one factor is not measured on an interval/ratio scale. The *Spearman correlation coefficient* is used to examine the relationship between two factors measured on an ordinal scale; the *phi correlation coefficient* is used to examine the relationship between two factors measured on a nominal scale; and the *point-biserial correlation coefficient* is used to examine the relationship between two factors when one factor is dichotomous (nominal) and a second factor is continuous (interval or ratio scale). Each alternative correlation coefficient was mathematically derived from, and is therefore equal to, the Pearson formula. For this reason, the Pearson correlation coefficient can be used to analyze data on any scale because its value will equal the value of the other coefficients—with some minor adjustments needed for data on ordinal and nominal scales.

Similarly, choosing an appropriate linear regression analysis will require that we know the scale of measurement of the data. In addition, we need to know how many predictor variables we will include in the model. For one predictor variable, we use *linear regression*. For two or more predictor variables, we use *multiple regression*. Choosing an appropriate regression analysis can also depend on whether the research question is exploratory or confirmatory. The details of exploratory and confirmatory factor analyses, however, go beyond the scope of this book and can be very complex—resources for applying factor analyses using regression models can be found in many upper-level textbooks (see Darlington & Hayes, 2017; Gelman & Hill, 2006).

Nonparametric Tests: Applying the Decision Tree

When the distribution in the population is not normally distributed or when data are measured on an ordinal or nominal scale, we apply **nonparametric tests** to analyze data in Step 4 of the research process (review Figure A.11). Nonparametric tests are tests of significance that can be used to test hypotheses about parameters in a population in which each of the following is true:

- Data in the population can have any type of distribution.

- Data are measured on a nominal or ordinal scale of measurement.

Nonparametric tests are often called *distribution-free tests* because the shape of the distribution in the population can be any shape. The reason that the variance and therefore the shape of a distribution in the population does not matter is that a test statistic for nonparametric tests will not measure variance to determine significance. Likewise, because variance is not computed in nonparametric test statistics, these tests can also be used to analyze ordinal and nominal data, which are scales in which the variance is not meaningful. In this section, we describe how to choose between nonparametric tests for ordinal and nominal data, and we introduce alternatives to the Pearson correlation.

Tests for Ordinal Data

Nonparametric tests for ordinal data are used as alternatives to parametric tests, which require that data be measured on an interval or ratio scale. Choosing an appropriate nonparametric test depends largely on how participants were observed (between subjects or within subjects) and the number of groups in the research design. Figure A.15 illustrates how to choose each nonparametric test for ordinal data for different research situations.

The structure of the decision tree for choosing an appropriate nonparametric test for ordinal data is similar to that for parametric tests with one factor—note the overlap between Figures A.14 and A.15 for one factor. We can require the use of nonparametric tests in two common situations. In the first situation, the data may be on an interval or ratio scale but are not normally distributed, which is an assumption that must be met for parametric tests. In these situations, we convert the data to ranks (ordinal data) and use the nonparametric alternative test to analyze the data. In the second situation, we record ranked

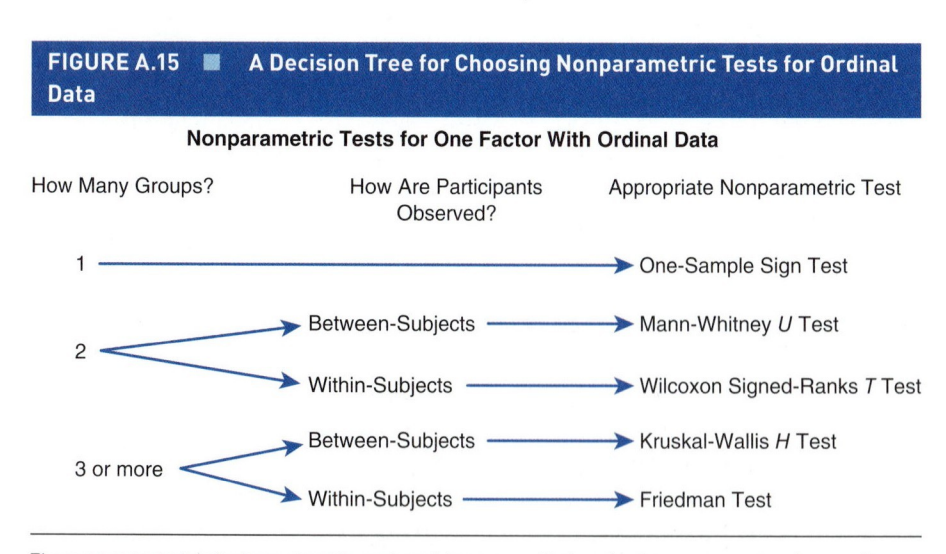

FIGURE A.15 ■ A Decision Tree for Choosing Nonparametric Tests for Ordinal Data

Nonparametric Tests for One Factor With Ordinal Data

How Many Groups?	How Are Participants Observed?	Appropriate Nonparametric Test
1		One-Sample Sign Test
2	Between-Subjects	Mann-Whitney *U* Test
2	Within-Subjects	Wilcoxon Signed-Ranks *T* Test
3 or more	Between-Subjects	Kruskal-Wallis *H* Test
3 or more	Within-Subjects	Friedman Test

These nonparametric tests are used to analyze data on an ordinal scale of measurement and as an alternative to parametric tests when one or more assumptions for those tests are violated.

data, in which case the variability of ranks (ordinal data) is not meaningful and so a nonparametric test is required.

The specific analysis of each nonparametric test for ordinal data given in Figure A.15 is beyond the scope of this book (for a full description of the analysis for each test, see Privitera, 2018).

Nonparametric Alternatives to Pearson *r*

The Pearson correlation, *r*, is a parametric statistic used to describe the relationship between two factors on an interval or ratio scale. There are many alternatives to the Pearson correlation—three of which are described in Table A.8, along with Pearson, and are the most commonly used:

- *Spearman correlation*. This correlation is used when we test the relationship between two ranked factors (ranks are an ordinal scale measurement). For example, we may identify the relationship in rankings between different polls for college sports teams, or how the order of completing a task is related from the first to the second trial.

- *Point-biserial correlation*. This correlation is used when we measure one factor that is continuous (on an interval or ratio scale of measurement) and a second factor that is dichotomous (on a nominal scale of measurement). For example, we may identify the relationship between sex (male, female) and job satisfaction, or between perceptions of happiness and pet ownership (yes, no).

- *Phi correlation*. This correlation is used when we measure two factors that are both dichotomous. For example, we may identify the relationship between branch of the military (Marines, Army) and troop morale (low, high) or between type of counseling (individual, family) and counseling outcome (completed, did not complete).

Deciding which nonparametric alterative to use depends largely on the scale of measurement of the data for each variable, and the nature of the variable (in terms of being scaled or dichotomous). Each alternative is mathematically equivalent to the Pearson. Hence, the formulas used to compute each alterative correlational test were derived from the Pearson correlation coefficient.

Tests for Nominal (Categorical) Data

In many research situations, we can use nonparametric tests to analyze nominal or categorical data using tests called *chi-square tests*. The chi-square test is used to evaluate the number of people counted in each of a finite set of categories for one or two categorical variables. The basic structure of such a research situation is to count the number of people in each category and then compare how the counts differed between the categories. For example, during an election, pollsters record the number of people who voted for each of two candidates; in business, marketers may count the number of customers who prefer one brand or another; in public health, clinicians may count the number of people who fall into various categories for health. In each example, the number of people in each category (candidates, brands, or health) are counted and compared. Using this test, the categories are the groups; the number of people counted in each category is the dependent variable. The null hypothesis for such a test is that the counts in each category are proportional; the alternative hypothesis states that the counts in each category are not proportional.

For one categorical factor, we can analyze the extent to which frequencies observed fit well with frequencies expected using the *chi-square goodness-of-fit test*. The chi-square goodness-of-fit test is a statistical procedure used to determine whether observed frequencies at each level of one categorical variable are similar to or different from frequencies expected. As an example, suppose a marketing team asks a group of children which of two products they prefer (one with or one without a picture of a cartoon character). We want to determine if children have a preference for one product. If there is no preference, then in this example, we expect the same number of children to choose each product. The chi-square goodness-of-fit test is used to determine if the proportion of children choosing each product fits well with this

TABLE A.8 ■ The Scales of Measurement for Factors Tested Using the Pearson, Spearman, Point-Biserial, and Phi Correlations

Correlation	Scale of Measurement for Correlated Variables
Pearson	Both factors are interval or ratio data.
Spearman	Both factors are ranked or ordinal data.
Point-biserial	One factor is dichotomous (nominal data), and the other factor is continuous (interval or ratio data).
Phi	Both factors are dichotomous (nominal data).

Each test is used to analyze data on different scales of measurement.

expectation. If it fits well, then there is no preference. If it does not fit well, then there is a preference.

For two categorical variables, we use a test called the *chi-square test for independence*. Using this test, we determine whether two categorical variables are independent or related (i.e., correlated). Specifically, the *chi-square test for independence* is a nonparametric statistical procedure used to determine whether two categorical variables are independent or related by comparing differences in frequencies observed across the levels of two categorical variables to frequencies expected if the two variables were independent. When two factors are related, such as activity levels and depression (yes, no), the frequencies displayed in a summary table will vary across the cells, as shown in Table A.9a. The decision is to reject the null hypothesis. When two factors are independent (not related), such as a preference (Coke or Pepsi) and depression (yes, no), the frequencies in a summary table will be the same or similar, as shown in Table A.9b. The decision is to retain the null hypothesis.

To illustrate a research situation in which we use this nonparametric test, suppose we test if the location that soccer players kick a ball (left, center, right) during a penalty kick in a professional tournament depends on which direction the goalie dives to block the ball (left, center, right). If it is dependent or related, then the location that a player kicked the ball is related to the direction the goalie dove to block the ball, and the result will be to reject the null hypothesis. If it is independent, then the location that a player kicked the ball is not related to the direction the goalie dove to block the ball, and the result will be to retain the null hypothesis.

Effect Size: How Big Is an Effect in the Population?

We use NHST to determine if the results observed in a sample are likely to occur in the population from which that sample was selected. In other words, we use NHST to determine if an effect exists in a population. An **effect** is a term used to describe the mean difference or discrepancy between what was observed in a sample and what was expected in the population as stated by the null hypothesis. When we reject a null hypothesis, an effect is significant and therefore does exist in a population; when we retain a null hypothesis, an effect is not significant and therefore does not exist in a population. The decision using NHST, however, indicates only if an effect exists but does not inform us of the size of that effect in the population.

To determine the size of an effect in a population, we compute an estimate called **effect size**, which is a measure of the size of an observed effect in a population. Effect size can describe how far scores shifted in a population, or it can describe the proportion of variance in a dependent variable that can be explained or accounted for by the levels of a factor. Effect size is often reported with many parametric and nonparametric tests for significance. Table A.10 lists common tests for significance and the corresponding effect size measure reported with each test. The following effect size measures listed in Table A.10 are described in this section:

- Cohen's d
- Proportion of variance: η^2, R^2
- Proportion of variance: Cramer's V

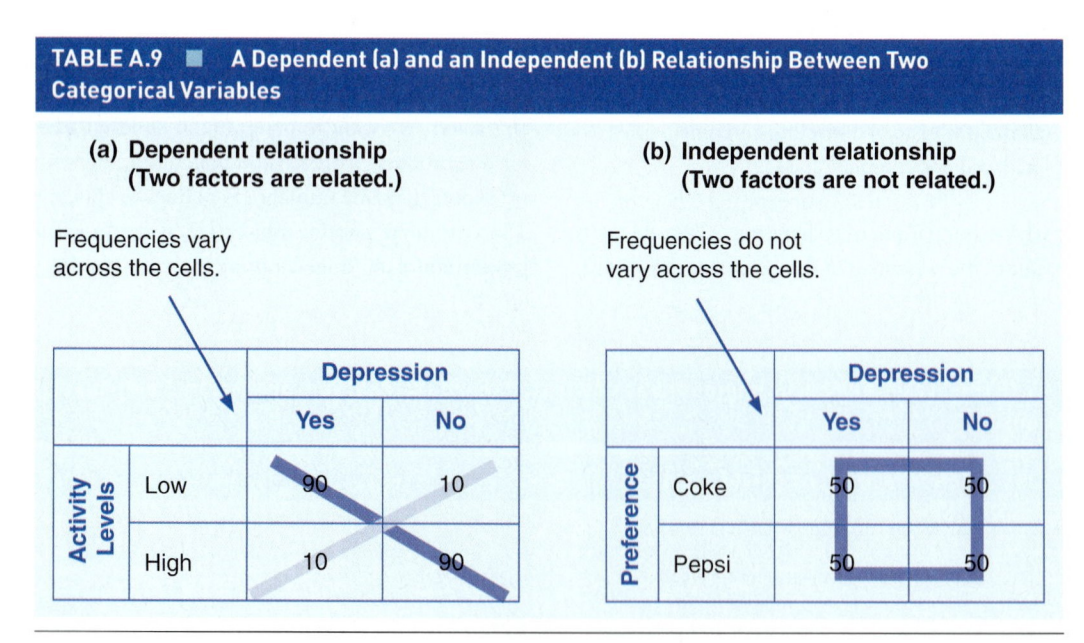

TABLE A.9 ■ **A Dependent (a) and an Independent (b) Relationship Between Two Categorical Variables**

(a) Dependent relationship
(Two factors are related.)

Frequencies vary across the cells.

Activity Levels	Depression Yes	Depression No
Low	90	10
High	10	90

(b) Independent relationship
(Two factors are not related.)

Frequencies do not vary across the cells.

Preference	Depression Yes	Depression No
Coke	50	50
Pepsi	50	50

Note that the interpretation for a chi-square test for independence is similar to that for a correlation.

TABLE A.10 ■ Measures of Effect Size That Correspond to Common Tests for Significance

Test for Significance	Effect Size — Corresponding Effect Size Measure	Interpretation of Effect Size Measure
t tests	Cohen's d	Its value represents the number of standard deviations that scores shift or fall above or below a value stated in a null hypothesis.
ANOVAs	η^2	Its value represents the proportion of variance in a dependent variable that can be explained by the levels of a factor.
Correlation and regression	R^2	Its value represents the proportion of variance in values of one factor that can be explained by changes in the values of a second factor.
Chi-square test for independence	Cramer's V	Same as R^2

The interpretation is also given for each effect size measure.

TABLE A.11 ■ The Size of an Effect Using Cohen's d, Eta Squared (η^2), and the Coefficient of Determination (R^2)

Description of Effect	d	$\eta^2 = R^2$
Trivial	—	$\eta^2, R^2 < .01$
Small	$d < 0.2$	$.01 < \eta^2, R^2 < .09$
Medium	$0.2 < d < 0.8$	$.09 < \eta^2, R^2 < .25$
Large	$d > 0.8$	$\eta^2, R^2 > .25$

Eta squared and the coefficient of determination are mathematically equivalent.

Cohen's d

When one or two groups are observed, we can describe effect size as a shift or mean difference between groups in a population using a measure called **Cohen's d** (Cohen, 1988). Cohen's d estimates the size of a shift in the population as the number of standard deviations by which scores shifted. This estimate is used with t tests. In each case, there is no effect size when $d = 0$, with larger values for d indicating a larger effect size in the population. We interpret the value of d in terms of standard deviations. The positive or negative sign indicates only the direction of an effect in the population. For example, if $d = +.36$, then scores shifted .36 standard deviations above the value stated in a null hypothesis; if $d = -.36$, then scores shifted .36 standard deviations below the value stated by a null hypothesis.

The size of an effect can be described as small, medium, or large. Conventions for interpreting the size of an effect using Cohen's d are identified by **Cohen's conventions**, which are given in Table A.11 under the d column heading. In our example, we would describe $d = ±.36$ as a medium effect size.

Proportion of Variance: η^2, R^2

An alternative measure of effect size is **proportion of variance**. Proportion of variance is a measure of effect size in terms of the proportion or percent of variability in a dependent variable that can be explained or accounted for by the levels of a factor or treatment. This type of effect size estimate is used when a study includes more than two groups or applies a correlational research design.

To estimate proportion of variance with ANOVA, we compute a measure called **eta squared**, symbolized as η^2. The value of eta squared can range between 0 and 1.0 and is interpreted as a proportion or percentage. For example, if $\eta^2 = .04$, then 4 percent of the variability in a dependent variable can be explained by the levels of a factor. The size of an effect for eta squared can be described as trivial, small, medium, or large. Conventions for interpreting the size of an effect using eta squared are given in Table A.11 under the $\eta^2 = R^2$ column heading. In our example, then, we would describe $\eta^2 = .04$ as a small effect size based on the conventions given in Table A.11.

A measure of proportion of variance that is used with a correlation or regression analysis is a measure called the **coefficient of determination**, symbolized as R^2. The coefficient of determination is the square of the *correlation coefficient, r*, and

TABLE A.12 ■ Effect Size Conventions for Cramer's V				
	Effect Size		
$df_{smaller}$	Small	Medium	Large
1	.10	.30	.50
2	.07	.21	.35
3	.06	.17	.29

Each value represents the smallest value for a given effect size category.

its value can range from 0 to 1.0. For example, suppose the correlation between mobile phone use and perceived stress is $r = .54$. Therefore, the coefficient of determination is $R^2 = (.54)^2 = .29$. To interpret R^2, we state that 29 percent of the variability in perceived stress can be explained by mobile phone use.

The coefficient of determination is mathematically equivalent to eta squared. For this reason, the size of an effect for R^2 is also described as trivial, small, medium, or large using the same conventions given in Table A.11 under the $\eta^2 = R^2$ column heading. In our example, then, we would describe $R^2 = .29$ as a large effect size based on the conventions given in Table A.11.

Proportion of Variance: Cramer's V

A measure of proportion of variance that is used with a chi-square test for independence is called **Cramer's V**. Its value can range from 0 to 1.0 and is interpreted the same as the coefficient of determination. For example, suppose the value for Cramer's $V = .16$ for the relationship between the direction a player kicks a soccer ball during a penalty kick and the direction a goalie dives to try to block the ball. To describe the size of the effect as small, medium, or large, we follow the conventions given in Table A.12. To interpret Cramer's V, we need to identify the factor with the smaller degrees of freedom, $df_{smaller}$. The degrees of freedom for a factor are the number of categories for a factor, minus one. In our example, there were three categories for each factor (left, center, and right). Hence, the smaller degrees of freedom in our example are 2. We can therefore describe $V = .16$ as a small effect size based on the conventions given in Table A.12.

Estimation: What Are the Possible Values of a Parameter?

As an alternative to NHST, we can also learn more about a parameter (e.g., a population mean) without ever stating a null hypothesis. This approach requires only that we set limits for the possible values of a population parameter within which it is likely to be contained. The goal of this approach, called **estimation**, is the same as that in significance testing—to learn more about the value of a mean or mean difference in a population of interest. To use estimation, we select a sample, measure a sample mean or mean difference, and then use that sample mean or mean difference to estimate the value of a population parameter.

We measure two types of estimates using estimation: a point estimate and an interval estimate. A **point estimate** is a sample mean for one group or mean difference between two groups. We use the sample mean (the statistic) to estimate the population mean (the parameter). An **interval estimate**, called the **confidence interval**, is the range of possible values for the parameter stated within a given **level of confidence**, which is the likelihood that a population mean is contained within that given interval.

Interval estimates are reported as a point estimate ± interval estimate. For example, you may read that "53% ± 3% of Americans believe that evolution is true," "34% ± 3% believe in ghosts," or "38% ± 3% believe that professional athletes are good role models for children." The "±3%," called the *margin of error*, is added to and subtracted from the point estimate to find the **confidence limits** of an interval estimate. If we add and subtract 3 percent from each point estimate, we can be confident that 50 to 56 percent of Americans believe evolution is true, 31 to 37 percent believe in ghosts, and 35 to 41 percent believe professional athletes are good role models for children, on average. Exactly how confident we are depends on the level of confidence, which is determined by the researcher. Typical levels of confidence are stated at 95 percent, or 99 percent in behavioral research. Figure A.16a illustrates an example of a 95 percent confidence interval for a hypothetical set of data in each of two studies.

A confidence interval states the range of possible values for a population parameter (e.g., a population mean) at a specified level of confidence. The process of computing a confidence interval is related to the process we used to retain or reject a null hypothesis using NHST. In fact, we can use the information conveyed by a confidence interval to determine the significance of an outcome. We apply the following rules to identify the significance of an outcome:

- If the null hypothesis were inside a confidence interval, the decision would have been to retain the null hypothesis (not significant).

FIGURE A.16 ■ The Informativeness of Confidence Intervals

Study 1

(a) Confidence intervals:

95% CI, −1 0 +3

(b) Inferring significance:

95% CI, −1 0 +3

Null hypothesis = 0 mean difference between the groups

(c) Inferring effect size:

95% CI, −1 0 +3

No effect: 0 is contained within the 95% CI.

Study 2

(a) Confidence intervals:

95% CI, 0 +1 +4

(b) Inferring significance:

95% CI, 0 +1 +4

(c) Inferring effect size:

95% CI, 0 +1 +4

The effects shifted between 1 to 4 points in the population.

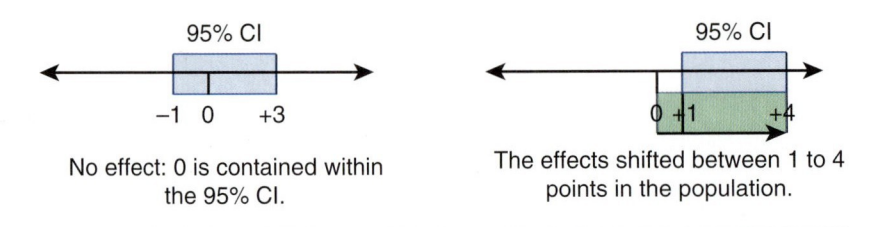

The 95 percent confidence interval (a), and interpretation of significance (b) and effect size (c) for each of two studies.

- If the null hypothesis were outside the confidence interval, the decision would have been to reject the null hypothesis (significant).

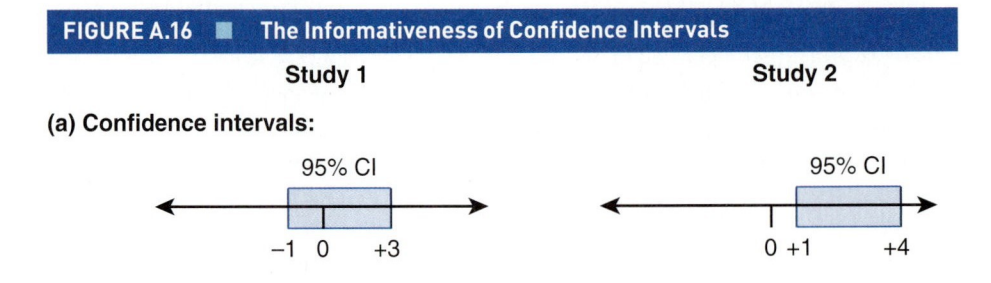

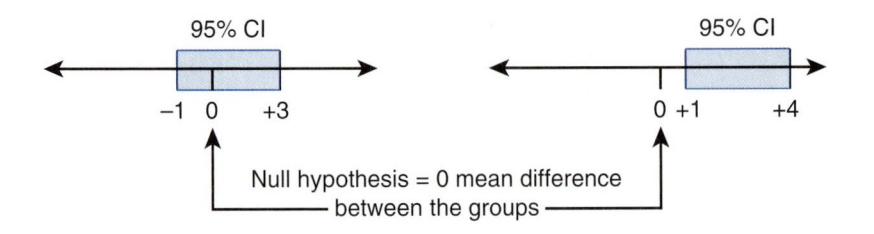

We can therefore compare a confidence interval with the decision for a significance test. To illustrate, suppose we tested the difference between two groups in each of two studies (Study 1 and Study 2). Figure A.16a gives the hypothetical results for each study. In Study 1, the 95 percent confidence interval is between −1 and +3. In Study 2, the 95 percent confidence interval is between +1 and +4. For studies in which we test the difference between two groups, the null hypothesis is typically that there is no difference between the groups—null hypothesis: mean difference = 0. To infer significance, we look to see if 0 difference is contained within the confidence interval. If 0 is contained within the 95 percent confidence interval, as shown for Study 1 in Figure A.16b, then 0 difference is a likely possible outcome in the population, and the decision is to retain the null hypothesis. If 0 is not contained within the 95 percent confidence interval (i.e., it is outside the interval), as shown for Study 2 in Figure A.16b, then 0 difference is not a likely possible outcome in the population, and the decision is to reject the null hypothesis.

We can also interpret effect size using the confidence limits of a confidence interval. The effect size for a confidence interval is a range or interval in which the lower effect size estimate is the difference between the value stated in the null hypothesis and the lower confidence limit, and the upper effect size estimate is the difference between the value stated in the null hypothesis and the upper confidence limit. Effect size can then be interpreted in terms of a shift in the population when the value of the null hypothesis is outside a given confidence interval. As illustrated in Figure A.16c, when the value stated in the null hypothesis (mean difference = 0) is contained within the confidence interval (as in Study 1), we do not interpret effect size. However, when the value stated in the null hypothesis (mean difference = 0) is outside the confidence interval (as in Study 2), we interpret effect size. In this case, the effect shifted between 1 to 4 points in the population.

Ethics in Focus: Full Disclosure of Data

When reporting statistical results, it is important to report data as thoroughly, yet concisely, as possible. Keep in mind that, as the author, you will have all the data in front of you. However, the reader will not. The reader will know only as much information as you provide. You need to be transparent: to make sure that the data you report in an article are thorough enough that they tell the whole story. For example, suppose you report that a treatment for a behavioral disorder is effective at alleviating symptoms. To support your claim, you provide all significant data, including test statistics and an effect size showing that the treatment is effective. However, suppose that your data also show that the treatment is effective for men, but not women. If you fail to provide all data for this outcome, then your report is misleading because you are selectively omitting data that could indicate limitations in the treatment's effectiveness.

Evidence of the failure to report all data can be found in the published peer-reviewed literature, with a strong commitment by peer-review journal editors to prevent this from happening (Bhaskar, 2017; DeVito, Bacon, & Goldacre, 2020). The failure to report all data is problematic, particularly for clinical trial research in which outcomes reported can mean the difference between life and death for patients. In the published scientific literature, many discrepancies in reporting have been identified, including a failure to report all trials for all results (particularly for results that do not show significance); missing data in published clinical trials (*dissemination bias*); selective removal of data and of patients (*data massaging*); and incomplete statistical reporting in some manner, such as data manipulation to obtain a desired result (*p-hacking*) and missing p values or effect size estimates (Bhaskar, 2017; Diong, Butler, Gandevia, & Héroux, 2018). Discrepancies such as these reflect a lack of transparency, which can lead to a lack of trust for the scientific outcomes reported in peer-reviewed scientific articles (Lee, 2017). To maximize transparency and instill trust is critically important—the simple solution: Always fully disclose data. Indeed, many peer-reviewed journals now require authors to fully disclose all aspects of the research they conduct as part of an "open access" movement that is growing and progressing (Piwowar et al., 2018; Privitera, 2020).

GLOSSARY

absolute threshold. The smallest amount of stimulation that can be detected.

accommodation. In Piaget's theory, the process of modifying existing cognitive structures in response to new information.

accommodation. The visual process by which lenses become rounded for viewing nearby objects and flatter for viewing remote objects.

acetylcholine (ACh). A neurotransmitter found throughout the nervous system that links the motor neurons and muscles.

achievement motivation. A strong desire to accomplish difficult tasks, outperform others, and excel.

acquisition. The formation of a learned response to a stimulus through the presentation of an unconditioned stimulus (classical conditioning) or reinforcement (operant conditioning).

action potential. An electrical impulse that surges along an axon, caused by an influx of positive ions in the neuron.

activation-synthesis theory. The theory that dreams result from the brain's attempt to make sense of random neural signals that fire during sleep.

adolescence. The period of life from puberty to adulthood, corresponding roughly to the ages of 13 to 20.

afterimage. A visual sensation that persists after prolonged exposure to and removal of a stimulus.

aggression. Behavior intended to inflict harm on someone who is motivated to avoid it.

agoraphobia. An anxiety disorder in which the main symptom is an intense fear of public places.

algorithm. A systematic, step-by-step problem-solving strategy that is guaranteed to produce a solution.

alternative hypothesis. A statement that directly contradicts a null hypothesis by stating that the actual value of a population parameter, such as the mean, is less than, greater than, or not equal to the value stated in the null hypothesis.

altruism. Helping behavior that is motivated primarily by a desire to benefit others, not oneself.

Alzheimer's disease. A progressive brain disorder that strikes older people, causing a failure to retrieve memory and other symptoms.

amygdala. A limbic structure that controls fear, anger, and aggression.

analogy. A problem-solving heuristic that involves using an old solution as a model for a new, similar problem.

anchoring effect. The tendency to use an initial value as an "anchor," or reference point, in making a new numerical estimate.

anorexia nervosa. An eating disorder in which the person limits eating and becomes emaciated.

anterograde amnesia. A memory disorder characterized by an inability to store new information in long-term memory.

antianxiety drugs. Tranquilizing medications used in the treatment of anxiety.

antidepressants. Drugs that relieve depression by increasing the supply of norepinephrine, serotonin, or dopamine.

antipsychotic drugs. Drugs that are used to control the positive symptoms of schizophrenia and other psychotic disorders.

antisocial personality disorder. A personality disorder involving a chronic pattern of self-centered, manipulative, and destructive behavior toward others.

applied research. Research that aims to solve practical human problems.

archival research. A form of research that relies on existing records of past behavior.

arousal theory. The notion that people are motivated to achieve and maintain an optimum level of bodily arousal.

assimilation. In Piaget's theory, the process of incorporating and, if necessary, changing new information to fit existing cognitive structures.

association cortex. Areas of the cortex that communicate with the sensory and motor areas and house the brain's higher mental processes.

attachment. A deep emotional bond that an infant develops with its primary caregiver.

attention. A state of awareness consisting of the sensations, thoughts, and feelings that one is focused on at a given moment.

attitude. A positive, negative, or mixed reaction to any person, object, or idea.

attribution. An explanation we create to explain a person's behavior.

attribution theory. A set of theories that describe how people explain the causes of behavior.

audition. The sense of hearing.

auditory localization. The ability to judge the direction a sound is coming from.

autobiographical memory. The recollections people have of their own personal experiences and observations.

autonomic nervous system. The branch of the peripheral nervous system that connects the CNS to the internal muscles, organs, and glands.

availability heuristic. A tendency to estimate the likelihood of an event in terms of how easily instances of it can be recalled.

aversion therapy. A behavioral therapy technique for classically conditioning people to react with aversion to alcohol and other harmful substances.

axon. The extension of the cell body of a neuron that sends impulses to other neurons.

babbling. Spontaneous vocalizations of basic speech sounds, which infants begin at about 4 months of age.

bar chart or bar graph. A graphical display used to summarize the frequency of discrete and categorical data using bars to represent each frequency.

basal ganglia. Masses of gray matter in the brain that help to initiate and coordinate deliberate movements.

basic research. "Pure science" research that tests theories and builds a foundation of knowledge.

behavioral neuroscience. A subfield of psychology that studies the links among the brain, nervous system, and behavior.

behavioral observation. A form of research based on the firsthand observation of a subject's behavior.

behavioral therapy. Techniques used to modify disordered thoughts, feelings, and behaviors through the principles of learning.

behaviorism. A school of thought that defines psychology as the scientific study of observable behavior.

beneficence. An ethical principle listed in the Belmont Report that states that it is the researcher's responsibility to minimize the potential risks and maximize the potential benefits associated with conducting a research study.

binge-eating disorder. An eating disorder marked by binge eating without chronic purging.

binocular disparity. A binocular cue for depth perception whereby the closer an object is to a perceiver, the more different the image is in each retina.

biofeedback. An operant procedure in which people learn to control physiological responses with the help of "feedback" about their internal states.

biological perspective. A perspective in psychology for evaluating the physical basis of animal and human behavior. It involves topics such as the brain, immune system, nervous system, and genetics.

biological rhythm. Any periodic, more or less regular fluctuation in a biological organism.

biomedical model. The perspective that health and illness can be explained solely on the basis of biological dysfunction.

biopsychosocial model. The holistic perspective that illness, health, and wellness can be best explained in the interactions of biological, psychological, and social factors.

bipolar disorder. A rare mood disorder characterized by wild fluctuations from mania (a euphoric, overactive state) to depression (a state of hopelessness and apathy).

blind spot. A part of the retina through which the optic nerve passes. Lacking rods and cones, this spot is not responsive to light.

borderline personality disorder. A type of personality characterized by instability in one's self-image, mood, and social relationships and a lack of clear identity.

brainstem. The inner core of the brain that connects to the spinal cord and contains the medulla, pons, and reticular formation.

Broca's area. A region in the left hemisphere of the brain that directs the muscle movements in the production and comprehension of speech.

bulimia nervosa. An eating disorder marked by cycles of binge eating followed by purging.

bystander effect. The finding that the presence of others inhibits helping in an emergency.

Cannon-Bard theory. The theory that an emotion-eliciting stimulus simultaneously triggers physiological arousal and the experience of emotion.

case study. A type of research that involves making in-depth observations of an individual person.

central limit theorem. A theorem that explains that regardless of the distribution of scores in a population, the sampling distribution of sample means selected at random from that population will approach the shape of a normal distribution, as the number of samples in the sampling distribution increases, or as sample size increases.

central nervous system (CNS). The network of nerves contained within the brain and spinal cord.

central route to persuasion. A process in which people think carefully about a message and are influenced by its arguments.

central tendency. Statistical measures for locating a single score that tends to be near the center of a distribution and is most representative or descriptive of all scores in a distribution.

cerebellum. A primitive brainstem structure that controls balance and coordinates complex voluntary movements.

cerebral cortex. The outermost covering of the brain, largely responsible for higher order mental processes.

cerebral lateralization. The tendency for each hemisphere of the brain to specialize in different functions.

childhood amnesia. The inability of most people to recall events from before the age of 3 or 4.

chromosomes. Rodlike structures, found in all biological cells, that contain DNA molecules in the form of genes

chunking. The process of grouping distinct bits of information into larger wholes, or chunks, to increase short-term-memory capacity.

circadian rhythm. A biological cycle, such as sleeping and waking, that occurs approximately every 24 hours.

classical conditioning. A type of learning in which an organism comes to associate one stimulus with another (also called Pavlovian conditioning).

clinical perspective. A perspective in psychology for evaluating the nature and treatment of dysfunction in human behavior. It involves topics of mental and physical health.

cocktail party phenomenon. The ability to attend selectively to one person's speech in the midst of competing conversations.

coding. The procedure of converting a categorical variable to numeric values.

coefficient of determination (R2). A measure of proportion of variance used to describe effect size for data analyzed using a correlation coefficient or regression. The coefficient of determination is mathematically equivalent to eta squared.

cognition. A general term that refers to mental processes such as thinking, knowing, and remembering.

cognitive dissonance. An unpleasant psychological state often aroused when people behave in ways that are discrepant with their attitudes.

cognitive perspective. A perspective in psychology for evaluating how mental processes such as memory, perception, thinking, and problem solving are related to behavior.

cognitive social-learning theory. An approach to personality that focuses on social learning (modeling), acquired cognitive factors (expectancies, values), and the person-situation interaction.

cognitive therapy. A form of psychotherapy in which people are taught to think in more adaptive ways.

cognitive-behavioral therapy. Techniques used to modify disordered thoughts, feelings, and behaviors through the principles of learning and cognition.

Cohen's conventions or effect size conventions. Standard rules for identifying small, medium, and large effects based on typical findings in behavioral research.

Cohen's d. A measure of effect size in terms of the number of standard deviations that mean scores shifted above or below the population mean stated by the null hypothesis. The larger the value of d, the larger the effect in the population.

collective unconscious. As proposed by Jung, a kind of memory bank that stores images and ideas that humans have accumulated over the course of evolution.

collectivism. A cultural orientation in which cooperation and group harmony take priority over the self.

comorbidity. The tendency for people diagnosed with one mental disorder to exhibit symptoms of other disorders as well.

computerized tomography (CT) scan. A series of X-rays taken from different angles and converted by computer into an image that depicts a horizontal slice of brain.

concept. A mental grouping of persons, ideas, events, or objects that share common properties.

conception. The fertilization of an egg cell by a sperm cell.

concrete operational stage. Piaget's third stage of cognitive development, when children become capable of logical reasoning.

concussion. An alteration in a person's mental state caused by trauma to the head.

conditional positive regard. A situation in which the acceptance and love one receives from significant others is contingent on one's behavior.

conditioned response (CR). A learned response (salivation) to a classically conditioned stimulus (bell).

conditioned stimulus (CS). A neutral stimulus (bell) that comes to evoke a classically conditioned response (salivation).

conductive hearing loss. Hearing loss caused by damage to the eardrum or bones in the middle ear.

cones. Cone-shaped photoreceptor cells in the retina that are sensitive to color.

confidence limits. The upper and lower boundaries of a confidence interval given within a specified level of confidence.

confirmation bias. The inclination to search only for evidence that will verify one's beliefs.

conformity. A tendency to alter one's opinion or behavior in ways that are consistent with group norms.

consciousness. An awareness of the sensations, thoughts, and feelings that one is attending to at a given moment.

conservation. The concept that physical properties of an object remain the same despite superficial changes in appearance.

construct. A conceptual variable that is known to exist but cannot be observed directly.

continuous data. Measured along a continuum at any place beyond the decimal point, meaning they can be measured in whole units or fractional units.

control group. The condition of an experiment in which participants are not exposed to the independent variable.

convergence. A binocular cue for depth perception involving the turning inward of the eyes as an object gets closer.

cornea. The clear outer membrane that bends light so that it is sharply focused in the eye.

corpus callosum. A bundle of nerve fibers that connects the left and right hemispheres of the brain.

correlation. A statistical measure of the extent to which two variables are associated.

counterfactual thinking. Imagining alternative scenarios and outcomes that might have happened but did not.

Cramer's V. A measure of proportion of variance used as an estimate of effect size for the chi-square test for independence.

critical period. A period of time during which an organism must be exposed to a certain stimulus for proper development to occur.

critical thinking. The process of solving problems and making decisions through a careful evaluation of evidence.

cross-cultural research. A body of studies designed to compare and contrast people of different cultures.

crystallized intelligence. A form of intelligence that reflects the accumulation of verbal skills and factual knowledge.

culture-bound syndromes. Recurring patterns of maladaptive behavior that are limited to a specific cultural group or location.

dark adaptation. A process of adjustment by which the eyes become more sensitive to light in a dark environment.

data. A set of scores, measurements, or observations that are typically numeric.

deception. A research procedure used to mislead participants about the true purposes of a study.

declarative memory. Stored long-term knowledge of facts about ourselves and the world.

defense mechanisms. Unconscious methods of minimizing anxiety by denying and distorting reality.

degrees of freedom (df) for sample variance. Equal to one less than the sample size, or $n - 1$.

delusions. False beliefs that often accompany schizophrenia and other psychotic disorders.

dendrites. Extensions from the cell body of a neuron that receive incoming impulses.

denial. A primitive form of repression in which anxiety-filled external events are barred from awareness.

deoxyribonucleic acid (DNA). The complex molecular structure of a chromosome that carries genetic information.

dependent variable. A variable that is being measured in an experiment (the proposed effect).

depression. A mood disorder characterized by sadness, despair, feelings of worthlessness, and low self-esteem.

depressive explanatory style. The tendency for depressed people to attribute negative events to factors that are internal, stable, and global.

depth perception. The use of visual cues to estimate the depth and distance of objects.

descriptive statistics. Procedures used to summarize, organize, and make sense of a set of scores called data, which are most often presented graphically, in tabular form, or as summary statistics.

developmental perspective. A perspective in psychology for evaluating change over the lifespan. It involves topics such as physical, cognitive, biological, and social development processes.

developmental psychology. The study of how people grow, mature, and change over the life span.

diagnosis. The process of identifying and grouping mental disorders with similar symptoms.

diathesis-stress model. The theory that certain mental disorders (such as schizophrenia) develop when people with a genetic or acquired vulnerability are exposed to high levels of stress.

diffusion of responsibility. In groups, a tendency for bystanders to assume that someone else will help.

discrete data. Measured in whole units or categories that are not distributed along a continuum.

discrimination. Behavior directed against persons because of their affiliation with a social group.

discrimination. In classical and operant conditioning, the ability to distinguish between different stimuli.

discriminative stimulus. A stimulus that signals the availability of reinforcement.

displacement. The property of language that accounts for the capacity to communicate about matters that are not in the here-and-now.

dissociation. A division of consciousness that permits one part of the mind to operate independently of another part.

dissociative amnesia. A dissociative disorder involving a partial or complete loss of memory.

dissociative disorder. A condition marked by a temporary disruption in one's memory, consciousness, or self-identity.

dissociative fugue. A specifier of dissociative amnesia in which a person "forgets" his or her identity, wanders from home, and develops new autobiographical memories.

dissociative identity disorder (DID). Formerly known as multiple personality disorder, it is a condition in which an individual develops two or more distinct identities.

distress. A stressor that one interprets as having harmful effects.

divided attention. The ability to distribute one's attention and simultaneously engage in two or more activities.

dopamine. A neurotransmitter that is involved in voluntary movements and with reward-seeking behaviors, such as eating, sex, and drug use.

drive theory. The notion that physiological needs arouse tension that motivates people to satisfy the need.

DSM-5. Acronym for the American Psychiatric Association's *Diagnostic and Statistical Manual of Mental Disorders* (5th edition).

dualism. The assumption that the body and mind are separate, though perhaps interacting, entities.

dualism. The perspective that the mind and the body are distinct.

echoic memory. A brief sensory memory for auditory input that lasts only 2 or 3 seconds.

eclectic. A therapeutic approach that uses a range of orientations instead of a single orientation.

effect size. A statistical measure of the size or magnitude of an observed effect in a population, which allows researchers to describe how far scores shifted in a population, or the proportion of variance in a dependent variable that can be explained by the levels of a factor.

effect. A mean difference or discrepancy between what was observed in a sample and what was expected to be observed in the population (stated by the null hypothesis).

ego. The part of personality that operates according to the reality principle and mediates the conflict between the id and superego.

egocentric. Self-centered, unable to adopt the perspective of another person.

elaborative rehearsal. A technique for transferring information into long-term memory by thinking about it in a deeper way.

electroconvulsive therapy (ECT). Electric shock treatments that often relieve severe depression by triggering seizures in the brain.

electroencephalograph (EEG). An instrument used to measure electrical activity in the brain through electrodes placed on the scalp.

embryo. The developing human organism, from two weeks to two months after conception.

emotion. A feeling state characterized by physiological arousal, expressive behaviors, and a cognitive interpretation.

empirical rule. A rule for normally distributed data that states that at least 99.7 percent of data fall within three standard deviations of the mean; at least 95 percent of data fall within two standard deviations of the mean; and at least 68 percent of data fall within one standard deviation of the mean.

encoding specificity. The principle that any stimulus encoded along with an experience can later jog one's memory of that experience.

endocrine system. A collection of ductless glands that regulate aspects of growth, reproduction, metabolism, and behavior by secreting hormones.

endorphin. A morphinelike neurotransmitter that is produced in the brain and is linked to pain control and pleasure.

epidemiology. The study of the distribution of illnesses in a population.

estimation. A statistical procedure in which a sample statistic is used to estimate the value of an unknown population parameter. Two types of estimation are point estimation and interval estimation.

eta squared (η^2). A measure of proportion of variance used to describe effect size for data analyzed using ANOVA.

ethogram. A grid of predetermined behaviors to watch for when collecting data during naturalistic observation.

ethologists. Scientists who study the behavior of animals in their natural habitats.

etiology. The origins or causes of disease or illness.

eustress. A stressor that one interprets as having beneficial effects.

experiment. A type of research in which the investigator varies some factors, keeps others constant, and measures the effects on randomly assigned participants.

experimental group. Any condition of an experiment in which participants are exposed to an independent variable.

explicit memory. The types of memory elicited through the conscious retrieval of recollections in response to direct questions.

extinction. The elimination of a learned response by removal of the unconditioned stimulus (classical conditioning) or reinforcement (operant conditioning).

extravert. A kind of person who seeks stimulation and is sociable and impulsive.

eye movement desensitization and reprocessing (EMDR). A blend of psychotherapeutic techniques that include desensitization, physiological response awareness, and the replacement of negative reactions, feelings, and thoughts with positive ones.

facial electromyograph (EMG). An electronic instrument used by emotion researchers to record activity in the facial muscles.

facial-feedback hypothesis. The hypothesis that changes in facial expression can produce corresponding changes in emotion.

family therapy. A form of psychotherapy that treats the members of a family as an interactive system.

feature detectors. Neurons in the visual cortex that respond to specific aspects of a visual stimulus (such as lines or angles).

fetal alcohol syndrome (FAS). A specific pattern of birth defects (stunted growth, facial deformity, and intellectual disability) often found in the offspring of mothers who have alcoholism.

fetus. The developing human organism, from nine weeks after conception to birth.

field research. Research conducted in real-world locations.

five-factor model. A model of personality that consists of five basic traits: neuroticism, extraversion, openness, agreeableness, and conscientiousness.

fixation. In psychoanalysis, a tendency to get "locked in" at early, immature stages of psychosexual development.

fixed action pattern. A species-specific behavior that is built into an animal's nervous system and triggered by a specific stimulus.

flashbulb memories. Highly vivid and enduring memories, typically for events that are dramatic and emotional.

flooding. A behavioral therapy technique in which the patient is saturated with a fear-provoking stimulus until the anxiety is extinguished.

fluid intelligence. A form of intelligence that involves the ability to reason logically and abstractly.

forgetting curve. A consistent pattern in which the rate of memory loss for input is steepest right after input is received and levels off over time.

formal operational stage. Piaget's fourth stage of cognitive development, when adolescents become capable of logic and abstract thought.

fovea. The center of the retina, where cones are clustered.

free association. A basic technique of psychoanalysis in which the patient says whatever comes to mind—freely and without censorship.

free recall. A type of explicit-memory task in which a person must reproduce information without the benefit of external cues (e.g., an essay exam).

frequency distribution table. A tabular summary display for a distribution of data organized or summarized in terms of how often a category, score, or range of scores occurs.

frequency. A value that describes the number of times or how often a category, score, or range of scores occurs.

frustration-aggression hypothesis. The theory that frustration causes aggression.

functional fixedness. The tendency to think of objects only in terms of their usual functions, a limitation that disrupts problem solving.

fundamental attribution error. A tendency to overestimate the impact of personal causes of behavior and to overlook the role of situations.

gate-control theory. The theory that the spinal cord contains a neurological "gate" that blocks pain signals from the brain when flooded by competing signals.

general adaptation syndrome. A three-stage process (alarm, resistance, and exhaustion) by which the body responds to stress.

general intelligence (g). A broad intellectual-ability factor used to explain why performances on different intelligence-test items are often correlated.

generalizability. The extent to which a finding applies to a broad range of subject populations and circumstances.

generalized anxiety disorder. A psychological disorder characterized by a constant state of anxiety not linked to an identifiable source.

generativity. The property of language that accounts for the capacity to use a limited number of words to produce an infinite variety of expressions.

genes. The biochemical units of heredity that govern the development of an individual life.

genetics. The branch of biology that deals with the mechanisms of heredity.

geropsychology. A subfield of developmental psychology dedicated to understanding and helping people with the mental and physical changes of aging.

Gestalt psychology. A school of thought rooted in the idea that the whole (perception) is different from the sum of its parts (sensation).

Gestalt therapy. A humanistic form of psychotherapy in which clients are aggressively prompted to express their feelings.

glial cells. Nervous system cells, also called neuroglia, that provide structural support, insulation, and nutrients to the neurons.

grasping reflex. In infants, an automatic tendency to grasp an object that stimulates the palm.

group therapy. The simultaneous treatment of several clients in a group setting.

gustatory system. The structures responsible for the sense of taste.

habituation. The tendency for attention to a stimulus to wane over time (often used to determine whether an infant has "learned" a stimulus).

habituation. The tendency of an organism to become familiar with a stimulus as a result of repeated exposure.

hallucinations. Sensory experiences that occur in the absence of actual stimulation.

hallucinogens. Psychedelic drugs that distort perceptions and cause hallucinations.

hardiness. A personality style that is characterized by commitment, challenge, and control. Hardiness acts as a buffer against stress.

health behaviors. The actions people take to achieve and maintain good health, promote wellness, and prevent illness.

health beliefs. The knowledge, attitudes, and expectations that people have about their personal health and how that health is cared for.

health promotion. Efforts to enable people to have greater control over, and to improve, their health and wellness.

health psychology. A subfield of psychology that examines psychosocial and behavioral processes related to health, illness, wellness, and health care in order to understand how such processes contribute to the landscape of health across the lifespan.

health. A state of physical, mental, and social well-being that is also affected by various psychological and social/cultural factors.

heuristic. A rule of thumb that allows one to make judgments that are quick but often in error.

hierarchy of needs. Maslow's list of basic needs that have to be satisfied before people can become self-actualized.

hippocampus. A limbic structure that plays a key role in the formation of new memories.

hippocampus. A portion of the brain in the limbic system that plays a key role in encoding and transferring new information into long-term memory.

histogram. A graphical display used to summarize the frequency of continuous data that are distributed in numeric intervals using bars connected at the upper limits of each interval.

hormones. Chemical messengers secreted from endocrine glands, into the bloodstream, to be carried to various organs throughout the body.

humanistic theory. An approach to personality that focuses on the self, subjective experience, and the capacity for fulfillment.

hypermnesia. A term referring to the unsubstantiated claim that hypnosis can be used to facilitate the retrieval of past memories.

hypnosis. Attention-focusing procedures in which changes in a person's behavior or mental state are suggested.

hypnotic susceptibility. The extent to which an individual is characteristically responsive to hypnosis.

hypothalamus. A tiny limbic structure in the brain that helps regulate the autonomic nervous system, endocrine glands, emotions, and basic drives.

hypothesis. A specific testable prediction, often derived from a theory.

iconic memory. A fleeting sensory memory for visual images that lasts only a fraction of a second.

id. A primitive and unconscious part of personality that contains basic drives and operates according to the pleasure principle.

identification. The process by which children internalize their parents' values and form a superego.

identity crisis. An adolescent's struggle to establish a personal identity, or self-concept.

illness. A disease or sickness over any length of time that can affect an individual.

illness-wellness continuum. A model for understanding health, ranging from illness and death to health and wellness.

image. A mental representation of visual information.

immune system. A biological surveillance system that detects and destroys "nonself" substances that invade the body.

Implicit Association Test (IAT). A measure of stereotyping that is derived from the speed at which people respond to pairings of concepts (such as *Blacks* or *Whites* with *good* or *bad*).

implicit memory. A nonconscious recollection of a prior experience that is revealed indirectly, by its effects on performance.

imprinting. Among newly hatched ducks and geese, an instinctive tendency to follow the mother.

incentive theory. The notion that people are motivated to behave in ways that produce a valued inducement.

incubation effect. Forming a solution to a problem as a result of taking a mental break from it.

independent variable. Any variable that the researcher manipulates in an experiment (the proposed cause).

individualism. A cultural orientation in which personal goals and preferences take priority over group allegiances.

industrial/organizational (I/O). An applied field of psychology that addresses issues related to individuals and groups in workplace settings.

inferential statistics. Procedures that allow researchers to infer or generalize observations made with samples to the larger population from which they were selected.

informational influence. Conformity motivated by the belief that others are correct.

information-processing model. A model of memory in which information must pass through discrete stages via the processes of attention, encoding, storage, and retrieval.

informed consent. The ethical requirement that prospective participants receive enough information to permit them to decide freely whether to participate in a study.

ingroup favoritism. The tendency to discriminate in favor of ingroups over outgroups.

insecure attachment. A parent-infant relationship in which the baby clings to the parent, cries at separation, and reacts with anger or apathy to reunion.

insight. A form of problem solving in which the solution seems to pop to mind all of a sudden.

insomnia. An inability to fall asleep, stay asleep, or get the amount of sleep needed to function during the day.

instinct. A fixed pattern of behavior that is unlearned, universal in a species, and "released" by specific stimuli.

intelligence quotient (IQ). A metric used to represent a child's intelligence, calculated by dividing mental age by chronological age.

intelligence. The capacity to learn from experience and adapt successfully to one's environment.

internalization. A process proposed by Vygotsky through which children absorb knowledge from the social-cultural context within which they live that can impact cognitive development.

interneurons. Central nervous system neurons that connect sensory inputs and motor outputs.

interval estimate or confidence interval (CI). The interval or range of possible values within which an unknown population parameter is likely to be contained.

interval scales. Measurements that have no true zero and are distributed in equal units.

introspection. Wundt's method of having trained observers report on their conscious, moment-to-moment reactions.

introvert. A kind of person who avoids stimulation and is low key and cautious.

iris. The ring of muscle tissue that gives eyes their color and controls the size of the pupil.

James-Lange theory. The theory that emotion stems from the physiological arousal that is triggered by an emotion-eliciting stimulus.

just noticeable difference (JND). The smallest amount of change in a stimulus that can be detected.

justice. An ethical principle listed in the Belmont Report that states that all participants should be treated fairly and equitably in terms of receiving the benefits and bearing the risks in research.

kinesthetic system. The structures distributed throughout the body that give us a sense of position and movement of body parts.

laboratory research. Research conducted in an environment that can be regulated and in which participants can be observed carefully.

language. A form of communication consisting of sounds, words, meanings, and rules for their combination.

latent content. According to Freud, the unconscious, censored meaning of a dream.

latent learning. Learning that occurs but is not exhibited in performance until there is an incentive to do so.

law of effect. A law stating that responses followed by positive outcomes are repeated, whereas those followed by negative outcomes are not.

learned helplessness. A learned expectation that one cannot control important life outcomes, resulting in apathy and depression.

learning. A relatively permanent change in knowledge or behavior that results from experience.

lens. A transparent structure in the eye that focuses light on the retina.

level of confidence. The probability or likelihood that an interval estimate will contain the value of an unknown population parameter (e.g., a population mean).

level of significance, or significance level. A criterion of judgment on which a decision is made regarding the value stated in a null hypothesis. The criterion is based on the probability of obtaining a statistic measured in a sample if the value stated in the null hypothesis is true.

life expectancy. The number of years that an average member of a species is expected to live.

life span. The maximum age possible for members of a given species.

light adaptation. The process of adjustment by which the eyes become less sensitive to light in a bright environment.

limbic system. A set of loosely connected structures in the brain that help to regulate motivation, emotion, and memory.

linguistic-relativity hypothesis. The hypothesis that language determines, or at least influences, the way we think.

lithium. A mineral prescribed as an effective treatment for bipolar disorder.

locus of control. The expectancy that one's reinforcements are generally controlled by internal or external factors.

long-term memory (LTM). A relatively permanent memory storage system that can hold vast amounts of information for many years.

lucid dreaming. A semiconscious dream state in which sleepers are aware that they are dreaming.

lymphocytes. Specialized white blood cells that secrete chemical antibodies and facilitate the immune response.

magnetic resonance imaging (MRI). A brain-scanning technique that uses magnetic fields and radio waves to produce clear, three-dimensional images.

maintenance rehearsal. The use of sheer repetition to keep information in short-term memory.

manifest content. According to Freud, the conscious dream content that is remembered in the morning.

means-end analysis. A problem-solving heuristic that involves breaking down a larger problem into a series of subgoals.

median. The middle value in a distribution of data listed in numeric order.

medical model. The perspective that mental disorders are caused by biological conditions and can be treated through medical intervention.

medulla. A brainstem structure that controls vital involuntary functions.

memory. The process by which information is retained for later use.

menarche. A girl's first menstrual period.

menopause. The end of menstruation and fertility.

mental age. The average age of children who passed the same number of items on the Stanford-Binet intelligence test.

mental models. Intuitive theories about the way things work.

mental set. Incorporating a strategy that worked in the past.

mere exposure effect. The attraction to a stimulus that results from increased exposure to it.

meta-analysis. A set of statistical procedures used to review a body of evidence by combining the results of individual studies.

microsleep. A brief episode of sleep that occurs in the midst of a wakeful activity.

mind-body relationship. The historical and philosophical debate over whether the mind and the body are one (part of the same system) or distinct (part of separate systems).

Minnesota Multiphasic Personality Inventory (MMPI). A large-scale test designed to measure a multitude of psychological disorders and personality traits.

misinformation effect. The tendency to incorporate false postevent information into one's memory of the event itself.

mode. The value in a data set that occurs most often or most frequently.

modeling. The social-learning process by which behavior is observed and imitated.

monism. The assumption that the body and mind are the same; the mind and body are part of one synergistic entity.

monism. The perspective that the mind and the body are the same.

monocular depth cues. Distance cues, such as linear perspective, that enable us to perceive depth with one eye.

mood disorder. A condition characterized by prolonged emotional extremes ranging from mania to depression.

moon illusion. The tendency for people to see the moon as larger when it is low on the horizon than when it is overhead.

moral reasoning. The way people think about and try to solve moral dilemmas.

morphemes. In language, the smallest units that carry meaning (e.g., prefixes, root words, suffixes).

motivation. An inner state that energizes people toward the fulfilment of a goal.

motor cortex. The area of the cortex that sends impulses to voluntary muscles.

motor (motion-producing) neurons. Neurons that transmit commands from the central nervous system to the muscles, glands, and organs.

Müller-Lyer illusion. An illusion in which the perceived length of a line is altered by the position of other lines that enclose it.

multicultural research. A body of studies designed to compare and contrast racial and ethnic minority groups within cultures.

multiple intelligences. Gardner's theory that there are seven types of intelligence (linguistic, logical-mathematical, spatial, musical, bodily-kinesthetic, interpersonal, intrapersonal).

myelin sheath. A layer of fatty cells that is wrapped tightly around the axon to insulate it and speed the movement of electrical impulses.

narcolepsy. A sleep disorder characterized by irresistible and sudden attacks of REM sleep during the day.

naturalistic observation. The observation of behavior as it occurs naturally in real-world settings.

need for affiliation. The desire to establish and maintain social contacts.

need for intimacy. The desire for close relationships characterized by open and intimate communication.

neural graft. A technique of transplanting healthy tissue from the nervous system of one animal into that of another.

neural networks. Clusters of densely interconnected neurons that form and strengthen as a result of experience.

neurogenesis. The production of new brain cells.

neurons. Nerve cells that serve as the building blocks of the nervous system.

neurotransmitters. Chemical messengers in the nervous system that transmit information by crossing the synapse from one neuron to another.

nominal scales. Measurements in which a number is assigned to represent something or someone. Numbers on a nominal scale are often coded values.

nonparametric tests. Significance tests used to test hypotheses about data that can have any type of distribution and to analyze data on a nominal or ordinal scale of measurement.

nonverbal communication. Conveying information without the use of spoken language, such as through gestures, facial expressions, and body posture.

normal distribution. A theoretical distribution with data that are distributed symmetrically around the mean, the median, and the mode.

normative influence. Conformity motivated by a fear of social rejection.

NREM sleep. The stages of sleep not accompanied by rapid eye movements.

null hypothesis significance testing (NHST). A method of evaluating statistics in a sample to test hypotheses about parameters in a given population; also called hypothesis testing. This method tests a hypothesis by determining the likelihood that a sample statistic would be selected if the null hypothesis regarding the population parameter were true.

null hypothesis. A statement about a population parameter, such as the population mean, that is assumed to be true. The null hypothesis is a starting point. We will test whether the value stated in the null hypothesis is likely to be true.

obesity. The state of having a surplus of body fat that causes a person to exceed his or her optimum weight by 20 percent.

object permanence. Developing at 6 to 8 months of age, an awareness that objects continue to exist after they disappear from view.

observational learning. Learning that takes place when one observes and models the behavior of others.

obsessive-compulsive disorder (OCD). An anxiety disorder defined by persistent thoughts (obsessions) and the need to perform repetitive acts (compulsions).

Oedipus complex. A tendency for young children to become sexually attracted to the parent of the opposite sex and hostile toward the parent of the same sex.

olfactory system. The structures responsible for the sense of smell.

operant conditioning. The process by which organisms learn to behave in ways that produce reinforcement.

operational definition. A concrete definition of a research variable in terms of the procedures needed to control and measure it.

opiates. A class of highly addictive drugs that depress neural activity and provide temporary relief from pain and anxiety.

opponent-process theory. The theory that color vision is derived from three pairs of opposing receptors. The opponent colors are blue and yellow, red and green, and black and white.

optic nerve. The pathway that carries visual information from the eyeball to the brain.

ordinal scales. Measurements that convey order or rank only.

outgroup-homogeneity bias. The tendency to assume that "they" (members of groups other than our own) are all alike.

ovulation. The release of a mature egg cell from a woman's ovary.

ovum. An unfertilized egg cell.

p value. The probability of obtaining a sample outcome if the value stated in the null hypothesis is true. The p value is compared to the level of significance to make a decision about a null hypothesis.

panic disorder. A disorder characterized by sudden and intense rushes of anxiety without an apparent reason.

parametric tests. Significance tests used to test hypotheses about parameters in a population in which the data in the population are normally distributed and measured on an interval or ratio scale of measurement.

parasympathetic nervous system. The division of the autonomic nervous system that reduces arousal and restores the body to its preenergized state.

partial-reinforcement effect. The tendency for a schedule of partial reinforcement to strengthen later resistance to extinction.

peak experience. A fleeting but intense moment of self-actualization in which people feel happy, absorbed, and extraordinarily capable.

perception. The processes by which people select, organize, and interpret sensations.

perceptual illusions. Patterns of sensory input that give rise to misperceptions.

perceptual set. The tendency to perceive or notice some aspects of the available information due to our past experiences or the context

peripheral nervous system (PNS). The network of nerves that radiate from the central nervous system to the rest of the body. The PNS comprises the somatic and autonomic nervous systems.

peripheral route to persuasion. A process in which people do not think carefully about a message and are influenced by superficial cues.

personality. An individual's distinct and relatively enduring pattern of thoughts, feelings, motives, and behaviors.

personality disorder. One of a group of disorders characterized by a personality that is highly inflexible and maladaptive.

person-centered therapy. A humanistic psychotherapy in which a warm and accepting environment is created to foster self-insight and acceptance.

pheromones. Chemicals secreted by animals that transmit signals—usually to other animals of the same species.

phonemes. The basic, distinct sounds of a spoken language.

phrase. A group of words that act as a unit to convey meaning. Phrases are formed from combinations of morphemes.

phrenology. The pseudoscientific theory that psychological characteristics are revealed by bumps on the skull.

physical dependence. A physiological addiction in which a drug is needed to prevent symptoms of withdrawal.

physiological measure. A type of measurement in which researchers record physical responses of the brain or body in a human or an animal.

pie chart. A graphical display in the shape of a circle that is used to summarize the relative percentages of discrete and categorical data as sectors.

pituitary gland. A tiny gland in the brain that regulates growth and stimulates hormones in other endocrine glands at the command of the hypothalamus.

placebo effect. The curative effect of an inactive treatment that results simply from the patient's belief in its therapeutic value.

plasticity. A capacity to change as a result of experience.

pleasure principle. The id's boundless drive for immediate gratification.

point estimate. A sample statistic (e.g., a sample mean) used to estimate a population parameter (e.g., a population mean).

pons. A portion of the brainstem that plays a role in sleep and arousal.

population parameter. A characteristic (usually numeric) that describes a population.

population. A set of all individuals, items, or data of interest. This is the group about which scientists will generalize.

positive psychological perspective. A perspective in psychology for evaluating human flourishing and wellness. It involves topics of maintaining optimal mental and physical health.

positron emission tomography (PET) scan. A visual display of brain activity, as measured by the amount of glucose being used.

posthypnotic amnesia. A reported tendency for hypnosis subjects to forget events that occurred during the induction.

posthypnotic suggestion. A suggestion made to a subject in hypnosis to be carried out after the induction session is over.

posttraumatic stress disorder (PTSD). A psychological disorder that develops as a result of exposure to a traumatic event.

posttraumatic stress disorder (PTSD). An anxiety disorder triggered by an extremely stressful event, such as combat.

power. In hypothesis testing, the probability of rejecting a false null hypothesis; specifically, the probability that we will detect an effect if an effect actually exists in a population.

prejudice. Negative feelings toward others based solely on their membership in a certain group.

preoperational stage. Piaget's second stage of cognitive development, when 2- to 6-year-olds become capable of reasoning in an intuitive, prelogical manner.

prevention. Efforts to avoid a disease entirely by taking actions that can stop a given disease from developing.

primacy effect. The tendency for impressions of others to be influenced heavily by information appearing early in an interaction.

priming. The tendency for a recently presented word or concept to facilitate, or "prime," responses in a subsequent situation.

proactive interference. The tendency for previously learned material to disrupt the recall of new information.

procedural memory. Stored long-term knowledge of learned habits and skills.

prodigy. Someone who is highly precocious in a specific domain of endeavor.

projection. A defense mechanism in which people attribute or "project" their own unacceptable impulses onto others.

projective tests. Psychoanalytic personality tests that allow people to "project" unconscious needs, wishes, and conflicts onto ambiguous stimuli.

proportion of variance. A measure of effect size in terms of the proportion or percent of variability in a dependent variable that can be explained or accounted for by the levels of a factor or treatment.

prototype. A "typical" member of a category, one that has most of the defining features of that category.

psychoactive drug. A chemical that alters perceptions, thoughts, moods, or behavior.

psychoanalysis. Freud's theory of personality and method of psychotherapy, both of which assume that our motives are largely unconscious.

psychological dependence. A condition in which drugs are needed to maintain a sense of well-being or relief from negative emotions.

psychological disorder. A condition in which a person's thoughts, feelings, or behavior is judged to be dysfunctional.

psychological model. The perspective that mental disorders are caused and maintained by one's life experiences.

psychology. The scientific study of behavior and the mind, and its biological bases.

psychoneuroimmunology. A subfield of psychology that examines the interactions among psychological factors, the nervous system, and the immune system.

psychopharmacology. The study of the effects of drugs on psychological processes and disorders.

psychophysics. The study of the relationship between physical stimulation and subjective sensations.

psychosexual stages. Freud's stages of personality development during which pleasure is derived from different parts of the body (oral, anal, phallic, and genital).

psychosurgery. The surgical removal of portions of the brain for the purpose of treating psychological disorders.

psychotherapy. A term used to describe any treatment in which a trained professional uses psychological techniques to help someone in need of assistance.

puberty. The onset of adolescence, as evidenced by rapid growth, rising levels of sex hormones, and sexual maturity.

punishment. In operant conditioning, any stimulus that decreases the likelihood of a prior response.

pupil. The small round hole in the iris of the eye through which light passes.

qualitative data. Varies by class. A qualitative variable is often a category or label for the behaviors and events researchers observe, and so describes nonnumeric aspects of phenomena.

quantitative data. Varies by amount or quantity. A quantitative variable is measured as a numeric value and is often collected by measuring or counting.

racism. A deep-seated form of prejudice that is based on the color of a person's skin.

random assignment. The procedure of assigning participants to conditions of an experiment in an arbitrary manner.

random sample. A method of selection in which everyone in a population has an equal chance of being chosen.

range. The difference between the largest (L) value and the smallest (S) value in a data set.

ratio scales. Measurements that have a true zero and are equidistant.

rational-emotive behavior therapy (REBT). A form of cognitive therapy in which people are confronted with their irrational, maladaptive beliefs.

rationalization. A defense mechanism that involves making excuses for one's failures and shortcomings.

reaction formation. A defense mechanism in which one converts an unacceptable feeling into its opposite.

realistic-conflict theory. The theory that prejudice stems from intergroup competition for limited resources.

reality principle. The ego's capacity to delay gratification.

receptive field. An area of the retina in which stimulation triggers a response in a cell within the visual system.

receptors. Specialized neural cells that receive neurotransmitters.

reciprocal determinism. The view that personality emerges from a mutual interaction of individuals, their actions, and their environments.

recognition. A form of explicit-memory retrieval in which items are presented to a person who must determine if they were previously encountered.

recovery. Following habituation to one stimulus, the tendency for a second stimulus to arouse new interest (often used to test whether infants can discriminate between stimuli).

reflex. An inborn automatic response to a sensory stimulus.

reinforcement. In operant conditioning, any stimulus that increases the likelihood of a prior response.

reliability. The extent to which a test yields consistent results over time or using alternate forms.

REM sleep behavior disorder (RBD). A condition in which the skeletal muscles are not paralyzed during REM sleep, enabling sleepers to act on their nightmares, often violently.

REM sleep. The rapid-eye-movement stage of sleep associated with dreaming.

replication. The process of repeating a study to determine if the results are reliable enough to be duplicated.

representativeness heuristic. A tendency to estimate the likelihood of an event in terms of how typical it seems.

repression. A defense mechanism in which personally threatening thoughts, memories, and impulses are banned from awareness.

research ethics. Identifies the actions that researchers must take to conduct responsible and moral research.

resistance. In psychoanalysis, the tendency for patients to actively block, or "resist," psychologically painful insights.

respect for persons. An ethical principle listed in the Belmont Report that states that participants in a research study must be autonomous agents capable of making informed decisions concerning whether to participate in research.

reticular formation. A group of nerve cells in the brainstem that helps to control sleep, arousal, and attention.

retina. The rear, multilayered part of the eye where rods and cones convert light into neural impulses.

retroactive interference. The tendency for new information to disrupt the memory of previously learned material.

retrograde amnesia. A memory disorder characterized by an inability to retrieve long-term memories from the past.

reversible figure. A drawing that one can perceive in different ways by reversing figure and ground.

rods. Rod-shaped photoreceptor cells in the retina that are highly sensitive to light.

rooting reflex. In response to contact on the cheek, an infant's tendency to turn toward the stimulus and open its mouth.

Rorschach. A projective personality test in which people are asked to report what they see in a set of inkblots.

sample mean. The sum of all scores divided by the number of scores summed in a sample, or in a subset of scores selected from a larger population.

sample standard deviation (SD). A measure of variability for the average distance that scores in a sample deviate from the sample mean; computed by taking the square root of the sample variance.

sample statistic. A characteristic (usually numeric) that describes a sample.

sample variance. A measure of variability for the average squared distance that scores in a sample deviate from the sample mean.

sample. A set of selected individuals, items, or data selected from a population of interest.

savant syndrome. A term used to describe a developmental condition in which a person is neurodiverse but extraordinarily talented in some ways.

scales of measurement. Rules for how the properties of numbers can change with different uses.

scatter plot. A graphical display of discrete data points (x, y) used to summarize the relationship between two factors.

scatterplot. A graph in which paired scores (X, Y) for many participants are plotted as single points to reveal the direction and strength of their correlation.

schemas. In Piaget's theory, mental representations of the world that guide the processes of assimilation and accommodation.

schemas. Preconceptions about persons, objects, or events that bias the way new information is interpreted and recalled.

schizophrenia spectrum disorders. Disorders involving gross distortions of thoughts and perceptions coupled with the loss of contact with reality.

secure attachment. A parent-infant relationship in which the baby is secure when the parent is present, distressed by separation, and delighted by reunion.

sedatives. A class of depressant drugs that slow down activity in the central nervous system.

selective attention. The ability to focus awareness on a single stimulus to the exclusion of other stimuli, as in the cocktail party phenomenon.

self-actualization. In humanistic personality theories, the need to realize and fulfill one's unique potential.

self-disclosure. The sharing of intimate details about oneself with another person.

self-discrepancy theory. The notion that discrepancies between one's self-concept and "ideal" and "ought" selves have negative emotional consequences.

self-efficacy. The belief that one is capable of performing the behaviors required to produce a desired outcome.

self-esteem. A positive or negative evaluation of the self.

self-fulfilling prophecy. The idea that a person's expectation can lead to its own fulfillment (as in the effect of teacher expectations on student performance).

self-report. A method of observation that involves asking people to describe their own thoughts, feelings, or behavior.

self-schemas. Specific beliefs about the self that influence how we interpret self-relevant information.

semantic network. A complex web of semantic associations that link items in memory such that retrieving one item triggers the retrieval of others as well.

semanticity. The property of language that accounts for the communication of meaning.

sensation. The processes by which our sense organs receive information from the environment.

sensorimotor stage. Piaget's first stage of cognitive development, from birth to 2 years old, when infants come to know the world through their own actions.

sensorineural hearing loss. Hearing loss caused by damage to the structures of the inner ear.

sensory adaptation. A decline in sensitivity to a stimulus as a result of constant exposure.

sensory memory. A memory storage system that records information from the senses for up to three seconds.

sensory neurons. Neurons that send signals from the senses, skin, muscles, and internal organs to the central nervous system.

sentence. An organized sequence of words that expresses a thought, a statement of fact, a proposition, an intention, a request, or a question.

separation anxiety. Among infants with object permanence, a fear reaction to the absence of their primary caregiver.

serial-position curve. A U-shape pattern indicating the tendency to recall more items from the beginning and end of a list than from the middle.

set point. A level of weight toward which a person's body gravitates.

shaping. A procedure in which reinforcements are used to gradually guide an animal or a person toward a specific behavior.

short-term memory (STM). A memory storage system that holds about seven items for up to 20 seconds before the material is transferred to long-term memory or is forgotten.

signal-detection theory. The theory that detecting a stimulus is jointly determined by the signal and the subject's response criterion.

significance or statistical significance. Describes a decision made concerning a value stated in the null hypothesis. When the null hypothesis is rejected, we reach significance. When the null hypothesis is retained, we fail to reach significance.

size constancy. The tendency to view an object as constant in size despite changes in the size of the retinal image.

skewed distribution. A distribution of scores that includes outliers or scores that fall substantially above or below most other scores in a data set.

Skinner box. An apparatus, invented by B. F. Skinner, used to study the effects of reinforcement on the behavior of laboratory animals.

sleep apnea. A disorder in which a person repeatedly stops breathing during sleep and awakens gasping for air.

social anxiety disorder. An intense fear of situations that invite public scrutiny.

social categorization. The classification of persons into groups based on common attributes.

social clock. A set of cultural expectations concerning the most appropriate ages for men and women to leave home, marry, start a career, have children, and retire.

social facilitation. The tendency for the presence of others to enhance performance on simple tasks and impair performance on complex tasks.

social loafing. The tendency for people to exert less effort in group tasks for which individual contributions are pooled.

social norms. Implicit rules of conduct according to which each culture operates.

social perception. The processes by which we come to know and evaluate other persons.

social psychological perspective. A perspective in psychology for evaluating the dynamics of social interaction and its effects on groups and the individual.

social psychology. The study of how individuals think, feel, and behave in social situations.

social skills training. A form of behavioral therapy used to teach interpersonal skills through modeling, rehearsal, and reinforcement (e.g., assertiveness training).

social support. The healthful coping resources provided by friends and other people.

social-identity theory. The theory that people favor ingroups and discriminate against outgroups in order to enhance their own self-esteem.

sociocultural model. The perspective that psychological disorders are influenced by cultural factors.

sociocultural perspective. A perspective in psychology for evaluating the dynamics of society and culture on human behavior. It involves topics such as the dynamics of stereotyping, prejudice, and discrimination.

soma. The cell body of a neuron.

somatic nervous system. The branch of the peripheral nervous system that transmits signals from the sensory organs to the CNS, and from the CNS to the skeletal muscles.

somatosensory cortex. The area of the cortex that receives sensory information from the touch receptors in the skin.

specific phobia. An intense, irrational fear of a specific object or situation.

split brain. A surgically produced condition in which the corpus callosum is severed, thus cutting the link between the left and right hemispheres of the brain.

split-half reliability. The degree to which alternate forms of a test yield consistent results.

spontaneous recovery. The reemergence of an extinguished conditioned response after a rest period.

standardization. The procedure by which existing norms are used to interpret an individual's test score.

Stanford-Binet. An individually administered test designed to measure intelligence.

Statistics. A branch of mathematics that is used for analyzing research data.

stereotype threat. The tendency for positive and negative performance stereotypes about a group to influence its members when they are tested in the stereotyped domain.

stereotype. A belief that associates a group of people with certain traits.

stimulants. A class of drugs that excite the central nervous system and energize behavior.

stimulus generalization. The tendency to respond to a stimulus that is similar to the conditioned stimulus.

strange-situation test. A parent-infant "separation and reunion" procedure that is staged in a laboratory to test the security of a child's attachment.

stress. An aversive state of arousal triggered by the perception that an event threatens our ability to cope effectively.

Stroop test. A color-naming task that demonstrates the automatic nature of highly practiced activities such as reading.

structuralism. Developed by Wilhelm Wundt and his student Edward Titchener as a theory of consciousness by breaking down consciousness into elements that constitute the mind.

sublimation. The channeling of repressed sexual and aggressive urges into socially acceptable substitute outlets.

subliminal message. A stimulus that is presented below the threshold for awareness.

sum of squares (SS). The sum of the squared deviations of scores from the mean; the value placed in the numerator of the sample variance formula.

superego. The part of personality that consists of one's moral ideals and conscience.

survey. A research method that involves interviewing or giving questionnaires to a large number of people.

sympathetic nervous system. A branch of the autonomic nervous system that controls the involuntary activities of various organs and mobilizes the body for fight or flight.

sympathetic nervous system. The division of the autonomic nervous system that heightens arousal and energizes the body for action.

synapse. The junction between the axon terminal of one neuron and the dendrites of another.

synesthesia. A rare condition in which stimulation in one sensory modality triggers sensations in another sensory modality.

syntax. Rules of grammar that govern the arrangement of words in a sentence.

systematic desensitization. A behavioral therapy technique used to treat phobias and other anxiety disorders by pairing gradual exposure to an anxiety-provoking situation with relaxation.

taste buds. Nets of taste-receptor cells.

telegraphic speech. The early short form of speech in which the child omits unnecessary words—as telegrams once did ("More milk").

telemental health and telepsychiatry. Types of mental health care delivered via technology such as video conferencing.

teratogens. Toxic substances that can harm the embryo or fetus during prenatal development.

test statistic. A mathematical formula that allows researchers to determine the likelihood of obtaining sample outcomes if the null hypothesis is true. The value of the test statistic can be used to make a decision regarding the null hypothesis.

test-retest reliability. The degree to which a test yields consistent results when readministered at a later time.

thalamus. A limbic structure that relays neural messages between the senses and areas of the cerebral cortex.

Thematic Apperception Test (TAT). A projective personality test in which people are asked to make up stories from a set of ambiguous pictures.

theory. An organized set of principles that describes, predicts, and explains some phenomenon.

threshold. The level of stimulation needed to trigger a neural impulse.

token economy. A large-scale behavior-change program in which participants earn valuable tokens for engaging in desired target behaviors.

trait. A relatively stable predisposition to behave in a certain way.

transduction. The process by which physical energy is converted into sensory neural impulses.

transference. In psychoanalysis, the tendency of patients to displace intense feelings for others onto the therapist.

trial and error. A problem-solving strategy in which several solutions are attempted until one is found that works.

trichromatic theory. A theory of color vision stating that the retina contains three types of color receptors—for red, blue, and green—and that these combine to produce all other colors.

true zero. The value 0 truly indicates nothing on a scale of measurement. Interval scales do not have a true zero.

two-factor theory of emotion. The theory that emotion is based on both physiological arousal and a cognitive interpretation of that arousal.

Type A personality. A personality characterized by an impatient, hard-driving, and hostile pattern of behavior.

Type B personality. A personality characterized by an easy-going, relaxed pattern of behavior.

Type I error. A "false positive" finding; the probability of rejecting a null hypothesis that is actually true. Researchers directly control for this error by stating the level of significance.

Type II error. A "false negative" finding; the probability of retaining a null hypothesis that is actually false. The researcher is reporting no effect in the population, when in truth there is an effect.

unbiased estimator. Any sample statistic obtained from a randomly selected sample that equals the value of its respective population parameter on average.

unconditional positive regard. A situation in which the acceptance and love one receives from significant others is unqualified.

unconditioned response (UR). An unlearned response (salivation) to an unconditioned stimulus (food).

unconditioned stimulus (US). A stimulus (food) that triggers an unconditioned response (salivation).

validity. The extent to which a test measures or predicts what it is designed to.

variability. A measure of the dispersion or spread of scores in a distribution, ranging from 0 to $+\infty$.

vestibular system. The inner ear and brain structures that give us a sense of equilibrium.

visual cliff. An apparatus used to test depth perception in infants and animals.

visual cortex. Located in the back of the brain, it is the main information-processing center for visual information.

Weber's law. The principle that the just noticeable difference of a stimulus is a constant proportion despite variations in intensity.

Wechsler Adult Intelligence Scale (WAIS). The most widely used IQ test for adults, it yields separate scores for verbal and performance subtests.

wellness. A physical state or condition to the right of the illness-wellness continuum that involves being in good physical and mental health, typically characterized by overt efforts aimed at maintaining this state or condition.

Wernicke's area. A region of the brain that is involved in the comprehension of language.

white noise. A hissing sound that results from a combination of all frequencies of the sound spectrum.

working memory. Term used to describe short-term memory as an active workspace where information is accessible for current use.

zygote. A fertilized egg that undergoes a two-week period of rapid cell division and develops into an embryo.

REFERENCES

Abba-Aji, A., Li, D., Hrabok, M., Shalaby, R., Gusnowski, A., Vuong, W., . . . Agyapong, V. (2020). COVID-19 pandemic and mental health: Prevalence and correlates of new-onset obsessive-compulsive symptoms in a Canadian province. *International Journal of Environmental Research and Public Health, 17*(19), e6986. doi:10.3390/ijerph17196986

Abbott, R. A., Whear, R., Rodgers, L. R., Bethel, A., Coon, J. T., Kuyken, W., . . . Dickens, C. (2014e). Effectiveness of mindfulness-based stress reduction and mindfulness based cognitive therapy in vascular disease: A systematic review and meta-analysis of randomised controlled trials. *Journal of Psychosomatic Research, 76*(5), 341–351. doi:10.1016/j.jpsychores.2014.02.012

ABC News. (2005). Restaurant shift turns into nightmare. Retrieved from http://abcnews.go.com/Primetime/story?id=1297922&page=1

Abedi, H., Salimi, S. J., Feizi, A., & Safari, S. (2013). Effect of self-efficacy enhancement program on self-care behaviors in chronic obstructive pulmonary disease. *Iranian Journal of Nursing and Midwifery Research, 18*(5), 421–424.

Ablon, J. S., & Jones, E. E. (2002). Validity of controlled clinical trials of psychotherapy: Findings from the NIMH Treatment of Depression Collaborative Research Program. *American Journal of Psychiatry, 159*, 775–783.

Abma, J. C., & Martinez, G. M. (2020, May). Activity and contraceptive use among teenagers aged 15-19 in the United States, 2015-2017. *National Health Statistics Reports*. cdc.gov/nchs/products/databriefs/db366.htm

Abramov, I., Gordon, J., Feldman, O., & Chavarga, A. (2012). Sex & vision I: Spatio-temporal resolution. *Biology of Sex Differences, 3*, 20.

Abrams, R. (1988). *Electroconvulsive therapy*. New York, NY: Oxford University Press

Abrams, R. (2002). *Electroconvulsive therapy* (4th ed.). New York, NY: Oxford University Press.

Abramson, L. Y., Metalsky, G., & Alloy, L. B. (1989). Hopelessness depression: A theory-based subtype. *Psychological Review, 96*, 358–372.

Abumrad, J., & Krulwich, R. (2007, June 6). Clive, Radiolab [Audio podcast]. Retrieved on from https://www.wnycstudios.org/story/91578-clive/

Abumrad, J., & Krulwich, R. (2011, April 18). Mirror, mirror: Radiolab. Retrieved from https://www.wnycstudios.org/podcasts/radiolab/segments/122613-mirror-mirror

Ackerman, D. (1990). *A natural history of the senses*. New York, NY: Random House.

Adams, P. R., & Adams, G. R. (1984). Mount Saint Helens's ashfall: Evidence for a disaster stress reaction. *American Psychologist, 39*, 252–260.

Adams, R. J., & Courage, M. L. (1998). Human newborn color vision: Measurement with chromatic stimuli varying in excitation purity. *Journal of Experimental Child Psychology, 68*, 22–34.

Adams, R. J., & Maurer, D. (1984). Detection of contrast by the newborn and 2-month-old infant. *Infant Behavior and Development, 7*, 415–422.

Addington, J., Liu, L., Buchy, L., Cadenhead, K. S., Cannon, T. D., Cornblatt, B. A., . . . McGlashan, T. H. (2015). North American Prodrome Longitudinal Study (NAPLS 2): The prodromal symptoms. *Journal of Nervous and Mental Disease, 203*(5), 328–335.

Adeponle, A. B., Groleau, D., & Kirmayer, L. J. (2015). Clinician reasoning in the use of cultural formulation to resolve uncertainty in the diagnosis of psychosis. *Culture, Medicine and Psychiatry, 39*(1), 16–42. doi:2126/10.1007/s11013-014-9408-5

Ader, R., & Cohen, N. (1985). CNS-immune system interactions: Conditioning phenomena. *Behavioral and Brain Sciences, 8*, 379–426.

Ader, R., & Cohen, N. (1993). Psychoneuroimmunology: Conditioning and stress. *Annual Review of Psychology, 44*, 53–85.

Ader, R., & Cohen, N. (2001). Conditioning and immunity. In R. Ader, D. L. Felton, & N. Cohen (Eds.), *Psychoneuroimmunology* (3rd ed., Vol. 2, pp. 3–34). San Diego, CA: Academic.

Ader, R., Felten, D. L., & Cohen, N. (Eds.).(1991). *Psychoneuroimmunology* (2nd ed.). San Diego, CA: Academic.

Ader, R., Felton, D. L., & Cohen, N. (Eds.).(2001). *Psychoneuroimmunology* (3rd ed.). New York, NY: Academic.

Adikari, A., de Silva, D., Ranasinghe, W., Bandaragoda, T., Alahakoon, O., Persad, R., . . . Bolton, D. (2020). Can online support groups address psychological morbidity of cancer patients? An artificial intelligence based investigation of prostate cancer trajectories. *PLOS ONE, 15*(3), e0229361. doi:10.1371/journal.pone.0229361

Adler, A. (1927). *The practice and theory of individual psychology*. New York, NY: Harcourt, Brace & World.

Adler, D. H., Wisse, L. E. M., Ittyerah, R., Pluta, J. B., Ding, S.-L., Xie, L., . . . Yushkevich, P. A. (2018). Characterizing the human hippocampus in aging and Alzheimer's disease using a computational atlas derived from ex vivo MRI and histology. *Proceedings of the National Academy of Sciences USA, 115*(16), 4252–4257. doi:10.1073/pnas.1801093115

Adolph, K. E., Vereijken, B., & Denny, M. A. (1998). Learning to crawl. *Child Development, 69*, 1299–1312.

Adolphs, R. (2013). The biology of fear. *Current Biology, 23*(2), R79–R93. doi:10.1016/j.cub.2012.11.055

Adolphs, R., Russell, J. A., & Tranel, D. (1999). The role for the human amygdala in recognizing emotional arousal from unpleasant stimuli. *Psychological Science, 10*, 167–171.

Advokat, C. D., Comaty, J. E., & Julien, R. M. (2014). *Julien's primer of drug action: A comprehensive guide to the actions, uses, and side effects of psychoactive drugs*. New York, NY: Worth.

Advokat, C. D., Comaty, J. E., & Julien, R. M. (2019). *Julien's primer of drug action: A comprehensive guide to the actions, uses, and side effects of psychoactive drugs*. New York, NY: Worth.

Agerström, J., & Rooth, D.-O. (2011). The role of automatic obesity stereotypes in real hiring discrimination. *Human Resource Management International Digest, 20*(1). doi:10.1108/hrmid.2012.04420aaa.006

Ahadzadeh, A. S., Sharif, S. P., & Ong, F. S. (2017). Self-schema and self-discrepancy mediate the influence of Instagram usage on body image satisfaction among youth. *Computers in Human Behavior, 68*, 8–16. doi:10.1016/j.chb.2016.11.011

Ahmadi, H., Daramadi, P. S., Asadi-Samani, M., & Sani, M. R. M. (2017). Effectiveness of group training of assertiveness on social anxiety among deaf and hard of hearing adolescents. *International Tinnitus Journal, 21*(1), 13–19.

Ahuja, K. K., Banerjee, D., Chaudhary, K., & Gidwani, C. (2020). Fear, xenophobia and collectivism as predictors of well-being during coronavirus disease 2019: An empirical study from India. *International Journal of Social Psychiatry*. doi:10.1177/0020764020936323

Ainsworth, M. D. S., Blehar, M. C., Waters, E., & Wall, S. (1978). *Patterns of attachment: A psychological study of the Strange Situation*. Hillsdale, NJ: Erlbaum.

Aizer, A. A., Chen, M. H., McCarthy, E. P., Mendu, M. L., Koo, S., Wilhite, T. J., . . . Nguyen, P. L. (2013). Marital status and survival in patients with cancer. *Journal of Clinical Oncology, 31*(31), 3869–3876. doi:10.1200/JCO.2013.49.6489

Ajilore, O. (2018). How civilian review boards can further police accountability and improve community relations. *Scholars Strategy Network*, Retrieved from https://scholars.org/brief/how-civilian-review-boards-can-further-police-accountability-and-improve-community-relations

Ajzen, I. (2001). Nature and operation of attitudes. *Annual Review of Psychology, 52*, 27–58.

Ajzen, I., & Fishbein, M. (1980). *Understanding attitudes and predicting social behavior*. Englewood Cliff, NJ: Prentice Hall.

Akil, L. (1982). On the role of endorphins in pain modulation. In A. L. Beckman (Ed.), *The neural bases of behavior* (pp. 311–333). New York, NY: Spectrum.

Akutsu, S., Yamaguchi, A., Kim, M. S., & Oshio, A. (2016). Self-construals, anger regulation, and life satisfaction in the United States and Japan. *Frontiers in Psychology, 7*, 768. doi:10.3389/fpsyg.2016.00768

Al-Lawati, N. M. (2018). Sleepy drivers: High time for action. *Sultan Qaboos University Medical Journal, 18*(2), e127–e129. doi:10.18295/squmj.2018.18.02.001

Alberti, R. E., & Emmons, M. L. (1986). *Your perfect right: A guide to assertive living* (5th ed.). San Luis Obispo, CA: Impact.

Alcántara, C., Casement, M. D., & Lewis-Fernández, R. (2013). Conditional risk for PTSD among Latinos: A systematic review of racial/ethnic differences and sociocultural explanations. *Clinical Psychology Review, 33*(1), 107–119. doi:10.1016/j.cpr.2012.10.005

Alcock, J. (1997). *Animal behavior: An evolutionary approach* (6th ed.). New York, NY: Sinauer.

Alegría, M., Álvarez, K., & DiMarzio, K. (2017). Immigration and mental health. *Current Epidemiology Reports, 4*(2), 145–155. doi:10.1007/s40471-017-0111-2

Alexander, F., & French, T. M. (1946). *Psychoanalytic therapy: Principles and application*. New York, NY: Ronald.

Alford, B. A., Freeman, A., Beck, A. T., & Wright, F. D. (1990). Brief focused cognitive therapy of panic disorder. *Psychotherapy, 27*, 230–234.

Alink, L. R. A., Mesman, J., Zeijl, J. V., Stolk, M. N., Juffer, F., Koot, H. M., . . . Ijzendoorn, M. H. V. (2006). The Early Childhood Aggression Curve: Development of physical aggression in 10- to 50-month-old children. *Child Development, 77*(4), 954–966. doi:10.1111/j.1467-8624.2006.00912.x

Alitto, H. J., & Usrey, W. M. (2015). Surround suppression and temporal processing of visual signals. *Journal of Neurophysiology, 113*(7), 2605–2617. doi:10.1152/jn.00480.2014

Allan, D. G. (2018). Peak experiences, perfect moments, and the extra-ordinary. *CNN*. Retrieved from https://www.cnn.com/2018/05/03/health/perfect-moments-wisdom-project/index.html

Allan, K., & Burridge, K. (1991). *Euphemism and dysphemism: Language used as shield and weapon*. New York, NY: Oxford University Press.

Allen, V. L., & Levine, J. M. (1971). Social support and conformity: The role of independent assessment of reality. *Journal of Experimental Social Psychology, 7*, 48–58.

Allison, K. R., & Bussey, K. (2016). Cyber-bystanding in context: A review of the literature on witnesses responses to cyberbullying. *Children and Youth Services Review, 65*, 183–194. doi:10.1016/j.childyouth.2016.03.026

Allison, T., & Cicchetti, D. V. (1976). Sleep in mammals: Ecological and constitutional correlates. *Science, 194*, 732–734.

Alloy, L. B., Abramson, L. Y., & Francis, E. L. (1999). Do negative cognitive styles confer vulnerability to depression? *Current Directions in Psychological Science, 8*, 128–132.

Allport, G. W. (1961). *Pattern and growth in personality*. New York, NY: Holt, Rinehart & Winston.

Allport, G. W. (1967). Gordon W. Allport. In E. G. Boring & G. Lindzey (Eds.), *A history of psychology in autobiography* (Vol. V). New York, NY: Appleton-Century-Crofts.

Allport, G. W., & Odbert, H. S. (1936). Trait-names: A psycholexical study. *Psychological Monographs, 47* (Whole No. 1).

Allport, G. W., & Postman, L. J. (1947). *The psychology of rumor*. New York, NY: Holt.

Almerigi, J. B., Carbary, T., & Harris, L. J. (2002). Most adults show opposite-side biases for the imagined holding of objects and infants. *Brain and Cognition, 48*, 258–263.

Álvaro, L., Moreira, H., Lillo, J., & Franklin, A. (2015). Color preference in red–green dichromats. *Proceedings of the National Academy of Sciences USA, 112*(30), 9316–9321. doi:10.1073/pnas.1502104112

Alzheimer's Association. (2019). *Alzheimer's and dementia*. Retrieved from https://www.alz.org/alzheimer_s_dementia

Amabile, T. M. (1996). *Creativity in context.* New York, NY: Westview.

Ambesh, P., Shetty, V., Ambesh, S., Gupta, S. S., Kamholz, S., & Wolf, L. (2018). Jet lag: Heuristics and therapeutics. *Journal of Family Medicine and Primary Care, 7*(3), 507–510.

American Academy of Neurology. (1997). Practice parameter: The management of concussion in sports (summary statement). *Neurology, 48*, 581–585.

American Addiction Centers. (2018). What is the success rate of AA? Retrieved from https://americanaddictioncenters.org/rehab-guide/12-step/whats-the-success-rate-of-aa

American Foundation for Suicide Prevention. (2014). *Suicide attempts among transgender and gender non-conforming adults: Findings of the National Transgender Discrimination Survey.* Retrieved from https://williamsinstitute.law.ucla.edu/wp-content/uploads/AFSP-Williams-Suicide-Report-Final.pdf

American Psychiatric Association & ATA. (2018). Best practices in videoconferencing-based telemental health. American Psychiatric Association. Retrieved from https://www.psychiatry.org/File%20Library/Psychiatrists/Practice/Telepsychiatry/APA-ATA-Best-Practices-in-Videoconferencing-Based-Telemental-Health.pdf

American Psychiatric Association Task Force. (2001). *Practice of electroconvulsive therapy: Recommendations for treatment, training, and privileging* (2nd ed.). Washington, DC: American Psychiatric Press.

American Psychiatric Association. (1994). *Diagnostic and statistical manual of mental disorders* (4th ed.). Washington, DC: American Psychiatric Association.

American Psychiatric Association. (2000). *Diagnostic and statistical manual of mental disorders* (4th ed., rev.). Washington, DC: American Psychiatric Press.

American Psychiatric Association. (2013). *Diagnostic and statistical manual of mental disorders,* 5th ed. Arlington, VA: American Psychiatric Association.

American Psychiatric Association. (2013). *Diagnostic and statistical manual of mental disorders* (5th ed.). Arlington, VA: American Psychiatric Publishing.

American Psychiatric Association. (2017). Addressing insomnia: Getting a good night's sleep without medication. Retrieved from https://www.psychiatry.org/news-room/apa-blogs/apa-blog/2017/01/addressing-insomnia

American Psychiatric Association. (2020). Help with sleep disorders. Retrieved from https://www.psychiatry.org/patients-families/sleep-disorders

American Psychological Association. (1990). *Guidelines for providers of psychological services to ethnic, linguistic, and culturally diverse populations.* Retrieved from www.apa.org/pi/oema/resources/policy/provider-guidelines

American Psychological Association (2013). Recognition of psychotherapy effectiveness. Retrieved from https://www.apa.org/about/policy/resolution-psychotherapy.aspx

American Psychological Association (2015). Guidelines for psychological practice with transgender and gender nonconforming people. *American Psychologist, 70*(9), 832–864. doi:10.1037/a0039906

American Psychological Association. (2021). *Diversity and accreditation.* Retrieved from https://www.apa.org/pi/oema/resources/brochures/accreditation

American Psychological Association. (n.d.). Personality. Retrieved from https://www.apa.org/topics/personality/

American Psychological Association. (2012). Fact sheet: Health disparities and stress. Retrieved from https://www.apa.org/topics/health-disparities/fact-sheet-stress

American Psychological Association. (2016). Mistaken identity. Retrieved from https://www.apa.org/monitor/2016/02/mistaken-identity

American Psychological Association. (2017a). *Ethical principles of psychologists and code of conduct.* Washington, DC: Author.

American Psychological Association. (2017b). *APA member profiles.* Retrieved from http://www.apa.org/workforce/publications/17-member-profiles/table-3.pdf

American Psychological Association. (2020a). Getting a good night's sleep. Retrieved from https://www.apa.org/helpcenter/sleep-disorders

American Psychological Association. (2020b). Hypnosis. Retrieved from https://www.apa.org/topics/hypnosis/

American Sleep Apnea Association. (2017). Sleep apnea information for clinicians. Retrieved from https://www.sleepapnea.org/learn/sleep-apnea-information-clinicians/

Ameringen, M. V., Turna, J., Khalesi, Z., Pullia, K., & Patterson, B. (2017). There is an app for that! The current state of mobile applications (apps) for DSM-5 obsessive-compulsive disorder, posttraumatic stress disorder, anxiety and mood disorders. *Depression and Anxiety, 34*(6), 526–539. doi:10.1002/da.22657

Amlung, M., Gray, J. C., & MacKillop, J. (2016). Delay discounting and addictive behavior: Review of the literature and identification of emerging priorities. In C. E. Kopetz, C. W. Lejuez, C. E. Kopetz, & C. W. Lejuez (Eds.), *Addictions: A social psychological perspective* (pp. 15–46). New York, NY: Routledge/Taylor & Francis.

Amoore, J. E., Johnston, J. W., & Rubin, M. (1964). The stereochemical theory of odor. *Scientific American, 210*, 42–49.

Anand, B. K., & Brobeck, J. R. (1951). Localization of a "feeding center" in the hypothalamus of the rat. *Proceedings of the Society for Experimental Biology and Medicine, 77*, 323–324.

Anastasi, A., & Urbina, S. (1997). *Psychological testing* (7th ed.). Upper Saddle River, NJ: Prentice-Hall.

Anders, C., Kivlighan, D. M., Porter, E., Lee, D., & Owen, J. (2021). Attending to the intersectionality and saliency of clients' identities: A further investigation of therapists' multicultural orientation. *Journal of Counseling Psychology, 68*(2), 139–148. doi:10.1037/cou0000447

Andersen, B. L., Kiecolt-Glaser, J. K., & Glaser, R. (1994). A biobehavioral model of cancer stress and disease course. *American Psychologist, 49*, 389–404.

Anderson, C. A., & Bushman, B. J. (2002). Human aggression. *Annual Review of Psychology, 53*(1), 27–51. doi:10.1146/annurev.psych.53.100901.135231

Anderson, C. A., Benjamin, A. J., & Bartholow, B. D. (1998). Does the gun pull the trigger? Automatic priming effects of weapon pictures and weapon names. *Psychological Science, 9*(4), 308–314. doi:10.1111/1467-9280.00061

Anderson, I. M., Haddad, P. M., & Scott, J. (2012). Bipolar disorder. *British Medical Journal, 345*. doi:10.1136/bmj.e8508

Anderson, J. R. (1983). *The architecture of cognition*. Cambridge, MA: Harvard University Press.

Anderson, J. R. (1990). *Cognitive psychology and its implications* (3rd ed.). New York, NY: Freeman.

Anderson, J. R., & Schooler, L. J. (1991). Reflections of the environment in memory. *Psychological Science, 2*, 396–408.

Anderson, M. J., Petros, T. V., Beckwith, B. E., Mitchell, W. W., & Fritz, S. (1991). Individual differences in the effect of time of day on long-term memory access. *American Journal of Psychology, 104*, 241–255.

Anderson, N. H. (1981). *Foundations of information integration theory*. New York, NY: Academic.

Andersson, G., & Titov, N. (2014). Advantages and limitations of Internet-based interventions for common mental disorders. *World Psychiatry, 13*(1), 4–11. doi:10.1002/wps.20083

Andrade, C., Arumugham, S. S., & Thirthalli, J. (2016). Adverse effects of electroconvulsive therapy. *Psychiatric Clinics of North America, 39*, 513–530.

Andrade, J., Baddeley, A., & Hitch, G. (Eds.).(2002). Working memory in perspective. Brighton, UK: Psychology Press.

Andreasen, N. C. (2001). *Brave new brain: Conquering mental illness in the era of the genome*. New York, NY: Oxford.

Angoff, W. H. (1988). The nature-nurture debate, aptitudes, and group differences. *American Psychologist, 43*, 713–720.

Angus, L., Watson, J. C., Elliott, R., Schneider, K., & Timulak, L. (2015). Humanistic psychotherapy research 1990–2015: From methodological innovation to evidence-supported treatment outcomes and beyond. *Psychotherapy Research, 25*(3), 330–347. doi:10.1080/10503307.2014.989290

Anisfeld, M. (1991). Neonatal imitation. *Developmental Review, 11*, 60–97.

Antrobus, J. (1991). Dreaming: Cognitive processes during cortical activation and high afferent thresholds. *Psychological Review, 98*(1), 96–121.

Appelbaum, P. S., Robbins, P. C., & Roth, L. H. (1999). Dimensional approach to delusions: Comparison across types and diagnoses. *American Journal of Psychiatry, 156*, 1938–1943.

Appleton, K. M., Hemingway, A., Rajska, J., & Hartwell, H. (2018). Repeated exposure and conditioning strategies for increasing vegetable liking and intake: Systematic review and meta-analyses of the published literature. *American Journal of Clinical Nutrition, 108*(4), 842–856. doi:10.1093/ajcn/nqy143

Archer, S. N., Djamgoz, M. B. A., Loew, E. R., Partridge, J. C., & Vallerga, S. (Eds.).(1999). *Adaptive mechanisms in the ecology of vision*. Dordrecht, Netherlands: Kluwer.

Ardiel, E. L., & Rankin, C. H. (2010). The importance of touch in development. *Paediatrics & Child Health, 15*(3), 153–156. doi:10.1093/pch/15.3.153

Arnon, Z., Maoz, G., Gazit, T., & Klein, E. (2011). Rorschach indicators of PTSD. *Rorschachiana, 32*(1), 5–26. doi:10.1027/1192-5604/a000013

Aron, E. N., & Aron, A. (1997). Sensory-processing sensitivity and its relation to introversion and emotionality. *Journal of Personality and Social Psychology, 73*, 345–368.

Aron, E. N., Aron, A., & Jagiellowicz, J. (2012). Sensory processing sensitivity. *Personality and Social Psychology Review, 16*(3), 262–282. doi:10.1177/1088868311434213

Aronson, E., & Mills, J. (1959). The effect of severity of initiation on liking for a group. *Journal of Abnormal and Social Psychology, 59*, 177–181.

Arora, R., & Rangnekar, S. (2016). The interactive effects of conscientiousness and agreeableness on career commitment. *Journal of Employment Counseling, 53*(1), 14–29. doi:10.1002/joec.12025

Asch, S. E. (1946). Forming impressions of personality. *Journal of Abnormal and Social Psychology, 41*, 258–290.

Asch, S. E. (1956). Studies of independence and conformity: A minority of one against a unanimous majority. *Psychological Monographs, 70*, 416.

Asch, S. E. (1956). Studies of independence and conformity: A minority of one against a unanimous majority. *Psychological Monographs, 70*, 416.

Asch, S. E. (1951). Effects of group pressure upon the modification and distortion of judgments. In H. Guetzkow (Ed.), *Groups, leadership, and men*. Pittsburgh, PA: Carnegie Press.

Aserinksy, E., & Kleitman, N. (1953). Regularly occurring periods of eye motility and concomitant phenomena during sleep. *Science, 118*, 273.

Ashby, F. G., Isen, A. M., & Turken, A. (1999). A neuropsychological theory of positive affect and its influence on cognition. *Psychological Review, 106*, 529–550.

Asher, S. R., & Coie, J. D. (1990). *Peer rejection in childhood*. New York, NY: Cambridge University Press.

Ashok, A. H., Marques, T. R., Jauhar, S., Nour, M. M., Goodwin, G. M., Young, A. H., & Howes, O. D. (2017). The dopamine hypothesis of bipolar affective disorder: The state of the art and implications for treatment. *Molecular Psychiatry, 22*(5), 666–679. doi:10.1038/mp.2017.16

Askenasy, H. (1978). *Are we all Nazis?* Secaucus, NJ: Lyle Stuart.

Aslin, R. N. (1989). Discrimination of frequency transitions by human infants. *Journal of the Acoustical Society of America, 86*, 582–590.

Association for Women in Psychology. (2019). *AWP Herstory*. Retrieved from https://www.awpsych.org/awp_herstory.php

Atkinson, J. W. (1964). *An introduction to motivation*. New York, NY: Van Nostrand.

Atkinson, J. W., (1957). Motivational determinants of risk-taking behavior. *Psychological Review, 64*, 359–372.

Atkinson, R. C., & Shiffrin, R. M. (1968). Human memory: A proposed system and its control processes. In K. Spence & J. Spence (Eds.), *The psychology of learning and motivation: Advances in research and theory* (Vol. 2). New York, NY: Academic Press.

Auld, F., Maschauer, E. L., Morrison, I., Skene, D. J., & Riha, R. L. (2017). Evidence for the efficacy of melatonin in the treatment of primary adult sleep disorder. *Sleep Medicine Reviews, 34*, 10–22. doi:10.1016/j.smrv.2016.06.005

Avramova, N. (2019, May 2). Do self-help books and apps really help? CNN. Retrieved https://www.cnn.com/2019/05/02/health/self-help-books-usefulness-intl/index.html

Axelrod, S., & Apsche, J. (Eds.).(1983). *The effects of punishment on human behavior.* New York, NY: Academic.

Ayllon, T. (1963). Intensive treatment of psychotic behaviour by stimulus satiation and food reinforcement. *Behaviour Research and Therapy, 1,* 53–61.

Ayllon, T., & Azrin, N. H. (1968). *The token economy.* New York, NY: Appleton-Century-Crofts.

Azar, B. (1996, January). Why is it that practice makes perfect? *APA Monitor,* p. 18.

Azuma, H. (1984). Secondary control as a heterogeneous category. *American Psychologist, 39,* 970–971.

Babbel. (2018). Ten most spoken languages in the world. *Babbel Magazine.* Retrieved from https://www.babbel.com/en/magazine/the-10-most-spoken-languages-in-the-world/

Bach, P., Becker, S., Kleinbohl, D., & Holzl, R. (2011). The thermal grill illusion and what is painful about it. *Neuroscience Letters, 505,* 31–35. doi:10.1016/j.neulet.2011.09.061.

Bachmann, M. F., Jennings, G. T., & Vogel, M. (2019). A vaccine against Alzheimer's disease: Anything left but faith? *Expert Opinion on Biological Therapy, 19*(1), 73–78. doi:10.1080/14712598.2019.1554646

Backlund, E. O., Grandburg, P. O., & Hamberger, B. (1985). Transplantation of adrenal medullary tissue to striatum in Parkinsonianism: First clinical trials. *Journal of Neurosurgery, 62,* 169–173.

Baddeley, A. (1966). Short-term memory for word sequences as a function of acoustic, semantic, and formal similarity. *Quarterly Journal of Experimental Psychology, 18,* 362–365.

Baddeley, A. (1992). Working memory. *Science, 255,* 556–559.

Baddeley, A. (1999). *Essentials of human memory.* Philadelphia: Psychology Press.

Baer, L., et al. (1995). Cingulotomy for intractable obsessive-compulsive disorder. *Archives of General Psychiatry, 52,* 384–392.

Baggs, K., & Spence, S. H. (1990). Effectiveness of booster sessions in the maintenance and enhancement of treatment gains following assertion training. *Journal of Consulting and Clinical Psychology, 58,* 845–854.

Bahrick, H. P. (1984). Semantic memory content in perma-store: Fifty years of memory for Spanish learned in school. *Journal of Experimental Psychology: General, 113,* 1–35.

Bahrick, H. P., & Hall, L. K. (1991). Lifetime maintenance of high school mathematics content. *Journal of Experimental Psychology: General, 120,* 20–33.

Bahrick, H. P., Bahrick, P. O., & Wittlinger, R. P. (1975). Fifty years of memory for names and faces: A cross-sectional approach. *Journal of Experimental Psychology: General, 104,* 54–75.

Bailes, J. E., Lovell, M. R., & Maroon, J. C. (1998). *Sports-related concussion.* St. Louis: Quality Medical Publishing.

Bailine, S. H., et al. (2000). Comparison of bifrontal and bitemporal ECT for major depression. *American Journal of Psychiatry, 157,* 121–123.

Baillargeon, R. (1986). Representing the existence and the location of hidden objects: Object permanence in 6- and 8-month-old infants. *Cognition, 23,* 21–41.

Baillargeon, R. (1994). How do infants learn about the physical world? *Current Directions in Psychological Science, 5,* 133–140.

Baillargeon, R. H., Zoccolillo, M., Keenan, K., Côté, S., Pérusse, D., Wu, H.-X., . . . Tremblay, R. E. (2007). Gender differences in physical aggression: A prospective population-based survey of children before and after 2 years of age. *Developmental Psychology, 43*(1), 13–26. doi:10.1037/0012-1649.43.1.13

Baioui, A., Ambach, W., Walter, B., & Vaitl, D. (2012). Psychophysiology of false memories in a Deese-Roediger-McDermott paradigm with visual scenes. *PLOS ONE, 7*(1), e30416. doi:10.1371/journal.pone.0030416

Baker, E. L. (1985). Psychoanalysis and psychoanalytic therapy. In S. J. Lynn & J. P. Garske (Eds.), *Contemporary psychotherapies: Models and methods.* Columbus, OH: Merrill.

Baldwin, M. W., & Sinclair, L. (1996). Self-esteem and "if-then" contingencies of interpersonal acceptance. *Journal of Personality and Social Psychology, 71,* 1130–1141.

Ball, H. A., Arseneault, L., Taylor, A., Maughan, B., Caspi, A., & Moffitt, T. E. (2008). Genetic and environmental influences on victims, bullies and bully-victims in childhood. *Journal of Child Psychology and Psychiatry, 49*(1), 104–112. doi:10.1111/j.1469-7610.2007.01821.x

Baltes, P. B., & Lindenberger, U. (1997). Emergence of a powerful connection between sensory and cognitive functions across the adult life span: A new window to the study of cognitive aging? *Psychology and Aging, 12,* 12–21.

Baltes, P. B., Staudinger, U. M., & Lindenberger, U. (1999). Lifespan psychology: Theory and application to intellectual functioning. *Annual Review of Psychology, 50,* 471–507.

Bandura, A. (1977). *Social learning theory.* Englewood Cliffs, NJ: Prentice-Hall.

Bandura, A. (1982). The psychology of chance encounters and life paths. *American Psychologist, 37,* 747–755.

Bandura, A. (1986). *Social foundations of thought and action: A social cognitive theory.* Englewood Cliffs, NJ: Prentice-Hall.

Bandura, A. (1997). *Self-efficacy: The exercise of control.* New York: Freeman.

Bandura, A. (1999). A sociocognitive analysis of substance abuse: An agentic perspective. *Psychological Science, 10,* 214–218.

Bandura, A. (2001). Social cognitive theory: An agentic perspective. *Annual Review of Psychology, 52,* 1–26.

Bandura, A. (2011). On the functional properties of perceived self-efficacy revisited. *Journal of Management, 38*(1), 9–44. doi:10.1177/0149206311410606

Bandura, A. (2016). The power of observational learning through social modeling. In R. J. Sternberg, S. T. Fiske, D. J. Foss, R. J. Sternberg, S. T. Fiske, & D. J. Foss (Eds.), *Scientists making a difference: One hundred eminent behavioral and brain scientists talk about their most important contributions* (pp. 235–239). New York, NY: Cambridge University Press.

Bandura, A., Blanchard, E. B., & Ritter, B. (1969). Relative efficacy of desensitization and modeling approaches for inducing behavioral, affective, and attitudinal changes. *Journal of Personality and Social Psychology, 13*, 173–199.

Bandura, A., Ross, D., & Ross, S. A. (1961). Transmission of aggression through imitation of aggressive models. *Journal of Abnormal and Social Psychology, 63*, 575–582.

Banks, M. S., & Salapatek, P. (1983). Infant visual perception. In M. M. Haith & J. J. Campos (Eds.), *Handbook of child psychology: Vol. 2. Infancy and developmental psychobiology* (4th ed., pp. 435–571). New York, NY: Wiley.

Banse, R., Seise, J., & Zerbes, N. (2001). Implicit attitudes towards homosexuality: Reliability, validity, and controllability of the IAT. *Zeitschrift für Experimentelle Psychologie, 48*, 145–160.

Bar, M., & Biederman, I. (1998). Subliminal visual priming. *Psychological Science, 9*, 464–469.

Barbosa, L. S., Vlassova, A., & Kouider, S. (2017). Prior expectations modulate unconscious evidence accumulation. *Consciousness and Cognition, 51*, 236–242. doi:10.1016/j.concog.2017.04.001

Barbosa, M., Guirro, E. C., & Nunes, F. R. (2013). Evaluation of sensitivity, motor and pain thresholds across the menstrual cycle through medium-frequency transcutaneous electrical nerve stimulation. *Clinics (Sao Paulo, Brazil), 68*(7), 901–908. doi:10.6061/clinics/2013(07)03

Barclay, P. (2010). Altruism as a courtship display: Some effects of third-party generosity on audience perceptions. *British Journal of Psychology, 101*(1), 123–135. doi:10.1348/000712609x435733

Bardeen, J. R., Stevens, E. N., Clark, C. B., Lahti, A. C., & Cropsey, K. L. (2015). Cognitive risk profiles for anxiety disorders in a high-risk population. *Psychiatry Research, 229* (1–2), 572–576. doi:10.1016/j.psychres.2015.05.020

Barfield, R. C., & Kane, J. R. (2009). Balancing disclosure of diagnosis and assent for research in children with HIV. *Journal of the American Medical Association, 300*, 576–578. doi:10.1001/jama.300.5.576

Bargh, J. A., McKenna, K. Y. A., & Fitzsimons, G. M. (2002). Can you see the real me? Activation and expression of the "true self" on the Internet. *Journal of Social Issues, 58*, 33–48.

Barker, S. L., Funk, S. C., & Houston, B. K. (1988). Psychological treatment versus nonspecific factors: A meta-analysis of conditions that engender comparable expectations for improvement. *Clinical Psychology Review, 8*, 579–594.

Barlow, D. H. (Ed.).(2001). *Anxiety and its disorders: The nature and treatment of anxiety and panic* (2nd ed.). New York, NY: Guilford.

Barlow, D. H. (1988). *Anxiety and its disorders*. New York, NY: Guilford.

Barnett, J. H., & Smoller, J. W. (2009). The genetics of bipolar disorder. *Neuroscience, 164*(1), 331–343.

Barnett, S. M., & Ceci, S. J. (2002). When and where do we apply what we learn? A taxonomy for far transfer. *Psychological Bulletin, 128*, 612–637.

Barnhill, J. W. (Ed.).(2014). *DSM-5 clinical cases*. Arlington, VA: American Psychiatric Publishing.

Barnier, A. J., & McConkey, K. M. (1998). Posthypnotic responding away from the hypnotic setting. *Psychological Science, 9*, 256–262.

Barrick, M. R., & Mount, M. K. (1991). The Big Five personality dimensions and job performance: A meta-analysis. *Personnel Psychology, 44*(1), 1–26. doi:10.1111/j.1744-6570.1991.tb00688.x

Barrick, M. R., Dustin, S. L., Giluk, T. L., Stewart, G. L., Shaffer, J. A., & Swider, B. W. (2012). Candidate characteristics driving initial impressions during rapport building: Implications for employment interview validity. *Journal of Occupational and Organizational Psychology, 85*, 330–352. doi:10.1111/j.2044-8325.2011.02036.x

Barron, G., & Yechiam, E. (2002). Private e-mail requests and the diffusion of responsibility. *Computers in Human Behavior, 18*(5), 507–520. doi:10.1016/s0747-5632(02)00007-9

Bartholomew, R. E., & Wessely, S. (2002). Protean nature of mass sociogenic illness: From possessed nuns to clinical and biological terrorism fears. *British Journal of Psychiatry, 180*, 300–306.

Bartholow, B. D., Anderson, C. A., Carnagey, N. L., & Benjamin, A. J. (2005). Interactive effects of life experience and situational cues on aggression: The weapons priming effect in hunters and nonhunters. *Journal of Experimental Social Psychology, 41*(1), 48–60. doi:10.1016/j.jesp.2004.05.005

Bartholow, B. D., Dickter, C. L., & Sestir, M. A. (2006). Stereotype activation and control of race bias: Cognitive control of inhibition and its impairment by alcohol. *Journal of Personality and Social Psychology, 90*(2), 272–287. doi:10.1037/0022-3514.90.2.272

Barthrop, R. W., Lazarus, L., Luckhurst, E., Kiloh, L. G., & Penny, R. (1977). Depressed lymphocyte function after bereavement. *Lancet, 1*, 834–839.

Bartlett, E. L. (2013). The organization and physiology of the auditory thalamus and its role in processing acoustic features important for speech perception. *Brain and Language, 126*(1), 29–48. doi:10.1016/j.bandl.2013.03.003

Bartley, E. J., & Fillingim, R. B. (2013). Sex differences in pain: A brief review of clinical and experimental findings. *British Journal of Anaesthesia, 111*(1), 52–58. doi:10.1093/bja/aet127

Barton, J. (1994). Choosing to work at night: A moderating influence on individual tolerance to shift work. *Journal of Applied Psychology, 79*, 449–454.

Bartoshuk, L. M., & Beauchamp, G. K. (1994). Chemical senses. *Annual Review of Psychology, 45*, 419–449.

Bashford, L., Rosenthal, I., Kellis, S., Pejsa, K., Kramer, D., Lee, B., . . . Andersen, R. A. (2021). The neurophysiological representation of imagined somatosensory percepts in human cortex. *Journal of Neuroscience, 41*(10), 2177–2185. doi:10.1523/JNEUROSCI.2460-20.2021

Bass, E., & Davis, L. (1988). *The courage to heal*. New York, NY: Harper & Row.

Bassetti C. L., & Bargiotas P. (2018). REM sleep behavior disorder. *Frontiers of Neurology and Neuroscience, 41*, 104-116. doi:10.1159/000478914

Batson, C. D. (1998). Altruism and prosocial behavior. In D. T. Gilbert, S. T. Fiske, & G. Lindzey (Eds.), *Handbook of social psychology* (4th ed., Vol. 2, pp. 282–316). New York, NY: McGraw-Hill.

Bauer, D. J., Goldfield, B. A., & Reznick, J. S. (2002). Alternative approaches to analyzing individual differences in the rate of early vocabulary development. *Applied Psycholinguistics, 23*, 313–335. doi:10.1017/S0142716402003016

Bauer, P. J., & Larkina, M. (2014). The onset of childhood amnesia in childhood: A prospective investigation of the course and determinants of forgetting of early-life events. *Memory (Hove, England), 22*(8), 907–924. doi:10.1080/09658211.2013.854806

Baumeister, R. F., Dale, K., & Sommer, K. L. (1998). Freudian defense mechanisms and empirical findings in modern social psychology: Reaction formation, projection, displacement, undoing, isolation, sublimation, and denial. *Journal of Personality, 66*, 1081–1124.

Baumrind, D., Larzelere, R. E., & Cowan, P. A. (2002). Ordinary physical punishment: Is it harmful? Comment on Gershoff (2002). *Psychological Bulletin, 128*, 580–589.

BBC News. (2018, April 17). Alex Skeel: Domestic abuse survivor was "days from death." Retrieved from https://www.bbc.com/news/uk-england-beds-bucks-herts-43799850

Beames, J. R., Schofield, T. P., & Denson, T. F. (2018). A meta-analysis of improving self-control with practice. In D. de_Ridder, M. Adriaanse, K. Fujita, D. de_Ridder, M. Adriaanse, & K. Fujita (Eds.), *The Routledge international handbook of self-control in health and well-being* (pp. 405–417). New York, NY: Routledge/Taylor & Francis.

Bechara, A., Tranel, D., Damasio, R., Adolphs, C. R., & Damasio, A. (1995). Double dissociation of conditioning and declarative knowledge relative to the amygdala and hippocampus in humans. *Science, 269*, 1115–1118.

Beck, A. T. (1967). *Cognitive therapy and the emotional disorders.* New York, NY: International Universities Press.

Beck, A. T. (1991). Cognitive therapy: A 30-year retrospective. *American Psychologist, 46*, 368–375.

Beck, A. T. (1999). *Prisoners of hate: The cognitive basis of anger, hostility, and violence.* New York, NY: Harper-Collins.

Beck, A. T., Brown, G., Berchick, R. J., Stewart, B. L., & Steer, R. A. (1990). Relationship between hopelessness and ultimate suicide: A replication with psychiatric outpatients. *American Journal of Psychiatry, 147*, 190–195.

Beck, A. T., Rector, N. A., Stolar, N., & Grant, P. (2011). *Schizophrenia: Cognitive theory, research, and therapy.* New York, NY: Guilford.

Beck, A. T., Rush, A. J., Shaw, B. F., & Emery, G. (1979). *Cognitive therapy of depression.* New York, NY: Guilford.

Beck, J. G., Freeman, J. B., Shipherd, J. C., Hamblen, J. L., & Lackner, J. M. (2001). Specificity of Stroop interference in patients with pain and PTSD. *Journal of Abnormal Psychology, 110*, 536–543.

Beck, J. G., Ohtake, P. J., & Shipherd, J. C. (1999). Exaggerated anxiety is not unique to CO2 in panic disorder: A comparison of hypercapnic and hypoxic challenges. *Journal of Abnormal Psychology, 108*, 473–482.

Becker, D., & Birkelbach, K. (2018). Social mobility and subjective well-being revisited: The importance of individual locus of control. *Research in Social Stratification and Mobility, 54*, 1–20. doi:10.1016/j.rssm.2018.01.001

Beckstead, D. J., Lambert, M. J., DuBose, A. P., &Linehan, M. (2015). Dialectical behavior therapy with American Indian/Alaska Native adolescents diagnosed with substance use disorders: Combining an evidence based treatment with cultural, traditional, and spiritual beliefs. *Addictive Behaviors, 51*, 84–87. doi:10.1016/j.addbeh.2015.07.018

Beekman, C., Neiderhiser, J. M., Buss, K. A., Loken, E., Moore, G. A., Leve, L. D., . . . Reiss, D. (2015). The development of early profiles of temperament: Characterization, continuity, and etiology. *Child Development, 86*(6), 1794–1811. doi:10.1111/cdev.12417

Begley, S., & Ramo, J. C. (1993, November 1). Not just a pretty face. *Newsweek, pp.* 63–67.

Beidel, D. C., & Turner, S. M. (1998). *Shy children, phobic adults: Nature and treatment of social phobia.* Washington, DC: American Psychological Association.

Beilin, H. (1992). Piaget's enduring contribution to developmental psychology. *Developmental Psychology, 28*, 191–204.

Beilock, S. L., Carr, T. H., MacMahon, C., & Starkes, J. L. (2002). When paying attention becomes counterproductive: Impact of divided versus skill-focused attention on novice and experienced performance of sensorimotor skills. *Journal of Experimental Psychology: Applied, 8*, 6–16.

Beitman, B. D., Goldfried, M. R., & Norcross, J. C. (1989). The movement toward integrating the psychotherapies: An overview. *American Journal of Psychiatry, 146*, 138–147.

Bekoff, M., Allen, C., & Burghardt, G. M. (Eds.).(2002). *The cognitive animal: Empirical and theoretical perspectives on animal cognition.* Cambridge, MA: MIT Press.

Bellack, A. S., & Hersen, M. (Eds.).(1985). *Dictionary of behavior therapy techniques.* New York, NY: Pergamon.

Belleville, S., Caza, N., & Peretz, I. (2003). A neuropsychological argument for a processing view of memory. *Journal of Memory and Language, 48*, 686–703.

Belli, B. (2020, October 27). Racial disparity in police shootings unchanged over 5 years. *Yale News* [online], Retrieved from https://news.yale.edu/2020/10/27/racial-disparity-police-shootings-unchanged-over-5-years

Belli, R. F., Lindsay, D. S., Gales, M. S., & McCarthy, T. T. (1994). Memory impairment and source misattribution in postevent misinformation experiments with short retention intervals. *Memory & Cognition, 22*, 40–54.

Bellisle, F., Dalix, A. M., & de Castro, J. M. (1999). Eating patterns in French subjects studied by the "weekly food diary" method. *Appetite, 32*, 46–52.

Bem, S. (1974). Measurement of psychological androgyny. *Journal of Consulting and Clinical Psychology, 42*(2), 155–162.

Benazon, N. R., & Coyne, J. C. (2000). Living with a depressed spouse. *Journal of Family Psychology, 14*, 71–79.

Benbow, C. P. (1988). Sex differences in mathematical reasoning ability in intellectually talented preadolescents: Their nature, effects, and possible causes. *Behavioral and Brain Sciences, 11*, 169–232.

Benca, R. M., Obermeyer, W. H., Thisted, R. A., & Gillin, J. C. (1992). Sleep and psychiatric disorders: A metaanalysis. *Archives of General Psychiatry, 49*, 651–658.

Bender, P. K., Plante, C., & Gentile, D. A. (2018). The effects of violent media content on aggression. *Current Opinion in Psychology, 19*, 104–108. doi:10.1016/j.copsyc.2017.04.003

Benjamin, A. J., Kepes, S., & Bushman, B. J. (2017). Effects of weapons on aggressive thoughts, angry feelings, hostile appraisals, and aggressive behavior: A meta-analytic review of the weapons effect literature. *Personality and Social Psychology Review, 22*(4), 347–377. doi:10.1177/1088868317725419

Benjamin, L. J., Whitaker, J. L., Ramsey, R. M., & Zeve, D. R. (2007). John B. Watson's alleged sex research: An appraisal of the evidence. *American Psychologist, 62*(2), 131–139. doi:10.1037/0003-066X.62.2.131

Benjamin, L. L., Jr. (1988). A history of teaching machines. *American Psychologist, 43*, 703–712.

Benjamin, L. T., Jr., Durkin, M., Link, M., Vestal, M., & Acord, J. (1992). Wundt's American doctoral students. *American Psychologist, 47*, 123–131.

Bennett, M. (2014). Confronting cognitive anchoring effect and blind spot biases in federal sentencing: A modest solution for reforming a fundamental flaw. *Journal of Criminal Law & Criminology, 104*(3), 489–534.

Bennett, R. J. (1998). Taking the sting out of the whip: Reactions to consistent punishment for unethical behavior. *Journal of Experimental Psychology: Applied, 4*, 248–262.

Benoit, D. (2004). Infant-parent attachment: Definition, types, antecedents, measurement and outcome. *Paediatrics & Child Health, 9*(8), 541–545. doi:10.1093/pch/9.8.541

Benson, H. (1975). *The relaxation response.* New York, NY: Morrow.

Benson, H. (1993). The relaxation response. In D. Goleman & J. Gurin (Eds.), *Mind body medicine: How to use your mind for better health* (pp. 233–257). Yonkers, NY: Consumer Reports Books.

Benton, T., Golden, S., Chamberlain, T., George, N., & Walker, F. (2010). *Tellus4 national report.* Slough, UK: National Foundation for Educational Research, Department for Children, Schools and Families.

Berger, A. A. (1995). Psychoanalytic theory and cultural criticism. In *Foundations of popular culture, Vol. 4: Cultural criticism: A primer of key concepts* (pp. 103–134). Thousand Oaks, CA: Sage.

Berghuis, J. P., & Stanton, A. L. (2002). Adjustment to a dyadic stressor: A longitudinal study of coping and depressive symptoms in infertile couples over an insemination attempt. *Journal of Consulting and Clinical Psychology, 70*, 433–138.

Bergin, A. E., & Lambert, M. J. (1978). The evaluation of therapeutic outcomes. In S. L. Garfield & A. E. Bergin (Eds.), *Handbook of psychotherapy and behavior change* (2nd ed., pp. 139–189). New York, NY: Wiley.

Bergman, E. T., & Roediger, H. L. (1999). Can Bartlett's repeated reproduction experiments be replicated? *Memory & Cognition, 27*, 937–947.

Bergner, R. M., & Bunford, N. (2017). Mental disorder is a disability concept, not a behavioral one. *Philosophy, Psychiatry, & Psychology, 24*(1), 25–40.

Berk, M. S., & Andersen, S. M. (2000). The impact of past relationships on interpersonal behavior: Behavioral confirmation in the social-cognitive process of transference. *Journal of Personality and Social Psychology, 79*, 546–562.

Berkely, K. J. (1997). Sex differences in pain. *Behavioral and Brain Sciences, 20*, 371–380.

Berkman, L., & Syme, S. L. (1979). Social networks, host resistance, and mortality: A nine-year follow-up study of Alameda County residents. *American Journal of Epidemiology, 109*, 186–204.

Berkowitz, B., & Alcantara, C. (2020, May 27). The terrible numbers that grow with each mass shooting. *Washington Post.* Retrieved from https://www.washingtonpost.com/graphics/2018/national/mass-shootings-in-america/

Berkowitz, L. (1993). *Aggression: Its causes, consequences, and control.* New York, NY: McGraw-Hill.

Berkowitz, L. (1983). Aversively stimulated aggression: Some parallels and differences in research with animals and humans. *American Psychologist, 38*, 1135–1144.

Berkowitz, L. (1989). Frustration-aggression hypothesis: Examination and reformulation. *Psychological Bulletin, 106*, 59–73.

Berkowitz, L., & LePage, A. (1967). Weapons as aggression-eliciting stimuli. *Journal of Personality and Social Psychology, 7*, 202–207.

Bernard, M. E., & DiGiuseppe, R. (Eds.).(1989). *Inside rational-emotive therapy.* New York, NY: Academic Press.

Berndt, T. J. (1996). Transitions in friendship and friends' influence. In J. A. Graber, J. Brooks-Gunn, & A. C. Petersen (Eds.), *Transitions through adolescence: Interpersonal domains and context* (pp. 57–84). Mahwah, NJ: Erlbaum.

Berndt, X. J. (1979). Developmental changes in conformity to peers and parents. *Developmental Psychology, 15*, 606–616.

Bernstein, I. L. (1985). Learned food aversions in the progression of cancer and its treatment. *Annals of the New York Academy of Sciences, 443*, 365–380.

Bernstein, I. L., & Borson, S. (1986). Learned food aversion: A component of anorexia syndromes. *Psychological Review, 93*, 462–472.

Berry, J. W., Segall, M.H., &Poortinga, Y. H. (Eds.), (2002). *Cross-cultural psychology: Research and applications* (2nd ed.). New York, NY: Cambridge University Press.

Berscheid, E., & Reis, H. T. (1998). Attraction and close relationships. In D. T. Gilbert, S. T. Fiske, & G. Lindzey (Eds.), *Handbook of social psychology* (4th ed.). New York, NY: McGraw-Hill.

Bershad, A. K., Mayo, L. M., Van Hedger, K., McGlone, F., Walker, S. C., & de it, H. (2019). Effects of MDMA on attention to positive social cues and pleasantness of affective touch. *Neuropsychopharmacology, 44*(10), 1698–1705. doi:10.1038/s41386-019-0402-z

Bertills, K., Granlund, M., & Augustine, L. (2021). Student self-efficacy and aptitude to participate in relation to perceived functioning and achievement in students in secondary school with and without disabilities. *Frontiers in Psychology, 6*(2), 607329. doi:10.3389/fpsyg.2021.607329

Best, P. J., White, A. M., & Minai, A. (2001). Spatial processing in the brain: The activity of hippocampal place cells. *Annual Review of Neuroscience, 24*, 459–486.

Bettencourt, B. A., & Miller, N. (1996). Gender differences in aggression as a function of provocation: A meta-analysis. *Psychological Bulletin, 119*, 422–447.

Bhaskar S. B. (2017). Concealing research outcomes: Missing data, negative results and missed publications. *Indian Journal of Anaesthesia, 61*(6), 453–455. 10.4103/ija.IJA_361_17

Bhatt, R. S., & Quinn, P. C. (2011). How does learning impact development in infancy? The case of perceptual organization. *Infancy, 16*, 2–38. doi:10.1111/j.1532-7078.2010.00048.x

Biddlestone, M., Green, R., & Douglas, K. (2020). Cultural orientation, powerlessness, belief in conspiracy theories, and intentions to reduce the spread of COVID-19. *British Journal of Social Psychology*. doi:10.1111/bjso.12397

Biederman, I. (1987). Recognition-by-components: A theory of human image understanding. *Psychological Review, 94*, 115–147.

Binet, A., & Simon, T. (1905). Methodes nouvelles pour le diagnostic du niveau intellectuel des anormaux. *L'Annee Psychologique, 11*, 191–244.

Binggeli, S., Krings, F., & Sczesny, S. (2014). Perceived competition explains regional differences in the stereotype content of immigrant groups. *Social Psychology, 45*(1), 62–70. doi:10.1027/1864-9335/a000160

Birnbaum, G. E. (2018). The fragile spell of desire: A functional perspective on changes in sexual desire across relationship development. *Personality and Social Psychology Review, 22*(2), 101–127.

Birren, J. E., & Fisher, L. M. (1995). Aging and speed of behavior: Possible consequences for psychological functioning. *Annual Review of Psychology, 46*, 329–353.

Bisson, J. I., Cosgrove, S., Lewis, C., & Robert, N. P. (2015). Post-traumatic stress disorder. *BMJ, 351*, h6161. doi:10.1136/bmj.h6161

Bisson, J., Ehlers, A., Matthews, R., Pilling, S., Richards, D., & Turner, S. (2007). Psychological treatments for chronic post-traumatic stress disorder: Systematic review and meta-analysis. *British Journal of Psychiatry, 190*, 97–104.

Bjork, D. W. (1997). *B. E Skinner: A life.* (Reprint edition). New York, NY: Basic Books.

Bjork, E. L., &Bjork, R. A. (Eds.). (1996). *Memory.* San Diego: Academic Press.

Black, D. W., Gunter, T., Loveless, P., Allen, J., & Sieleni, B. (2010). Antisocial personality disorder in incarcerated offenders: Psychiatric comorbidity and quality of life. *Annals of Clinical Psychiatry, 22*(2), 113–120.

Blair, I. V., Ma, J. E., & Lenton, A. P. (2001). Imagining stereotypes away: The moderation of implicit stereotypes through mental imagery. *Journal of Personality and Social Psychology, 81*, 828–841.

Blair, R. J. R., Jones, L., Clark, F., & Smith, M. (1997). The psychopathic individual: A lack of responsiveness to distress cues? *Psychophysiology, 34*, 192–198.

Blakeslee, S. (1993, June 1). Scanner pinpoints sites of thoughts as people see or speak. *The New York Times*, pp. C1, C3.

Blakeslee, S. (2000, January 4). A decade of discovery yields a shock about the brain. *New York Times*, pp. D1, D4.

Blanchard, E. B., et al. (1982). Biofeedback and relaxation training with three kinds of headache: Treatment effects and their prediction. *Journal of Consulting and Clinical Psychology, 50*, 562–575.

Blascovich, J., Spencer, S. J., Quinn, D., & Steele, C. (2001). African Americans and high blood pressure: The role of stereotype threat. *Psychological Science, 12*, 225–229.

Blass, E. M., & Camp, C. A. (2001). The ontogeny of face recognition: Eye contact and sweet taste induce face preference in 9- and 12-week-old human infants. *Developmental Psychology, 37*, 762–774.

Blass, T. (Ed.).(2000). *Obedience to authority: Current perspectives on the Milgram paradigm.* Mahwah, NJ: Erlbaum.

Bleidorn, W., Arslan, R. C., Denissen, J. J. A., Rentfrow, P. J., Gebauer, J. E., Potter, J., & Gosling, S. D. (2016). Age and gender differences in self-esteem?A cross-cultural window. *Journal of Personality and Social Psychology, 111*(3), 396–410. doi:10.1037/pspp0000078

Bleuler, E. (1911). *Dementia praecox oder gruppe der schizophrenien.* Leipzig, Germany: F. Deuticke.

Bloom, A. (1981). *The linguistic shaping of thought.* Hillsdale, NJ: Erlbaum.

Bloom, S. G. (2005, September). Lesson of a lifetime. *Smithsonian*. Retrieved from https://www.smithsonianmag.com/science-nature/lesson-of-a-lifetime-72754306/

Blow, F. C., Zeber, J. E., McCarthy, J. F., Valenstein, M., Gillon, L., & Bingham, C. R. (2004). Ethnicity and diagnostic patterns in veterans with psychoses. *Social Psychiatry and Psychiatric Epidemiology, 30*(10), 841–851.

Blue Cross Blue Shield Association. (2018). Blue Cross Blue Shield Association study shows surge in major depression diagnoses. Retrieved fromhttps://www.bcbs.com/press-releases/blue-cross-blue-shield-association-study-shows-surge-major-depression-diagnoses%09

Blue, S. N., Kazama, A. M., & Bachevalier, J. (2013). Development of memory for spatial locations and object/place associations in infant rhesus macaques with and without neonatal hippocampal lesions. *Journal of the International Neuropsychological Society, 19*(10), 1053–1064. doi:10.1017/s1355617713000799

Blumenstein, B., & Hung, E. T. (2016). Biofeedback in sport. In R. J. Schinke, K. R. McGannon, B. Smith, R. J. Schinke, K. R. McGannon, & B. Smith (Eds.), *The Routledge international handbook of sport psychology* (pp. 429–438). New York, NY: Routledge/Taylor & Francis.

Bocage-Barthélémy, Y., Selimbegović,L., & Chatard, A. (2018). Evidence that social comparison with the thin ideal affects implicit self-evaluation. *International Review of Social Psychology, 31*(1). doi:10.5334/irsp.114

Bockting, C. L. H., Klein, N. S., Elgersma, H. J., Rijsbergen, G. D. V., Slofstra, C., Ormel, J., . . . Burger, H. (2018). Effectiveness of preventive cognitive therapy while tapering antidepressants versus maintenance antidepressant treatment versus their combination in prevention of depressive relapse or recurrence (DRD study): A three-group, multicentre, randomised controlled trial. *Lancet Psychiatry, 5*(5), 401–410. doi:10.1016/s2215-0366(18)30100-7

Bodenhausen, G. V. (1990). Stereotypes as judgmental heuristics: Evidence of circadian variations in discrimination. *Psychological Science, 1*, 319–322.

Bohanek, J. G., & Fivush, R. (2010). Personal narratives, well-being, and gender in adolescence. *Cognitive Development, 25*, 368–379.

Bolles, R. C. (1970). Species-specific defense reactions and avoidance learning. *Psychological Review, 77,* 32–48.

Bollu, P. C., Goyal, M. K., Thakkar, M. M., & Sahota, P. (2018). Sleep medicine parasomnias. *Missouri Medicine, 115*(2), 169–175.

Bond, R., & Smith, P. B. (1996). Culture and conformity: A meta-analysis of studies using Asch's (1952b, 1956) line judgment task. *Psychological Bulletin, 119,* 111–137.

Bondolfi, G., Jermann, F., Linden, M. V. D., Gex-Fabry, M., Bizzini, L., Rouget, B. W., . . . Bertschy, G. (2010). Depression relapse prophylaxis with Mindfulness-Based Cognitive Therapy: Replication and extension in the Swiss health care system. *Journal of Affective Disorders, 122*(3), 224–231. doi:10.1016/j.jad.2009.07.007

Bonivento, C., Urquijo, M. F., Borgwardt, S., Meisenzahl, E., Rosen, M., Salokangas, R., . . . Brambilla, P. (2018). Diagnostic and neurocognitive correlates of schizotypy within and across the pronia study groups. *Schizophrenia Bulletin, 44*(Suppl. 1), S144.

Boon, S., & Draijer, N. (1993). Multiple personality disorder in the Netherlands: A clinical investigation of 71 patients. *American Journal of Psychiatry, 150,* 489–494.

Boring, E. G. (1923). Intelligence as the tests test it. *New Republic, 35,* 35–37.

Bornstein, M. H. (1989). Information processing (habituation) in infancy and stability in cognitive development. *Human Development, 32,* 129–136.

Bornstein, R. F. (1992). Subliminal mere exposure effects. In R. F. Bornstein & T. S. Pittman (Eds.), *Perception without awareness: Cognitive, clinical, and social perspectives* (pp. 191–210). New York, NY: Guilford Press.

Bornstein, R. F., & Pittman, T. S. (Eds.).(1992). *Perception without awareness: Cognitive, clinical, and social perspectives.* New York, NY: Guilford Press.

Borum, R., & Fulero, S. M. (1999). Empirical research on the insanity defense and attempted reforms: Evidence toward informed policy. *Law and Human Behavior, 23,* 117–135.

Botella, C., Fernández-Álvarez, J., Guillén, V., García-Palacios, A., & Baños, R. (2017). Recent progress in virtual reality exposure therapy for phobias: A systematic review. *Current Psychiatry Reports, 19*(7). doi:10.1007/s11920-017-0788-4

Both, S., Brauer, M., & Laan, E. (2011). Classical conditioning of sexual response in women: A replication study. *Journal of Sexual Medicine, 8*(11), 3116–3131. doi:10.1111/j.1743-6109.2011

Bouhassira, D., Kern, D., Rouaud, J., Pelle-Lancien, E., & Morain, F. (2005). Investigation of the paradoxical painful sensation ("illusion of pain") produced by a thermal grill. *Pain, 114,* 160–167. doi:10.1016/j.pain.2004.12.014

Bousfield, W. A. (1953). The occurrence of clustering in the recall of randomly arranged associates. *Journal of General Psychology, 49,* 229–240.

Bouton, M. E., Mineka, S., & Barlow, D. H. (2001). A modern learning theory perspective on the etiology of panic disorder. *Psychological Review, 108,* 4–32.

Bovbjerg, D. H., Redd, W. H., Holland, J. C., Lesko, L. M., Niedzwiecki, D., Rubin, S. C., & Hakes, T. B. (1990). Anticipatory immune suppression in women receiving cyclic chemotherapy for ovarian cancer. *Journal of Consulting and Clinical Psychology, 58,* 153–157.

Bovbjerg, D. H., Redd, W. H., Jacobsen, P. B., Manne, S. L., Taylor, K. L., Surbone, A., et al. (1992). An experimental analysis of classically conditioned nausea during cancer chemotherapy. *Psychosomatic Medicine, 54,* 623–637.

Bowdle, B. F., & Gentner, D. (2005). The career of metaphor. *Psychological Review, 112,* 193–216.

Bower, G. H. (1970). Organizational factors in memory. *Cognitive Memory, 1,* 18–46.

Bower, G. H. (1981). Mood and memory. *American Psychologist, 36,* 129–148.

Bower, G. H., & Winzenz, D. (1970). Comparison of associative learning strategies. *Psychonomic Science, 20,* 119–120.

Bower, T. G. R. (1982). *Development in infancy* (2nd ed.). San Francisco, CA: Freeman.

Bowers, K. S. (1992). Imagination and dissociation in hypnotic responding. *International Journal of Clinical and Experimental Hypnosis, 40,* 253–275.

Bowers, K. S., & Farvolden, R (1996). Revisiting a century-old Freudian slip: From suggestion disavowed to the truth repressed. *Psychological Bulletin, 119,* 355–380.

Bowers, K. S., & Woody, E. Z. (1996). Hypnotic amnesia and the paradox of intentional forgetting. *Journal of Abnormal Psychology, 105,* 381–390.

Bowlby, J. (1969). *Attachment and loss: Vol. 1. Attachment.* London, UK: Hogarth.

Bowlby, J. (1988). *A secure base.* New York, NY: Basic Books.

Braaksma, M. A. H., Rijlaarsdam, G., & van den Bergh, H. (2002). Observational learning and the effects of model-observer similarity. *Journal of Educational Psychology, 94,* 405–415.

Brabender, V. (2002). *Introduction to group therapy.* New York, NY: Wiley.

Bradbury, J. C. (2010). *How do baseball players age? Investigating the age-27 theory.* Retrieved from https://www.baseballprospectus.com/news/article/9933/how-do-baseball-players-age-investigating-the-age-27-theory/

Bradley, R., Doolittle, J., & Bartolotta, R. (2008). Building on the data and adding to the discussion: The experiences and outcomes of students with emotional disturbance. *Journal of Behavioral Education, 17*(1), 4–23.

Bradshaw, J. L., & Nettleton, N. C. (1981). The nature of hemispheric specialization in man. *Behavioral and Brain Sciences, 4,* 51–91.

Brasted, P. J., Watts, C., Torres, E., Robbins, T., & Dunnett, S. B. (2000). Behavioral recovery after transplantation into a rat model of Huntington's disease dependence on anatomical connectivity and extensive postoperative training. *Behavioral Neuroscience, 114,* 431–436.

Braun, A. R., Balkin, T. J., Wesensten, N., Gwadry, F., Carson, R. E., Varga, M., . . . Herscovitch, P. (1998). Dissociated pattern of activity in visual cortices and their projections during human rapid eye movement sleep. *Science, 279,* 91–95. doi:10.1126/science.279.5347.91

Braveman, P., & Gottlieb, L. (2014). The social determinants of health: It's time to consider the causes of the causes. *Public Health Reports, 129*(1, Suppl. 2), 19–31. doi:10.1177/00333549141291s206

Braverman, B. (2020). The coronavirus is taking a huge toll on workers' mental health across America. CNBC. Retrieved from https://www.cnbc.com/2020/04/06/coronavirus-is-taking-a-toll-on-workers-mental-health-across-america.html

Breedlove, S. M., & Watson, N. V. (2017). *Behavioral neuroscience* (8th ed.). Oxford, UK: Oxford University Press.

Breedlove, S. M., & Watson, N. V. (2017). *Behavioral neuroscience* (8th ed.). Sunderland, MA: Sinauer Associates.

Breggin, P. (2001). *The anti-depressant fact book: What your doctor won't tell you about Prozac, Zoloft, Paxil, Celexa, and Luvox.* New York, NY: Perseus.

Bregman, A. S. (1990). *Auditory scene analysis.* Cambridge, MA: MIT Press.

Brehm, S. S., Miller, R., Perlman, D., & Campbell, S. M. (2001). *Intimate relationships* (3rd ed.). New York, NY: McGraw-Hill.

Breland, K., & Breland, M. (1961). The misbehavior of organisms. *American Psychologist, 16,* 681–684.

Bremner, J. D., Innis, R. B., White, T., Fujita, M., Silbersweig, D., Goddard, A. W., . . . Charney, D. S. (2000). SPECT [I-123] iomazenil measurement of the benzodiazepine receptor in panic disorder. *Biological Psychiatry, 47,* 96–106.

Bremner, J. G. (2002). The nature of imitation by infants. *Infant Behavior & Development, 25,* 65–67.

Brenner, C. (1982). *The mind in conflict.* New York, NY: International Universities Press.

Breslau, N., & Schultz, L. (2013). Neuroticism and post-traumatic stress disorder: A prospective investigation. *Psychological Medicine, 43*(8), 1697–1702. doi:10.1017/S0033291712002632

Breuer, J., & Freud, S. (1895). Studies on hysteria. In J. Strachey (Ed.), *The standard edition of the complete psychological works of Sigmund Freud.* London: Hogarth Press. (Reprinted in 1955.)

Breuer, J., & Freud, S. (1895). Studies on hysteria. In J. Strachey (Ed.), *The standard edition of the complete psychological works of Sigmund Freud.* London: Hogarth.

Breuer, M. E., McGinnis, M. Y., Lumia, A. R., & Possidente, B. P. (2001). Aggression in male rats receiving anabolic androgenic steroids: Effects of social and environmental provocation. *Hormones and Behavior, 40,* 409–418.

Brewer, M. B., & Brown, R. J. (1998). Intergroup relations. In D. T. Gilbert, S. T. Fiske, & G. Lindzey (Eds.), *Handbook of social psychology* (4th ed., Vol. 2, pp. 554–594). New York, NY: McGraw-Hill.

Brewer, P., & Venaik, S. (2010). GLOBE practices and values: A case of diminishing marginal utility? *Journal of International Business Studies, 41*(8), 1316–1324. doi:10.1057/jibs.2010.23

Brewer, W. F., & Treyens, J. C. (1981). Role of schemata in memory for places. *Cognitive Psychology, 13,* 207–230.

Brewin, C. R., & Andrews, B. (2017). Creating memories for false autobiographical events in childhood: A systematic review. *Applied Cognitive Psychology, 31,* 2–23. doi:10.1002/Acp.3220

Brewin, C. R., Andrews, B., & Valentine, J. D. (2000). Meta-analysis of risk factors for posttraumatic stress disorder in trauma-exposed adults. *Journal of Consulting and Clinical Psychology, 68*(5), 748–766.

Brewin, C., Reynolds, M., & Tata, P. (1999). Autobiographical memory processes and the course of depression. *Journal of Abnormal Psychology, 108,* 511–517.

Bridge, L., Smith, P., & Rimes, K. A. (2019). Sexual orientation differences in the self-esteem of men and women: A systematic review and meta-analysis. *Psychology of Sexual Orientation and Gender Diversity, 6*(4), 433–446. doi:10.1037/sgd0000342

Brito, C. (2018, May 18). "It's America": Video of man's racist tirade at NYC restaurant goes viral. CBS News. Retrieved from https://www.cbsnews.com/news/man-threatens-ice-new-york-city-fresh-kitchen-spanish-emily-serrano/

Brix, N., Ernst, A., Lauridsen, L. L. B., Parner, E., Støvring, H., Olsen, J. . . . Ramlau-Hansen, C. H. (2019). Timing of puberty in boys and girls: A population-based study. *Paediatrics and Perinatal Epidemiology, 33*(1), 70–78. doi:10.1111/ppe.12507

Brocas, I., & Carrillo, J. D. (Eds.).(2003). *The psychology of economic decisions (Vol. 1: Rationality and well-being).* New York, NY: Oxford University Press.

Brockner, J. (1983). Low self-esteem and behavioral plasticity: Some implications. In L. Wheeler & P. Shaver (Eds.), *Review of personality and social psychology* (Vol. 4, pp. 237–271). Beverly Hills, CA: Sage.

Bronchain, J., Raynal, P., & Chabrol, H. (2020). Heterogeneity of adaptive features among psychopathy variants. *Personality Disorders: Theory, Research, and Treatment, 11*(1), 63–68. doi:10.1037/per0000366

Brooks-Gunn, J., & Warren, M. P. (1985). The effects of delayed menarche in different contexts: Dance and non-dance students. *Journal of Youth and Adolescence, 14,* 163–189.

Brooks, N. (2017). Understanding the manifestation of psychopathic personality characteristics across populations [doctoral dissertation]. Retrieved from https://research.bond.edu.au/en/studentTheses/understanding-the-manifestation-of-psychopathic-personality-chara

Brown, A. S. (1991). A review of the tip-of-the-tongue experience. *Psychological Bulletin, 109,* 204–223.

Brown, A. S., & Murphy, D. R. (1989). Cryptomnesia: Delineating inadvertent plagiarism. *Journal of Experimental Psychology: Learning, Memory, and Cognition, 15,* 432–442.

Brown, B. B., Clasen, D. R., & Eicher, S. A. (1986). Perceptions of peer pressure, peer conformity dispositions, and self-reported behavior among adolescents. *Developmental Psychology, 22,* 521–530.

Brown, C. M., & Hagoort, P. (1999). *The neurocognition of language.* New York, NY: Oxford University Press.

Brown, E. L., Deffenbacher, K. A., & Sturgill, W. (1977). Memory for faces and the circumstances of encounter. *Journal of Applied Psychology, 62,* 311–318.

Brown, J. D. (1998). *The self.* New York, NY: McGraw-Hill.

Brown, J. D., & Dutton, K. A. (1995). The thrill of victory, the complexity of defeat: Self-esteem and people's emotional reactions to success and failure. *Journal of Personality and Social Psychology, 68,* 712–722.

Brown, J. W. (2017). Microgenetic theory of perception, memory, and the mental state: A brief review. *Journal of Consciousness Studies, 24* (11–12), 51–70.

Brown, M. Z., Comtois, K. A., & Linhan, M. M. (2002). Reasons for suicide attempts and nonsuicidal self-injury in women with borderline personality disorder. *Journal of Abnormal Psychology, 111*, 198–202.

Brown, R. (1973). *A first language: The early stages.* Cambridge, MA: Harvard University Press.

Brown, R., & Kulik, J. (1977). Flashbulb memories. *Cognition, 5*, 73–99.

Brown, R., & McNeill, D. (1966). The "tip of the tongue" phenomenon. *Journal of Verbal Learning and Verbal Behavior, 5*, 325–337.

Brown, T. A., & Barlow, D. H. (1992). Comorbidity among anxiety disorders: Implications for treatment and DSM-IV. *Journal of Consulting and Clinical Psychology, 60*, 835–844.

Brown, T. A., Campbell, L. A., Lehman, C. L., Grisham, J. R., & Mancill, R. B. (2001). Current and lifetime comorbidity of the DSM-IV anxiety and mood disorders in a large clinical sample. *Journal of Abnormal Psychology, 110*, 585–599.

Brown, T. L., Gore, C. L., & Carr, T. H. (2002). Visual attention and word recognition in Stroop color naming: Is word recognition "automatic?" *Journal of Experimental Psychology: General, 131*, 220–240.

Brown, W. A. (1998, January). The placebo effect. *Scientific American*, pp. 90–95.

Brownley, K. A., Berkman, N. D., Peat, C. M., Lohr, K. N., Cullen, K. E., Bann, C. M., & Bulik, C. M. (2016). Binge-eating disorder in adults: A systematic review and meta-analysis. *Annals of Internal Medicine, 165*(6), 409–420. doi:10.7326/M15-2455

Bruijnzeel, H., Ziylan, F., Stegeman, I., Topsakal, V., & Grolman, W. (2016). A systematic review to define the speech and language benefit of early (<12 months) pediatric cochlear implantation. *Audiology and Neurotology, 21*, 113–126.

Bruner, J. S., & Potter, M. C. (1964). Interference in visual recognition. *Science, 144*, 424–425.

Brunner, D. P., Kijk, D. J., Tobler, L., & Borbely, A. A. (1990). Effect of partial sleep stages and EEG power spectra: Evidence for non-REM and REM sleep homeostasis. *Electroencephalography and Clinical Neurophysiology, 75*, 492–499.

Bryan, J. H., & Test, M. A. (1967). Models and helping: Naturalistic studies in aiding behavior. *Journal of Personality and Social Psychology, 6*, 400–407.

Bryant, R. A., & Harvey, A. G. (2003). Gender differences in the relationship between acute stress disorder and post-traumatic stress disorder following motor vehicle accidents. *Australian & New Zealand Journal of Psychiatry, 37*(2), 226–229. doi:10.1046/j.1440-1614.2003.01130.x

Buck, L. B. (2000). Smell and taste: The chemical senses. In E. R. Kandel, J. H. Schwartz, & T. M. Jessell (Eds.), *Principles of neural science* (4th ed., pp. 625–647). New York, NY: McGraw-Hill.

Bullis, J. R., & Sauer-Zavala, S. (2018). The unified protocol for insomnia disorder. In D. H. Barlow, T. J. Farchione, D. H. Barlow, & T. J. Farchione (Eds.), *Applications of the unified protocol for transdiagnostic treatment of emotional disorder* (pp. 164–178). New York, NY: Oxford University Press.

Bullock, W. A., & Gilliland, K. (1993). Eysenck's arousal theory of introversion-extraversion: A converging measures investigation. *Journal of Personality and Social Psychology, 64*, 113–123.

Burger, J. M. (1991). Control. In V. Derlega, B. Winstead, & W. Jones (Eds.), *Personality* (pp. 287–312). Chicago, IL: Nelson-Hall.

Burgess, D. J., Ding, Y., Hargreaves, M., van Ryn, M., & Phelan, S. (2008). The association between perceived discrimination and underutilization of needed medical and mental health care in a multi-ethnic community sample. *Journal of Health Care for the Poor and Underserved, 19*(3), 894–911. doi:10.1353/hpu.0.0063

Burnham, C. A., & Davis, K. G. (1969). The nine-dot problem: Beyond perceptual organization. *Psychonomic Science, 17*, 321–323.

Burns, J. C., & Corwin, J. T. (2013). A historical to present-day account of efforts to answer the question: "What puts the brakes on mammalian hair cell regeneration?" *Hearing Research, 297*, 52–67.

Burns, M. D., Monteith, M. J., & Parker, L. R. (2017). Training away bias: The differential effects of counterstereotype training and self-regulation on stereotype activation and application. *Journal of Experimental Social Psychology, 73*, 97–110. doi:10.1016/j.jesp.2017.06.003

Burton, H., & Sinclair, R. (1996). Somatosensory cortex and tactile perceptions. In L. Kruger (Ed.), *Pain and touch* (pp. 105–177). San Diego, CA: Academic Press.

Bushman, B. J. (2016). Violent media and hostile appraisals: A meta-analytic review. *Aggressive Behavior, 42*(6), 605–613. doi:10.1002/ab.21655

Bushman, B. J., & Huesmann, L. R. (2001). Effects of televised violence on aggression. In D. G. Singer & J. L. Singer (Eds.), *Handbook of children and the media* (pp. 223–254). Thousand Oaks, CA: Sage.

Buske-Kirschbaum, A., Kirschbaum, C., Stierle, H., Jabaij, L., & Hellhammer, D. (1994). Conditioned manipulation of natural killer (NK) cells in humans using a discriminative learning protocol. *Biological Psychology, 38*, 143–155.

Buske-Kirschbaum, A., Kirschbaum, C., Stierle, H., Lehnert, H., & Hellhammer, D. (1992). Conditioned increase in natural killer cell activity (NKCA) in humans. *Psychosomatic Medicine, 54*, 123–132.

Butcher, J. N., & Williams, C. J. (2000). *Essentials of MMPI-2 and MMPI-A interpretation* (2nd ed.). Minneapolis: University of Minnesota Press.

Butcher, J. N., Hass, G. A., Greene, R. L., & Nelson, L. D. (2015). Cultural factors in forensic assessment with the MMPI-2. In *Using the MMPI-2 in forensic assessment* (pp. 69–89). Washington, DC: American Psychological Association.

Byrne, D. (1971). *The attraction paradigm.* New York, NY: Academic.

Byrne, D. (1997). An overview (and underview) of research and theory within the attraction paradigm. *Journal of Social and Personal Relationships, 14*, 417–431.

Byrne, D., Clore, G. L., & Smeaton, G. (1986). The attraction hypothesis: Do similar attitudes attract anything? *Journal of Personality and Social Psychology, 51*, 1167–1170.

Byrne, D., Kelley, K., & Fisher, W. A. (1993). Unwanted teenage pregnancies: Incidence, interpretation, and intervention. *Applied and Preventive Psychology, 2*, 101–113.

Byrne, R. M. J., & McEleney, A. (2000). Counterfactual thinking about actions and failures to act. *Journal of Experimental Psychology: Learning Memory, and Cognition, 26*, 1318–1331.

Cabeza, R. (2002). Hemispheric asymmetry reduction in older adults: The HAROLD model. *Psychology & Aging, 17*, 85–100.

Cacioppo, J. T., & Gardner, W. L. (1999). Emotion. *Annual Review of Psychology, 50*, 191–214.

Cacioppo, J. T., & Petty, R. E. (1982). Electromyograms as measures of extent and affectivity of information processing. *American Psychologist, 36*, 441–456.

Cai, D., Aharoni, D., Shuman, T., Shobe, J., Biane, J., Song, W., . . . Silva, A. J. (2016). A shared neural ensemble links distinct contextual memories encoded close in time. *Nature, 534*, 115–118. doi:10.1038/nature17955

Calvo, S., & Egan, J. (2015). The endocrinology of taste receptors. *Nature Reviews Endocrinology, 11*, 213–227. doi:10.1038/nrendo.2015.7

Campbell, J. D., & Fairey, P. J. (1989). Informational and normative routes to conformity. *Journal of Personality and Social Psychology, 57*, 457–468.

Campbell, J. M., Amerikaner, M., Swank, P., & Vincent, K. (1989). The relationship between the Hardiness Test and the Personal Orientation Inventory. *Journal of Research in Personality, 23*, 373–380.

Campbell, S. S., & Murphy, P. J. (1998). Extraocular circadian phototransduction in humans. *Science, 279*, 396–399.

Campfield, L., Arthur, S., Francoise, J., Rosenbaum, M., & Hirsch, J. (1996). Human eating: Evidence for a physiological basis using a modified paradigm. *Neuroscience & Biobehavioral Reviews, 20*, 1133–1137.

Campos, J. J., Langer, A., & Krowtiz, A. (1970). Cardiac responses on the visual cliff in prelocomotor infants. *Science, 170*, 196–197.

Canadian Psychological Association. (2013, October). The efficacy and effectiveness of psychological treatments. Retrieved from https://cpa.ca/docs/File/Practice/TheEfficacyAndEffectivenessOfPsychologicalTreatments_web.pdf

Canfield, R. L., & Smith, E. G. (1996). Number-based expectations and sequential enumeration by 5-month-old infants. *Developmental Psychology, 32*, 269–279.

Cannito, L., Anzani, S., Bortolotti, A., Palumbo, R., Ceccato, I., Di Crosta, A., . . . Palumbo, R. (2021). Temporal discounting of money and face masks during the COVID-19 pandemic: The role of hoarding level. *Frontiers in Psychology, 12*, 642102. doi:10.3389/fpsyg.2021.642102

Cannon, W. B. (1927). The James-Lange theory of emotion: A critical examination and an alternative theory. *American Journal of Psychology, 39*, 106–124.

Cannon, W. B. (1932). *The wisdom of the body.* New York, NY: Norton.

Cannon, W. B., & Washburn, A. L. (1912). An explanation of hunger. *American Journal of Physiology, 29*, 441–454.

Capozza, D., & Brown, R. (2000). *Social identity processes: Trends in theory and research.* London, UK: Sage.

Cappagli, G., Cocchi, E., & Gori, M. (2017). Auditory and proprioceptive spatial impairments in blind children and adults. *Developmental Science, 20*(3), 10.1111/desc.12374. https://doi.org/10.1111/desc.12374

Cappagli, G., Cocchi, E., & Gori, M. (2015). Auditory and proprioceptive spatial impairments in blind children and adults. *Developmental Science, 20*(3). doi:10.1111/desc.12374

Capuano, N., Gaeta, M., Ritrovato, P., & Salerno, S. (2014). Elicitation of latent learning needs through learning goals recommendation. *Computers in Human Behavior, 30*, 663–673. doi:10.1016/j.chb.2013.07.036

Caramazza, A., & Hillis, A. E. (1991). Lexical organization of nouns and verbs in the brain. *Nature, 349*, 788–790.

Carey, B. (1997). Don't face stress alone. *Health*, pp. 74–76, 78.

Carhart-Harris, R. L., Kaelen, M., Whalley, M. G., Bolstridge, M., Feilding, A., & Nutt, D. J. (2015). LSD enhances suggestibility in healthy volunteers. *Psychopharmacology, 232*, 785–794.

Carl, E., Stein, A. T., Levihn-Coon, A., Pogue, J. R., Rothbaum, B., Emmelkamp, P., . . . Powers, M. B. (2019). Virtual reality exposure therapy for anxiety and related disorders: A meta-analysis of randomized controlled trials. *Journal of Anxiety Disorders, 61*, 27–36. doi:10.1016/j.janxdis.2018.08.003

Carmichael, L., Hogan, H. P., & Walter, A. (1932). An experimental study of the effect of language on the reproduction of visually perceived form. *Journal of Experimental Psychology, 15*, 73–86.

Carone, N., Bos, H., Shenkman, G., & Tasker, F. (2021). Editorial: LGBTQ parents and their children during the family life cycle. *Frontiers in Psychology, 12*, 643647. doi:10.3389/fpsyg.2021.643647

Carpenter, S. (1999, July/August). Freud's dream theory gets boost from imaging work. *APA Monitor*, p. 19.

Carpenter, S. (2002, February). Plagiarism or memory glitch? *APA Monitor, 33*, 25–26.

Carstensen, L. L., Isaacowitz, D. M., & Charles, S. T. (1999). Taking time seriously: A theory of socioemotional selectivity. *American Psychologist, 54*, 165–181.

Casalin, S., Luyten, P., Vliegen, N., & Meurs, P. (2012). The structure and stability of temperament from infancy to toddlerhood: A one-year prospective study. *Infant Behavior and Development, 35*(1), 94–108. doi:10.1016/j.infbeh.2011.08.004

Casanova, C., & Ptito, M. (Eds.).(2001). *Vision: From neurons to cognition.* Amsterdam, Netherlands: Elsevier Science.

Case, R. (1992). *The mind's staircase.* Hillsdale, NJ: Erlbaum.

Caselli, R. J., Langlais, B. T., Dueck, A. C., Henslin, B. R., Johnson, T. A., Woodruff, B. K., . . . Locke, D. E. C. (2018). Personality changes during the transition from cognitive health to mild cognitive impairment. *Journal of the American Geriatrics Society, 66*(4), 671–678. doi:10.1111/jgs.15182

Casey, K. L., & Bushnell, M. C. (Eds.).(2000). *Pain imaging.* Seattle, WA: IASP Press.

Caspi, A. (2000). The child is the father of man: Personality continuities from childhood to adulthood. *Journal of Personality and Social Psychology, 78*, 158–172.

Cassidy, J., Kirsh, S. J., Scolton, K. L., & Parke, R. D. (1996). Attachment and representations of peer relationships. *Developmental Psychology, 32*, 892–904.

Cassidy, J., Shaver, P. R., & Main, M. (Eds.).(1999). *Handbook of attachment: Theory, research, and clinical applications.* New York, NY: Guilford.

Cassidy, W., Faucher, C., & Jackson, M. (2013). Cyberbullying among youth: A comprehensive review of current international research and its implications and application to policy and practice. *School Psychology International, 34*(6), 575–612. doi:10.1177/0143034313479697

Cate, C. T. (2009). Niko Tinbergen and the red patch on the herring gull's beak. *Animal Behaviour, 77*(4), 785–794. doi:10.1016/j.anbehav.2008.12.021

Cate, C. T., Bruins, W. S., den Ouden, J., Egberts, T., Neevel, H., Spierings, M., . . . Brokerhof, A. W. (2009). Tinbergen revisited: A replication and extension of experiments on the beak colour preferences of herring gull chicks. *Animal Behaviour, 77*(4), 795–802. doi:10.1016/j.anbehav.2008.12.020

Cattell, R. B. (1949). *The culture-free intelligence test.* Champaign, IL: Institute for Personality and Ability Testing.

Cattell, R. B. (1963). Theory of crystallized and fluid intelligence: A critical experiment. *Journal of Educational Psychology, 54,* 1–22.

Cattell, R. B. (1965). *The scientific analysis of personality.* Baltimore, MD: Penguin Books.

Cavanagh, K., & Davey, G. C. L. (2000). The development of a measure of individual differences in disgust. Paper presented to the British Psychological Society.

Cavazza, N., Guidetti, M., & Butera, F. (2015). Ingredients of gender-based stereotypes about food. Indirect influence of food type, portion size and presentation on gendered intentions to eat. *Appetite, 91,* 26–272. doi:10.1016/j.appet.2015.04.068

CBS News. (2014). Adrian Peterson says NFL discipline is unfair. Retrieved from https://www.cbsnews.com/news/adrian-peterson-says-nfl-discipline-is-unfair/

Ceci, S. J. (1991). How much does schooling influence general intelligence and its cognitive components? A reassessment of the evidence. *Developmental Psychology, 27,* 703–722.

Centers for Disease Control. (2019). *Table 39. Prescription drug use in the past 30 days, by sex, race and Hispanic origin, and age: United States, selected years 1988-1994 through 2015-2018.* Retrieved from https://www.cdc.gov/nchs/data/hus/2019/039-508.pdf

Centers for Disease Control and Prevention. (2009). The power of prevention. Retrieved from http://www.cdc.gov/chronicdisease/pdf/2009-Power-of-Prevention.pdf

Centers for Disease Control and Prevention. (2015). QuickStats: Percentage of adults aged 18–64 years who have seen or talked with a mental health professional in the past 12 months, by health insurance status and age group—National Health Interview Survey, United States, 2012–2013. Retrieved from https://www.cdc.gov/mmwr/preview/mmwrhtml/mm6407a12.htm

Centers for Disease Control and Prevention. (2017). *ART success rates.* Retrieved from https://www.cdc.gov/art/artdata/index.html

Centers for Disease Control and Prevention. (2017). Leading causes of death. Retrieved from https://www.cdc.gov/nchs/fastats/leading-causes-of-death.htm

Centers for Disease Control and Prevention. (2018, February 4). Pregnancy mortality surveillance system. Retrieved from https://www.cdc.gov/reproductivehealth/maternal-mortality/pregnancy-mortality-surveillance-system.htm

Centers for Disease Control and Prevention. (2019). Heart disease facts. Retrieved from https://www.cdc.gov/heartdisease/facts.htm

Centers for Disease Control and Prevention. (2019a). Reproductive health: Teen pregnancy. Retrieved from https://www.cdc.gov/teenpregnancy/about/index.htm

Centers for Disease Control and Prevention. (2019b). Alzheimer's disease. Retrieved from https://www.cdc.gov/aging/aginginfo/alzheimers.htm

Centers for Disease Control and Prevention. (2020, June 10). Using telehealth to expand access to essential health services during the COVID-19 pandemic. Retrieved from https://www.cdc.gov/coronavirus/2019-ncov/hcp/telehealth.html

Centers for Disease Control Vietnam Experience Study. (1988). Health status of Vietnam veterans: I. Psychosocial characteristics. *Journal of the American Medical Association, 259,* 2701–2707.

Centers for Disease Control Vietnam Experience Study. (1988). Health status of Vietnam veterans: I. Psychosocial characteristics. *Journal of the American Medical Association, 259,* 2701–2707.

Cerullo, M. (2019, January 29). Kendall Jenner and top models can be subpoenaed over Fyre Festival. Retrieved from https://www.cbsnews.com/news/fyre-festival-subpoenas-kendall-jenner-top-models-to-be-subpoenaed-in-fyre-festival-bankruptcy-case/

Cervone, D., & Shoda, Y. (Eds.).(1999). *The coherence of personality: Social-cognitive bases of consistency, variability, and organization.* New York, NY: Guilford.

Ceylan, M. E., Dönmez, A., Ünsalver, B. Ö., & Evrensel, A. (2016). Neural synchronization as a hypothetical explanation of the psychoanalytic unconscious. *Consciousness and Cognition, 40,* 34–44. doi:10.1016/j.concog.2015.12.011

Chafe, W. H., Gavins, R., & Korstad, R. (2002). *Remembering Jim Crow: African Americans tell about life in the segregated South.* New York, NY: Norton.

Chance, P. (2013). *Learning and behavior* (7th ed.). Belmont, CA: Wadsworth.

Chandler, C. C. (1991). How memory for an event is influenced by related events: Interference in modified recognition tests. *Journal of Experimental Psychology: Learning, Memory, and Cognition, 17,* 115–125.

Chandra, A., Copen, C. E., & Stephen, E. H. (2014). Infertility service use in the United States: Data from the National Survey of Family Growth, 1982–2010. *National Health Statistics Reports, 73,* 1–21. Retrieved from https://www.cdc.gov/nchs/data/nhsr/nhsr073.pdf

Chaplin, T. (2015). Gender and emotion expression: A developmental contextual perspective. *Emotion Review, 7*(1), 14–21.

Chapman University Survey of American Fears Wave 4. (2017). *Paranormal America 2017.* Retrieved from https://blogs.chapman.edu/wilkinson/2017/10/11/paranormal-america-2017/

Charles, L., Gaillard, R., Amado, I., Krebs, M.-O., Bendjemaa, N., & Dehaene, S. (2017). Conscious and unconscious performance monitoring: Evidence from patients with schizophrenia. *NeuroImage, 144,* 153–163. doi:10.1016/j.neuroimage.2016.09.056

Chartier, F. (2012). *Taste buds and molecules: The art and science of food, wine, and flavor* (L Reiss, Trans.). Hoboken, NJ: Wiley.

Chartrand, T. L., & Bargh, J. A. (1999). The chameleon effect: The perception-behavior link and social interaction. *Journal of Personality and Social Psychology, 76,* 893–910.

Chartrand, T. L., & Bargh, J. A. (1999). The chameleon effect: The perception-behavior link and social interaction. *Journal of Personality and Social Psychology, 76,* 893–910.

Chase, M. H., & Morales, F. R. (1983). Subthreshold excitatory activity and motorneuron discharge during REM periods of active sleep. *Science, 221,* 1195–1198.

Chase, W. G., & Simon, H. A. (1973). Perception in chess. *Cognitive Psychology, 4,* 55–81.

Chaudhuri, P., Bhattacharya, K., & Sengupta, P. (2016). Co-education with environmental cues may kindle early onset of female puberty. *International Journal of Preventive Medicine, 7*, 29. doi:10.4103/2008-7802.175452

Cheit, R. E. (2014). Research ethics and case studies in psychology. *Journal of Interpersonal Violence, 29*(18), 3290–3307. doi:10.1177/0886260514534987

Chen, E., Brody, G. H., & Miller, G. E. (2017). Childhood close family relationships and health. *American Psychologist, 72*(6), 555–566. doi:10.1037/amp0000067

Chen, R., Gillespie, A., Zhao, Y., Xi, Y., Ren, Y., & Mclean, L. (2018). The efficacy of eye movement desensitization and reprocessing in children and adults who have experienced complex childhood trauma: A systematic review of randomized controlled trials. *Frontiers in Psychology, 9*. doi:10.3389/fpsyg.2018.00534

Chen, Z. (2002). Analogical problem solving: A hierarchical analysis of procedural similarity. *Journal of Experimental Psychology: Learning, Memory, and Cognition, 28*, 81–98.

Cheney, D. L., & Seyfarth, R. M. (1990). *How monkeys see the world.* Chicago, IL: University of Chicago Press.

Cherry, E. C. (1953). Some experiments on the recognition of speech, with one and with two ears. *Journal of the Acoustical Society of America, 25*, 975–979.

Chiao, J. Y., & Immordino-Yang, M. H. (2013). Modularity and the cultural mind: Contributions of cultural neuroscience to cognitive theory. *Perspectives on Psychological Science, 8*(1), 56–61. doi:10.1177/1745691612469032

Chiao, J. Y., Iidaka, T., Gordon, H. L., Nogawa, J., Bar, M., Aminoff, E., . . . Ambady, N. (2008). Cultural specificity in amygdala response to fear faces. *Journal of Cognitive Neuroscience, 20*(12), 2167–2174. doi:10.1162/jocn.2008.20151

Chichirez, C. M., & Purcărea, V. L. (2018). Interpersonal communication in healthcare. *Journal of Medicine and Life, 11*(2), 119–122.

Child Trends Data Bank. (2016). *Condom use: Indicators of child and youth well-being.* Retrieved from https://www.childtrends.org/wp-content/uploads/2016/10/28_Condom_Use.pdf

Chivers-Wilson, K. A. (2006). Sexual assault and posttraumatic stress disorder: A review of the biological, psychological and sociological factors and treatments. *McGill Journal of Medicine, 9*(2), 111–118.

Chmielewski, M., Clark, L. A., Bagby, R. M., & Watson, D. (2015). Method matters: Understanding diagnostic reliability in DSM-IV and DSM-5. *Journal of Abnormal Psychology, 124*(3), 764–769.

Chomsky, N. (1959). A review of B. F. Skinner's "Verbal behavior." *Language, 35*, 26–58.

Chomsky, N. (1972). *Language and mind.* New York, NY: Harcourt Brace Jovanovich.

Chorpita, B. F., Daleiden, E. L., Ebesutani, C., Young, J., Becker, K. D., Nakamura, B. J., . . . Starace, N. (2011). Evidence-based treatments for children and adolescents: An updated review of indicators of efficacy and effectiveness. *Clinical Psychology: Science and Practice, 18*, 154–172. doi:10.1111/j.1468-2850.2011.01247.x

Chow, P. I., Wagner, J., Lüdtke, O., Trautwein, U., & Roberts, B. W. (2017). Therapy experience in naturalistic observational studies is associated with negative changes in personality. *Journal of Research in Personality, 68*, 88–95. doi:10.1016/j.jrp.2017.02.002

Chow, R. M., Tiedens, L. Z., & Govan, C. L. (2008). Excluded emotions: The role of anger in antisocial responses to ostracism. *Journal of Experimental Social Psychology, 44*(3), 896–903. doi:10.1016/j.jesp.2007.09.004

Christensen, A., & Jacobson, N. S. (1994). Who (or what) can do psychotherapy: The status and challenge of nonprofessional therapies. *Psychological Science, 5*, 8–14.

Christiansen, N. D., Tozek, R. F., & Burns, G. (2010). Effects of social desirability scores on hiring judgments. *Journal of Personnel Psychology, 9*(1).

Chu, J., & Leino, A. (2017). Advancement in the maturing science of cultural adaptations of evidence-based interventions. *Journal of Consulting and Clinical Psychology, 85*(1), 45–57.

Chumlea, W. C., Schubert, C. M., Roche A. F., Kulin, H. E., Lee, P. A., Himes, J. H., & Sun, S. S. (2003). Age at menarche and racial comparisons in US girls. *Pediatrics, 111*, 110–113.

Church, A. T. (2001). Personality measurement in cross-cultural perspective. *Journal of Personality, 69*, 979–1006.

Cialdini, R. (2009). *Influence: The psychology of persuasion.* New York, NY: Harper Collins.

Cialdini, R. B., & Trost, M. R. (1998). Influence, social norms, conformity, and compliance. In D. T. Gilbert, S. T. Fiske, & G. Lindzey (Eds.), *Handbook of social psychology* (4th ed.). New York, NY: Oxford University Press.

Cioffi, D., & Holloway, J. (1993). Delayed costs of suppressed pain. *Journal of Personality and Social Psychology, 64*, 274–282.

Cipolletta, S., Votadoro, R., & Faccio, E. (2017). Online support for transgender people: An analysis of forums and social networks. *Health and Social Care in the Community, 25*(5), 1542–1551. doi:10.1111/hsc.12448

Cipolli, C., Bolzani, R., Cornoldi, C., DeBeni, R., & Fagioli, I. (1993). Bizarreness effect in dream recall. *Sleep, 16*, 163–170.

Cipriani, A., Furukawa, T. A., Salanti, G., Geddes, J. R., Higgins, J. P., Churchill, R., . . . Barbui, C. (2009). Comparative efficacy and acceptability of 12 new-generation antidepressants: A multiple-treatments meta-analysis. *Lancet, 373*(9665), 746–758. doi:10.1016/s0140-6736(09)60046-5

Clark, D. M., Salkovskis, P. M., Ost, L. G., Breitholtz, E., Koehler, K. A., Westling, B. E., . . . & Gelder, M. (1997). Misinterpretation of body sensations in panic disorder. *Journal of Consulting and Clinical Psychology, 65*, 203–213.

Clark, L. A. (1999). Introduction to the special section on the concept of disorder. *Journal of Abnormal Psychology, 108*, 371–373.

Classen, C., Howes, D., & Synnott, A. (1994). *Aroma: The cultural history of smell.* London, UK: Routledge.

Clay, R. A. (2017). Trends report: Psychology is more popular than ever. Retrieved from http://www.apa.org/monitor/2017/11/trends-popular.aspx

Clearfield, M. W., & Mix, K. S. (1999). Number versus contour length in infants' discrimination of small visual sets. *Psychological Science, 10*, 408–411.

Cleckley, H. (1976). *The mask of sanity* (5th ed.). St. Louis, MO: Mosby.

Cleeremans, A., Allakhverdov, V., & Kuvaldina, M. (2019). *Implicit learning: 50 years on.* London, UK: Routledge.

Clements, C. B., Althouse, R., Ax, R. K., Magaletta, P. R., Fagan, T. J., & Wormith, J. S. (2007). Systematic issues and correctional outcomes: Expanding the scope of correctional psychology. *Criminal Justice and Behavior, 34*, 919–932.

Clower, W. T., & Finger, S. (2001). Discovering trepanation: The contribution of Paul Broca. *Neurosurgery, 49*(6), 1417–1426. doi:10.1097/00006123-200112000-00021

Coccaro, E. F., Cremers, H., Fanning, J., Nosal, E., Lee, R., Keedy, S., & Jacobson, K. C. (2018). Reduced frontal grey matter, life history of aggression, and underlying genetic influence. *Psychiatry Research: Neuroimaging, 271*, 126–134. doi:10.1016/j.pscychresns.2017.11.007

Cochran, J. C., Toman, E. L., Mears, D. P., & Bales, W. D. (2017). Solitary confinement as punishment: Examining in-prison sanctioning disparities. *Justice Quarterly, 35*(3), 381–411. doi:10.1080/07418825.2017.1308541

Coe, C. L. (1993). Psychosocial factors and immunity in nonhuman primates: A review. *Psychosomatic Medicine, 55*, 298–308.

Coffey, C. E., Weiner, R. D., & Djang, W. T. (1991). Brain anatomic effects of electroconvulsive therapy: A prospective magnetic resonance imaging study. *Archives of General Psychiatry, 48*, 1013–1021.

Cohen, A. (2016). *Imbeciles: The Supreme Court, American eugenics, and the sterilization of Carrie Buck.* New York, NY: Penguin.

Cohen, J. (1988). *Statistical power analysis for the behavioral sciences.* Hillsdale, NJ: Erlbaum.

Cohen, J. (1994). The earth is round (p < .05). *American Psychologist, 49*, 997–1003.

Cohen, S., & Herbert, T. B. (1996). Health psychology: Psychological factors and physical disease from the perspective of human psychoneuroimmunology. *Annual Review of Psychology, 47*, 113–142.

Cohen, S., & Williamson, G. (1991). Stress and infectious disease in humans. *Psychological Bulletin, 109*, 5–24.

Cohen, S., Frank, E., Doyle, W. J., Skoner, D. P., Rabin, B. S., & Gwaltney, J. M. (1998). Types of stressors that increase susceptibility to the common cold in healthy adults. *Health Psychology, 17*, 214–223.

Cohen, S., Hamrick, N., Rodriguez, M. S., Feldman, P. J., Rabin, B. S., & Manuck, S. B. (2002). Reactivity and vulnerability to stress-associated risk for upper respiratory illness. *Psychosomatic Medicine.*

Cohen, S., Tyrrell, D. A. J., & Smith, A. P. (1991). Psychological stress and susceptibility to the common cold. *New England Journal of Medicine, 325*, 606–612.

Cohen, Y. (1964). *The transition from childhood to adolescence: Cross-cultural studies of initiation ceremonies, legal systems, and incest taboos.* Chicago, IL: Aldine.

Coile, D. C., & Miller, N. E. (1984). How radical animal activists try to mislead humane people. *American Psychologist, 39*, 700–701.

Colangelo, A. M., Cirillo, G., Alberghina, L., Papa, M., & Westerhoff, H. V. (2019). Neural plasticity and adult neurogenesis: The deep biology perspective. *Neural Regeneration Research, 14*(2), 201–205. doi:10.4103/1673-5374.244775

Colby, A., Kohlberg, L., Gibbs, J., & Lieberman, M. (1983). A longitudinal study of moral judgment. *Monographs of the Society for Research in Child Development, 48*(1–2, Serial No. 200).

Cole, S. F., Greenwald-O'Brien, J., Gadd, M. G., Ristuccia, J., Wallace, D. L., & Gregory, M. (2005). *Helping traumatized children learn: Supportive school environments for children traumatized by family violence. A report and policy agenda.* Boston, MA: Massachusetts Advocates for Children. Retrieved from https://traumasensitiveschools.org/wp-content/uploads/2013/06/Helping-Traumatized-Children-Learn.pdf

Coleman, R. M. (1986). *Wide awake at 3:00 a.m.: By choice or by chance?* New York, NY: Freeman.

College Board. (2015). *Total group profile report: 2015 College-bound seniors.* New York, NY: The College Board. Retrieved from https://secure-media.collegeboard.org/digitalServices/pdf/sat/total-group-2015.pdf

Collier, J. (2017). Could Alzheimer's be prevented with a vaccine? Retrieved from https://www.medicalnewstoday.com/articles/319857.php

Collins, A. M., & Loftus, E. F. (1975). A spreading activation theory of semantic processing. *Psychological Review, 82*, 407–428.

Colloca, L., & Miller, F. G. (2011). The nocebo effect and its relevance for clinical practice. *Psychosomatic Medicine, 73*, 598.

Coltheart, V. (Ed.).(1999). *Fleeting memories: Cognition of brief visual stimuli.* Cambridge, MA: MIT Press.

Comedy Central. (2016, Exclusive - Tomi Lahren extended interview. *The Daily Show with Trevor Noah* [Video]. Retrieved from http://www.cc.com/video-clips/m9ds7s/the-daily-show-with-trevor-noah-exclusive---tomi-lahren-extended-interviewNovermber 30).

Compère, L., Rari, E., Gallarda, T., Assens, A., Nys, M., Coussinoux, S., Machefaux, S., & Piolino, P. (2018). Gender identity better than sex explains individual differences in episodic and semantic components of autobiographical memory and future thinking. *Consciousness and Cognition, 57*, 1–19. doi:10.1016/j.concog.2017.11.001.

Compo, N. S., Carol, R. N., Evans, J. R., Piementel, P., Holness, H., Nichols-Lopez, K., . . . Furton, K. G. (2017). Witness memory and alcohol: The effects of state-dependent recall. *Law and Human Behavior, 41*(2), 202–215. doi:10.1037/lhb0000224

Conger, R. D., Reuter, M. A., & Elder, G. H., Jr. (1999). Couple resilience to economic pressure. *Journal of Personality and Social Psychology, 76*, 54–71.

Conger, R. D., Wallace, L. E., Sun, Y., Simons, R. L., McLoyd, V. C., & Brody, G. H. (2002). Economic pressure in African American families: A replication and extension of the family stress model. *Developmental Psychology, 38*, 179–193.

Congressional Budget Office. (2012, February). *The Veterans Health Administration's treatment of PTSD and traumatic brain injury among recent combat veterans.* Washington, DC: Congress of the United States. Retrieved from https://www.cbo.gov/sites/default/files/cbofiles/attachments/02-09-PTSD.pdf

Conrad, R. (1964). Acoustic confusions in immediate memory. *British Journal of Psychology, 55*, 75–84.

Conti, R. (2001). Time flies: Investigating the connection between intrinsic motivation and the experience of time. *Journal of Personality, 69*(1), 1–26. doi:10.1111/1467-6494.00134

Conversano, C., Rotondo, A., Lensi, E., Della Vista, O., Arpone, F., & Reda, M. A. (2010). Optimism and its impact on mental and physical well-being. *Clinical Practice and Epidemiology in Mental Health, 6*, 25–29. doi:10.2174/1745017901006010025

Conway, B. R. (2002). *Neural mechanisms of color vision: Double-opponent cells in the visual cortex.* Dordrecht, Netherlands: Kluwer.

Conway, B. R. (2013). Color signals through dorsal and ventral visual pathways. *Visual Neuroscience, 31*(2), 197–209. doi:10.1017/s0952523813000382

Conway, M. A. (2013). On being a memory expert witness: Three cases. *Memory, 21*, 566–575. doi:10.1080/09658211.2013.794241.

Conway, M., Cohen, G., & Stanhope, N. (1991). On the very long-term retention of knowledge acquired through formal education: Twelve years of cognitive psychology. *Journal of Experimental Psychology: General, 120*, 395–109.

Conway, M., Collins, A. F., Gatheicole, S. E., & Anderson, S. J. (1996). Recollections of true and false autobiographical memories. *Journal of Experimental Psychology: General, 125*, 69–95.

Cook, B. L., Liu, Z., Lessios, A. S., Loder, S., & McGuire, T. (2015). The costs and benefits of reducing racial-ethnic disparities in mental health care. *Psychiatric Services, 66*(4), 389–396. doi:10.1176/appi.ps.201400070

Cook, L. G., & Mitschow, L. C. (2019). Beyond the polygraph: Deception detection and the autonomic nervous system. *Federal Practitioner, 36*(7), 316–321.

Cook, M., & Mineka, S. (1990). Selective association in the observational conditioning of fear in monkeys. *Behaviour Research and Therapy, 25*, 349–364.

Cook, T. D., Cooper, H., Cordray, D. S., Hartmann, H., Hedges, L. V., Light, R. J., . . . Mosteller, F. (1992). *Meta-analysis for explanation: A casebook.* New York, NY: Russell Sage Foundation.

Cooke, M., Emery, H., Brimelow, R., & Wollin, J. (2016). The impact of therapeutic massage on adult residents living with complex and high level disabilities: A brief report. *Disability and Health Journal, 9*(4), 730–734. doi:10.1016/j.dhjo.2016.04.009

Cooper, J. R., Bloom, F. E., & Roth, R. H. (2002). *The biochemical basis of neuropharmacology* (8th ed.). New York, NY: Oxford University Press.

Cooper, J., Bloom, F., & Roth, R. (1995). *The biochemical basis of neuropharmacology* (7th ed.). New York, NY: Oxford University Press.

Cooper, L. A., Roter, D. L., Carson, K. A., Beach, M. C., Sabin, J. A., Greenwald, A. G., & Inui, T. S. (2012). The associations of clinicians' implicit attitudes about race with medical visit communication and patient ratings of interpersonal care. *American Journal of Public Health, 102*(5), 979–987. doi:10.2105/ajph.2011.300558

Coopersmith, S. (1967). *The antecedents of self-esteem.* San Francisco, CA: Freeman.

Corballis, M. C. (2014). Left brain, right brain: Facts and fantasies. *PLoS Biology, 12*(1), e1001767. doi:10.1371/journal.pbio.1001767

Corballis, P. M., Funnell, M. G., & Gazzaniga, M. S. (2002). Hemispheric asymmetries for simple visual judgments in the split brain. *Neuropsychologia, 40*, 401–410.

Coren, S. (1996). *Sleep thieves: An eye-opening exploration into science and mysteries of sleep.* New York, NY: Free Press.

Coren, S., & Aks, D. J. (1990). Moon illusion in pictures: A multimechanism approach. *Journal of Experimental Psychology: Human Perception and Performance, 16*, 365–380.

Corina, D. P., Vaid, J., & Belugi, U. (1992). The linguistic basis of left-hemisphere specialization. *Science, 255*, 1258–1260.

Corthay, A. (2014). Does the immune system naturally protect against cancer? *Frontiers in Immunology, 5*, 197. doi:10.3389/fimmu.2014.00197

Corwin, D. L., & Olafson, E. (1997). Videotaped discovery of a reportedly unrecallable memory of child sexual abuse: Comparison with a childhood interview videotaped 11 years before. *Child Maltreatment, 2*(2), 91–112. doi:10.1177/1077559597002002001

Costa, P. T., Jr., & McCrae, R. M. (1992). *Revised NEO personality inventory: NEO PI and NEO Five Factor Inventory (NEO FFI professional manual).* Odessa, FL: Psychological Assessment Resources.

Cote, K. A., De Lugt, D. R., & Campbell, K. B. (2002). Changes in the scalp topography of event-related potentials and behavioral responses during the sleep onset period. *Psychophysiology, 39*, 29–37.

Cousins, N. (1989). *Head first: The biology of hope.* New York, NY: Dutton.

Couzin-Frankel, J. (2017, November 16). Scientists are learning to predict psychosis years in advance-and possibly prevent it. *Science.* Retrieved from http://www.sciencemag.org/news/2017/11/scientists-are-learning-predict-psychosis-years-advance-and-possibly-prevent-it

Cowan, N. (1988). Evolving concepts of memory storage, selective attention, and their mutual constraints within the human information-processing system. *Psychological Bulletin, 104*, 163–191.

Cowan, N. (2000). The magical number 4 in short-term memory: A reconsideration of mental storage capacity. *Behavioral and Brain Sciences, 24*, 87–185.

Cowan, N. (2010). The magical mystery four: How is working memory capacity limited, and why? *Current Directions in Psychological Science, 19*(1), 51–57. doi:10.1177/0963721409359277

Cowan, N. (2016). The many faces of working memory and short-term storage. *Psychonomic Bulletin & Review, 24*(4), 1158–1170. doi:10.3758/s13423-016-1191-6

Cowley, G. (1996, June 3). The biology of beauty. *Newsweek*, pp. 61–69.

Cox, M. J., & Paley, B. (1997). Families as systems. *Annual Review of Psychology, 48*, 243–267.

Coyne, J. C. (1976). Depression and the responses of others. *Journal of Abnormal Psychology, 85*, 186–193.

Coyne, J. C., Thompson, R., & Palmer, S. C. (2002). Marital quality, coping with conflict, marital complaints, and affection in couples with a depressed wife. *Journal of Family Psychology, 16*, 26–37.

Craig, J. C., & Rollman, G. B. (1999). Somesthesis. *Annual Review of Psychology, 50*, 305–331.

Craig, J. C., Reiman, E. M., Evans, A., & Bushnell, M. C. (1996). Functional imaging of an illusion of pain. *Nature, 384*, 258–260.

Craik, F. I. M. (1992). Human memory and cognitive capabilities. In F. Craik & T. A. Salthouse (Eds.), *Handbook of aging and cognition.* Hillsdale, NJ: Erlbaum.

Craik, F. I. M., & Tulving, E. (1975). Depth of processing and the retention of words in episodic memory. *Journal of Experimental Psychology: General, 104*, 268–294.

Cralley, E. L., & Ruscher, J. B. (2005). Lady, girl, female, or woman. Sexism and cognitive busyness predict use of gender-biased nouns. *Journal of Language and Social Psychology, 24*(3), 300–314. doi:10.1177/0261927x05278391

Cramer, P. (1996). *Storytelling, narrative, and the Thematic Apperception Test.* New York, NY: Guilford.

Cramer, P. (1998). Coping and defense mechanisms: What's the difference? *Journal of Personality, 66*, 919–946.

Cramer, P. (2000). Defense mechanisms in psychology today: Further processes for adaptation. *American Psychologist, 55*, 637–646.

Cramer, P. (2015). Using the TAT to assess the relation between gender identity and the use of defense mechanisms. *Journal of Personality Assessment, 99*(3), 265–274. doi:10.1080/00223891.2015.1055358

Cramer, P. (2017). Defense mechanism card pull in TAT stories. *Journal of Personality Assessment, 99*(1), 15–24. doi:10.1080/00223891.2016.1207080

Craske, M. G., & Barlow, D. H. (2001). Panic disorder and agoraphobia. In D. H. Barlow (Ed.), *Anxiety and its disorders: The nature and treatment of anxiety and panic* (2nd ed., pp. 1–59). New York, NY: Guilford.

Craske, M. G., Lang, A. J., Rowe, M., DeCola, J. P., Simmons, J., Mann, C., . . . Bystritsky, A. (2002). Presleep attributions about arousal during sleep: Nocturnal panic. *Journal of Abnormal Psychology, 111*, 53–62.

Crawford, H. J., Kitner-Triolo, M., Clarke, S. W., & Otesko, B. (1992). Transient positive and negative experiences accompanying stage hypnosis. *Journal of Abnormal Psychology, 101*, 663–667.

Criss, D. (2018, May 16). A White woman sees a Black man inspecting a house and calls the cops. But there's a twist. CNN. Retrieved from https://www.cnn.com/2018/05/16/us/investor-memphis-police-trnd/index.html

Crits-Christoph, P., & Barber, J. (Eds.).(1991). *Handbook of short-term dynamic psychotherapy.* New York, NY: Basic Books.

Crosby, E., Bromley, S., & Saxe, L. (1980). Recent unobtrusive studies of black and white discrimination and prejudice: A literature review. *Psychological Bulletin, 87*, 546–563.

Crowder, R. G. (1993). Short-term memory: Where do we stand? *Memory & Cognition, 21*, 142–145.

Crowley, R., Kirschner, N., Dunn, A. S., & Bornstein, S. S. (2017). Health and public policy to facilitate effective prevention and treatment of substance use disorders involving illicit and prescription drugs: An American College of Physicians position paper. *Annals of Internal Medicine, 166*(10), 733–736. doi:10.7326/M16-2953

Crowson, M. G., Semenov, Y. R., Tucci, D. L., & Niparko, J. K. (2017). Quality of life and cost-effectiveness of cochlear implants: A narrative review. *Audiology and Neurotology, 22* (4–5), 236–258. doi:10.1159/000481767

Csikszentmihalyi, M. (1990). *Flow: The psychology of optimal experience.* New York, NY: Harper & Row.

Csikszentmihalyi, M. (1997). *Finding flow.* New York, NY: Basic Books.

Cuellar, I., & Paniagua, F. A. (Eds.).(2000). *Handbook of multicultural mental health: Assessment and treatment of diverse populations.* San Diego: Academic.

Cuijpers, P., Andersson, G., Donker, T., & Van Straten, A. (2011). Psychological treatment of depression: Results of a series of meta-analyses. *Nordic Journal of Psychiatry, 65*, 354–364.

Cullum, J., O'Grady, M., & Tennen, H. (2011). Affiliation goals and health behaviors. *Social and Personality Psychology Compass, 5*(10), 694–705. doi:10.1111/j.1751-9004.2011.00376.x

Cumming, B. G., & DeAngelis, G. C. (2001). The physiology of stereopsis. *Annual Review of Neuroscience, 24*, 203–238.

Cummings, J. L. (2019). Assessing U.S. racial and gender differences in happiness, 1972–2016: An intersectional approach. *Journal of Happiness Studies.* doi:10.1007/s10902-019-00103-z

Cummings, J., Lee, G., Zhong, K., Fonseca, J., & Taghva, K. (2021). Alzheimer's disease drug development pipeline: 2021. *Alzheimer's & Dementia, 7*(1), e12179. doi:10.1002/trc2.12179

Cunha, D. (2014, July 8). This is what happened when I drove my Mercedes to pick up food stamps. *Washington Post.* Retrieved from https://www.washingtonpost.com/posteverything/wp/2014/07/08/this-is-what-happened-when-i-drove-my-mercedes-to-pick-up-food-stamps/

Cunningham, L. (2012, December 14). Myers-Briggs: Does it pay to know your type? *Washington Post.* Retrieved from https://www.washingtonpost.com/national/on-leadership/myers-briggs-does-it-pay-to-know-your-type/2012/12/14/eaed51ae-3fcc-11e2-bca3-aadc9b7e29c5_story.html

Curran, J. P., & Monti, P. M. (1982). *Social skills training: A practical handbook for assessment and treatment.* New York, NY: Guilford.

Curtis, G. C., Magee, W. J., Eaton, W. W., Wittchen, H. C., & Kessler, R. C. (1998). Specific fears and phobias. Epidemiology and classification. *The British Journal of Psychiatry: The Journal of Mental Science, 173*, 212–217.

Cusack, K., Jonas, D. E., Forneris, C. A., Wines, C., Sonis, J., Middleton, J. C., . . . Gaynes, B. N. (2016). Psychological treatments for adults with posttraumatic stress disorder: A systematic review and meta-analysis. *Clinical Psychology Review, 43*, 128–141. doi:10.1016/j.cpr.2015.10.003

Cyranowski, J. M., Frank, E., Young, E., & Shear, M. K. (2000). Adolescent onset of the gender difference in lifetime rates of major depression. *Archives of General Psychiatry, 57*, 21–27.

Cytowic, R. E. (1999). *The man who tasted shapes.* Cambridge, MA: MIT Press.

Cytowic, R. E. (2002). *Synesthesia: A union of the senses* (2nd ed.). Cambridge, MA: MIT Press.

Czeisler, C. A., Johnson, M. P., Duffy, J. F., Brown, E. N., Ronda, J. M., & Kronauer, R. E. (1990). Exposure to bright light and darkness to treat physiologic maladaptation to night work. *New England Journal of Medicine, 322*, 1253–1259.

Czopp, S. T., & Zeligman, R. (2016). The Rorschach Comprehensive System (CS) psychometric validity of individual variables. *Journal of Personality Assessment, 98*(4), 335–342. doi:10.1080/00223891.2015.1131162

D'Esposito, M. (Ed.).(2002). *Neurological foundations of cognitive neuroscience.* Cambridge, MA: MIT Press.

Dabbs, J. B. (2000). *Heroes, rogues, and lovers: Testosterone and behavior.* New York, NY: McGraw-Hill.

Dahlgren, G., & Whitehead, M. (1991). *Policies and strategies to promote social equity in health: Background document to WHO-Strategy paper for Europe.* Stockholm, Sweden: Institute for Future Studies.

Dalenberg, C. J. (2014). Protecting scientists, science, and case protagonists. *Journal of Interpersonal Violence, 29*(18), 3308–3319. doi:10.1177/0886260514534991

Dalenberg, C. J., Brand, B. L., Gleaves, D. H., Dorah, M. J., Loewenstein, R. L., Cardena, E., . . . Spiegel, D. (2012). Evaluation of the evidence for the trauma and fantasy models of dissociation. *Psychological Bulletin, 138*(3), 550–588.

Dallenbach, K. M. (1927). The temperature spots and end organs. *American Journal of Psychology, 54*, 431–433.

Dalton, P., & Wysocki, C. J. (1996). The nature and duration of adaptation following long-term odor exposure. *Perception & Psychophysics, 58*, 781–792.

Dalton, P., Doolittle, N., & Breslin, P. A. (2002). Gender-specific induction of enhanced sensitivity to odors. *Nature Neuroscience, 5*, 199–200.

Daly, M., & Wilson, M. (1990). Is parent-offspring conflict sex-linked? Freudian and Darwinian models. *Journal of Personality, 58*, 163–189.

Damasio, A. R. (1994). *Descartes' error: Emotion, reason, and the human brain.* New York, NY: Avon Books.

Damasio, H., Grabowski, T., Frank, R., Galaburda, A. M., & Damasio, A. R. (1994). The return of Phineas Gage: The skull of a famous patient yields clues about the brain. *Science, 264*, 1102–1105.

Damon, W. (1999, December). The moral development of children. *Scientific American*, pp. 72–78.

Dana, R. H. (2013). Culture and methodology in personality assessment. In F. A. Paniagua & A. Yamada (Eds.), *Handbook of multicultural mental health: Assessment and treatment of diverse populations* (2nd ed., pp. 205–224). San Diego, CA: Elsevier Academic.

Dantzer, R., Cohen, S., Russo, S. J., & Dinan, T. G. (2018). Resilience and immunity. *Brain, Behavior, and Immunity, 74*, 28–42. doi:10.1016/j.bbi.2018.08.010

Darbyshire, D., Kirk, C., Wall, H. J., & Kaye, L. (2016). Don't judge a (Face)book by its cover: Exploring judgement accuracy of others' personality on Facebook. *Computers in Human Behavior, 58*, 380–387.

Darley, J. M., & Latané, B. (1968). Bystander intervention in emergencies: Diffusion of responsibility. *Journal of Personality and Social Psychology, 8*, 377–383.

Darlington, R. B., & Hayes, A. F. (2017). *Regression analysis and linear models: Concepts, applications, and implementation (methodology in the social sciences).* New York, NY: Guilford.

Darwin, C. (1859). *On the origin of species.* London: John Murray.

Darwin, C. (1872). *The expression of the emotions in man and animals.* London, UK: John Murray.

Darwin, C. J., Turvey, M. T., & Crowder, R. G. (1972). An auditory analogue of the Sperling partial report procedure: Evidence for brief auditory storage. *Cognitive Psychology, 3*, 255–267.

Davey, G. C. L. (1995). Preparedness and phobias: Specific evolved associations or a generalized expectancy bias? *Behavioral and Brain Sciences, 18*, 289–325.

Davidai, S., & Gilovich, T. (2018). The ideal road not taken: The self-discrepancies involved in people's most enduring regrets. *Emotion, 18*(3), 439–452. doi:10.1037/emo0000326

Davidson, J., Hughes, D., Blazer, D., & George, L. (1991). Posttraumatic stress disorder in the community: An epidemiological study. *Psychological Medicine, 21*(3), 713–721. doi:10.1017/S0033291700022352

Davidson, R. J., & Hugdahl, K. (Eds.).(1995). *Brain asymmetry.* Cambridge, MA: MIT Press.

Davis, M. (1992). The role of the amygdala in fear and anxiety. *Annual Review of Neuroscience, 15*, 353–375.

Davis, M. C., Matthews, K. A., & McGrath, C. (2000). Hostile attitudes predict elevated vascular resistance during interpersonal stress in men and women. *Psychosomatic Medicine, 62*, 17–25.

Davison, K. P., Pennebaker, J. W., & Dickerson, S. S. (2000). Who talks? The social psychology of illness support groups. *American Psychologist, 55*, 205–217.

Dawes, R. M. (1994). *House of cards: Psychology and psychotherapy built on myth.* New York, NY: Free Press.

Dawes, R. M., Faust, D., & Meehl, P. E. (1989). Clinical versus actuarial judgment. *Science, 243*, 1668–1674.

de Castro, J. M. (1994). Family and friends produce greater social facilitation of food intake than other companions. *Physiology and Behavior, 56*, 445–455.

de Castro, J. M., & Brewer, F. M. (1992). The amount eaten in meals by humans is a power function of the number of people present. *Physiology and Behavior, 51*, 121–125.

De Groot, A. D. (1965). *Thought and chance in chess.* The Hague: Moulton.

De Houwer, J., Thomas, S., & Baeyens, F. (2001). Association learning of likes and dislikes: A review of 25 years of research on human evaluative conditioning. *Psychological Bulletin, 127*, 853–869.

De Raad, B. (2000). *The Big Five factors.* Seattle, WA: Hogrefe & Huber.

de Rivera, J. (1997). The construction of false memory syndrome: The experience of retractors. *Psychological Inquiry, 8*, 271–292.

De Ruddere, L., Goubert, L., Prkachin, K. M., Stevens, M. A., Van Ryckeghem, D. M., & Crombez, G. (2011). When you dislike patients, pain is taken less seriously. *Pain, 152*(10), 2342–2347. doi:10.1016/j.pain.2011.06.028

Deacon, T. W. (1998). *The symbolic species: The co-evolution of language and the brain.* New York, NY: Norton.

Deary, I. J., Ramsay, H., Wilson, J. A., & Riad, M. (1988). Stimulated salivation: Correlations with personality and time of day effects. *Personality and Individual Differences, 9*, 903–909.

Debeuf, T., Verbeken, S., Van Beveren, M. L., Michels, N., & Braet, C. (2018). Stress and eating behavior: A daily diary study in youngsters. *Frontiers in Psychology, 9*, 2657. doi:10.3389/fpsyg.2018.02657

Debrosse, R., Rossignac-Milon, M., & Taylor, D. M. (2017). When "who we are" and "who I desire to be" appear disconnected: Introducing collective/personal self-discrepancies and investigating their relations with minority students' psychological health. *European Journal of Social Psychology, 48*(3), 255–268. doi:10.1002/ejsp.2320

DeFazio, P. D., Gaetano, R., Caroleo, M., Cerminara, G., Maida, F., Bruno, A., . . . Segura-Garcìa, C. (2015). Rare and very rare adverse effects of clozapine. *Neuropsychiatric Disease and Treatment,* 1995. doi:10.2147/ndt.s83989

DelBello, M. P. (2002). Effects of ethnicity on psychiatric diagnosis: A developmental perspective. *Psychiatric Times, 19.*

DeLoache, J. S., & Brown, A. L. (1983). Very young children's memory for the location of objects in a large-scale environment. *Child Development, 54,* 888–897.

Dement, W. C. (1992). *The sleepwatchers.* Stanford, CA: Stanford Alumni Association.

Dement, W. C., & Kleitman, N. (1957). The relation of eye movements during sleep to dream activity: An objective method for the study of dreaming. *Journal of Experimental Psychology, 53,* 339–346.

Dement, W. C., & Vaughan, C. (1999). *The promise of sleep.* New York, NY: Delacorte.

Dempster, F. N. (1988). The spacing effect: A case study in the failure to apply the results of psychological research. *American Psychologist, 43,* 627–634.

DePaulo, B. M., & Kashy, D. A. (1998). Everyday lies in close and casual relationships. *Journal of Personality and Social Psychology, 74,* 63–79.

Deregowski, J. B. (1989). Real space and represented space: Cross-cultural perspectives. *Brain and Behavioral Sciences, 12,* 51–119.

Deroy, O., & Spence, C. (2013). Why we are not all synesthetes (not even weakly so). *Psychonomic Bulletin & Review, 20*(4), 643–664. doi:10.3758/s13423-013-0387-2

DeRubeis, R. J., & Hollon, S. D. (2014). Explanatory style in the treatment of depression. In G. M. Buchanan & M. E. P. Seligman (Eds.), *Explanatory style* (pp. 99–112). New York, NY: Routledge.

DeRubeis, R. J., Siegle, G. J., & Hollon, S. D. (2008). Cognitive therapy versus medication for depression: Treatment outcomes and neural mechanisms. *Nature Reviews Neuroscience, 9*(10), 788–796.

Deubert, C. R., Cohen, I. G., & Lynch, H. F. (2017). Comparing health-related policies & practices in sports: The NFL and other professional leagues. Retrieved from https://footballplayershealth.harvard.edu/wp-content/uploads/2017/05/03_Exec_Summary.pdf

Deutsch, M., & Gerard, H. B. (1955). A study of normative and informational social influences upon individual judgment. *Journal of Abnormal and Social Psychology, 51,* 629–636.

Devanand, D. P., Dwork, A. J., Hutchinson, M. S. E., Bolwig, T. G., & Sackeim, H. A. (1994). How does ECT alter brain structure? *American Journal of Psychiatry, 151,* 957–970.

Devine, P. G., Forscher, P. S., Austin, A. J., & Cox, W. T. (2012). Long-term reduction in implicit race bias: A prejudice habit-breaking intervention. *Journal of Experimental Social Psychology, 48*(6), 1267–1278. doi:10.1016/j.jesp.2012.06.003

DeVito, N., Bacon, S., & Goldacre, B. (2020). Compliance with legal requirement to report clinical trial results on ClinicalTrials.gov: A cohort study. *Lancet, 395*(10221), 361–369. doi:10.1016/S0140-6736(19)33220-9

Devitt, P. (2018). *13 Reasons Why and suicide contagion: What science shows about the dangers of suicide depiction. Scientific American.* Retrieved from https://www.scientificamerican.com/article/13-reasons-why-and-suicide-contagion1/

Devonport, T. J., Nicholls, W., & Fullerton, C. (2017). A systematic review of the association between emotions and eating behaviour in normal and overweight adult populations. *Journal of Health Psychology, 24*(1), 3–24. doi:10.1177/1359105317697813

Dhabhar, F. S. (2014). Effects of stress on immune function: The good, the bad, and the beautiful. *Immunology Research, 58* (2–3), 193–210. doi:10.1007/s12026-014-8517-0

Dhabhar, F., & McEwen, B. (1995). Effects of stress on immune cell distribution. Dynamics and hormonal mechanisms. *Journal of Immunology, 154,* 5511–5527.

Dickens, W. T., & Flynn, J. R. (2001). Heritability estimates versus large environmental effects: The IQ paradox resolved. *Psychological Review, 108,* 346–369.

Dickens, W. T., & Flynn, J. R. (2006). Black Americans reduce the racial IQ gap: Evidence from standardization samples. *Psychological Science, 17*(10), 913–920. doi:10.1111/j.1467-9280.2006.01802.x

Dickey, L. M., & Budge, S. L. (2020). Suicide and the transgender experience: A public health crisis. *American Psychologist, 75*(3), 380–390. doi:10.1037/amp0000619

Dielenberg, R. A., & McGregor, I. S. (1999). Habituation of the hiding response to car odor in rats. *Journal of Comparative Psychology, 113,* 376–387.

Diener, E., & Suh, E. M. (Eds.).(2000). *Culture and subjective well-being.* Cambridge, MA: MIT Press.

Diener, E., Emmons, R. A., Larsen, R. J., & Griffin, S. (1984). The Satisfaction with Life Scale. *Journal of Personality Assessment, 49,* 71–75.

Diener, E., Suh, E. M., Lucas, R. E., & Smith, H. L. (1999). Subjective well-being: Three decades of progress. *Psychological Bulletin, 125,* 276–302.

Diergaarde, B., & Kurta, M. L. (2014). Use of fertility drugs and risk of ovarian cancer. *Current Opinion in Obstetrics & Gynecology, 26*(3), 125–129. doi:10.1097/GCO.0000000000000060

Dijksterhuis, A., & Bargh, J. A. (2001). The perception-behavior expressway: Automatic effects of social perception on social behavior. *Advances in Experimental Social Psychology, 33,* 1–40.

Dijksterhuis, A., & Smith, P. (2002). Affective habituation: Subliminal exposure to extreme stimuli decreases their extremity. *Emotion, 2,* 203–214.

DiLalla, L. F., & Gottesman, I. I. (1991). Biological and genetic contributions to violence? Widom's untold tale. *Psychological Bulletin, 109,* 125–129.

Dillon, K. P., & Bushman, B. J. (2017). Effects of exposure to gun violence in movies on children's interest in real guns. *JAMA Pediatrics, 171*(11), 1057. doi:10.1001/jamapediatrics.2017.2229

Dimberg, U. (1990). Facial electromyography and emotional reactions. *Psychophysiology, 27,* 481–494.

Dimberg, U., & Ohman, A. (1996). Behold the wrath: Psychophysiological responses to facial stimuli. *Motivation and Emotion, 20*, 149–181.

Dimberg, U., Thunberg, M., & Elmehed, K. (2000). Unconscious facial reactions to emotional facial expressions. *Psychological Science, 11*, 86–89.

Dindia, K., & Allen, M. (1992). Sex differences in self-disclosure: A meta-analysis. *Psychological Bulletin, 112*, 106–124.

Dinges, D. F., Whitehouse, W. G., Orne, E. C., Powell, J. W., Orne, M. T., & Erdelyi, M. H. (1992). Evaluating hypnotic memory enhancement (hypermnesia and reminiscence) using multitrial forced recall. *Journal of Experimental Psychology: Learning, Memory, and Cognition, 18*, 1139–1147.

Dingfelder, S. (2012, October). Psychologist testifies on the risks of solitary confinement. American Psychological Association. Retrieved from https://www.apa.org/monitor/2012/10/solitary.aspx

Diong, J., Butler, A. A., Gandevia, S. C., & Héroux, M. E. (2018). Poor statistical reporting, inadequate data presentation and spin persist despite editorial advice. *PLOS ONE, 13*(8), e0202121. doi:10.1371/journal.pone.0202121

Dixon De Silva, L. E., Pointing, C., Ramos, G., Cornejo Guevara, M. V., & Chavira, D. A. (2020). Urban Latinx parent's attitudes towards mental health: Mental health literacy and service use. *Children and Youth Services Review, 109*, 104719. doi:10.1016/j.childyouth.2019.104719

Dixson, B. J., Dixson, A., Bishop, P., & Parish, A. (2009). Human physique and sexual attractiveness in men and women: A New Zealand–U.S. comparative study. *Archives of Sexual Behavior, 39*(3), 798–806.

Dixson, B. J., Dixson, A., Morgan, B., & Anderson, M. (2007). Human physique and sexual attractiveness: Sexual preferences of men and women in Bakossiland, Cameroon. *Archives of Sexual Behavior, 36*(3), 369–375.

Dobbs, S., Furnham, A., & McClelland, A. (2011). The effect of background music and noise on the cognitive test performance of introverts and extraverts. *Applied Cognitive Psychology, 25*(2), 307–313. doi:10.1002/acp.1692

Dobson, K. S. (1989). A meta-analysis of the efficacy of cognitive therapy for depression. *Journal of Consulting and Clinical Psychology, 57*, 414–419.

Docherty, A. R., Moscati, A., Peterson, R., Edwards, A. C., Adkins, D. E., Bacanu, S. A., . . . Kendler, K. S. (2016). SNP-based heritability estimates of the personality dimensions and polygenic prediction of both neuroticism and major depression: Findings from CONVERGE. *Translational Psychiatry, 6*(10), e926. doi:10.1038/tp.2016.177

Dodson, C., & Reisberg, D. (1991). Indirect testing of eyewitness memory: The (non)effect of misinformation. *Bulletin of the Psychonomic Society, 29*, 333–336.

Doidge, N. (2007). *The brain that changes itself: Stories of personal triumph from the frontiers of brain science.* London, UK: Penguin Books.

Doliński, D., Grzyb, T., Folwarczny, M., Grzybała, P., Krzyszycha, K., Martynowska, K., & Trojanowski, J. (2017). Would you deliver an electric shock in 2015? Obedience in the experimental paradigm developed by Stanley Milgram in the 50 years following the original studies. *Social Psychological and Personality Science, 8*(8), 927–933.

Dollard, J., Doob, L. W., Miller, N. E., Mowrer, O. H., & Sears, R. R. (1939). *Frustration and aggression.* New Haven, CT: Yale University Press.

Domhoff, G. W. (1996). *Finding meaning in dreams: A quantitative approach.* New York, NY: Plenum.

Domhoff, G. W. (2001). A new neurocognitive theory of dreams. *Dreaming, 11*, 13–33.

Domingue, B. W., Belsky, D. W., Fletcher, J. M., Conley, D., Boardman, J. D., & Harris, K.M. (2018). The social genome of friends and schoolmates in the National Longitudinal Study of Adolescent to Adult Health. *Proceedings of the National Academy of Sciences USA, 115*(4), 702–707. doi:10.1073/pnas.1711803115

Domingue, B. W., Fletcher, J., Conley, D., & Boardman, J. D. (2014.) Genetic and educational assortative mating among US adults. *Proceedings of the National Academy of Sciences USA, 111*, 7996–8000.

Domjan, M. (2018a). Habituation and sensitization. In *The essentials of conditioning and learning* (4th ed., pp. 27–41). Washington, DC: American Psychological Association.

Domjan, M. (2018b). *The essentials of conditioning and learning* (4th ed.). Washington, DC: American Psychological Association.

Domjan, M. (2018c). Punishment. In *The essentials of conditioning and learning* (pp. 161–174). Washington, DC: American Psychological Association.

Domjan, M., Blesbois, E., & Williams, J. (1998). The adaptive significance of sexual conditioning: Pavlovian control of sperm release. *Psychological Science, 9*, 411–415.

Donde, S. D., & Ragsdale, S. K. A. (2017). Assuming personal responsibility for sexual victimization: Harmful but potentially adaptive for college women? *Journal of Interpersonal Violence*, 88626051773422. doi:10.1177/0886260517734223

Dong, P., & Wyer, R. S. (2013). How time flies: The effects of conversation characteristics and partner attractiveness on duration judgments in a social interaction. *Journal of Experimental Social Psychology, 50*, 1–14.

Donley, R. D., & Ashcraft, M. H. (1992). The methodology of testing naive beliefs in the physics classroom. *Memory & Cognition, 20*, 381–391.

Donnelly, C., & McDaniel, M. (1993). Use of analogy in learning scientific concepts. *Journal of Experimental Psychology: Learning, Memory, and Cognition, 19*, 975–986.

Doorey, M. (2020). Lawrence Kohlberg: American psychologist. *Encyclopedia Britannica.* Retrieved from https://www.britannica.com/biography/Lawrence-Kohlberg

Dorahy, M. J., Brand, B. L., Şar, V., Krüger, C., Stavropoulos, P., Martínez-Taboas, A., . . . Middleton, W. (2014). Dissociative identity disorder: An empirical overview. *Australian & New Zealand Journal of Psychiatry, 48*(5), 402–417. doi:10.1177/0004867414527523

Dorrington, S., Zavos, H., Ball, H., McGuffin, P., Sumathipala, A., Siribaddana, S., . . . Hotopf, M. (2019). Family functioning, trauma exposure and PTSD: A cross sectional study. *Journal of Affective Disorders, 245*, 645–652. doi:10.1016/j.jad.2018.11.056

Dosher, B., & Lu, Z.-L. (2017). Visual perceptual learning and models. *Annual Review of Vision Science, 3*(1), 343–363. doi:10.1146/annurev-vision-102016-061249

Doty, R. L. (Ed.).(1995). *Handbook of olfaction and gustation*. New York, NY: Marcel Dekker.

Doty, R. L. (2001). Olfaction. *Annual Review of Psychology, 52*, 423–452.

Dougherty, T. W., Turban, D. B., & Callender, J. C. (1994). Confirming first impressions in the employment interview: A field study of interviewer behavior. *Journal of Applied Psychology, 79*, 659–665.

Douglas, N. J. (1998). The psychosocial aspects of narcolepsy. *Neurology, 50*, S27–S30.

Dovidio, J. F., & Fiske, S. T. (2012). Under the radar: How unexamined biases in decision-making processes in clinical interactions can contribute to health care disparities. *American Journal of Public Health 102*(5), 945–952.

Dovidio, J. F., Kawakami, K., Johnson, C., Johnson, B., & Howard, A. (1997). On the nature of prejudice: Automatic and controlled processes. *Journal of Experimental Social Psychology, 33*, 510–540.

Drake, R. E., & Whitley, R. (2014). Recovery and severe mental illness: Description and analysis. *Canadian Journal of Psychiatry, 59*(5), 236–242. doi:10.1177/070674371405900502

Drewnowski, A., Mennella, J. A., Johnson, S. L., & Bellisle, F. (2012). Sweetness and food preference. *Journal of Nutrition, 142*(6), 1142S–1148S. doi:10.3945/jn.111.149575

Driskell, J. E., Willis, R. P., & Copper, C. (1992). Effect of overlearning on retention. *Journal of Applied Psychology, 77*, 615–622.

Drouin, M., O'Connor, K. W., Schmidt, G. B., & Miller, D. A. (2015). Facebook fired: Legal perspectives and young adults' opinions on the use of social media in hiring and firing decisions. *Computers in Human Behavior, 46*, 123–128. doi:10.1016/j.chb.2015.01.011

Dubé, K., Sylla, L., Dee, L., Taylor, J., Evans, D., Bruton, C. D., . . . Rennie, S. (2017). Research on HIV cure: Mapping the ethics landscape. *PLoS Medicine, 14*, e1002470. doi:10.1371/journal.pmed.1002470

Dubovsky, S. L. (1997). *Mind-body deceptions: The psychosomatics of everyday life*. New York: Norton.

Duclos, S. E., Laird, J. D., Schneider, E., Sexter, M., Stern, L., & Lighten, O. V. (1989). Emotion-specific effects of facial expressions and postures on emotional experience. *Journal of Personality and Social Psychology, 57*, 100–108.

Dudycha, G. J., & Dudycha, M. M. (1941). Childhood memories: A review of the literature. *Psychological Bulletin, 38*, 668–682.

Duncombe, M. E., Havighurst, S. S., Holland, K. A., & Frankling, E. J. (2012). The contribution of parenting practices and parent emotion factors in children at risk for disruptive behavior disorders. *Child Psychiatry and Human Development, 43*(5), 715–733. doi:10.1007/s10578-012-0290-5

Dupre, M. E., & Nelson, A. (2016). Marital history and survival after a heart attack. *Social Science & Medicine, 170*, 114–123. doi:10.1016/j.socscimed.2016.10.013

Duval, S., & Wicklund, R. A. (1972). *A theory of objective self-awareness*. New York, NY: Academic.

Dweck, C.S. (2012). Mindsets and malleable minds: Implications for giftedness and talent. In R. F. Subotnik, A. Robinson, C. M. Callahan, & E. J. Gubbins (Eds). *Malleable minds: Translating insights from psychology and neuroscience to gifted education* (pp. 7–18). Storrs: National Research Center on the Gifted and Talented, University of Connecticut.

Dysart, J. E., Lindsay, R. C. L., Hammond, R., & Dupuis, P. (2001). Mug shot exposure prior to lineup identification: Interference, transference, and commitment effects. *Journal of Applied Psychology, 86*(6), 1280–1284. doi:10.1037/0021-9010.86.6.1280

Eacott, M. J., & Crawley, R. A. (1998). The offset of childhood amnesia: Memory for events that occurred before age 3. *Journal of Experimental Psychology: General, 127*, 22–33.

Eagly, A. H., & Chaiken, S. (1998). Attitude structure and function. In D. Gilbert, S. Fiske, & G. Lindzey (Eds.), *Handbook of social psychology* (4th ed.). New York, NY: McGraw-Hill.

Eagly, A. H., & Steffen, V. J. (1986). Gender and aggressive behavior: A meta-analytic review of the social psychology literature. *Psychological Bulletin, 100*, 309–330.

Earl, P. E. (2017). The evolution of behavioural economics. In R. Frantz, S. Chen, K. Dopfer, F. Heukelom, S. Mousavi, R. Frantz, (Eds.), *The Routledge handbook of behavioral economics* (pp. 5–17). New York, NY: Routledge/Taylor & Francis.

Ebbinghaus, H. (1913). *Memory: A contribution to experimental psychology* (H. Roger & C. Bussenius, Trans.). New York, NY: Teachers College Press. (Original work published 1885.)

Eccleston, C., & Crombez, G. (1999). Pain demands attention: A cognitive-affect model of the interruptive function of pain. *Psychological Bulletin, 125*, 356–366.

Education Northwest. (2017, August). *Trauma-informed practices for post-secondary education: A guide*. Retrieved from https://educationnorthwest.org/resources/trauma-informed-practices-post secondary-education-guide

Efron, R. (1990). *The decline and fall of hemispheric specialization*. Hillsdale, NJ: Erlbaum.

Egalite, A. J., & Kisida, B. (2018). The effects of teacher match on students' academic perceptions and attitudes. *Educational Evaluation and Policy Analysis, 40*(1), 59–81.

Ehlers, A., & Breuer, P. (1992). Increased cardiac awareness in panic disorder. *Journal of Abnormal Psychology, 101*, 371–382.

Eich, E. (1995). Mood as a mediator of place dependent memory. *Journal of Experimental Psychology: General, 124*(3), 293–308. doi:10.1037/0096-3445.124.3.293

Eich, E., Macaulay, D., Loewenstein, R. J., & Dihle, P. H. (1997). Memory, amnesia, and dissociative identity disorder. *Psychological Science, 8*, 417–422.

Eisenberger, R., & Cameron, J. (1996). Detrimental effects of reward: Reality or myth? *American Psychologist, 51*, 1153–1166.

Eisenberger, R., & Rhoades, L. (2001). Incremental effects of reward on creativity. *Journal of Personality and Social Psychology, 81*, 728–741.

Ekman, P., & Friesen, W. V. (1974). Detecting deception from the body or face. *Journal of Personality and Social Psychology, 29*, 288–298.

Ekman, P., Friesen, W. V., O'Sullivan, M., Chan, A., Diacoyanni-Tarlatzis, I., Heider, K., . . . Tzavaras, A. (1987). Universals and cultural differences in the judgments of facial expressions of emotion. *Journal of Personality and Social Psychology, 53*, 712–717.

Ekman, P., Levenson, R. W., & Friesen, W. V. (1983). Autonomic nervous system activity distinguishes among emotions. *Science, 221*, 1208–1210.

Ekselius L. (2018). Personality disorder: A disease in disguise. *Upsala Journal of Medical Sciences, 123*(4), 194-204. doi:10.1080/03009734.2018.1526235

Eldridge, L. L., Masterman, D., & Knowlton, B. J. (2002). Intact implicit habit learning in Alzheimer's disease. *Behavioral Neuroscience, 116,* 722-726.

Elfenbein, H. A., & Ambady, N. (2002). On the universality and cultural specificity of emotion recognition: A meta-analysis. *Psychological Bulletin, 128,* 203-235.

Elkin, I., Shea, M. T., & Watkins, J. T. (1989). National Institute of Mental Health Treatment of Depression Collaborative Research Program: General effectiveness of treatments. *Archives of General Psychiatry, 46,* 971-983.

Elkind, D. (1989). *Miseducation: Preschoolers at risk.* New York, NY: Knopf.

Elkins, R. L., Richards, T. L., Nielsen, R., Repass, R., Stahlbrandt, H., & Hoffman, H. G. (2017). The neurobiological mechanism of chemical aversion (emetic) therapy for alcohol use disorder: An fMRI study. *Frontiers in Behavioral Neuroscience, 11,* 182. doi:10.3389/fnbeh.2017.00182

Ellis, A. (1962). *Reason and emotion in psychotherapy.* New York, NY: Lyle Stuart.

Ellis, A. (1999). Why rational emotive therapy to rational emotive behavior therapy? *Psychotherapy, 36,* 154-159.

Ellison, K., & Martin, N. (2019, March 9). Severe complications for women during childbirth are skyrocketing—and could often be prevented. ProPublica. Retrieved from https://www.propublica.org/article/severe-complications-for-women-during-childbirth-are-skyrocketing-and-could-often-be-prevented

Ellsworth, P. C. (1994). William James and emotion: Is a century of fame worth a century of misunderstanding? *Psychological Review, 101,* 222-229.

Emde, R. N., Gaensbauer, T. J., & Harmon, R. J. (1976). Emotional expression in infancy: A biobehavioral study. *Psychological Issues,* 10 (Monograph 37).

Endicott, J., Nee, J., Harrison, W., & Blumenthal, R. (1993). Quality of Life Enjoyment and Satisfaction Questionnaire: A new measure. *Psychopharmacology Bulletin, 29,* 321-326.

Endler, N. S., & Persad, E. (1988). *Electroconvulsive therapy: The myths and the realities.* Toronto: Hans Huber Publishers.

Engels, G. I., Garnefski, N., & Diekstra, R. (1993). Efficacy of rational-emotive therapy: A quantitative analysis. *Journal of Consulting and Clinical Psychology, 61,* 1083-1090.

Epstein, R., Kirshnit, C. E., Lanza, R. P., & Rubin, L. C. (1984). "Insight" in the pigeon: Antecedents and determinants of an intelligent performance. *Nature, 308,* 61-62.

Epstein, S. (1979). The stability of behavior: On predicting most of the people much of the time. *Journal of Personality and Social Psychology, 37,* 1097-1126.

Epstude, K., & Roese, N. J. (2008). The functional theory of counterfactual thinking. *Personality and Social Psychology Review, 12*(2), 168-192. doi:10.1177/1088868308316091

Erbil, N. (2018). Attitudes towards menopause and depression, body image of women during menopause. *Alexandria Journal of Medicine, 54*(3), 241-246. doi:10.1016/j.ajme.2017.05.012

Erdelyi, M. H. (1992). Psychodynamics and the unconscious. *American Psychologist, 47,* 784-787.

Erdelyi, M. H. (1996). *The recovery of unconscious memories: Hypermnesia and reminiscence.* Chicago, IL: University of Chicago Press.

Ericsson, K. A., & Chase, W. G. (1982). Exceptional memory. *American Scientist, 70,* 607-615.

Ericsson, K. A., Chase, W. G., & Faloon, S. (1980). Acquisition of a memory skill. *Science, 208,* 1181-1182.

Erikson, E. H. (1959). Identity and the life cycle. *Psychological Issues* (Monograph 1).

Erikson, E. H. (1963). *Childhood and society.* New York, NY: Norton.

Eriksson, M., Marschik, P. B., Tulviste, T., Almgren, M., Pérez Pereira, M., Wehberg, S., . . . Gallego, C. (2012). Differences between girls and boys in emerging language skills: Evidence from 10 language communities. *British Journal of Developmental Psychology, 30*(Pt. 2), 326-343.

Ernst, E., & Abbot, N. (1999). I shall please: The mysterious power of placebos. In S. D. Sala (Ed.), *Mind myths: Exploring popular assumptions about the mind and brain* (pp. 209-213). Chichester, UK: Wiley.

Erol, R. Y., & Orth, U. (2011). Self-esteem development from age 14 to 30 years: A longitudinal study. *Journal of Personality and Social Psychology, 101*(3), 607-619. doi:10.1037/a0024299

Eron, L. D. (1987). The development of aggressive behavior from the perspective of a developing behaviorism. *American Psychologist, 42,* 435-442.

Eschweiler, G. W., Vonthein, R., Bode, R., Huell, M., Conca, A., Peters, O., . . . Schlotter, W. (2007). Clinical efficacy and cognitive side effects of bifrontal versus right unilateral electroconvulsive therapy (ECT): A short-term randomised controlled trial in pharmaco-resistant major depression. *Journal of Affective Disorders, 101* (1-3), 149-157. doi:10.1016/j.jad.2006.11.012

Esterson, A. (2001). The mythologizing of psychoanalytic history: Deception and self-deception in Freud's accounts of the seduction theory episode. *History of Psychiatry, 12,* 329-352.

Ethnologue. (2018). How many languages are there in the world? Ethnologue. Retrieved from https://www.ethnologue.com/guides/how-many-languages

Ethnologue.com. (n.d.). Browse by language name. Retrieved from https://www.ethnologue.com/browse/names

Etzersdorfer, E., & Sonneck, G. (1998). Preventing suicide by influencing mass-media reporting. The Viennese experience 1980-1996. *Archives of Suicide Research, 4*(67). doi:10.1023/A:1009691903261

Evans, J. R., & Aberbanel, A. (Eds.).(1999). *Introduction to quantitative EEG and neurofeedback.* San Diego, CA: Academic.

Evenson, K. R., Goto, M. M., & Furberg, R. D. (2015). Systematic review of the validity and reliability of consumer-wearable activity trackers. *International Journal of Behavioral Nutrition and Physical Activity, 12,* 159. doi:10.1186/s12966-015-0314-1

Everson, S. A., Goldberg, D. E., Kaplan, G. A., Cohen, R. D., Pukkala, E., Tuomilehto, J., & Salonen, J. (1996). Hopelessness and risk of mortality and incidence of myocardial infarction and cancer. *Psychosomatic Medicine, 58,* 103-121.

Exelmans, L., Custers, K., & Bulck, J. V. D. (2015). Violent video games and delinquent behavior in adolescents: A risk factor perspective. *Aggressive Behavior, 41*(3), 267–279. doi:10.1002/ab.21587

Exner, J. E., Jr. (1996). *The Rorschach: A comprehensive system* A critical examination". *Psychological Science, 7*, 11–13.

Exner, J. E., Jr. (1993). *The Rorschach: A comprehensive system* (Vol. 1: *Basic foundations*; 3rd ed.). New York, NY: Wiley.

Eysenck, H. (1952). The effects of psychotherapy: An evaluation. *Journal of Consulting Psychology, 16*, 319–324.

Eysenck, H. (2002). *Decline and fall of the Freudian empire.* New York, NY: Routledge.

Eysenck, H. J. (1967). *The biological basis of personality.* Springfield, IL: Thomas.

Eysenck, H. J. (1982). *A model for intelligence.* Berlin, Germany: Springer-Verlag.

Eysenck, H. J., & Eysenck, S. G. B. (1964). *Manual of the Eysenck personality inventory.* London, UK: University of London Press.

Eysenck, H. J. (1990). Biological dimensions of personality. In L. A. Pervin (Ed.), *Handbook of personality theory and research* (pp. 244–276). New York, NY: Guilford.

Eysenck, H. J., & Eysenck, M. W. (1985). *Personality and individual differences: A natural science approach.* New York: Plenum.

Fabes, R. A., Martin, C. L., & Hanish, L. D. (2003). Young children's play qualities in same-, other-, and mixed-sex peer groups. *Child Development, 74*(3), 921–932.

Fallon, J. (2013). *The psychopath inside: A neuroscientist's personal journey into the dark side of the brain.* New York, NY: Current.

Fanelli Kuczmarski, M., Cotugna, N., Pohlig, R. T., Beydoun, M. A., Adams, E. L., Evans, M. K., . . . Zonderman, A. B. (2017). Snacking and diet quality are associated with the coping strategies used by a socioeconomically diverse urban cohort of African-American and White adults. *Journal of the Academy of Nutrition and Dietetics, 117*(9), 1355–1365. doi:10.1016/j.jand.2017.02.010

Fantz, R. L. (1961). The origin of form perception. *Scientific American, 204*, 66–72.

Farber, B. A., Brink, D. C., & Raskin, P. M. (Eds.).(1996). *The psychotherapy of Carl Rogers: Cases and commentary.* New York, NY: Guilford.

Fardouly, J., Diedrichs, P. C., Vartanian, L. R., & Halliwell, E. (2015). Social comparisons on social media: The impact of Facebook on young women's body image concerns and mood. *Body Image, 13*, 38–45. doi:10.1016/j.bodyim.2014.12.002

Farley, H. (2019). Promoting self-efficacy in patients with chronic disease beyond traditional education: A literature review. *Nursing Open, 7*(1), 30–41. doi:10.1002/nop2.382

Farrell, P. A., Gates, W. K., Maksud, M. G., & Morgan, W. P. (1982). Increases in plasma beta endorphin/ beta-lipotropin immunoreactivity after treadmill running in humans. *Journal of Applied Psychology, 52*, 1245–1249.

Farrelly, D., Clemson, P., & Guthrie, M. (2016). Are women's mate preferences for altruism also influenced by physical attractiveness? *Evolutionary Psychology, 14*(1), 147470491562369. doi:10.1177/1474704915623698

Farrelly, D., Lazarus, J., & Roberts, G. (2007). Altruists attract. *Evolutionary Psychology, 5*(2), 147470490700500. doi:10.1177/147470490700500205

Fawcett, J., Rosser, A. E., & Dunnett, S. B. (Eds.).(2001). *Brain damage and brain repair.* New York, NY: Oxford University Press.

Fazel, S., & Danesh, J. (2002). Serious mental disorder in 23,000 prisoners: A systematic review of 62 surveys. *Lancet, 359*, 545–550.

Fearnow, B. (2018, May 10). A Black family's Sunday barbecue was interrupted after a woman called out their charcoal grill and phoned the cops. *Newsweek.* Retrieved from http://www.newsweek.com/lake-merritt-bbq-barbecue-video-oakland-racist-charcoal-east-bay-black-family-919355

Fechner, G. T. (1860). *Elements of psychophysics* (H. E. Alder, Trans.). New York, NY: Holt, Rinehart & Winston. (Translated edition 1966.)

Feehan, M., McGee, R., Stanton, W. R., & Silva, P. A. (1991). Strict and inconsistent discipline in childhood: Consequences for adolescent mental health. *British Journal of Clinical Psychology, 30*(4), 325–331. doi:10.1111/j.2044-8260.1991.tb00953.x

Feigenson, L., Carey, S., & Spelke, E. (2002). Infant discrimination of number and spatial extent. *Cognitive Psychology, 44*, 33–66.

Feixas, G., & Botella, L. (2004). Psychotherapy integration: Reflections and contributions from a constructivist epistemology. *Journal of Psychotherapy Integration, 142*, 192–222. doi:10.1037/1053-0479.14.2.192

Feld, B. (2012). *Kids, cops, and interrogation: Inside the interrogation room.* New York, NY: New York University Press.

Felitti, V. J., Anda, R. F., Nordenberg, D., Williamson, D. F., Spitz, A. M., Edwards, V., . . . Marks, J. S. (1998). Relationship of childhood abuse and household dysfunction to many of the leading causes of death in adults. The Adverse Childhood Experiences (ACE) Study. *American Journal of Preventive Medicine, 14*(4), 245–258. doi:10.1016/s0749-3797(98)00017-8

Ferdenzi, C., Delplanque, S., Atanassova, R., & Sander, D. (2016). Androstadienone's influence on the perception of facial and vocal attractiveness is not sex specific. *Psychoneuroendocrinology, 66*, 166–175. doi:10.1016/j.psyneuen.2016.01.016

Fernald, A. (1985). Four-month-old infants prefer to listen to motherese. *Infant Behavior and Development, 8*, 181–195.

Fernald, A., Taeschner, T., Dunn, J., Papousek, M., Boysson-Bardies, B. D., & Fukui, I. (1989). A cross-linguistic study of prosodic modifications in mothers' and fathers' speech to preverbal infants. *Journal of Child Language, 16*, 477–501.

Ferrell, D. R., & Silverman, M. A. (2014). A dangerous movie? Hollywood does psychoanalysis. *Journal of Religion and Health, 53*(6), 1841–1856. doi:10.1007/s10943-014-9930-3

Ferster, C. B., & Skinner, B. F. (1957). *Schedules of reinforcement.* New York, NY: Appleton-Century-Crofts.

Fessel, J. (2021). A vaccine to prevent initial loss of cognition and eventual Alzheimer's disease in elderly persons. *Alzheimers Dement, 7*(1), e12126. doi:10.1002/trc2.12126

Festinger, L. (1957). *A theory of cognitive dissonance.* Stanford, CA: Stanford University Press.

Festinger, L., & Carlsmith, J. M. (1959). Cognitive consequences of forced compliance. *Journal of Abnormal and Social Psychology, 58*, 203–210.

Fidler Mis, N., Braegger, C., Bronsky, J., Campoy, C., Domellöf, M., Embleton, N. D., ... Fewtrell, M. (2017). Sugar in infants, children and adolescents: A position paper of the European Society for Paediatric Gastroenterology, Hepatology and Nutrition Committee on Nutrition. *Journal of Pediatric Gastroenterology and Nutrition, 65*(6), 681–696. doi:10.1097/MPG.0000000000001733

Field, T. (2001). *Touch.* Cambridge, MA: MIT Press.

Field, T., Woodson, R., Greenberg, R., & Cohen, D. (1982). Discrimination and imitation of facial expressions by neonates. *Science, 218,* 179–181.

Filippopulos, F. M., Albers, L., Straube, A., Gerstl, L., Blum, B., Langhagen, T., ... Landgraf, M. N. (2017). Vertigo and dizziness in adolescents: Risk factors and their population attributable risk. *PLOS ONE, 12*(11), e0187819. doi:10.1371/journal.pone.0187819

Fink, M. (1999). *Electroshock: Restoring the mind.* New York, NY: Oxford University Press.

Finucane, A., & Mercer, S. W. (2006). An exploratory mixed methods study of the acceptability and effectiveness of mindfulness-based cognitive therapy for patients with active depression and anxiety in primary care. *BMC Psychiatry, 6*(1). doi:10.1186/1471-244x-6-14

Fischer-Tenhagen, C., Theby, V., Krömker, V., & Heuwieser, W. (2018). Detecting *Staphylococcus aureus in milk from dairy cows using sniffer dogs. Journal of Dairy Science, 101*(5), 4317–4324. doi:10.3168/jds.2017-14100

Fischer, J. S. (2000, January 24). Taking the shock out of electroshock. *U.S. News & World Report,* p. 46.

Fischer, P., Krueger, J. I., Greitemeyer, T., Vogrincic, C., Kastenmüller, A., Frey, D., ... Kainbacher, M. (2011). The bystander-effect: A meta-analytic review on bystander intervention in dangerous and non-dangerous emergencies. *Psychological Bulletin, 137*(4), 517–537. doi:10.1037/a0023304

Fisher, G. H. (1968). Ambiguity of form: Old and new. *Perception & Psychophysics, 4,* 189–192.

Fisher, S., & Greenberg, R. P. (1977). *The scientific credibility of Freud's theories and therapy.* New York, NY: Columbia University Press.

Fiske, D. W., & Maddi, S. R. (1961). *The functions of varied experience.* Homewood, IL: Dorsey.

Fitzgerald, J. M. (1988). Vivid memories and the reminiscence phenomenon: The role of self-narrative. *Human Development, 31,* 261–273.

Flavell, J. H. (1996). Piaget's legacy. *Psychological Science, 7,* 200–203.

Flavell, J. H. (1999). Cognitive development: Children's knowledge about the mind. *Annual Review of Psychology, 50,* 21–45.

Flavell, J. H., Miller, P. H., & Miller, S. A. (1993). *Cognitive development* (3rd ed.). Englewood Cliffs, NJ: Prentice-Hall.

Flayelle, M., Maurage, P., Di Lorenzo, K. R., Vögele, C., Gainsbury, S. M., & Billieux, J. (2020). Binge-watching: What do we know so far? A first systematic review of the evidence. *Current Addition Reports, 7,* 44–60. doi:10.1007/s40429-020-00299-8

Fleischman, J. (2002). *Phineas Gage: A gruesome but true story about brain science.* Boston: Houghton Mifflin.

Flieller, A. (1999). Comparison of the development of formal thought in adolescent cohorts aged 10 to 15 years (1967–1996 and 1972–1993). *Developmental Psychology, 35,* 1048–1058.

Flinker, A., Korzeniewska, A., Shestyuk, A. Y., Franaszczuk, P. J., Dronkers, N. F., Knight, R. T., & Crone, N. E. (2015). Redefining the role of Broca's area in speech. *Proceedings of the National Academy of Science USA, 112*(9), 2871–2875. doi:10.1073/pnas.1414491112

Flor, H., Elbert, T., Knecht, S., Wienbruch, C., Pantev, C., Birbaumers, N., ... Taub, E. (1995). Phantom-limb pain as a perceptual correlate of cortical reorganization following arm amputation. *Nature, 375,* 482–484.

Flore, P. C., & Wicherts, J. M. (2015). Does stereotype threat influence performance of girls in stereotyped domains? A meta-analysis. *Journal of School Psychology, 53*(1), 25–44.

Flynn, J. R. (1987). Massive IQ gains in 14 nations: What IQ tests really measure. *Psychology Bulletin, 101,* 171–191.

Foa, E. B., & Franklin, M. E. (2001). Obsessive-compulsive disorder. In D. H. Barlow (Ed.), *Clinical handbook of psychological disorders* (3rd ed., pp. 209–263). New York, NY: Guilford.

Foa, E. B., Kozak, M. J., Salkovskis, P. M., Coles, M. E., & Amir, N. (1999). The validation of a new obsessive-compulsive disorder scale: The Obsessive-Compulsive Inventory. *Psychological Assessment, 10,* 206–214.

Foa, E. B., Riggs, D. S., & Gershuny, B. S. (1995). Arousal, numbing, and intrusion: Symptom structure of PTSD following assault. *American Journal of Psychiatry, 152*(1), 116–120. doi:10.1176/ajp.152.1.116

Folch, J., Petrov, D., Ettcheto, M., Abad, S., Sánchez-López, E., García, M. L., ... Camins, A. (2016). Current research therapeutic strategies for Alzheimer's disease treatment. *Neural Plasticity, 2016,* 1–15. doi:10.1155/2016/8501693

Folsom, D. P., Fleisher, A. S., & Depp, C. A. (2006). Schizophrenia. In D. V. Jeste & J. H. Friedman (Eds.), *Psychiatry for neurologists* (pp. 59–66). Totowa, NJ: Humana.

Fond, G., Pauly, V., Leone, M., Llorca, P. M., Orleans, V., Loundou, A., ... Boyer, L. (2021). Disparities in intensive care unit admission and mortality among patients with schizophrenia and COVID-19: A national cohort study. *Schizophrenia Bulletin, 47*(3), 624–634. doi:10.1093/schbul/sbaa158

Fontaine, J. R. J., Scherer, K. R., Roesch, E. B., & Ellsworth, P. C. (2007). The world of emotions is not two-dimensional. *Psychological Science, 18,* 1050–1057. doi:10.1111/j.1467-9280.2007.02024.x

Fontana, L., & Partridge, L., (2015). Promoting health and longevity through diet: From model organisms to humans. *Cell, 161*(1), 106–118. doi:10/1016/j.cell.2015.02.020

Forbes, H., Fichera, E., Rogers, A., & Sutton, M. (2017). The effects of exercise and relaxation on health and wellbeing. *Health Economics, 26*(12), e67–e80. doi:10.1002/hec.3477

Ford, M. R., & Widiger, T. A. (1989). Sex bias in the diagnosis of histrionic and antisocial personality disorders. *Journal of Consulting and Clinical Psychology, 57,* 301–305.

Ford, T. E., Lappi, S. K., & Holden, C. J. (2016). Personality, humor styles and happiness: Happy people have positive humor styles. *Europe's Journal of Psychology, 12*(3), 320–337. doi:10.5964/ejop.v12i3.1160

Forrest, D. (2001). *Hypnotism: A history.* New York, NY: Penguin.

Forscher, P. S., Mitamura, C., Dix, E. L., Cox, W. T., & Devine, P. G. (2017). Breaking the prejudice habit: Mechanisms, timecourse, and longevity. *Journal of Experimental Social Psychology, 72,* 133–146. doi:10.1016/j.jesp.2017.04.009

Forsyth, D. R., Zyzniewski, L. E., & Giammanco, C. A. (2002). Responsibility diffusion in cooperative collectives. *Personality and Social Psychology Bulletin, 28,* 54–65.

Foster, J. K., & Jelicic, M. (Eds.).(1999). *Memory: Systems, process, or function?* New York, NY: Oxford University Press.

Foulke, E. (1991). Braille. In M. A. Heller & W. Schiff (Eds.), *The psychology of touch* (pp. 219–233). Hillsdale, NJ: Erlbaum.

Foulkes, D. (1962). Dream reports from different states of sleep. *Journal of Abnormal and Social Psychology, 65,* 14–25.

Foulkes, D. (1999). *Children's dreaming and the development of consciousness.* Cambridge, MA: Harvard University Press.

Fowler, M. J., Sullivan, M. J., & Ekstrand, B. R. (1973). Sleep and memory. *Science, 179,* 302–304.

Fowler, R. D. (1986, May). Howard Hughes: A psychological autopsy. *Psychology Today,* pp. 22–33.

Fowles, D. C. (1992). Schizophrenia: Diathesis-stress revisited. *Annual Review of Psychology, 43,* 303–336.

Fraley, R. C., & Roisman, G. I. (2015). Early attachment experiences and romantic functioning. In: *Attachment theory and research: New directions and emerging themes.* (p. 9).

Fraley, R. C., & Marks, M. J. (2010). Westermarck, Freud, and the incest taboo: Does familial resemblance activate sexual attraction? *Personality and Social Psychology Bulletin, 36*(9), 1202–1212. doi:10.1177/0146167210377180

Franceschini, C., Pizza, F., Cavalli, F., & Plazzi, G. (2021). A practical guide to the pharmacological and behavioral therapy of Narcolepsy. *Neurotherapeutics: The Journal of the American Society for Experimental NeuroTherapeutics, 18*(1), 6–19. doi:10.1007/s13311-021-01051-4

Frank, D. L., Khorshid, L., Kiffer, J. F., Moravec, C. S., & McKee, M. G. (2010). Biofeedback in medicine: Who, when, why and how? *Mental Health in Family Medicine, 7*(2), 85–91.

Frazier, J. A., & Morrison, F. J. (1998). The influence of extended-year schooling on growth of achievement and perceived competence in early elementary school. *Child Development, 69,* 495–517.

Fréchette, S., & Romano, E. (2017). How do parents label their physical disciplinary practices? A focus on the definition of corporal punishment. *Child Abuse & Neglect, 71,* 92–103. doi:10.1016/j.chiabu.2017.02.003

Frederickson, B. L., Maynard, K. E., Helms, M. J., Haney, T. L., Siegler, I. C., & Barefoot, J. C. (2000). Hostility predicts magnitude and duration of blood pressure response to anger. *Journal of Behavioral Medicine, 23,* 229–243.

Freedman, B. J. (1974). The perceptual experience of perpetual and cognitive disturbances in schizophrenia: A review of autobiographical accounts. *Archives of General Psychiatry, 30,* 333–340.

Freedman, J. L. (1988). Television violence and aggression: What the evidence shows. *Applied Social Psychology Annual, 8,* 144–162.

Freedman, R., Adler, L. E., Gerhardt, G. A., Waldo, M., Baker, N., Rose, G. M., . . . Franks, R. (1987). Neurobiological studies of sensory gating in schizophrenia. *Schizophrenia Bulletin, 13,* 669–678.

Freud, S. (1900). *The interpretation of dreams.* Vols. 4 and 5 of the Standard Edition. London, UK: Hogarth.

Freud, S. (1909). Analysis of a phobia in a five-year-old boy. In *Collected works of Sigmund Freud* (Vol. 10). London, UK: Hogarth.

Freud, S. (1940). *An outline of psychoanalysis.* Vol. 2Vol. 23 of the Standard Edition. London, UK: Hogarth.

Freud, S. (1917). Mourning and melancholia. In J. Riviere (Trans.), *Collected papers* (Vol. 4). London, UK: Hogarth Press.

Fridlund, A. J. (1994). *Human facial expression: An evolutionary view.* San Diego, CA: Academic.

Friedman, H. S. (1991). *The self-healing personality.* New York, NY: Holt.

Friedman, H. S., & Booth-Kewley, S. (1987). The "disease-prone personality": A meta-analytic view of the construct. *American Psychologist, 42,* 539–555.

Friedman, L. E., Aponte, C., Perez Hernandez, R., Velez, J. C., Gelaye, B., Sánchez, S. E., . . . & Peterlin, B. L. (2017). Migraine and the risk of post-traumatic stress disorder among a cohort of pregnant women. *Journal of Headache and Pain, 18*(1), 67. doi:10.1186/s10194-017-0775-5

Friedman, M., & Ulmer, D. (1984). *Treating Type A behavior–and your heart.* New York, NY: Knopf.

Friedman, S. L., & Boyle, D. E. (2008). Attachment in US children experiencing nonmaternal care in the early 1990s. *Attachment & Human Development, 10*(3), 225–261.

Friedrich, M. J. (2002). Epidemic of obesity expands its spread to developing countries. *Journal of the American Medical Association, 287,* 1382–1386.

Frieske, D. A., & Park, D. C. (1999). Memory for news in young and old adults. *Psychology and Aging, 14,* 90–98.

Fromm, E. (1941). *Escape from freedom.* New York, NY: Farrar & Rinehart.

Frosh, S. (2016). Towards a psychosocial psychoanalysis. *American Imago, 73*(4), 469–482. doi:10.1353/aim.2016.0025

Fry, J. M. (1998). Treatment modalities for narcolepsy. *Neurology, 50,* S43–S48.

Fuchs, E., & Flügge, G. (2014). Adult neuroplasticity: More than 40 years of research. *Neural Plasticity.* doi:10.1155/2014/541870

Fukuwatari, T., Kawada, T., Tsuruta, M., Hiraoka, T., Iwanaga, T., Sugimoto, E., & Fushiki, T. (1997). Expression of the putative membrane fatty acid transporter (FAT) in taste buds of the circumvallate papillae in rats. *FEBS Letters, 414*(2), 461–464. doi:10.1016/s0014-5793(97)01055-7

Funder, D. C. (2001). Personality. *Annual Review of Psychology, 52,* 197–221.

Funk, S. C. (1992). Hardiness: A review of theory and research. *Health Psychology, 11,* 335–345.

Furman, W., & Shaffer, L. A. (1999). A story of adolescence: The emergence of other-sex relationships. *Journal of Youth and Adolescence, 28,* 513–522.

Furr, S. R., Westefeld, J. S., McConnell, G. N., & Jenkins, J. M. (2001). Suicide and depression among college students: A decade later. *Professional Psychology: Research and Practice, 32*, 97–100.

Gabrieli, J. D., Desmond, J. E., Demb, J. B., Wagner, A. D., Stone, M. V., Vaidya, C. J., & Glover, G. H. (1996). Functional magnetic resonance imaging of semantic memory processes in the frontal lobes. *Psychological Science, 7*, 278–283.

Gacono, C. B., Gacono, L. A., & Evans, F. B. (2008). Essential issues in the forensic use of the Rorschach. In C. B. Gacono & F. B. Evans (Eds.) *The handbook of forensic Rorschach assessment* (pp. 3–20). New York, NY: Routledge.

Gaertner, S. L., & McLaughlin, J. P. (1983). Racial stereotypes: Associations and ascriptions of positive and negative characteristics. *Social Psychology Quarterly, 46*, 23–30.

Gaffney, A., & McCormick, D. (2017). The Affordable Care Act: Implications for health-care equity. *Lancet, 389*(10077), 1442–1452. doi:10.1016/s0140-6736(17)30786-9

Gafford, G. M., Parsons, R. G., & Helmstetter, F. J. (2011). Consolidation and reconsolidation of contextual fear memory requires mammalian target of rapamycin-dependent translation in the dorsal hippocampus. *Neuroscience, 182*, 98–104.

Gage, N., & Baars, B. (2018). *Fundamentals of cognitive neuroscience* (2nd ed.). Cambridge, MA: Academic Press.

Galanter, M. (1999). *Cults: Faith, healing, and coercion* (2nd ed.). New York, NY: Oxford University Press.

Galinsky, A. D., & Moskowitz, G. B. (2000). Perspective-taking: Decreasing stereotype expression, stereotype accessibility, and in-group favoritism. *Journal of Personality and Social Psychology, 78*, 708–724.

Gallagher, A. M., De Lisi, R., Holst, P. C., McGillicuddy-De Lisi, A. V., & Cahalan, C. (2000). Gender differences in advanced mathematical problem solving. *Journal of Experimental Child Psychology, 75*, 165–190.

Galmiche, M., Déchelotte, P., Lambert, G., & Tavolacci, M. P. (2019). Prevalence of eating disorders over the 2000–2018 period: A systematic literature review. *American Journal of Clinical Nutrition, 109*(5), 1402–1413. doi:10.1093/ajcn/nqy342

Galton, F. (1883). *Inquiries into human faculty and its development*. London, UK: Dent.

Gamwell, L., & Tomes, N. (1995). *Madness in America: Cultural and medical perceptions of mental illness before 1914*. Ithaca, NY: Cornell University Press.

Gansberg, M. (1964, March 27). 37 Who saw murder didn't call police. *New York Times*.

Gara, M. A., Woolfolk, R. L., Cohen, B. D., Goldston, R. B., Allen, L. A., & Novalany, J. (1993). Perception of self and other in major depression. *Journal of Abnormal Psychology, 102*, 93–100.

Garb, H. N., Florio, C. M., & Grove, W. M. (1998). The validity of the Rorschach and the Minnesota Multiphasic Personality Inventory: Results from metaanalyses. *Psychological Science, 9*, 402–404.

García-Lizana, F., & Muñoz-Mayorga, I. (2010). What about telepsychiatry? *Primary Care Companion to the Journal of Clinical Psychiatry*. doi:10.4088/pcc.09m00831whi

Garcia, J. (1981). The logic and limits of mental aptitude testing. *American Psychologist, 36*, 1172–1180.

Garcia, J. R., Reiber, C., Massey, S. G., & Merriwether, A. M. (2012). Sexual hookup culture: A review. *Review of General Psychology, 16*(2), 161–176. doi:10.1037/a0027911

Garcia, J., Vargas, N., Clark, J.L., Magaña Álvarez, M., Nelons, D. A., & Parker, R.G. (2020). Social isolation and connectedness as determinants of well-being: Global evidence mapping focused on LGBTQ youth. *Global Public Health, 15*(4), 497–519. doi:10.1080/17441692.2019.1682028

Garcia, J., & Koelling, R. A. (1966). The relation of cue to consequence in avoidance learning. *Psychonomic Science, 4*, 123–124.

Gardner, E. P., & Martin, J. H. (2000). Coding of sensory information. In E. R. Kandel, J. H. Schwartz, & T. M. Jessell (Eds.), *Principles of neural science* (4th ed., pp. 411–429). New York, NY: McGraw-Hill.

Gardner, H. (1983). *Frames of mind: The theory of multiple intelligences*. New York: Basic Books.

Gardner, H. (2000). *Intelligence reframed: Multiple intelligences for the 21st century*. New York: Basic Books.

Garner, W. H., & Garner, M. H. (2016). Protein disulfide levels and lens elasticity modulation: applications for presbyopia. *Investigative Ophthalmology & Visual Science, 57*(6), 2851. doi:10.1167/iovs.15-18413

Gatchel, R. J., & Turk, D. C. (Eds.).(1999). *Psychosocial factors in pain: Critical perspectives*. New York, NY: Guilford.

Gatchel, R. J., Peng, Y. B., Peters, M. L., Fuchs, P. N., & Turk, D. C. (2007). The biopsychosocial approach to chronic pain: Scientific advances and future directions. *Psychological Bulletin, 133*(4), 581–624. doi:10.1037/0033-2909.133.4.581

Gathercole, S. E. (Ed.).(2001). *Short-term and working memory*. Brighton, UK: Psychology Press.

Gavin, L., & Furman, W. (1989). Age differences in adolescents' perceptions of their peer groups. *Developmental Psychology, 25*, 827–834.

Gazzaniga, M. S. (Ed.).(1984). *Handbook of cognitive neuroscience*. New York, NY: Springer.

Gazzaniga, M. S. (1967). The split brain in man. *Scientific American*, 24–29.

Gazzaniga, M. S. (1985). *The social brain*. New York, NY: Basic Books.

Gazzaniga, M. S. (1992). *Nature's mind: The roots of thinking, emotions, sexuality, language, and intelligence*. New York, NY: Basic Books.

Geen, R. G., & Donnerstein, E. (1998). *Human aggression: Theories, research, and implications for social policy*. San Diego, CA: Academic.

Geer, J. G. (2004). *Public opinion and polling around the world: A historical encyclopedia, Vol. 1*, Santa Barbara, CA: ABC-CLIO.

Geers, A. L., Rose, J. P., Fowler, S. L., Rasinski, H. M., Brown, J. A., & Helfer, S. G. (2013). Why does choice enhance treatment effectiveness? Using placebo treatments to demonstrate the role of personal control. *Journal of Personality and Social Psychology, 105*(4), 549–566. doi:10.1037/a0034005

Geher, G. (2000). Perceived and actual characteristics of parents and partners: A test of a Freudian model of mate selection. *Current Psychology, 19*(3), 194–214.

Gelman, A., & Hill, J. (2006). *Data analysis using regression and multilevel/hierarchical models (analytical methods for social research)*. Cambridge, UK: Cambridge University Press.

Gelman, R. (1979). Preschool thought. *American Psychologist, 34*, 900–905.

Gendreau, P., & Goggin, C. (2014). Practicing psychology in correctional settings. In I. B. Weiner & R. K. Otto (Eds.), *The handbook of forensic psychology* (4th ed.). Hoboken, NJ: Wiley.

Genetics of Personality Consortium, de Moor, M. H., van den Berg, S. M., Verweij, K. J., Krueger, R. F., Luciano, M., . . . Boomsma, D. I. (2015). Meta-analysis of genome-wide association studies for neuroticism, and the polygenic association with major depressive disorder. *JAMA Psychiatry, 72*(7), 642–650. doi:10.1001/jamapsychiatry.2015.0554

Gentner, D., & Stevens, A. L. (Eds.).(1983). *Mental models*. Hillsdale, NJ: Erlbaum.

George, T. P., & Hartmann, D. P. (1996). Friendship networks of unpopular, average, and popular children. *Child Development, 67*, 2301–2316.

Gerrard, M. (1987). Sex, sex guilt, and contraceptive use revisited: The 1980s. *Journal of Personality and Social Psychology, 52*, 975–980.

Gershkoff-Stowe, L., Thal, D. J., Smith, L. B., & Namy, L. L. (1997). Categorization and its developmental relation to early language. *Child Development, 68*, 843–859.

Gershoff, E. T. (2002). Corporal punishment by parents and associated child behaviors and experiences: A meta-analytic and theoretical review. *Psychological Bulletin, 128*, 539–579.

Gershoff, E. T. (2013). Spanking and child development: We know enough now to stop hitting our children. *Child Development Perspectives, 7*(3), 133–137.

Gescheider, G. A. (1997). *Psychophysics: The fundamentals* (3rd ed.). Mahwah, NJ: Erlbaum.

Geschwind, N. (1979). Specializations of the human brain. *Scientific American, 241*, 180–199.

Giakoumatos, C. I., Nanda, P., Mathew, I. T., Tandon, N., Shah, J., Bishop, J. R., . . . Keshavan, M. S. (2015). Effects of lithium on cortical thickness and hippocampal subfield volumes in psychotic bipolar disorder. *Journal of Psychiatric Research, 61*, 180–187. doi:10.1016/j.jpsychires.2014.12.008

Gibbons, F. X., Gerrard, M., Blanton, H., & Russell, D. W. (1998). Reasoned action and social reaction: Willingness and intention as independent predictors of health risk. *Journal of Personality and Social Psychology, 74*, 1164–1180.

Gibbs, W. W. (2001, October). Fact or artifact? The placebo effect may be a little of both. *Scientific American*, p. 1.

Gibson, E. J., & Walker, A. S. (1984). Development of knowledge of visual-tactual affordances of substance. *Child Development, 55*, 453–461.

Gibson, E., & Walk, R. D. (1960). The visual cliff. *Scientific American, 202*, 80–92.

Gibson, H. B. (1991). Can hypnosis compel people to commit harmful, immoral and criminal acts? A review of the literature. *Contemporary Hypnosis, 8*, 129–140.

Gibson, J. (2015). *The ecological approach to visual perception*. New York, NY: Psychology Press.

Gibson, J. J. (1962). Observations on active touch. *Psychological Review, 69*, 477–491.

Gibson, J. J. (1979). *The ecological approach to visual perception*. Boston, MA: Houghton Mifflin.

Gieser, L., & Stein, M. I. (1999). *Evocative images: The Thematic Apperception Test and the art of projection*. Washington, DC: American Psychological Association.

Gilbert, D. T., & Hixon, J. G. (1991). The trouble of thinking: Activation and application of stereotypic beliefs. *Journal of Personality and Social Psychology, 60*, 509–517.

Gilbert, D. T., & Malone, P. S. (1995). The correspondence bias. *Psychological Bulletin, 117*, 21–38.

Gilboa, A., & Bodner, E. (2009). What are your thoughts when the national anthem is playing? An empirical exploration. *Psychology of Music, 37*(4), 459–484. doi:10.1177/0305735608097249

Gillespie, J. J., & Privitera, G. J. (2018). *Patient-centric analytics in health care: Driving value in clinical settings and psychological practice*. Lanham, MD: Lexington.

Gillham, N. W. (2001). *A life of Sir Francis Galton: From African exploration to the birth of eugenics*. New York, NY: Oxford University Press.

Gilligan, C. (1982). *In a different voice: Psychological theory and women's development*. Cambridge, MA: Harvard University Press.

Gillum, R. F., King, D. E., Obisesan, T. O., & Koenig, H. G. (2008). Frequency of attendance at religious services and mortality in a U.S. national cohort. *Annals of Epidemiology, 18*(2), 124–129. doi:10.1016/j.annepidem.2007.10.015

Gilmore, J. H., Knickmeyer, R. C., & Gao, W. (2018). Imaging structural and functional brain development in early childhood. *Nature Reviews Neuroscience, 19*(3), 123–137. doi:10.1038/nrn.2018.1

Ginsburg, H., & Opper, S. (1988). *Piaget's theory of intellectual development* (3rd ed.). Englewood Cliffs, NJ: Prentice-Hall.

Gitlin, M. J. (1996). *The psychotherapist's guide to psychopharmacology* (2nd ed.). New York, NY: Free Press.

Glanzer, M., & Cunitz, A. (1966). Two storage mechanisms in free recall. *Journal of Verbal Learning and Verbal Behavior, 5*, 351–360.

Glaser, R. (1990). The reemergence of learning theory within instructional research. *American Psychologist, 45*, 29–39.

Glaser, T., Dickel, N., Liersch, B., Rees, J., Süssenbach, P., & Bohner, G. (2015). Lateral attitude change. *Personality and Social Psychology Review, 19*(3), 257–276. doi:10.1177/1088868314546489

Glazzard, J., & Stones, S. (2021). Running scared? A critical analysis of LGBTQ+ inclusion policy in schools. *Frontiers in Sociology, 6*, 613283. doi:10.3389/fsoc.2021.613283

Gleaves, D. H., & Hernandez, E. (1999). Recent reformulations of Freud's development and abandonment of his seduction theory: Historical/scientific clarification or a continued assault on the truth? *History of Psychology, 2*, 324–354.

Gleeson, G., & Fitzgerald, A. (2014). Exploring the association between adult attachment styles in romantic relationships, perceptions of parents from childhood and relationship satisfaction. *Health, 6*(13), 1643–1661. doi:10.4236/health.2014.613196

Glick, I. D., Clarkin, J. F., Rait, D. S., & Berman, E. M. (2000). *Marital and family therapy* (4th ed.). Washington, DC: American Psychiatric Association.

Gobet, F. (2016). *Understanding expertise: A multi-disciplinary approach.* London: Palgrave Macmillan Education.

Gobet, F., & Simon, H. A. (1996). Recall of random and distorted chess positions: Implications for the theory of expertise. *Memory & Cognition, 24,* 493–503.

Godden, D. R., & Baddeley, A. D. (1975). Context-dependent memory in two natural environments: On land and underwater. *British Journal of Psychology, 66,* 325–332.

Goebel, B. L., & Brown, D. (1981). Age differences in motivation related to Maslow's need hierarchy. *Developmental Psychology, 17,* 809–815.

Goh, D., & Chi, J. (2017). Central or peripheral? Information elaboration cues on childhood vaccination in an online parenting forum. *Computers in Human Behavior, 69,* 181–188. doi:10.1016/j.chb.2016.11.066

Gold, L. H., & Simon, R. I. (Eds.).(2016). *Gun violence and mental illness.* Arlington, VA: American Psychiatric Association Publishing.

Goldberg, L. R. (1999). The Curious Experiences Survey, a revised version of the Dissociative Experiences Scale: Factor structure, reliability, and relations to demographic and personality variables. *Psychological Assessment, 11,* 134–145.

Golder, S., Ahmed, S., Norman, G., & Booth, A. (2017). Attitudes toward the ethics of research using social media: A systematic review. *Journal of Medical Internet Research, 19*(6), e195. doi:10.2196/jmir.7082

Goldhagen, D. J. (1996). *Hitler's willing executioners: Ordinary Germans and the Holocaust.* New York, NY: Knopf.

Golomb, J., de Leon, M. J., Kluger, A., George, A. E., Tarshish, C., & Ferris, S. H. (1993). Hippocampal atrophy in normal aging: An association with recent memory impairment. *Archives of Neurology, 50,* 967–973.

Golombok, S., Zadeh, S., Freeman, T., Lysons, J., & Foley, S. (2021). Single mothers by choice: Parenting and child adjustment in middle childhood. *Journal of Family, 35*(2), 192–202. doi:10.1037/fam0000797

Gómez-López, M., Viejo, C., & Ortega-Ruiz, R. (2019). Well-being and romantic relationships: A systematic review in adolescence and emerging adulthood. *International Journal of Environmental Research and Public Health, 16*(13), 2415. doi:10.3390/ijerph16132415

Gonzales, A. L., & Hancock, J. T. (2011). Mirror, mirror on my Facebook wall: Effects of exposure to Facebook on self-esteem. *Cyberpsychology, Behavior, & Social Networking, 14,* 79–83.

Good, B. J., & Kleinman, A. M. (1985). Culture and anxiety: Cross-cultural evidence for the patterning of anxiety disorders. In A. H. Tuma & J. D. Maser (Eds.), *Anxiety and the anxiety disorders.* Hillsdale, NJ: Erlbaum.

Good, K., & Chanoff, D. (1991). *Into the heart.* New York, NY: Simon & Schuster.

Good, P. I., & Hardin, J. W. (2003). *Common errors in statistics (and how to avoid them).* New York, NY: Wiley.

Goodall, J. (1986). *The chimpanzees of Gombe: Patterns of behavior.* Cambridge, MA: Harvard University Press.

Goodall, J. (2000, Reissue). *Through a window: My thirty years with the chimpanzees of Gombe.* Boston: Houghton Mifflin.

Goodkind, D. M. (1991). Creating new traditions in modern Chinese populations: Aiming for birth in the Year of the Dragon. *Population and Development Review, 17,* 663–686.

Goodman, N. D., & Lassiter, D. (2014). Probabilistic semantics and pragmatics: Uncertainty in language and thought. In S. Lappin & C. Fox (Eds.), *Handbook of contemporary semantics* (2nd ed.). New York, NY: Wiley-Blackwell.

Goodwin, F. K., & Jamison, K. R. (1990). *Manic depressive illness.* New York, NY: Oxford University Press.

Gopnik, A. (2016). *The gardener and the carpenter.* New York, NY: Farrar, Straus and Giroux.

Gopnik, A., Meltzoff, A. N., & Kuhl, P. K. (1999). *The scientist in the crib: Minds, brains, and how children learn.* New York, NY: Morrow.

Gorman, J. M., Liebowitz, M. R., Fyer, A. J., & Stein, J. (1989). A neuroanatomical hypothesis for panic disorder. *American Journal of Psychiatry, 146,* 148–161.

Gosselin, P., Kirouac, G., & Dore, F. Y. (1995). Components and recognition of facial expression in the communication of emotion by actors. *Journal of Personality and Social Psychology, 68,* 83–96.

Gottesman, I. I. (1991). *Schizophrenia genesis: The origins of madness.* San Francisco, CA: Freeman.

Gottesman, I. I., & Shields, J. (1982). *Schizophrenia: The epigenetic puzzle.* New York, NY: Cambridge University Press.

Gould, J. L., & Marler, P. (1987). Learning by instinct. *Scientific American, 256*(1), 74–75.

Graber, J. A., Brooks-Gunn, J., Paikoff, R. L., & Warren, M. P. (1994). Prediction of eating problems: An 8-year study of adolescent girls. *Developmental Psychology, 30,* 823–834.

Graffin, N. F., Ray, W. J., & Lundy, R. (1995). EEG concomitants of hypnosis and hypnotic susceptibility. *Journal of Abnormal Psychology, 104,* 123–131.

Graham, J. R. (2000). *MMPI-2: Assessing personality and psychopathology* (3rd ed.). New York, NY: Oxford University Press.

Graham, S. (2005). Scans show how hypnosis affects brain activity. Retrieved from https://www.scientificamerican.com/article/scans-show-how-hypnosis-a/

Grammer, K., & Thornhill, R. (1994). Human facial attractiveness and sexual selection: The role of average-ness and symmetry. *Journal of Comparative Psychology, 108,* 233–242.

Grandner, M. A. (2019). *Sleep and health.* Cambridge, MA: Academic Press.

Granrud, C. E. (2006). Size constancy in infants: 4-month-olds responses to physical versus retinal image size. *Journal of Experimental Psychology: Human Perception and Performance, 32*(6), 1398–1404. doi:10.1037/0096-1523.32.6.1398

Graveline, Y. M., & Wamsley, E. J. (2015). Dreaming and waking cognition. *Translational Issues in Psychological Science, 1*(1), 97–105. doi:10.1037/tps0000018

Gray-Little, B., & Hafdahl, A. R. (2000). Factors influencing racial comparisons of self-esteem: A quantitative review. *Psychological Bulletin, 126,* 26–54.

Green, A. E., Cohen, M. S., Kim, J. U., & Gray, J. R. (2012). An explicit cue improves creative analogical reasoning. *Intelligence, 40,* 598–603.

Green, D. M., & Swets, J. A. (1966). *Signal detection theory and psychophysics.* New York, NY: Wiley.

Green, J. P. (1999). Hypnosis and the recall of early auto-biographical memories. *International Journal of Clinical and Experimental Hypnosis, 47*.

Green, L., Myerson, J., & Vanderveldt, A. (2014). Delay and probability discounting. In F. K. McSweeney, E. S. Murphy, F. K. McSweeney, & E. S. Murphy (Eds.), *The Wiley Blackwell handbook of operant and classical conditioning* (pp. 307–337). Hoboken, NJ: Wiley-Blackwell. doi:10.1002/9781118468135.ch13

Greenberg, L. S., & Malcolm, W. (2002). Resolving unfinished business: Relating process to outcome. *Journal of Consulting and Clinical Psychology, 70*, 406–416.

Greenberg, R. P., Constantino, M. J., & Bruce, N. (2006). Are patient expectations still relevant for psychotherapy process and outcome? *Clinical Psychology Review, 26*(6), 657–678. doi:10.1016/j.cpr.2005.03.002

Greenough, W. T., Black, J. E., & Wallace, C. S. (1987). Experience and brain development. *Child Development, 58*, 539–559.

Greenough, W. T., Withers, G. S., & Wallace, C. S. (1990). Morphological changes in the nervous system arising from behavioral experience: What is the evidence they are involved in learning and memory? In L. R. Squire & E. Lindenlaub (Eds.), *The biology of memory* (pp. 159–185). Stuttgart: Schattauer.

Greenspan, J. D., & Bolanowski, S. J. (1996). The psychophysics of tactile perception and its peripheral physiological basis. In L. Kruger (Ed.), *Pain and touch* (pp. 25–103). San Diego, CA: Academic Press.

Greenwald, A. G. (1992). New look 3: Unconscious cognition reclaimed. *American Psychologist, 47*, 766–779.

Greenwald, A. G., & Farnham, S. D. (2001). Using the Implicit Association Test to measure self-esteem and self-concept. *Journal of Personality and Social Psychology, 79*, 1022–1038.

Greenwald, A. G., McGhee, D. E., & Schwartz, J. L. K. (1998). Measuring implicit differences in implicit cognition: The Implicit Association Test. *Journal of Personality and Social Psychology, 74*, 1464–1480.

Greenwald, A. G., Poehlman, T. A., Uhlmann, E. L., & Banaji, M. R. (2009). Understanding and using the Implicit Association Test: III. Meta-analysis of predictive validity. *Journal of Personality and Social Psychology, 97*(1), 17–41. doi:10.1037/a0015575

Greenwald, A. G., Spangenberg, E. R., Pratkanis, A. R., & Eskenazi, J. (1991). Double-blind tests of subliminal self-help audiotapes. *Psychological Science, 2*, 119–122.

Gregory, R. L. (1998). *Eye and brain: The psychology of seeing* (5th ed.). Princeton, NJ: Princeton University Press.

Greif, E. B., & Ulman, K. J. (1982). The psychological impact of menarche on early adolescent females: A review of the literature. *Child Development, 53*, 1413–1430.

Greil, A. L., Slauson-Blevins, K., & McQuillan, J. (2010). The experience of infertility: A review of recent literature. *Sociology of Health & Illness, 32*(1), 140–162. doi:10.1111/j.1467-9566.2009.01213.x

Griffiths, M. (1998). Internet addiction: Does it really exist? In J. Gackenbach (Ed.), *Psychology and the Internet: Intrapersonal, interpersonal, and transpersonal implications* (pp. 61–75). San Diego, CA: Academic.

Grilo, C. M., & Pogue-Geile, M. (1991). The nature of environmental influences in weight and obesity: A behavior genetic analysis. *Psychological Bulletin, 110*, 520–537.

Gritti, E. S., Marino, D. P., Lang, M., & Meyer, G. J. (2017). Assessing narcissism using Rorschach-based imagery and behavior validated by clinician reports: Studies with adult patients and nonpatients. *Assessment, 25*(7), 898–916. doi:10.1177/1073191117715728

Grønli, J., & Mrdalj, J. (2018). Can night shift workers benefit from light exposure? *Journal of Physiology, 596*(12), 2269–2270. doi:10.1113/JP276043

Gross, A. E., & Crofton, C. (1977). What is good is beautiful. *Sociometry, 40*, 85–90.

Gross, S. R., & Shaffer, M. (2012). *Exonerations in the United States, 1989–2012: Report by the National Registry of Exoneration.* Retrieved from http://www.law.umich.edu/special/exoneration/Documents/exonerations_us_1989_2012_full_report.pdf

Gross, T. (Producer). (2017, March 24). The Supreme Court ruling that led to 70,000 forced sterilizations. National Public Radio *Fresh Air [podcast]*. Retrieved from https://www.npr.org/2017/03/24/521360544/the-supreme-court-ruling-that-led-to-70-000-forced-sterilizations

Grossmann, I., & Jowhari, N. (2017). Cognition and the self: Attempt of an independent close replication of the effects of self-construal priming on spatial memory recall. OSF. doi:10.31219/osf.io/t34kf

Groth-Marnat, H. (2003). *Handbook of psychological assessment* (4th ed.). New York, NY: Wiley.

Grover, V. P., Tognarelli, J. M., Crossey, M. M., Cox, I. J., Taylor-Robinson, S. D., & McPhail, M. J. (2015). Magnetic resonance imaging: Principles and techniques: Lessons for clinicians. *Journal of Clinical and Experimental Hepatology, 5*(3), 246–255. doi:10.1016/j.jceh.2015.08.001

Gruber, N. (2017). Is the achievement motive gender-biased? The validity of TAT/PSE in women and men. *Frontiers in Psychology, 8*. doi:10.3389/fpsyg.2017.00181

Grunwald, L., & Goldberg, J. (1993, July). The amazing minds of infants. *Life*, pp. 46–56.

Gruwez, A., Bruyneel, A. V., & Bruyneel, M. (2019). The validity of two commercially-available sleep trackers and actigraphy for assessment of sleep parameters in obstructive sleep apnea patients. *PLOS ONE, 14*(1), e0210569. doi:10.1371/journal.pone.0210569

Grysman, A., & Hudson, J. A. (2013). Gender differences in autobiographical memory: Developmental and methodological considerations. *Developmental Review, 33*(3), 239–272. doi:10.1016/j.dr.2013.07.004.

Grysman, A., Fivush, R., Merrill, N. A., & Graci, M. (2016). The influence of gender and gender typicality on autobiographical memory across event types and age groups. *Memory & Cognition, 44*(6) 856–868. doi:10.3758/s13421-016-0610-2.

Guénolé, F., Marcaggi, G., & Baleyte, J.-M. (2013). Do dreams really guard sleep? Evidence for and against Freuds theory of the basic function of dreaming. *Frontiers in Psychology, 4*. doi:10.3389/fpsyg.2013.00017

Guilford, J. P. (1967). *The nature of human intelligence.* New York, NY: McGraw-Hill.

Guilford, J. P. (1985). The structure-of-intellect model. In B. B. Wolman (Ed.), *Handbook of intelligence: Theories, measurements, and applications* (pp. 225–266). New York, NY: Wiley.

Guilleminault, C., & Roth, T. (1993). Hypersomnia. In M. A. Carskadon (Ed.), *Encyclopedia of sleep and dreaming* (pp. 287–288). New York, NY: Macmillan.

Guion, R. M. (1965). *Personnel testing.* New York, NY: McGraw-Hill.

Guiso, L., Monte, F. Sapienza, P., & Zingales, L. (2008). Culture, gender, and math. *Science, 320,* 1164–1165.

Guivarch, J., Murdymootoo, V., Elissalde, S. N., Salle-Collemiche, X., Tardieu, S., Jouve, E., & Poinso, F. (2017). Impact of an implicit social skills training group in children with autism spectrum disorder without intellectual disability: A before-and-after study. *PLOS ONE, 12*(7), e0181159. doi:10.1371/journal.pone.0181159

Gullion, C. L., Orrick, E. A., & Bishopp, S. A. (2021). Who is at-risk? an examination of the likelihood and time variation in the predictors of repeated police misconduct. *Police Quarterly.* doi:10.1177/10986111211013048

Gulliver, A., Farrer, L., Bennett, K., Ali, K., Hellsing, A., Katruss, N., & Griffiths, K. M. (2018). University staff experiences of students with mental health problems and their perceptions of staff training needs. *Journal of Mental Health, 27*(3), 247–256. doi:10.1080/09638237.2018.1466042

Gumbrecht, J. (2014, March 6). Major changes coming to 2016 SAT test: Here's what, how, and why. CNN. Retrieved from https://www.cnn.com/2014/03/05/living/sat-test-changes-schools/index.html

Gumperz, J. J., & Levinson, S. C. (Eds.).(1996). *Rethinking linguistic relativity.* Cambridge, UK: Cambridge University Press.

Gunderson, J. G. (1984). *Borderline personality disorder.* Washington, DC: American Psychiatric Press.

Gunderson, J. G. (2001). *Borderline personality disorder: A clinical guide.* Washington, DC: American Psychiatric Press.

Guo, G., Wang, L., Liu, H., & Randall, T. (2014). Genomic assortative mating in marriages in the United States. *PLOS One, 9,* e112322.

Gurtman, M. B. (1987). Depressive affect and disclosures as factors in interpersonal rejection. *Cognitive Therapy and Research, 11,* 87–100.

Guthrie, J. P., Ash, R. A., & Bendapudi, V. (1995). Additional validity evidence for measures of morningness. *Journal of Applied Psychology, 80,* 186–190.

Gutman, R. (May 15, 2018). A linguist explains why "Laurel" sounds like "Yanny." *The Atlantic.* Retrieved from https://www.theatlantic.com/technology/archive/2018/05/dont-rest-on-your-laurels/560483/

Gutner, C. A., Pineles, S. L., Griffin, M. G., Bauer, M. R., Weierich, M. R., & Resick, P. A. (2010). Physiological predictors of posttraumatic stress disorder. *Journal of Traumatic Stress, 23*(6), 775–784. doi:10.1002/jts.20582

Gutteling, B. M., de Weerth, C., Zandbelt, N., Mulder, E. J., Visser, G. H., & Buitelaar, J. K. (2006). Does maternal prenatal stress adversely affect the child's learning and memory at age six? *Journal of Abnormal Child Psychology, 34,* 789–798.

Guttman, N., & Kalish, H. (1956). Discriminability and stimulus generalization. *Journal of Experimental Psychology, 51,* 79–88.

Guttmann, M. G. (2001). *The enigma of Anna O.: A biography of Bertha Pappenheim.* Wickford, RI: Moyer Bell.

Haag, M., & Fortin, J. (2017, May 27). Two killed in Portland while trying to stop anti-Muslim rant, police say. *New York Times.* Retrieved from https://www.nytimes.com/2017/05/27/us/portland-train-attack-muslim-rant.html

Haaga, D. A., Dyck, M. J., & Ernst, D. (1991). Empirical status of cognitive theory of depression. *Psychological Bulletin, 110,* 215–236.

Hackett, C., & McClendon, D. (2017, April 5). World's largest religion by population is still Christianity. Pew Research Center. Retrieved from https://www.pewresearch.org/fact-tank/2017/04/05/christians-remain-worlds-largest-religious-group-but-they-are-declining-in-europe/

Hagen, M. A. (1997). *Whores of the court: The fraud of psychiatric testimony and the rape of American justice.* New York, NY: HarperCollins.

Hagen, R., Turkingon, D., Berge, T., & Gawe, R. W. (Eds.) (2011). *CBT for psychosis: A symptom-based approach. International Society for the Treatment of Schizophrenia and Other Psychosis.* New York, NY: Routledge/Taylor & Francis Group.

Haidt, J. (2001). The emotional dog and its rational tail: The social intuitist approach to moral judgment. *Psychological Review, 108,* 814–834.

Haist, F., Shimamura, A. P., & Squire, L. R. (1992). On the relationship between recall and recognition memory. *Journal of Experimental Psychology: Learning, Memory, and Cognition, 18,* 691–702.

Haith, M. M. (1998). Who put the cog in infant cognition? Is rich interpretation too costly? *Infant Behavior and Development, 21,* 167–179.

Hall, H. V., & Pritchard, D. A. (1996). *Detecting malingering and deception: Forensic distortion analysis (FDA).* Delray Beach, FL: St. Lucie Press.

Hamermesh, D. S., & Biddle, J. E. (1994). Beauty and the labor market. *American Economic Review, 84,* 1174–1195.

Hamilton, B. E., Martin, J. A., Osterman, M. J. K., Curtin, S. C., & Mathews, T. J. (2015). Births: Final data for 2014. *National Vital Statistics Reports, 64*(12), 1–63.

Hamilton, D. L., & Zanna, M. P. (1974). Context effects in impression formation: Changes in connotative meaning. *Journal of Personality and Social Psychology, 29,* 649–654.

Hamilton, M. (1960). A rating scale for depression. *Journal of Neurology, Neurosurgery, and Psychiatry, 163,* 28–40.

Hammond, S. I. (2014). Children's early helping in action: Piagetian developmental theory and early prosocial behavior. *Frontiers in Psychology, 5,* 759. doi:10.3389/fpsyg.2014.00759

Hampton, R. R., & Shettleworth, S. J. (1996). Hippocampus and memory in a food-storing and in a nonstoring bird species. *Behavioral Neuroscience, 110,* 946–964.

Hamrick, N., Cohen, S., & Rodriguez, M. S. (2002). Being popular can be healthy or unhealthy: Stress, social network diversity, and incidence of upper respiratory infection. *Health Psychology, 21,* 294–298.

Handel, A. (1987). Personal theories about the life-span development of one's self in autobiographical self-presentations of adults. *Human Development, 30,* 83–98.

Hankin, B. L., & Abramson, L. Y. (2001). Development of gender differences in depression: An elaborated cognitive vulnerability-transactional stress theory. *Psychological Bulletin, 127,* 773–796.

Hanna, E., & Meltzoff, A. N. (1993). Peer imitation by toddlers in laboratory, home, and day-care contexts: Implications for social learning and memory. *Developmental Psychology, 29,* 701–710.

Hannover, B., Birkner, N., & Pohlmann, C. (2006). Ideal selves and self-esteem in people with independent or interdependent self-construal. *European Journal of Social Psychology, 36,* 119–133. doi:10.1002/ejsp.289

Hardin, C., & Banaji, M. R. (1993). The influence of language on thought. *Social Cognition, 11,* 277–308.

Hare, R. D. (1993). *Without conscience: The disturbing world of the psychopaths among us.* New York, NY: Pocket Books.

Hare, R. D., McPherson, L. M., & Forth, A. E. (1988). Male psychopaths and their criminal careers. *Journal of Consulting and Clinical Psychology, 56,* 710–714.

Hargadon, R., Bowers, K. S., & Woody, E. Z. (1995). Does counter-pain imagery mediate hypnotic responding? *Journal of Abnormal Psychology, 104,* 508–516.

Hariri, A. G., Gulec, M. Y., Orengul, F. F. C., Sumbul, E. A., Elbay, R. Y., & Gulec, H. (2015). Dissociation in bipolar disorder: Relationships between clinical variables and childhood trauma. *Journal of Affective Disorders, 184,* 104–110. doi:10.1016/j.jad.2015.05.023

Harkins, D. A., & Uzgiris, I. C. (1991). Hand-use matching between mothers and infants during the first year. *Infant Behavior and Development, 14,* 289–298.

Harlow, H. F. (1958). The nature of love. *American Psychologist, 13,* 673–685.

Harlow, H. F. (1971). *Learning to love.* San Francisco, CA: Albion.

Harlow, J. M. (1868). Recovery from the passage of an iron bar through the head. *Massachusetts Medical Society Publication, 2,* 327–347.

Harmon-Jones, E., & Allen, J. B. (2001). The role of affect in the mere exposure effect: Evidence from psychophysiological and individual differences approaches. *Personality and Social Psychology Bulletin, 27,* 889–898.

Harmon-Jones, E., Brehm, J. W., Greenberg, J., Simon, L., & Nelson, D. E. (1996). Evidence that the production of aversive consequences is not necessary to create cognitive dissonance. *Journal of Personality and Social Psychology, 70,* 5–16.

Harrington, A. (Ed.).(1997). *The placebo effect: An interdisciplinary exploration.* Cambridge, MA: Harvard University Press.

Harris, B. (1979). Whatever happened to Little Albert? *American Psychologist, 34,* 151–160.

Harris, D. J., Wilson, M. R., & Vine, S. J. (2018). A systematic review of commercial cognitive training devices: Implications for use in sport. *Frontiers in Psychology, 9,* 709. doi:10.3389/fpsyg.2018.00709

Harris, J. R. (1995). Where is the child's environment? A group socialization theory of development. *Psychological Review, 102,* 458–489.

Harris, L. J. (2002). Lateral biases for holding infants: Early opinions, observations, and explanations, with some possible lessons for theory and research today. *Brain and Cognition, 48,* 392–394.

Harris, M. A., & Brett, C. E. (2016). Personality stability from age 14 to 77 years. *Psychology and Aging, 31*(8), 862–874.

Harris, P. L., & Kavanaugh, R. D. (1993). Young children's understanding of pretense. *Monographs of the Society for Research in Child Development, 58*(1, Serial No. 231).

Harris, R. A., & Koob, G. F. (2017). The future is now: A 2020 view of alcoholism research. *Neuropharmacology, 122,* 1–2. doi:10.1016/j.neuropharm.2017.06.001

Harris, R. J., & Monaco, G. E. (1978). Psychology of pragmatic implication: Information processing between the lines. *Journal of Experimental Psychology: General, 107,* 1–22.

Harrison, J. (2001). *Synaesthesia: The strangest thing.* Oxford, UK: Oxford University Press.

Hartshorne, H., & May, M. (1928). *Studies in deceit.* New York, NY: Macmillan.

Hartung, C. M., & Widiger, T. A. (1998). Gender differences in the diagnosis of mental disorders: Conclusions and controversies of the DSM-IV. *Psychological Bulletin, 123,* 260–278.

Hartup, W. W., & Stevens, N. (1999). Friendships and adaptation across the life span. *Current Directions in Psychological Science, 8,* 76–79.

Harvath, T. A. (2008). What if Maslow was wrong? *American Journal of Nursing, 108*(4), 11. doi:10.1097/01.NAJ.0000315243.00587.2f

Harvey, A. G. (2002). A cognitive model of insomnia. *Behaviour Research and Therapy, 40,* 869–894.

Hasan, S., Santhi, N., Lazar, A. S., Slak, A., Lo, J., von Schantz, M., . . . Dijk, D. J. (2012). Assessment of circadian rhythms in humans: Comparison of real-time fibroblast reporter imaging with plasma melatonin. *FASEB Journal, 26*(6), 2414–2423.

Haskell, R. (2018, January 16). Serena Williams on motherhood, marriage, and making her comeback. *Vogue.* Retrieved from https://www.vogue.com/article/serena-williams-vogue-cover-interview-february-2018

Hassett, J. (1978). *A primer of psychophysiology.* San Francisco, CA: Freeman.

Hatch, J. P., Fisher, J. G., & Rugh, J. D. (1987). *Biofeedback: Studies in clinical efficacy.* New York, NY: Plenum.

Hathaway, S. R., & McKinley, J. C. (1983). *Minnesota Multiphasic Personality Inventory: Manual for administration and scoring.* New York, NY: Psychological Corporation.

Hattersley, G. (2018, July). Ariana Grande: The year that changed everything. *British Vogue.* Retrieved from https://www.vogue.co.uk/article/july-cover-vogue-2018

Häuser, W., Hagl, M., Schmierer, A., & Hansen, E. (2016). The efficacy, safety and applications of medical hypnosis. *Deutsches Arzteblatt International, 113*(17), 289–296.

Havard, C., Memon, A., & Humphries, J. E. (2017). The own-race bias in child and adolescent witnesses. *International Journal of Police Science & Management, 19*(4), 261–272. doi:10.1177/1461355717731579

Hawkins, S. A., & Hastie, R. (1990). Hindsight: Biased judgments of past events after the outcomes are known. *Psychological Bulletin, 107*, 311–327.

Haworth, C. M. A., & Plomin, R. (2011). Genetics and education: Towards a genetically sensitive classroom. In K. R. Harris, S. Graham, & T. Urdan (Eds.), *The American Psychological Association handbook of educational psychology* (pp. 529–559). Washington, DC: American Psychological Association.

Haworth, C. M. A., Wright, M. J., Luciano, M., Martin, N. G., de Geus, E. J. C., van Beijsterveldt, C. E. M., . . . Plomin, R. (2010). The heritability of general cognitive ability increases linearly from childhood to young adulthood. *Molecular Psychiatry, 15*, 1112–1120. doi:10.1038/mp.2009.55

Hawton, K., & van Heeringen, K. (2000). *The international handbook of suicide and attempted suicide*. New York, NY: Wiley.

Hay, J. L., Okkerse, P., van Amerongen, G., & Groeneveld, G. J. (2016). Determining pain detection and tolerance thresholds using an integrated, multi-modal pain task battery. *Journal of Visualized Experiments, 110*, 53800. doi:10.3791/53800

Hayes, S. (2018). Acceptance and commitment therapy (ACT). Association for Contextual Behavioral Science. Retrieved from https://contextualscience.org/act#

Hazelrigg, M. D., Cooper, H. M., & Borduin, C. (1987). Evaluating the effectiveness of family therapies: An integrative review and analysis. *Psychological Bulletin, 101*, 428–442.

HealthyPeople.gov. (2021). *Social determinants of health*. https://www.healthypeople.gov/2020/topics-objectives/topic/social-determinants-of-healthexternalicon

Healy, D. (2002). *The creation of psychopharmacology*. Cambridge, MA: Harvard University Press.

Hearing Voices Network. (2018). Hearing Voices Network England's position statement on DSM-5 and psychiatric diagnoses. Retrieved from http://www.hearing-voices.org/wp-content/uploads/2013/05/HVN-Position-Statement-on-DSM5-and-Diagnoses.pdf.

Heatherton, T. F., & Polivy, J. (1991). Development and validation of a scale for measuring state self-esteem. *Journal of Personality and Social Psychology, 60*, 895–910.

Hecht, H., & Proffitt, D. R. (1995). The price of expertise: Effects of experience on the water-level task. *Psychological Science, 6*, 90–95.

Hedges, L. B., & Nowell, A. (1995). Sex differences in mental test scores, variability, and numbers of high-scoring individuals. *Science, 269*, 41–45.

Hedman, E., Axelsson, E., Andersson, E., Lekander, M., & Ljótsson, B. (2016). Exposure-based cognitive-behavioural therapy via the Internet and as bibliotherapy for somatic symptom disorder and illness anxiety disorder: Randomised controlled trial. *British Journal of Psychiatry, 209*(5), 407–413. doi:10.1192/bjp.bp.116.181396

Hehman, E., Graber, E. C., Hoffman, L. H., & Gaertner, S. L. (2012). Warmth and competence: A content analysis of photographs depicting American presidents. *Psychology of Popular Media Culture, 1*(1), 46–52. doi:10.1037/a0026513

Heider, F. (1958). *The psychology of interpersonal relations*. New York, NY: Wiley.

Heijnen, S., Hommel, B., Kibele, A., & Colzato, L. S. (2016). Neuromodulation of aerobic exercise: A review. *Frontiers in Psychology, 6*, 1890. doi:10.3389/fpsyg.2015.01890

Heimberg, R. G., Liebowitz, M. R., Hope, D. A., & Schneier, F. R. (Eds.).(1995). *Social phobia: Diagnosis, assessment, and treatment*. New York, NY: Guilford.

Heine, M. K., Ober, B. A., & Shenaut, G. K. (1999). Naturally occurring and experimentally induced tip-of-the-tongue experiences in three adult age groups. *Psychology and Aging, 14*, 445–457.

Heine, S. J. (2008). *Cultural psychology*. New York, NY: Norton.

Heinrich, M. D., Bryant, N. B., Jones, A. P., Robert, B., Clark, V. P., & Pilly, P. K. (2018). Extroverts outperform introverts on a learning task under conditions of acute sleep deficit. *Sleep, 41*(Suppl. 1). doi:10.1093/sleep/zsy061.100

Helander, E. E., Wansink, B., & Chieh, A. (2016). Weight gain over the holidays in three countries. *New England Journal of Medicine, 375*(12), 1200–1202. doi:10.1056/NEJMc1602012

Heller, M. A., & Schiff, W. (Eds.).(1991). *The psychology of touch: Theory and application*. Hillsdale, NJ: Erlbaum.

Helliwell, J. F., & Wang, S. (2015). How was the weekend? How the social context underlies weekend effects in happiness and other emotions for US workers. *PLOS ONE, 10*(12), e0145123. doi:10.1371/journal.pone.0145123

Helliwell, J. F., Layard, R., & Sachs, J. D. (2019). *World happiness report*. Retrieved from https://worldhappiness.report/ed/2019/

Helliwell, J. F., Layard, R., Sachs, J. D., & De Neve, J-E. (2020). World happiness report, 2020. Retrieved from https://happiness-report.s3.amazonaws.com/2020/WHR20.pdf

Hellwig, T., & Sinno, A. (2016). Different groups, different threats: Public attitudes towards immigrants. *Journal of Ethnic and Migration Studies, 43*(3), 339–358. doi:10.1080/1369183x.2016.1202749

Helms, J. E. (1992). Why is there no study of cultural equivalence in standardized cognitive ability testing? *American Psychologist, 47*, 1083–1101.

Henderlong, J., & Lepper, M. R. (2002). The effects of praise on children's intrinsic motivation: A review and synthesis. *Psychological Bulletin, 128*, 774–795.

Henry, J. D., Hippel, W. V., & Baynes, K. (2009). Social inappropriateness, executive control, and aging. *Psychology and Aging, 24*(1), 239–244. doi:10.1037/a0013423

Henry, W. P., Strupp, H. H., Schacht, T. E., & Gaston, L. (1994). Psychodynamic approaches. In A. E. Bergin & S. L. Garfield (Eds.), *Handbook of psychotherapy and behavior change* (4th ed., pp. 467–508). New York, NY: Wiley.

Hensel, H. (1981). *Thermoreception and temperature regulation*. London, UK: Academic Press.

Herbert, C., Platte, P., Wiemer, J., Macht, M., & Blumenthal, T. D. (2014). Supertaster, super reactive: Oral sensitivity for bitter taste modulates emotional approach and avoidance behavior in the affective startle paradigm. *Physiology & Behavior, 135*, 198–207. doi:10.1016/j.physbeh.2014.06.002

Herculano-Houzel, S. (2014). The glia/neuron ratio: How it varies uniformly across brain structures and species and what that means for brain physiology and evolution. *Glia, 62*, 1377–1391. https://doi.org/10.1002/glia.22683

Herculano-Houzel, S. (2009). The human brain in numbers: A linearly scaled-up primate brain. *Frontiers in Human Neuroscience, 3*, 31. doi:10.3389/neuro.09.031.2009

Hering, E. (1878). *Outlines of a theory of the light sense* (L. M. Hurvich & D. Jameson, Trans.). Cambridge, MA: Harvard University Press.

Herman-Giddens, M. E., Wang, L., & Koch, G. (2001). Secondary sexual characteristics in boys. *Archives of Pediatric and Adolescent Medicine, 155*, 1022–1028.

Hernnstein, R., & Murray, C. (1994). *The bell curve: Intelligence and class structure in American life.* New York, NY: Free Press.

Herrera, B. M., & Lindgren, C. M. (2010). The genetics of obesity. *Current Diabetes Reports, 10*(6), 498–505. doi:10.1007/s11892-010-0153-z

Herrera, B. M., Keildson, S., & Lindgren, C. M. (2011). Genetics and epigenetics of obesity. *Maturitas, 69*(1), 41–49. doi:10.1016/j.maturitas.2011.02.018

Herrnstein, R. J. (1970). On the law of effect. *Journal of the Experimental Analysis of Behavior, 7*, 243–266.

Hess, E. H. (1959). Imprinting. *Science, 130*, 133–144.

Hetherington, A. W., & Ranson, S. W. (1942). The spontaneous activity and food intake of rats with hypothalamic lesions. *American Journal of Physiology, 136*, 609–617.

Heyes, C. M., & Galef, B. G., Jr. (1996). *Social learning in animals: The roots of culture.* New York, NY: Academic.

Hibbard, W. S., & Worring, R. W. (1996). *Forensic hypnosis: The practical application of hypnosis in criminal investigation.* Springfield, IL: Charles C. Thomas.

Higgins, E. T. (1989). Self-discrepancy theory: What patterns of self-beliefs cause people to suffer? In L. Berkowitz (Ed.), *Advances in experimental social psychology* (Vol. 22, pp. 93–136). New York, NY: Academic.

Hilgard, E. R. (1965). *Hypnotic susceptibility.* New York, NY: Harcourt, Brace, & World.

Hilgard, E. R. (1982). Hypnotic susceptibility and implications for measurement. *International Journal of Clinical and Experimental Hypnosis, 30*, 394–403.

Hilgard, E. R. (1986). *Divided consciousness: Multiple controls in human thought and action.* New York, NY: Wiley-Interscience.

Hilgard, E. R. (1987). *Psychology in America: A historical survey.* San Diego: Harcourt Brace Jovanovich.

Hilgard, E. R. (1992). Divided consciousness and dissociation. *Consciousness and Cognition, 1*, 16–31.

Hilgard, E. R., Morgan, A. H., & MacDonald, H. (1975). Pain and dissociation in the cold pressor test: A study of "hidden reports" through automatic key-pressing and automatic talking. *Journal of Abnormal Psychology, 84*, 280–289.

Hill, C. E., Spiegel, S. B., Hoffman, M. A., Kivlighan, D. M., & Gelso, C. J. (2017). Therapist expertise in psychotherapy revisited. *Counseling Psychologist, 45*(1), 7–53. doi:10.1177/0011000016641192

Hilton, J. L., & von Hippel, W. (1996). Stereotypes. *Annual Review of Psychology, 47*, 237–271.

Hilts, P. J. (1995). *Memory's ghost: The strange tale of Mr. M and the nature of memory.* New York, NY: Simon & Schuster.

Hirst, W. (2016, November 15). Collective memory: A psychologist explains how emotional memories of Trump's victory will divide Americans for years to come. Quartz. Retrieved from https://qz.com/837271/flashbulb-memories-and-the-collective-consciousness-a-psychologist-explains-how-emotional-memories-of-donald-trumps-victory-will-divide-americans-for-years-to-come/

Hirst, W., Phelps, E. A., Buckner, R. L., Budson, A. E., Cuc, A., Gabrieli, J. D. E., . . . Vaidya, C. J. (2009). Long-term memory for the terrorist attack of September 11: Flashbulb memories, event memories, and the factors that influence their retention. *Journal of Experimental Psychology. General, 138*(2), 161–176. doi:10.1037/a0015527

Hoaglin, D. C., Mosteller, F., & Tukey, J. W. (1991). *Fundamentals of exploratory analysis of variance.* New York, NY: Wiley.

Hobson, A. (2013). The ancient art of memory. *Behavioral and Brain Sciences, 36*(6), 621–621. doi:10.1017/s0140525x13001350

Hobson, J. A. (1988). *The dreaming brain.* New York, NY: Basic Books.

Hobson, J. A. (2003). *Dreaming: An introduction to the science of sleep.* New York, NY: Oxford University Press.

Hobson, J. A., & Friston K. J. (2012). Waking and dreaming consciousness: Neurobiological and functional considerations. *Progress in Neurobiology, 98*, 82–98. doi:10.1016/j.pneurobio.2012.05.003

Hobson, J. A., & McCarley, R. W. (1977). The brain as a dream state generator: An activational-synthesis hypothesis of the dream process. *American Journal of Psychiatry, 134*, 1335–1348.

Hockenberry, J. M., Joski, P., Yarbrough, C., & Druss, B. G. (2019). Trends in treatment and spending for patients receiving outpatient treatment of depression in the United States, 1998–2015. *JAMA Psychiatry, 76*(8), 810. doi:10.1001/jamapsychiatry.2019.0633

Hofbauer, R. K., Rainville, P., Duncan, G. H., & Bushnell, M. V. (2001). Cortical representation of the sensory dimension of pain. *Journal of Neurophysiology, 86*, 402–411.

Hoffman, D. D. (1998). *Visual intelligence: How we create what we see.* New York, NY: Norton.

Hoffman, E. (1989). *Lost in translation: A life in a new language.* New York, NY: Dutton.

Hoffman, H. J., Dobie, R. A., Losonczy, K. G., Themann, C. L., & Flamme, G. A. (2017). Declining prevalence of hearing loss in US adults aged 20 to 69 years. *JAMA Otolaryngology: Head & Neck Surgery, 143*(3), 274–285. doi:10.1001/jamaoto.2016.3527

Hoffman, K. M., Trawalter, S., Axt, J. R., & Oliver, M. N. (2016). Racial bias in pain assessment and treatment recommendations, and false beliefs about biological differences between Blacks and Whites. *Proceedings of the National Academy of Sciences USA, 113*(16), 4296–4301. doi:10.1073/pnas.1516047113

Hoffman, M., Gneezy, U., & List, J. A. (2011). Nurture affects gender differences in spatial abilities. *Proceedings of the National Academy of Sciences USA, 108*(36), 14786–14788. doi:10.1073/pnas.1015182108

Hoffmann, H., Peterson, K., & Garner, H. (2012). Field conditioning of sexual arousal in humans. *Socioaffective Neuroscience & Psychology, 2*, 17336. doi:10.3402/snp.v2i0.17336

Hofmann, A. (1980). *LSD: My problem child.* New York, NY: McGraw-Hill.

Hofmann, S. G., & Hinton, D. E. (2014). Cross-cultural aspects of anxiety disorders. *Current Psychiatry Reports, 16*(6), 450.

Hofmann, S. G., Asnaani, A., Vonk, I. J. J., Sawyer, A. T., & Fang, A. (2012). The efficacy of cognitive behavioral therapy: A review of meta-analyses. *Cognitive Therapy and Research, 36*(5), 427–440. doi:10.1007/s10608-012-9476-1

Hofmann, S. G., Asnaani, M. A., & Hinton, D. E. (2010). Cultural aspects in social anxiety and social anxiety disorder. *Depression and Anxiety, 27*(12), 1117–1127. doi:10.1002/da.20759

Hofstede, G. (1980). *Culture's consequences.* Beverly Hills, CA: Sage.

Hofstede, G. (2013). *Culture's consequences: Comparing values, behaviors, institutions, and organizations across nations.* Thousand Oaks, CA: Sage.

Hogg, M. A., & Abrams, D. (1990). Social motivation, self-esteem and social identity. In D. Abrams & M. Hogg (Eds.), *Social identity theory: Constructive and critical advances* (pp. 28–47). New York, NY: Springer-Verlag.

Holder, R. W. (2002). *How not to say what you mean: A dictionary of euphemisms* (3rd ed.). New York, NY: Oxford University Press.

Holding, D. H. (1989). *Human skills* (2nd ed.). New York, NY: Wiley.

Hollands, J. G., & Spence, I. (1992). Judgments of change and proportion in graphical perception. *Human Factors, 34*, 313–334.

Hollands, J. G., & Spence, I. (1998). Judging proportions with graphs: The summation model. *Applied Cognitive Psychology, 12*, 173–190. doi:10.1002/(SICI)1099-0720(199804)12:2<173::AID-ACP499>3.0.CO;2-K

Hollon, S. D., Shelton, R. C., & Loosen, P. T. (1991). Cognitive therapy and pharmacotherapy for depression. *Journal of Consulting and Clinical Psychology, 59*, 88–99.

Holmes, T. H., & Rahe, R. H. (1967). The social readjustment rating scale. *Journal of Psychosomatic Research, 11*, 213.

Holyoak, K. J., & Thagard, P. (1997). The analogical mind. *American Psychologist, 52*, 35–44.

Holzman, P. S., & Matthysse, S. (1990). The genetics of schizophrenia: A review. *Psychological Science, 1*, 279–286.

Hope, L., & Wright, D. (2007). Beyond unusual? Examining the role of attention in the weapon focus effect. *Applied Cognitive Psychology, 21*(7), 951–961. doi:10.1002/acp.1307

Hoppen, T. H., Heinz-Fischer, I., & Morina, N. (2020). If only ? a systematic review and meta-analysis of social, temporal and counterfactual comparative thinking in PTSD. *European Journal of Psychotraumatology, 11*(1), 1737453. doi:10.1080/20008198.2020.1737453

Hopthrow, T., Hooper, N., Mahmood, L., Meier, B. P., & Weger, U. (2017). Mindfulness reduces the correspondence bias. *Quarterly Journal of Experimental Psychology, 70*(3), 351–360. doi:10.1080/17470218.2016.1149498

Hopthrow, T., Hooper, N., Mahmood, L., Meier, B. P., & Weger. U. (2016). Mindfulness reduces the correspondence bias. *Quarterly Journal of Experimental Psychology, 70*(3), 351–360. doi:10.1080/17470218.2016.1149498

Hor, K., & Taylor, M. (2010). Suicide and schizophrenia: A systematic review of rates and risk factors. *Journal of Psychopharmacology, 24*(4 Suppl.), 81–90. doi:10.1177/1359786810385490

Horgen, K. B., & Brownell, K. D. (2002). Confronting the toxic environment: Environmental and public health actions in a world crisis. In T. A. Wadden & A. J. Stunkard (Eds.), *Handbook of obesity treatment* (pp. 95–106). New York, NY: Guilford.

Horn, J. L. (1982). The aging of human abilities. In B. B. Wolman (Ed.), *Handbook of developmental psychology* (pp. 847–870). Englewood Cliffs, NJ: Prentice-Hall.

Horn, J. L., & Cattell, R. C. (1966). Refinement and test of the theory of fluid and crystallized general intelligences. *Journal of Educational Psychology, 57*, 253–270.

Horne, J. A. (1988). *Why we sleep: The functions of sleep in humans and other animals.* Oxford, U.K.: Oxford University Press.

Horne, J. A., & Reyner, L. A. (1996). Counteracting driver sleepiness: Effects of napping, caffeine, and placebo. *Psychophysiology, 33*, 306–309.

Horney, K. (1935). The problem of feminine masochism. *Psychoanalytic Review, 22*, 241.

Horney, K. (1936). Culture and neurosis. *American Sociological Review, 1*(2), 221–230. doi:10.1037/11305-044

Horney, K. (1945). *Our inner conflicts.* New York, NY: Norton.

Horney, K. (1967). *Feminine psychology.* H. Kelman (Ed.). New York, NY: Norton.

Horvath, A. O., & Luborsky, L. (1993). The role of the therapeutic alliance in psychotherapy. *Journal of Consulting and Clinical Psychology, 61*, 561–573.

Horvath, A. O., & Symonds, B. D. (1991). Relation between working alliance and outcome in psychotherapy: A meta-analysis. *Journal of Counseling Psychology, 38*, 139–149.

Hoscheidt, S. M., LaBar, K. S., Ryan, L., Jacobs, W. J., & Nader, L. (2014). Encoding negative events under stress: High subjective arousal is related to accurate emotional memory despite misinformation exposure. *Neurobiology of Learning and Memory, 112*, 237–247. doi:10.1016/j.nlm.2013.09.008

Hothersall, D. (1990). *History of psychology* (2nd ed.). New York, NY: McGraw-Hill.

Houk, J. C., Buckingham, J. T., & Barto, A. G. (1996). Models of the cerebellum and motor learning. *Behavioral and Brain Sciences, 19*, 368–383.

House, J. S., Landis, K. R., & Umberson, D. (1988). Social relationships and health. *Science, 241*, 540–545.

Househam, A. M., Peterson, C. T., Mills, P. J., & Chopra, D. (2017). The effects of stress and meditation on the immune system, human microbiota, and epigenetics. *Advances in Mind-Body Medicine, 31*(4), 10–25.

Hovland, C. I., & Sears, R. R. (1940). Minor studies in aggression: VI. Correlation of lynchings with economic indices. *Journal of Psychology, 9*, 301–310.

Howard, I. P. (1986). The perception of posture, self-motion, and the visual vertical. In K. R. Boff, L. Kaufman, & J. P. Thomas (Eds.), *Handbook of perception and human performance* (Vol. 1). New York, NY: Wiley.

Howard, K. I., Kopta, S. M., Krause, M. S., & Orlinsky, D. E. (1986). The dose-effect relationship in psychotherapy. *American Psychologist, 41*, 159–164.

Howe, M. L., & Courage, M. L. (1993). On resolving the enigma of infantile amnesia. *Psychological Bulletin, 113*, 305–326.

Howells, F. M., Temmingh, H. S., Hsieh, J. H., van Dijen, A. V., Baldwin, D. S., & Stein, D. J. (2018). Electroencephalographic delta/alpha frequency activity differentiates psychotic disorders: A study of schizophrenia, bipolar disorder and methamphetamine-induced psychotic disorder. *Translational Psychiatry, 8*, 75. doi:10.1038/s41398-018-0105-y

Howes, J. L., & Katz, A. N. (1988). Assessing remote memory with an improved public events questionnaire. *Psychology and Aging, 3*, 142–150.

Hoyer, W. J., Rybash, J. M., & Roodin, P. A. (1999). *Adult development and aging* (4th ed.). New York, NY: McGraw-Hill.

Hoyt, L. T., Niu, L., Pachucki, M. C., & Chaku, N. (2020). Timing of puberty in boys and girls: Implications for population health. *SSM - Population Health, 10*, 100549. doi:10.1016/j.ssmph.2020.100549

Hrobjartsson, A., & Gotzsche, P. C. (2001). Is the placebo powerless? An analysis of clinical trials comparing placebo with no treatment. *New England Journal of Medicine, 344*, 1594–1602.

Hsiang, S. M., Burke, M., & Miguel, E. (2013). Quantifying the influence of climate on human conflict. *Science, 341*(6151). doi:10.1126/science.1235367

Hsieh, L. (2012). A queer sex, or, can feminism and psychoanalysis have sex without the phallus. *Feminist Review, 102*(1), 97–115. doi:10.1057/fr.2011.52

Hu, Z., Oh, S., Ha, T. W., Hong, J. T., & Oh, K. W. (2018). Sleep-aids derived from natural products. *Biomolecules & Therapeutics, 26*(4), 343–349.

Huang, J. L., Ryan, A. M., Zabel, K. L., & Palmer, A. (2014). Personality and adaptive performance at work: A meta-analytic investigation. *Journal of Applied Psychology, 99*(1), 162–179. doi:10.1037/a0034285

Huang, Y. F., & Hsieh, P. J. (2013). The mere exposure effect is modulated by selective attention but not visual awareness. *Vision Research, 91*, 56–61. doi:10.1016/j.visres.2013.07.017

Hubel, D. H. (1996). A big step along the visual pathway. *Nature, 380*, 197–198.

Hubel, D. H., & Wiesel, T. N. (1962). Receptive fields, binocular interaction and functional architecture in the cat's visual cortex. *Journal of Physiology, 160*, 106–154.

Hubel, D. H., & Wiesel, T. N. (1979). Brain mechanisms of vision. *Scientific American, 241*, 150–162.

Hubley, S., Lynch, S. B., Schneck, C., Thomas, M., & Shore, J. (2016). Review of key telepsychiatry outcomes. *World Journal of Psychiatry, 6*(2), 269–282. doi:10.5498/wjp.v6.i2.269

Hudson, W. (1960). Pictorial depth perception in sub-cultural groups in Africa. *Journal of Social Psychology, 52*, 183–208.

Hudspeth, A. J. (2000). Hearing. In E. R. Kandel, J. H. Schwartz, & T. M. Jessell (Eds.), *Principles of neural science* (4th ed., p. 590–613). New York, NY: McGraw-Hill.

Huesmann, L. R., & Eron, L. D. (Eds.).(1986). *Television and the aggressive child: A cross-national comparison*. Hillsdale, NJ: Erlbaum.

Hughes, A. K., & Cummings, C. E. (2020). Grief and loss associated with stroke recovery: A qualitative study of stroke survivors and their spousal caregivers. *Journal of Patient Experience*. doi:10.1177/2374373520967796

Hull, C. L. (1943). *Principles of behavior*. New York, NY: Appleton-Century-Crofts.

Hulsebusch, J., Hasenbring, M. I., & Rusu, A. C. (2016). Understanding pain and depression in back pain: The role of catastrophizing, help-/hopelessness, and thought suppression as potential mediators. *International Journal of Behavioral Medicine, 23*(3), 251–259.

Hummer, T. A., Phan, K. L., Kern, D. W., & Mcclintock, M. K. (2017). A human chemosignal modulates frontolimbic activity and connectivity in response to emotional stimuli. *Psychoneuroendocrinology, 75*, 15–25. doi:10.1016/j.psyneuen.2016.09.023

Humphries, T., Kushalnagar, P., Mathur, G., Napoli, D. J., Padden, C., & Rathmann, C. (2014). Ensuring language acquisition for deaf children: What linguists can do. *Language 90*(2), e31–e52.

Hunsley, J., & Bailey, J. M. (2001). Wither the Rorschach? An analysis of the evidence. *Psychological Assessment, 13*, 472–185.

Hunt, E., & Agnoli, F. (1991). The Whorfian hypothesis: A cognitive psychology perspective. *Psychological Review, 9*, 377–389.

Hunt, M. (1997). *How science takes stock: The story of meta-analysis*. New York, NY: Russell Sage Foundation.

Hunter, J. A., Hollands, G. J., Couturier, D., & Marteau, T. M. (2018). Effect of snack-food proximity on intake in general population samples with higher and lower cognitive resource. *Appetite, 121*, 337–347. doi:10.1016/j.appet.2017.11.101

Hunyady, O., Josephs, L., & Jost, J. T. (2008). Priming the primal scene: Betrayal trauma, narcissism, and attitudes toward sexual infidelity. *Self and Identity, 7*(3), 278–294. doi:10.1080/15298860701620227

Hupka, R. B., Lemon, A. P., & Hutchison, K. A. (1999). Universal development of emotion categories in natural language. *Journal of Personality and Social Psychology, 77*, 247–278.

Hutchinson, C. (2010, April 27). Why homeless hero Hugo Alfredo Tale-Yax died on NYC street. ABC News. Retrieved from https://abcnews.go.com/Health/Wellness/dying-good-samaritan-hugo-alfredo-tale-yax-symptom/story?id=10488434

Huttenlocher, J., Levine, S., & Vevea, J. (1998). Environmental input and cognitive growth: A study using time-period comparisons. *Child Development, 69*, 1012–1029.

Huttenlocher, J., Waterfall, H., Vasilyeva, M., Vevea, J., & Hedges, L. V. (2010). Sources of variability in children's language growth. *Cognitive Psychology, 61*(4), 343–365.

Huttenlocher, P. R. (2002). *Neural plasticity: The effects of environment on the development of the cerebral cortex*. Cambridge, MA: Harvard University Press.

Huxley, A. (1932). *Brave new world*. London, UK: Chatto & Windus.

Hyde, J. S., & Linn, M. C. (1988). Gender differences in verbal ability: A meta-analysis. *Psychological Bulletin, 104*, 53–69.

Hyde, J. S., Fennema, E., & Lamon, S. (1990). Gender differences in mathematics performance: A meta-analysis. *Psychological Bulletin, 107*, 139–155.

Hyde, M. (2020). America's most common recurring dreams. Retrieved from https://amerisleep.com/blog/americas-common-recurring-dreams/

Iceland, J., & Ludwig-Dehm, S. (2019). Black-White differences in happiness, 1972–2014. *Social Science Research, 77*, 16–29. doi:10.1016/j.ssresearch.2018.10.004

Inal, S., & Kelleci, M. (2012). Distracting children during blood draw: Looking through distraction cards is effective in pain relief of children during blood draw. *International Journal of Nursing Practice, 18*(2), 210–219. doi:10.1111/j.1440-172x.2012.02016.x

Ingham, A. G., Levinger, G., Graves, J., & Peckham, V. (1974). The Ringelmann effect: Studies of group size and group performance. *Journal of Experimental Social Psychology, 10*, 371–384.

Inhelder, B., & Piaget, J. (1958). *The growth of logical thinking from childhood to adolescence.* New York, NY: Basic Books.

Inman, A. G., & Kreider, E. D. (2013). Multicultural competence: Psychotherapy practice and supervision. *Psychotherapy, 50*(3), 346–350. doi:10.1037/a0032029

Innocence Project. (2017). Ronald Cotton. Retrieved from https://www.innocenceproject.org/cases/ronald-cotton/

Insel, T. R. (Ed.). (1984). *New findings in obsessive-compulsive disorder.* Washington, DC: American Psychiatric Press.

Inslicht, S. S., Metzler, T. J., Garcia, N. M., Pineles, S. L., Milad, M. R., Orr, S. P., . . . Neylan, T. C. (2013). Sex differences in fear conditioning in posttraumatic stress disorder. *Journal of Psychiatric Research, 47*(1), 64–71. doi:10.1016/j.jpsychires.2012.08.027

Institute of Medicine, Committee on Leading Health Indicators for Healthy People 2020. (2011). Leading health indicators for Healthy People 2020: Letter report. Washington, DC: National Academies Press.

Insurance Information Institute. (2016). Facts + statistics: Mortality risk. Retrieved from https://www.iii.org/fact-statistic/facts-statistics-mortality-risk

Intons-Peterson, M. (1993). Imaginal priming. *Journal of Experimental Psychology: Learning, Memory, and Cognition, 19*, 223–235.

Intons-Peterson, M. J., Rocchi, P., West, T., McLellan, K., & Hackney, A. (1999). Age, testing at preferred or nonpreferred times (testing optimally), and false memory. *Journal of Experimental Psychology: Learning, Memory, & Cognition, 25*, 23–40.

Intraub, H., Gortesman, C. V., & Bills, A. J. (1998). Effects of perceiving and imagining scenes on memory for pictures. *Journal of Experimental Psychology: Learning, Memory, and Cognition, 24*, 186–201.

Ironson, G., Wynings, C., Schneiderman, N., Baum, A., Rodriguez, M., Greenwood, D., . . . Fletcher, M. A. (1997). Posttraumatic stress symptoms, intrusive thoughts, loss, and immune function after Hurricane Andrew. *Psychosomatic Medicine, 59*, 128–141.

Irwin, M., Mascovich, S., Gillin, J. C., Willoughby, R., Pike, J., & Smith, T. L. (1994). Partial sleep deprivation reduces natural killer cell activity in humans. *Psychosomatic Medicine, 56*, 493–498.

Isaacson, J. S. (2010). Odor representations in mammalian cortical circuits. *Current Opinion in Neurobiology, 20*(3), 328–331. doi:10.1016/j.conb.2010.02.004

Isabella, R. A., & Belsky, J. (1991). Interactional synchrony and the origins of infant-mother attachment: A replication study. *Child Development, 62*, 373–384.

Israel, S., Moffitt, T. E., Belsky, D. W., Hancox, R. J., Poulton, R., Roberts, B., . . . Caspi, A. (2014). Translating personality psychology to help personalize preventive medicine for young adult patients. *Journal of Personality and Social Psychology, 106*(3), 484–498. doi:10.1037/a0035687

Ito, T. A., Miller, N., & Pollock, V. E. (1996). Alcohol and aggression: A meta-analysis on the moderating effects of inhibitory cues, triggering events, and self-focused attention. *Psychological Bulletin, 120*, 60–82.

Izard, C. E. (1990). Facial expressions and the regulation of emotions. *Journal of Personality and Social Psychology, 58*, 487–498.

Izard, C. E. (2009). Emotion theory and research: Highlights, unanswered questions, and emerging issues. *Annual Review of Psychology, 60*, 1–25. doi:10.1146/annurev.psych.60.110707.163539

Jack, R. E., Garrod, O. G. B, Yu, H., Caldara, R., & Schyns, P. G. (2012). Facial expressions of emotion are not culturally universal. *Proceedings of the National Academy of Sciences USA, 109*(19), 7241–7244. doi:10.1073/pnas.1200155109

Jackman, P. C., Swann, C., & Crust, L. (2016). Exploring athletes perceptions of the relationship between mental toughness and dispositional flow in sport. *Psychology of Sport and Exercise, 27*, 56–65. doi:10.1016/j.psychsport.2016.07.007

Jackson, S. A., & Csikzentmihalyi, M. (1999). *Flow in sports.* Champaign, IL: Human Kinetics.

Jacob, K. S. (2013). Employing psychotherapy across cultures and contexts. *Indian Journal of Psychological Medicine, 35*(4), 323–325. doi:10.4103/0253-7176.122218

Jacobs, B., Schall, M., Scheibel, A. B. (1993). A quantitative dendritic analysis of Wernicke's area. II. Gender, hemispheric, and environmental factors. *Journal of Comparative Neurology, 237*, 97–111.

Jacobs, G. H. (1993). The distribution and nature of color vision among mammals. *Biological Review, 68*, 413–471.

Jacobs, G. H. (2014). The discovery of spectral opponency in visual systems and its impact on understanding the neurobiology of color vision. *Journal of the History of the Neurosciences, 23*(3), 287–314. doi:10.1080/0964704x.2014.896662

Jacobs, T. (1999). On the question of self-disclosure by the analyst: Error or advance in technique? *Psychoanalytic Quarterly, 68*, 159–183.

Jacobson, S. W., Jacobson, J. L., Sokol, R. J., Martier, S. S., & Ager, J. W. (1993). Prenatal alcohol exposure and infant information processing ability. *Child Development, 64*, 1706–1721.

Jacoby, L. L., Toth, J. P., & Yonelinas, A. P. (1993). Separating conscious and unconscious influences on memory: Measuring recollection. *Journal of Experimental Psychology: General, 122*, 139–154.

James, W. (1884). What is an emotion? *Mind, 9*, 188–205.

James, W. (1890). *Principles of psychology* (Vols. 1–2). New York, NY: Holt.

Jamison, C., & Scogin, F. (1995). The outcome of cognitive bibliotherapy with adults. *Journal of Consulting and Clinical Psychology, 63*, 644–650.

Jamison, K. R. (1993). *Touched with fire: Manic-depressive illness and the artistic temperament.* New York, NY: Free Press.

Jamison, K. R. (1995). *An Unquiet Mind: A Memoir of Moods and Madness.* New York, NY: Knopf.

Jamison, K. R. (1999). *Night falls fast: Understanding suicide.* New York, NY: Knopf.

Janata, P., Tomic, S. T., & Rakowski, S. K. (2007). Characterisation of music-evoked autobiographical memories. *Memory, 15,* 845–860. doi:10.1080/09658210701734593

Jang, K., Taylor, S., Stein, M., & Yamagata, S. (2007). Trauma exposure and stress response: Exploration of mechanisms of cause and effect. *Twin Research and Human Genetics, 10*(4), 564–572. doi:10.1375/twin.10.4.564

Janjhua, Y., & Chandrakanta (2012). Behavior of personality type toward stress and job performance: A study of healthcare professionals. *Journal of Family Medicine and Primary Care, 1*(2), 109–113. doi:10.4103/2249-4863.104969

Janovcová, M., Rádlová, S., Polák, J., Sedláčková, K., Peléšková, Š., Žampachová, B., . . . Landová, E. (2019). Human attitude toward reptiles: A relationship between fear, disgust, and aesthetic preferences. *Animals (Basel), 9*(5), E238. doi:10.3390/ani9050238

Jansari, A., & Parkin, A. J. (1996). Things that go bump in your life: Explaining the reminiscence bump in autobiographical memory. *Psychology and Aging, 11,* 85–91.

Jáuregui-Garrido, B., & Jáuregui-Lobera, I. (2012). Sudden death in eating disorders. *Vascular Health and Risk Management, 8,* 91–98.

Jendrny, P., Schulz, C., Twele, F., Meller, S., von Köckritz-Blickwede, M., Osterhaus, A., . . . et al. (2020). Scent dog identification of samples from COVID-19 patients: A pilot study. *BMC Infectious Diseases, 20*(1), 536. doi:10.1186/s12879-020-05281-3

Jenkins, J. G., & Dallenbach, K. M. (1924). Oblivescence during sleep and waking. *American Journal of Psychology, 35,* 605–612.

Jenkins, S. (2017). Not your same old story: New rules for Thematic Apperceptive Techniques (TATs). *Journal of Personality Assessment, 99*(3), 238–253. doi:10.1080/00223891.2016.1248972

Jensen, A. R. (1980). *Bias in mental testing.* New York, NY: Free Press.

Jensen, A. R. (1998). *The g factor: The science of mental ability.* Westport, CT: Praeger.

Jensen, M. P., Adachi, T., Tomé-Pires, C., Lee, J., Osman, Z. J., & Miró, J. (2015). Mechanisms of hypnosis: Toward the development of a biopsychosocial model. *International Journal of Clinical and Experimental Hypnosis, 63*(1), 34–75.

Jerry Media (Producer) & Smith, C. (Director). (2019). FYRE: The greatest party that never happened [video]. Netflix. Retrieved from https://www.netflix.com/title/81035279

Jessor, R. (Ed.).(1998). *New perspectives on adolescent risk behavior.* New York, NY: Cambridge University Press.

Jiang, W., Zhao, F., Guderley, N., & Manchaiah, V. (2016). Daily music exposure dose and hearing problems using personal listening devices in adolescents and young adults: A systematic review. *International Journal of Audiology, 55*(4), 197–205. doi:10.3109/14992027.2015.1122237

Joëls, M., & Krugers, H. J. (2007). LTP after stress: Up or down? *Neural Plasticity, 2007,* 1–6. doi:10.1155/2007/93202

Johns, M., Cullum, J., Smith, T., & Freng, S. (2008). Internal motivation to respond without prejudice and automatic egalitarian goal activation. *Journal of Experimental Social Psychology, 44*(6), 1514–1519. doi:10.1016/j.jesp.2008.07.003

Johnsen, S. (2017). Test of nonverbal intelligence: A language-free measure of cognitive ability. In R. S. McCalllum (Ed.) *Handbook of nonverbal assessment* (pp. 185–206). New York, NY: Springer. doi:10.1007/978-3-319-50604-3_11.

Johnson-Laird, P. N. (1983). *Mental models.* Cambridge, MA: Harvard University Press.

Johnson-Laird, P. N. (2001). Mental models and deduction. *Trends in Cognitive Science, 5,* 434–442.

Johnson, B. T., & Eagly, A. H. (1989). Effects of involvement on persuasion: A meta-analysis. *Psychological Bulletin, 106,* 290–314.

Johnson, D. (1990). Animal rights and human lives: Time for scientists to right the balance. *Psychological Science, 1,* 213–214.

Johnson, J. L., & Cameron, M. C. (2001). Barriers to providing effective mental health services to American Indians. *Mental Health Services Research, 3,* 215–223. doi:10.1023/A:1013129131627

Johnson, J. S., & Newport, E. L. (1989). Critical period effects in second language learning: The influence of maturational state on the acquisition of English as a second language. *Cognitive Psychology, 21,* 60–99.

Johnson, M. H., Dziurawiec, S., Ellis, H. D., & Morton, J. (1991). Newborns' preferential tracking of faces and its subsequent decline. *Cognition, 40,* 1–19.

Johnson, M. K., Hashtroudi, S., & Lindsay, D. S. (1993). Source monitoring. *Psychological Bulletin, 114,* 3–28.

Johnson, R. C., McClearn, G. E., Yuen, S., Nagoshi, C. T., Ahern, F. M., & Cole, R. E. (1985). Galton's data a century later. *American Psychologist, 40,* 875–892.

Johnson, W. B., Barnett, J. E., Elman, N. S., Forrest, L., & Kaslow, N. J. (2012). The competent community: Toward a vital reformulation of professional ethics. *American Psychologist, 67,* 557–569. doi:10.1037/a0027206

Joiner, T., & Coyne, J. C. (Eds.).(1999). *The interactional nature of depression.* Washington, DC: American Psychological Association.

Jonauskaite, D., Parraga, C. A., Quiblier, M., & Mohr, C. (2020). Feeling blue or seeing red? Similar patterns of emotion associations with colour patches and colour terms. *i-Perception, 11*(1), 2041669520902484. doi:10.1177/2041669520902484

Jones, C. L., Jensen, J. D., Scherr, C. L., Brown, N. R., Christy, K., & Weaver, J. (2015). The health belief model as an explanatory framework in communication research: Exploring parallel, serial, and moderated mediation. *Health Communication, 30*(6), 566–576. doi:10.1080/10410236.2013.873363

Jones, E. (1953). *The life and work of Sigmund Freud.* New York, NY: Basic Books.

Jones, K. L., Smith, D. W., Ulleland, C. N., & Streissguth, A. P. (1973). Patterns of malformation in the offspring of chronic alcoholic mothers. *Lancet, 1,* 1267–1271.

Jones, M. C. (1924). A laboratory study of fear: The case of Peter. *Journal of Genetic Psychology, 31,* 308–315.

Jones, M. N., Willits, J., & Dennis, S. (2015). Models of semantic memory. In J. R. Busemeyer (Ed.), *The Oxford handbook of computational and mathematical psychology.* Oxford, UK: Oxford University Press.

Jones, M. R., Viswanath, O., Peck, J., Kaye, A. D., Gill, J. S., & Simopoulos, T. T. (2018). A brief history of the opioid epidemic and strategies for pain medicine. *Pain and Therapy, 7*(1), 13-21. doi:10.1007/s40122-018-0097-6

Jones, T. F., Craig, A., Hoy, D., Gunter, E. W., Ashley, D. L., Barr, D. B.,...Schaffner, W. (2000). Mass psychogenic illness attributed to toxic exposure at a high school. *New England Journal of Medicine, 342*, 96-100.

Jones, T. L., Baxter, M. A., & Khanduja, V. (2013). A quick guide to survey research. *Annals of the Royal College of Surgeons of England, 95*(1), 5-7. doi:10.1308/003588413X13511609956372

Jordan, C. (2018). The hidden meanings behind 50 of the world's most recognizable logos. Retrieved from https://www.canva.com/learn/hidden-meanings-behind-50-worlds-recognizable-logos/

Jordan, C. H., Wang, W., Donatoni, L., & Meier, B. P. (2014). Mindful eating: Trait and state mindfulness predict healthier eating behavior. *Personality and Individual Differences, 68*, 107-111.

Josephs, R. A., Bosson, J. K., & Jacobs, C. G. (2003). Self-esteem maintenance processes: Why low self-esteem may be resistant to change. *Personality and Social Psychology Bulletin, 29*(7), 920-933. doi:10.1177/0146167203029007010

Josselyn, S. A., Kohler, S., & Frankland, P. W. (2017). Heroes of the engram. *Journal of Neuroscience, 37*(18), 4647-4657.

Julien, R. M. (1992). *A primer of drug action* (6th ed.). New York, NY: Freeman.

Jung, C. G. (1928). *Contributions to analytical psychology.* New York, NY: Harcourt Brace.

Jussim, L., Crawford, J. T., Anglin, S. M., Stevens, S. T., & Duarte, J. (2016). Interpretations and methods: Towards a more effectively self-correcting social psychology. *Journal of Experimental Social Psychology, 66*, 116-133. doi:10.1016/j.jesp.2015.10.003

Jutzeler, C. R., Warner, F. M., Wanek, J., Curt, A., & Kramer, J. L. K. (2017). Thermal grill conditioning: Effect on contact heat evoked potentials. *Scientific Reports, 7*(1). doi:10.1038/srep40007

Kagan, J. (1994). *Galen's prophecy: Temperament in human nature.* New York, NY: Basic Books.

Kagan, J. (2018). Perspectives on two temperamental biases. *Philosophical Transactions of the Royal Society Biological Sciences, 373*(1744). doi:10.1098/rstb.2017.0158

Kagan, J., Snidman, N., & Arcus, D. M. (1992). Initial reactions to unfamiliarity. *Current Directions in Psychological Science, 1*, 171-174.

Kahn, D., Stickgold, R., Pace-Schott, E. F., & Hobson, A. (2008). Dreaming and waking consciousness: A character recognition study. *Journal of Sleep Research, 9*(4), 317-325. doi:10.1046/j.1365-2869.2000.00213.x

Kahn, M. (1991). *Between therapist and client: The new relationship.* New York, NY: Freeman.

Kahneman, D., & Miller, D. T. (1986). Norm theory: Comparing reality to its alternatives. *Psychological Review, 93*, 136-153.

Kahneman, D., & Tversky, A. (1973). On the psychology of prediction. *Psychological Review, 80*, 237-251.

Kahneman, D., Diener, E., & Schwarz, N. (Eds.).(1999). *Well-being: The foundations of hedonic psychology.* New York, NY: Russell Sage Foundation.

Kahneman, D., Slovic, P., & Tversky, A. (Eds.).(1982). *Judgment under uncertainty: Heuristics and biases.* New York, NY: Cambridge University Press.

Kail, R. (1990). *The development of memory in children* (3rd ed.). New York, NY: Freeman.

Kaiser Family Foundation. (2018). Adults who report they are overweight or obese by gender. Retrieved from https://www.kff.org/other/state-indicator/adult-overweightobesity-rate-by-gender/?currentTimeframe=0&sortModel=%7B%22colId%22:%22Location%22,%22sort%22:%22asc%22%7D

Kaiser, P. K., & Boynton, R. M. (1996). *Human color vision* (2nd ed.). Washington, DC: Optical Society of America.

Kajonius, P. J., & Johnson, J. (2018). Sex differences in 30 facets of the five factor model of personality in the large public. *Personality and Individual Differences, 129*(15), 126-130.

Kalali, A. H., Williams, J. B., Kobak, K. A., Engelhardt, N., Evans, K. R., Olin, J., ... Bech, P. (2002). The new GRID HAM-D pilot testing and international field trials. *International Journal of Neuropsychopharmacology, 5*, S147.

Kalish, R. A. (1981). *Death, grief, and caring relationships.* Monterey, CA: Wadsworth.

Kaliterna-Lipovčan, L., & Prizmić-Larsen, Z. (2016). What differs between happy and unhappy people?. *SpringerPlus, 5*, 225. doi:10.1186/s40064-016-1929-7

Kammers, M. P., de Vignemont, F., & Haggard, P. (2010). Cooling the thermal grill illusion through self-touch. *Current Biology, 20*, 1819-1822. doi:10.1016/j.cub.2010.08.038

Kanagawa, C., Cross, S. E., & Markus, H. R. (2001). "Who am I?" The cultural psychology of the conceptual self. *Personality and Social Psychology Bulletin, 27*, 90-103.

Känd, E. (2020). 8 myths about hypnosis. Retrieved from https://hypnosisevents.com/myths-about-hypnosis/

Kandel, E. R. (1979). Small systems of neurons. *Scientific American, 241*, 66-87.

Kandel, E. R. (1999). Biology and the future of psychoanalysis: A new intellectual framework for psychiatry revisited. *American Journal of Psychiatry, 156*, 505-524.

Kandel, E. R., Dudai, Y., & Mayford, M. R. (2014). The molecular and systems biology of memory. *Cell, 157*(1), 163-186. doi:10.1016/j.cell.2014.03.001

Kandel, E. R., Schwartz, J. H., & Jessell, T. M. (Eds.).(2000). *Principles of neural science* (4th ed.). New York, NY: McGraw-Hill.

Kandler, C., Bleidorn, W., Riemann, R., Angleitner, A., & Spinath, F. (2011). The genetic links between the Big Five personality traits and general interest domains. *Personality and Social Psychology Bulletin. 37*, 1633-1643. doi:10.1177/0146167211414275

Kann, L. (2016). Youth risk behavior surveillance?United States, 2015. *MMWR Surveillance Summaries, 63*(4). Retrieved from https://www.cdc.gov/healthyyouth/data/yrbs/pdf/2015/ss6506_updated.pdf

Kanner, A. D., Feldman, S. S., Weinberger, D. A., & Ford, M. F. (1991). Uplifts, hassles, and adaptational outcomes in early adolescents. In A. Monat & R. S. Lazarus (Eds.), *Stress and coping: An anthology* (pp. 158-181). New York, NY: Columbia University Press.

Kaplan, J. (2006). Islamophobia in America? September 11 and Islamophobic hate crime. *Terrorism and Political Violence, 18*(1), 1-33.

Kaplan, R. M. (1985). The controversy related to the use of psychological tests. In B. B. Wolman (Ed.), *Handbook of intelligence: Theories, measurements, and applications* (pp. 465-504). New York, NY: Wiley.

Kaptchuk, T. J., Friedlander, E., Kelley, J. M., Sanchez, M. N., Kokkotou, E., Singer, J. P., . . . Lembo, A. J. (2010). Placebos without deception: A randomized controlled trial in irritable bowel syndrome. *PLOS ONE, 5*(12): e15591. doi:10.1371/journal.pone.0015591

Karl, A., Birbaumer, N., Lutzenberger, W., Cohen, L., & Flor, H. (2001). Reorganization of motor and somatosensory cortex in upper extremity amputees with phantom limb pain. *Journal of Neuroscience, 21*, 3609-3618.

Karni, A., & Ungerleider, L. (1996). Comorbidity and treatment implications. *Journal of Consulting and Clinical Psychology, 60*, 833-834.

Kashima, Y., & Kerekes, A. R. Z. (1994). A distributed memory model of averaging phenomena in person impression formation. *Journal of Experimental Social Psychology, 30*, 407-455.

Kassin, S., Fein, S., & Markus, H. R. (2017). *Social psychology.* Boston, MA: Cengage Learning.

Kassin, S. M., Goldstein, C. J., & Savitsky, K. (2003). Behavioral confirmation in the interrogation room: On the dangers of presuming guilt. *Law and Human Behavior, 27*, 187-203.

Kataoka, S., Langley, A. K., Wong, M., Baweja, S., & Stein, B. D. (2012). Responding to students with posttraumatic stress disorder in schools. *Child and Adolescent Psychiatric Clinics of North America, 21*(1), 119-133. doi:10.1016/j.chc.2011.08.009

Kaufman, A. S. (2001). WAIS-III IQs, Horn's theory, and generational changes from young adulthood to old age. *Intelligence, 29*, 131-167.

Kaufman, A. S., & Lichtenberger, E. O. (1999). *Essentials of WAIS-III assessment.* New York, NY: Wiley.

Kavanaugh, R. D., Eizenman, D. R., & Harris, P. L. (1997). Young children's understanding of pretense expressions of independent agency. *Developmental Psychology, 33*, 764-770.

Kazdin, A. E. (1982). The token economy: A decade later. *Journal of Applied Behavior Analysis, 15*, 431-445.

Kazdin, A. E. (2001). *Behavior modification in applied settings* (6th ed.). Belmont, CA: Wadsworth.

Kecklund, G., & Akerstedt, T. (1993). Sleepiness in long distance truck driving: An ambulatory EEG study of night driving. *Ergonomics, 36*, 1007-1017.

Keenan, G. S., Brunstrom, J. M., & Ferriday, D. (2015). Effects of meal variety on expected satiation: Evidence for a 'perceived volume' heuristic. *Appetite, 89*, 10-15. doi:10.1016/j.appet.2015.01.010

Keesey, R. E. (1995). A set-point model of weight regulation. In K. D. Brownell & C. G. Fairburn (Eds.), *Eating disorders and obesity* (pp. 46-50). New York, NY: Guilford.

Kefeli, M. C., Turow, R. G., Yıldırım, A., & Boysan, M. (2018). Childhood maltreatment is associated with attachment insecurities, dissociation and alexithymia in bipolar disorder. *Psychiatry Research, 260*, 391-399. doi:10.1016/j.psychres.2017.12.026

Keith, J. R., Rapgay, L., Theodore, D., Schwartz, J. M., & Ross, J. L. (2015). An assessment of an automated EEG biofeedback system for attention deficits in a substance use disorders residential treatment setting. *Psychology of Addictive Behaviors, 29*(1), 17-25.

Keller, J. (2005). In genes we trust: The biological component of psychological essentialism and its relationship to mechanisms of motivated social cognition. *Journal of Personality and Social Psychology, 88*(4), 686-702. doi:10.1037/0022-3514.88.4.686

Kelley, H. H. (1967). Attribution theory in social psychology. In D. Levine (Ed.), *Nebraska symposium on motivation* (Vol. 15, pp. 192-241). Lincoln: University of Nebraska Press.

Kelly, A. E., & McKillop, K. J. (1996). Consequences of revealing personal secrets. *Psychological Bulletin, 120*, 450-465.

Kelly, R. E., Dodd, A. L., & Mansell, W. (2017). "When my moods drive upward there is nothing I can do about it": A review of extreme appraisals of internal states and the bipolar spectrum. *Frontiers in Psychology, 8.* doi:10.3389/fpsyg.2017.01235

Kelman, H. C., & Hamilton, V. L. (1989). *Crimes of obedience: Toward a social psychology of authority and responsibility.* New Haven, CT: Yale University Press.

Kendall, P. C., & Clarkin, J. F. (1992). Introduction to special section: Comorbidity and treatment implications. *Journal of Consulting and Clinical Psychology, 60*, 833-834.

Kendler, K. S., Neale, M. C., Kessler, R. C., Heath, A. C., & Eaves, L. J. (1993). The lifetime history of major depression in women. Reliability of diagnosis and heritability. *Archives of General Psychiatry, 50*, 863-870.

Kenealy, P. M. (1997). Mood-state-dependent retrieval: The effects of induced mood on memory reconsidered. *Quarterly Journal of Experimental Psychology: Human Experimental Psychology, 50*, 290-317.

Kenrick, D. T., Gutierres, S. E., & Goldberg, L. L. (1989). Influence of popular erotica on judgments of strangers and mates. *Journal of Experimental Social Psychology, 25*, 159-167.

Kensinger, E. A., & Giovanello, K. S. (2006). The status of semantic and episodic memory in amnesia. In F. J. Chen (Ed.), *Brain mapping and language* (pp. 1-14). Hauppauge, NY: Nova Science Publishers.

Keogh, E., & Herdenfeldt, M. (2002). Gender, coping, and the perception of pain. *Pain, 97*, 195-201.

Kergoat, M., Meyer, T., & Merot, A. (2017). Picture-based persuasion in advertising: The impact of attractive pictures on verbal ad's content. *Journal of Consumer Marketing, 34*(7), 624-635. doi:10.1108/jcm-01-2016-1691

Kesner, R. P., & Rolls, E. T. (2015). A computational theory of hippocampal function, and tests of the theory: New developments. *Neuroscience & Biobehavioral Reviews, 48*, 92-147. doi:10.1016/j.neubiorev.2014.11.009

Kessler, R. C., & Wang, P. S. (2008). The descriptive epidemiology of commonly occurring mental disorders in the United States. *Annual Review of Public Health, 29*, 115-129.

Kessler, R. C., Angermeyer, M., Anthony, J. C., De Graaf, R., Demyttenaere, K., Gasquet, I., . for the WHO World Mental Health Survey Consortium. (2007). Lifetime prevalence and age-of-onset distributions of mental disorders in the World Health Organization's World Mental Health Survey Initiative. *World Psychiatry, 6*(3), 168-176.

Kessler, R. C., McGonagle, K. A., Zhao, S., Nelson, C. B., Hughes, M., Eshleman, S., . . . Kendler, K. S. (1994). Lifetime and 12-month prevalence of DSM-III-R psychiatric disorders in the United States. *Archives of General Psychiatry, 51,* 8–19.

Kessler, R. C., Mickelson, K. D., & Zhao, S. (1997). Patterns and correlates of self-help group membership in the United States. *Social Policy, 27,* 27–46.

Khadilkar, V. V., Stanhope, R. G., & Khadilkar, V. (2006). Secular trends in puberty. *Indian Pediatrics, 43,* 475–478.

Khan, S. H. (2011). Duration of adolescent technology use and closeness with parents. *Columbia University Academic Commons.* doi:10.7916/D8765NBH

Kheirkhah, M., Shayegan, F., Haghani, H., & Jafar Jalal, E. (2018). The relationship between job stress, personality traits and the emotional intelligence of midwives working in health centers of Lorestan University of Medical Sciences in 2017. *Journal of Medicine and Life, 11*(4), 365–370. doi:10.25122/jml-2018-0022

Khorsandi, M., Vakilian, K., Salehi, B., Goudarzi, M. T., & Abdi, M. (2016). The effects of stress inoculation training on perceived stress in pregnant women. *Journal of Health Psychology, 21*(12), 2977–2982. doi:10.1177/1359105315589800

Kiecolt-Glaser, J. K., & Glaser, R. (1993). Mind and immunity. In D. Goleman & J. Gurin (Eds.), *Mind body medicine* (pp. 39–61). Yonkers, NY: Consumer Reports Books.

Kiecolt-Glaser, J. K., McGuire, I., Rubles, T. F., & Glaser, R. (2002). Emotions, morbidity, and mortality: New perspectives from psychoneuroimmunology. *Annual Review of Psychology, 53,* 83–107.

Kiefer, R. A. (2008). An integrative review of the concept of well-being. *Holistic Nursing Practice, 22*(5), 244–252. doi:10.1097/01.HNP.0000334915.16186.b2

Kieseppa, T., Partonen, T., Haukka, J., Kaprio, J., & Lonnqvist, J. (2004). High concordance of bipolar I disorder in a nationwide sample of twins. *American Journal of Psychiatry, 161,* 1814–1821.

Kihlstrom, J. F. (2013). Unconscious processes. In D. Reisberg & D. Reisberg (Eds.), *The Oxford handbook of cognitive psychology* (pp. 176–186). New York, NY: Oxford University Press. doi:10.1093/oxfordhb/9780195376746.013.0012

Kihlstrom, J. F., Barnhardt, T. M., & Tataryn, D. J. (1992). The psychological unconscious: Found, lost, and regained. *American Psychologist, 47,* 788–791.

Kilgour, A., & Lederman, S. J. (2002). Face recognition by hand. *Perception & Psychophysics, 64,* 339–352.

Killian, N. J., Jutras, M. J., & Buffalo, E. A. (2012). A map of visual space in the primate entorhinal cortex. *Nature, 491*(7426), 761–764. doi:10.1038/nature11587

Killingsworth, M. A. (2021). Experienced well-being rises with income, even above $75,000 per year. *Proceedings of the National Academy of Sciences, 118*(4), e2016976118. doi:10.1073/pnas.2016976118

Kim, J. W., & Chock, T. M. (2015). Body image 2.0: Associations between social grooming on Facebook and body image concerns. *Computers in Human Behavior, 48,* 331–339.

Kim, S. F. (2012). Animal models of eating disorders. *Neuroscience, 211,* 2–12. doi:10.1016/j.neuroscience.2012.03.024

Kim, S., & Lee, Y. (2018). Why do women want to be beautiful? A qualitative study proposing a new "human beauty values" concept. *PLOS ONE, 13*(8), e0201347. doi:10.1371/journal.pone.0201347

Kimmel, A. J. (1991). Predictable biases in the ethical decision-making of American psychologists. *American Psychologist, 46,* 786–788.

Kimmig, A. S., Andringa, G., & Derntl, B. (2018). Potential adverse effects of violent video gaming: Interpersonal-affective traits are rather impaired than disinhibition in young adults. *Frontiers in Psychology, 9,* 736. doi:10.3389/fpsyg.2018.00736

King, G., Graham, B., & Richardson, R. (2018). Individual differences in fear relapse. *Behaviour Research and Therapy, 100,* 37–43. doi:10.1016/j.brat.2017.11.003

Kinnunen, T., Zamanksi, H. S., & Block, M. L. (1994). Is the hypnotized subject lying? *Journal of Abnormal Psychology, 103,* 184–191.

Kinsey, A. C., Pomeroy, W. B., & Martin, C. E. (1948). *Sexual behavior in the human male.* Philadelphia, PA: Saunders.

Kinsey, A. C., Pomeroy, W. B., Martin, C. E., & Gebhard, P. H. (1953). *Sexual behavior in the human female.* Philadelphia, PA: Saunders.

Kirby, K. N. (1997). Bidding on the future: Evidence against normative discounting of delayed rewards. *Journal of Experimental Psychology: General, 126,* 54–70.

Kirby, K. N., Petry, N. M., & Bickel, W. K. (1999). Heroin addicts have higher discount rates for delayed rewards than non-drug-using controls. *Journal of Experimental Psychology: General, 128,* 78–87.

Kirmayer, L. J., Jarvis, G. E., & Guzder, J. (2013). The process of cultural consultation. *Cultural Consultation International and Cultural Psychology,* 47–69. doi:10.1007/978-1-4614-7615-3_3

Kirsch, I. (2019). Placebo effect in the treatment of depression and anxiety. *Frontiers in Psychiatry, 10,* 407. doi:10.3389/fpsyt.2019.00407

Kirsch, I., & Lynn, S. J. (1995). Altered state of hypnosis: Changes in theoretical landscape. *American Psychologist, 50,* 846–858.

Kirsch, I., & Lynn, S. J. (1999). Automaticity in clinical psychology. *American Psychologist, 54,* 504–515.

Kirsch, I., & Sapirstein, G. (1999). Listening to Prozac but hearing placebo: A meta-analysis of antidepressant medication. In I. Kirsch (Ed.), *How expectancies shape experience* (pp. 303–320). Washington, DC: American Psychological Association. doi:10.1037/10332-012

Kirsch, I., Montgomery, G., & Sapirstein, G. (1995). Hypnosis as an adjunct cognitive-behavioral psychotherapy: A meta-analysis. *Journal of Consulting and Clinical Psychology, 63,* 214–220.

Kirsner, K., Speelman, C., Mayberry, M., O'Brien-Malone, A., Anderson, M., & MacLeod, C. (Eds.). (1998). *Implicit and explicit mental processes.* Mahwah, NJ: Erlbaum.

Kirwin, B. R. (1997). *The mad, the bad, and the innocent: The criminal mind on trial.* Boston, MA: Little, Brown.

Kivimäki, M., Jokela, M., Nyberg, S. T., Singh-Manoux, A., Fransson, E. I., Alfredsson, L., & . . . Virtanen, M. (2015). Long working hours and risk of coronary heart disease and stroke: A systematic review and meta-analysis of published and unpublished data for 603,838 individuals. *Lancet, 386*(10005), 1739–1746. doi:10.1016/S0140-6736(15)60295-1

Klassen, R. M. (2004). A cross-cultural investigation of the efficacy beliefs of south Asian immigrant and Anglo Canadian nonimmigrant early adolescents. *Journal of Educational Psychology, 96*(4), 731–742. doi:10.1037/0022-0663.96.4.731

Klatsky, R. A., & Lederman, S. J. (1992). Stages of manual exploration in haptic object identification. *Perception & Psychophysics, 52*, 661–670.

Klein, D. F. (1993). False suffocation alarms, spontaneous panics, and related conditions: An integrative hypothesis. *Archives of General Psychiatry, 50*, 306–317.

Kleiner, K. A. (1987). Amplitude and phase spectra as indices of infants' pattern preferences. *Infant Behavior and Development, 10*, 49–59.

Kleinke, C. L., Peterson, T. R., & Rutledge, T. R. (1998). Effects of self-generated facial expressions on mood. *Journal of Personality and Social Psychology, 74*, 272–279.

Kleinman, A. (2004). Culture and depression. *New England Journal of Medicine, 351*(10), 951–953.

Kleitman, N. (1963). *Sleep and wakefulness.* Chicago, IL: University of Chicago Press.

Kline, P. (1991). *Intelligence: The psychometric view.* New York, NY: Routledge, Chapman & Hall.

Klinger, R., Blasini, M., Schmitz, J., & Colloca, L. (2017). Nocebo effects in clinical studies: Hints for pain therapy. *Pain Reports, 2*: e586. doi:10.1097/PR9.0000000000000586

Kluemper, D. H., Mclarty, B. D., & Bing, M. N. (2015). Acquaintance ratings of the Big Five personality traits: Incremental validity beyond and interactive effects with self-reports in the prediction of workplace deviance. *Journal of Applied Psychology, 100*(1), 237–248. doi:10.1037/a0037810

Kluft, R. P. (1996). Dissociative identity disorder. In L. K. Michetson & W. J. Ray (Eds.), *Handbook of dissociation: Theoretical, empirical, and clinical perspectives* (pp. 337–366). New York, NY: Plenum.

Knapp, R. R. (1976). *Handbook for the Personal Orientation Inventory.* San Diego, CA: Edits Publishers.

Knoblich, G., & Ohlsson, S. (1999). Constraint relaxation and chunk decomposition in insight problem solving. *Journal of Experimental Psychology: Learning, Memory, and Cognition, 25*, 1534–1556.

Kobasa, S. C. (1979). Stressful life events, personality, and health: An inquiry into hardiness. *Journal of Personality and Social Psychology, 37*, 1–11.

Kocab, K., & Sporer, S. L. (2016). The weapon focus effect for person identifications and descriptions: A meta-analysis. *Advances in Psychology and Law, 1*, 71–117. doi:10.1007/978-3-319-29406-3_3

Koch, S. (Ed.).(1959). *Psychology: A study of a science* (Vol. 2). New York, NY: McGraw-Hill.

Koch, S. (1993). "Psychology" or "the psychological studies"? *American Psychologist, 48*, 902–904.

Kochendorfer, L. B., & Kerns, K. A. (2020). A meta-analysis of friendship qualities and romantic relationship outcomes in adolescence. *Journal of Research on Adolescence, 30*(1), 4–25. doi:10.1111/jora.12505

Koenig, H. G. (2012). Religion, spirituality, and health: The research and clinical implications. *ISRN Psychiatry, 2012*, 278730. doi:10.5402/2012/278730

Koffka, K. (1935). *Principles of Gestalt psychology.* New York, NY: Harcourt, Brace & World.

Kohlberg, L. (1981). *Essays on moral development: 1: The philosophy of moral development.* New York, NY: Harper & Row.

Kohlberg, L. (1984). *Essays on moral development: Vol. 1. The philosophy of moral development.* New York, NY: Harper & Row.

Kohlberg, L. (1969). Stage and sequence: The cognitive-developmental approach to socialization. In D. A. Goslin (Ed.), *Handbook of socialization theory and research.* Chicago, IL: Rand McNally.

Köhler, W. (1925). *The mentality of apes.* London, UK: Pelican.

Kohler, W. (1947). *Gestalt psychology.* New York, NY: Liveright.

Kohn, P. M., Lafreniere, K., & Gurevich, M. (1991). Hassles, health, and personality. *Journal of Personality and Social Psychology, 61*, 478–482.

Kojima, T., Karino, S., Yumoto, M., & Funayama, M. (2012). A stroke patient with impairment of auditory sensory (echoic) memory. *Neurocase, 20*(2), 133–143. doi:10.1080/13554794.2012.732091

Kolb, B., & Whishaw, I. Q. (1990). *Fundamentals of human neuropsychology* (3rd ed.). New York, NY: Freeman.

Kolb, B., & Whishaw, I. Q. (1998). Brain plasticity and behavior. *Annual Review of Psychology, 49*, 43–64.

Kõlves, K., Kõlves, K. E., & De Leo, D. (2013). Natural disasters and suicidal behaviours: A systematic literature review. *J Affect Disord, 146*(1), 1–14. doi:10.1016/j.jad.2012.07.037

Konishi, M. (1993). Listening with two ears. *Scientific American, 268*, 66–73.

Koppel, J., & Berntsen, D. (2014). The reminiscence bump in autobiographical memory and for public events: A comparison across different cueing methods. *Memory, 24*(1), 44–62. doi:10.1080/09658211.2014.985233

Kopta, S. M., Lueger, R. J., Saunders, S. M., & Howard, K. I. (1999). Individual psychotherapy outcome and process research: Challenges leading to greater turmoil or a positive transition? *Annual Review of Psychology, 50*, 441–469.

Korcha, R. A., Polcin, D. L., Bond, J. C., Lapp, W. M., & Galloway, G. (2011). Substance use and motivation: A longitudinal perspective. *American Journal of Drug and Alcohol Abuse, 37*(1), 48–53. doi:10.3109/00952990.2010.535583

Koren, D., Norman, D., Cohen, A., Barman, J., & Klein, E. M. (2005). Increased PTSD risk with combat-related injury: A matched comparison study of injured an uninjured soldiers experiencing the same combat events. *American Journal of Psychiatry, 162*(2), 276–282.

Korkmaz, A. G., Kulakçı, A. H., Özen, Ç. İ., & Veren, F. (2019). Attitudes to ageing and their relationship with quality of life in older adults in Turkey. *Psychogeriatrics, 19*(2), 157–164. doi:10.1111/psyg.12378

Korn, J. H., Davis, R., & Davis, S. F. (1991). Historians' and chairpersons judgments of eminence among psychologists. *American Psychologist, 46*, 789–792.

Kornfield, S. L., Hantsoo, L., & Epperson, C. N. (2018). What does sex have to do with it? The role of sex as a biological variable in the development of posttraumatic stress disorder. *Current Psychiatry Reports, 20*(6), 39. doi:10.1007/s11920-018-0907-x

Koskinen, A., Bachour, A., Vaarno, J., Koskinen, H., Rantanen, S., Bäck, L., & Klockars, T. (2018). A detection dog for obstructive sleep apnea. *Sleep and Breathing, 23*(1), 281–285. doi:10.1007/s11325-018-1659-x

Kosslyn, S. M. (1980). *Image and mind.* Cambridge, MA: Harvard University Press.

Kosslyn, S. M., Leone-Pascual, A., Felician, O., Camposano, S., Keenan, J. P., Thompson, W. L., . . . Alpert, N. M. (1999). The role of Area 17 in visual imagery: Convergent evidence from PET and rTMS. *Science, 284,* 167–170.

Kotovsky, K., Hayes, J. R., & Simon, H. A. (1985). Why are some problems hard? Evidence from Tower of Hanoi. *Cognitive Psychology, 17,* 248–294.

Kotre, J., & Hall, E. (1990). *Seasons of life.* Boston: Little, Brown.

Kovecses, Z. (1990). *Emotion concepts.* New York, NY: Springer-Verlag.

Kozhevnikov, M., & Hegarty, M. (2001). Impetus beliefs as default heuristics: Dissociation between explicit and implicit knowledge about motion. *Psychonomic Bulletin and Review, 8,* 439–453.

Kramer, A. D. I., Guillory, J. E., & Hancock, J. T. (2014). Experimental evidence of massive-scale emotional contagion through social networks. *Proceedings of the National Academy of Sciences USA, 111,* 8788–8790. doi:10.1073/pnas.1320040111

Kramer, P. D. (1993). *Listening to Prozac.* New York, NY: Viking.

Krantz, D. S., & McCeney, M. K. (2002). Effects of psychological and social factors on organic disease: A critical assessment of research on coronary heart disease. *Annual Review of Psychology, 53,* 341–369.

Krasne, F. B., & Glanzman, D. L. (1995). What we can learn from invertebrate learning. *Annual Review of Psychology, 46,* 585–624.

Krebs, D. L., Denton, K. L., Vermeulen, S. C., Carpendale, J. I., & Bush, A. (1991). Structural flexibility in moral judgment. *Journal of Personality and Social Psychology, 61,* 1012–1023.

Kruger, I., (Ed.).(1996). *Pain and touch.* San Diego, CA: Academic Press.

Krumhansl, C. L. (1991). Music psychology: Tonal structures in perception and memory. *Annual Review of Psychology, 42,* 277–303.

Krumhansl, C. L., & Zupnick, J. A. (2013). Cascading reminiscence bumps in popular music. *Psychological Science, 24*(10), 2057–2068.

Kryter, K. D. (1994). *The handbook of hearing and the effects of noise.* San Diego, CA: Academic Press.

Kübler-Ross, E. (1969). *On death and dying.* New York, NY: Macmillan.

Kubricht, J. R., Holyoak, K. J., & Lu, H. (2017). Intuitive physics: Current research and controversies. *Trends in Cognitive Sciences, 21*(10), 749–759. doi:10.1016/j.tics.2017.06.002

Kubzansky, L. D., Sparrow, D., Vokonas, P., & Kawachi, I. (2001). Is the glass half empty or half full? A prospective study of optimism and coronary heart disease in the Normative Aging Study. *Psychosomatic Medicine, 63,* 910–916.

Kuffler, S. W. (1953). Discharge patterns and functional organization of mammalian retina. *Journal of Neurophysiology, 16,* 37–68.

Kuhn, M. H., & McPartland, T. S. (1954). An empirical investigation of self-attitudes. *American Sociological Review, 19*(1), 68. doi:10.2307/2088175

Kuhnen, U., Hannover, B., & Schubert, B., (2001). The semantic procedural interface model of the self: The role of self-knowledge for context-dependent versus context-independent modes of thinking. *Journal of Personality and Social Psychology, 80,* 397–409.

Kumar, A., & Ekavali, A. S. (2015). A review on Alzheimer's disease pathophysiology and its management: An update. *Pharmacological Reports, 67*(2), 195–203. doi:10.1016/j.pharep.2014.09.004

Kumar, A., Pareek, V., Faiq, M. A., Ghosh, S. K., & Kumari, C. (2019). Adult neurogenesis in humans: A review of basic concepts, history, current research, and clinical implications. *Innovations in Clinical Neuroscience, 16*(5-6), 30–37.

Kung, F. Y. H., Chao, M. M., Yao, J., Adair, W. L., Fu, J. H., & Tasa, K. (2017). Bridging racial divides: Social constructionist (vs. essentialist) beliefs facilitate trust in intergroup contexts. OSF. doi:10.31234/osf.io/2s3qr

Kuppens, S., & Ceulemans, E. (2019). Parenting styles: A closer look at a well-known concept. *Journal of Child and Family Studies, 28*(1), 168–181. doi:10.1007/s10826-018-1242-x

Kurkela, K. A., & Dennis, N. A. (2016). Event-related fMRI studies of false memory: An activation likelihood estimation meta-analysis. *Neuropsychologia, 81,* 149–167. doi:10.1016/j.neuropsychologia.2015.12.006

Kuroda, S., & Yamamoto, I. (2018). Why do people overwork at the risk of impairing mental health? *Journal of Happiness Studies.* doi:10.1007/s10902-018-0008-x

Kurtzleben, D. (2014). AP test shows wide gender gap in computer science, physics. *U.S. News & World Report.* Retrieved from https://www.usnews.com/news/blogs/data-mine/2014/01/14/ap-test-shows-wide-gender-gap-in-computer-science-physics

Kutchins, H., & Kirk, S. A. (1997). *Making us crazy: DSM, the psychiatric bible and the creation of mental disorders.* New York, NY: Free Press.

Kuwert, P., Glaesmer, H., Eichhorn, S., Grundke, E., Pietrzak, R. H., Freyberger, H. J., & Klauer, T. (2014). Long-term effects of conflict-related sexual violence compared with non-sexual war trauma in female World War II survivors: A matched pairs study. *Archives of Sexual Behavior, 43,* 1059–1064. doi:10.1007/s10508-014-0272-8

LaBerge, S. P. (1992). *Physiological studies of lucid dreaming.* Hillsdale, NJ: Erlbaum.

Lai, S. K. L., & Craig, A. (2002). Driver fatigue: Electroenchephalography and psychological assessment. *Psychophysiology, 39,* 313–321.

Lai, Y. H., & Carr, S. (2018). A critical exploration of child-parent attachment as a contextual construct. *Behavioral Sciences (Basel, Switzerland), 8*(12), 112. doi:10.3390/bs8120112

Laird, J. D. (1974). Self-attribution of emotion: The effects of expressive behavior on the quality of emotional experience. *Journal of Personality and Social Psychology, 33,* 475–486.

Lamb, M., Sternberg, K. J., & Prodromidis, M. (1992). Nonmaternal care and the security of the infant-mother attachment: A reanalysis of the data. *Infant Behavior and Development, 15,* 71–83.

Lambert, M. J., & Bergin, A. E. (1994). The effectiveness of psychotherapy. In A. Bergin & S. Garfield (Eds.), *Handbook of psychotherapy and behavior change* (4th ed., pp. 143–189). New York, NY: Wiley.

Lambracht-Washington, D., & Rosenberg, R. N. (2013). Advances in the development of vaccines for Alzheimer's disease. *Discovery Medicine, 15*(84), 319–326.

Lamm, H., Wiesmann, U., & Keller, K. (1997). Subjective attributes of attraction: How people characterize their liking, their love, and their being in love. *Personal Relationships, 4*(3), 271–284. doi:10.1111/j.1475-6811.1997.tb00145.x

Lampinen, J. M., Copeland, S. M., & Neuschatz, J. S. (2001). Recollections of things schematic: Room schemas revisited. *Journal of Experimental Psychology: Learning, Memory, & Cognition, 27*, 1211–1222.

Land, M. F., & Fernald, R. D. (1992). The evolution of eyes. *Annual Review of Neuroscience, 15*, 1–29.

Landay, K., Harms, P. D., & Credé, M. (2019). Shall we serve the dark lords? A meta-analytic review of psychopathy and leadership. *Journal of Applied Psychology, 104*(1), 183–196. doi:10.1037/apl0000357

Landová, E., Bakhshaliyeva, N., Janovcová, M., Pelešková, á., Suleymanova, M., Polák, J., . . . Frynta, D. (2018). Association between fear and beauty evaluation of snakes: Cross-cultural findings. *Frontiers in Psychology, 9*: 333. doi:10.3389/fpsyg.2018.00333

Lang, F. R., & Carstensen, L. L. (2002). Time counts: Future time perspective, goals, and social relationships. *Psychology & Aging, 17*, 125–139.

Lang, P. J. (1995). The emotion probe: Studies of motivation and attention. *American Psychologist, 50*, 372–385.

Langer, E. J. (1975). The illusion of control. *Journal of Personality and Social Psychology, 32*, 311–328.

Langevin, B., Sukkar, F., Leger, P., Guez, A., & Robert, D. (1992). Sleep apnea syndromes (SAS) of specific etiology: Review and incidence from a sleep laboratory. *Sleep, 15*, S25–S32.

Langley, G. (Ed.).(1989). *Animal experimentation: The consensus changes*. New York, NY: Chapman & Hall.

Langlois, J. H., & Roggman, L. A. (1990). Attractive faces are only average. *Psychological Science, 1*, 115–121.

Langlois, J. H., Kalakanis, L., Rubenstein, A. J., Larson, A., Hallam, M., & Smoot, M. (2000). Maxims or myths of beauty? A meta-analytic and theoretical review. *Psychological Bulletin, 126*, 390–423.

Langlois, J. H., Ritter, J. M., Roggman, L. A., & Vaughn, L. S. (1991). Facial diversity and infant preferences for attractive faces. *Developmental Psychology, 27*, 79–84.

Langlois, J. H., Roggman, L. A., & Musselman, L. (1994). What is average and what is not average about attractive faces? *Psychological Science, 5*, 214–220.

Lansford, J. E., Cappa, C., Putnick, D. L., Bornstein, M. H., Deater-Deckard, K., & Bradley, R. H. (2017). Change over time in parents' beliefs about and reported use of corporal punishment in eight countries with and without legal bans. *Child Abuse & Neglect, 71*, 44–55. doi:10.1016/j.chiabu.2016.10.016

Lansing, A. K. (1959). General biology of senescence. In J. E. Birren (Ed.), *Handbook of aging and the individual*. Chicago, IL: University of Chicago Press.

Laplante, D. P., Brunet, A., Schmitz, N., Ciampi, A., & King, S. (2008). Project Ice Storm: Prenatal maternal stress affects cognitive and linguistic functioning in 5 1/2-year-old children. *Journal of the American Academy of Child and Adolescent Psychiatry 47*, 1063–1072.

Lara-Carrasco, J., Simard, V., Saint-Onge, K., Lamoureux-Tremblay, V., & Nielsen, T. (2013). Maternal representations in the dreams of pregnant women: A prospective comparative study. *Frontiers in Psychology, 4*, 551. doi:10.3389/fpsyg.2013.00551

Larsen, K. S. (1990). The Asch conformity experiment: Replication and transhistorical comparisons. *Journal of Social Behavior and Personality, 5*, 163–168.

Larsen, R. J., & Diener, E. (1992). Promises and problems with the circumplex model of emotion. *Review of Personality and Social Psychology, 13*, 25–59.

Larson, R. W., Richards, M. H., Moneta, G., Holmbeck, G., & Duckett, E. (1996). Changes in adolescents' daily interactions with their families from ages 10 to 18: Disengagement and transformation. *Developmental Psychology, 32*, 744–754.

Lashley, K. S. (1950). In search of the engram. *Society for Experimental Biology, Symposium 4*, 454–482.

Latané, B. (1981). The psychology of social impact. *American Psychologist, 36*, 343–356.

Latané, B., & Darley, J. M. (1970). *The unresponsive bystander: Why doesn't he help?* New York, NY: Appleton-Century-Crofts.

Latané, B., & Nida, S. (1981). Ten years of research on group size and helping. *Psychological Bulletin, 89*, 308–324.

Latané, B., & Werner, C. (1978). Regulation of social contact in laboratory rats: Time, not distance. *Journal of Personality and Social Psychology, 36*, 1128–1137.

Latané, B., Williams, K., & Harkins, S. (1979). Many hands make light the work: The causes and consequences of social loafing. *Journal of Personality and Social Psychology, 37*, 822–832.

Lattal, K. A., & Perone, M. (Eds.).(1998). *Handbook of research methods in human operant behavior*. New York, NY: Plenum.

Lavie, P. (2001). Sleep-wake as a biological rhythm. *Annual Review of Psychology, 52*, 277–303.

Lawrence, E. M., Rogers, R. G., & Wadsworth, T. (2015). Happiness and longevity in the United States. *Social Science & Medicine, 145*, 115–119. doi:10.1016/j.socscimed.2015.09.020

Lawson, W. B. (2008). Schizophrenia in African Americans. In K. T. Mueser & D. V. Jeste (Eds.), *Clinical handbook of schizophrenia* (pp. 616–623). New York, NY: Guilford.

Lazarev, V. V. (2006). The relationship of theory and methodology in EEG studies of mental activity. *International Journal of Psychophysiology, 62*(3), 384-393. doi:10.1016/j.ijpsycho.2006.01.006

Lazarus, R. S. (1984). On the primacy of cognition. *American Psychologist, 39*, 124–129.

Lazarus, R. S. (1991). Cognition and motivation in emotion. *American Psychologist, 46*, 352–367.

Lazarus, R. S. (1993). From psychological stress to the emotions: A history of changing outlooks. *Annual Review of Psychology, 44*, 1–21.

Lazarus, R. S., & Folkman, S. (1984). *Stress, appraisal, and coping*. New York, NY: Springer.

Leader, L. R. (2016). The potential value of habituation in the fetus. In N. Reissland, B. S. Kisilevsky, N. Reissland, & B. S. Kisilevsky (Eds.), *Fetal development: Research on brain and behavior, environmental influences, and emerging technologies* (pp. 189–209). New York, NY: Springer Science + Business Media. doi:10.1007/978-3-319-22023-9_11

Leary, D. E. (1992). William James and the art of human understanding. *American Psychologist, 47*, 152–160.

Leary, M. R., & Kowalski, R. M. (1995). *Social anxiety.* New York, NY: Guilford.

Leaver, A. M., & Rauschecker, J. P. (2016). Functional topography of human auditory cortex. *Journal of Neuroscience, 36*(4), 1416–1428. doi:10.1523/jneurosci.0226-15.2016

Lebois, E. P., Schroeder, J. P., Esparza, T. J., Bridges, T. M., Lindsley, C. W., Conn, P. J., . . . Levey, A. I. (2017). Disease-modifying effects of M1 muscarinic acetylcholine receptor activation in an Alzheimer's disease mouse model. *ACS Chemical Neuroscience, 8*(6), 1177–1187. doi:10.1021/acschemneuro.6b00278

LeDoux, J. E. (1996). *The emotional brain: The mysterious underpinnings of emotional life.* New York, NY: Simon & Schuster.

Lee, C. T., Beckert, T. E., & Goodrich, T. R. (2010). The relationship between individualistic, collectivistic, and transitional cultural value orientations and adolescents' autonomy and identity status. *Journal of Youth and Adolescence, 39*(8), 882–893. doi:10.1007/s10964-009-9430-z

Lee, H., Shimizu, Y., & Uleman, J. S. (2015). Cultural differences in the automaticity of elemental impression formation. *Social Cognition, 33*, 1–19.

Lee, S. (2017). Can we trust the results of scientific papers? *Korean Journal of Anesthesiology, 70*(5), 491–492. doi:10.4097/kjae.2017.70.5.491

Lefcourt, H. M. (1982). *Locus of control: Current trends in theory and research.* Hillsdale, NJ: Erlbaum.

Lefèbvre, P., Malgrange, M. B., & Moonen, M. G. (2008). Regeneration of hair cells and auditory neurons in the ear. *Bulletin de l'Academie Royale de Medecine de Belgique, 163* (7–9), 391–396.

Leichsenring, F., & Schauenburg, H. (2014). Empirically supported methods of short-term psychodynamic therapy in depression: Towards an evidence-based unified protocol. *Journal of Affective Disorders, 169*, 128–143. doi:10.1016/j.jad.2014.08.007

Leigh, B. C., & Stacy, A. W. (1993). Alcohol outcome expectancies: Scale construction and predictive utility in higher-order confirmatory models. *Psychological Assessment, 5*, 216–229.

Lemann, N. (1999). *The big test: The secret history of the American meritocracy.* New York, NY: Farrar, Straus & Giroux.

Lemesle, B., Planton, M., Pagès, B., & Pariente, J. (2017). Accelerated long-term forgetting and autobiographical memory disorders in temporal lobe epilepsy: One entity or two? *Revue Neurologique, 173* (7–8), 498–505. doi:10.1016/j.neurol.2017.07.004

Lenneberg, E. H. (1967). *Biological foundations of language.* New York, NY: Wiley.

Lennie, P. (2000). Color vision. In E. R. Kandel, J. H. Schwartz, & T. M. Jessell (Eds.), *Principles of neural science* (4th ed., pp. 572–589). New York, NY: McGraw-Hill.

Lennon, R. T. (1985). Group tests of intelligence. In B. Wolman (Ed.), *Handbook of intelligence: Theories, measurement, and applications* (pp. 825–845). New York, NY: Wiley.

Lenzenweger, M. E., & Dworkin, R. H. (Eds.).(1998). *Origins and development of schizophrenia.* Washington, DC: American Psychological Association.

Leon, M. (1992). The neurobiology of filial learning. *Annual Review of Psychology, 43*, 377–398.

Leotti, L. A., Iyengar, S. S., & Ochsner, K. N. (2010). Born to choose: The origins and value of the need for control. *Trends in Cognitive Sciences, 14*(10), 457–463. doi:10.1016/j.tics.2010.08.001

Lepper, M. R., Greene, D., & Nisbett, R. E. (1973). Undermining children's intrinsic interest with extrinsic reward: A test of the "overjustification" hypothesis. *Journal of Personality and Social Psychology, 28*, 129–137.

Leucht, S., Cipriani, A., Spineli, L., Mavridis, D., Orey, D., Richter, F., . . . Davis, J. M. (2013). Comparative efficacy and tolerability of 15 antipsychotic drugs in schizophrenia: A multiple-treatments meta-analysis. In *Database of Abstracts of Reviews of Effects (DARE): Quality-assessed reviews.* York, UK: Centre for Reviews and Dissemination.

Levanen, S., Jousmaki, V., & Hari, R. (1998). Vibration-induced auditory-cortex activation in a congenitally deaf adult. *Current Biology, 8*, 869–872.

Levenson, R. W., Carstensen, L. L., & Gottman, J. M. (1993). Long-term marriage: Age, gender, and satisfaction. *Psychology and Aging, 8*, 301–313.

Levine, J. D., Gordon, N. C., & Fields, H. L. (1978). The mechanism of placebo analgesia. *Lancet, 2*, 654–657.

Levine, J. M. (1989). Reaction to opinion deviance in small groups. In P. B. Paulus (Ed.), *Psychology of group influence* (2nd ed., pp. 187–231). Hillsdale, NJ: Erlbaum.

Levine, J. M., & Tindale, R. S. (2015). Social influence in groups. In M. Mikulincer & P. R. Shaver (Eds.), *APA handbook of personality and social psychology* (Vol. 2, pp. 3–34). Washington, DC: American Psychological Association.

Levine, R. A., & Campbell, D. T. (1972). *Ethnocentrism: Theories of conflict, ethnic attitudes, and group behavior.* New York, NY: Wiley.

Levinson, D. J. (1996). *The seasons of a woman's life.* New York, NY: Knopf.

Levinson, D. J., Darrow, C. N., Klein, E. B., Levinson, M. H., & McKee, B. (1978). *The seasons of a man's life.* New York, NY: Knopf.

Levy, B. R., Slade, M. D., Kunkel, S. R., & Kasl, S. V. (2002). Longevity increased by positive self-perceptions of aging. *Journal of Personality and Social Psychology, 83*, 261–270.

Levy, J., Trevarthen, C., & Sperry, R. W. (1972). Perception of bilateral chimeric figures following hemispheric-disconnection. *Brain, 95*, 61–78.

Lewinsohn, P. M. (1974). A behavioral approach to depression. In R. Friedman & M. Katz (Eds.), *The psychology of depression: Contemporary theory and research.* Washington, DC: Winston-Wiley.

Lewinsohn, P. M., Duncan, E. M., Stanton, A. K., & Hautzinger, M. (1986). Age at first onset for nonbipolar depression. *Journal of Abnormal Psychology, 95*, 378–383.

Lewis, J. G. (2012, August). The neuroscience of déjà vu. *Psychology Today.* Retrieved from https://www.psychologytoday.com/us/blog/brain-babble/201208/the-neuroscience-d-j-vu

Lewis, P., & Boylan, P. (1979). Fetal breathing: A review. *American Journal of Obstetrics and Gynecology, 134*, 587–598.

Li, M., Yao, X., Sun, L., Zhao, L., Xu, W., Zhao, H., . . . Cui, R. (2020). Effects of electroconvulsive therapy on depression and its potential mechanism. *Frontiers in Psychology, 11*, 80. doi:10.3389/fpsyg.2020.00080

Li, W., Liu, Q., Deng, X., Chen, Y., Liu, S., & Story, M. (2017). Association between obesity and puberty timing: A systematic review and meta-analysis. *International Journal of Environmental Research and Public Health, 14*(10), 1266. doi:10.3390/ijerph14101266

Li, W., Ma, L., Yang, G., & Gan, W. B. (2017). REM sleep selectively prunes and maintains new synapses in development and learning. *Nature Neuroscience, 20*, 427–437. doi:10.1038/nn.4479

Liberman, Z., Woodward, A. L., & Kinzler, K. D. (2017). The origins of social categorization. *Trends in Cognitive Sciences, 21*(7), 556–568. doi:10.1016/j.tics.2017.04.004

Lichstein, K. L., & Morin, C. M. (Eds.).(2000). *Treatment of late life insomnia*. Thousand Oaks, CA: Sage.

Lichtman, S. W., Pisarska, K., Berman, E. R., Pestone, M., Dowling, H., Offenbacher, E., . . . Heymsfield, S. B. (1992). Discrepancy between self-reported and actual caloric intake and exercise in obese subjects. *New England Journal of Medicine, 327*, 1893–1898.

Lick, D. J., Alter, A. L., & Freeman, J. B. (2018). Superior pattern detectors efficiently learn, activate, apply, and update social stereotypes. *Journal of Experimental Psychology: General, 147*(2), 209–227. doi:10.1037/xge0000349

Lickey, M. E., & Gordon, B. (1991). *Medicine and mental illness*. New York, NY: Freeman.

Liechti, M. E. (2017). Modern clinical research on LSD. *Neuropsychopharmacology, 42*(11), 2114–2127. doi:10.1038/nnp.2017.86

Light, L. L. (1991). Memory and aging: Four hypotheses in search of data. *Annual Review of Psychology, 42*, 333–376.

Lightfoot, C. (1999). *The culture of adolescent risk-taking*. New York, NY: Guilford.

Lilienfeld, S. O., & Arkowitz, H. (2008). Facts and fictions in mental health: Altered states. *Scientific American Mind, 19*(6), 80–81. doi:10.1038/scientificamericanmind1208-80

Lilienfeld, S. O., Lynn, S. J., Kirsch, I., Chaves, J. F., Sarbin, T. R., Ganaway, G. K., & Powell, R. A. (1999). Dissociative identity disorder and the sociocognitive model: Recalling the lessons of the past. *Psychological Bulletin, 125*, 507–523.

Lima, M. P., Moret-Tatay, C., & Irigaray, T. Q. (2021). Locus of control, personality, and depression symptoms in cancer: Testing a moderated mediation model. *Clinical Psychology & Psychotherapy*. doi:10.1002/cpp.2604

Lin, E. L., & Murphy, G. L. (2001). Thematic relations in adults' concepts. *Journal of Experimental Psychology: General, 130*, 3–28.

Lin, H., & Hwang, G. (2018). Research trends of flipped classroom studies for medical courses: A review of journal publications from 2008 to 2017 based on the technology-enhanced learning model. *Interactive Learning Environments*. doi:10.1080/10494820.2018.1467462

Lin, J. Y., Arthurs, J., & Reilly, S. (2017). Conditioned taste aversions: From poisons to pain to drugs of abuse. *Psychonomic Bulletin & Review, 24*(2), 335–351.

Lin, L. yi, Sidani, J. E., Shensa, A., Radovic, A., Miller, E., Colditz, J. B., . . . Primack, B. A. (2016). Association between social media use and depression among U.S. young adults. *Depression and Anxiety, 33*(4), 323–331. doi:10.1002/da.22466

Lin, R., & Utz, S. (2017). Self-disclosure on SNS: Do disclosure intimacy and narrativity influence interpersonal closeness and social attraction? *Computers in Human Behavior, 70*, 426–436. doi:10.1016/j.chb.2017.01.012

Lin, T. E., & Honey, R. C. (2016). Learning about stimuli that are present and those that are not: Separable acquisition processes for direct and mediated learning. In R. A. Murphy, R. C. Honey, R. A. Murphy, & R. C. Honey (Eds.), *The Wiley handbook on the cognitive neuroscience of learning* (pp. 69–85). Hoboken, NJ: Wiley-Blackwell. doi:10.1002/9781118650813.ch4

Lindquist, K. A., Wager, T. D., Kober, H., Bliss-Moreau, E., & Barrett, L. F. (2012). The brain basis of emotion: A meta-analytic review. *Behavioral and Brain Sciences, 35*(3), 121–143. doi:10.1017/S0140525X11000446

Lindstedt, F., Johansson, B., Martinsen, S., Kosek, E., Fransson, P., & Ingvar, M. (2011). Evidence for thalamic involvement in the thermal grill illusion: An fMRI study. *PLOS ONE, 6*(11): e27075. doi:10.1371/journal.pone.0027075

Linn, M. C., & Petersen, A. (1985). Emergence and characterization of sex differences in spatial ability: A metaanalysis. *Child Development, 56*, 1479–1498.

Linn, R. L. (1982). Ability testing: Individual differences, prediction, and differential prediction. In A. K. Wigdor & W. R. Garner (Eds.), *Ability testing: Uses, consequences, and controversies (Part II)*. Washington, DC: National Academies Press.

Linton, M. (1982). Transformations of memory in everyday life. In U. Neisser (Ed.), *Memory observed: Remembering in natural contexts* (pp. 77–91). San Francisco, CA: Freeman.

Linville, P. W., & Jones, E. E. (1980). Polarized appraisals of outgroup members. *Journal of Personality and Social Psychology, 38*, 689–703.

Lipsey, M. W., & Wilson, D. B. (1993). The efficacy of psychological, educational, and behavioral treatment: Confirmation from meta-analysis. *American Psychologist, 48*, 1181–1209.

Lipsitt, L. (1971, December). Babies: They're a lot smarter than they look. *Psychology Today*, p. 23.

Lissek, S., & van Meurs, B. (2015). Learning models of PTSD: Theoretical accounts and psychobiological evidence. *International Journal of Psychophysiology, 98*(3), 594–605. doi.org/10.1016/j.ijpsycho.2014.11.006

Litt, M. D., & Kadden, R. M. (2015). Willpower versus "skillpower": Examining how self-efficacy works in treatment for marijuana dependence. *Psychology of Addictive Behaviors, 29*(3), 532–540. doi:10.1037/adb0000085

Little, A. C., DeBruine, L. M., & Jones, B. C. (2011). Exposure to visual cues of pathogen contagion changes preferences for masculinity and symmetry in opposite-sex faces. *Proceedings of the Royal Society of London B: Biological Sciences, 278*(1714), 2032–2039. doi:10.1098/rspb.2010.1925.

Liu, J., Lee, M., & Gershenson, S. (2020). The short- and long-run impacts of secondary school absences (EdWorkingPaper: 20-125). doi:10.26300/xg6s-z169

Livesley, W. J. (Ed.).(2001). *Handbook of personality disorders: Theory, research, and treatment.* New York, NY: Guilford.

Livingstone, M. (2002). *Vision and art: The biology of seeing.* New York, NY: Harry N. Abrams.

Livingstone, M., & Hubel, D. (1988). Segregation of form, color, movement, and depth: Anatomy, physiology, and perception. *Science, 240,* 740–749.

Llamas, J. D., Consoli, M. L. M., Hendricks, K., & Nguyen, K. (2018). Latino/a freshman struggles: Effects of locus of control and social support on intragroup marginalization and distress. *Journal of Latina/o Psychology, 6*(2), 131–148. doi:10.1037/lat0000089

Lo, M., Hinds, D. A., Tung, J. Y., Franz, C., Fan, C., Wang, Y., . . . Chen, C.-H. (2016). Genome-wide analyses for personality traits identify six genomic loci and show correlations with psychiatric disorders. *Nature Genetics, 49,* 152–156. doi:10.1038/ng.3736

Loeber, R., & Hay, D. (1997). Key issues in the development of aggression and violence from childhood to early adulthood. *Annual Review of Psychology, 48,* 371–410.

Loftus, E. F. (1979). *Eyewitness testimony.* Cambridge, MA: Harvard University Press.

Loftus, E. F. (1993). The reality of repressed memories. *American Psychologist, 48,* 518–537.

Loftus, E. F. (1993a). The reality of repressed memories. *American Psychologist, 48,* 518–537.

Loftus, E. F. (1993b). Desperately seeking memories of the first few years of childhood: The reality of early memories. *Journal of Experimental Psychology: General, 122,* 274–277.

Loftus, E. F. (1997). Creating false memories. *Scientific American, 277*(3), 70–75.

Loftus, E. F., & Guyer, M. J. (2002). Who abused Jane Doe? The hazards of the single case study. *Skeptical Inquirer, 26,* 24–32.

Loftus, E. F., & Loftus, G. R. (1980). On the permanence of stored information in the human brain. *American Psychologist, 35,* 409–420.

Loftus, E. F., Donders, K., Hoffman, H. G., & Schooler, J. W. (1989). Creating new memories that are quickly accessed and confidently held. *Memory & Cognition, 17,* 607–616.

Loftus, E. F., Loftus, G. R., & Messo, J. (1987). Some facts about "weapon focus." *Law and Human Behavior, 11*(1), 55–62.

Loftus, E. F., Miller, D. G., & Burns, H. J. (1978). Semantic integration of verbal information into visual memory. *Journal of Experimental Psychology: Human Learning and Memory, 4,* 19–31.

Logue, A. W. (2014). The psychology of eating and drinking (4th ed.). London, UK: Routledge.

Longden, E. (2013). The voices in my head [video]. Retrieved from https://www.ted.com/talks/eleanor_longden_the_voices_in_my_head?language=en#t-250672

Lopez-Gonzalez, H., Estévez, A., & Griffiths, M. D. (2017). Controlling the illusion of control: A grounded theory of sports betting advertising in the UK. *International Gambling Studies, 18*(1), 39–55. doi:10.1080/14459795.2017.1377747

Lopez, S. R., & Guarnaccia, P. J. (2000). Cultural psychopathology: Uncovering the social world of mental illness. *Annual Review of Psychology, 51,* 571–598.

Lor, M. (2018). Systematic review: Health promotion and disease prevention among Hmong adults in the USA. *Journal of Racial and Ethnic Health Disparities, 5*(3), 638–661. doi:10.1007/s40615-017-0410-9

Lorenz, K. (1937). Imprinting. *The Auk, 54,* 245–273.

Lourenco, O., & Machado, A. (1996). In defense of Piaget's theory: A reply to 10 common criticisms. *Psychological Review, 103,* 143–164.

Lu, Z.-L., Williamson, S. J., & Kaufman, L. (1992). Behavioral lifetime of human auditory sensory memory predicted by physiological measures. *Science, 258,* 1668–1670.

Lubbe, M., van Walbeek, C., & Vellios, N. (2017). The prevalence of fetal alcohol syndrome and its impact on a child's classroom performance: A case study of a rural South African school. *International Journal of Environmental Research and Public Health, 14*(8), 896. doi:10.3390/ijerph14080896

Luborsky, L. (1984). *Principles of psychoanalytic psychotherapy.* New York, NY: Basic Books.

Lucy, J. A. (1992). *Language diversity and thought: A reformulation of the linguistic relativity hypothesis.* New York, NY: Cambridge University Press.

Ludwig, A. M. (1995). *The price of greatness: Resolving the creativity and madness controversy.* New York, NY: Guilford.

Lundstrom, J. N., & Hummel, T. (2006). Sex-specific hemispheric differences in cortical activation to a bimodal odor. *Behavioral Brain Research, 166,* 197–203.

Lundy, B. L., Jones, N. A., Field, T., Nearing, G., Davalos, M., Pietro, P. A., . . . Kuhn, C. (1999). Prenatal depression effects on neonates. *Infant Behavior and Development, 22,* 119–129.

Luria, A. R. (1968). *The mind of a mnemonist.* New York, NY: Basic Books.

Lutz, W. (1996). *The new doublespeak: Why no one knows what anyone's saying anymore.* New York, NY: HarperCollins.

Lykken, D. (2000). *Happiness: The nature and nurture of joy and contentment.* New York, NY: St. Martin's.

Lykken, D. T. (1995). *The antisocial personalities.* Mahwah, NJ: Erlbaum.

Lykken, D. T., & Tellegen, A. (1996). Happiness is a stochastic phenomenon. *Psychological Science, 7,* 186–189.

Lymburner, J. A., & Roesch, R. (1999). The insanity defense: Five years of research (1993–1997). *International Journal of Law and Psychiatry, 22,* 213–240.

Lynn, S. J., Rhue, J. W., & Weekes, J. R. (1990). Hypnotic involuntariness: A social cognitive analysis. *Psychological Review, 97,* 169–184.

Lynn, S. K., & Barrett, L. F. (2014). "Utilizing" signal detection theory. *Psychological Science, 25*(9), 1663–1673. doi:10.1177/0956797614541991

Lyons, L. C., & Woods, P. J. (1991). The efficacy of rational-emotive therapy: A quantitative review of outcome research. *Clinical Psychology Review, 11,* 357–369.

Ma, Z., Zhao, J., Li, Y., Chen, D., Wang, T., Zhang, Z., . . . Liu, X. (2020). Mental health problems and correlates among 746 217 college students during the coronavirus disease 2019 outbreak in China. *Epidemiology and Psychiatric Sciences, 29*, e181. doi:10.1017/S2045796020000931

Maas, J. B. (1998). *Power sleep: How to prepare your mind for peak performance.* New York, NY: Random House.

MacCabe, J. H., Sariaslan, A., Almqvist, C., Lichtenstein, P., Larsson, H., & Kyaga, S. (2018). Artistic creativity and risk for schizophrenia, bipolar disorder and unipolar depression: A Swedish population-based case–control study and sib-pair analysis. *British Journal of Psychiatry, 212*(6), 370–376. doi:10.1192/bjp.2018.23

Maccoby, E. E. (1998). *The two sexes: Growing up apart, coming together.* New York, NY: Belknap.

Maccoby, E. E., & Jacklin, C. N. (1974). *The psychology of sex differences.* Palo Alto, CA: Stanford University Press.

Maccoby, E. E., & Jacklin, C. N. (1987). Gender segregation in childhood. In H. W. Reese (Ed.), *Advances in child development and behavior* Vol. 20, pp. 239–287).

MacGregor, J. N., Ormerod, T. C., & Chronicle, E. P. (2001). Information processing and insight: A process model of performance on the nine-dot and related problems. *Journal of Experimental Psychology: Learning, Memory, and Cognition, 27*, 176–201.

Macionis, J. J. (2001). *Sociology* (8th ed.). Upper Saddle-River, NJ: Prentice-Hall.

Mack, C. C., Cinel, C., Davies, N., Harding, M., & Ward, G. (2017). Serial position, output order, and list length effects for words presented on smartphones over very long intervals. *Journal of Memory and Language, 97*, 61–80. doi:10.1016/j.jml.2017.07.009

Mackavey, W. R., Malley, J. E., & Stewart, A. J. (1991). Remembering autobiographically consequential experiences: Content analysis of psychologists' accounts of their lives. *Psychology and Aging, 6*, 50–59.

MacLean, P. S., Blundell, J. E., Mennella, J. A., & Batterham, R. L. (2017). Biological control of appetite: A daunting complexity. *Obesity, 25* (Suppl. 1), S8–S16. doi:10.1002/oby.21771

MacLeod, C. M. (1991). Half a century of research on the Stroop effect: An integrative review. *Psychological Bulletin, 109*, 163–203.

MacMillan, M. (2000). *An odd kind of fame: Stories of Phineas Gage.* Cambridge, MA: MIT Press.

Macrae, C. N., & Bodenhausen, G. V. (2000). Social cognition: Thinking categorically about others. *Annual Review of Psychology, 51*, 93–120.

Macrae, C. N., Bodenhausen, G. V., & Calvini, G. (1999). Contexts of cryptomnensia: May the source be with you. *Social Cognition, 17*, 273–297.

MacWhinney, B. (1998). Models of the emergence of language. *Annual Review of Psychology, 49*, 199–227.

Madani, D. (2018, October 11). Fyre Festival organizer Billy McFarland sentenced to 6 years on fraud charges. NBC News. Retrieved from https://www.nbcnews.com/news/us-news/fyre-festival-organizer-billy-mcfarland-sentenced-6-years-fraud-charges-n919086

Madden, K. S., Boehm, G. W., Lee, S. C., Grota, L. J., Cohen, N., & Ader, R. (2001). One-trial conditioning of the antibody response to hen egg lysozyme in rats. *Journal of Neuroimmunology, 113*, 236–239.

Maddi, S. R., Bartone, P. T., & Puccetti, M. C. (1987). Stressful events are indeed a factor in physical illness: Reply to Schroeder and Costa (1984). *Journal of Personality and Social Psychology, 52*, 833–843.

Maddux, J. E. (1991). Self-efficacy. In C. R. Snyder & D. R. Forsyth (Eds.), *Handbook of social and clinical psychology: The health perspective* (pp. 57–78). New York, NY: Pergamon.

Madigan, S., & O'Hara, R. (1992). Short-term memory at the turn of the century: Mary Whiten Calkins's memory research. *American Psychologist, 47*, 170–174.

Madigan, S., Racine, N., Cooke, J. E., & Korczak, D. J. (2020). COVID-19 and telemental health: Benefits, challenges, and future directions. *Canadian Psychology/Psychologie Canadienne.* doi:10.1037/cap0000259

Mahmood, T., & Silverstone, T. (2001). Serotonin and bipolar disorder. *Journal of Affective Disorders, 66*(1), 1–11. doi:10.1016/s0165-0327(00)00226-3

Mahmoodian-sani, M.-R., & Mehri-Ghafarrokhi, A. (2017). The potential of miR-183 family expression in inner ear for regeneration, treatment, diagnosis and prognosis of hearing loss. *Journal of Otology, 12*(2), 55–61. doi:10.1016/j.joto.2017.03.003

Mahoney, M. J. (1991). *Human change processes.* New York, NY: Basic Books.

Maier, S. F., & Seligman, M. E. (2016). Learned helplessness at fifty: Insights from neuroscience. *Psychological Review, 123*(4), 349–367.

Maj, M., Veltro, F., Pirozzi, R., Lobrace, S., & Magliano, L. (1992). Pattern of recurrence of illness after recovery from an episode of major depression: A prospective study. *Journal of Personality and Social Psychology, 62*, 795–800.

Major, R. J., Whelton, W. J., & Duff, C. T. (2016). Secure your buffers or stare at the sun? Terror management theory and psychotherapy integration. *Journal of Psychotherapy Integration, 26*(1), 22–35. doi:10.1037/a0039631

Maliepaard, E. (2017). Bisexual safe space(s) on the Internet: Analysis of an online forum for bisexuals. *Tijdschrift Voor Economische en Sociale Geografie, 108*(3), 318–330.

Malinoski, P. T., & Lynn, S. J. (1999). The plasticity of early memory reports: Social pressure, hypnotizability, compliance, and interrogative suggestibility. *International Journal of Clinical and Experimental Hypnosis, 47*.

Mallers, M. H., Claver, M., & Lares, L. A. (2013). Perceived control in the lives of older adults: The influence of Langer and Rodins work on gerontological theory, policy, and practice. *Gerontologist, 54*(1), 67–74. doi:10.1093/geront/gnt051

Malloy, K. M., & Milling, L. S. (2010). The effectiveness of virtual reality distraction for pain reduction: A systematic review. *Clinical Psychology Review, 30*(8), 1011–1018. doi:10.1016/j.cpr.2010.07.001

Malone, S. K., Patterson, F., Lozano, A., & Hanlon, A. (2017). Differences in morning-evening type and sleep duration between Black and White adults: Results from a propensity-matched UK Biobank sample. *Chronobiology International, 34*(6), 740–752.

Malooley, J. (2019, February 13). Jill Abramson plagiarized my writing. So I interviewed her about it. *Rolling Stone.* Retrieved from https://www.rollingstone.com/culture/culture-features/jill-abramson-jake-malooley-plagiarism-interview-794257/amp/

Maltsberger, J. T., & Goldblatt, M. J. (Eds.).(1996). *Essential papers on suicide.* New York, NY: New York University Press.

Mandel, D. R., Jusczyk, P. W., & Pisoni, D. B. (1995). Infants' recognition of the sound patterns of their own names. *Psychological Science, 6,* 314–317.

Mandel, N. (2003). Shifting selves and decision making: The effects of self-construal priming on consumer risk-taking. *Journal of Consumer Research, 30*(1), 30–40. doi:10.1086/374700

Mandler, G. (1980). Recognizing: The judgment of previous occurrence. *Psychological Review, 87,* 252–271.

Mandolesi, L., Polverino, A., Montuori, S., Foti, F., Ferraioli, G., Sorrentino, P., & Sorrentino, G. (2018). Effects of physical exercise on cognitive functioning and wellbeing: Biological and psychological benefits. *Frontiers in Psychology, 9,* 509. doi:10.3389/fpsyg.2018.00509

Mann, F. D., Tackett, J. L., Tucker-Drob, E. M., & Harden, K. P. (2017). Callous-unemotional traits moderate genetic and environmental influences on rule-breaking and aggression: Evidence for gene × trait interaction. *Clinical Psychological Science, 6*(1), 123–133. doi:10.1177/2167702617730889

Manning, R., Levine, M., & Collins, A. (2007). The Kitty Genovese murder and the social psychology of helping: The parable of the 38 witnesses. *American Psychologist, 62*(6), 555–562. doi:10.1037/0003-066x.62.6.555

Mansell, W., Morrison, A. P., Reid, G., Lowens, I., & Tai, S. (2007). The interpretation of, and responses to, changes in internal states: An integrative cognitive model of mood swings and bipolar disorders. *Behavioural and Cognitive Psychotherapy, 35,* 515–539. 10.1017/S1352465807003827

Mansouri, M., Elalaoui, S. C., Bencheikh, B. O. A., Alloussi, M. E., Dion, P. A., Sefiani, A., & Rouleau, G. A. (2014). A novel nonsense mutation in SCN9A in a Moroccan child with congenital insensitivity to pain. *Pediatric Neurology, 51*(5), 741–744. doi:10.1016/j.pediatrneurol.2014.06.009

Marcel, A. J. (1983). Conscious and unconscious perception: Experiments on visual masking and word recognition. *Cognitive Psychology, 15,* 197–237.

Marcus-Newhall, A., Pedersen, W. C., Carlson, M., & Miller, N. (2000). Displaced aggression is alive and well: A meta-analytic review. *Journal of Personality and Social Psychology, 78,* 670–689.

Maren, S. (2001). Neurobiology of Pavlovian fear conditioning. *Annual Review of Neuroscience, 24,* 897–931.

Mares, D. (2013). Climate change and levels of violence in socially disadvantaged neighborhood groups. *Journal of Urban Health, 90*(4), 768–783. doi:10.1007/s11524-013-9791-1

Marigold, D. C., Cavallo, J. V., Holmes, J. G., & Wood, J. V. (2014). You can't always give what you want: The challenge of providing social support to low self-esteem individuals. *Journal of Personality and Social Psychology, 107,* 56–80. doi:10.1037/a0036554

Maris, R. W., Berman, A. L., & Silverman, M. M. (2001). *Comprehensive textbook of suicidology.* New York, NY: Guilford.

Marist Poll. (2016, May 3). 5/3: 65 stands strong as "middle-aged." Retrieved from http://maristpoll.marist.edu/53-65-stands-strong-as-middle-aged/

MaristPoll. (2017). *Yahoo News/Marist Poll: Weed & the American family.* Retrieved from http://maristpoll.marist.edu/wp-content/misc/Yahoo%20News/20170417_Summary%20Yahoo%20News-Marist%20Poll_Weed%20and%20The%20American%20Family.pdf

Mark, V. H., & Ervin, F. R. (1970). *Violence and the brain.* New York, NY: Harper & Row.

Markey, P. M. (2000). Bystander intervention in computer-mediated communication. *Computers in Human Behavior, 16,* 183–188.

Markman, A. B. (1999). *Knowledge representation.* Mahwah, NJ: Erlbaum.

Marks, G. A., Shaffrey, J. P., Oksenberg, A., Speciale, S. G., & Roffwarg, H. P. (1995). A functional role for the REM sleep in brain maturation. *Behavioural Brain Research, 69,* 1–11.

Markus, H. (1977). Self-schemata and processing information about the self. *Journal of Personality and Social Psychology, 35,* 63–78.

Markus, H. R., & Kitayama, S. (1991). Culture and the self: Implications for cognition, emotion, and motivation. *Psychological Review, 98,* 224–253.

Markus, H. R., & Kitayama, S. (2010). Cultures and selves. *Perspectives on Psychological Science, 5*(4), 420–430. doi:10.1177/1745691610375557

Marlowe, F., & Wetsman, A. (2001). Preferred waist-to-hip ratio and ecology. *Personality and Individual Differences, 30*(3), 481–489.

Maroon, J., & Bost, J. (2018). Review of the neurological benefits of phytocannabinoids. *Surgical Neurology International, 9,* 91. doi:10.4103/sni.sni_45_18

Marques, T. R., Bloomfield, P., Owen, D., Gunn, R., Rabiner, E., Veronese, M., & Howes, O. (2017). 117.4 Pet imaging of neuroinflammation in schizophrenia. *Schizophrenia Bulletin, 43*(Suppl 1), S64–S65. doi:10.1093/schbul/sbx021.171

Marr, J., & Wilcox, S. (2015). Self-efficacy and social support mediate the relationship between internal health locus of control and health behaviors in college students. *American Journal of Health Education, 46*(3), 122–131. doi:10.1080/19325037.2015.1023477

Marriott, T. C., & Buchanan, T. (2014). The true self online: Personality correlates of preference for self-expression online, and observer ratings of personality online and offline. *Computers in Human Behavior, 32,* 171–177.

Marsh, R. L., & Bower, G. H. (1993). Eliciting cryptomnesia: Unconscious plagiarism in a puzzle task. *Journal of Experimental Psychology: Learning, Memory, and Cognition, 19,* 673–688.

Marsh, R. L., Landau, J. D., & Hicks, J. L. (1997). Contributions of inadequate source monitoring to unconscious plagiarism during idea generation. *Journal of Experimental Psychology: Learning, Memory, and Cognition, 23,* 886–897.

Marshall, D. A., & Moulton, D. G. (1981). Olfactory sensitivity to xionone in humans and dogs. *Chemical Senses, 6,* 53–61.

Marshall, G. N. (1991). A multidimensional analysis of internal health locus of control belief: Separating the wheat from the chaff? *Journal of Personality and Social Psychology, 61,* 483–491.

Marshall, G. N., Schell, T. L., & Miles, J. N. V. (2009). Ethnic differences in posttraumatic distress: Hispanics' symptoms differ in kind and degree. *Journal of Consulting and Clinical Psychology, 77*(6), 1169–1178. doi:10.1037/a0017721

Marti, M. W., & Wissler, R. L. (2000). Be careful what you ask for: The effect of anchors in personal-injury damages awards. *Journal of Experimental Psychology: Applied, 6,* 91–103.

Martin, C. L., & Fabes, R. A. (2001). The stability and consequences of young children's same-sex peer interactions. *Developmental Psychology, 37,* 431–446.

Martin, C., Passilly-Degrace, P., Gaillard, D., Merlin, J.-F., Chevrot, M., & Besnard, P. (2011). The lipid-sensor candidates CD36 and GPR120 are differentially regulated by dietary lipids in mouse taste buds: Impact on spontaneous fat preference. *PLOS ONE, 6*(8). doi:10.1371/journal.pone.0024014

Martin, J. A., Hamilton, B. E., Osterman, M. J., Driscoll, A. K., & Drake, P. (2018). *Births: Final data for 2016.* Hyattsville, MD: National Center for Health Statistics. Retrieved from https://www.cdc.gov/nchs/data/nvsr/nvsr67/nvsr67_01.pdf

Martin, P. (1998). *The healing mind.* New York, NY: St. Martin's.

Martin, S., Bhatt, R., Payne, L., Seidman, L., Coates, T., & Zeltzer, L. (2018). The effects of pain-related anxiety on hypnosis treatment responses in adults with and without sickle cell disease. *Journal of Pain, 19*(3). doi:10.1016/j.jpain.2017.12.097

Martino, G., & Marks, L. E. (2001). Synesthesia: Strong and weak. *Current Directions in Psychological Science, 10,* 61–65.

Masdeu, J. C. (2011). Neuroimaging in psychiatric disorders. *Neurotherapeutics, 8*(1), 93–102. doi:10.1007/s13311-010-0006-0

Maser, J. D. (1985). List of phobias. In A. H. Tuma & J. D. Maser (Eds.), *Anxiety and the anxiety disorders.* Hillsdale, NJ: Erlbaum.

Maslach, C., & Leiter, M. P. (2016). Understanding the burnout experience: Recent research and its implications for psychiatry. *World Psychiatry, 15*(2), 103–111. doi:10.1002/wps.20311

Maslow, A. (1954). *Motivation and personality.* New York, NY: Harper.

Maslow, A. (1968). *Toward a psychology of being.* New York, NY: Van Nostrand.

Master, M. S. (1998). The gender difference on the mental rotations test is not due to performance factors. *Memory & Cognition, 26,* 444–448.

Masui, K., Nomura, M., & Ura, M. (2012). Psychopathy, reward, and punishment. In M. Balconi, M. Balconi (Eds.), *Psychology of rewards* (pp. 55–86). Hauppauge, NY: Nova Biomedical Books.

Materna, L., Halfter, H., Heidbreder, A., Boentert, M., Lippert, J., Koch, R., & Young, P. (2018). Idiopathic hypersomnia patients revealed longer circadian period length in peripheral skin fibroblasts. *Frontiers in Neurology, 9,* 424. doi:10.3389/fneur.2018.00424

Mathes, E. W., (2019). An evolutionary perspective on Kohlberg's theory of moral development. *Current Psychology.* doi:10.1007/s12144-019-00348-0

Matousek, M. (2018, April 25). Electric cars are eerily quiet—and US regulators are worried this could make them dangerous. *Business Insider.* Retrieved from https://www.businessinsider.com/why-electric-cars-have-noise-feature-2018-4

Matsumoto, D., & Juang, L. (2008). *Culture and psychology* (4th ed). Australia: Thompson Wadworth.

Matthews, K. A. (1988). CHD and Type A behavior: Update on and alternative to the Booth-Kewley and Friedman quantitative review. *Psychological Bulletin, 104,* 373–380.

Maurer, D., & Maurer, C. (1988). *The world of the newborn.* New York, NY: Basic Books.

May, C. P., & Hasher, L. (1998). Synchrony effects in inhibitory control over thought and action. *Journal of Experimental Psychology: Human Perception and Performance, 24,* 363–379.

Mayberg, H. S., Silva, J. A., Brannan, S. K., Tekell, J. L., Mahurin, R. K., McGinnis, S., & Jerabek, P. A. (2002). The functional neuroanatomy of the placebo effect. *American Journal of Psychiatry, 159,* 728–737.

Mayo Clinic. (2019). Alzheimer's treatments: What's on the horizon? Retrieved from https://www.mayoclinic.org/diseases-conditions/alzheimers-disease/in-depth/alzheimers-treatments/art-20047780

Mayo Clinic. (2019, May). Post-traumatic stress disorder. Diseases and conditions. Retrieved from https://www.mayoclinic.org/diseases-conditions/post-traumatic-stress-disorder/symptoms-causes/syc-20355967

Mazur, J. E. (1998). Choice and self-control. In K. A. Lattal & M. Perone (Eds.), *Handbook of research methods in human operant behavior* (pp. 131–161). New York, NY: Plenum.

McAdams, D. P. (1989). *Intimacy: The need to be close.* New York, NY: Doubleday.

McAdams, D. P., &de_St. Aubin, E. (Eds.). (1998). *Generativity and adult development: How and why we care for the next generation.* Washington, DC: American Psychological Association.

McAdams, D. P., Jackson, R. J., & Kirshnit, C. (1984). Looking, laughing, and smiling in dyads as a function of intimacy motivation and reciprocity. *Journal of Personality, 52,* 261–273.

McAleavey, A. A., & Castonguay, L. G. (2015). The process of change in psychotherapy: Common and unique factors. In O. Gelo, A. Pritz, & B. Rieken (Eds.), *Psychotherapy research.* New York, NY: Springer.

McBurnett, K., Lahey, B. B., Rathouz, P. J., & Loeber, R. (2000). Low salivary cortisol and persistent aggression in boys referred for disruptive behavior. *Archives of General Psychiatry, 57,* 38–43.

McCartney, K., Harris, M. J., & Bernieri, F. (1990). Growing up and growing apart: A developmental metaanalysis of twin studies. *Psychological Bulletin, 107,* 226–237.

McClelland, D. C. (1985). *Human motivation.* Glenview, IL: Scott, Foresman.

McClelland, D. C. (1998). Identifying competencies with behavioral-event interviews. *Psychological Science, 9,* 331–339.

McClelland, D. C., Atkinson. J. W., Clark, R. A., & Lowell, E. (1953). *The achievement motive.* New York, NY: Appleton-Century-Crofts.

McClelland, D. C., Koestner, R., & Weinberger, J. (1989). How do self-attributed and implicit motives differ? *Psychological Review, 96,* 690–702.

McCloskey, M., & Kuhl, D. (1983). Naive physics: The curvilinear impetus principle and its role in interactions with moving objects. *Journal of Experimental Psychology: Learning, Memory, and Cognition, 9,* 146–156.

McCloskey, M., & Zaragoza, M. (1985). Misleading postevent information and memory for events: Arguments and evidence against memory impairment hypotheses. *Journal of Experimental Psychology, 114,* 3–18.

McCluskey, M. (2018, December). "I'm upset I even have to say this." Pete Davidson addresses struggle with borderline personality disorder. *Time.* Retrieved from http://time.com/5469557/pete-davidson-bpd/

McConkey, K. M., & Sheehan, P. W. (1995). *Hypnosis, memory, and behavior in criminal investigation.* New York, NY: Guilford Press.

McConnachie, A. L., Ayed, N., Foley, S., Lamb, M. E., Jadva, V., Tasker, F., & Golombok, S. (2020). Adoptive gay father families: A longitudinal study of children's adjustment at early adolescence. *Child Development, 92*(1), 425–443. doi:10.1111/cdev.13442

McCormick, D. A., & Thompson, R. F. (1984). Cerebellum: Essential involvement in the classically conditioned eyelid response. *Science, 223,* 296–299.

McCrae, R. R., & Costa, P. T., Jr. (1990). *Personality in adulthood.* New York, NY: Guilford.

McCrae, R. R., & Costa, P. T., Jr. (1997). Personality trait structure as a human universal. *American Psychologist, 52,* 509–516.

McCreery, D., Han, M., Pikov, V., Yadav, K., & Pannu, S. (2013). Encoding of the amplitude modulation of pulsatile electrical stimulation in the feline cochlear nucleus by neurons in the inferior colliculus: Effects of stimulus pulse rate. *Journal of Neural Engineering, 10*(5):056010.

McFall, R. M., & Treat, T. A. (1999). Quantifying the information value of clinical assessments with signal detection theory. *Annual Review of Psychology, 50,* 215–241.

McFarland, S. (2012, March 20). Job seekers getting asked for Facebook passwords. *USA Today.* Retrieved from http://usatoday30.usatoday.com/tech/news/story/2012-03-20/job-applicants-facebook/53665606/1

McGhie, A., & Chapman, J. (1961). Disorders of attention and perception in early schizophrenia. *British Journal of Medical Psychology, 34,* 102–116.

McGinnis, A. L. (1987). *The power of optimism.* San Francisco: Harper & Row.

McGlynn, S. M., & Kaszniak, A. W. (1991). When metacognition fails: Impaired awareness of deficit in Alzheimer's disease. *Journal of Cognitive Neuroscience, 3,* 183–189.

McGuffin, P., Katz, R., Watkins, S., & Rutherford, J. (1996). A hospital-based twin register of the heritability of DSM-IV unipolar depression. *Archives of General Psychiatry, 53,* 129–136.

McGuffin, P., Rijsdijk, F., Andrew, M., Sham, P., Katz, R., & Cardno, A. (2003). The heritability of bipolar affective disorder and the genetic relationship to unipolar depression. *Archives of General Psychiatry, 60*(5), 497–502.

McGuire, A. M. (1994). Helping behaviors in the natural environment: Dimensions and correlates of helping. *Personality and Social Psychology Bulletin, 20,* 45–56.

McIntosh, D. N. (1996). Facial feedback hypothesis: Evidence, implications, and directions. *Motivation and Emotion, 20,* 121–147.

McKenna, K. Y. A., & Bargh, J. A. (1998). Coming out in the age of the Internet: "Demarginalization" through virtual group participation. *Journal of Personality and Social Psychology, 75,* 681–694.

McLeod, S. A. (2010). *SRRS—stress of life events.* Simply Psychology. Retrieved from https://www.simplypsychology.org/SRRS.html

McMullin, R. E. (2000). *The new handbook of cognitive therapy techniques.* New York, NY: Norton.

McNally, R. J. (1987). Preparedness and phobias: A review. *Psychological Bulletin, 101,* 283–303.

McNally, R. J. (1994). *Panic disorder: A critical analysis.* New York, NY: Guilford.

McNally, R. J. (2011). Searching for repressed memory. *True and False Recovered Memories Nebraska Symposium on Motivation, 121–*147. doi:10.1007/978-1-4614-1195-6_4

McNamara, T. P. (1994). Theories of priming: IL types of primes. *Journal of Experimental Psychology: Learning, Memory, and Cognition, 20,* 507–520.

McNatt, D. B. (2000). Ancient Pygmalion joins contemporary management: A meta-analysis of the result. *Journal of Applied Psychology, 85,* 314–322.

McNeill, D. (1970). *The acquisition of language: The study of developmental psycholinguistics.* New York, NY: Harper & Row.

McParland, A., & Hicks, C. (2018). LO39: Stress inoculation training: A critical review for emergency medicine. *Canadian Journal of Emergency Medicine, 20*(S1), S20. doi:10.1017/cem.2018.101

McPherson, M., Smith-Lovin, L., & Cook, J. M. (2001). Birds of a feather: Homophily in social networks. *Annual Review of Sociology, 27,* 415–444.

McReynolds, P. (1997). *Lightner Witmer: His life and times.* Washington, DC: American Psychological Association.

McSweeney, F. K. & Murphy, E. S. (2014). *The Wiley Blackwell handbook of operant and classical conditioning.* Hoboken, NJ: Wiley-Blackwell.

McSweeney, F. K., & Swindell, S. (1999). General-process theories of motivation revisited: The role of habituation. *Psychological Bulletin, 125,* 437–457.

Mealey, L., Bridgstock, R., & Townsend, G. C. (1999). Symmetry and perceived facial attractiveness: A monozygotic co-twin comparison. *Journal of Personality and Social Psychology, 76,* 151–158.

Meaney, R., Hasking, P., & Reupert, A. (2016). Prevalence of borderline personality disorder in university samples: Systematic review, meta-analysis and meta-regression. *PLOS ONE, 11*(5). doi:10.1371/journal.pone.0155439

Medina, J. J. (1996). *The clock of ages: Why we age-how we age-winding back the clock.* New York, NY: Cambridge University Press.

Medvec, V. H., & Savitsky, K. (1997). When doing better means feeling worse: The effects of categorical cutoff points on counterfactual thinking and satisfaction. *Journal of Personality and Social Psychology, 72,* 1284–1296.

Medvec, V. H., Madey, S. E, & Gilovich, T. (1995). When less is more: Counterfactual thinking and satisfaction among Olympic medalists. *Journal of Personality and Social Psychology, 69,* 603–610.

Meehl, P. E. (1962). Schizotaxia, schizotypy, schizophrenia. *American Psychologist, 17,* 827–838.

Meerwijk, E. L., & Sevelius, J. M. (2017). Transgender population size in the United States: A meta-regression of population-based probability samples. *American Journal of Public Health, 107*(2), e1–e8. doi:0.2105/AJPH.2016.303578

Mehdizadeh, S. (2010). Self-presentation 2.0: Narcissism and self-esteem on Facebook. *Cyberpsychology, Behavior & Social Networking, 13*, 357–364.

Meichenbaum, D. (1985). *Stress inoculation training*. New York, NY: Pergamon.

Meissner, C. A., & Brigham, J. C. (2001). 30 years of investigating the own-race bias in memory for faces: A meta-analytic review. *Psychology, Public Policy, & Law, 7*, 3–35.

Melamed, O. C., Hahn, M. K., Agarwal, S. M., Taylor, V. H., Mulsant, B. H., & Selby, P. (2020). Physical health among people with serious mental illness in the face of COVID-19: Concerns and mitigation strategies. *General Hospital Psychiatry, 66*, 30–33.

Meltzer, H. Y. (2000). Genetics and etiology of schizophrenia and bipolar disorder. *Biological Psychiatry, 47*, 171–173.

Meltzoff, A. N., & Moore, M. K. (1983). Imitation of facial and manual gestures by human neonates. *Child Development, 54*, 702–709.

Meltzoff, A. N., & Moore, M. K. (1992). Early imitation within a functional framework: The importance of person identity, movement, and development. *Infant Behavior and Development, 15*, 479–505.

Meltzoff, A. N., & Moore, M. K. (1998). Object representation, identity, and the paradox of early permanence: Steps toward a new framework. *Infant Behavior and Development, 21*, 201–235.

Melzack, R., & Wall, P. (1965). Pain mechanisms: A new theory. *Science, 150*, 971–979.

Melzack, R., & Wall, P. D. (2001). *The challenge of pain* (2nd updated ed.). London, UK: Penguin.

Mendell, L. M. (2014). Constructing and deconstructing the gate theory of pain. *Pain, 155*(2), 210–216. doi:10.1016/j.pain.2013.12.010

Mendoza, M. M., Dmitrieva, J., Perreira, K. M., Hurwich-Reiss, E., & Watamura, S. E. (2017). The effects of economic and sociocultural stressors on the well-being of children of Latino immigrants living in poverty. *Cultural Diversity and Ethnic Minority Psychology, 23*(1), 15–26. doi:10.1037/cdp0000111

Mennella, J. A. (2014). Ontogeny of taste preferences: Basic biology and implications for health. *American Journal of Clinical Nutrition, 99*(3), 704S–711S. doi:10.3945/ajcn.113.067694

Mercer, T. (2014). Wakeful rest alleviates interference-based forgetting. *Memory, 23*(2), 127–137. doi:10.1080/09658211.2013.872279

Meredith, S. E., Juliano, L. M., Hughes, J. R., & Griffiths, R. R. (2013). Caffeine use disorder: A comprehensive review and research agenda. *Journal of Caffeine Research, 3*(3), 114–130.

Merikle, P. M., Smilek, D., & Eastwood, J. D. (2001). Perception without awareness: Perspectives from cognitive psychology. *Cognition, 79*, 115–134.

Merikle, P., & Skanes, H. E. (1992). Subliminal self-help audiotapes: A search for placebo effects. *Journal of Applied Psychology, 77*, 772–776.

Merzenich, M., Kass, J. H., Wall, J., Nelson, R. J., Sur, M., & Felleman, D. (1983). Topographic reorganization of somatosensory cortical areas 3b and 1 in adult monkeys following restricted deafferentiation. *Neuroscience, 8*, 33–55.

Mesa, R. R., & Monteiro, T. (2018). Continuous transitional focus (CTF): A new concept in ophthalmic surgery. *Ophthalmology and Therapy, 7*(2), 223–231. doi:10.1007/s40123-018-0134-x

Messinger, D. S., Fogel, A., & Dickson, K. L. (1999). What's in a smile? *Developmental Psychology, 35*, 701–708.

Metalsky, G. I., Joiner, T. E., Hardin, T. S., & Abramson, L. Y. (1993). Depressive reactions to failure in a naturalistic setting: A test of the hopelessness and self-esteem theories of depression. *Journal of Abnormal Psychology, 102*, 101–109.

Metcalfe, J., & Mischel, W. (1999). A hot/cool system analysis of delay of gratification: Dynamics of willpower. *Psychological Review, 106*, 3–19.

Metcalfe, J., & Wiebe, D. (1987). Intuition in insight and non-insight problem solving. *Memory & Cognition, 15*, 238–246.

Meyer, D. E., & Schvaneveldt, R. W. (1971). Facilitation in recognizing pairs of words: Evidence of a dependence between retrieval operations. *Journal of Experimental Psychology, 90*, 227–234.

Meyer, J. R., & Reppucci, N. D. (2007). Police practices and perceptions regarding juvenile interrogation and interrogative suggestibility. *Behavioral Sciences & the Law, 25*(6), 757–780. doi:10.1002/bsl.774

Mezzich, J. E., Kleinman, A., Fabrega, H., & Parron, D. L. (Eds.).(1996). *Culture and psychiatric diagnosis: A DSM-IV perspective*. Washington, DC: American Psychiatric Press.

Middlebrooks, J. C., & Green, D. M. (1991). Sound localization by human listeners. *Annual Review of Psychology, 42*, 135–159.

Miele, F. (2002). *Intelligence, race, and genetics: Conversations with Arthur R. Jensen*. New York, NY: Westview.

Mihura, J. L., Meyer, G. J., Dumitrascu, N., & Bombel, G. (2013). The validity of individual Rorschach variables: Systematic reviews and meta-analyses of the comprehensive system. *Psychological Bulletin, 139*(3), 548–605. doi:10.1037/a0029406

Miles, A. N., Fischer-Mogensen, L., Nielsen, N. H., Hermansen, S., & Berntsen, D. (2013). Turning back the hands of time: Autobiographical memories in dementia cued by a museum setting. *Consciousness and Cognition, 22*(3), 1074–1081. doi:10.1016/j.concog.2013.07.008

Miles, D. R., & Carey, G. (1997). Genetic and environmental architecture of human aggression. *Journal of Personality and Social Psychology, 72*, 207–217.

Milgram, S. (1963). Behavioral study of obedience. *Journal of Abnormal and Social Psychology, 67*, 371–378.

Milgram, S. (1974). *Obedience to authority: An experimental view*. New York, NY: Harper & Row.

Milgram, S., Bickman, L., & Berkowitz, L. (1969). Note on the drawing power of crowds of different size. *Journal of Personality and Social Psychology, 13*, 79–82.

Millar, S., & Al-Attar, Z. (2002). The Muller-Lyer illusion in touch and vision: Implications for multisensory processes. *Perception & Psychophysics, 64*, 353–365.

Miller-Jones, D. (1989). Culture and testing. *American Psychologist, 44*, 360–366.

Miller, C. W., Zwickl, B. M., Posselt, J. R., Silvestrini, R. T., & Hodapp, T. (2019). Typical physics Ph.D. admissions criteria limit access to underrepresented groups but fail to predict doctoral completion. *Science Advances, 5*(1). doi:10.1126/sciadv.aat7550

Miller, C., & Stassun, K. (2014, June 11). A test that fails. *Nature, 510*, 303–304. doi:10.1038/nj7504-303a

Miller, F. G., Colloca, L., & Kaptchuk, T. J. (2009). The placebo effect: Illness and interpersonal healing. *Perspectives in Biology and Medicine, 52*(4), 518–539. doi:10.1353/pbm.0.0115

Miller, G. (1991). *The science of words*. New York, NY: Freeman.

Miller, G. A. (1956). The magical number seven plus or minus two: Some limits on our capacity for processing information. *Psychological Review, 63*, 81–97.

Miller, G. E., & Cohen, S. (2001). Psychological interventions and the immune system: A meta-analytic review and critique. *Health Psychology, 20*, 47–63.

Miller, I. J., & Reedy, F. E. (1990). Variations in human taste bud density and taste intensity perception. *Physiology & Behavior, 47*, 1213–1219.

Miller, J. G. (1984). Culture and the development of everyday social explanation. *Journal of Personality and Social Psychology, 46*, 961–978.

Miller, L. J., & Lu, W. (2019, February 24). These are the world's healthiest nations. Bloomberg. https://www.bloomberg.com/news/articles/2019-02-24/spain-tops-italy-as-world-s-healthiest-nation-while-u-s-slips

Miller, N. E. (1969). Learning of visceral and glandular responses. *Science, 163*, 434–445.

Miller, N. E. (1985). The value of behavioral research on animals. *American Psychologist, 40*, 423–440.

Miller, T. Q., Smith, T. W., Turner, C. W., Guijarro, M. L., & Hallet, A. J. (1996). A meta-analytic review of research on hostility and physical health. *Psychological Bulletin, 119*, 322–348.

Miller, W. I. (1997). *The anatomy of disgust*. Cambridge, MA: Harvard University Press.

Miller, Z. F., Fox, J. K., Moser, J. S., & Godfroid, A. (2017). Playing with fire: Effects of negative mood induction and working memory on vocabulary acquisition. *Cognition and Emotion, 32*(5), 1105–1113. doi:10.1080/02699931.2017.1362374

Millon, T. (1995). *Disorders of personality: DSM-IV and beyond* (2nd ed.). New York, NY: Wiley Interscience.

Millon, T., Simonsen, E., Birket-Smith, M., & Davis, R. (1998). *Psychopathy: Antisocial, criminal, and violent behavior*. New York, NY: Guilford.

Milner, B., Corkin, S., & Teuber, H. L. (1968). Further analysis of the hippocampal amnesic syndrome: 14-year follow-up study of H. M. *Neuropsychologia, 6*, 215–234.

Mimeault, V., & Morin, C. M. (1999). Self-help treatment for insomnia: Bibliotherapy with and without professional guidance. *Journal of Consulting and Clinical Psychology, 67*, 511–519.

Miñarro, S., Reyes-García, V., Aswani, S., Selim, S., Barrington-Leigh, C. P., & Galbraith, E. D. (2021). Happy without money: Minimally monetized societies can exhibit high subjective well-being. *PLoS One, 16*(1), e0244569. doi:10.1371/journal.pone.0244569

Mineka, S., & Cook, M. (1993). Mechanisms involved in the observational conditioning of fear. *Journal of Experimental Psychology: General, 122*, 23–38.

Mineka, S., Mystkowski, J. L., Hladek, D., & Rodriguez, B. I. (1999). The effects of changing contexts on return of fear following exposure therapy for spider fear. *Journal of Consulting and Clinical Psychology, 67*, 599–604.

Minhas, R. A., Walsh, D., & Bull, R. (2016). Developing a scale to measure the presence of possible prejudicial stereotyping in police interviews with suspects: The Minhas Investigative Interviewing Prejudicial Stereotyping Scale (MIIPSS). *Police Practice and Research, 18*(2), 132–145. doi:10.1080/15614263.2016.1249870

Minkov, M., Dutt, P., Schachner, M., Morales, O., Sanchez, C., Jandosova, J., . . . Mudd, B. (2017). A revision of Hofstede's individualism-collectivism dimension: A new national index from a 56-country study. *Cross Cultural & Strategic Management, 24*(3), 386–404. doi:10.1108/CCSM-11-2016-0197

Minuchin, S. (1974). Families and family therapy. Cambridge, MA: Harvard University Press.

Mireault G. C. (2017). Laughing MATTERS. *Scientific American Mind, 28*(3), 33–37.

Mischel, W. (1968). *Personality and assessment*. New York, NY: Wiley.

Mischel, W. (1973). Toward a cognitive social-learning reconceptualization of personality. *Psychological Review, 80*, 252–283.

Mischel, W. (2014). *The marshmallow test: Mastering self-control*. New York, NY: Hachette.

Mischel, W., Shoda, Y., & Rodriguez, M. L. (1989). Delay of gratification in children. *Science, 244*, 933–938.

Mita, T. H., Dermer, M., & Knight, J. (1977). Reversed facial images and the mere-exposure hypothesis. *Journal of Personality and Social Psychology, 35*, 597–601.

Mitchell, S. H. (1999). Measures of impulsivity in cigarette smokers and non-smokers. *Psychopharmacology, 146*, 455–464.

Mitler, M. M., Miller, J. C., Lipsitz, J. J., Walsh, J. K., & Wylie, C. D. (1997). The sleep of long-haul truck drivers. *New England Journal of Medicine, 337*, 755–761.

Mix, K. S., Huttenlocher, J., & Levine, S. C. (2002). Multiple cues for quantification in infancy: Is number one of them? *Psychological Bulletin, 128*, 278–294.

Miyake, A., & Shah, P. (Eds.).(1999). *Models of working memory: Mechanisms of active maintenance and executive control*. New York, NY: Cambridge University Press.

Mizuno, K., Matsumoto, A., Aiba, T., Abe, T., Ohshima, H., Takahashi, M., & Inoue, Y. (2016). Sleep patterns among shift-working flight controllers of the International Space Station: An observational study on the JAXA Flight Control Team. *Journal of Physiological Anthropology, 35*(1), 19. doi:10.1186/s40101-016-0108-4

Moagi, M. M., van Der Wath, A. E., Jiyane, P. M., & Rikhotso, R. S. (2021). Mental health challenges of lesbian, gay, bisexual and transgender people: An integrated literature review. *Health SA = SA Gesondheid, 26*, 1487. doi:10.4102/hsag.v26i0.1487

Mocan, N. H., & Yu, H. (2017). Can superstition create a self-fulfilling prophecy? School outcomes of Dragon children of China. *National Bureau of Economic Research, Working Paper Series 23709*. doi:10.3386/w23709

Moffitt, T. E. (1993). Adolescence-limited and life-course persistent antisocial behavior: A developmental taxonomy. *Psychological Review, 100*, 674–701.

Moffitt, T. E., Arseneault, L., Belsky, D., Dickson, N., Hancox, R. J., Harrington, H., . . . Caspi, A. (2011). A gradient of childhood self-control predicts health, wealth, and public safety. *Proceedings of the National Academy of Sciences USA, 108*(7), 2693–2698. doi:10.1073/pnas.1010076108

Moffitt, T., Poulton, R., & Caspi, A. (2013). Lifelong impact of early self-control. *American Scientist, 100*(5), 352. doi:10.1511/2013.104.1

Mohr, C. D., Armeli, S., Tennen, H., Carney, M. A., Affleck, G., & Hromi, A. (2001). Daily interpersonal experiences, context, and alcohol consumption: Crying in your beer and toasting good times. *Journal of Personality and Social Psychology, 80*, 489–500.

Molgora, M., Cortez, V. S., & Colonna, M. (2021). Killing the invaders: NK cell impact in tumors and anti-tumor therapy. *Cancers (Basel), 13*(4), 595. doi:10.3390/cancers13040595

Mondloch, C. J., Lewis, T. L., Budreau, D. R., Maurer, D., Dannemiller, J. L., Stephens, B. R., & Kleiner-Gathercoal, K. A. (1999). Face perception during early infancy. *Psychological Science, 10*, 419–422.

Mongeluzi, D. L., Rosellini, R. A., Caldarone, B. J., Stock, H. S., & Abrahamson, G. C. (1996). Pavlovian aversive conditioning using carbon dioxide as the unconditioned stimulus. *Journal of Experimental Psychology: Animal Behavior Processes, 22*, 244–257.

Montepare, J. M., & Lachman, M. E. (1989). "You're only as old as you feel": Self perceptions of age, fears of aging, and life satisfaction from adolescence to old age. *Psychology and Aging, 4*, 73–78.

Mooijman, M., Hoover, J., Lin, Y., Ji, H., & Dehghani, M. (2018). Moralization in social networks and the emergence of violence during protests. *Nature Human Behaviour*. doi:10.1038/s41562-018-0353-0

Moore, K. L., Persaud, T. V. N., & Tochia, M. G. (2013). *The developing human: Clinically oriented embryology* (9th ed.). Philadelphia, PA: Elsevier.

Moore, M. K., & Meltzoff, A. N. (1999). New findings on object permanence: A developmental difference between two types of occlusion. *British Journal of Developmental Psychology, 17*(4), 623–644. doi:10.1348/026151099165410

Moore, T. J., & Mattison, D. R. (2017). Adult utilization of psychiatric drugs and differences by sex, age, and race. *JAMA Internal Medicine, 177*(2), 274. doi:10.1001/jamainternmed.2016.7507

Moos, R. H., & Moos, B. S. (2006). Participation in treatment and Alcoholics Anonymous: A 16-year follow-up of initially untreated individuals. *Journal of Clinical Psychology, 62*(6), 735–750. doi:10.1002/jclp.20259

Moran, C. A., Southwick, S., Steffian, G., Hazlett, G. A., & Loftus, E. F. (2013). Misinformation can influence memory for recently experienced, highly stressful events. *International Journal of Law and Psychiatry, 36*, 11–17.

Moray, N. (1959). Attention in dichotic listening: Affective cues and the influence of instructions. *Quarterly Journal of Experimental Psychology, 11*, 56–60.

Morgan, E. R., Rowhani-Rahbar, A., Azrael, D., & Miller, M. (2018). Public perceptions of firearm- and non-firearm-related violent death in the United States: A national study. *Annals of Internal Medicine, 169*(10), 734–737. doi:10.7326/M18-1533

Morgan, M., & Nickson, D. (2001). Uncivil aviation: A review of the air rage phenomenon. *International Journal of Tourism Research, 3*(6), 443. Retrieved from https://onlinelibrary.wiley.com/doi/abs/10.1002/jtr.327

Morris, D. Z. (2017). *New French law bars work emails after hours*. Retrieved from http://fortune.com/2017/01/01/french-right-to-disconnect-law/

Morrison, D. C. (1988). Marine mammals join the navy. *Science, 242*, 1503–1504.

Mortimer, A., & Shepherd, E. (1999). Frames of mind: Schemata guiding cognition and conduct in the interviewing of suspected offenders. In A. Memon & R. Bull (Eds.), *Handbook of the psychology of interviewing* (pp. 293–315). Chichester, UK: Wiley.

Morton, J., & Johnson, M. H. (1991). CONSPEC and CONLERN: A two-process theory of infant face recognition. *Psychological Review, 98*, 164–181.

Moskowitz, G. B., & Li, P. (2011). Egalitarian goals trigger stereotype inhibition: A proactive form of stereotype control. *Journal of Experimental Social Psychology, 47*(1), 103–116. doi:10.1016/j.jesp.2010.08.014

Moston, S., Stephenson, G. M., & Williamson, T. (1992). The effects of case characteristics on suspect behaviour during police questioning. *British Journal of Criminology, 32*, 23–40.

Moullin, S., Waldfogel, J., & Washbrook, E. (2014). *Baby bonds: Parenting, attachment, and a secure base for children*. Retrieved from https://www.suttontrust.com/wp-content/uploads/2014/03/baby-bonds-final.pdf

Moulton, S. T., & Kosslyn, S. M. (2009). Imagining predictions: Mental imagery as mental emulation. *Philosophical Transactions of the Royal Society B: Biological Sciences, 364*(1521), 1273–1280. doi:10.1098/rstb.2008.0314

Moynihan, J. A., & Ader, R. (1996). Psychoneuroimmunology: Animal models of disease. *Psychosomatic Medicine, 58*, 546–558.

Mozell, M. M., Smith, B., Smith, P., Sullivan, R., & Swender, P. (1969). Nasal chemoreception in flavor identification. *Archives of Otolaryngology, 90*, 367–373.

Mrklas, K., Shalaby, R., Hrabok, M., Gusnowski, A., Vuong, W., Surood, S., . . . Agyapong, V. (2020). Prevalence of perceived stress, anxiety, depression, and obsessive-compulsive symptoms in health care workers and other workers in Alberta during the COVID-19 pandemic: Cross-sectional survey. *JMIR Mental Health, 7*(9), e22408. doi:10.2196/22408

Mroz, J. E., Pullen, C. H., & Hageman, P. A. (2018). Health and appearance reasons for weight loss as predictors of long-term weight change. *Health Psychology Open, 5*(2), 2055102918816606. doi:10.1177/2055102918816606

Mueller, C. M., & Dweck, C. S. (1998). Praise for intelligence can undermine children's motivation and performance. *Journal of Personality and Social Psychology, 75*, 33–52.

Mulla, Z. R., Govindaraj, K., Polisetti, S. R., George, E., & More, N. R. S. (2017). Mindfulness-based stress reduction for executives: Results from a field experiment. *Business Perspectives and Research, 5*(2), 113–123. doi:10.1177/2278533717692906

Mullington, J., & Broughton, R. (1993). Scheduled naps in the management of daytime sleepiness in narcolepsy-cataplexy. *Sleep, 16*, 444–456.

Murdoch, M., Spoont, M. R., Kehle-Forbes, S. M., Harwood, E. M., Sayer, N. A., Clothier, B. A., & Bangerter, A. K. (2017). Persistent serious mental illness among former applicants for VA PTSD disability benefits and long-term outcomes: Symptoms, functioning, and employment. *Journal of Traumatic Stress, 30*(1), 36–44. doi:10.1002/jts.22162

Murray, G., & Johnson, S. L. (2010). The clinical significance of creativity in bipolar disorder. *Clinical Psychology Review, 30*(6), 721–732.

Murray, H. A. (1943). *Thematic Apperception Test: Pictures and manual.* Cambridge, MA: Harvard University Press.

Murray, I. J., Parry, N. R., McKeefry, D. J., & Panorgias, A. (2012). Sex-related differences in peripheral human color vision: A color matching study. *Journal of Vision, 12.*

Myers & Briggs Foundation. (2019). MBTI basics. Retrieved from https://www.myersbriggs.org/my-mbti-personality-type/mbti-basics/home.htm

Myers, M. G., Stewart, D. G., & Brown, S. A. (1998). Progression from conduct disorder to antisocial personality disorder following treatment for adolescent substance abuse. *American Journal of Psychiatry, 155*, 479–485.

Myerson, J., Rank, M. R., Raines, F. Q., & Schintzler, M. A. (1998). Race and general cognitive ability: The myth of diminishing returns to education. *Psychological Science, 9*, 139–142.

Na, J., & Kitayama, S. (2011). Spontaneous trait inference is culture-specific behavioral and neural evidence. *Psychological Science, 22*, 1025–1032. doi:10.1177/0956797611414727

Nabawy, G. E. L., Moawad, A., & Ebrahem, G. G. S. (2016). The relationship between use of technology and parent-adolescent social relationship. *Journal of Education and Practice, 7*(14), 168–178.

Nadon, R., Hoyt, I. P., Register, P. A., & Kihlstrom, J. F. (1991). Absorption and hypnotizability: Context effects reexamined. *Journal of Personality and Social Psychology, 60*, 144–153.

Nahari, G., & Pazuelo, M. (2015). Telling a convincing story: Richness in detail as a function of gender and information. *Journal of Applied Research in Memory and Cognition, 4*(4), 363–367.

Narrow, W. E., Rae, D. S., Robins, L. N., & Regier, D. A. (2002). Revised prevalence estimates of mental disorders in the United States: Using a clinical significance criterion to reconcile 2 surveys' estimates. *Archives of General Psychiatry, 59*, 115–123.

Nash, M. R., & Benham, G. (2005). The truth and the hype of hypnosis. *Scientific American Mind, 16*(2), 46–53.

Nason, E. E., Rinehart, J. K., Yeater, E. A., Newlands, R. T., & Crawford, J. N. (2018). Prior sexual relationship, gender and sexual attitudes affect the believability of a hypothetical sexual assault vignette. *Gender Issues, 36*(3), 319–338. doi:10.1007/s12147-018-9227-z.

Nasser, M. (1988). Culture and weight consciousness. *Journal of Psychosomatic Research, 32*(6), 573–577. doi:10.1016/0022-3999(88)90005-0

Nathan, P. E., & Langenbucher, J. W. (1999). Psychopathology: Description and classification. *Annual Review of Psychology, 50*, 79–107.

Nathans, J. (1989). The genes for color vision. *Scientific American, 260*, 42–49.

National Cancer Institute. (2017). Treatment-related nausea and vomiting (PDQ®)–Health professional version. Retrieved from https://www.cancer.gov/about-cancer/treatment/side-effects/nausea/nausea-hp-pdq

National Center for Health Statistics. (2017). Exercise of physical activity. Retrieved from https://www.cdc.gov/nchs/fastats/exercise.htm

National Commission on Correctional Health Care. (2018). Solitary confinement (isolation). Standards and resources. Retrieved from https://www.ncchc.org/solitary-confinement

National Eating Disorders Association. (2018). Bulimia nervosa. Retrieved from https://www.nationaleatingdisorders.org/learn/by-eating-disorder/bulimia

National Highway Traffic Safety Administration. (2018). NHTSA studies vehicle safety and driving behavior to reduce vehicle crashes. Retrieved from https://www.nhtsa.gov/research-data

National Institute of Mental Health. (2016, November). Overview: Psychotherapies. Retrieved from https://www.nimh.nih.gov/health/topics/psychotherapies/index.shtml

National Institute of Mental Health. (2017). Eating disorders. Retrieved from https://www.nimh.nih.gov/health/statistics/eating-disorders.shtml#part_155060

National Institute on Deafness and Other Communication Disorders. (2016). Quick statistics about hearing. Retrieved from https://www.nidcd.nih.gov/health/statistics/quick-statistics-hearing

National Institute on Deafness and Other Communication Disorders. (2018, June 15). Cochlear implants. Retrieved from https://www.nidcd.nih.gov/health/cochlear-implants

National Institutes of Health. (2018). Genetics home reference: 22q11.2 deletion syndrome. Retrieved from https://ghr.nlm.nih.gov/condition/22q112-deletion-syndrome#sourcesforpage

National Public Radio. (2005). Frequently asked questions about lobotomies. Retrieved on from https://www.npr.org/templates/story/story.php?storyId=5014565

National Public Radio. (2017, December 27). The haunting effects of going days without sleep. Retrieved from https://www.npr.org/2017/12/27/573739653/the-haunting-effects-of-going-days-without-sleep

National Sleep Foundation. (2018). National Sleep Foundation's 2018 Sleep in America® poll shows Americans failing to prioritize sleep. Retrieved from https://www.sleepfoundation.org/press-release/national-sleep-foundations-2018-sleep-americar-poll-shows-americans-failing

NCAA Sport Science Institute. (2020). Concussion diagnosis and management best practices. Retrieved from http://www.ncaa.org/sport-science-institute/concussion-diagnosis-and-management-best-practices

Needham, T., Lambrechts, H., & Hoffman, L. (2017). Castration of male livestock and the potential of immunocastration to improve animal we. *South African Journal of Animal Science, 47*(6), 731. doi:10.4314/sajas.v47i6.1

Neisser, U. (1967). *Cognitive psychology.* New York, NY: Appleton-Century-Crofts.

Neisser, U., & Becklen, R. (1975). Selective looking: Attending to visually specified events. *Cognitive Psychology, 7*, 480–494.

Nelson, C. A. (1999). Neural plasticity and human development. *Current Directions in Psychological Science, 8*, 42–45.

Nelson, K. (1973). Structure and strategy in learning to talk. *Monographs of the Society for Research in Child Development, 38*(Whole No. 149).

Nesse, R. M. (2000). Is depression an adaptation? *Archives of General Psychiatry, 57*, 14–20.

Neubauer, D. N., Pandi-Perumal, S. R., Spence, D. W., Buttoo, K., & Monti, J. M. (2018). Pharmacotherapy of insomnia. *Journal of Central Nervous System Disease, 10*, 1179573518770672. doi:10.1177/1179573518770672

Neuenschwander, R., & Blair, C. (2017). Zooming in on children's behavior during delay of gratification: Disentangling impulsigenic and volitional processes underlying self-regulation. *Journal of Experimental Child Psychology, 154*, 46–63. doi:10.1016/j.jecp.2016.09.007

Neugarten, B. L. (1979). Time, age, and the life cycle. *American Journal of Psychiatry, 136*, 887–894.

Newcomb, A. F., & Bagwell, C. L. (1995). Children's friendship relations: A meta-analytic review. *Psychological Bulletin, 117*, 306–347.

Newcomb, A. F., Bukowski, W. M., & Pattee, L. (1993). Children's peer relations: A meta-analytic review of popular, rejected, neglected, controversial, and average sociometric status. *Psychological Bulletin, 113*, 99–128.

Newcombe, E., & Ratcliff, G. (1990). Disorders of visuospatial analysis. In H. Goodglass & A. R. Damasio (Eds.), *Handbook of neuropsychology* (Vol. 2). Amsterdam, Netherlands: Elsevier.

Newell, A., & Simon, H. (1972). *Human problem solving.* Englewood Cliffs, NJ: Prentice-Hall.

Newell, A., Shaw, J. G., & Simon, H. A. (1958). Elements of a theory of human problem solving. *Psychological Review, 65*, 151–166.

Newman, C. (2000, January). The enigma of beauty. *National Geographic*, pp. 94–121.

Newman, M. (July 26, 2006). Yates found not guilty by reason of insanity. *New York Times.* Retrieved from https://www.nytimes.com/2006/07/26/us/26cnd-yates.html

Newport, F. (2013, July 25). In U.S., 87% approve of Black-White marriage, vs. 4% in 1958. Gallup. Retrieved from http://news.gallup.com/poll/163697/approve-marriage-blacks-whites.aspx

Ng, B. (2018). The neuroscience of growth mindset and intrinsic motivation. *Brain Sciences, 8*(2), 20. doi:10.3390/brainsci8020020

Ng, Q. X., Soh, A., Loke, W., Venkatanarayanan, N., Lim, D. Y., & Yeo, W. S. (2019). Systematic review with meta-analysis: The association between post-traumatic stress disorder and irritable bowel syndrome. *Journal of Gastroenterology and Hepatology, 34*(1), 68–73. doi:10.1111/jgh.14446

Nickerson, R. S. (1998). Confirmation bias: A ubiquitous phenomenon in many guises. *Review of General Psychology, 2*, 175–220.

Nickerson, R. S. (2000). Null hypothesis significance testing: A review of an old and continuing controversy. *Psychological Methods, 5*, 241–301.

Nickerson, R. S., & Adams, M. J. (1979). Long-term memory for a common object. *Cognitive Psychology, 11*, 287–307.

Nieder, A. (2012). Neurobiology of perception of illusory contours in animals. In O. F. Lazareva, T. Shimizu, & E. A. Wasserman (Eds.), *How animals see the world: comparative behavior, biology, and evolution of vision.* Oxford, UK: Oxford University Press.

Nieuwsma, J. A., Trivedi, R. B., McDuffie, J., Kronish, I., Benjamin, D., & Williams, J. W. (2012). Brief psychotherapy for depression: A systematic review and meta-analysis. *International Journal of Psychiatry in Medicine, 43*, 129–151.

Nijhawan, R. (1991). Three-dimensional Müller-Lyer illusion. *Perception & Psychophysics, 49*, 333–341.

Nikles, C., Brecht, D., Klinger, E., & Bursell, A. (1998). The effects of current concern- and nonconcern-related waking suggestions and nocturnal dream content. *Journal of Personality and Social Psychology, 75*, 242–255.

Nisbett, R. E., & Wilson, T. D. (1977). Telling more than we can know: Verbal reports on mental processes. *Psychological Review, 84*, 231–259.

Noah, T., Schul, Y., & Mayo, R. (2018). When both the original study and its failed replication are correct: Feeling observed eliminates the facial-feedback effect. *Journal of Personality and Social Psychology, 114*(5), 657–664. doi:10.1037/pspa0000121

Noble, J., & McConkey, K. M. (1995). Hypnotic sex change: Creating and challenging a delusion in the laboratory. *Journal of Abnormal Psychology, 104*, 69–74.

Nolen-Hoeksema, S., & Girgus, J. S. (1994). The emergence of gender differences in depression during adolescence. *Psychological Bulletin, 115*, 424–443.

Norberg, P. A. (2017). Employee incentive programs: Recipient behaviors in points, cash, and gift card programs. *Performance Improvement Quarterly, 29*(4), 375–388. doi:10.1002/piq.21233

Norcross, J. C. (1991). Prescriptive matching in psychotherapy: An introduction. *Psychotherapy, 28*, 439–443.

Norcross, J. C., Karpiak, C. P., & Lister, K. M. (2005). What's an integrationist? A study of self-identified integrative and (occasionally) eclectic psychologists. *Journal of Clinical Psychology, 61*(12), 1587–1594. doi:10.1002/jclp.20203

Nordell, J. (2018, May 3). Does Starbucks understand the science of racial bias? *The Atlantic.* Retrieved from https://www.theatlantic.com/science/archive/2018/05/starbucks-unconscious-bias-training/559415/

Norman, P. (2007, March 29). Halle Berry admits to suicide attempt. *People.* Retrieved from https://people.com/celebrity/halle-berry-admits-to-suicide-attempt/

Norman, S. (2006). The use of telemedicine in psychiatry. *Journal of Psychiatric and Mental Health Nursing, 13*(6), 771–777. doi:10.1111/j.1365-2850.2006.01033.x

Northoff, G. (2016). *Neuro-philosophy and the healthy mind: Learning from the unwell brain.* New York, NY: Norton.

Norton, K. I., Olds, T. S., Olive, S., & Dank, S. (1996). Ken and Barbie at life size. *Sex Roles, 34*, 287–294.

Novins, D. K., Croy, C. D., Moore, L. A., & Rieckmann, T. (2016). Use of evidence-based treatments in substance abuse treatment programs serving American Indian and Alaska Native communities. *Drug and Alcohol Dependence, 161*, 214–221. doi:10.1016/j.drugalcdep.2016.02.007

Novotney, A. (2018). *Psychology job forecast: Partly sunny.* Retrieved from http://www.apa.org/gradpsych/2011/03/cover-sunny.aspx

Nowicki, S. (2016). *Choice or chance: Understanding your locus of control and why it matters.* Amherst, NY: Prometheus.

Noyes, E. T., Levine, J. A., Schlauch, R. C., Crane, C. A., Connors, G. J., Maisto, S. A., & Dearing, R. L. (2018). Impact of pretreatment change on mechanism of behavior change research: An applied example using alcohol abstinence self-efficacy. *Journal of Studies on Alcohol and Drugs, 79*(2), 223–228. doi:10.15288/jsad.2018.79.223

NPR. (2015). Timeline: What we know about the Freddie Gray arrest. Retrieved from https://www.npr.org/sections/thetwo-way/2015/05/01/403629104/baltimore-protests-what-we-know-about-the-freddie-gray-arrest

Nyklíček, I., Mommersteeg, P. M. C., Beugen, S. V., Ramakers, C., & Boxtel, G. J. V. (2013). Mindfulness-based stress reduction and physiological activity during acute stress: A randomized controlled trial. *Health Psychology, 32*(10), 1110–1113. doi:10.1037/a0032200

O'Connell, A. N. (1980). Karen Horney: Theorist in psychoanalysis and feminine psychology. *Psychology of Women Quarterly, 5*(1), 81–93.

O'Connell, A. N., & Russo, N. F. (Eds.).(1990). *Women in psychology: A bio-bibliographic sourcebook*. Westport, CT: Greenwood.

O'Connor, S. C., & Rosenblood, L. K. (1996). Affiliation motivation in everyday experience: A theoretical comparison. *Journal of Personality and Social Psychology, 70*, 513–522.

O'Leary, A. (1990). Stress, emotion, and human immune function. *Psychological Bulletin, 108*, 363–382.

O'Reilly, J., Robinson, S. L., Berdahl, J. L., & Banki, S. (2014). Is negative attention better than no attention? The comparative effects of ostracism and harassment at work. *Organizational Science*. doi:10.1287/orsc.2014.0900

Ogbu, J. U. (1978). *Minority education and caste: The American system in cross-cultural perspective*. New York, NY: Academic.

Ohlsson, S. (2011). *Deep learning: How the mind overrides experience*. Cambridge, UK: Cambridge University Press.

Ohman, A., & Mineka, S. (2001). Fears, phobias, and preparedness: Toward an evolved module of fear and fear learning. *Psychological Review, 108*, 483–522.

Ohman, A., & Mineka, S. (2001). Fears, phobias, and preparedness: Toward an evolved module of fear and fear learning. *Psychological Review, 108*, 483–522.

Ohman, A., & Soares, J. J. F. (1998). Emotional conditioning to masked stimuli: Expectancies for aversive outcomes following nonrecognized fear-relevant stimuli. *Journal of Experimental Psychology: General, 127*, 69–82.

Oishi, S., Diener, E. E, Lucas, R. E., & Suh, E. M. (1999). Cross-cultural variations in predictors of life satisfaction: Perspectives from needs and values. *Personality and Social Psychology Bulletin, 25*, 980–990.

Oitzl, M. S., Champagne, D. L., van der Veen, R., & de Kloet, E. R. (2010). Brain development under stress: Hypotheses of glucocorticoid actions revisited. *Neuroscience & Biobehavioral Reviews, 34*, 853–866.

Okbay, A., Baselmans, B. M., De Neve, J. E., Turley, P., Nivard, M. G., Fontana, M. A., . . . Cesarini, D. (2016). Genetic variants associated with subjective well-being, depressive symptoms, and neuroticism identified through genome-wide analyses. *Nature Genetics, 48*(6), 624–633. doi:10.1038/ng.3552

Olafson, E. (2014). A review and correction of the errors in Loftus and Guyer on Jane Doe. *Journal of Interpersonal Violence, 29*(18), 3245–3259. doi:10.1177/0886260514534988

Olds, J., & Milner, P. M. (1954). Positive reinforcement produced by electrical stimulation of septal area and other regions of the rat brain. *Journal of Comparative and Physiological Psychology, 47*, 419–427.

Olff, M. (2017). Sex and gender differences in post-traumatic stress disorder: An update. *European Journal of Psychotraumatology, 8*(Supppl. 4), 1351204. http://doi.org/10.1080/20008198.2017.1351204

Oliver, G., & Wardle, J. (1999). Perceived effects of stress on food choice. *Physiology & Behavior, 66*, 511–515.

Öllinger, M., Jones, G., & Knoblich, G. (2014). The dynamics of search, impasse, and representational change provide a coherent explanation of difficulty in the nine-dot problem. *Psychological Research, 78*(2), 266–275. doi:10.1007/s00426-013-0494-8

Olness, K. (1993). Hypnosis: The power of attention. In D. Goleman & J. Gurin (Eds.), *Mind body medicine* (pp. 277–290). Yonkers, NY: Consumer Reports Books.

Olweus, D. (2012). Cyberbullying: An overrated phenomenon? *European Journal of Developmental Psychology, 9*, 520–538. doi:10.1080/17405629.2012.682358

Omura, M., Maguire, J., Levett-Jones, T., & Stone, T. E. (2017). The effectiveness of assertiveness communication training programs for healthcare professionals and students: A systematic review. *International Journal of Nursing Studies, 76*, 120–128. doi:10.1016/j.ijnurstu.2017.09.001

Ones, D. S., Viswesvaran, C., & Reiss, A. D. (1996). Role of social desirability in personality testing for personnel selection: The red herring. *Journal of Applied Psychology, 81*, 660–679.

Oomen, C. A., Soeters, H., Audureau, N., Vermunt, L., van Hasselt, F., Manders, E. M., . . . Krugers, H. (2010). Severe early life stress hampers spatial learning and neurogenesis, but improves hippocampal synaptic plasticity and emotional learning under high-stress conditions in adulthood. *Journal of Neuroscience, 30*, 6635–6645.

Opitz, B. (2014). Memory function and the hippocampus. *Frontiers in Neurology and Neuroscience, 34*, 51–59. doi:10.1159/000356422

Orehek, E., Sasota, J. A., Kruglanski, A. W., Dechesne, M., & Ridgeway, L. (2014). Interdependent self-construals mitigate the fear of death and augment the willingness to become a martyr. *Journal of Personality and Social Psychology, 107*(2), 265–275. doi:10.1037/a0036675

Orne, M. T., & Evans, F. J. (1965). Social control in the psychological experiment: Antisocial behavior and hypnosis. *Journal of Personality and Social Psychology, 1*, 189–200.

Ornstein, R., & Sobel, D. (1987). *The healing brain*. New York, NY: Simon & Schuster.

Ortega, A. N., & Rosenheck, R. (2000). Posttraumatic stress disorder among Hispanic Vietnam veterans. *American Journal of Psychiatry, 157*, 615–619.

Orth, U., & Robins, R. W. (2014). The development of self-esteem. *Current Directions in Psychological Science, 23*(5), 381–387. doi:10.1177/0963721414547414

Osmanski, B., Martin, C., Montaldo, G., Lanièce, P., Pain, F., Tanter, M., & Gurden, H. (2014). Functional ultrasound imaging reveals different odor-evoked patterns of vascular activity in the main olfactory bulb and the anterior piriform cortex. *NeuroImage, 95*, 176–184. doi:10.1016/j.neuroimage.2014.03.054

Osofsky, H., Osofsky, J., Kronenberg, M., Brennan, A., & Hansel, T. (2009). Posttraumatic stress symptoms in children after Hurricane Katrina: Predicting the need for mental health services. *American Journal of Orthopsychiatry, 79*, 212–220.

Ost, L.-G. (1992). Blood and injection phobia: Background and cognitive, physiological, and behavioral variables. *Journal of Abnormal Psychology, 101*, 68–74.

Ostafin, B. D., & Kassman, K. T. (2012). Stepping out of history: Mindfulness improves insight problem solving. *Consciousness and Cognition, 21*, 1031–1036 10.1016/j.concog.2012.02.014

Oswald, F. L., Mitchell, G., Blanton, H., Jaccard, J., & Tetlock, P. E. (2013). Predicting ethnic and racial discrimination: A meta-analysis of IAT criterion studies. *Journal of Personality and Social Psychology, 105*(2), 171–192. doi:10.1037/a0032734

Ouirdi, M. E., Segers, J., Ouirdi, A. E., & Pais, I. (2015). Predictors of job seekers' self-disclosure on social media. *Computers in Human Behavior, 53*, 1–12. doi:10.1016/j.chb.2015.06.039

Oxenham, A. J. (2018). How we hear: The perception and neural coding of sound. *Annual Review of Psychology, 69*, 27–50. doi:10.1146/annurev-psych-122216-011635

Oyserman, D., & Lee, S. W. S. (2008). Does culture influence what and how we think? Effects of priming individualism and collectivism. *Psychological Bulletin, 134*(2), 311–342. doi:10.1037/0033-2909.134.2.311

Oz, M., Petroianu, G., & Lorke, D. E. (2016). α7-Nicotinic acetylcholine receptors: New therapeutic avenues in Alzheimer's disease. In M. Li (Ed.), *Neuromethods* (Vol. 117: *Nicotinic acetylcholine receptor technologies*). New York, NY: Humana Press.

Özçalişkan, S., & Goldin-Meadow, S. (2010). Sex differences in language first appear in gesture. *Development Science, 13*(5), 752–760.

Pacheco, D., & Verschure, P. F. M. J. (2017). Long-term spatial clustering in free recall. *Memory, 26*(6), 798–806. doi:10.1080/09658211.2017.1409768

Paffenbarger, R. S., Jr., Hyde, R. T., Wing, A. L., & Hsieh, C. (1986). Physical activity, all-cause mortality, and longevity of college alumni. *New England Journal of Medicine, 314*, 605–613.

Page, A., & Morrison, N. (2018). The effects of gender, personal trauma history and memory continuity on the believability of child sexual abuse disclosure among psychologists. *Child Abuse & Neglect, 80*, 1–8. doi:10.1016/j.chiabu.2018.03.014

Paiva, W., Soares, Fonoff, E., Zanetti, Amorim, R., Bernardo, L., . . . Teixeira. (2013). Psychosurgery for schizophrenia: History and perspectives. *Neuropsychiatric Disease and Treatment, 509*. doi:10.2147/ndt.s35823

Paivio, A. (1969). Mental imagery in associative learning and memory. *Psychological Review, 76*, 241–263.

Paivio, A. (1986). *Mental representations: A dual coding approach.* New York, NY: Oxford University Press.

Palfai, T., & Jankiewicz, H. (1991). *Drugs and human behavior.* Dubuque, IA: William C. Brown.

Palmer, B. W., Friend, S., Huege, S., Mulvaney, M., Badawood, A., Almaghraby, A., & Lohr, J. B. (2019). Aging and trauma: Post traumatic stress disorder among Korean War veterans. *Federal Practitioner, 36*(12), 554–562.

Palmer, S. E. (1999). *Vision science: Photons to phenomenology.* Cambridge, MA: MIT Press.

Palmore, E. B. (1982). Predictors of the longevity difference: A 25-year follow-up. *Gerontologist, 22*, 513–518.

Panagopoulou-Koutnatzi, F. (2014). The practice of naming and shaming through the publicizing of "culprit" lists. In C. M. Akrivopoulou, N. Garipidis, C. M. Akrivopoulou, & N. Garipidis (Eds.), *Human rights and the impact of ICT in the public sphere: Participation, democracy, and political autonomy* (pp. 145–155). Hershey, PA: Information Science Reference/IGI Global. doi:10.4018/978-1-4666-6248-3.ch008

Panskepp, J. (1986). The anatomy of emotions. In R. Plutchik & H. Kellerman (Eds.), *Emotion: Theory, research, and experience-biological foundations of emotion* (Vol. 3, pp. 91–124). San Diego, CA: Academic.

Pantic, I. (2014). Online social networking and mental health. *Cyberpsychology, Behavior, & Social Networking, 17*(10), 652–657. doi:10.1089/cyber.2014.0070

Pappa, S., Ntella, V., Giannakas, T., Giannakoulis, V. G., Papoutsi, E., & Katsaounou, P. (2020). Prevalence of depression, anxiety, and insomnia among healthcare workers during the COVID-19 pandemic: A systematic review and meta-analysis. *Brain, Behavior, and Immunity, 88*, 901–907.

Paradies, Y., Ben, J., Denson, N., Elias, A., Priest, N., Pieterse, A., . . . Gee, G. (2015). Racism as a determinant of health: A systematic review and meta-analysis. *PLOS ONE, 10*(9), e0138511. doi:10.1371/journal.pone.0138511

Paris, J. (2017). Is psychoanalysis still relevant to psychiatry? *Canadian Journal of Psychiatry. Revue canadienne de psychiatrie, 62*(5), 308–312.

Parks, R. W., Zee, R. F., & Wilson, R. S. (Eds.).(1993). *Neuropsychology of Alzheimer's disease and other dementias.* New York, NY: Oxford University Press.

Parma, V., Ohla, K., Veldhuizen, M. G., Niv, M. Y., Kelly, C. E., Bakke, A. J., . . . Hayes, J. E., GCCR Group. (2020, June). More than smell—COVID-19 is associated with severe impairment of smell, taste, and chemesthesis. *Chemical Senses.* doi:10.1093/chemse/bjaa041

Parmelee, A. H., Jr., & Sigman, M. D. (1983). Perinatal brain development and behavior. In P. H. Mussen (Ed.), *Handbook of child psychology: Vol. 2. Infancy and developmental psychobiology.* New York, NY: Wiley.

Parsons, L. M., & Fox, P. T. (1998). The neural basis of implicit movements used in recognizing hand shape. *Cognitive-Neuropsychology, 15*, 583–615.

Pascalis, O., de Schonen, S., Morton, J., DeRuelle, C., & Fabre-Grenet, M. (1995). Mother's face recognition by neonates: A replication and an extension. *Infant Behavior and Development, 18*, 79–85.

Pashler, H. E. (1998). *The psychology of attention.* Cambridge, MA: MIT Press.

Pashler, H., Johnston, J. C., & Ruthruff, E. (2001). Attention and performance. *Annual Review of Psychology, 52*, 629–651.

Passman, R. H. (1987). Attachments to inanimate objects: Are children who have security blankets insecure? *Journal of Consulting and Clinical Psychology, 55*, 825–830.

Patel, K. A., & Schlundt, D. G. (2001). Impact of moods and social context on eating behavior. *Appetite, 36*, 111–118.

Patrick, C. J., Bradley, M. M., & Lang, P. J. (1993). Emotion in the criminal psychopath: Startle reflex modulation. *Journal of Abnormal Psychology, 102*, 82–92.

Paul, E. S., Sher, S., Tamietto, M., Winkielman, P., & Mendl, M. T. (2020). Towards a comparative science of emotion: Affect and consciousness in humans and animals. *Neuroscience and Biobehavioral Reviews, 108*, 749–770. doi:10.1016/j.neubiorev.2019.11.014

Paulesu, E., Harrison, J., Baron-Cohen, S., Watson, J. D. G., Goldstein, L., Heather, J., . . . Frith, C. D. (1995). The physiology of coloured hearing: A PET activation study of colour-word synesthesia. *Brain, 118*, 661–676.

Paulson, S., Azzarelli, K. K., McMahon, D. M., & Schwartz, B. (2016). A new science of happiness: The paradox of pleasure. *Annals of the New York Academy of Sciences, 1384*(1), 12–31. doi:10.1111/nyas.13068

Pavlov, I. (1927). *Conditioned reflexes*. Oxford, UK: Oxford University Press.

Pavot, W., & Diener, E. (1993). Review of the Satisfaction with Life Scale. *Psychological Assessment, 5*, 164–172.

Pearce, J. M. (1987). A model for stimulus generalization in Pavlovian conditioning. *Psychological Review, 94*, 61–73.

Pearce, J. M., & Bouton, M. E. (2001). Theories of associative learning in animals. *Annual Review of Psychology, 52*, 111–139.

Pederson, D. R., & Moran, G. (1996). Expressions of the attachment relationship outside the strange situation. *Child Development, 67*, 915–927.

Peever, J., & Fuller, P. M. (2016). Neuroscience: A distributed neural network controls REM sleep. *Current Biology, 26*(1), R34–R35.

Pelham, B. W. (1995). Self-investment and self-esteem: Evidence for a Jamesian model of self-worth. *Journal of Personality and Social Psychology, 69*, 1141–1150.

Pelham, B. W., & Swann, W. B., Jr. (1989). From self-conceptions to self-worth: The sources and structure of self-esteem. *Journal of Personality and Social Psychology, 57*, 672–680.

Pellegrino, R., Sinding, C., Wijk, R. D., & Hummel, T. (2017). Habituation and adaptation to odors in humans. *Physiology & Behavior, 177*, 13–19. doi:10.1016/j.physbeh.2017.04.006

Penfield, W., & Perot, P. (1963). The brain's record of auditory and visual experience. *Brain, 86*, 595–696.

Peng, X. D., Huang, C. Q., Chen, L. J., & Lu, Z. C. (2009). Cognitive behavioural therapy and reminiscence techniques for the treatment of depression in the elderly: A systematic review. *Journal of International Medical Research, 37*, 975–982.

Pennebaker, J. W. (1997). Writing about emotional experiences as a therapeutic process. *Psychological Science, 8*, 162–166.

Pereira, P. J., & Lerner, E. A. (2017). Gate control theory springs a leak. *Neuron, 93*(4), 723–724. doi:10.1016/j.neuron.2017.02.016

Peri, T., Ben-Shakhar, G., Orr, S. P., & Shalev, A. Y. (2000). Psychophysiologic assessment of aversive conditioning in post-traumatic stress disorder. *Biological Psychiatry, 47*(6), 512–519. doi:10.1016/s0006-3223(99)00144-4

Perilla, J. L., Norris, F. H., & Lavizzo, E. A. (2002). Ethnicity, culture, and disaster response: Identifying and explaining ethnic differences in PTSD six months after Hurricane Andrew. *Journal of Social and Clinical Psychology, 21*(1), 20–45.

Perillo, J. T., & Kassin, S. M. (2011). Inside interrogation: The lie, the bluff, and false confessions. *Law and Human Behavior, 35*(4), 327–337. doi:10.1007/s10979-010-9244-2

Perilloux, C., Duntley, J. D., & Buss, D. M. (2014). Blame attribution in sexual victimization. *Personality and Individual Differences, 63*, 81–86. doi:10.1016/j.paid.2014.01.058

Perlow, M. J., Freed, W. J., Hoffer, B. J., Seiger, A., Olson, L., & Wyatt, R. J. (1979). Brain grafts reduce motor abnormalities produced by destruction of nigrostriatal dopamine system. *Science, 204*, 643–646.

Perls, F. S. (1969). *Gestalt therapy verbatim*. Lafayette, CA: Real People Press.

Perls, F. S., Heffertine, R. E, & Goodman, P. (1951). *Gestalt therapy*. New York, NY: Julian Press.

Perogamvros, L., & Schwartz, S. (2012). The roles of the reward system in sleep and dreaming. *Neuroscience and Biobehavioral Reviews, 36*, 1934–1951. doi:10.1016/j.neubiorev.2012.05.010

Perrin, D. (2018). A case for procedural causality in episodic recollection 1. In K. Michaelian, D. Debus, & D. Perrin (Eds.), *New directions in the philosophy of memory* (pp. 33–51). New York, NY: Routledge. doi:10.4324/9781315159591-3

Perry, M. (2016, September 27). 2016 SAT test results confirm pattern that's persisted for 50 years—high school boys are better at math than girls. *AEIdeas*. Retrieved from http://www.aei.org/publication/2016-sat-test-results-confirm-pattern-thats-persisted-for-45-years-high-school-boys-are-better-at-math-than-girls/

Persky, V. W., Kempthorne-Rawson, J., & Shekelle, R. B. (1987). Personality and risk of cancer: 20-year follow-up of the Western Electric Study. *Psychosomatic Medicine, 49*, 435–449.

Pert, C. B., & Snyder, S. H. (1973). Opiate receptor: Demonstration in nervous tissue. *Science, 179*, 1011–1014.

Perugini, E. M., Kirsch, I., Allen, S. T., Coldwell, E., Meredith, J. M., Montgomery, G. H., & Sheehan, J. (1998). Surreptitious observations of responses to hypnotically suggested hallucinations: A test of the compliance hypothesis. *International Journal of Clinical and Experimental Hypnosis, 46*, 191–203.

Peter-Hagene, L. C., & Ullman, S. E. (2016). Longitudinal effects of sexual assault victims' drinking and self-blame on posttraumatic stress disorder. *Journal of Interpersonal Violence, 33*(1), 83–93. doi:10.1177/0886260516636394

Peterhänsel, C., Linde, K., Wagner, B., Dietrich, A., & Kersting, A. (2017). Subtypes of personality and 'locus of control' in bariatric patients and their effect on weight loss, eating disorder and depressive symptoms, and quality of life. *European Eating Disorders Review, 25*(5), 397–405. doi:10.1002/erv.2534

Peterlin, B. L., Nijjar, S. S., & Tietjen, G. E. (2011). Post-traumatic stress disorder and migraine: Epidemiology, sex differences, and potential mechanisms. *Headache, 51*(6), 860–868. doi:10.1111/j.1526-4610.2011.01907.x

Petersen, A. C. (1984). The early adolescence study: An overview. *Journal of Early Adolescence, 4*, 103–106.

Peterson, C, Seligman, M. E. P., Yurko, K. H., Martin, L. R., & Friedman, H. S. (1998). Catastrophizing and untimely death. *Psychological Science, 9*, 127–130.

Peterson, C. (2000). The future of optimism. *American Psychologist, 55*, 44–55.

Peterson, C., Seligman, M. E. P., & Vaillant, G. E. (1988). Pessimistic explanatory style is a risk factor for physical illness: A thirty-five-year longitudinal study. *Journal of Personality and Social Psychology, 55*, 23–27.

Peterson, K. M., Piazza, C. C., & Volkert, V. M. (2016). A comparison of a modified sequential oral sensory approach to an applied behavior-analytic approach in the treatment of food selectivity in children with autism spectrum disorder. *Journal of Applied Behavior Analysis, 49*(3), 485–511. doi:10.1002/jaba.332

Peterson, L. R., & Peterson, M. J. (1959). Short-term retention of individual verbal items. *Journal of Experimental Psychology, 58*, 193–198.

Peterson, S. E., & Fiez, J. A. (1993). The processing of single words studied with positron emission tomography. *Annual Review of Neuroscience, 16*, 509–530.

Peterson, S. E., Fox, P. T., Mintun, M. A., Posner, J. I., & Raichle, M. E. (1989). Studies of the processing of single words using averaged positron emission tomographic measurements of cerebral blood flow change. *Journal of Cognitive Neuroscience, 1*, 153–170.

Petty, R. E., & Cacciopo, J. T. (2019). *Attitudes and persuasion: Classic and contemporary approaches.* New York, NY: Routledge.

Petty, R. E., & Cacioppo, J. T. (1986). *Communication and persuasion: Central and peripheral routes to attitude change.* New York, NY: Springer-Verlag.

Petty, R. E., & Cacioppo, J. T. (1990). Involvement and persuasion: Tradition versus integration. *Psychological Bulletin, 107*, 367–374.

Petty, R. E., & Wegener, D. T. (1999). The elaboration likelihood model: Current status and controversies. In S. Chaiken & Y. Trope (Eds.), *Dual process theories in social psychology* (pp. 41–72). New York, NY: Guilford.

Petty, R. E., Wegener, D. T., & Fabrigar, L. R. (1997). Attitudes and attitude change. *Annual Review of Psychology, 48*, 609–647.

Pew Research Center. (2012). The global religious landscape. Retrieved from https://www.pewforum.org/2012/12/18/global-religious-landscape-exec/

Pezdek, K., Whetstone, T., Reynolds, K., Askari, N., & Dougherty, T. (1989). Memory for real-world scenes: The role of consistency with schema expectation. *Journal of Experimental Psychology: Learning, Memory, and Cognition, 15*, 587–595.

Pflum, S. R., Testa, R. J., Balsam, K. F., Goldblum, P. B., & Bongar, B. (2015). Social support, trans community connectedness, and mental health symptoms among transgender and gender nonconforming adults. *Psychology of Sexual Orientation and Gender Diversity, 2*(3), 281–286. doi:10.1037/sgd0000122

Phares, E. J. (1976). *Locus of control in personality.* Morristown, NJ: General Learning Press.

Phillips, A. (2019). *Attention seeking.* London, UK: Penguin Press.

Phillips, A. P., & Dipboye, R. L (1989). Correlational tests of predictions from a process model of the interview. *Journal of Applied Psychology, 74*, 41–52.

Phillips, D. P. (1982). The impact of fictional television stories on U.S. adult fatalities: New evidence on the effect of the mass media on violence. *American Journal of Sociology, 87*, 1340–1359.

Phillips, D. P., & Lesyna, K. (1995). Suicide and the media: Research and policy implications. In R. F. W. Diekstra, W. Gulbinat, I. Kienhorst, & D. De Leo (Eds.), *Preventive strategies on suicide* (pp. 231–261). Leiden, Netherlands: Brill.

Phillips, J. O., Ling, L., Nie, K., Jameyson, E., Phillips, C. M., Nowack, A. L., . . . Rubinstein, J. T. (2015). Vestibular implantation and longitudinal electrical stimulation of the semicircular canal afferents in human subjects. *Journal of Neurophysiology, 113*(10), 3866–3892. doi:10.1152/jn.00171.2013

Piaget, J. (1932). *The moral judgment of the child.* New York, NY: Harcourt, Brace & World.

Piaget, J. (1936). *The origins of intelligence in children.* New York, NY: International University Press.

Piaget, J. (1976). *The grasp of consciousness: Action and concept in the young child.* Cambridge, MA: Harvard University Press.

Piaget, J., & Inhelder, B. (1969). *The psychology of the child.* New York, NY: Basic Books.

Piccione, C., Hilgard, E. R., & Zimbardo, P. G. (1989). On the degree of stability of measured hypnotizability over a 25-year period. *Journal of Personality and Social Psychology, 56*(2), 289–295. doi:10.1037//0022-3514.56.2.289

Piccirillo, J. F., Duntley, S., & Schotland, H. (2000). Obstructive sleep apnea. *Journal of the American Medical Association, 284*, 1492–1494.

Pickel, K. L. (1999). The influence of context on the "weapon focus" effect. *Law and Human Behavior, 23*, 299–311.

Pickel, K. L. (2009). The weapon focus effect on memory for female versus male perpetrators. *Memory, 17*, 664–678. doi:10.1080/09658210903029412.

Pieles, G. E., Husk, V., Blackwell, T., Wilson, D., Collin, S. M., Williams, C. A., & Stuart, A. G. (2017). High g-force rollercoaster rides induce sinus tachycardia but no cardiac arrhythmias in healthy children. *Pediatric Cardiology, 38*(1), 15–19. doi:10.1007/s00246-016-1477-5

Pierre, J. M. (2010). The borders of mental disorder in psychiatry and the DSM: Past, present, and future. *Journal of Psychiatric Practice, 16*(6), 375–386.

Pietkiewicz, I. J., Bańbura-Nowak, A., Tomalski, R., & Boon, S. (2021). Revisiting false-positive and imitated dissociative identity disorder. *Frontiers in Psychology, 12*, 637929. doi:10.3389/fpsyg.2021.637929

Pillemer, D. B., Picariello, M. L., & Pruett, J. C. (1994). Very long-term memories of a salient preschool event. *Applied Cognitive Psychology, 8*, 95–106.

Pillemer, D. B., Picariello, M. L., Law, A. B., & Reichman, J. S. (1996). Memories of college: The importance of educational episodes. In D. C. Rubin (Ed.), *Remembering our past: Studies in autobiographical memory* (pp. 318–337). New York, NY: Cambridge University Press.

Pilorz, V., Helfrich-Förster, C., & Oster, H. (2018). The role of the circadian clock system in physiology. *Pflugers Archiv, 479*(2), 227–239. doi:10.1007/s00424-017-2103-y

Pinderhughes, H., Davis, R. A., & Williams, M. (2015). *Adverse community experiences and resilience: A framework for addressing and preventing community trauma.* Oakland, CA: Prevention Institute.

Pine, A., Mendelsohn, A., & Dudai, Y. (2014). Unconscious learning of likes and dislikes is persistent, resilient, and reconsolidates. *Frontiers in Psychology, 5*, 1051. doi:10.3389/fpsyg.2014.01051

Pinel, J. P., Assanand, S., Lehman, D. R. (2000). Hunger, eating, and ill health. *American Psychologist, 55*, 1105–1116.

Pink, D. (2011). *Drive: The surprising truth about what motivates us.* New York, NY: Riverhead Books.

Pinker, S. (1994). *The language instinct: How the mind creates language.* New York, NY: HarperCollins.

Pinker, S. (1999). *Words and rules: The ingredients of language.* New York, NY: Basic Books.

Pinnell, C. M., & Covino, N. M. (2000). Empirical findings on the use of hypnosis in medicine: A critical review. *International Journal of Clinical and Experimental Hypnosis, 48*, 170–194.

Pinquart, M., & Duberstein, P. R. (2010). Depression and cancer mortality: A meta-analysis. *Psychological Medicine, 40*(11), 1797–1810. doi:10.1017/S0033291709992285

Pinsker, E. A., Hennrikus, D. J., Erickson, D. J., Call, K. T., Forster, J. L., & Okuyemi, K. S. (2018). Trends in self-efficacy to quit and smoking urges among homeless smokers participating in a smoking cessation RCT. *Addictive Behaviors, 78*, 43–50. doi:10.1016/j.addbeh.2017.10.025

Piwowar, H., Priem, J., Larivière, V., Alperin, J. P., Matthias, L., Norlander, B., . . . Haustein, S. (2018). The state of OA: A large-scale analysis of the prevalence and impact of Open Access articles. *PeerJ, 6*, e4375. doi:10.7717/peerj.4375

Platt, J. J. (2000). *Cocaine addiction: Theory, research, and treatment.* Cambridge, MA: Harvard University Press.

Plomin, R. (1988). The nature and nurture of cognitive abilities. In R. J. Sternberg (Ed.), *Advances in the psychology of human intelligence* (Vol. 4, pp. 1–33). Hillsdale, NJ: Erlbaum.

Plomin, R., & Deary, I. J. (2015). Genetics and intelligence differences: Five special findings. *Molecular Psychiatry, 20*, 98–108.

Plomin, R., Shakeshaft, N. G., Mcmillan, A., & Trzaskowski, M. (2014). Nature, nurture, and expertise: Response to Ericsson. *Intelligence, 45*, 115–117. doi:10.1016/j.intell.2014.01.003

Plutchik, R. (1980). *Emotion: A psychoevolutionary synthesis.* New York, NY: Harper & Row.

Pole, N., Best, S. R., Metzler, T., & Marmar, C. R. (2005). Why are hispanics at greater risk for PTSD? *Cultural Diversity and Ethnic Minority Psychology, 11*(2), 144–161.

Pole, N., Best, S. R., Weiss, D. S., Metzler, T., Liberman, A. M., Fagan, J., & Marmar, C. R. (2001). Effects of gender and ethnicity on duty-related posttraumatic stress symptoms among urban police officers. *Journal of Nervous and Mental Disease, 189*, 442–448.

Poling, A., Schlinger, H. D., Jr., Starin, S., & Blakely, E. (1990). *Psychology: A behavioral overview.* New York, NY: Plenum.

Pollet, T. V., Roberts, S. G. B., & Dunbar, R. I. M. (2011). Extraverts have larger social network layers but do not feel emotionally closer to individuals at any layer. *Journal of Individual Differences, 32*, 161–169.

Popova, S., Lange, S., Probst, C., Gmel, G., & Rehm, J. (2017). Estimation of national, regional, and global prevalence of alcohol use during pregnancy and fetal alcohol syndrome: A systematic review and meta-analysis. *Lancet Global Health, 5*, e290–e299. doi:10.1016/S2214-109X(17)30021-9

Popper, K. R. (1963). *Conjectures and refutations: The growth of scientific knowledge.* London, UK: Routledge, Kegan Paul.

Porte, H. S., & Hobson, J. A. (1996). Physical motion in dreams: One measure of three theories. *Journal of Abnormal Psychology, 105*, 329–335.

Posner, M. I., & Raichle, M. E. (1997). *Images of mind.* New York, NY: Scientific American Library.

Post, R. M., Ballenger, J. C., & Goodwin, F. K. (1980). Cerebrospinal fluid studies of neurotransmitter function in manic and depressive illness. In J. H. Wood (Ed.), *The neurobiology of cerebrospinal fluid* (Vol. 1). New York, NY: Plenum.

Post, R. M., Lake, C. R., Jimerson, D. C., Bunney, J. H., Ziegler, M. G., & Goodwin, F. K. (1978). Cerebrospinal fluid norepinephrine in affective illness. *American Journal of Psychiatry, 135*(8), 907–912.

Poulin-Dubois, D. (1995). Object parts and the acquisition of the meaning of names. In K. Nelson & Z. Re'ger (Eds.), *Children's language* (Vol. 8). Mahwah, NJ: Erlbaum.

Poulson, C. L., Kymissis, E., Reeve, K. F., Andreatos, M., & Reeve, L. (1991). Generalized vocal imitation in infants. *Journal of Experimental Child Psychology, 51*, 267–279.

Power, R. A., & Pluess, M. (2015). Heritability estimates of the Big Five personality traits based on common genetic variants. *Translational Psychiatry, 5*(7), e604. doi:10.1038/tp.2015.96

Powers, M., Halpern, J., Ferenschak, M., Gillihan, S., & Foa, E. (2010). A meta-analytic review of prolonged exposure or posttraumatic stress disorder. *Clinical Psychology Review, 30*(6), 625–641.

Practice Committee of the American Society for Reproductive Medicine in collaboration with the Society for Reproductive Endocrinology and Infertility.(2013). Optimizing natural fertility: A committee opinion.*Fertility and Sterility,* 100(3), 631–637.

Pratto, F., & Bargh, J. A. (1991). Stereotyping based on apparently individuating information: Trait and global components of sex stereotypes under attention overload. *Journal of Experimental Social Psychology, 27*, 26–47.

Pratto, F., Liu, J. H., Levin, S., Sidanius, J., Shih, M., Bachrach, H., & Hegarty, P. (2000). Social dominance orientation and the legitimization of inequality across cultures. *Journal of Cross-Cultural Psychology, 31*, 369–409.

Pressman, J. (1998). *The last resort: Psychosurgery and the limits of medicine.* New York, NY: Cambridge University Press.

Previde, E. P., & Poli, M. D. (1996). Social learning in the golden hamster *(Mesocricetus auratus). Journal of Comparative Psychology, 110*, 203–208.

Price, R. A. (2002). Genetics and common obesities: Background, current status, strategies and future prospects. In T. A. Wadden & A. J. Stunkard (Eds.), *Handbook of obesity treatment* (pp. 73–94). New York, NY: Guilford.

Prioleau, L., Murdock, M., & Brody, N. (1983). An analysis of psychotherapy versus placebo studies. *Behavioral and Brain Sciences, 6*, 275–310.

Privette, G. (1983). Peak experience, peak performance, and flow: A comparative analysis of positive human experiences. *Journal of Personality and Social Psychology, 45*, 1361–1368.

Privitera, G. J. (2008). *The psychology of eating: It's not all about the calories.* Lanham, MD: University Press of America.

Privitera, G. J. (2018). *Statistics for the Behavioral Sciences* (3rd ed.). Thousand Oaks, CA: Sage.

Privitera, G. J. (2019). *Essential statistics for the behavioral sciences* (2nd ed.). Thousand Oaks, CA: SAGE.

Privitera, G. J. (2020). *Research methods for the behavioral sciences* (3rd ed.). Thousand Oaks, CA: Sage.

Privitera, G. J. (2016). Health psychology. In C. McCarthy, M. DeLisi, A. Getzfeld, G. J. Privitera, C. Spence, J. Walker, . . . C. Youssef-Morgan (Eds.), *Introduction to applied behavioral science* (pp. 32–54). San Diego, CA: Bridgepoint Education.

Privitera, G. J., & Dickinson, E. K. (2015). Control your cravings: Self-control varies by eating attitudes, sex, and food type among Division I collegiate athletes. *Psychology of Sport and Exercise, 19*, 18–22. doi:10.1016/j.psychsport.2015.02.004

Privitera, G. J., & Zuraikat, F. M. (2014). Proximity of foods in a competitive food environment influences consumption of a low calorie and a high calorie food. *Appetite, 76*(1), 175–179. doi:10.1016/j.appet.2014.02.004

Privitera, G. J., Welling, D., Tejada, G., Sweazy, N., Cuifolo, K., King-Shepard, Q., & Doraiswamy, P. M. (2018). No calorie comfort: Viewing and drawing "comfort foods" similarly augment positive mood for those with depression. *Journal of Health Psychology, 23*(4), 598–607. doi:10.1177/1359105316681861

Prochaska, J. O., & DiClemente, C. C. (1982). Transtheoretical therapy: Toward a more integrative model of change. *Psychotherapy: Theory, Research, and Practice, 19*, 276–288. doi:10.1037/h0088437

Pruessner, M., Cullen, A. E., Aas, M., & Walker, E. F. (2017). The neural diathesis-stress model of schizophrenia revisited: An update on recent findings considering illness stage and neurobiological and methodological complexities. *Neuroscience & Biobehavioral Reviews, 73*, 191–218. doi:10.1016/j.neubiorev.2016.12.013

Przybylski, A. K., Murayama, K., Dehaan, C. R., & Gladwell, V. (2013). Motivational, emotional, and behavioral correlates of fear of missing out. *Computers in Human Behavior, 29*(4), 1841–1848. doi:10.1016/j.chb.2013.02.014

Putnam, F. W., Guroff, J. J., Silberman, E. K., Barban, L., & Post, R. M. (1986). The clinical phenomenology of multiple personality disorder: 100 recent cases. *Journal of Clinical Psychiatry, 47*, 285–293.

Pyszczynski, T., Solomon, S., & Greenberg, J. (2015). Thirty years of terror management theory. *Advances in Experimental Social Psychology*, 1–70. doi:10.1016/bs.aesp.2015.03.001

Qeadan, F., VanSant-Webb, E., Tingey, B., Rogers, T. N., Brooks, E., Mensah, N. A., & Rogers, C. R. (2021). Racial disparities in COVID-19 outcomes exist despite comparable Elixhauser comorbidity indices between Blacks, Hispanics, Native Americans, and Whites. *Scientific Reports, 11*, 8738. doi:10.1038/s41598-021-88308-2

Quartana, P. J., & Burns, J. W. (2010). Emotion suppression affects cardiovascular responses to initial and subsequent laboratory stressors. *British Journal of Health Psychology, 15*(Pt. 3), 511–528. doi:10.1348/135910709X474613

Quigley, E. (2015, October 22). The woman who can smell Parkinson's disease. BBC News. Retrieved from https://www.bbc.com/news/uk-scotland-34583642

Quinn, P. C., Burke, S., & Rush, A. (1993). Part-whole perception in early infancy: Evidence for perceptual grouping produced by lightness similarity. *Infant Behavior and Development, 16*, 19–42.

Quittkat, H. L., Düsing, R., Holtmann, F. J., Buhlmann, U., Svaldi, J., & Vocks, S. (2020). Perceived impact of Covid-19 across different mental disorders: A study on disorder-specific symptoms, psychosocial stress and behavior. *Frontiers in Psychology, 11*, 586246. doi:10.3389/fpsyg.2020.586246

Rachlin, H. (1995). Self-control: Beyond commitment. *Behavioral and Brain Sciences, 18*, 109–159.

Rachman, S. J. (1990). *Fear and courage* (2nd ed.). San Francisco, CA: Freeman.

Rachman, S., & Maser, J. D. (Eds.).(1988). *Panic: Psychological perspectives.* Hillsdale, NJ: Erlbaum.

Rahman, R. (2018). Building brand awareness: The role of celebrity endorsement in advertisements. *Journal of Global Scholars of Marketing Science, 28*(4), 363–384. doi:10.1080/21639159.2018.1509366

Rainville, P., Hofbauer, R. K., Paus, T., Duncan, G. H., Bushnell, M. C, & Price, D. P. (1999). Cerebral mechanisms of hypnotic induction and suggestion. *Journal of Cognitive Neuroscience, 11*, 110–125.

Rajan, A. M., Srikrishna, G., & Romate, J. (2018). Resilience and locus of control of parents having a child with intellectual disability. *Journal of Developmental and Physical Disabilities, 30*(3), 297–306. doi:10.1007/s10882-018-9586-0

Ramnani, N., & Passingham, R. E. (2001). Changes in the human brain during rhythm learning. *Journal of Cognitive Neuroscience, 13*, 952–966.

Rana, M., Varan, A. Q., Davoudi, A., Cohen, R. A., Sitaram, R., & Ebner, N. C. (2016). Real-time fMRI in neuroscience research and its use in studying the aging brain. *Frontiers in Aging Neuroscience, 8*, 239. doi:10.3389/fnagi.2016.00239

Rapoport, J. L. (1989). *The boy who couldn't stop washing: The experience and treatment of obsessive-compulsive disorder.* New York, NY: Plume.

Raskin, N. J. (1985). Client-centered therapy. In S. Lynn & J. Garske (Eds.), *Contemporary psychotherapies: Models and methods* (pp. 155–190). Columbus, OH: Charles E. Merrill.

Raven, J. C., Court, J. H., & Raven, J. (1985). *A manual for Raven's progressive matrices and vocabulary scales.* London, UK: H. K. Lewis.

Ray, W. J. (1996). Dissociation in normal populations. In L. K. Michelson & W. J. Ray (Eds.), *Handbook of dissociation: Theoretical, empirical, and clinical perspectives* (pp. 51–68). New York, NY: Plenum.

Razinsky, L. (2014). *Freud, psychoanalysis and death.* Cambridge, UK: Cambridge University Press.

Read, D. J., & Lindsay, D. S. (Eds.).(1997). *Recollections of trauma: Scientific research and clinical practice.* New York, NY: Plenum.

Read, S. C., Carrier, M., Boucher, M., Whitley, R., Bond, S., & Zelkowitz, P. (2014). Psychosocial services for couples in infertility treatment: What do couples really want? *Patient Education and Counseling, 94*(3), 390–395. doi:10.1016/j.pec.2013.10.025

Reardon, D. C. (2018). The abortion and mental health controversy: A comprehensive literature review of common ground agreements, disagreements, actionable recommendations, and research opportunities. *SAGE Open Medicine, 6*, 2050312118807624. doi:10.1177/2050312118807624

Reay, R. E., Looi, J. C., & Keightley, P. (2020). Telehealth mental health services during COVID-19: Summary of evidence and clinical practice. *Australasian Psychiatry, 28*(5), 514–516. doi:10.1177/1039856220943032

Reber, A. S. (1993). *Implicit learning and tacit knowledge: An essay on the cognitive unconscious.* New York, NY: Oxford University Press.

Reber, P. J., (2013). The neural basis of implicit learning and memory: A review of neuropsychological and neuroimaging research. *Neuropsychologia, 51*(10), 2026–2042. doi:10.1016/j.neuropsychologia.2013.06.019

Reblin, M., & Uchino, B. N. (2008). Social and emotional support and its implication for health. *Current Opinion in Psychiatry, 21*(2), 201–205. doi:10.1097/YCO.0b013e3282f3ad89

Redish, A. D. (1999). *Beyond the cognitive map: From place ceils to episodic memory.* Cambridge, MA: MIT Press.

Reed, C. F., & Krupinski, E. A. (1992). The target in the celestial (moon) illusion. *Journal of Experimental Psychology: Human Perception and Performance, 18*, 247–256.

Reed, J. L., Gallagher, N. M., Sullivan, M., Callicott, J. H., & Green, A. E. (2017). Sex differences in verbal working memory performance emerge at very high loads of common neuroimaging tasks. *Brain and Cognition, 113*, 56–64. doi:10.1016/j.bandc.2017.01.001

Regier, D. A., Boyd, J. H., & Burke, J. D. (1988). One-month prevalence of mental disorders in the United States: Based on five epidemiologic catchment area sites. *Archives of General Psychiatry, 45*, 977–986.

Reich, D. A., & Mather, R. D. (2008). Busy perceivers and ineffective suppression goals: A critical role for distracter thoughts. *Personality and Social Psychology Bulletin, 34*(5), 706–718. doi:10.1177/0146167207313732

Reilly, K. (2018, May 14). Yale: Black student calls for accountability after 911 call. *Time.* Retrieved from http://time.com/5276309/yale-police-sarah-braasch-lolade-siyonbola/

Reisenzein, R. (1983). The Schachter theory of emotion: Two decades later. *Psychological Bulletin, 94*, 239–264.

Reiser, M. (1980). *Handbook of investigative hypnosis.* Los Angeles, CA: LEHI.

Reith, T. P. (2018). Burnout in United States healthcare professionals: A narrative review. *Cureus, 10*(12), e3681. doi:10.7759/cureus.3681

Rendell, L., & Whitehead, H. (2001). Culture in whales and dolphins. *Behavioral and Brain Sciences, 24*, 309–382.

Renfrew, J. W. (1997). *Aggression and its causes: A biosocial approach.* New York, NY: Oxford University Press.

Reniers, R. L. E. P., Murphy, L., Lin, A., Bartolomé, S. P., & Wood, S. J. (2016). Risk perception and risk-taking behaviour during adolescence: The influence of personality and gender. *PLOS ONE, 11*(4), e0153842. doi:10.1371/journal.pone.0153842

Renn, B. N., Hoeft, T. J., Lee, H. S., Bauer, A. M., & Areán, P. A. (2019). Preference for in-person psychotherapy versus online psychotherapy options for depression: Survey of adults in the U.S. *NPJ Digital Medicine, 11*(2), 6. doi:10.1038/s41746-019-0077-1

Rennemark, M., Jogréus, C., Elmståhl, S., Welmer, A. K., Wimo, A., & Sanmartin-Berglund, J. (2018). Relationships between frequency of moderate physical activity and longevity: An 11-year follow-up study. *Gerontology & Geriatric Medicine, 4.* doi:10.1177/2333721418786565

Reppucci, N. D., Meyer, J., & Kostelnik, J. (2010). Police interrogation of juveniles: Results from a national survey of police. In G. D. Lassiter & C. Meissner (Eds.), *Interrogations and confessions: Current research, practices, and policy.* Washington, DC: American Psychological Association.

Rescorla, A. (1987). A Pavlovian analysis of goal-directed behavior. *American Psychologist, 42*, 119–129.

Rescorla, R. A. (1980). *Pavlovian second-order conditioning.* Hillsdale, NJ: Erlbaum.

Rescorla, R. A. (1996). Preservation of Pavlovian associations through extinction. *Quarterly Journal of Experimental Psychology, 49B*, 245–258.

Rescorla, R. A. (2001). Retraining of extinguished Pavlovian stimuli. *Journal of Experimental Psychology: Animal Behavior Processes, 27*, 115–124.

Résibois, M., Verduyn, P., Delaveau, P., Rotgé, J. Y., Kuppens, P., Van Mechelen, I., & Fossati, P. (2017). The neural basis of emotions varies over time: Different regions go with onset- and offset-bound processes underlying emotion intensity. *Social Cognitive and Affective Neuroscience, 12*(8), 1261–1271. doi:10.1093/scan/nsx051

Resnick, L. R. (1989). Developing mathematical knowledge. *American Psychologist, 44*, 162–169.

Rest, J. R. (1986). *Moral development: Advances in research and theory.* New York, NY: Praeger.

Restak, R. M. (1988). *The mind.* New York, NY: Bantam.

Reuter-Lorenz, P. A., & Miller, A. C. (1998). The cognitive neuroscience of human laterality: Lessons from the bisected brain. *Current Directions in Psychological Science, 7*, 15–20.

Rhee, E., Uleman, J. S., Lee, H. K., & Roman, R. J. (1995). Spontaneous self-descriptions and ethnic identities in individualistic and collectivistic cultures. *Journal of Personality and Social Psychology, 69*, 142–152.

Rhodes, G. A., & Zebrowitz, L. A. (Eds.).(2001). *Physical attractiveness: Evolutionary, cognitive, and social perspectives.* Westport, CT: Greenwood Publishing.

Rhodes, G., Sumich, A., & Byatt, G. (1999). Are average facial configurations attractive only because of their symmetry? *Psychological Science, 10*, 52–58.

Rice, A. N., & Harris, S. C. (2021). Issues of cultural competence in mental health care. *Journal of the American Pharmacists Association, 61*(1), e65–e68. doi:10.1016/j.japh.2020.10.015

Rice, M. L. (1989). Children's language acquisition. *American Psychologist, 44*, 149–156.

Rice, M. L., Huston, A. C., Truglio, R., & Wright, J. (1990). Words from "Sesame Street": Learning vocabulary while viewing. *Developmental Psychology, 26*, 421–428.

Richards, C. (2008, September 23). My Bloody Valentine plays loudest show ever! *Vulture.* Retrieved October 3, 2020 from https://www.vulture.com/2008/09/my_bloody_valentine_play_loude.html

Richards, M. H., Crowe, P. A., Larson, R., & Swarr, A. (1998). Developmental patterns and gender differences in the experiences of peer companionship during adolescence. *Child Development, 69*, 154–163.

Richardson, J. T. E., & Zucco, G. M. (1989). Cognition and olfaction: A review. *Psychological Bulletin, 105*, 352–360.

Richetin, J., Richardson, D. S., & Mason, G. D. (2010). Predictive validity of IAT aggressiveness in the context of provocation. *Social Psychology, 41*(1), 27–34. doi:10.1027/1864-9335/a000005

Rico-Uribe, L. A., Caballero, F. F., Martín-María, N., Cabello, M., Ayuso-Mateos, J. L., & Miret, M. (2018). Association of loneliness with all-cause mortality: A meta-analysis. *PLOS ONE, 13*(1), e0190033. doi:10.1371/journal.pone.0190033

Rieckmann, T., Moore, L. A., Croy, C. D., Novins, D. K., & Aarons, G. (2016). A national study of American Indian and Alaska Native substance abuse treatment: Provider and program characteristics. *Journal of Substance Abuse Treatment, 68*, 46–56. doi:10.1016/j.jsat.2016.05.007

Rilling, M. (2000). John Watson's paradoxical struggle to explain Freud. *American Psychologist, 55*, 301–312.

Rimmele, C. T., Howard, M. O., & Hilfrink, M. L. (1995). Aversion therapies. In R. K. Hester & W. R. Miller (Eds.), *Handbook of alcoholism treatment approaches: Effective alternatives* (pp. 134–147). Allyn & Bacon.

Rinck, M. (1999). Memory for everyday objects: Where are the digits on numerical keypads? *Applied Cognitive Psychology, 13*, 329–350.

Rindermann, H., Becker, D., & Coyle, T. R. (2017). Survey of expert opinion on intelligence: The Flynn effect and the future of intelligence. *Personality and Individual Differences, 106*, 242–247. doi:10.1016/j.paid.2016.10.061

Rink, F., Kane, A. A., Ellemers, N., & van der Vegt, G. S. (2013). Team receptivity to newcomers: Five decades of evidence and future research themes. *Academy of Management Annals, 7*, 245–291. doi:10.1080/19416520.2013.766405

Rips, L. J. (1975). Inductive judgments about natural categories. *Journal of Verbal Learning and Verbal Behavior, 14*, 665–681.

Ritchie, H., & Roser, M. (2018, January 20). Mental health. Our World in Data. Retrieved from https://ourworldindata.org/mental-health

Rivas-Vazquez, R. A., Johnson, S. L., Rey, G. J., Blais, M. A., & Rivas-Vazquez, A. (2002). Current treatments for bipolar disorder: A review and update for psychologists. *Professional Psychology: Research & Practice, 33*, 212–223.

Rizzolo, G. S. (2016). The critique of regression. *Journal of the American Psychoanalytic Association, 64*(6), 1097–1131. doi:10.4324/9780429460876

Robins, R. W., Gosling, S. D., & Craik, K. H. (1999). An empirical analysis of trends in psychology. *American Psychologist, 54*, 117–128.

Robinson, K. J., & Cameron, J. J. (2012). Self-esteem is shared relationship resources: Additive effects of dating partners' self-esteem levels predict relationship quality. *Journal of Research in Personality, 46*, 227–230. doi:10.1016/j.jrp.2011.12.002

Robinson, M. R., Kleinman, A., Graff, M., Vinkhuyzen, A. A. E., Couper, D., Miller, M. B., . . . Visscher, P. M. (2017). Genetic evidence of assortative mating in humans. *Nature, Human Behavior: Letters, 1* (0016). doi:10.1038/s41562-016-0016

Robles, T. F., Slatcher, R. B., Trombello, J. M., & McGinn, M. M. (2014). Marital quality and health: A meta-analytic review. *Psychological Bulletin, 140*(1), 140–187. doi:10.1037/a0031859

Robson, D. (2013, January 14). There really are 50 Eskimo words for "snow." *Washington Post.* Retrieved from https://www.washingtonpost.com/national/health-science/there-really-are-50-eskimo-words-for-snow/2013/01/14/e0e3f4e0-59a0-11e2-beee-6e38f5215402_story.html

Roca, M., Gili, M., Garcia-Campayo, J., Armengol, S., Bauza, N., & García-Toro, M. (2013). Stressful life events severity in patients with first and recurrent depressive episodes. *Social Psychiatry and Psychiatric Epidemiology, 48*(12), 1963–1969. doi:10.1007/s00127-013-0691-1

Rochat, P. (1989). Object manipulation and exploration in 2- to 5-month-old infants. *Developmental Psychology, 25*, 871–884.

Rock, I. (1997). *Indirect perception.* Cambridge, MA: MIT Press.

Roddenberry, A., & Renk, K. (2010). Locus of control and self-efficacy: Potential mediators of stress, illness, and utilization of health services in college students. *Child Psychiatry and Human Development, 41*, 353–370. doi:10.1007/s10578-010-0173-6.

Rodenbush, K. (2015). *The effects of trauma on behavior in the classroom [presentation materials].* Monterey County Office of Education. Retrieved from http://www.montereycoe.org/Assets/selpa/Files/Presentation-Materials/The%20 Effects%20of%20Trauma%20on%20Behavior%20in%20the%20Classroom.pdf

Rodgers, J. E. (1992). *Psychosurgery: Damaging the brain to save the mind.* New York, NY: HarperCollins.

Rodgers, N. (1998). *Incredible optical illusions.* New York, NY: Barnes & Noble Books.

Rodin, J. (1986). Aging and health: Effects of the sense of control. *Science, 233*, 1271–1276.

Rodkey, E. N. (2015). The visual cliffs forgotten menagerie: Rats, goats, babies, and myth-making in the history of psychology. *Journal of the History of the Behavioral Sciences, 51*(2), 113–140. doi:10.1002/jhbs.21712

Roediger, H. L., III, & McDermott, K. B. (1995). Creating false memories: Remembering words not presented in lists. *Journal of Experimental Psychology: Learning, Memory, and Cognition, 21*, 803–814.

Roediger, H. L., III. (1990). Implicit memory: Retention without remembering. *American Psychologist, 45*, 1043–1056.

Roediger, H. L., Meade, M. L., Gallo, D. A., & Olson, K. (2014). Bartlett revisited: Direct comparison of repeated reproduction and serial reproduction techniques. *Journal of Applied Research in Memory and Cognition, 3*(4), 266–271.

Roese, N. J. (1997). Counterfactual thinking. *Psychological Bulletin, 121*, 133–148.

Roese, N. J., & Olson, J. M. (Eds.).(1995). *What might have been: The social psychology of counterfactual thinking.* Mahwah, NJ: Erlbaum.

Rogers, C. R. (1942). *Counseling and psychotherapy: New concepts in practice.* Boston, MA: Houghton Mifflin.

Rogers, C. R. (1961). *On becoming a person.* Boston, MA: Houghton Mifflin.

Rogers, C. R. (1974). In retrospect: Forty-six years. *American Psychologist, 29*, 115–123.

Rogers, R. (Ed.). (1997). *Clinical assessment of malingering and deception* (2nd ed.). New York, NY: Guilford.

Rogoff, B. (1990). *Apprenticeship in thinking: Cognitive development in social context*. New York, NY: Oxford University Press.

Rogoff, B. (2002). *The cultural nature of human development*. New York, NY: Oxford University Press.

Rogoff, B., & Chavajay, P. (1995). What's become of research on the cultural basis of cognitive development? *American Psychologist, 50*, 859–877.

Rogoff, B., & Morelli, G. (1989). Perspectives on children's development from cultural psychology. *American Psychologist, 44*, 343–348.

Rolls, E. T. (1999). *The brain and emotion*. New York, NY: Oxford University Press.

Rolls, E. T. (2000). Memory systems in the brain. *Annual Review of Psychology, 51*, 599–630.

Rolls, E. T. (2008). Functions of the orbitofrontal and pregenual cingulate cortex in taste, olfaction, appetite and emotion. *Acta Physiologica Hungarica, 95*, 131–164. doi:10.1556/APhysiol.95.2008.2.1

Romney, A. K., Brewer, D. D., & Batchelder, W. H. (1993). Predicting clustering from semantic structure. *Psychological Science, 4*, 28–34.

Romo, V. (2018, October 3). Las Vegas shooting investigation closed. No motive found. NPR. Retrieved from https://www.npr.org/2018/08/03/635507299/las-vegas-shooting-investigation-closed-no-motive-found

Romo, V. (2020, November 13). Father and son charged with murder in Ahmaud Arbery killing are denied bond. NPR. Retrieved from https://www.npr.org/2020/11/13/934862159/father-and-son-charged-with-murder-in-ahmaud-arbery-killing-are-denied-bond

Rosa-Alcazar, A., Sanchez-Meca, J., Gomez-Conesa, & Marin-Martinez, F. (2008). Psychological treatment of obsessive-compulsive disorder: A meta-analysis. *Clinical Psychology Review, 28*, 1310–1325.

Rosch, E. (1975). Cognitive representations of semantic categories. *Journal of Experimental Psychology: General, 104*, 192–223.

Rosenberg, M. (1965). *Society and the adolescent self-image*. Princeton, NJ: Princeton University Press.

Rosenfeld, D. S., & Elhajjar, A. J. (1998). Sleepsex: A variant of sleepwalking. *Archives of Sexual Behavior, 27*, 269–278.

Rosenman, R. H., Brand, R. J., Jenkins, C. D., Friedman, M., Straus, R., & Wurm, M. (1975). Coronary heart disease in the Western Collaborative Group Study: Final follow-up experience of 8 years. *Journal of the American Medical Association, 233*, 872–877.

Rosenstock, I. M., Strecher, V. J., & Becker, M. H. (1988). Social learning theory and the Health Belief Model. *Health Education Behavior, 15*, 175–183. doi:10.1177/109019818801500203

Rosenthal, R. (1985). From unconscious experimenter bias to teacher expectancy effects. In J. B. Dusek, V. C. Hall, & W. J. Meyer (Eds.), *Teacher expectancies*. Hillsdale, NJ: Erlbaum.

Rosenthal, R., & Jacobson, L. (1968). *Pygmalion in the classroom: Teacher expectation and pupils' intellectual development*. New York, NY: Holt, Rinehart & Winston.

Rosenzweig, M. R. (1984). Experience, memory, and the brain. *American Psychologist, 39*, 365–376.

Rosenzweig, M. R. (1996). Aspects of the search for neural mechanisms of memory. *Annual Review of Psychology, 47*, 1–32.

Rosnow, R. L., Rotheram-Borus, M. J., Ceci, S. J., Blanck, P. D., & Koocher, G. P. (1993). The institutional review board as a mirror of scientific and ethical standards. *American Psychologist, 48*, 821–826.

Ross, C. A. (1997). *Dissociative identity disorder*. New York, NY: Wiley.

Ross, C. A., Joshi, S., & Currie, R. (1990a). Dissociative experiences in the general population. *American Journal of Psychiatry, 147*, 1547–1552.

Ross, C. A., Miller, S. D., Reagor, P. L., Bjornson, L., Fraser, G. A., & Anderson, G. (1990b). Structured interview data on 102 cases of multiple personality disorder from four centers. *American Journal of Psychiatry, 147*, 596–601.

Ross, D. E., Ceci, S. J., Dunning, D., & Toglia, M. P. (1994). Unconscious transference and mistaken identity: When a witness misidentifies a familiar but innocent person. *Journal of Applied Psychology, 79*, 918–930.

Ross, L. (1977). The intuitive psychologist and his shortcomings: Distortions in the attribution process. In L. Berkowitz (Ed.), *Advances in experimental social psychology* (Vol. 10). New York, NY: Academic.

Ross, M., & Sicoly, F. (1979). Egocentric biases in availability and attribution. *Journal of Personality and Social Psychology, 37*, 322–336.

Ross, R. T., & LoLordo, V. M. (1987). Evaluation of the relation between Pavlovian occasion-setting and instrumental discriminative stimuli. *Journal of Experimental Psychology: Animal Behavior Processes, 13*, 3–16.

Rossen, E., & Cowan, K. (2013). The role of schools in supporting traumatized students. *Principal's Research Review, 8*(6), 1–8.

Rosso, M. S., & Bäärnhielm, S. (2012). Use of the Cultural Formulation in Stockholm: A qualitative study of mental illness experience among migrants. *Transcultural Psychiatry, 49*(2), 283–301. doi:10.1177/1363461512442344

Rotenberg, K. J., & Chase, N. (1992). Development of the reciprocity of self-disclosure. *Journal of Genetic Psychology, 153*(1), 75–86. doi:10.1080/00221325.1992.10753703

Rotenberg, V. S. (2015). Lucid dreams: Their advantage and disadvantage in the frame of search activity concept. *Frontiers in Psychology, 6*, 1472. doi:10.3389/fpsyg.2015.01472

Rothbaum, B. O., Hodges, L., Anderson, P. L., Price, L., & Smith, S. (2002). Twelve-month follow-up of virtual reality and standard exposure therapies for the fear of flying. *Journal of Consulting and Clinical Psychology, 70*, 428–432.

Rotter, J. B. (1954). *Social learning and clinical psychology*. Englewood Cliffs, NJ: Prentice-Hall.

Rotter, J. B. (1966). Generalized expectancies for internal versus external control of reinforcement. *Psychological Monographs, 80* (No. 609).

Rotter, J. B. (1990). Internal versus external control of reinforcement: A case history of a variable. *American Psychologist, 45*, 489–493.

Rotter, J. B., Chance, J. E., & Phares, E. J. (Eds.).(1972). *Applications of a social learning theory of personality*. New York, NY: Holt, Rinehart & Winston.

Rousseau, P., Khoury-Malhame, M. E., Reynaud, E., Boukezzi, S., Cancel, A., Zendjidjian, X., . . . Khalfa, S. (2019). Fear extinction learning improvement in PTSD after EMDR therapy: An fMRI study. *European Journal of Psychotraumatology, 10*(1), 1568132. doi: 10.1080/20008198.2019.1568132

Rovee-Collier, C. (2001). Information pick-up by infants: What is it, and how can we tell? *Journal of Experimental Child Psychology, 78*, 35–49.

Rovee-Collier, C. (1988). The joy of kicking: Memories, motives, and mobiles. In P. Solomon, G. Goethals, C. Kelley, & B. Stephens (Eds.), *Memory: Interdisciplinary approaches*. New York, NY: Springer-Verlag.

Rovee-Collier, C., Hankins, E., & Bhatt, R. (1992). Textons, visual pop-out effects, and object recognition in infancy. *Journal of Experimental Psychology: General, 121*, 435–445.

Rowe, M. L. (2012). A longitudinal investigation of the role of quantity and quality of child-directed speech in vocabulary development. *Child Development, 83*(5), 1762–1774.

Rozin, P. (1999). The process of moralization. *Psychological Science, 10*(3), 218–221. doi:10.1111/ 1467-9280.00139

Rozin, P., Dow, S., Moscovitch, M., & Rajaram, S. (1998). What causes humans to begin and end a meal? A role for memory for what has been eaten, as evidenced by a study of multiple meal eating in amnesic patients. *Psychological Science, 9*, 392–396.

Rubenstein, A. J., Kalakanis, L., & Langlois, J. H. (1999). Infant preferences for attractive faces: A cognitive explanation. *Developmental Psychology, 35*, 848–855.

Rubin, D. C. (Ed.).(1996). *Remembering our past: Studies in autobiographical memory*. New York, NY: Cambridge University Press.

Rubin, D. C., & Kozin, M. (1986). Vivid memories. *Cognition, 16*, 81–95.

Rubin, D. C., & Wenzel, A. E. (1996). One hundred years of forgetting: A quantitative description of retention. *Psychological Review, 103*, 734–760.

Rubin, D. C., Hinton, S., & Wenzel, A. (1999). The precise time course of retention. *Journal of Experimental Psychology: Learning, Memory, and Cognition, 25*, 1161–1176.

Ruby, P. M. (2011). Experimental research on dreaming: State of the art and neuropsychoanalytic perspectives. *Frontiers in Psychology, 2*. doi:10.3389/fpsyg.2011.00286

Ruch, S., Züst, M. A., & Henke, K. (2016). Subliminal messages exert long-term effects on decision-making. *Neuroscience of Consciousness, 2016*(1), niw013. doi:10.1093/nc/niw013

Rudgley, R. (1999). *The encyclopedia of psychoactive substances*. New York, NY: St. Martin's.

Ruiter, N. M. P. D., Geert, P. L. C. V., & Kunnen, E. S. (2017). Explaining the "how" of self-esteem development: The self-organizing self-esteem model. *Review of General Psychology, 21*(1), 49–68. doi:10.1037/gpr0000099

Runtagh, J. (2016, June 25). Songs on trial: 12 Landmark music copyright cases. *Rolling Stone*. Retrieved from www.rollingstone.com/politics/politics-lists/songs-on-trial-12-landmark-music-copyright-cases-166396/

Runtagh, J. (2018, June 25). Songs on trial: 12 Landmark music copyright cases. *Rolling Stone*. Retrieved from www.rollingstone.com/politics/politics-lists/songs-on-trial-12-landmark-music-copyright-cases-166396/

Rush, S. E., & Sharma, M. (2016). Mindfulness-based stress reduction as a stress management intervention for cancer care. *Journal of Evidence-Based Complementary & Alternative Medicine, 22*(2), 348–360. doi:10.1177/2156587216661467

Rushton, J. P., & Ankney, C. D. (1996). Brain size and cognitive ability: Correlations with age, sex, social class, and race. *Psychonomic Bulletin & Review, 3*, 21–36.

Russell, B. (2018). Police perceptions in intimate partner violence cases: The influence of gender and sexual orientation. *Journal of Crime and Justice, 41*(2), 193–205. doi:10.1080/0735648x.2017.1282378

Russell, J. A. (1980). A circumplex model of affect. *Journal of Personality and Social Psychology, 39*, 1161–1178.

Russell, J. A. (1991). Culture and the categorization of emotions. *Psychological Bulletin, 110*, 426–450.

Russell, J. A. (1994). Is there universal recognition of emotion from facial expression? A review of cross-cultural studies. *Psychological Bulletin, 115*, 102–141.

Russell, J. A., & Carroll, J. M. (1999). On the bipolarity of positive and negative affect. *Psychological Bulletin, 125*, 3–30.

Russell, R. L., & Orlinsky, D. E. (1996). Psychotherapy research in historical perspective: Implications for mental health care policy. *Archives of General Psychiatry, 53*, 708–715.

Ruvolo, A., & Markus, H. (1992). Possible selves and performance: The power of self-relevant imagery. *Social Cognition, 9*, 95–124.

Ruzek, E., Burchinal, M., Farkas, G., & Duncan, G. J. (2014). The quality of toddler child care and cognitive skills at 24 months: Propensity score analysis results from the ECLS-B. *Early Childhood Research Quarterly, 28*(1). doi:10.1016/j.ecresq.2013.09.002

Ryan, C. (2009). *Helping families support their lesbian, gay, bisexual, and transgender (LGBT) children*. Washington, DC: National Center for Cultural Competence, Georgetown University Center for Child and Human Development.

Ryan, C., Huebner, D., Diaz, R. M., & Sanchez, J. (2009). Family rejection as a predictor of negative health outcomes in White and Latino lesbian, gay and bisexual young adults. *Pediatrics, 123*(1): 346–352.

Ryckeghem, D. M. V., Damme, S. V., Eccleston, C., & Crombez, G. (2018). The efficacy of attentional distraction and sensory monitoring in chronic pain patients: A meta-analysis. *Clinical Psychology Review, 59*, 16–29. doi:10.1016/j.cpr.2017.10.008

Ryff, C. D. (1989). In the eye of the beholder: Views of psychological well-being among middle-aged and older adults. *Psychology and Aging, 4*, 195–210.

Ryff, C. D. (2014). Psychological well-being revisited: Advances in the science and practice of eudaimonia. *Psychotherapy and Psychosomatics, 83*, 10–28. doi:10.1159/000353263

Sacco, W. P., & Dunn, V. K. (1990). Effect of actor depression on observer attributions: Existence and impact of negative attributions toward the depressed. *Journal of Personality and Social Psychology, 59*, 517–524.

Sachs-Ericsson, N. J., Sheffler, J. L., Stanley, I. H., Piazza, J. R., & Preacher, K. J. (2017). When emotional pain becomes physical: Adverse childhood experiences, pain, and the role of mood and anxiety disorders. *Journal of Clinical Psychology, 73*(10), 1403–1428. doi:10.1002/jclp.22444

Sachs, J. (1967). Recognition memory for syntactic and semantic aspects of connected discourse. *Perception and Psychophysics, 2*, 437–442.

Sackett, P. R., Hardison, C. M., & Cullen, M. J. (2004). On interpreting stereotype threat as accounting for African American–White differences on cognitive tests. *American Psychologist, 59*, 7–13.

Sacks, O. (1985). *The man who mistook his wife for a hat and other clinical tales*. New York, NY: Summit Books.

Sacks, O. (1995). *An anthropologist on Mars: Seven paradoxical tales*. New York, NY: Knopf.

Sadato, N., Pascual-Leone, A., Grafman, J., Ibanez, V., Deiber, M. P., Dold, G., & Hallett, M. (1999). Left-hemisphere dominance for motion processing in deaf signers. *Psychological Science, 10*, 256–262.

Sakai, K. L., Tatsuno, Y., Suzuki, K., Kimura, H., & Ichida, Y. (2005). Sign and speech: Amodal commonality in left hemisphere dominance for comprehension of sentences. *Brain, 128*(6), 1407–1417. doi:10.1093/brain/awh465

Saklofske, D. H., van de Vijver, F. J. R., Oakland, T., Mpofu, E., & Suzuki, L. A. (2015). Intelligence and culture: History and assessment. In S. Goldstein, D. Princiotta, & J. Naglieri (Eds.), *Handbook of intelligence*. New York, NY: Springer.

Sala, G., & Gobet, F. (2016). Experts' memory superiority for domain-specific random material generalizes across fields of expertise: A meta-analysis. *Memory & Cognition, 45*(2), 183–193. doi:10.3758/s13421-016-0663-2

Salk, L. (1962). Mothers' heartbeat as an imprinting stimulus. *Transactions of the New York Academy of Sciences, 24*, 753–763.

Salleh, M. R. (2008). Life event, stress and illness. *Malaysian Journal of Medical Sciences, 15*(4), 9–18.

Salthouse, T. A. (1996). The processing-speed theory of adult age differences in cognition. *Psychological Review, 103*, 403–428.

Salthouse, T. A., Berish, D. E., & Miles, J. D. (2002). The role of cognitive stimulation on the relations between age and cognitive functioning. *Psychology & Aging, 17*, 548–557.

Sampson, E. E. (2000). Reinterpreting individualism and collectivism: Their religious roots and monologic versus dialogic person-other relationship. *American Psychologist, 55*, 1425–1432.

Sams, M., Hari, R., Rif, J., & Knuutila, J. (1993). The human auditory memory trace persists about 10 sec: Neuromagnetic evidence. *Journal of Cognitive Neuroscience, 5*, 363–370.

Samuelson, M., Carmody, J., Kabat-Zinn, J., & Bratt, M. A. (2007). Mindfulness-based stress reduction in Massachusetts correctional facilities. *Prison Journal, 87*(2), 254–268. doi:10.1177/0032885507303753

Sanchis-Segura, C., Aguirre, N., Cruz-Gómez, Á. J., Solozano, N., & Forn, C. (2018). Do gender-related stereotypes affect spatial performance? Exploring when, how and to whom using a chronometric two-choice mental rotation task. *Frontiers in Psychology, 9*, 1261. doi:10.3389/fpsyg.2018.01261

Sandberg, K., Timmermans, B., Overgaard, M., & Cleeremans, A. (2010). Measuring consciousness: Is one measure better than the other? *Consciousness and Cognition, 19*(4), 1069–1078. doi:10.1016/j.concog.2009.12.013

Sanderson, W. C., DiNardo, P. A., Rapee, R. M., & Barlow, D. H. (1990). Syndrome comorbidity in patients diagnosed with a DSM-III-R anxiety disorder. *Journal of Abnormal Psychology, 99*, 308–312.

Sandstrom, M. J., & Coie, J. D. (1999). A developmental perspective on peer rejection: Mechanisms of stability and change. *Child Development, 70*, 955–966.

Sanger, G. J., Hellström, P. M., & Näslund, E. (2011). The hungry stomach: Physiology, disease, and drug development opportunities. *Frontiers in Pharmacology, 1*, 145. doi:10.3389/fphar.2010.00145

Sanjosé-Cabezudo, R., Gutiérrez-Arranz, A. M., & Gutiérrez-Cillán, J. (2009). The combined influence of central and peripheral routes in the online persuasion process. *CyberPsychology & Behavior, 12*(3), 299–308. doi:10.1089/cpb.2008.0188

Sansavini, A., Bertoncini, J., & Giovanelli, G. (1997). Newborns discriminate the rhythm of multisyllabic stressed words. *Developmental Psychology, 33*, 3–11.

Santa-Cruz Calvo, S., & Egan, J. M. (2015). The endocrinology of taste receptors. *Nature Reviews Endocrinology, 11*(4), 213–227. doi:10.1038/nrendo.2015.7

Santos, H. C., Varnum, M. E. W., & Grossman, I. (2017). Global increases in individualism. *Psychological Science, 28*(9), 1228–1239.

Santosa, C. M., Strong, C. M., Nowakowska, C., Wang, P. W., Rennicke, C. M., & Ketter, T. A. (2007). Enhanced creativity in bipolar disorder patients: A controlled study. *Journal of Affective Disorders, 100*(1–3), 31–39. doi:10.1016/j.jad.2006.10.013

Saper, C. B., Iverson, S., & Frackowiak, R. (2000). Integration of sensory and motor function: The association areas of the cerebral cortex and the cognitive capabilities of the brain. In E. R. Kandel, J. H. Schwartz, & T. M. Jessell (Eds.), *Principles of neural science* (4th ed., pp. 349–380). New York, NY: McGraw-Hill.

Sapolsky, R. M. (1994). *Why zebras don't get ulcers: A guide to stress, diseases, and coping*. New York, NY: Freeman.

Sar, V., Dorahy, M., & Krüger, C. (2017). Revisiting the etiological aspects of dissociative identity disorder: A biopsychosocial perspective. *Psychology Research and Behavior Management, 10*, 137–146. doi:10.2147/prbm.s113743

Sareen, J. (2014). Posttraumatic stress disorder in adults: Impact, comorbidity, risk factors, and treatment. *Canadian Journal of Psychiatry, 59*(9), 460–467. doi:10.1177/070674371405900902

Sareen, J., Erickson, J., Medved, M. I., Asmundson, G. J. G., Enns, M. W., Stein, M., . . . Logsetty, S. (2013). Risk factors for post-injury mental health problems. *Depression & Anxiety, 30*(4), 321–327.

Sava, F. A., Yates, B. T., Lupu, V., Szentagotai, A., & David, D. (2009). Cost-effectiveness and cost-utility of cognitive therapy, rational emotive behavioral therapy, and fluoxetine (Prozac) in treating depression: A randomized clinical trial. *Journal of Clinical Psychology, 65*(1), 36–52. doi:10.1002/jclp.20550

Sawyer, S. M., Azzopardi, P. S., Wickremarathne, D., & Patton, G. C. (2018). The age of adolescence. *Lancet Child and Adolescent Health, 2*(3), 223–228. doi:10/1016/S2352-4642(18)30022-1

Sawyer, T. F. (2000). Francis Cecil Sumner: His views and influence on African American higher education. *History of Psychology, 3*, 122–141.

Saylor, C. F., Nida, S. A., Williams, K. D., Taylor, L. A., Smyth, W., Twyman, K. A., . . . Spratt, E. G. (2012). Bullying and Ostracism Screening Scales (BOSS): Development and applications. *Children's Health Care, 41*, 322–343.

Saylor, C. F., Williams, K. D., Nida, S. A., McKenna, M. E., Twomey, K. E., & Macias, M. M. (2013). Ostracism in pediatric populations: Review of theory and research. *Journal of Developmental & Behavioral Pediatrics, 34*, 279–287.

Scarpelli, S., Alfonsi, V., Gorgoni, M., Giannini, A. M., & De Gennaro, L. (2021). Investigation on neurobiological mechanisms of dreaming in the new decade. *Brain Sciences, 11*(2), 220. doi:10.3390/brainsci11020220

Scarpina, F., & Tagini, S. (2017). The Stroop Color and Word Test. *Frontiers in Psychology, 8*, 557. doi:10.3389/fpsyg.2017.00557

Scarr, S., & Weinberg, R. A. (1976). I.Q. test performance of Black children adopted by White families. *American Psychologist, 31*, 726–739.

Schachter, S. (1959). *The psychology of affiliation*. Palo Alto, CA: Stanford University Press.

Schachter, S. (1964). The interaction of cognitive and physiological determinants of emotional state. In L. Berkowitz (Ed.), *Advances in experimental social psychology* (Vol. 1, pp. 49–80). New York, NY: Academic.

Schachter, S., & Gross, L. (1968). Manipulated time and eating behavior. *Journal of Personality and Social Psychology, 10*, 98–106.

Schachter, S., & Singer, J. E. (1962). Cognitive, social, and physiological determinants of emotional state. *Psychological Review, 69*, 379–399.

Schacter, D. L. (1986). Amnesia and crime: How much do we really know? *American Psychologist, 41*, 286–295.

Schacter, D. L. (1992). Understanding implicit memory: A cognitive neuroscience approach. *American Psychologist, 47*, 559–569.

Schacter, D. L. (1996). *Searching for memory*. New York, NY: Basic Books.

Schacter, D. L. (1999). The seven sins of memory: Insights from psychology and cognitive neuroscience. *American Psychologist, 54*, 182–203.

Schacter, D. L. (2001). *The seven sins of memory: How the mind forgets and remembers*. Boston: Houghton Mifflin.

Schaie, K. W., & Willis, S. L. (Eds.).(2016). *Handbook of the psychology of aging* (8th ed.). San Diego, CA: Academic. doi:10.1016/C2012-0-07221-3

Schaie, K. W., & Willis, S. L. (1993). Age difference patterns of psychometric intelligence in adulthood: Generalizability within and across ability domains. *Psychology and Aging, 8*, 44–55.

Schanberg, S. M., & Field, T. M. (1987). Sensory deprivation stress and supplemental stimulation in the rat pup and preterm human neonate. *Child Development, 58*, 1431–1447.

Schatzberg, A. F., & Nemeroff, C. B. (Eds.).(1998). *The American Psychiatric Press textbook of psychopharmacology* (2nd ed.). Washington, DC: American Psychiatric Pass.

Scheibel, A. B. (1995). Structural and functional changes in the aging brain. In J. E. Birren & K. W. Schaie (Eds.), *Handbook of the psychology of aging* (4th ed., pp. 78–128). San Diego, CA: Academic.

Scheier, M. F., & Carver, C. S. (1985). Optimism, coping, and health: Assessment and implications of generalized outcome expectancies. *Health Psychology, 4*, 219–247.

Scheier, M. F., & Carver, C. S. (1992). Effects of optimism on psychological and physical well-being: Theoretical overview and empirical update. *Cognitive Therapy and Research, 16*, 201–228.

Schenck, C. H. (1993). REM sleep behavior disorder. In M. A. Carskadon (Ed.), *Encyclopedia of sleep and dreaming* (pp. 499–505). New York, NY: Macmillan.

Schiffman, S. S., Graham, B. G., Sattely-Miller, E. A., & Warwick, Z. S. (1998). Orosensory perception of dietary fat. *Current Directions in Psychological Science, 7*, 137–143.

Schiller, F. (1992). *Paul Broca*. New York, NY: Oxford University Press.

Schimel, J., Arndt, J., Pyszczynski, T., & Greenberg, J. (2001). Being accepted for who we are: Evidence that social validation of the intrinsic self reduces general defensiveness. *Journal of Personality and Social Psychology, 80*, 35–52.

Schindler, A., Herdener, M., & Bartels, A. (2013). Coding of melodic gestalt in human auditory cortex. *Cerebral Cortex, 23*(12), 2987–2993. doi:10.1093/cercor/bhs289

Schlam, T. R., Wilson, N. L., Shoda, Y., Mischel, W., & Ayduk, O. (2013). Preschoolers' delay of gratification predicts their body mass 30 years later. *Journal of Pediatrics, 162*(1), 90–93.

Schlarb, A. A., Friedrich, A., & Claßen, M. (2017). Sleep problems in university students: An intervention. *Neuropsychiatric Disease and Treatment, 13*, 1989–2001. doi:10.2147/NDT.S142067

Schlichting, A., & Bäuml, K. (2017). Brief wakeful resting can eliminate directed forgetting. *Memory, 25*(2), 254–260. doi:10.1080/09658211.2016.1153659

Schmidt, G. B., & O'Connor, K. W. (2015). Fired for Facebook: Using NLRB guidance to craft appropriate social media policies. *Business Horizons, 58*(5), 571–579. doi:10.1016/j.bushor.2015.05.008

Schmidt, H. G., Peeck, V. H., Paas, E., & van Breukelen, G. (2000). Remembering the street names of one's childhood neighbourhood: A study of very long-term retention. *Memory, 8*, 37–49.

Schmidt, N. B., & Trakowski, J. H. (1997). Body vigilance in panic disorder: Evaluating attention to bodily perturbations. *Journal of Consulting and Clinical Psychology, 65*, 214–220.

Schnapf, J. L., Kraft, T. W., & Baylor, D. A. (1987). Spectral sensitivity of human cone photoreceptors. *Nature, 325*, 439–441.

Schneider, B. H., Atkinson, L., & Tardif, C. (2001). Child-parent attachment and children's peer relations: A quantitative review. *Developmental Psychology, 37*, 86–100.

Schneider, D. M., & Watkins, M. J. (1996). Response conformity in recognition testing. *Psychonomic Bulletin & Review, 3*, 481–485.

Schneider, E. C., Zaslavsky, A. M., & Epstein, A. M. (2002). Racial disparities in the quality of care for enrollees in Medicare managed care. *Journal of the American Medical Association, 287*(10), 1288–1294.

Schneider, P. (2000, February 13). Saving Konrad Latte. *New York Times*, pp. 52–57, 72–73, 90, 95.

Schneider, P., Scherg, M., Dosch, H. G., Specht, H. J., Gutschalk, A., & Rupp, A. (2002). Morphology of Heschl's gyrus reflects enhanced activation in the auditory cortex of musicians. *Nature Neuroscience, 5*, 688–694.

Schneider, T. J., Goffin, R. D., & Daljeet, K. N. (2015). "Give us your social networking site passwords": Implications for personnel selection and personality. *Personality and Individual Differences, 73*, 78–83. doi:10.1016/j.paid.2014.09.026

Schooler, J. W., & Engstler-Schooler, T. Y. (1990). Verbal overshadowing of visual memories: Some things are better left unsaid. *Cognitive Psychology, 17*, 36–71.

Schooler, J. W., Ohlsson, S., & Brooks, K. (1993). Thoughts beyond words: When language overshadows insight. *Journal of Experimental Psychology: General, 122*, 166–183.

Schou, M. (1997). Forty years of lithium treatment. *Archives of General Psychiatry, 54*, 9–13.

Schrauf, R. W., & Rubin, D. C. (2001). Effects of voluntary immigration on the distribution of autobiographical memory over the lifespan. *Applied Cognitive Psychology, 29*, S75–S88.

Schroeder, D. A., Dovidio, J. F., Sibicky, M. A., Matthews, L. L., & Allen, J. L. (1995). *The psychology of helping and altruism: Problems and puzzles.* New York, NY: McGraw-Hill.

Schultchen, D., Reichenberger, J., Mittl, T., Weh, T., Smyth, J. M., Blechert, J., & Pollatos, O. (2019). Bidirectional relationship of stress and affect with physical activity and healthy eating. *British Journal of Health Psychology, 24*(2), 315–333. doi:10.1111/bjhp.12355

Schultz, W. (2017). Electrophysiological correlates of reward processing in dopamine neurons. In J. Dreher, L. Tremblay, J. Dreher, & L. Tremblay (Eds.), *Decision neuroscience: An integrative perspective* (pp. 21–31). San Diego, CA: Elsevier Academic. doi:10.1016/B978-0-12-805308-9.00002-6

Schuppe, J., & Morrison, J. (2017, January 11). Dylann Roof sentenced to death for Charleston church massacre. NBC News. Retrieved from https://www.nbcnews.com/storyline/charleston-church-shooting/dylann-roof-sentenced-death-charleston-church-massacre-n705376

Schwabe, L., Joëls, M., Roozendaal, B., Wolf, O. T., & Oitzl, M. S. (2012). Stress effects on memory: An update and integration. *Neuroscience & Biobehavioral Reviews, 36*(7), 1740–1749. doi:10.1016/j.neubiorev.2011.07.002

Schwartz, B. L. (2002). *Tip-of-the-tongue states: Phenomenology, mechanism, and lexical retrieval.* Mahwah, NJ: Erlbaum.

Schwartz, B., & Reisberg, D. (1991). *Learning and memory.* New York, NY: Norton.

Schwartz, J. M. (1996). *Brain lock.* New York, NY: Harper-Collins.

Schwartz, J. M., Stoessel, P. W., Baxter, L. R., Martin, K. M., & Phelps, M. E. (1996). Systematic changes in cerebral glucose metabolic rate after successful behavior modification treatment of obsessive-compulsive disorder. *Archives of General Psychiatry, 53*, 109–113.

Schwartz, M. S., et al. (1999). *Biofeedback: A practitioner's guide* (2nd ed.). New York, NY: Guilford.

Schwarz, N. (1999). Self-reports: How the questions shape the answers. *American Psychologist, 54*, 93–105.

Scoboria, A., Mazzoni, G., Kirsch, I., & Milling, L. S. (2002). Immediate and persisting effects of misleading questions and hypnosis on memory reports. *Journal of Experimental Psychology: Applied, 8*, 26–32.

Scoville, W. B., & Milner, B. (1957). Loss of recent memory after bilateral hippocampal lesions. *Journal of Neurology, Neurosurgery, and Psychiatry, 20*, 11–21.

Seabrook, E. M., Kern, K. L., & Rickard, N. S. (2016). Social networking sits, depression, and anxiety: A systematic review. *JMIR Mental Health, 3*(4): e50. doi:10.2196/mental.5842

Seawell, A. H., Cutrona, C. E., & Russell, D. W. (2014). The effects of general social support and social support for racial discrimination on African American women's well-being. *Journal of Black Psychology, 40*(1), 3–26. doi:10.1177/0095798412469227

Seawell, M. (Ed.).(1998). *National Television Violence Study*, Vol. 2. Thousand Oaks, CA: Sage.

Sedlacek, W. E. (2004). Why we should use noncognitive variables with graduate and professional students. *The Advisor: The Journal of the National Association of Advisors for the Health Professions, 24*(2), 32–39.

Seeman, P., Guan, H.-C., & Van Tol, H. H. M. (1993). Dopamine D4 receptors elevated in schizophrenia. *Nature, 365*, 441–445.

Segal, N. L. (2000). Virtual twins: New findings on within-family environmental influences on intelligence. *Journal of Educational Psychology, 92*, 442–448.

Segal, Z. V., Bieling, P., Young, T., Macqueen, G., Cooke, R., Martin, L., . . . Levitan, R. D. (2010). Antidepressant monotherapy vs sequential pharmacotherapy and mindfulness-based cognitive therapy, or placebo, for relapse prophylaxis in recurrent depression. *Archives of General Psychiatry, 67*(12), 1256. doi:10.1001/archgenpsychiatry.2010.168

Segerberg, O. (1982). *Living to be 100: 1200 who did and how they did it.* New York, NY: Scribner.

Segerstrom, S. C., & Sephton, S. E. (2010). Optimistic expectancies and cell-mediated immunity: The role of positive affect. *Psychological Science, 21*(3), 448–455. doi:10.1177/0956797610362061

Segrin, C., & Abramson, L. Y. (1994). Negative reactions to depressive behaviors: A communications theories analysis. *Journal of Abnormal Psychology, 103*, 655–668.

Sekar, A., Bialas, A. R., Rivera, H. D., Davis, A., Hammond, T. R., Kamitaki, N., . . . McCarroll, S. A. (2016). Schizophrenia risk from complex variation of complement component 4. *Nature, 530*(7589), 177–183. doi:10.1038/nature16549

Seligman, M. E. P. (1971). Phobias and preparedness. *Behavior Therapy, 2*, 307–320.

Seligman, M. E. P. (1975). *Helplessness: On depression, development, and death.* San Francisco, CA: Freeman.

Seligman, M. E. P. (1991). *Learned optimism.* New York, NY: Knopf.

Seligman, M. E. P., & Csikszentmihalyi, M. (2000). Positive psychology: An introduction. *American Psychologist, 55*, 5–14. doi:10.1037/0003-066X.55.1.5

Selvi, Y., Besiroglu, L., Aydin, A., Gulec, M., Atli, A., Boysan, M., & Celik, C. (2012). Relations between childhood traumatic experiences, dissociation, and cognitive models in obsessive compulsive disorder. *International Journal of Psychiatry and Clinical Practice, 16*(1), 53–59.

Selye, H. (1936). A syndrome produced by diverse nocuous agents. *Nature, 138*, 32.

Selye, H. (1976). *The stress of life*. New York, NY: McGraw-Hill.

Semb, G. B., Ellis, J. A., & Araujo, J. (1993). Long-term memory for knowledge learned in school. *Journal of Educational Psychology, 85*, 305–316.

Sepple, C. P., & Read, N. W. (1989). Gastrointestinal correlates of the development of hunger in man. *Appetite, 13*, 183–191.

Serpell, R., & Boykin, A. W. (1994). Cultural dimensions of cognition: A multiplex, dynamic system of constraints and possibilities. In R. J. Sternberg (Ed.), *Handbook of perception and cognition: Vol. 2. Thinking and problem solving* (pp. 369–408). New York, NY: Academic. doi:10.1016/B978-0-08-057299-4.50018-9

Shadish, W. R., Matt, G. E., Navarro, A. M., Siegle, G., Crits-Christoph, P., Hazelrigg, M. D., . . . Weiss, B. (1997). Evidence that therapy works in clinically representative conditions. *Journal of Consulting and Clinical Psychology, 65*, 355–365.

Shams, T. (2015). The declining significance of race or the persistent racialization of Blacks? A conceptual, empirical, and methodological review of today's race debate in America. *Journal of Black Studies, 46*(3), 282–296. doi:10.1177/0021934714568566

Shan, H. P., Yang, X. H., Zhan, X. L., Feng, C. C., Li, Y. Q., Guo, L. L., & Jin, H. M. (2017). Overwork is a silent killer of Chinese doctors: A review of Karoshi in China 2013–2015. *Public Health, 147*, 98–100. doi:10.1016/j.puhe.2017.02.014

Shanafelt, T., Trockel, M., Ripp, J., Murphy, M. L., Sandborg, C., & Bohman, B. (2019). Building a program on well-being: Key design considerations to meet the unique needs of each organization. *Academic Medicine, 94*(2), 156–161. doi:10.1097/ACM.0000000000002415

Shapiro, F., Kaslow, F. W., & Maxfield, L. (2007). *Handbook of EMDR and family therapy processes*. Hoboken, NJ: Wiley.

Shastry, B. S. (2005). Bipolar disorder: An update. *Neurochemistry International, 46*(4), 273–279.

Shaw, M. A., & DiClemente, C. (2016). Temptation minus self-efficacy in alcohol relapse: A project MATCH follow-up. *Journal of Studies on Alcohol and Drugs, 77*(3), 521–525.

Shedler, J. (2010). The efficacy of psychodynamic psychotherapy. *American Psychologist, 65*, 98–109. doi:10.1037/a0018378

Sheehan, P. W., Statham, D., & Jamieson, G. A. (1991). Pseudomemory effects and their relationship to level of susceptibility to hypnosis and state instruction. *Journal of Personality and Social Psychology, 60*, 130–137.

Sheeran, P., Maki, A., Montanaro, E., Avishai-Yitshak, A., Bryan, A., Klein, W. M. P., . . . Rothman, A. J. (2016). The impact of changing attitudes, norms, and self-efficacy on health-related intentions and behavior: A meta-analysis. *Health Psychology, 35*(11), 1178–1188. doi:10.1037/hea0000387

Sheffler, Z. M., Reddy, V., & Pillarisetty, L. S. (2021). Physiology, neurotransmitters. In: *StatPearls* [Internet]. Treasure Island, FL: StatPearls Publishing. Retrieved from https://www.ncbi.nlm.nih.gov/books/NBK539894/

Shepard, R. N., & Cooper, L. A. (1982). *Mental images and their transformations*. Cambridge, MA: MIT Press.

Sheppard, J. A. (1993). Productivity loss in performance groups: A motivation analysis. *Psychological Bulletin, 113*, 67–81.

Sheridan, L. P. (2006). Islamophobia pre- and post-September 11, 2001. *Journal of Interpersonal Violence, 21*(3), 317–336.

Sherif, M. (1963). *The psychology of social norms*. New York, NY: Harper.

Sherman, R. A., Rauthmann, J. F., Brown, N. A., Serfass, D. G., & Jones, A. B. (2015). The independent effects of personality and situations on real-time expressions of behavior and emotion. *Journal of Personality and Social Psychology, 109*(5), 872–888. doi:10.1037/pspp0000036

Sherry, D. F. (1992). Memory, the hippocampus, and natural selection: Studies of food-storing birds. In L. Squire & N. Butters (Eds.), *Neuropsychology of memory* (2nd ed., pp. 521–532). New York, NY: Guilford.

Shibata, K., Sasaki, Y., Bang, J. W., Walsh, E. G., Machizawa, M. G., Tamaki. M., . . . Watanabe, T. (2017). Overlearning hyperstabilizes a skill by rapidly making neurochemical processing inhibitory-dominant. *Nature Neuroscience, 20*, 470–475. doi:10.1038/nn.4490

Shields, G. S., Spahr, C. M., & Slavich, G. M. (2021). Psychosocial interventions and immune system function: A systematic review and meta-analysis of randomized clinical trials. *JAMA Psychiatry, 77*(10), 1031–1043. doi:10.1001/jamapsychiatry.2020.0431

Shields, G. S., Sazma, M. A., McCullough, A. M., & Yonelinas, A. P. (2017). The effects of acute stress on episodic memory: A meta-analysis and integrative review. *Psychological Bulletin, 143*(6), 636–675. doi:10.1037/bul0000100

Shimamura, A. P., Berry, J. M., Mangels, J. A., Rusting, C. L., & Jurica, P. J. (1995). Memory and cognitive abilities in university professors: Evidence for successful aging. *Psychological Science, 6*, 271–277.

Shiraev, E. B., & Levy, D. A. (2016). *Cross-cultural psychology: Critical thinking and contemporary applications* (6th ed.). New York, NY: Routledge.

Shiraev, E., & Levy, D. (2001). *Introduction to cross-cultural psychology: Critical thinking and contemporary applications*. Boston, MA: Allyn & Bacon.

Shneidman, E. (Ed.).(1984). *Death: Current perspectives*. Palo Alto, CA: Mayfield.

Shneidman, E. S. (1996). *The suicidal mind*. New York, NY: Oxford University Press.

Shorer, Z., Wajsbrot, E., Liran, T.-H., Levy, J., & Parvari, R. (2014). A novel mutation in SCN9A in a child with congenital insensitivity to pain. *Pediatric Neurology, 50*(1), 73–76. doi:10.1016/j.pediatrneurol.2013.09.007

Shostrom, E. (1965). An inventory for the measurement of self-actualization. *Educational and Psychological Measurement, 24*, 207–218.

Shpigelman, C. (2018). Leveraging social capital of individuals with intellectual disabilities through participation on Facebook. *Journal of Applied Research in Intellectual Disabilities, 31*(1), e79-e91.

Shum, M. S. (1998). The role of temporal landmarks in autobiographical memory processes. *Psychological Bulletin, 124*, 423–442.

Sidani, J. E., Shensa, A., Hoffman, B., Hanmer, J., & Primack, B. A. (2016). The Association between Social Media Use and Eating Concerns among US Young Adults. *Journal of the Academy of Nutrition and Dietetics, 116*(9), 1465–1472. doi:10.1016/j.jand.2016.03.021

Sidanius, J., Levin, S., Liu, J., & Pratto, F. (2000). Social dominance orientation, anti-egalitarianism, and the political psychology of gender: An extension and cross-cultural replication. *European Journal of Social Psychology, 30*, 41–67.

Siegel, J. M. (2001). The REM sleep-memory consolidation hypothesis. *Science, 294*, 1058–1063.

Siegel, J. M., Nienhuis, R., Fahringer, H. M., Paul, R., Shiromani, P., Dement, W. C., . . . Chiu, C. (1991). Neuronal activity in narcolepsy: Identification of cataplexy related cells in the medial medulla. *Science, 252*, 1315–1318.

Siegel, R. (2018, May 3). Two Black men arrested at Starbucks settle with Philadelphia for $1 each. *Washington Post*. Retrieved from https://www.washingtonpost.com/news/business/wp/2018/05/02/african-american-men-arrested-at-starbucks-reach-1-settlement-with-the-city-secure-promise-for-200000-grant-program-for-young-entrepreneurs/

Siegler, I. C. (1994). Hostility and risk: Demographic and lifestyle variables. In A. W. Siegman & T. W. Smith (Eds.), *Anger, hostility, and the heart* (pp. 199–214). Mahwah, NJ: Erlbaum.

Siegler, R. S. (1996). *Emerging minds: The process of change in children's thinking*. New York, NY: Oxford University Press.

Siegler, R. S. (1998). *Children's thinking* (3rd ed.). Upper Saddle River, NJ: Prentice-Hall.

Siegler, R. S., & Ellis, S. (1996). Piaget on childhood. *Psychological Science, 7*, 211–215.

Siekanska, M., Blecharz, J., & Wojtowicz, A. (2013). The athlete's perception of coaches' behavior towards competitors with a different sports level. *Journal of Human Kinetics, 39*(1), 231–242. doi:10.2478/hukin-2013-0086

Sigafoos, J., Ramdoss, S., Kagohara, D., Pennington, R. C., Lancioni, G. E., & O'Reilly, M. F. (2014). Computer-based instruction. In J. K. Luiselli & J. K. Luiselli (Eds.), *Children and youth with autism spectrum disorder (ASD): Recent advances and innovations in assessment, education, and intervention* (pp. 76–89). New York, NY: Oxford University Press. doi:10.1093/med:psych/9780199941575.003.0005

Silberg, J. L., Copeland, W., Linker, J., Moore, A. A., Roberson-Nay, R., & York, T. P. (2016). Psychiatric outcomes of bullying victimization: A study of discordant monozygotic twins. *Psychological Medicine, 46*(9), 1875–1883. doi:10.1017/s0033291716000362

Silbersweig, D. A., Stern, E., Frith, C., Cahill, C., Holmes, A., Grootoonk, S., Seaward, J., et al. (1995). A functional neuroanatomy of hallucinations in schizophrenia. *Nature, 378*, 176–179.

Silva, H. (2013). Ethnopsychopharmacology and pharmacogenomics. In: R. D. Alarcón & R. D. Alarcón (Eds.), *Cultural psychiatry: Advanced psychosomatic medicine.* (Vol. 33, pp. 88–96). doi:doi:10.1159/000348741

Silveira, J. (1971). Incubation: The effect of interruption timing and length on problem solution and quality of problem processing. Unpublished doctoral dissertation. University of Oregon, Eugene.

Silver, E., Cirincione, C., & Steadman, H. J. (1994). Demythologizing inaccurate perceptions of the insanity defense. *Law and Human Behavior, 18*, 63–70.

Silverman, D. H. S., Mosconi, L., Ercoli, L., Chen, W., & Small, G. W. (2008). PET scans obtained for evaluation of cognitive dysfunction. *Seminars in Nuclear Medicine, 38*(4), 251–261. doi:10.1053/j.semnuclmed.2008.02.006

Silverman, H., & Moon, S. (2020, March 23). Crowds packed California beaches despite shelter in place order. CNN. Retrieved from https://www.cnn.com/2020/03/23/us/california-stay-at-home-beach-goers/index.html

Sim, N. (2015). Astronomics in action: The graduate earnings premium and the dragon effect in Singapore. *Economic Inquiry, 53*, 922–939.

Simcock, G., Garrity, K., & Barr, R. (2011). The effect of narrative cues on infants' imitation from television and picture books. *Child Development, 82*(5), 1607–1619. doi:10.1111/j.1467-8624.2011.01636.x

Šimleša, M., Guegan, J., Blanchard, E., Tarpin-Bernard, F., & Buisine, S. (2018). The flow engine framework: A cognitive model of optimal human experience. *Europe's Journal of Psychology, 14*(1), 232–253. doi:10.5964/ejop.v14i1.1370

Simmons, J. V. (1981). *Project sea hunt: A report on prototype development and tests*. Technical Report 746, Naval Ocean Systems Center, San Diego.

Simner, J., & Bain, A. E. (2013). A longitudinal study of grapheme-color synesthesia in childhood: 6/7 years to 10/11 years. *Frontiers in Human Neuroscience, 7*. doi:10.3389/fnhum.2013.00603

Simner, J., Harrold, J., Creed, H., Monro, L., & Foulkes, L. (2009). Early detection of markers for synaesthesia in childhood populations. *Brain, 132*(1), 57–64. doi:10.1093/brain/awn292

Simon, H. A. (1975). The functional equivalence of problem solving skills. *Cognitive Psychology, 7*, 268–288.

Simon, H. A. (1989). The scientist as a problem solver. In D. Kiahr & K. Kotovsky (Eds.), *Complex information processing: The impact of Herbert Simon*. Hillsdale, NJ: Erlbaum.

Simon, P., Connell, C., Kong, G., Morean, M. E., Cavallo, D. A., Camenga, D., & Krishnan-Sarin, S. (2015). Self-efficacy mediates treatment outcome in a smoking cessation program for adolescent smokers. *Drug and Alcohol Dependence, 146*. doi:10.1016/j.drugalcdep.2014.09.639

Simonds, G. R., Marvin, E. A., Apfel, L. S., Elias, Z., Howes, G. A., Witcher, M. R., . . . Sontheimer, H. (2018). Clinical neuroscience in practice: An experiential learning course for undergraduates offered by neurosurgeons and neuroscientists. *Journal of Undergraduate Neuroscience Education, 16*(2), A112–A119.

Simons-Morton, B., & Ehsani, J. P. (2016). Learning to drive safely: Reasonable expectations and future directions for the learner period. *Safety (Basel, Switzerland), 2*(4), 20.

Simons, D. J. (Ed.).(2000). Change blindness and visual memory: A special issue. *Visual Cognition*.

Simons, D. J., & Levin, D. T. (1998). Failure to detect changes to people during a real-world interaction. *Psychonomic Bulletin & Review, 4*, 644–649.

Simons, R. C., & Hughes, C. C. (1986). *The culture-bound syndromes: Folk illnesses of psychiatric and anthropological interest*. Boston, MA: D. Reidel.

Simonton, D. K. (2002). *Great psychologists and their time: Scientific insights into psychology's history*. Washington, DC: American Psychological Association.

Simpson, E. H., & Balsam, P. D. (2016). The behavioral neuroscience of motivation: An overview of concepts, measures, and translational applications. *Current Topics in Behavioral Neurosciences, 27*, 1–12.

Simpson, R., Byrne, S., Wood, K., Mair, F. S., & Mercer, S. W. (2017). Optimising mindfulness-based stress reduction for people with multiple sclerosis. *Chronic Illness*, *14*(2), 154–166. doi:10.1177/1742395317715504

Simunovic, M. P. (2016). Acquired color vision deficiency. *Survey of Ophthalmology*, *61*(2), 132–155. doi:10.1016/j.survophthal.2015.11.004

Singelis, T. M. (1994). The measurement of independent and interdependent self-construals. *Personality and Social Psychology Bulletin*, *20*, 580–591.

Singh, D. (1993). Adaptive significance of female physical attractiveness: Role of waist-to-hip ratio. *Journal of Personality and Social Psychology*, *65*(2), 293–307.

Singh, K., Drouin, K., Newmark, L. P., Lee, J., Faxvaag, A., Rozenblum, R., . . . Bates, D. W. (2016). Many mobile health apps target high-need, high-cost populations, but gaps remain. *Health Affairs*, *35*(12), 2310–2318. doi:10.1377/hlthaff.2016.0578

Skahill, P., & DesRoches, D. (2019, May 19). Connecticut students with "emotional disturbances" face high rate of suspensions. NPR. Retrieved from https://www.wnpr.org/post/connecticut-students-emotional-disturbances-face-high-rate-suspensions

Skinner, B. F. (1948). *Walden two*. New York, NY: Macmillan.

Skinner, B. F. (1957). *Verbal behavior*. New York, NY: Appleton-Century-Crofts.

Skinner, B. F. (1988). *The school of the future*. Paper presented at the annual meeting of the American Psychological Association, Atlanta, GA.

Skinner, B. F. (1990). Can psychology be a science of mind? *American Psychologist*, *45*, 1206–1210.

Skinner, E. A. (1996). A guide to constructs of control. *Journal of Personality and Social Psychology*, *71*, 549–570.

Skitka, L. J., & Morgan, G. S. (2014). The social and political implications of moral conviction. *Political Psychology*, *35*(Suppl. 1), 95–110. doi:10.1111/pops.12166

Skitka, L. J., Hanson, B. E., & Wisneski, D. C. (2017). Utopian hopes or dystopian fears? Exploring the motivational underpinnings of moralized political engagement. *Personality and Social Psychology Bulletin*, *43*(2), 177–190. doi:10.1177/0146167216678858

Sklar, L. S., & Anisman, H. (1981). Stress and cancer. *Psychological Bulletin*, *89*, 369–406.

Skoog, G., & Skoog, I. (1999). A 40-year follow-up of patients with obsessive-compulsive disorder. *Archives of General Psychiatry*, *56*, 121–127.

Skora, L. I., Yeomans, M. R., Crombag, H. S., & Scott, R. B. (2021). Evidence that instrumental conditioning requires conscious awareness in humans. *Cognition*, *208*, 104546. Retrieved from https://doi.org/10.1016/j.cognition.2020.104546

Slater, G., & Steier, J. (2012). Excessive daytime sleepiness in sleep disorders. *Journal of Thoracic Disease*, *4*(6), 608–616.

Slovic, P. (2000). *The perception of risk*. London, UK: Earthscan.

Slovic, P., Fischoff, B., & Lichtenstein, S. (1982). Facts versus fears: Understanding perceived risk. In D. Kahneman, P. Slovic, & A. Tversky (Eds.), *Judgment under uncertainty: Heuristics and biases* (pp. 463–489). New York, NY: Cambridge University Press.

Smetana, J. G. (1988). Concepts of self and social convention: Adolescents' and parents' reasoning about hypothetical and actual family conflicts. In M. R. Gunnar & W. A. Collins (Eds.), *Development during the transition to adolescence: Minnesota Symposia on Child Psychology* (Vol. 21, pp. 79–122). Hillsdale, NJ: Erlbaum.

Smilek, D., Dixon, M. J., Cudahy, C., & Merikle, P. M. (2002). Concept driven color experiences in digit-color synesthesia. *Brain and Cognition*, *48*, 570–573.

Smillie, L. D., & Gokcen, E. (2010). Caffeine enhances working memory for extraverts. *Biological Psychology*, *85*, 496–498.

Smith, A. M., & Cutler, B. L. (2013). Introduction: Identification procedures and conviction of the innocent. In B. L. Cutler (Ed.), *Reform of eyewitness identification procedures* (pp. 3–21). Washington, DC: American Psychological Association.

Smith, A. P. (2012). Caffeine, extraversion and working memory. *Journal of Psychopharmacology*, *27*(1), 71–76. doi:10.1177/0269881112460111

Smith, A., Graham, L., & Senthinathan, S. (2007). Mindfulness-based cognitive therapy for recurring depression in older people: A qualitative study. *Aging & Mental Health*, *11*(3), 346–357. doi:10.1080/13607860601086256

Smith, D. (1982). Trends in counseling and psychotherapy. *American Psychologist*, *37*, 802–809.

Smith, D. (2002). *Report from Ground Zero: The story of the rescue efforts at the World Trade Center*. New York, NY: Viking.

Smith, D. E., Thompson, J. K., Raczynski, J. M., & Hilner, J. E. (1999). Body image among men and women in a biracial cohort: The CARDIA Study. *International Journal of Eating Disorders*, *25*, 71–82.

Smith, D. J., Escott-Price, V., Davies, G., Bailey, M. E., Colodro-Conde, L., Ward, J., . . . O'Donovan, M. C. (2016). Genome-wide analysis of over 106 000 individuals identifies 9 neuroticism-associated loci. *Molecular Psychiatry*, *21*(6), 749–757. doi:10.1038/mp.2016.49

Smith, E. E., Shoben, E. J., & Ripps, L. J. (1974). Structure and processes in semantic memory: A featural model for semantic decisions. *Psychological Review*, *81*, 214–241.

Smith, M. C. (1983). Hypnotic memory enhancement of witnesses: Does it work? *Psychological Bulletin*, *94*, 387–407.

Smith, M. L., Glass, G. V., & Miller, T. I. (1980). *The benefits of psychotherapy*. Baltimore, MD: Johns Hopkins University Press.

Smith, R. W., & Kounios, J. (1996). Sudden insight: All-or-none processing revealed by speed-accuracy decomposition. *Journal of Experimental Psychology: Learning, Memory, and Cognition*, *22*, 1443–1462.

Smoller, J. (2016). The genetics of stress-related disorders: PTSD, depression, and anxiety disorders. *Neuropsychopharmacology*, *41*, 297–319. doi:10.1038/npp.2015.266

Smoller, J. W., & Finn, C. T. (2003). Family, twin, and adoption studies of bipolar disorder. *American Journal of Medical Genetics C: Seminars in Medical Genetics*, *123*, 48–58. doi:10.1002/ajmg.c.20013

Smyth, J. M. (1998). Written emotional expression: Effect sizes, outcome types, and moderating variables. *Journal of Consulting and Clinical Psychology*, *66*, 174–184.

Snarey, J. R. (1985). Cross-cultural universality of social-moral development: A critical review of Kohlbergian research. *Psychological Bulletin, 97*, 202–233.

Söderlund, H., Moscovitch, M., Kumar, N., Daskalakis, Z. J., Flint, A., Herrmann, N., & Levine, B. (2014). Autobiographical episodic memory in major depressive disorder. *Journal of Abnormal Psychology, 123*(1), 51–60. doi:10.1037/a0035610.

Soeliman, F. A., & Azadbakht, L. (2014). Weight loss maintenance: A review on dietary related strategies. *Journal of Research in Medical Sciences, 19*(3), 268–275.

Sohn, H. (2016). Racial and ethnic disparities in health insurance coverage: Dynamics of gaining and losing coverage over the life-course. *Population Research and Policy Review, 36*(2), 181–201.

Sokolov, E. M. (1963). Higher nervous functions: The orienting reflex. *Annual Review of Physiology, 25*, 545–580.

Solms, M. (1997). *The neuropsychology of dreams: A clinico-anatomical study*. Mahwah, NJ: Erlbaum.

Sompayrac, L. (1999). *How the immune system works*. Malden, MA: Blackwell Science.

Souleymanov, R. Kuzmanović, D., Marshall, Z., Scheim, A. I., Mikiki, M., Worthington, C., & Millson, M. P. (2016). The ethics of community-based research with people who use drugs: Results of a scoping review. *BMC Medical Ethics, 17*: 25. doi:10.1186/s12910-016-0108-2

Spangler, W. D. (1992). Validity of questionnaire and TAT measures of need for achievement: Two meta-analyses. *Psychological Bulletin, 112*, 140–154.

Spanos, N. P. (1996). *Multiple identities and false memories: A sociocognitive perspective*. Washington, DC: American Psychological Association.

Sparkman, D. J., & Hamer, K. (2020). Seeing the human in everyone: Multicultural experiences predict more positive intergroup attitudes and humanitarian helping through identification with all humanity. *International Journal of Intercultural Relations, 79*, 121–134.

Spearman, C. (1904). General intelligence objectively determined and measured. *American Journal of Psychology, 15*, 201–293.

Spector, F., & Maurer, D. (2011). The colors of the alphabet: Naturally-biased associations between shape and color. *Journal of Experimental Psychology: Human Perception and Performance, 37*(2), 484–495.

Spelke, E. S., Breinlinger, K., Macomber, J., & Jacobson, K. (1992). Origins of knowledge. *Psychological Review, 99*, 605–632.

Spence, C. (2015). Multisensory flavor perception. *Cell, 161*(1), 24–35. doi:10.1016/j.cell.2015.03.007

Spencer, S. J., Steele, C. M., & Quinn, D. M. (1999). Stereotype threat and women's math performance. *Journal of Experimental Social Psychology, 35*, 4–28.

Sperling, G. (1960). The information available in brief visual presentations. *Psychological Monographs, 74*(Whole No. 11), 1–29.

Sperry, R. W. (1968). Hemisphere deconnection and unity in conscious awareness. *American Psychologist, 23*, 723–733.

Spiegel, D. (1993). Social support: How friends, family, and groups can help. In D. Goleman & J. Gurin (Eds.), *Mind, body, medicine: How to use your mind for better health* (pp. 331–350). Yonkers, NY: Consumer Reports Books.

Spielberg, J. M., Stewart, J. L., Levin, R. L., Miller, G. A., & Heller, W. (2008). Prefrontal cortex, emotion, and approach/withdrawal motivation. *Social and Personality Psychology Compass, 2*(1), 135–153. doi:10.1111/j.1751-9004.2007.00064.x

Spiro, A., III., Schnurr, P. P., & Aldwin, C. M. (1994). Combat-related posttraumatic stress disorder symptoms in older men. *Psychology and Aging, 9*, 17–26.

Spitz, H. H. (1999). Beleaguered Pygmalion: A history of the controversy over claims that teacher expectancy raises intelligence. *Intelligence, 27*, 199–234.

Spradley, B. W., Spradley, J. P., & McCurdy, D. W. (Eds.).(2000). *Conformity and conflict: Readings in cultural anthropology* (10th ed.). Needham Heights, MA: Allyn & Bacon.

Springer, S. P., & Deutsch, G. (1998). *Left brain right brain: Perspectives from cognitive neuroscience* (5th ed.). New York, NY: Freeman.

Sprouse-Blum, A. S., Smith, G., Sugai, D., & Parsa, F. D. (2010). Understanding endorphins and their importance in pain management. *Hawaii Medical Journal, 69*(3), 70–71.

Squier, L. H., & Domhoff, G. W. (1998). The presentation of dreaming and dreams in introductory psychology textbooks: A critical examination with suggestions for textbook authors and course instructors. *Dreaming, 8*, 149–168.

Squire, L. R. (1992). Memory and the hippocampus: A synthesis from findings with rats, monkeys, and humans. *Psychological Review, 99*, 195–231.

Squire, L. R., & Schacter, D. L. (Eds.).(2002). *Neuropsychology of memory* (3rd ed.). New York, NY: Guilford.

Squire, L. R., & Zola-Morgan, S. (1991). The medial temporal lobe memory system. *Science, 253*, 1380–1386.

Squitieri, J. (2017, October 6). Doctor canoes through flood to perform emergency surgery. CNN. Retrieved from https://www.cnn.com/2017/08/30/us/doctor-canoes-flood-to-perform-emergency-surgery-cnntv/index.html

Staats, A. W., & Staats, C. K. (1958). Attitudes established by classical conditioning. *Journal of Abnormal and Social Psychology, 57*, 37–40.

Stangor, C., & Lange, J. E. (1994). Mental representations of social groups: Advances in understanding stereotypes and stereotyping. *Advances in Experimental Social Psychology, 26*, 357–416.

Stark, E. (1986, October). Young, innocent, and pregnant. *Psychology Today*, pp. 28–35.

Starr, K. E., & Aron, L. (2011). Women on the couch: Genital stimulation and the birth of psychoanalysis. *Psychoanalytic Dialogues, 21*(4), 373–392. doi:10.1080/10481885.2011.595316

Staub, E. (1996). Cultural-societal roots of violence: The examples of genocidal violence and of contemporary youth violence in the United States. *American Psychologist, 51*, 117–132.

Steblay, N. K., & Dysart, J. E. (2016). Repeated eyewitness identification procedures with the same suspect. *Journal of Applied Research in Memory and Cognition, 5*(3), 284–289. doi:10.1016/j.jarmac.2016.06.010

Steblay, N. M. (1992). A meta-analytic review of the weapon-focus effect. *Law and Human Behavior, 16*, 413–124.

Steele, C. M. (1997). A threat in the air: How stereotypes shape the intellectual identities and performance of women and African Americans. *American Psychologist, 52*(6), 613–629.

Steele, C. M., & Aronson, J. (1995). Stereotype threat and the intellectual test performance of African Americans. *Journal of Personality and Social Psychology, 69*, 797–811.

Steele, C. M., & Josephs, R. A. (1990). Alcohol myopia: Its prized and dangerous effects. *American Psychologist, 45*, 921–933.

Steele, C. M., Spencer, S. J., & Aronson, J. (2002). Contending with group image: The psychology of stereotype and social identity. *Advances in Experimental Social Psychology, 34*, 384–406.

Steele, S. (1990). *The content of our character.* New York, NY: St. Martin's.

Steiger, A. E., Fend, H. A., & Allemand, M. (2015). Testing the vulnerability and scar models of self-esteem and depressive symptoms from adolescence to middle adulthood and across generations. *Developmental Psychology, 51*(2), 236–247. doi:10.1037/a0038478

Stein, B. E., & Meredith, M. A. (1993). *The merging of the senses.* Cambridge, MA: MIT Press.

Stein, D. J. (2009). Social anxiety disorder in the West and in the East. *Annals of Clinical Psychiatry, 21*(2), 109–117.

Stein, J. H., & Reiser, L. W. (1994). A study of White middle-class adolescent boys' responses to "semenarche" (the first ejaculation). *Journal of Youth and Adolescence, 23*, 373–384.

Stein, M. B., Jang, K. L., Taylor, S., Vernon, P. A., & Livesley, W. J. (2002). Genetic and environmental influences on trauma exposure and posttraumatic stress disorder symptoms: A twin study. *American Journal of Psychiatry, 159*, 1675–1681.

Stein, M. B., Walker, J. R., & Forde, D. R. (1996). Public-speaking fears in a community sample. *Archives of General Psychiatry, 53*, 169–174.

Stein, M. B., Walker, J. R., & Forde, D. R. (2000). Gender differences in susceptibility to posttraumatic stress disorder. *Behaviour Research and Therapy, 38*(6), 619–628. doi:10.1016/s0005-7967(99)00098-4

Stein, R., & Swan, A. B. (2019). Evaluating the validity of Myers-Briggs Type Indicator theory: A teaching tool and window into intuitive psychology. *Social and Personality Psychological Compass, 13*, 123–134. doi:10.1111/spc3.12434

Steinberg, L. (1987, September). Bound to bicker. *Psychology Today*, pp. 36–39.

Steinberg, L. (2010). A dual systems model of adolescent risk-taking. *Developmental Psychobiology, 52*, 216–224. doi:10.1002/dev.20445

Steiner, K. L., Pillemer, D. B., Thomsen, D. K., & Minigan, A. P. (2013). The reminiscence bump in older adults' life story transitions. *Memory, 22*(8), 1002–1009. doi:10.1080/09658211.2013.863358

Stellar, E. (1954). The physiology of motivation. *Psychological Review, 61*, 5–22.

Stephan, W. G., Ybarra, O., & Bachman, G. (1999). Prejudice toward immigrants. *Journal of Applied Social Psychology, 29*, 2221–2237.

Steptoe, A. (2019). Happiness and health. *Annual Review of Public Health, 40*, 339–359. doi:10.1146/annurev-publhealth-040218-044150

Sternbach, R. A. (1964). The effects of instructional sets of autonomic responsivity. *Psychophysiology, 1*, 67–72.

Sternberg, R. J. (Ed.).(2000). *Handbook of intelligence.* New York, NY: Cambridge University Press.

Sternberg, R. J., & Davidson, J. E. (1999). Insight. In M. A. Runco & S. R. Pritzker (Eds.), *Encyclopedia of creativity* (Vol. 2). San Diego, CA: Academic.

Sternberg, R. J., & Lubart, T. I. (1991). An investment theory of creativity and its development. *Human Development, 34*, 1–31.

Sterpenich, V., Schmidt, C., Albouy, G., Matarazzo, L., Vanhaudenhuyse, A., Boveroux, P., . . . Maquet, P. (2014). Memory reactivation during rapid eye movement sleep promotes its generalization and integration in cortical stores. *Sleep, 37*, 1061–1075. doi:10.5665/sleep.3762

Stevens, J. C., Foulke, E., & Patterson, M. Q. (1996). Tactile acuity, aging, and Braille reading in long-term blindness. *Journal of Experimental Psychology: Applied, 2*, 91–106.

Stevens, S. S. (1946). On the theory of scales of measurement. *Science, 103*, 677–680.

Stewart, B. D., Hippel, W. V., & Radvansky, G. A. (2009). Age, race, and implicit prejudice. Using process dissociation to separate the underlying components. *Psychological Science, 20*(2), 164–168. doi:10.1111/j.1467-9280.2009.02274.x

Stewart, S. L., Moodley, R., & Hyatt, A. (2016). *Indigenous cultures and mental health counselling.* New York, NY: Routledge

Stieg, C. (2019). Half of millennials and 75% of Gen-Zers have left jobs for mental health reasons. CNBC. Retrieved from https://www.cnbc.com/2019/10/08/millennials-gen-z-have-quit-jobs-due-to-mental-health-issues-survey.html

Stiles, W. B., Agnew-Davies, R., Hardy, G. E., Barkham, M., & Shapiro, D. A. (1998). Relations of the alliance with psychotherapy outcome: Findings in the second Sheffield Psychotherapy Project. *Journal of Consulting and Clinical Psychology, 66*, 791–802.

Stiles, W. B., Shapiro, D. A., & Elliott, R. (1986). Are all psychotherapies equivalent? *American Psychologist, 41*, 165–180.

Stinchfield, R., McCready, J., Turner, N. E., Jimenez-Murcia, S., Petry, N. M., Grant, J., . . . Winters, K. C. (2015). Reliability, validity, and classification accuracy of the DSM-5 diagnostic criteria for gambling disorder and comparison to DSM-IV. *Journal of Gambling Studies, 32*(3), 905–922.

Stoker, T. B., Blair, N. F., & Barker, R. A. (2017). Neural grafting for Parkinson's disease: Challenges and prospects. *Neural Regeneration Research, 12*(3), 389–392. doi:10.4103/1673-5374.202935

Stone, A. A., Neale, J. M., Cox, D. S., Napoli, A., Valdimarsdottir, H., & Kennedy-Moore, E. (1994). Daily events are associated with a secretory immune response to an oral antigen in men. *Health Psychology, 13*, 440–446.

Stone, J., Lynch, C. L., Sjomeling, M., & Darley, J. M. (1999). Stereotype threat effects on Black and White athletic performance. *Journal of Personality and Social Psychology, 77*, 1213–1227.

Stone, M. H. (1997). *Healing the mind: A history of psychiatry from antiquity to present.* New York, NY: Norton.

Stopfer, J. M., Egloff, B., Nestler, S., & Back, M. D. (2014). Personality expression and impression formation in online social networks: An integrative approach to understanding the processes of accuracy, impression management and meta-accuracy. *European Journal of Personality, 28*(1), 73–94.

Straneva, P. A., Maixner, W., Light, K. C., Pedersen, C. A., Costello, N. L., & Girdler, S. S. (2002). Menstrual cycle, beta-endorphins, and pain sensitivity in premenstrual dysphoric disorder. *Health Psychology, 21*, 358–367.

Strange, D., Wade, K., & Hayne, H. (2008). Creating false memories for events that occurred before versus after the offset of childhood amnesia. *Memory, 16*, 475–484. doi:10.1080/09658210802059049.

Straub, R. H., & Cutolo, M. (2018). Psychoneuroimmunology—Developments in stress research. *Wiener Medizinische Wochenschrift, 168*(3–4), 76–84. doi:10.1007/s10354-017-0574-2

Straube, E. R., & Oades, R. D. (1992). *Schizophrenia: Empirical research and findings.* San Diego, CA: Academic.

Strawbridge, W. J., Shema, S. J., Cohen, R. D., & Kaplan, G. A. (2001). Religious attendance increases survival by improving and maintaining good health behaviors, mental health, and social relationships. *Annals of Behavioral Medicine, 23*, 68–74.

Street, A. E., & Dardis, C. M. (2018). Using a social construction of gender lens to understand gender differences in posttraumatic stress disorder. *Clinical Psychology Review, 66*, 97–105. doi:10.1016/j.cpr.2018.03.001

Streissguth, A. P., Barr, H. M., Bookstein, F. L., & Sampson, P. D. (1993). *The enduring effects of prenatal alcohol exposure on child development: Birth through 7 years.* Ann Arbor: University of Michigan Press.

Streissguth, A. P., Barr, H. M., Bookstein, F. L., Sampson, P. D., & Olson, H. C. (1999). The long-term neurocognitive consequences of prenatal alcohol exposure: A 14-year study. *Psychological Science, 10*, 186–190.

Streissguth, A. P., Brookstein, F. L., Barr, H. M., Sampson, P. D., O'Malley, K., & Young, J. K. (2004). Risk factors for adverse life outcomes in fetal alcohol syndrome and fetal alcohol effects. *Journal of Developmental & Behavioral Pediatrics, 25*, 228–238. doi:10.1097/00004703-200408000-00002

Streri, A., & Pecheux, M. G. (1986). Tactual habituation and discrimination of form in infancy: A comparison with vision. *Child Development, 57*, 100–104.

Strickland, B. R. (1989). Internal-external control expectancies: From contingency to creativity. *American Psychologist, 44*, 1–12.

Stromberg, J. (2015, January 28). 9 surprising facts about the sense of touch. *Vox.* Retrieved from https://www.vox.com/2015/1/28/7925737/touch-facts

Stroop, J. R. (1935). Studies of interference in serial verbal reactions. *Journal of Experimental Psychology, 18*, 643–662.

Strupp, H. H. (1989). Psychotherapy: Can the practitioner learn from the researcher? *American Psychologist, 44*, 717–724.

Strupp, H. H. (1996). The tripartite model and the *Consumer Reports* study. *American Psychologist, 51*, 1017–1024.

Stuart, H. (2006). Media portrayal of mental illness and its treatments: What effect does it have on people with mental illness? *CNS Drugs, 20*(2), 99.

Stults-Kolehmainen, M. A., & Sinha, R. (2014). The effects of stress on physical activity and exercise. *Sports Medicine (Auckland, N.Z.), 44*(1), 81–121. doi:10.1007/s40279-013-0090-5

Stumpf, H., & Stanley, J. C. (1996). Gender-related differences on the College Board's Advanced Placement and achievement tests, 1982–1992. *Journal of Educational Psychology, 88*, 353–364.

Stunkard, A. J., Harris, J. R., Pedersen, N. L., & McClearn, G. E. (1990). The body-mass index of twins who have been reared apart. *New England Journal of Medicine, 332*, 1483–1487.

Substance Abuse and Mental Health Service Administration (SAMHSA). (2016). *Key substance use and mental health indicators in the United States: Results from the 2016 National Survey on Drug Use and Health.* Center for Behavioral Health Statistics. Retrieved from www.samhsa.gov/data/sites/default/files/NSDUH-FFR1-2016/NSDUH-FFR1-2016.htm#summary

Sue, D. W., & Sue, D. (1999). *Counseling the culturally different: Theory and practice* (3rd ed.). New York, NY: Wiley.

Sue, D. W., & Sue, D. (2002). *Counseling the culturally diverse: Theory and practice* (4th ed.). New York, NY: Wiley.

Sullivan, R. M., Taborsky-Barbar, S., Mendoza, R., Itino, A., Leon, M., Cotman, C. W., . . . Lott, I. (1991). Olfactory classical conditioning in neonates. *Pediatrics, 87*, 511–518.

Suls, J. (2013). Anger and the heart: Perspectives on cardiac risk, mechanisms and interventions. *Progress in Cardiovascular Diseases, 55*(6), 538–547. doi:10.1016/j.pcad.2013.03.002

Suls, J., & Rothman, A. (2004). Evolution of the biopsychosocial model: Prospects and challenges for health psychology. *Health Psychology, 23*, 119–125. doi:10.1037/0278-6133.23.2.119

Sun, S., Xu, Q., Guo, C., Guan, Y., Liu, Q., & Dong, X. (2017). Leaky gate model: Intensity-dependent coding of pain and itch in the spinal cord. *Neuron, 93*(4). doi:10.1016/j.neuron.2017.01.012

Suzuki, K. (1991). Moon illusion simulated in complete darkness: Planetarium experiment reexamined. *Perception & Psychophysics, 49*, 349–354.

Suzuki, K. (1998). The role of binocular viewing in a spacing illusion arising in a darkened surround. *Perception, 27*, 355–361.

Swain, K. D., Pillay, B. J., & Kliewer, W. (2017). Traumatic stress and psychological functioning in a South African adolescent community sample. *South African Journal of Psychiatry, 23*, 1008. doi:10.4102/sajpsychiatry.v23i0.1008

Swayze, V. W. (1995). Frontal leukotomy and related psychosurgical procedures in the era before antipsychotics (1935–1954): A historical overview. *American Journal of Psychiatry, 152*(4), 505–515.

Swets, J. A. (1996). *Signal detection theory and ROC analysis in psychology and diagnostics.* Mahwah, NJ: Erlbaum.

Swider, B. W., Barrick, M. R., & Harris, T. B. (2016). Initial impressions: What they are, what they are not, and how they influence structured interview outcomes. *Journal of Applied Psychology, 101*(5), 625–638. doi:10.1037/ap10000077

Swift, A. (2020, January 6). Americans' worries about race relations at record high. Gallup. Retrieved from http://news.gallup.com/poll/206057/americans-worry-race-relations-record-high.aspx

Swift, D. L., Johannsen, N. M., Lavie, C. J., Earnest, C. P., & Church, T. S. (2014). The role of exercise and physical activity in weight loss and maintenance. *Progress in Cardiovascular Diseases, 56*(4), 441–447. https://doi.org/10.1016/j.pcad.2013.09.012

Swift, D. L., Johannsen, N. M., Lavie, C. J., Earnest, C. P., & Church, T. S. (2013). The role of exercise and physical activity in weight loss and maintenance. *Progress in Cardiovascular Diseases, 56*(4), 441–447.

Syurina, E. V., Bood, Z. M., Ryman, F., & Muftugil-Yalcin, S. (2018). Cultural phenomena believed to be associated with orthorexia nervosa: Opinion study in Dutch health professionals. *Frontiers in Psychology, 9*, 1419. doi:10.3389/fpsyg.2018.01419

Szasz, T. (1961). *The myth of mental illness*. New York, NY: Harper & Row.

Szasz, T. (1987). *Insanity: The idea and its consequences*. New York, NY: Wiley.

Tajfel, H. (Ed.).(1982). *Social identity and intergroup relations*. London, UK: Cambridge University Press.

Tajfel, H., Billig, M. G., Bundy, R. P., & Flament, C. (1971). Social categorization and intergroup behavior. *European Journal of Social Psychology, 1*, 149–178.

Takeuchi, A. H., & Hulse, S. H. (1993). Absolute pitch. *Psychological Bulletin, 113*, 345–361.

Talamini, F., Altoè, G., Carretti, B., & Grassi, M. (2017). Musicians have better memory than nonmusicians: A meta-analysis. *PLOS ONE, 12*(10). doi:10.1371/journal.pone.0186773

Talarico, J. M., & Rubin, D. C. (2007). Flashbulb memories are special after all; In phenomenology, not accuracy. *Applied Cognitive Psychology, 21*, 557–578. doi:10.1002/acp.1293

Talbot, K. (2019, January 22). What the Fyre Festival documentaries reveal about millennials. *Forbes*. Retrieved from https://www.forbes.com/sites/katetalbot/2019/01/21/what-the-fyre-festival-documentaries-revealed-about-millennials/

Talih, F., Ajaltouni, J., Ghandour, H., Abu-Mohammad, A. S., & Kobeissy, F. (2018). Insomnia in hospitalized psychiatric patients: Prevalence and associated factors. *Neuropsychiatric Disease and Treatment, 14*, 969–975. doi:10.2147/NDT.S160742

Talwar, S. K., Xu, S., Hawley, E. S., Weiss, S. A., Moxon, K. A., & Chapin, J. K. (2002). Behavioural neuroscience: Rat navigation guided by remote control. *Nature, 417*, 37–38.

Tamir, D. I., & Mitchell, J. P. (2012). Disclosing information about the self is intrinsically rewarding. *Proceedings of the National Academy of Sciences USA, 109*(21), 8038–8043. doi:10.1073/pnas.1202129109

Tannenbaum, M. B., Hepler, J., Zimmerman, R. S., Saul, L., Jacobs, S., Wilson, K., & Albarracín, D. (2015). Appealing to fear: A meta-analysis of fear appeal effectiveness and theories. *Psychological Bulletin, 141*(6), 1178–1204.

Taormina, R. J., & Gao, J. H. (2013). Maslow and the motivation hierarchy: Measuring satisfaction of the needs. *American Journal of Psychology, 126*(2), 155–177. doi:10.5406/amerjpsyc.126.2.0155

Taras, V., Steel, P., & Kirkman, B. L. (2010). Negative practice-value correlations in the GLOBE data: Unexpected findings, questionnaire limitations and research directions. *Journal of International Business Studies, 41*(8), 1330–1338. doi:10.1057/jibs.2010.30

Tay, L., & Diener, E. (2011). Needs and subjective well-being around the world. *Journal of Personality and Social Psychology, 101*, 354–365. doi:10.1037/a0023779

Taylor, C. B., Sheikh, J., Agras, W. S., Roth, W. T., Margraf, J., Ehlers, A., . . . & Gossard, D. (1986). Ambulatory heart rate changes in patients with panic attacks. *American Journal of Psychiatry, 143*(4), 478–482. doi:10.1176/ajp.143.4.478

Taylor, D. M., & Moghaddam, F. M. (1994). *Theories of intergroup relations* (2nd ed.). Westport, CT: Praeger.

Taylor, S. E., & Armor, D. A. (1996). Positive illusions and coping with adversity. *Journal of Personality, 64*, 873–898.

Teitelbaum, P., & Epstein, A. N. (1962). The lateral hypothalamic syndrome: Recovery of feeding and drinking after lateral hypothalamic lesions. *Psychological Review, 69*, 74–90.

Teixeira, P. J., Silva, M. N., Mata, J., Palmeira, A. L., & Markland, D. (2012). Motivation, self-determination, and long-term weight control. *International Journal of Behavioral Nutrition and Physical Activity, 9*, 22. doi:10.1186/1479-5868-9-22

Tekampe, J., van Middendorp, H., Meeuwis, S. H., van Leusden, J. R., Pacheco-López, G., Hermus, A. M., & Evers, A. M. (2017). Conditioning immune and endocrine parameters in humans: A systematic review. *Psychotherapy and Psychosomatics, 86*(2), 99–107. doi:10.1159/000449470

Telner, J. I., Lapierre, Y. D., Horn, E., & Browne, M. (1986). Rapid reduction of mania by means of reserpine therapy. *American Journal of Psychiatry, 143*(8), 1058. doi:10.1176/ajp.143.8.aj14381058

Ten Kate, J., de Koster, W., & van der Waal, J. (2017). The effect of religiosity on life satisfaction in a secularized context: Assessing the relevance of believing and belonging. *Review of Religious Research, 59*(2), 135–155. doi:10.1007/s13644-016-0282-1

Tenpenny, P. L., Keriazakos, M. S., Lew-Gavin, S., & Phelan, T. P. (1998). In search of inadvertent plagiarism. *American Journal of Psychology, 111*, 529–559.

Tepper, B. J., White, E. A., Koelliker, Y., Lanzara, C., Dadamo, P., & Gasparini, P. (2009). Genetic variation in taste sensitivity to 6-n-propylthiouracil and its relationship to taste perception and food selection. *Annals of the New York Academy of Sciences, 1170*(1), 126–139. doi:10.1111/j.1749-6632.2009.03916.x

Terman, L. M. (1916). *The measurement of intelligence*. Boston, MA: Houghton Mifflin.

Terracciano, A., Stephan, Y., Luchetti, M., & Sutin, A. R. (2018). Cognitive impairment, dementia, and personality stability among older adults. *Assessment, 25*(3), 336–347. doi:10.1177/1073191117691844

Terry, R. D., Katzman, R., Sisodia, S. S., & Bick, K. L. (Eds.).(1999). *Alzheimer's disease*. Philadelphia, PA: Lippincott, Williams & Wilkins.

Thanawala, S., & Nakashima, R. (2018, April 3). Woman shoots 3, self at YouTube headquarters in possible domestic dispute. *Denver Post*. Retrieved from https://www.denverpost.com/2018/04/03/youtube-shooting/

Thatcher, R. W., Walker, R. A., & Giudice, S. (1986). Human cerebral hemispheres develop at different rates and different ages. *Science, 236*, 1110–1113.

The Economist. (2017, September 4). Why Chinese children born in the Year of the Dragon are more successful. *The Economist.* Retrieved from https://www.economist.com/graphic-detail/2017/09/04/why-chinese-children-born-in-years-of-the-dragon-are-more-successful

The Innocence Project. (2021). *Eyewitness misidentification.* Retrieved from http://www.innocenceproject.org/understand/Eyewitness-Misidentification.php

The Innocence Project. (2014). *Eyewitness misidentification.* Retrieved from http://www.innocenceproject.org/understand/Eyewitness-Misidentification.php

Theeuwes, J., Kramer, A. F., Hahn, S., & Irwin, D. E. (1998). Our eyes do not always go where we want them to go: Capture of the eyes by new objects. *Psychological Science, 9,* 379–385.

Thessing, V. C., Anch, A. M., Muelbach, M. J., Schweitzer, P. K., & Walsh, J. K. (1994). Two- and 4-hour bright-light exposure differentially affect sleepiness and performance the subsequent night. *Sleep, 17,* 140–145.

Thiebaut de Schotten, M., Dell'Acqua, F., Ratiu, P., Leslie, A., Howells, H., Cabanis, E., . . . Catani, M. (2015). From Phineas Gage and Monsieur Leborgne to H.M.: Revisiting disconnection syndromes. *Cerebral Cortex, 25*(12), 4812–4827. doi:10.1093/cercor/bhv173

Thomas, P. (2017, October 7). Investigators believe Las Vegas gunman had severe undiagnosed mental illness: Sources. ABC News. Retrieved from https://abcnews.go.com/US/investigators-las-vegas-gunman-severe-undiagnosed-mental-illness/story?id=50346433

Thomas, R. (2001). Reoccurring errors among recent history of psychology textbooks. *American Journal of Psychology, 120*(3), 477–495.

Thompson, J. K., Heinberg, L. J., Altabe, M., & Tantleff-Dunn, S. (1999). *Exacting beauty: Theory, assessment, and treatment of body image disturbance.* Washington, DC: American Psychological Association.

Thompson, N. L., & Keable, H. (2016). The psychoanalytic study of the child: A narrative of postwar psychoanalysis. *American Imago, 73*(3), 343–365. doi:10.1353/aim.2016.0018

Thompson, P., & Mikellidou, K. (2011). Applying the Helmholtz illusion to fashion: Horizontal stripes won't make you look fatter. *I-Perception, 2*(1), 69–76. doi:10.1068/i0405

Thompson, T. L., & Amedee, R. (2009). Vertigo: A review of common peripheral and central vestibular disorders. *The Ochsner Journal, 9*(1), 20–26.

Thorley, C., Baxter, R. E., & Lorek, J. (2015). The impact of note taking style and note availability at retrieval on mock jurors' recall and recognition of trial information. *Memory, 24*(4), 560–574. doi:10.1080/09658211.2015.1031250

Thorndike, E. L. (1898). Animal intelligence: An experimental study of the associative processes in animals. *Psychological Monographs, 2*(No. 8).

Thorndike, E. L. (1911). *Animal intelligence: Experimental studies.* New York, NY: Macmillan.

Thurstone, L. L. (1938). *Primary mental abilities.* Chicago, IL: University of Chicago Press.

Tidbury, L. P., Black, R. H., & O'Connor, A. R. (2015). Clinical assessment of stereoacuity and 3-d stereoscopic entertainment. *Strabismus, 23*(4), 164–169. doi:10.3109/09273972.2015.1107600

Tiggemann, M., & Slater, A. (2013). NetGirls: The Internet, Facebook, and body image concern in adolescent girls. *International Journal of Eating Disorders, 46*(6), 630–633.

Tobe, B. T. D., Crain, A. M., Winquist, A. M., Calabrese, B., Makihara, H., Zhao, W.-N., . . . & Snyder, E. Y. (2017). Probing the lithium-response pathway in hiPSCs implicates the phosphoregulatory set-point for a cytoskeletal modulator in bipolar pathogenesis. *Proceedings of the National Academy of Sciences USA, 114*(22). doi:10.1073/pnas.1700111114

Tobisch, A., & Dresel, M. (2017). Negatively or positively biased? Dependencies of teachers' judgments and expectations based on students' ethnic and social backgrounds. *Social Psychology of Education, 20*(4), 731–752.

Tolin, D. F., & Foa, E. B. (2006). Sex differences in trauma and post-traumatic stress disorder: A quantitative review of 25 years of research. *Psychological Bulletin, 132*(6):959–992.

Tolman, E. C. (1948). Cognitive maps in rats and men. *Psychological Review, 55,* 189–208.

Tolman, E. C., & Honzik, C. H. (1930). Introduction and removal of reward and maze performance in rats. *University of California Publications in Psychology, 4,* 257–275.

Torrey, E. F. (1988). *Surviving schizophrenia: A family manual.* New York, NY: Harper & Row.

Tosun, L. P., & Lajunen, T. (2009). Why do young adults develop a passion for Internet activities? The associations among personality, revealing "true self" on the Internet, and passion for the Internet. *CyberPsychology & Behavior, 12,* 401–406.

Totterdell, P., Spelten, E., Smith, L., Barton, J., & Folkard, S. (1995). Recovery from work shifts: How long does it take? *Journal of Applied Psychology, 80,* 43–57.

Town, R., Hayes, D., Fonagy, P., & Stapley, E. (2021). A qualitative investigation of LGBTQ+ young people's experiences and perceptions of self-managing their mental health. *European Child & Adolescent Psychiatry,* 1–14. doi:10.1007/s00787-021-01783-w, Advance online publication

Trabulsi, J. C., & Mennella, J. A. (2012). Diet, sensitive periods in flavour learning, and growth. *International Review of Psychiatry, 24*(3), 219–230.

Trafimow, D., Silverman, E. S., Fan, R. M.-T., & Law, J. S. F. (1997). The effects of language and priming on the relative accessibility of the private self and the collective self. *Journal of Cross-Cultural Psychology, 28*(1), 107–123. doi:10.1177/0022022197281007

Trafimow, D., Triandis, H. C., & Goto, S. G. (1991). Some tests of the distinction between the private and collective self. *Journal of Personality and Social Psychology, 60,* 649–655.

Trainor, L. J., & Heinmiller, B. M. (1998). The development of evaluative responses to music: Infants prefer to listen to consonance over dissonance. *Infant Behavior and Development, 21,* 77–88.

Trainor, L. J., & Zacharias, C. A. (1998). Infants prefer higher-pitched singing. *Infant Behavior and Development, 21,* 799–806.

Treisman, A., Viera, A., & Hayes, A. (1992). Automaticity and preattentive processes. *American Journal of Psychology, 105,* 341–362.

Tremblay, K. L. (2015). The ear-brain connection: Older ears and older brains. *American Journal of Audiology, 24*(2), 117–120.

Triandis, H. C. (1994). *Culture and social behavior.* New York, NY: McGraw-Hill.

Triandis, H. C. (1995). *Individualism and collectivism: New directions in social psychology.* Boulder, CO: Westview.

Triandis, H. C., Chen, X. P., & Chan, D. K. (1998). Scenarios for the measurement of collectivism and individualism. *Journal of Cross-Cultural Psychology, 29*, 275–289.

Trinh, N. H. T., Bernard-Negron, R., & Ahmed, I. (2019). Mental health issues in racial and ethnic minority elderly. *Current Psychiatry Reports, 21*, 102. doi:10.1007/s11920-019-1082-4

Trujillo, M. A., Perrin, P. B., Sutter, M., Tabaac, A., & Benotsch, E. G. (2017). The buffering role of social support on the associations among discrimination, mental health, and suicidality in a transgender sample. *International Journal of Transgenderism, 18*(1), 39–52. doi:10.1080/15532739.2016.1247405

Tryon, W. W. (2014). Evaluation, criticisms, and rebuttals. *Cognitive Neuroscience and Psychotherapy*, 311–366. doi:10.1016/b978-0-12-420071-5.00007-7

Tseng, W. (2001). *Handbook of cultural psychiatry.* San Diego, CA: Academic.

Tsirigotis, K., Gruszczynski, W., & Tsirigotis, M. (2011). Gender differentiation in methods of suicide attempts. *Medical Science Monitor, 17*(8), 65–70.

Tsuang, M. T., & Faraone, S. V. (1990). *The genetics of mood disorders.* Baltimore, MD: Johns Hopkins University Press.

Tsukamoto, S., & Fiske, S. T. (2017). Perceived threat to national values in evaluating stereotyped immigrants. *Journal of Social Psychology, 158*(2), 157–172. doi:10.1080/00224545.2017.1317231

Tubaldi, F., Ansuini, C., Tirindelli, R., & Castiello, U. (2008). Odours grab his hand but not hers. *Perception, 37*, 1886–1889.

Tucker, J. K. (June, 2020). Mental health effects of the COVID-19 pandemic. Harvard Medical School: Thought Leadership. Retrieved from https://postgraduateeducation.hms.harvard.edu/thought-leadership/mental-health-effects-covid-19-pandemic.

Tuerlinckx, E., De Boeck, P., & Lens, W. (2002). Measuring needs with the Thematic Apperception Test: A psychometric study. *Journal of Personality and Social Psychology, 82*, 448–461.

Tukey, J. W. (1977). *Exploratory data analysis.* Reading, MA: Addison-Wesley.

Tulving, E. (1983). *Elements of episodic memory.* Oxford, UK: Clarendon Press.

Tulving, E. (1985). How many memory systems are there? *American Psychologist, 40*, 385–398.

Tulving, E. (2002). Episodic memory: From mind to brain. *Annual Review of Psychology, 53*, 1–25.

Turiel, E. (1983). *The development of social knowledge: Morality and convention.* New York, NY: Cambridge University Press.

Turk, C. L., Heimberg, R. G., & Hope, D. A. (2001). Social anxiety disorder. In D. H. Barlow (Ed.), *Anxiety and its disorders: The nature and treatment of anxiety and panic* (2nd ed., pp. 114–153). New York, NY: Guilford.

Turkkan, J. S. (1989). Classical conditioning: The new hegemony. *Behavioral and Brain Sciences, 12*, 121–179.

Turnbull, C. M. (1961). *The forest people: A study of the Pygmies of the Congo.* New York, NY: Clarion.

Turner, J. C. (1987). *Rediscovering the social group: A self-categorization theory.* Oxford, England: Basil Blackwell.

Turner, J. C., & Reynolds, K. J. (2003). Why social dominance theory has been falsified. *British Journal of Social Psychology, 42*(2), 199–206. doi:10.1348/014466603322127184

Turner, J. C., Oakes, P. J., Haslam, S. A., & McGarty, C. (1994). Self and collective: Cognition and social context. *Personality and Social Psychology Bulletin, 20*, 454–463.

Tversky, A., & Kahneman, D. (1973). Availability: A heuristic for judging frequency and probability. *Cognitive Psychology, 5*, 207–232.

Twenge, J. M., & Crocker, J. (2002). Race and self-esteem: Meta-analyses comparing Whites, Blacks, Hispanics, Asians, and American Indians. *Psychological Bulletin, 128*, 371–408.

Twenge, J. M., Baumeister, R. E., Tice, D. M., & Stucke, T. S. (2001). If you can't join them, beat them: Effects of social exclusion on aggressive behavior. *Journal of Personality and Social Psychology, 81*, 1058–1069.

Twenge, J. M., Joiner, T. E., Rogers, M. L., & Martin, G. N. (2017). Increases in depressive symptoms, suicide-related outcomes, and suicide rates among U.S. adolescents after 2010 and links to increased new media screen time. *Clinical Psychological Science, 6*(1), 3–17. doi:10.1177/2167702617723376

Tyng, C. M., Amin, H. U., Saad, M., & Malik, A. S. (2017). The influences of emotion on learning and memory. *Frontiers in Psychology, 8*, 1454. doi:10.3389/fpsyg.2017.01454

Tyrer, P., Reed, G. M., & Crawford, M. J. (2015). Classification, assessment, prevalence, and effect of personality disorder. *Lancet, 385*(9969), 717–726.

U. S. Census Bureau. (2017). Facts for features: Older Americans. Month: May 2017. Retrieved from https://www.census.gov/newsroom/facts-for-features/2017/cb17-ff08.html

U.S. Bureau of Labor Statistics. (2020). Databases, tables & calculators by subject. Retrieved from http://data.bls.gov/timeseries/LNS14000000

U.S. Census Bureau. (2019). QuickFacts: United States. Retrieved from https://www.census.gov/quickfacts/fact/table/US/INC110218

U.S. Census Bureau. (2019, December 23). International Data Base (IDB). Retrieved from https://www.census.gov/programs-surveys/international-programs/about/idb.html

U.S. Department of Health and Human Services. (2017). *Key substance use and mental health indicators in the united states: Results from the 2015 National Survey on Drug Use and Health.* Retrieved from https://www.samhsa.gov/data/report/key-substance-use-and-mental-health-indicators-united-states-results-2015-national-survey-0

U.S. Department of Health and Human Services. (2018). Does depression increase the risk for suicide? Retrieved from https://www.hhs.gov/answers/mental-health-and-substance-abuse/does-depression-increase-risk-of-suicide/index.html

U.S. Department of Veterans Affairs. (2019, October 17). PTSD: National Center for PTSD. Retrieved from https://www.ptsd.va.gov/understand/common/common_adults.asp

U.S. Energy Information Administration. (2015). Independent statistics and analysis. Retrieved from https://www.eia.gov/todayinenergy/detail.php?id=30132

U.S. Equal Employment Opportunity Commission, Select Task Force on the Study of Harassment in the Workplace. (2016). Report of co-chairs Chai R. Feldblum & Victoria A. Lipnic. Retrieved from https://www.eeoc.gov/select-task-force-study-harassment-workplace

Uchino, B. N., Cacioppo, J. T., & Kiecolt-Glaser, J. K. (1996). The relationship between social support and physiological processes: A review with emphasis on underlying mechanisms and implications for health. *Psychological Bulletin, 119*, 488–531.

Uga, V., Lemut, M. C., Zampi, C., Zilli, L., & Salzarulo, P. (2006). Music in dreams. *Consciousness and Cognition, 15*(2), 351–357. doi:10.1016/j.concog.2005.09.003

Uleman, J. S., Saribay, S. A., & Gonzalez, C. M. (2008). Spontaneous inferences, implicit impressions, and implicit theories. *Annual Review of Psychology, 59*, 329–360. doi:10.1146/annurev.psych.59.103006.093707

Umeda, T., Isa, T., & Nishimura, Y. (2019). The somatosensory cortex receives information about motor output. *Science Advances, 5*(7), eaaw5388. doi:10.1126/sciadv.aaw5388

Umesh, S., & Bose, S. (2019). Binge-watching: A matter of concern? *Indian Journal of Psychological Medicine, 41*(2), 182–184. doi:10.4103/IJPSYM.IJPSYM_279_18

Underwood, B. J. (1957). Interference and forgetting. *Psychological Review, 64*, 49–60.

Unsworth, N., & Spillers, G. J. (2010). Working memory capacity: Attention control, secondary memory, or both? A direct test of the dual-component model. *Journal of Memory and Language, 62*, 392–406.

Urdan, T., & Bruchmann, K. (2018). Examining the academic motivation of a diverse student population: A consideration of methodology. *Educational Psychologist, 53*(2), 114–130.

Ursano, R. J., McCarroll, J. E., & Fullerton, C. S. (2003). Traumatic death in terrorism and disasters: The effects of posttraumatic stress and behavior. In R. J. Ursano, C. S. Fullerton, & A. E. Norwood (Eds.), *Terrorism and disaster: Individual and community mental health interventions* (pp. 308–332). New York, NY: Cambridge University Press.

Usher, J. A., & Neisser, U. (1993). Childhood amnesia and the beginnings of memory for four early life events. *Journal of Experimental Psychology: General, 122*, 155–165.

Vahia, V. M., & Vahia, I. V. (2008). Schizophrenia in developing countries. In K. T. Mueser & D. V. Jeste (Eds.), *Clinical handbook of schizophrenia* (pp. 549–555). New York, NY: Guilford.

Valarmathi, A., Suresh, A., Venkatesh, L., & Santhanam, T. (2021). Visual-perceptual function of children using the developmental test of visual perception-3. *Clinical and Experimental Optometry*. doi:10.1080/08164622.2021.1878823

Valenstein, E. S. (1986). *Great and desperate cures: The rise and decline of psychosurgery and other radical treatments for mental illness*. New York, NY: Basic Books.

Valenza, E., Simion, F., Cassia, V. M., & Umilta, C. (1996). Face preference at birth. *Journal of Experimental Psychology: Human Perception and Performance, 22*, 892–903.

Vallar, G. (1998). Spatial hemineglect in humans. *Trends in Cognitive Science, 2*, 87–97.

Vallee, B. L. (1998, June). Alcohol in the Western world. *Scientific American*, 80–85.

Van de Castle, R. L. (1994). *Our dreaming mind*. New York, NY: Ballantine Books.

van Emmerik, A. A. P. V., Jong, K. D., & Hofmann, S. G. (2018). The evidence for cognitive behavioral therapy. *Journal of the American Medical Association, 319*(8), 832. doi:10.1001/jama.2017.20838

Van Loocke, P. (1999). *The nature of concepts: Evolution, structure and representation*. New York, NY: Routledge.

Van Petten, C. (2004). Relationship between hippocampal volume and memory ability in healthy individuals across the lifespan: Review and meta-analysis. *Neuropsychologia, 42*(10), 1394–1413. doi:10.1016/j.neuropsychologia.2004.04.006

vanMarle, K., & Wynn, K. (2011). Tracking and quantifying objects and non-cohesive substances. *Developmental Science, 14*(3), 502–515. doi:10.1111/j.1467-7687.2010.00998.x

Vaquero, J. J., & Kinahan, P. (2015). Positron emission tomography: Current challenges and opportunities for technological advances in clinical and preclinical imaging systems. *Annual Review of Biomedical Engineering, 17*, 385–414. doi:10.1146/annurev-bioeng-071114-040723

Vedantam, S. (2017, December 11). How labels can affect people's personalities and potential. National Public Radio. Retrieved from https://www.npr.org/2017/12/11/569983801/how-labels-can-affect-peoples-personalities-and-potential

Velasco-Mondragon, E., Jimenez, A., Palladino-Davis, A. G., Davis, D., & Escamilla-Cejudo, J. A. (2016). Hispanic health in the USA: A scoping review of the literature. *Public Health Reviews, 37*, 31. doi:10.1186/s40985-016-0043-2

Ventriglio, A., Gentile, A., Bonfitto, I., Stella, E., Mari, M., Steardo, L., & Bellomo, A. (2016). Suicide in the early stage of schizophrenia. *Frontiers in Psychiatry, 7*, 116. doi:10.3389/fpsyt.2016.00116

Venturini, E., & Roques, M. (2016). Évaluation des processus de changement des femmes atteintes d'un cancer pelvien: à propos des qualités de test/retest du Thematic Apperception Test. *Annales Médico-Psychologiques, Revue Psychiatrique, 174*(6), 499–502. doi:10.1016/j.amp.2016.04.004

Vera, A., Abdelaziz, S., & Mahmood, Z. (2020, June 15). Black protestor who carried injured White man through angry crowd says he was trying to avoid catastrophe. CNN. Retrieved from https://www.cnn.com/2020/06/14/uk/london-blm-protester-injured-man-photo-trnd/index.html

Vercillo, T., Burr, D., & Gori, M. (2016). Early visual deprivation severely compromises the auditory sense of space in congenitally blind children. *Developmental Psychology, 52*(6), 847–853. doi:10.1037/dev0000103

Vere, J. P. (2008). Dragon children: Identifying the causal effect of the first child on female labor supply with the Chinese lunar calendar. *Oxford Bulletin of Economics and Statistics, 70*, 303–325.

Verma, I. M. (2014). Editorial expression of concern and correction. *Proceedings of the National Academy of Sciences USA, 111*, 10779. doi:10.1073/pnas.1412583111

Vicente, K. J., & Wang, J. H. (1998). An ecological theory of expertise effects in memory recall. *Psychological Review, 105*, 33–57.

Villalobos, J. G., & Davis, D. (2016). Interrogation and the minority suspect: Pathways to true and false confession. In M. Miller & B. Bornstein (Eds.), *Advances in psychology and law* (Vol. 1). New York, NY: Springer.

Villemure, C., & Bushnell, M. C. (2002). Cognitive modulation of pain: How do attention and emotion influence pain processing? *Pain, 95*, 195–199.

Vimal, R. L. P., Pokorny, J., & Smith, V. C. (1987). Appearance of steadily viewed lights. *Vision Research, 27*, 1309–1318.

Virani, S. S., Alonso, A., Benjamin, E. J., Bittencourt, M. S., Callaway, C. W., Carson, A. P., . . . Tsao, C. W. (2020). Heart disease and stroke statistics—2020 update: A report from the American Heart Association. *Circulation, 141*, e139–e596. doi:10.1161/CIR.0000000000000757

Visintainer, M., Volpicelli, J., & Seligman, M. (1982). Tumor rejection in rats after inescapable or escapable shock. *Science, 216*, 437–439.

Vlachakis, C., Dragoumani, K., Raftopoulou, S., Mantaiou, M., Papageorgiou, L., Champeris Tsaniras, S., . . . Vlachakis, D. (2018). Human emotions on the onset of cardiovascular and small vessel related diseases. *In Vivo (Athens, Greece), 32*(4), 859–870. doi:10.21873/invivo.11320

Voelpel, S. C., Eckhoff, R. A., & Förster, J. (2008). David against Goliath? Group size and bystander effects in virtual knowledge sharing. *Human Relations, 61*(2), 271–295. doi:10.1177/0018726707087787

Volz, L. J., & Gazzaniga, M. S. (2017). Interaction in isolation: 50 years of insights from split-brain research. *Brain, 140*(7), 2051–2060. doi:10.1093/brain/awx139

Von Gehlen, J., & Sachse, P. (2015). Benefits of distraction. *Social Behavior and Personality, 43*(4), 601–612.

von Helmholtz, H. (1852). On the theory of compound colours. *Philosophical Magazine, 4*, 519–534.

von Hippel, W., Sekaquaptewa, D., & Vargas, P. (1995). On the role of encoding processes in stereotype maintenance. *Advances in Experimental Social Psychology, 27*, 177–254.

von Hippel, W., Silver, L. A., & Lynch, M. E. (2000). Stereotyping against your will: The role of inhibitory ability in stereotyping and prejudice among the elderly. *Personality and Social Psychology Bulletin, 26*, 523–532.

von Soest, T. V., Wichstrøm, L., & Kvalem, I. L. (2016). The development of global and domain-specific self-esteem from age 13 to 31. *Journal of Personality and Social Psychology, 110*(4), 592–608. doi:10.1037/pspp0000060

Vonk J. (2016). Advances in animal cognition. *Behavioral Sciences (Basel, Switzerland), 6*(4), 27. doi:10.3390/bs6040027

Vosniadou, S., & Brewer, W. F. (1992). Mental models of the earth: A study of conceptual change in childhood. *Cognitive Psychology, 24*, 535–585.

Voss, U., Tuin, I., Schermelleh, K., & Hobson, A. (2011). Waking and dreaming: Related but structurally independent. Dream reports of congenitally paraplegic and deaf-mute persons. *Consciousness and Cognition, 20*(3), 673–687. doi:10.1016/j.concog.2010.10.020

Vukasović, T., & Bratko, D. (2015). Heritability of personality: A meta-analysis of behavior genetic studies. *Psychological Bulletin, 141*(4), 769–785. doi:10.1037/bul0000017

Wade, K. A., Garry, M., Read, J. D., & Lindsay, D. S. (2002). A picture is worth a thousand lies: Using false photographs to create false childhood memories. *Psychonomic Bulletin & Review, 9*, 597–603. doi:10.3758/bf03196318.

Wade, M. G., & Whiting, H. T. A. (Eds.). (1986). *Motor development in children: Aspects of coordination and control*. Dordrecht, Netherlands: Martinus Nijhoff.

Wade, N. (1990). *Visual allusions: Pictures of perception*. Hillsdale, NJ: Erlbaum.

Wagemans, J., Elder, J. H., Kubovy, M., Palmer, S. E., Peterson, M. A., Singh, M., & von der Heydt, R. (2012). A century of Gestalt psychology in visual perception. I. Perceptual grouping and figure-ground organization. *Psychological Bulletin, 138*(6), 1172–1217. doi:10.1037/a0029333

Wagner, J., Hoppmann, C., Ram, N., & Gerstorf, D. (2015). Self-esteem is relatively stable late in life: The role of resources in the health, self-regulation, and social domains. *Developmental Psychology, 51*(1), 136–149. doi:10.1037/a0038338

Wald, G. (1964). The receptors of human color vision. *Science, 145*, 1007–1017.

Walk, R. D. (1981). *Perceptual development*. Monterey, CA: Brooks/Cole.

Walker, E. E., & Diforio, D. (1997). Schizophrenia: A neural diathesis-stress model. *Psychological Review, 104*, 667–685.

Walker, E., & Lewine, R. J. (1990). Prediction of adult-onset schizophrenia from childhood home movies of the patients. *American Journal of Psychiatry, 147*, 1052–1056.

Walker, L. J. (1984). Sex differences in the development of moral reasoning: A critical review. *Child Development, 55*, 677–691.

Wall, H. J., Taylor, P. J., Dixon, J., Conchie, S. M., & Ellis, D. A. (2013). Rich contexts do not always enrich the accuracy of personality judgments. *Journal of Experimental Social Psychology, 49*(6), 1190–1195.

Walther, E. (2002). Guilty by mere association: Evaluative conditioning and the spreading attitude effect. *Journal of Personality and Social Psychology, 82*, 919–934.

Walton, G. E., Bower, N. J. A., & Bower, T. G. R. (1992). Recognition of familiar faces by newborns. *Infant Behavior and Development, 15*, 265–269.

Wang, J., Otgarr, H., Santtila, P., Shen, X., & Zhou, C. (2021). How culture shapes constructive false memory. *Journal of Applied Research in Memory and Cognition, 10*(1), 24–32. doi:10.1016/j.jarmac.2020.12.002

Wang, M. T., Degol, J. L., Amemiya, J., Parr, A., & Guo, J. (2020). Classroom climate and children's academic and psychological wellbeing: A systematic review and meta-analysis. *Developmental Review, 57*, 100912. doi:10.1016/j.dr.2020.100912

Wang, Q., & Peterson, C. (2014). Your earliest memory may be earlier than you think: Prospective studies of children's dating of earliest childhood memories. *Developmental Psychology, 50*(6), 1680–1686. doi:10.1037/a0036001.

Wang, Y. (2002). Is obesity associated with early sexual maturation? A comparison of the association in American boys versus girls. *Pediatrics, 110*, 903–910.

Wang, Y., Wang, G., Zhang, D., Wang, L., Cui, X., Zhu, J., & Fang, Y. (2017). Learning to dislike chocolate: Conditioning negative attitudes toward chocolate and its effect on chocolate consumption. *Frontiers in Psychology, 8*, 1468. doi:10.3389/fpsyg.2017.01468

Warburton, D. E., Nicol, C. W., & Bredin, S. S. (2006). Health benefits of physical activity: The evidence. *Canadian Medical Association Journal, 174*(6), 801–809. doi:10.1503/cmaj.051351

Wark, G. R., & Krebs, D. L. (1996). Gender and dilemma differences in real-life moral judgment. *Developmental Psychology, 32*, 220–230.

Warrington, E. K., & Weiskrantz, L. (1970). Amnesic syndrome: Consolidation or retrieval? *Nature, 228*, 629–630.

Wason, P. C. (1960). On the failure to eliminate hypotheses in a conceptual task. *Quarterly Journal of Experimental Psychology, 12*, 129–140.

Wasserstein, R. L., & Lazar, N. A. (2016). The ASA's statement on p-values: Context, process, and purpose. *American Statistician, 70*, 129–133. doi:10.1080/00031305.2016.1154108

Watanabe, S., Sakamoto, J., & Wakita, M. (1995). Pigeons' discrimination of painting by Monet and Picasso. *Journal of the Experimental Analysis of Behavior, 63*, 165–174.

Wathen, C. N., & Macmillan, H. L. (2013). Children's exposure to intimate partner violence: Impacts and interventions. *Paediatrics & Child Health, 18*(8), 419–422.

Watkins, L. E., Sprang, K. R., & Rothbaum, B. O. (2018). Treating PTSD: A review of evidence-based psychotherapy interventions. *Frontiers in Behavioral Neuroscience, 12*, 258. doi:10.3389/fnbeh.2018.00258

Watkins, M. J., & Peynircioglu, Z. F. (1984). Determining perceived meaning during impression formation: Another look at the meaning change hypothesis. *Journal of Personality and Social Psychology, 46*, 1005–1016.

Watson, D., & Pennebaker, J. W. (1989). Health complaints, stress, and distress: Exploring the central role of negative affectivity. *Psychological Review, 96*, 234–254.

Watson, D., Wiese, D., Vaidya, J., & Tellegen, A. (1999). The two general activation systems of affect: Structural findings, evolutionary considerations, and psychobiological evidence. *Journal of Personality and Social Psychology, 76*, 820–838.

Watson, J. B. (1913). Psychology as the behaviorist views it. *Psychological Review, 20*, 158–177.

Watson, J. B. (1925). *Behaviorism*. New York, NY: Norton.

Watson, J. B. (1927). The myth of the unconscious. *Harper's, 155*, 502–508.

Watson, J. B., & Rayner, R. (1920). Conditioned emotional reactions. *Journal of Experimental Psychology, 3*, 1–14. doi:10.1037/h0069608

Watson, J. D., & Crick, E. H. C. (1953). Molecular structure of nucleic acids. A structure for deoxyribose nucleic acids. *Nature, 171*, 737–738.

Watson, R. L., & Evans, R. B. (1991). *The great psychologists: A history of psychological thought*. New York, NY: HarperCollins.

Watt, H. (2017, September 23). "Some days I think I was molested and others I'm sure it didn't happen": A controversial case of repressed memory. *Guardian*. Retrieved from https://www.theguardian.com/science/2017/sep/23/inside-case-of-repressed-memory-nicole-kluemper

Watts, T. W., Duncan, G. J., & Quan, H. (2018). Revisiting the marshmallow test: A conceptual replication investigating links between early delay of gratification and later outcomes. *Psychological Science, 29*(7), 1159–1177. doi:10.1177/0956797618761661

Wax, A. (2009). Stereotype threat: A case of overclaim syndrome? In C. H. Sommers (Ed.), *The science on women and science* (pp. 132–169). Washington, DC: AIE Press.

Weaver, M. F. (2015). Prescription sedative misuse and abuse. *Yale Journal of Biology and Medicine, 88*(3), 247–256.

Webb, C. E., Turney, I. C., & Dennis, N. A. (2016). What's the gist? The influence of schemas on the neural correlates underlying true and false memories. *Neuropsychologia, 93*(Pt A), 61–75. doi:10.1016/j.neuropsychologia.2016.09.023

Weber, D., Dekhtyar, S., & Herlitz, A. (2017). The Flynn effect in Europe—Effects of sex and region. *Intelligence, 60*, 39–45.

Weber, E. H. (1834). *De pulen, resorptione, auditu et tactu: Annotationes anatomicae et physiologicae*. Leipzig, Germany: Kohler.

Webster, D. M., Richter, L., & Kruglanski, A. W. (1996). On leaping to conclusions when feeling tired: Mental fatigue effects on impressional primacy. *Journal of Experimental Social Psychology, 32*, 181–195.

Wechsler, D. (1939). *The measurement of adult intelligence*. Baltimore, MD: Williams & Wilkins.

Weger, U. W., Hooper, N., Meier, B. P., & Hopthrow, T. (2012). Mindful maths: Reducing the impact of stereotype threat through a mindfulness exercise. *Consciousness and Cognition, 21*, 471–475.

Wegner, D. M. (1989). *White bears and other unwanted thoughts: Suppression, obsession, and the psychology of mental control*. New York, NY: Viking.

Wegner, D. M. (1994). Ironic processes of mental control. *Psychological Review, 101*, 34–52.

Wegner, D. M. (1997). When the antidote is the poison: Ironic mental control processes. *Psychological Science, 8*, 148–153.

Wegner, D. M., Ansfield, M., & Pilloff, D. (1998). The putt and the pendulum: Ironic effects of the mental control of action. *Psychological Science, 9*, 196–199.

Weidner, R., Plewan, T., Chen, Q., Buchner, A., Weiss, P. H., & Fink, G. R. (2014). The moon illusion and size-distance scaling—Evidence for shared neural patterns. *Journal of Cognitive Neuroscience, 26*(8), 1871–1882. doi:10.1162/jocn_a_00590

Weil, A., & Rosen, W. (1993). *From chocolate to morphine: Everyday mind-altering drugs*. Boston, MA: Houghton Mifflin.

Weinberg, R. A. (1989). Intelligence and IQ: Landmark issues and great debates. *American Psychologist, 44*, 98–104.

Weinberg, R. A., Scarr, S., & Waldman, I. D. (1992). The Minnesota Transracial Adoption Study: The follow-up of IQ test performance at adolescence. *Intelligence, 16*, 117–135.

Weiner, B. (1989). *Human motivation*. Mahwah, NJ: Erlbaum.

Weingardt, K. R., Loftus, E. F., & Lindsay, D. S. (1995). Misinformation revisited: New evidence on the suggestibility of memory. *Memory & Cognition, 23*, 72–82.

Weingartner, H., Grafman, J., Boutelle, W., Kaye, W., & Martin, R. R. (1983). Forms of memory failure. *Science, 221*, 380–382.

Weinstein, S. (1968). Intensive and extensive aspects of tactile sensitivity as a function of body part, sex, and laterality. In D. R. Kenshalo (Ed.), *The skin senses* (pp. 195–218). Springfield, IL: Thomas.

Weintraub, K. (2018, May 16). Blue or white dress? Why we see colors differently. *National Geographic.* Retrieved from https://www.nationalgeographic.com.au/science/blue-or-white-dress-why-we-see-colours-differently.aspx

Weisberg, R. W. (1986). *Creativity: Genius and other myths.* New York, NY: Freeman.

Weisberg, R. W. (1992). Metacognition and insight during problem solving: Comment on Metcalfe. *Journal of Experimental Psychology: Learning, Memory, and Cognition, 18*, 426–431.

Weisberg, R. W. (2015). Toward an integrated theory of insight in problem solving. *Thinking & Reasoning, 21*(1), 5–39. doi:10.1080.13546783.2014.886625

Weiss, L., Saklofske, D. H., Coalson, D. L., & Engi Raiford, S. (Eds.) (2010). *WAIS-IV: Clinical uses and interpretation.* London, UK: Elsevier Academic.

Weissberg, M. (1993). Multiple personality disorder and iatrogenesis: The cautionary tale of Anna O. *International Journal of Clinical and Experimental Hypnosis, 41*, 15–34.

Weisz, J. R., Suwanlert, S., Chaiyasit, W., Weiss, B., Achenbach, T. M., & Eastman, K. L. (1993). Behavioral and emotional problems among Thai and American adolescents: Parent reports for ages 12–16. *Journal of Abnormal Psychology, 102*, 395–403.

Wenzlaff, R. M., & Wegner, D. M. (2000). Thought suppression. *Annual Review of Psychology, 51*, 59–91.

Wernicke, C. (1874). *Das aphasische symptomenkomplex.* Breslau, Poland: Cohn und Weigart.

West, P. D. B., & Evans, E. F. (1990). Early detection of hearing damage in young listeners resulting from exposure to amplified music. *British Journal of Audiology, 24*, 89–103.

Westerhof, G. J., & Bohlmeijer, E. T. (2014). Celebrating fifty years of research and applications in reminiscence and life review: State of the art and new directions. *Journal of Aging Studies, 29*, 107–114. doi:10.1016/j.jaging.2014.02.003.

Westerhof, G. J., Miche, M., Brothers, A. F., Barrett, A. E., Diehl, M. K., Montepare, J. M., . . . & Wurm, S. (2014). The influence of subjective aging on health and longevity: A meta-analysis of longitudinal data. *Psychology and Aging, 29*(4), 793–802. doi:10.1037/a0038016

Westerlund, M., & Lagerberg, D. (2008). Expressive vocabulary in 18-month-old children in relation to demographic factors, mother and child characteristics, communication style and shared reading. *Child Care and Health Development, 34*(2), 257–266.

Wetherford, R. (2019). Francine Shapiro on the evolution of EMDR therapy. Psychotherapy.net Retrieved from https://www.psychotherapy.net/interview/francine-shapiro-emdr

Wheeler, M. A. (1995). Improvement in recall over time without repeated testing: Spontaneous recovery revisited. *Journal of Experimental Psychology: Learning, Memory, and Cognition, 21*, 173–184.

Whitbourne, S. K. (2002). *The aging individual: Physical and psychological perspectives* (2nd ed.). New York, NY: Springer.

White, H., Jubran, R., Heck, A., Chroust, A., & Bhatt, R. S. (2018). The role of shape recognition in figure/ground perception in infancy. *Psychonomic Bulletin & Review, 25*(4), 1381–1387. doi:10.3758/s13423-018-1476-z

White, R. W. (1975). *Lives in progress* (3rd ed.). New York, NY: Holt, Rinehart & Winston.

Whiting, B. B., & Edwards, C. P. (1988). *Children of different worlds.* Cambridge, MA: Harvard University Press.

Whitley, B. E., Jr. (1999). Right-wing authoritarianism, social dominance orientation, and prejudice. *Journal of Personality and Social Psychology, 77*, 126–134.

Whitney, P. (1986). Processing category terms in context: Instantiations as inferences. *Memory & Cognition, 14*, 39–48.

Whorf, B. L. (1956). Science and linguistics. In J. B. Carroll (Ed.), *Language, thought, and reality: Selected writings of Benjamin Lee Whorf* (pp. 207–219). Cambridge, MA: MIT Press.

Wickens, C. D., Hollands, J. G., Banbury, S., & Parasuraman, R. (2016). *Engineering psychology and human performance.* New York, NY: Routledge.

Wickens, C. D., Rice, S., Keller, D., Hutchins, S., Hughes, J., & Clayton, K. D. (2009). False alerts in air traffic control conflict alerting system: Is there a "cry wolf" effect? *Human Factors, 51*(4), 446–462.

Wickens, T. D. (2001). *Elementary signal detection theory.* New York, NY: Oxford University Press.

Wiens, A. N., & Menustik, C. E. (1983). Treatment outcome and patient characteristics in an aversion therapy program for alcoholism. *American Psychologist, 38*, 1089–1096.

Wiggins, J. S. (Ed.).(1996). *The five-factor model of personality: Theoretical perspectives.* New York, NY: Guilford.

Wilder, D. A. (1986). Social categorization: Implications for creation and reduction of intergroup bias. In L. Berkowitz (Ed.), *Advances in experimental social psychology* (Vol. 19, pp. 291–355). New York, NY: Academic.

Williams, D. R., & Sternthal, M. (2010). Understanding racial-ethnic disparities in health: Sociological contributions. *Journal of Health and Social Behavior, 51*(Suppl.), S15–S27. doi:10.1177/0022146510383838

Williams, J. M. G., Mathews, A., & MacLeod, C. (1996). The emotional Stroop task and psychopathology. *Psychological Bulletin, 120*, 3–24.

Williams, K. D., Cheung, C. K. T., & Choi, W. (2000). Cyberostracism: Effects of being ignored over the internet. *Journal of Personality and Social Psychology, 79*, 748–762.

Williams, K. D., Govan, C. L., Croker, V., Tynan, D., Cruickshank, M., & Lam, A. (2002). Investigations into differences between social- and cyberostracism. *Group Dynamics: Theory, Research, and Practice, 6*, 65–77.

Williams, M. T., Mugno, B., Franklin, M., & Faber, S. (2013). Symptom dimensions in obsessive-compulsive disorder: Phenomenology and treatment outcomes with exposure and ritual revention. *Psychopathology, 46*(6), 365–376.

Wilson, T. D., Houston, C. E., Brekke, N., & Etling, K. M. (1996). A new look at anchoring effects: Basic anchoring and its antecedents. *Journal of Experimental Psychology: General, 125*, 387–402.

Wimber, M., Alink, A., Charest, I., Kriegeskorte, N., & Anderson, M. C. (2015). Retrieval induces adaptive forgetting of competing memories via cortical pattern suppression. *Nature Neuroscience, 18*(4), 582–589. doi:10.1038/nn.3973

Windschitl, P. D. (1996). Memory for faces: Evidence of retrieval-based impairment. *Journal of Experimental Psychology: Learning, Memory, and Cognition, 22*, 1101–1122.

Wingenbach, T., Brosnan, M., Pfaltz, M. C., Peyk, P., & Ashwin, C. (2020). Perception of discrete emotions in others: Evidence for distinct facial mimicry patterns. *Scientific Reports, 10*(1), 4692. doi:10.1038/s41598-020-61563-5

Winokur, G., Coryell, W., Keller, M., Endicott, J., & Akiskall, H. S. (1993). A prospective follow-up of patients with bipolar and primary unipolar affective disorder. *Archives of General Psychiatry, 50*, 457–465.

Wise, R. A. (1996). Addictive drugs and brain stimulation reward. *Annual Review of Neuroscience, 19*, 319–340.

Wise, R. A. (2006). Role of brain dopamine in food reward and reinforcement. *Philosophical Transactions of the Royal Society B: Biological Sciences, 361*(1471), 1149–1158. doi:10.1098/rstb.2006.1854

Wise, R. A., Sartori, G., Magnussen, S., & Safer, M. A. (2014). An examination of the causes and solutions to eyewitness error. *Frontiers in Psychiatry, 5*, 102. doi:10.3389/fpsyt.2014.00102

Witelson, S. F., Kigar, D. L., & Harvey, T. (1999). The exceptional brain of Albert Einstein. *Lancet, 353*, 2149–2153.

Wittmann, M. (2015). Modulations of the experience of self and time. *Consciousness and Cognition, 38*, 172–181. doi:10.1016/j.concog.2015.06.008

Wixted, J. T., & Mickes, L. (2014). A signal-detection-based diagnostic-feature-detection model of eyewitness identification. *Psychological Review, 121*(2), 262–276.

Woidneck, M. R., Morrison, K. L., & Twohig, M. P. (2013). Acceptance and commitment therapy for the treatment of post-traumatic stress among adolescents. *Behavior Modification, 38*(4), 451–476.

Wolf, A., Renner, B., Tomazic, P. V., & Mueller, C. A. (2018). Gustatory function in patients with chronic rhinosinusitis. *Annals of Otology, Rhinology & Laryngology, 127*(4), 229–234. doi:10.1177/0003489418754583

Wolff, H. G., Weikamp, J. G., & Batinic, B. (2018). Implicit motives as determinants of networking behaviors. *Frontiers in Psychology, 9*, 411. doi:10.3389/fpsyg.2018.00411

Wolitzky-Taylor, K. B., Horowitz, J. D., Powers, M. B., & Telch, M. J. (2008). Psychological approaches in the treatment of specific phobias: A meta-analysis. *Clinical Psychology Review, 28*(6), 1021–1037. doi:10.1016/j.cpr.2008.02.007

Wolke, D., & Lereya, S. T. (2015). Long-term effects of bullying. *Archives of Disease in Childhood, 100*(9), 879–885. doi:10.1136/archdischild-2014-306667

Wolpe, J. (1958). *Psychotherapy by reciprocal inhibition*. Palo Alto, CA: Stanford University Press.

Wolpe, J. (1982). *The practice of behavior therapy* (3rd ed.). New York, NY: Pergamon.

Wolpow, R., Johnson, M. M., Hertel, R., & Kincaid, S. O. (2009). *The heart of learning and teaching: Compassion, resiliency, and academic success*. Office of Superintendent of Public Instruction, Compassionate Schools. Retrieved from http://www.k12.wa.us/compassionateschools/pubdocs/TheHeartofLearningandTeaching.pdf

Wolverton, B. (2019, February 21). As students struggle with stress and depression, colleges act as counselors. *New York Times*. Retrieved from https://www.nytimes.com/2019/02/21/education/learning/mental-health-counseling-on-campus.html

Wong, D. F., Wagner, H. N., Jr., Tune, L. E., Dannals, R. F., Pearlson, G. D., Links, J. M., . . . Gjedde, A. (1986). Positron emission tomography reveals elevated D-2 dopamine receptors in drug-naive schizophrenics. *Science, 234*, 1558–1563.

Wood, J. M., Lilienfeld, S. O., Nezworski, M. T., Garb, H. N., Allen, K. H., & Wildermuth, J. L. (2010). Validity of Rorschach Inkblot scores for discriminating psychopaths from nonpsychopaths in forensic populations: A meta-analysis. *Psychological Assessment, 22*(2), 336–349. doi:10.1037/a0018998

Wood, N. L., & Cowan, N. (1995). The cocktail parry phenomenon revisited: Attention and memory in the classic selective learning procedure of Cherry (1953). *Journal of Experimental Psychology: General, 124*, 243–262.

Wood, W. (2000). Attitude change: Persuasion and social influence. *Annual Review of Psychology, 51*, 539–570.

Wood, W., Wong, F. Y., & Chachere, J. G. (1991). Effects of media violence on viewers' aggression in unconstrained social interaction. *Psychological Bulletin, 109*, 371–383.

Woods, D. L., Arbogast, T., Doss, Z., Younus, M., Herron, T. J., & Yund, E. W. (2015). Aided and unaided speech perception by older hearing impaired listeners. *PLOS ONE, 10*(3):e0114922.

Woods, S. A., Patterson, F. C., Koczwara, A., & Sofat, J. A. (2016). The value of being a conscientious learner. *Journal of Workplace Learning, 28*(7), 424–434. doi:10.1108/jwl-10-2015-0073

Woodward, A. L., Markman, E. M., & Fitzsimmons, C. M. (1994). Rapid word-learning in 13- and 18-month-olds. *Developmental Psychology, 30*, 553–566.

Woodward, S. A., McManis, M. H., Kagan, J., Deldin, P., Snidman, N., Lewis, M., & Kahn, V. (2001). Infant temperament and the brainstem auditory evoked response in later childhood. *Developmental Psychology, 37*, 533–538.

Woog, A. (2008). *Jennifer Lopez: The great Hispanic heritage*. New York, NY: Chelsea House.

Wool, J., & Saragoza, P. (2012). Conflicting expert opinions concerning insanity. *Journal of the American Academy of Psychiatry and the Law, 40*(4), 581–583.

World Health Organization. (1948). *Preamble to the Constitution of the WHO as adopted by the International Health Conference*, New York, 19–22 June, 1946; signed on 22 July 1946 by the representatives of 61 States (Official Records of the World Health Organization, no. 2, p. 100) and entered into force on 7 April 1948.

World Health Organization. (2013, August 6). WHO releases guidance on mental health care after trauma. Retrieved from https://www.who.int/mediacentre/news/releases/2013/trauma_mental_health_20130806/en/

World Health Organization. (2019, July 4). Suicide data. Retrieved from https://www.who.int/mental_health/prevention/suicide/estimates/en/

World Health Organization. (2020). Controlling the global obesity epidemic. Retrieved from https://www.who.int/nutrition/topics/obesity/en/

Woudenberg, C. V., Voorendonk, E. M., Bongaerts, H., Zoet, H. A., Verhagen, M., Lee, C. W., . . . Jongh, A. D. (2018). Effectiveness of an intensive treatment programme combining prolonged exposure and eye movement desensitization and reprocessing for severe post-traumatic stress disorder. *European Journal of Psychotraumatology, 9*(1), 1487225. doi:10.1080/20008198.2018.1487225

Woytowicz, E. J., Sainburg, R. L., Westlake, K. P., & Whitall, J. (2020). Competition for limited neural resources in older adults leads to greater asymmetry of bilateral movements than in young adults. *Journal of Neurophysiology, 123*(4), 1295–1304. doi:10.1152/jn.00405.2019

Wrenn, J. M. (2012). TV stars, travel bloggers not immune to fear of flying. CNN. Retrieved from https://www.cnn.com/travel/article/fear-of-flying/index.html

Wright, K. P., & Czeisler, C. A. (2002). Absence of circadian phase resetting in response to bright light behind the knees. *Science, 297*, 571.

Wygant, D. B., & Lareau, C. R. (2015). Civil and criminal forensic psychological assessment: similarities and unique challenges. *Psychological Injury and Law, 8*(1), 11–26. doi:10.1007/s12207-015-9220-8

Wynn, K. (1992). Addition and subtraction by human infants. *Nature, 358*, 749–750.

Wynn, K. (1996). Infants' individuation and enumeration of actions. *Psychological Science, 7*, 164–169.

Wyrwicka, W., & Dobrzecka, C. (1960). Relationship between feeding and satiation centers of the hypothalamus. *Science, 132*, 805–806.

Xiong, A., & Proctor, R. W. (2018). Information processing: the language and analytical tools for cognitive psychology in the information age. *Frontiers in Psychology, 9*, 1270. doi:10.3389/fpsyg.2018.01270

Yagi, Y., & Inoue, K. (2018). The contribution of attention to the mere exposure effect for parts of advertising images. *Frontiers in Psychology, 9*, 1635. doi:10.3389/fpsyg.2018.01635

Yalom, I. D. (1989). *Love's executioner and other tales of psychotherapy*. New York, NY: HarperCollins.

Yan, J. (2017, September 15). Percentage of Americans taking antidepressants climbs. *Psychiatric News*. Retrieved from https://psychnews.psychiatryonline.org/doi/full/10.1176/appi.pn.2017.pp9b2

Yang, C., Sun, B., & Shanks, D. R. (2017). The anchoring effect in metamemory monitoring. *Memory & Cognition, 46*(3), 384–397. doi:10.3758/s13421-017-0772-6

Yang, H. C., & Schuler, T. A. (2009). Marital quality and survivorship: Slowed recovery for breast cancer patients in distressed relationships. *Cancer, 115*(1), 217–228. doi:10.1002/cncr.23964

Yang, Y. (2008). Long and happy living: Trends and patterns of happy life expectancy in the U.S., 1970–2000. *Social Science Research, 37*(4), 1235–1252. doi:10.1016/j.ssresearch.2007.07.004

Yaribeygi, H., Panahi, Y., Sahraei, H., Johnston, T. P., & Sahebkar, A. (2017). The impact of stress on body function: A review. *EXCLI Journal, 16*, 1057–1072. doi:10.17179/excli2017-480

Yau, J., & Smetana, J. G. (1996). Adolescent-parent conflict among Chinese adolescents in Hong Kong. *Child Development, 67*, 1262–1275.

Yeager, D. S., & Dweck, C. S. (2012). Mindsets that promote resilience: When students believe that personal characteristics can be developed. *Educational Psychologist, 47*(4), 302–314. doi:10.1080/00461520.2012.722805

Yeager, D. S., Hanselman, P., Walton, G. M., Murray, J. S., Crosnoe, R., Muller, C., . . . Dweck, C. S. (2019). A national experiment reveals where a growth mindset improves achievement. *Nature, 573*(7774), 364–369. doi:10.1038/s41586-019-1466-y

Yeh, V. M., Schnur, J. B., & Montgomery, G. H. (2014). Disseminating hypnosis to health care settings: Applying the RE-AIM framework. *Psychology of Consciousness (Washington, D.C.), 1*(2), 213–228.

Yoder, W. M., Larue, A. K., Rosen, J. M., Aggarwal, S., Shukla, R. M., Monir, J., & Smith, D. W. (2014). Evidence of rapid recovery from perceptual odor adaptation using a new stimulus paradigm. *Attention, Perception, & Psychophysics, 76*(4), 1093–1105. doi:10.3758/s13414-013-0620-0

Yoon, J., Ericsson, K. A., & Donatelli, D. (2018). Effects of 30 years of disuse on exceptional memory performance. *Cognitive Science, 42*, 884–903. doi:10.1111/cogs.12562

Young, T. (1802). On the theory of light and colors. *Philosophical Transactions of the Royal Society of London, 92*, 12–48.

Yu, D. W., & Shepard, G. H. (1998). Is beauty in the eye of the beholder? *Nature, 396*(6709), 321–322.

Yudofsky, S. C., & Hales, R. E. (Eds.).(2002). *American Psychiatric Press textbook of neuropsychiatry and clinical neurosciences*. Washington, DC: American Psychiatric Press.

Yurkovich, E. E., & Lattergrass, I. (2008). Defining health and unhealthiness: Perceptions held by Native American Indians with persistent mental illness. *Mental Health, Religion & Culture, 11*(5), 437–459. doi:10.1080/13674670701473751

Zajonc, R. B. (1965). Social facilitation. *Science, 149*, 269–274.

Zajonc, R. B. (1968). Attitudinal effects of mere exposure. *Journal of Personality and Social Psychology Monograph, 9*(2), 1–27.

Zajonc, R. B. (1984). On the primacy of affect. *American Psychologist, 39*, 117–123.

Zajonc, R. B. (2001). Mere exposure: A gateway to the subliminal. *Current Directions in Psychological Science, 10*, 224–228.

Zajonc, R. B. (1993). Brain temperature and subjective emotional experience. In M. Lewis & J. M. Haviland (Eds.), *Handbook of emotions* (pp. 209–220). New York, NY: Guilford.

Zajonc, R. B., Murphy, S. T., & Inglehart, M. (1989). Feeling and facial efference: Implications of the vascular theory of emotion. *Psychological Review, 96*, 395–416.

Zárate, M. A., Uleman, J. S., & Voils, C. I. (2001). Effects of culture and processing goals on the activation and binding of trait concepts. *Social Cognition, 19*, 295–323.

Zarbo, C., Tasca, G. A., Cattafi, F., & Compare, A. (2016). Integrative psychotherapy works. *Frontiers in Psychology, 6*, 2021. doi:10.3389/fpsyg.2015.02021

Zaval, L., Li, Y., Johnson, E. J., & Weber, E. U. (2015). Complementary contributions of fluid and crystallized intelligence to decision making across the life span. *Aging and Decision Making*, 149–168. doi:10.1016/b978-0-12-417148-0.00008-x

Zebrowitz, L. A., & Franklin, R. G. (2014). The attractiveness halo effect and the babyface stereotype in older and younger adults: Similarities, own-age accentuation, and older adult positivity effects. *Experimental Aging Research, 40*(3), 375–393. doi:10.1080/0361073x.2014.897151

Zeigler-Hill, V., Li, H., Masri, J., Smith, A., Vonk, J., Madson, M. B., & Zhang, Q. (2013). Self-esteem instability and academic outcomes in American and Chinese college students. *Journal of Research in Personality, 47*, 455–463. doi:10.1016/j.jrp.2013.03.010

Zeltins, A., West, J., Zabel, F., Turabi, A. E., Balke, I., Haas, S. . . . Bachmann, M. F. (2017). Incorporation of tetanus-epitope into virus-like particles achieves vaccine responses even in older recipients in models of psoriasis, Alzheimer's and cat allergy. *NPJ Vaccines, 2*, 30. doi:10.1038/s41541-017-0030-8

Zentall, T. R., Sutton, J. E., & Sherburne, L. M. (1996). True imitative learning in pigeons. *Psychological Science, 7*, 343–346.

Zentner, M., & Kagan, J. (1998). Infants' perception of consonance and dissonance in music. *Infant Behavior and Development, 21*, 483–492.

Zhai, Y. (2017). Values of deference to authority in Japan and China. *International Journal of Comparative Sociology, 58*(2), 120–139. doi:10.1177/0020715217694078

Zhang, L. L. (2015). Stereotypes of Chinese by American college students: Media use and perceived realism. *International Journal of Communication, 9*, 1–18.

Zhang, Y. B., Lin, M.-C., Nonaka, A., & Beom, K. (2005). Harmony, hierarchy and conservatism: A cross-cultural comparison of Confucian values in China, Korea, Japan, and Taiwan. *Communication Research Reports, 22*(2), 107–115. doi:10.1080/00036810500130539

Zhang, Y., Wang, Y., Shen, C., Ye, Y., Shen, S., Zhang, B., . . . Wang, W. (2017). Relationship between hypnosis and personality trait in participants with high or low hypnotic susceptibility. *Neuropsychiatric Disease and Treatment, 13*, 1007–1012. doi:10.2147/NDT.S134930

Zhang, Y., Wu, C., Chang, H., Yan, Q., Wu, L., Yuan, S., . . . Yu, Y. (2018). Genetic variants in oxytocin receptor gene (OXTR) and childhood physical abuse collaborate to modify the risk of aggression in Chinese adolescents. *Journal of Affective Disorders, 229*, 105–110. doi:10.1016/j.jad.2017.12.024

Zhao, S., Grasmuch, S., & Martin, J. (2008). Identity construction on Facebook: Digital empowerment in anchored relationships. *Computers in Human Behavior, 24*(5), 1816–1836.

Zhou, H., Zhou, Q., & Xu, L. (2016). Unilateral hippocampal inactivation or lesion selectively impairs remote contextual fear memory. *Psychopharmacology, 233* (19–20), 3639–3646. doi:10.1007/s00213-016-4394-7

Zhu, C., Huang, S., Evans, R., & Zhang, W. (2021). Cyberbullying among adolescents and children: A comprehensive review of the global situation, risk factors, and preventive measures. *Frontiers in Public Health, 9*, 634909. doi:10.3389/fpubh.2021.634909

Zigler, E. (1987). Formal schooling for 4-year-olds? No. *American Psychologist, 42*, 254–260.

Zimmerman, A., Bai, L., & Ginty, D. D. (2014). The gentle touch receptors of mammalian skin. *Science, 346*(6212), 950–954. doi:10.1126/science.1254229

Zola-Morgan, S. (1995). Localization of brain function: The legacy of Franz Gall (1758–1828). *Annual Review of Neuroscience, 18*, 359–383.

Zoroya, G. (1999, November 18). Passengers behaving badly.*USA Today*.

Zou, J. Y., Park, D. S., Burchard, E. G., Torgerson, D. G., Pino-Yanes, M., Song, Y. S., . . . & Zaitlen, N. (2015). Genetic and socioeconomic study of mate choice in Latinos reveals novel assortment patterns. *Proceedings of the National Academy of Sciences USA, 112*(44), 13621–13626. doi:10.1073/pnas.1501741112

Zuckerman, M., Li, C., & Hall, J. A. (2016). When men and women differ in self-esteem and when they don't: A meta-analysis. *Journal of Research in Personality, 64*, 34–51. doi:10.1016/j.jrp.2016.07.007

Zunic, A., Corcoran, P., & Spasic, I. (2020). Sentiment analysis in health and well-being: Systematic review. *JMIR Medical Informatics, 8*(1):e16023. doi:10.2196/16023

NAME INDEX

Ackerman, Diane, 108
Adams, Gerald, 500
Adams, Marilyn, 242
Adams, Neal, 98
Adams, Paul, 500
Adams, Russell, 357
Agostini, Evan, 551
Ainsworth, Mary, 16, 370
Ali, Muhammad, 79, 350, 439
Allen, Ian, 197
Allenden, Ian, 62
Amabile, Teresa, 203
Aserinksy, Eugene, 141
Asher, Jay, 407
Atwood, Margaret, 283–84
Auburtin, Ernest, 68
Aurelius, Marcus, 481
Austen, Jane, 282
Axtell, Daniel G., 48

Barbour, Scott, 217
Barnier, Amanda, 156
Bass, Ellen, 581
Bell, Kristen, 534
Berkman, Lisa, 515
Bieber, Justin, 237
Bizzotto, Milla, 451
Bleuler, Eugene, 560
Bohannon, Brian, 414
Bolles, Robert, 200
Bouchard, Sylvie, 303
Bourdain, Anthony, 534
Brady, Tom, 77
Breland, Marian, 199
Brown, Alan, 237
Brown, Michael, 14
Brown, Roger, 233
Brown, Walter, 496
Bruner, Jerome S., 124
Burns, John, 510
Bush, George W., 22

Camazine, Scott, 45
Carrey, Jim, 534
Carskadon, Mary, 149
Carver, Charles, 512
Cerletti, Ugo, 608
Cheney, Dorothy, 26
Cherry, Colin, 133
Chomsky, Noam, 269, 272
Cioffi, Delia, 509
Clapton, Eric, 106
Clearfield, Melissa, 361
Cobain, Kurt, 534
Coie, John, 373

Coile, Caroline, 35
Connor, Kris, 283
Cotton, Ronald, 246
Courage, Mary, 357
Cousins, Norman, 496
Crick, Francis, 352
Crocker, Jennifer, 328
Crow, Sheryl, 534
Crowe, Russell, 560
Czeisler, Charles, 139–40

Dack, Simon, 545
Damon, William, 377
Davison, Kathryn, 600
Dawn, Walter, 190
Deacon, Terrence, 269
DeGeneres, Ellen, 98, 534
Delevingne, Cara, 534
Deniker, Pierre, 603
Dipasupil, Dia, 283
Dix, Dorothea, 454
Dollard, John, 424
Dorsett, Sybil, 564
Dray, Luke, 427
Dubovsky, Steven, 495
Dumper, Kathryn, 231

Elfenbein, Hillary, 472
Elliot, Jane, 296
Elmore, Steven, 562
Etchart, Julio, 219
Everson, Susan, 514

Falk, Sam, 198
Farnham, Shelly, 329
Feingold, Russell, 14
Fisher, Carrie, 552
Floyd, George, 15, 439
Folkman, Susan, 509
Frazier, Julie, 287
Fridlund, Alan, 470
Furr, Susan, 538

Gabrieli, John, 225
Gaye, Marvin, 237
Genovese, Kitty, 427
Gibbons, Frederick, 380
Gilbert, Daniel, 400
Goldhagen, Daniel, 412
Gonzales, Amy, 515
Goodall, Jane, 26
Gopnik, Alison, 357
Gotzsche, Peter, 496

Graveline, Yvette, 149
Graves, Anthony, 586
Gray, Freddie, 14
Gray-Little, Bernadette, 328
Gross, Larry, 457
Gross, Terry, 276
Guyer, Melvin, 312

Hafdahl, Adam, 328
Haidt, John, 377
Haith, Marshall, 358
Hamrick, Natalie, 516
Handel, George Frideric, 552
Haney, Craig, 586
Harris, Kamala, 440
Healy, David, 603
Hefner, Hugh, 542
Heller, Joseph, 270
Higgins, Tory, 330, 338
Hobbes, Thomas, 4, 39
Holloway, James, 509
Hoover, Joseph, 15
Horn, John, 281–82
House, James, 515
Hupka, Ralph, 481
Hustace, Billy, 22
Hutton, Kurt, 609

Ironson, Gail, 500
Ives, Thomas, 138

Jacklin, Carol, 290
Jackson, Jesse, 439
James, LeBron, 227
James, William, 5–6, 9, 16, 39, 133, 136, 238, 357, 466, 469
Jefferson, Thomas, 280, 481
Jemison, Mae, 282
Jendrny, Paula, 107
Jenner, Kendall, 416
Jones, Jim, 412
Judd, Ashley, 534

Kamen, Dean, 282–83
Karni, Avi, 75
Kashy, Deborah, 462
Kavanaugh, Brett, 213
Kaysen, Susanna, 533
Ken, Carol, 461
Kennedy, Rosemary, 529
Kerouac, Jack, 167
Khayyam, Omar, 282
Kilgour, Andrea, 110
King, Martin Luther, Jr., 284, 439
Kleinke, Chris, 473
Kline, Paul, 282
Kuhl, Patricia, 357

Lacombe, Arlene, 231
Lady Gaga, 534
Lanzano, Louis, 397
Lederman, Susan, 110
Leen, Nina, 195, 369
Lichtman, Steven, 460
Linden, David, 110
Longden, Eleanor, 592
Lopez, Jennifer, 440
Lovato, Demi, 552
Lovett, Marilyn, 231
Lutz, William, 273

Maccoby, Eleanor, 290, 372
Mackavey, William, 248
Mandolesi, Laura, 511 284, 439
Maslow, Abraham, 8, 326, 331, 338, 345, 453
Maurer, Charles, 358
Maurer, Daphne, 358
McClendon, David, 432
McConkey, Kevin, 156
McCormick, David, 231
McDermott, Kathleen, 212
McNew, David, 155, 398
Mehdizadeh, Soraya, 515
Meichenbaum, Donald, 591
Meltzoff, Andrew, 357, 359
Merzenich, Michael, 76
Millington, Ollie, 419
Minturn, Leigh, 124
Mita, Theodore, 403
Mix, Kelly, 361
Molaison, Henry, 229
Monroe, Marilyn, 555
Münsterberg, Hugo, 4
Myerson, Joel, 289

Nasar, Sylvia, 560
Nasim Najafi Aghdam, 422
Newcomb, Andrew, 372
Nix, Walter, 414

O'Connor, Shawn, 462
Ogborn, Louise, 413–14, 444
O'Neill, Eugene, 552
Osaka, Naomi, 217

Pappenheim, Bertha, 578
Parant, Dimitri, 99
Pavlov, Ivan, 1, 6, 9, 178, 188
Perlmutter, Marion, 231
Perry, Katy, 534
Pert, Candace, 56
Phares, Jerry, 201
Pickrell, Jacqueline, 581
Pinel, John, 459

Pissarova, Marina, 121
Pizzello, Chris, 552
Plath, Sylvia, 552
Poole, Bobby, 246

Quartana, Phillip, 510

Rapaport, David, 315
Raynor, Rosalie, 7, 186
Reaves, Michael, 283
Reiser, Martin, 157
Rentz, Lee, 140
Rips, Lance, 258
Roberson, Jeff, 501
Robson, David, 274
Rock, Irvin, 126
Rogers, Carl, 8, 326–27, 334, 338, 344, 593–94
Rolls, Barbara, 16
Rovee-Collier, Carolyn, 234, 358, 361
Rush, Benjamin, 576

Sachs, Jacqueline, 226
Sakuma, Paul, 582
Salé, Jamie, 476
Sandstrom, Marlene, 373
Schaie, Warner, 281
Schanberg, Saul, 370
Scheier, Michael, 512
Seaman, Tricia, 451
Sellers, Robert M., 16
Seyfarth, Robert, 26
Shereshevskii, Solomon, 239
Shockey, Gwen, 109
Silver, Eric, 558
Simons, Daniel, 242
Sinton, Christopher M., 59
Skeel, Alex, 422
Skoog, Gunnar, 549
Skoog, Ingmar, 549
Snarey, John, 376
Snyder, Evan, 554
Snyder, Solomon, 56
Spade, Kate, 534
Sternbach, Robert, 496

Stone, Arthur, 506
Stone, Jeff, 296
Strawbridge, William, 516
Stubblefield, Katie, 539
Stunkard, Albert, 459
Stupak, Bart, 440
Syme, Leonard, 515

Tama, Mario, 397
Terrazes, Jacob, 426
Thatcher, Robert, 368
Theeuwes, Jan, 134
Thicke, Robin, 237
Titchener, Edward, 4
Tomasikiewicz, Amanda, 474
Townshend, Pete, 106
Treanor, Peter, 599
Trevor Noah, 440
Turiel, Eliot, 375
Twain, Mark, 58, 143, 552
Tweed, Michael, 473

Uchino, Bert, 515
Ungerleider, Leslie, 75
Ut, Nick, 473

Vaccaro, Tony, 283
Vallecillos, Lucas, 85
Vallee, Bert, 162
Visintainer, Madeline, 507
Vosniadou, Stella, 363

Walk, Richard, 122
Walther, Eva, 189
Wamsley, Erin, 149
Wason, Peter, 266
Watson, John, 6–7, 39, 185, 320–21
Wax, Amy, 295
Webster, Donna, 402
Weisz, John, 530
Wiebe, David, 263
Wilkinson, Kendra, 542
Worth, Jordan, 422

SUBJECT INDEX

Abnormal psychology, 160, 536
Academic performance, 18, 278, 280, 293, 296, 299, 547
Acetylcholine, 55–56, 81, 83, 231
Achievement motivation, 136, 463, 465, 484, 487
Acquisition of language, 8, 269, 272
Action potentials, 54, 81
Activation-synthesis theory, 145, 148–49, 170, 172
Adolescence, 248, 253, 286, 330–31, 347, 351, 373–75, 377, 379–80, 382, 386, 389, 391–93
Adulthood, 10, 27, 343–44, 347, 351, 373–74, 381, 383–84, 386, 389, 391–92
   late, 281, 386, 389
   young, 286, 368, 386
Affluence, 433–34, 446, 482
African American students, 294–95
Afterimages, 99–100, 128, 130
Aggression, 11, 13, 27–28, 30–31, 34–35, 64, 396, 398, 421–26, 431, 442, 444–45, 447
Aging, 2, 37, 41, 98, 382–84, 386, 392
Agoraphobia, 541, 543, 568, 571, 583
Agreeableness, 304, 335–36, 340, 345
AIDS, 166, 189, 354, 512, 595, 600–601
Alcohol, 59, 64, 139–40, 150–51, 161–65, 167, 171, 354–56, 380, 384, 505, 507, 585
Alcohol consumption, 164, 355, 491, 585
Alcoholics Anonymous, 595–96
Alcoholism, 35, 354–55, 512, 585, 596, 600–601
Algorithms, 34, 261–62, 264, 296–97, 301
Alfred Binet, 6, 13, 276
Altered states of consciousness, 161–62, 171–72
Altruism, 11, 398, 421, 426–27, 430, 444, 446–47
Alzheimer's disease, 35, 56, 79, 81, 166, 230–31, 236, 384, 392–93, 498, 506
American Psychiatric Association, 149–51, 460, 528, 530–33, 535, 544, 546–47, 553, 555, 612
American Psychological Association (APA), 4–6, 9, 16, 32–33, 35–36, 140–41, 154, 158, 305, 494, 499, 597–99, 602
Amphetamines, 163, 165, 167, 171, 561
Amplitude, 59, 91, 102–3, 106, 127–28
Amygdala, 64, 69, 82–83, 146, 184, 230–31, 467–68, 477–78, 485
Anchoring effects, 267–68, 298, 301
Anger, 64, 371, 388, 466, 468–74, 477, 479, 481, 483, 485–86, 504, 577, 579
Animal behavior, 5, 10, 26, 175, 207–8
Animal intelligence, 7, 190
Animal research, 7, 34, 35, 122, 183, 209, 355, 467, 477
Anorexia nervosa, 460, 484, 487, 530
Antianxiety drugs, 603–4, 606, 612–13
Antidepressants, 496, 569, 573, 591, 604–7, 612–13
Antipsychotic drugs, 561, 604, 606, 609, 612–13
Antisocial personality disorder, 531, 555–56, 566, 569–71
Anxiety, 163–66, 312, 315, 318, 327–30, 342–43, 510–11, 516, 527–28, 530–31, 540–42, 545, 547–48, 550–51, 555, 567–68, 583–84, 587–89, 591, 603
Anxiety disorders, 525, 531, 533, 540–41, 545, 549, 551, 568, 583, 590, 597
APA. *See* American Psychological Association

Applied research, 9, 39, 42
Archival research, 22, 40, 42
Arousal, 49, 56–57, 62–63, 69, 82, 420, 425, 467–70, 474–76, 481, 484–86, 499
   autonomic, 467, 469, 474, 481, 485
Arousal theory, 453, 465, 484, 487
Assimilation, 244, 363, 390, 393
Association cortex, 66–67, 82–83
Association for Humanistic Psychology, 326
Association for Psychological Science, 16, 36
Association for Women in Psychology, 16
Attachment, 369–72, 390–91, 393
Attitude change, 414–15, 445
Attraction, 11, 136, 317, 359, 398, 403–4, 444, 472
Attractiveness halo effect, 405
Attributions, 399–401, 444, 447, 464, 475–76, 486, 514
Auditory inputs, 69–70, 216, 221
Auditory localization, 104–5, 128, 130
Auditory nerve, 103–5, 114, 128
Auditory system, 91, 103, 105
Authority, 13, 156, 245, 317, 337, 376, 396–97, 412–14, 419, 444–45
Autobiographical memory, 211, 247–50, 253–54, 389, 392
Autonomic nervous system, 49, 65, 67, 80, 82–83, 92, 456, 467–69
Availability heuristic, 267–68, 298, 301
Aversion therapy, 585, 611, 613
Award for Outstanding Lifetime Contribution to psychology, 195
Awareness, 132–33, 135–36, 167, 169, 174, 232, 235–36, 308, 312, 318, 344, 364, 472, 509–10, 563
Axons, 53–55, 57, 63, 77–78, 80–81, 83, 95–96, 103, 108

Barbiturates, 163–64, 167, 171, 603, 606
Basic types of emotions, 468, 479
Basic units of personality, 334–35, 345
Behavior, 6–12, 20–23, 25–27, 37–42, 53–55, 57–59, 160–62, 174–76, 190–93, 195–202, 204–9, 319–26, 340–45, 372–73, 399–400, 407–9, 444–46, 452–53, 504–8, 528–31
   abnormal, 11, 527, 530
   aggressive, 205, 395, 421, 425, 447
   antisocial, 424, 557
   attitude-discrepant, 416–18
   attribute, 400
   bizarre, 18, 606
   compulsive, 525, 549, 569
   desirable, 196, 586, 611
   destructive, 556, 566, 569
   distressing, 611
   expressive, 466, 470, 474, 478–79, 485
   goal-directed, 189, 208
   health-related, 490
   healthy, 324, 492
   helping, 421, 426, 446
   ineffective, 261
   instinctual, 175, 452
   maladaptive, 189, 530, 567, 582, 589
   observable, 3, 7–8, 39, 320, 326, 532
   observed, 410, 429

Behavior (*Continued*)
   operant, 197, 199
   past, 22, 40, 325
   people's, 304, 444
   person's, 154, 399, 444, 463
   predetermined, 26
   reward-seeking, 56
   sleep-related, 150
   unhealthful, 507, 516
Behavioral changes, 353, 395, 407, 460
Behavioral-confirmation biases, 402-3, 444
Behavioral expressions of emotion, 470, 485
Behavioral neuroscience, 37, 41-42, 45-83, 231, 382, 456, 467, 606
Behavioral observations, 20, 22, 40, 42, 325, 344
Behavioral therapies, 576, 582, 587, 591-92, 611, 613
Behavior change, 209
Behavior control, 58, 195
Behavior in response to social norms, 445
Behavior in response to social pressure, 414
Behaviorism, 6-9, 39, 42, 183, 207, 320-21, 326, 530
Behavior modification, 199, 582
Behavior of laboratory animals, 190
Behavior patterns, 321, 528
Behavior springs, 342, 345
Beliefs, 11-12, 211, 213, 223, 265, 287-88, 324, 327, 344-45, 402-3, 436, 446, 492, 559, 588-90
   cultural, 288, 545, 568
   existing, 402, 441
   false, 403, 442, 553, 559, 566, 569
Belongingness, 331, 453-54, 461, 484
Beneficence, 32-33, 42
Benzodiazepines, 163-64, 167, 171, 603, 606, 612
Biases, 127, 246, 250, 255, 257, 265-68, 275, 280, 393, 399-400, 402, 443-45, 446
Binge-eating disorder, 460, 484, 487
Biofeedback, 49, 199, 586-88, 611, 613
Biological perspective, 10, 39, 42
Biological rhythms, 137, 161, 170, 172
Biomedical model, 491-92, 518, 521
Biopsychosocial model, 112, 489, 491, 497, 518, 521
Bipolar disorder, 533-34, 547, 552-55, 564, 569, 571, 602, 605-6, 608, 612
Black patients, 442
Blind spots, 95-96, 127, 130, 260, 264, 268, 297, 300
Bloomberg Healthiest Country Index, 385, 520
BMI (body mass index), 322, 457-59
Body dissatisfaction, 328, 330
Body fat, 457, 484
Body image, 66, 374, 382, 391
Body mass index. *See* bmi
Body's response to stress, 519
Body temperature, 21, 49, 137-38, 456, 470
Body weight, 33, 456, 459
Borderline personality disorder, 555-56, 566, 569-71
Brain and behavior, 37, 41, 58-59, 97, 100, 105, 108, 143, 603
Brain damage, 23, 58, 74, 76-77, 81, 236, 284, 355, 384
Brain disorders, 77, 235
   degenerative, 56
   irreversible, 384
   progressive, 384
   rare, 467
Brain structures, 58, 60, 75, 113, 467, 485
Brain tissue, 48, 65, 105, 384, 562
Brain-wave patterns, 140, 177, 510, 565, 586

Breuer, 307, 422, 510, 578
Broca's area, 68-69, 73, 82-83
Building blocks of personality, 334-35, 345
Bulimia nervosa, 460, 484, 487, 530
Bystander effect, 427-30, 446-47
Bystander intervention, 427-28, 446

Canadian Psychological Association. *See* CPA
Cancer, 135, 137, 489, 491, 495, 498, 505, 507-8, 511-12, 514-15, 530, 533, 595
Caregivers, 19-20, 33, 195-98, 206, 210, 309-10, 362, 367, 370-72, 377, 379
   primary, 364, 368-69, 391
Carl Rogers, 8, 326-27, 334, 338, 344, 593-94
Case studies, 23, 31, 40, 42, 47, 58, 64, 122, 129, 216, 236
Catatonic behavior, 560, 569
CBT (cognitive-behavioral therapy), 591-92, 596, 598, 611, 613
Central nervous system. *See* CNS
Cerebellum, 62-63, 75, 82-83, 113, 231
Cerebral cortex, 62, 64-67, 69, 80-83, 128, 161, 230-31, 467-68, 478, 485, 562
Cerebral lateralization, 71-72, 82-83
CHD (coronary heart disease), 465, 504-5, 512, 519
Cheap-necklace problem, 263, 266
Cheating, 32, 146, 579
Chemical treatment for psychological disorders, 574
Chemotherapy treatments, 184, 189
Child development researchers, 8, 273, 342
Childhood, 146, 149, 284, 286, 311, 314, 361-62, 373-74, 386, 389-91, 548, 557, 560
Childhood experiences, 247, 546
Childhood friendships, 379
Childhood memories, 247, 251
   false, 247
   inaccurate, 581
Chinese culture, 287
Chromosomes, 336, 351-52, 389, 393
Chunking, 218-20, 225, 241, 252, 254
Circadian rhythm, 137-38, 140, 161, 170, 172
Classical conditioning, 173, 178-91, 193, 197, 200, 207-10, 231, 236, 320, 541, 543, 582-83, 585
Clients, 17, 308, 326-27, 570, 576-77, 584, 588-95, 597-99, 601-2, 610-11, 613
Clinical case studies, 58, 72, 81, 527
Clinical neuroscience, 37, 41
Clinical perspective, 12, 40, 42
Clinical psychologists, 12-13, 24, 90, 305, 498, 526, 532, 558, 575, 577, 591
Clinical researchers, 597
Clinicians, 36, 442, 526, 528, 532, 547, 552-53, 592, 598-600, 602
CNS (central nervous system), 49, 52, 56-57, 79-81, 83, 92, 110, 163, 165, 171, 236
Cocaine, 161-67, 171, 307, 354-55
Cochlea, 87, 103-5, 115, 128
Cocktail party phenomenon, 133-34, 169, 172
Cognition, 8, 12, 39, 42, 245, 358, 368-69, 474, 477, 591-93, 598
Cognitive-behavioral therapy. *See* CBT
Cognitive development, 271, 362-69, 375-76, 381, 390-91
Cognitive dissonance, 416-17, 445, 447
Cognitive factors in emotion, 474, 485
Cognitive map, 200-202, 231
Cognitive neuroscience, 37, 41, 61
Cognitive social-learning approach, 303, 306, 319, 325, 341

Cognitive social-learning theory, 319, 322, 325, 342–44, 346, 530
Cognitive stages, 8–9, 363
Cognitive therapy, 551, 576, 589–91, 598, 601, 607, 611, 613
Collectivism, 431–34, 446–47
Color vision, 4, 95, 98–101, 127–28
Combat, 402, 415, 500–501, 503
Communication, 42, 51, 55, 269–70, 298, 301, 346, 351, 379, 442, 461–62
Community relations officer (CROs), 448
Complete loss of memory, 563, 570
Comprehension, 67–69, 82, 277
Comprehension of language, 68–69, 82
Compulsions, 337, 549–51, 569
Computerized tomography. *See* CT
Concrete operational stage, 365–66, 390, 393
Conditional positive regard, 326–27, 345–46
Conditioned response. *See* CR
Conditioned stimulus. *See* CS
Conditioning, 7, 173, 180–81, 186–87, 189, 191, 209, 543
Conduct, 22, 31–34, 38, 432, 577
Confederate flag, 187, 439
Confirmation biases, 265, 268, 296, 298, 301
Conformity, 11, 379, 391, 408–11, 414, 444–45, 448
Conscientiousness, 304–5, 335, 340, 342, 345
Consciousness, 4–5, 10, 76, 82, 131–72, 214–15, 217, 221, 319, 491, 495, 509–10, 549–50
Control group, 29–31, 41–42, 114, 137, 235, 293, 409, 417–18, 488, 511
    no-treatment, 150
Controlled research, 155, 317, 344
Controlled studies, 552, 575, 589, 600
Control of habitual behaviors, 551
Control subjects, 114, 156, 159–60, 235, 246, 305, 443–44, 552–53, 555, 588, 597
    healthy elderly, 236
    normal, 235
    no-treatment, 597–98
Cornea, 92–93, 101, 127, 130
Coronary heart disease. *See* CHD
Corporal punishment, 196
Corporations, 443–45, 557
Corpus callosum, 62, 69–72, 82–83
Correctional treatment specialist, 520
Correlational studies, 23, 27, 30–31, 40, 42, 232, 422, 425
Correlations, 27–28, 31, 40, 42, 279–80, 282, 304, 424–25, 488, 511–12, 516
    positive, 27
Cortex, 64–69, 104, 107–8, 114, 128, 138, 145–46, 148, 468, 478, 485
    auditory, 66, 73, 75, 104, 128, 360
Cost-benefit trade-offs of medical interventions for psychological disorders, 573, 603
Counterfactual thinking, 474, 476–78, 486–87
CPA (Canadian Psychological Association), 36, 597–98, 611
CR (conditioned response), 179–83, 185–86, 188–89, 193, 208, 210, 320, 585
CROs (community relations officer), 448
Cross-cultural studies, 122, 369, 481, 568
Crystallized intelligence, 281–82, 299, 301, 389
CS (conditioned stimulus), 179–83, 185–89, 193, 208, 210, 320, 585
CT (computerized tomography), 60, 81, 83, 442, 534
Cultural differences in emotion, 480
Cultural influences, 397–448, 568
Cultural orientations, 432–34, 448
Culture-bound syndromes, 530, 567, 571

Cultures, 10–11, 38, 108–9, 184, 273–75, 280–81, 284, 290, 367–70, 373, 376, 386–88, 404–6, 431–38, 444–46, 457–58, 479–82, 530–31, 568–69, 607
    collectivistic, 400–401
    gender-equal, 290–91
    individualistic, 329, 399–401, 433, 435
    non-individualistic, 400

Deaf children, 272
Death, 14, 56, 146–47, 188, 267, 308–9, 316–18, 382, 387–89, 397–98, 429, 490–91, 498–500, 503–4, 527–28, 537, 540
Deception, 26, 33–34, 41–42
Declarative memory, 227–28, 252, 254
Defense mechanisms, 312–13, 315, 318, 343–44, 346, 530
Delusions, 531, 553, 559–61, 566, 569, 571, 575, 592–93, 604, 606
Dementia, 230, 305, 384, 392
Demographics, 25, 37, 546, 573–74
Dendrites, 52–55, 75, 77, 80–81, 83, 108, 362
Denial, 76, 312, 318–19, 344, 346, 388, 392
Department of Health and Human Services, 164, 535
Dependent variable, 29–30, 41–42
Depression, 21, 24–25, 38, 55–57, 328–30, 388, 490, 492, 511, 516, 526–28, 533–40, 547–48, 552–53, 566–69, 588–91, 598, 605, 608–9
    experienced, 538
    oriented psychologists trace, 537
    research linking, 612
Depressive disorders, 525, 531, 533–34, 538, 552, 567
    minor, 538
Depressive explanatory style, 537, 567, 571
Depressive symptoms, 330–31
Depth perception, 85, 120, 122, 129–30
Descriptive studies, 23, 31, 40, 42
Development, 2, 4, 185–86, 229, 309, 311, 348–51, 353–54, 356, 358, 361–69, 381–83, 386–91, 494–95, 593
    healthy, 372, 377
    human, 39, 75, 301, 309, 349–50, 386
    interpersonal relationship, 130, 210, 254
Developmental changes, 282, 361, 392
Developmental perspective, 10, 12, 40, 42
Developmental psychology, 37, 349–50, 393
Diagnosis, 33, 39, 527, 531–33, 535, 556, 558, 563–64, 566–67, 570–71, 577, 592–93
Dichotic listening task, 133–34, 169
Diet, 28, 374–75, 381–82, 459–60, 484, 490, 492, 507, 510, 513, 518
Difference thresholds, 90, 127
Diffusion of responsibility, 428, 446–47
Discipline, 2, 4–5, 9, 11–13, 18, 37–39, 132, 196, 317, 489
Discrimination, 11–13, 16, 180, 182, 185, 197, 208–10, 320, 435–36, 438, 443–445, 446–48, 494
Discriminative stimulus, 196–97, 204, 209–10
Disease Control and Prevention Vietnam Experience Study, 500
Disgust, 21, 184, 445, 466, 468–73, 477, 479, 481, 483, 486
Dislikes, 108, 180, 187, 189, 332, 437
Disordered thoughts, 529, 582, 591
Disorders, 151–52, 525–27, 529–33, 540–42, 545–46, 549, 551–53, 555–59, 562–63, 565–70, 575, 583, 591, 602–3, 607, 611–13
    autism spectrum, 582, 587, 602
    behavioral, 196, 321
    degenerative nerve, 79
    substance abuse, 526
Displacement, 269–70, 296, 298, 301, 426
Dissociation, 159–61, 171–72, 232, 236, 564, 566

Dissociative amnesia, 563–64, 566, 570–71
Dissociative disorders, 243, 531, 555, 563–64, 570–71
Dissociative fugue, 564, 566, 570–71
Dissociative identity disorder, 531–32, 559, 563–66, 570–71
Divided attention, 134–35, 169, 172
DNA, 158, 351–52, 389, 393, 561
Dopamine, 56, 79, 81, 83, 165, 232, 554, 561, 605–6
Dreams, 2, 5–6, 132–33, 137, 143, 146–49, 152, 167, 169–70, 172, 307–8, 312–13, 320, 578, 610–11
Drugs, 9–10, 34–35, 55–56, 163–66, 171, 188, 307, 354–55, 375–76, 496, 507–8, 536, 540–42, 585, 603–7, 612
    chemotherapy, 188–89
    illicit, 156, 161, 163, 166
    mind-altering, 162, 169
    mood-stabilizing, 605–6
Drug therapies, 603, 607–8, 612–13
DSM-5, 528, 530–33, 546–47, 552–53, 555–56, 567, 571, 602
DSM-IV, 532, 564
Dualism, 4, 39, 42, 491, 497, 521

Early intervention systems, 443–45
Eating disorders, 38, 374, 452, 454, 460–61, 484, 486, 530, 590, 605
Ebbinghaus, 6, 220, 225, 232, 239–41, 247, 253
Echoic memory, 211, 215–16, 251, 254
Educational Testing Service (ETS), 278
Education Northwest, 547
Edward Thorndike, 5–7, 261–62
EEG, 59–60, 83, 141–43, 587
Efferent neuron, 52
Einstein's brain, 58, 75
Electroconvulsive therapy, 603, 608, 612–13
Embryo, 353–54, 356, 389–90, 393
EMDR, 588, 611, 613
EMDR therapy, 588
Emotional responses, 62, 251, 468, 485
Emotional states, 72, 234, 355, 473, 476–77, 485
    negative, 491, 504, 507–8, 511
Emotion-focused coping, 509, 519
Emotions, 10, 12, 34, 48–49, 62, 64–65, 67, 82, 149, 451–87, 509–10, 559–60, 566, 588, 605–6
    basic, 65, 471–72, 479, 481, 483, 485
    negative, 64, 163, 196, 199, 424, 445, 468, 472–73
Endocrine system, 50–51, 57, 65, 80, 83
Endorphins, 56–57, 81, 83, 128, 496
ENIGMA Bipolar Disorder Working Group, 554
Environment, 7–8, 12, 19, 133, 190–91, 234–35, 275, 286–88, 298–301, 325, 336, 344, 368, 392, 434–35
    new, 177, 602
    quiet, 339
Environmental factors, 10, 287, 297, 300, 330, 343, 374, 519, 528, 536, 548
Epinephrine, 49, 232, 466, 468–69, 475–76
Ethics, 13, 32, 34, 340, 609, 613
Ethnographies, 481
ETS (Educational Testing Service), 278
Exercise, 27–28, 30, 322, 324, 457, 460, 491–92, 494, 503–5, 507, 509–11, 514, 516, 518
Exhaustion, 502–3, 508, 519, 541
Expectations, 124, 129, 204, 206, 293–94, 323–24, 492, 496–97, 518, 530, 537
    parental, 287–88
    person's, 293, 496

Experimental group, 29–30, 41, 43, 409, 488
Experimental interventions, 58
Experimental psychology, 83, 220, 224, 240, 245, 268
Experimenter, 89, 131–32, 137, 141–42, 173–74, 212, 245–47, 266–67, 395–96, 408–9, 412, 417, 427–29
Experiments, 7–8, 28–31, 41–42, 64, 174, 177–79, 208, 212–13, 241–42, 247, 296, 396, 411–12, 417, 424–27, 467, 473
    controlled, 383, 410
Explanatory styles, 512–14, 520, 538
Explicit memory, 232–35, 243, 252, 254
Exposure effect, 136, 403, 444, 450
External locus of control, 202–3, 319, 323, 492
Extinction, 180–81, 185, 192–94, 196, 208–10, 320, 583, 588
Extraversion, 304–6, 335, 338–39, 345

Facebook, 18, 329–30, 411, 515
Facial electromyograph, 472–73, 478, 485, 487
Facial expressions, 358, 368, 467, 470–73, 477–78, 480, 485–86, 539, 566
Factor analysis, 335, 338, 345
Fallopian tube, 352–53, 356, 389
False memories, 158, 171, 212, 244, 246–47, 581
Familiarity, 119, 121, 236–37, 403, 444
Family therapies, 595, 611, 613
Fantasy measure, 463, 484
FAS (fetal alcohol syndrome), 354–55, 390, 393
Fear, 64–65, 177, 184–86, 210, 267, 399, 419, 466–72, 474–75, 478–79, 481, 485–86, 541–45, 558, 568, 582–84, 588, 592–93
    intense, 184, 541, 544–45
    irrational, 186, 314, 542, 551
Fear response, 467, 548, 588, 611
    context-dependent, 234
Feature detectors, 96, 98, 127, 130
Fertility, 347, 353, 356, 382, 386, 390, 392
Fetal alcohol syndrome. See FAS
Fetus, 136, 353–56, 389–90, 393
Field research, 20, 40, 43
First impressions, 9, 189, 293, 398, 401–3, 444
Five-factor model, 335–36, 341, 345–46
Fixed action patterns, 175–76, 207–8, 210
Flashbulb memories, 249, 253–54
Flooding, 583, 588, 611, 613
Fluid intelligence, 281, 299, 301, 389
Forgetting curve, 239–40, 244, 253–54
Fraternal twins, 286, 356, 459, 483, 536, 553, 561
Free recall, 223, 235, 238, 252, 254
Freud's ideas, 318, 344
Freud's theory, 148, 306, 310, 312, 317–18
Friendships, 322–23, 372–73, 379, 391, 480, 509, 530
Frontal lobes, 48, 58, 62, 65, 67, 73, 149, 381, 529, 608
Frustration, 196, 312, 324, 327, 424–25, 430–31, 445, 476, 481, 530, 539
Fyre Festival, 416, 418–20

GAM (General Aggression Model), 425
Ganglion cells, 93–96, 127
    retinal, 94
Gate-control theory, 112, 128, 130
Gender differences, 286, 289–91, 300, 328–29, 545, 570
Gender gaps, 290, 300, 328
Gender identity, 16, 35, 39, 248, 251, 379, 437, 494–95
General adaptation syndrome, 502–3, 508, 519, 521

General Aggression Model (GAM), 425
Generalized anxiety disorder, 540–41, 551, 566, 568, 571, 603–4
Generations, 5, 251, 256–57, 352, 361, 378–79, 387, 392, 437, 443, 535
Generativity, 269–70, 296, 298, 301, 386
Genes, 57, 273, 287, 300, 347, 350–53, 389, 392–93, 548, 553, 561–62
Genetic research, 105, 404
Genital stage, 311, 343
Germinal stage, 353–54, 389
Geropsychology, 36–37, 41, 43
Gestalt psychology, 6–7, 116, 118, 129–30
Gestalt therapy, 593, 601, 611, 613
GMAT (Graduate Management Admission Test), 278
Graduate Management Admission Test (GMAT), 278
Grief, 474, 479, 481, 527, 534, 537, 613
Group therapy, 595, 609, 611, 613

Habituation, 119, 175–78, 207–8, 210, 357, 390, 393
Hallucinations, 55, 163, 553, 559–61, 566, 569, 571, 575, 592–93, 604, 606
Hallucinogens, 163–67, 171–72
Happiness, 19, 25, 326, 328, 385–86, 434, 469, 472, 479, 481–83, 486–87, 491
Hardiness, 511, 517, 519, 521
Health, 9, 11–14, 32–33, 35, 39–40, 140, 164, 169–70, 322–24, 326, 382, 385–86, 465, 489–521, 599
Health and Human Services (HHS), 164, 535
Health and illness, 491–92, 517–18, 527
Health belief model, 489, 492, 499, 518
Health onion, 489, 493
Health psychology, 489–90, 493, 498–99, 518–19, 521
Health risks, 140, 312, 355, 380, 416, 458
Hearing Voices Network, 592–93
Heredity, 287–88, 351, 389, 562
Heritability, 286–87, 336, 392, 548
Heroin, 162–63, 166–67, 171, 198
HHS (Health and Human Services), 164, 535
Hierarchy, 8, 331, 345, 453–54, 461, 484, 487, 583–84
Hindbrain, 63, 145
Hippocampus, 64–65, 69, 77, 80, 82–83, 213, 219, 229–32, 238, 245, 252–54
Histrionic personality, 532, 555
Hopelessness, 514, 537, 540, 552, 558, 567–68
Human behavior, 2–3, 10–13, 17–18, 39–40, 172, 175, 178, 207, 210, 321–22, 325, 431–32, 452
  complex, 452
  explained, 452
  guiding, 42
Humanistic approach, 8, 306, 325, 331, 334, 341, 343–44, 576, 593, 598
Hypersomnia, 149, 151, 170
Hypnosis, 4, 6, 113, 131–33, 153–61, 169, 171–72, 307–8, 575, 582
Hypothalamus, 50–51, 62, 64–65, 69, 80, 82–83, 170, 456, 467–68, 484
Hypothesis, 18–19, 29–33, 40, 43, 273, 293, 296, 424, 470, 473, 502, 504, 507

IAT (Implicit Association Test), 441–43, 446–47
Iconic memory, 215–16, 251, 254
Identity, 329, 377, 386, 410, 434–35, 438–39, 556, 558, 564–65, 569–70, 578
Identity crisis, 38, 377, 386, 391, 393

Illusion, 6–7, 98, 112, 116, 120, 124–26, 129, 253, 260, 318, 323
Illusory memories, 246–47, 253
Immune system, 10, 186, 188–89, 488–89, 491, 499, 502, 505–8, 511, 517, 519–21
Implicit Association Test. See IAT
Implicit memory, 232, 234–38, 250, 252–54
Impulses, 50, 53–55, 81, 106, 113, 309, 312, 318, 322, 338, 344
Incentive, 56, 200, 204, 453, 457
Incentive theory, 453, 465, 484, 487
Incubation effect, 263, 297, 301
Independent variable, 28–31, 41, 43
Individual differences, 4, 30, 98, 155, 251, 305, 338–39, 375, 432, 452
Influencers, 329, 416, 418–19
Information-processing model, 214, 217, 222, 251, 254
Ingroup favoritism, 438, 443, 446, 450
Inkblots, 10, 315–16, 325, 344
Insecure attachment, 370–72, 391, 393
Insight, 21, 23–24, 237, 243, 260–61, 263–64, 296–97, 300–301, 575, 578–80, 595, 600, 610
  personal, 285, 578
Insomnia, 149–52, 157, 163–64, 170, 172, 196–97, 496, 518, 545
Instincts, 175–76, 183, 269, 309, 325, 422, 451–52, 465, 484, 487
Intelligence, 2, 10, 22–23, 123, 221, 255–301, 383, 389, 402, 404, 464
Intelligence tests, 164, 275, 277–78, 280–81, 289, 299, 363
Internal locus of control, 202–3, 492
Internal states, 22, 49, 191, 234, 253, 425, 555, 569, 586
Interpersonal form of psychotherapy, 607
Interpersonal intelligence, 285
Intimacy, 317, 386, 451, 454, 461–62, 465, 484, 487
Intrapersonal, 282, 284, 299
Introversion, 306, 337–38, 345–46
IQ, 256–57, 277, 280, 285–86, 289, 293, 297–300
IQ scores, 256–57, 280, 282, 287, 342, 355, 402
IQ tests, 229, 256, 275, 279–81, 284, 286, 293, 297, 300

James-Lange theory, 466–67, 478, 485, 487
JND (just noticeable difference), 90, 127, 130
John Watson, 23, 185, 543
Journal of Personality and Social Psychology, 159, 295, 328, 421, 428

Laboratory research, 19–20, 40, 43, 429
Latent learning, 200, 202, 209–10
Lateral hypothalamus, 456
Law, 8–9, 11–12, 14, 39–40, 117–18, 190, 192, 208, 210, 376, 432, 435, 558
Law enforcement, 12, 402, 443–45, 494, 533
Law School Admission Test (LSAT), 278
Learning, 2, 7–8, 10–12, 62, 64, 136, 138, 173–210, 234, 236, 242–43, 319–21, 548–49, 568, 582
  animal, 5–6
  human, 11–12
  implicit, 174, 318
  perceptual, 122
Learning and memory, 56, 62–63, 80, 169, 361
Learning problems, 11–12
Left hemisphere, 46–47, 67–72, 74–75, 77, 82
Life events, 520, 548
  major, 392, 499, 501, 519
  stressful, 323, 575
Life expectancy, 381, 386, 392–93
Lifespan, 10–12, 282, 350–51, 353, 381, 386, 389, 392–93, 405, 490, 497, 518

Lifespan development, 271, 305, 347, 349–93
Limbic system, 62, 64–65, 80–83, 229, 467, 477, 485
Linguistic-relativity hypothesis, 273–74, 298, 301
Listeners, 102–3, 116, 250, 271, 600
Lithium, 554, 604–6, 612–13
Lived experiences, 2, 350, 494
Lobotomy, 529, 608–9, 612
Locus of control, 201–3, 210, 322–24, 341, 344, 346, 492
Longevity, 27–28, 383, 511, 514, 516, 519
Long-term memory (LTM), 214, 221–24, 226–30, 233, 235, 238, 241–42, 244, 251–52, 254, 258
LSAT (Law School Admission Test), 278
LSD, 162–63, 165–67, 171
LTM. *See* long-term memory
Lucid dreaming, 148, 170, 172

Magnetic resonance imaging. *See* MRI
Major depressive disorder, 534–35, 567, 589
Mania, 535, 537, 552–53, 566, 569, 608
Marijuana, 161, 163–67, 171, 354
Master of Social Work (MSW), 571
MBCT (mindfulness-based cognitive therapy), 591
MBTI (Myers-Briggs Type Indicator), 305–6
MCAT (Medical College Admission Test), 278
Medical College Admission Test (MCAT), 278
Medical model, 529, 551, 567, 571
Medulla, 62–63, 69, 82–83
Memories, 2, 6, 8–10, 61–65, 67, 132–33, 157–59, 211–54, 257–58, 273–74, 296–97, 308, 312, 314–15, 318, 383–84, 563, 565–66, 578, 581
Memory disorder, 55, 229, 235
Memory performance, 223, 234, 243, 246, 267
Memory researchers, 5, 214, 249
Memory tests, 132, 235
Menarche, 374–75, 386, 391, 393
Menopause, 382, 386, 392–93
Mental age, 276–77, 285, 298, 301
Mental disorders, 35, 150, 528–34, 536, 547, 551, 562, 567, 575, 578, 580
Mental health, 460, 498, 501, 516–18, 538, 541, 570, 573–74, 577, 581, 586, 602, 607
Mental health professionals, 213, 531, 533, 538, 573, 577, 601, 607
Mental illness, 317, 510, 526, 530, 560, 576, 608
Microsleeps, 140, 170, 172
Midbrain, 62–63
Milgram's research, 412, 445
Mind-body relationship, 489, 491, 521
Mindfulness, 323–24, 402, 547, 601
Mindfulness-based cognitive therapy (MBCT), 591
Minnesota Multiphasic Personality Inventory, 336, 341, 345–46
Misinformation effect, 245–46, 253–54
MMPI, 336–38, 341, 345–46
MMPI-2, 336–38
Modern psychology, 4, 6, 136, 190
Monism, 4, 43, 491, 497, 521
Monocular depth cues, 120–21, 129–30
Mood disorders, 35, 533, 535, 554, 558, 566–67, 571, 603
Mood stabilizers, 604–6, 612
Moral reasoning, 373, 375–77, 391, 393, 557
Morphine, 56–57, 163, 166–67, 171
Motivation, 7, 10, 12, 62, 64, 203–4, 206–7, 209, 294, 415, 417, 451–54, 464–65, 483–84, 487
Motor areas, 66–67, 69, 82, 113, 128

Motor behavior, 168, 407, 467, 559
Motor cortex, 66–69, 82–83, 145, 284, 381
Motor neurons, 52–53, 55–57, 81, 148
MRI (magnetic resonance imaging), 60, 62, 81, 83
MSW (Master of Social Work), 571
Multicultural research, 38, 41, 43
Multiple intelligences, 282, 285, 292, 299–301
Multiple personality disorder, 531, 564–65, 570
Myers-Briggs Type Indicator. *See* MBTI

Narcolepsy, 151, 161, 165, 170, 172
National Child Traumatic Stress Network, 547
National Football League. *See* NFL
Negative correlation, 27
Negative self-images, 327
Neo-Freudian theorists, 313, 580
Nervous system, 10, 34, 37, 41, 47–52, 54–58, 63, 75–76, 79–81, 175, 362, 382–84, 489
Neural signals, 52–53, 81, 87, 115, 127, 138
Neurogenesis, 77, 82, 84
Neuroglia, 52
Neurons, 51–56, 58–59, 63, 65, 75–78, 81, 83–84, 96, 98, 100, 231, 234, 362, 381, 553–54
Neuroscientists, 23, 54, 61, 79–80, 229, 245, 252
Neuroticism, 304–5, 335–36, 345, 548
Neurotransmitters, 45, 51, 54–57, 59, 80–81, 84, 231, 536–37, 553–54, 603, 605–6, 612
Neutral stimulus, 179–84, 186, 188–89, 243, 320, 548
New York Times, 238, 427, 496
NFL (National Football League), 77–79, 349
Nightmares, 24, 148, 152, 170, 172, 500, 527, 608
Nine-dot problem, 264–66
Nocebo effects, 496–97
Non associative learning, 173, 175, 207
Non-REM sleep stages, 153
Normal brain, 48, 231
NREM sleep, 143, 152, 172
Nurture, 39, 257, 272, 277, 286–87, 297, 299–300, 303, 334, 350, 369

Obesity, 19, 35, 157, 165, 410, 442, 454, 457–59, 484, 487, 504
Object permanence, 364, 367, 369, 388, 390, 393
Observational learning, 173, 178, 204–7, 209–10
Obsessions, 337, 549–51, 569
Obsessive-compulsive disorder. *See* OCD
OCD (obsessive-compulsive disorder), 525, 549–51, 566, 569, 571, 590
OCF (Outline for Cultural Formulation), 532
Operant conditioning, 173, 178, 180–81, 189, 191–93, 196, 198–99, 207–10, 319–21, 582, 585, 588–89
Operational definitions, 18–19, 40, 43
Opiates, 163, 166–67, 171–72
Opponent-process theory, 98–100, 128, 130
Optic chiasm, 70, 96–97, 101, 127
Optic nerve, 64, 70, 94–97, 101, 114, 127, 130, 138
Optimism, 27–28, 481, 509, 512–14, 516, 519–20, 600
Oral stage, 309, 311
Outgroup-homogeneity bias, 436, 443, 446, 450
Outline for Cultural Formulation (OCF), 532
Outstanding Lifetime Contribution, 195
Overlearning, 225, 252
Overweight, 375, 457–58, 460, 486, 530

Pain, 48–49, 57, 76, 112–14, 128, 130, 155–56, 159–60, 163–64, 166, 180–81, 183, 477, 496–97, 504–5, 509–10
  chronic, 112–13, 156, 496, 518, 546, 600–601
Panic disorder, 541–42, 551, 568, 571, 590
Paranoid personality, 555
Parasympathetic nervous system, 49, 57, 80, 84, 468, 485, 487
Parents, 243, 250, 286–88, 309–11, 318–21, 326, 330–31, 342–43, 350–51, 359, 362–63, 370–80, 391–92, 548–49, 556–57, 561–63
  opposite-sex, 310, 318
Parkinson's disease, 56, 79, 81, 606
Partial-reinforcement effect, 194–95, 209–10
Pavlov's work on classical conditioning, 173, 178
Perceivers, 115, 118, 120, 126, 403, 436
Perception psychologists, 124, 126
Perceptions, 10, 12, 15, 37, 85–89, 91–130, 132, 162, 166, 216–17, 288, 402, 404, 499, 559
Perceptual illusions, 115, 124–25, 127, 129–30
Peripheral nervous system. *See* PNS
Personality, 6, 48, 303–46, 381, 384, 488–89, 504, 508, 521, 555–56, 558, 564–65, 567, 578, 580
Personality Consortium, 336, 548
Personality development, 309, 314, 321, 326, 343–44
Personality disorders, 525, 531, 555–56, 558, 569, 571
Personality inventories, 336, 345
Personality psychologists, 326, 342–43
Personality questionnaires, 335, 340
Personality style, 511, 517, 519
Personality tests, 304–6, 313, 334, 336, 340, 342
Personality traits, 9, 13, 310, 336, 342, 511
Personality types, 4, 306, 311
Personal Orientation Inventory, 331
Person-centered therapy, 593, 596, 611, 613
Persuasion, 11, 306, 415–17, 419, 444–45, 448, 487
Pessimism, 512–14, 520, 537
PET scans, 60–61, 63, 72–73, 114, 226
Pew Research Center, 432, 516
Phallic personality types, 318
Phallic stages, 309, 343
Phobias, 206, 511, 541–44, 551, 566, 568, 571, 582–83, 592
Photoreceptors, 93–94, 127–28
Physical activity, 37, 509–11, 529, 535, 602
Physiological arousal, 49, 177, 184, 249, 340, 466–69, 475, 478, 485, 502
Piaget's theory, 93, 244, 363, 367
Pituitary gland, 50–51, 62, 80, 84
Placebo control group, 475, 607
Placebo effect, 489, 495–97, 518, 600, 612–13
Plasticity, 45, 74–76, 82, 84
Pleasure, 3, 48, 57, 65, 163, 309, 432, 481–82, 556–57
PNS (peripheral nervous system), 49, 80, 84
Police officers, 14, 140, 157, 195, 403, 413–14, 501
Posthypnotic suggestion, 156–57, 171–72
Posttraumatic stress disorder, 316, 324, 500–501, 508, 519, 521, 531, 545–47, 551, 568, 571
Predators, 120, 145, 170, 502
Prejudice, 11–13, 21, 38, 318, 328, 395, 402, 435, 437–39, 443, 446–47
Premature infants, 146, 370
Prenatal development, 347, 353–54, 389
Preoperational stage, 365, 390, 393
Presleep, 141, 153, 170
Primacy effect, 401–2, 414, 444, 450
Priming, 136, 161, 170, 172

Prison, 12, 355, 414, 422, 557–58, 581–82, 586
Proactive interference, 242–44, 253–54
Problem-focused coping, 509, 517, 519
Problem solving, 10, 18, 130, 260, 263–65, 268, 276, 297, 301, 367, 380
Procedural memory, 227–28, 231, 236, 252, 254
Productivity, 42, 140, 192, 501
Projective personality tests, 315–16
Projective tests, 307, 315–16, 344, 346
Prozac, 537, 589, 604–6, 612
Psychiatric drugs, 573–75
Psychoactive drugs, 133, 162–63, 165–66, 168, 171–72, 605, 612
Psychoanalysis, 6–9, 39, 154, 157, 306–8, 311–12, 314–15, 317–19, 321, 325–26, 341–44, 346, 577–80
Psychological dependence, 163, 171–72, 607, 612
Psychological disorders, 9, 12, 34, 37, 60, 336, 343, 525–71, 573–77, 601–3, 608, 610, 612
  heritable, 569
  severe, 591
Psychological measurements, 20, 40
Psychologists, 1–5, 7–9, 12–20, 33–35, 38–39, 41–42, 88–90, 169, 207, 278–82, 296, 312–13, 338, 369–71, 385–86, 451–53, 479–81, 485–86, 536–38, 586–87
  budding, 443–45
  cognitive, 23, 214–15, 221, 226, 229, 232, 235, 246, 248, 251, 483
  developmental, 348, 357–58, 369–70, 377, 388
  first, 35, 85, 88, 275, 466
  gestalt, 116–17, 129
  humanistic, 334, 345
  male, 213
  minority, 9, 16
  oriented, 36, 315
  trait, 341
Psychology
  clinical, 6, 558, 567, 577
  cognitive, 8, 134, 241, 319
  counseling, 577
  defined, 6
  studied, 363
Psychology coursework, 254, 346
Psychology degrees, 42, 195
Psychology graduates, 210, 448, 487
Psychology students, 42, 83, 130, 172, 210, 254, 301, 334, 346, 393
Psychoneuroimmunology, 489, 506, 508, 519, 521
Psychosexual development, 309, 311
Psychosexual stages, 309, 311, 318, 341, 343, 346
Psychosurgery, 65, 603, 608–9, 612–13
Psychotherapy, 6, 308, 315, 318, 573, 575–77, 580, 589, 593, 595, 597–601, 603, 607, 610–13
PTSD (post-traumatic stress disorder), 500, 508, 519, 521, 525, 545–49, 568, 571, 588

Race, 24–25, 281, 288, 294, 317, 320, 380, 384–85, 403–4, 436–37, 440, 442–43
Racism, 38, 187, 422, 439–41, 443–45, 446–47
Rational-emotive behavior therapy. *See* REBT
Rationalization, 313, 319, 344, 346
Realistic-conflict theory, 437–38, 443, 446, 447
REBT (rational-emotive behavior therapy), 589, 596, 611, 613
Recognition, 22, 72, 133, 233, 235, 238, 252, 254, 331, 454, 470
Recollections, 158, 213–14, 232, 238, 248–49, 252, 488
Recurring dreams, 146–47

Reinforcement, 7–9, 180–81, 189–204, 206–10, 321–23, 325–26, 343–44, 582, 585, 587, 589
Reinforcement schedules, 193–95, 209, 320–21
Reinforcers, 191–95, 208
Relationships, 18, 89, 95, 298, 370–72, 389, 391, 462, 504, 506, 509, 535, 537, 579, 594
   first, 369–71
   parent-infant, 371
   therapist-patient, 579–80
Relaxation training, 542, 583, 592, 611
Reliability, 278–79, 285, 299, 301, 316–17, 338, 532
Religion, 32, 112, 270, 317, 332, 399, 404, 432–33, 436–38, 516, 520
REM sleep, 59, 137, 142–43, 145–49, 151–53, 161, 164, 170, 172
REM sleep behavior disorder, 152, 170, 172
Representativeness heuristic, 266, 268, 298, 301
Repressed memories, 158, 313, 581, 588
Repression, 241, 243–44, 253, 312–13, 319, 343, 346
Reprocessing therapy, 588, 613
Research, 16–20, 22–23, 25–28, 31–34, 36–37, 40, 82–83, 138–40, 155–58, 261–63, 304–5, 318, 321–24, 329–32, 401–3, 459–63, 467–69, 482–85, 518–20, 605–7
Research ethics, 32, 43
Research findings, 18, 289, 477, 515
Research methods, 9, 18, 24, 39, 58
Research participants, 19, 29, 31, 41–42, 238, 401
Resistance, 194, 209, 308–9, 317–18, 488, 502–3, 508, 519, 578–80, 610, 613
Response to light, 88, 95, 99
Retention, 206–7, 209, 224–25, 232, 235–36, 239, 241, 244, 252–53
Retina, 88, 93–96, 98–101, 118–20, 127–30, 138, 170
Rewards, 8, 168, 177, 190–92, 197–99, 202–4, 209, 309, 321–22, 325, 586
Right hemisphere, 46–47, 65, 69–74, 82, 284, 292

Sadness, 55, 466, 468–73, 479, 481, 483, 486, 528, 534–35, 558, 567
SAMHSA (Substance Abuse and Mental Health Services Administration), 164, 526–27
Schizophrenia, 56, 60, 532–33, 553, 555, 559–63, 566, 569–70, 590–93, 603–4, 606, 608–9, 611–12
Schizophrenia spectrum disorders, 559–61, 569, 571
Scientific methods, 10, 17–18, 32, 35, 39–40, 330, 346
Sedatives, 151, 163–65, 167, 171–72, 573
Selective attention, 114, 129, 133–34, 169, 172
Selective serotonin reuptake inhibitors (ssris), 605–6
Self-actualization, 8, 303, 325–27, 331–32, 334, 341, 343–46, 453–54, 483–84, 530
Self-concept, 250, 326–27, 330, 334, 344–45, 377, 385–86, 391, 530
Self-control, 197, 209, 322, 337
Self-disclosure, 462, 484, 487, 600
Self-discrepancy theory, 330, 346
Self-distraction, 509–10, 519
Self-efficacy, 130, 172, 324, 344, 346, 520, 613
   high, 324–25
Self-esteem, 10, 21, 132, 327–31, 345–46, 429, 438–39, 446, 508, 511, 516
   lower, 515
Self-fulfilling prophecy, 293–94, 297, 300–301, 402, 555
Self-help groups, 595–96
Self-report measures, 21–22
Self-schemas, 327, 345–46
Sensation and perception, 10, 87–129, 169, 264, 456
Sensorimotor stage, 363–64, 390, 393
Sensory adaptation, 114, 126, 129–30

Sensory information, 63, 66–67, 69, 82, 116, 128, 220
Sensory memory, 214–16, 251, 254
Sensory neurons, 52–53, 57, 81, 84, 110, 148
Sensory register, 215–17, 251
Sensory systems, 87–89, 91, 106, 110, 114–15, 128, 560
Separation anxiety, 364, 385, 390, 393
Shootings, mass, 532–33, 545–46, 601
Short-term memory (stm), 149, 211, 214, 216–18, 220–23, 230, 251–52, 254, 391
Signal-detection theory, 89–90, 127, 130
Situational attributions, 400–401, 444
Situational cues, 197, 424, 445, 541
Sleep, 20, 59, 62–63, 65, 131–33, 137–46, 148–54, 164, 169–70, 212–13, 242, 492, 505–7, 546, 566–67
Sleep and arousal, 62–63, 69, 82
Sleep apnea, 107, 152, 161, 170, 172, 458
Sleep disorders, 140, 151, 566
Sleep disturbances, 149, 170, 537
Sleep-wake cycle, 137, 139, 170
Sleepwalkers, 152
Social anxiety disorder, 541, 544–45, 568, 571
Social contacts, 337–38, 388, 461–62, 465, 484, 516–17, 520
Social development, 347, 361–62, 364, 368–69, 372, 379, 381, 385, 390–92
Social-identity theory, 438–39, 446, 449
Social influence, 159, 161, 171, 407–8, 411, 415, 445
Social-learning theory, 319, 321, 344
Social loafing, 420–21, 445, 449
Social media, 2–3, 15, 25, 28, 34, 38, 328–29, 340–41, 373, 379, 461, 515–16, 583–84
Social norms, 432, 445–46, 450
Social perception, 398–99, 414, 444, 450
Social psychological perspective, 11, 40, 43
Social-psychological theories, 171
Social psychology, 159, 295, 328, 346, 397–98, 420–21, 428, 444, 450
Social Readjustment Rating Scale (SRRS), 500–501
Social responsibility, 13, 337, 377
Social situations, 11, 380, 398, 444, 505, 605
Social skills training, 587–88, 611, 613
Social support, 324, 411, 491, 509, 515–17, 520–21, 538, 575, 595, 599–600
Social workers, 501, 570, 577, 609
Society, 11, 13, 290–91, 296, 310, 318, 404, 433–34, 557, 563, 565
Sociocultural perspectives, 11, 38, 41, 43
Somatosensory cortex, 66, 76, 82, 84, 110
Spatial intelligence, 283–85, 291–92
Specialization, 2–3, 36, 39, 74
Spinal cord, 49, 52–54, 61–63, 76, 80, 110, 112, 362
Split brain, 69, 84, 559
Split-brain patients, 46, 70–72, 80
SRRS (Social Readjustment Rating Scale), 500–501
SSRIs (selective serotonin reuptake inhibitors), 605–6
Stages of cognitive development, 367–68
Stages of prenatal development, 347, 353
Stages of sleep, 137, 141–43, 151, 153
Stanford-Binet Intelligence Test, 276–77
Stereotypes, 248, 290–91, 294, 296, 372, 383, 436–37, 443, 446, 449, 532–33
   negative, 296, 300, 402, 446
Stereotype threat, 294–96, 300–301
Stereotype threat effect, 295, 300
Stereotyping, 11–12, 436, 441
Stimulants, 163, 165–67, 171–72
Stimulus generalization, 182, 197, 208, 210, 320, 543, 583

Stimulus-response connections, 7, 96, 589
STM. *See* short-term memory
Stories, 48, 156–57, 223, 235–36, 244, 264, 281–82, 293, 316–17, 375–76, 426–28, 434, 463, 484, 580–81, 592
Strange-situation test, 370, 372, 391, 393
Stress, 2, 33–34, 49, 232, 246, 453, 456, 462, 488–89, 491–521, 562–63, 565, 567, 588, 591–92
   emotional, 465, 491
   high, 516–17
   low, 516–17
   psychological, 498, 503, 519
   research guidelines, 41
   work-related, 465, 504
Stress-inoculation training, 591
Stressor-related disorder, 545–46, 568
Stressors, 140, 246, 499, 501–3, 507, 509, 512, 519
Stroop test, 135, 169, 172
Subjective ages, 348–49, 389
Subjective experience, 7, 22, 326, 470
Subjective sensations, 4, 89, 128
Substance Abuse and Mental Health Services Administration. *See* SAMHSA
Suicide, 377, 379, 491, 494, 498, 533, 535–40, 553, 555–57, 559, 568, 570
Sunlight, 92, 138, 170
Superego, 309–10, 313, 315, 319, 343, 346, 557
Supertasters, 109
Support groups, 600–601, 610
Supportive relationship, 599, 612
Surgery, 35, 46–47, 69, 81, 88, 105, 156, 229–30, 426, 490, 495
Survival, 105, 110, 112, 176, 331, 453, 516, 535
Survivors, 397–98, 500, 581, 595
Sympathetic nervous system, 49, 57, 80, 84, 468, 485, 487, 503
Systematic desensitization, 583–84, 588, 611, 613

TAT (Thematic Apperception Test), 316–17, 338, 341, 344, 346
Teen birth rates, 380
telemental health, 602, 612–13
Temporal lobe, 64–66, 68, 229–30
Test anxiety, 24, 582
Testosterone, 374, 422, 430–31
Test-retest reliability, 279, 299, 301
Thalamus, 63–64, 69, 82, 84, 96–97, 100–101, 104, 107–8, 110–11, 115, 127–28, 467, 477–78
Thematic Apperception Test. *See* TAT
Theories of depression, 535, 567
Theories of emotion, 474, 485
Theories of Obsessive-Compulsive Disorder, 550, 569
Theories of personality, 570
Theory of personality, 6, 23, 316–17, 326–27
Therapy, 153, 243, 247, 569, 575, 577–78, 580, 582, 584–85, 587–91, 593, 595–601, 610–13
Therapy group, 575, 595
Threat, 112, 184, 294, 438, 462, 477–78, 502–4, 519, 566
Tools of behavioral neuroscience, 58, 81
Touch, 64, 66–67, 71, 75, 88–89, 91, 109–11, 113–15, 122, 128, 179–80, 358
   active, 110, 128
Transference, 307, 578–80, 610, 613
Transgender, 410, 494–95, 515, 539
Transition to adolescence, 347, 373

Trauma, 77, 213, 308, 312, 460, 500, 545–48, 551, 568, 580, 588
Treatment, 11–12, 39–41, 151, 154, 184, 493–96, 518–19, 528–32, 534–35, 549, 551, 554, 573, 575–78, 580, 583, 585, 591, 597–602, 607–13
   chemical, 574
   psychological, 551, 573, 575
Treatment for depression, 535, 601
Treatment of posttraumatic stress disorder, 588, 611
Treatment of psychological disorders, 343, 602–3, 612
Trichromatic theory, 98–100, 128, 130
TV violence, 28, 425
Twins, 286, 299, 356, 400, 422, 459, 561, 570
   identical, 286–87, 352, 389, 459, 483, 536, 553, 561–62
Two-factor theory of emotion, 474–75, 478, 486–87

Unconditional positive regard, 303, 325–27, 341, 345–46, 593, 596, 611
Unconditioned response. *See* UR
Unconditioned stimulus. *See* US
Unconscious forces, 6, 136, 241, 307–8, 317
UR (unconditioned response), 179–80, 183, 185–86, 188, 208, 210, 585
US (unconditioned stimulus), 179–81, 183, 185–89, 193, 208–10, 320, 582, 585

Valium, 164, 167, 603–4, 606–7
Vestibular system, 113, 115, 128, 130
Victims, 413, 422–23, 427, 429, 431, 435, 559–60, 562, 564, 581, 590
Violence, 14–15, 42, 64, 90, 165, 196, 209, 422, 424–25, 445, 472
   acceptability of, 15
Virtual reality (VR), 120, 194, 584
Visual cliff, 122–23, 129–30
Visual cortex, 64, 66, 68, 70, 73, 75, 88, 95–98, 100–101, 127, 130, 358, 362
Visual field, 69–70, 85, 93, 96
Visual pathways, 96–97
VR (virtual reality), 120, 194, 584
VRET (virtual reality exposure therapy), 584

WAIS (Wechsler Adult Intelligence Scale), 277, 279, 281, 285, 299, 301
Washington Post, 274, 306, 443–45, 545
Wechsler Adult Intelligence Scale. *See* WAIS
Wellness, 2, 11–12, 319, 453, 489–521, 547, 550, 600
Wernicke's area, 66, 68–69, 75, 82, 84
WHO. *See* World Health Organization
Work-health balance, 464–65
Working memory, 135, 221–22, 241, 252, 254, 339
Work-life balance, 13, 465
World Health Organization (WHO), 457, 489, 499, 527, 539, 586, 588, 611
World War II, 13, 198, 412, 424, 500

X-rays, 60, 91–92, 183, 354

Zygote, 353–54, 356, 389, 393